I0824412

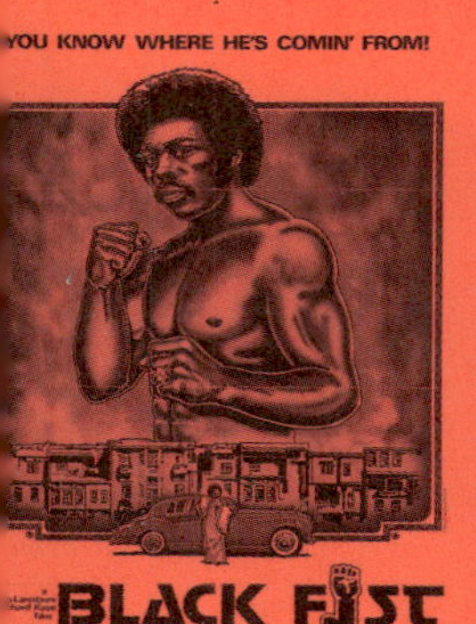

YOU KNOW WHERE HE'S COMIN' FROM!
BLACK FIST
A WORLDWIDE FILMS RELEASE

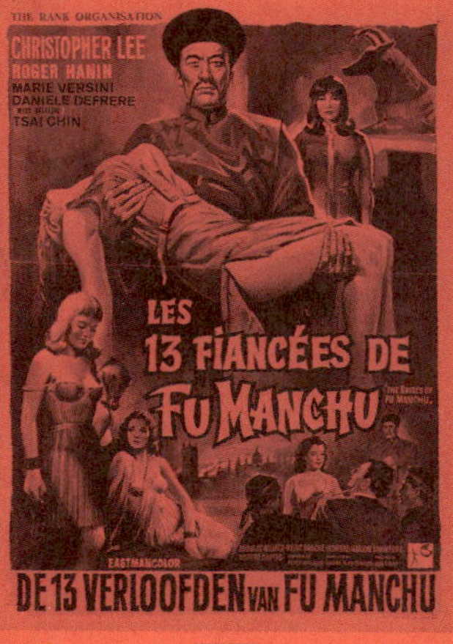

THE RANK ORGANISATION
CHRISTOPHER LEE
LES 13 FIANCÉES DE FU MANCHU
DE 13 VERLOOFDEN van FU MANCHU

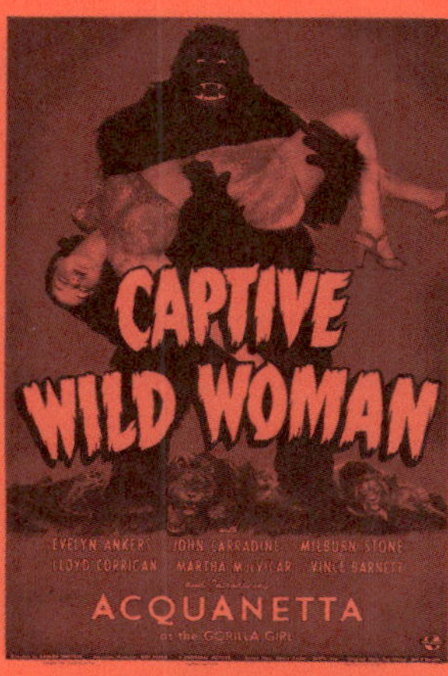

CAPTIVE WILD WOMAN
ACQUANETTA

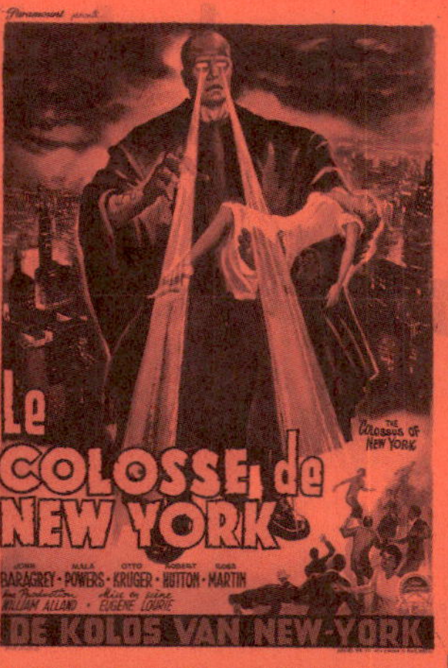

Le COLOSSE de NEW YORK
DE KOLOS VAN NEW-YORK

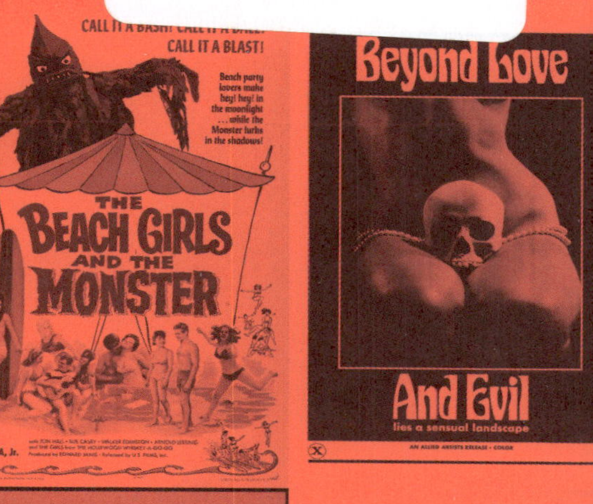

CALL IT A BLAST!
THE BEACH GIRLS AND THE MONSTER
Beyond Love And Evil
lies a sensual landscape

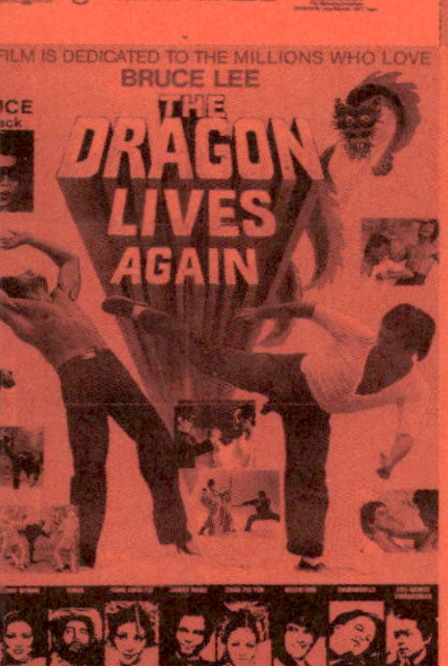

THIS FILM IS DEDICATED TO THE MILLIONS WHO LOVE BRUCE LEE
THE DRAGON LIVES AGAIN
THE UNDERWORLD ASSASINS TRAINED TO FIND AND KILL BRUCE!

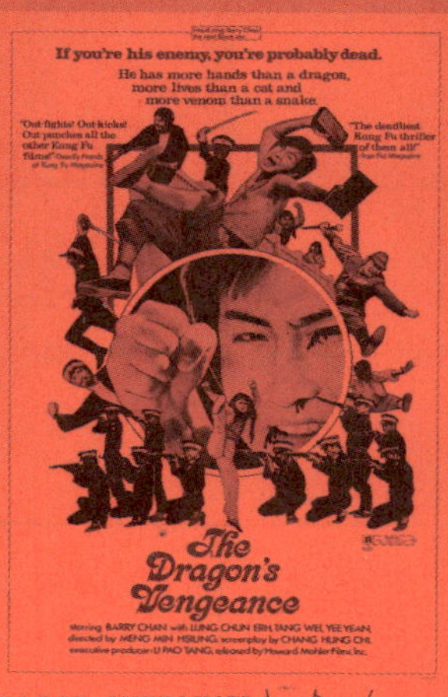

If you're his enemy, you're probably dead.
He has more hands than a dragon, more lives than a cat and more venom than a snake.
The Dragon's Vengeance

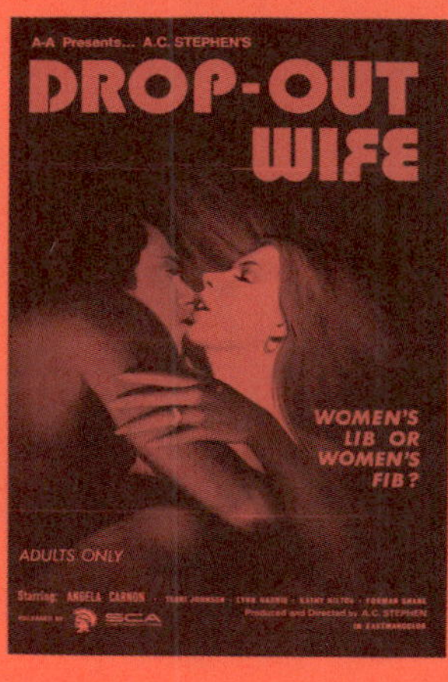

DROP-OUT WIFE
WOMEN'S LIB OR WOMEN'S FIB?
ADULTS ONLY

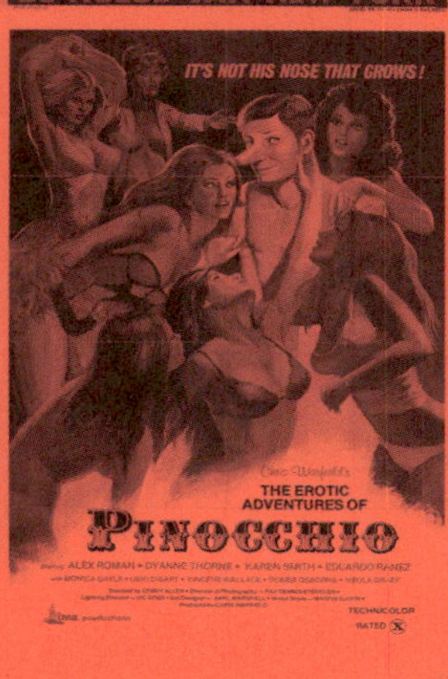

IT'S NOT HIS NOSE THAT GROWS!
THE EROTIC ADVENTURES OF
PINOCCHIO

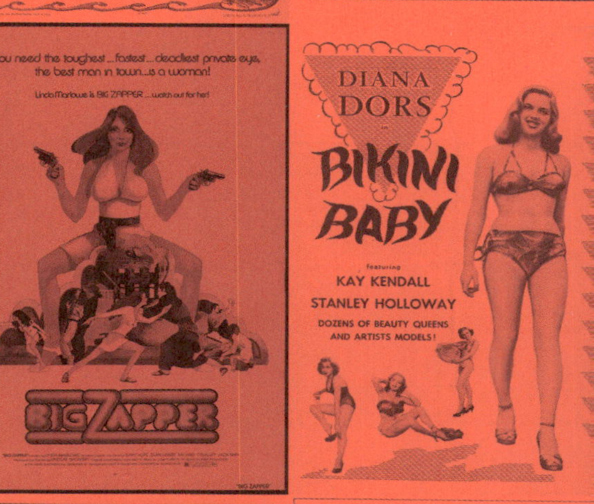

If you need the toughest... fastest... deadliest private eye, the best man in town...is a woman!
BIG ZAPPER
DIANA DORS
BIKINI BABY
featuring
KAY KENDALL
STANLEY HOLLOWAY
DOZENS OF BEAUTY QUEENS AND ARTISTS MODELS!

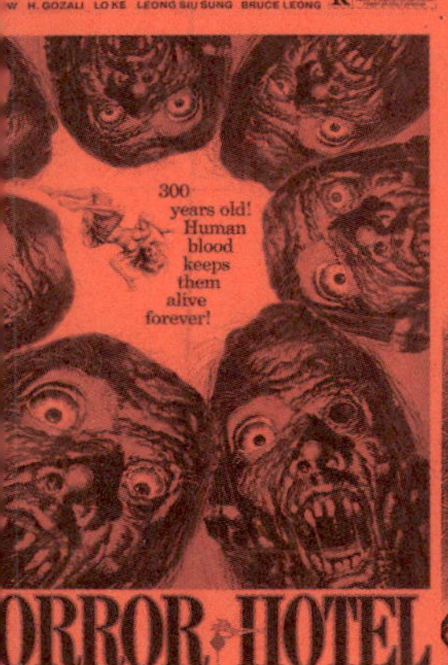

300 years old! Human blood keeps them alive forever!
HORROR HOTEL
Just ring for doom service!

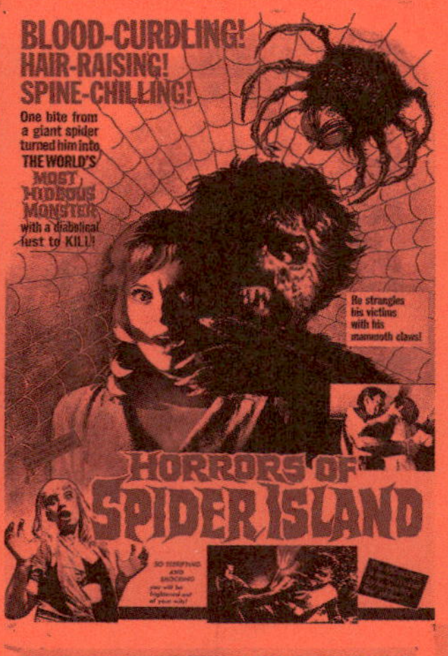

BLOOD-CURDLING! HAIR-RAISING! SPINE-CHILLING!
One bite from a giant spider turned him into THE WORLD'S MOST HIDEOUS MONSTER with a relentless lust to KILL!
HORRORS OF SPIDER ISLAND

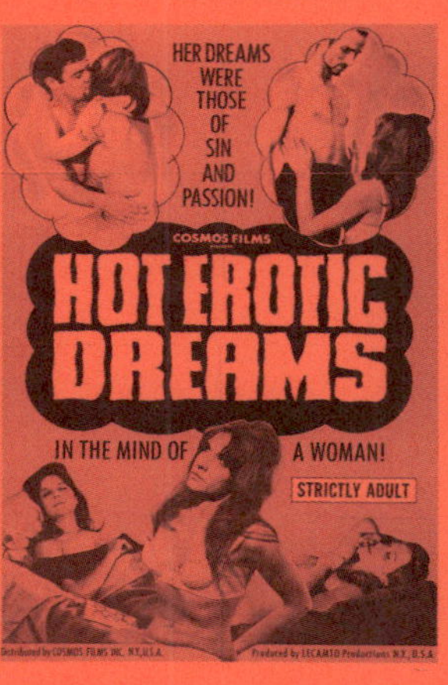

HER DREAMS WERE THOSE OF SIN AND PASSION!
COSMOS FILMS
HOT EROTIC DREAMS
IN THE MIND OF A WOMAN!
STRICTLY ADULT

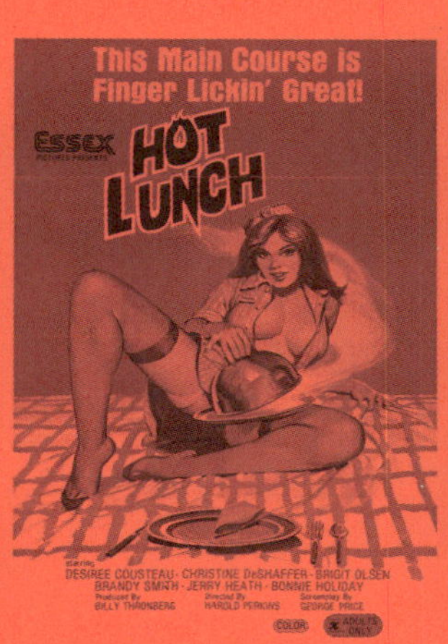

This Main Course is Finger Lickin' Great!
ESSEX
HOT LUNCH

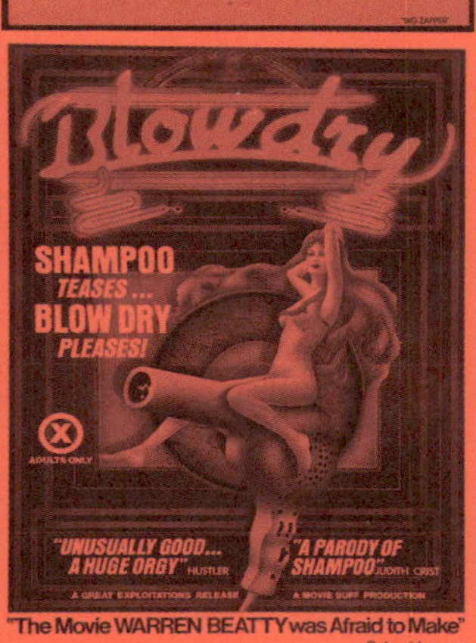

Blowdry
SHAMPOO TEASES... BLOW DRY PLEASES!
"The Movie WARREN BEATTY was Afraid to Make"

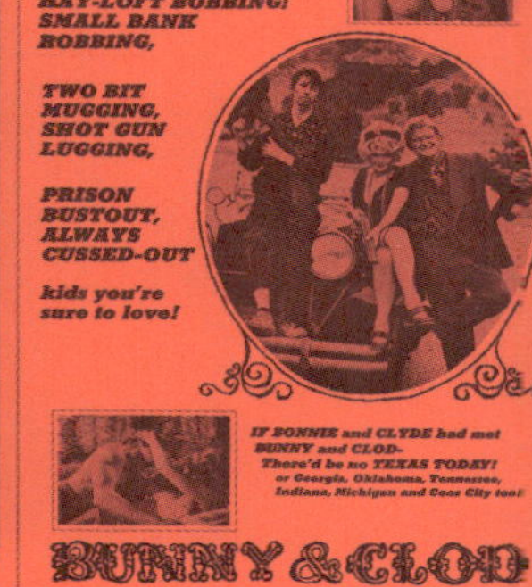

They were a couple of... TRIGGER PUMPING, BACK WOODS HUMPING,
HAY-LOFT BOBBING; SMALL BANK ROBBING,
TWO BIT MUGGING, SHOT GUN LUGGING,
PRISON BUSTOUT, ALWAYS CUSSED-OUT
kids you're sure to love!
BUNNY & CLOD

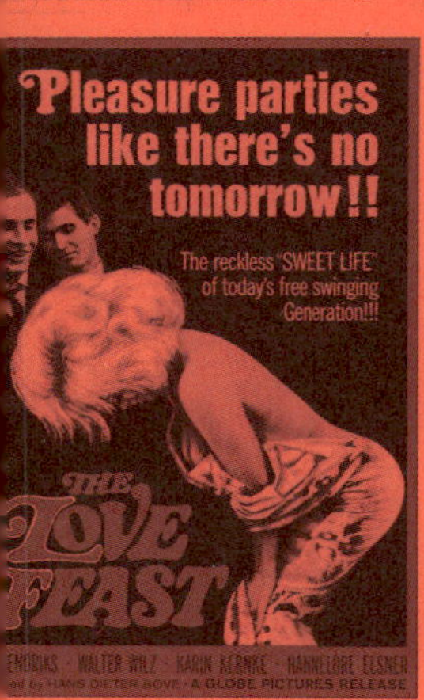

"Pleasure parties like there's no tomorrow!!
The reckless 'SWEET LIFE' of today's free swinging Generation!!!
THE LOVE FEAST

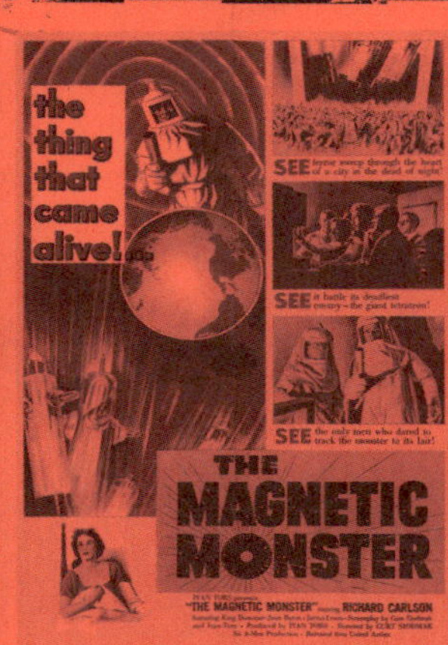

the thing that came alive!
THE MAGNETIC MONSTER

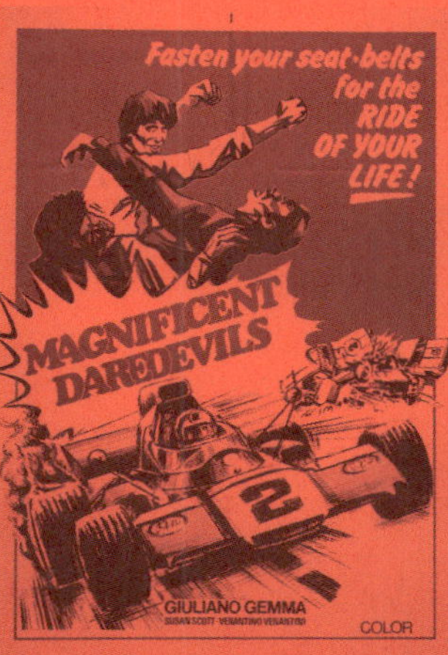

Fasten your seat-belts for the RIDE OF YOUR LIFE!
MAGNIFICENT DAREDEVILS
GIULIANO GEMMA
COLOR

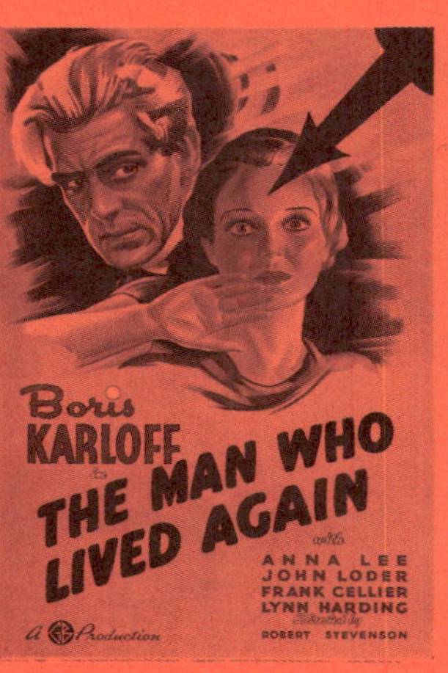

Boris KARLOFF
THE MAN WHO LIVED AGAIN
ANNA LEE
JOHN LODER
FRANK CELLIER
LYNN HARDING

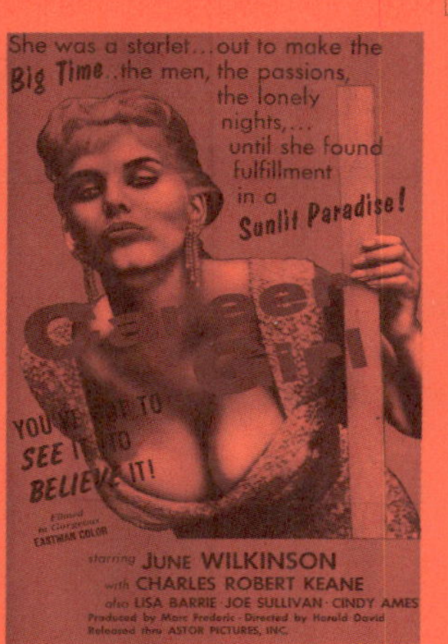

She was a starlet...out to make the Big Time...the men, the passions, the lonely nights,... until she found fulfillment in a Sunlit Paradise!
starring JUNE WILKINSON

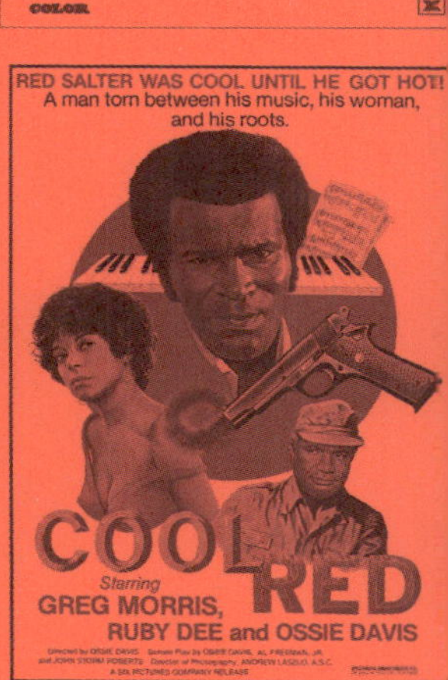

RED SALTER WAS COOL UNTIL HE GOT HOT!
A man torn between his music, his woman, and his roots.
COOL RED
Starring GREG MORRIS, RUBY DEE and OSSIE DAVIS

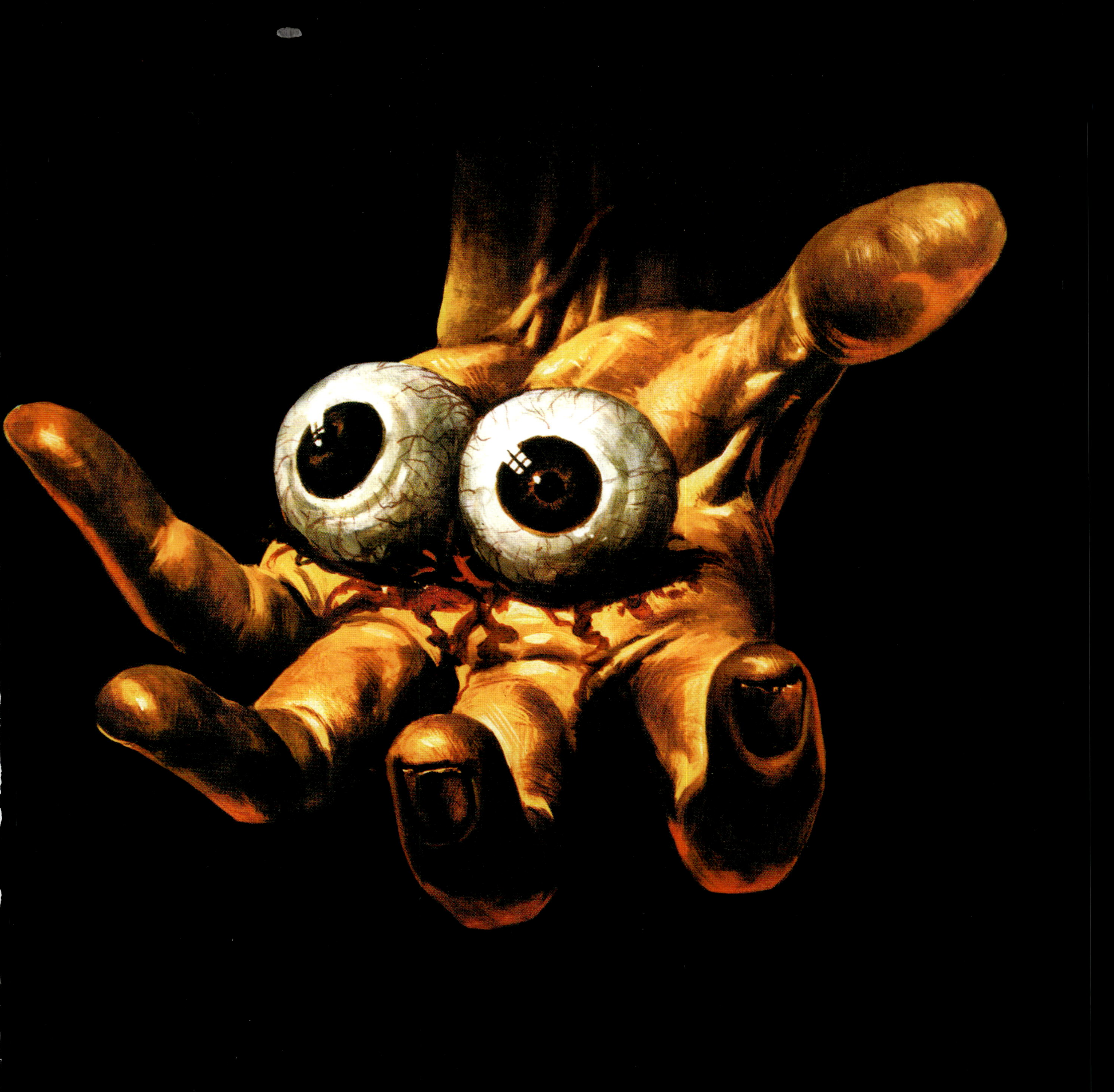

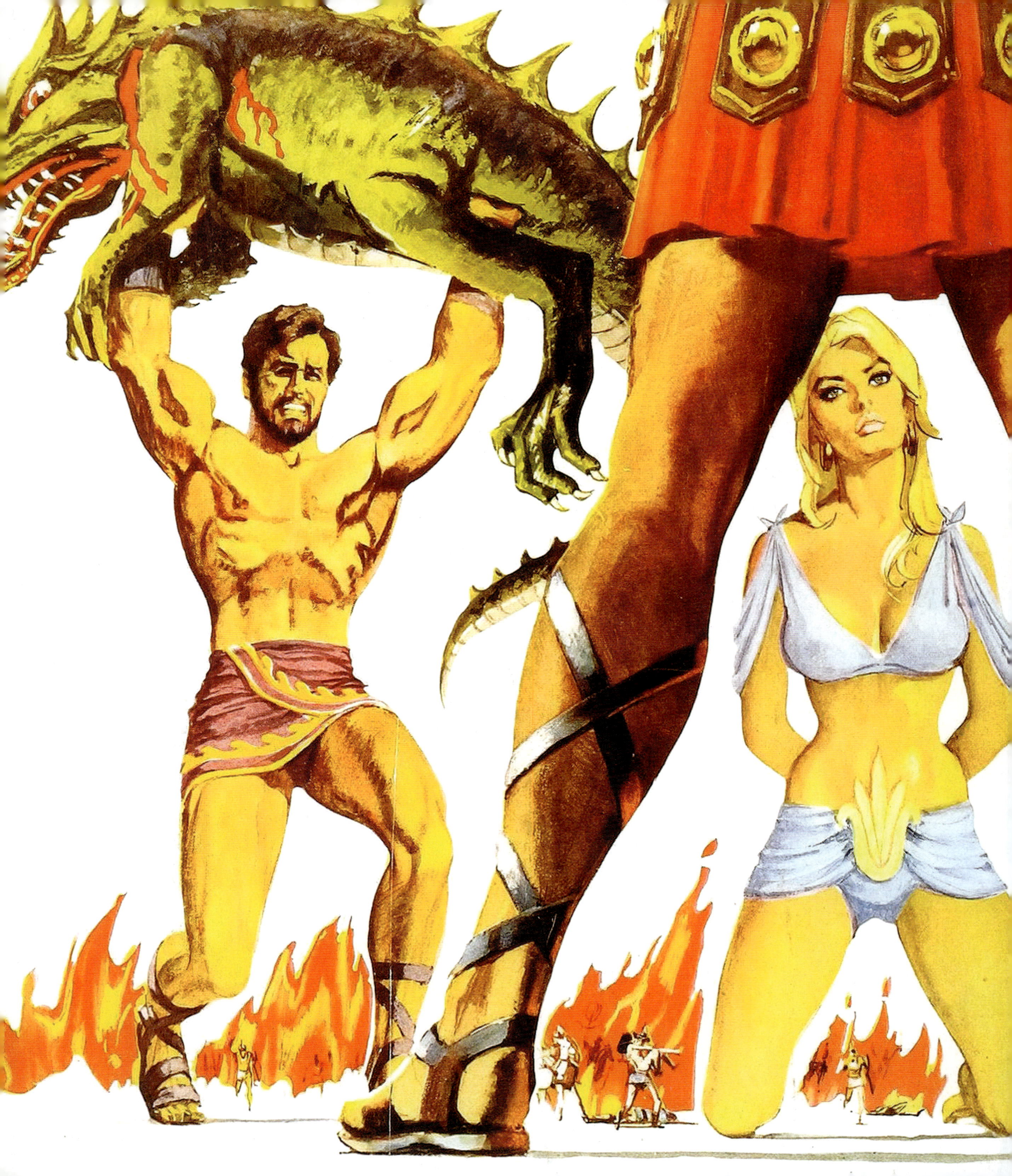

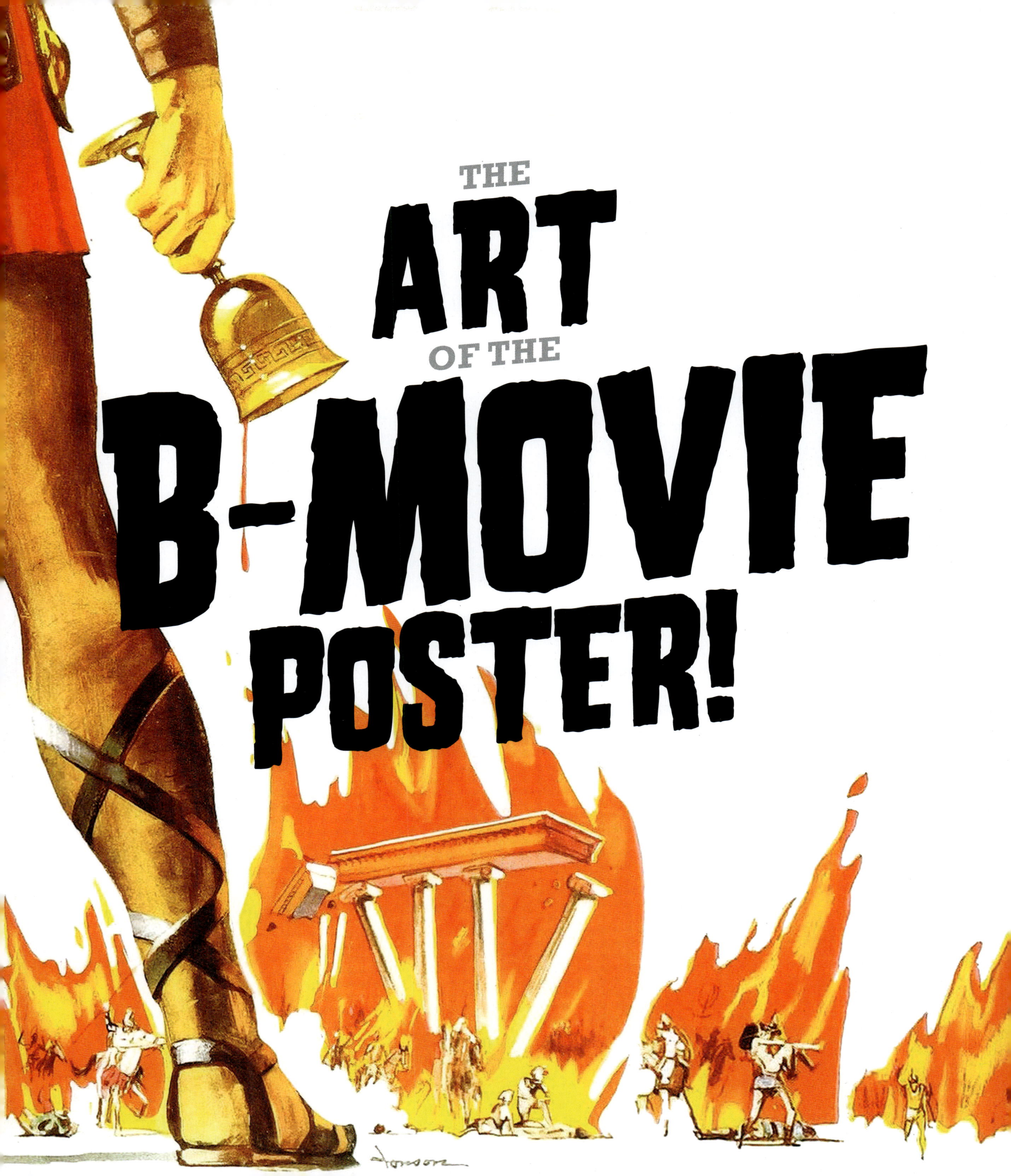
THE
ART
OF THE
B-MOVIE
POSTER!

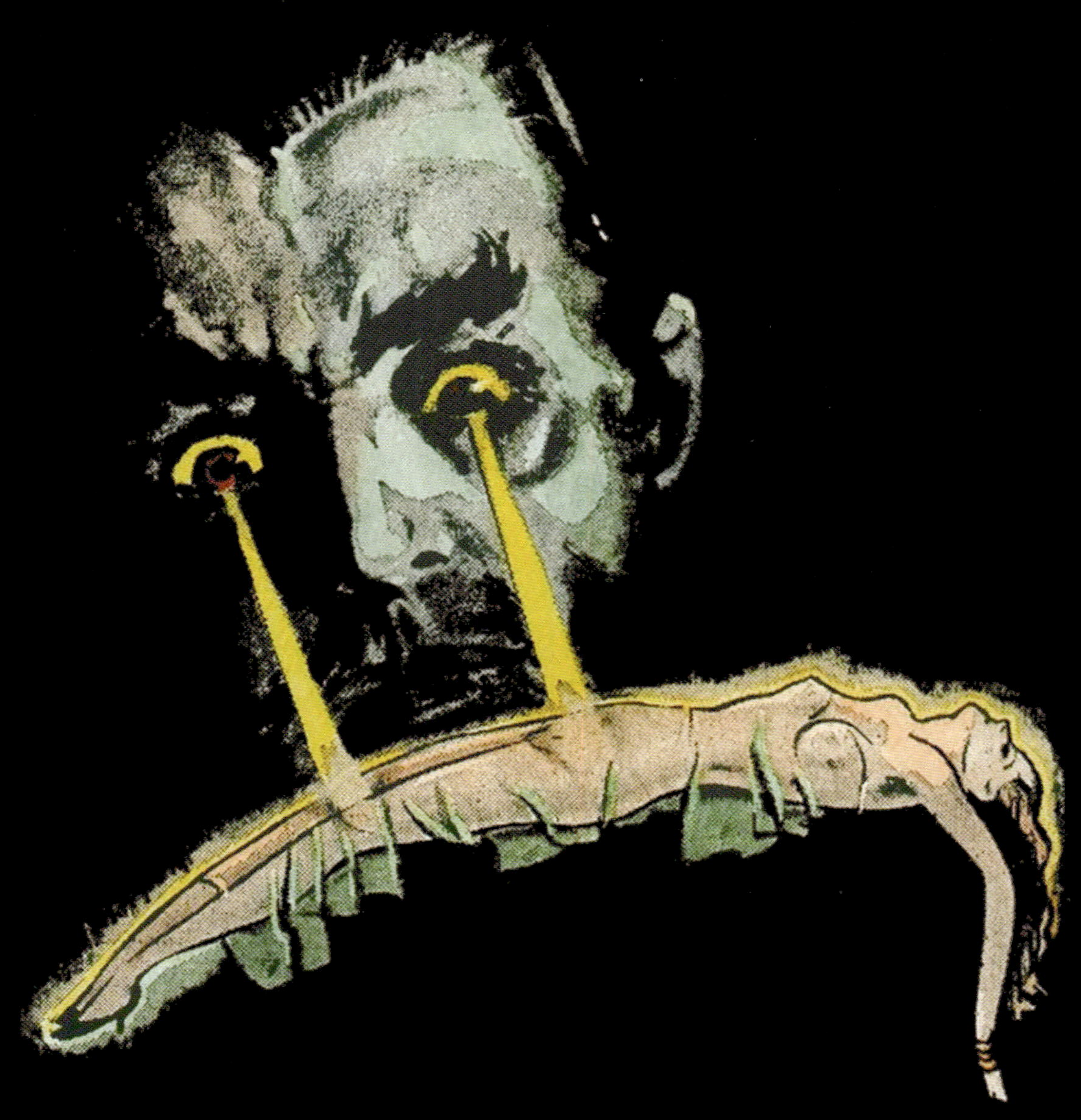

FRONT COVER: Detail from the unsigned US one-sheet art for *Eyeball* (1975), director Umberto Lenzi's *giallo* originally released in Italy as *Gatti rossi in un labirinto di vetro*.

BACK COVER (LEFT TO RIGHT): US one-sheet for *Mondo Mod* (1967); Italian *foglio* for *The Mad Magician* (1954), art by Vittorio Pisani; US one-sheet for *A*P*E* (1976).

PAGE 1: Detail from the Italian *locandina* for *Cinque dita di violenza* (aka *Five Fingers of Death*, aka *King Boxer*, 1972), art by Mos (Mario de Berardinis).

PAGES 2 & 3: Detail from the US half-sheet for *Hercules and the Captive Women* (aka *Ercole alla conquista di Atlantide*, 1961), art by Jim Jonson.

PAGE 4: Detail from a US one-sheet for *White Zombie* (1932).

PAGE 5: Detail from the US double bill one-sheet for *Beast of Blood* (1970) and *Curse of the Vampires* (aka *Whisper to the Wind*, 1966).

First Published in the United States of America, September 2016
Third Printing, October 2024

Gingko Press, Inc., 217 W. Richmond Ave, Suite B, Richmond, CA 94801, USA
www.gingkopress.com

ISBN: 978-1-58423-803-4

Printed in China

Editorial director: Will Steeds
Book design: Martin Stiff at Amazing 15. www.amazing15.com

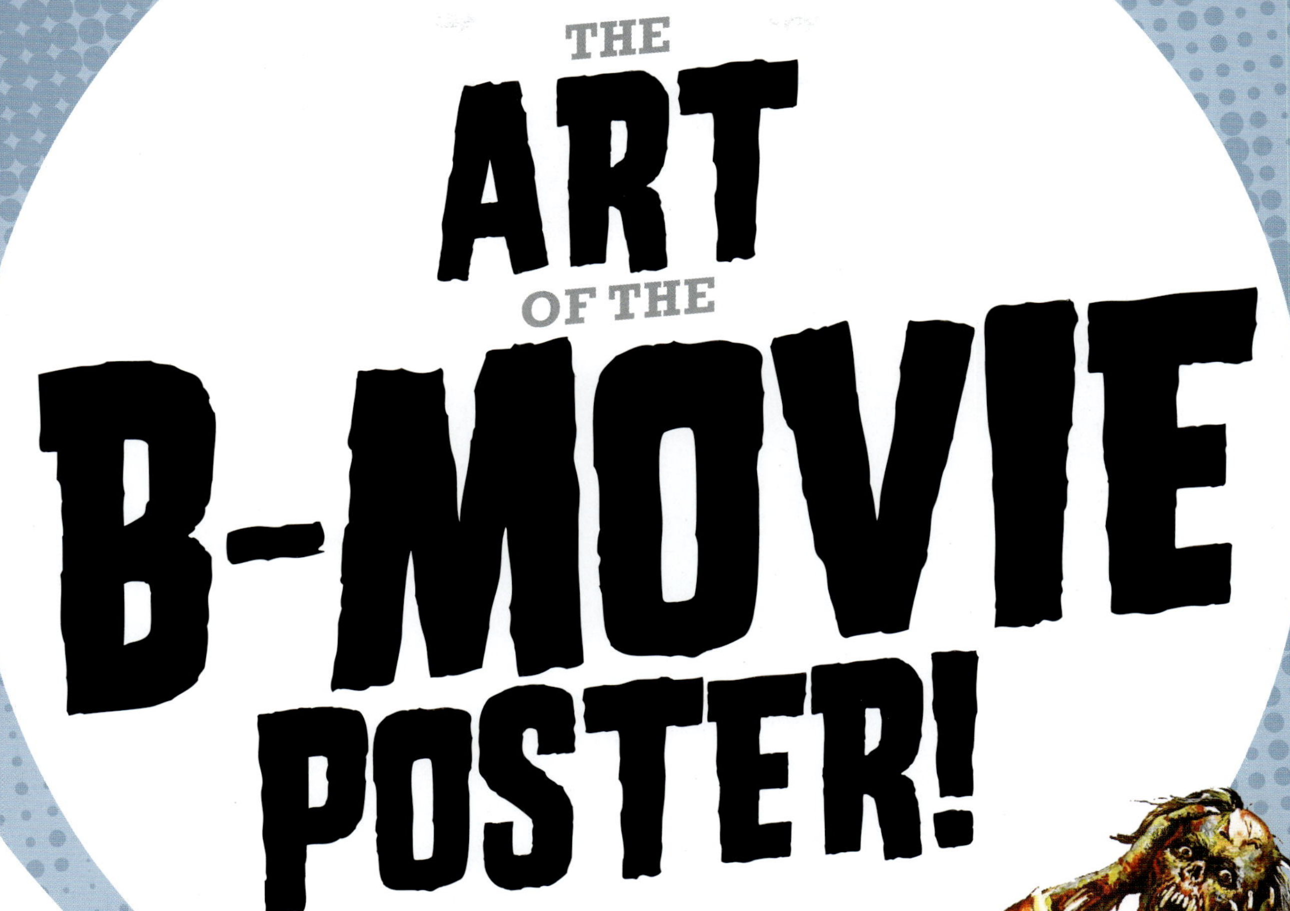

THE ART OF THE B-MOVIE POSTER!

Edited by **ADAM NEWELL**

Introduction by **PETE TOMBS**

With Contributions from
STEPHEN JONES
KIM NEWMAN
ERIC SCHAEFER
SIMON SHERIDAN
VERN

GINGKO PRESS

CONTENTS

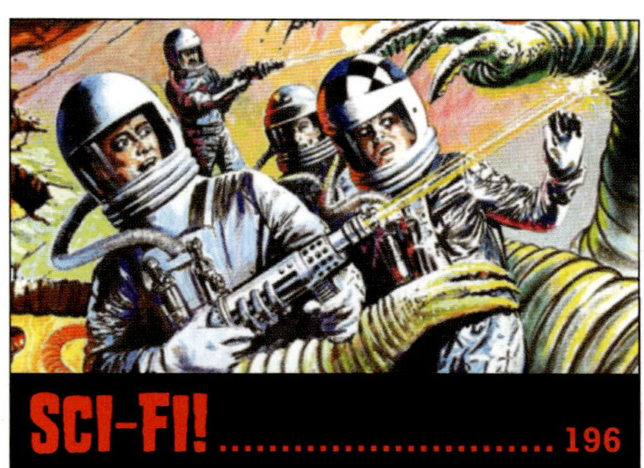

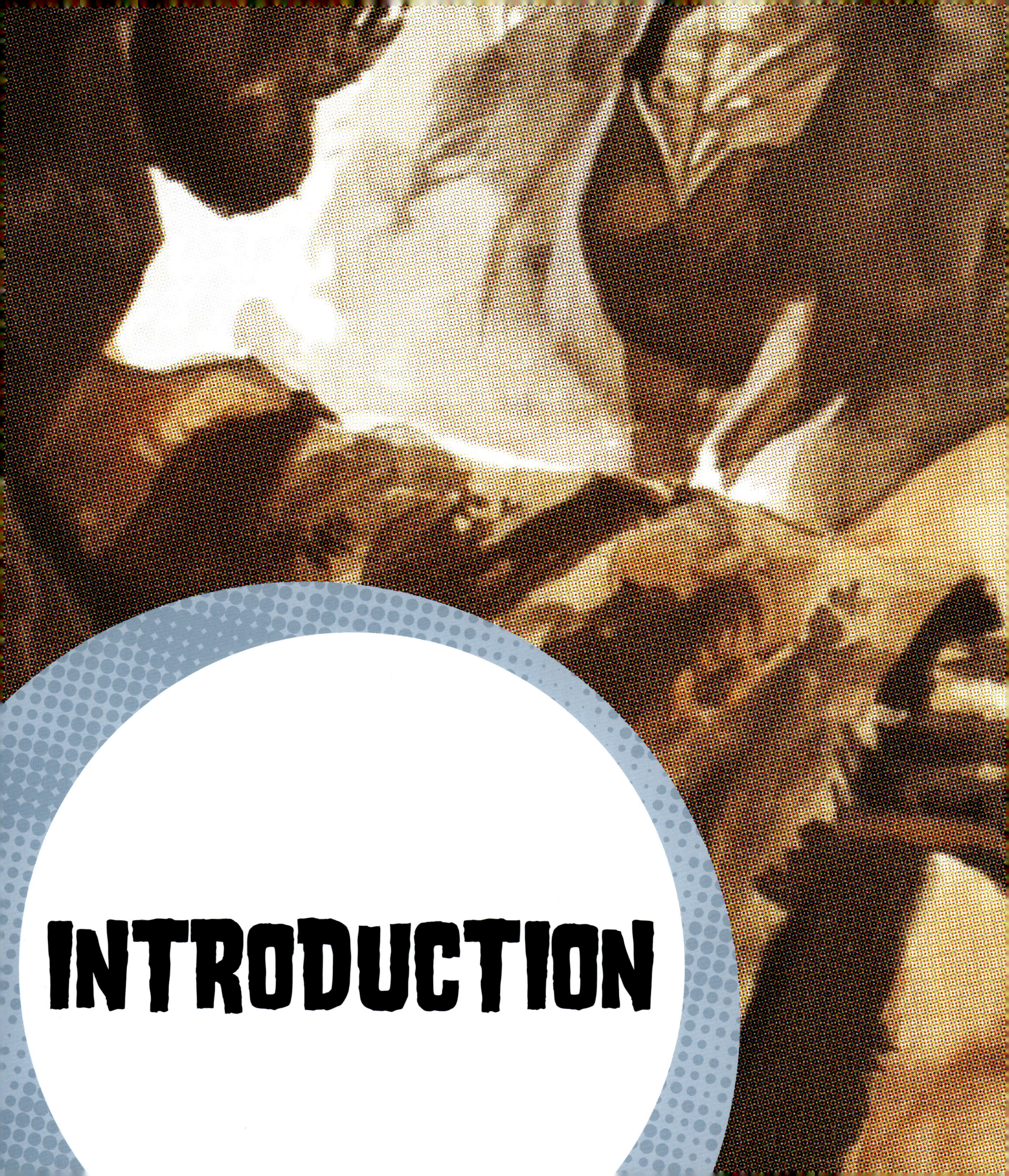

INTRODUCTION

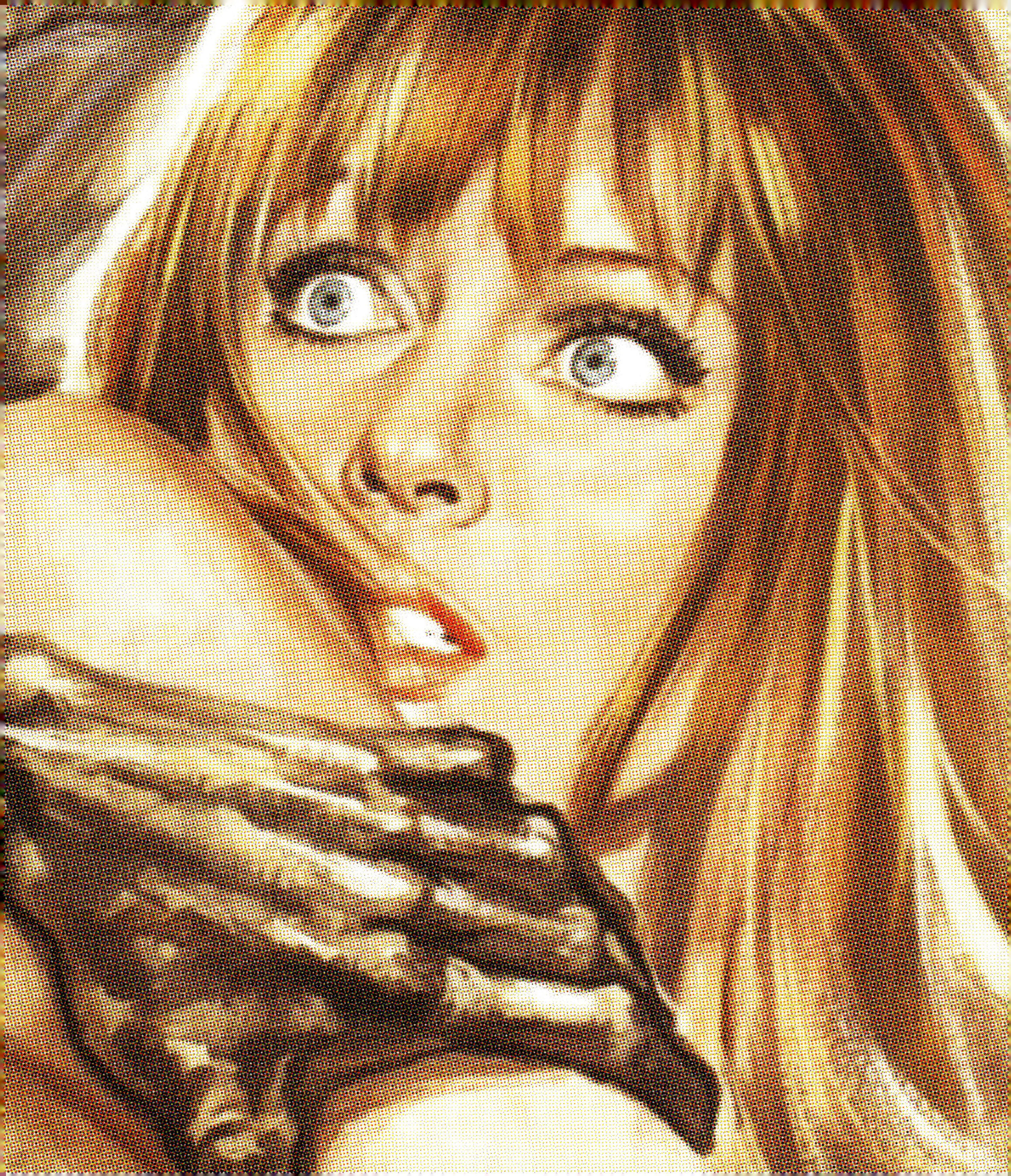

THE LURE OF THE LURID
By Pete Tombs

PREVIOUS SPREAD: Detail from the Italian *foglio* for *Tombs of the Blind Dead* (1971), art by Renato Casaro.

BELOW: Director León Klimovsky's Spanish sex-swap drama *Odio mi cuerpo* had a dubbed US release as *I Hate My Body* (1974), with stars Alexandra Bastedo and Eva León given the Anglicized names Alexandra Bass and Eve Leigh on the poster.

OPPOSITE: The action-packed poster for 1976's *King Kong* rip-off *A*P*E* promised that ten tons of animal fury would leap from the screen. Given that the movie's entire budget was reportedly only $23,000, it was bound to disappoint. A legal battle with the producers of the same year's official *King Kong* remake meant the poster had to carry the "Not to be confused with" disclaimer.

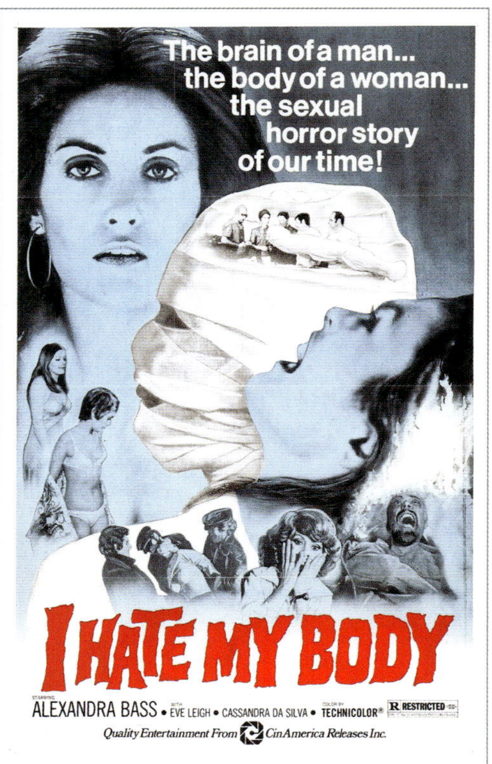

Exploitation is a dirty word. But not always. For fans of non-mainstream cinema, connoisseurs of the B-movie, it opens a Pandora's box of horror, sex-action-monsters-sex-thrills-chills-drugs . . . and more sex, with a couple of cannibals and maybe a giant ape or two dropped into the mix. It signals the lure of the lurid, an unmistakeable come-on to the jaded thrill-seeker looking to spice up a boring day. And, let's face it, if a movie doesn't contain at least some of the elements listed above, it's probably not going to be much of a show. As Sam Fuller said, in Jean-Luc Godard's *Pierrot le Fou* (1965), "A film is like a battleground. It's love, hate, action, violence, death. In one word: emotion."

These days, the tag "Exploitation" has a retro vibe. As so often happens over time, things once deemed taboo and infra dig become safely nostalgic, framed and hung on the wall or reprinted in glossy art books. With its original use, the exploitation movie poster induced a frisson of danger in the adventurous filmgoer. It meant that the story you were about to see would be exploiting not only your prurient interest but also some currently taboo or newsworthy topic. Something ripped from the day's headlines. Something that the public was interested in, even if they would rather not admit it in polite company. Something, therefore, that could be "exploited" to bring a certain type of viewer into the cinema.

Our vicarious enjoyment of thrills and spills and the desire of creative entities to exploit this for personal gain is not new. The artistic types among our ancient ancestors who produced the cave paintings were probably not averse to throwing in a particularly exciting bison hunt or a daringly skimpy loin cloth if it meant they got an extra bowl of stew that night round the camp fire. Even church paintings could be said to be "exploiting" something—in their case, the public's need for spiritual satisfaction, which would later be expressed via the full collection box. And art galleries—didn't they invent the "exit through the gift shop" strategy?

Ten Tons of Animal Fury Leaps from the Screen

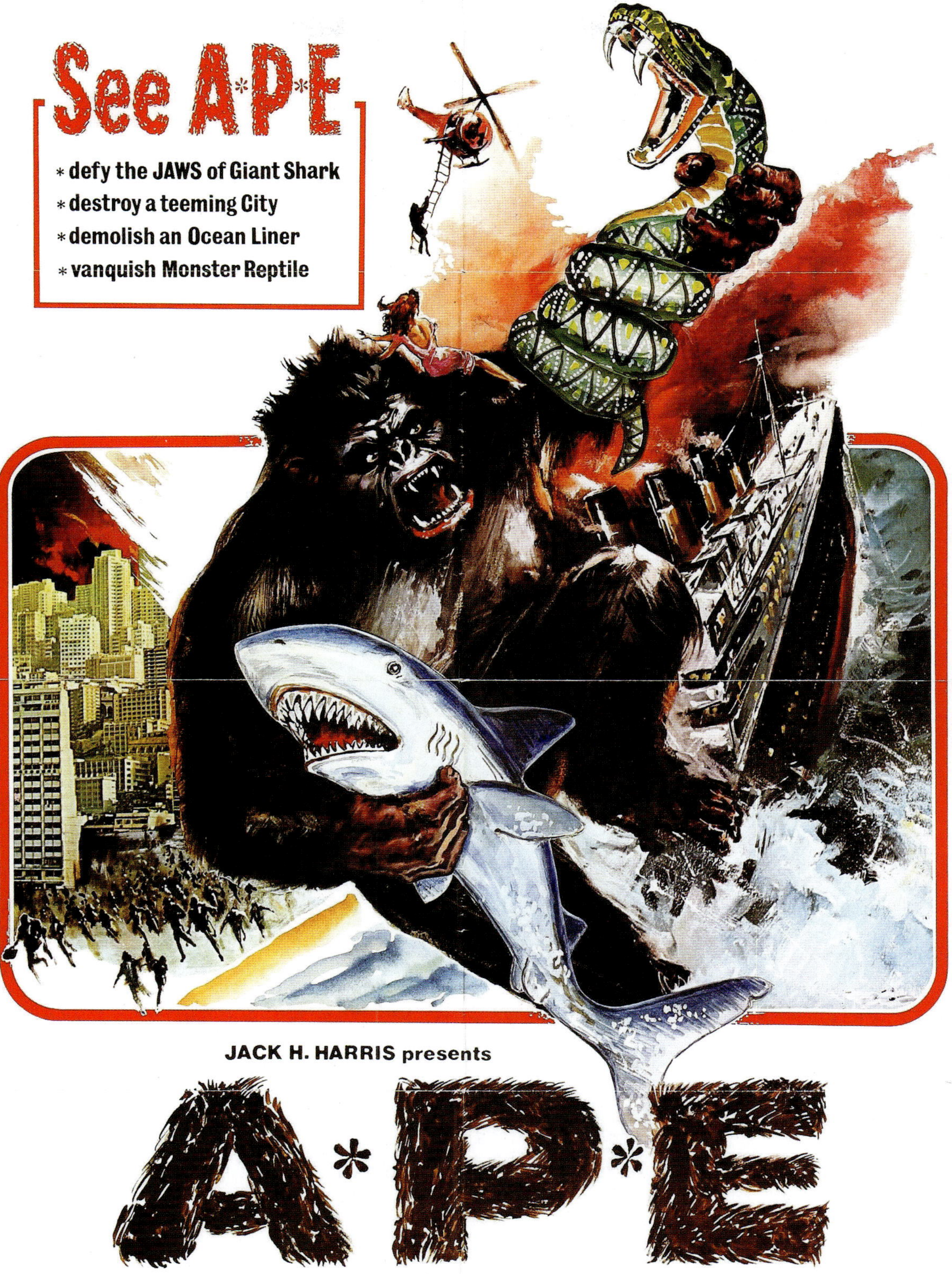

NOT TO BE CONFUSED WITH **KING KONG**

Starring ROD ARRANTS * JOANNA DE VARONA * ALEX NICOL * Directed by Paul Leder * Produced by K. M. Yeung and Paul Leder * LEE MING FILM CO.

PG PARENTAL GUIDANCE SUGGESTED   WIDESCREEN • COLOR   WORLDWIDE ENTERTAINMENT CORPORATION release

76/208

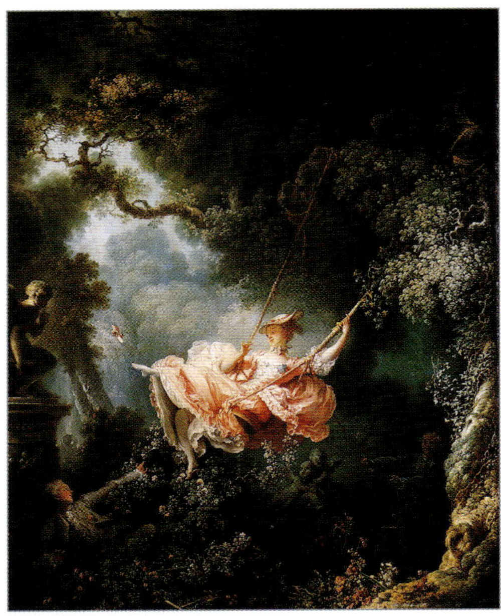

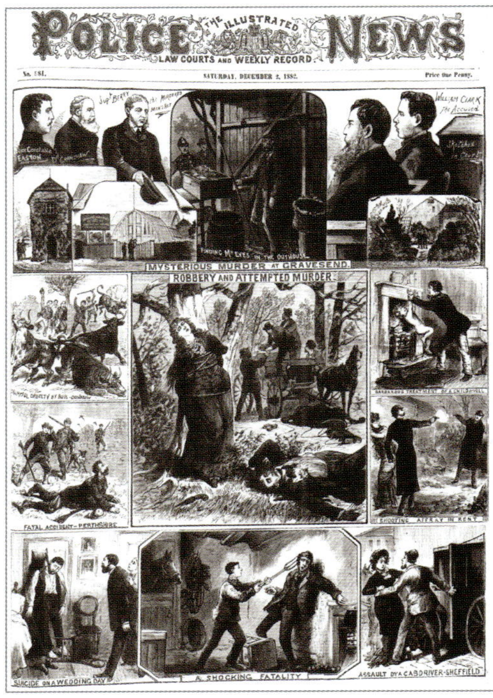

THE ILLUSTRATED POLICE NEWS
LAW COURTS AND WEEKLY RECORD.

SATURDAY, DECEMBER 2, 1882. Price One Penny.

TOP: *The Swing* (circa 1767) by Jean-Honoré Fragonard. This Rococo celebration of voyeurism was used as visual reference and inspiration by Disney animators during the production of their Rapunzel movie *Tangled*.

ABOVE: Nefarious activities galore, as presented by *The Illustrated Police News* for Saturday, December 2, 1882.

OPPOSITE: Though this re-release poster for *Teen Lust* (1979) bills him as "James Hall," the director is actually James Hong, who is better known as an actor—*Blade Runner* and *Big Trouble in Little China* are two of his more high-profile credits.

Commissioned art, outside its utilitarian or religious use, was for many centuries reserved for the elite—those with disposable income to spare. It was "owned" by the man (usually) who had paid for it. And so it was kept under lock and key, in private chambers, far from the curious gaze of the peasants whose labor had helped pay for it. Witness the fabulous eighteenth-century Fragonard painting *The Swing*, showing a rich suitor hiding in the bushes so he can gaze up the skirts of his favorite girl. It was titillation for the master's eyes only. Is it art? Or is it exploitation? Actually, it's a bit of both. The same can be said for a surprising number of the works contained in this present collection.

Sadly, movie posters were generally not signed, and some of the best ones in this book are from the prolific hand of "Anonymous." But that should not blind us to the fact that there is real wit, economy of means, and genuine inspiration in many of the works in the pages that follow. That's one of the reasons why they've lasted and still have impact today. That's what art should do—move, inspire, and entertain—and occasionally startle too, for that's all part of the plan. Remove the shock of the new and art becomes little more than wallpaper—and one thing that film posters must never do is fade into the background. Like the best art, the best exploitation movie posters should make a statement. It's why we stop to look; it's what impels us to make sense of what we are seeing. In the case of the movie poster, the ultimate act of making sense of it is to buy a ticket and go see the film.

To pass from Fragonard to the poster for the 1979 movie *Teen Lust* might seem something of a leap. But think on: the rich had art—genuine paintings—on their walls, the poor had reproductions. And of course, in this instance, both painting and poster celebrate the joys of voyeurism. And cinema *is* voyeurism.

When cheap paper and mass-printing techniques became affordable, so did the use of art and illustration to lure in the paying punters. Look at the ballad sheets, the penny dreadfuls, *The Illustrated Police News* of days gone by. And note there the use of the word "illustrated." For that was what the public wanted—eye candy. Even if they couldn't read the accompanying text, they could pore over the pictures and get a vicarious thrill from the nefarious activities being displayed.

The large-sized poster most commonly used to sell films is a direct descendent of the theatrical posters created in the nineteenth century to promote live shows, circus performances, and burlesque acts. In their earliest incarnations (the *Belle Époque* posters of 1860s France, perfected by Jules Chéret), these were elaborate artistic creations that made full use of the latest techniques of color lithography. Advertising designed for films of the silent era followed suit and early twentieth-century movie posters were largely painterly affairs, well–balanced compositions, with tasteful typography: the title, maybe a strap line, the names of the stars, and a synopsis of the plot.

The desire to sell and the need to exploit was still there, although only rarely expressed in the strong visual terms that became commonplace in the following decades. In the late 1920s, with the arrival of sound pictures, a moral crusade inspired by religious leaders against the alleged turpitude of Hollywood folk led to the introduction in 1930 of the Motion Picture Production Code. This attempt to tame the mainstream cinema and ban a list of activities and storylines in fact created a counter reaction. Sin and skin became fashionable subjects for

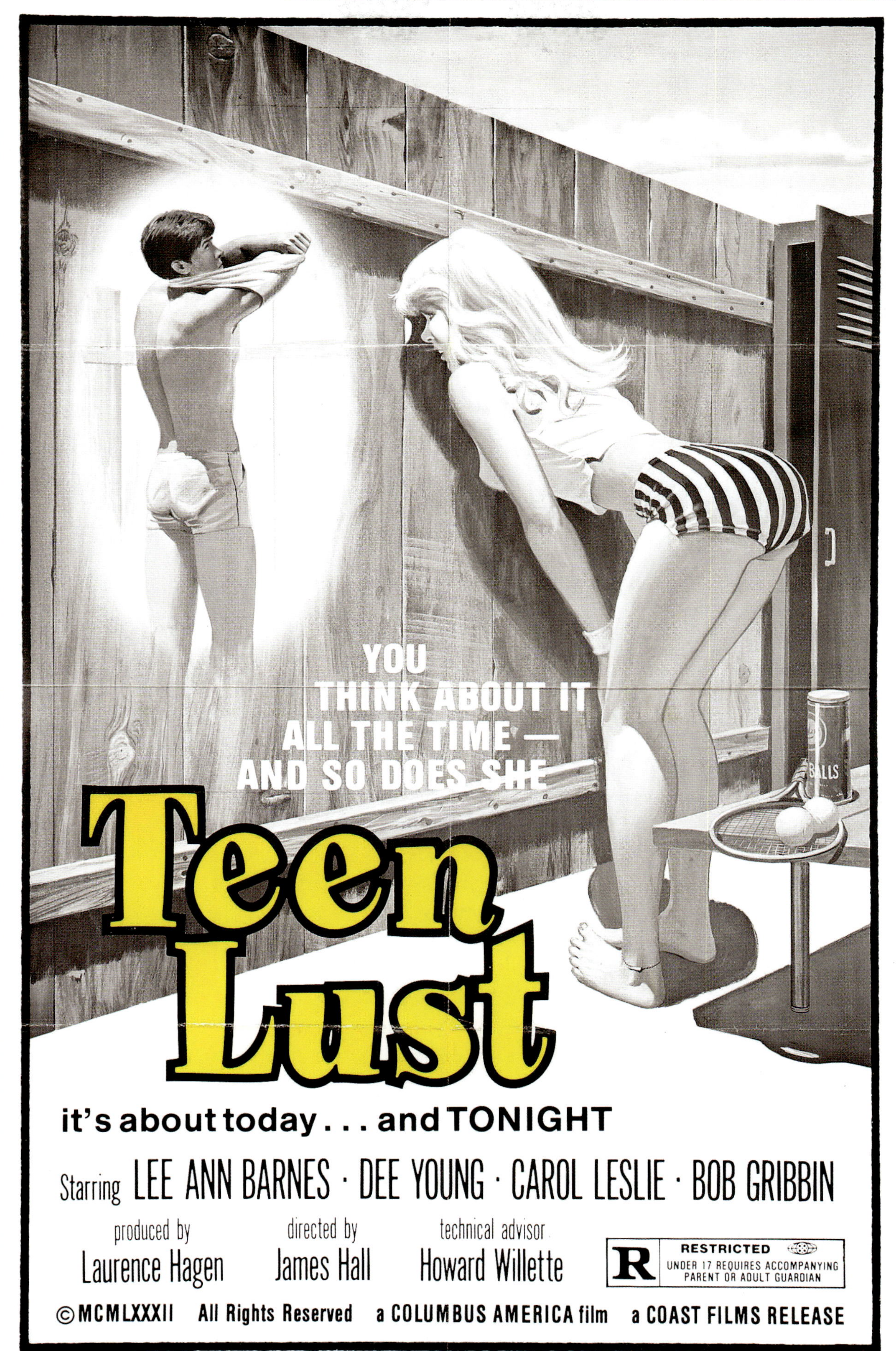

YOU
THINK ABOUT IT
ALL THE TIME —
AND SO DOES SHE
Teen
Lust
it's about today . . . and TONIGHT
Starring LEE ANN BARNES · DEE YOUNG · CAROL LESLIE · BOB GRIBBIN
produced by
Laurence Hagen
directed by
James Hall
technical advisor
Howard Willette
R
RESTRICTED
UNDER 17 REQUIRES ACCOMPANYING PARENT OR ADULT GUARDIAN
©MCMLXXXII All Rights Reserved a COLUMBUS AMERICA film a COAST FILMS RELEASE
BALLS

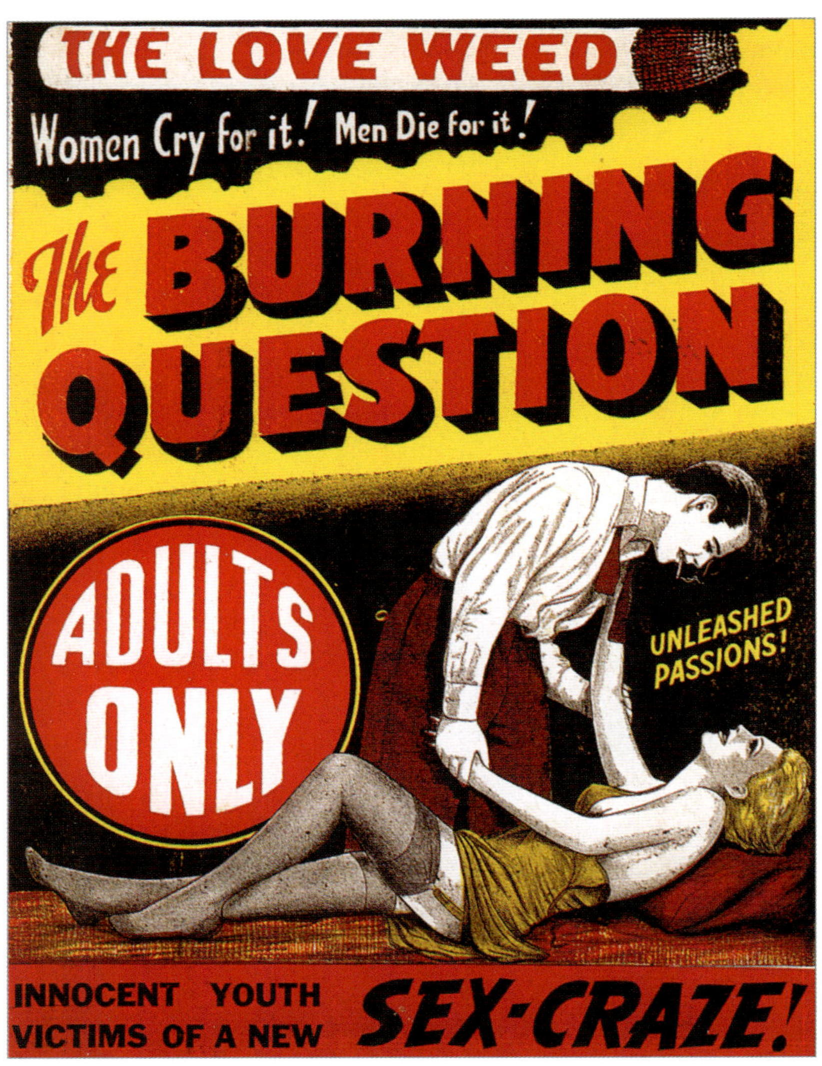

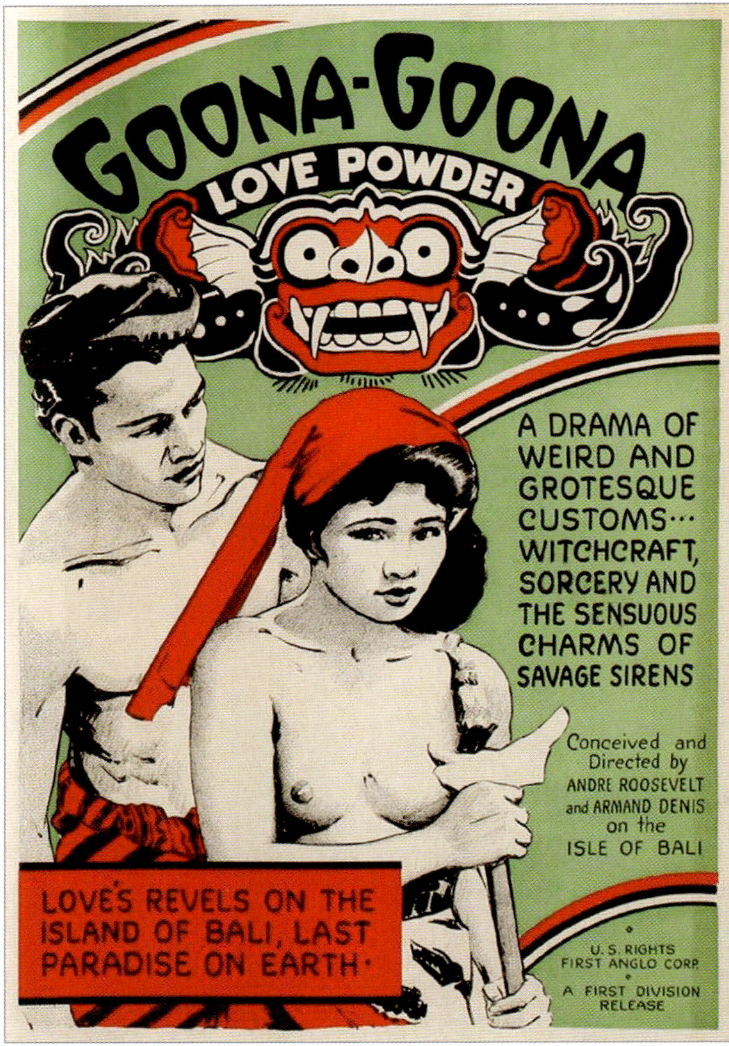

ABOVE LEFT: *Reefer Madness,* originally produced in 1936, was released under several titles over its many years on the exploitation circuit, including *The Burning Question, Doped Youth,* and *Tell Your Children.*

ABOVE RIGHT: While *Goona-Goona: An Authentic Melodrama of the Isle of Bali* (1932) didn't technically claim to be a documentary, "goona-goona" became a catch-all term for the subgenre of travelogues and purported documentaries which usually focused on bare-breasted "savages" and weird rituals.

exploitation, in particular for those lower budget B-movies destined for the bottom half of the bill. It was the time of the Great Depression and audiences wanted to be entertained. Crime, violence, sex, horror, drugs, juvenile delinquency, jungle love—all were grist to the mill of cinematic exploitation, with posters to match. The moral guardians were swamped, left like King Canute trying to hold back a tidal wave of filth. As the actual content of the films was restricted by law and the moral codes of the time, it was largely down to the poster artists to draw in audiences seeking the forbidden pleasures that the films promised, but were mostly unable to deliver.

Here began that constant complaint that the worst movies often had the best posters. A natural fallout from the fact that while big films had a star cast to put bums on seats, with the cheaper exploitation releases the bums were largely on screen (no pun intended).

In 1934, Joseph Breen was appointed head of the new Production Code Administration, which required all films to receive a certificate of approval before they could be released. The rigorous enforcement of this rule by the moralistic Mr. Breen had the studios in a headlock that lasted decades. This unwittingly created a burgeoning commercial underground of exploitation film pioneers who worked outside the system, screening their movies in road shows, burlesque houses, and, if all else failed, in tents on the outskirts of town. The

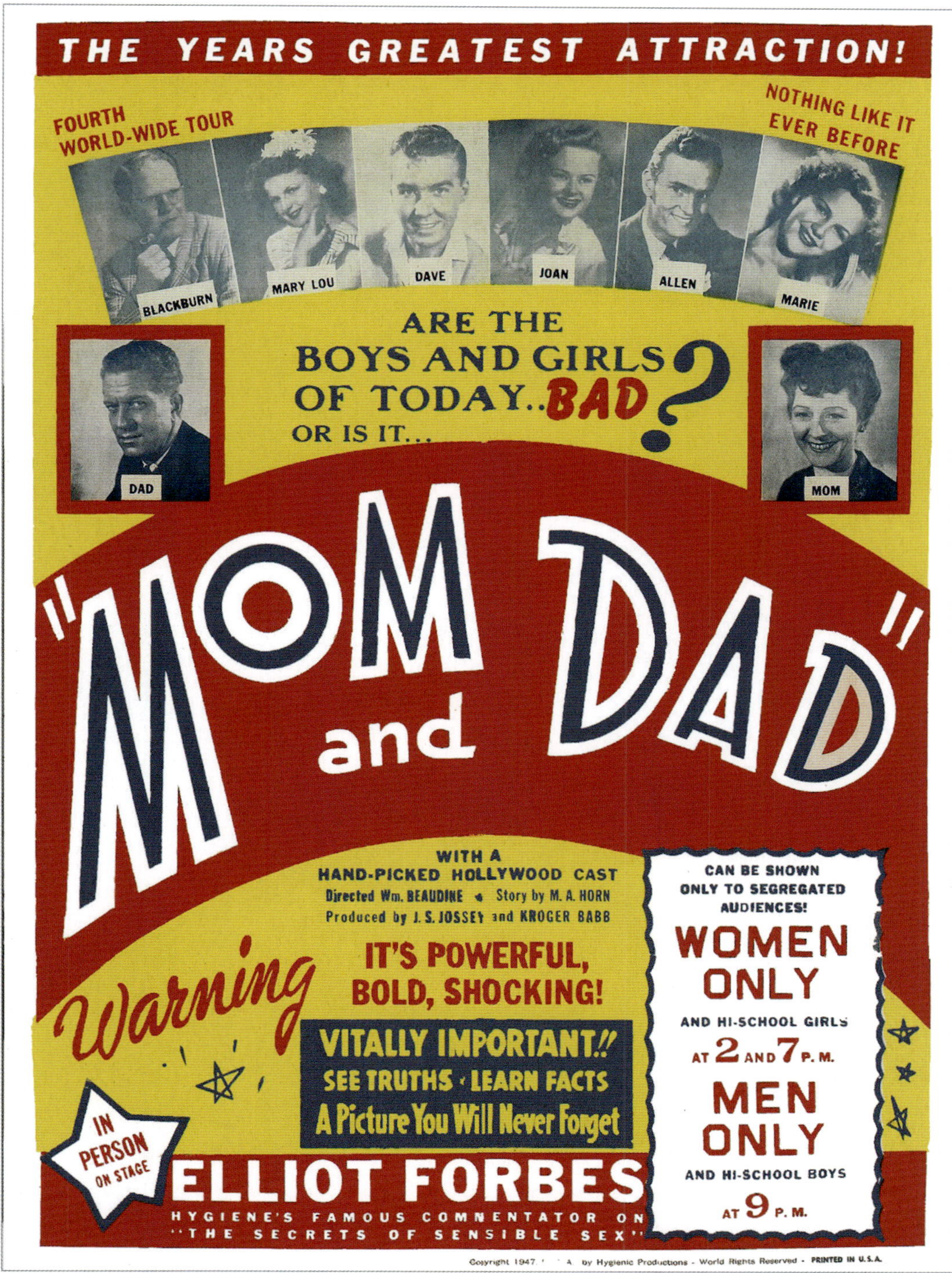

"Grindhouse" circuit was born and these pioneers became known as the "Forty Thieves." To stay just inside the law, their films would often claim an educational or documentary aspect, as seen in "anti-drug" films such as *Reefer Madness* (1936) or in "goona-goona" movies—fake documentaries filled with semi-nude "natives" performing weird rituals.

This was exploitation cinema at its commercial height, with lurid posters lining the punters up outside the movie houses, all of them eager to part with their ten cents for a promised evening of vicarious pleasures. The legendary Howard W. "Kroger" Babb, a mainstay of this commercial underground, promoted *Mom and Dad*, a supposed sex-education film, so successfully that it became the third highest-grossing movie of the 1940s.

ABOVE: *Mom and Dad* was originally released in 1945, but remained a box-office draw for years. This poster is for its "Fourth World-wide Tour," and mentions the sex-segregated screenings that were part of its presentation. Also promised is an "in person" lecture by "hygiene's famous commentator" Elliot Forbes. There was no such person. At any one time, multiple "Elliot Forbes" would be appearing simultaneously around the country—all played by actors hired by canny promoter Kroger Babb.

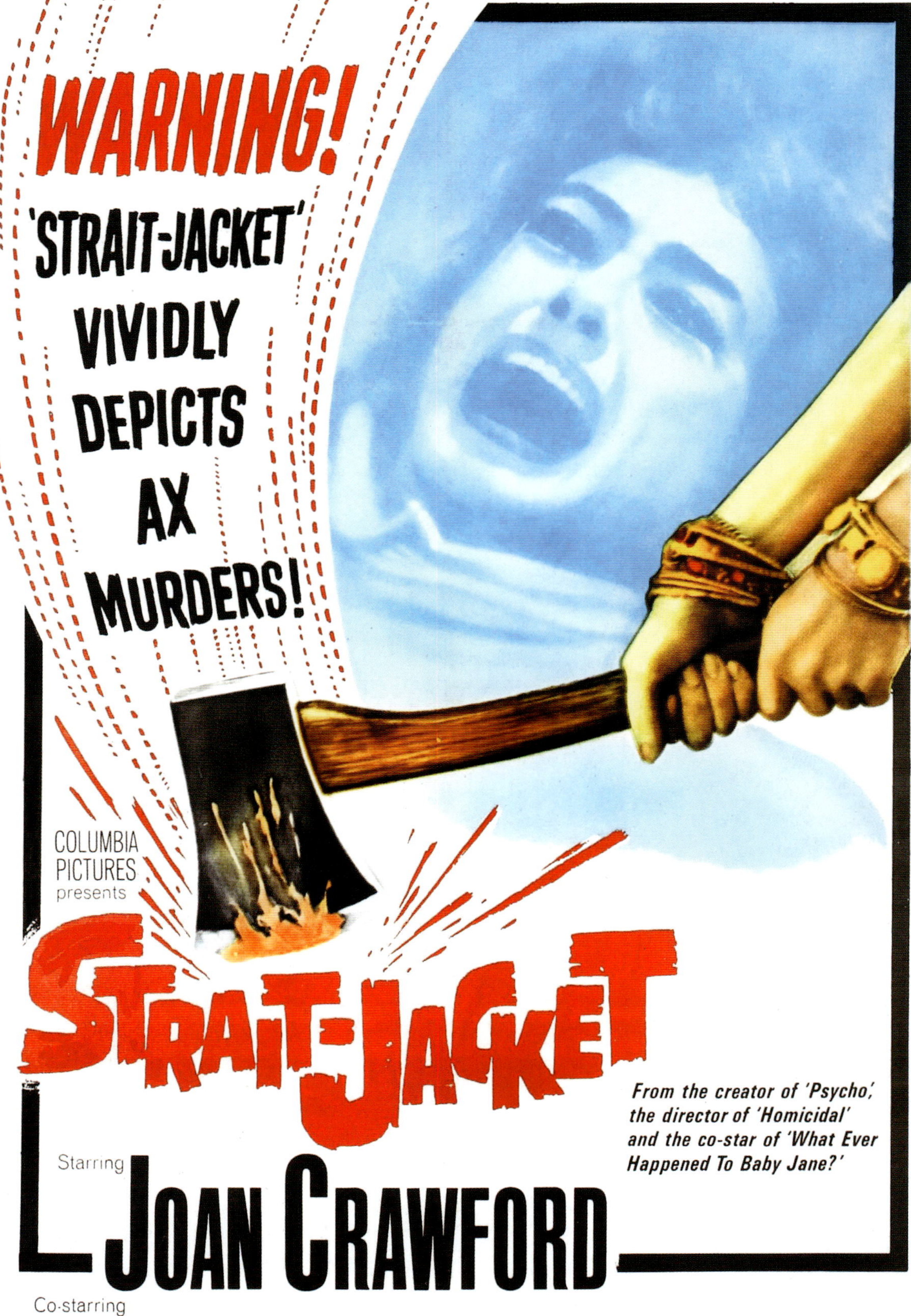
WARNING!
'STRAIT-JACKET'
VIVIDLY
DEPICTS
AX
MURDERS!
COLUMBIA
PICTURES
presents
STRAIT-JACKET
From the creator of 'Psycho,'
the director of 'Homicidal'
and the co-star of 'What Ever
Happened To Baby Jane?'
Starring
JOAN CRAWFORD
Co-starring
DIANE BAKER · LEIF ERICKSON · HOWARD ST. JOHN
with JOHN ANTHONY HAYES · ROCHELLE HUDSON · Written by ROBERT BLOCH · Produced and Directed by WILLIAM CASTLE A WILLIAM CASTLE PRODUCTION

As a passing aside, maybe we need to spell out the difference between an exploitation film and one that explores a social problem that might reasonably concern any right-minded citizen. *The Snake Pit* (1948) was a star-cast film dealing with the serious subject of mental illness. Olivia de Havilland, on the tasteful poster, looks perplexed and in need of enlightened care. *Strait-Jacket* (1964) is the exploitation version, a film produced by one of the masters of cinematic hucksterism—William Castle. No perplexity on the poster for this movie, as a screaming Joan Crawford (at the tail end of her career) wields a blood-splattered axe. The serious film leaves us feeling better about ourselves and optimistic about society. The exploitation film, more often than not, would leave us feeling like we needed a cold shower.

By the 1950s the landscape had changed. The mainstream had caught up. The rigorous enforcement of the Code had begun to falter following the retirement of Joseph Breen in 1954. Then came various legal challenges, citing constitutional guarantees of freedom of speech, which opened the way for more nudity and sexual expression on screen. Imported films from Europe, armed with the double threat of being both risqué and artistic, pushed censorship barriers and were shown in the same circuit as the 1940s exploiters. Even Ingmar Bergman, that doyen of the art house, was drawn into the maelstrom when Kroger Babb re-edited Bergman's 1953 *Summer with Monika* to highlight the sex and nudity, re-titled it *Monika, the Story of a Bad Girl*, then re-released it in the US in 1955. His promo copy included the strap line: "The Devil Controls Her by Radar!"

The 1950s was a time of affluence and new-found freedoms, and not just in the US. In the shadow of the bomb and to a soundtrack of rock 'n' roll and Martin Denny-style exotica, the citizens of the free world wanted to have fun and explore the far side. The movies fed off this new energy with independent production houses popping up to meet the demand. This period, from the early 1950s up to the late 1970s, was a golden age for exploitation movies and movie posters. As this book lovingly illustrates, there was not a genre or subgenre that wasn't out there being promoted by wonderfully wilful, gaudy, and often totally shameless art. The influences of comic book covers and pulp paperbacks (and sometimes the same artists) were all over these masterpieces of the hard sell. Even if the films have been lost or forgotten, the posters linger on with an allure that is still hard to resist. As Alan Adler wrote, "These posters are ideals, dreams of how great their movies could be."

If the viewer felt cheated by the film, it was only *after* they had paid for their ticket. Filled with disappointment as they were, they would still come back the next week to go through it all again with a new double bill. Eternal optimists, that's what we moviegoers are. And it's largely down to the hypnotic lure of the images created by poster designers that we agree to forgo our cynicism yet again and take that plunge into the all-enveloping anonymity of the dark room, where we discover whether that "beast" really has a million eyes (it doesn't!), or whether Chesty Morgan's breasts really are that big (they were!).

Today, with marketing departments, stylists, media specialists, and trend analysts all playing their part, little is left to chance and inspiration is perhaps the last thing to squeeze through the cracks of a very narrow brief. The majority of post-1980 movie posters tend to be based around photographic images—of

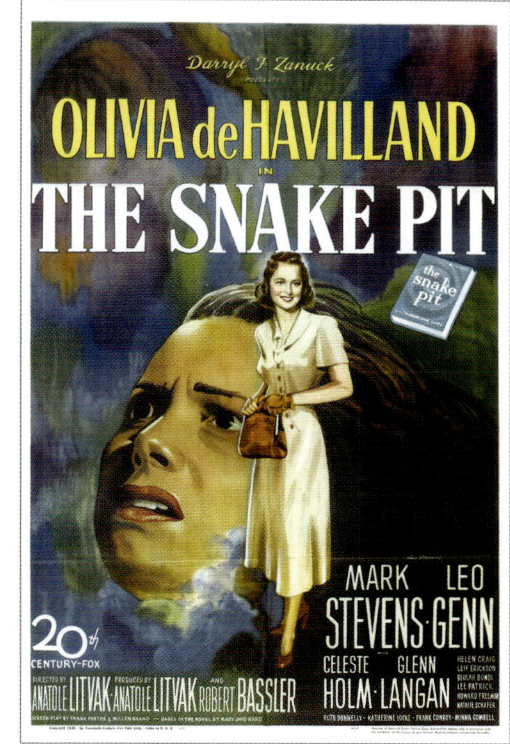

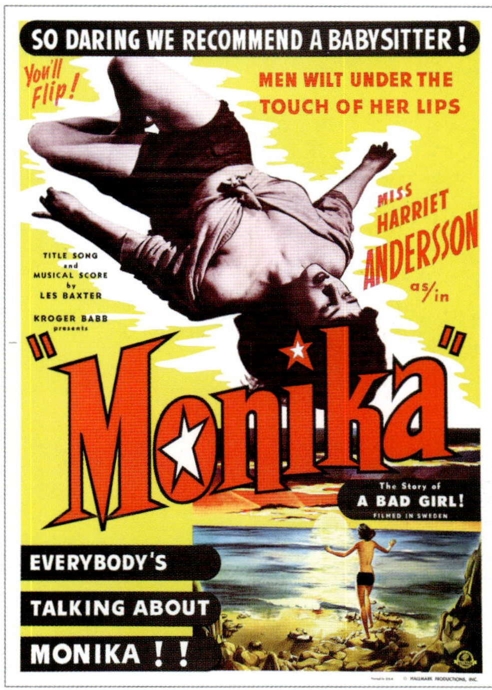

OPPOSITE: The blood-spattered one-sheet for the unashamedly exploitative *Strait-Jacket* (1964).

TOP: The somewhat more tasteful poster for *Strait-Jacket*'s major studio drama forebear, *The Snake Pit* (1948).

ABOVE: "You'll flip!" promises the poster for *Monika, the Story of a Bad Girl* (1955), the re-edited exploitation release of Ingmar Bergman's *Summer with Monika* (1953).

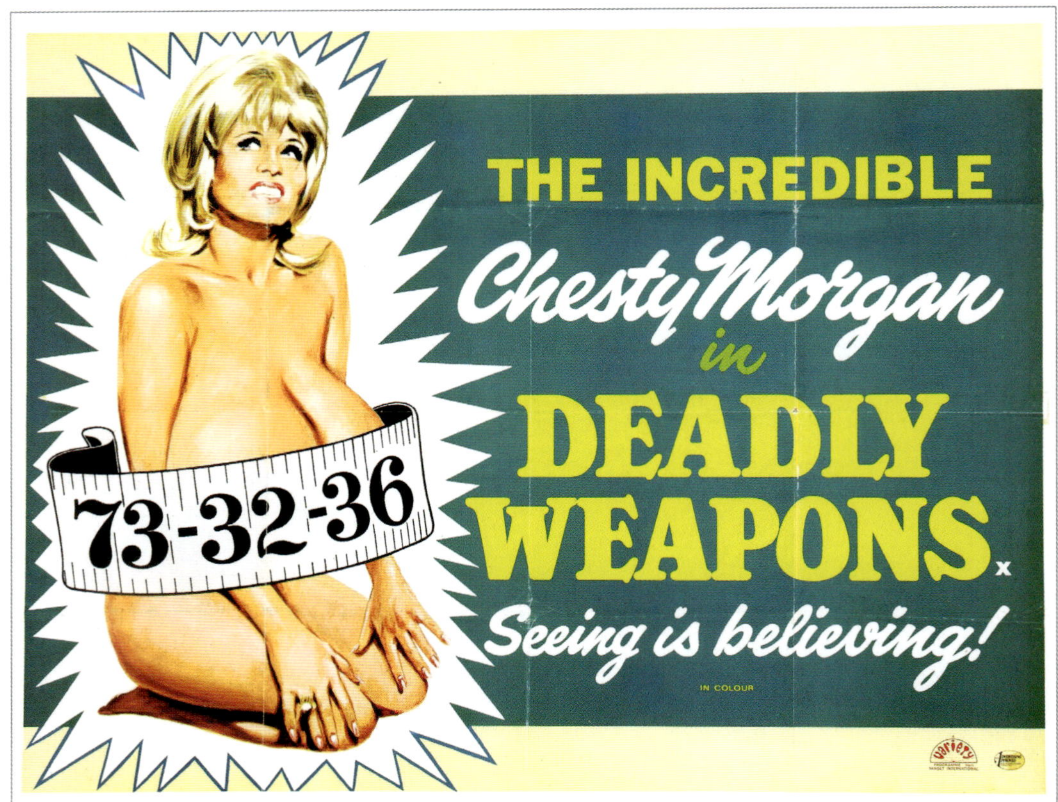

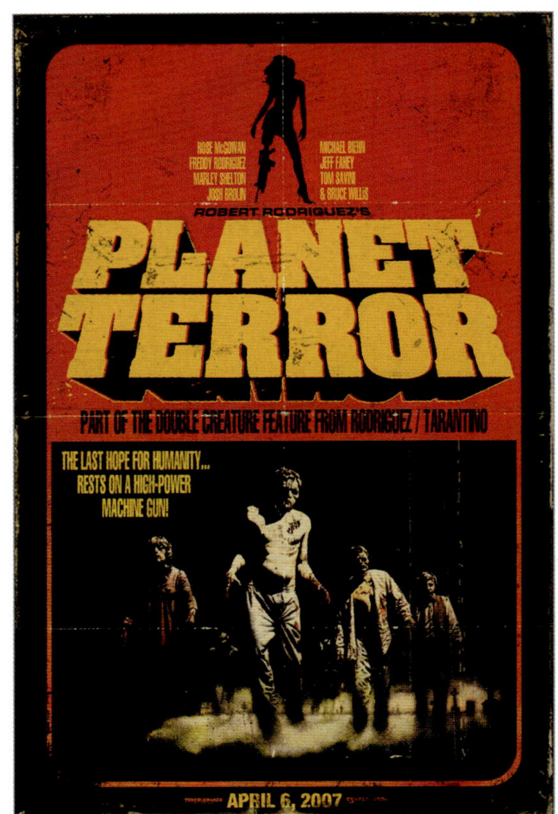

the star cast and maybe a key location. Illustrated posters featuring originally created artwork are rare now, and often produced to have a deliberately retro feel, as in the teaser poster for *Planet Terror* (2007), recalling the glory days of the double bill and the B-movie.

One of the factors behind the rise of movie poster collecting is the nostalgia market developed to service the affluent baby boomers of the 1960s. As they came of age and accumulated surplus income, they began to spend some of it on the things they remembered from their reckless youth. And what better than a garish poster of that first-date drive-in film where you met the girl who is now your wife? If it was an outrageous example of 1950s cheesecake, then so much the better—and if your wife didn't want it in the house, well, there was always the man cave in the basement. What den could be complete without a bunch of lurid one-sheets for your buddies to drool over while they watched the game and schlurped cold beer on a Saturday night?

The huge gulf between thought and expression that is so often the sad lot of low-budget moviemakers is poignantly expressed in poster form with the micro-budget, non "epic" from 1974 known variously as *The Beauties and the Beast*, *Desperately Seeking Yeti*, and *The Beast and the Vixens*. There's something almost heroic in the way the anonymous artist created a mind-boggling image to sell (oversell?) this late-era nudie cutie that endlessly replays, over a library music score, the "Me Tarzan, you Jane!" gambit that was probably never even uttered in the first place.

Perhaps the best possible comment would be the one actually submitted by a satisfied Amazon.com customer: "EVERY GOOD MOVIE. I WOULD LIKE IT A LITTLE BITE SCAREY AND MORE NUDE FEMALE AND SEX."

But he still gave it four out of five stars, folks . . . Maybe he never got beyond the poster. Now *That's* Exploitation! ●

ABOVE LEFT: The poster for *Deadly Weapons* (1974) highlights its star's vital statistics—they really were that big, and all natural to boot.

ABOVE RIGHT: A deliberately retro teaser poster for Robert Rodriguez's grindhouse tribute, *Planet Terror* (2007).

OPPOSITE: The one-sheet for *The Beast and the Vixens* (1974) sells its product hard, with no less than five taglines, including, "The unbelievable erotic adventure!" One IMDB.com reviewer did find it unbelievable, but not in a good way, remarking that, "The creature looks more like a guy wearing a black bathroom rug and false teeth."

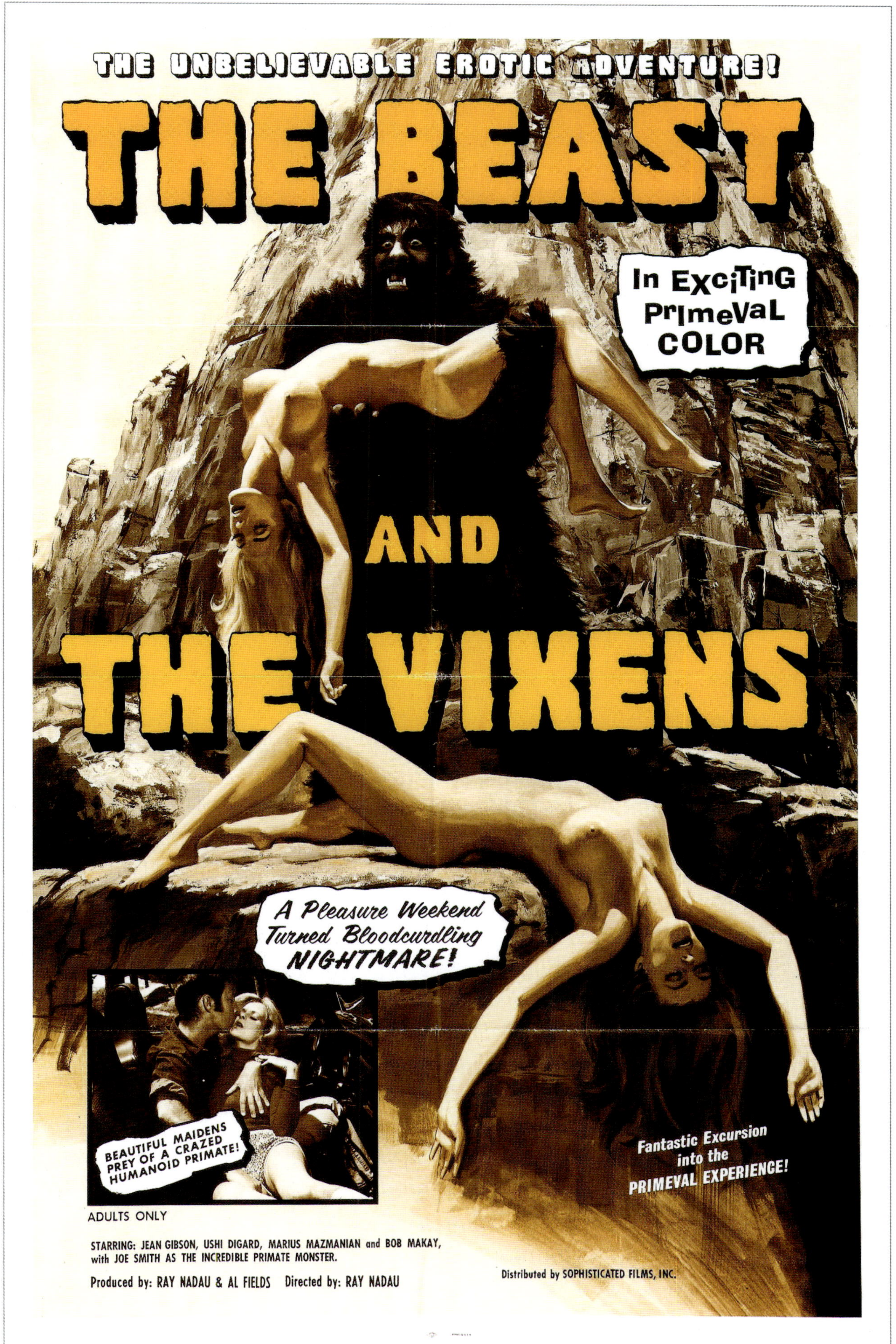
THE UNBELIEVABLE EROTIC ADVENTURE!
THE BEAST
In EXCITING PRIMEVAL COLOR
AND
THE VIXENS
A Pleasure Weekend Turned Bloodcurdling NIGHTMARE!
BEAUTIFUL MAIDENS PREY OF A CRAZED HUMANOID PRIMATE!
Fantastic Excursion into the PRIMEVAL EXPERIENCE!
ADULTS ONLY
STARRING: JEAN GIBSON, USHI DIGARD, MARIUS MAZMANIAN and BOB MAKAY, with JOE SMITH AS THE INCREDIBLE PRIMATE MONSTER.
Produced by: RAY NADAU & AL FIELDS Directed by: RAY NADAU
Distributed by SOPHISTICATED FILMS, INC.

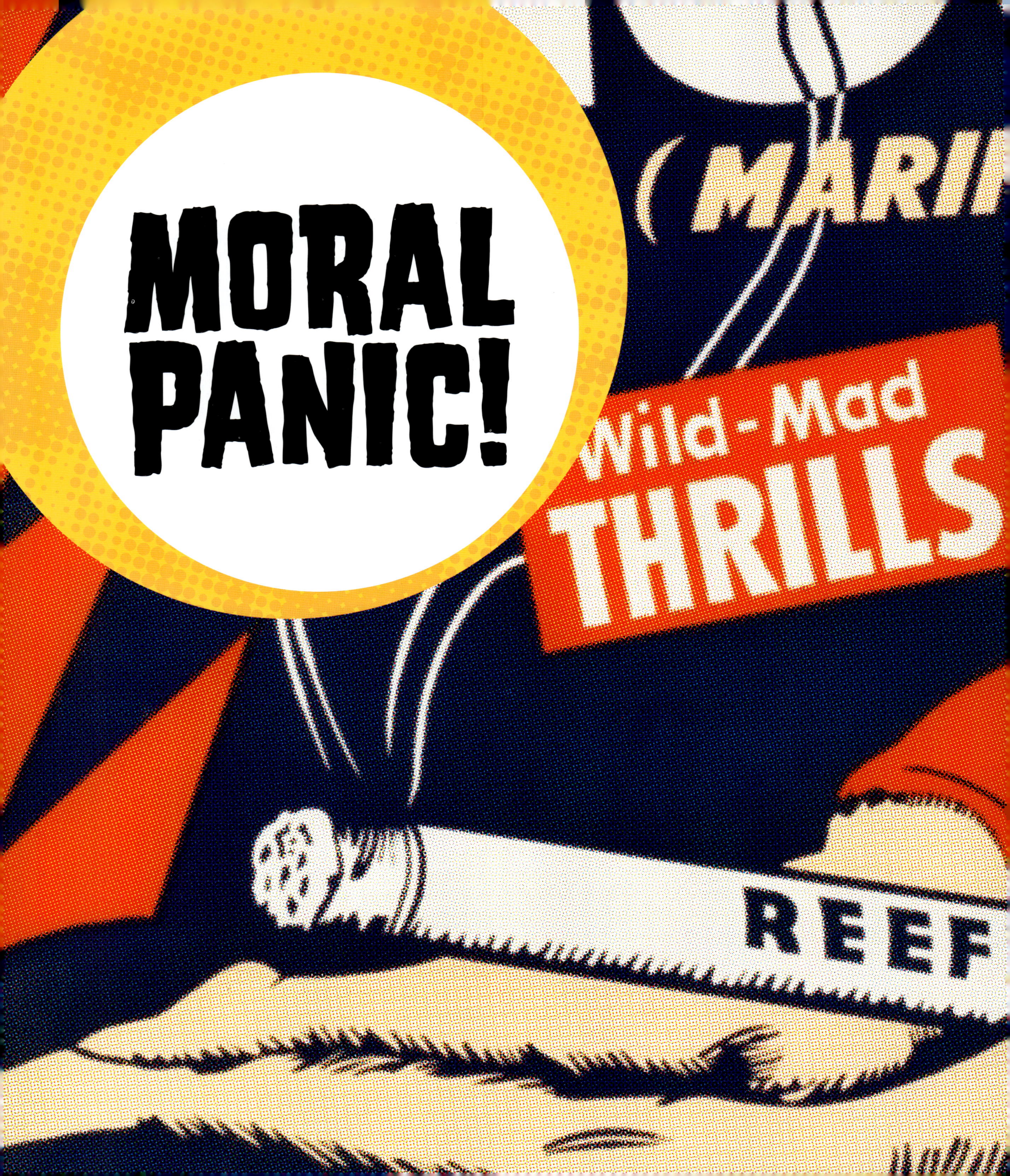
MORAL PANIC!
(MARI
Wild-Mad
THRILLS
REEF

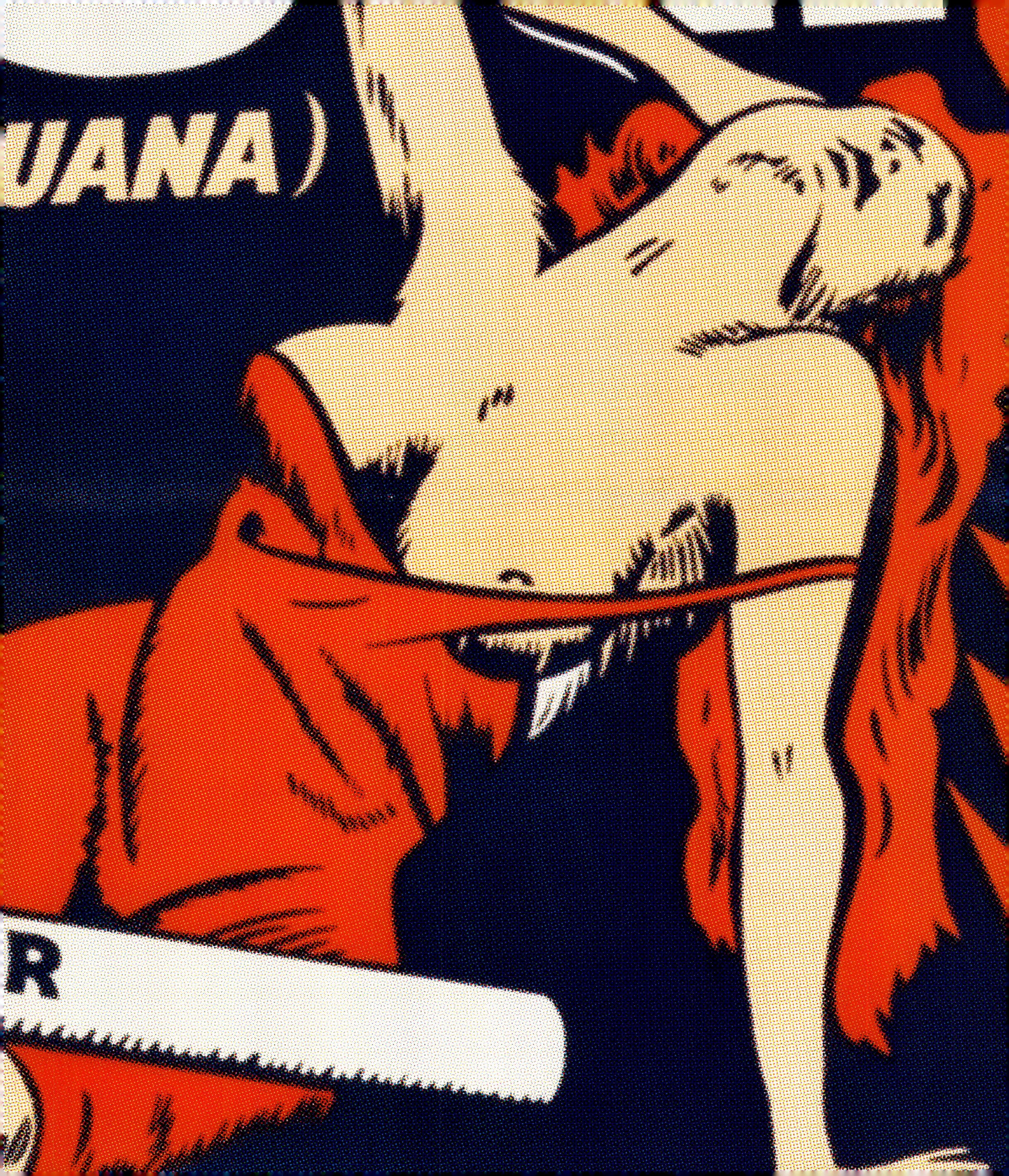
UANA)
R

Eric Schaefer on

SKID ROW and SOCK IT TO ME BABY

Exploitation movies emerged in the years around World War I. As concern mounted about the risks of venereal disease that faced the United States expeditionary forces in Europe, several films were produced by independent companies and the government to keep the troops "Fit to Fight," as the title of a 1919 film counseled.

When the movies were disseminated to the general public, the sordid stories and graphic images of the damage caused by syphilis and gonorrhea led to a backlash, quickly driving them out of the mainstream. Exploitation films, as they came to be known, flourished on the fringes of the movie business for the next four decades, taking on subjects forbidden by state censors and the Production Code: sex hygiene, drug use, prostitution, nudity, and a range of other vices. If there was a moral panic to be mined, a hysteria to be hyped, the low-rent makers of exploitation movies were there to dig deep and sell hard—stressing all the while that they were providing education to a public starved for the unvarnished truth about taboo topics. The movies were advertised and shown for "adults only," differentiating them from the family friendly fare of the Hollywood studios.

The term "exploitation film" originally referred to movies without recognizable stars that had to be exploited in ways beyond the usual posters and trailers to attract audiences. Hence, ballyhoo and sensationalism were at the core of advertising strategy for any exploitation film, something always reflected in posters. *Skid Row* is a good case in point. The movie was originally called *Confessions of a Vice Baron* and released by Willis Kent around 1942. The film is almost entirely made up of clips from Kent's prior threadbare productions including *The Pace That Kills* (1935), *Race Suicide* (1937), *Smashing the Vice Trust* (1937), *The Wages of Sin* (1938), and *Mad Youth* (1939). Willy Castello, who had appeared in most of those earlier efforts, plays Lucky Lombardi, the titular vice baron, who recounts his sordid career for the newspapers while awaiting execution on death row. Explaining that he frequently changed his name and appearance, clips from the older movies were presented as a series of flashbacks. These included some of the choice bits from the older movies such as a sideshow hoochie-coochie dance, scenes in a brothel, and a nude woman awaiting a medical exam.

PREVIOUS SPREAD: Detail from the poster for *Assassin of Youth* (1937).

BELOW: The more restrained one-sheet for *Skid Row's* original release, as *Confessions of a Vice Baron*.

OPPOSITE: Bold primary colors, ballyhoo, and provocative photos on Mack Enterprises' *Skid Row* poster.

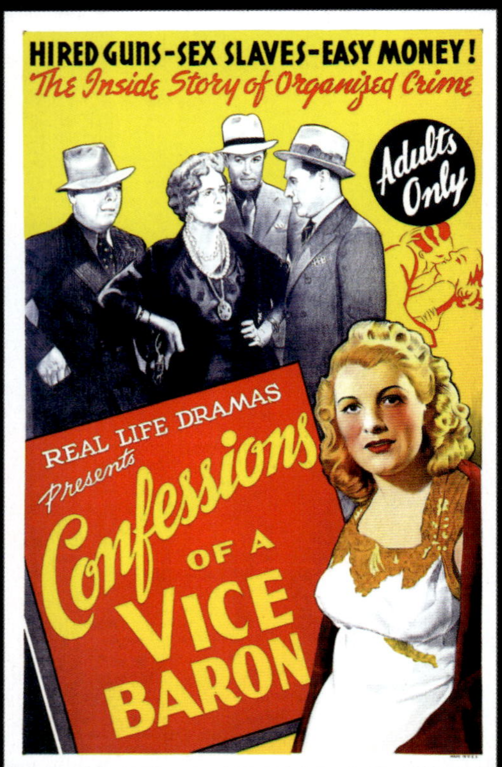

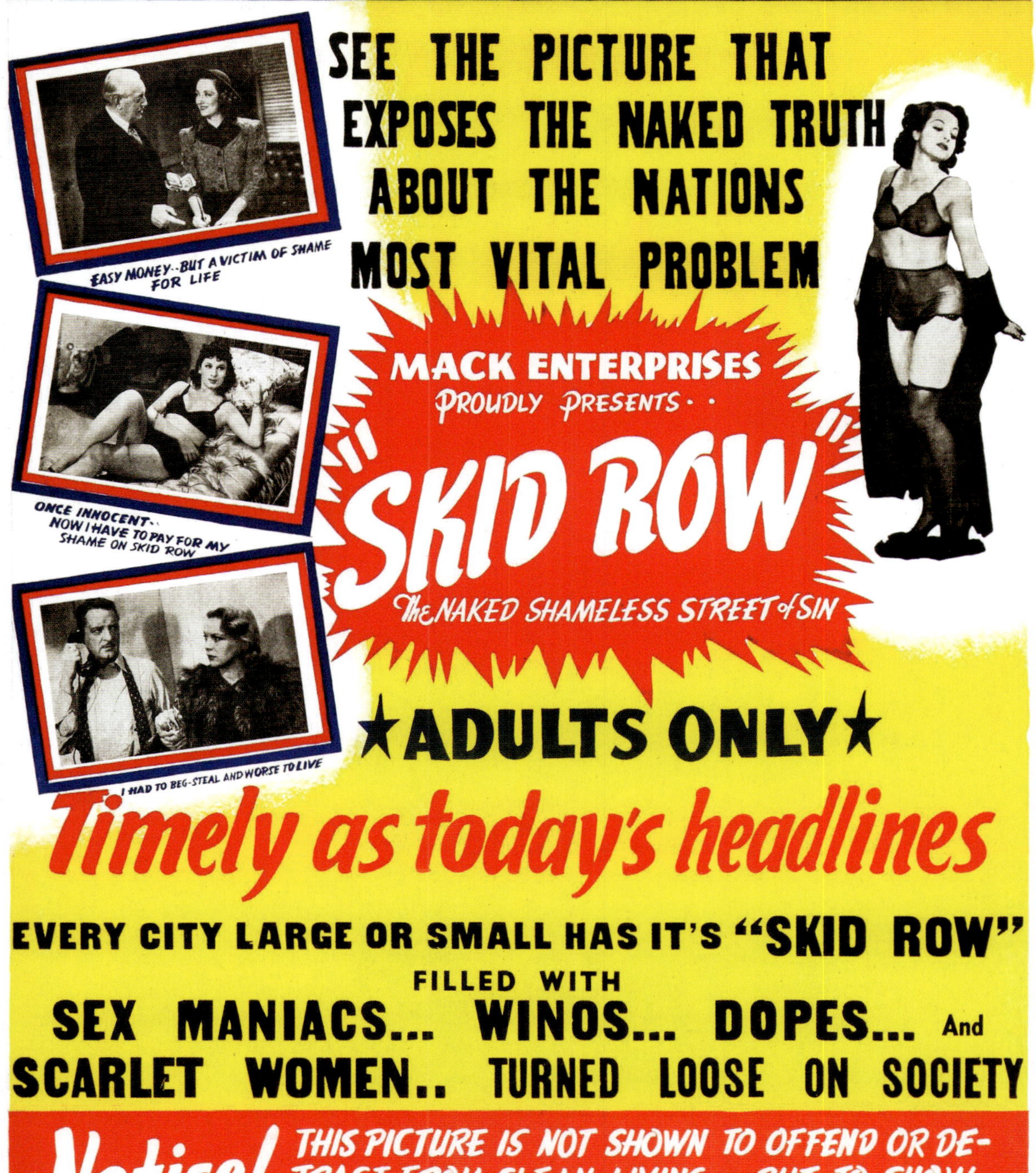
SCOOP!!
WAKE UP . . . .
MR. & MRS. AMERICA
SEE THE PICTURE THAT
EXPOSES THE NAKED TRUTH
ABOUT THE NATIONS
MOST VITAL PROBLEM
EASY MONEY..BUT A VICTIM OF SHAME FOR LIFE
ONCE INNOCENT..
NOW I HAVE TO PAY FOR MY SHAME ON SKID ROW
I HAD TO BEG-STEAL AND WORSE TO LIVE
MACK ENTERPRISES
PROUDLY PRESENTS..
"SKID ROW"
The NAKED SHAMELESS STREET of SIN
★ADULTS ONLY★
Timely as today's headlines
EVERY CITY LARGE OR SMALL HAS IT'S "SKID ROW"
FILLED WITH
SEX MANIACS... WINOS... DOPES... And
SCARLET WOMEN.. TURNED LOOSE ON SOCIETY
Notice!
THIS PICTURE IS NOT SHOWN TO OFFEND OR DETRACT FROM CLEAN LIVING.. BUT TO SHOW YOU THE TRUE FACTS ABOUT "SKID ROW"

When *Confessions* was picked up by the Oklahoma-based Mack Enterprises around 1950 the company was faced with selling a film from the early 1940s that was cobbled together with clips from the 1930s. Title changes were a common way of extending the life of exploitation films, and the lurid *Skid Row* filled that bill. For the poster, images of scantily clad women were complemented by vivid primary colors and the promise of seeing sex maniacs, scarlet women, and "dopes" on screen, enough to entice the most jaded moviegoer in search of thrills. And if that wasn't enough, seeing the film was framed as a civic imperative in order to expose "the naked truth about the nation's most vital problem"—presumably the existence of skid row itself.

By the late 1950s movies from Hollywood and Europe were taking an increasingly adult approach. Many of the moral panics that had prompted exploitation movies were subsiding and old exploitation subjects started turning up in films made for the classroom. Exploitation outfits moved into "sexploitation," first focusing on nudity as courts determined that the naked human body was not in itself obscene. Filmmakers Russ Meyer, David F. Friedman and Herschell Gordon Lewis, Doris Wishman and others ushered in the "nudies"—movies that displayed copious amounts of female skin in a non-erotic, often comic, context. They made no pretense to education. Other films with titles like *Sin in the Suburbs* (1964) and *Suburban Pagans* (1968) began to appear that featured less nudity but dealt with seduction, sexual dissatisfaction and dysfunction, and a variety of fetishes. While not necessarily focused on moral panics, these melodramas frequently served as titillating warnings about the dangers of marital infidelity or promiscuity.

Lou Campa's 1968 *Sock It to Me Baby* stands as a typical example. The title was topical, the same as a 1967 Top 40 hit for Mitch Ryder, a refrain in Aretha Franklin's recording of "Respect," and a catchphrase on the top-rated NBC television show *Rowan and Martin's Laugh-In* where Judy Carne, Goldie Hawn, and others proclaimed "It's sock it to me time!" The poster image presents an attractive, scantily clad woman dancing with the title suggestively splayed across her torso, as if an eager sexual invitation. However, the seedy film was anything but inviting. Ron Baker (Larry Hunter) is a doughy middle-aged suburbanite in a loveless relationship with his shrewish wife, June. He lusts after Susan, June's 18-year-old niece, but resists temptation before she embarks on a trip to Europe. This compounds Ron's frustration as he concludes he needs "some of this young blood." He begins to "sock it to" a local teenage babysitter, Tina. But his initial excitement turns to frustration with Tina's annoying behavior and the growing realization that he is being hustled. Ron confides to his old girlfriend Betty that he is going to confess his transgressions with the underage girl to the police and take his medicine. Susan, back from Europe, reveals to Ron that June is a lesbian, and that she has been using their marriage as a front in order to seduce young girls—just as she did with Susan! Ron confronts June and Tina *in flagrante delicto* and announces he is turning himself in and will marry Betty when he is released from jail. It is difficult to come away from the film without feeling sullied—not only by Ron and June's illicit desires, but also by the movie itself, which is poorly acted and haphazardly executed, complete with muddy sound and numerous out-of-focus shots.

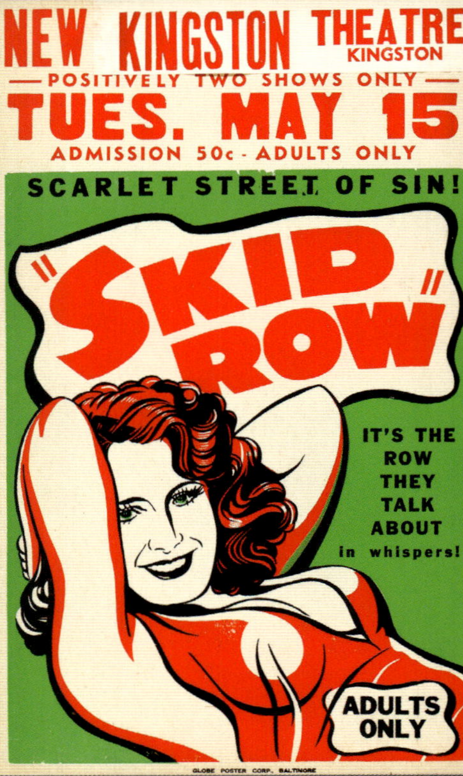

ABOVE: Another *Skid Row* poster, circa 1950s, with simple but eye-catching artwork that was also employed on a one-sheet for *Reefer Madness* (see page 32).

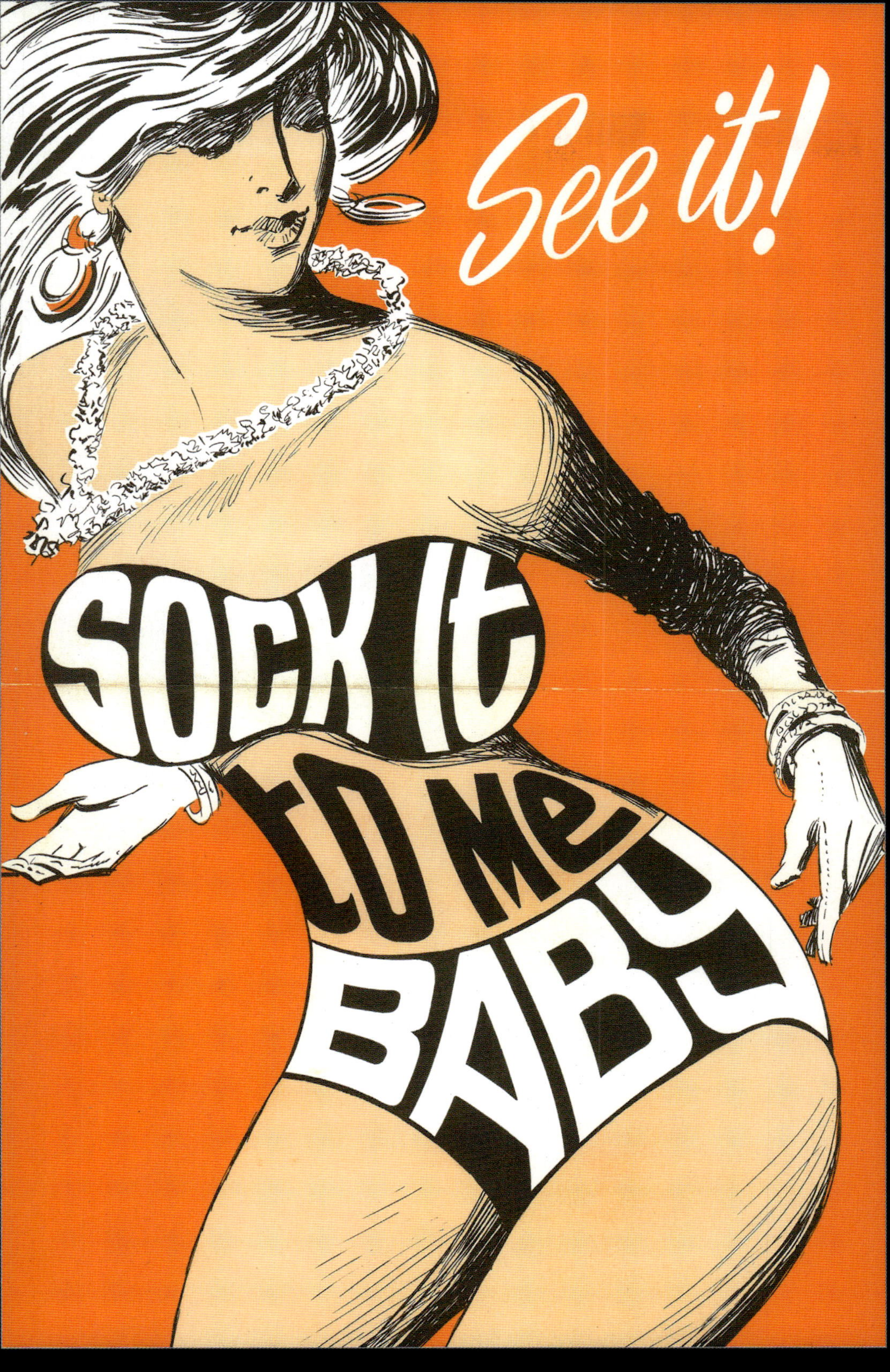

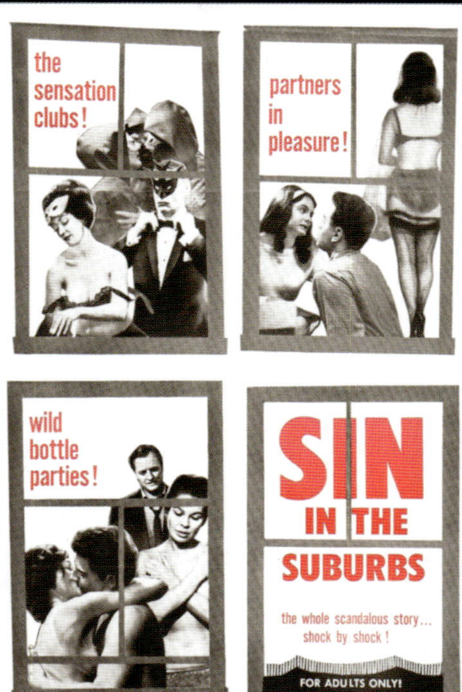

Whether it was the exploitation films that were focused on moral panics from the teens to the 1950s or the sexploitation films that followed in the 1960s and 1970s that served as cautionary tales, the advertising for both promised ticket-buyers that these tawdry little movies would provide provocative and arousing imagery. Even if they did not always deliver, they spoke to the taboos and tensions of their times. ●

ABOVE LEFT: The key art for *Sock It to Me Baby* (1968), taken from the cover of the movie's pressbook, a brochure featuring items local exhibitors could use to promote the film.

ABOVE RIGHT: With promises on the poster of "sensation clubs" and "wild bottle parties," the wife-swapping drama *Sin in the Suburbs* (1964) was an early writing/directing credit for sexploitation pioneer Joseph Sarno.

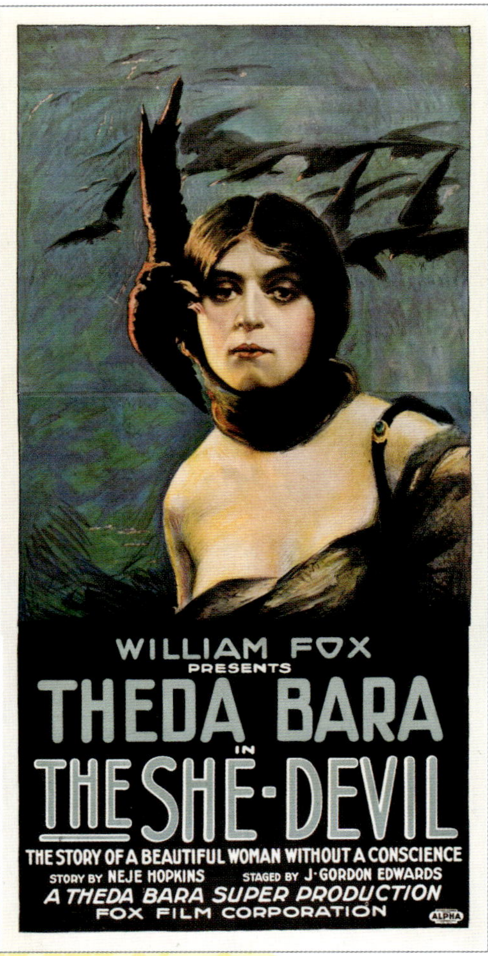

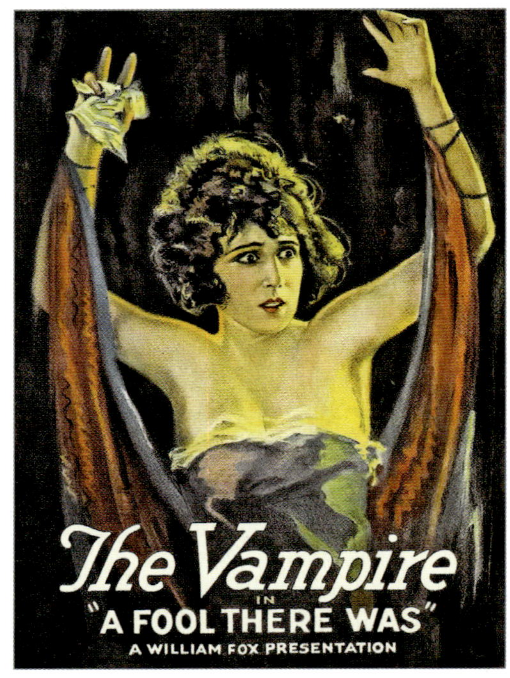

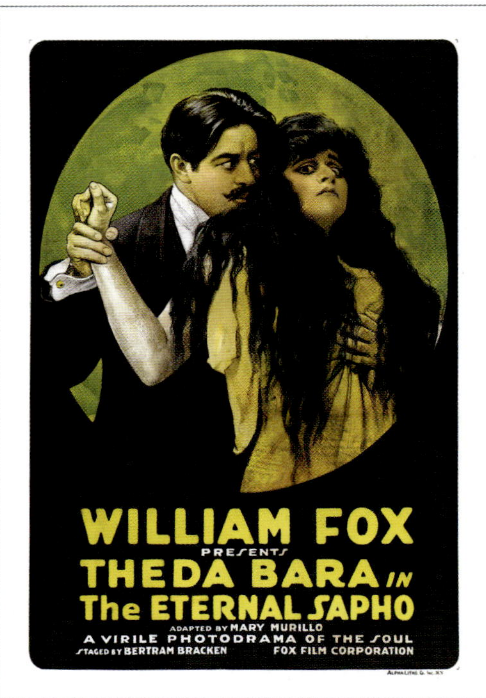

THE ORIGINAL SINNER

She was one of cinema's very first sex symbols, a *femme fatale* who popularized the term "vamp" for portraying the kind of wanton woman who, while not literally a bloodsucker, would lead good men astray. The studio promoted her as exotic Egyptian-born Theda Bara, but she was actually Theodosia Goodman (1885–1955), from Cincinnati. "I submerge myself in each role . . . losing my own identity utterly, living the part," she once wrote of her approach to playing characters, however immoral. "The rest must be left on the lap of the National Board of Censorship." Alas, still images, such as these stunning posters, are pretty much all that is left of her legacy: prints of just six of her 40 films survive.

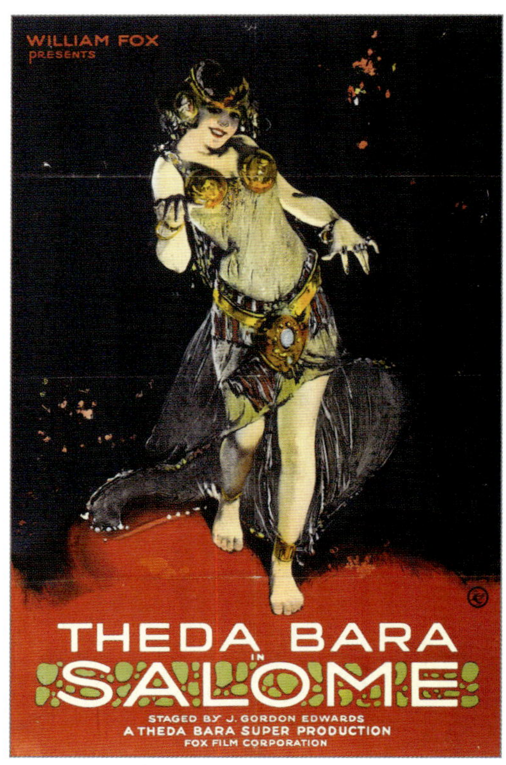

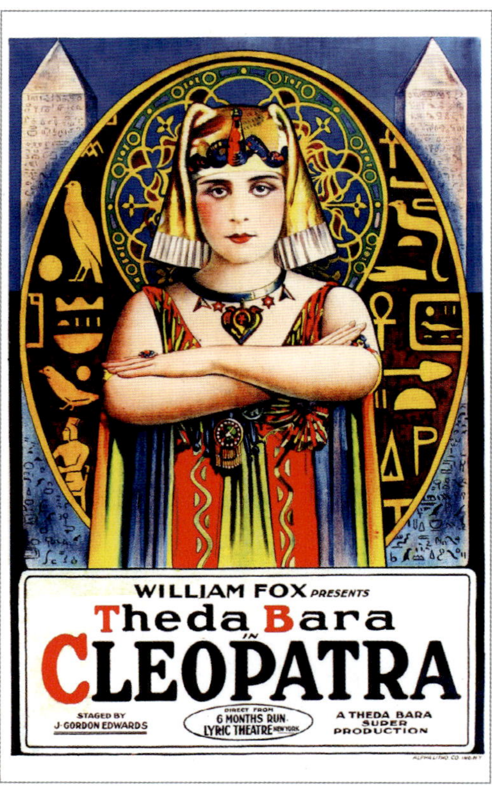

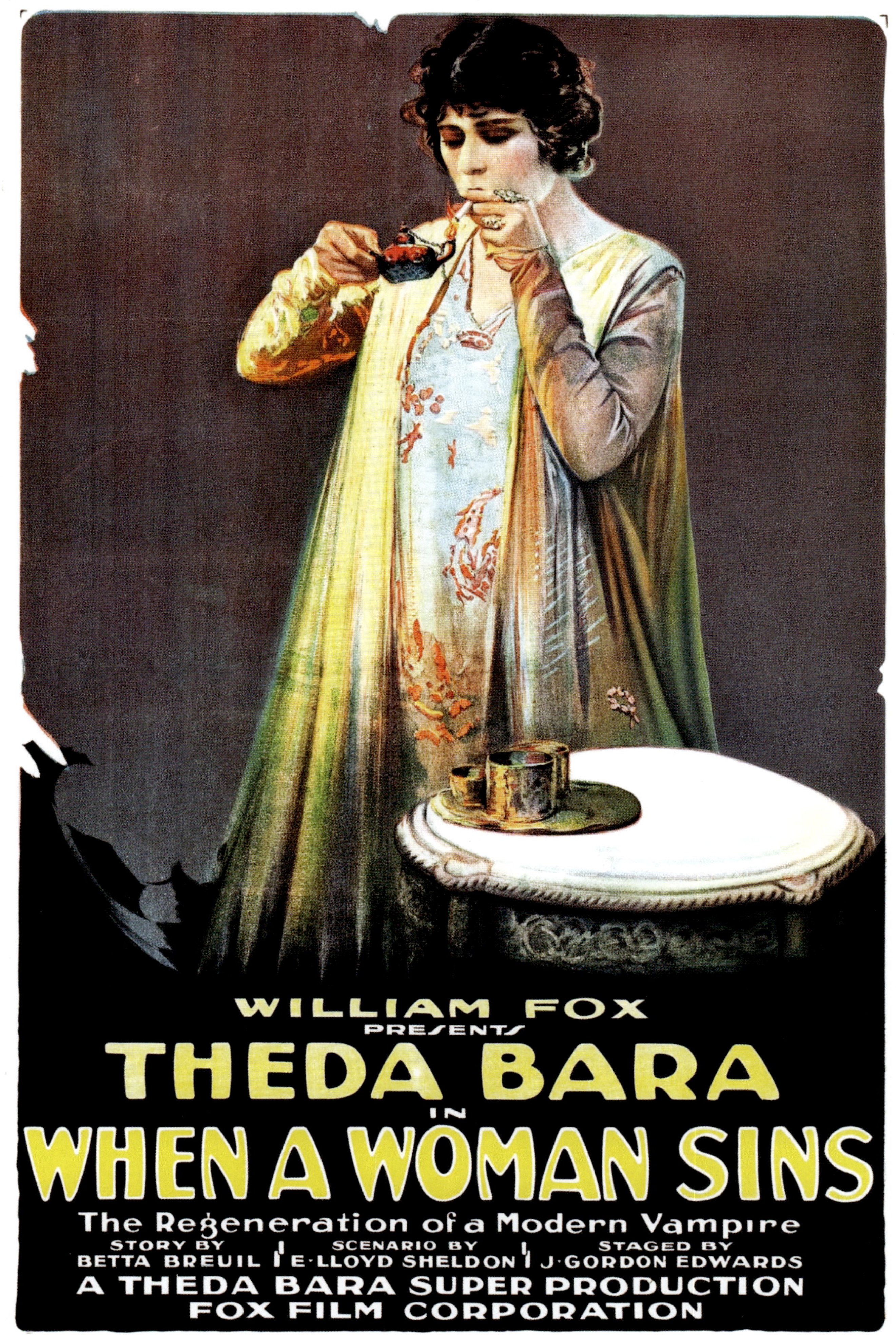
WILLIAM FOX
PRESENTS
THEDA BARA
IN
WHEN A WOMAN SINS
The Regeneration of a Modern Vampire
STORY BY
BETTA BREUIL
SCENARIO BY
E·LLOYD SHELDON
STAGED BY
J·GORDON EDWARDS
A THEDA BARA SUPER PRODUCTION
FOX FILM CORPORATION

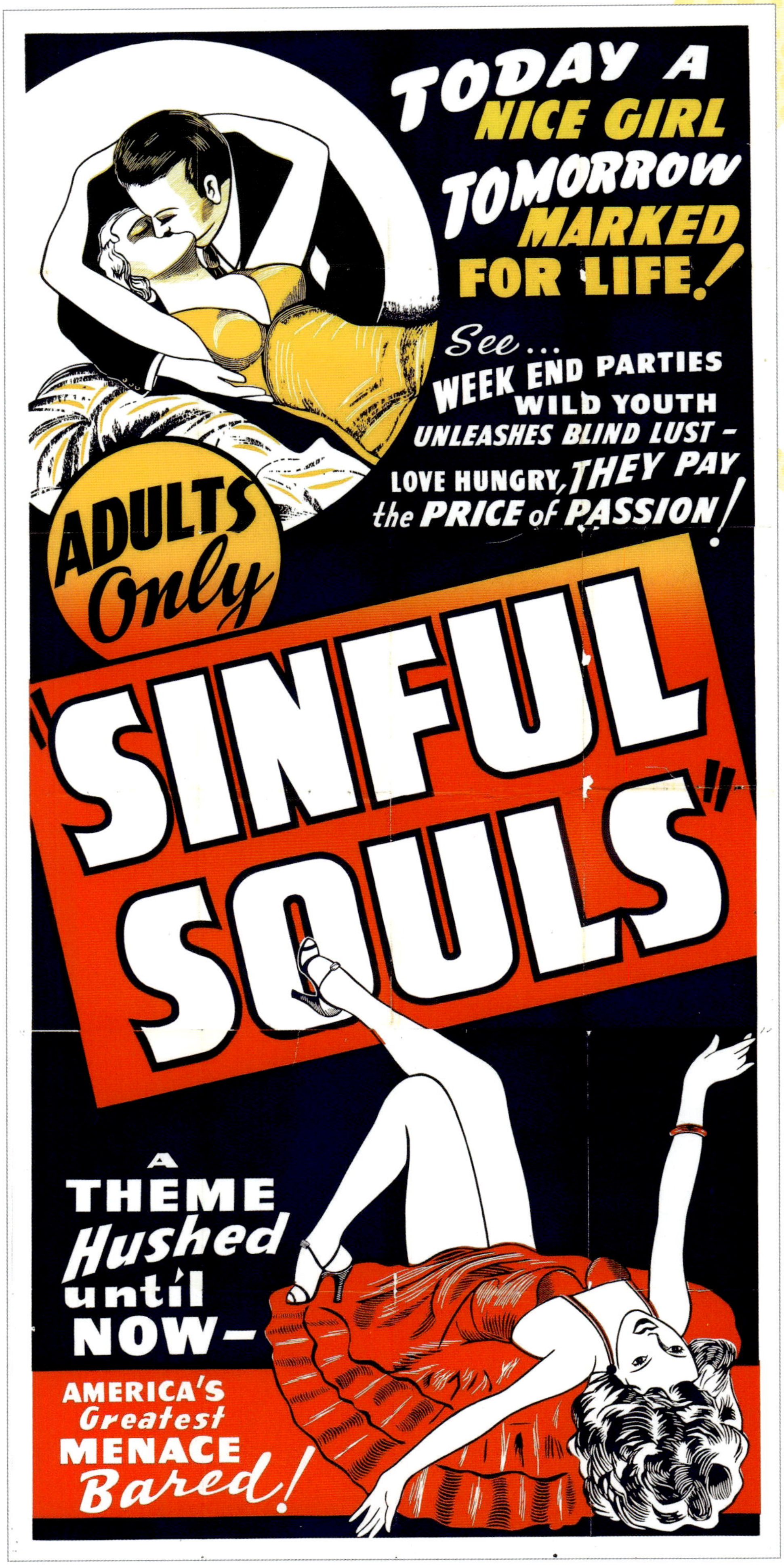

SCARLET WOMEN

Exploitation movie distributors had to walk a fine line with their promotional efforts. On the one hand, their tales of predatory men and fallen women were presented as nothing less than crusading public service: "A searing indictment of today's moral standards!" announces the poster for *Bootleg Babies* (aka *Souls in Pawn*, 1940); "Lifts the Iron Curtain of fear and ignorance!" promises *Street Corner* (1948), with its "educational" single-sex screenings. On the other hand, titillation sells tickets: "Thrill to the most exciting exposé of sex crimes, sin, and vice . . ." the same *Bootleg Babies* poster adds, while an on-screen caption in the movie's trailer goes even further: "A picture that shows everything—Sexsational!" *Sinful Souls* is a re-release of a 1939 anti-abortion polemic that originally went by the more accurate if less enticing title *Unborn Souls*. A poster highlighting sin, "wild youth," and "blind lust" was deemed a better bet.

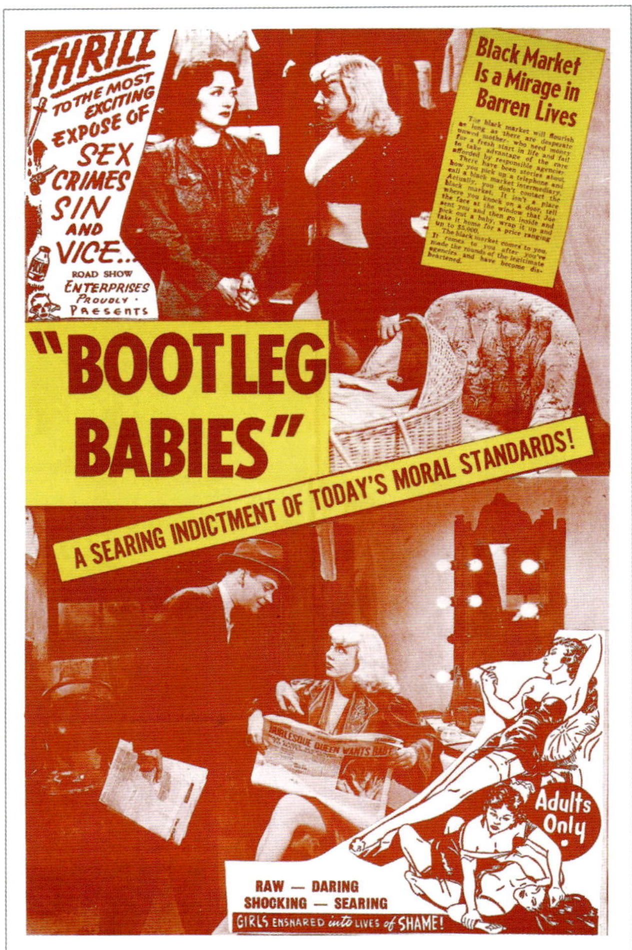

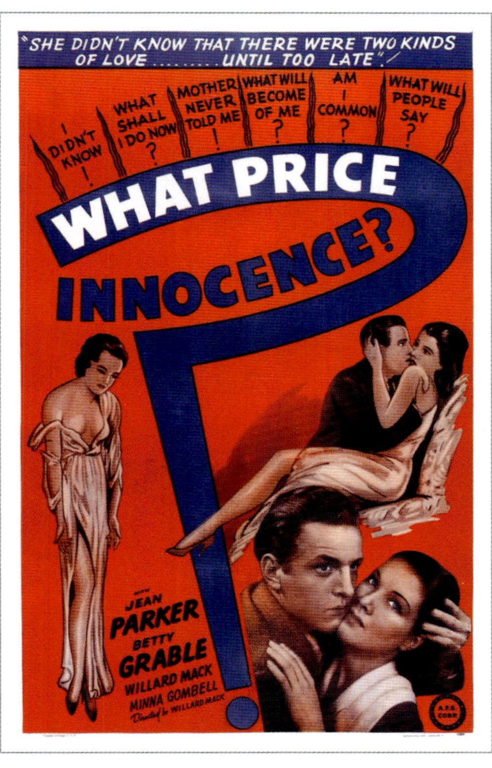
"SHE DIDN'T KNOW THAT THERE WERE TWO KINDS OF LOVE .... UNTIL TOO LATE"
I DIDN'T KNOW !
WHAT SHALL I DO NOW ?
MOTHER NEVER TOLD ME !
WHAT WILL BECOME OF ME ?
AM I COMMON ?
WHAT WILL PEOPLE SAY ?
WHAT PRICE INNOCENCE?
JEAN PARKER
BETTY GRABLE
WILLARD MACK
MINNA GOMBELL

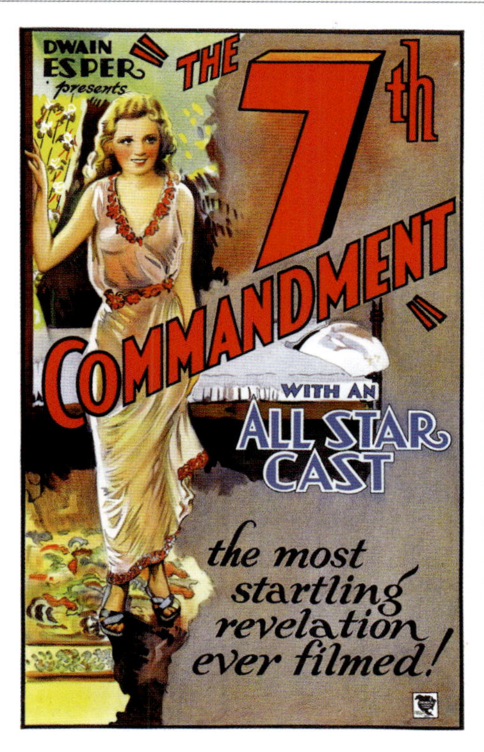
DWAIN ESPER presents
"THE 7th COMMANDMENT"
WITH AN ALL STAR CAST
the most startling revelation ever filmed!

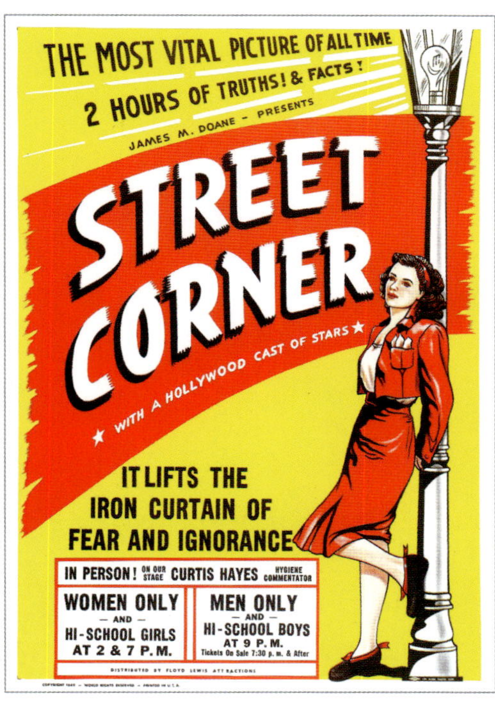
THE MOST VITAL PICTURE OF ALL TIME
2 HOURS OF TRUTHS! & FACTS!
JAMES M. DOANE - PRESENTS
STREET CORNER
★ WITH A HOLLYWOOD CAST OF STARS ★
IT LIFTS THE IRON CURTAIN OF FEAR AND IGNORANCE
IN PERSON! ON OUR STAGE CURTIS HAYES HYGIENE COMMENTATOR
WOMEN ONLY — AND — HI-SCHOOL GIRLS AT 2 & 7 P.M.
MEN ONLY — AND — HI-SCHOOL BOYS AT 9 P.M.

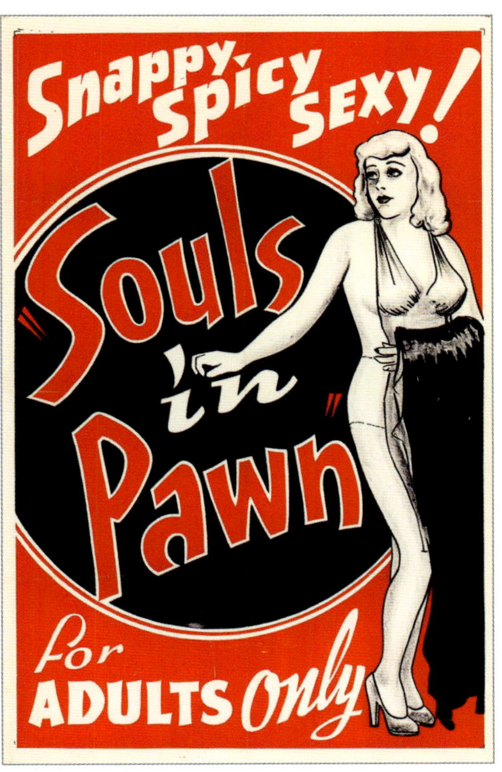
Snappy, Spicy, Sexy!
"Souls in Pawn"
for ADULTS Only

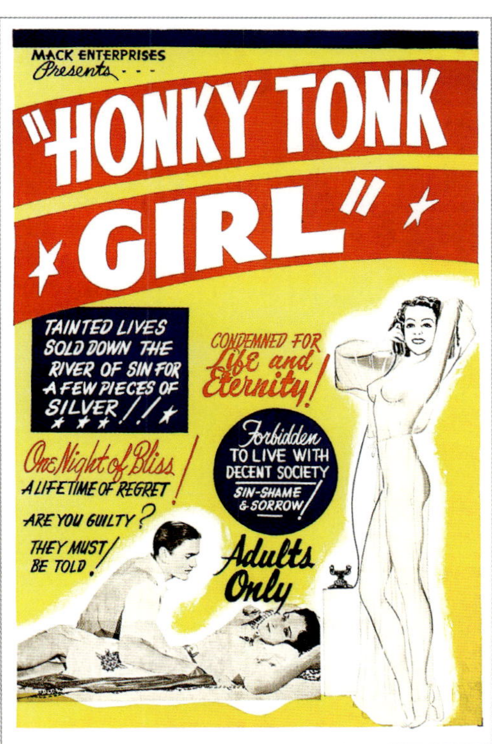
MACK ENTERPRISES Presents - - -
"HONKY TONK GIRL"
TAINTED LIVES SOLD DOWN THE RIVER OF SIN FOR A FEW PIECES OF SILVER!!
CONDEMNED FOR Life and Eternity!
One Night of Bliss! A LIFETIME OF REGRET!
ARE YOU GUILTY?
THEY MUST BE TOLD!
Forbidden TO LIVE WITH DECENT SOCIETY SIN-SHAME & SORROW!
Adults Only

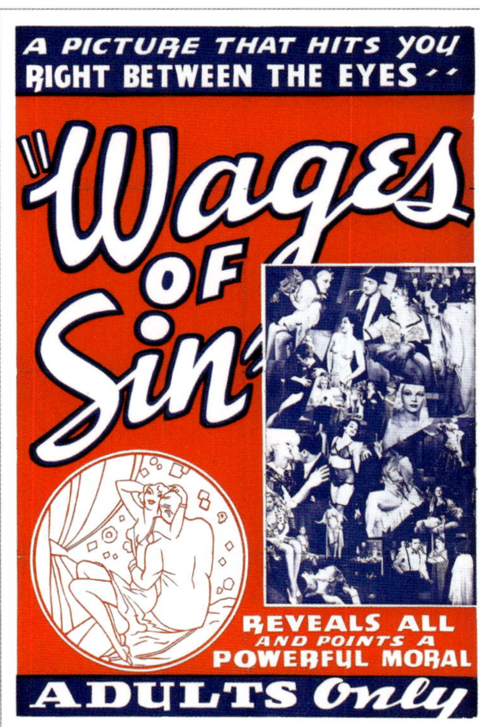
A PICTURE THAT HITS YOU RIGHT BETWEEN THE EYES - -
"Wages of Sin"
REVEALS ALL AND POINTS A POWERFUL MORAL
ADULTS Only

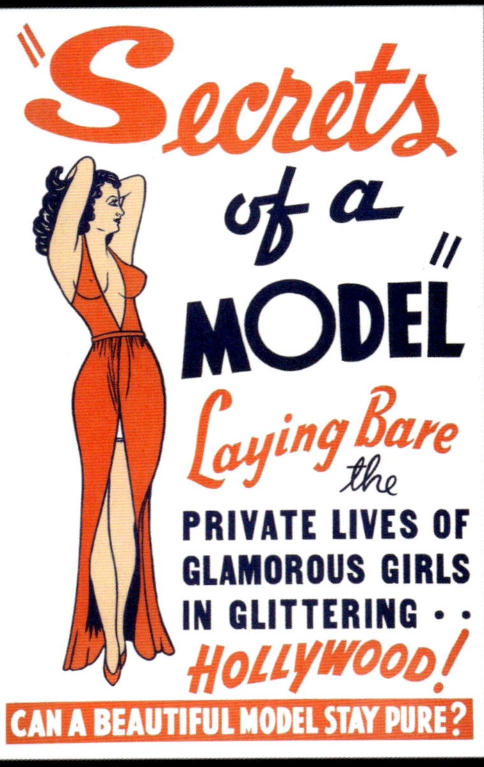
"Secrets
of a
MODEL"
Laying Bare
the
PRIVATE LIVES OF
GLAMOROUS GIRLS
IN GLITTERING . .
HOLLYWOOD!
CAN A BEAUTIFUL MODEL STAY PURE?

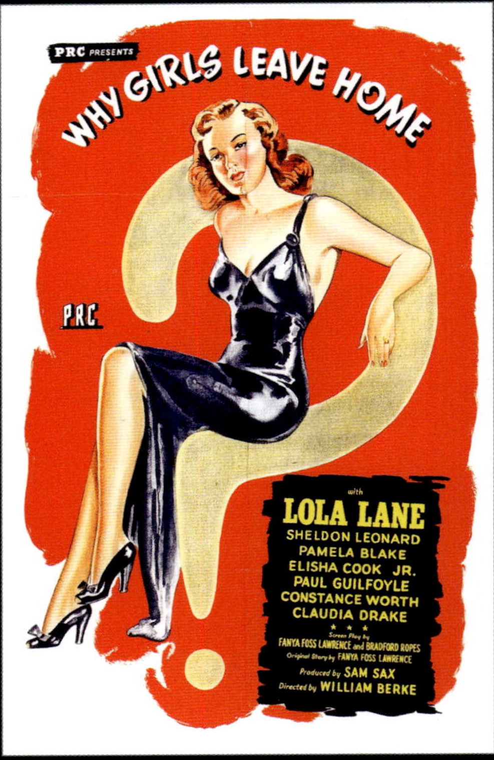
PRC PRESENTS
WHY GIRLS LEAVE HOME
P.R.C.
with
LOLA LANE
SHELDON LEONARD
PAMELA BLAKE
ELISHA COOK JR.
PAUL GUILFOYLE
CONSTANCE WORTH
CLAUDIA DRAKE
Screen Play by
FANYA FOSS LAWRENCE and BRADFORD ROPES
Original Story by FANYA FOSS LAWRENCE
Produced by SAM SAX
Directed by WILLIAM BERKE

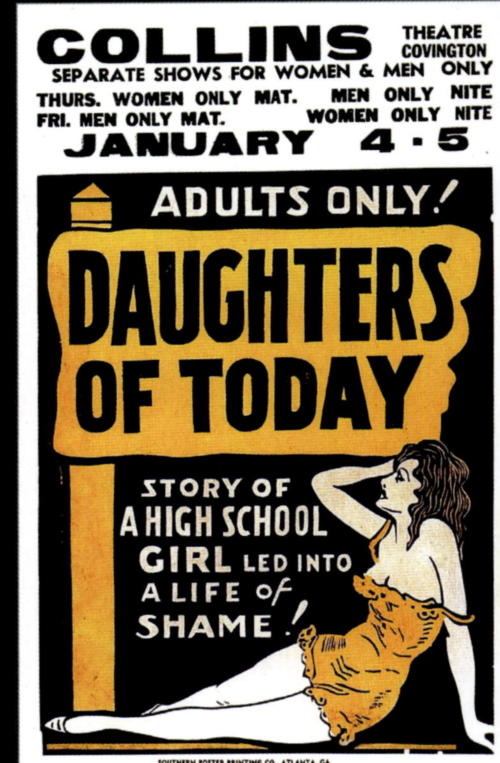
COLLINS THEATRE COVINGTON
SEPARATE SHOWS FOR WOMEN & MEN ONLY
THURS. WOMEN ONLY MAT. MEN ONLY NITE
FRI. MEN ONLY MAT. WOMEN ONLY NITE
JANUARY 4 · 5
ADULTS ONLY!
DAUGHTERS
OF TODAY
STORY OF
A HIGH SCHOOL
GIRL LED INTO
A LIFE OF
SHAME!
SOUTHERN POSTER PRINTING CO., ATLANTA, GA.

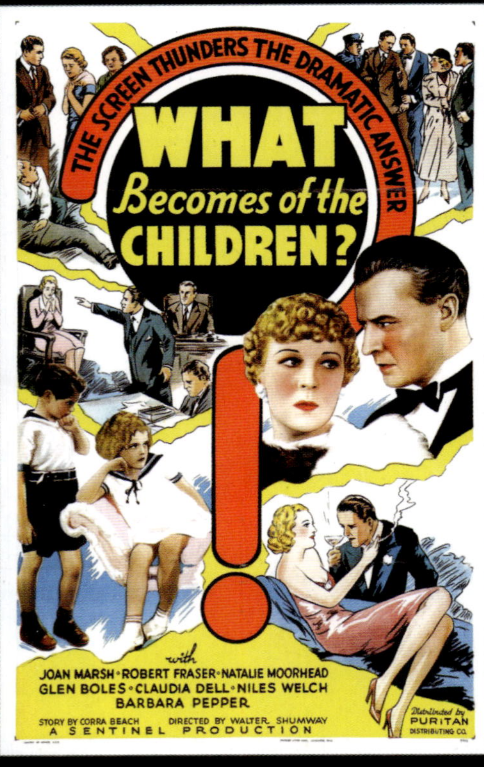
THE SCREEN THUNDERS THE DRAMATIC ANSWER
WHAT
Becomes of the
CHILDREN?
with
JOAN MARSH · ROBERT FRASER · NATALIE MOORHEAD
GLEN BOLES · CLAUDIA DELL · NILES WELCH
BARBARA PEPPER
STORY BY CORRA BEACH
DIRECTED BY WALTER SHUMWAY
A SENTINEL PRODUCTION
Distributed by
PURITAN
DISTRIBUTING CO.

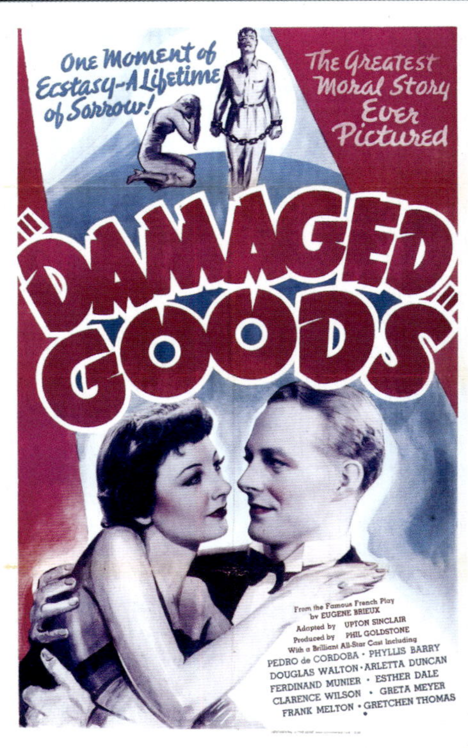
One Moment of Ecstasy—A Lifetime of Sorrow!
The Greatest Moral Story Ever Pictured
"DAMAGED" GOODS
From the Famous French Play
by EUGENE BRIEUX
Adapted by UPTON SINCLAIR
Produced by PHIL GOLDSTONE
With a Brilliant All-Star Cast Including
PEDRO de CORDOBA · PHYLLIS BARRY
DOUGLAS WALTON · ARLETTA DUNCAN
FERDINAND MUNIER · ESTHER DALE
CLARENCE WILSON · GRETA MEYER
FRANK MELTON · GRETCHEN THOMAS

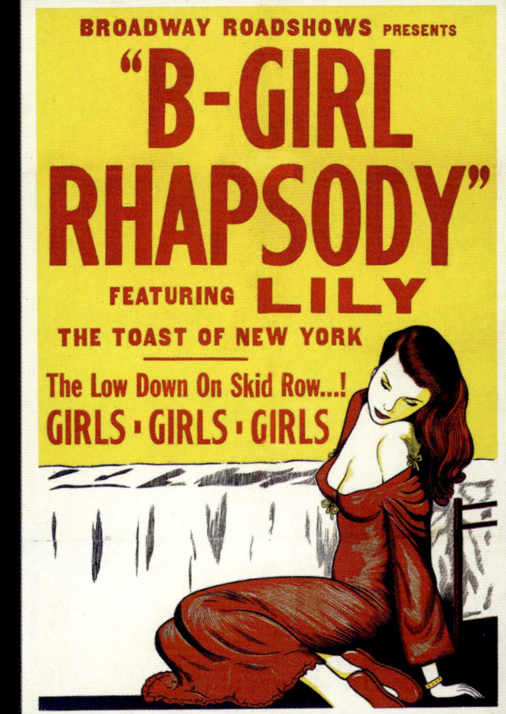
BROADWAY ROADSHOWS PRESENTS
"B-GIRL
RHAPSODY"
FEATURING LILY
THE TOAST OF NEW YORK
The Low Down On Skid Row...!
GIRLS · GIRLS · GIRLS

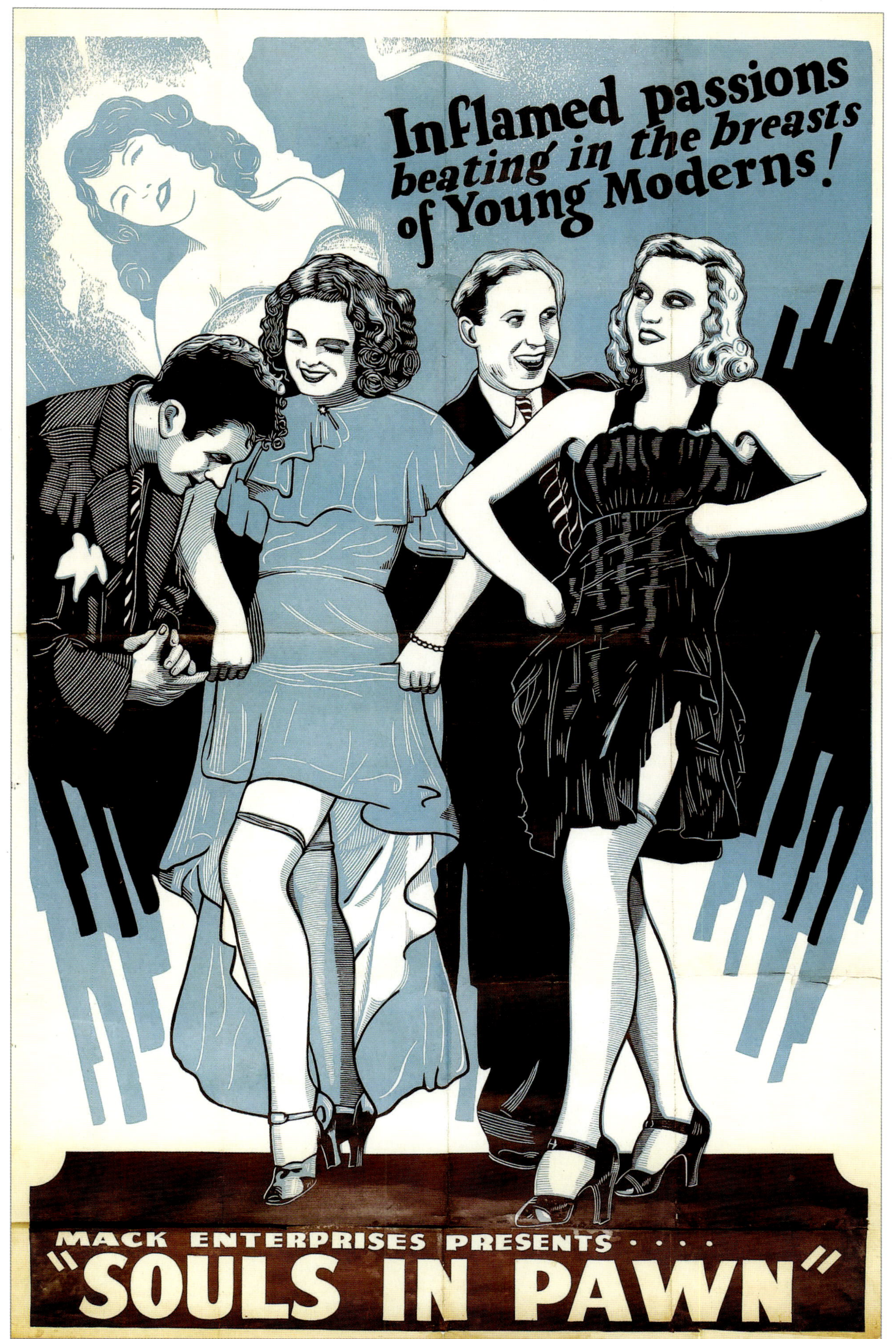
Inflamed passions
beating in the breasts
of Young Moderns!
MACK ENTERPRISES PRESENTS . . . .
"SOULS IN PAWN"

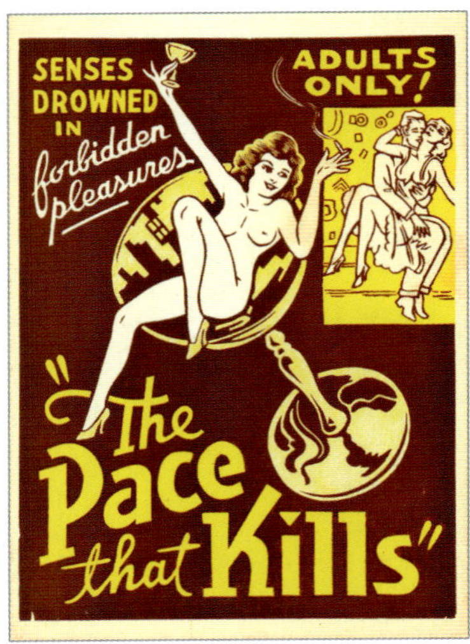

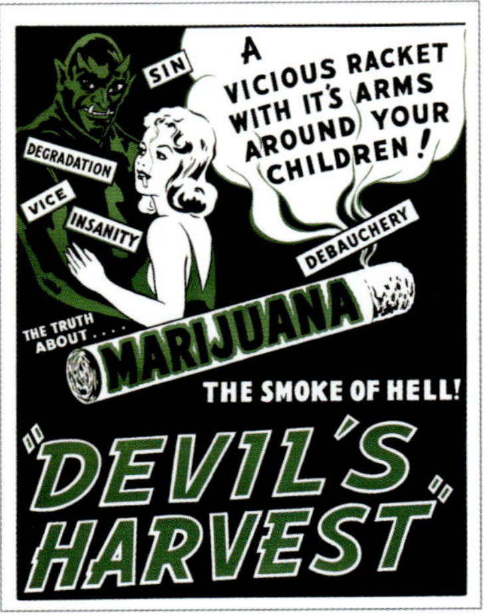

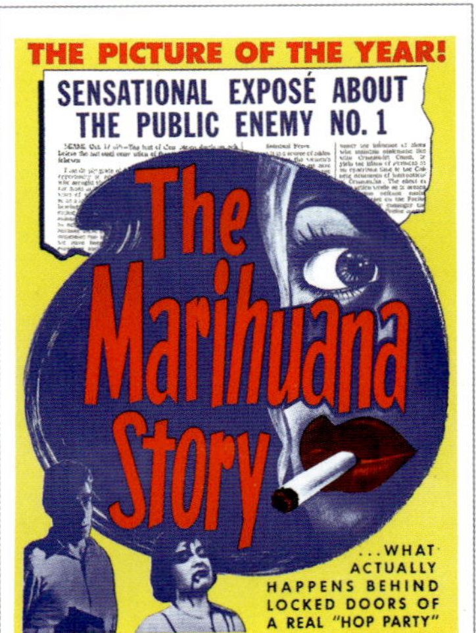

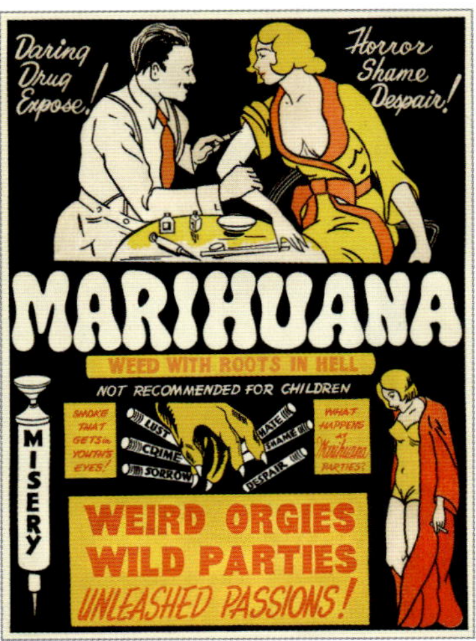

JUST SAY NO

Though pills and cocaine got a look-in, from the 1930s to '50s marijuana was the main focus of exploitationers' fear-mongering when it came to drugs. As its fabulously sleazy poster is keen to highlight, *The Devil's Weed* (aka *"She Shoulda Said 'No!'"*, 1949) had an enviable USP: starlet Lila Leeds had sensationally been busted for possessing pot the previous year, alongside a big star—Robert Mitchum. While Mitchum's career as a Hollywood tough guy was if anything enhanced, when Leeds emerged from 60 days in jail she "only had one offer . . . which was an obvious attempt to capitalize on the Mitchum case notoriety. I took it. I was broke." Thanks to the marketing guile of promoter Kroger Babb, who announced that the release had been endorsed by the US government as a public service (it hadn't), the film did well, but Leeds's career never recovered.

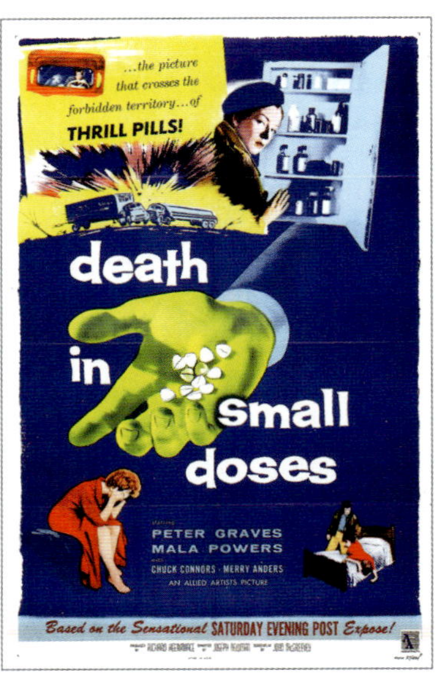

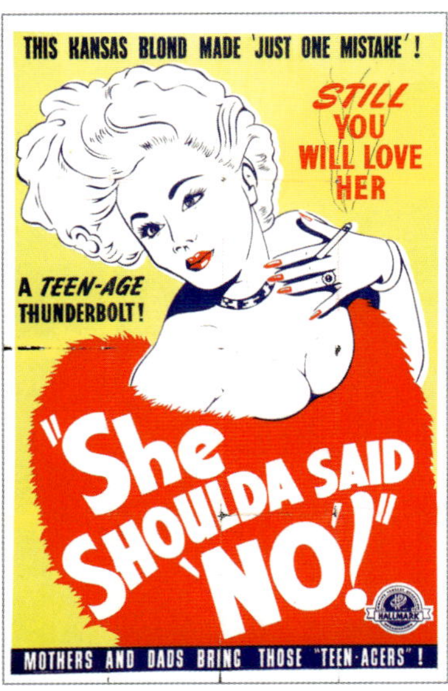

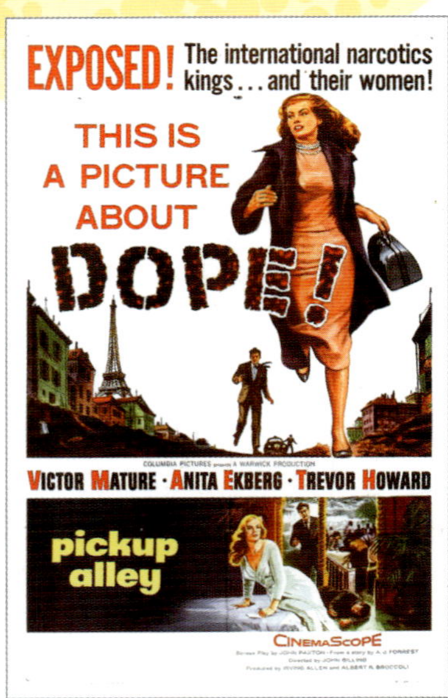

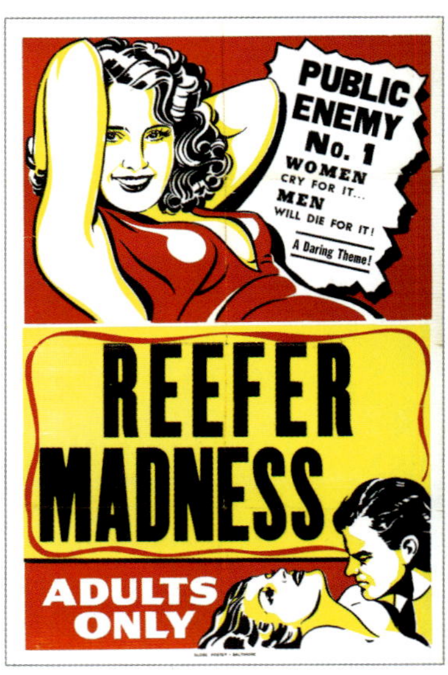

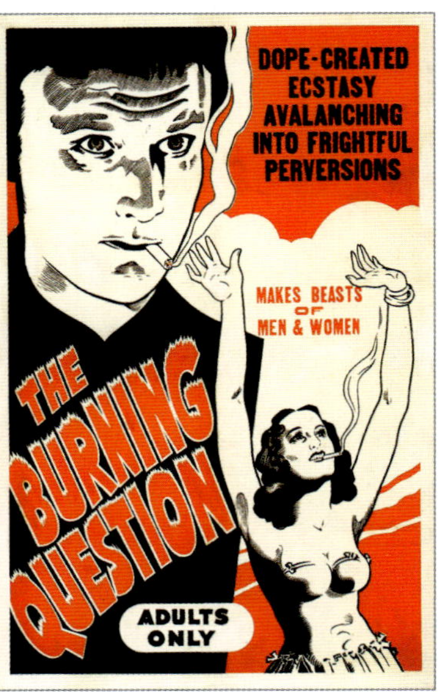

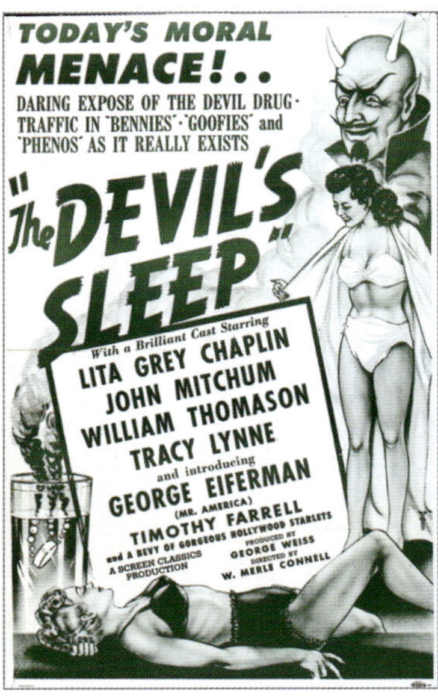

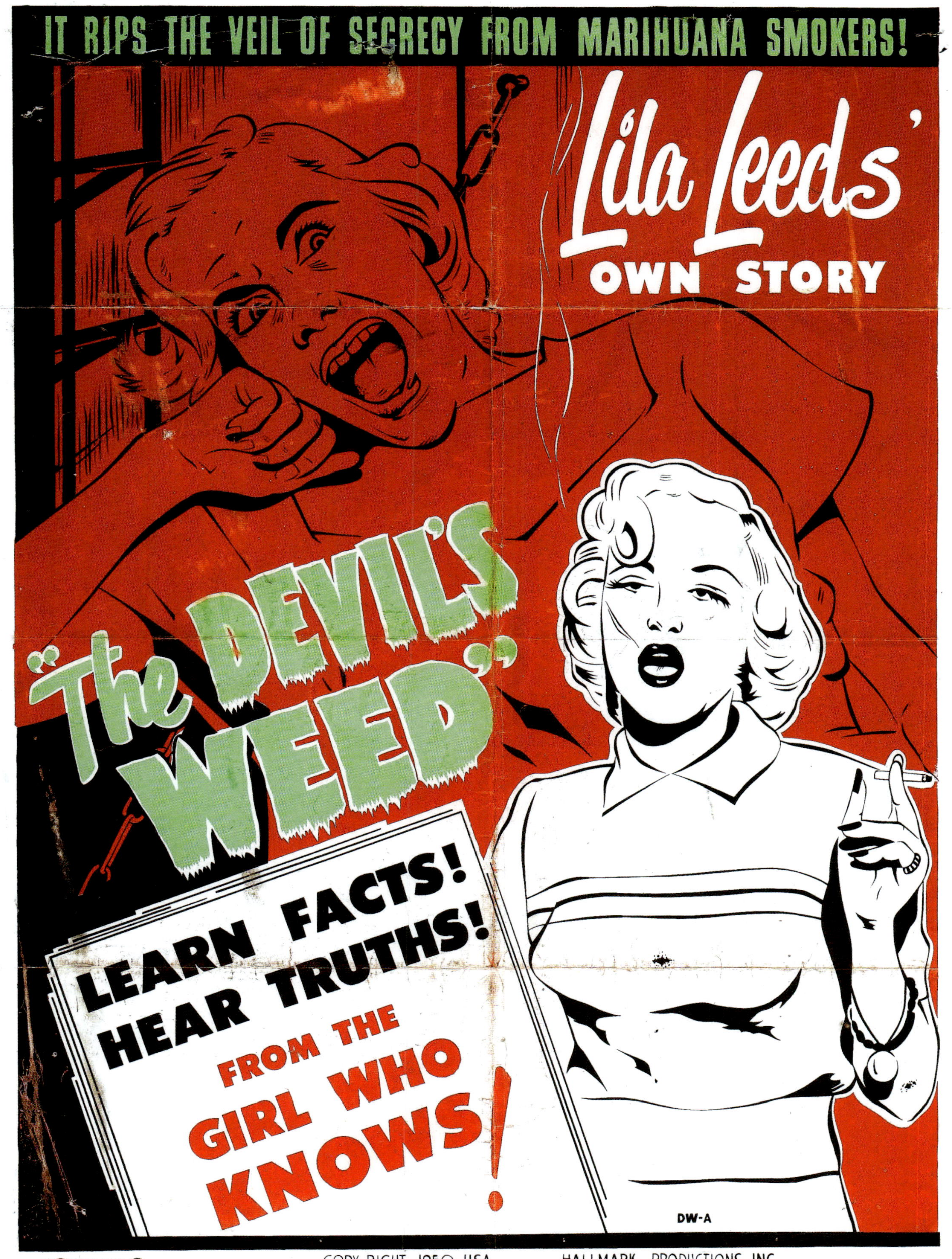
IT RIPS THE VEIL OF SECRECY FROM MARIHUANA SMOKERS!
Lila Leeds' OWN STORY
"The DEVIL'S WEED"
LEARN FACTS! HEAR TRUTHS!
FROM THE GIRL WHO KNOWS!
DW-A
MODERN BLAN.
COPY RIGHT 1950 USA
HALLMARK PRODUCTIONS INC.

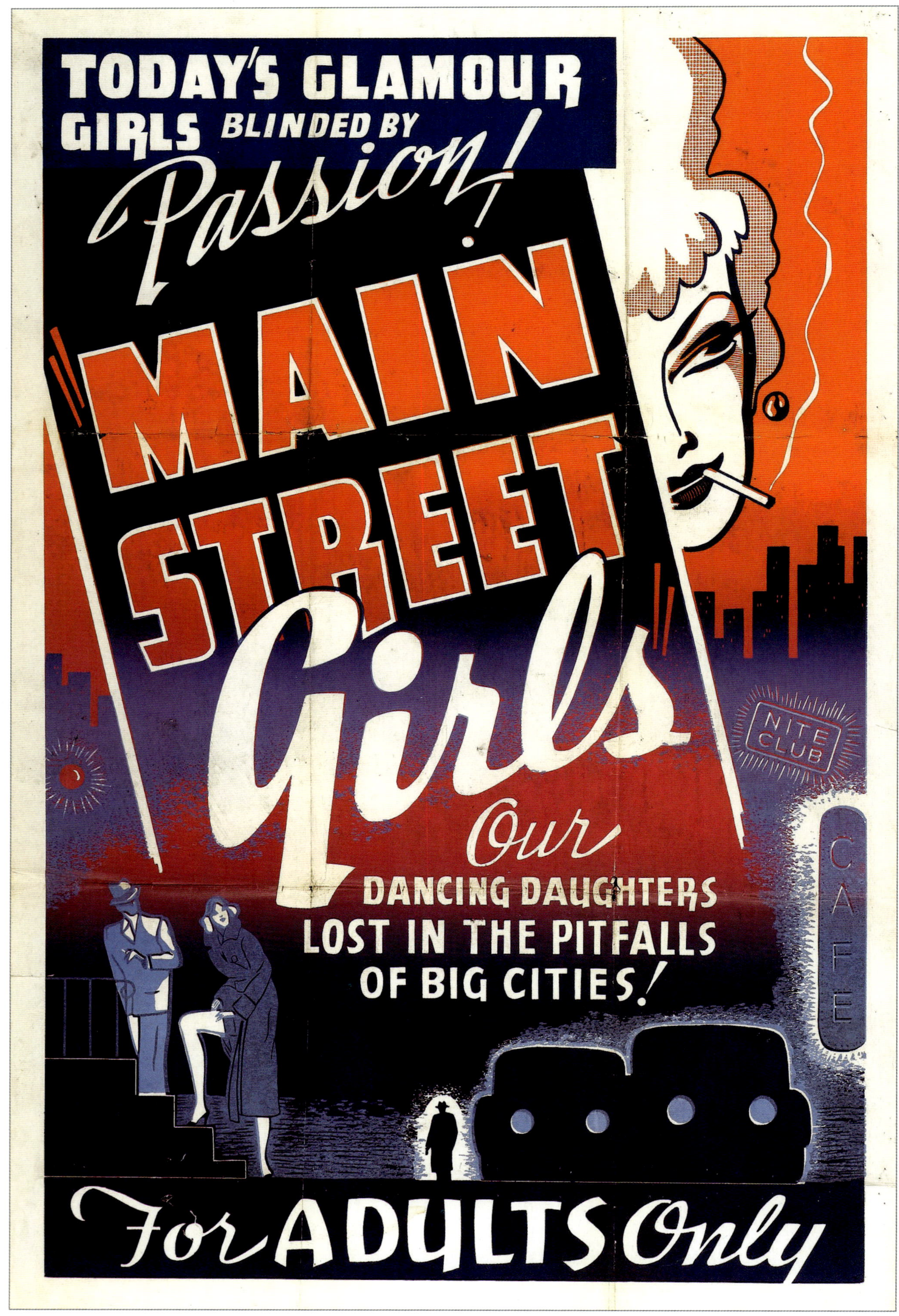
TODAY'S GLAMOUR
GIRLS BLINDED BY
Passion!
MAIN
STREET
Girls
NITE CLUB
CAFE
Our
DANCING DAUGHTERS
LOST IN THE PITFALLS
OF BIG CITIES!
For ADULTS Only

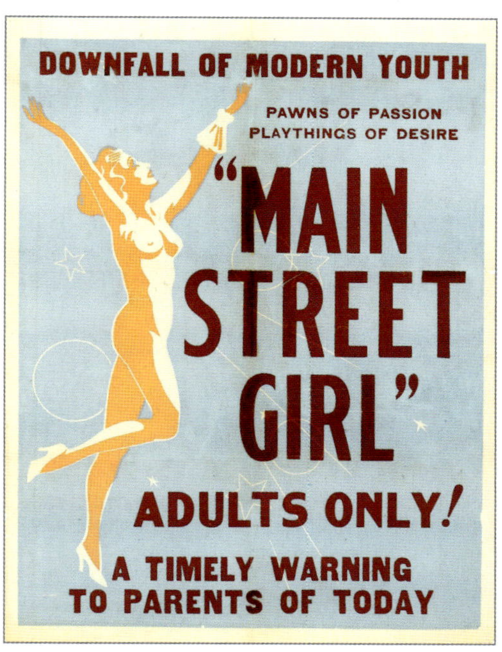

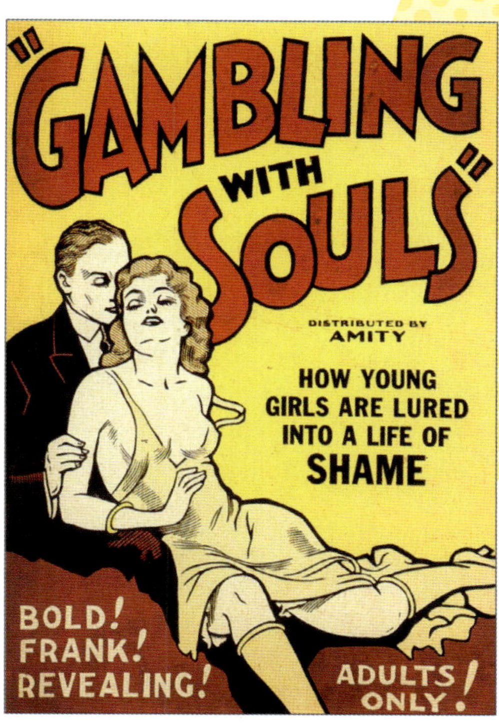

DIRECTED BY ELMER CLIFTON

"An epic picture is produced, I believe, when a great thought is told in a simple and understandable way by expert motion picture technicians," Elmer Clifton (1890–1949) told *Motion Picture Magazine* in 1926. Clifton had certainly started out pretty epic—he acted in D. W. Griffith's *The Birth of a Nation* and helmed early films featuring Clara Bow and Rudolph Valentino—but after leading actress Martha Mansfield sustained fatal burns following an accident on the set of *The Warrens of Virginia* in 1924, he found his directing career declining into B-Westerns and exploitation pictures. *Main Street Girls* is better known as *Paroled from The Big House* (1938), though that version is reportedly missing the undressing and striptease scenes that make the exploitation edit an "epic" in its own way.

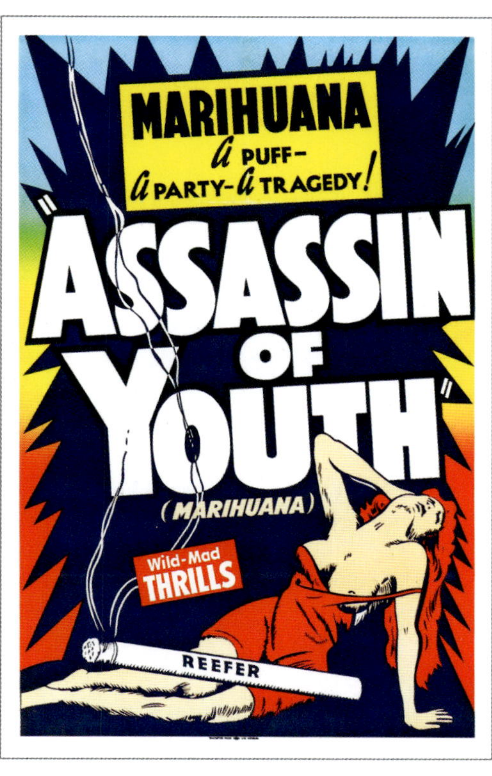

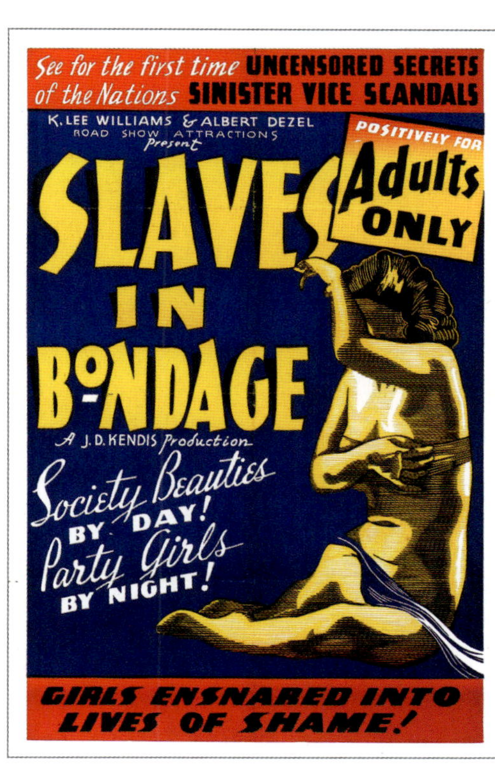

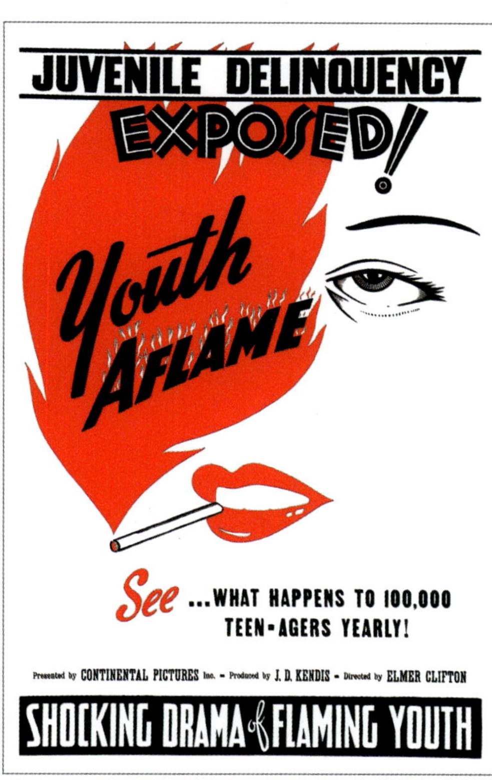

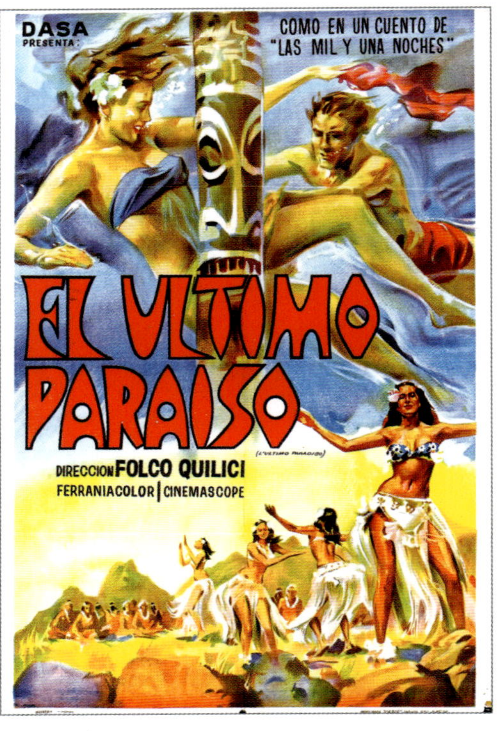

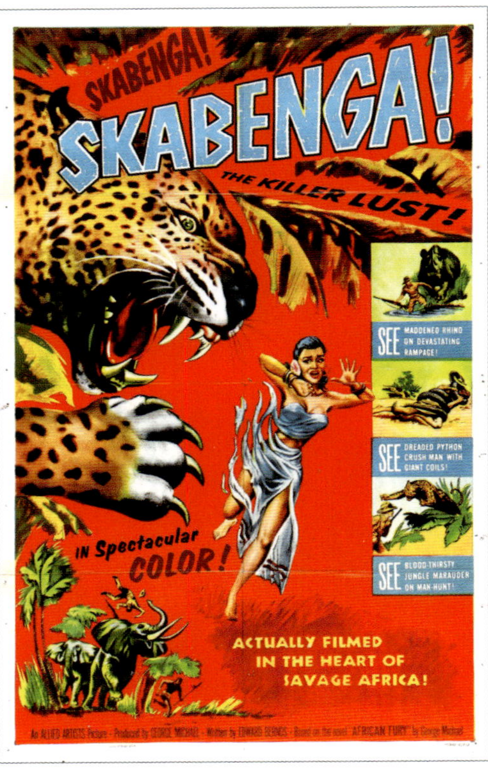

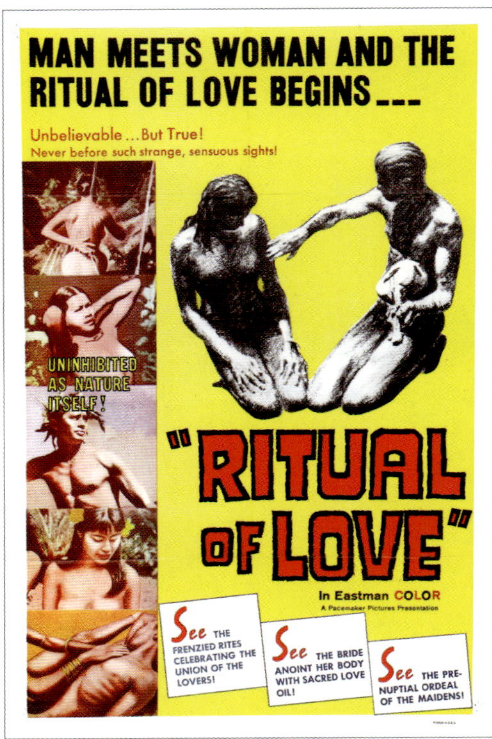

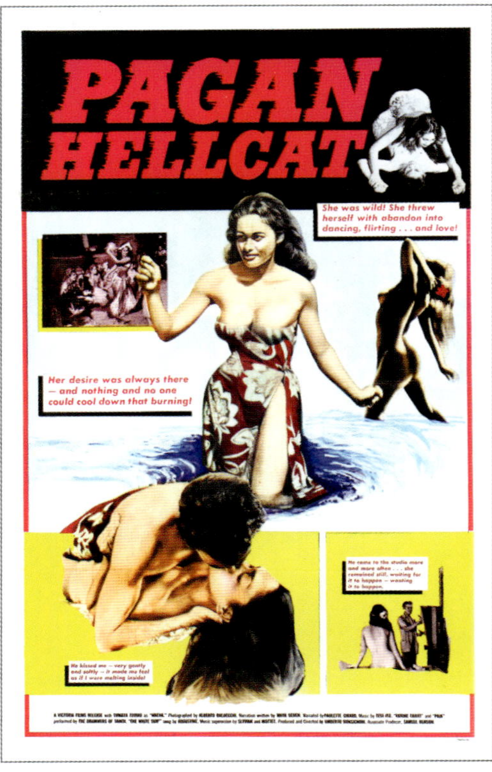

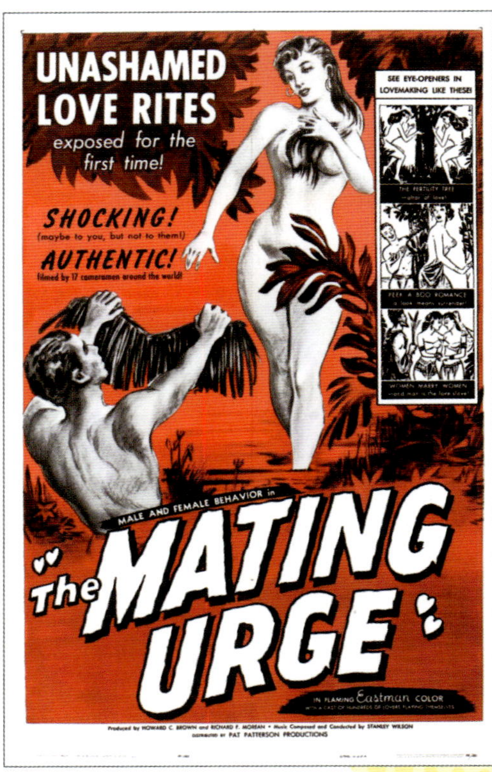

"PRIMITIVE RITES!"

When is a film including bare-breasted or nude women perfectly respectable? When it's an educational travelogue documentary of course, detailing customs and lifestyles of ethnographic interest in a measured, professional way. Or you could shout about a woman breastfeeding a suckling piglet, like the poster for *Primitive Paradise* (1961), which also highlights the overriding interest of ethnography exploitation style: "See courtship rites of maidens in all their native glory." Sex sells, especially sex in exotic countries. These "goona-goona" documentaries (and rudimentary dramas) are a reminder of the time when nobody batted an eyelid at a level of racism that by today's standards is breathtakingly blatant.

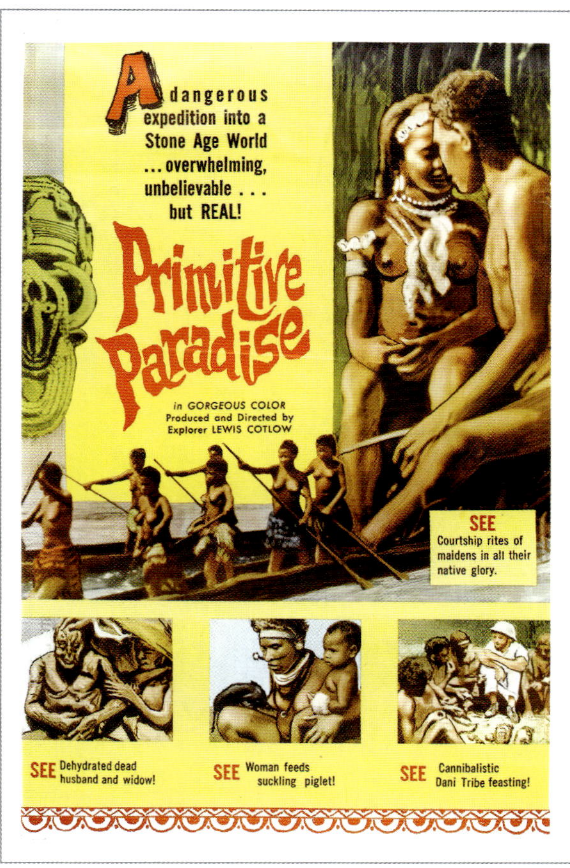

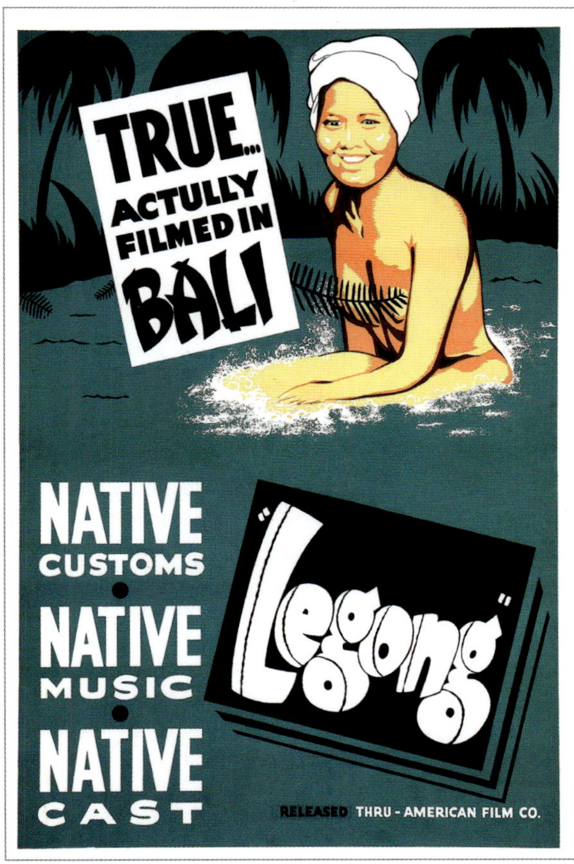

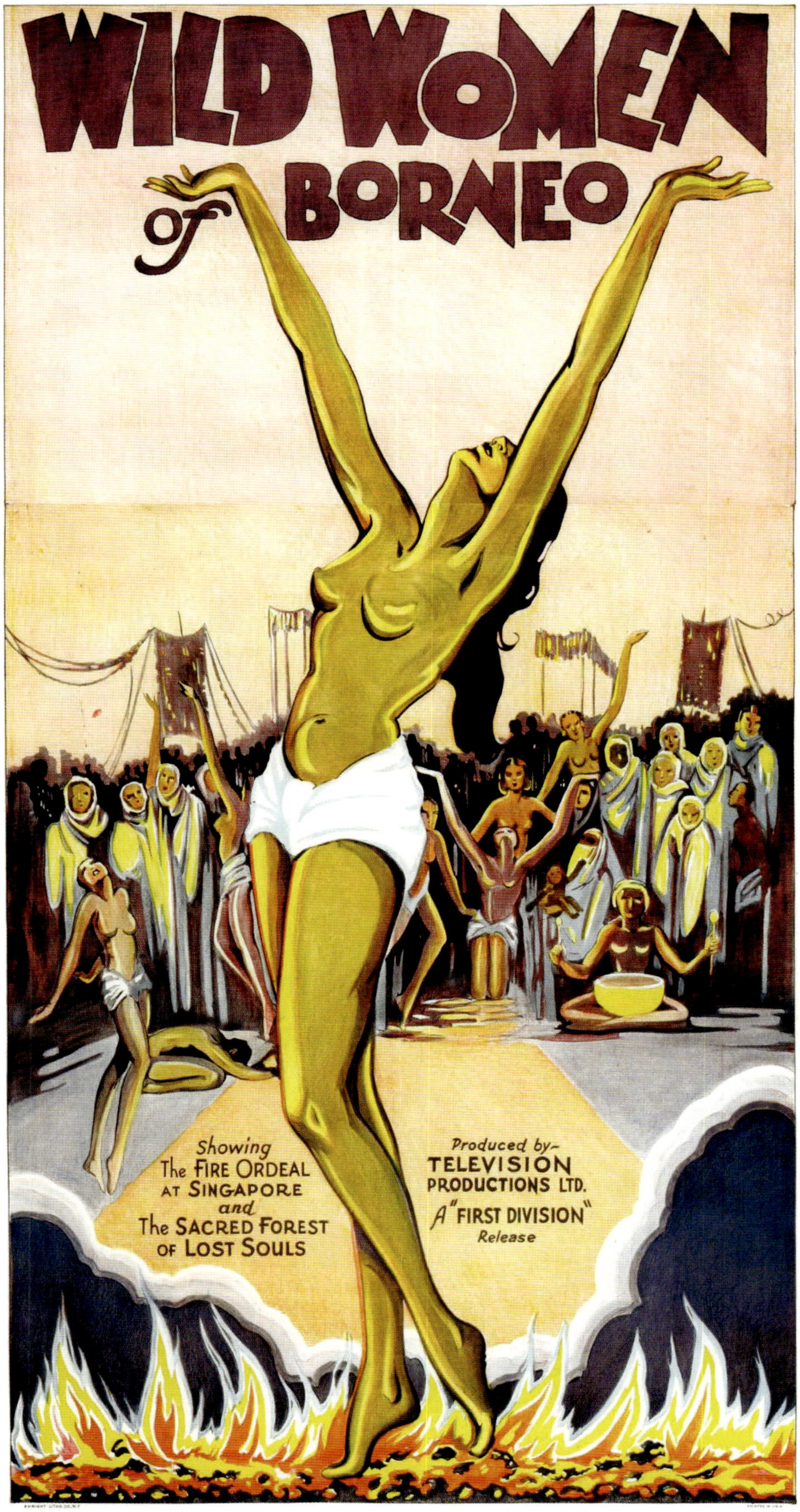

WILD WOMEN of BORNEO

Showing The FIRE ORDEAL AT SINGAPORE and The SACRED FOREST OF LOST SOULS

Produced by- TELEVISION PRODUCTIONS LTD.
A "FIRST DIVISION" Release

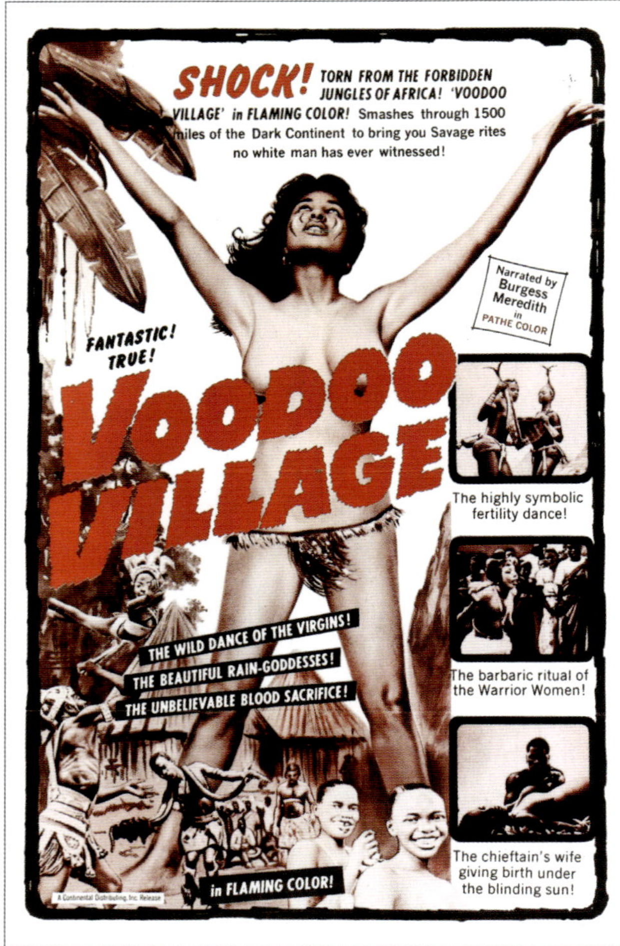
SHOCK! TORN FROM THE FORBIDDEN JUNGLES OF AFRICA! 'VOODOO VILLAGE' in FLAMING COLOR! Smashes through 1500 miles of the Dark Continent to bring you Savage rites no white man has ever witnessed!
Narrated by Burgess Meredith in PATHE COLOR
FANTASTIC! TRUE!
VOODOO VILLAGE
The highly symbolic fertility dance!
THE WILD DANCE OF THE VIRGINS!
THE BEAUTIFUL RAIN-GODDESSES!
THE UNBELIEVABLE BLOOD SACRIFICE!
The barbaric ritual of the Warrior Women!
The chieftain's wife giving birth under the blinding sun!
in FLAMING COLOR!

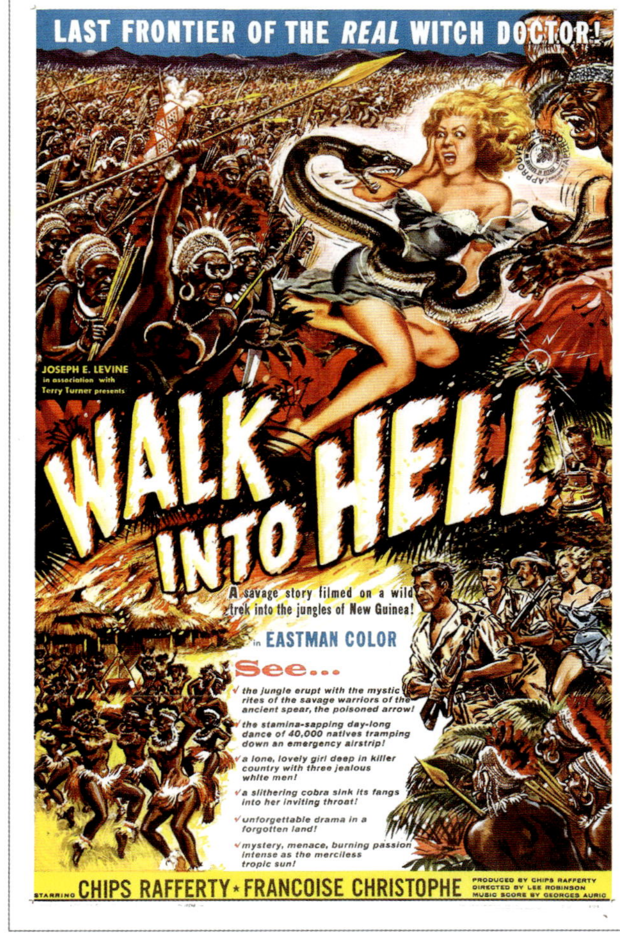
LAST FRONTIER OF THE REAL WITCH DOCTOR!
JOSEPH E. LEVINE in association with Terry Turner presents
WALK INTO HELL
A savage story filmed on a wild trek into the jungles of New Guinea!
in EASTMAN COLOR
See...
the jungle erupt with the mystic rites of the savage warriors of the ancient spear, the poisoned arrow!
the stamina-sapping day-long dance of 40,000 natives tramping down an emergency airstrip!
a lone, lovely girl deep in killer country with three jealous white men!
a slithering cobra sink its fangs into her inviting throat!
unforgettable drama in a forgotten land!
mystery, menace, burning passion intense as the merciless tropic sun!
STARRING CHIPS RAFFERTY ★ FRANCOISE CHRISTOPHE
PRODUCED BY CHIPS RAFFERTY DIRECTED BY LEE ROBINSON MUSIC SCORE BY GEORGES AURIC

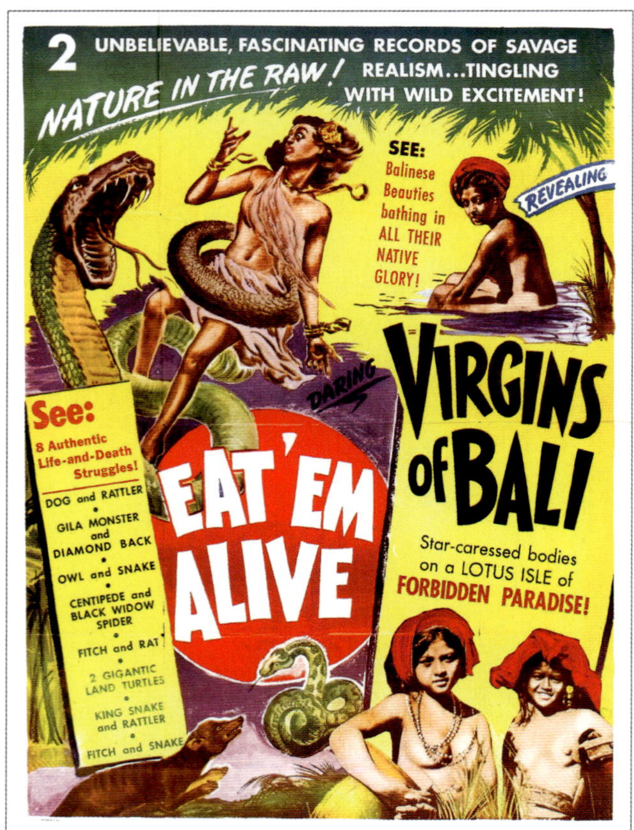
2 UNBELIEVABLE, FASCINATING RECORDS OF SAVAGE
NATURE IN THE RAW! REALISM...TINGLING WITH WILD EXCITEMENT!
SEE: Balinese Beauties bathing in ALL THEIR NATIVE GLORY!
REVEALING
DARING
See: 8 Authentic Life-and-Death Struggles!
DOG and RATTLER
GILA MONSTER and DIAMOND BACK
OWL and SNAKE
CENTIPEDE and BLACK WIDOW SPIDER
FITCH and RAT
2 GIGANTIC LAND TURTLES
KING SNAKE and RATTLER
FITCH and SNAKE
EAT 'EM ALIVE
VIRGINS of BALI
Star-caressed bodies on a LOTUS ISLE of FORBIDDEN PARADISE!

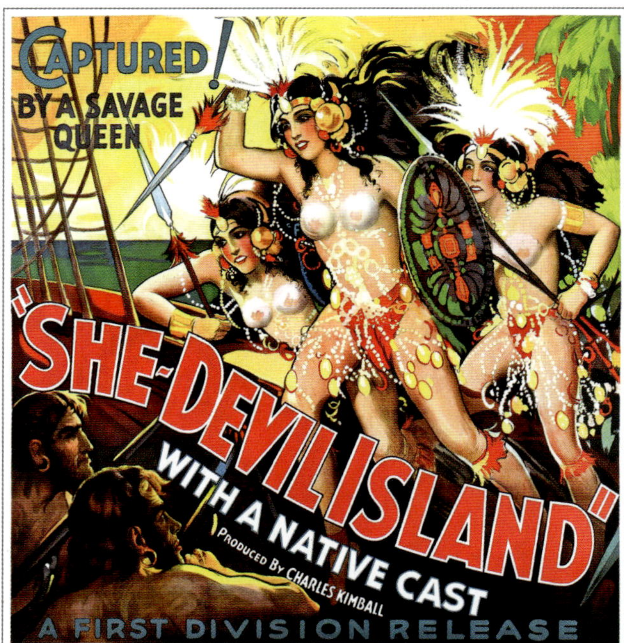
CAPTURED! BY A SAVAGE QUEEN
"SHE-DEVIL ISLAND"
WITH A NATIVE CAST
PRODUCED BY CHARLES KIMBALL
A FIRST DIVISION RELEASE

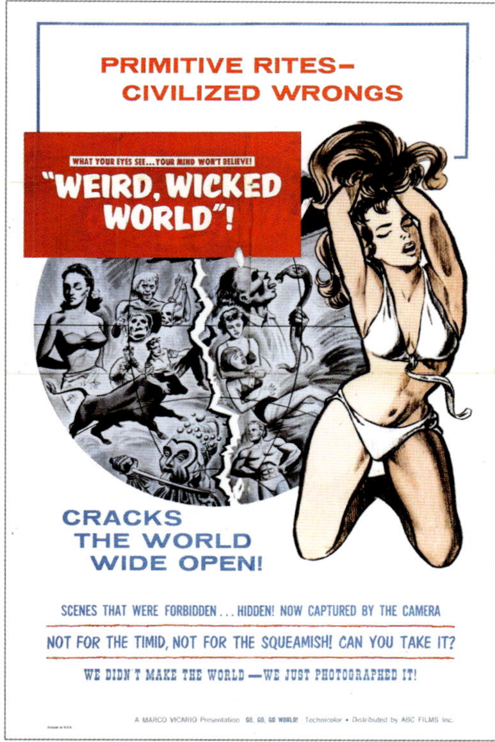
PRIMITIVE RITES–
CIVILIZED WRONGS
WHAT YOUR EYES SEE... YOUR MIND WON'T BELIEVE!
"WEIRD, WICKED WORLD"!
CRACKS THE WORLD WIDE OPEN!
SCENES THAT WERE FORBIDDEN... HIDDEN! NOW CAPTURED BY THE CAMERA
NOT FOR THE TIMID, NOT FOR THE SQUEAMISH! CAN YOU TAKE IT?
WE DIDN'T MAKE THE WORLD —WE JUST PHOTOGRAPHED IT!

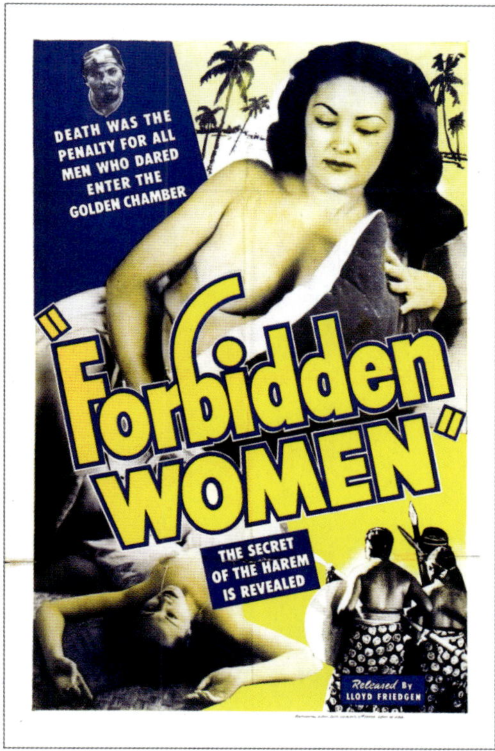
DEATH WAS THE PENALTY FOR ALL MEN WHO DARED ENTER THE GOLDEN CHAMBER
"Forbidden WOMEN"
THE SECRET OF THE HAREM IS REVEALED
Released by LLOYD FRIEDGEN

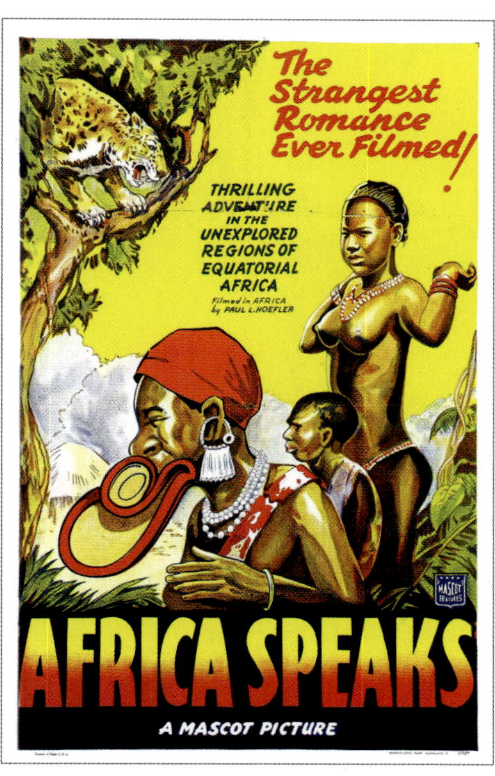
The Strangest Romance Ever Filmed!
THRILLING ADVENTURE IN THE UNEXPLORED REGIONS OF EQUATORIAL AFRICA
Filmed in AFRICA by PAUL L. HOEFLER
AFRICA SPEAKS
A MASCOT PICTURE

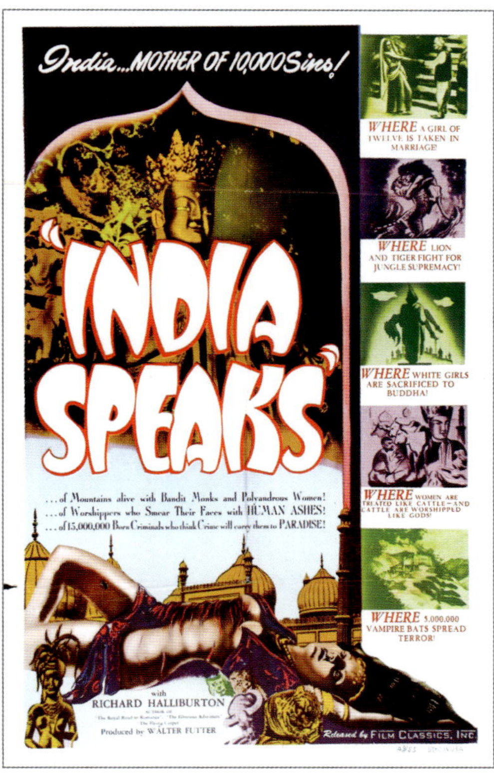
India...MOTHER OF 10,000 Sins!
"INDIA SPEAKS"
WHERE A GIRL OF TWELVE IS TAKEN IN MARRIAGE!
WHERE LION AND TIGER FIGHT FOR JUNGLE SUPREMACY!
WHERE WHITE GIRLS ARE SACRIFICED TO BUDDHA!
WHERE WOMEN ARE TREATED LIKE CATTLE—AND CATTLE ARE WORSHIPPED LIKE GODS!
WHERE 5,000,000 VAMPIRE BATS SPREAD TERROR!
...of Mountains alive with Bandit Monks and Polyandrous Women!
...of Worshippers who Smear Their Faces with HUMAN ASHES!
with RICHARD HALLIBURTON
Produced by WALTER FUTTER
Released by FILM CLASSICS, INC.

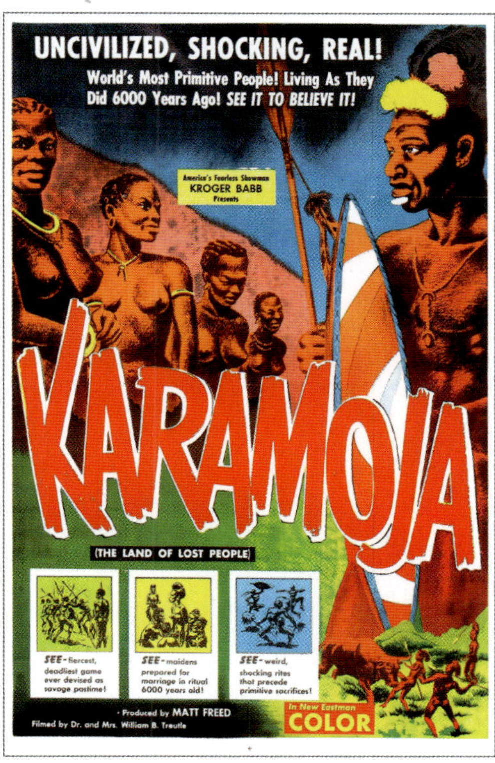
UNCIVILIZED, SHOCKING, REAL!
World's Most Primitive People! Living As They Did 6000 Years Ago! SEE IT TO BELIEVE IT!
America's Fearless Showman KROGER BABB Presents
KARAMOJA
(THE LAND OF LOST PEOPLE)
SEE–fiercest, deadliest game ever devised as savage pastime!
SEE–maidens prepared for marriage in ritual 6000 years old!
SEE–weird, shocking rites that precede primitive sacrifices!
Produced by MATT FREED
Filmed by Dr. and Mrs. William B. Treutle
In New Eastman COLOR

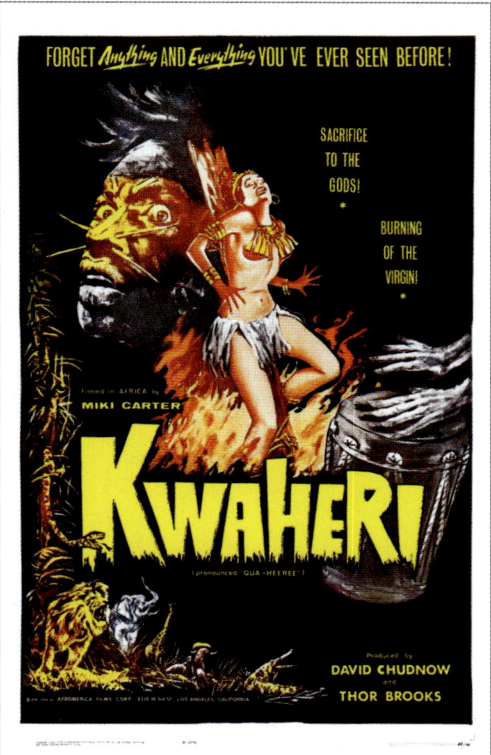
FORGET Anything AND Everything YOU'VE EVER SEEN BEFORE!
SACRIFICE TO THE GODS!
BURNING OF THE VIRGIN!
MIKI CARTER
KWAHERI
Produced by DAVID CHUDNOW and THOR BROOKS

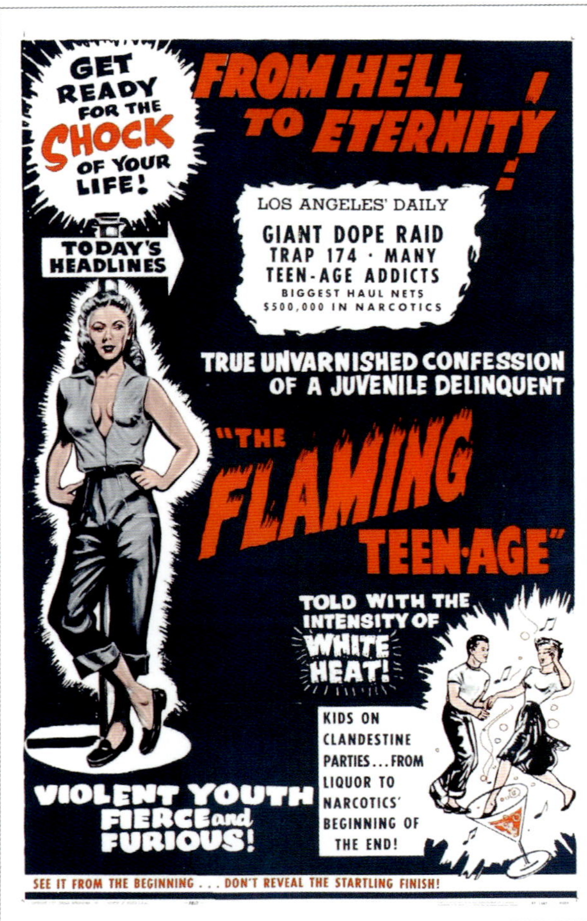
GET READY FOR THE SHOCK OF YOUR LIFE!
FROM HELL TO ETERNITY!
TODAY'S HEADLINES
LOS ANGELES' DAILY
GIANT DOPE RAID TRAP 174 · MANY TEEN-AGE ADDICTS
BIGGEST HAUL NETS $500,000 IN NARCOTICS
TRUE UNVARNISHED CONFESSION OF A JUVENILE DELINQUENT
"THE FLAMING TEEN-AGE"
TOLD WITH THE INTENSITY OF WHITE HEAT!
KIDS ON CLANDESTINE PARTIES... FROM LIQUOR TO NARCOTICS' BEGINNING OF THE END!
VIOLENT YOUTH FIERCE and FURIOUS!
SEE IT FROM THE BEGINNING . . . DON'T REVEAL THE STARTLING FINISH!

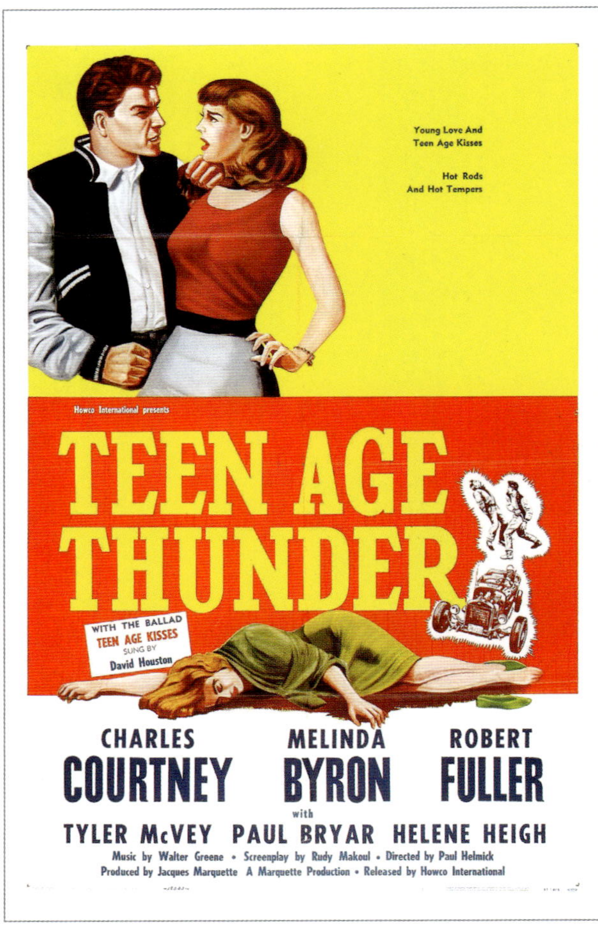
Young Love And Teen Age Kisses
Hot Rods And Hot Tempers
Howco International presents
TEEN AGE THUNDER
WITH THE BALLAD TEEN AGE KISSES SUNG BY David Houston
CHARLES COURTNEY
MELINDA BYRON
ROBERT FULLER
with
TYLER McVEY PAUL BRYAR HELENE HEIGH
Music by Walter Greene • Screenplay by Rudy Makoul • Directed by Paul Helmick
Produced by Jacques Marquette A Marquette Production • Released by Howco International

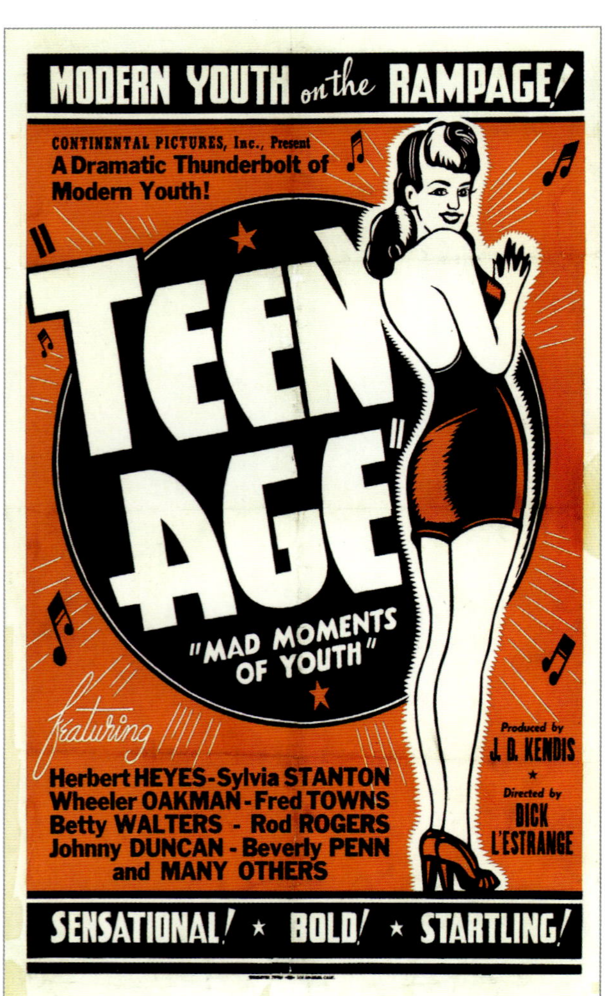
MODERN YOUTH on the RAMPAGE!
CONTINENTAL PICTURES, Inc., Present
A Dramatic Thunderbolt of Modern Youth!
"TEEN AGE"
"MAD MOMENTS OF YOUTH"
featuring
Herbert HEYES - Sylvia STANTON
Wheeler OAKMAN - Fred TOWNS
Betty WALTERS - Rod ROGERS
Johnny DUNCAN - Beverly PENN
and MANY OTHERS
Produced by J. D. KENDIS
Directed by DICK L'ESTRANGE
SENSATIONAL! ★ BOLD! ★ STARTLING!

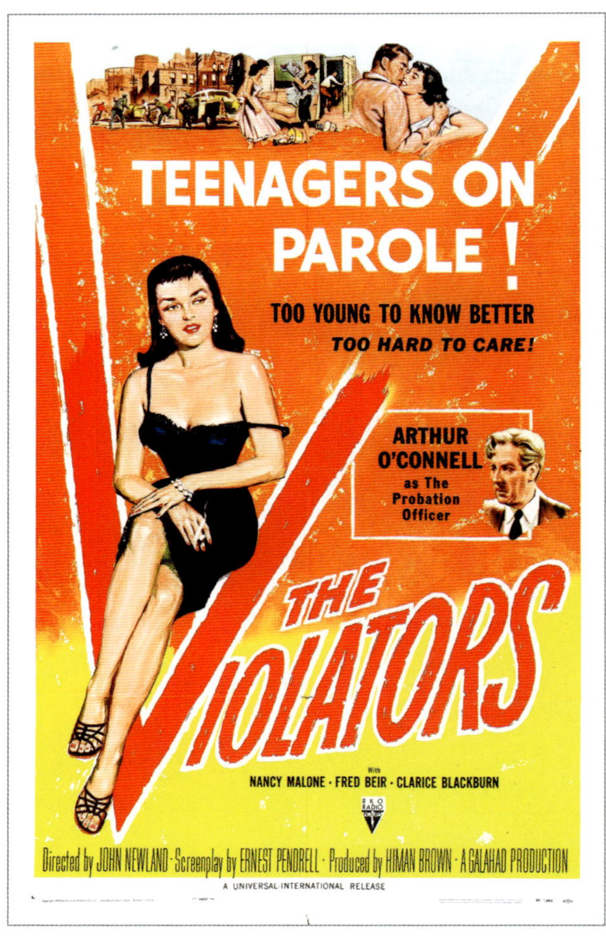
TEENAGERS ON PAROLE!
TOO YOUNG TO KNOW BETTER
TOO HARD TO CARE!
ARTHUR O'CONNELL as The Probation Officer
THE VIOLATORS
With
NANCY MALONE · FRED BEIR · CLARICE BLACKBURN
RKO RADIO PICTURES
Directed by JOHN NEWLAND · Screenplay by ERNEST PENDRELL · Produced by HIMAN BROWN · A GALAHAD PRODUCTION
A UNIVERSAL-INTERNATIONAL RELEASE

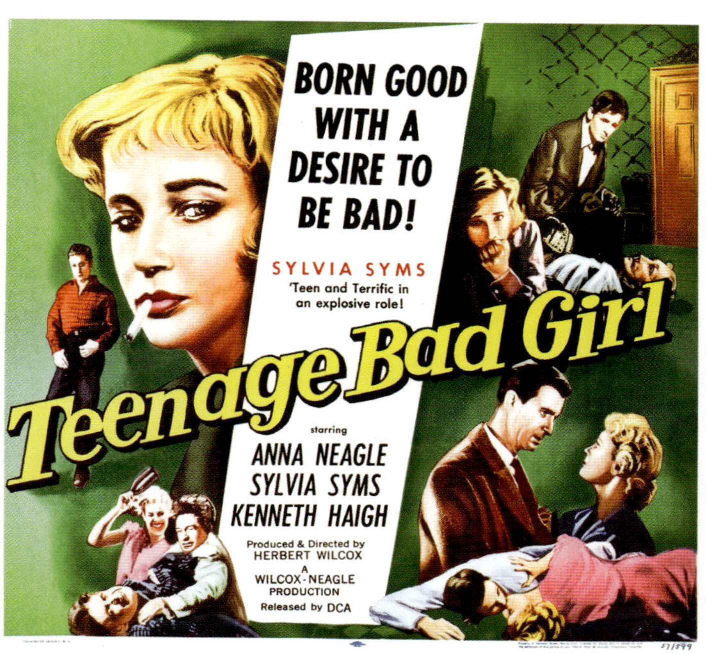

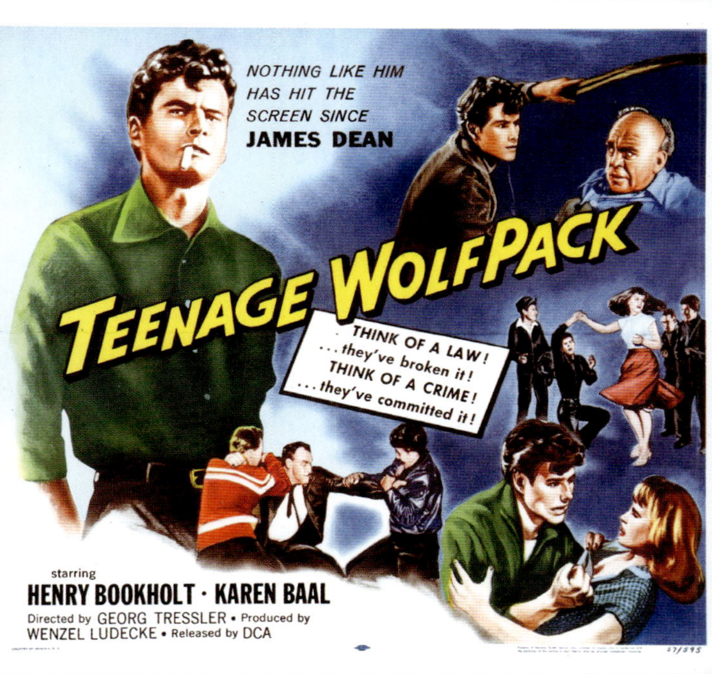

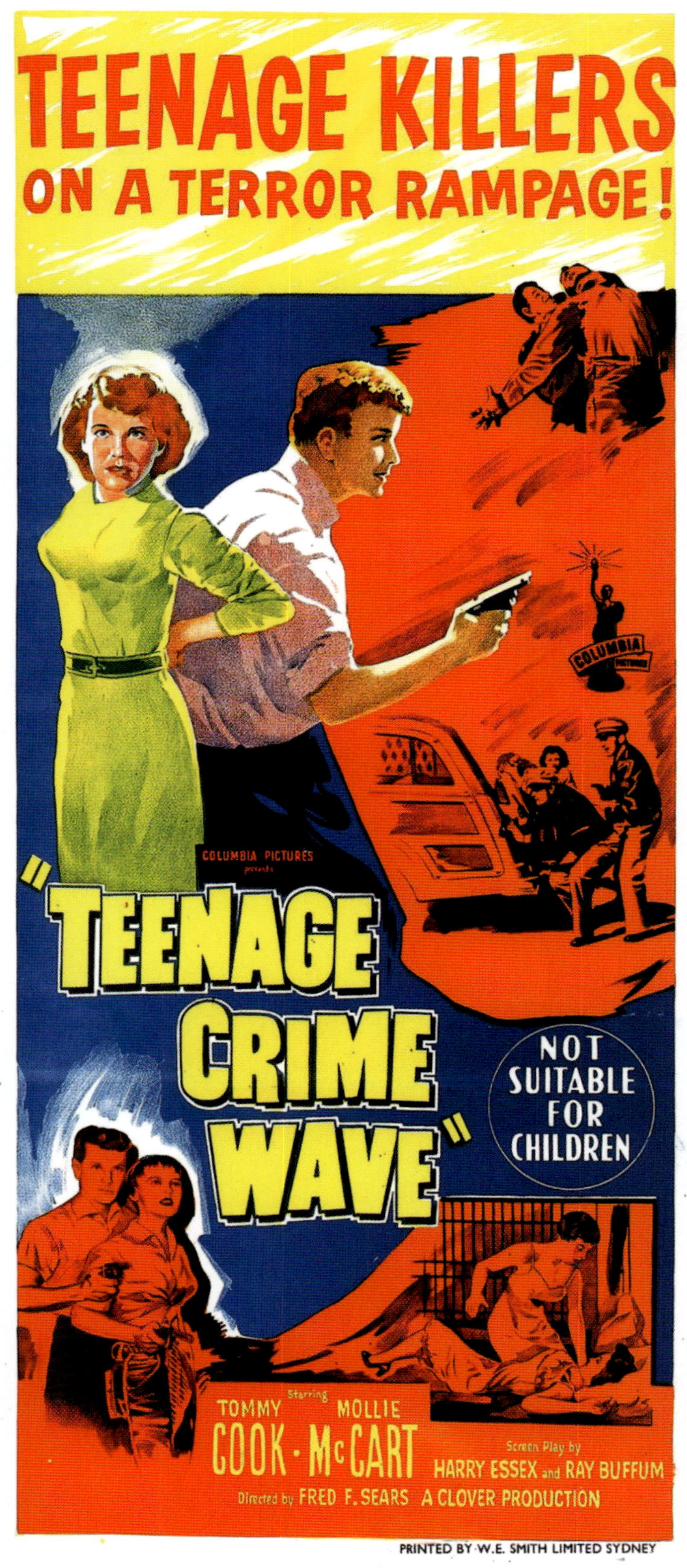

FEAR OF TEENAGERS

Though the researchers at Merriam-Webster have traced the first use of the word back to 1921, it was the '50s when "teenagers" became a cultural force. "Parents! Do you actually know what your sons and daughters do for thrills and kicks?" warns the trailer for *The Flaming Teenage* (1956), homing in on the fear and paranoia surrounding this new source of evil and chaos—the "juvenile delinquent." A year after James Dean tore the screen apart as the ultimate teen *Rebel Without a Cause*, the star of *Teenage Wolfpack* (1956) was promoted as his successor. "Henry Bookholt" was really Horst Buchholz, renamed to hide the movie's origins—it's actually a dubbed version of the German gang drama *Die Halbstarken*.

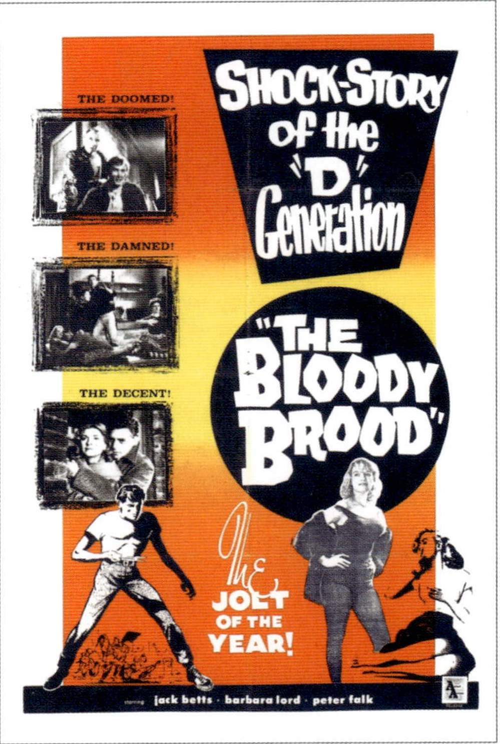

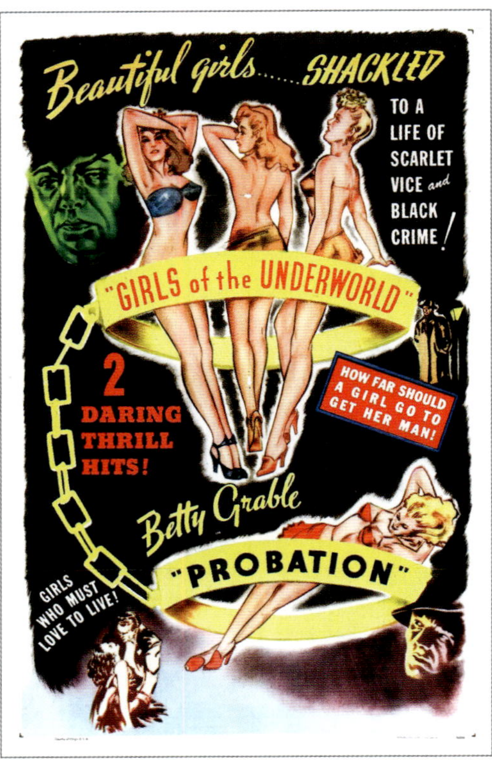

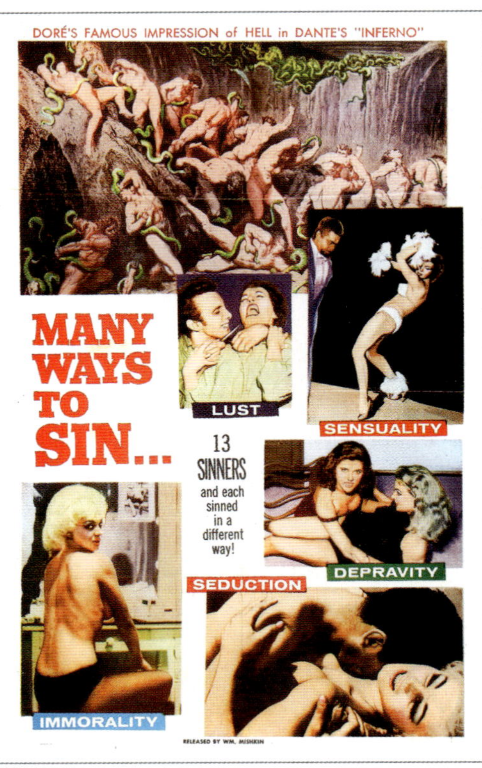

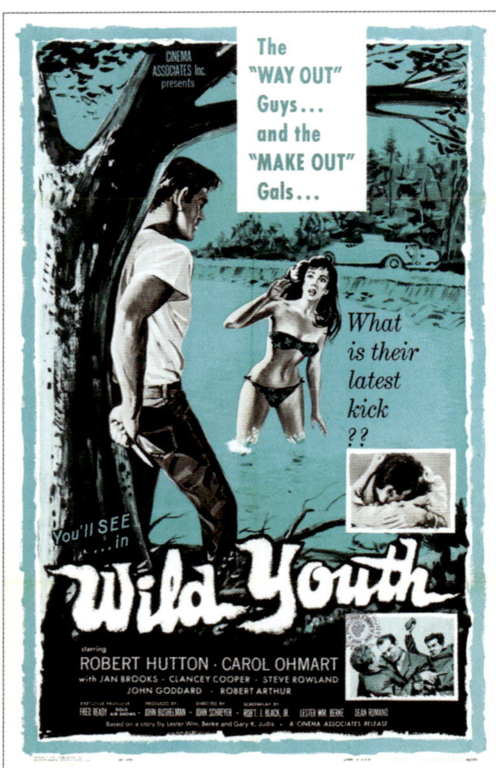

TOO MUCH TOO YOUNG

As the '50s progressed, American promoters continued to highlight—as a public service, you understand—the depths of moral turpitude that young women were sinking to, with posters that increasingly left less and less to the imagination. Some of the films were foreign imports given an exploitation makeover—thus Jeanne Moreau in *M'sieur La Caille* (1955) had *No Morals* in the dubbed US version, and the worthy Swedish drama *Ogift fader sökes* (Unmarried Father Wanted, 1953) became the luridly advertised *Unmarried Mothers* for its Stateside debut three years later. Homegrown effort *Blonde Pickup* (1951) starred, "The most exciting body in Hollywood," professional wrestler Peaches Page. The trailer made sure to include a *very* lengthy shot of her with a skipping rope, jumping up and down, up and down . . .

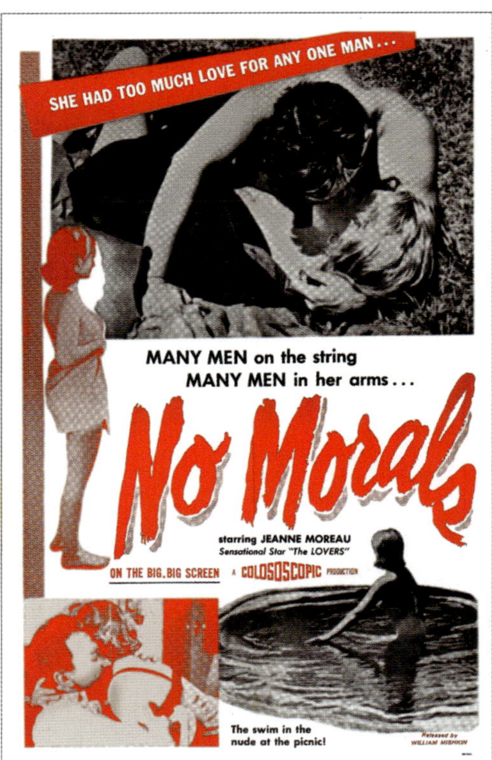

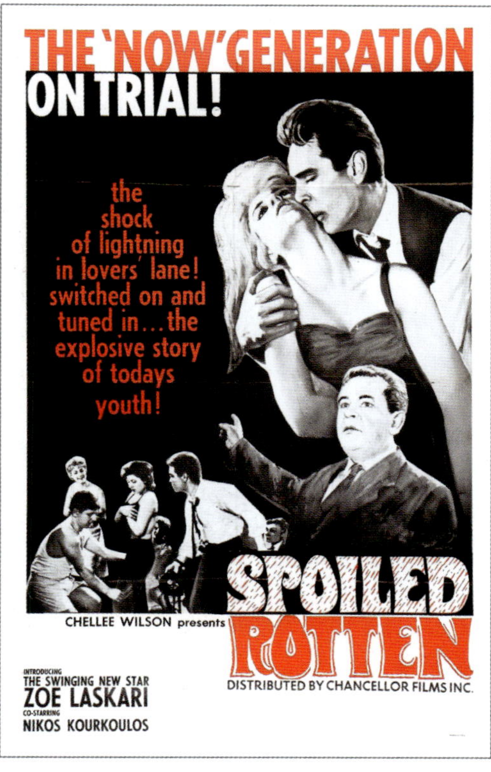
THE 'NOW' GENERATION
ON TRIAL!
the shock of lightning in lovers' lane! switched on and tuned in… the explosive story of todays youth!
CHELLEE WILSON presents
SPOILED ROTTEN
DISTRIBUTED BY CHANCELLOR FILMS INC.
INTRODUCING
THE SWINGING NEW STAR
ZOE LASKARI
CO-STARRING
NIKOS KOURKOULOS

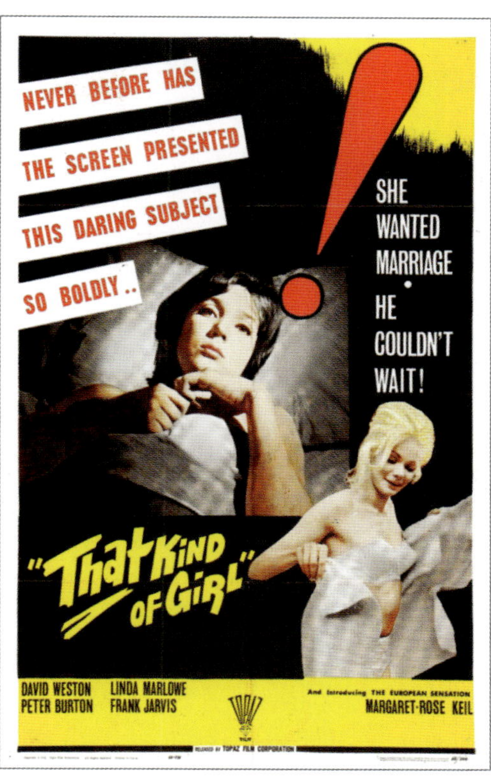
NEVER BEFORE HAS
THE SCREEN PRESENTED
THIS DARING SUBJECT
SO BOLDLY..
SHE WANTED MARRIAGE • HE COULDN'T WAIT!
"That Kind of Girl"
DAVID WESTON
PETER BURTON
LINDA MARLOWE
FRANK JARVIS
And introducing THE EUROPEAN SENSATION
MARGARET-ROSE KEIL

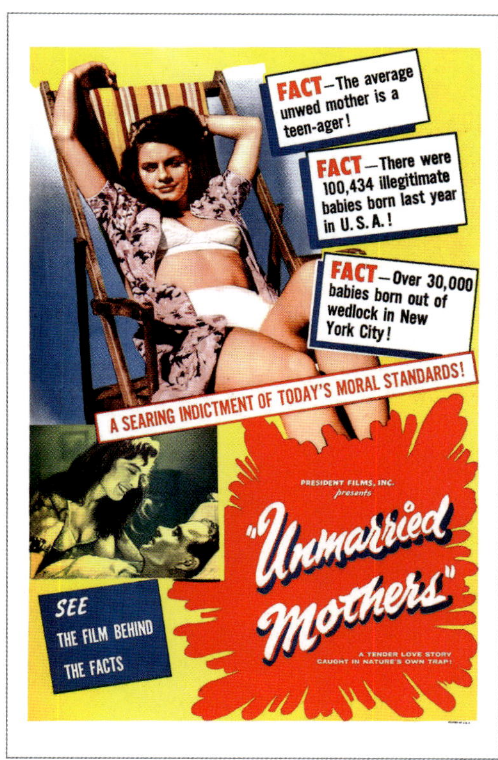
FACT—The average unwed mother is a teen-ager!
FACT—There were 100,434 illegitimate babies born last year in U.S.A.!
FACT—Over 30,000 babies born out of wedlock in New York City!
A SEARING INDICTMENT OF TODAY'S MORAL STANDARDS!
PRESIDENT FILMS, INC. presents
"Unmarried Mothers"
A TENDER LOVE STORY CAUGHT IN NATURE'S OWN TRAP!
SEE THE FILM BEHIND THE FACTS

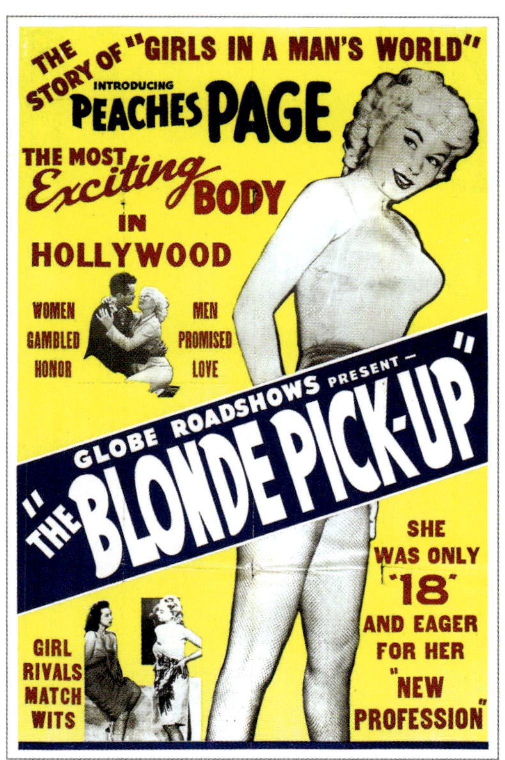
THE STORY OF "GIRLS IN A MAN'S WORLD"
INTRODUCING
PEACHES PAGE
THE MOST Exciting BODY IN HOLLYWOOD
WOMEN GAMBLED HONOR
MEN PROMISED LOVE
GLOBE ROADSHOWS PRESENT—
"THE BLONDE PICK-UP"
SHE WAS ONLY "18" AND EAGER FOR HER "NEW PROFESSION"
GIRL RIVALS MATCH WITS

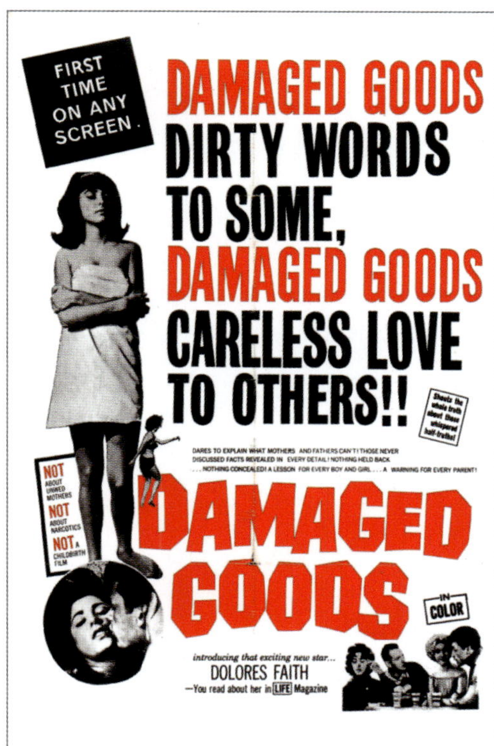
FIRST TIME ON ANY SCREEN.
DAMAGED GOODS
DIRTY WORDS
TO SOME,
DAMAGED GOODS
CARELESS LOVE
TO OTHERS!!
NOT ABOUT UNWED MOTHERS
NOT ABOUT NARCOTICS
NOT A CHILDBIRTH FILM
DAMAGED GOODS
IN COLOR
introducing that exciting new star...
DOLORES FAITH
—You read about her in LIFE Magazine

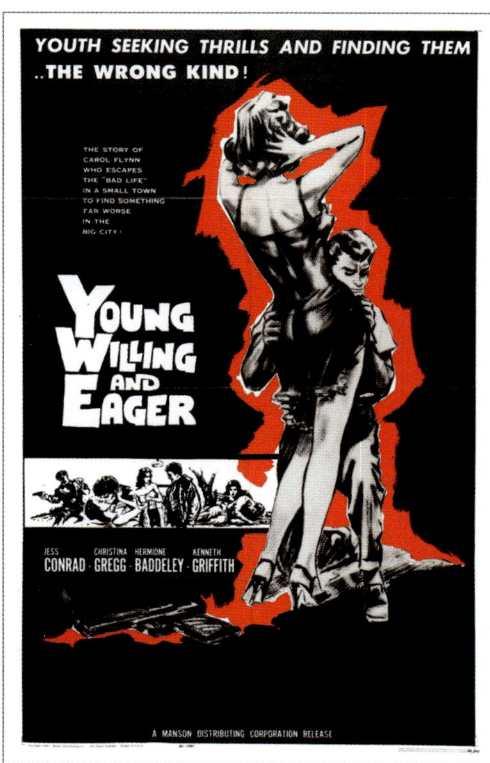
YOUTH SEEKING THRILLS AND FINDING THEM
..THE WRONG KIND!
THE STORY OF CAROL FLYNN WHO ESCAPES THE "BAD LIFE" IN A SMALL TOWN TO FIND SOMETHING FAR WORSE IN THE BIG CITY!
YOUNG WILLING AND EAGER
JESS CONRAD · CHRISTINA GREGG · HERMIONE BADDELEY · KENNETH GRIFFITH
A MANSON DISTRIBUTING CORPORATION RELEASE

This Film Is So UNUSUAL and INTIMATE, Details Are Too Obvious To Print!

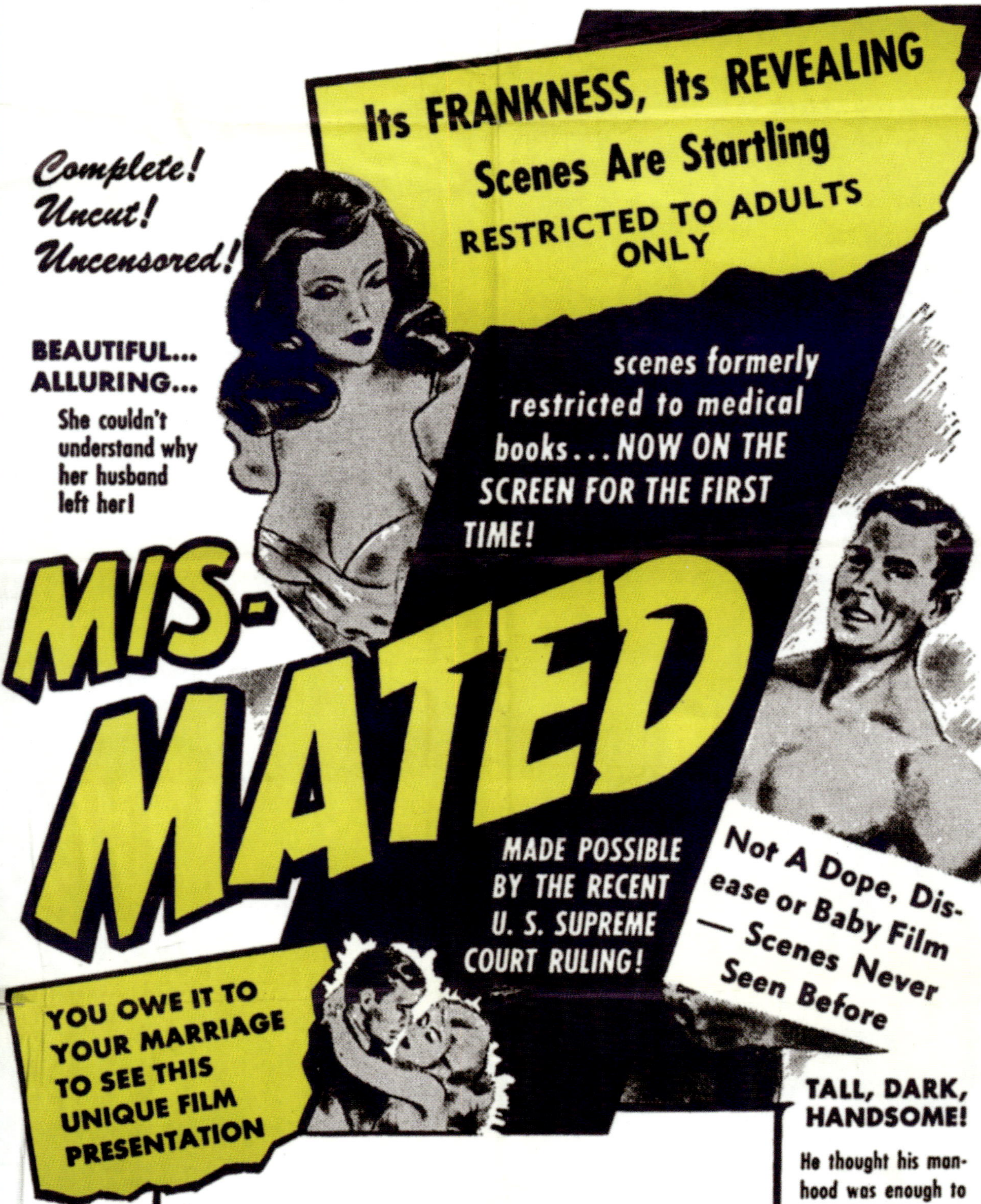

SEX ED

When Alfred Kinsey published his snappily titled academic report *Sexual Behavior in the Human Male* in 1948, he probably didn't expect it to end up on *The New York Times* best seller list for 27 weeks. The general public really, really wanted to talk about sex, and the exploitation showmen were happy to ramp up their supply of "educational" fodder for filmgoers, sometimes mixing cautionary tales with actual childbirth footage, often with a "hygiene commentator" live on stage to provide a lecture. The ubiquitous Kroger Babb was typically ahead of the curve with his blockbuster *Mom and Dad*, originally released in 1945, but still grossing millions of dollars well into the '50s. As *Time* magazine pointed out, Babb's saturation-level publicity wherever the film played left "only the livestock unaware of the chance to learn the facts of life." Such was the preponderance of filmed births that twins and even triplets were sought out to up the ante. The poster for *Mis-Mated* (1952) meanwhile was at pains to clarify that it was, "Not a Dope, Disease or Baby Film," and was, "Made possible by the recent U. S. Supreme Court ruling" (1952's *Joseph Burstyn, Inc. v. Wilson* to be precise, which dented censors' powers forever by confirming that motion pictures were worthy of free speech protection under the First Amendment). *Mis-Mated*'s trailer voiceover gave a taste of the movie's important revelations: "You will see the latest hygienic discoveries demonstrated and explained, among them the results of using hormone creams for bust development purposes."

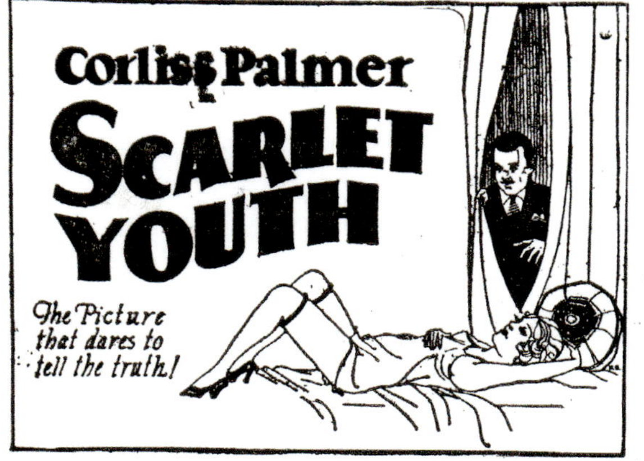

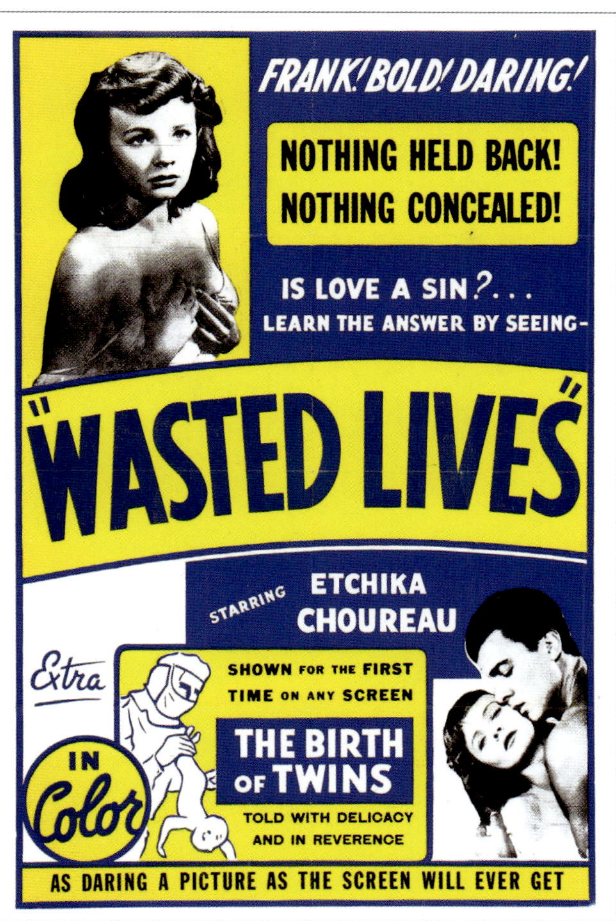

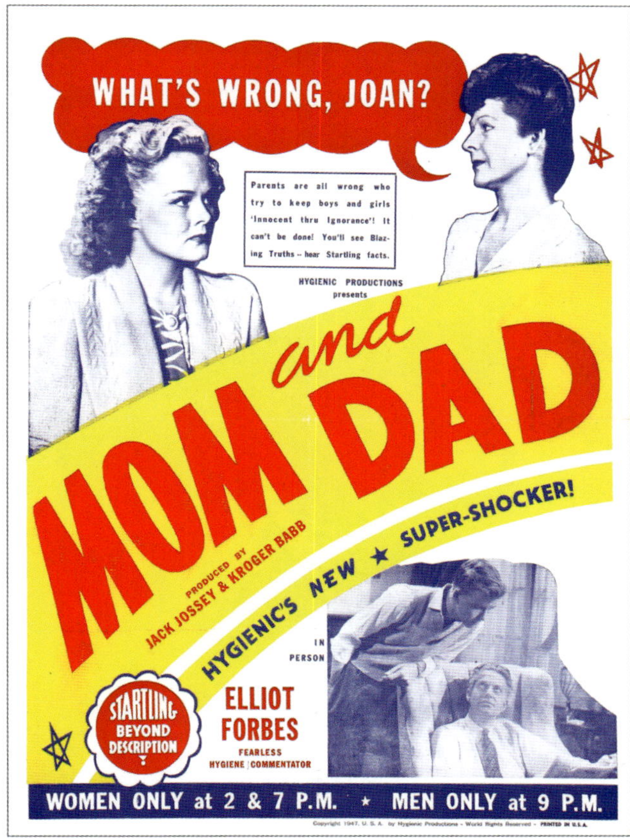

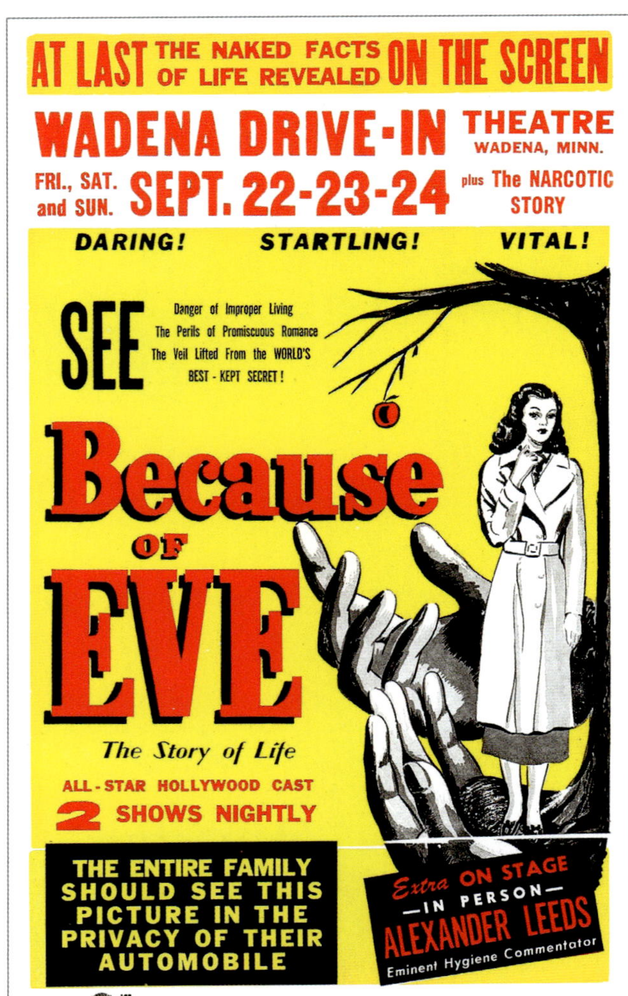
AT LAST THE NAKED FACTS OF LIFE REVEALED ON THE SCREEN
WADENA DRIVE-IN THEATRE
WADENA, MINN.
FRI., SAT. and SUN. SEPT. 22-23-24
plus The NARCOTIC STORY
DARING! STARTLING! VITAL!
SEE
Danger of Improper Living
The Perils of Promiscuous Romance
The Veil Lifted From the WORLD'S BEST-KEPT SECRET!
Because of EVE
The Story of Life
ALL-STAR HOLLYWOOD CAST
2 SHOWS NIGHTLY
THE ENTIRE FAMILY SHOULD SEE THIS PICTURE IN THE PRIVACY OF THEIR AUTOMOBILE
Extra ON STAGE
—IN PERSON—
ALEXANDER LEEDS
Eminent Hygiene Commentator

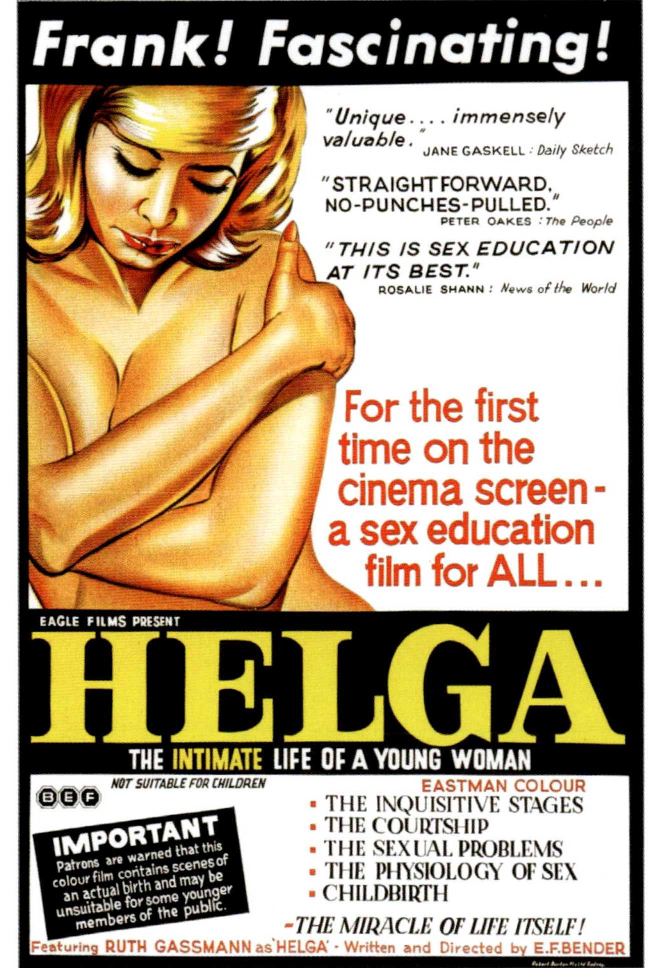
Frank! Fascinating!
"Unique.... immensely valuable." JANE GASKELL : Daily Sketch
"STRAIGHTFORWARD, NO-PUNCHES-PULLED." PETER OAKES : The People
"THIS IS SEX EDUCATION AT ITS BEST." ROSALIE SHANN : News of the World
For the first time on the cinema screen - a sex education film for ALL...
EAGLE FILMS PRESENT
HELGA
THE INTIMATE LIFE OF A YOUNG WOMAN
NOT SUITABLE FOR CHILDREN
EASTMAN COLOUR
IMPORTANT
Patrons are warned that this colour film contains scenes of an actual birth and may be unsuitable for some younger members of the public.
THE INQUISITIVE STAGES
THE COURTSHIP
THE SEXUAL PROBLEMS
THE PHYSIOLOGY OF SEX
CHILDBIRTH
-THE MIRACLE OF LIFE ITSELF!
Featuring RUTH GASSMANN as 'HELGA' · Written and Directed by E.F.BENDER

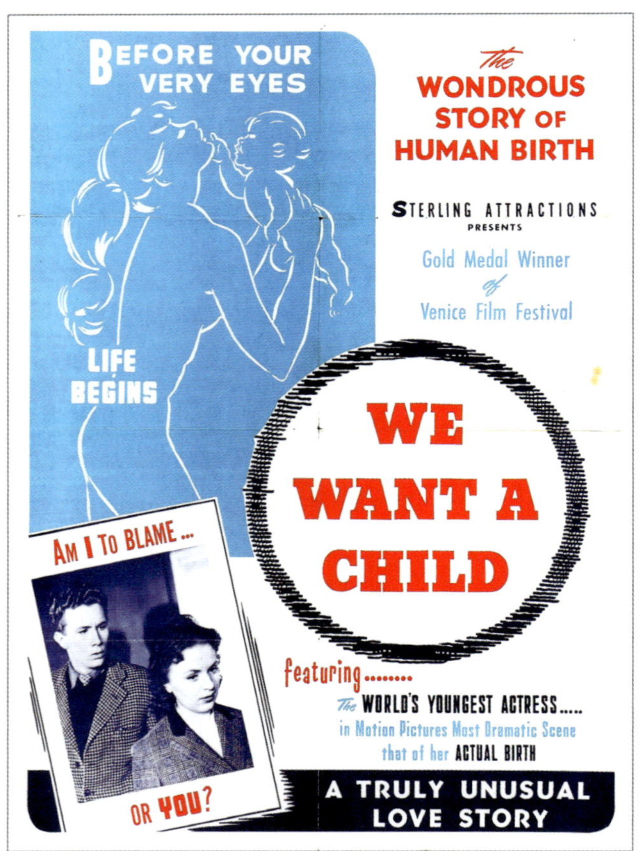
BEFORE YOUR VERY EYES
The WONDROUS STORY OF HUMAN BIRTH
STERLING ATTRACTIONS
PRESENTS
Gold Medal Winner of Venice Film Festival
LIFE BEGINS
WE WANT A CHILD
AM I TO BLAME...
OR YOU?
featuring.........
The WORLD'S YOUNGEST ACTRESS.....
in Motion Pictures Most Dramatic Scene
that of her ACTUAL BIRTH
A TRULY UNUSUAL LOVE STORY

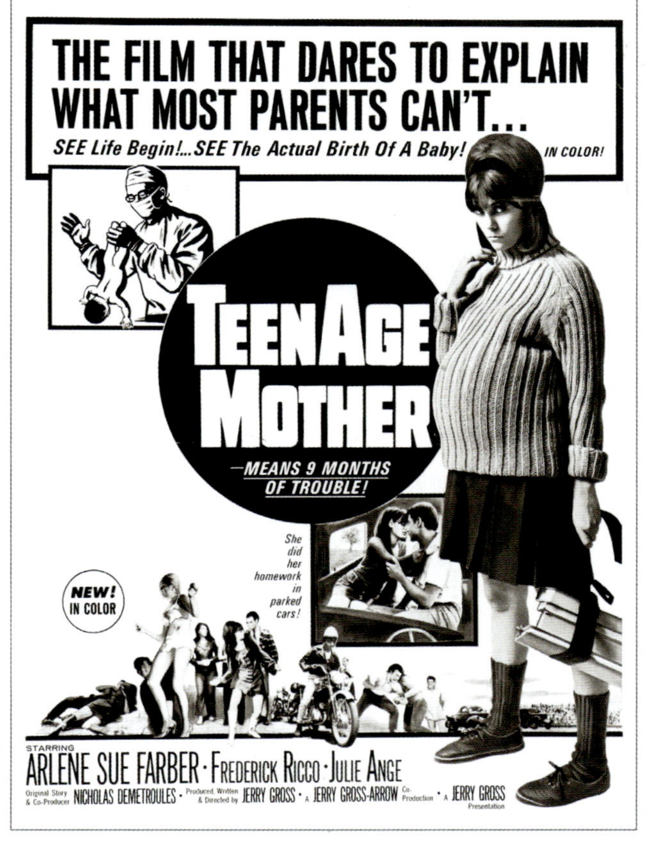
THE FILM THAT DARES TO EXPLAIN WHAT MOST PARENTS CAN'T...
SEE Life Begin!...SEE The Actual Birth Of A Baby!
IN COLOR!
TEENAGE MOTHER
—MEANS 9 MONTHS OF TROUBLE!
She did her homework in parked cars!
NEW! IN COLOR
STARRING
ARLENE SUE FARBER · FREDERICK RICCO · JULIE ANGE
NICHOLAS DEMETROULES · JERRY GROSS · A JERRY GROSS-ARROW · A JERRY GROSS

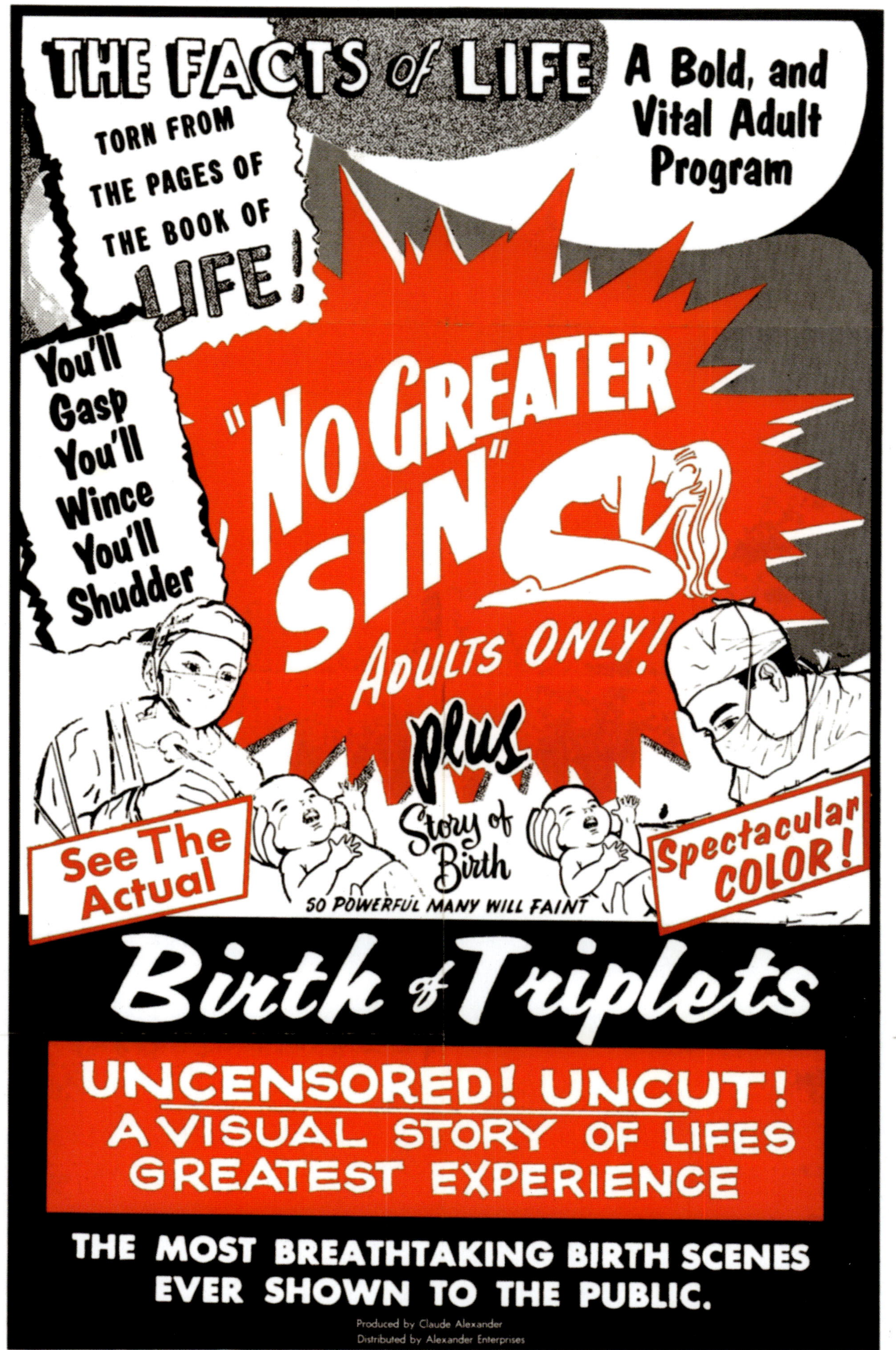
THE FACTS of LIFE
A Bold, and Vital Adult Program
TORN FROM THE PAGES OF THE BOOK OF LIFE!
You'll Gasp You'll Wince You'll Shudder
"NO GREATER SIN"
ADULTS ONLY!
plus
See The Actual
Story of Birth
SO POWERFUL MANY WILL FAINT
Spectacular COLOR!
Birth of Triplets
UNCENSORED! UNCUT!
A VISUAL STORY OF LIFES GREATEST EXPERIENCE
THE MOST BREATHTAKING BIRTH SCENES EVER SHOWN TO THE PUBLIC.
Produced by Claude Alexander
Distributed by Alexander Enterprises

TABOO

Seen today, these tales of biracial romance and "passing" for white have crossed the line from "taboo-busting" to uncomfortably racist. *The New York Times* found the drama *Night of the Quarter Moon* "sincere" but "misguided" when it opened in 1959, but its re-release campaign under the title *The Color of Her Skin* is simply misguided. *I Spit on Your Grave* (1959, no relation to the 1978 rape revenge shocker) presents the bizarre sight of Spanish/Arab actor Christian Marquand playing a light-skinned African-American in a Mississippi-set drama shot in France! *Quadroon* (1971) has a storyline based on historical events, but its poster design and tagline "¼ Black, ¾ White . . . ALL Woman" make clear that the movie's aim is to exploit, not educate.

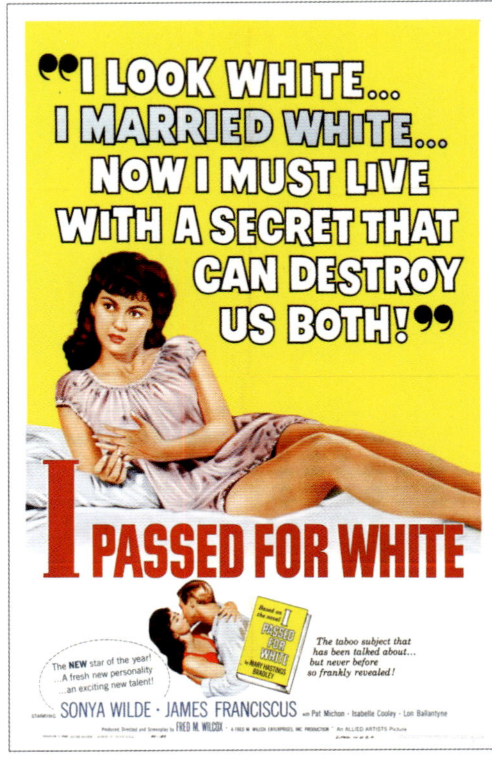

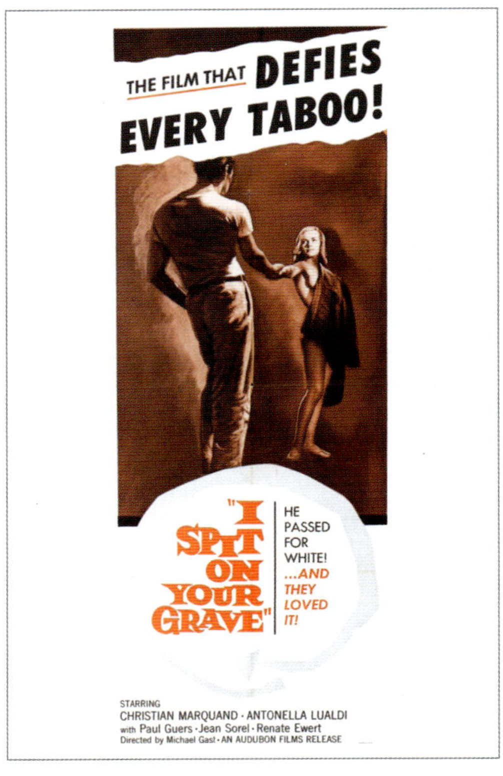

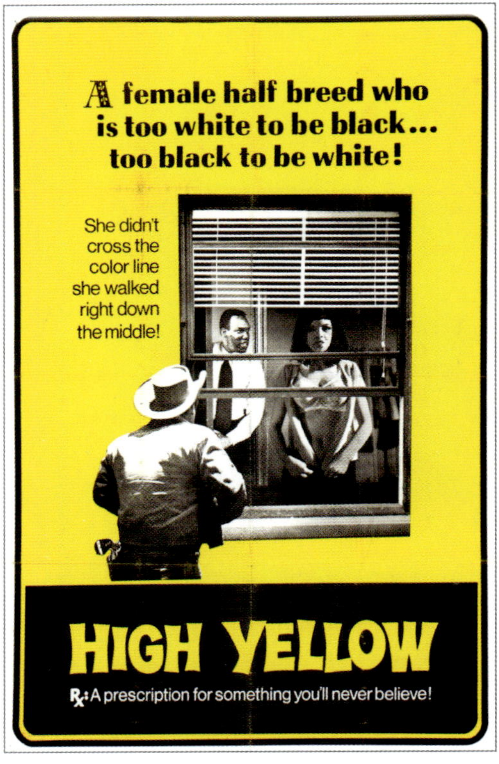

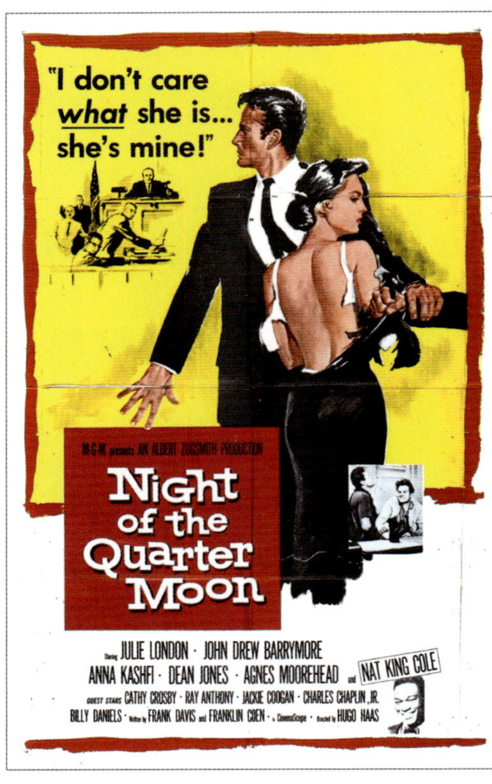

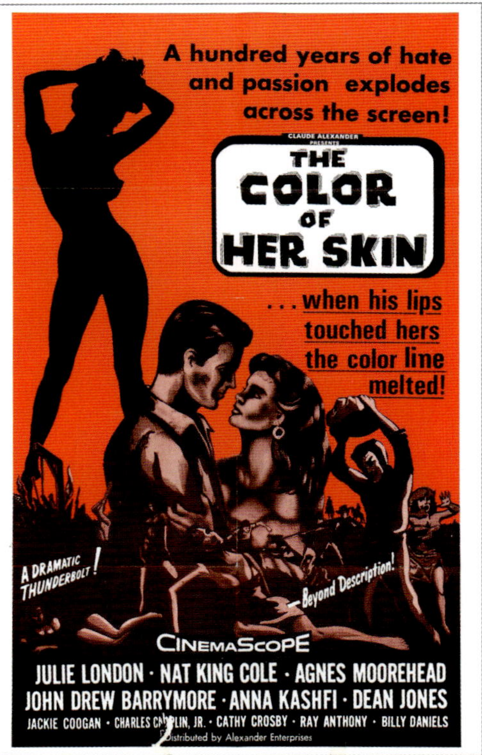

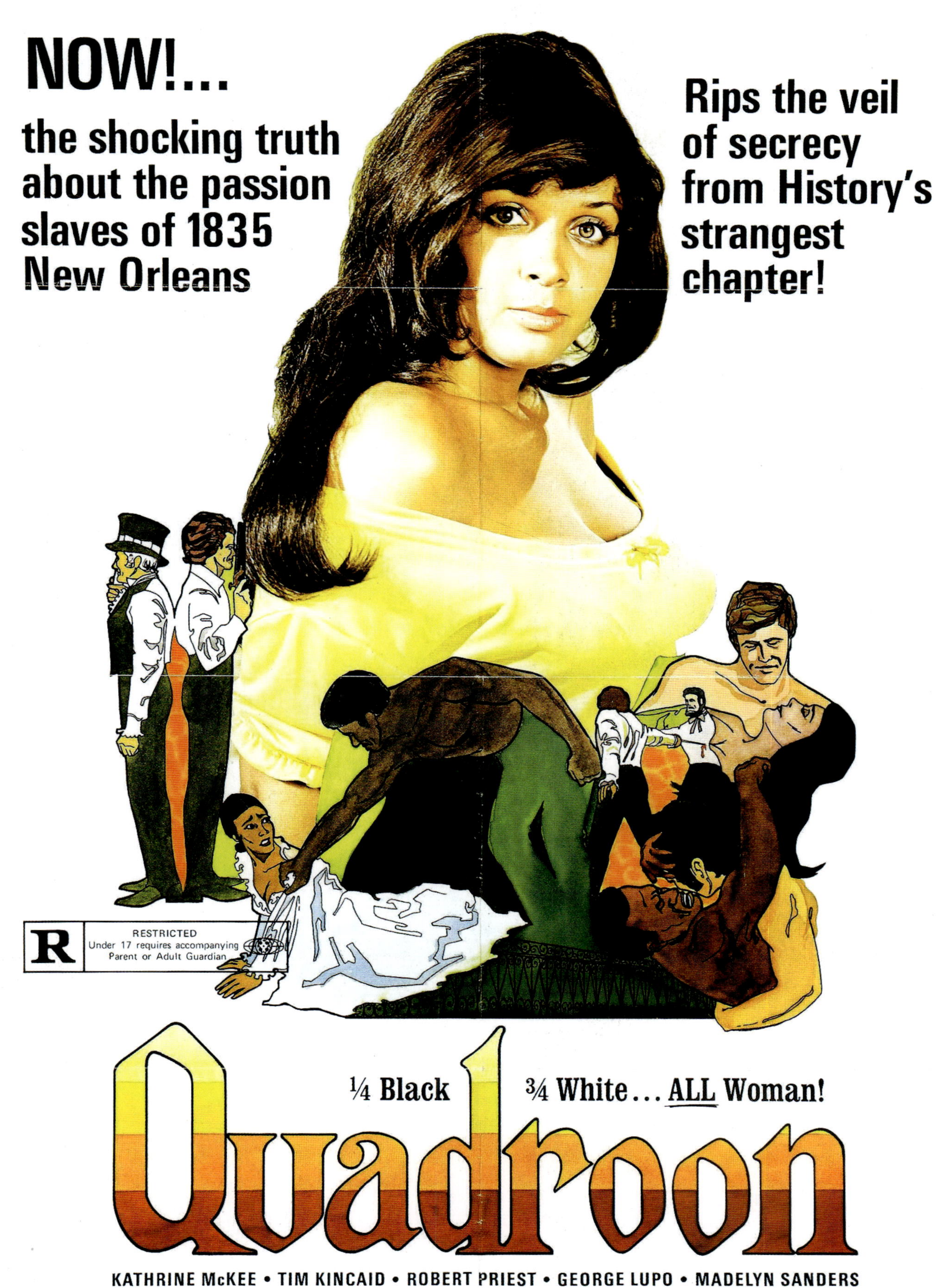
NOW!...
the shocking truth about the passion slaves of 1835 New Orleans
Rips the veil of secrecy from History's strangest chapter!
R
RESTRICTED
Under 17 requires accompanying Parent or Adult Guardian
¼ Black ¾ White... ALL Woman!
Quadroon
KATHRINE McKEE • TIM KINCAID • ROBERT PRIEST • GEORGE LUPO • MADELYN SANDERS
Color by Consolidated • Sound by Glen-Glen • A Presidio Production • Produced and Directed by Jack Weis
Executive Producer R. B. McGowen, Jr. • Screenplay by Sarah Riggs, from original story by R. B. McGowen, Jr.

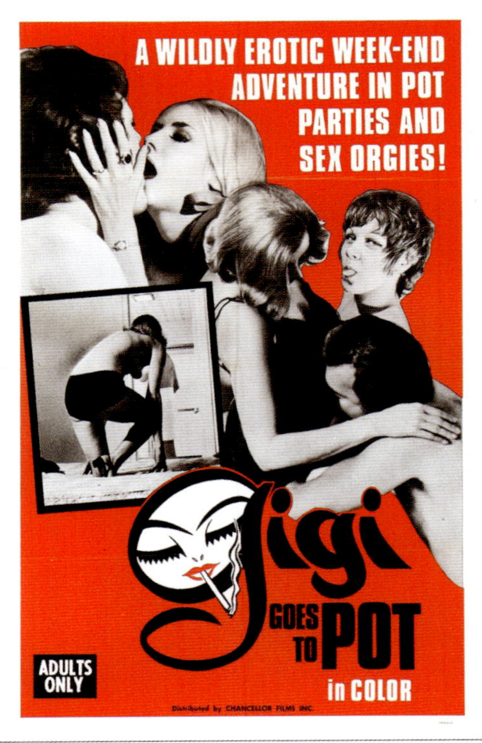

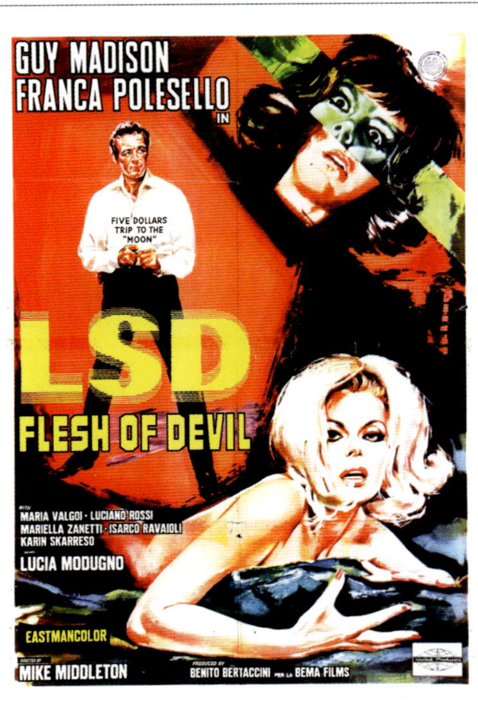

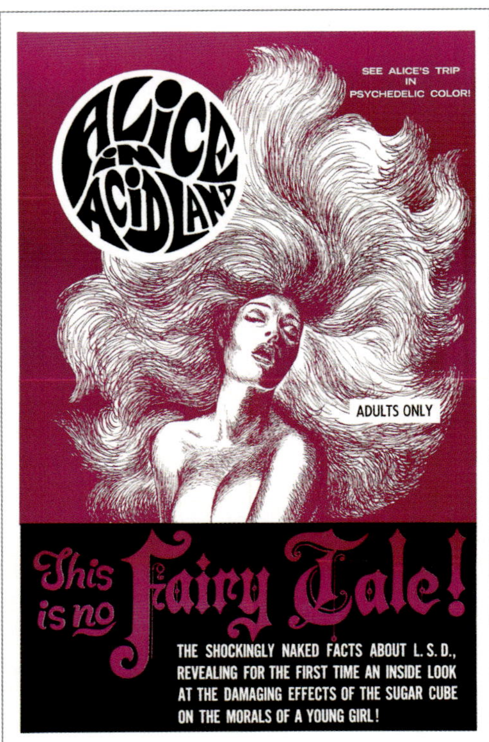

TUNE IN . . .

Around the time lysergic acid diethylamide joined the party, anti-drug exploitation films started to lose the "anti." In 1968, the year possession of the drug was finally made illegal in the US, the psychedelic one-sheet for *The Acid Eaters* was cheerily promoting "LSD orgies" as one of "the things that make life worthwhile" (alongside "motor-cycle mayhem" and "nude beach parties" of course). Similarly, while the tagline on the poster for *Alice in Acidland* (1968) soberly promises to "look at the damaging effects of the [LSD-laced] sugar cube on the morals of a young girl," the orgasmic art tells a somewhat different story.

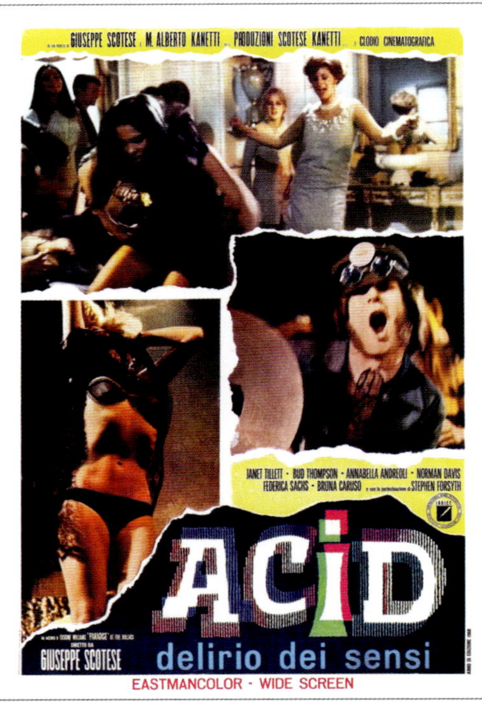

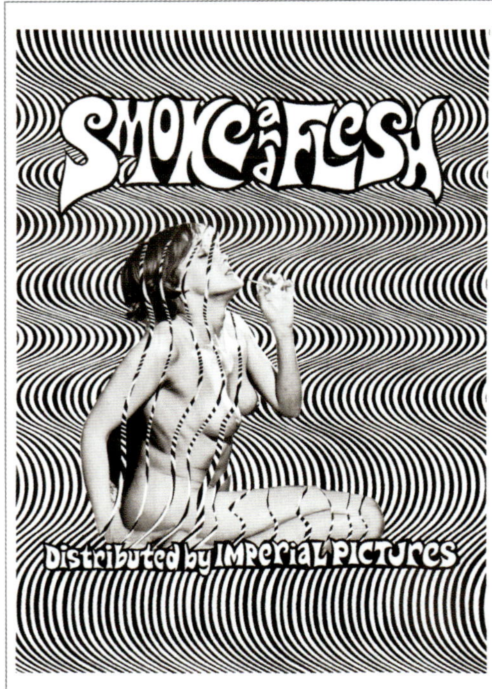

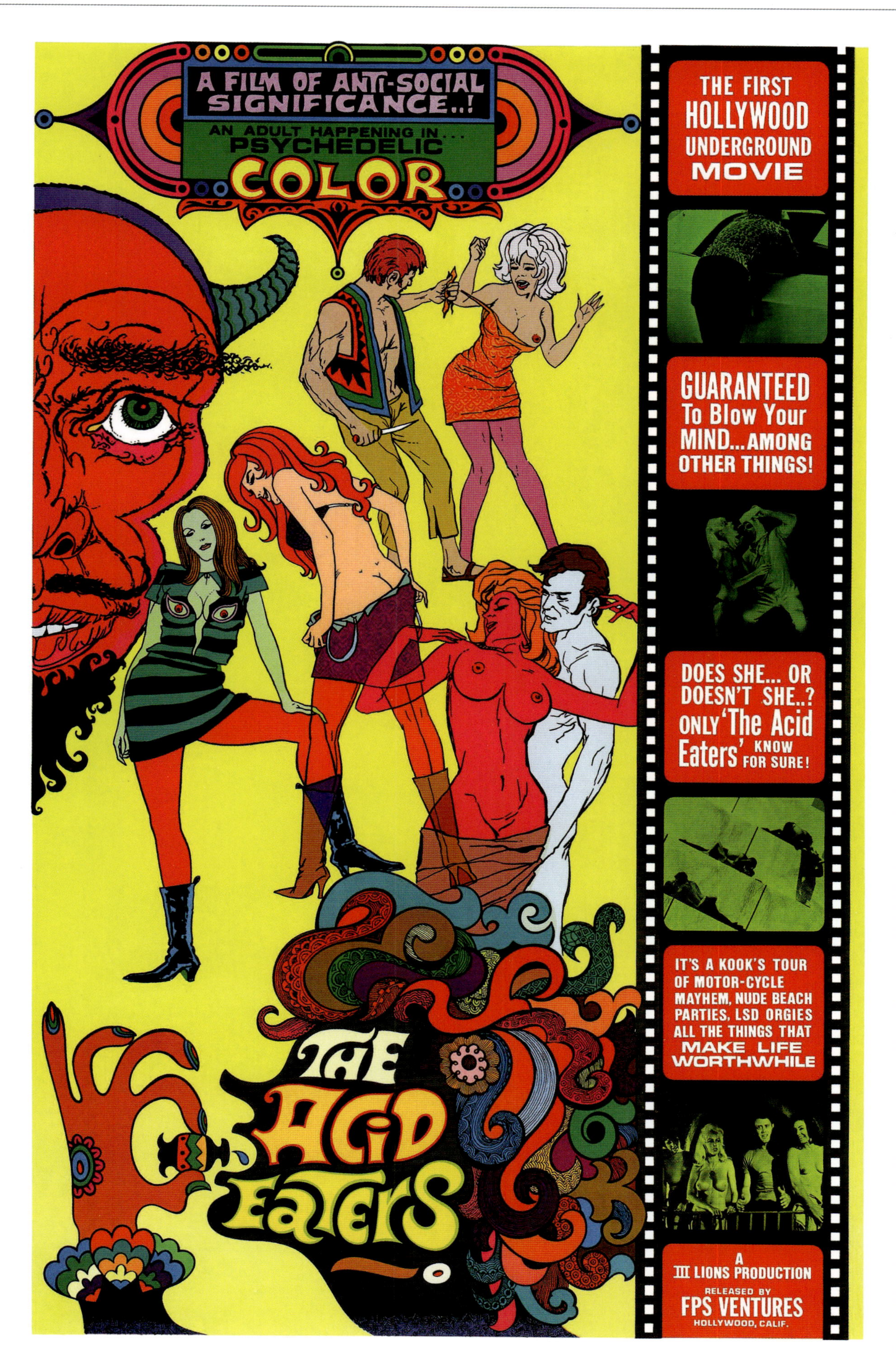
A FILM OF ANTI-SOCIAL SIGNIFICANCE..!
AN ADULT HAPPENING IN... PSYCHEDELIC
COLOR
THE FIRST HOLLYWOOD UNDERGROUND MOVIE
GUARANTEED To Blow Your MIND...AMONG OTHER THINGS!
DOES SHE... OR DOESN'T SHE..? ONLY 'The Acid Eaters' KNOW FOR SURE!
IT'S A KOOK'S TOUR OF MOTOR-CYCLE MAYHEM, NUDE BEACH PARTIES, LSD ORGIES ALL THE THINGS THAT MAKE LIFE WORTHWHILE
THE ACID EATERS
A III LIONS PRODUCTION
RELEASED BY FPS VENTURES HOLLYWOOD, CALIF.

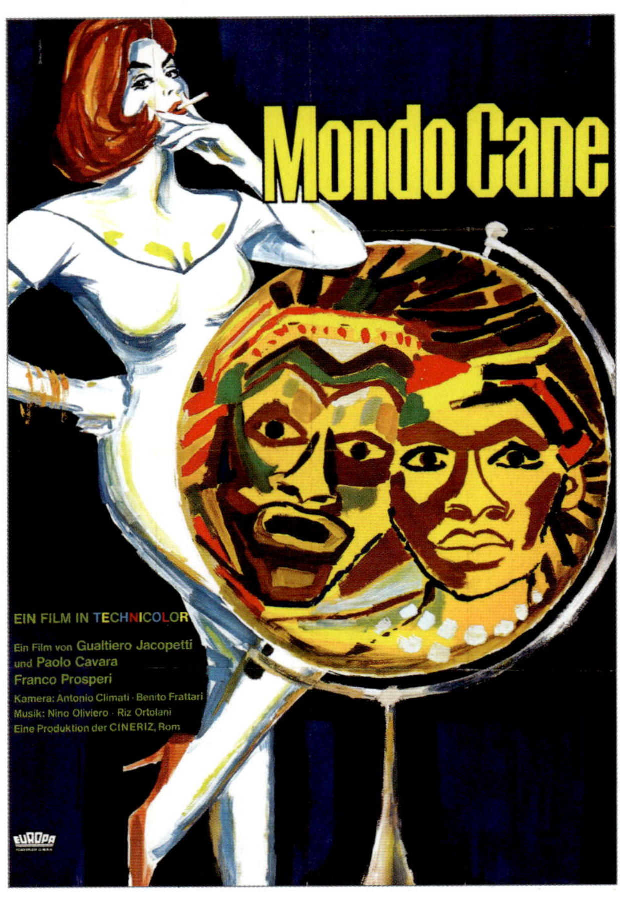
Mondo Cane
EIN FILM IN TECHNICOLOR
Ein Film von Gualtiero Jacopetti
und Paolo Cavara
Franco Prosperi
Kamera: Antonio Climati · Benito Frattari
Musik: Nino Oliviero · Riz Ortolani
Eine Produktion der CINERIZ, Rom
EUROPA

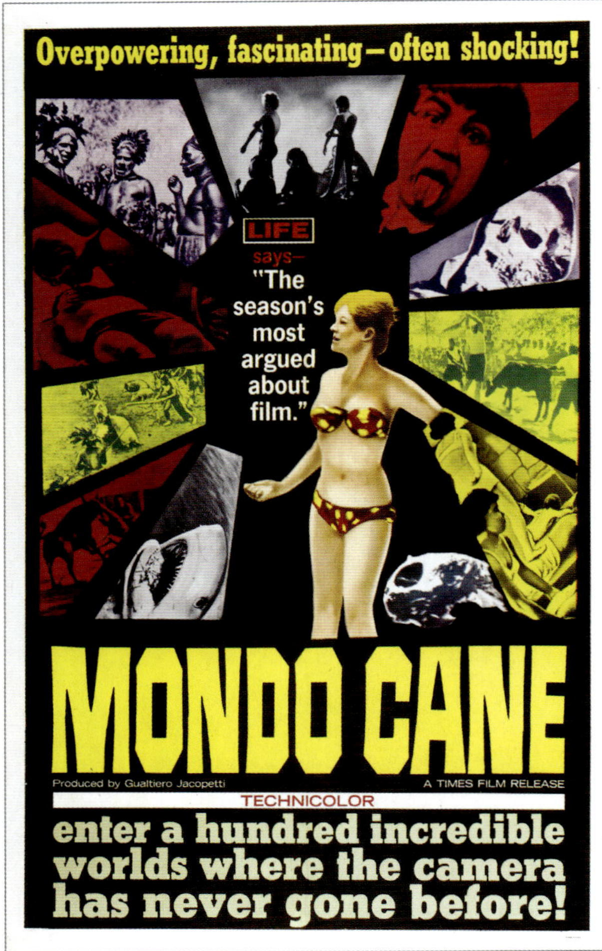
Overpowering, fascinating—often shocking!
LIFE
says—
"The season's most argued about film."
MONDO CANE
Produced by Gualtiero Jacopetti
A TIMES FILM RELEASE
TECHNICOLOR
enter a hundred incredible worlds where the camera has never gone before!

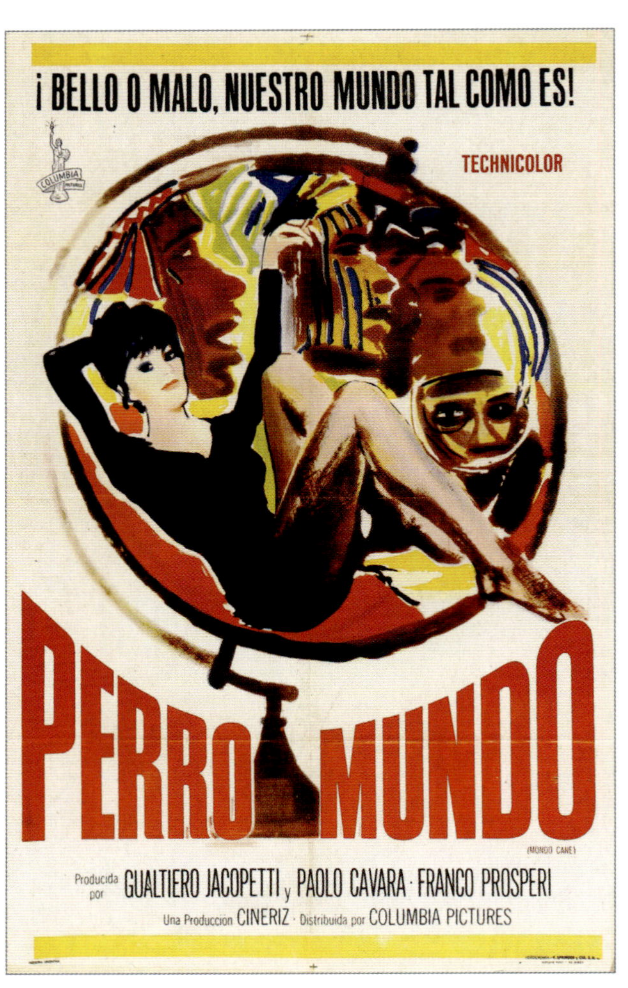
¡ BELLO O MALO, NUESTRO MUNDO TAL COMO ES!
TECHNICOLOR
COLUMBIA PICTURES
PERRO MUNDO
(MONDO CANE)
Producida por GUALTIERO JACOPETTI y PAOLO CAVARA · FRANCO PROSPERI
Una Produccion CINERIZ · Distribuida por COLUMBIA PICTURES

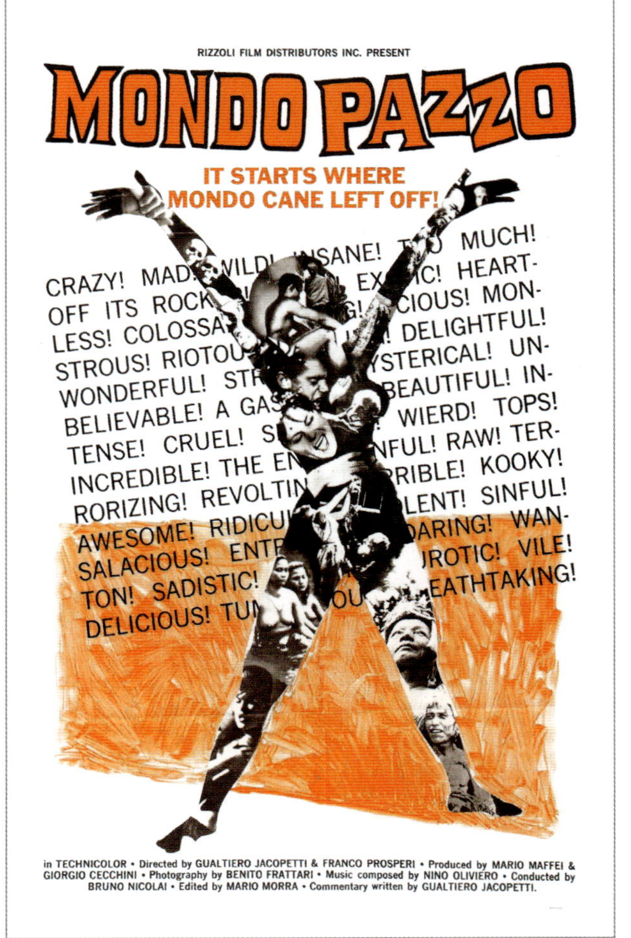
RIZZOLI FILM DISTRIBUTORS INC. PRESENT
MONDO PAZZO
IT STARTS WHERE MONDO CANE LEFT OFF!
CRAZY! MAD WILD INSANE! MUCH!
OFF ITS ROCK EX IC! HEART-
LESS! COLOSSA CIOUS! MON-
STROUS! RIOTOU ! DELIGHTFUL!
WONDERFUL! STR YSTERICAL! UN-
BELIEVABLE! A GA BEAUTIFUL! IN-
TENSE! CRUEL! S WIERD! TOPS!
INCREDIBLE! THE E NFUL! RAW! TER-
RORIZING! REVOLTIN RIBLE! KOOKY!
AWESOME! RIDICU LENT! SINFUL!
SALACIOUS! ENT DARING! WAN-
TON! SADISTIC! UROTIC! VILE!
DELICIOUS! TU EATHTAKING!
in TECHNICOLOR • Directed by GUALTIERO JACOPETTI & FRANCO PROSPERI • Produced by MARIO MAFFEI & GIORGIO CECCHINI • Photography by BENITO FRATTARI • Music composed by NINO OLIVIERO • Conducted by BRUNO NICOLAI • Edited by MARIO MORRA • Commentary written by GUALTIERO JACOPETTI.

MONDO

Mondo Cane (1962) is a remarkable production for many reasons—for a start, how many movies featuring graphic, real-life footage of animal butchery can boast an Academy Award nomination for Best Song? ("More" didn't win, alas, but was later covered by Frank Sinatra.) This Italian "shockumentary," which translates as "A Dog's World," or perhaps rather "A World Gone to the Dogs," was a kaleidoscopic mix of weird, wonderful, and often downright disturbing vignettes from around the globe: bikini-clad girls cavorting on the Riviera, dogs being skinned alive for food in Taipei, drunk Germans, cars being crushed in an LA junkyard, transvestite Nepalis, geese being force-fed for *foie gras*, et cetera. Unlikely to be to be nominated for the Palme d'Or at the Cannes Film Festival you'd think, and yet it was. *Mondo Cane* didn't win that award either, but it did spawn a whole subgenre of exploitation films with "Mondo" in the title. Some had slightly narrower horizons—*Mondo Freudo* (1966) had only one thing on its mind—others, as the arresting art by Mos (aka Mario de Berardinis) for *Mondo Balordo* (1964) shows, could incorporate everything from strange rituals, to marijuana use, to dwarf love. For animal cruelty fans, the promotional copy for the US release of *Mondo Balordo* (which was narrated by horror icon Boris Karloff) assures viewers that it also features footage of "needless dog surgery."

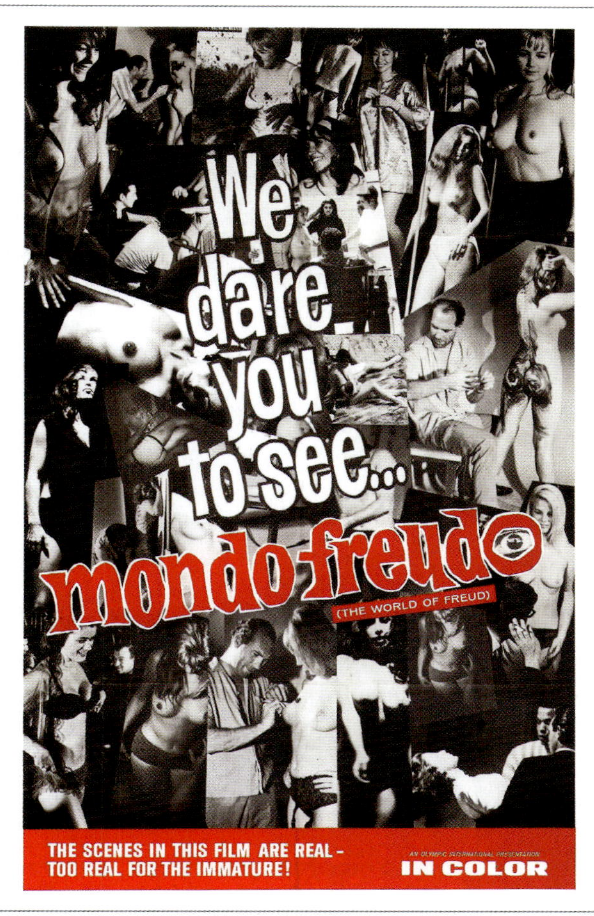

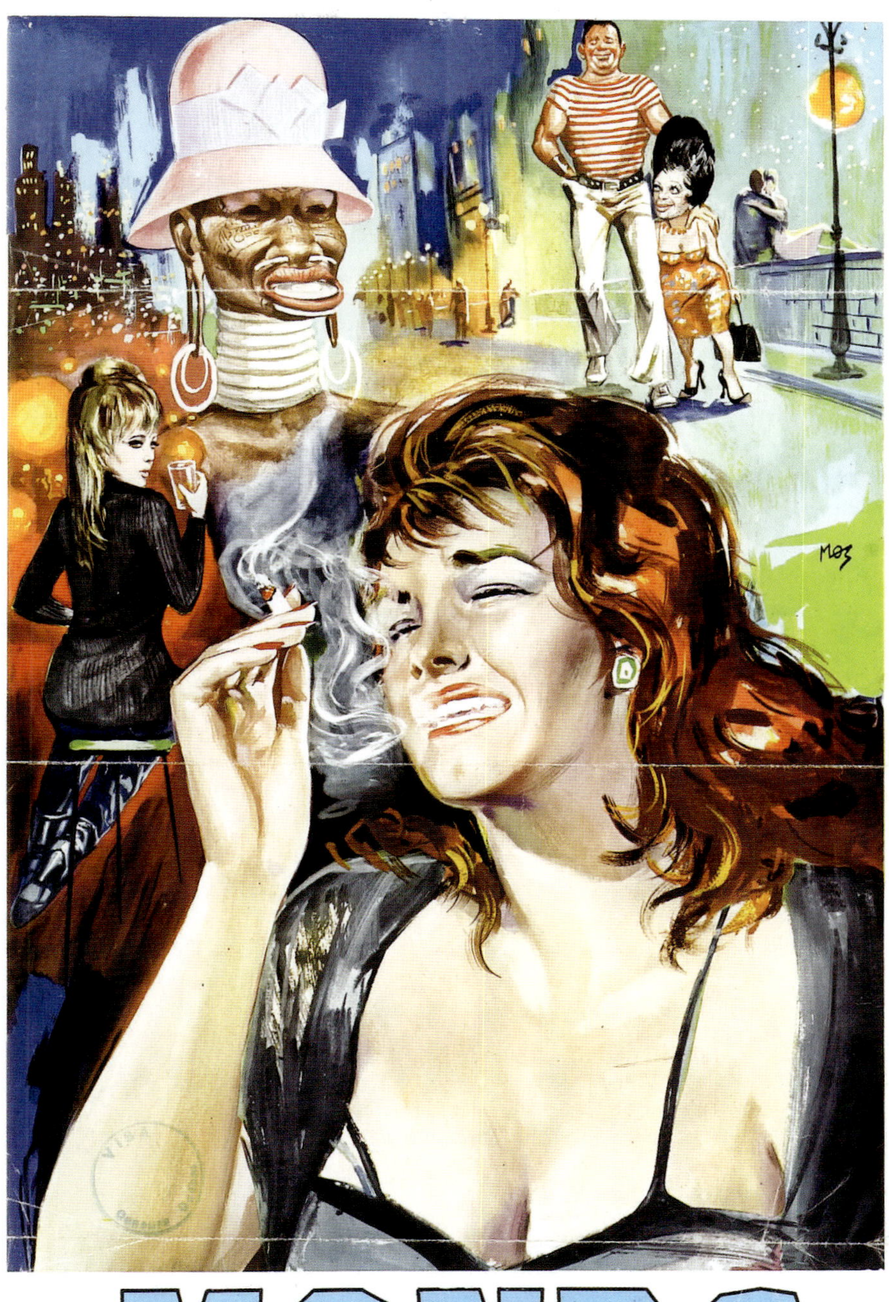

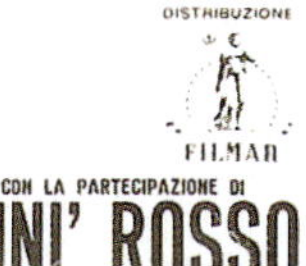

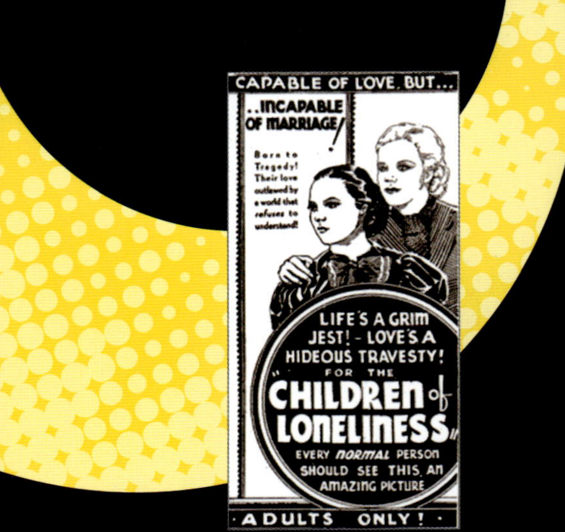

"STRANGE LOVE"

The poster for the first exploitation film to deal with homosexuality, *Children of Loneliness* (1934), doesn't mince its words: "Love's a hideous travesty!" for its lesbian characters. By 1957, when Julien Duvivier's girls' reformatory drama *Au royaume des cieux* (1949) got a US release as *The Sinners*, it's a kind of shocked fascination on the poster, while those for *The Fourth Sex* (1961) and *Monique* (1970) tip over into blatant titillation. The classically inspired *Sappho Darling* (1968) boasts a script by an Academy Award winner. This is what's technically known as "a barefaced lie": the closest Albert Zugsmith ever got to an Oscar was producing Douglas Sirk's *Written on the Wind*, which won the statuette for Best Supporting Actress. Any mention of Oscars on modern posters is accompanied by details of the precise award in the small print, to avoid exactly this kind of misdirection.

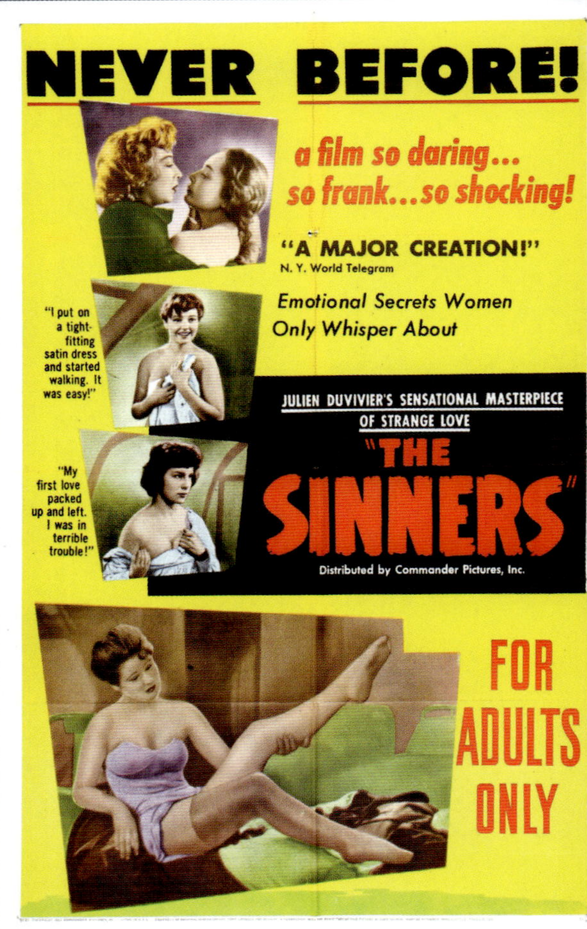

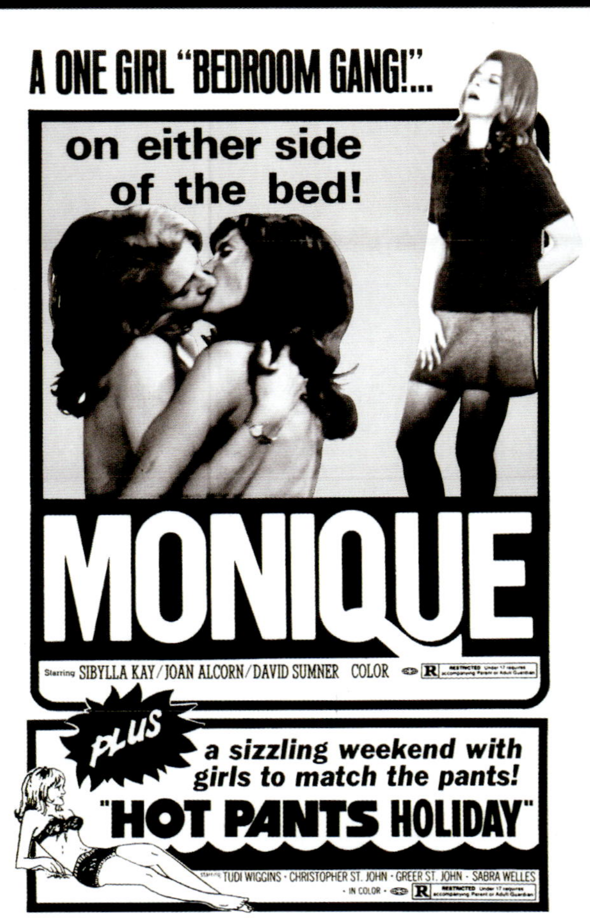

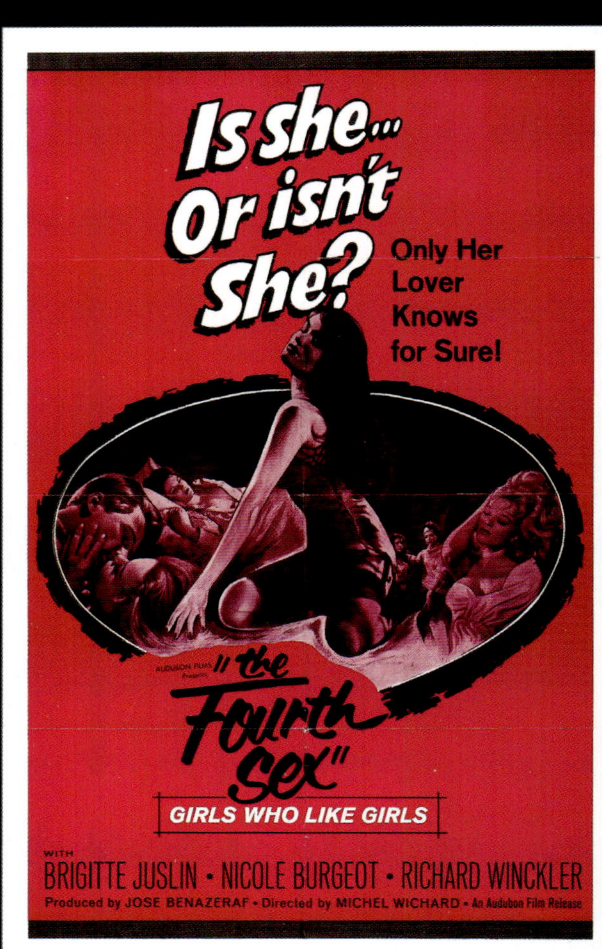

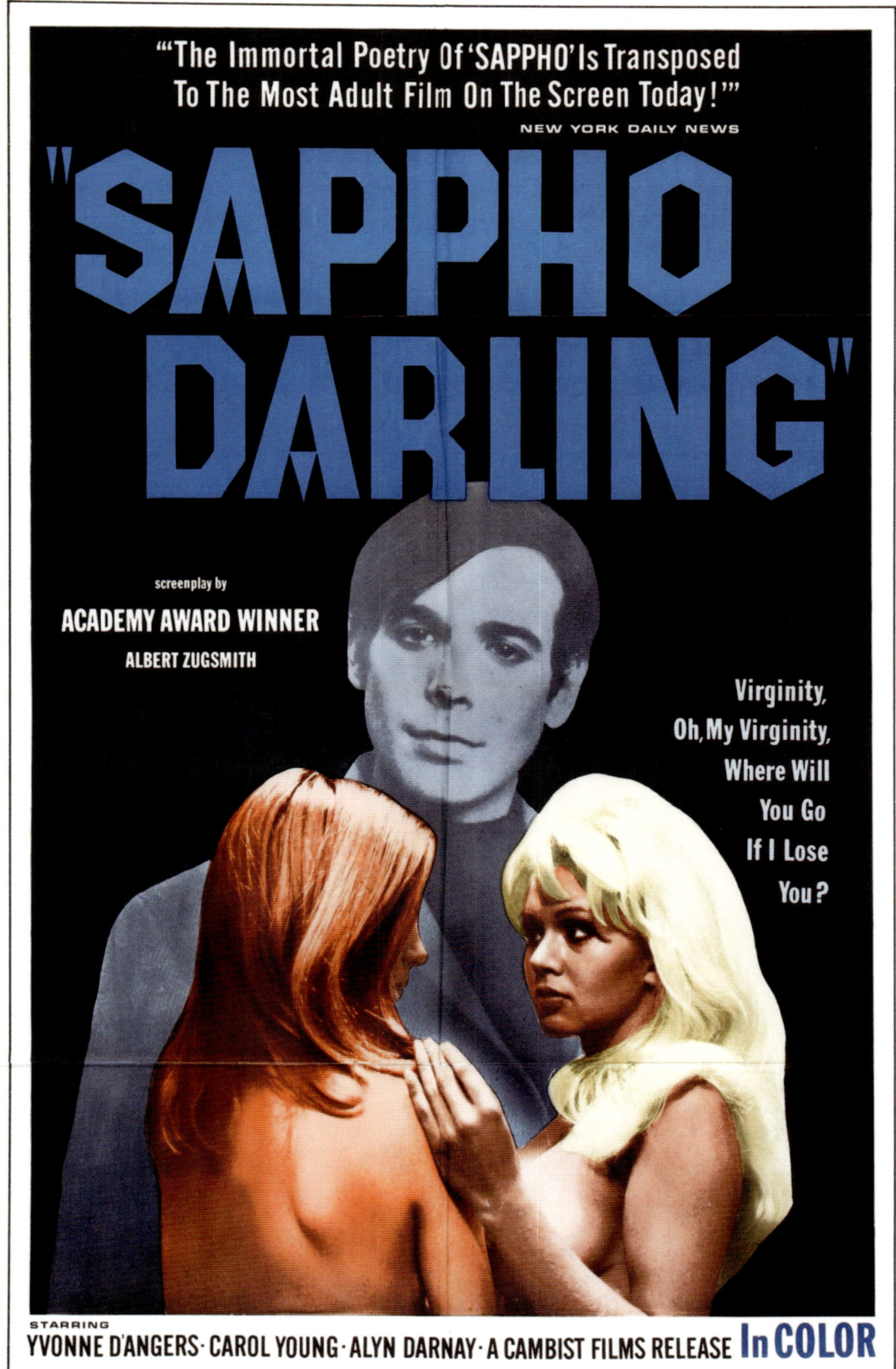
"'The Immortal Poetry Of 'SAPPHO' Is Transposed
To The Most Adult Film On The Screen Today!'"
NEW YORK DAILY NEWS
"SAPPHO
DARLING"
screenplay by
ACADEMY AWARD WINNER
ALBERT ZUGSMITH
Virginity,
Oh, My Virginity,
Where Will
You Go
If I Lose
You?
STARRING
YVONNE D'ANGERS · CAROL YOUNG · ALYN DARNAY · A CAMBIST FILMS RELEASE In COLOR

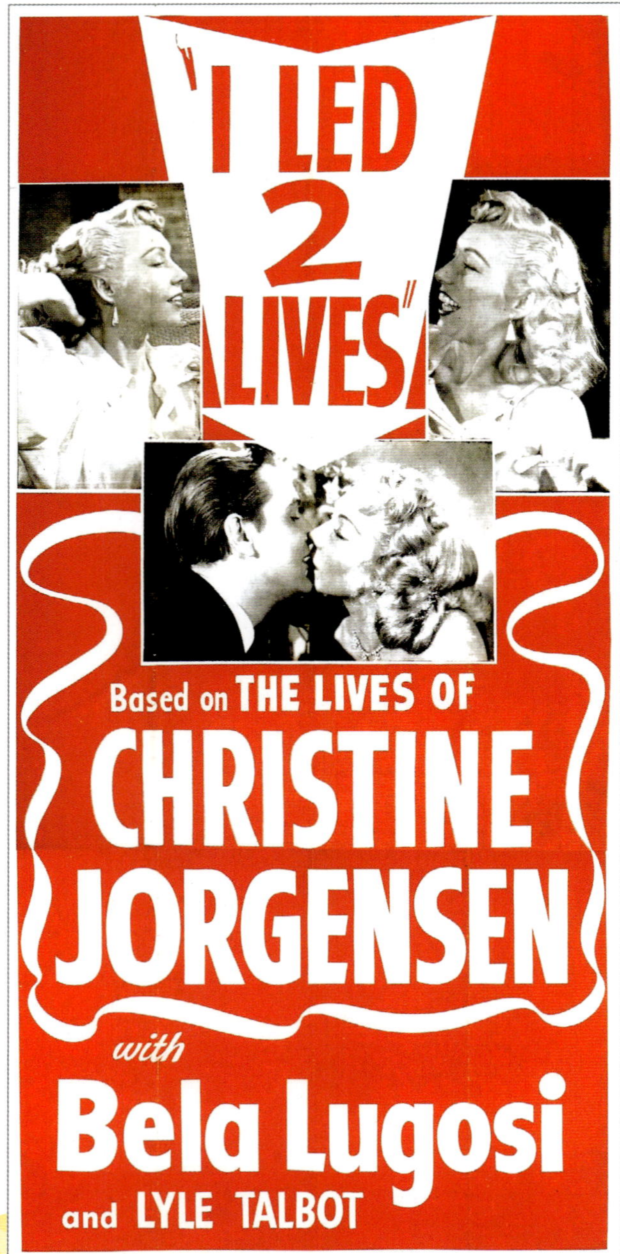

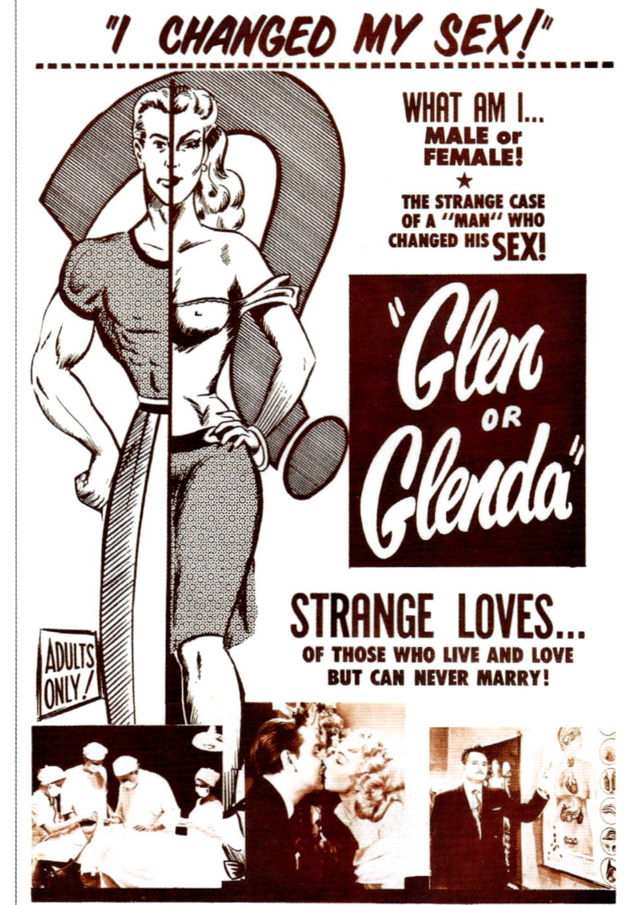

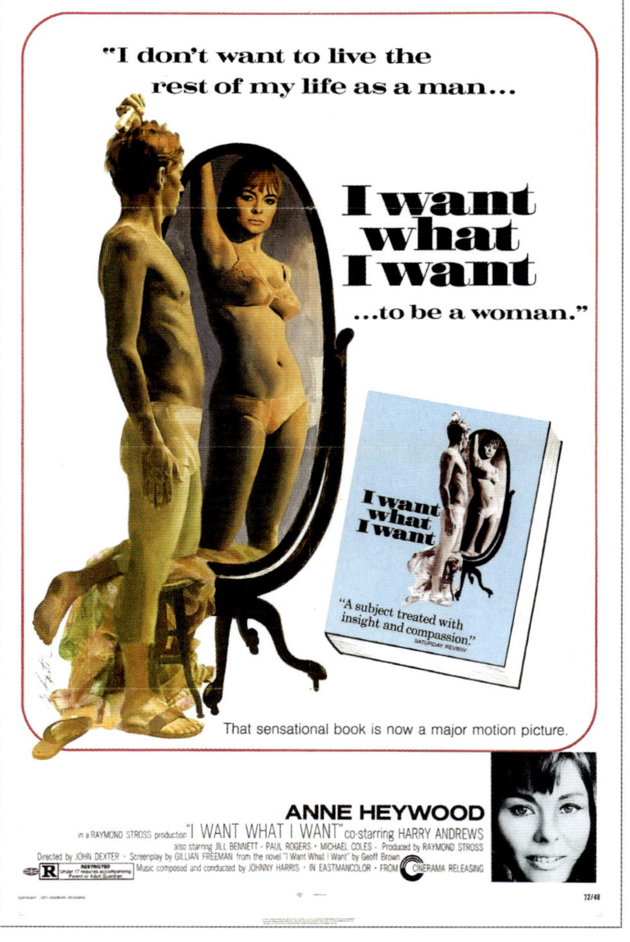

TRANSSEXUALS

As you might expect, exploitation cinema's dealings with transgender people and transsexuality tend to be based more on gawping prurience than a genuine desire to sympathetically examine a community within society. The notorious *Glen or Glenda* (aka *I Led 2 Lives*, 1953) was designed to cash in on the story of Christine Jorgensen, a trans woman who received widespread press attention in the early '50s, though it's actually more about the transvestism of its director/star Ed Wood. Leonard Maltin called it "possibly the worst film ever made," and most viewers would agree with him. The British drama *I Want What I Want* (1971) is a more restrained tale of a man successfully transitioning to life as a woman, while 1977's explicit docudrama *Let Me Die a Woman* got its widest audience when its footage of a sex change operation was later incorporated into a *South Park* episode entitled "Mr Garrison's Fancy New Vagina."

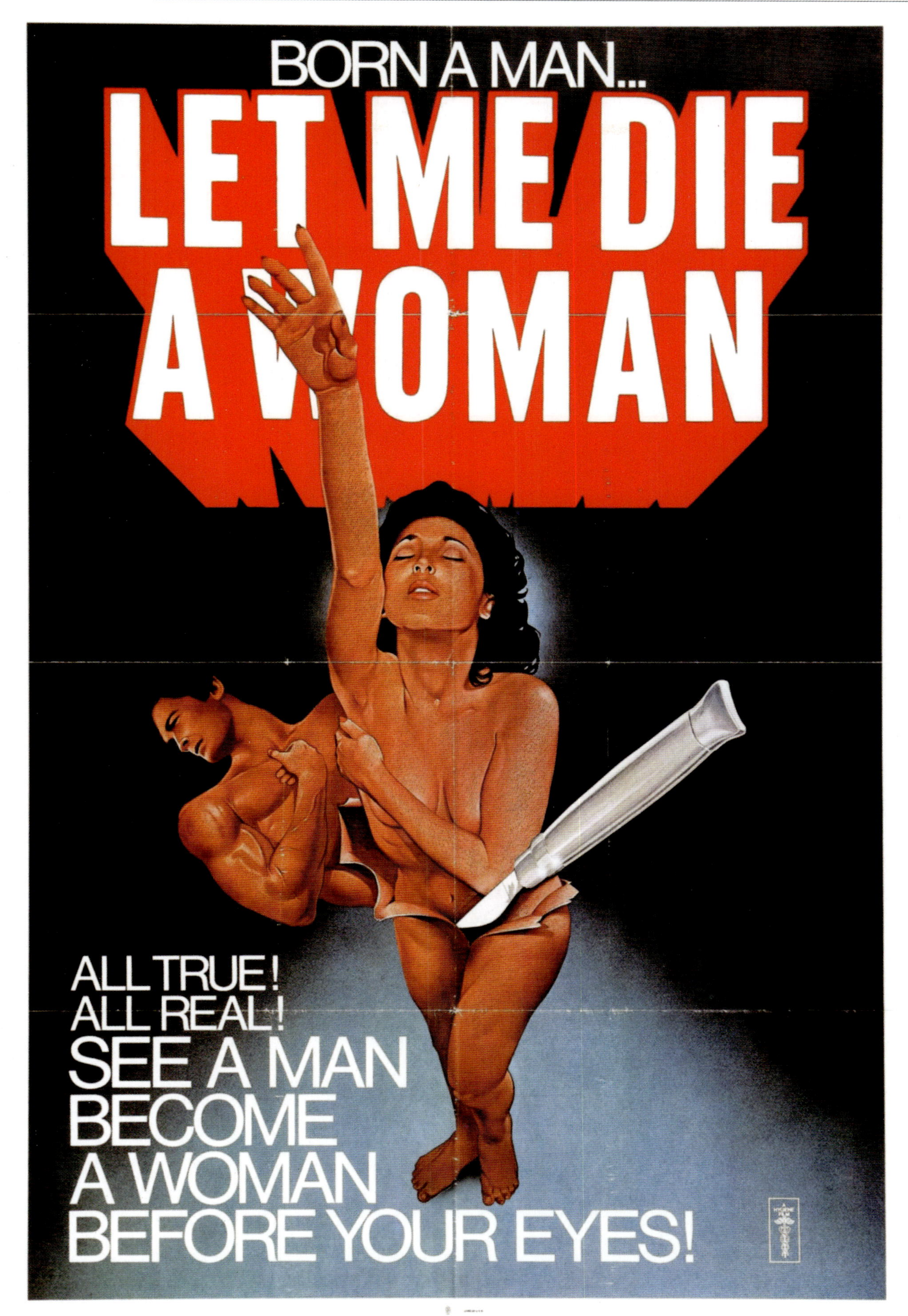
BORN A MAN...
LET ME DIE
A WOMAN
ALL TRUE!
ALL REAL!
SEE A MAN
BECOME
A WOMAN
BEFORE YOUR EYES!

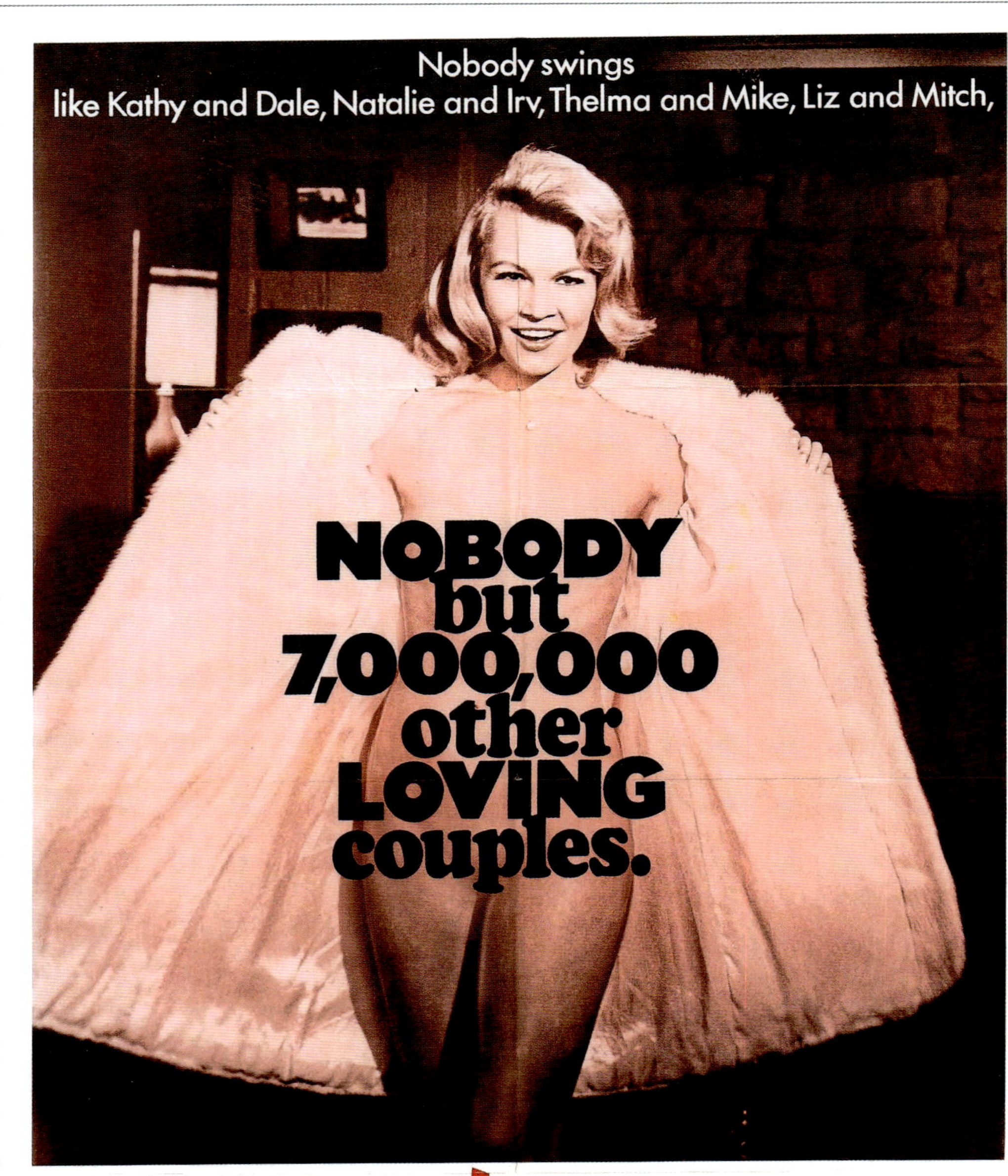

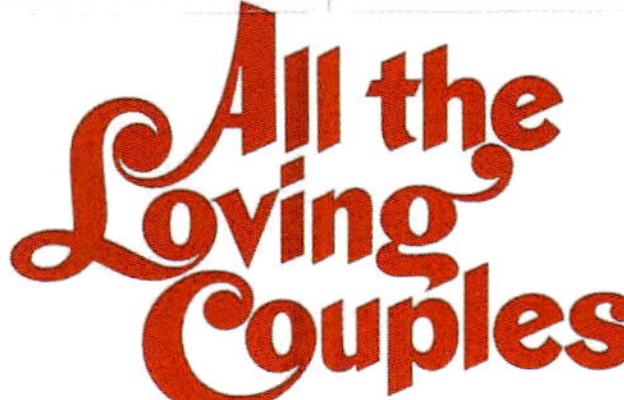

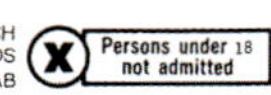

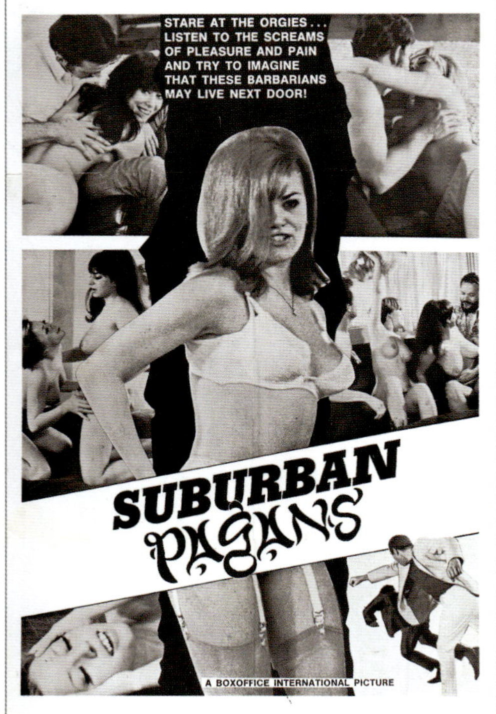

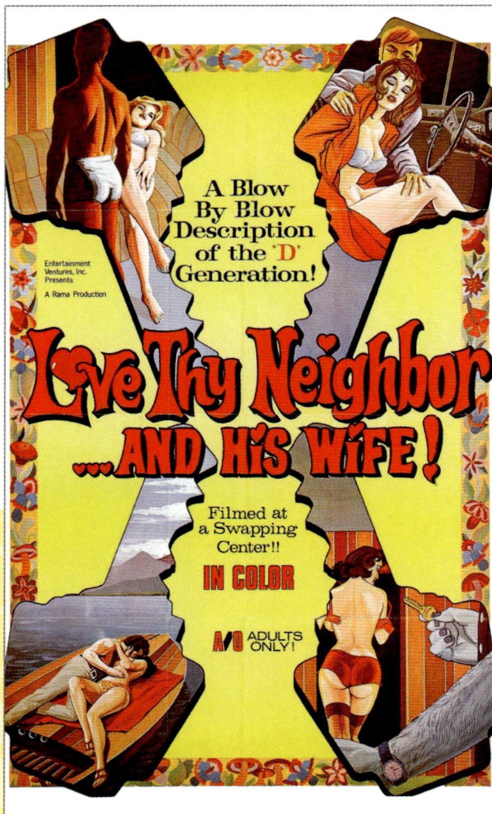

SWINGING IN THE SUBURBS

By the end of the '60s, with the contraceptive pill freely available, the sexual revolution had turned the inhabitants of entire city suburbs into phalanxes of sex-mad swingers, frantically bed-hopping from key party to swapping club. Not really, of course, but filmmakers were happy to peddle that impression. Exploitation specialists Boxoffice International's faux documentary *Suburban Pagans* (1968) had a suitably seedy, black-and-white *vérité* approach (with a basic, cut-and-paste poster to match). *All The Loving Couples* (1969), in the opinion of a young Roger Ebert, was "one of the most innocent of the recent skin-flicks, and so socially redeeming you'll walk out thinking wife-swapping is second only to scouting in making our nation strong." Though he had to admit, "the ad campaign is sort of sleazy." By the time the German sex comedy *Der neue heiße Sex-Report* was released in the US as *Swinging Wives* (1971), viewers were entering X-rated territory, of which more—much more—later in this book . . .

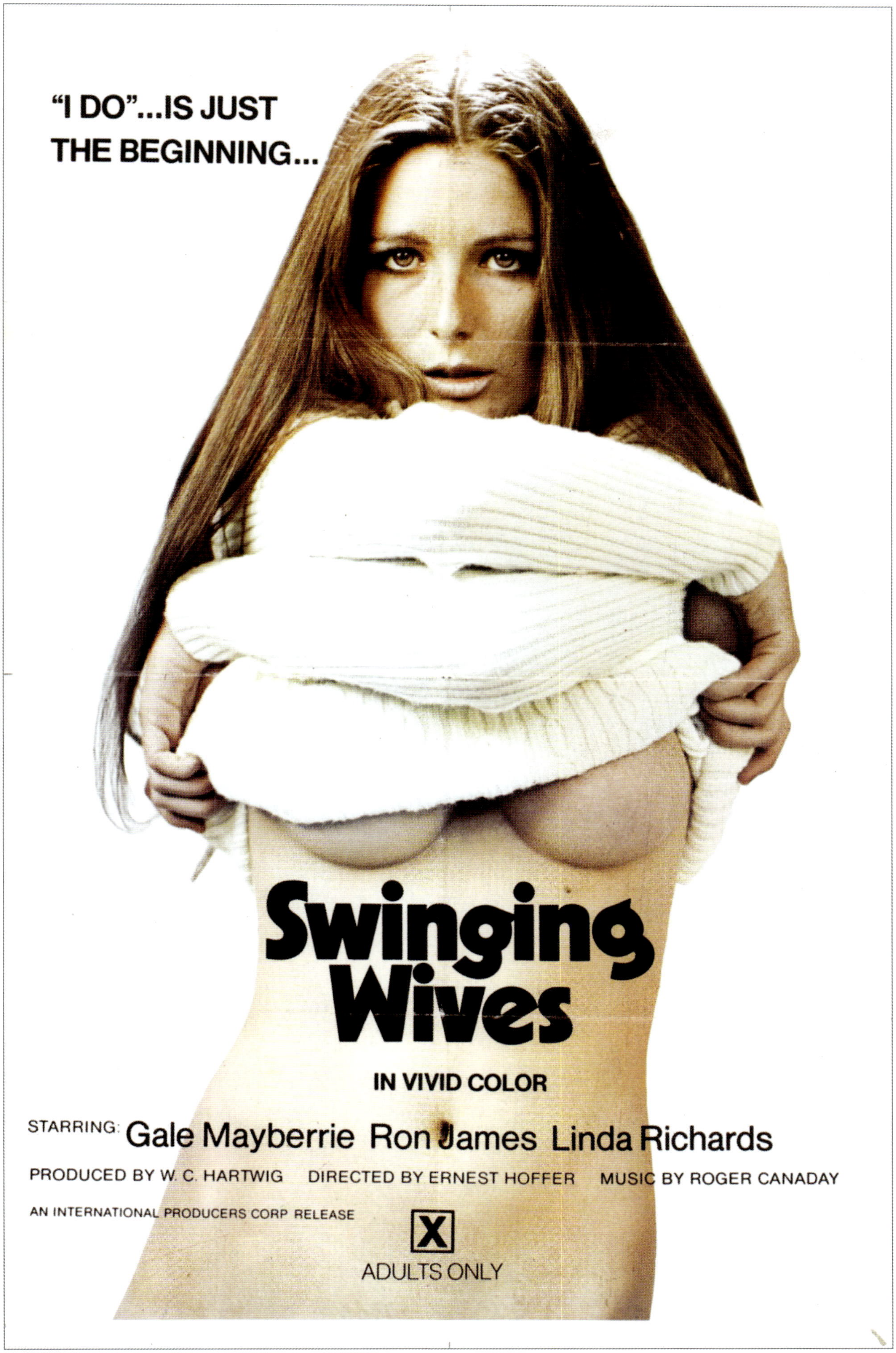

"I DO"...IS JUST
THE BEGINNING...

Swinging
Wives

IN VIVID COLOR

STARRING: Gale Mayberrie Ron James Linda Richards

PRODUCED BY W. C. HARTWIG DIRECTED BY ERNEST HOFFER MUSIC BY ROGER CANADAY

AN INTERNATIONAL PRODUCERS CORP RELEASE

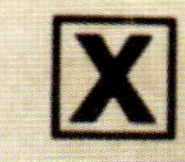

ADULTS ONLY

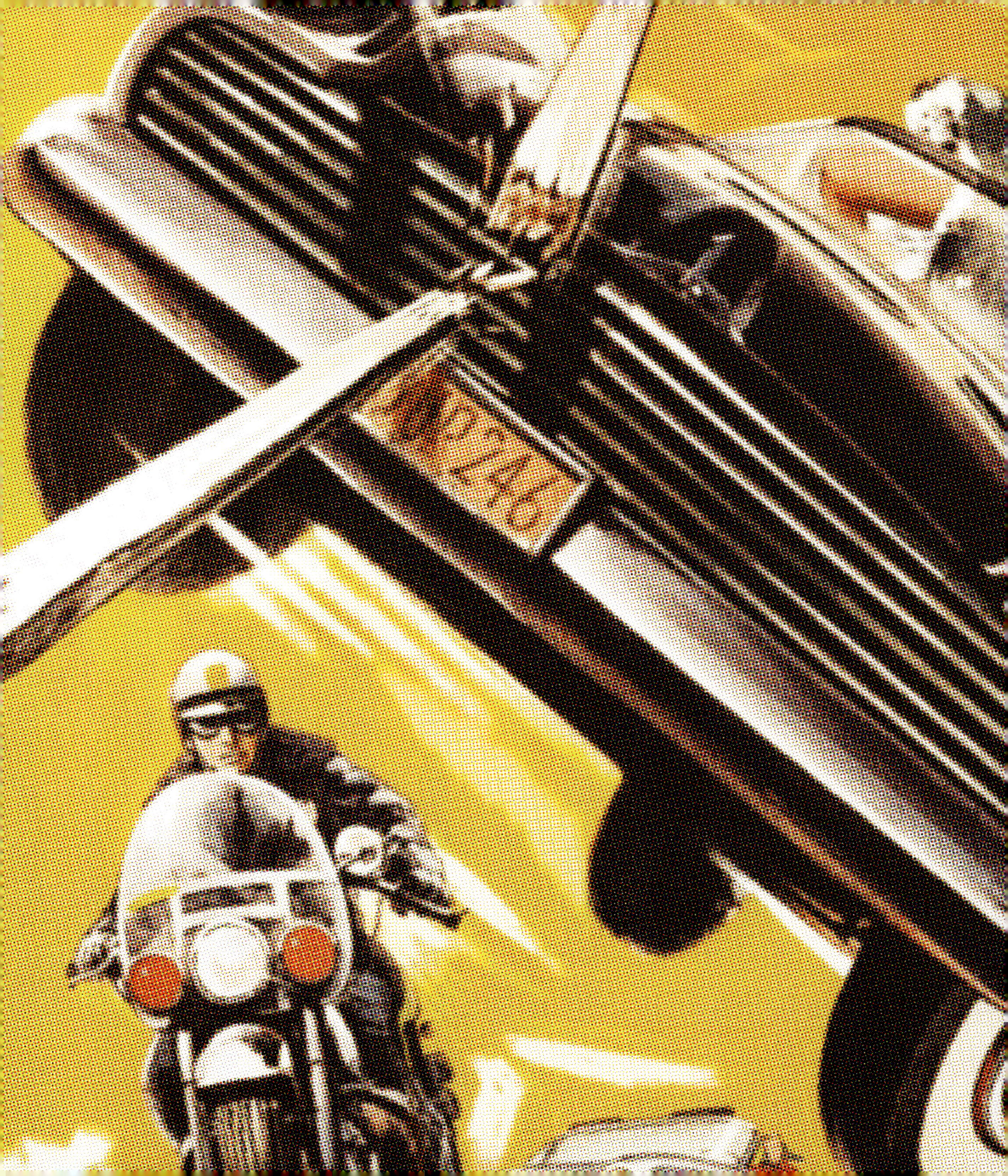

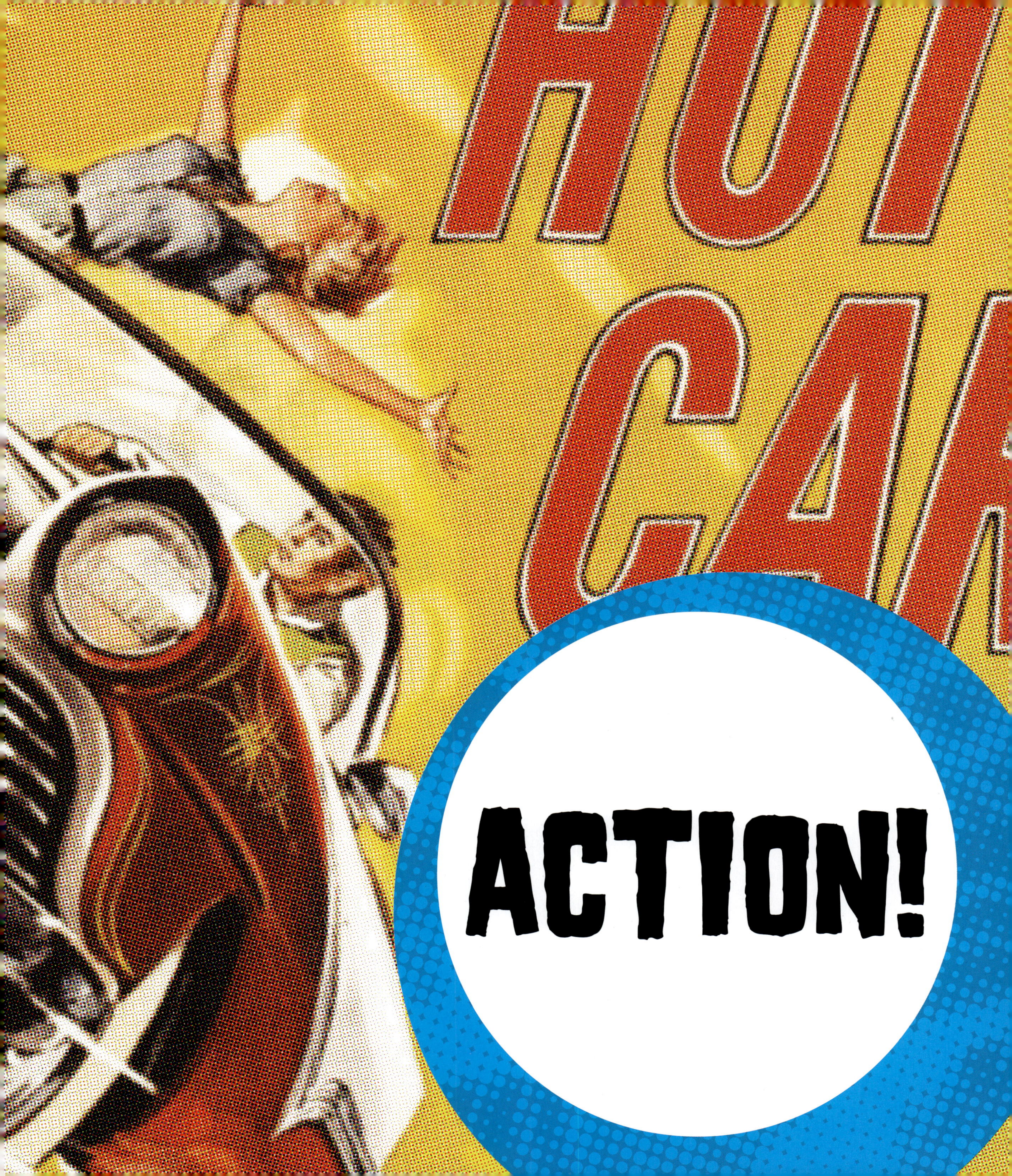
ACTION!

Vern on BLACK BELT JONES and THE MASTER GUNFIGHTER

When you slap the guts of an action movie onto a poster, all the crucial parts stick. Even when the film itself is dull, the poster knows how to entice us. Somewhere in the middle is our lead, who may be a pants-less *femme fatale*, or a man who is either accompanied by or being assaulted by some. Guns of all sizes are hefted, aimed, cocked, or firing. On the fringes we have our crashing/rolling/flipping/jumping/exploding cars, or perhaps a jumping motorcycle, or men who have just been thrown through windows or windshields. Faceless thugs—or sometimes we, the viewers—stand in the paths of flying fists, feet, knives, swords, darts, nunchakas, or throwing stars.

PREVIOUS SPREAD: Detail from the poster for *Hot Car Girl* (1958).

BELOW: A European poster for *Black Belt Jones* (1974), featuring both the French and Dutch titles.

OPPOSITE: The US one-sheet makes sure to refer back to Jim Kelly's appearance in the previous year's *Enter the Dragon.*

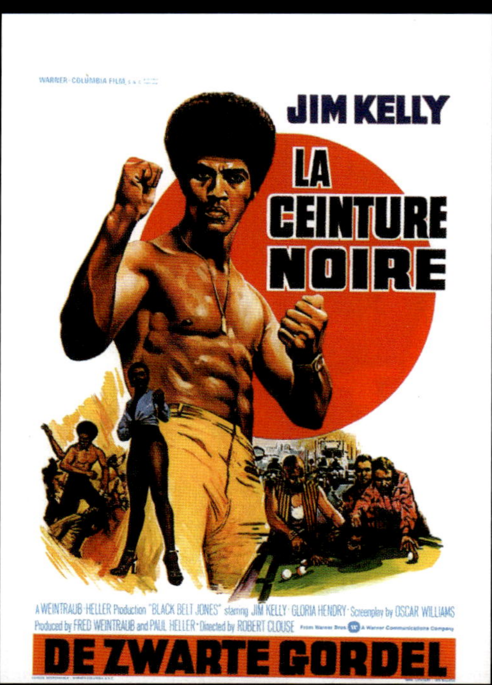

Many of the subjects of this chapter are suave secret agents, weathered street cops, public domain Spaghetti Western anti-heroes, or vaunted martial arts masters. Perhaps they are presumptuous would-be successors to Bruce Lee (sometimes pictured beside tasteless depictions of the original Dragon in his coffin), or muscled gladiators breaking chains, spines, or snakes with their bare hands. Quite a few of them wear masks to hide their identities as superheroes, master criminals, or professional wrestlers.

Hovering above these larger-than-life figures might be a series of all-caps adjectives followed by exclamation points, or an audacious tagline, sometimes in rhyme, sometimes wooing us with colorful phrases like "zany crash smash," "fiendish tigress of the jungle," "Hong Kong hell-cat," "at the mercy of a crazed killer!" or "a fury of blood and burning rubber!" That sounds like my kinda movie. I *love* zany crash smashes!

A favorite movie of mine that encompasses many of these elements is *Black Belt Jones* (1974). One year after *Enter the Dragon*, director Robert Clouse and co-star Jim Kelly re-teamed for this absurd and entertaining blaxploitation/martial arts hybrid.

Black Belt Jones (or B.B. for short) is an ex-CIA badass who wages war on the mafia after they muscle in on an all-black karate school owned by Pop Byrd

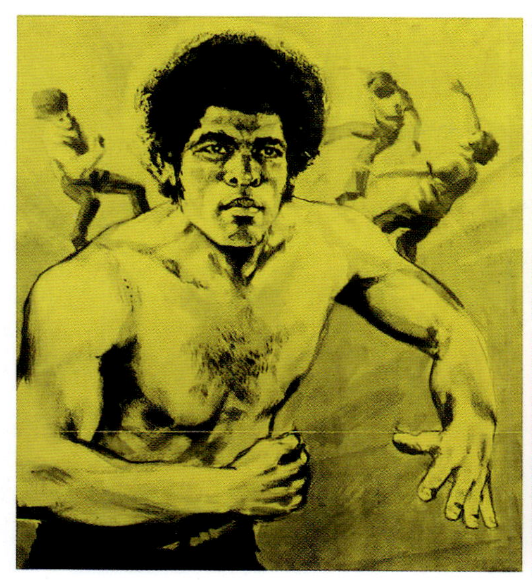

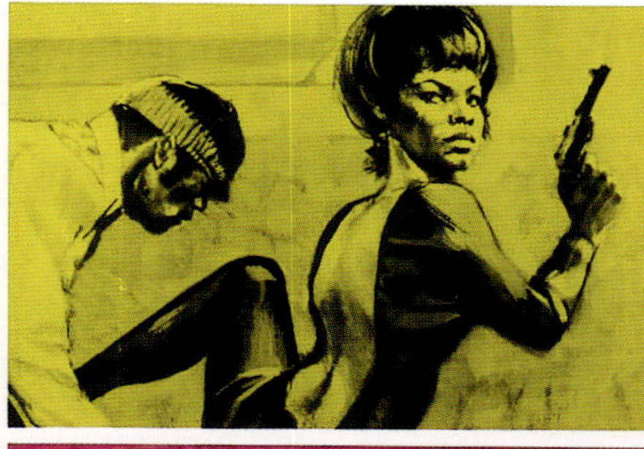

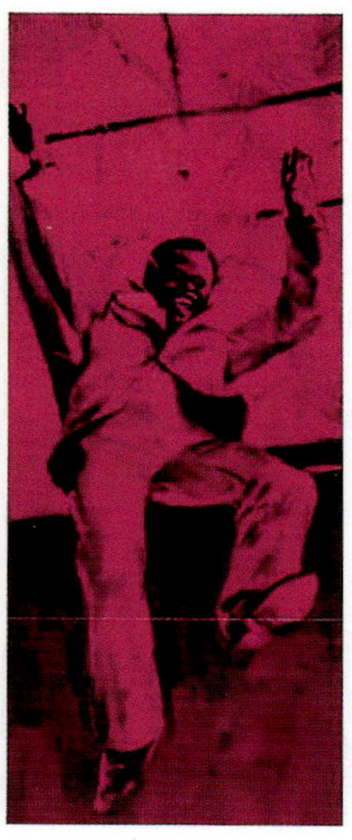

ENTER

JIM

"DRAGON"

KELLY

HE CLOBBERS THE MOB AS

BLACK BELT JONES

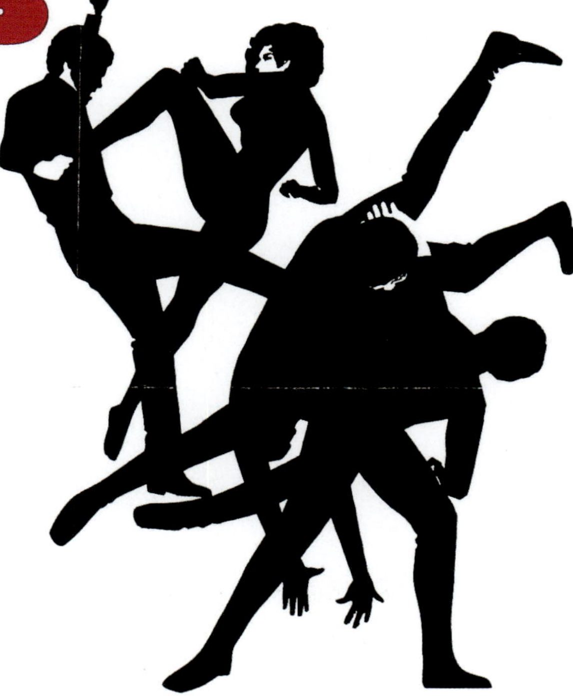

R RESTRICTED

A WEINTRAUB-HELLER Production "BLACK BELT JONES" starring JIM KELLY · GLORIA HENDRY · Screenplay by OSCAR WILLIAMS
Produced by FRED WEINTRAUB and PAUL HELLER · Directed by ROBERT CLOUSE

From Warner Bros. A Warner Communications Company

74/43

"BLACK BELT JONES"

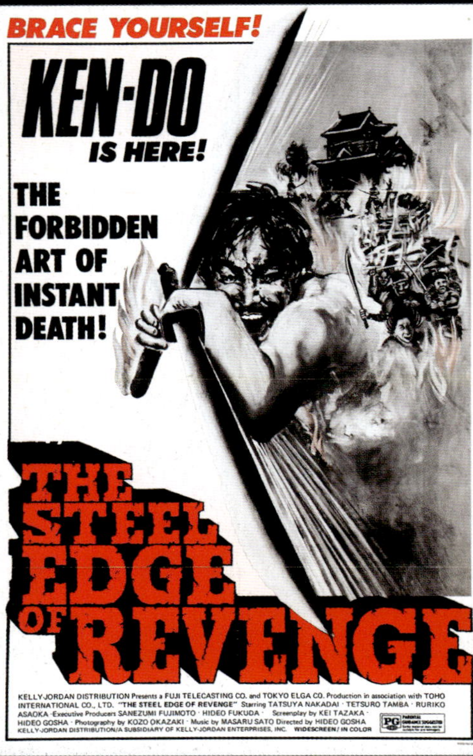

ABOVE: *Gyokin* (1969), the samurai drama remade six years later as *The Master Gunfighter*, was released in the US as *The Steel Edge of Revenge*. Given this choice of title, it's ironic that the poster trumpets the arrival of "Ken-do" on Western screens—kendo is a martial art usually associated with swords made of bamboo. *The Bamboo Edge of Revenge* doesn't sound as good though.

(Scatman Crothers). This is the only movie I know of where 20 minutes in you find out that the hero teaches a beachfront, all-female trampoline-jumping class. Later he has his students use their skills in a *Mission: Impossible*-style caper. But the love interest, Sydney (*Black Caesar*'s Gloria Hendry), is not so compliant. She makes B.B. duel her before she'll have sex with him, and when he tries to keep her out of danger by telling her to stay home and do the dishes, she shoots several bullets into them and says, "They're done."

Like many of Clouse's films, *Black Belt Jones* has an incredible theme song, this time performed by the Funk Brothers guitarist and first-white-performer-on-*Soul-Train* Dennis Coffey. Some of the action highlights include a fight on a train (where he manages to kick each opponent through a different window) and one at a car wash, knee-deep in suds.

Trivia: The director of photography was Kent Wakeford (who shot *Mean Streets* the year before) and the editor was longtime Spielberg collaborator Michael Kahn. It gives me joy to think that the guy who edited *Schindler's List* may have also been the one who put Clouse's director's credit over a shot of a guy running right before he gets hit in the ass by a bullet.

Although it's not required, some of these movies have more on their mind than kicking and shooting. A more serious-minded cross-cultural adventure is *The Master Gunfighter* (1975) starring, produced, and written by *Billy Jack*'s Tom Laughlin, and directed by him too, unless you believe the credits, which say it was Laughlin's nine-year-old son Frank.

If it was the little boy directing then he shares his old man's indignation about the treatment of indigenous people and his admiration for whistleblowers and conscientious objectors. Like all of Laughlin's films it's a little on the self-serious side, but his sincerity has always been his main charm. That, and he makes sure to play a righteous badass with exotic weapons and skills. Though the title and opening narration by Burgess Meredith refer to "the unsubstantiated legend of a remarkable six-chambered, double-action pistol that fired 12 repeating bullets and which was brought from the East by the son of one of the last great land-owning Spanish dons," it really puts more emphasis on the hero Finley's "mastery of the technique of the samurai sword." Even when he travels as a performing gunfighter his demonstration starts with a sword trick, and whenever someone attacks him it's with swords. The bullets only fly as an afterthought.

That's because, like so many better-known Westerns, this one is a pretty close remake of a samurai film, Hideo Gosha's *Goyokin* (1969), or as some of the English language posters would have it, *The Steel Edge of Revenge*. Both stories revolve around a conscientious warrior trying to stop the massacre of villagers for knowing about a plot to intentionally crash a government boat carrying gold. Weirdly, Laughlin's version is also based on an incident in California history that later inspired the shipwreck backstory to John Carpenter's *The Fog* (1980).

Though Laughlin was a pioneer in independent film distribution, *The Master Gunfighter* was a major flop, and was never seen enough to be considered forgotten like the *Billy Jack* series. But I really appreciate that it's a Western from a unique perspective, in a novel coastal setting, with some dynamic

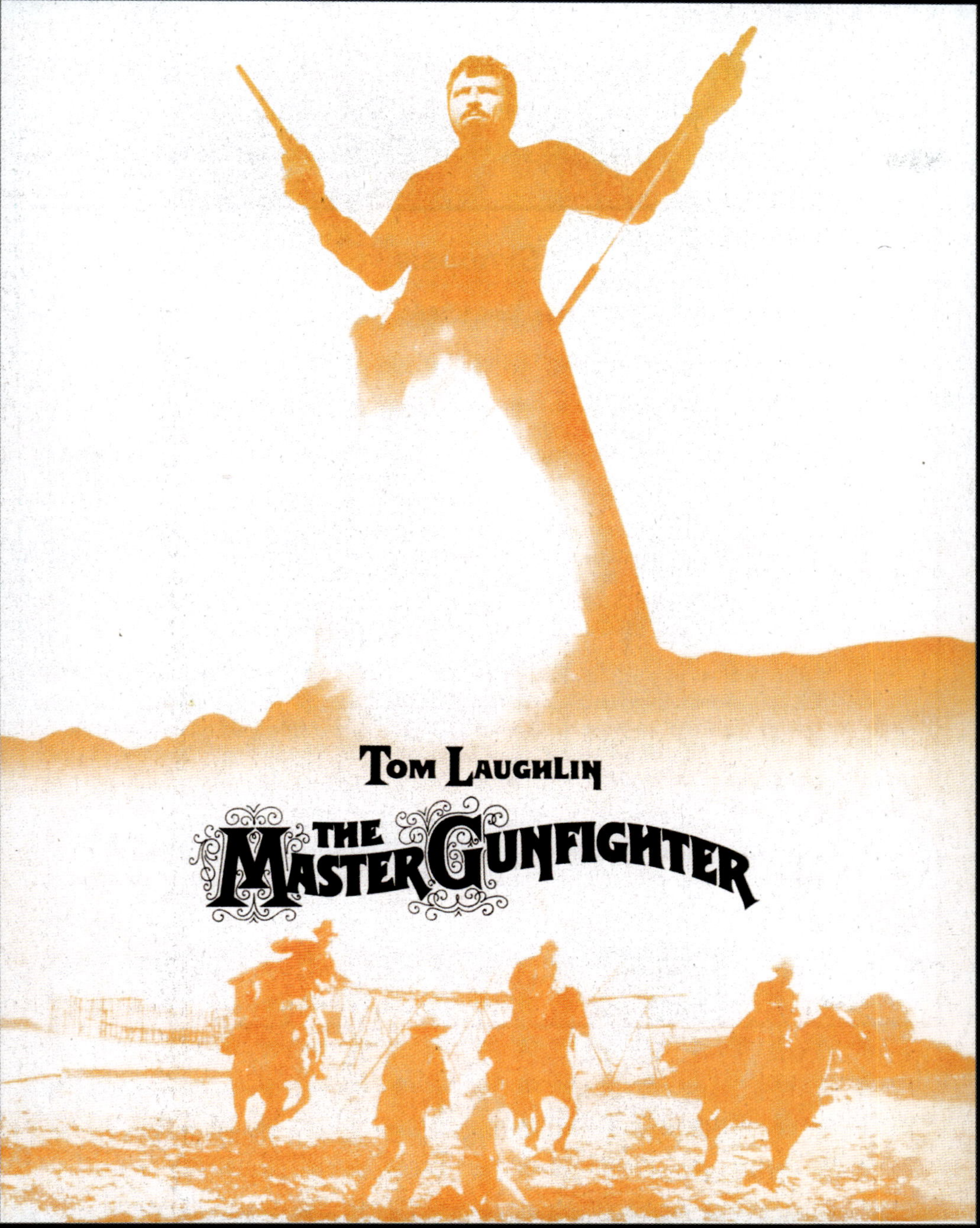

Tom Laughlin

The Master Gunfighter

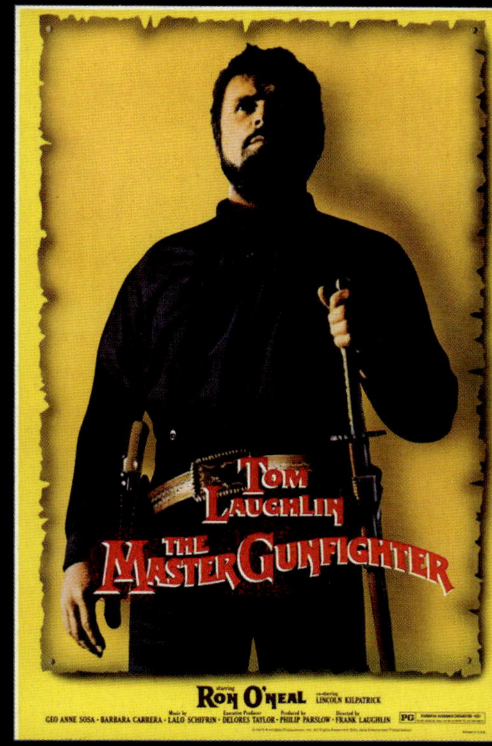

action beats (one guy gets shot on a chair and flies back into a saloon like something out of a Sam Raimi movie), and effective themes of honor. Finley has a complex relationship with the villain, Paulo (*Super Fly*'s Ron O'Neal), who really believes that massacring a village of Chumash Indians is the right thing to do when it's protecting his Spanish brethren from being taxed to death by the American government.

One part that's better in the original: both have a scene where the hero is hanging from a tree and the villain tries to convince him of his position. In *Master Gunfighter* the villain shoots the rope to let him down, but in the original he had to do an amazing Harry Houdini-style escape.

Whether or not these movies have something going on beneath the surface, they do look pretty on a wall. Please join me in enjoying a few of the ol' furies of blood and burning rubber. ●

ABOVE LEFT AND RIGHT: Tom Laughlin stands tall in the promotional posters for *The Master Gunfighter* (1975). Laughlin (1931–2013) was best known for his *Billy Jack* films, but he also wrote books of Jungian philosophy, founded a successful preschool, and ran for President of the United States, telling the press in 1992 that he was "the least qualified person I know to be President, except George Bush."

SERIAL THRILLS

In the days before TV and video games, many kids spent their Saturdays at the local movie theater, where the full program of entertainment might include (on top of the newsreel, cartoons, B-movie, and main feature) the latest chapter of a movie serial. These low-budget but action-packed, cliff-hanger-ridden adventures would often feature a hero battling wave after wave of opponents and henchmen before finally besting the Big Boss/main villain in the final installment. Not so different from video games, really. Market leaders Republic Pictures' espionage outing *Radar Patrol vs. Spy King* (1949) starred Kirk Alyn, fresh from playing the first on-screen Man of Steel in another serial: *Superman* (1948).

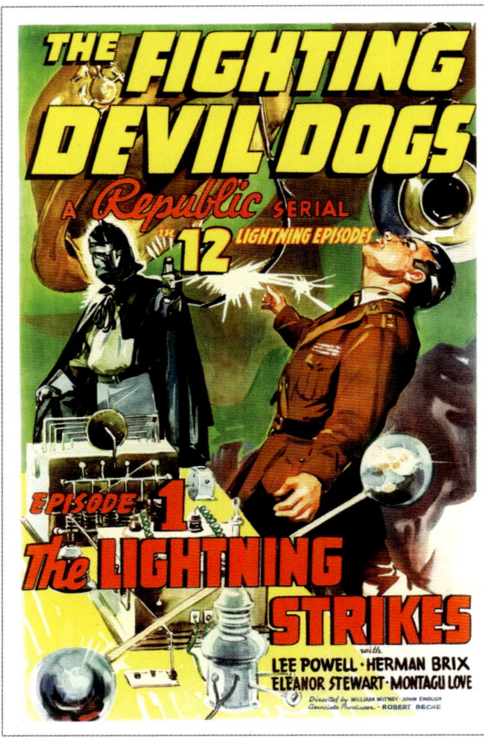

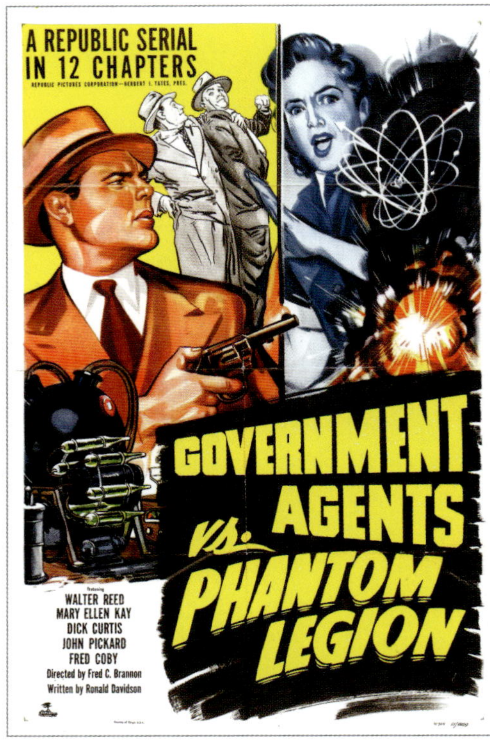

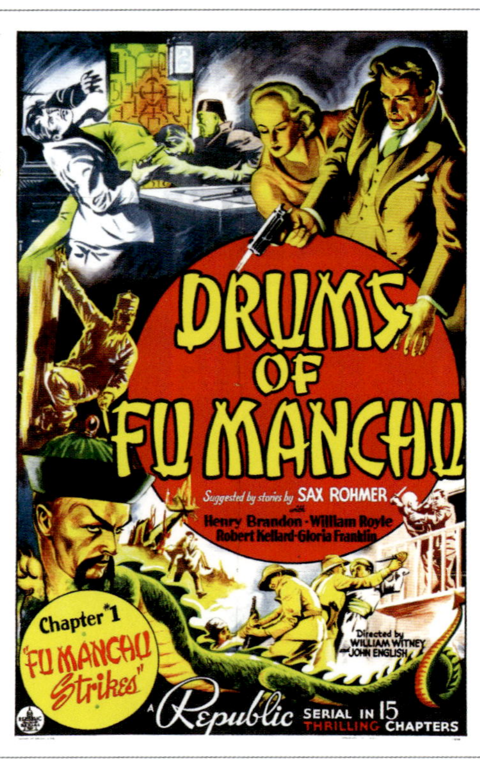

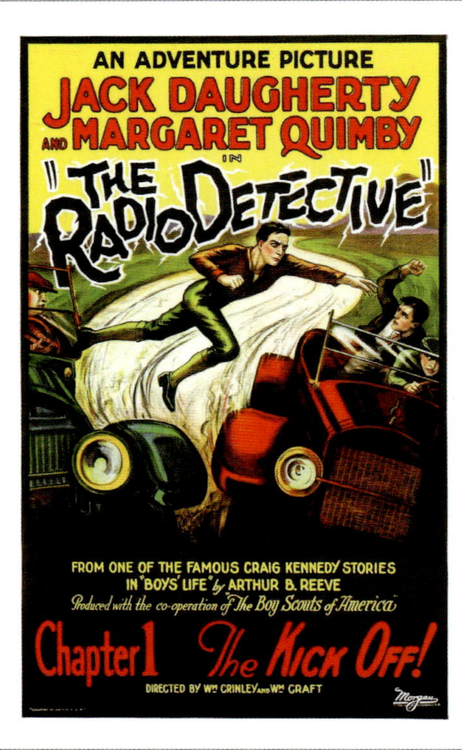

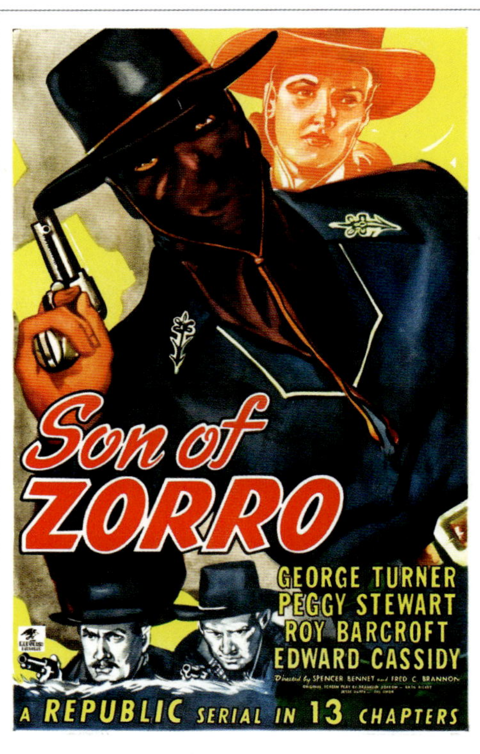

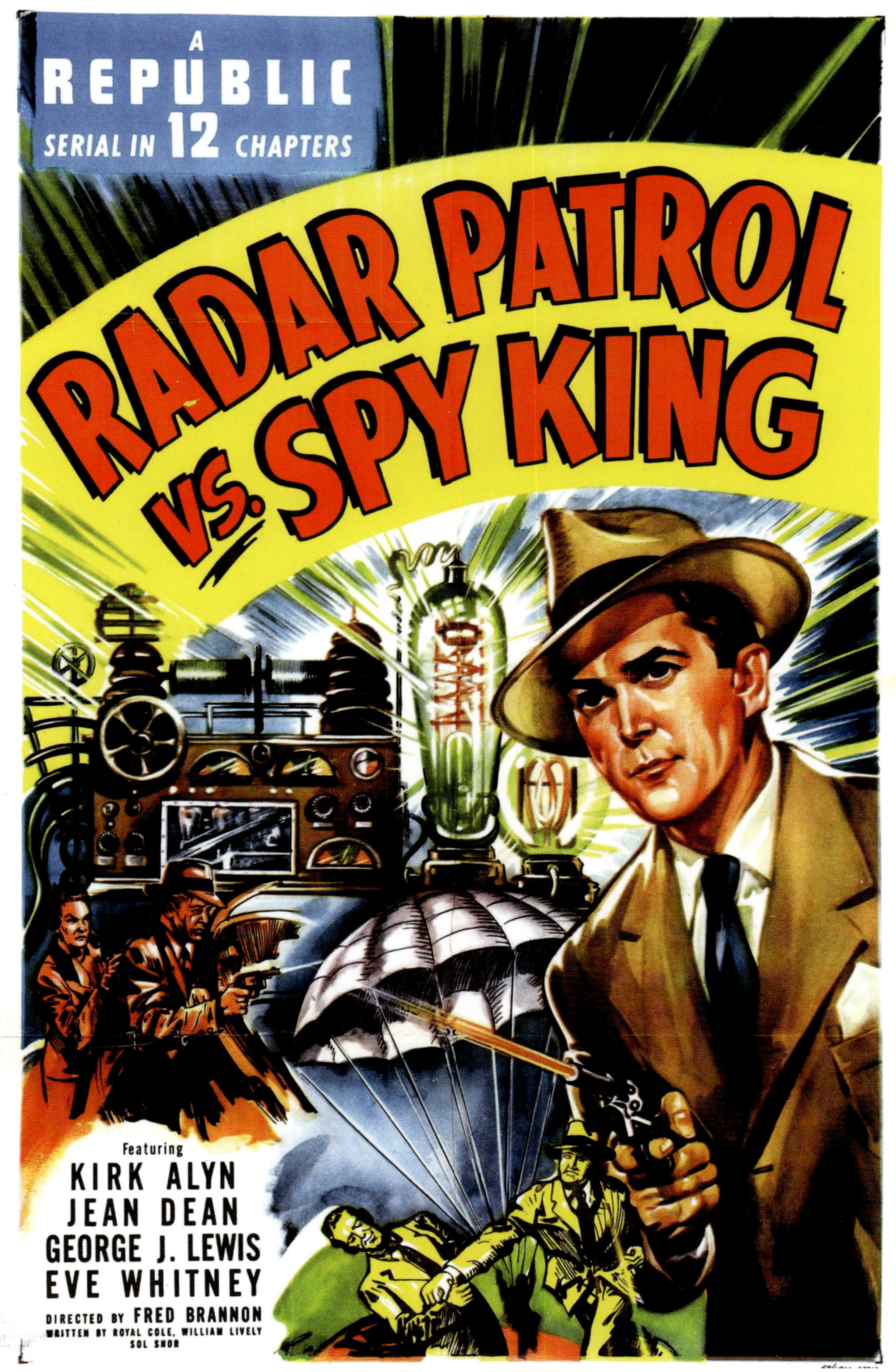
A
REPUBLIC
SERIAL IN 12 CHAPTERS
RADAR PATROL
VS. SPY KING
Featuring
KIRK ALYN
JEAN DEAN
GEORGE J. LEWIS
EVE WHITNEY
DIRECTED BY FRED BRANNON
WRITTEN BY ROYAL COLE, WILLIAM LIVELY
SOL SHOR

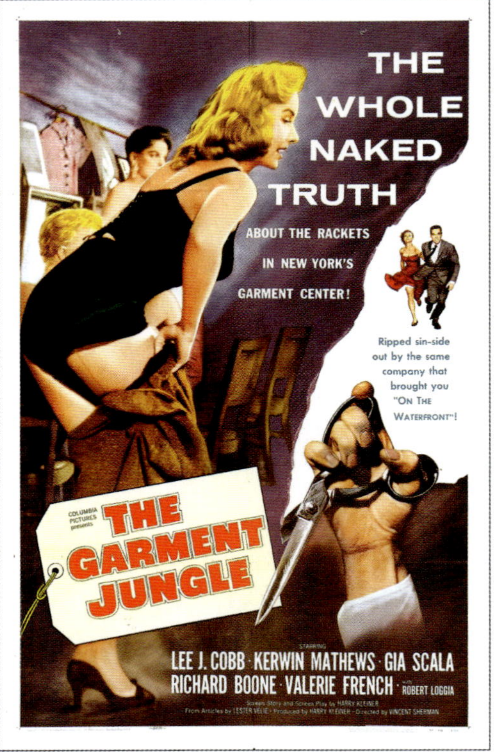

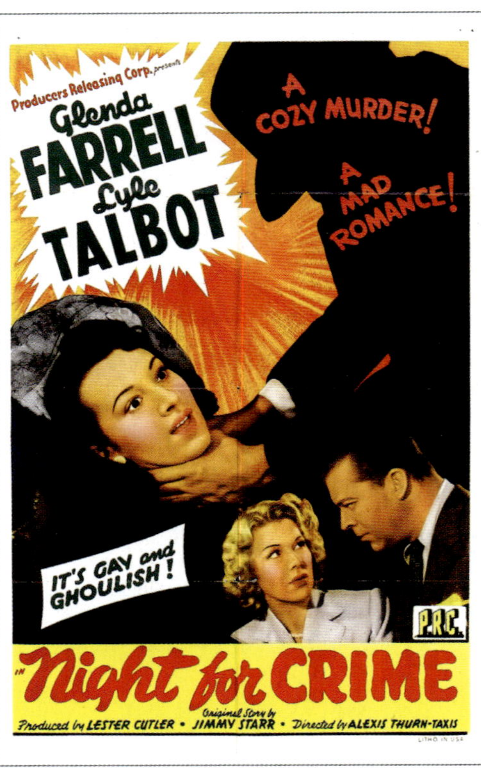

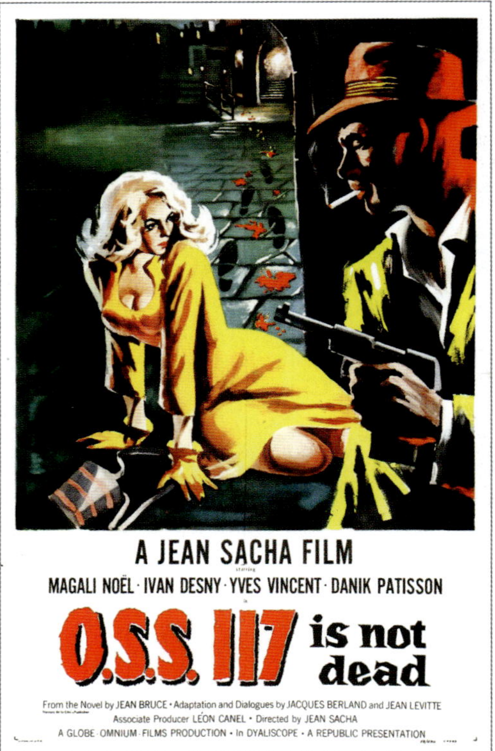

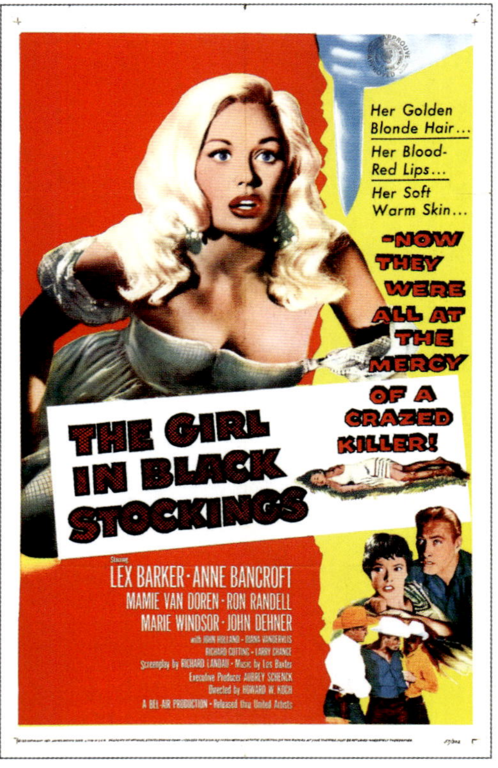

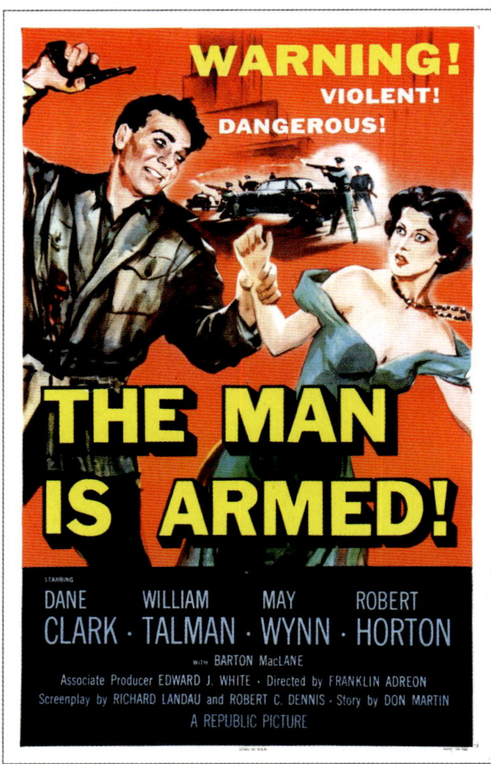

B-NOIR

Even today, highfalutin critics argue about the exact definition of film noir—is it a true genre in and of itself, or simply a visual approach? Does it have to be oneiric? Et cetera . . . Graphic novelist Frank Miller summed up the basic appeal with the title of one of his *Sin City* stories: "Booze, Broads & Bullets." What's not to like? Pulpy noir stories were a gift to B-movie producers, and their poster designers. *The Girl Hunters* (1963), an adaptation of the previous year's Mickey Spillane novel, bizarrely features the author himself playing his own private dick character, Mike Hammer. The poster nevertheless chooses to concentrate on the charms of upcoming starlet Shirley Eaton (who encountered 007 and some gold paint the following year).

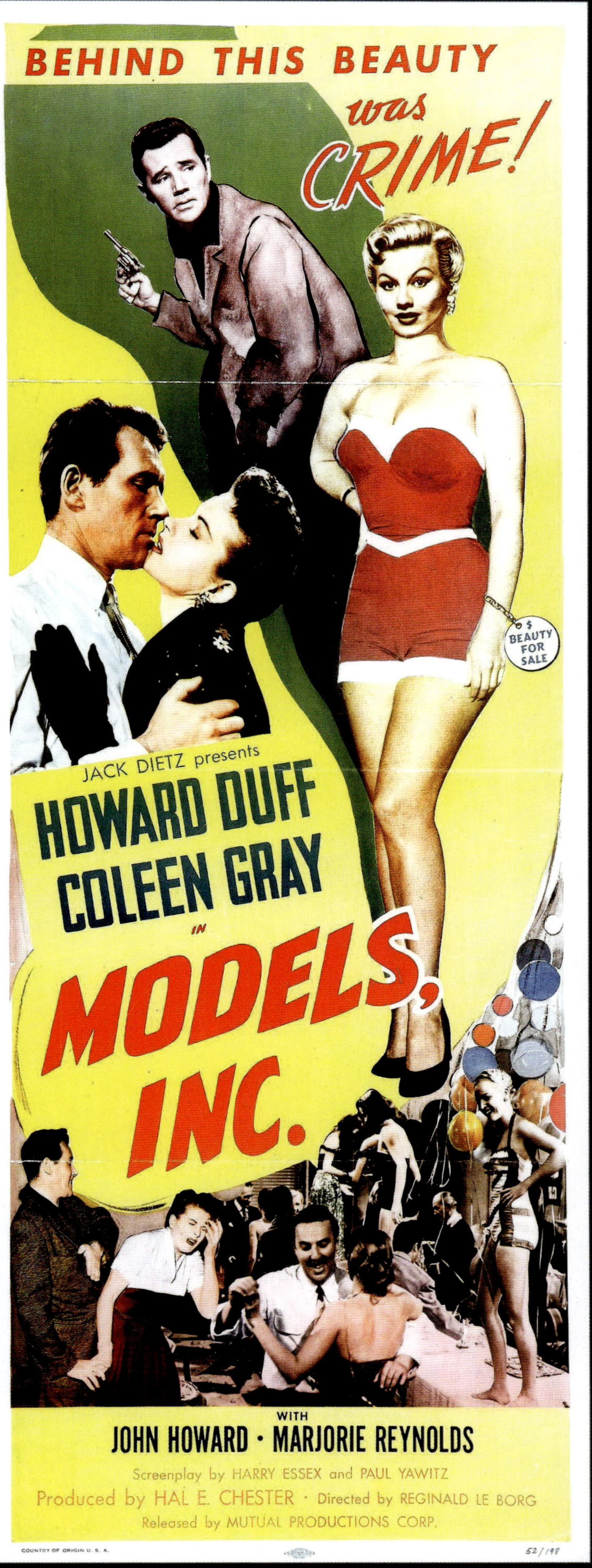

BEHIND THIS BEAUTY
was
CRIME!

$ BEAUTY FOR SALE

JACK DIETZ presents

HOWARD DUFF
COLEEN GRAY
in

MODELS, INC.

WITH
JOHN HOWARD · MARJORIE REYNOLDS

Screenplay by HARRY ESSEX and PAUL YAWITZ
Produced by HAL E. CHESTER · Directed by REGINALD LE BORG
Released by MUTUAL PRODUCTIONS CORP.

COUNTRY OF ORIGIN U. S. A.   52/198

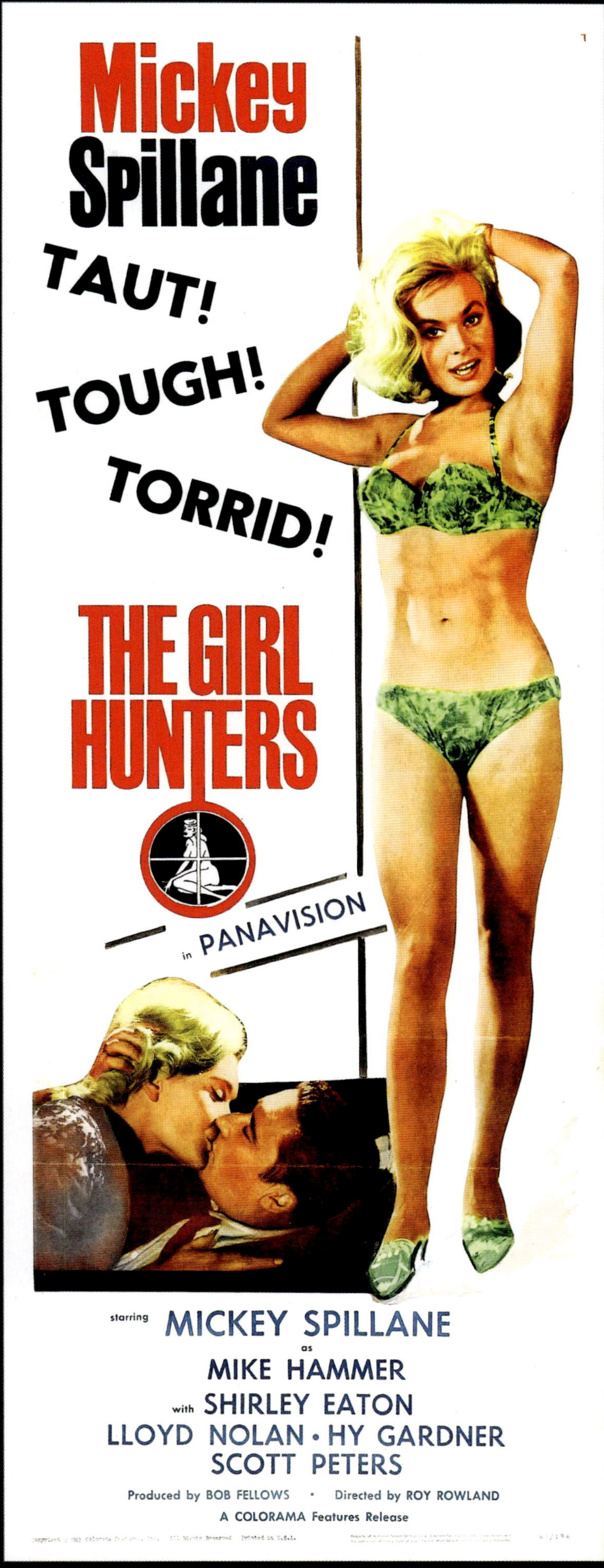

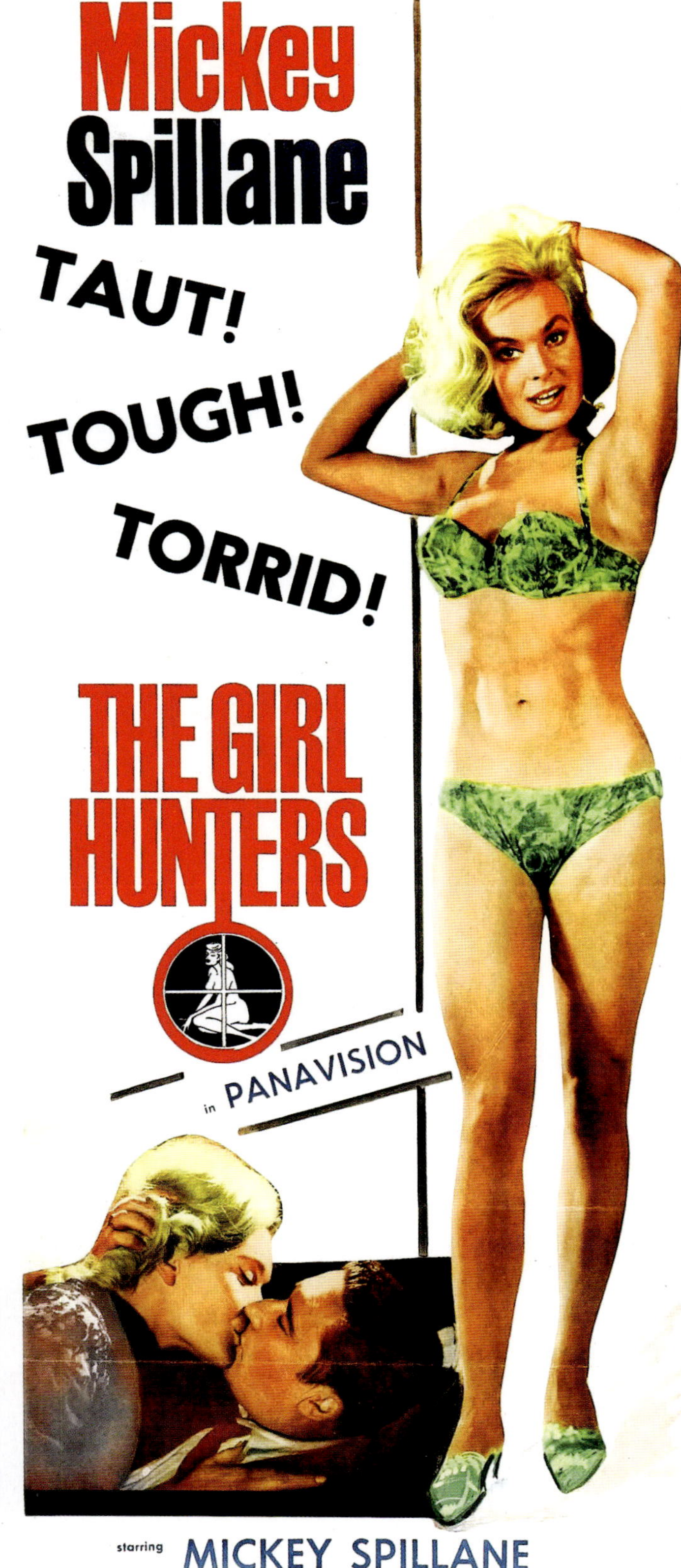

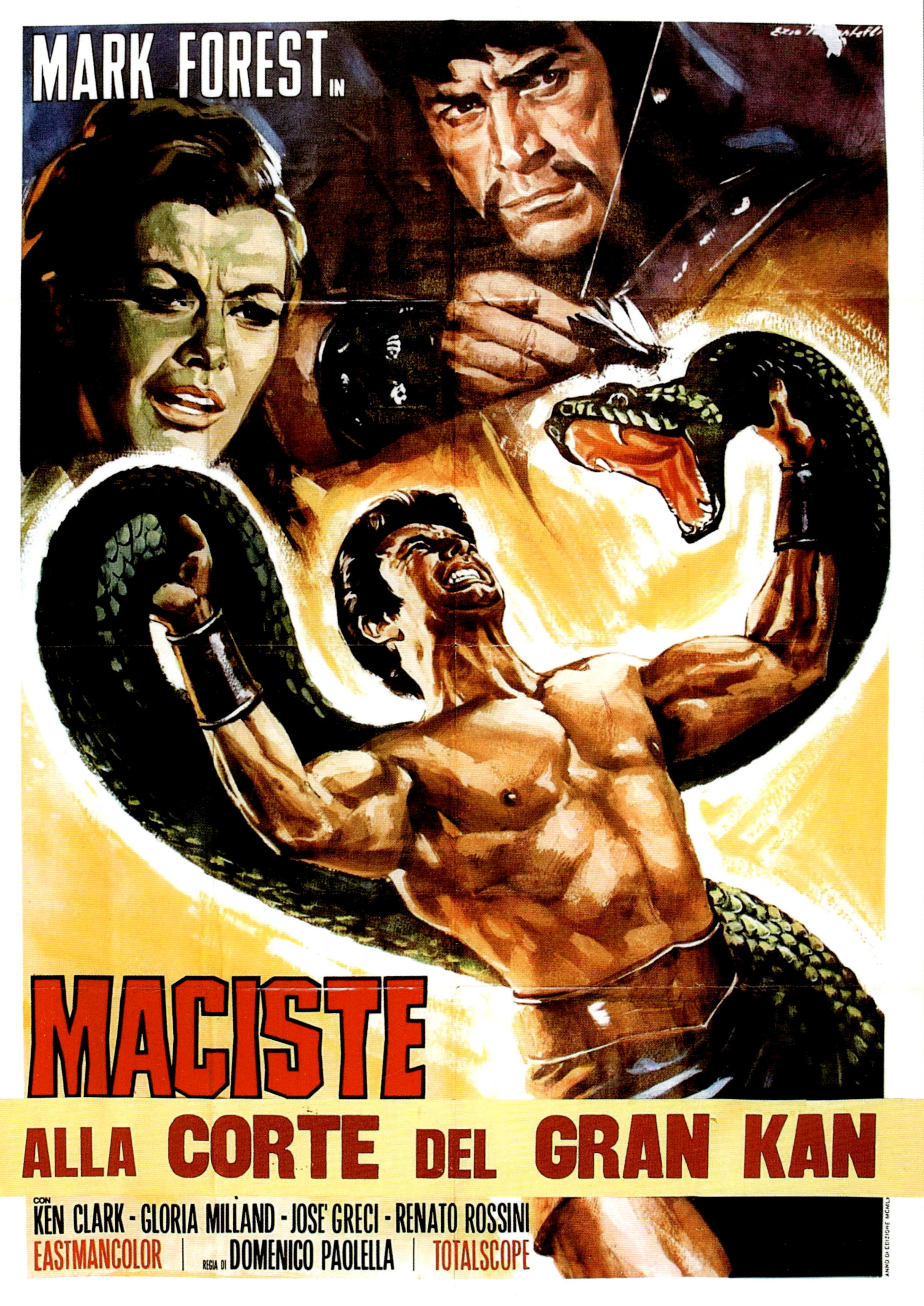
MARK FOREST IN
MACISTE
ALLA CORTE DEL GRAN KAN
CON
KEN CLARK - GLORIA MILLAND - JOSE' GRECI - RENATO ROSSINI
EASTMANCOLOR
REGIA DI DOMENICO PAOLELLA
TOTALSCOPE

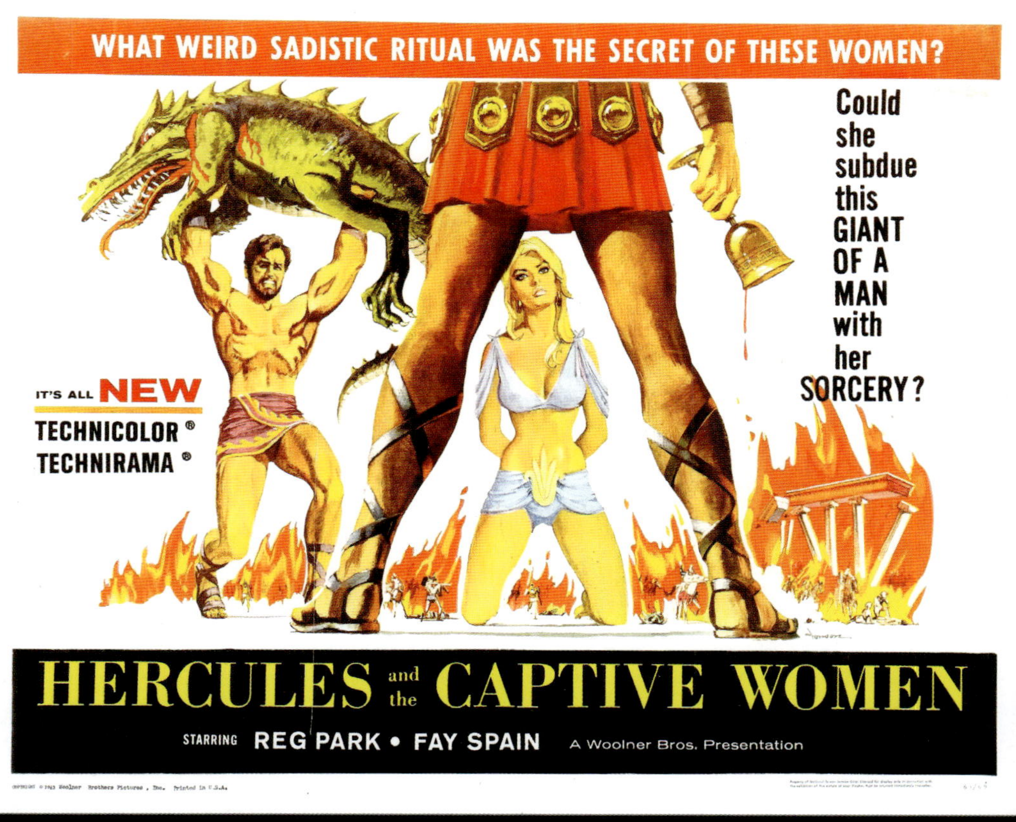

SWORDS, SORCERY, AND SANDALS

So-called *peplum* films, named after the Greek word for tunic, tried hard to compete with Hollywood's costume epics in the '50s and '60s, and while these (usually) Italian productions couldn't match the onscreen grandeur of *The Ten Commandments* or *Spartacus*, who cared, if the poster—like Ezio Tarantelli's superb example opposite—had a giant snake? The one-sheet for the US production *Hercules in New York* (1969) promises their aptly named star will "toss tough men like toothpicks." Newcomer Arnold Strong soon reverted to using his real surname, even if it took a while for people to be able to pronounce it properly: Schwarzenegger.

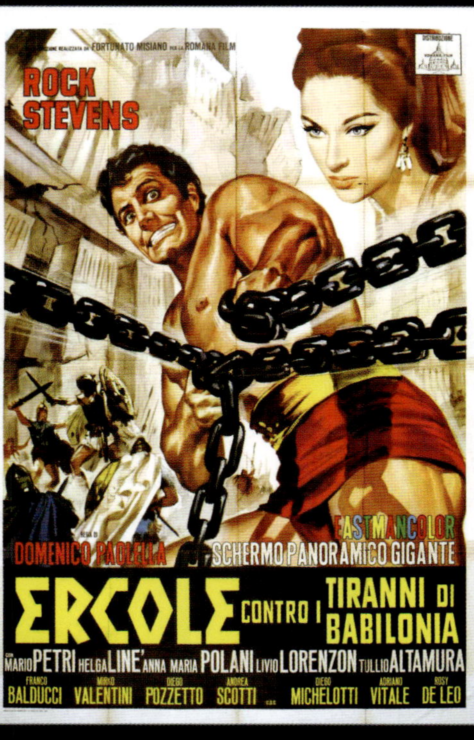

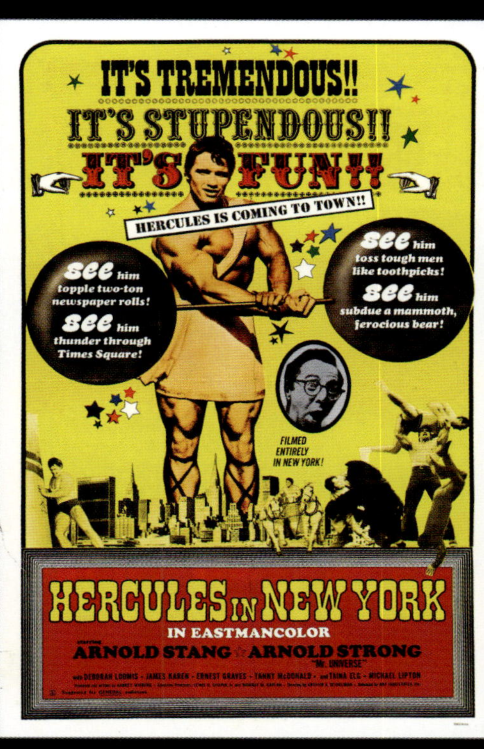

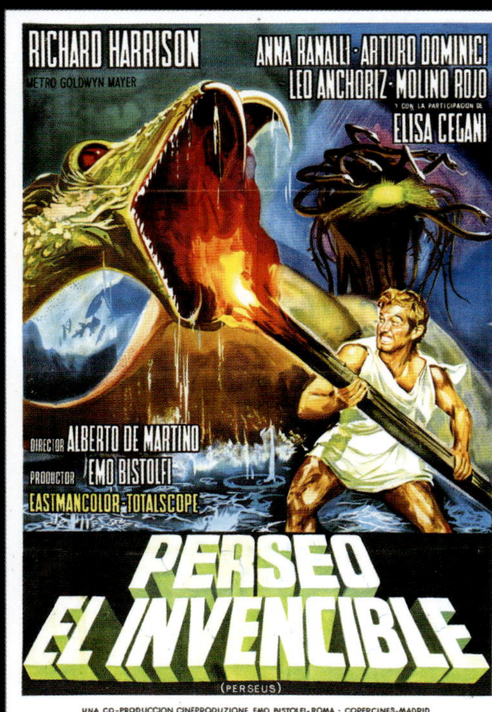

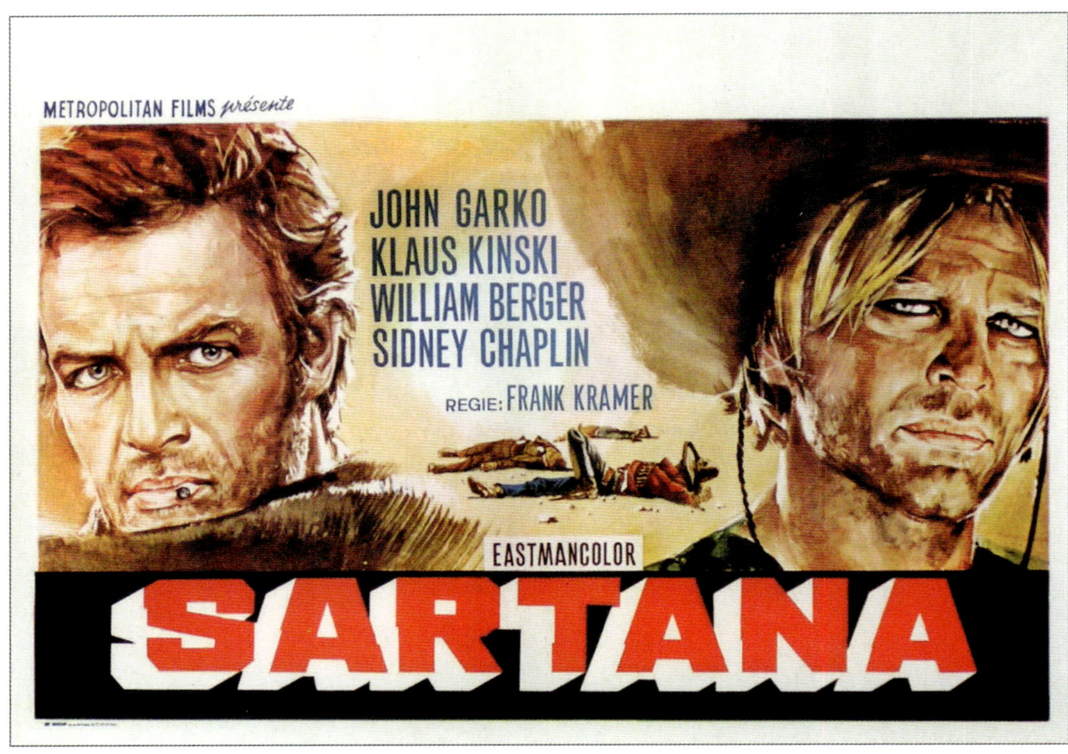
METROPOLITAN FILMS présente
JOHN GARKO
KLAUS KINSKI
WILLIAM BERGER
SIDNEY CHAPLIN
REGIE: FRANK KRAMER
EASTMANCOLOR
SARTANA

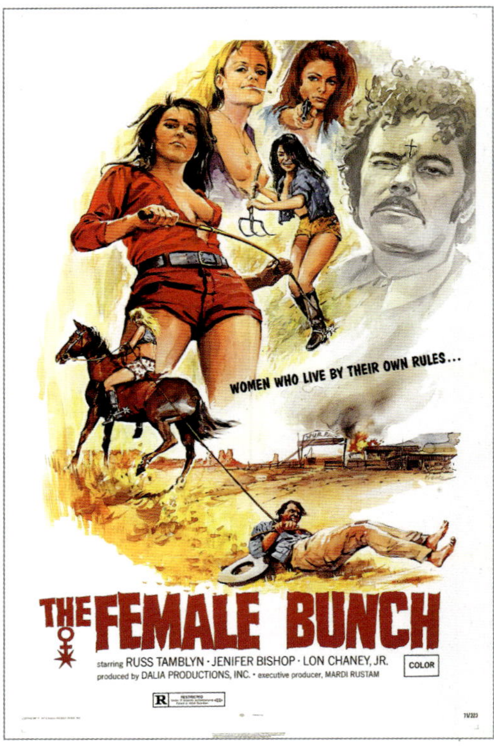
WOMEN WHO LIVE BY THEIR OWN RULES...
THE FEMALE BUNCH
starring RUSS TAMBLYN · JENIFER BISHOP · LON CHANEY, JR.
produced by DALIA PRODUCTIONS, INC. · executive producer, MARDI RUSTAM
COLOR

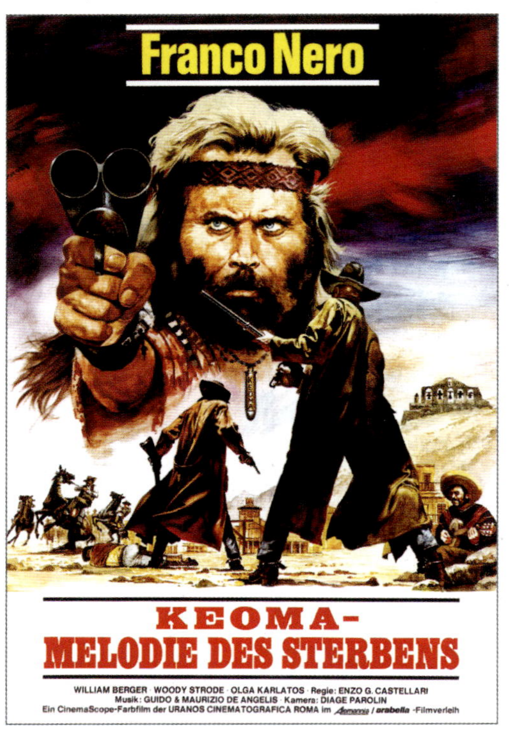
Franco Nero
KEOMA-
MELODIE DES STERBENS
WILLIAM BERGER · WOODY STRODE · OLGA KARLATOS · Regie: ENZO G. CASTELLARI
Musik: GUIDO & MAURIZIO DE ANGELIS · Kamera: DIAGE PAROLIN
Ein CinemaScope-Farbfilm der URANOS CINEMATOGRAFICA ROMA im / arabella -Filmverleih

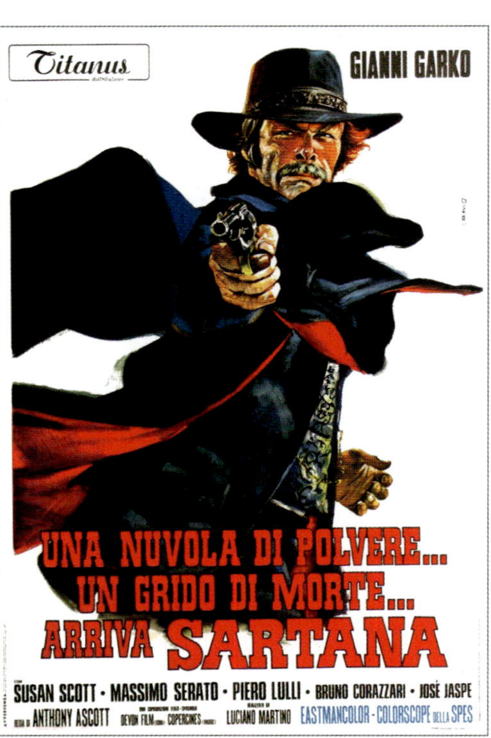
Titanus
GIANNI GARKO
UNA NUVOLA DI POLVERE...
UN GRIDO DI MORTE...
ARRIVA SARTANA
SUSAN SCOTT · MASSIMO SERATO · PIERO LULLI · BRUNO CORAZZARI · JOSÉ JASPE
ANTHONY ASCOTT
LUCIANO MARTINO
EASTMANCOLOR · COLORSCOPE

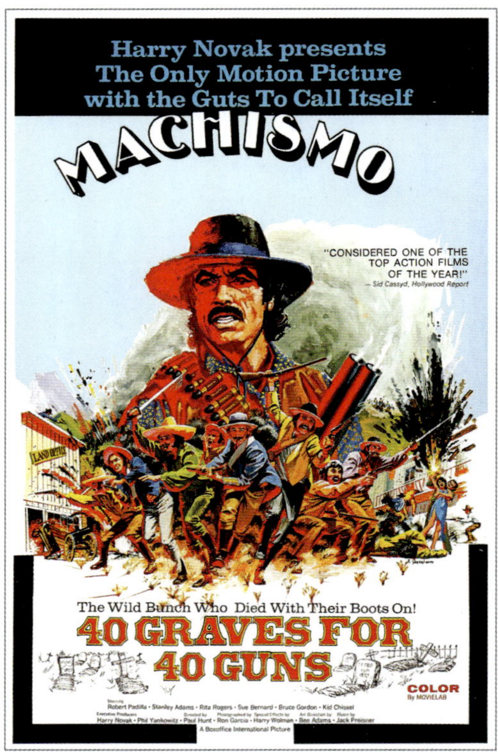
Harry Novak presents
The Only Motion Picture
with the Guts To Call Itself
MACHISMO
"CONSIDERED ONE OF THE TOP ACTION FILMS OF THE YEAR!"
– Sid Cassyd, Hollywood Report
The Wild Bunch Who Died With Their Boots On!
40 GRAVES FOR 40 GUNS
COLOR
A Boxoffice International Picture

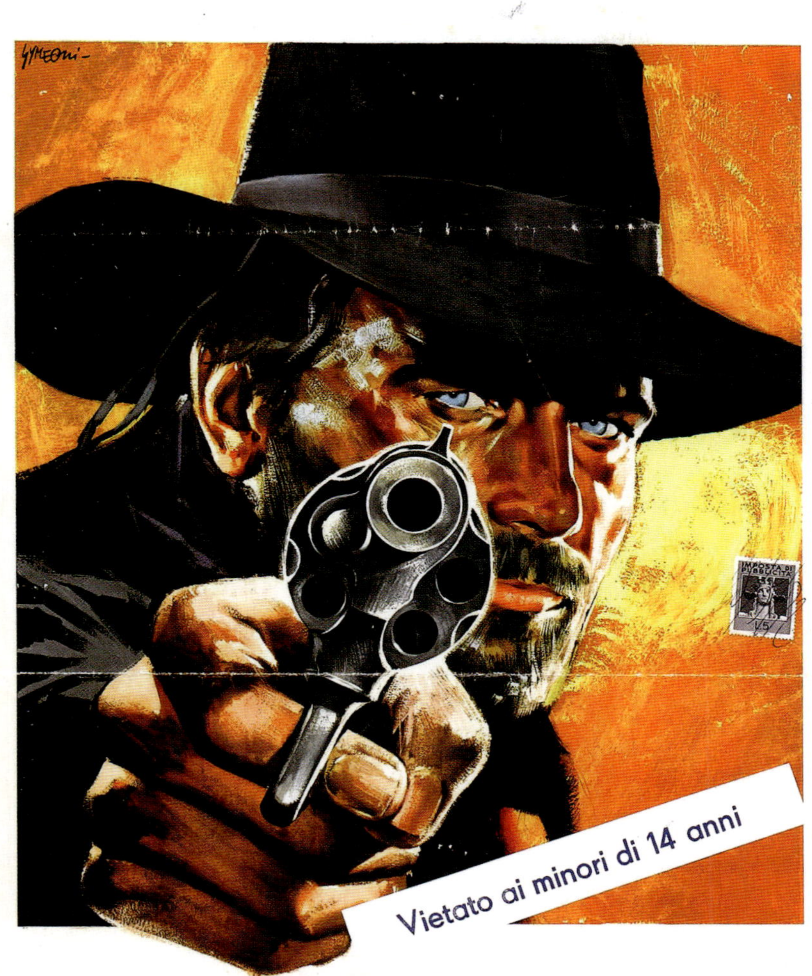

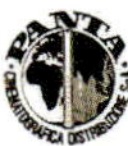

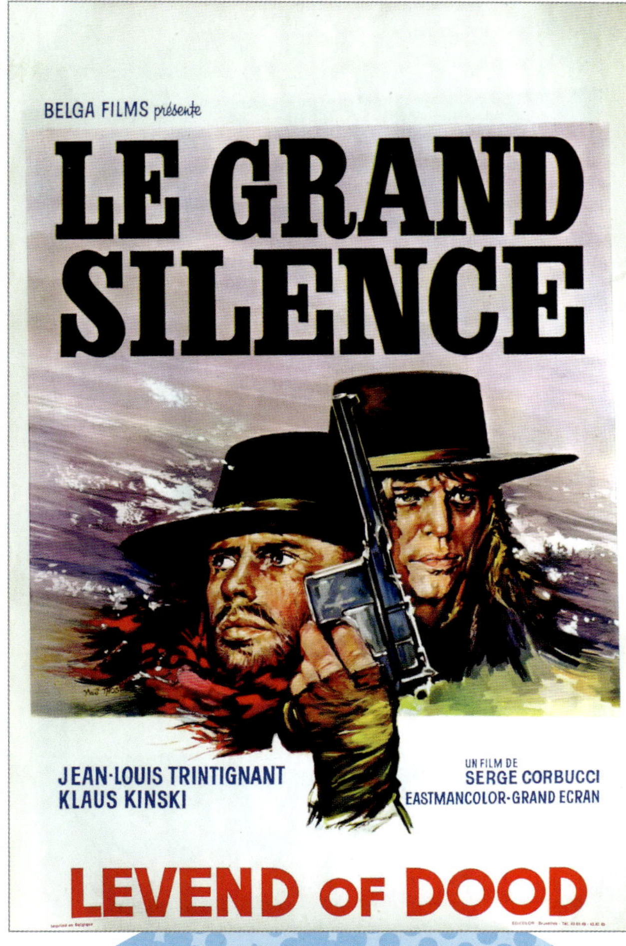

A FEW DOLLARS FOR THE WILD BUNCH

Clint Eastwood's Man with No Name is far from the only anti-hero to stare fixedly out of a Spaghetti Western movie poster. Gianni Garko played Sartana in four films, and Franco Nero made an indelible impression as *Django* (1966), despite appearing in just one of the 30-odd, mainly unofficial sequels (he starred in plenty of other Westerns though, and Tarantino gave him a thank you cameo in *Django Unchained*). The huge success of *The Wild Bunch* in 1969 ensured demand for violent oaters continued into the 1970s, both in the US and Europe. James Coburn toplined the Italian production *A Reason to Live, a Reason to Die* in 1972 (overleaf), but he could have been in the Spaghetti business years earlier if he hadn't turned down the lead in *A Fistful of Dollars*.

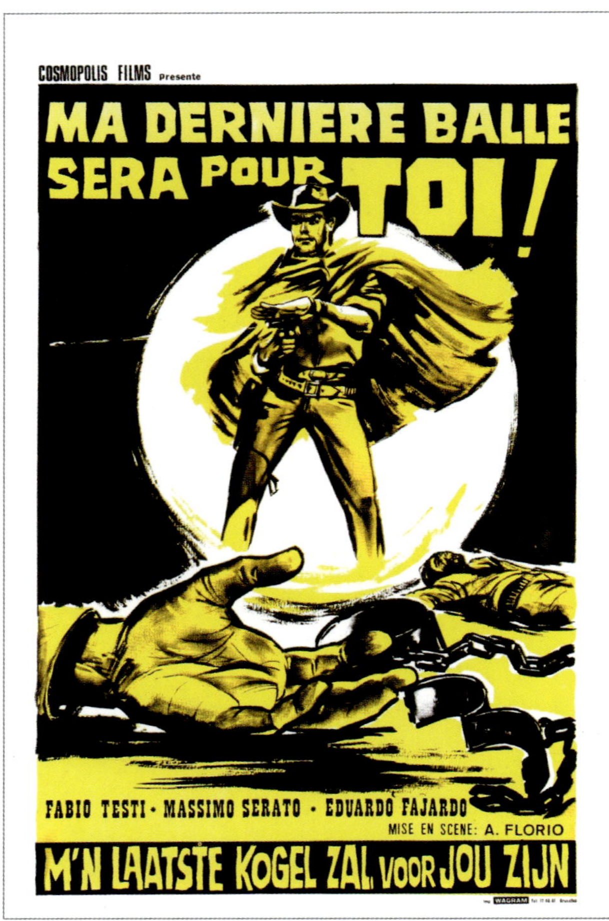
COSMOPOLIS FILMS presente
MA DERNIERE BALLE SERA POUR TOI!
FABIO TESTI · MASSIMO SERATO · EDUARDO FAJARDO
MISE EN SCENE: A. FLORIO
M'N LAATSTE KOGEL ZAL VOOR JOU ZIJN

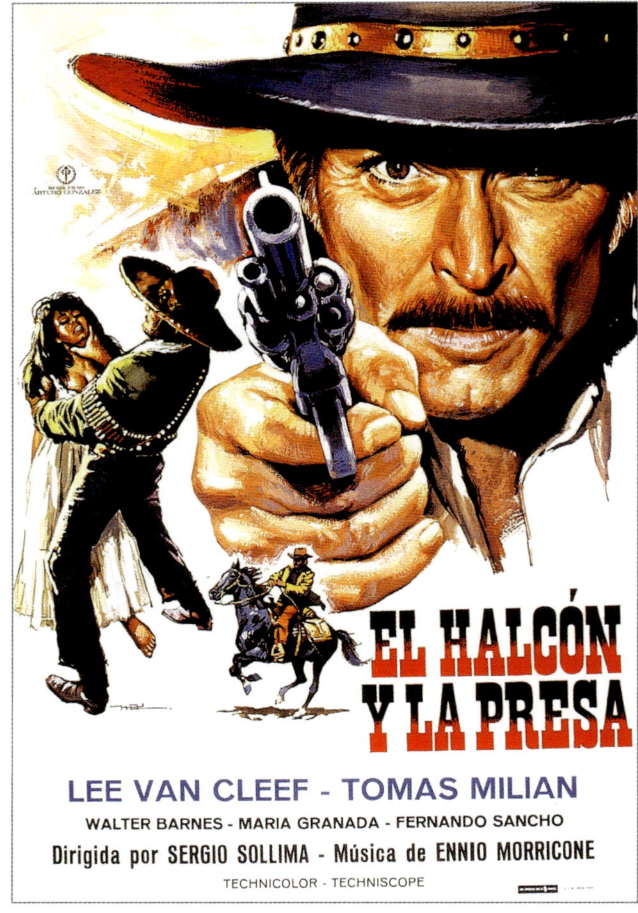
EL HALCÓN Y LA PRESA
LEE VAN CLEEF - TOMAS MILIAN
WALTER BARNES - MARIA GRANADA - FERNANDO SANCHO
Dirigida por SERGIO SOLLIMA - Música de ENNIO MORRICONE
TECHNICOLOR - TECHNISCOPE

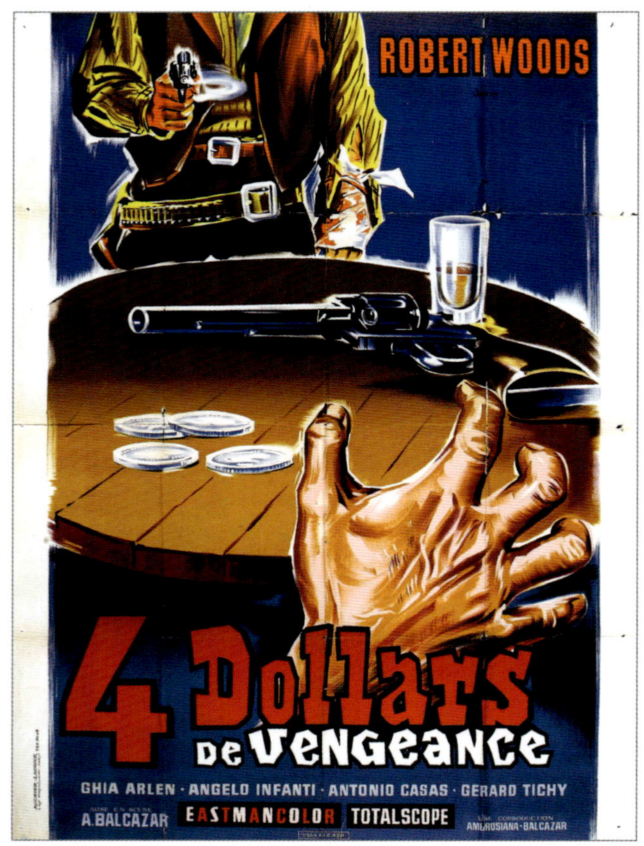
ROBERT WOODS
4 Dollars de vengeance
GHIA ARLEN · ANGELO INFANTI · ANTONIO CASAS · GERARD TICHY
MISE EN SCENE A. BALCAZAR
EASTMANCOLOR
TOTALSCOPE
UNE COPRODUCTION AMBROSIANA-BALCAZAR

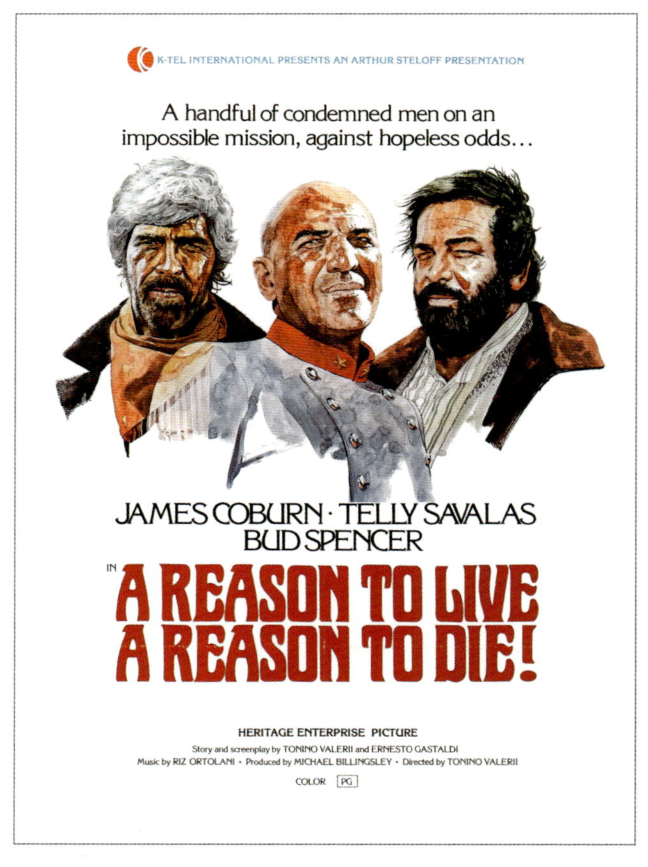
K-TEL INTERNATIONAL PRESENTS AN ARTHUR STELOFF PRESENTATION
A handful of condemned men on an impossible mission, against hopeless odds…
JAMES COBURN · TELLY SAVALAS
BUD SPENCER
IN
A REASON TO LIVE A REASON TO DIE!
HERITAGE ENTERPRISE PICTURE
Story and screenplay by TONINO VALERII and ERNESTO GASTALDI
Music by RIZ ORTOLANI · Produced by MICHAEL BILLINGSLEY · Directed by TONINO VALERII
COLOR
PG

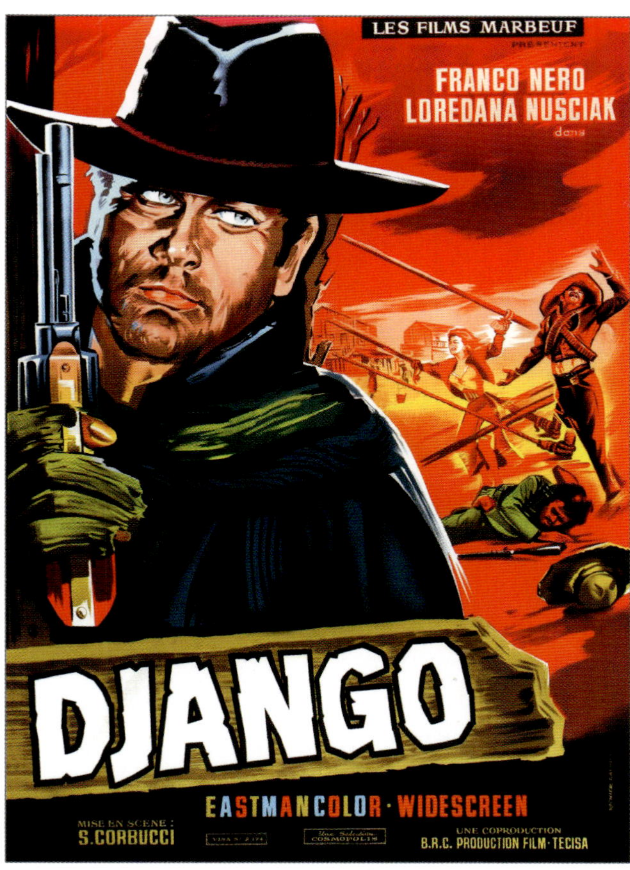
LES FILMS MARBEUF
FRANCO NERO
LOREDANA NUSCIAK
DJANGO
EASTMANCOLOR · WIDESCREEN
MISE EN SCENE :
S. CORBUCCI
UNE COPRODUCTION
B.R.C. PRODUCTION FILM · TECISA

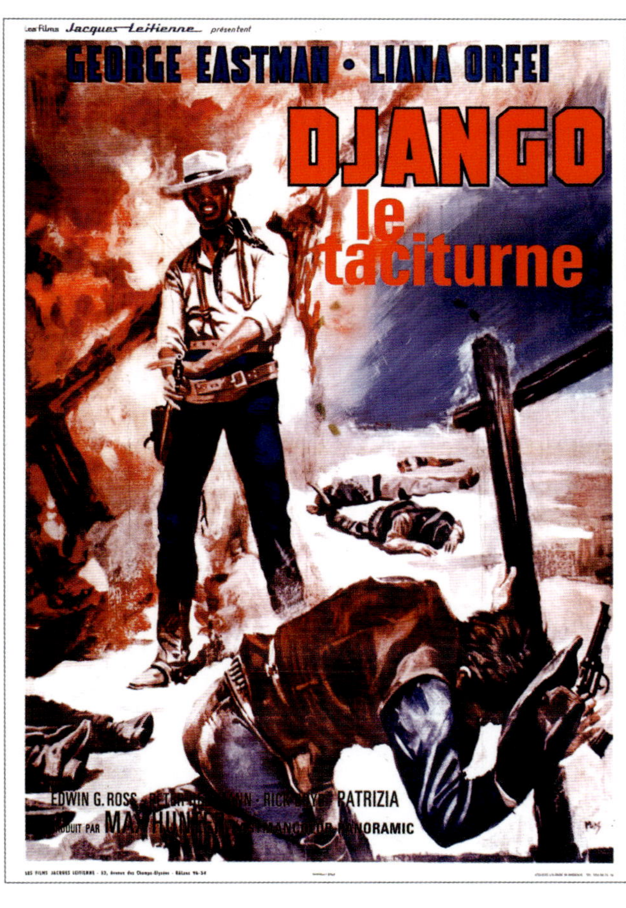
GEORGE EASTMAN · LIANA ORFEI
DJANGO
le
taciturne

MESTIZO-HALFBREED

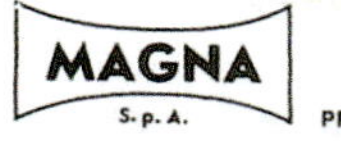
MAGNA
S. p. A.
PRESENTA

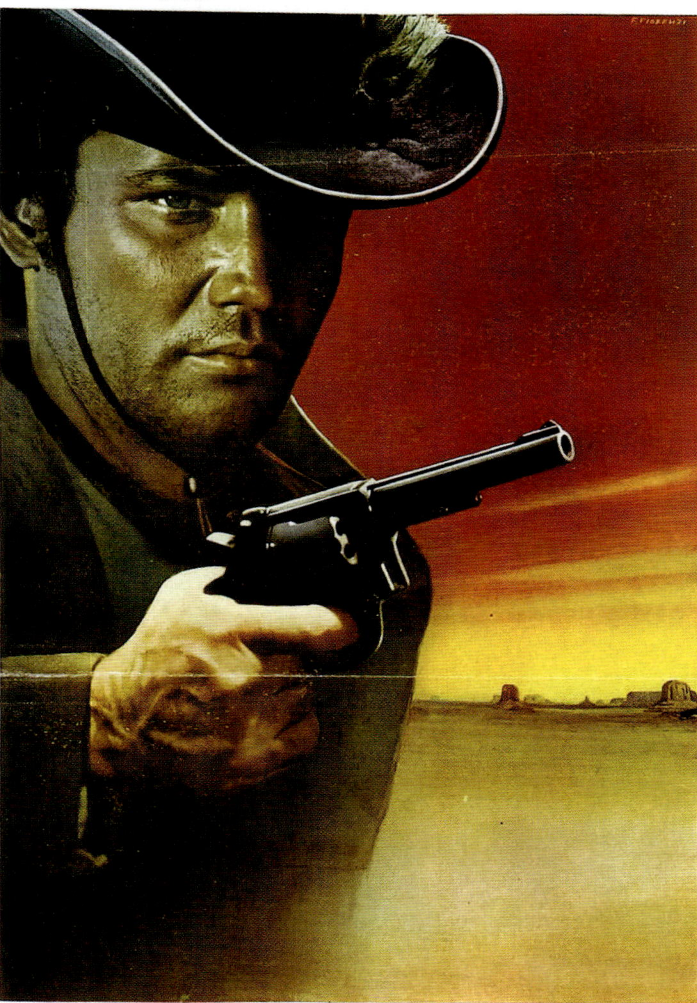

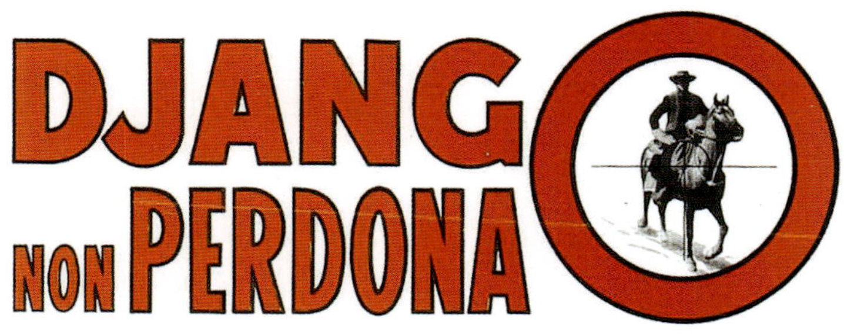
DJANGO
NON PERDONA
JOHN CLARK - EVELIN THERENS
GUSTAVO ROJO
REGIA DI J. BUCHS
UNA PRODUZIONE ATLANTIDA FILM

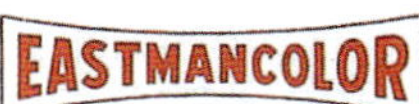
EASTMANCOLOR
SCOPE

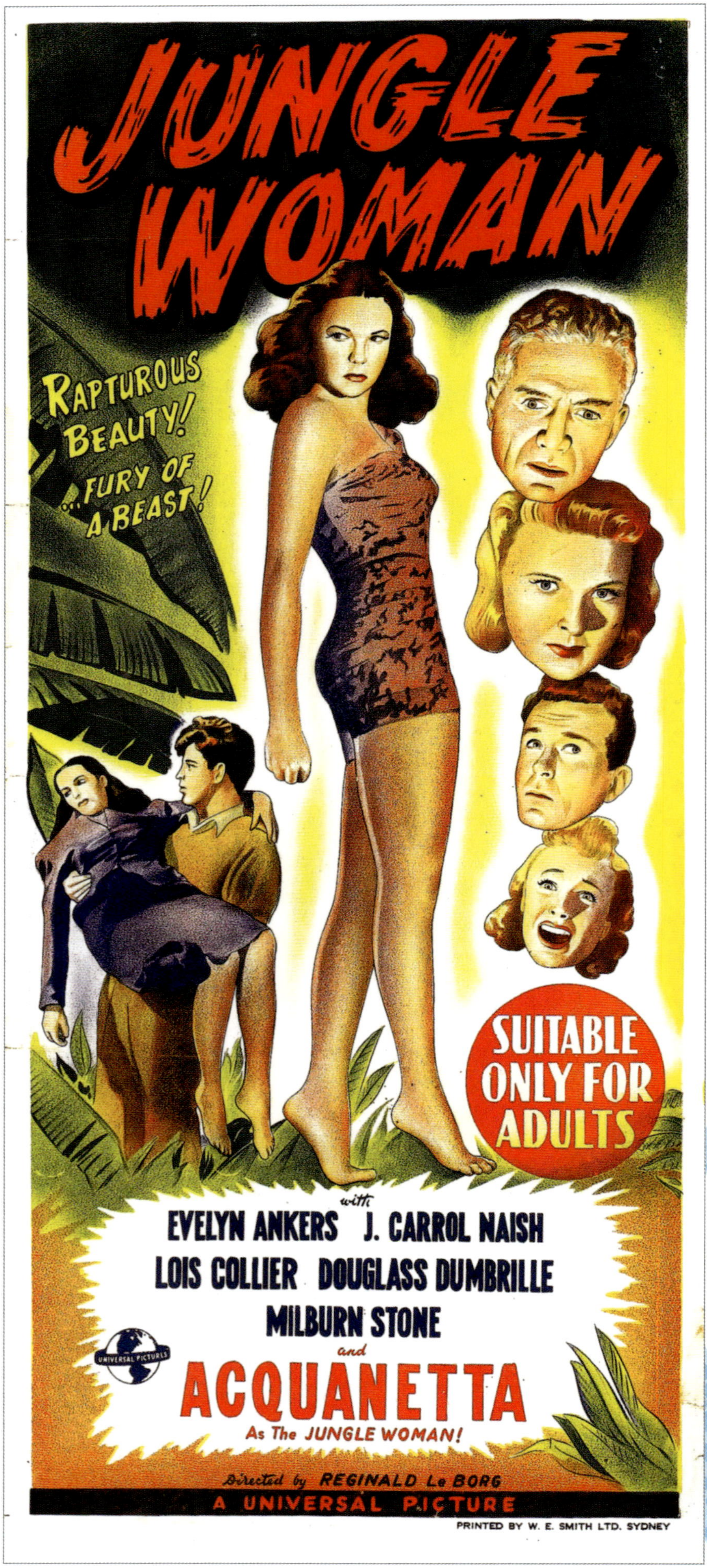

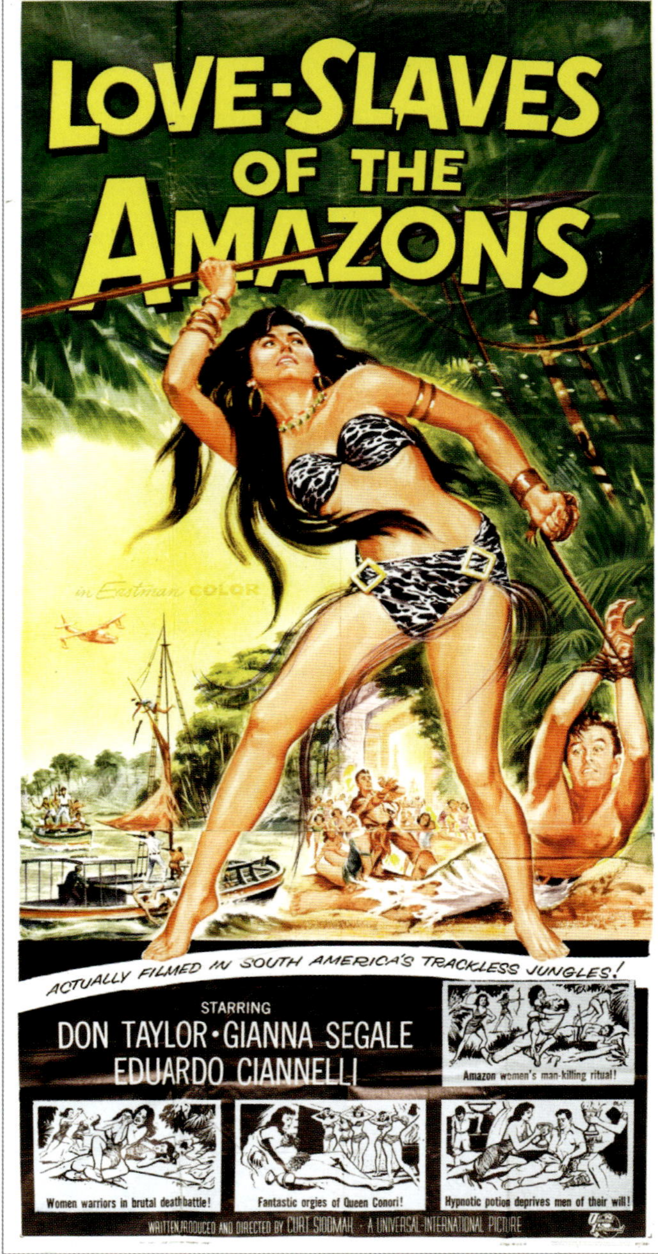

JUNGLE GIRLS

Exotic, wild, and usually dressed in only a few scraps of fur, the "jungle girl" archetype was an obvious choice for exploitation filmmakers. "She Fought Lust with the Clawing Fury of a Tormented Tigress" pants the poster for 1956's *Liane, Jungle Goddess* (starring Marion Michaels, "Germany's answer to Brigitte Bardot"), laying bare the essential appeal of such characters: raw sexuality, unfiltered by civilization. Acquanetta, the star of *Jungle Woman* (1944) was unusual in that unlike most of her counterparts she was not Caucasian, though she did have to suffer the indignity of her character turning into a gorilla. Initially promoted as "the Venezuelan Volcano," Acquanetta (aka Mildred Davenport) later revealed she was actually born on an Arapaho reservation in Wyoming.

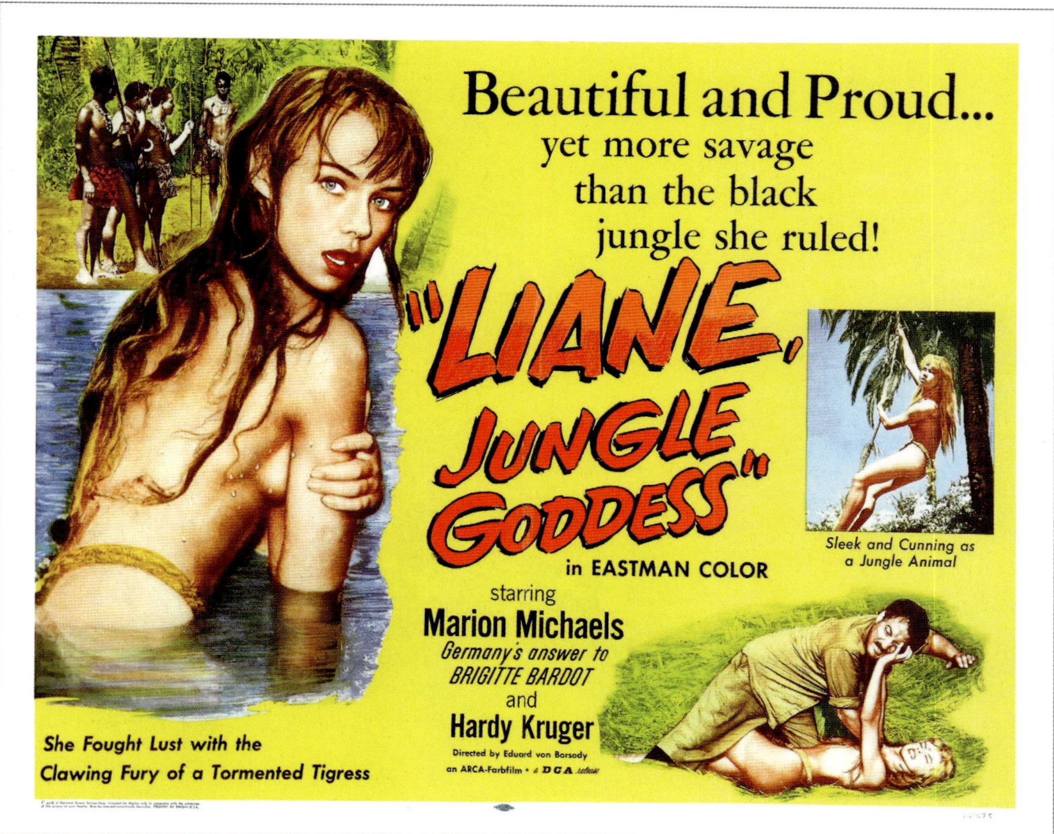
Beautiful and Proud...
yet more savage
than the black
jungle she ruled!
"LIANE, JUNGLE GODDESS"
in EASTMAN COLOR
Sleek and Cunning as a Jungle Animal
starring
Marion Michaels
Germany's answer to BRIGITTE BARDOT
and
Hardy Kruger
Directed by Eduard von Borsody
an ARCA-Farbfilm • a DCA release
She Fought Lust with the
Clawing Fury of a Tormented Tigress

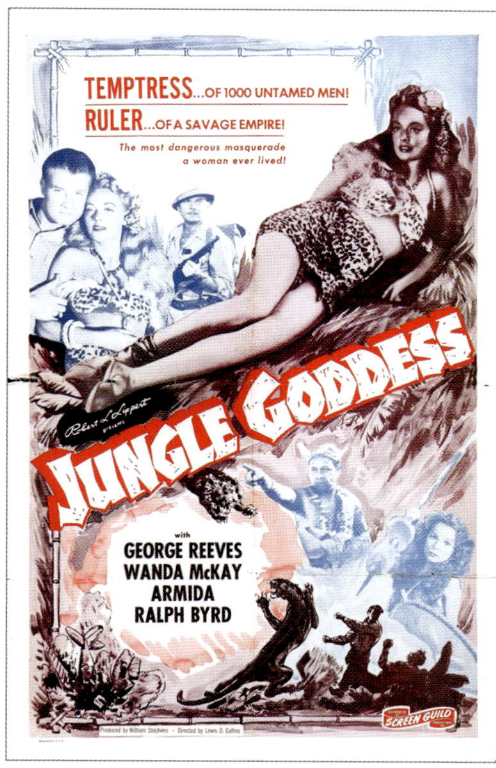
TEMPTRESS...OF 1000 UNTAMED MEN!
RULER...OF A SAVAGE EMPIRE!
The most dangerous masquerade a woman ever lived!
JUNGLE GODDESS
with
GEORGE REEVES
WANDA McKAY
ARMIDA
RALPH BYRD
SCREEN GUILD

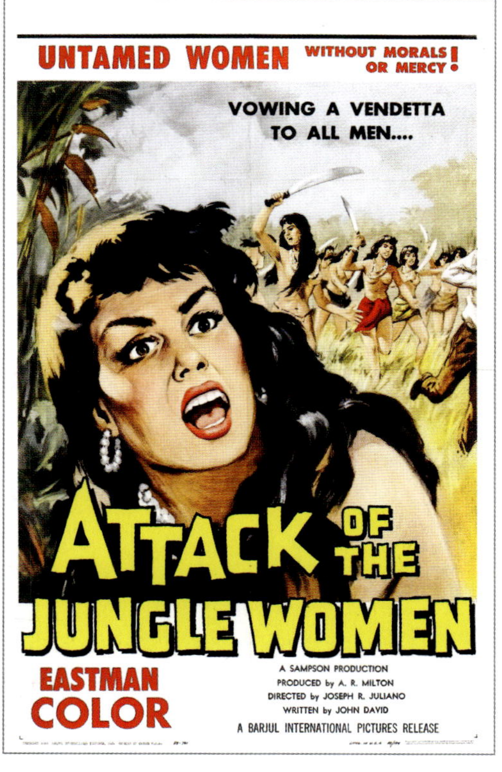
UNTAMED WOMEN WITHOUT MORALS OR MERCY!
VOWING A VENDETTA TO ALL MEN....
ATTACK OF THE JUNGLE WOMEN
EASTMAN COLOR
A SAMPSON PRODUCTION
PRODUCED by A. R. MILTON
DIRECTED by JOSEPH R. JULIANO
WRITTEN by JOHN DAVID
A BARJUL INTERNATIONAL PICTURES RELEASE

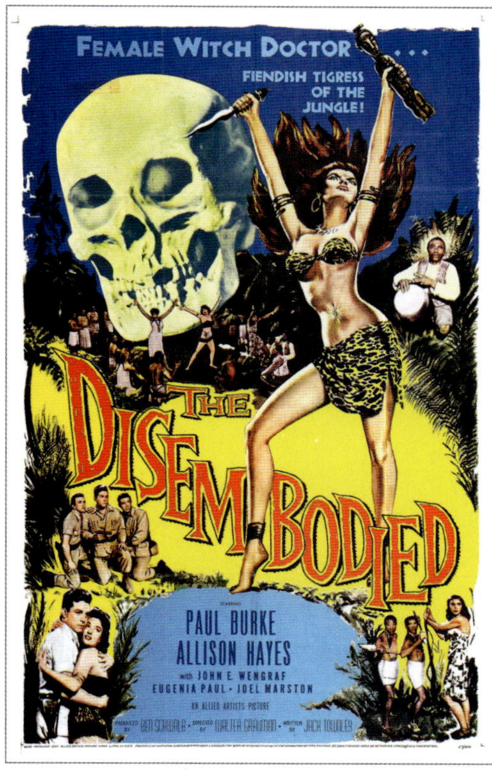
FEMALE WITCH DOCTOR . . .
FIENDISH TIGRESS OF THE JUNGLE!
THE DISEMBODIED
PAUL BURKE
ALLISON HAYES
with JOHN E. WENGRAF
EUGENIA PAUL • JOEL MARSTON
AN ALLIED ARTISTS PICTURE

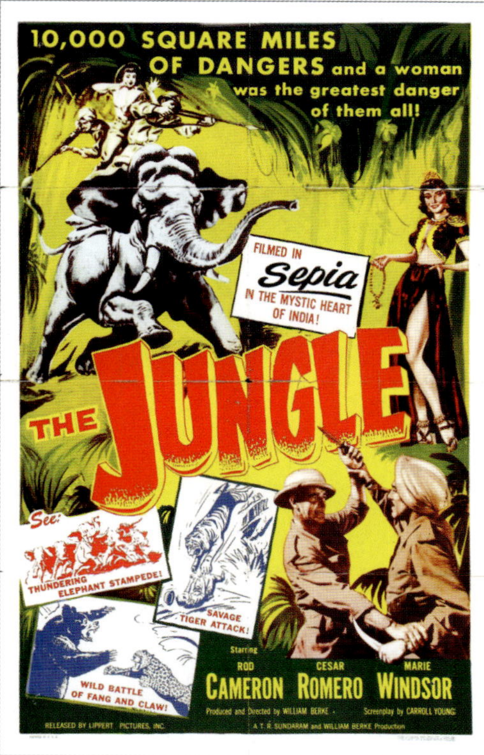
10,000 SQUARE MILES OF DANGERS and a woman was the greatest danger of them all!
FILMED IN Sepia IN THE MYSTIC HEART OF INDIA!
THE JUNGLE
See:
THUNDERING ELEPHANT STAMPEDE!
SAVAGE TIGER ATTACK!
WILD BATTLE OF FANG AND CLAW!
Starring
ROD CAMERON
CESAR ROMERO
MARIE WINDSOR
RELEASED BY LIPPERT PICTURES, INC.

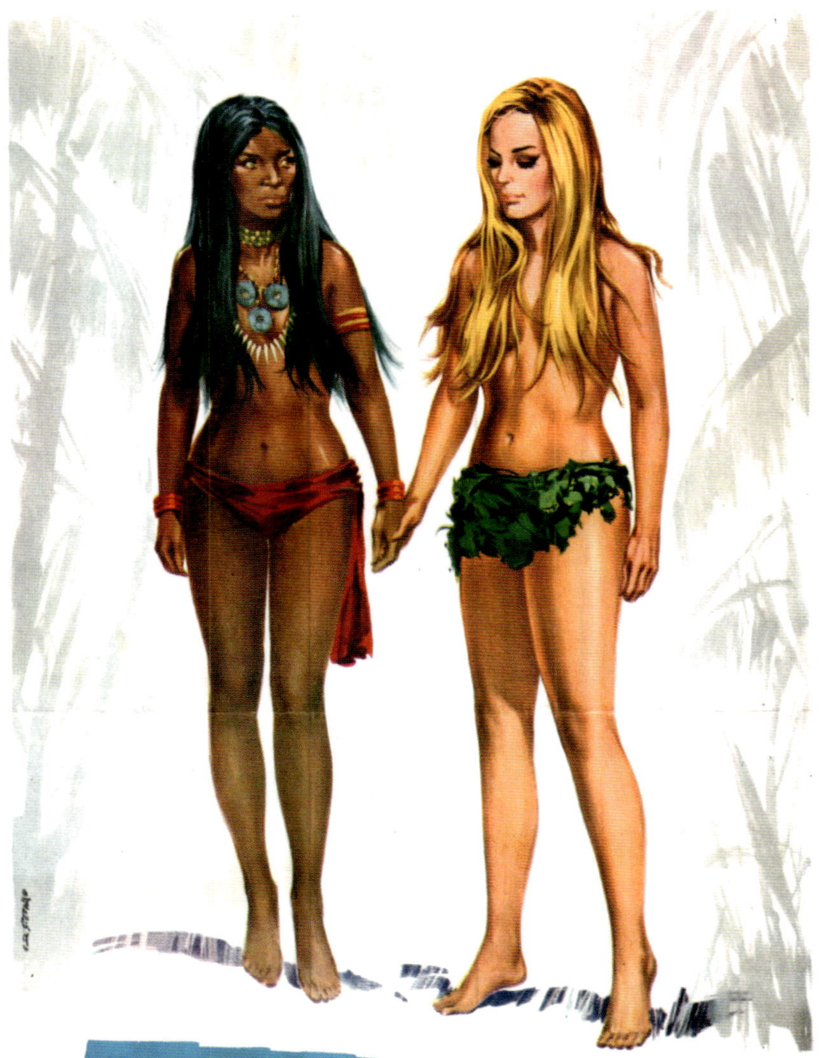
UN FILM PRODOTTO DA FORTUNATO MISIANO PER LA ROMANA FILM
TARZANA
SESSO SELVAGGIO
KEN CLARK
FRANCA POLESELLO
FRANK RESSEL
RAF BALDASSARRE - ANDREW RAY - ALFRED THOMAS - FURIO MENICONI
E CON LA PARTECIPAZIONE DI
BERYL CUNNINGHAM
E CON FEMI BENUSSI
REGIA DI
JAMES REED
EASTMANCOLOR
WIDE SCREEN
PRIMA EDIZIONE ITALIANA 1969
Printed in Italy - By ROTOLITO

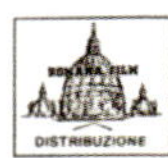

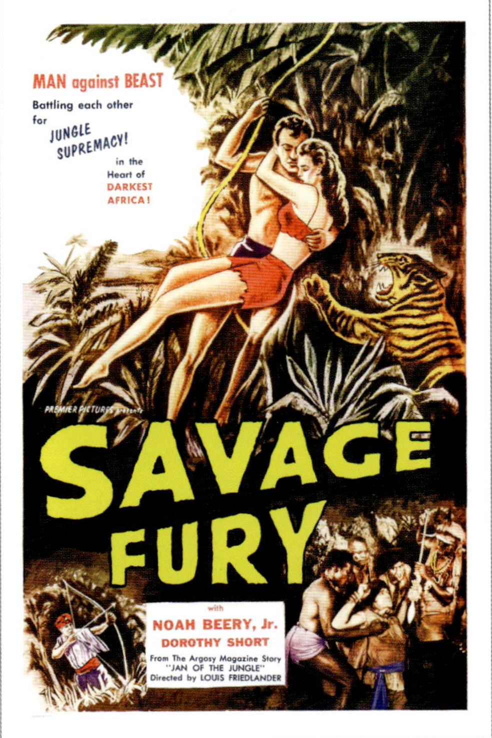
MAN against BEAST
Battling each other for JUNGLE SUPREMACY! in the Heart of DARKEST AFRICA!
SAVAGE FURY
with
NOAH BEERY, Jr.
DOROTHY SHORT
From The Argosy Magazine Story "JAN OF THE JUNGLE"
Directed by LOUIS FRIEDLANDER

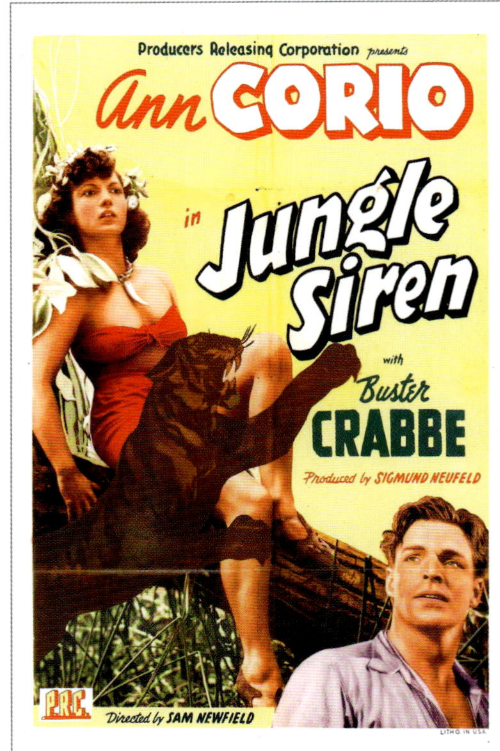
Producers Releasing Corporation presents
Ann CORIO
in
Jungle Siren
with
Buster CRABBE
Produced by SIGMUND NEUFELD
PRC
Directed by SAM NEWFIELD

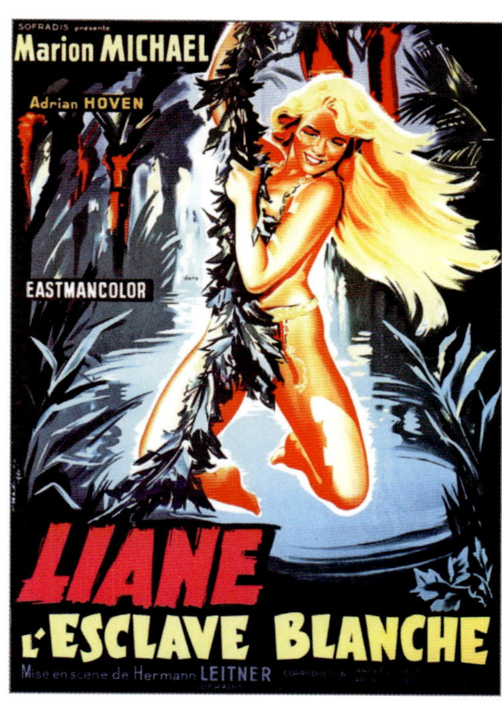

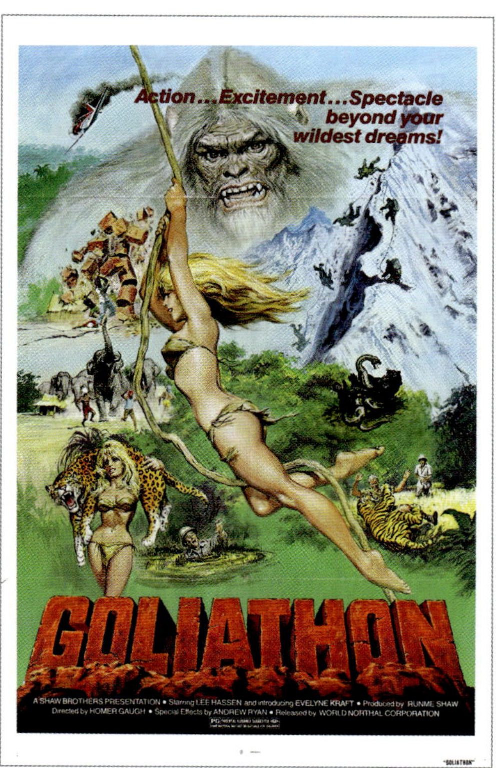

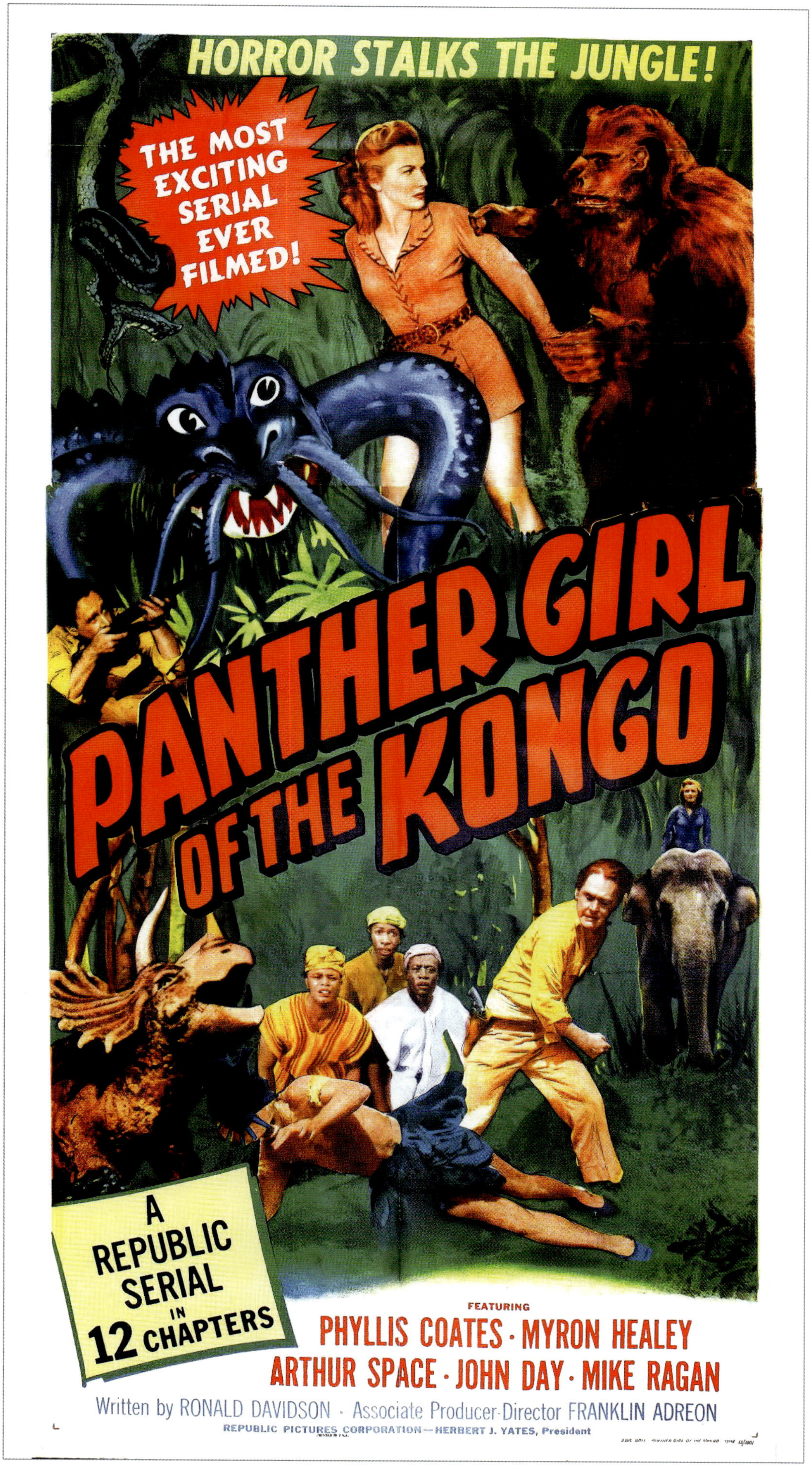

HORROR STALKS THE JUNGLE!

THE MOST EXCITING SERIAL EVER FILMED!

PANTHER GIRL OF THE KONGO

A REPUBLIC SERIAL IN 12 CHAPTERS

FEATURING

PHYLLIS COATES · MYRON HEALEY

ARTHUR SPACE · JOHN DAY · MIKE RAGAN

Written by RONALD DAVIDSON · Associate Producer-Director FRANKLIN ADREON

REPUBLIC PICTURES CORPORATION—HERBERT J. YATES, President

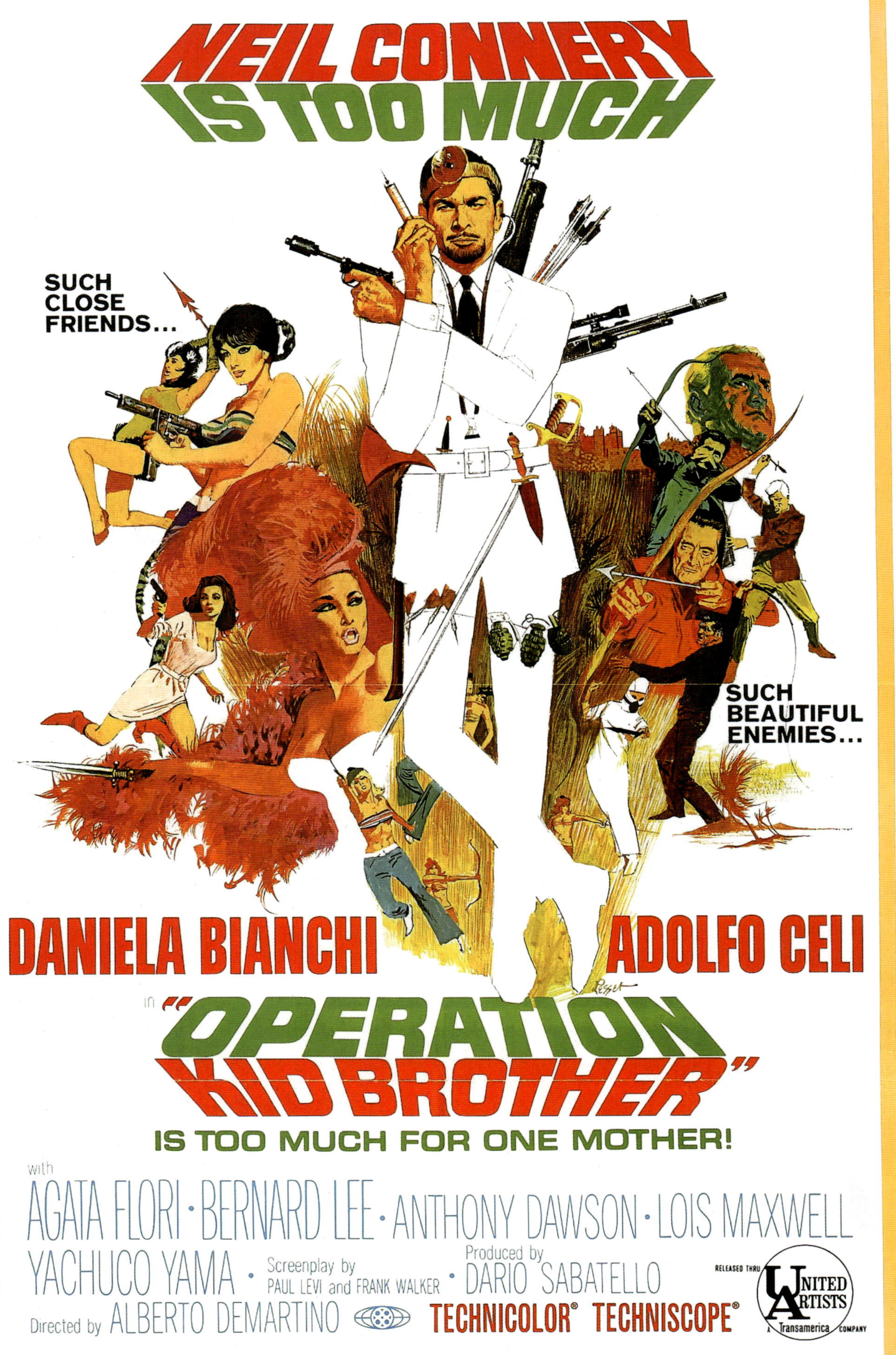
NEIL CONNERY
IS TOO MUCH
SUCH CLOSE FRIENDS...
SUCH BEAUTIFUL ENEMIES...
DANIELA BIANCHI
ADOLFO CELI
in "OPERATION KID BROTHER"
IS TOO MUCH FOR ONE MOTHER!
with
AGATA FLORI · BERNARD LEE · ANTHONY DAWSON · LOIS MAXWELL
YACHUCO YAMA · Screenplay by PAUL LEVI and FRANK WALKER · Produced by DARIO SABATELLO
Directed by ALBERTO DEMARTINO
TECHNICOLOR® TECHNISCOPE®
RELEASED THRU UNITED ARTISTS A Transamerica COMPANY

67/349

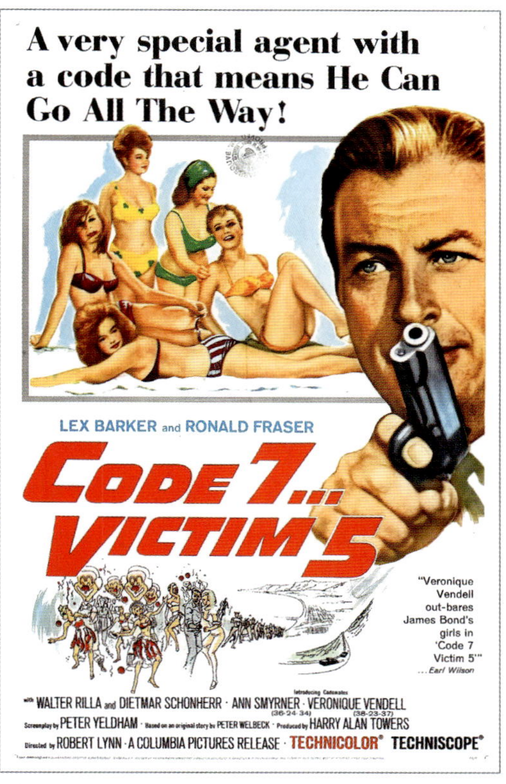

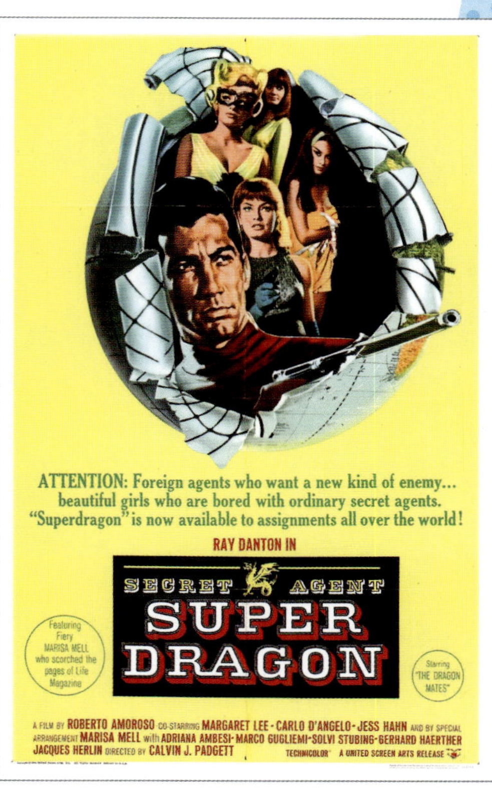

NOT BOND, JAMES BOND

If you adjust its earnings to twenty-first-century prices, 1965's *Thunderball* made a *billion* dollars. No wonder then that by the mid-'60s, Bond knock-offs were more numerous than 007's female conquests. While big US studios cashed in with stars like the über-cool James Coburn (as the homegrown agent Derek Flint), European producers with lower budgets had to make do with also-rans like Ray Danton, ex-Tarzan Lex Barker, and Sean Connery's younger sibling Neil. The latter appeared in the difficult-to-believe-it-actually-exists *Operation Kid Brother* (1967), aided and abetted by several imported "proper" Bond actors (including Bernard Lee, Lois Maxwell and *Thunderball*'s villain Adolfo Celi) and a poster by Ron Lesser which successfully aped Robert McGinnis's art for the official series.

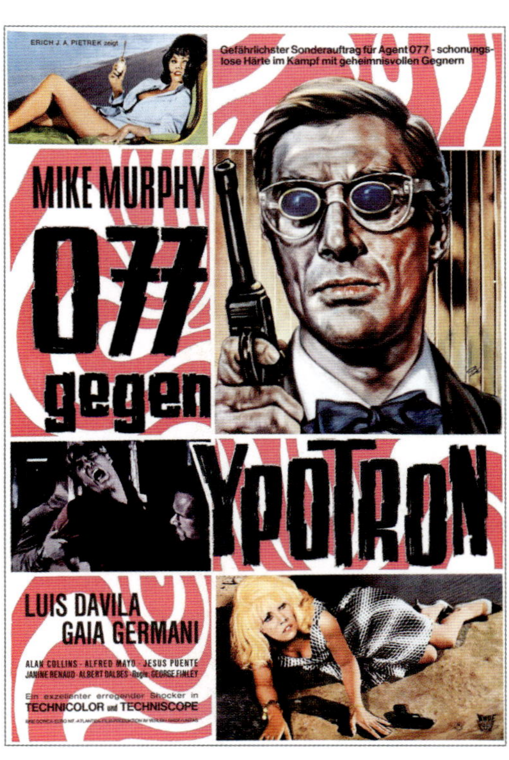

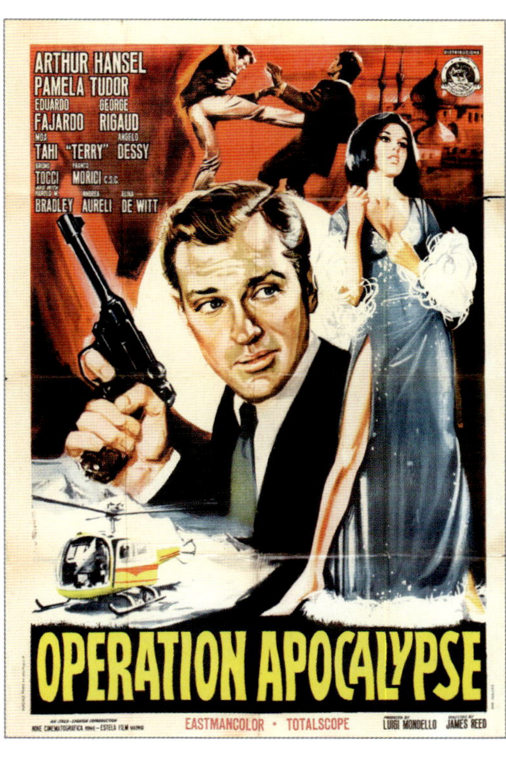

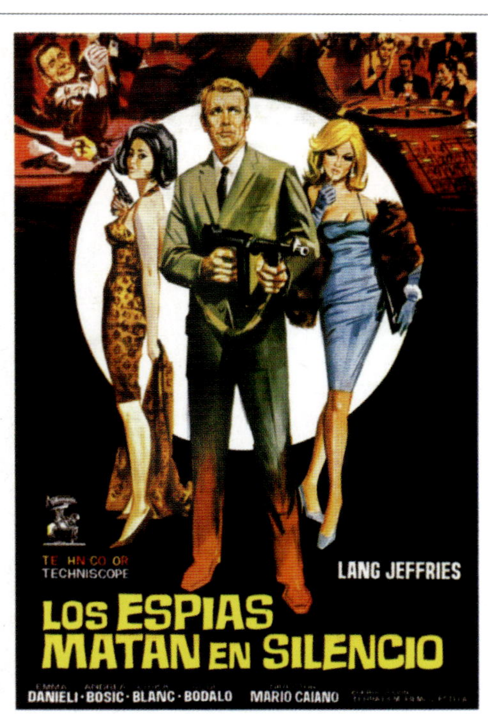

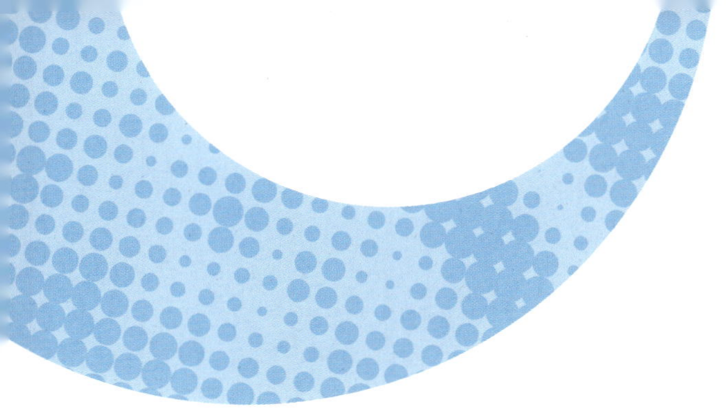

CATSUITS!

Catsuits were everywhere as the '60s really started to swing, especially when it came to action heroines. The TV trailblazers were Honor Blackman and Diana Rigg in *The Avengers*, and movies were quick to emulate their look. To be fair, even though the title translates as "The Masked Avengers," Kitty de Hoyos and Dacia Gonzalez in Mexico's *Las vengadoras enmascaradas* (1963) probably weren't inspired by Blackman's character Cathy Gale, though the poster art by the prolific Armando Martinez Cacho shows they were certainly her match. However, there are definitely shades of Rigg's Mrs Peel in the posters for the 1966 Euro flicks *Lightning Bolt* and *Il grande colpo dei 7 uomini d'oro* (aka *Seven Golden Men Strike Again*). Meanwhile the Japanese poster for the same year's *Modesty Blaise*, a free-wheeling adaptation of the British comic strip character, made sure to feature her in a catsuit, even though star Monica Vitti is dressed differently (and indeed is blonde) in all but one scene of the film. For *The Avengers*' continuing influence when it comes to kick-ass agents in tight black catsuits, one need only look at Scarlett Johansson in that other *The Avengers* . . .

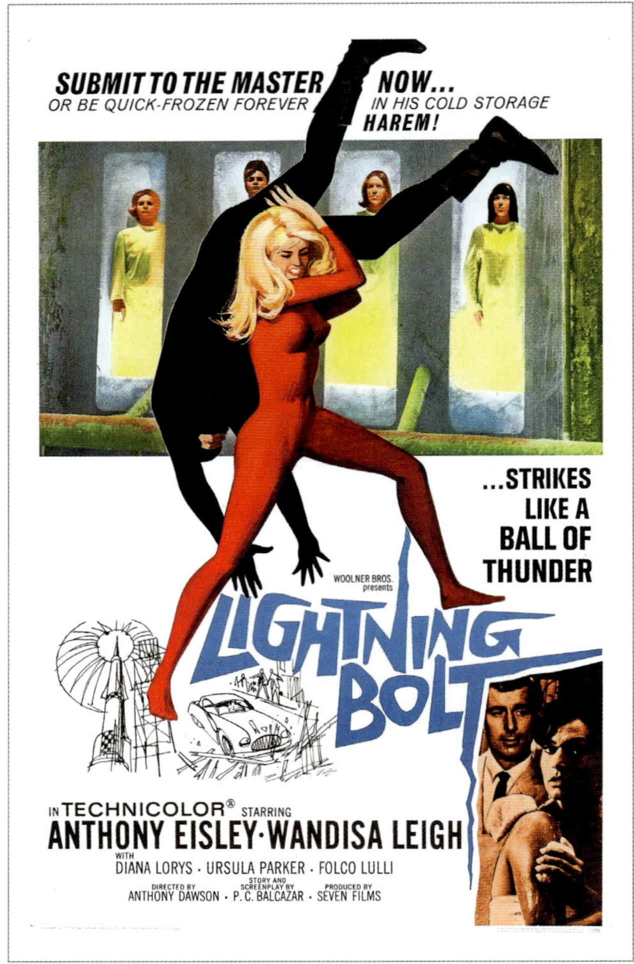

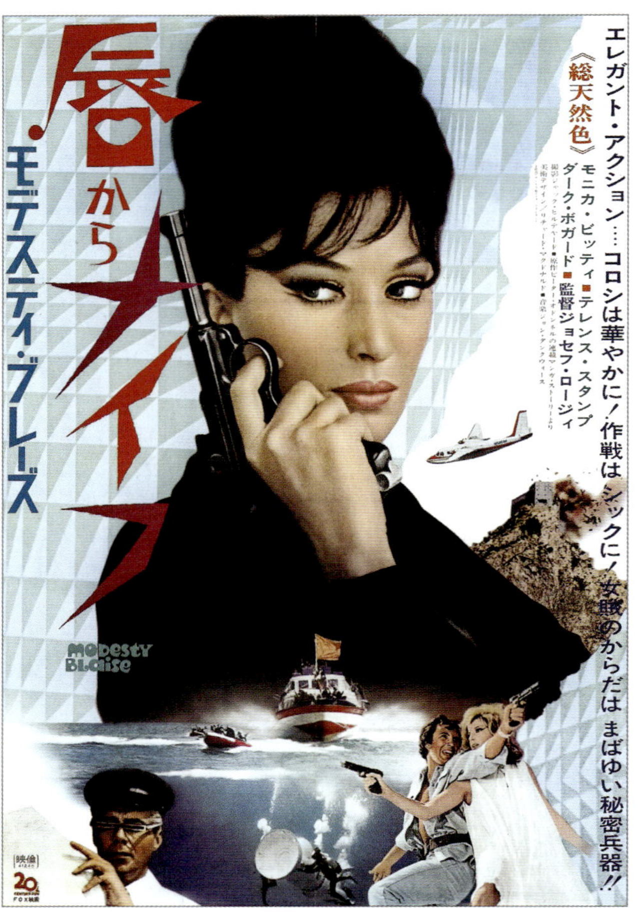

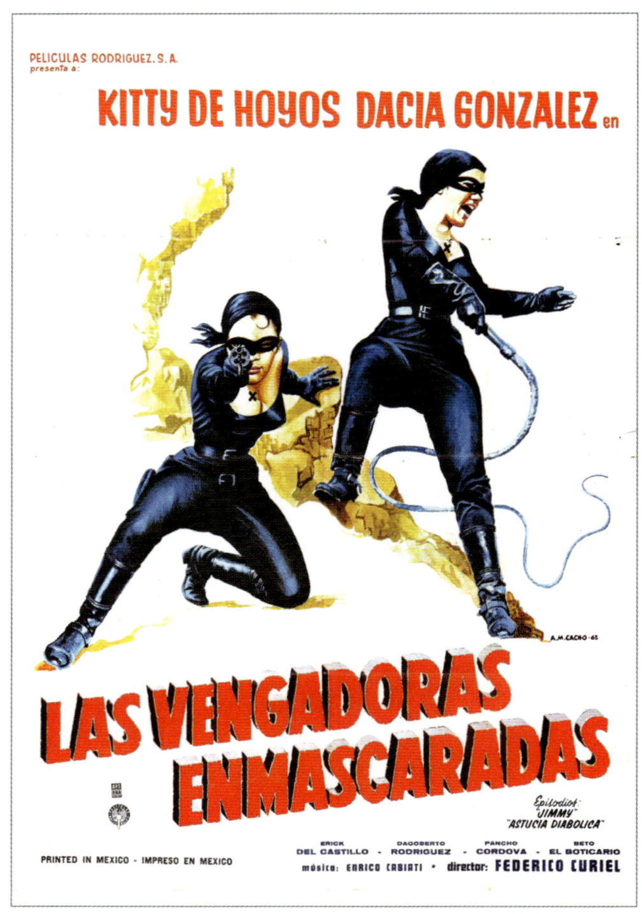

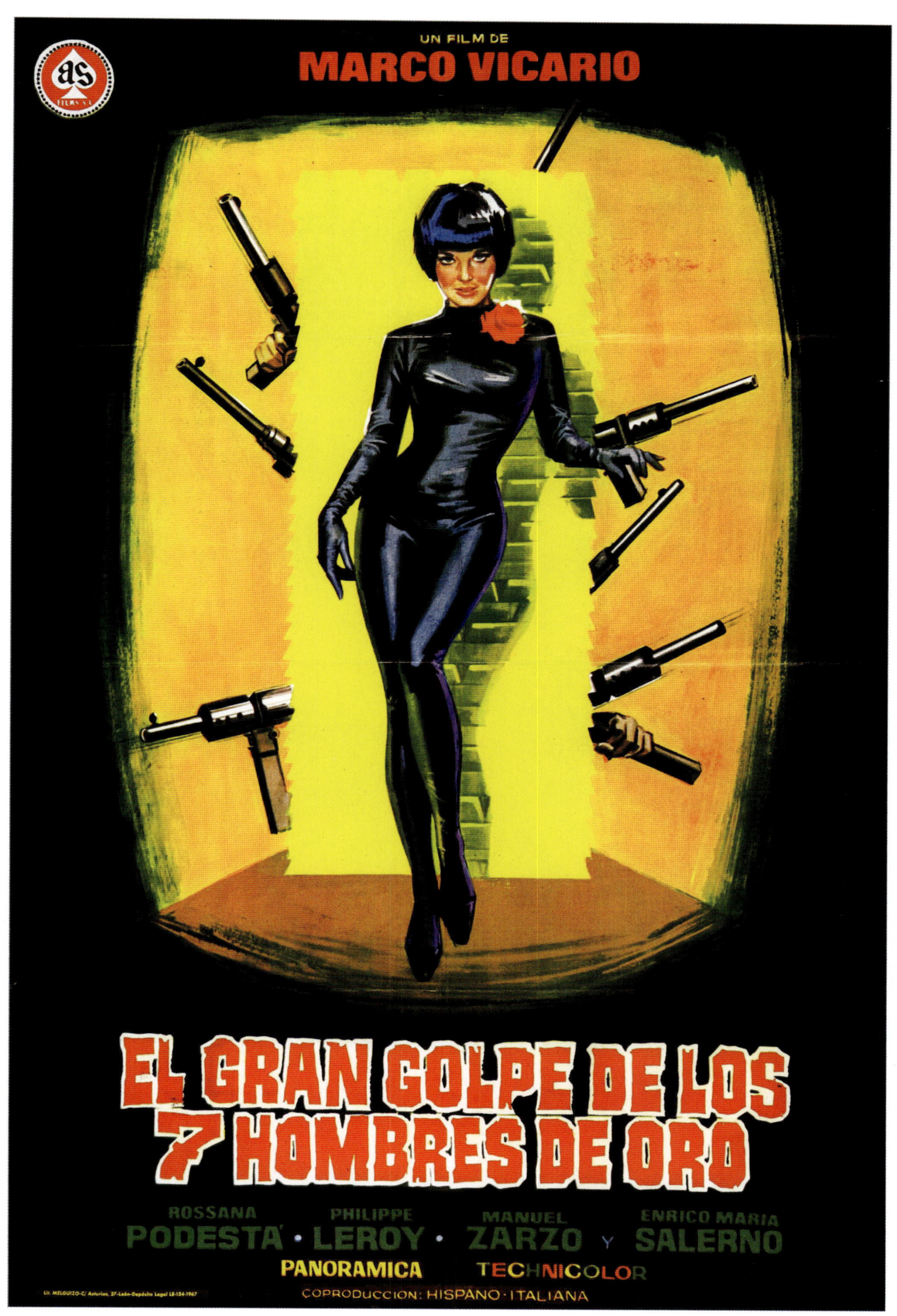
UN FILM DE
MARCO VICARIO
EL GRAN GOLPE DE LOS
7 HOMBRES DE ORO
ROSSANA PODESTA · PHILIPPE LEROY · MANUEL ZARZO Y ENRICO MARIA SALERNO
PANORAMICA
TECHNICOLOR
Lit. MELGUIZO-C/ Asturias, 27-León-Depósito Legal LE-134-1967
COPRODUCCION: HISPANO-ITALIANA

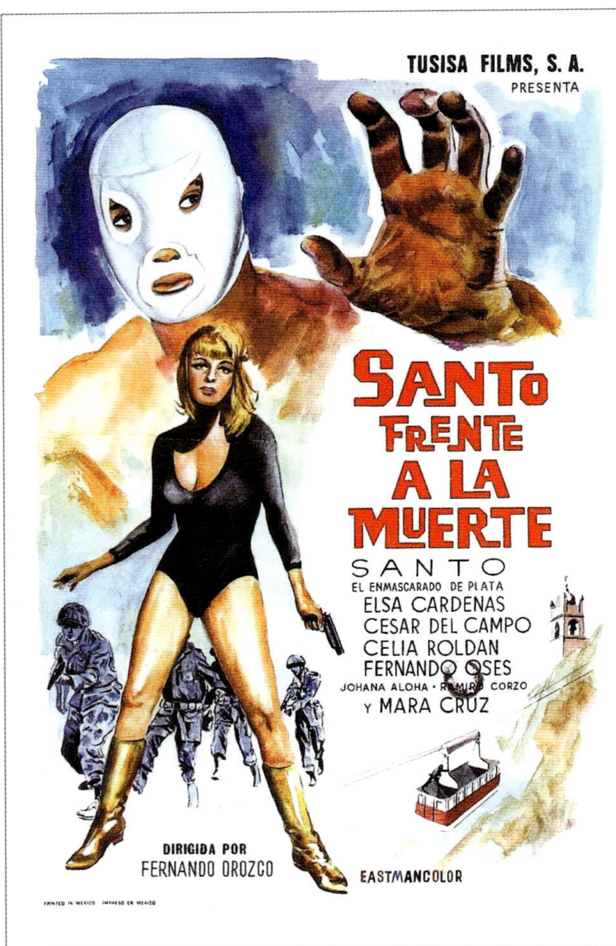

MEXICO!

As even this tiny sampling of wonderfully colorful posters suggests, the exuberantly bizarre world of Mexploitation cinema and its inextricable link to the sport of *lucha libre* (masked wrestling), can be somewhat overwhelming. To the uninitiated, it's best just to dive in and enjoy the action. You'll soon encounter the legendary El Santo (aka Rodolfo Guzmán Huerta), who fought injustice and crime in over 50 movies, shot alongside his real-life career as the nation's foremost *luchador*. While the films' style is uniquely Mexican, the local poster artists sometimes looked elsewhere for inspiration: if the pose of the woman on the poster for *Santo frente a la muerte* (1969) looks familiar, it's because it's a direct lift of the iconic image of Raquel Welch in *One Million Years B.C.*

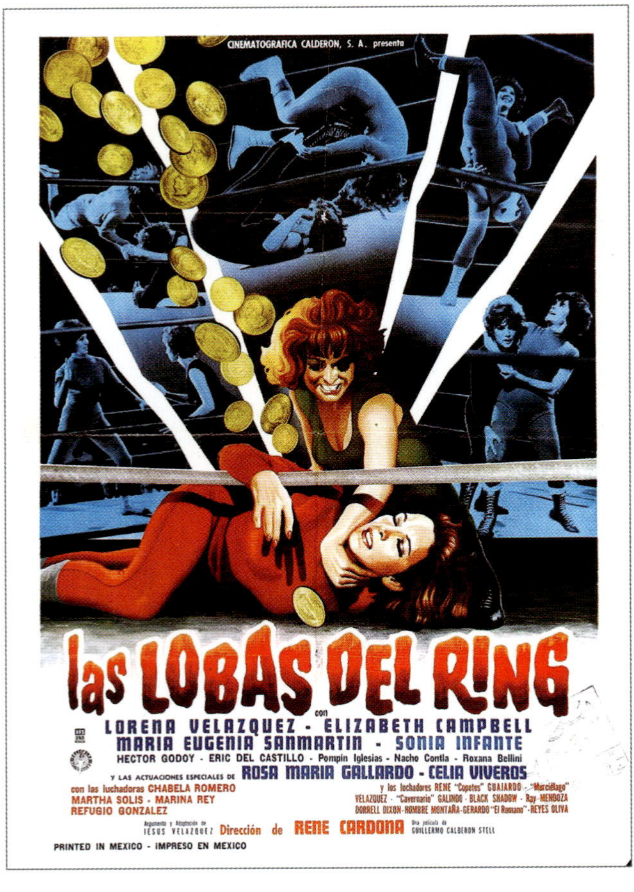

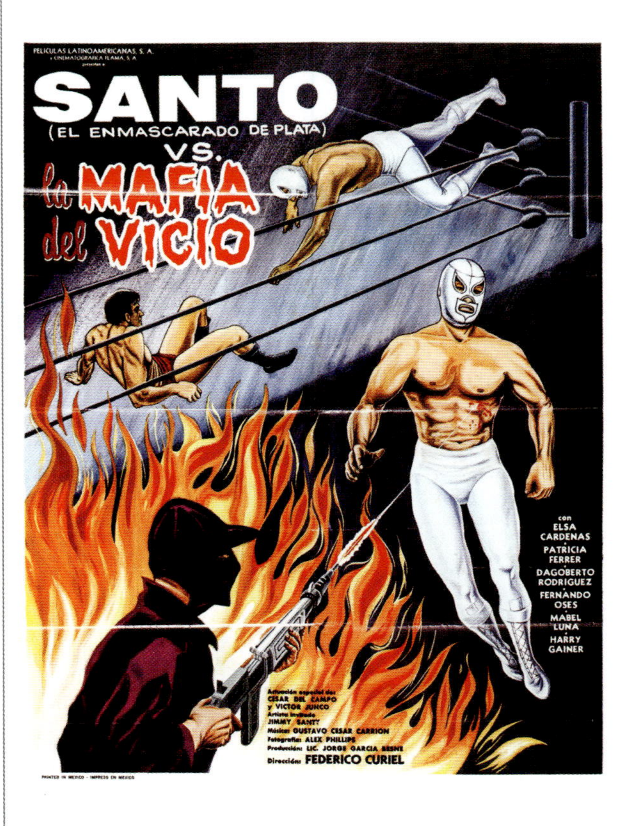

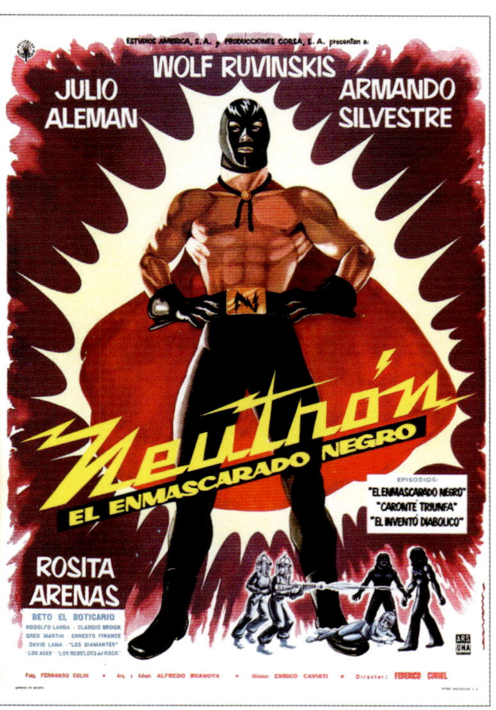
ESTUDIOS AMERICA, S. A. y PRODUCCIONES COREA, S. A. presentan a:
WOLF RUVINSKIS
JULIO ALEMAN
ARMANDO SILVESTRE
Neutrón
EL ENMASCARADO NEGRO
EPISODIOS:
"EL ENMASCARADO NEGRO"
"CARONTE TRIUNFA"
"EL INVENTO DIABOLICO"
ROSITA ARENAS
BETO EL BOTICARIO

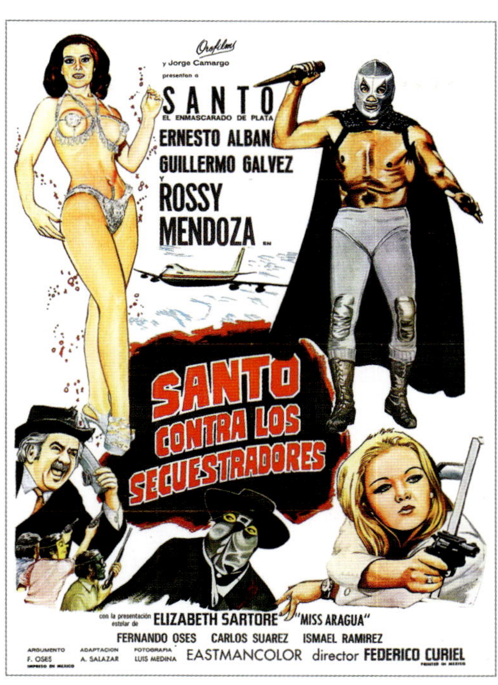
y Jorge Camargo
presentan a
SANTO
EL ENMASCARADO DE PLATA
ERNESTO ALBAN
GUILLERMO GALVEZ
y
ROSSY MENDOZA
SANTO CONTRA LOS SECUESTRADORES
ELIZABETH SARTORE "MISS ARAGUA"
FERNANDO OSES CARLOS SUAREZ ISMAEL RAMIREZ
EASTMANCOLOR director FEDERICO CURIEL

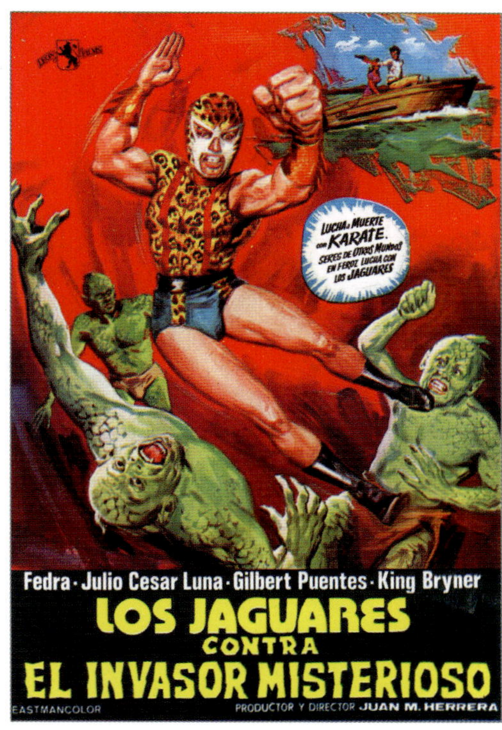
Lucha a Muerte con KARATE.
Fedra · Julio Cesar Luna · Gilbert Puentes · King Bryner
LOS JAGUARES
CONTRA
EL INVASOR MISTERIOSO
EASTMANCOLOR
PRODUCTOR Y DIRECTOR JUAN M. HERRERA

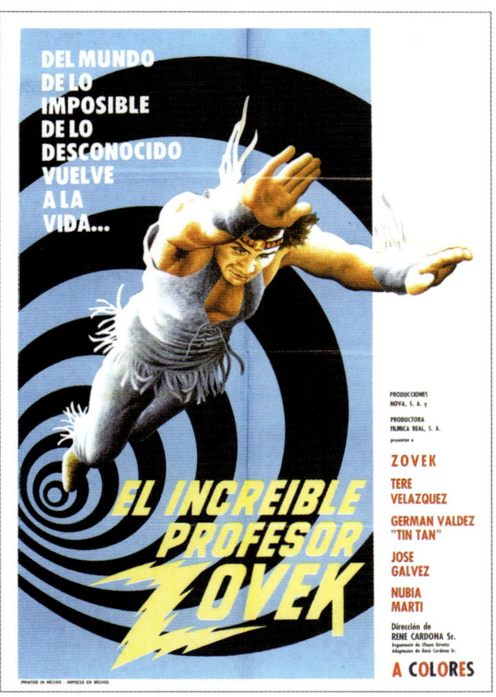
DEL MUNDO
DE LO
IMPOSIBLE
DE LO
DESCONOCIDO
VUELVE
A LA
VIDA...
EL INCREIBLE PROFESOR ZOVEK
ZOVEK
TERE VELAZQUEZ
GERMAN VALDEZ "TIN TAN"
JOSE GALVEZ
NUBIA MARTI
Dirección de
RENE CARDONA Sr.
A COLORES

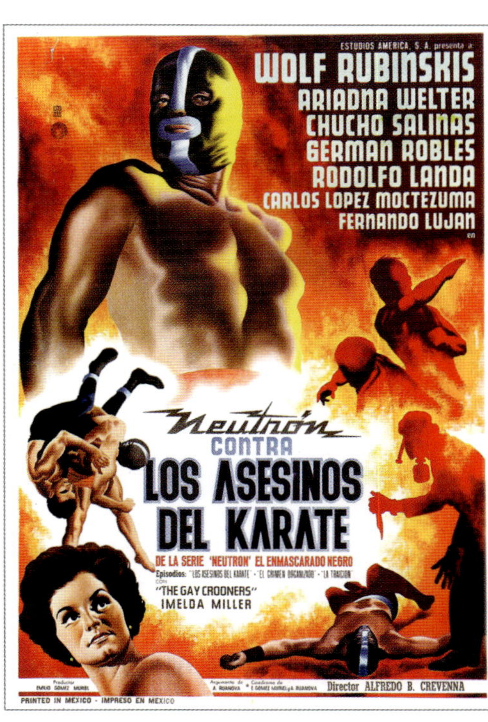
ESTUDIOS AMERICA, S. A. presenta a:
WOLF RUBINSKIS
ARIADNA WELTER
CHUCHO SALINAS
GERMAN ROBLES
RODOLFO LANDA
CARLOS LOPEZ MOCTEZUMA
FERNANDO LUJAN
Neutrón
CONTRA
LOS ASESINOS DEL KARATE
DE LA SERIE "NEUTRON" EL ENMASCARADO NEGRO
"THE GAY CROONERS"
IMELDA MILLER
Director ALFREDO B. CREVENNA
PRINTED IN MEXICO · IMPRESO EN MEXICO

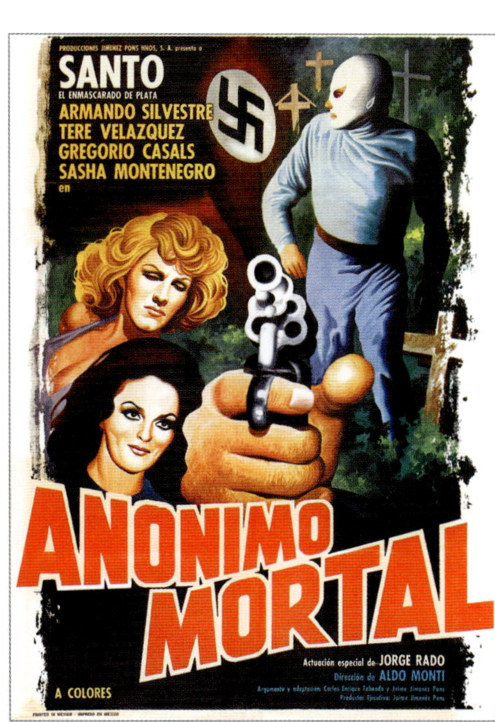
SANTO
EL ENMASCARADO DE PLATA
ARMANDO SILVESTRE
TERE VELAZQUEZ
GREGORIO CASALS
SASHA MONTENEGRO
en
ANONIMO MORTAL
Actuación especial de JORGE RADO
Dirección de ALDO MONTI
A COLORES

LEGION OF LOW BUDGET SUPERHEROES

Superhero movies weren't always a succession of A-list blockbusters queuing up to get into multiplexes. Among the modest beginnings of the genre is the Republic serial *Captain America* (1944), which ignored the comic book's super soldier character Steve Rogers, and had Dick Purcell play Cap as Grant Gardner, a revolver-toting District Attorney. Though the serial was technically licensed, Timely Comics (Marvel's forerunner) was not impressed. Most definitely *un*licensed was the balls-out crazy Turkish production *3 dev adam* (3 Giant Men, 1973) in which Captain America teams up with Mexican wrestler Santo to fight the evil crime-lord Spider-Man (this is not made up, honest). Similarly, the makers of both Mexico's *The Batwoman* (1968) and Turkey's *Uçan Kiz* (aka *Batgirl*, 1972), both seen overleaf, didn't trouble themselves with contacting DC Comics' clearance department.

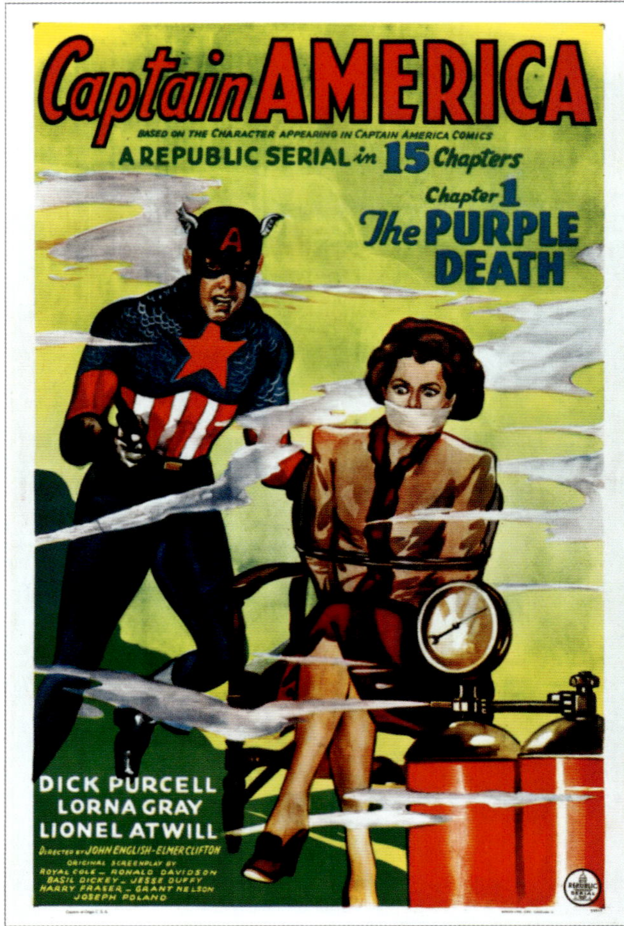

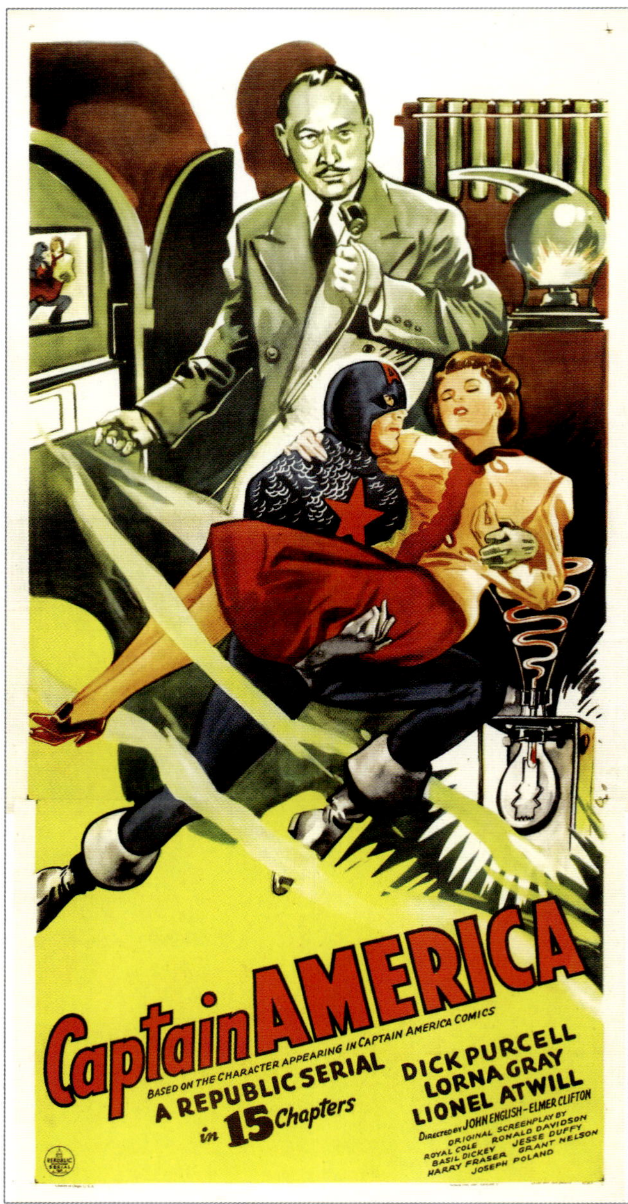

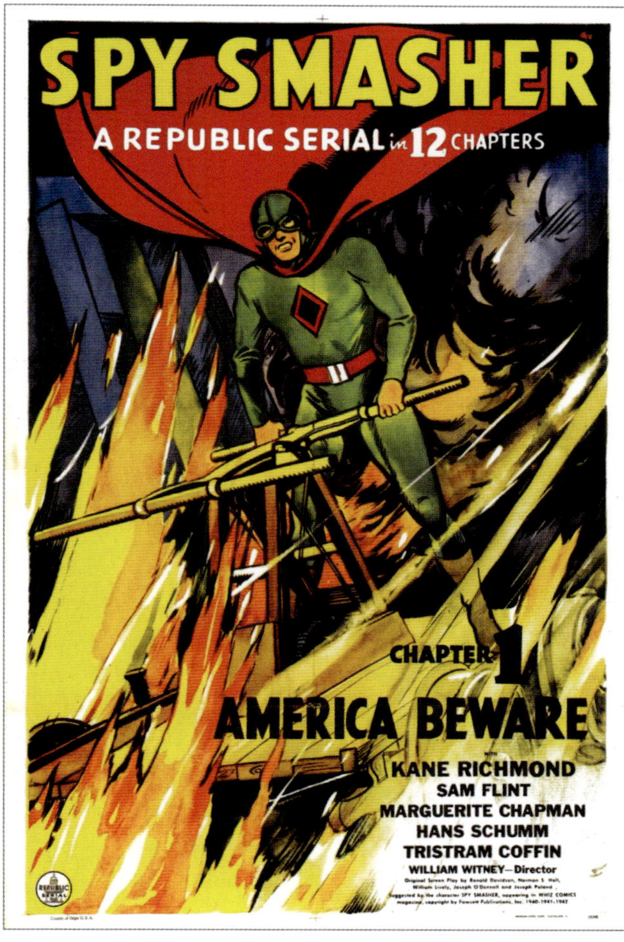
SPY SMASHER
A REPUBLIC SERIAL in 12 CHAPTERS
CHAPTER 1
AMERICA BEWARE
KANE RICHMOND
SAM FLINT
MARGUERITE CHAPMAN
HANS SCHUMM
TRISTRAM COFFIN
WILLIAM WITNEY—Director

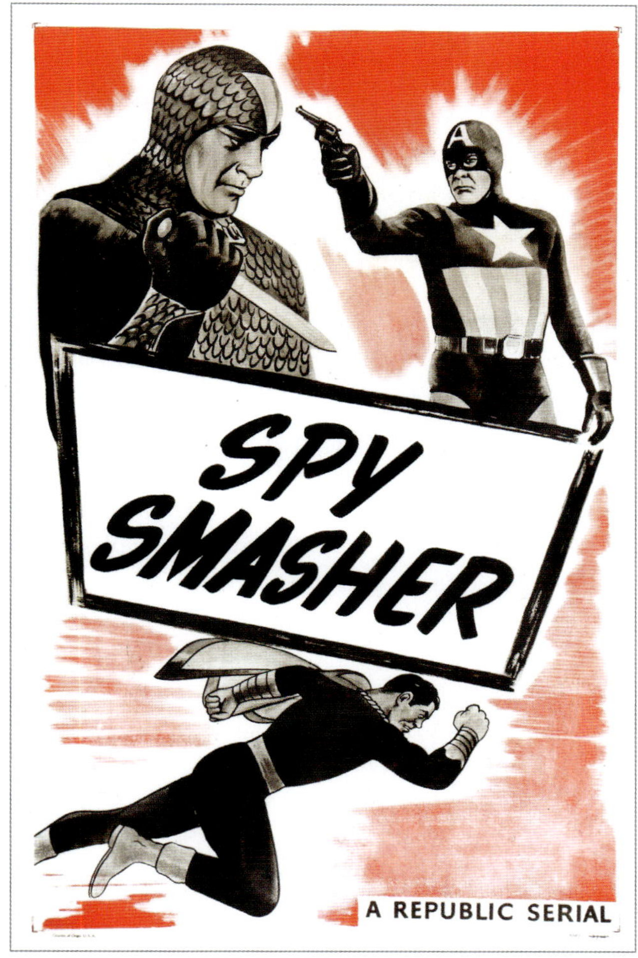
SPY SMASHER
A REPUBLIC SERIAL

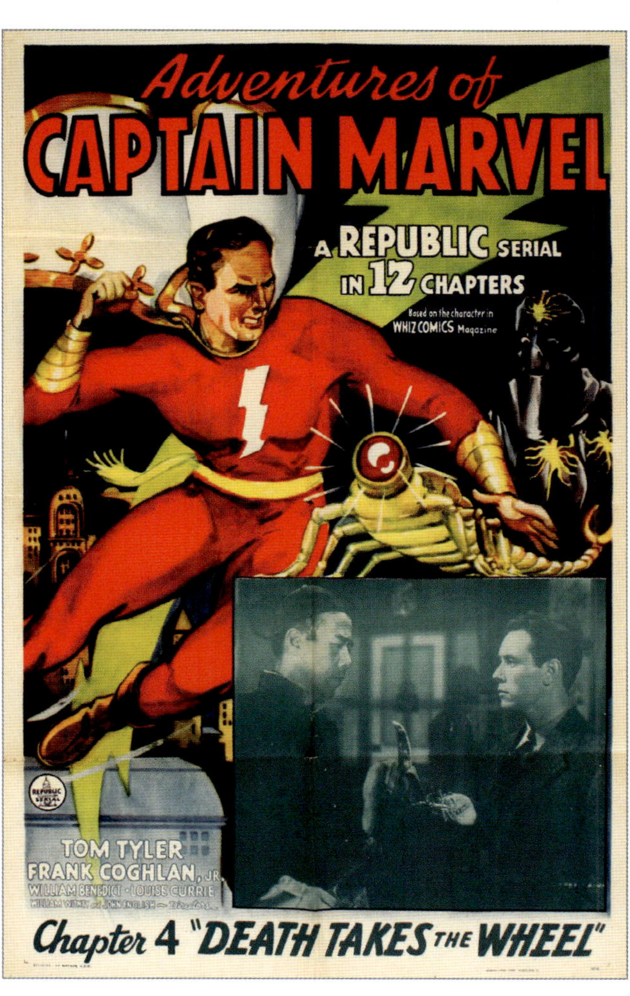
Adventures of
CAPTAIN MARVEL
A REPUBLIC SERIAL
IN 12 CHAPTERS
Based on the character in
WHIZ COMICS Magazine
TOM TYLER
FRANK COGHLAN, JR.
Chapter 4 "DEATH TAKES THE WHEEL"

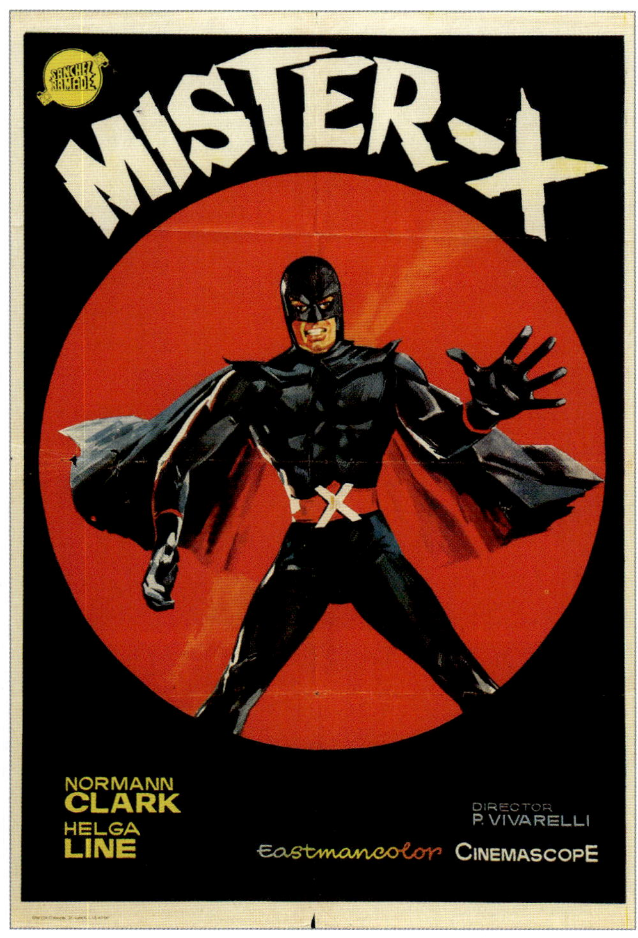
MISTER-X
NORMANN
CLARK
HELGA
LINE
DIRECTOR
P. VIVARELLI
Eastmancolor
CINEMASCOPE

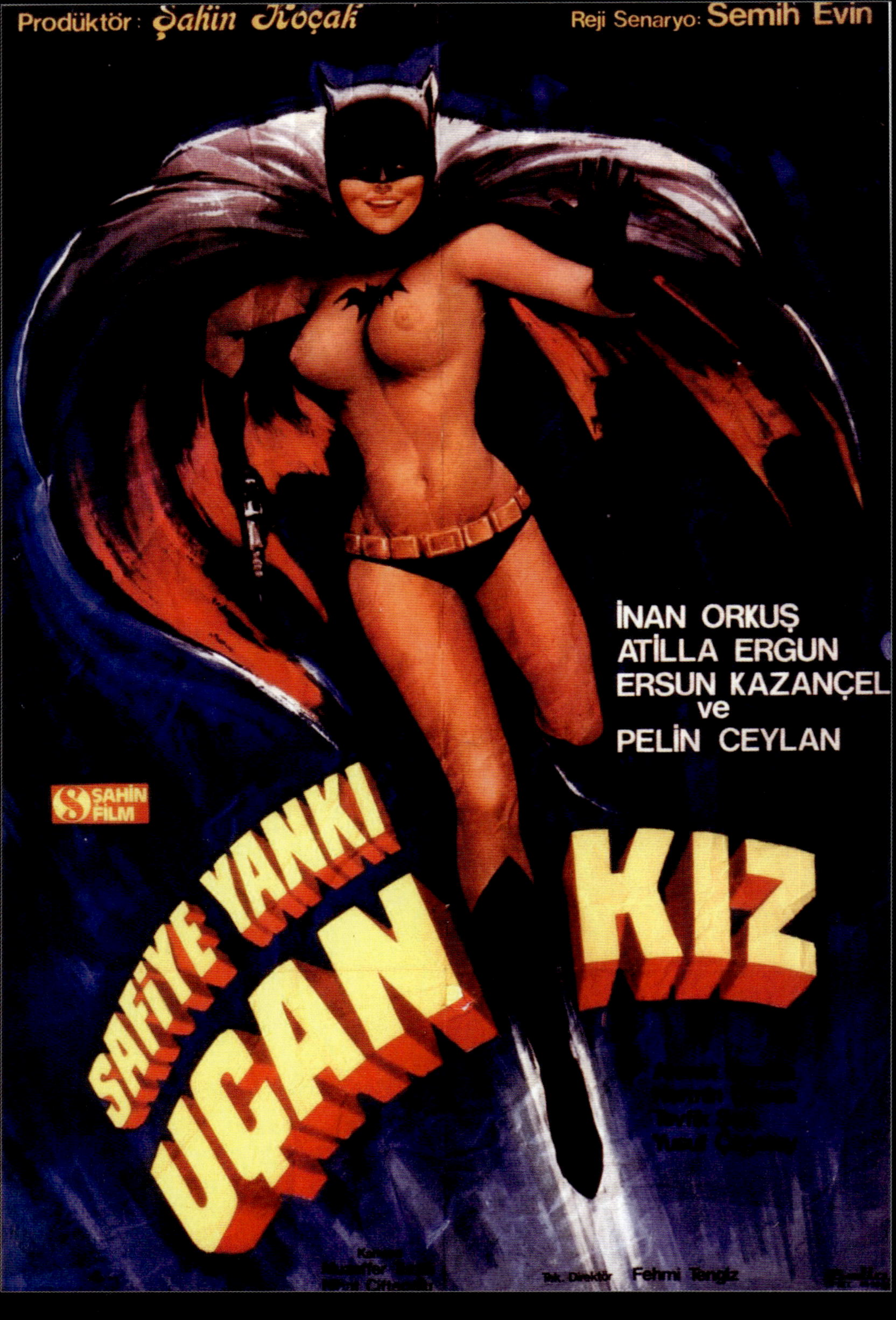

Prodüktör: Şahin Koçak
Reji Senaryo: Semih Evin

İNAN ORKUŞ
ATİLLA ERGUN
ERSUN KAZANÇEL
ve
PELİN CEYLAN

ŞAHİN FİLM

SAFİYE YANKI
UÇAN KIZ

Tek. Direktör Fehmi Tengiz

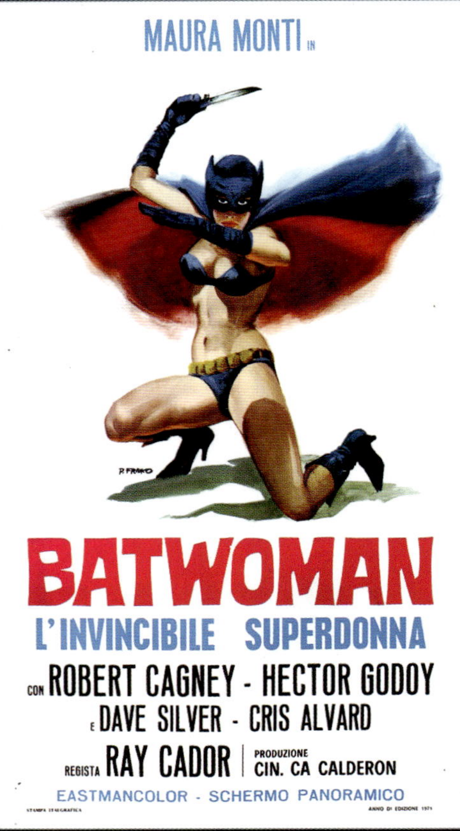

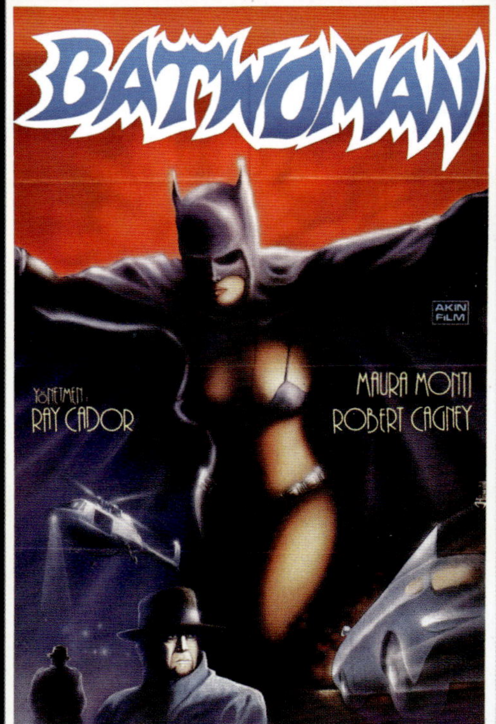

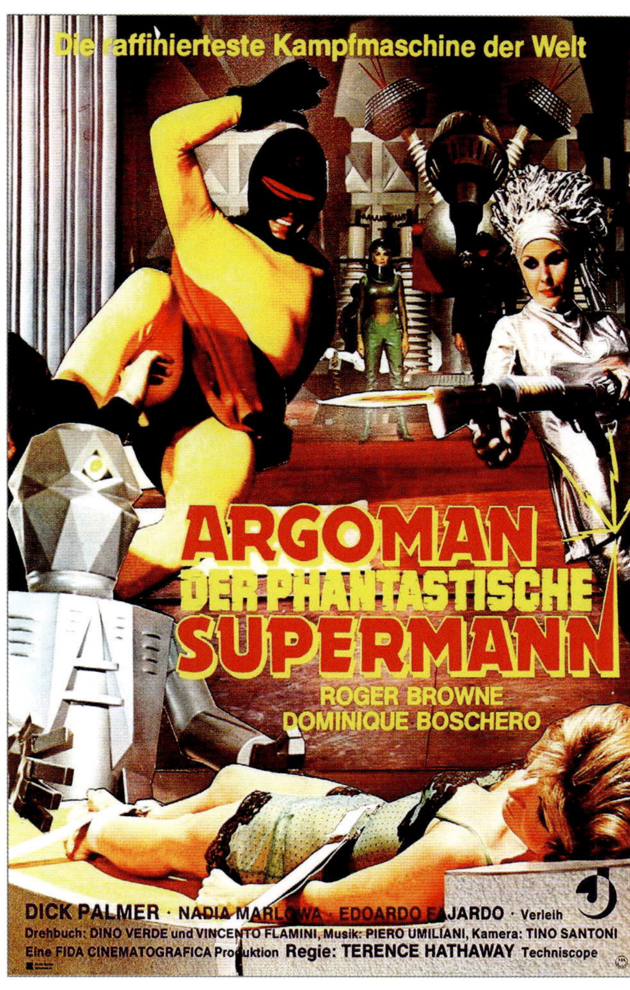
Die raffiniierteste Kampfmaschine der Welt
ARGOMAN
DER PHANTASTISCHE
SUPERMANN
ROGER BROWNE
DOMINIQUE BOSCHERO
DICK PALMER · NADIA MARLOWA · EDOARDO FAJARDO · Verleih
Drehbuch: DINO VERDE und VINCENTO FLAMINI, Musik: PIERO UMILIANI, Kamera: TINO SANTONI
Eine FIDA CINEMATOGRAFICA Produktion Regie: TERENCE HATHAWAY Techniscope

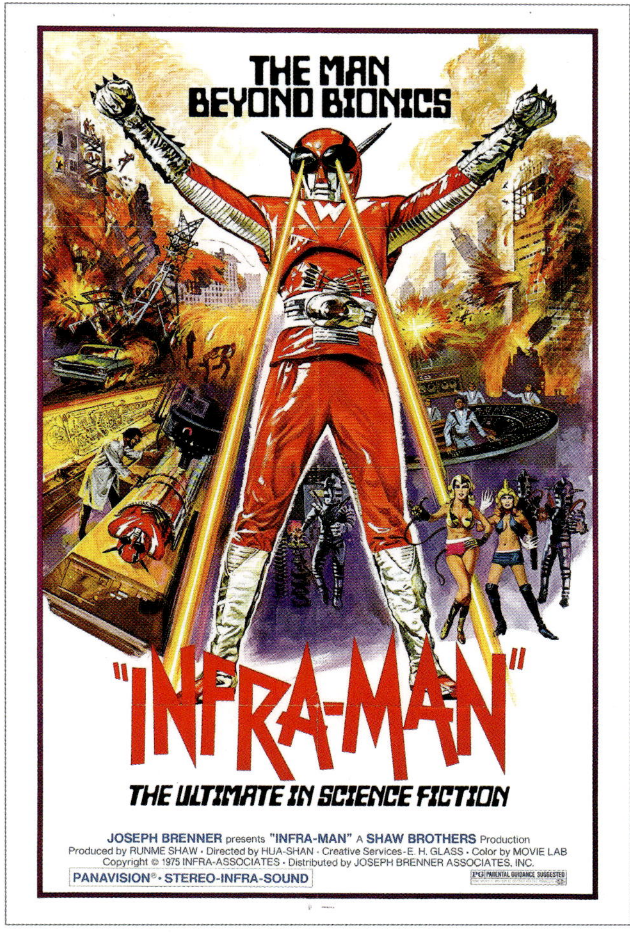
THE MAN
BEYOND BIONICS
"INFRA-MAN"
THE ULTIMATE IN SCIENCE FICTION
JOSEPH BRENNER presents "INFRA-MAN" A SHAW BROTHERS Production
Produced by RUNME SHAW · Directed by HUA-SHAN · Creative Services-E. H. GLASS · Color by MOVIE LAB
Copyright © 1975 INFRA-ASSOCIATES · Distributed by JOSEPH BRENNER ASSOCIATES, INC.
PANAVISION® · STEREO-INFRA-SOUND
PG PARENTAL GUIDANCE SUGGESTED

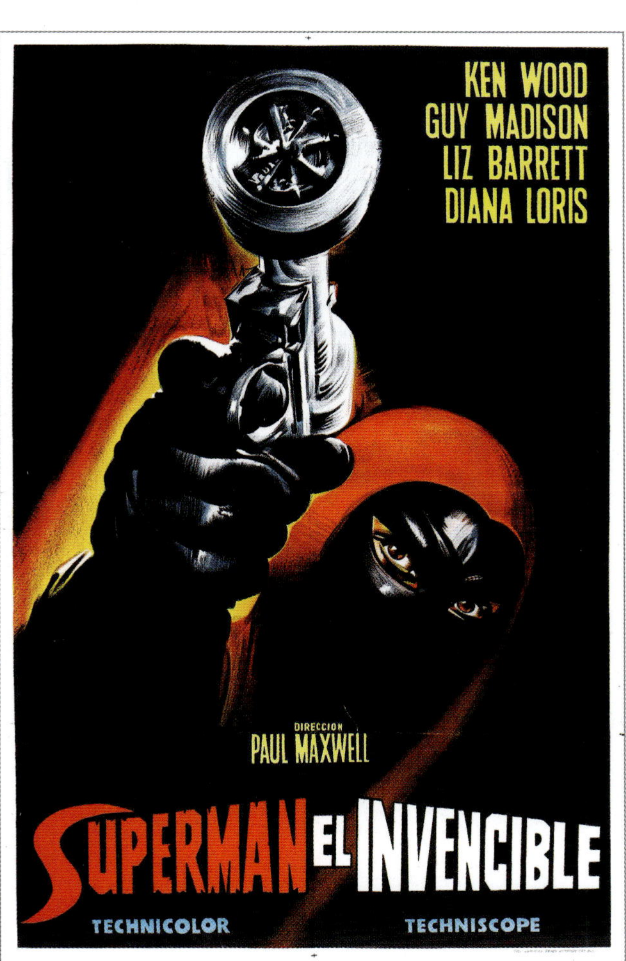
KEN WOOD
GUY MADISON
LIZ BARRETT
DIANA LORIS
DIRECCION
PAUL MAXWELL
SUPERMAN EL INVENCIBLE
TECHNICOLOR
TECHNISCOPE

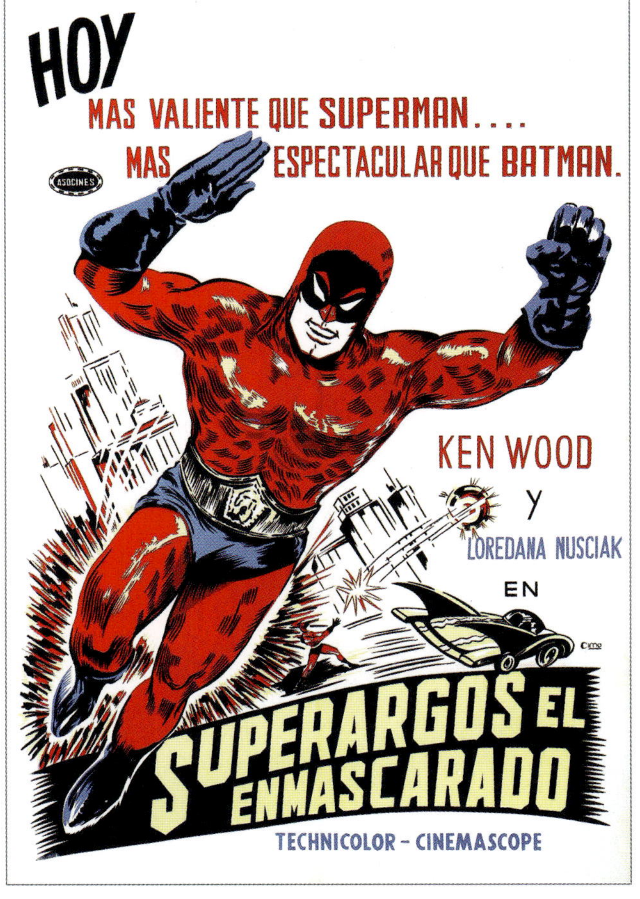
HOY
MAS VALIENTE QUE SUPERMAN....
MAS ESPECTACULAR QUE BATMAN.
ASDCINES
KEN WOOD
Y
LOREDANA NUSCIAK
EN
SUPERARGOS EL ENMASCARADO
TECHNICOLOR – CINEMASCOPE

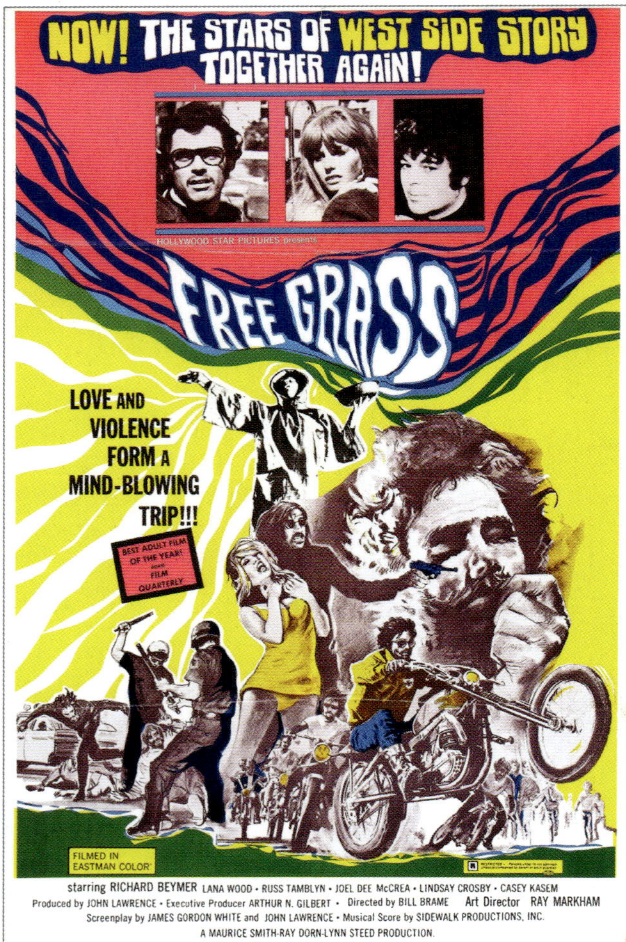

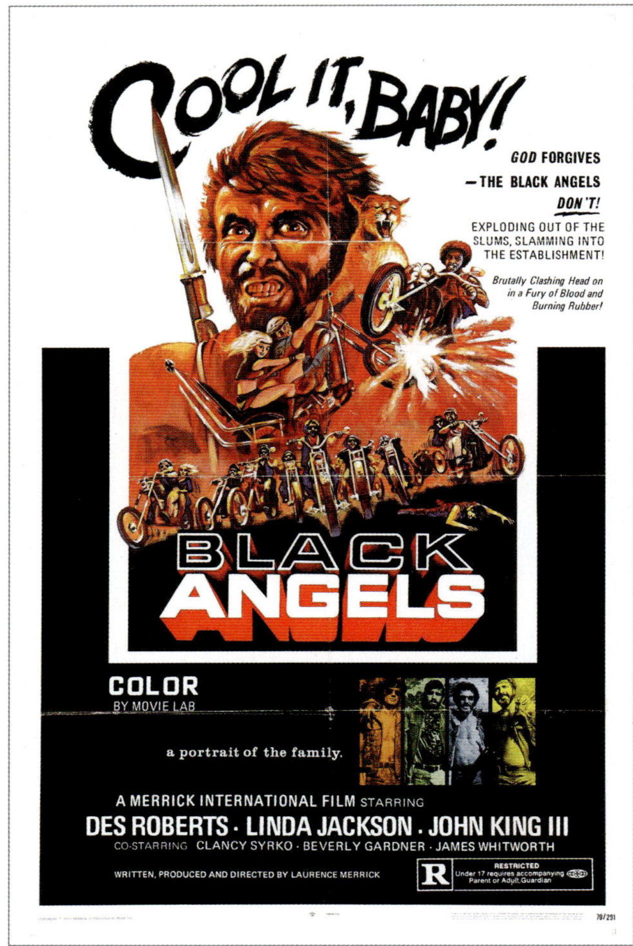

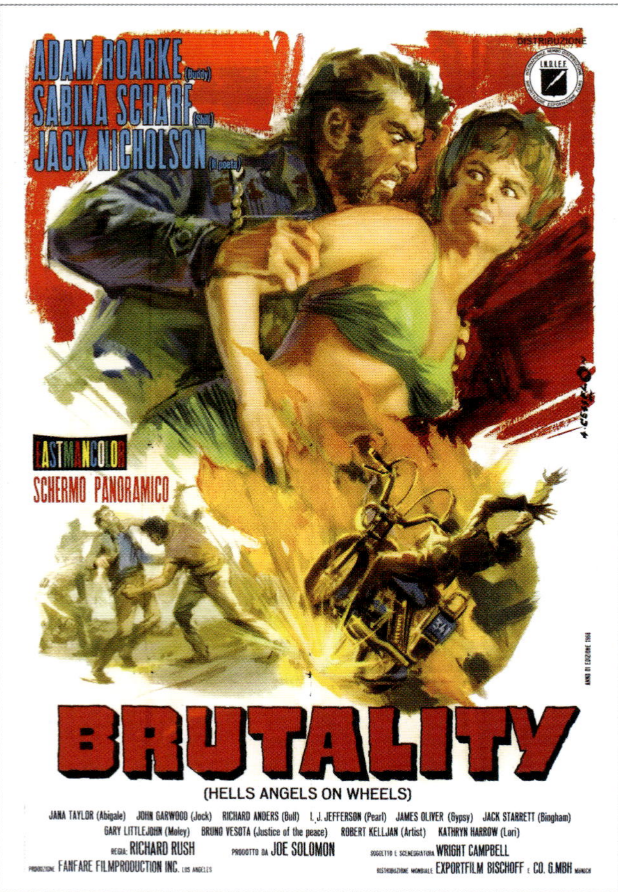

BIKERS

In 1967, Jack Nicholson was not a star. He was working though: writing an LSD exploitation film, *The Trip*, and acting (in very much a supporting role) in what he himself described as "an improvisational movie," *Rebel Rousers*. This was an example of that exploitation standby, the outlaw biker flick, but frankly not a very good one (though Nicholson's stripy pants, a nod to Lee Marvin's costume in biker urtext *The Wild One*, are memorable). *Rebel Rousers* ended up on the shelf, unreleased. A couple of years later, Nicholson appeared in another outlaw biker flick. Not only was this one very good indeed, it somewhat revolutionized Hollywood filmmaking, and won Jack an Oscar nomination to boot. For Nicholson, *Easy Rider* was "a progression in the genre, like *Stagecoach* to the Western—kicked it up one more notch." Few if any of the slew of biker movies that followed in its tracks troubled Academy voters, however. The likes of *Hell's Bloody Devils* (1970) and *Savage Abduction* (1973) are unlikely to join *Easy Rider* on the Library of Congress National Film Register. *Rebel Rousers* earned an inevitable cash-in release in 1970, with the Argentinean poster (opposite) brazenly promoting Nicholson as the star. The actor later admitted, "I think it's the only movie of mine I've never seen."

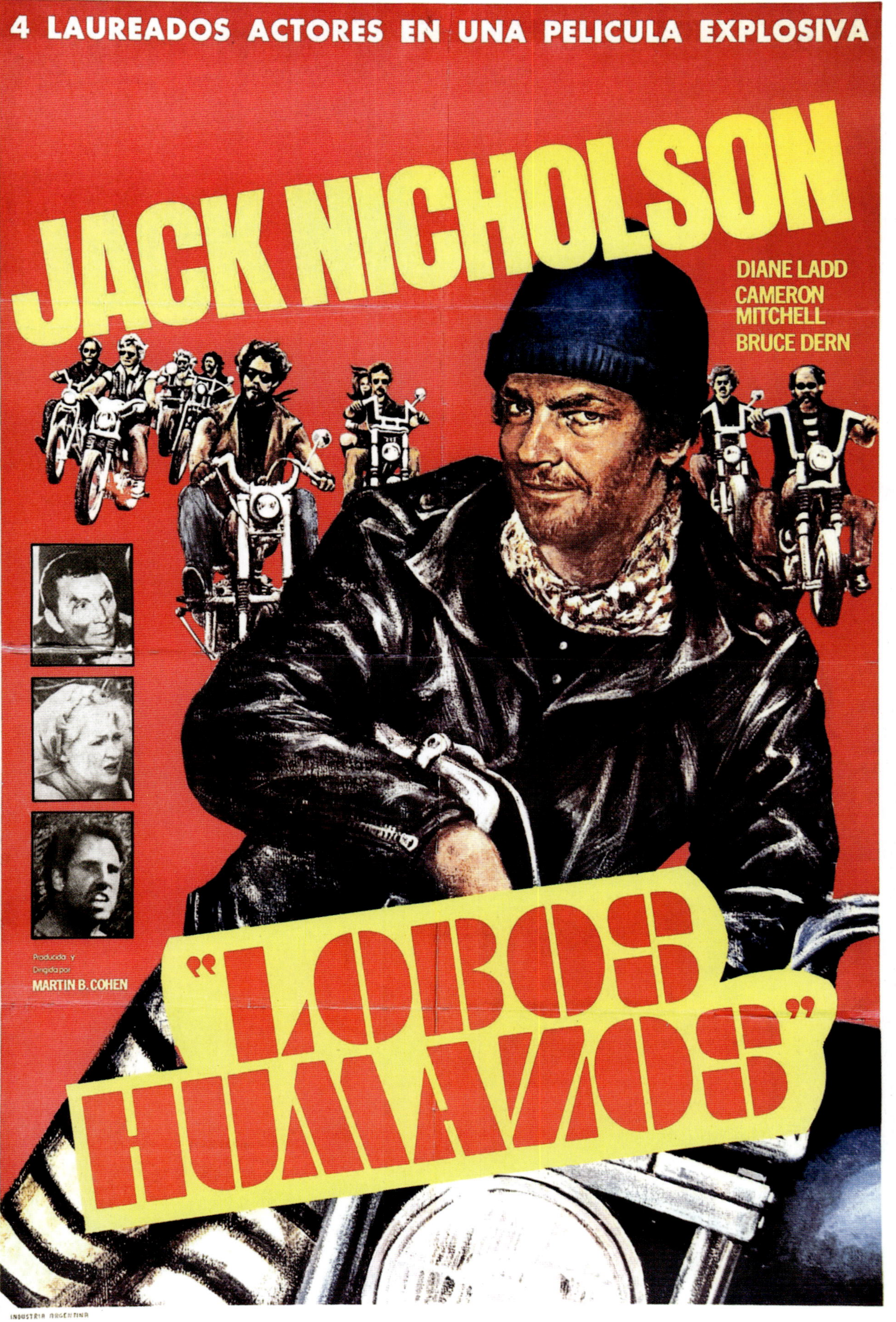
4 LAUREADOS ACTORES EN UNA PELICULA EXPLOSIVA
JACK NICHOLSON
DIANE LADD
CAMERON MITCHELL
BRUCE DERN
Producida y
Dirigida por
MARTIN B. COHEN
"LOBOS HUMANOS"
INDUSTRIA ARGENTINA

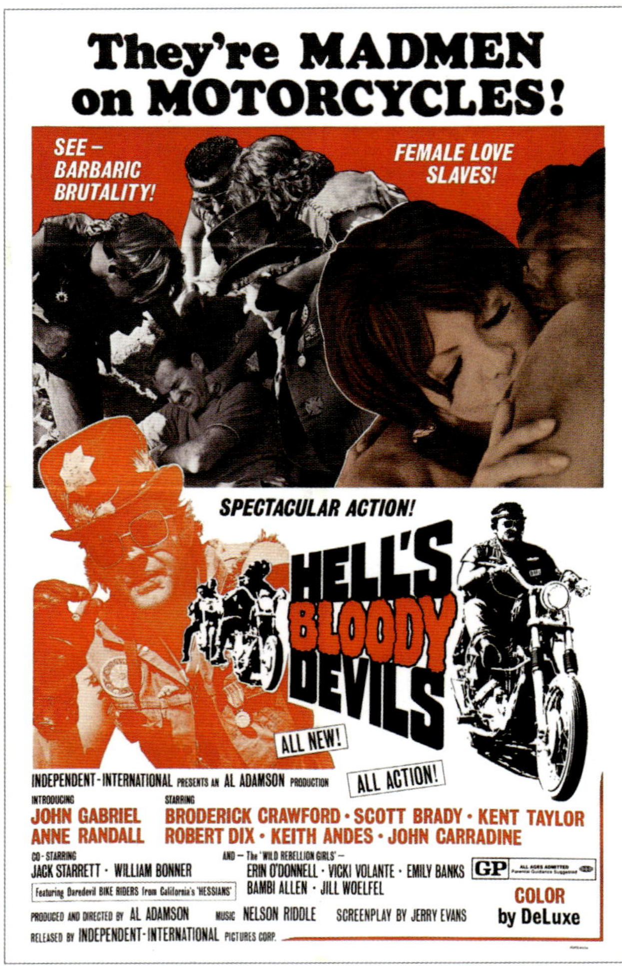
They're MADMEN on MOTORCYCLES!
SEE – BARBARIC BRUTALITY!
FEMALE LOVE SLAVES!
SPECTACULAR ACTION!
HELL'S BLOODY DEVILS
ALL NEW!
ALL ACTION!
INDEPENDENT-INTERNATIONAL PRESENTS AN AL ADAMSON PRODUCTION
INTRODUCING JOHN GABRIEL ANNE RANDALL
STARRING BRODERICK CRAWFORD · SCOTT BRADY · KENT TAYLOR ROBERT DIX · KEITH ANDES · JOHN CARRADINE
CO-STARRING JACK STARRETT · WILLIAM BONNER
AND – The 'WILD REBELLION GIRLS' – ERIN O'DONNELL · VICKI VOLANTE · EMILY BANKS BAMBI ALLEN · JILL WOELFEL
Featuring Daredevil BIKE RIDERS from California's 'HESSIANS'
GP
PRODUCED AND DIRECTED BY AL ADAMSON MUSIC NELSON RIDDLE SCREENPLAY BY JERRY EVANS
COLOR by DeLuxe
RELEASED BY INDEPENDENT-INTERNATIONAL PICTURES CORP.

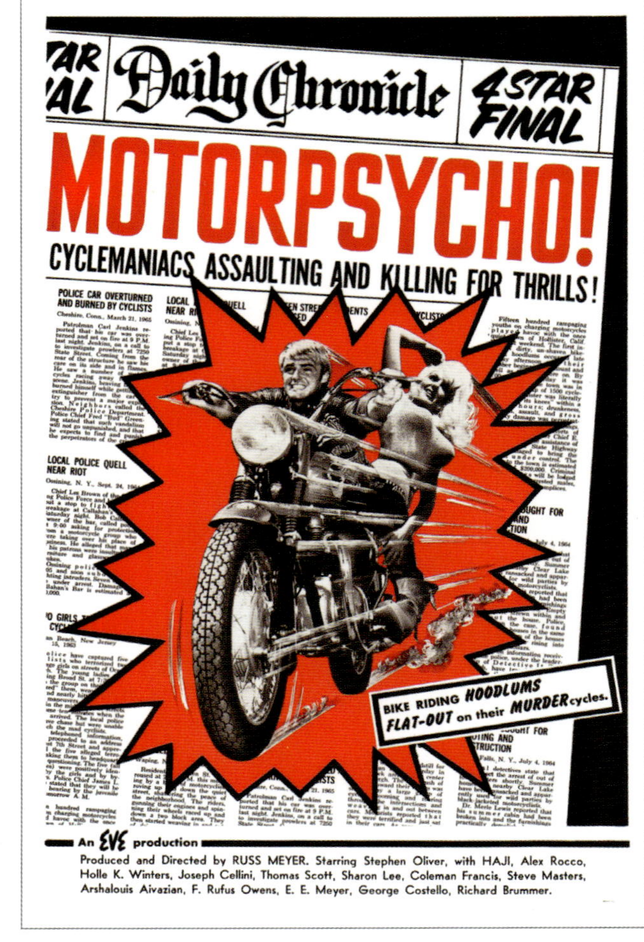
Daily Chronicle
4 STAR FINAL
MOTORPSYCHO!
CYCLEMANIACS ASSAULTING AND KILLING FOR THRILLS!
POLICE CAR OVERTURNED AND BURNED BY CYCLISTS
LOCAL POLICE QUELL NEAR RIOT
BIKE RIDING HOODLUMS FLAT-OUT on their MURDERcycles.
An EVE production
Produced and Directed by RUSS MEYER. Starring Stephen Oliver, with HAJI, Alex Rocco, Holle K. Winters, Joseph Cellini, Thomas Scott, Sharon Lee, Coleman Francis, Steve Masters, Arshalouis Aivazian, F. Rufus Owens, E. E. Meyer, George Costello, Richard Brummer.

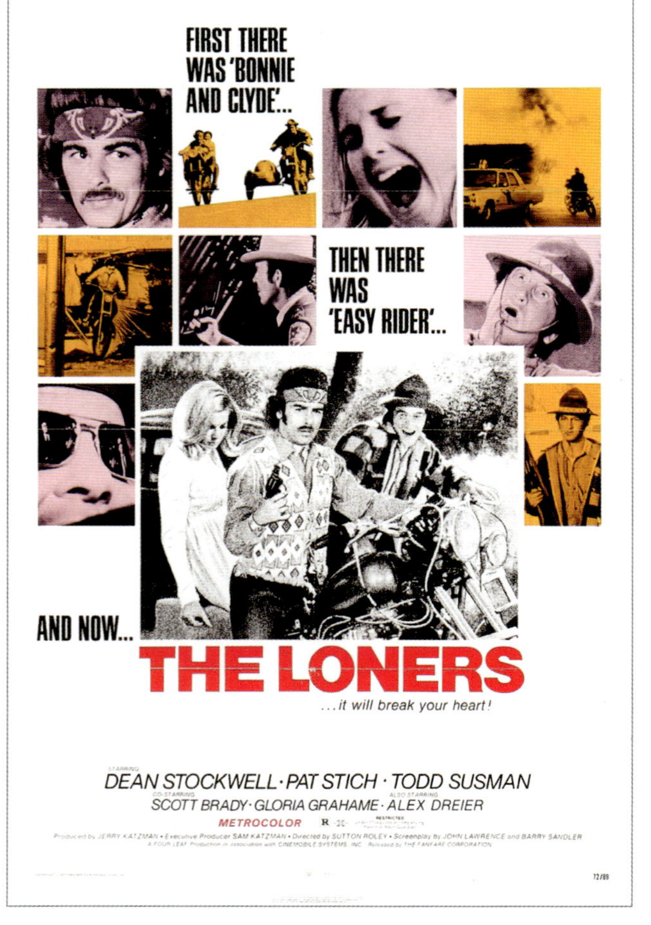
FIRST THERE WAS 'BONNIE AND CLYDE'...
THEN THERE WAS 'EASY RIDER'...
AND NOW... THE LONERS
...it will break your heart!
DEAN STOCKWELL · PAT STICH · TODD SUSMAN
SCOTT BRADY · GLORIA GRAHAME · ALEX DREIER
METROCOLOR

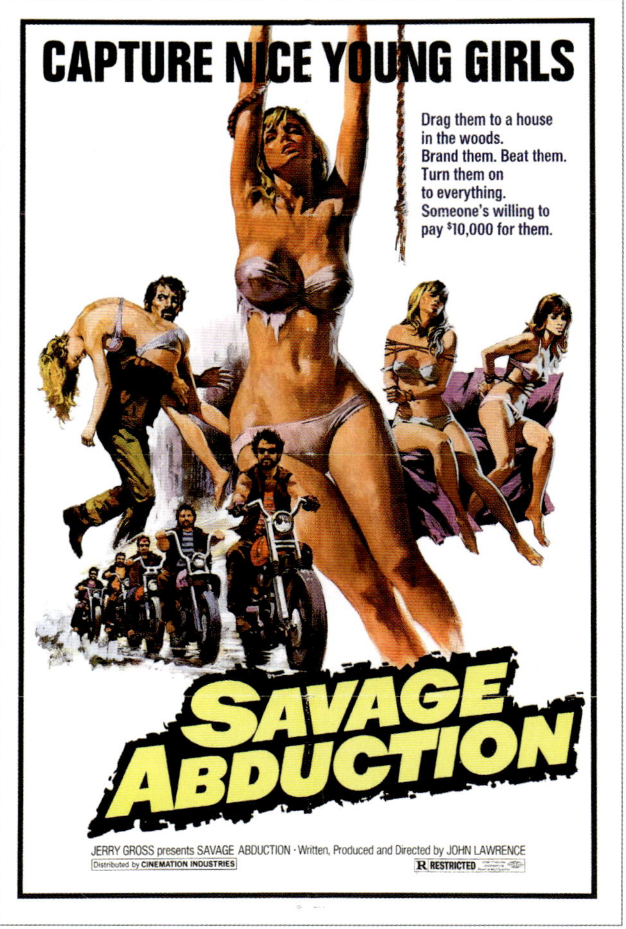
CAPTURE NICE YOUNG GIRLS
Drag them to a house in the woods. Brand them. Beat them. Turn them on to everything. Someone's willing to pay $10,000 for them.
SAVAGE ABDUCTION
JERRY GROSS presents SAVAGE ABDUCTION · Written, Produced and Directed by JOHN LAWRENCE
Distributed by CINEMATION INDUSTRIES
R RESTRICTED

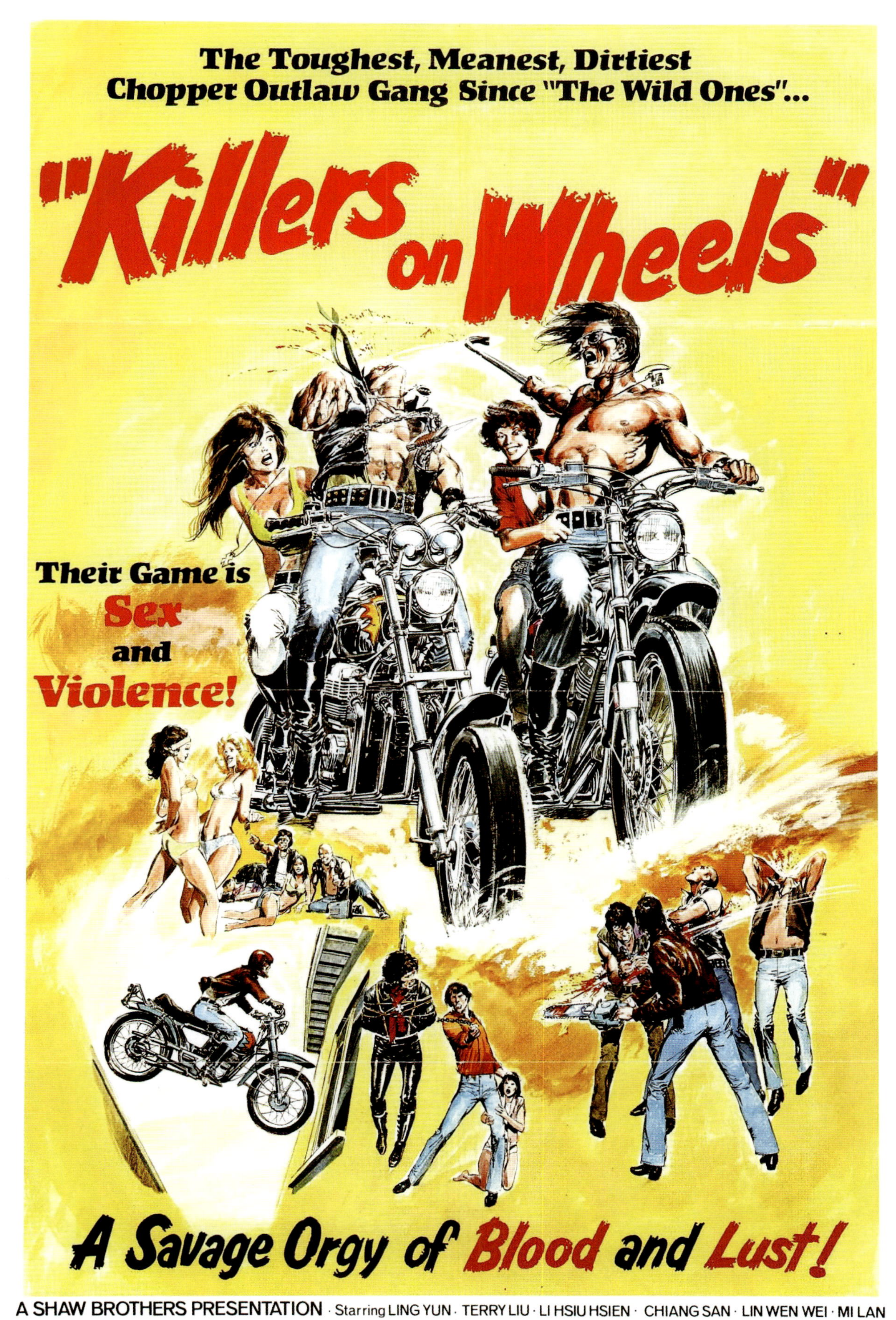
The Toughest, Meanest, Dirtiest
Chopper Outlaw Gang Since "The Wild Ones"...
"Killers on Wheels"
Their Game is
Sex
and
Violence!
A Savage Orgy of Blood and Lust!
A SHAW BROTHERS PRESENTATION · Starring LING YUN · TERRY LIU · LI HSIU HSIEN · CHIANG SAN · LIN WEN WEI · MI LAN
Directed by KUEI CHIH HUNG · Written by SZU TU AN · HOWARD MAHLER FILMS RELEASE · COLOR
R RESTRICTED

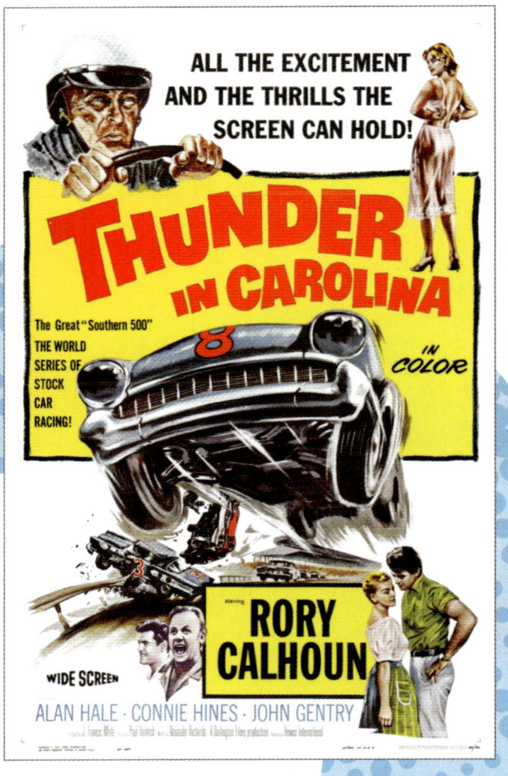

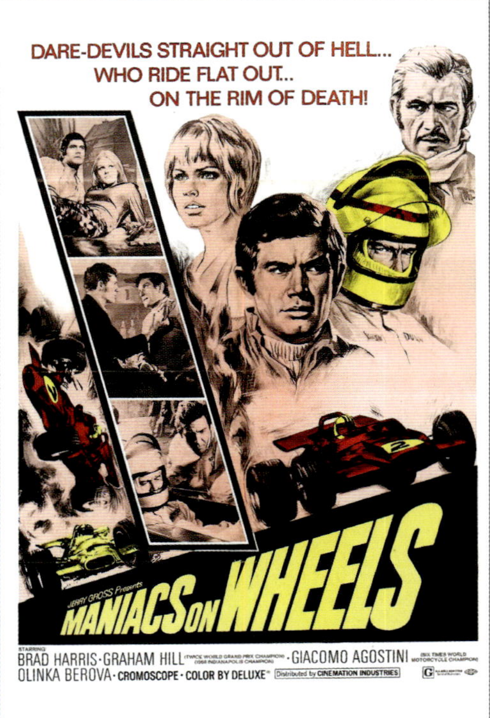

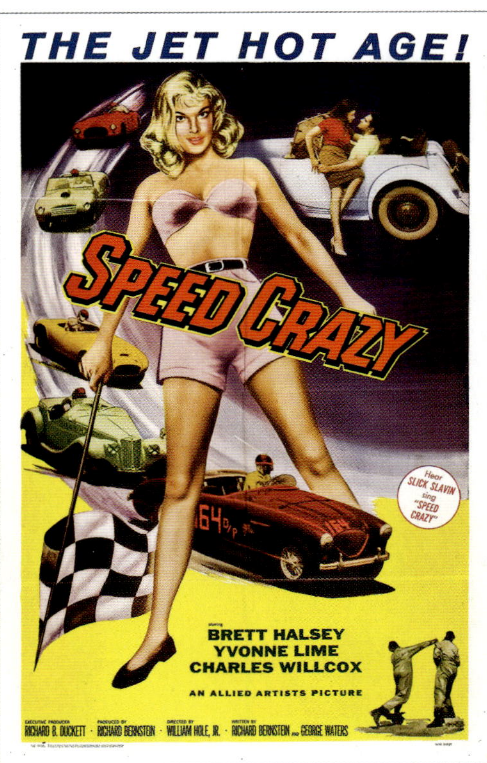

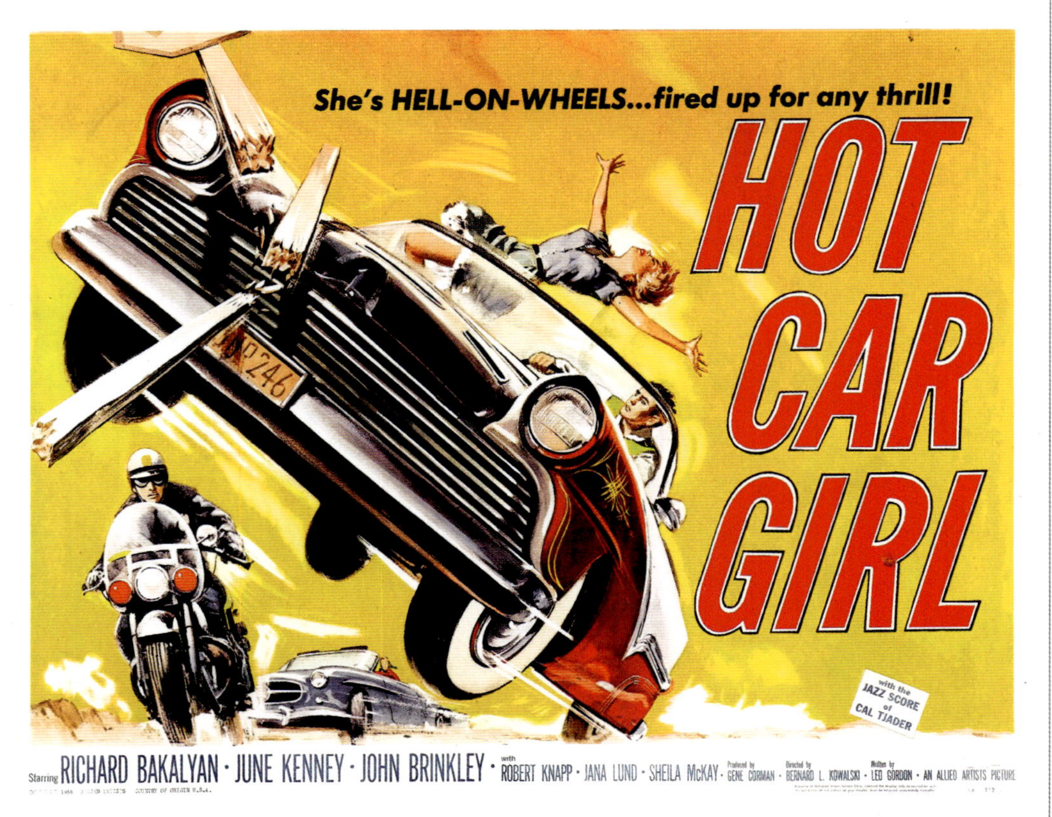

CARSPLOITATION

As the continuing success of a certain billion-dollar franchise amply demonstrates, viewers love the fast and furious action of movies where the car is the star. If they're paired with beautiful women and scenes where vehicles get smashed up real good, then so much the better. *Joyride to Nowhere* (1977) aims to tick both those boxes, and while its albeit skimpy plot of two girls on the run is intriguing as a kind of proto-*Thelma and Louise*, the film's one-sheet is more interested in letting viewers know what type of car they can expect to see "totally flattened!" on screen. *Speedtrap* (1977) is notable for having probably the only film poster to feature the cult British car the Jensen Interceptor. Plus, thanks to a rudimentary multi-angle camera setup used to capture a crash sequence, it arguably invented "bullet time," 22 years before *The Matrix*!

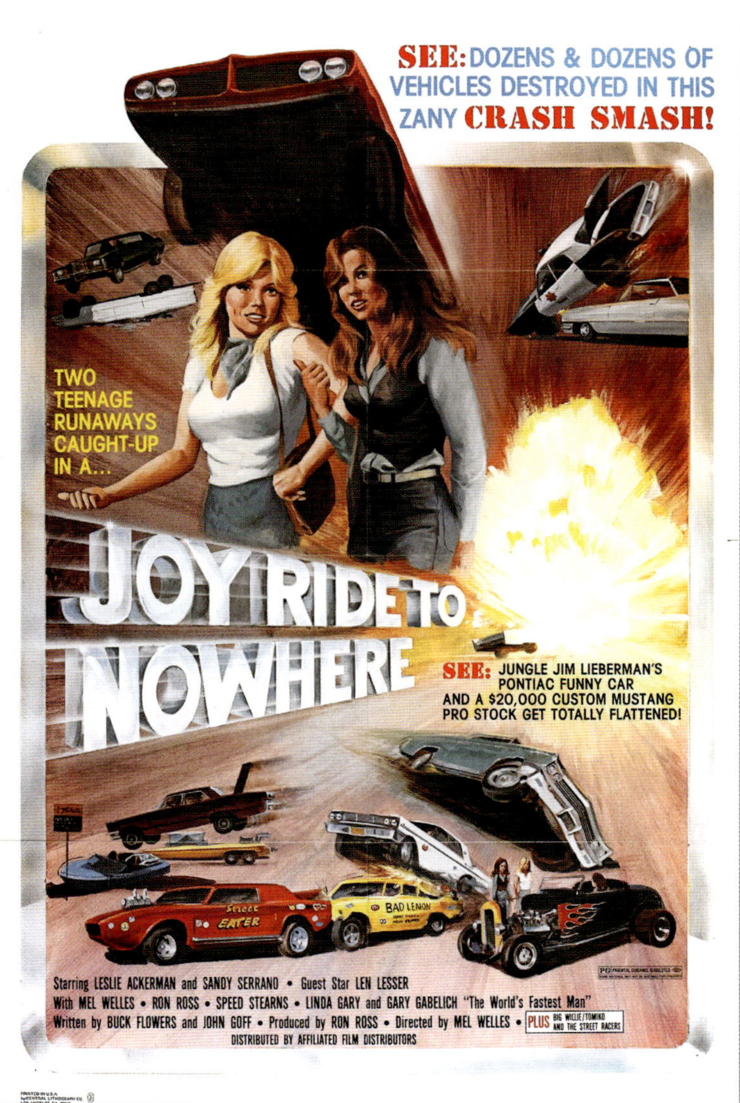
SEE: DOZENS & DOZENS OF VEHICLES DESTROYED IN THIS ZANY CRASH SMASH!
TWO TEENAGE RUNAWAYS CAUGHT-UP IN A...
JOY RIDE TO NOWHERE
SEE: JUNGLE JIM LIEBERMAN'S PONTIAC FUNNY CAR AND A $20,000 CUSTOM MUSTANG PRO STOCK GET TOTALLY FLATTENED!
Starring LESLIE ACKERMAN and SANDY SERRANO • Guest Star LEN LESSER
With MEL WELLES • RON ROSS • SPEED STEARNS • LINDA GARY and GARY GABELICH "The World's Fastest Man"
Written by BUCK FLOWERS and JOHN GOFF • Produced by RON ROSS • Directed by MEL WELLES • PLUS
DISTRIBUTED BY AFFILIATED FILM DISTRIBUTORS

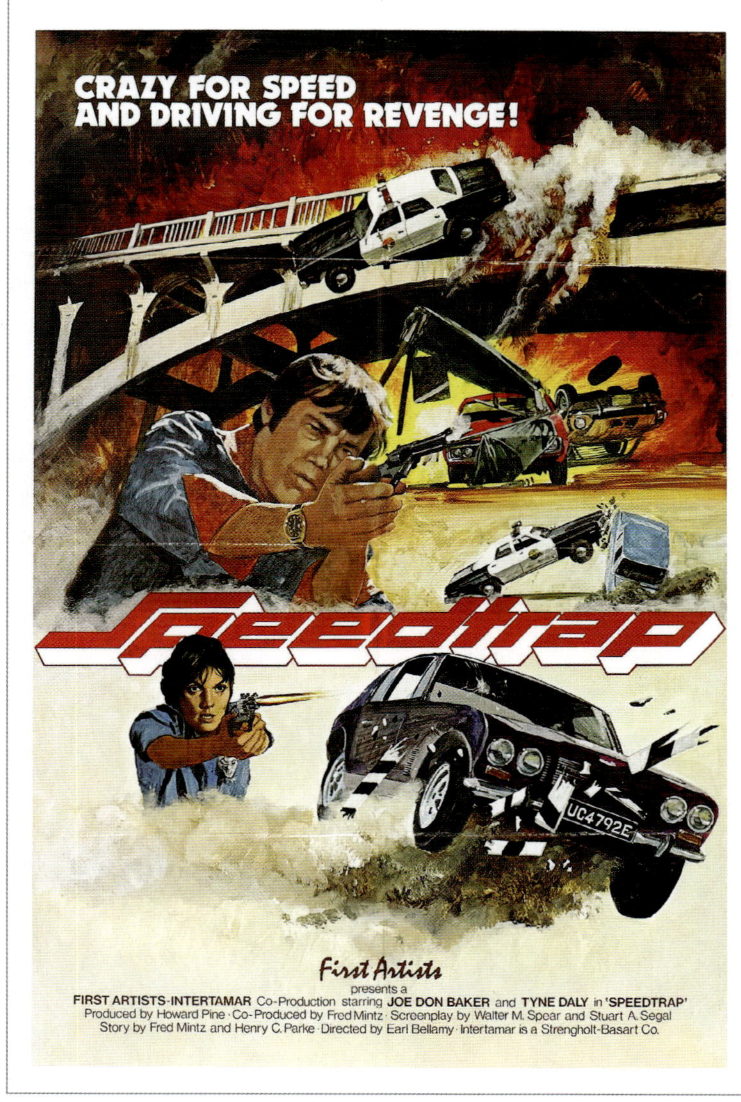
CRAZY FOR SPEED AND DRIVING FOR REVENGE!
Speedtrap
UC4792E
First Artists
presents a
FIRST ARTISTS-INTERTAMAR Co-Production starring JOE DON BAKER and TYNE DALY in 'SPEEDTRAP'
Produced by Howard Pine · Co-Produced by Fred Mintz · Screenplay by Walter M. Spear and Stuart A. Segal
Story by Fred Mintz and Henry C. Parke · Directed by Earl Bellamy · Intertamar is a Strengholt-Basart Co.

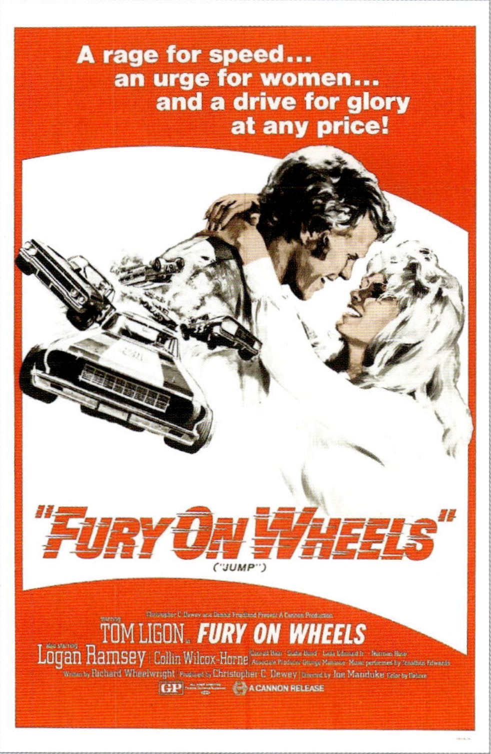
A rage for speed...
an urge for women...
and a drive for glory
at any price!
"FURY ON WHEELS"
("JUMP")
TOM LIGON FURY ON WHEELS
Logan Ramsey Collin Wilcox-Horne
GP
A CANNON RELEASE

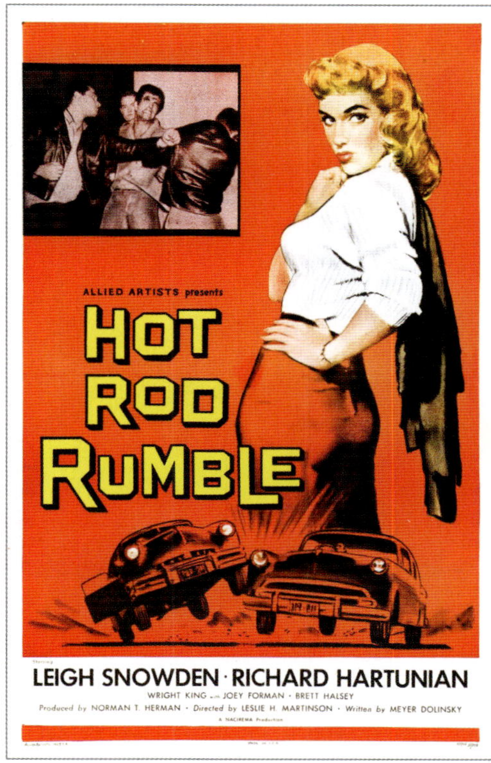
ALLIED ARTISTS presents
HOT ROD RUMBLE
LEIGH SNOWDEN · RICHARD HARTUNIAN
WRIGHT KING · JOEY FORMAN · BRETT HALSEY
Produced by NORMAN T. HERMAN · Directed by LESLIE H. MARTINSON · Written by MEYER DOLINSKY

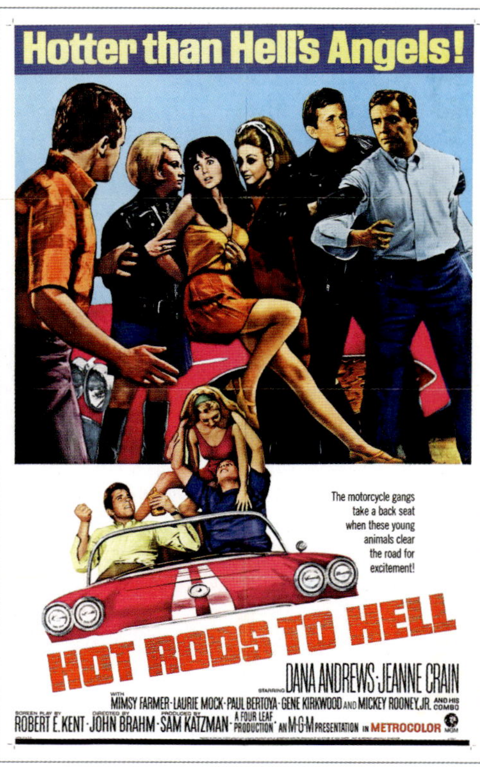
Hotter than Hell's Angels!
The motorcycle gangs take a back seat when these young animals clear the road for excitement!
HOT RODS TO HELL
DANA ANDREWS · JEANNE CRAIN
MIMSY FARMER · LAURIE MOCK · PAUL BERTOYA · GENE KIRKWOOD AND MICKEY ROONEY, JR.
ROBERT E. KENT · JOHN BRAHM · SAM KATZMAN · A FOUR LEAF PRODUCTION · AN M-G-M PRESENTATION IN METROCOLOR

BRUCEPLOITATION

The sudden death of martial arts pioneer Bruce Lee on July 20, 1973 shocked the world. Just six days later, *Enter the Dragon* was released, which quickly became a mainstream blockbuster, making him even more of a superstar. Lee's final "official" film, *Game of Death*, didn't emerge until 1978, but in the meantime plenty of low rent filmmakers rushed in to meet the demand, and "Bruceploitation" was born. A bewildering parade of lookalikes and "anointed successors" was introduced, from Bruce Li, via Bruce Le, Bruce Lai, Bruce Lei, Bruce Lie, Bruce Leong, and the inevitable Lee Bruce to a female version, Judy Lee (let's face it, these were probably not their real names). Some productions boasted they had footage of the "real" Lee; one film rather desperately claimed added authenticity because Bruce's brother Robert had provided the music.

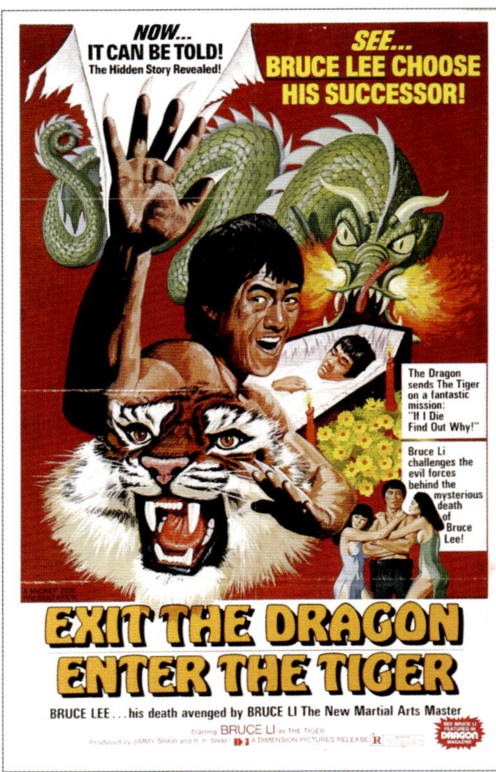

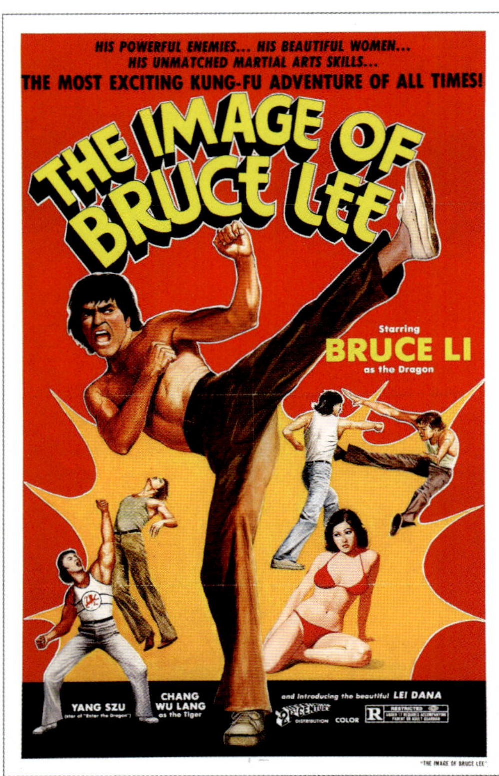

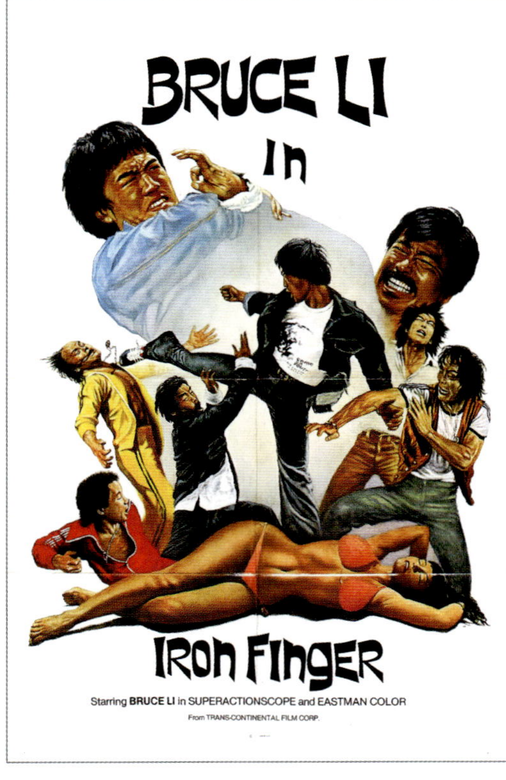

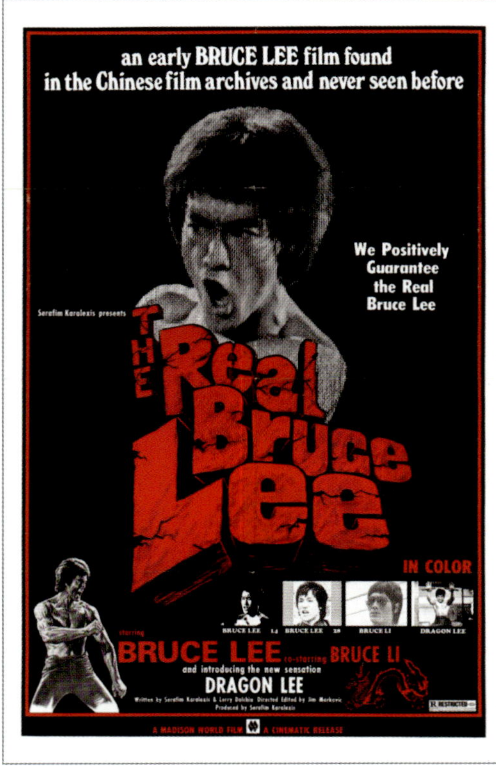

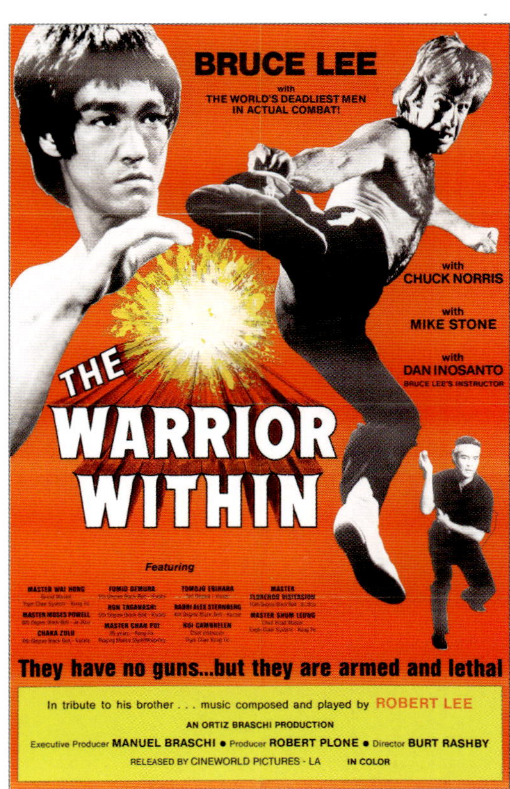

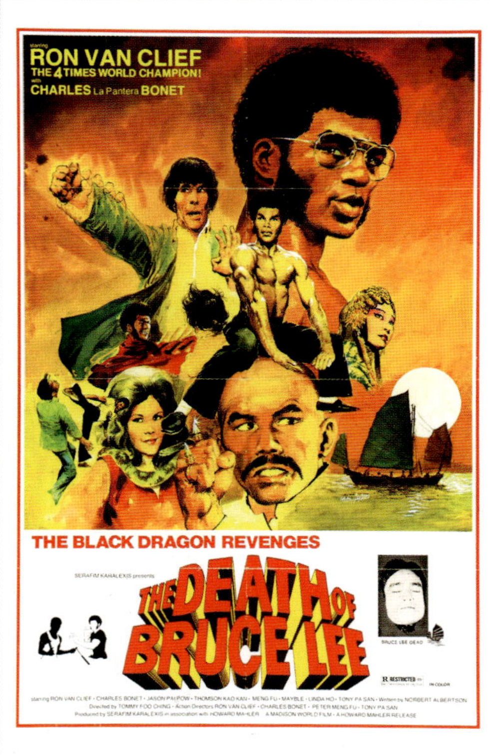

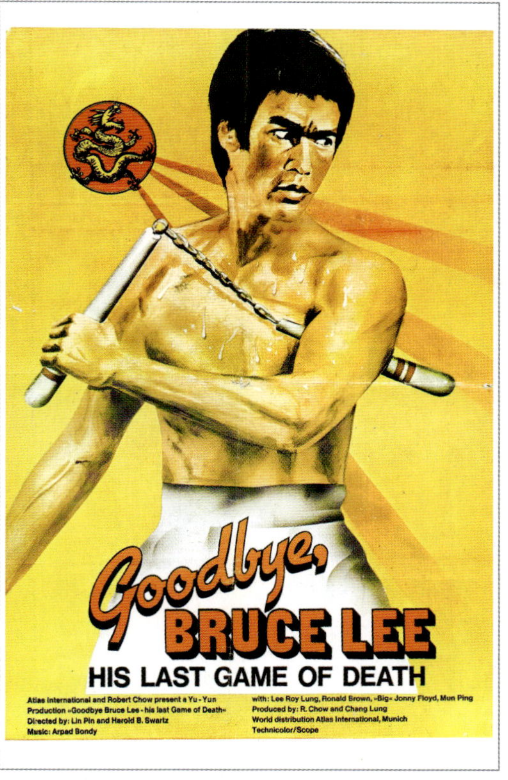

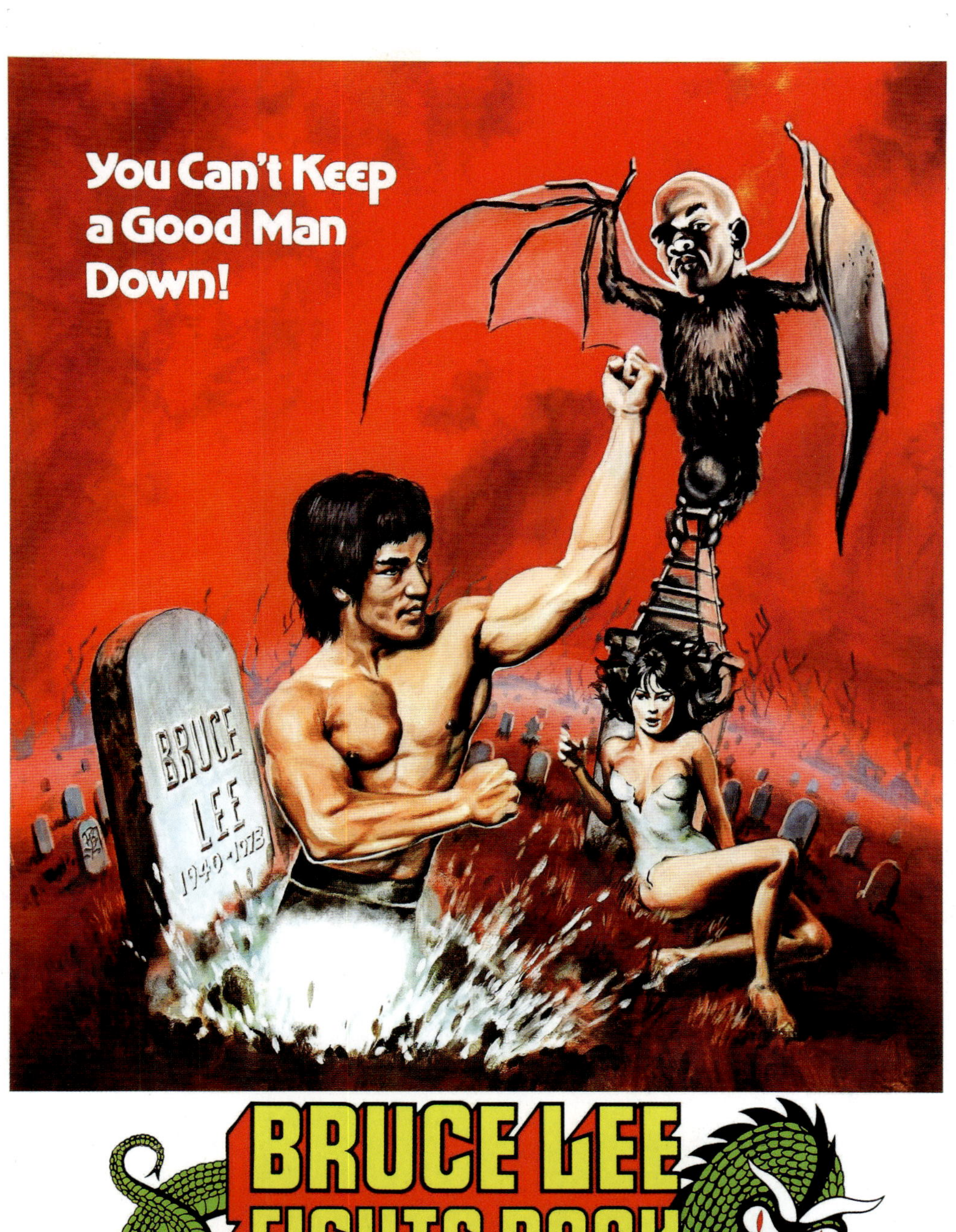

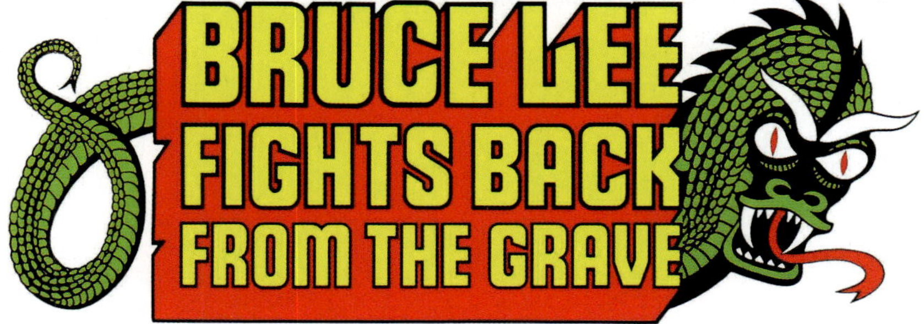

R RESTRICTED
Under 17 requires accompanying Parent or Adult Guardian

also starring DEBORAH CHAPLIN ANTHONY BRONSON STEVE MACK

directed by BERT LENZI music by MAURICE SARLI HEAD GORILLA RELEASING, INC. © 1976 HEAD GORILLA INC.

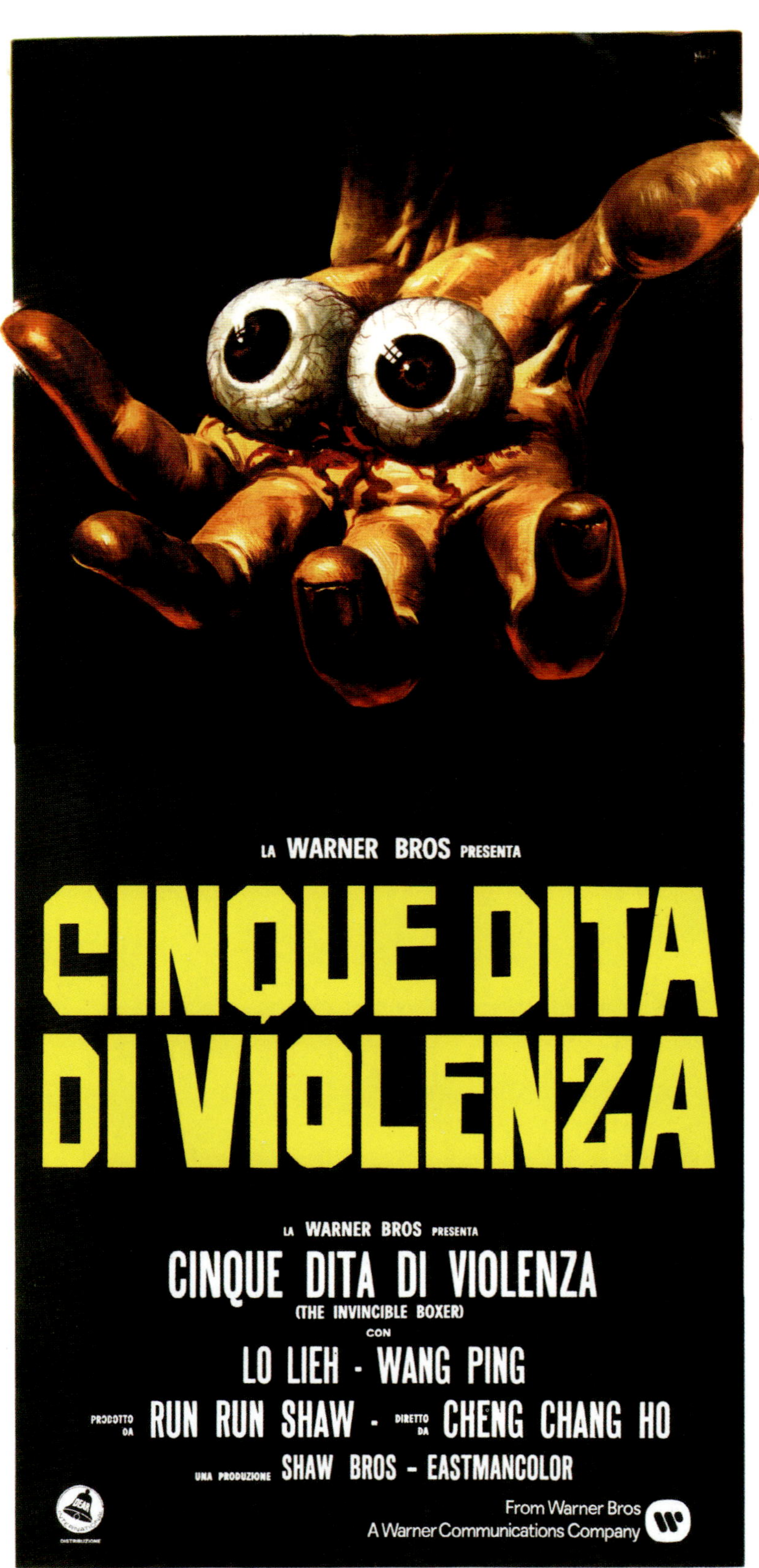

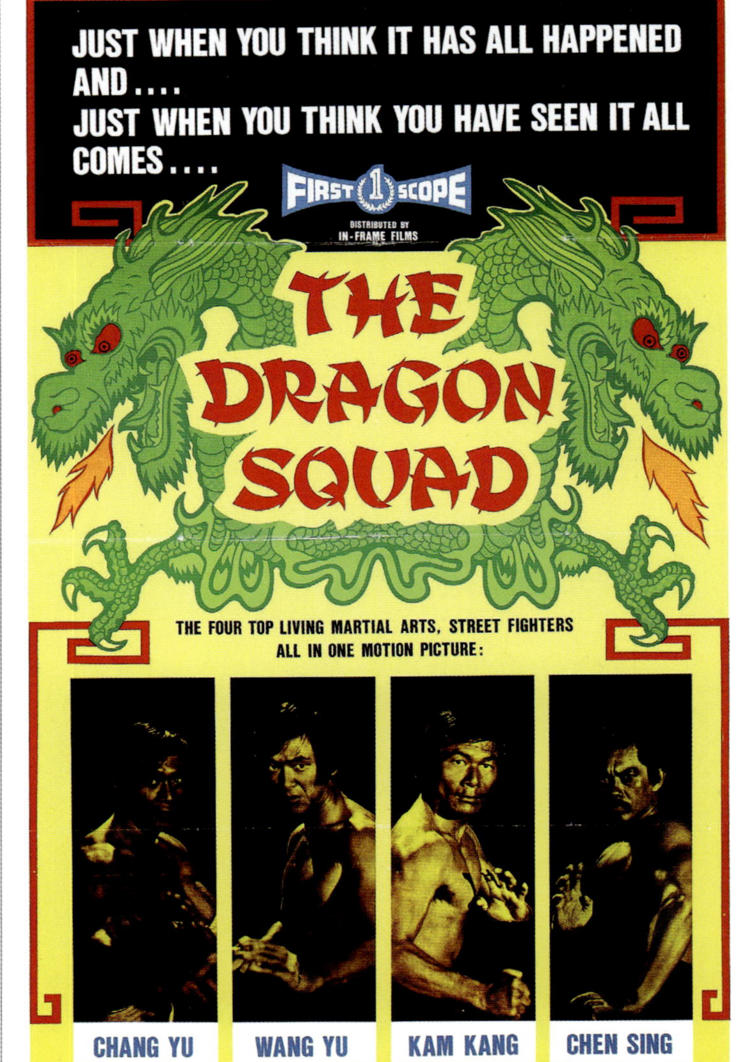

FURIOUS FISTS

Enter the Dragon's mainstream success only increased demand in the West for what trade paper *Variety* called "chop-socky" movies. Asian filmmakers were very happy to oblige throughout the '70s with an explosion of product, introducing new stars such as Jackie Chan and "The Bad Man from Japan," Sonny Chiba. The English language names for these films often seem to have appeared from some kind of Martial Arts Movie Title Generator, with endless variations on the same words, especially if, like "fist," "fury," and "dragon," they were previously associated with a Bruce Lee film.

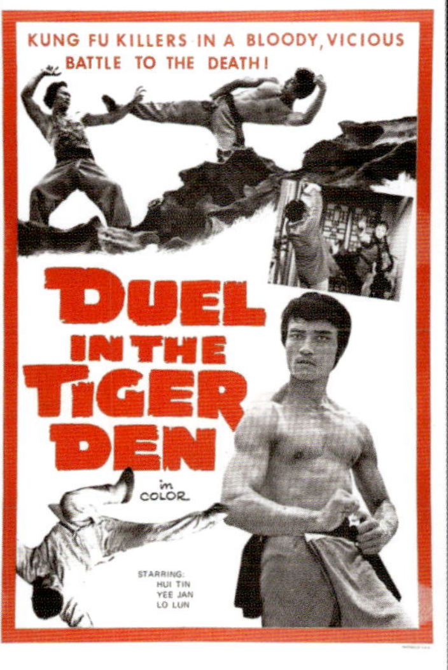
KUNG FU KILLERS IN A BLOODY, VICIOUS BATTLE TO THE DEATH!
DUEL IN THE TIGER DEN
in COLOR
STARRING: HUI TIN YEE JAN LO LUN

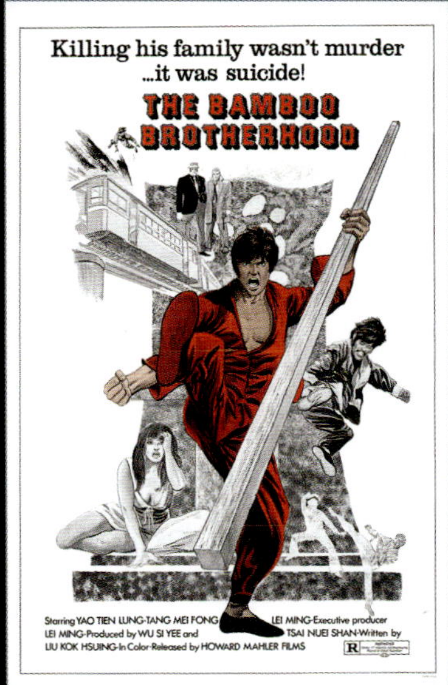
Killing his family wasn't murder ...it was suicide!
THE BAMBOO BROTHERHOOD
Starring YAO TIEN LUNG·TANG MEI FONG·LEI MING·Executive producer LEI MING·Produced by WU SI YEE and TSAI NUEI SHAN·Written by LIU KOK HSUING·In Color·Released by HOWARD MAHLER FILMS
R

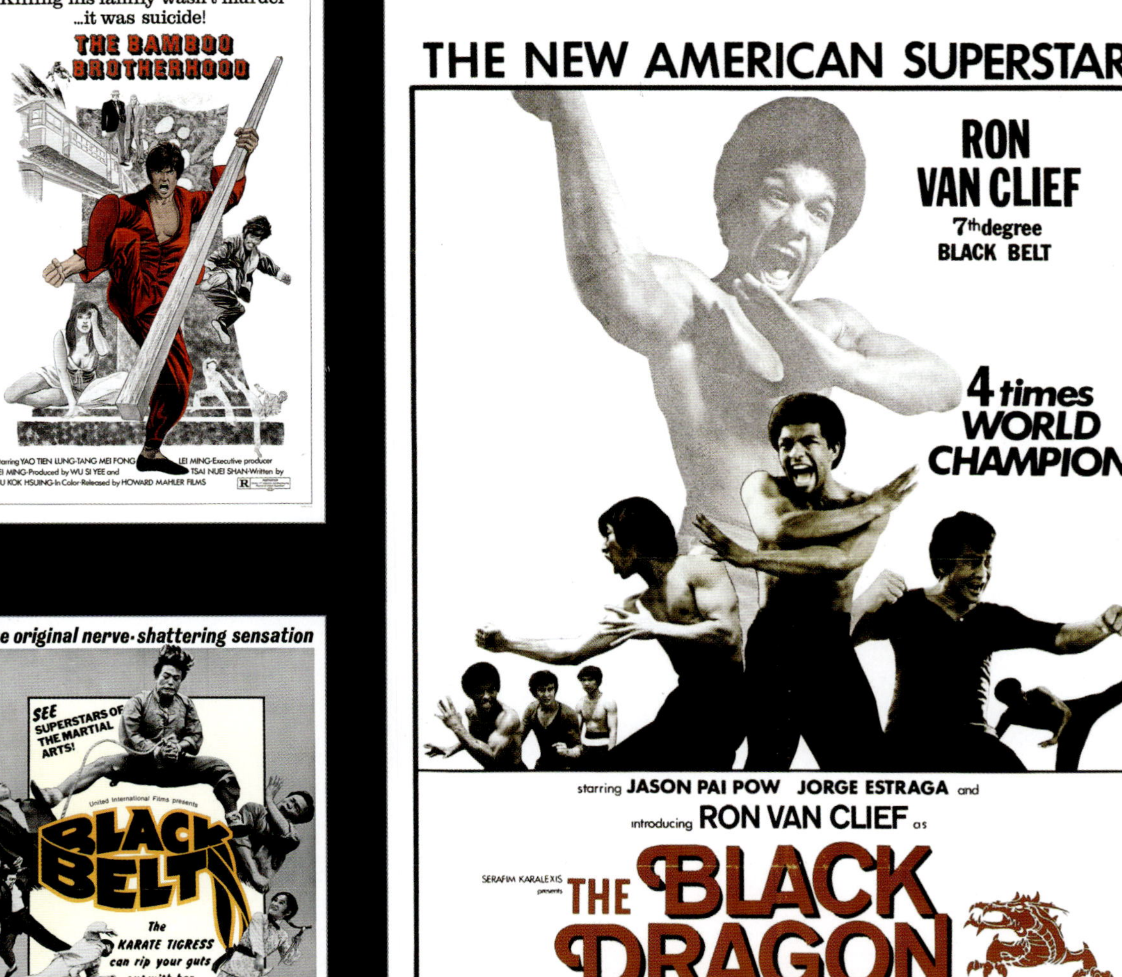
THE NEW AMERICAN SUPERSTAR
RON VAN CLIEF
7th degree BLACK BELT
4 times WORLD CHAMPION
starring JASON PAI POW JORGE ESTRAGA and
introducing RON VAN CLIEF as
SERAFIM KARALEXIS presents
THE BLACK DRAGON
IN COLOR R
starring JASON PAI POW • RON VAN CLIEF • JORGE ESTRAGA • NANCY VERONICA
MENG FU • THOMSON KAO KANG • CHANG LAU CHU • Screenplay by TOMMY LOO CHUNG
Directed by TOMMY LOO CHUNG • Action Directors JASON PAI POW, MENG FU, CHEN LAW
A co-production by SERAFIM KARALEXIS & YEO BAN YEE
A MADISON WORLD FILM A HOWARD MAHLER Release

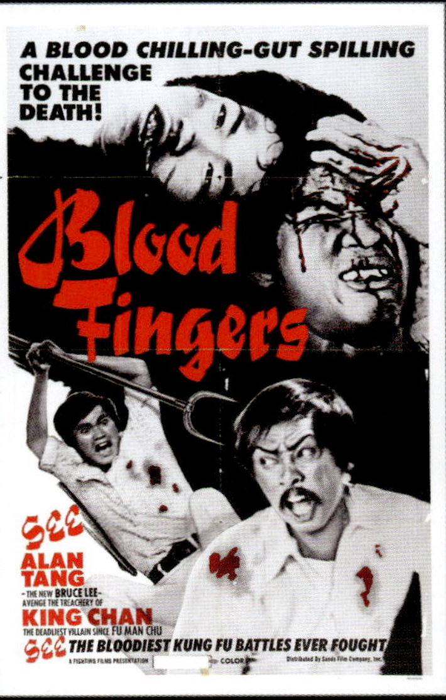
A BLOOD CHILLING-GUT SPILLING CHALLENGE TO THE DEATH!
Blood Fingers
SEE ALAN TANG
- THE NEW BRUCE LEE - AVENGE THE TREACHERY OF
KING CHAN
SEE THE BLOODIEST KUNG FU BATTLES EVER FOUGHT!
COLOR

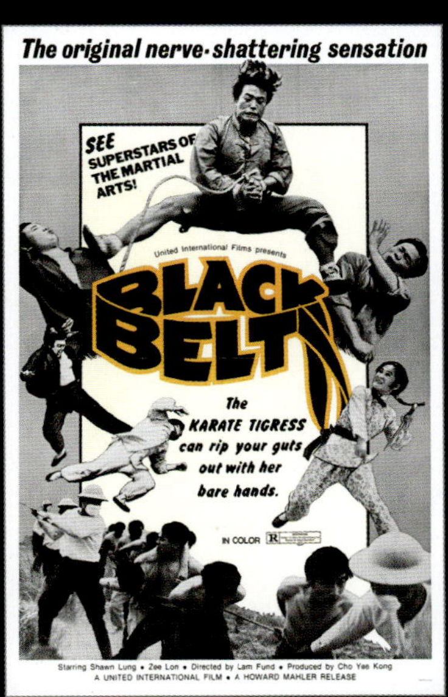
The original nerve-shattering sensation
SEE SUPERSTARS OF THE MARTIAL ARTS!
United International Films presents
BLACK BELT
The KARATE TIGRESS can rip your guts out with her bare hands.
IN COLOR R
Starring Shawn Lung • Zee Lon • Directed by Lam Fund • Produced by Cho Yee Kong
A UNITED INTERNATIONAL FILM • A HOWARD MAHLER RELEASE

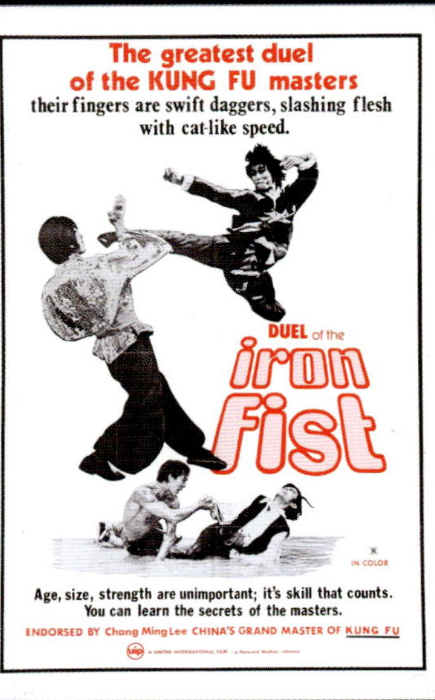
The greatest duel of the KUNG FU masters
their fingers are swift daggers, slashing flesh with cat-like speed.
DUEL of the iron fist
IN COLOR
Age, size, strength are unimportant; it's skill that counts.
You can learn the secrets of the masters.
ENDORSED BY Chang Ming Lee CHINA'S GRAND MASTER OF KUNG FU

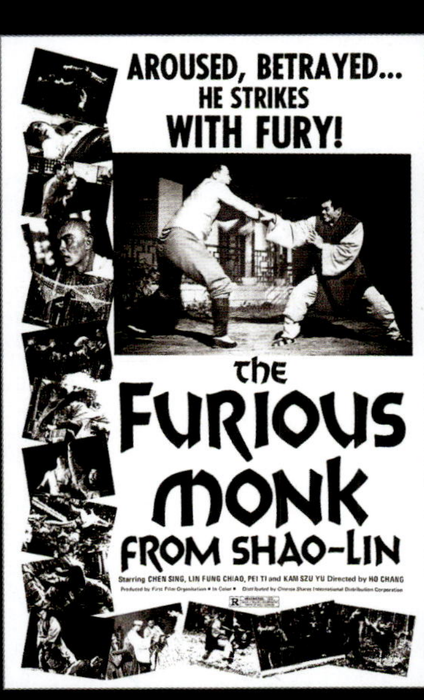
AROUSED, BETRAYED... HE STRIKES WITH FURY!
The FURIOUS MONK FROM SHAO-LIN
Starring CHEN SING, LIN FUNG CHIAO, PEI TI and KAM SZU YU Directed by HO CHANG

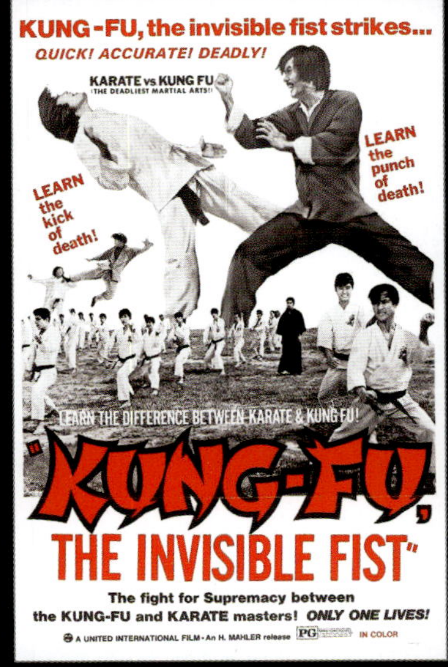
KUNG-FU, the invisible fist strikes...
QUICK! ACCURATE! DEADLY!
KARATE vs KUNG FU
(THE DEADLIEST MARTIAL ARTS!)
LEARN the kick of death!
LEARN the punch of death!
LEARN THE DIFFERENCE BETWEEN KARATE & KUNG FU!
"KUNG-FU, THE INVISIBLE FIST"
The fight for Supremacy between the KUNG-FU and KARATE masters! ONLY ONE LIVES!
A UNITED INTERNATIONAL FILM • An H. MAHLER release PG IN COLOR

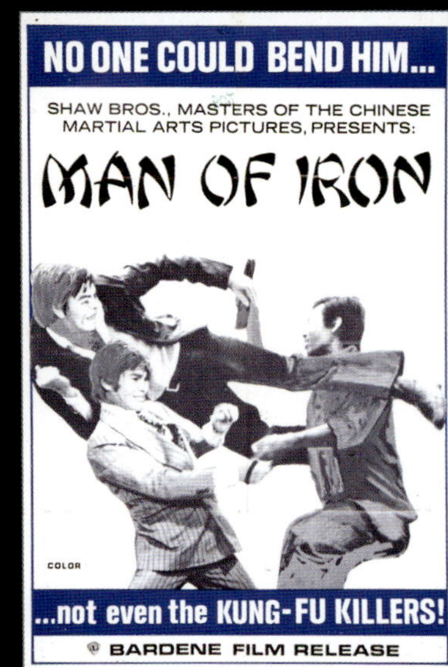
NO ONE COULD BEND HIM...
SHAW BROS., MASTERS OF THE CHINESE MARTIAL ARTS PICTURES, PRESENTS:
MAN OF IRON
COLOR
...not even the KUNG-FU KILLERS!
BARDENE FILM RELEASE

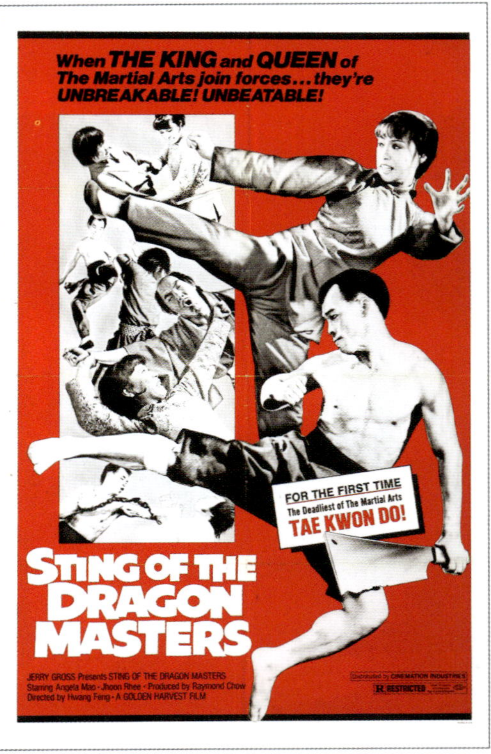
When THE KING and QUEEN of
The Martial Arts join forces... they're
UNBREAKABLE! UNBEATABLE!
FOR THE FIRST TIME
The Deadliest of The Martial Arts
TAE KWON DO!
STING OF THE
DRAGON
MASTERS

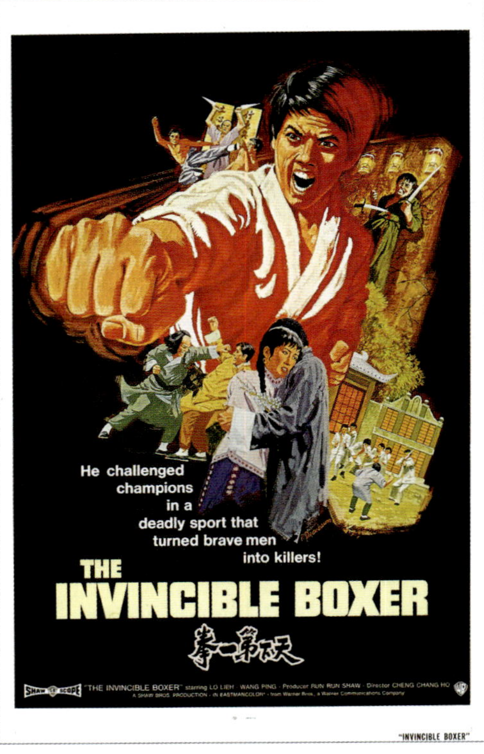
He challenged
champions
in a
deadly sport that
turned brave men
into killers!
THE
INVINCIBLE BOXER

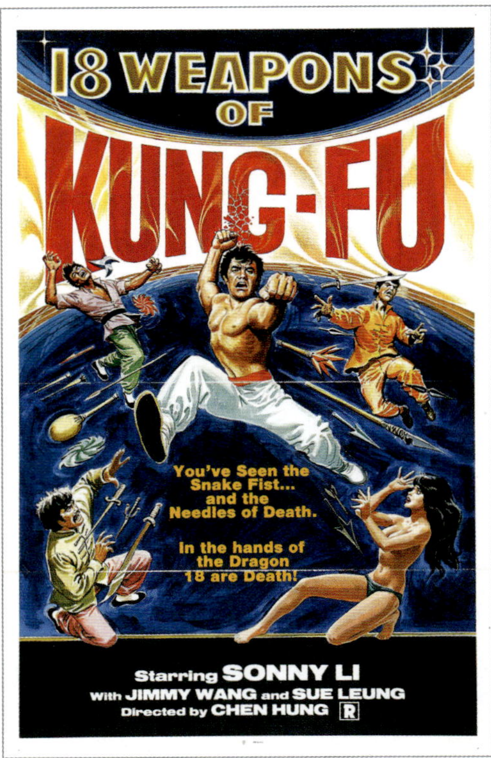
18 WEAPONS
OF
KUNG-FU
You've Seen the
Snake Fist...
and the
Needles of Death.
In the hands of
the Dragon
18 are Death!
Starring SONNY LI
With JIMMY WANG and SUE LEUNG
Directed by CHEN HUNG

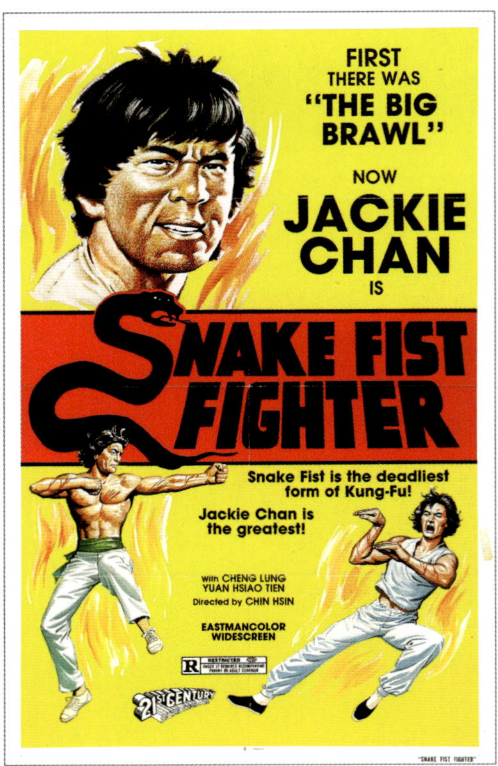
FIRST
THERE WAS
"THE BIG
BRAWL"
NOW
JACKIE
CHAN
IS
SNAKE FIST
FIGHTER
Snake Fist is the deadliest
form of Kung-Fu!
Jackie Chan is
the greatest!
with CHENG LUNG
YUAN HSIAO TIEN
Directed by CHIN HSIN
EASTMANCOLOR
WIDESCREEN

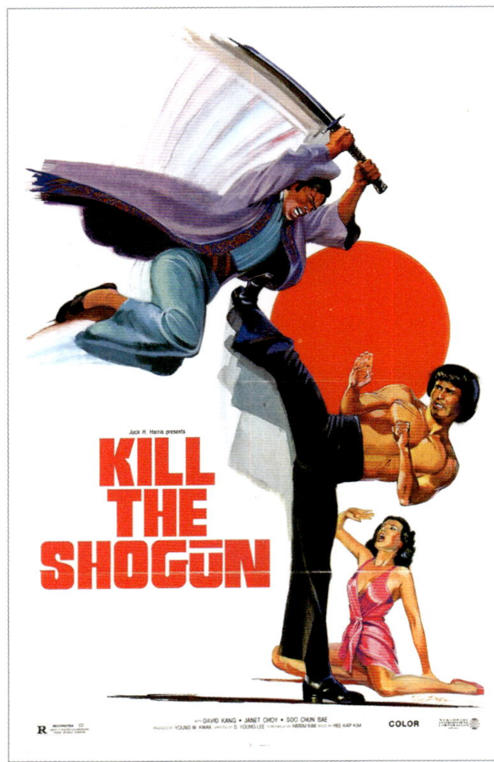
KILL
THE
SHOGUN
COLOR

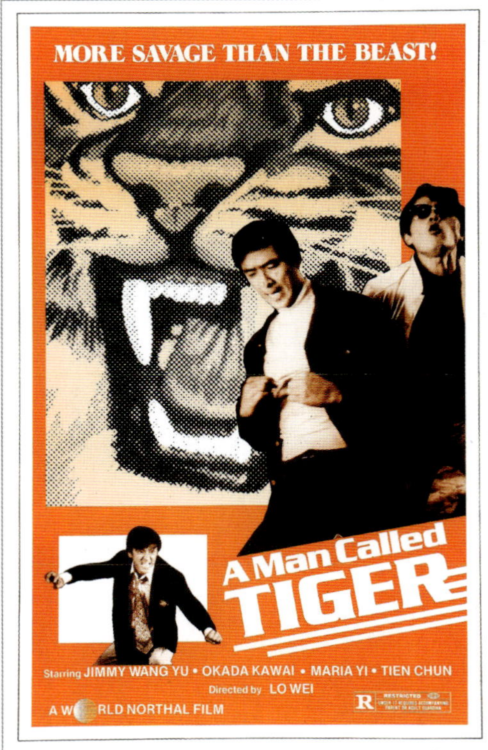
MORE SAVAGE THAN THE BEAST!
A Man Called
TIGER
Starring JIMMY WANG YU • OKADA KAWAI • MARIA YI • TIEN CHUN
Directed by LO WEI

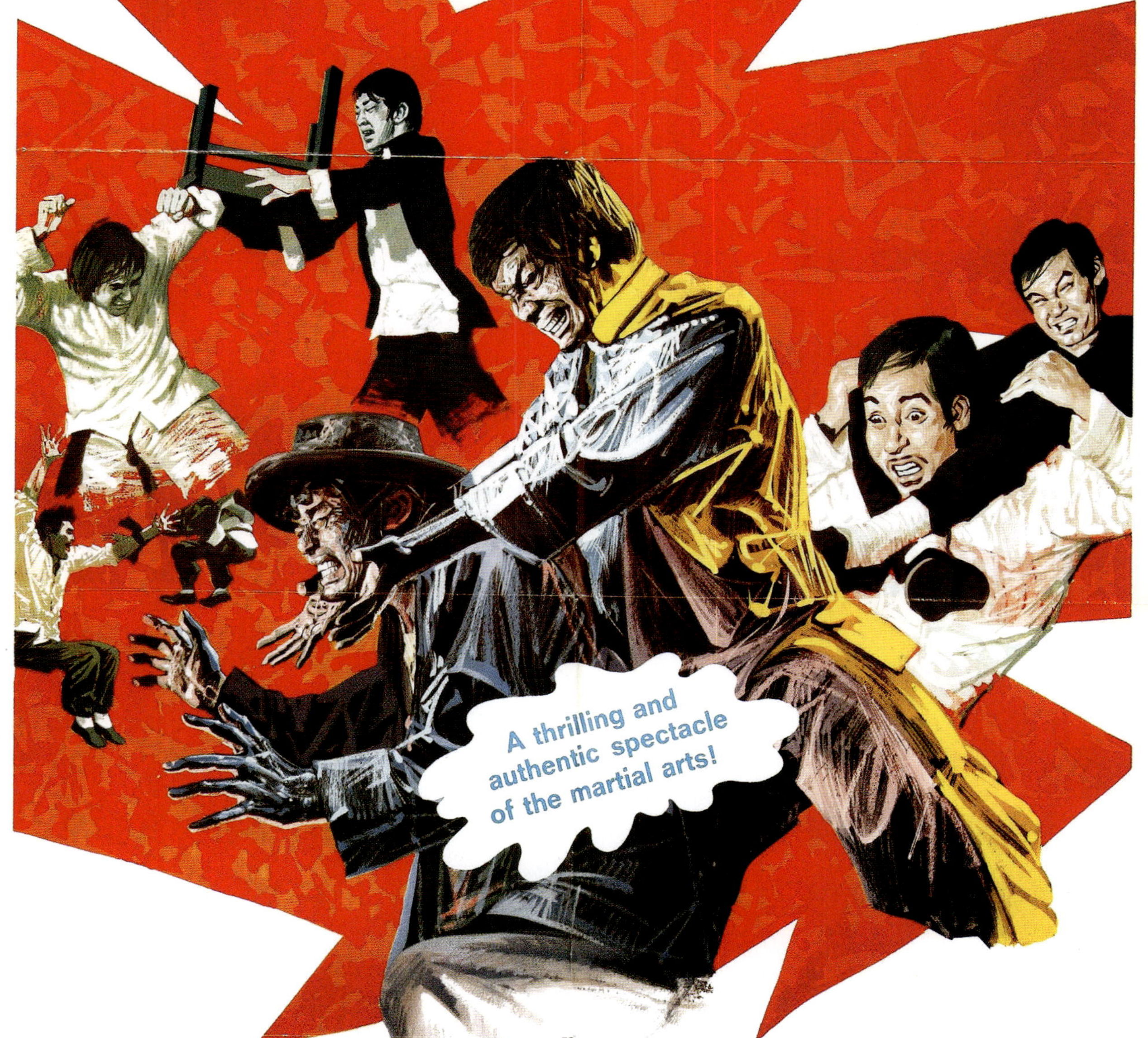
See the power, violence and excitement
of the Black Belt !
A thrilling and
authentic spectacle
of the martial arts!
THE FURY OF
THE BLACK BELT
with
HENRY YUE YONG · SHIUE JIA IAN · YANG PEY SHAN
TYAN FENG Director FANG LONG SIANG · COLOR · CINEMASCOPE
Distributed by L.A.N.A. FILMS, INC.
R RESTRICTED Under 17 Requires accompanying Parent or Adult Guardian

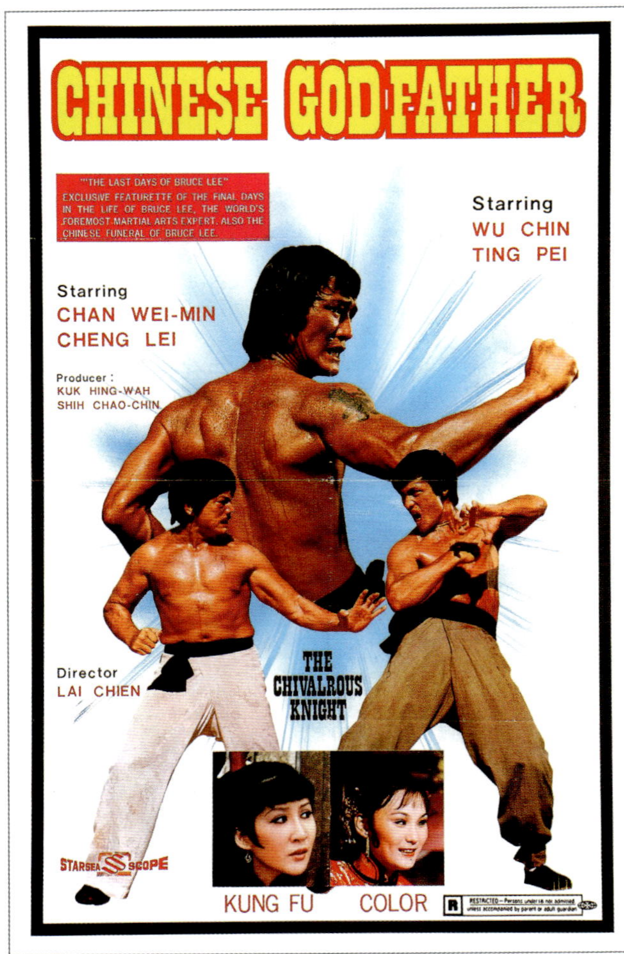
CHINESE GODFATHER
"THE LAST DAYS OF BRUCE LEE"
EXCLUSIVE FEATURETTE OF THE FINAL DAYS IN THE LIFE OF BRUCE LEE, THE WORLD'S FOREMOST MARTIAL ARTS EXPERT. ALSO THE CHINESE FUNERAL OF BRUCE LEE.
Starring
WU CHIN
TING PEI
Starring
CHAN WEI-MIN
CHENG LEI
Producer:
KUK HING-WAH
SHIH CHAO-CHIN
Director
LAI CHIEN
THE CHIVALROUS KNIGHT
STARSEA SCOPE
KUNG FU
COLOR

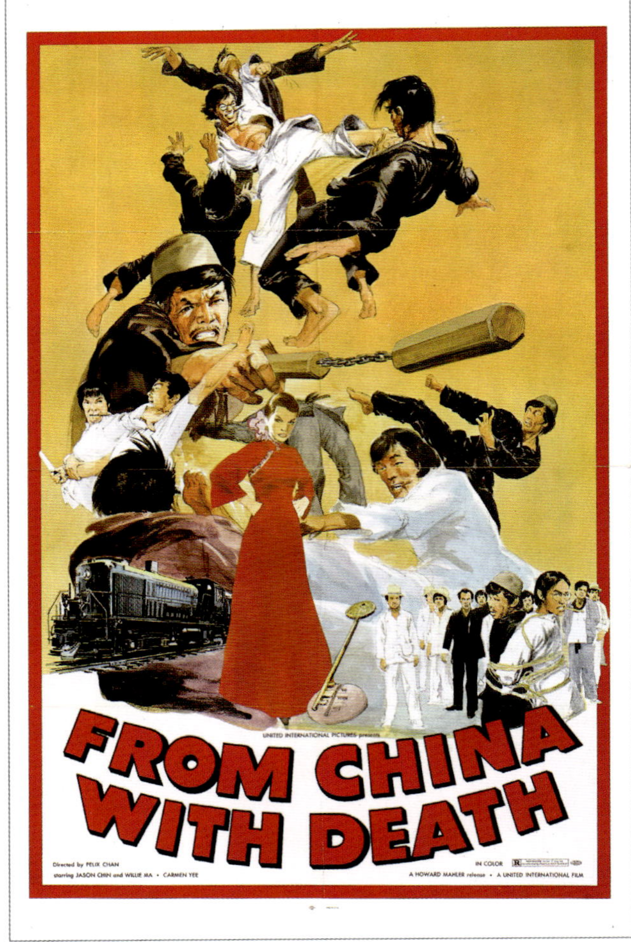
UNITED INTERNATIONAL PICTURES presents
FROM CHINA WITH DEATH
Directed by FELIX CHAN
starring JASON CHIN and WILLIE MA • CARMEN YEE
IN COLOR
A HOWARD MAHLER release • A UNITED INTERNATIONAL FILM

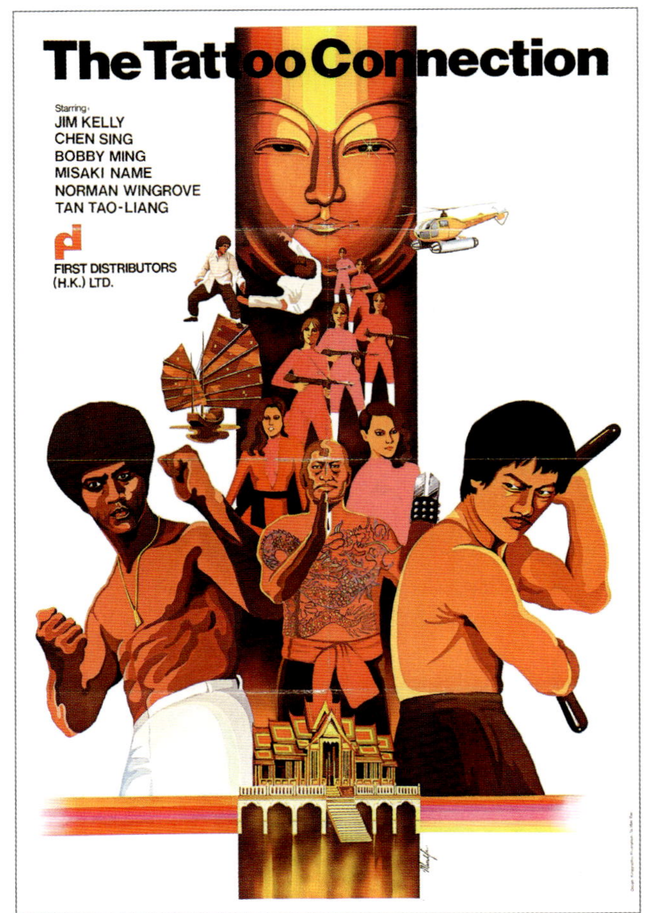
The Tattoo Connection
Starring:
JIM KELLY
CHEN SING
BOBBY MING
MISAKI NAME
NORMAN WINGROVE
TAN TAO-LIANG
FIRST DISTRIBUTORS (H.K.) LTD.

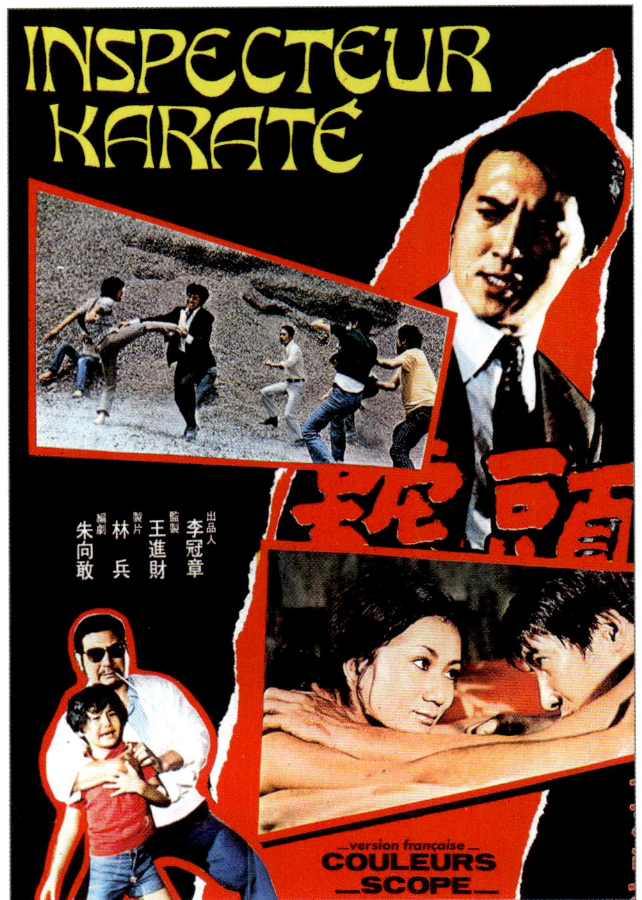
INSPECTEUR KARATÉ
出品人 李冠章
監製 王進財
製片 林兵
編劇 朱向敢
version française
COULEURS
SCOPE

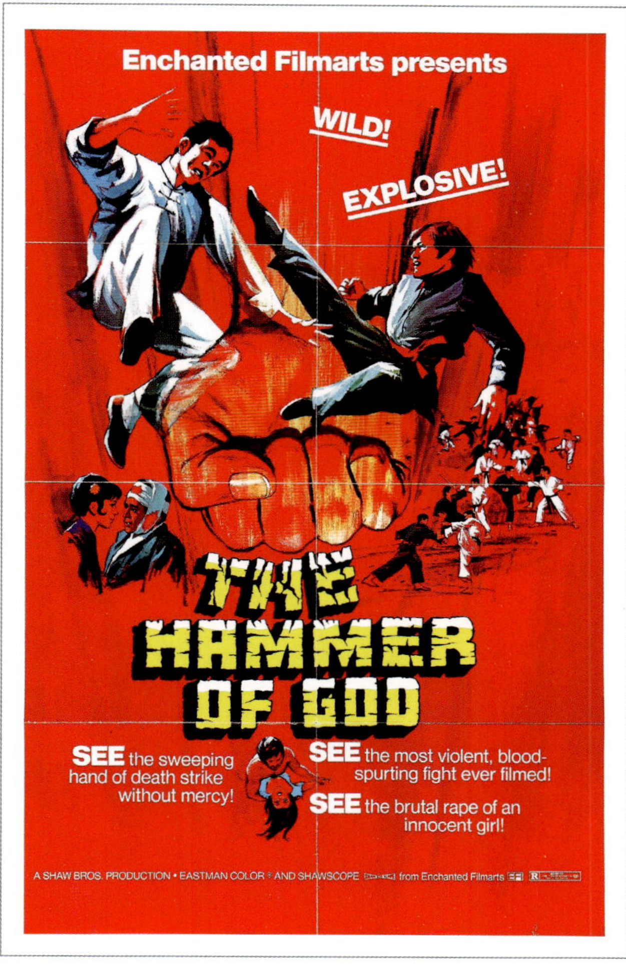
Enchanted Filmarts presents
WILD!
EXPLOSIVE!
THE HAMMER OF GOD
SEE the sweeping hand of death strike without mercy!
SEE the most violent, blood-spurting fight ever filmed!
SEE the brutal rape of an innocent girl!
A SHAW BROS. PRODUCTION • EASTMAN COLOR AND SHAWSCOPE from Enchanted Filmarts R

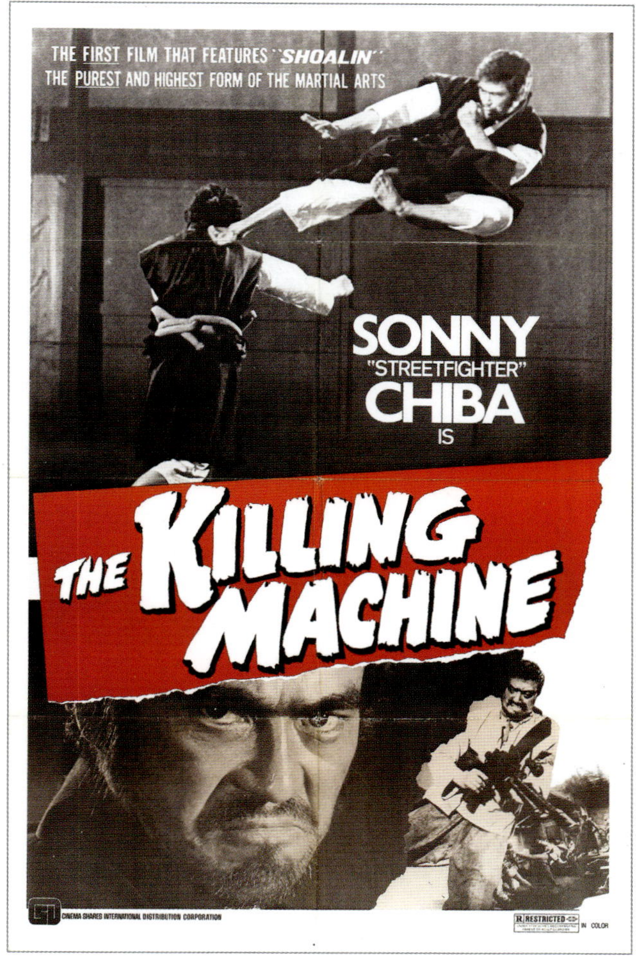
THE FIRST FILM THAT FEATURES "SHOALIN"
THE PUREST AND HIGHEST FORM OF THE MARTIAL ARTS
SONNY "STREETFIGHTER" CHIBA IS
THE KILLING MACHINE
CINEMA SHARES INTERNATIONAL DISTRIBUTION CORPORATION
R RESTRICTED IN COLOR

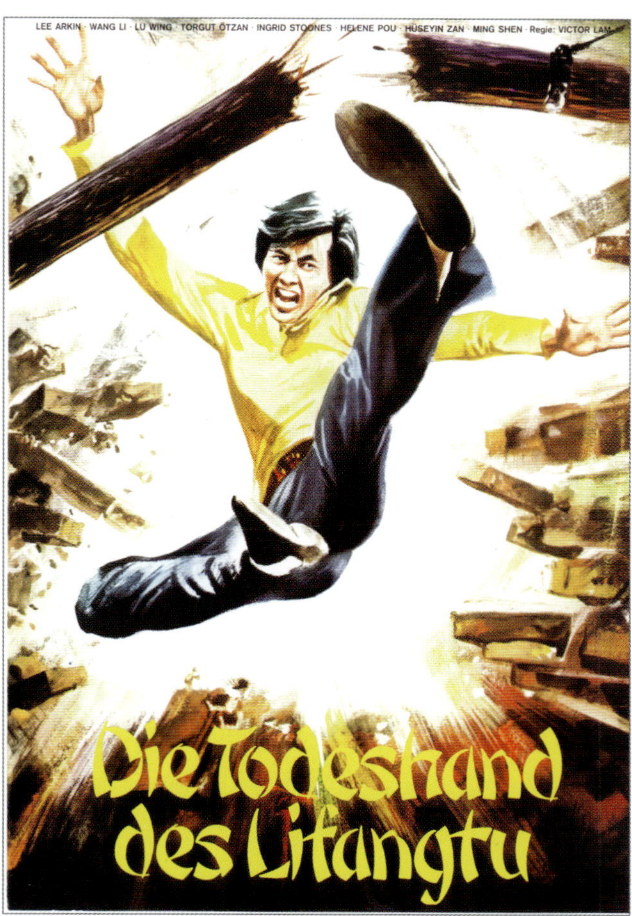
LEE ARKIN · WANG LI · LU WING · TORGUT ÖTZAN · INGRID STOONES · HELENE POU · HÜSEYIN ZAN · MING SHEN · Regie: VICTOR LAM
Die Todeshand des Lifangtu

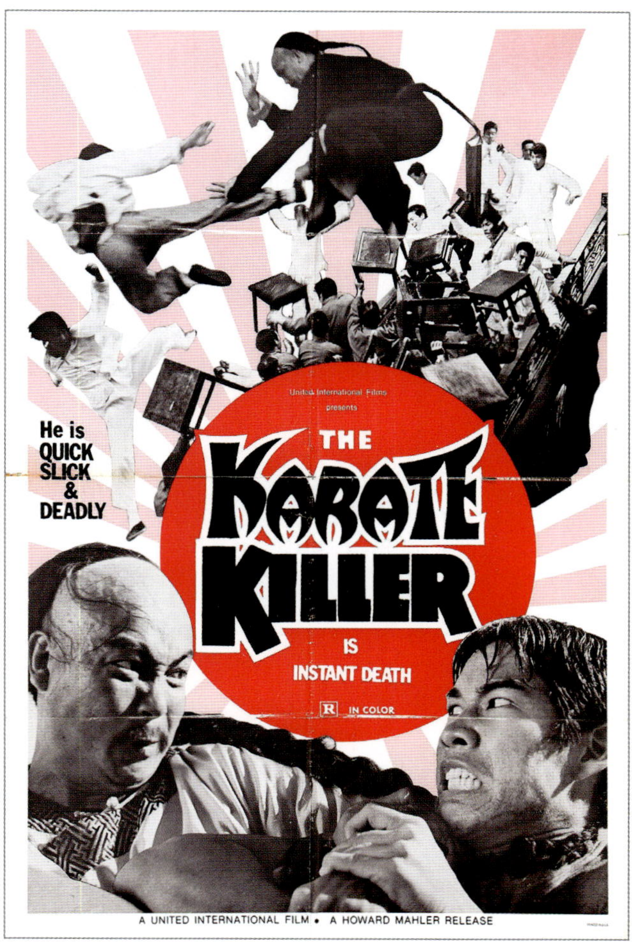
He is QUICK SLICK & DEADLY
United International Films presents
THE KARATE KILLER
IS INSTANT DEATH
R IN COLOR
A UNITED INTERNATIONAL FILM • A HOWARD MAHLER RELEASE

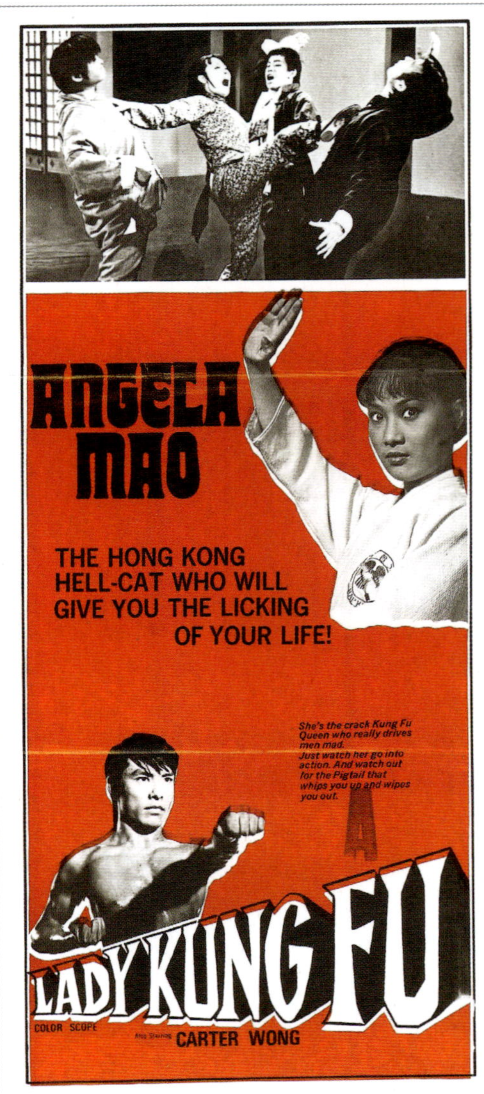

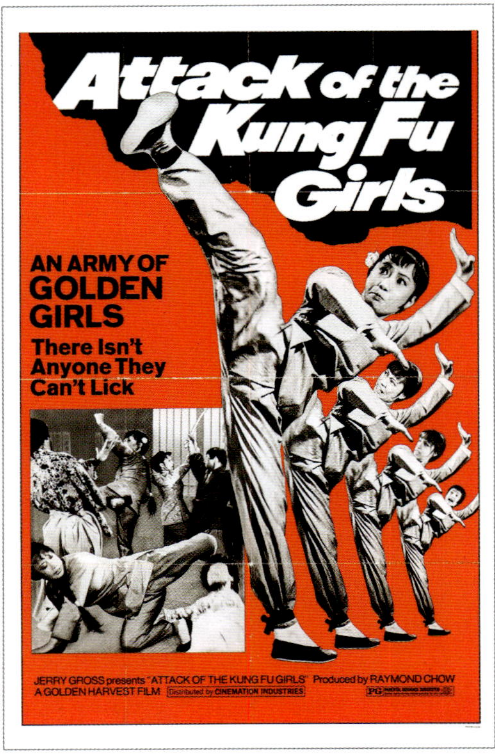

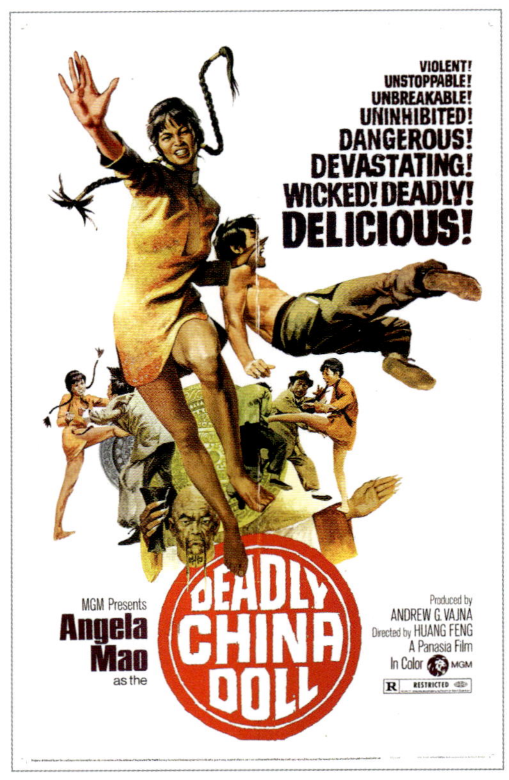

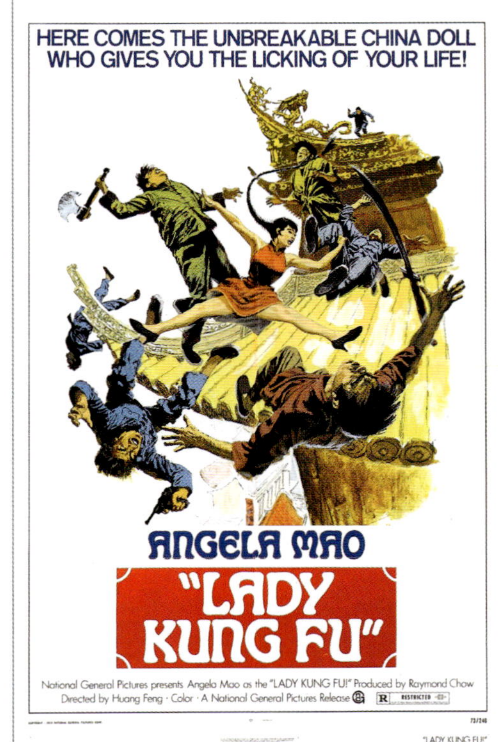

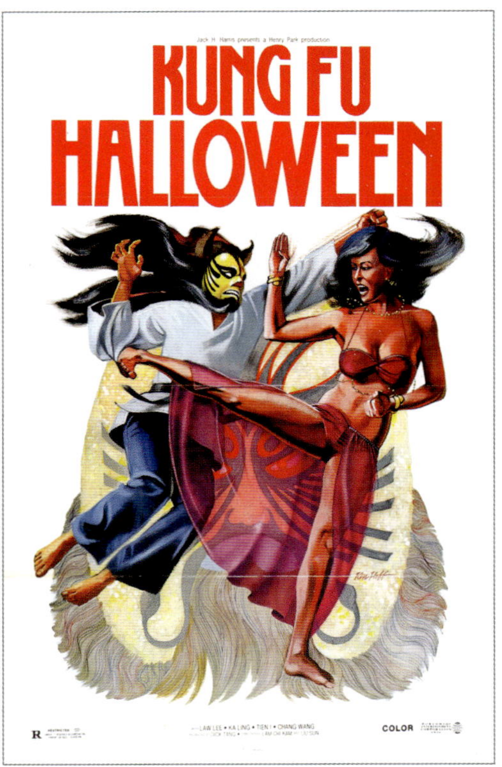

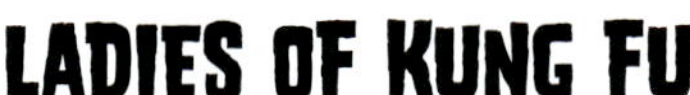

LADIES OF KUNG FU

Female kung fu stars also had a chance to shine in the '70s, including "the Hong Kong Hell-cat" Angela Mao (who was actually from Taiwan). Mao reportedly earned the dizzying sum of $100 for playing Bruce Lee's sister in *Enter the Dragon*; one hopes she was better paid as *Lady Kung Fu* (1972) and the *Deadly China Doll* (1973). Doris Lung starred in *Shi men wei feng* (1972). Its English title was *Brave Girl Boxer in Shanghai*, though the poster designer had trouble copying that out . . .

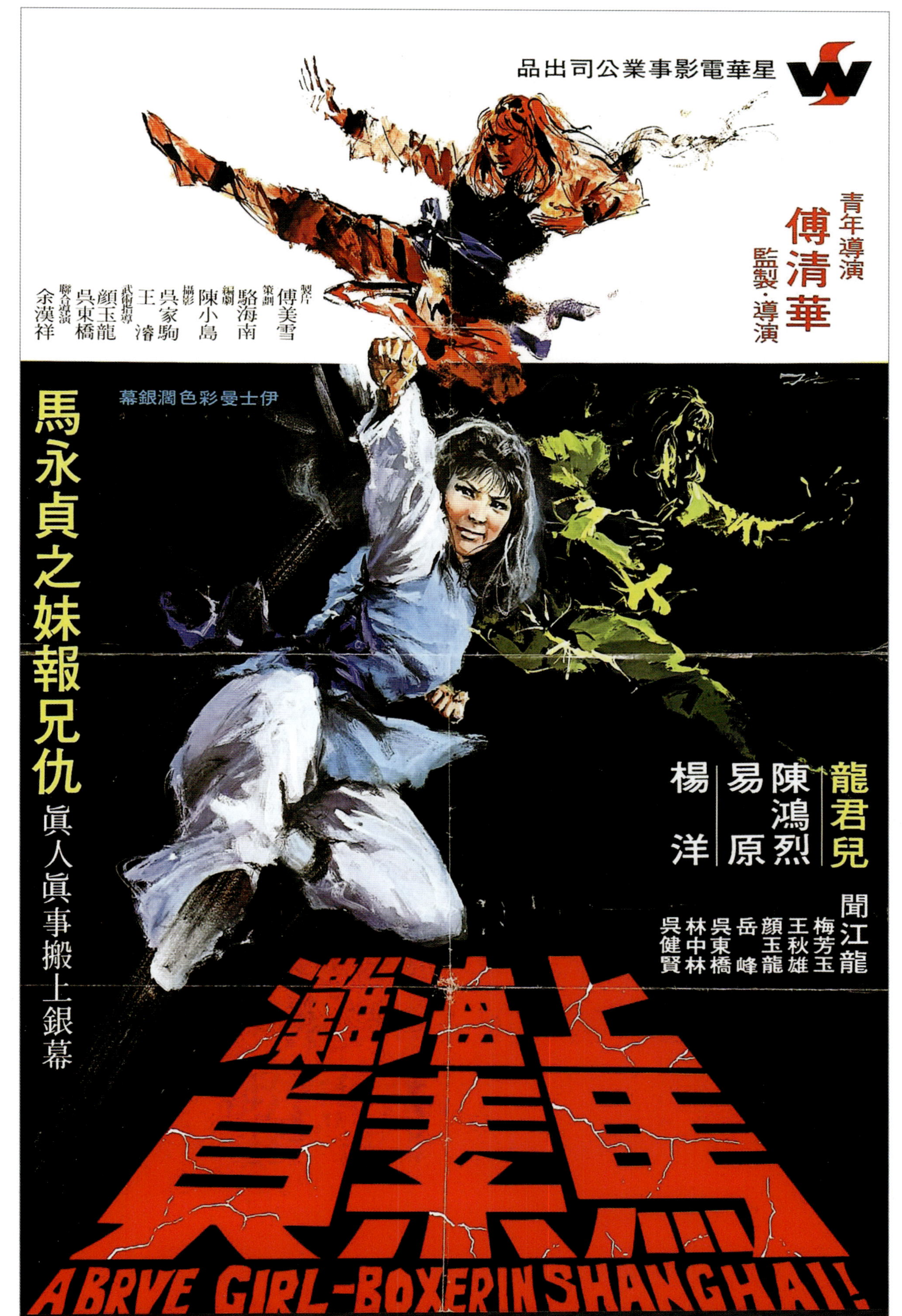
星華電影事業公司出品
青年導演
傅清華
監製‧導演
製片 傅美雪
策劃 駱海南
編劇 陳小島
攝影 吳家駒
王湷
武術指導 顏玉龍
吳東橋
聯合導演 余漢祥
伊士曼彩色潤銀幕
馬永貞之妹報兄仇
眞人眞事搬上銀幕
龍君兒
陳鴻烈
易原
楊洋
聞江龍
梅芳玉
王秋雄
顏玉龍
岳峰
吳東橋
林中林
吳健賢
上海灘
馬素貞
A BRVE GIRL-BOXER IN SHANGHAI!

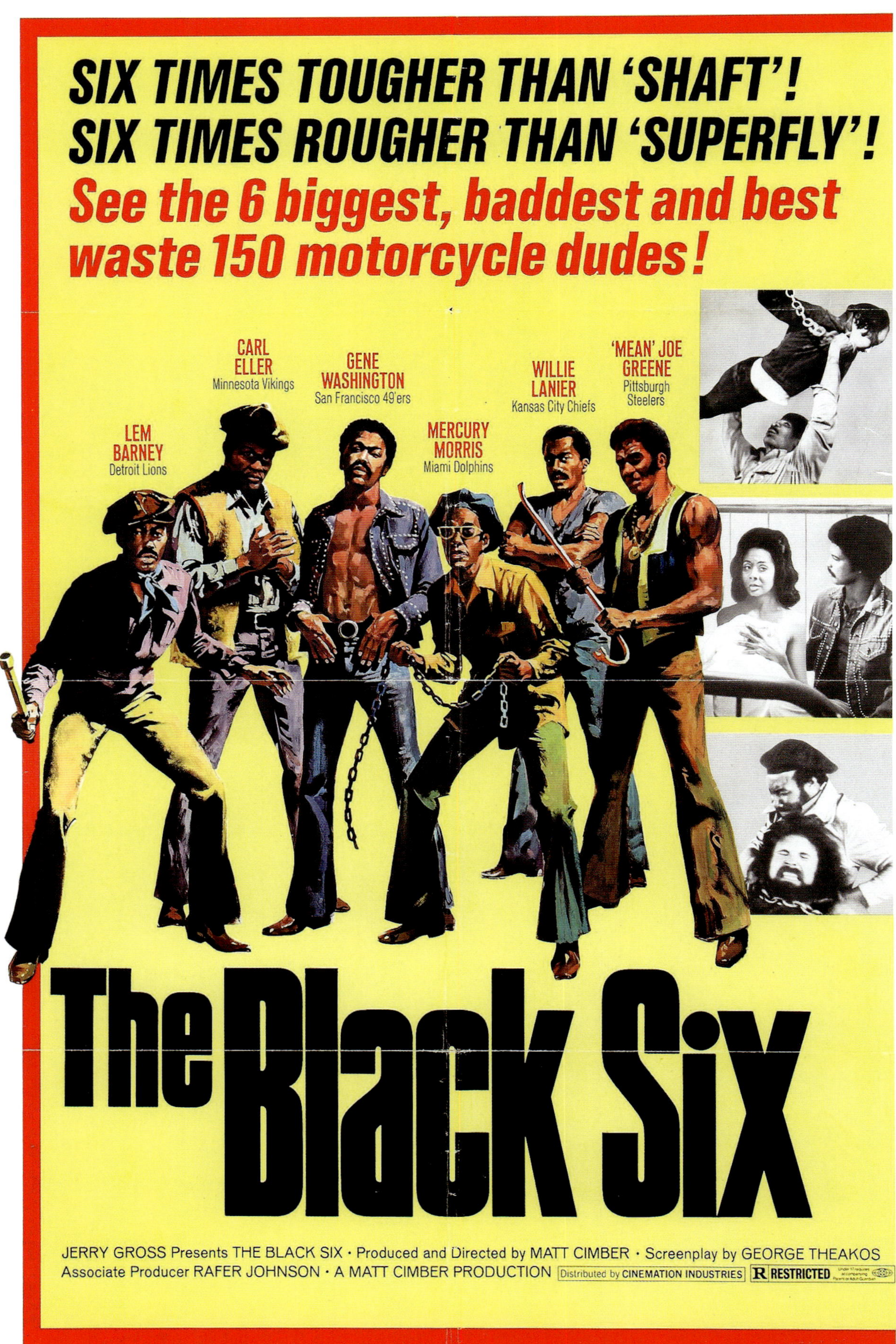
SIX TIMES TOUGHER THAN 'SHAFT'!
SIX TIMES ROUGHER THAN 'SUPERFLY'!
See the 6 biggest, baddest and best waste 150 motorcycle dudes!
CARL ELLER Minnesota Vikings
GENE WASHINGTON San Francisco 49'ers
WILLIE LANIER Kansas City Chiefs
'MEAN' JOE GREENE Pittsburgh Steelers
LEM BARNEY Detroit Lions
MERCURY MORRIS Miami Dolphins
The Black Six
JERRY GROSS Presents THE BLACK SIX · Produced and Directed by MATT CIMBER · Screenplay by GEORGE THEAKOS
Associate Producer RAFER JOHNSON · A MATT CIMBER PRODUCTION
Distributed by CINEMATION INDUSTRIES
R RESTRICTED

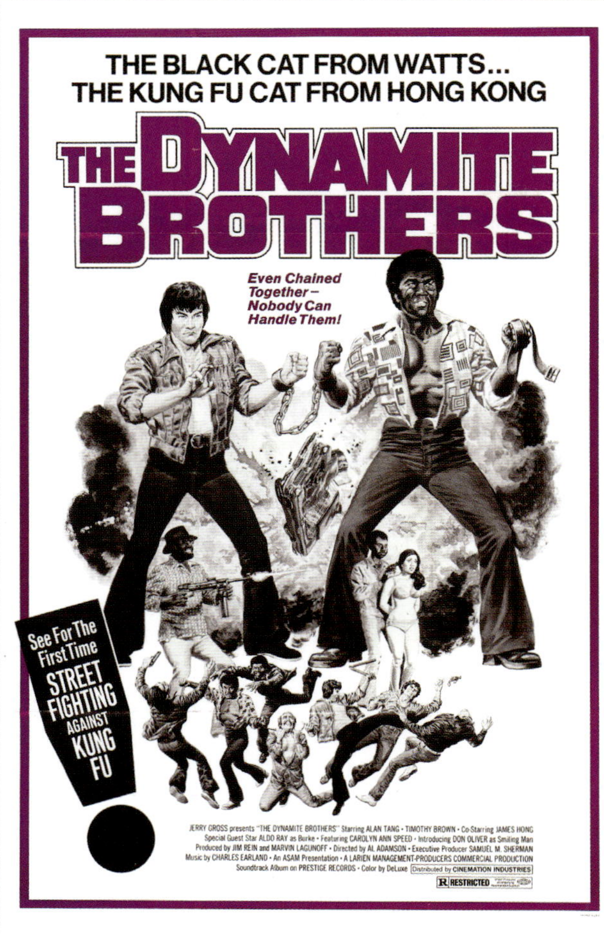

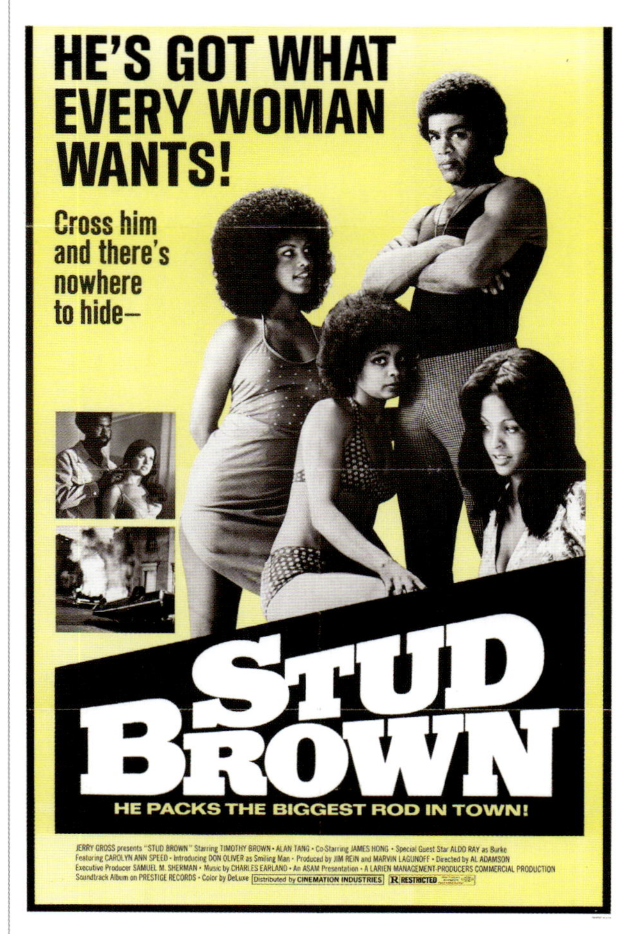

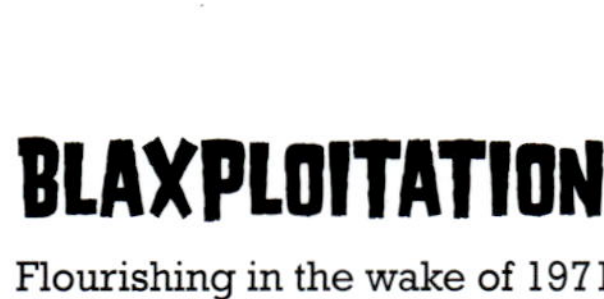

BLAXPLOITATION

Flourishing in the wake of 1971's smash hits *Sweet Sweetback's Baadasssss Song* and *Shaft*, blaxploitation was a subgenre milked by major studios and tiny independents alike. At the lower end of the budget scale, the posters were not always as slick, but they still got the message across: "He packs the biggest rod in town!" the one-sheet for *Stud Brown* points out somewhat superfluously, considering the bulge in Timothy Brown's pants. This is actually a later poster for the film originally released in 1974 as *Dynamite Brothers*, then marketed as the martial arts/blaxploitation crossover it actually is. Overleaf includes a selection from Fred Williamson, who as star, director, producer, and often writer of his movies, can perhaps be forgiven for not having time to notice that the poster for *Mean Johnny Barrows* (1976) misspells the names of co-stars Roddy McDowall and Elliott Gould.

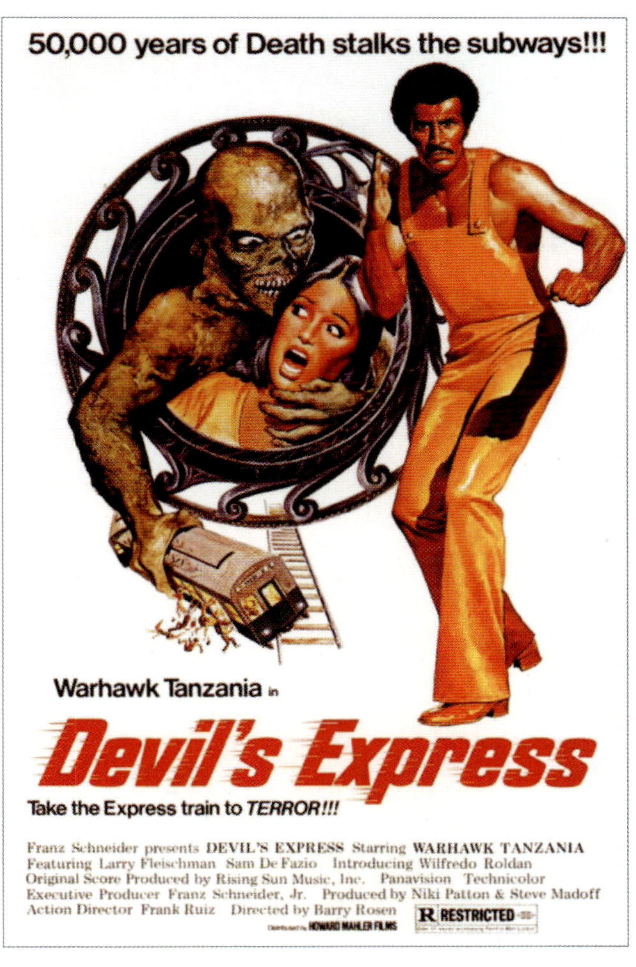

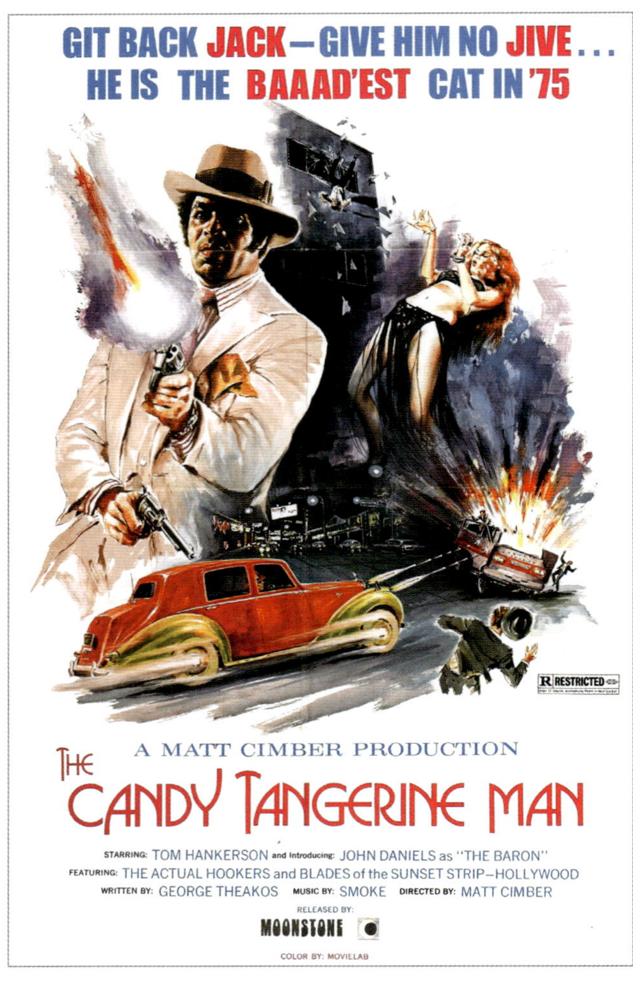
GIT BACK JACK—GIVE HIM NO JIVE . . .
HE IS THE BAAAD'EST CAT IN '75
R RESTRICTED
A MATT CIMBER PRODUCTION
THE CANDY TANGERINE MAN
STARRING: TOM HANKERSON and Introducing: JOHN DANIELS as "THE BARON"
FEATURING: THE ACTUAL HOOKERS and BLADES of the SUNSET STRIP—HOLLYWOOD
WRITTEN BY: GEORGE THEAKOS MUSIC BY: SMOKE DIRECTED BY: MATT CIMBER
RELEASED BY:
MOONSTONE
COLOR BY: MOVIELAB

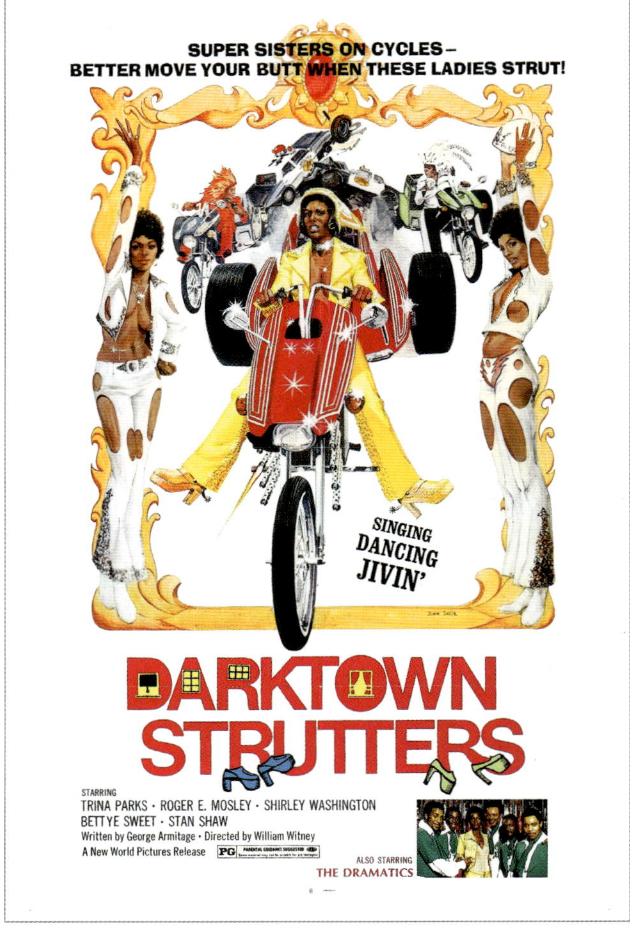
SUPER SISTERS ON CYCLES—
BETTER MOVE YOUR BUTT WHEN THESE LADIES STRUT!
SINGING
DANCING
JIVIN'
DARKTOWN
STRUTTERS
STARRING
TRINA PARKS · ROGER E. MOSLEY · SHIRLEY WASHINGTON
BETTYE SWEET · STAN SHAW
Written by George Armitage · Directed by William Witney
A New World Pictures Release
PG PARENTAL GUIDANCE SUGGESTED
ALSO STARRING
THE DRAMATICS

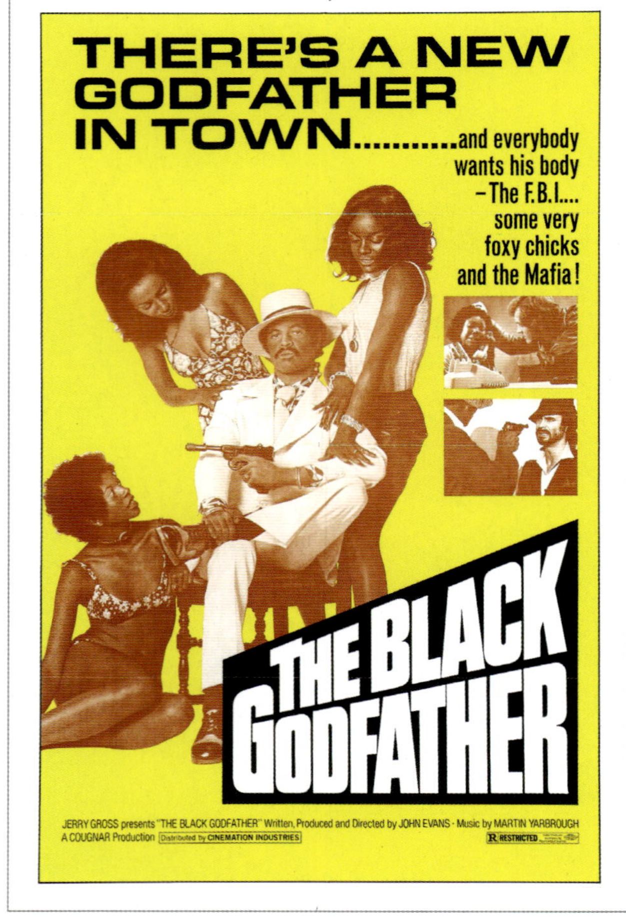
THERE'S A NEW
GODFATHER
IN TOWN..........and everybody
wants his body
–The F.B.I....
some very
foxy chicks
and the Mafia!
THE BLACK
GODFATHER
JERRY GROSS presents "THE BLACK GODFATHER" Written, Produced and Directed by JOHN EVANS · Music by MARTIN YARBROUGH
A COUGNAR Production
Distributed by CINEMATION INDUSTRIES
R RESTRICTED

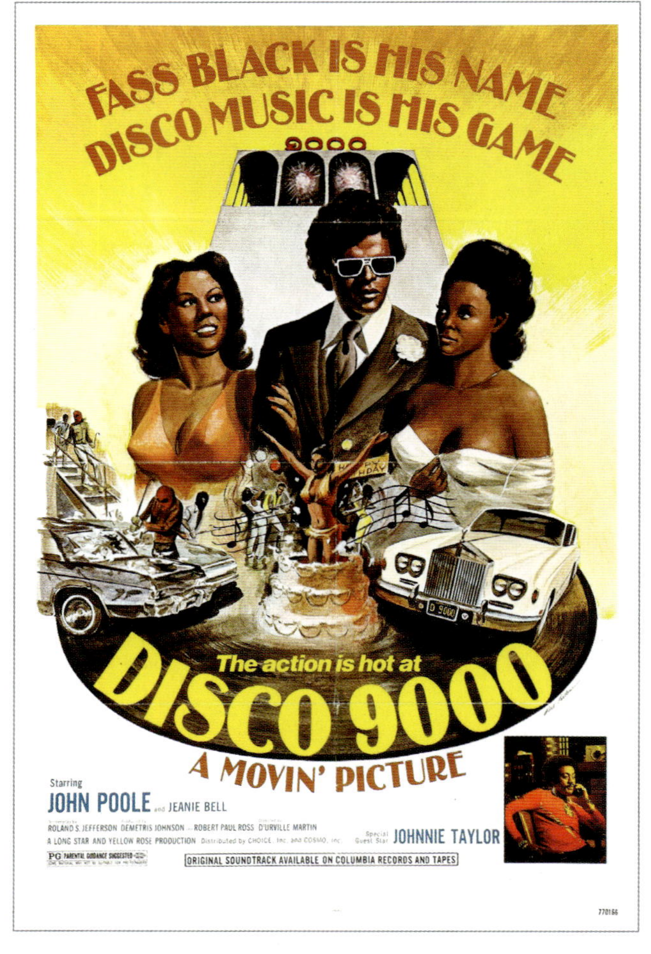
FASS BLACK IS HIS NAME
DISCO MUSIC IS HIS GAME
The action is hot at
DISCO 9000
A MOVIN' PICTURE
Starring
JOHN POOLE and JEANIE BELL
ROLAND S. JEFFERSON DEMETRIS JOHNSON ROBERT PAUL ROSS D'URVILLE MARTIN
A LONG STAR AND YELLOW ROSE PRODUCTION Distributed by CHOICE, Inc. and COSMO, Inc.
Special Guest Star JOHNNIE TAYLOR
PG PARENTAL GUIDANCE SUGGESTED
ORIGINAL SOUNDTRACK AVAILABLE ON COLUMBIA RECORDS AND TAPES
770166

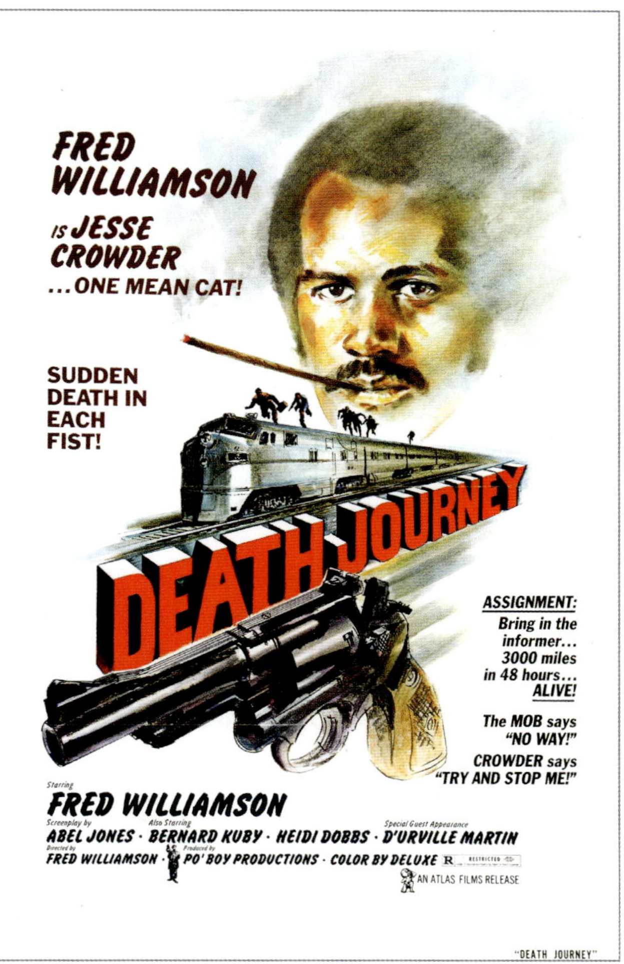
FRED WILLIAMSON
IS JESSE CROWDER
...ONE MEAN CAT!
SUDDEN DEATH IN EACH FIST!
DEATH JOURNEY
ASSIGNMENT:
Bring in the informer... 3000 miles in 48 hours... ALIVE!
The MOB says "NO WAY!"
CROWDER says "TRY AND STOP ME!"
FRED WILLIAMSON
ABEL JONES · BERNARD KUBY · HEIDI DOBBS · D'URVILLE MARTIN
FRED WILLIAMSON · PO' BOY PRODUCTIONS · COLOR BY DELUXE
AN ATLAS FILMS RELEASE
"DEATH JOURNEY"

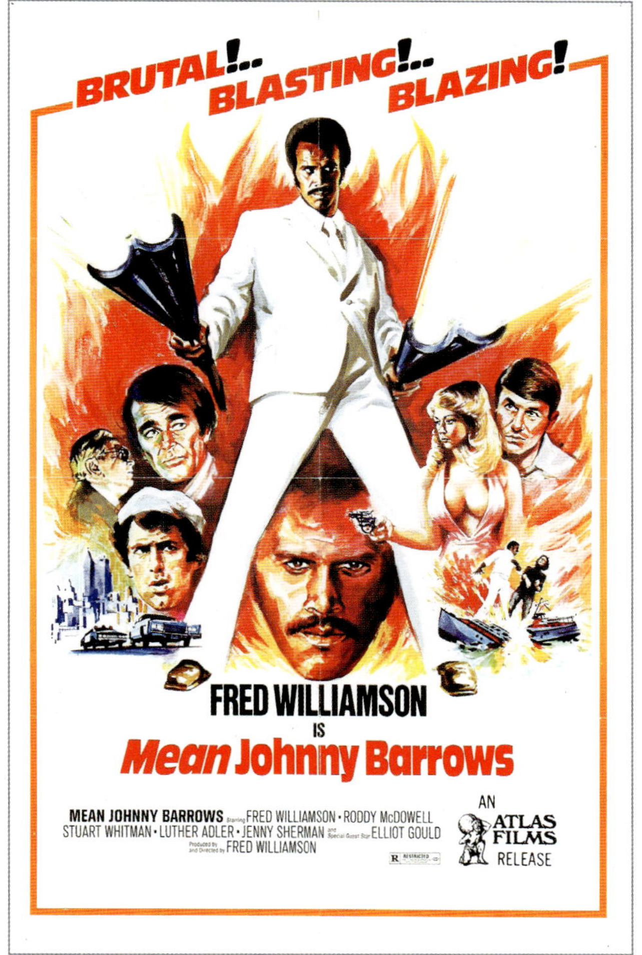
BRUTAL!.. BLASTING!.. BLAZING!
FRED WILLIAMSON
IS
Mean Johnny Barrows
MEAN JOHNNY BARROWS FRED WILLIAMSON · RODDY McDOWELL
STUART WHITMAN · LUTHER ADLER · JENNY SHERMAN ELLIOT GOULD
FRED WILLIAMSON
AN ATLAS FILMS RELEASE

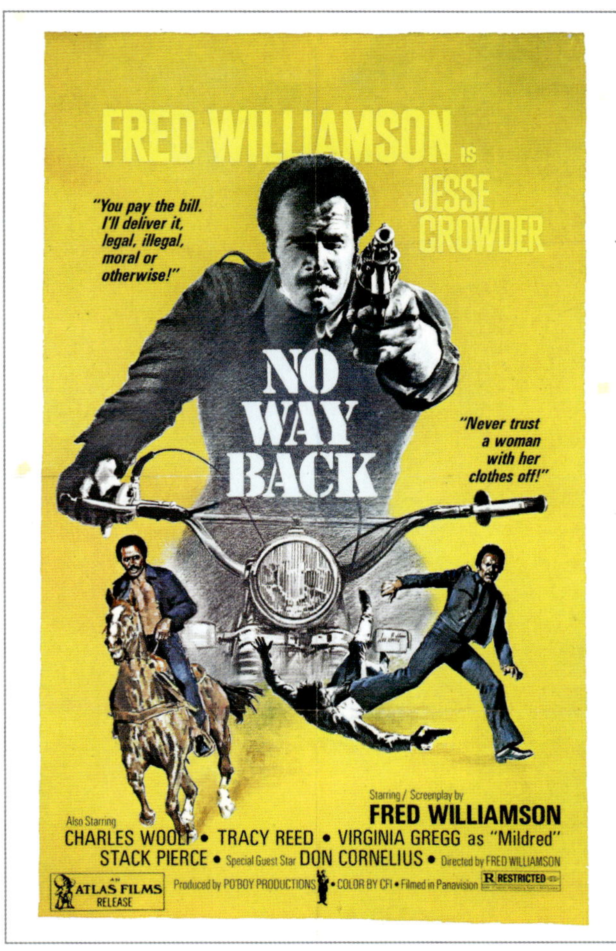
FRED WILLIAMSON IS
JESSE CROWDER
"You pay the bill. I'll deliver it, legal, illegal, moral or otherwise!"
NO WAY BACK
"Never trust a woman with her clothes off!"
Starring / Screenplay by
FRED WILLIAMSON
Also Starring
CHARLES WOOLF • TRACY REED • VIRGINIA GREGG as "Mildred"
STACK PIERCE • Special Guest Star DON CORNELIUS • Directed by FRED WILLIAMSON
ATLAS FILMS RELEASE
Produced by PO'BOY PRODUCTIONS · COLOR BY CFI · Filmed in Panavision
R RESTRICTED

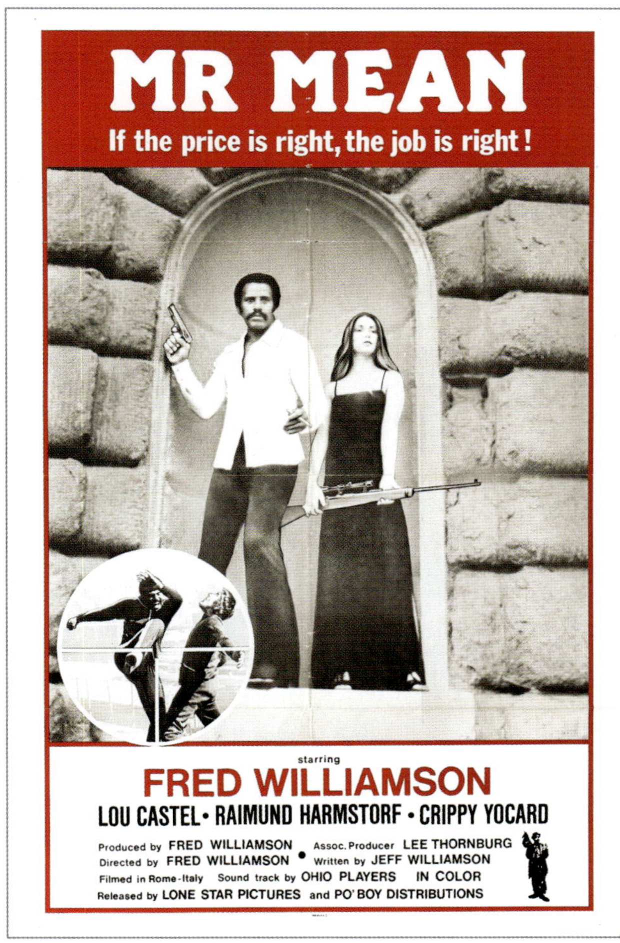
MR MEAN
If the price is right, the job is right!
starring
FRED WILLIAMSON
LOU CASTEL · RAIMUND HARMSTORF · CRIPPY YOCARD
Produced by FRED WILLIAMSON Assoc. Producer LEE THORNBURG
Directed by FRED WILLIAMSON • Written by JEFF WILLIAMSON
Filmed in Rome-Italy Sound track by OHIO PLAYERS IN COLOR
Released by LONE STAR PICTURES and PO' BOY DISTRIBUTIONS

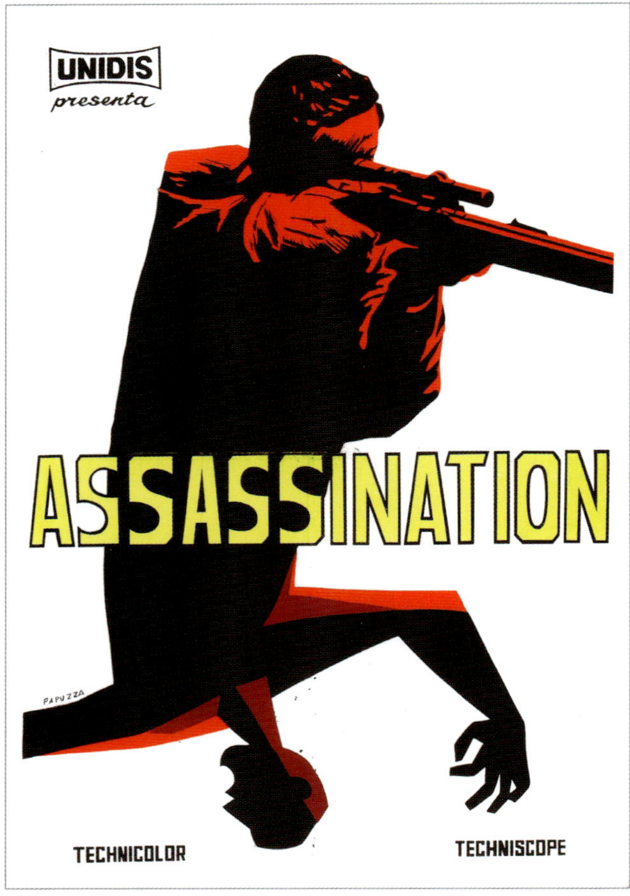

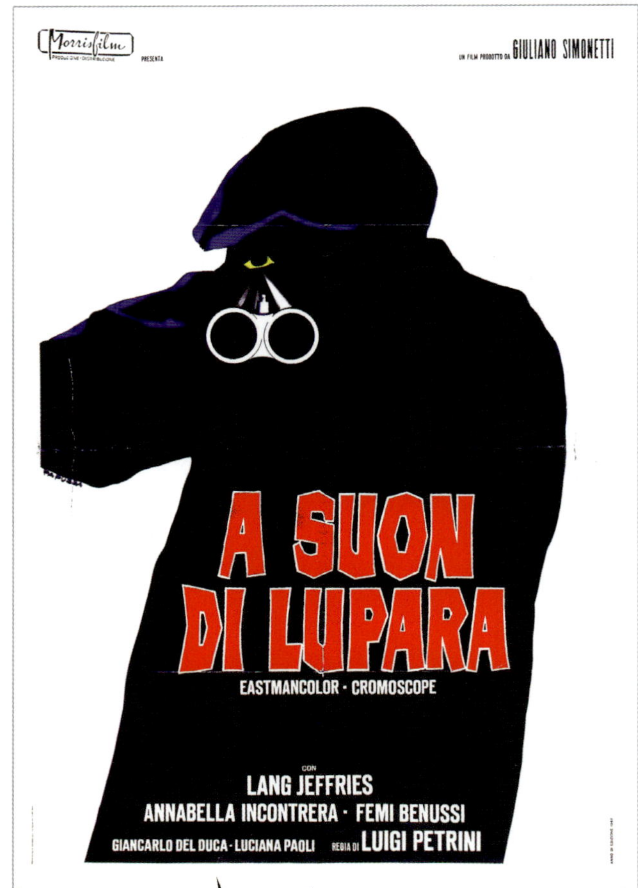

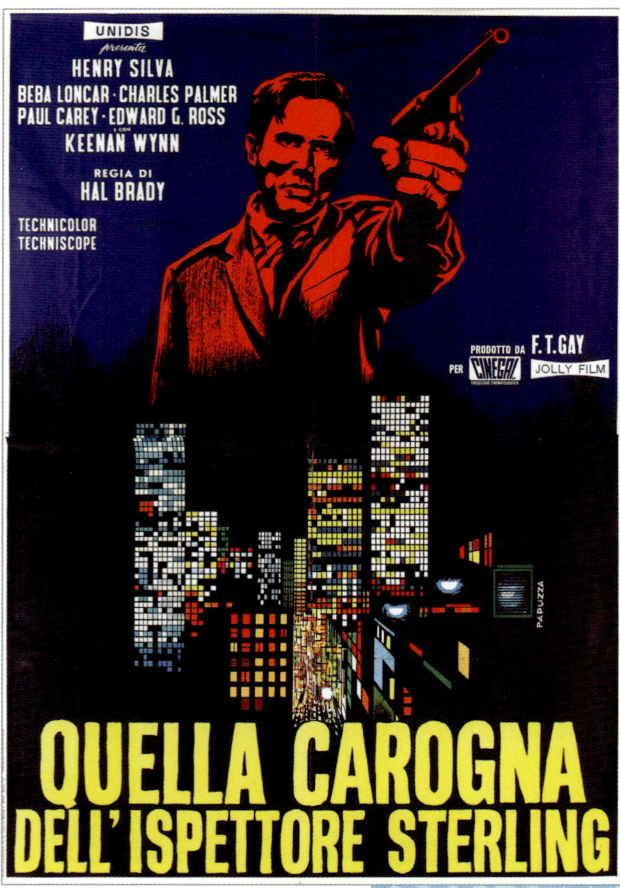

EURO CRIME

Like their Spaghetti Western counterparts, the tough, Italian-produced crime/police thrillers known as *poliziotteschi* have a style all of their own. The same goes for their domestic posters. Artist Michelangelo Papuzza uses a graphically stripped back but very effective approach in the three examples of his work seen here. The star of both *Assassination* (1967) and *Quella carogna dell'ispettore Sterling* (aka *The Falling Man,* 1968) was Henry Silva, an American actor typecast in villainous roles who had a good reason to work with foreigners: "Funny thing," he once told a US reporter, "over here they see me as a bad guy; in Europe they see me as a hero." The uncredited art for 1976's *Roma a mano armata* is suitably over the top. At one point in the film, the hunchback with the machine gun (played by Tomas Milian) is forced to swallow a bullet by the detective hero (Maurizio Merli). After nature takes its course, the hunchback retrieves the projectile and vows to shoot the detective in the face with it. Nice.

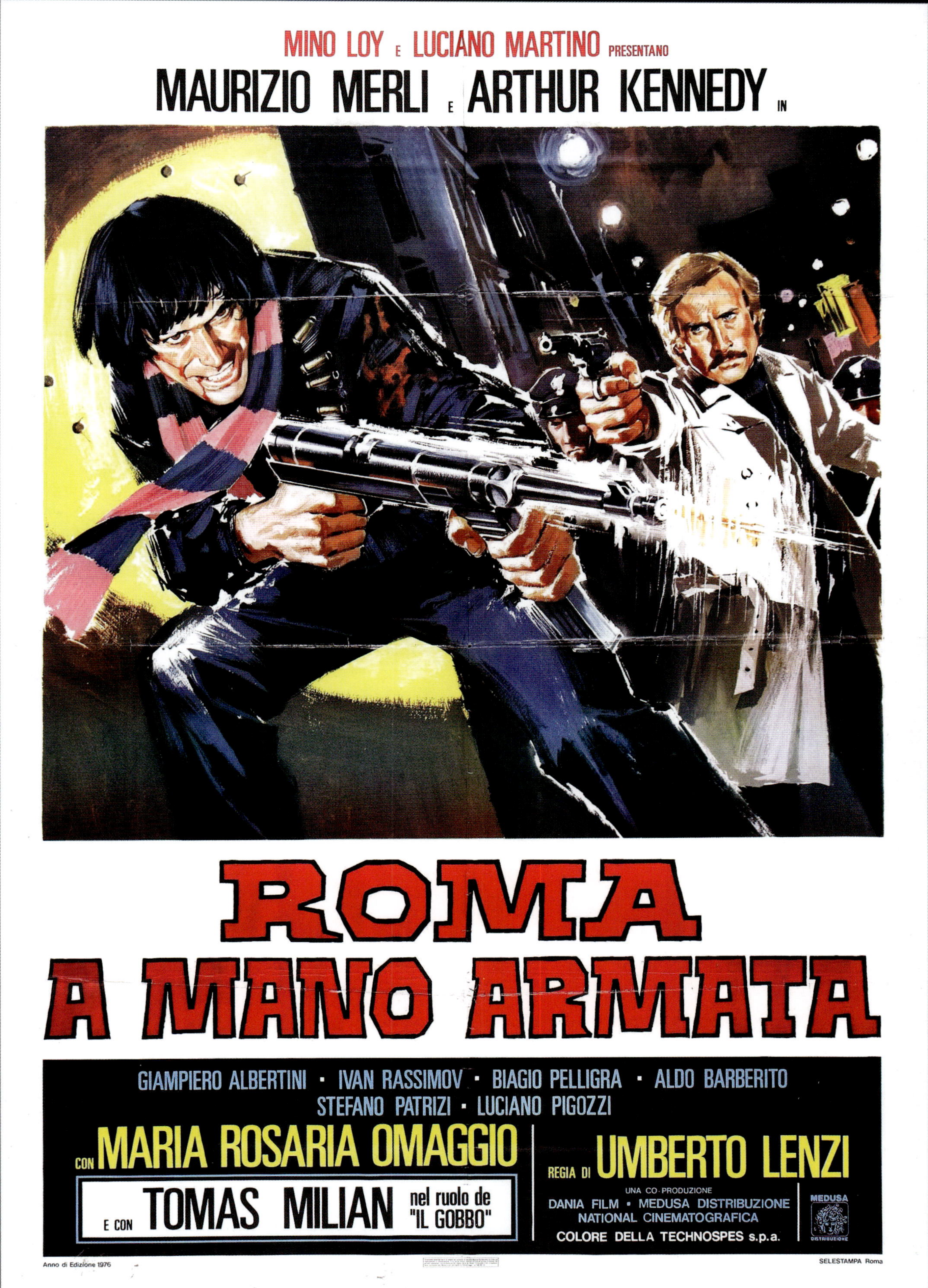

MINO LOY e LUCIANO MARTINO PRESENTANO

MAURIZIO MERLI e ARTHUR KENNEDY in

ROMA A MANO ARMATA

GIAMPIERO ALBERTINI · IVAN RASSIMOV · BIAGIO PELLIGRA · ALDO BARBERITO
STEFANO PATRIZI · LUCIANO PIGOZZI

con MARIA ROSARIA OMAGGIO

e con TOMAS MILIAN nel ruolo de "IL GOBBO"

regia di UMBERTO LENZI

UNA CO-PRODUZIONE
DANIA FILM · MEDUSA DISTRIBUZIONE
NATIONAL CINEMATOGRAFICA
COLORE DELLA TECHNOSPES s.p.a.

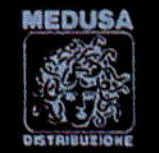

Anno di Edizione 1976

SELESTAMPA Roma

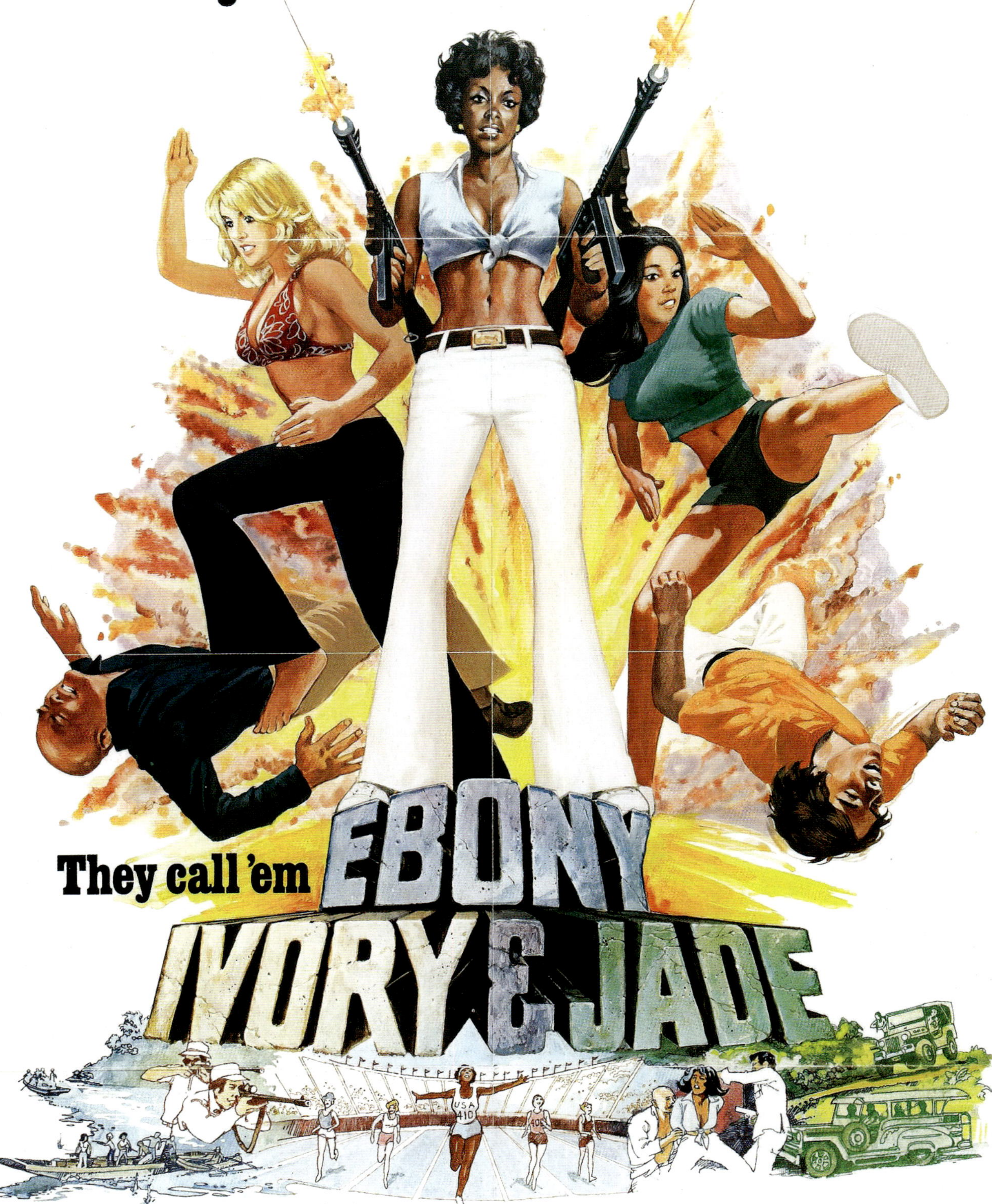
3 Foxy Mama's Turned Loose...
They call 'em
EBONY IVORY & JADE
They Can Lick Any Man Ever Made!
Starring
ROSANNE KATON • COLLEEN CAMP • SYLVIA ANDERSON
Story and Screenplay by HENRY BARNES • Music by EDDIE NOVA • Produced and Directed by CIRIO H. SANTIAGO
COLOR A DIMENSION PICTURES Release PG
© 1976 Dimension Pictures Inc.
PARENTAL GUIDANCE SUGGESTED

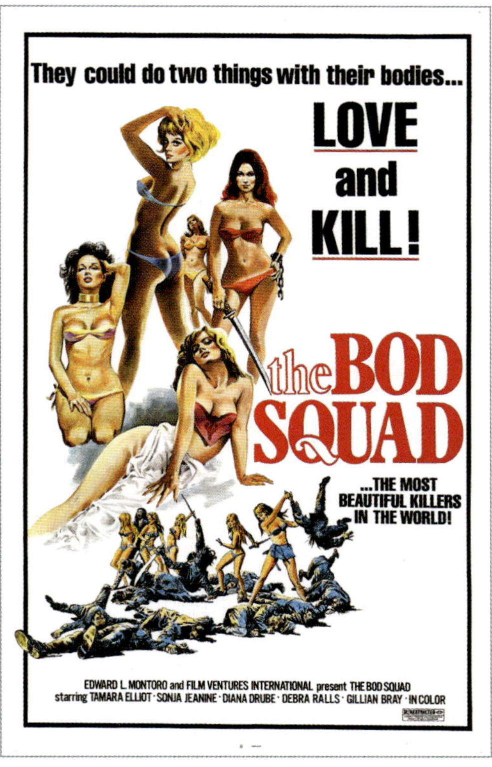

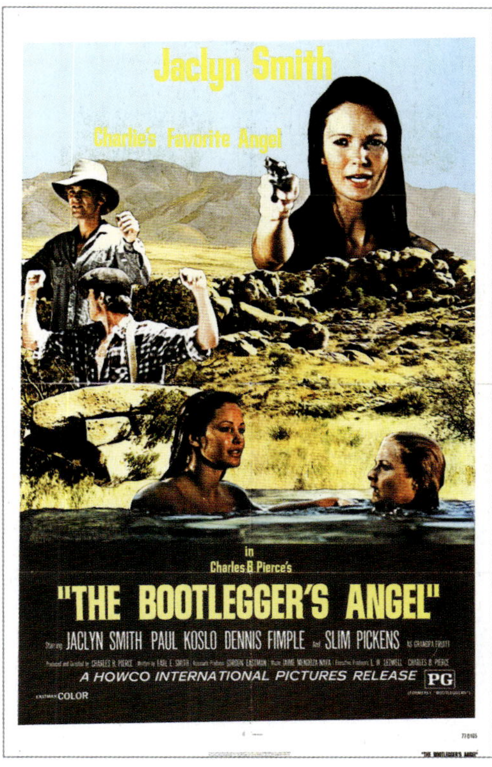

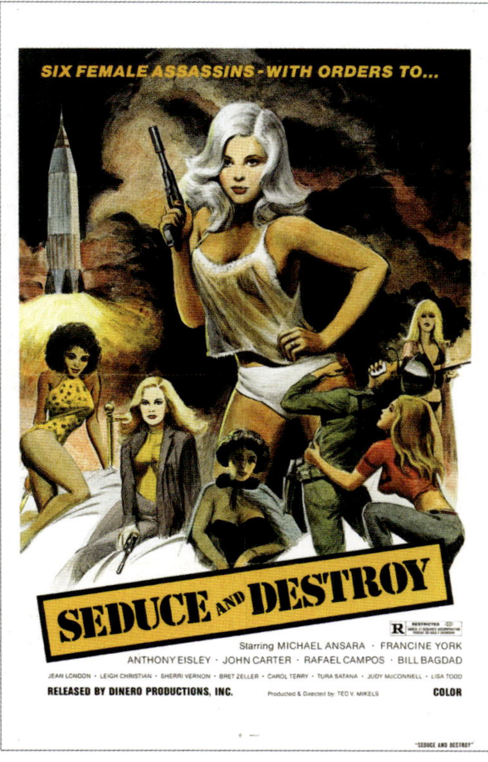

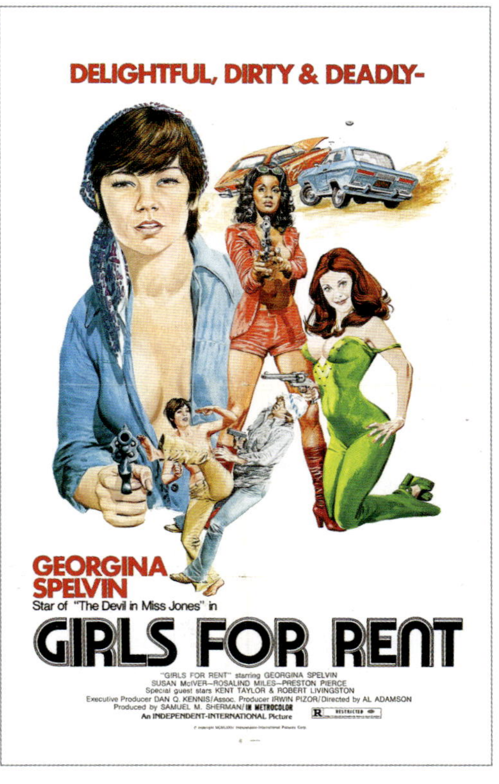

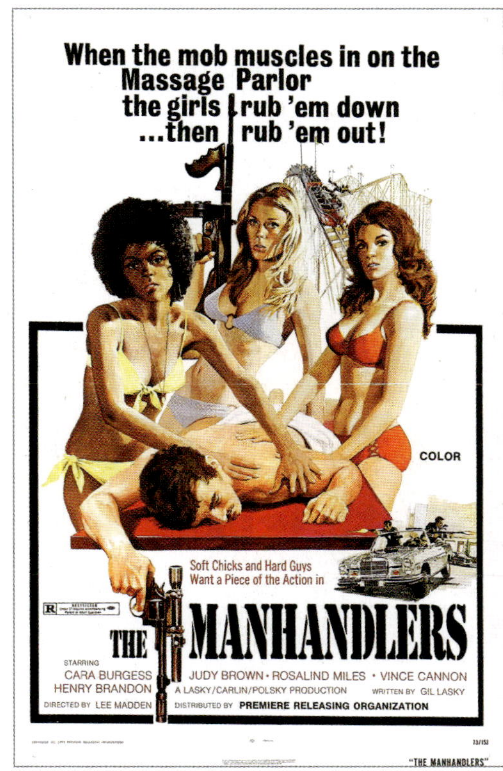

BEFORE CHARLIE'S ANGELS

There are several "girl team" exploitation movies that can be seen as possible inspirations for that landmark of jiggle television, *Charlie's Angels* (1976–81). Ted V. Mikels's *The Doll Squad* (aka *Seduce and Destroy*, 1973) even featured a lead character called Sabrina, like Kate Jackson's in the show. Mikels's *Squad* was certainly an influence on Tarantino's Deadly Viper Assassination Squad in *Kill Bill*, and that film's memorable tagline, "A roaring rampage of revenge," was first heard in the trailer for another *Angels* antecedent, 1976's *Ebony, Ivory & Jade*. The moonshine comedy *Bootleggers* (1974) had nothing to do with a girl team, but it did boast Angel-to-be Jaclyn Smith in a supporting role, leading to a blatant cash-in re-release in 1977 as *The Bootlegger's Angel*, with Smith top-billed on the poster.

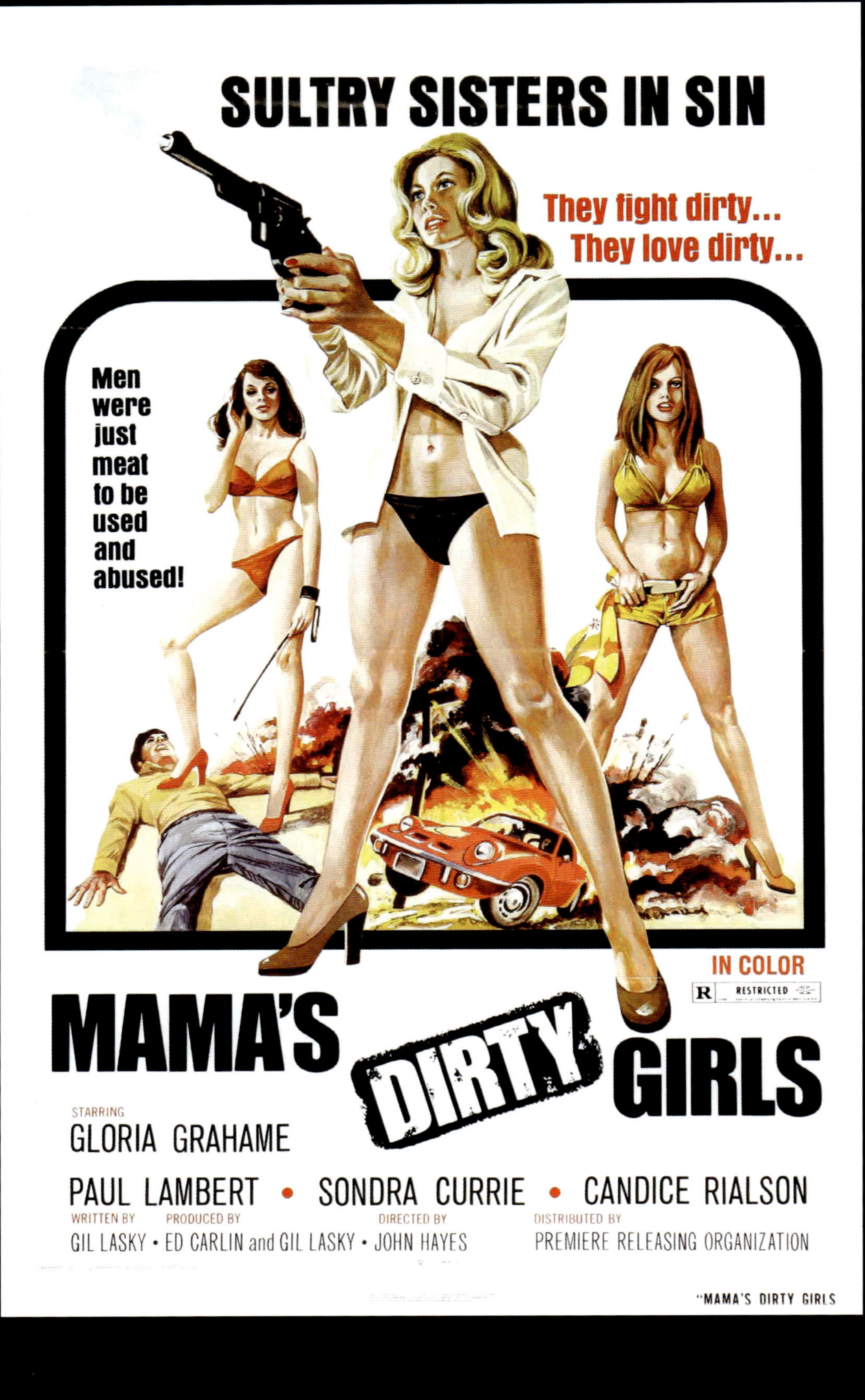

SULTRY SISTERS IN SIN

They fight dirty...
They love dirty...

Men were just meat to be used and abused!

IN COLOR

R RESTRICTED

MAMA'S DIRTY GIRLS

STARRING
GLORIA GRAHAME

PAUL LAMBERT • SONDRA CURRIE • CANDICE RIALSON

WRITTEN BY GIL LASKY • PRODUCED BY ED CARLIN and GIL LASKY • DIRECTED BY JOHN HAYES

DISTRIBUTED BY PREMIERE RELEASING ORGANIZATION

"MAMA'S DIRTY GIRLS

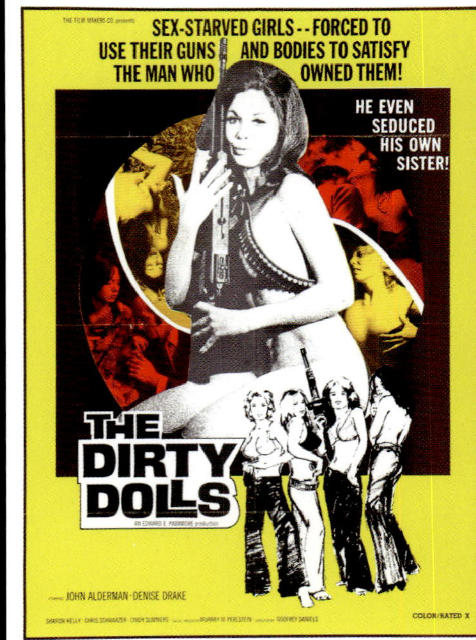

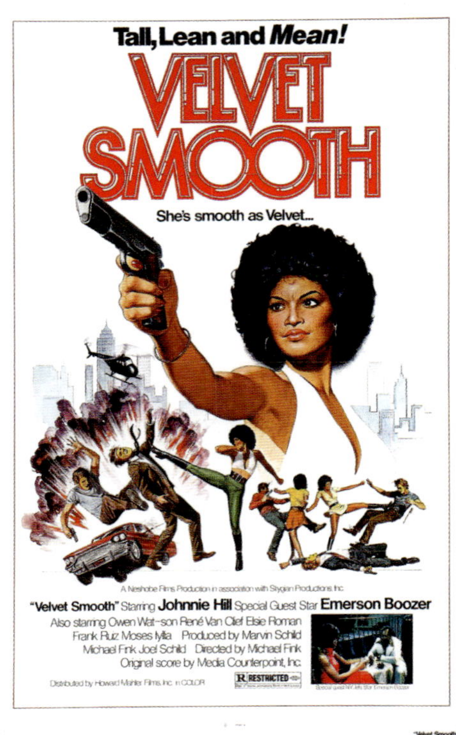

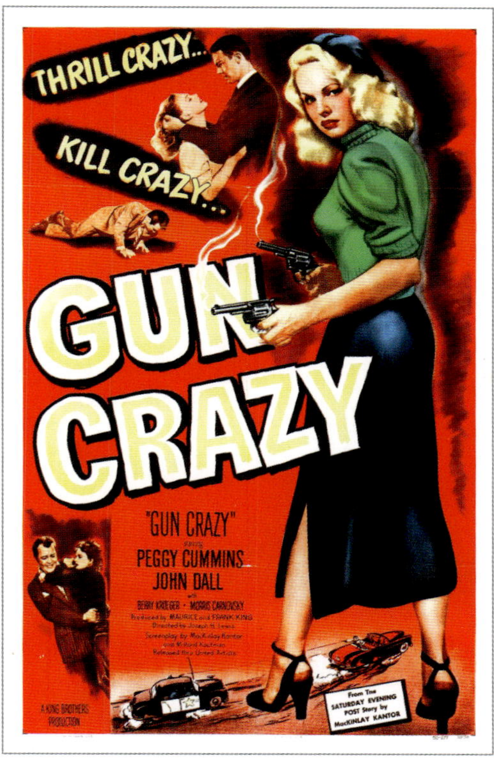

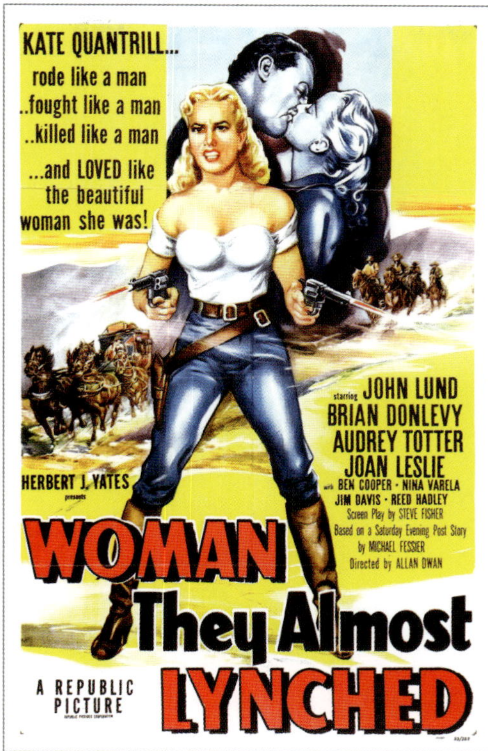

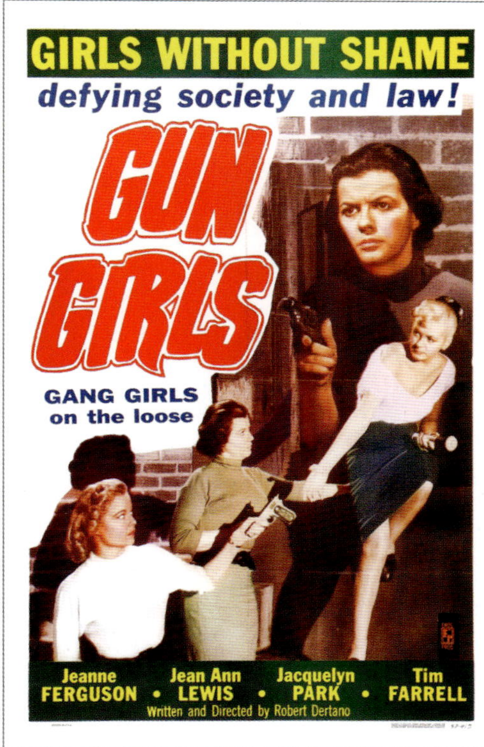

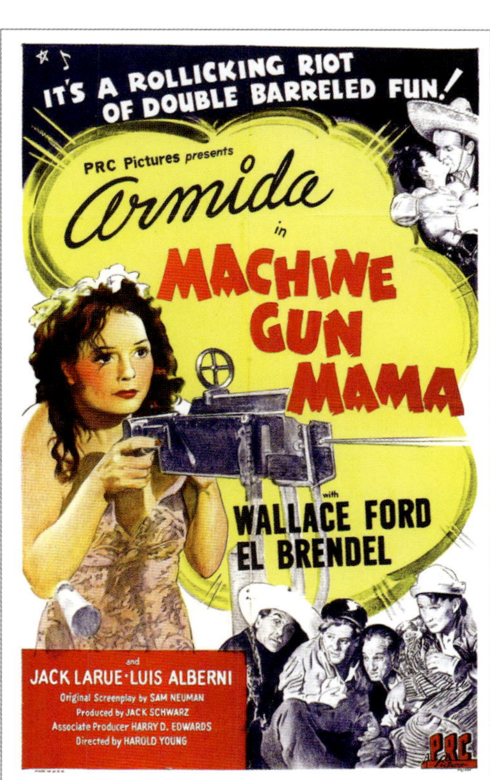

GIRLS WITH GUNS

It doesn't take Sigmund Freud to point out that a girl caressing a big, powerful gun is a loaded image. Women and weaponry on screen has been a potent combination since the earliest days of Westerns and noir, and when Clint Eastwood's turn as trigger-happy cop Harry Callahan added the word "dirty" into the mix, you can't blame filmmakers for jumping on it. The one-sheet for *Mama's Dirty Girls* (1974) apes both Clint's pose and the .44 Magnum from *Dirty Harry*'s poster (though strictly the arms should be straight and knees bent if you want to avoid being blown backward off your feet while smashing yourself in the face with the gun when it goes off). The poster for the X-rated *The Dirty Dolls* (1973) simply leaves very little to the imagination.

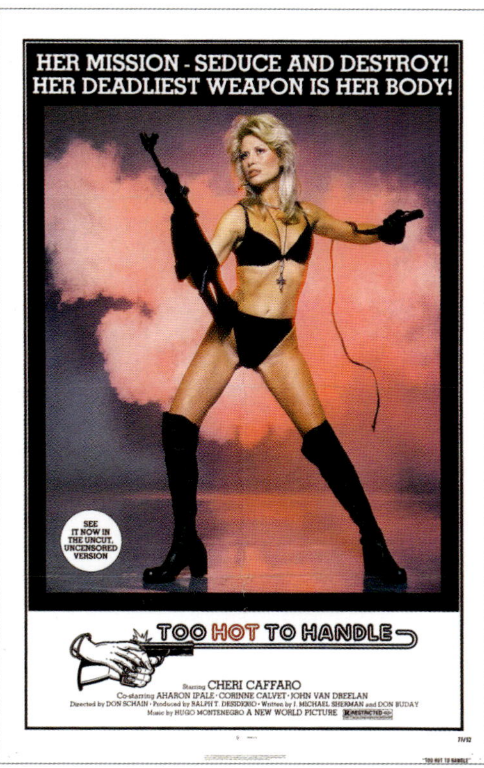

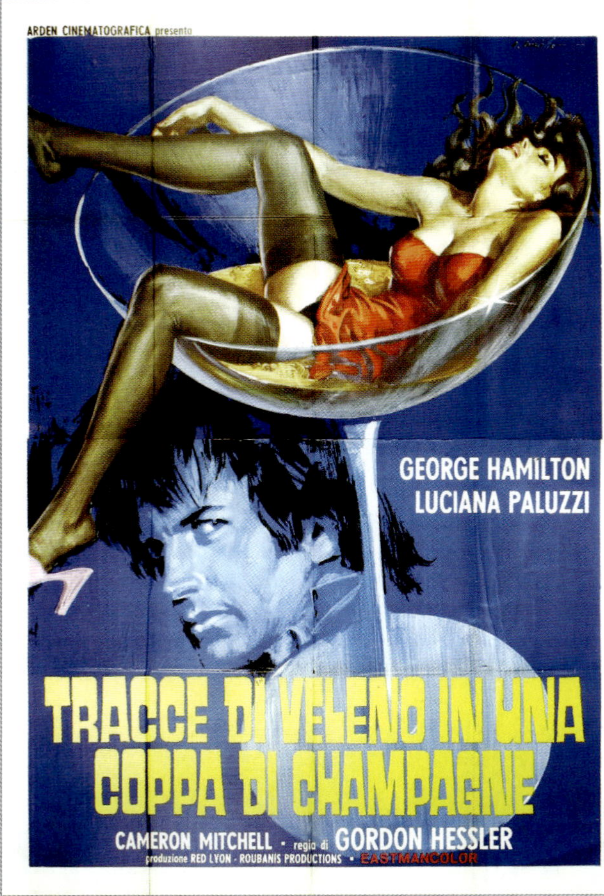

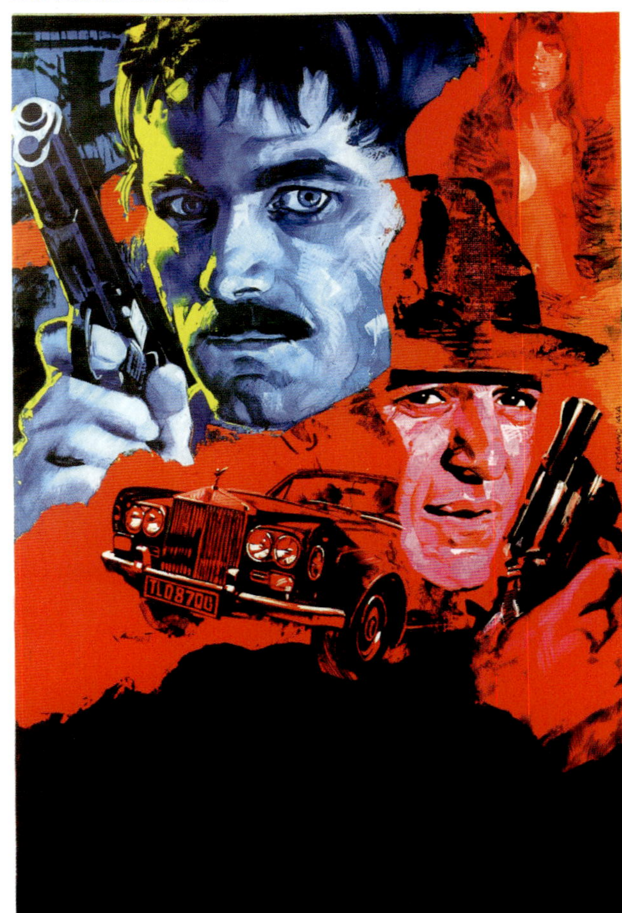

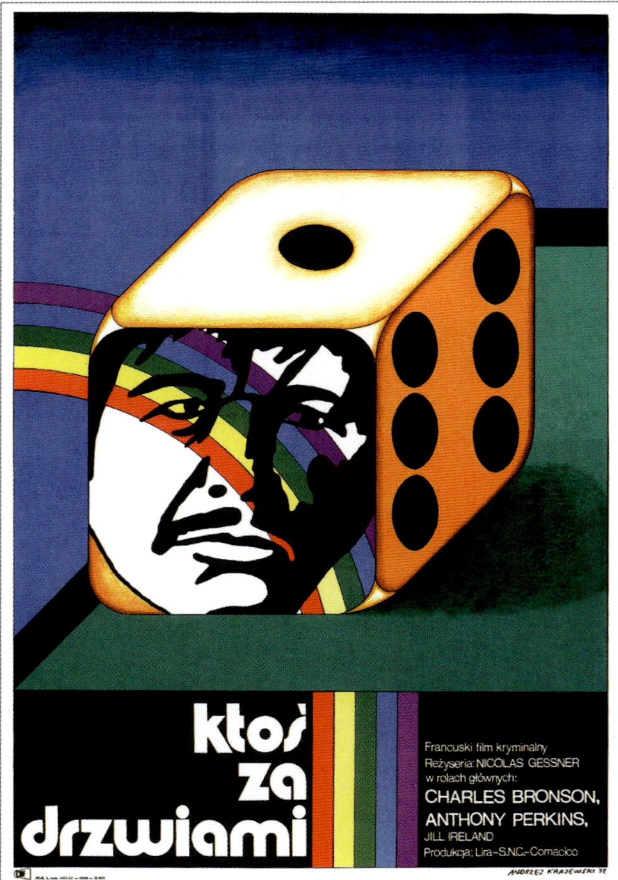

NICE POSTER, SHAME ABOUT THE FILM

Never judge a book by its cover, or a film by its poster. Presented here are both the eye-catching US one-sheet and Andrzej Krajewski's fabulous Polish design for *Someone Behind the Door* (1971), a plodding suspenser that despite being re-released as both *Two Minds for Murder* and *Brainkill*, remains a poorly received and now largely forgotten entry in Charles Bronson's filmography. Similarly, Ermanno Iaia's excellent poster for *Senza ragione* (aka *Redneck*, 1973) won't change the fact that this Italian-British cop thriller is far from Telly Savalas's finest hour. A. Giniello's evocative art on the *quattro fogli* for *Medusa* (1973) takes its inspiration from the Italian title, which translates as "Traces of poison in a glass of champagne," with a variation on the "girl in a giant glass" idea that's been around for over a century. Sadly, there's nothing remotely as exciting on screen in the actual film, shot in Greece and produced by its star. One recent online critic summarized his thoughts in the title of his review: "Please Make George Hamilton Go Away."

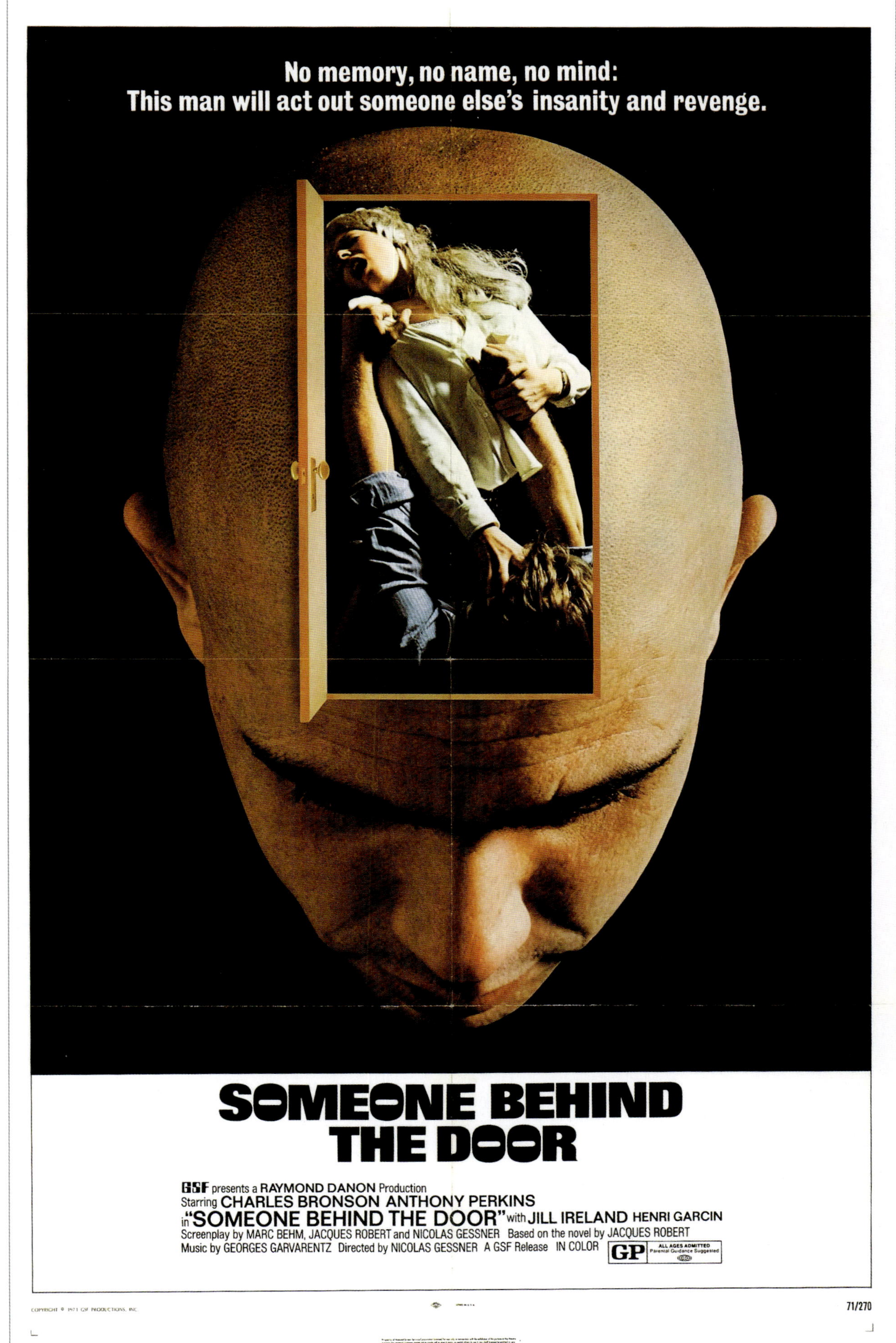
No memory, no name, no mind:
This man will act out someone else's insanity and revenge.
SOMEONE BEHIND THE DOOR
GSF presents a RAYMOND DANON Production
Starring CHARLES BRONSON ANTHONY PERKINS
in "SOMEONE BEHIND THE DOOR" with JILL IRELAND HENRI GARCIN
Screenplay by MARC BEHM, JACQUES ROBERT and NICOLAS GESSNER Based on the novel by JACQUES ROBERT
Music by GEORGES GARVARENTZ Directed by NICOLAS GESSNER A GSF Release IN COLOR
GP
ALL AGES ADMITTED
Parental Guidance Suggested
COPYRIGHT © 1971 GSF PRODUCTIONS, INC.
71/270

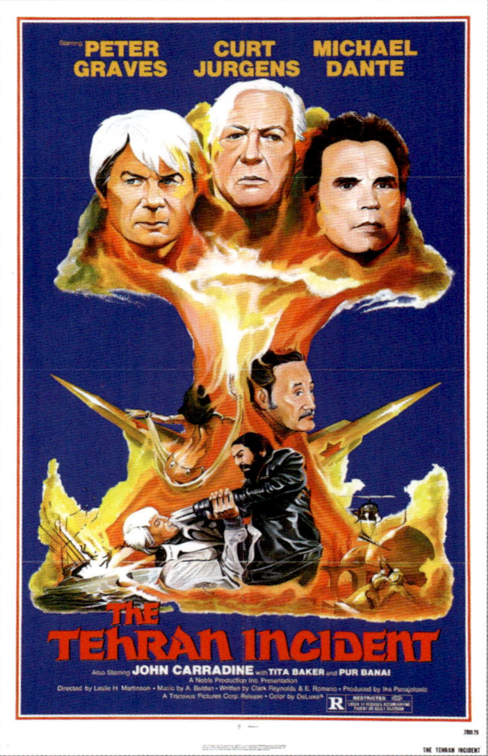

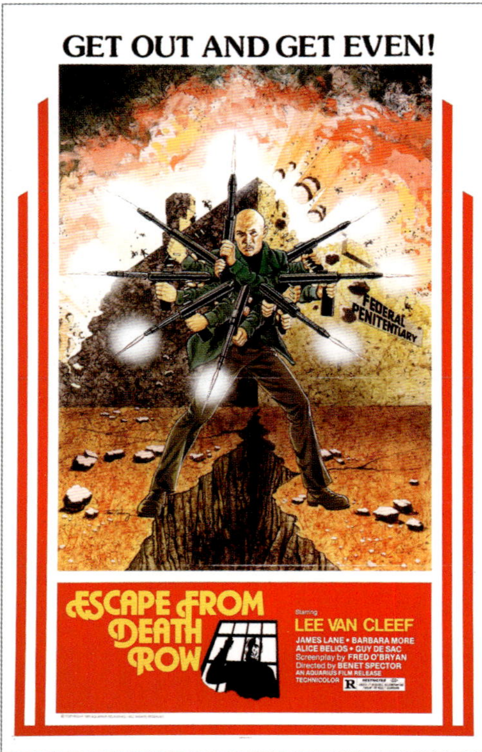

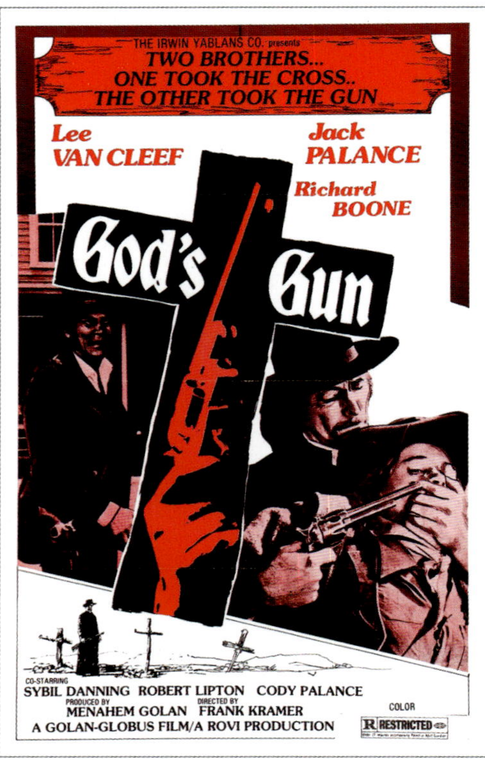

YOU MAY REMEMBER ME FROM

It could be that there's a gap in their schedule and they really like to work. It's more likely that Hollywood has stopped calling, or they have an urgent tax bill. That's when "big" names of yesteryear end up in low-budget exploitation movies, often for European filmmakers. "Ursula Andress's biggest role since James Bond!" trumpets the poster for the Italian production *Africa Express* (1975), just in case viewers couldn't place the name, 13 years after *Dr. No*. Yul Brynner gets top billing in *Death Rage* (1976, another Italian film, represented here by its Danish poster), while fellow import Martin Balsam gets his name printed slightly higher than his European co-stars, in a box. A triumph for the negotiation skills of Balsam's agent, but it just ends up looking like sloppy design.

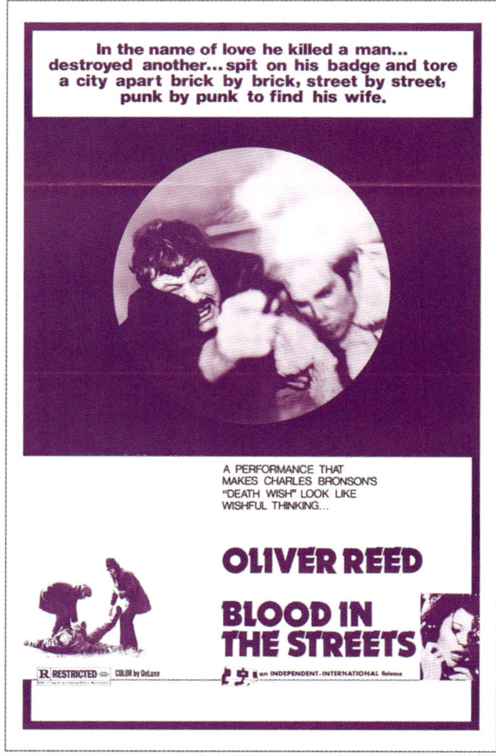

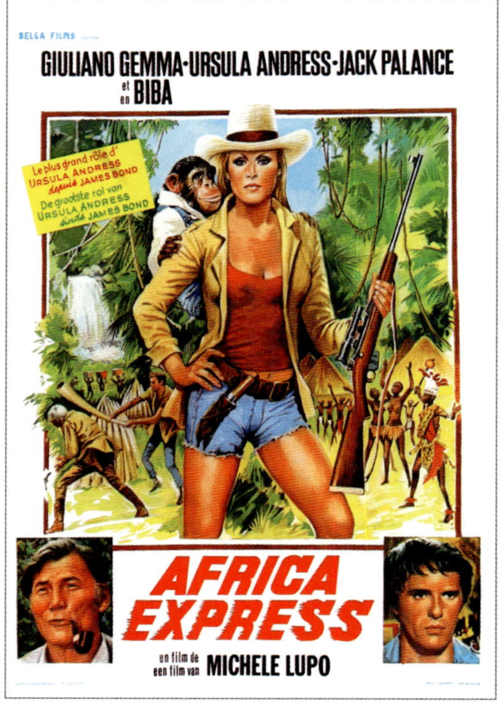

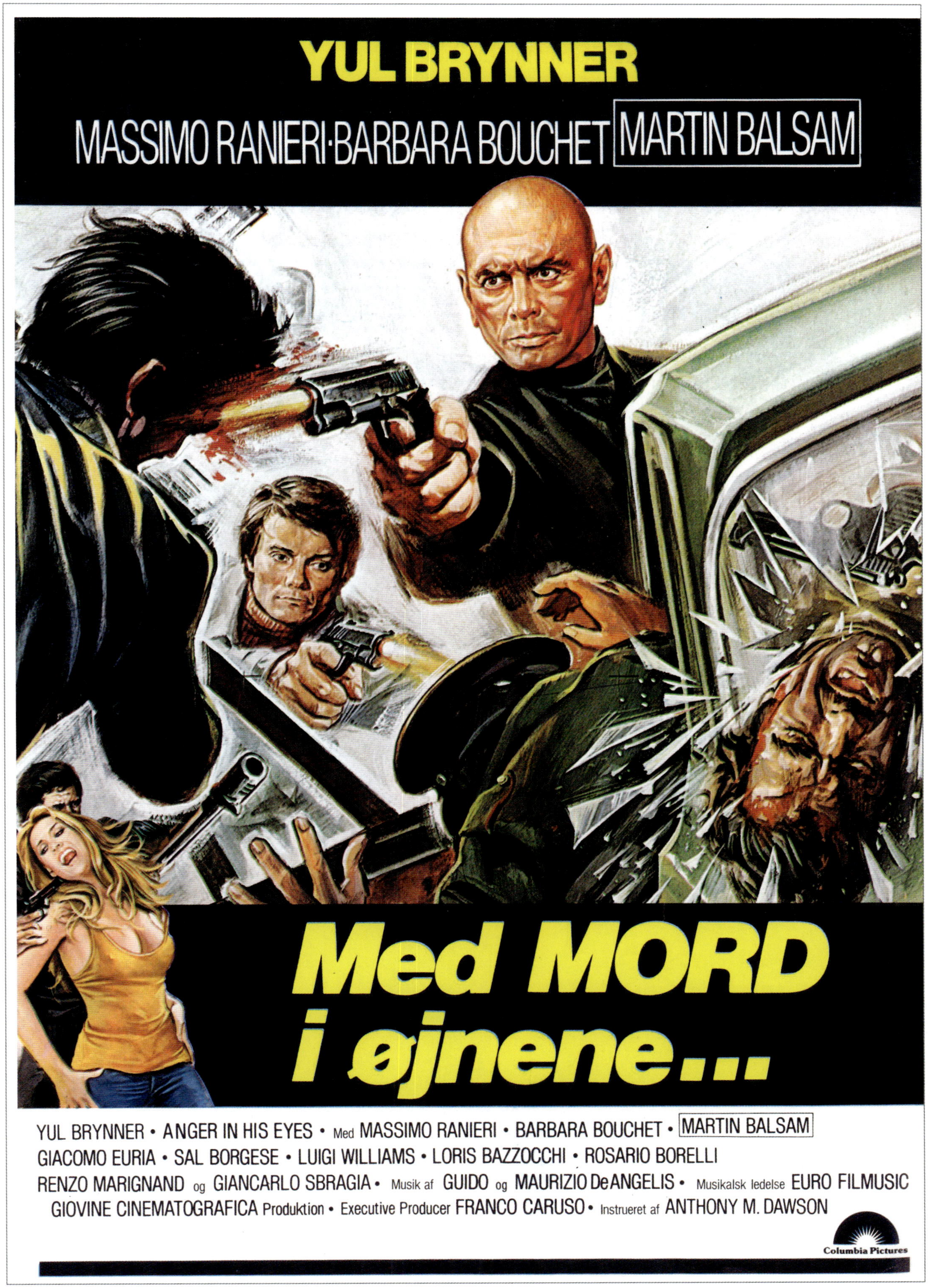

YUL BRYNNER

MASSIMO RANIERI·BARBARA BOUCHET MARTIN BALSAM

Med MORD i øjnene...

YUL BRYNNER • ANGER IN HIS EYES • Med MASSIMO RANIERI • BARBARA BOUCHET • MARTIN BALSAM
GIACOMO EURIA • SAL BORGESE • LUIGI WILLIAMS • LORIS BAZZOCCHI • ROSARIO BORELLI
RENZO MARIGNAND og GIANCARLO SBRAGIA • Musik af GUIDO og MAURIZIO De ANGELIS • Musikalsk ledelse EURO FILMUSIC
GIOVINE CINEMATOGRAFICA Produktion • Executive Producer FRANCO CARUSO • Instrueret af ANTHONY M. DAWSON

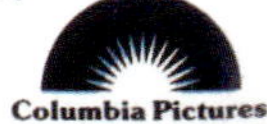

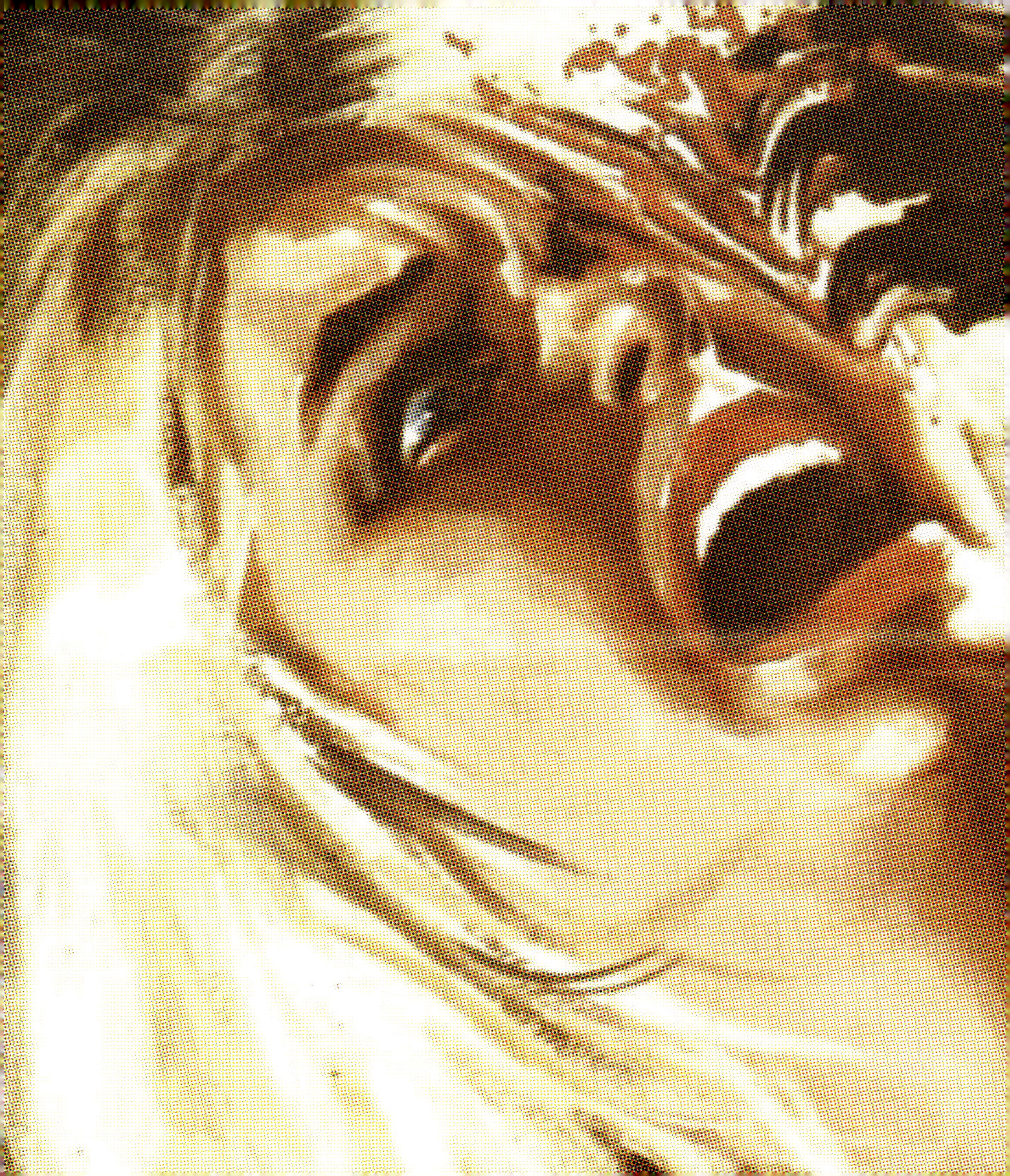

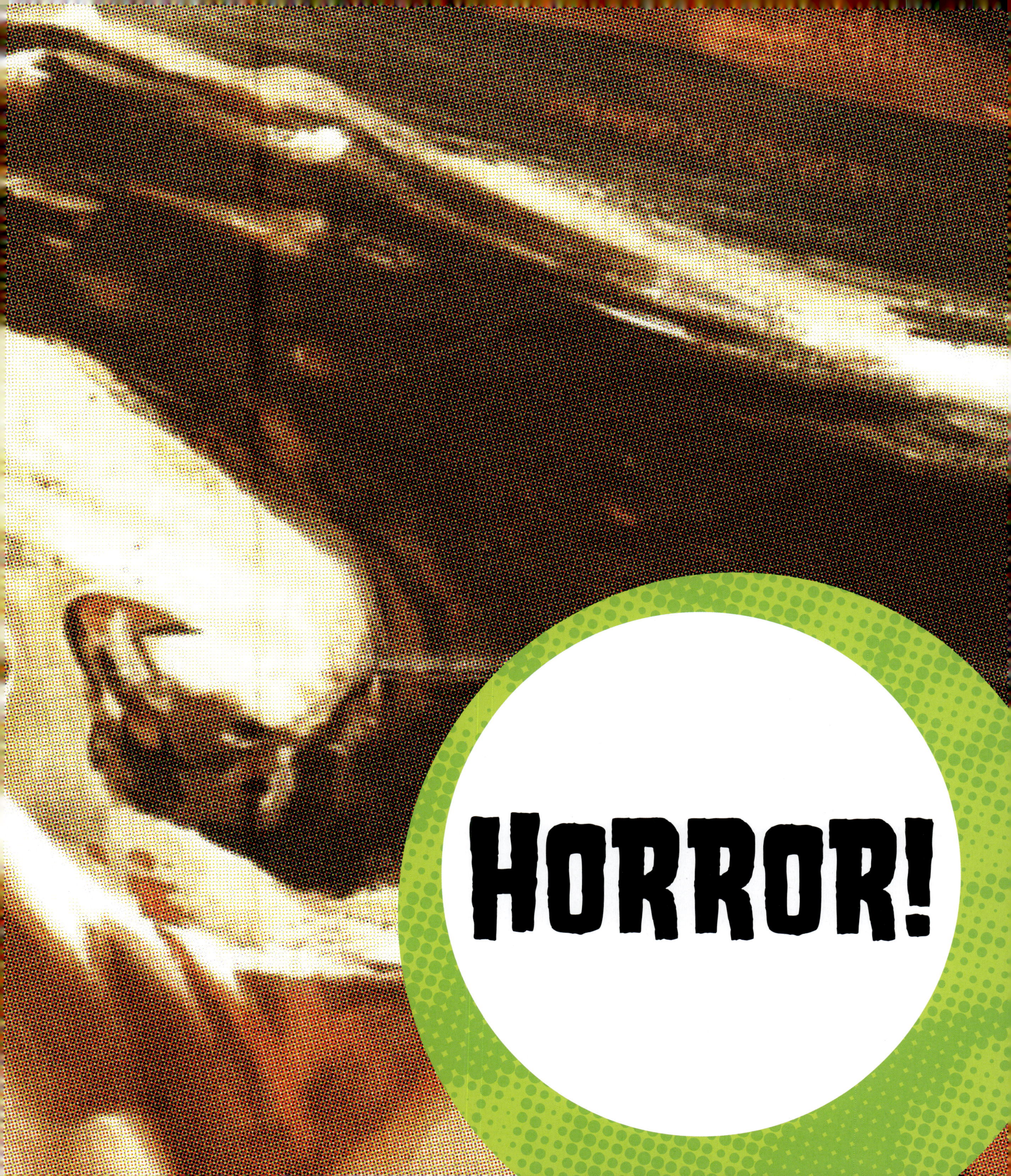
HORROR!

Stephen Jones on
THE BLACK SLEEP and HILLBILLYS IN A HAUNTED HOUSE

PREVIOUS SPREAD: Detail from the Italian *foglio* for *The Uncanny* (1977), art by Mafé.

OPPOSITE: The original American one-sheet poster for *The Black Sleep* highlighted its horror credentials by emphasizing the monstrously deformed results of the mad Dr. Cadman's experiments with the eponymous drug.

BELOW: In 1962, *The Black Sleep* was reissued in America by Cari Releasing Corp. under the new title *Dr. Cadman's Secret* on a double bill with *Voodoo Island*, which was retitled *Silent Death*.

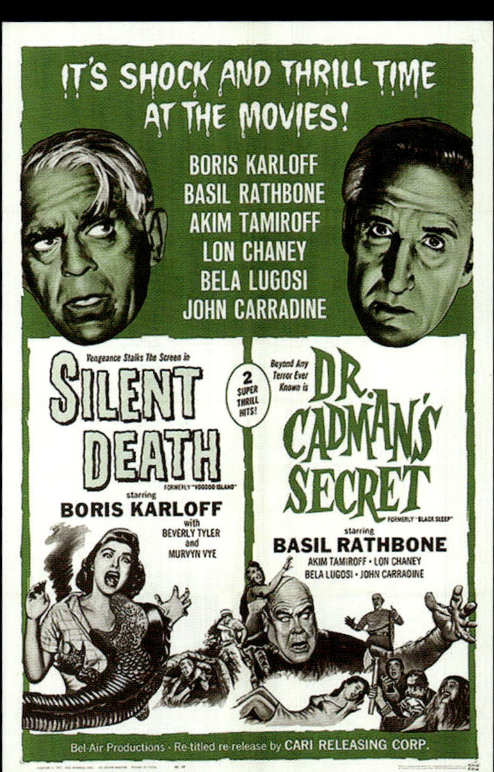

With audiences still weary of the all-too-real horrors of World War II, the golden age of movie monsters that had dominated the box office for around 20 years soon began to slip away during the late 1940s.

The radioactive atrocities of Hiroshima and Nagasaki were still fresh in people's minds as the new decade ushered in the atomic age with movies about giant behemoths, alien invaders, and science gone wrong, before cinema once again rediscovered its Gothic roots.

For the classic Hollywood horror stars of the preceding 20 years, things did not always end well with their careers. As they grew older and the popularity of horror movies waned with a fickle public, they were often forced to appear in low-budget projects that must have seemed demeaning to actors who had once had their names emblazoned above the titles of major studio productions.

In America, particularly, the horror film was kept alive during the 1950s by small, independent companies such as Bel-Air Productions, which was co-founded in 1953 by Howard W. Koch, Aubrey Schenck, and Edwin F. Zabel to make mostly low-budget Westerns and crime thrillers for distribution through United Artists.

Over the next few years they churned out almost a dozen movies that utilized the skills of actors and filmmakers whose careers were perhaps no longer at their peak and, when the company decided to make its first horror film, it continued with this commercially viable formula.

The Black Sleep (1956) was filmed over 12 days in budget-conscious black and white for an estimated cost of just $235,000. Although Allen Miner was originally announced as the director, he was replaced by the more experienced Reginald Le Borg, whose credits included two of Universal's "Inner Sanctum" mysteries and the sequels *Jungle Woman* and *The Mummy's Ghost* (both 1944).

Based on a story by Gerald Drayson Adams, the screenplay by fellow Canadian John C. Higgins was ambitiously set in 1872 England. On the eve of his execution for a murder that he didn't commit, Dr. Gordon Ramsay is visited in his cell by his old mentor, Sir Joel Cadman. The eminent surgeon gives Ramsay a sleeping powder, an East Indian drug called *nind andhera* (the

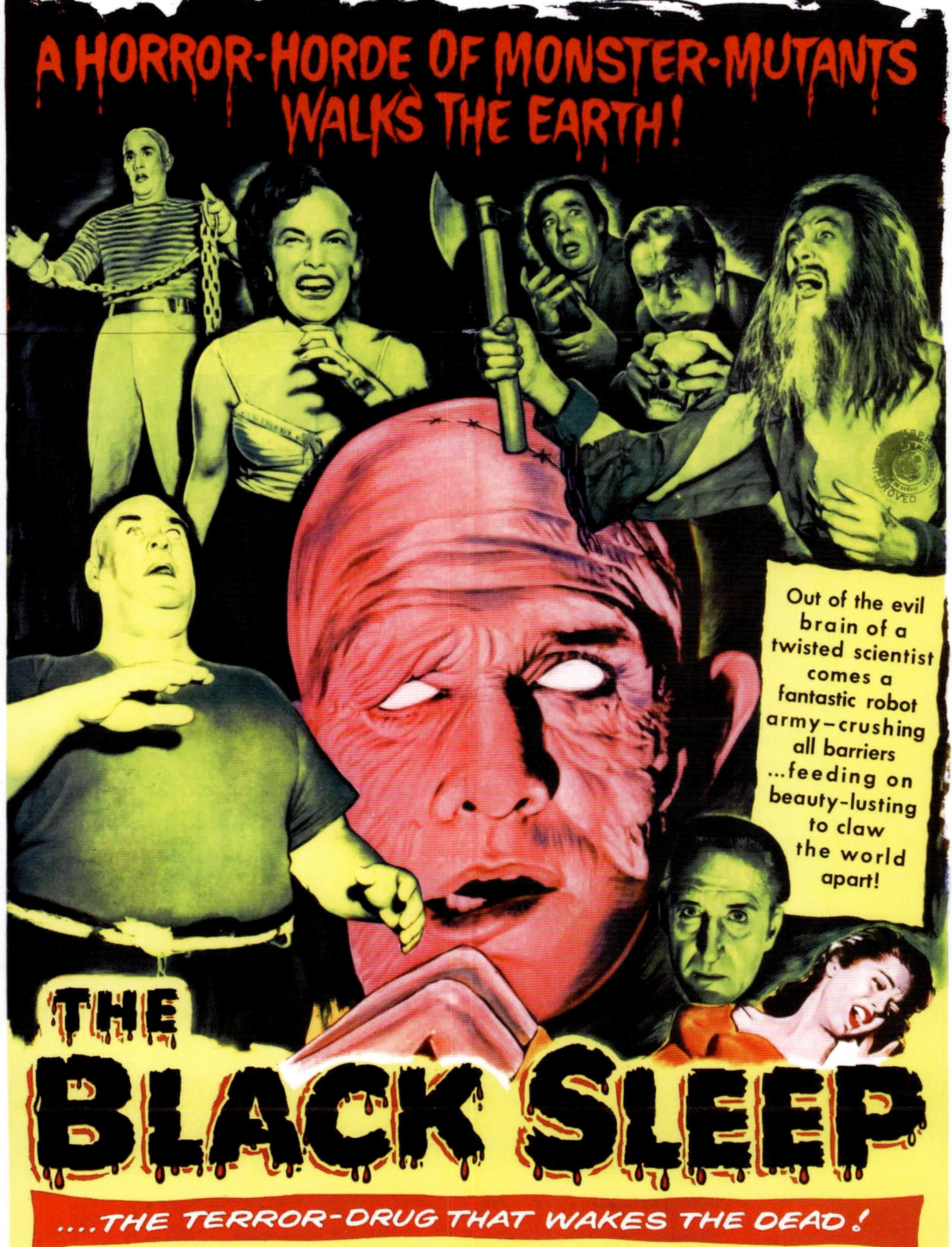
A HORROR-HORDE OF MONSTER-MUTANTS WALKS THE EARTH!
Out of the evil brain of a twisted scientist comes a fantastic robot army—crushing all barriers ...feeding on beauty-lusting to claw the world apart!
THE BLACK SLEEP
....THE TERROR-DRUG THAT WAKES THE DEAD!
Co-Starring
BASIL RATHBONE · AKIM TAMIROFF · LON CHANEY · JOHN CARRADINE · BELA LUGOSI
with Herbert RUDLEY · Patricia BLAKE · Phyllis STANLEY · Tor JOHNSON · Sally YARNELL · George SAWAYA · Claire CARLETON · Screenplay by John C. HIGGINS
Music by Les BAXTER · Executive Producer Aubrey SCHENCK · Produced by Howard W. KOCH · Directed by Reginald Le BORG
A BEL-AIR Production · Released thru United Artists
Property of National Screen Service Corp. Licensed for display only in connection with the exhibition of this picture at your theatre. Must be returned immediately thereafter.
56/247
Copyright 1956 United Artists Corporation. Country of Origin U.S.A.

"black sleep" of the title), which induces a death-like trance.

Pronounced dead and his body turned over to the care of Cadman and his creepy assistant Odo, the young doctor is revived and discovers that the obsessed surgeon is experimenting on the brains of others kept alive by the mysterious drug. Even worse, during a wild night of terror the crazed and horribly disfigured results of his experiments break free of their cells seeking revenge . . .

Except for its period setting, *The Black Sleep* is a mostly routine B-movie. However, what lifts it out of the ordinary is the exploitative casting of so many declining horror stars in key roles.

As the driven Cadman, Basil Rathbone gives his coldly arrogant performance a much-needed touch of pathos. A wild John Carradine is the maniacal leader of the escaped monstrosities, and Lon Chaney, Jr. (who had worked with director Le Borg before) reprises his Lennie routine from *Of Mice and Men* (1939) as the homicidal Mungo. The surgeon's mute butler Casimir is played by a sick-looking Bela Lugosi in his last completed role (he died in August that same year), and the other failed experiments are rounded out by big Swedish wrestler Tor Johnson, stuntman George Sawaya, and actress Sally Yarnell. When Peter Lorre's salary demands were considered too high for the limited budget, he was replaced by Akim Tamiroff as the scheming gypsy, Odo.

Given a major release by United Artists in June 1956 on a double bill with Hammer's *The Creeping Unknown* (aka *The Quatermass Xperiment*), *The Black Sleep* did well enough at the box office for Bel-Air to release two further horror films the following year: *Voodoo Island* and *Pharaoh's Curse*.

Eleven years after the initial release of *The Black Sleep*, three of its stars were reunited for one final time in a movie that shared striking similarities with its predecessor.

Despite the intermediary box office success of such specialist companies as Hammer Films, American International Pictures, and Amicus Productions, horror and exploitation movies during much of the 1960s were still perceived by audiences and critics alike as nothing more than B-movie fodder.

Woolner Brothers Pictures, Inc., founded by brothers Bernard and Lawrence Woolner, had started out as a production company in the late 1950s. By the following decade it was better known as the distributor of re-dubbed foreign films, such as Mario Bava's *Hercules in the Haunted World* (1961) and Sergio Corbucci's *Castle of Blood* (1964), into the American drive-in market.

In 1966 they decided to create their own product for the lucrative Southern regional market with the low-budget musical comedy *The Las Vegas Hillbillys*. Notwithstanding the spelling error in the title, it did well enough in its limited market for the producers to rush a follow-up into production. Shot on an estimated budget of $200,000, *Hillbillys in a Haunted House* was released in May 1967.

It was the final movie credit for workmanlike director Jean Yarbrough, who had been responsible for such Poverty Row programmers as *The Devil Bat* (1940) and *King of the Zombies* (1941). Country performer Woody Wetherby (Ferlin Husky, reprising his role from the first film), busty singer Boots Malone (Joi Lansing, replacing Mamie Van Doren), and irritating comedy-relief manager Jeepers (singer Don Bowman) are forced to spend the night in a reputedly haunted mansion on their way to a musical jamboree in Nashville.

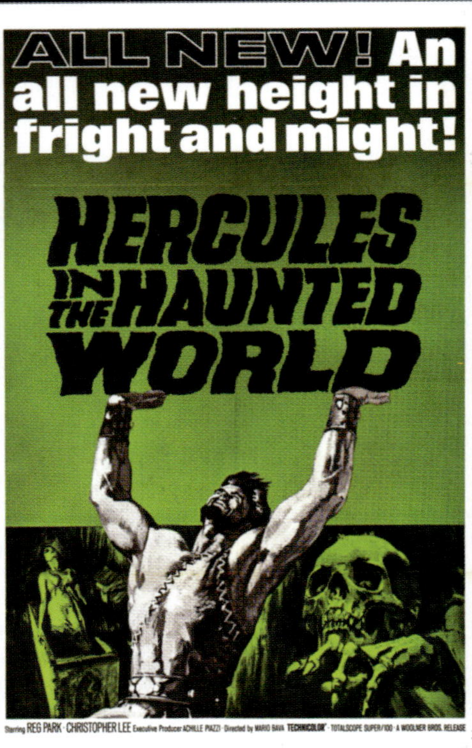

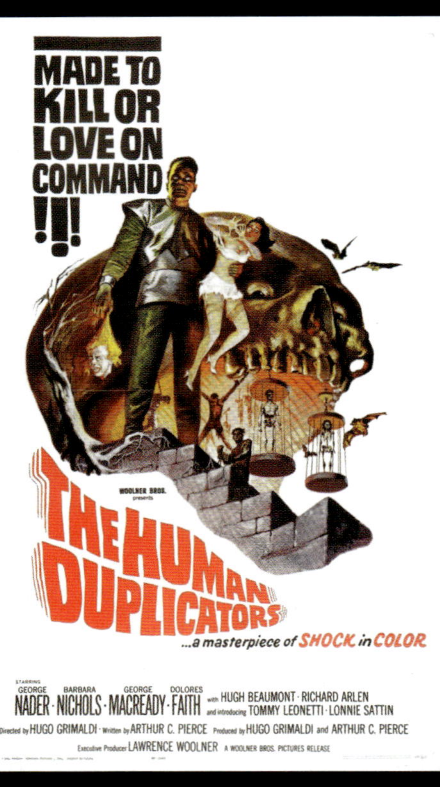

TOP: Released in America in 1964 by Woolner Bros., *Hercules in the Haunted World* was a belated attempt to cash in on the popular *peplum* movies that Italy had been churning out since the late 1950s.

ABOVE: This terrific poster design from Woolner Bros. for the low budget US/Italian co-production *The Human Duplicators* (1964) was much better than the movie, which featured Richard (Jaws) Kiel as an alien scientist.

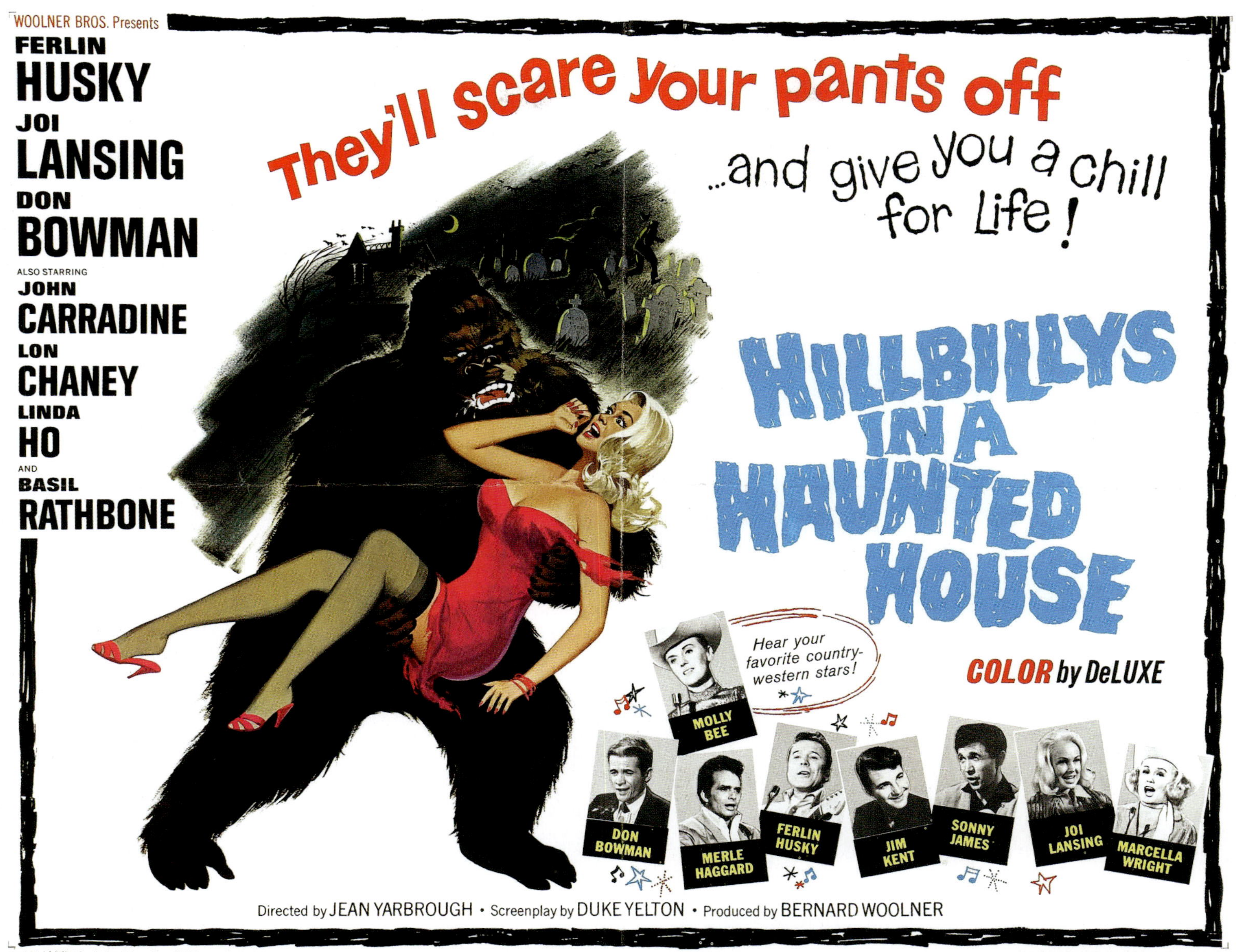

However, unknown to the stranded travelers, the old house is the secret headquarters for a gang of international spies who are after a top-secret formula for rocket fuel.

Once again, the only reason to watch this movie is because the spies are portrayed by faded horror stars John Carradine, Lon Chaney, Jr., and Basil Rathbone (in his final American film), under the command of Linda Ho's ruthless Madame Wong. Veteran stuntman George Barrows is beneath the shaggy ape-suit as Chaney's pet gorilla, and the real ghost of a Confederate General eventually turns up to put a scare into everyone.

However, the main attraction of the film for its intended audience was the inclusion of many popular country music acts, and when the already thin plot finally runs out of steam, the remainder of the short running time is padded out with a series of forgettable performances. After its initial release, the movie quickly disappeared and became an almost mythical credit in the careers of its trio of horror stars. It finally resurfaced again on tape during the video boom of the 1980s. ●

ABOVE: Instead of its cast of fading horror stars, the American half-sheet poster for *Hillbillys in a Haunted House* emphasized the inclusion of many country music acts well known to its intended audience.

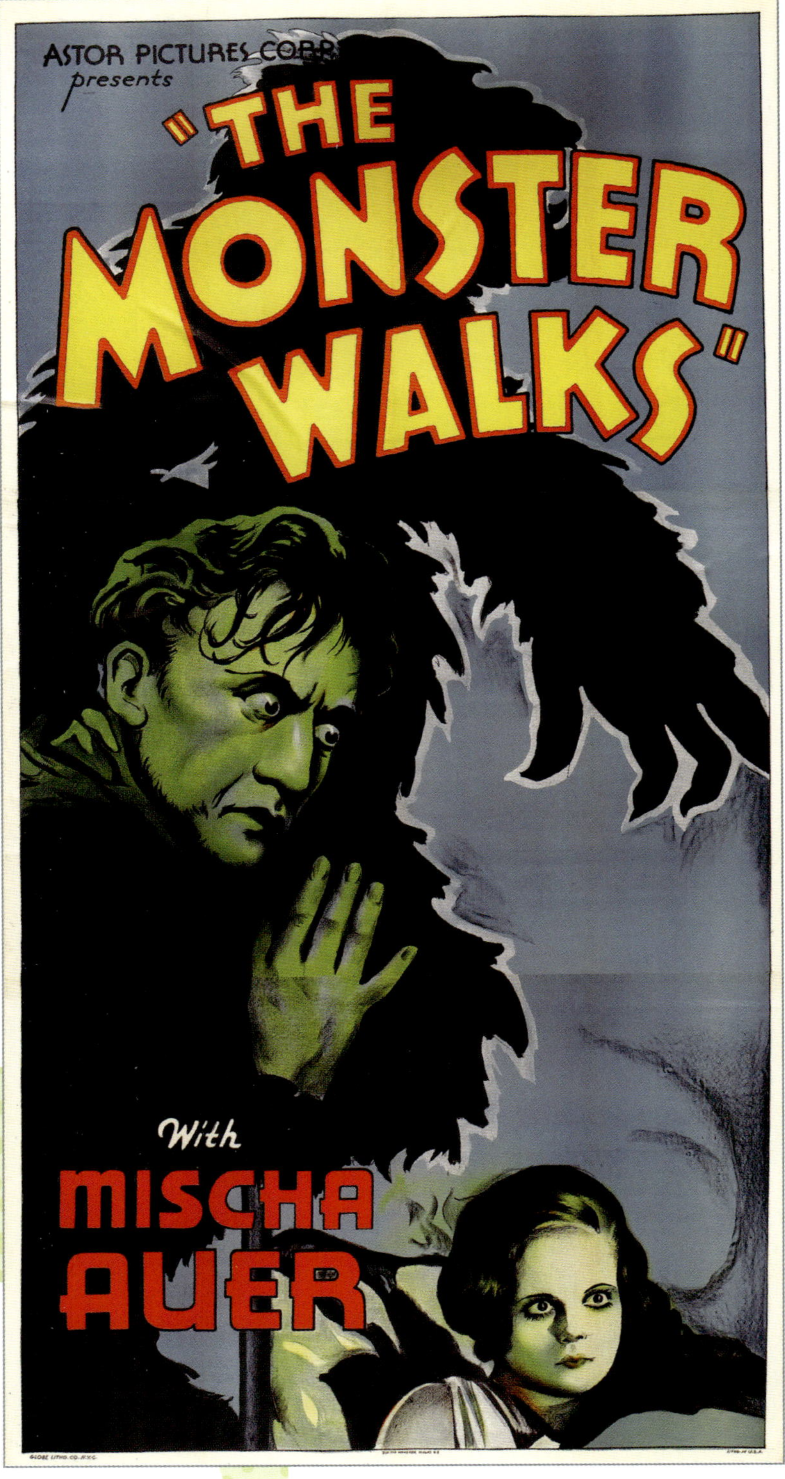

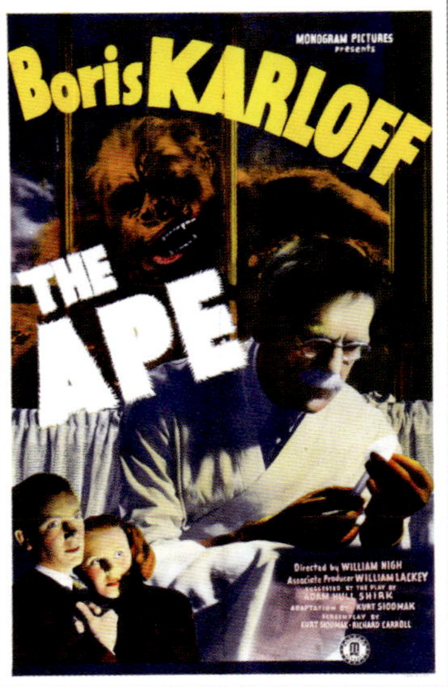

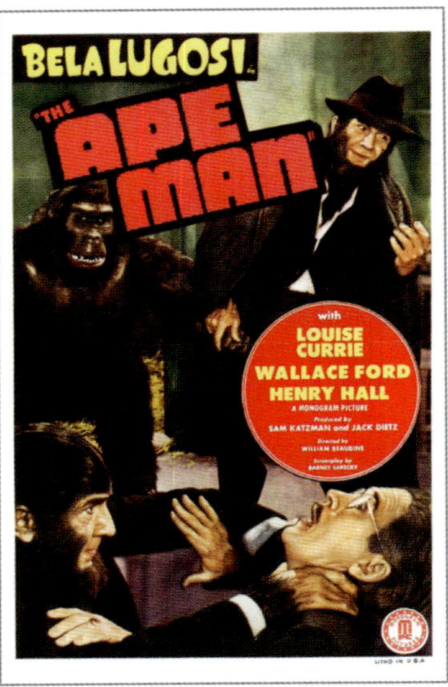

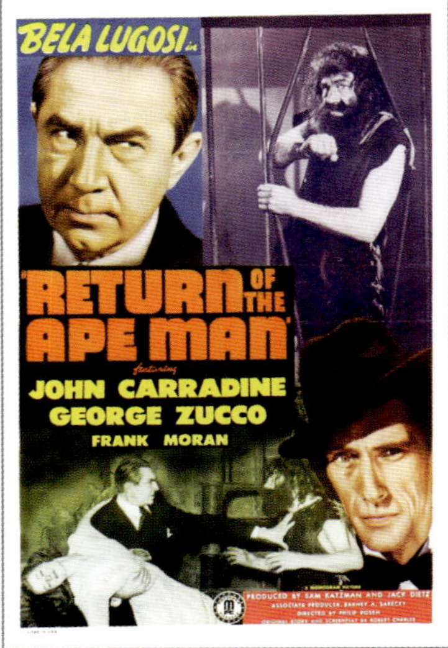

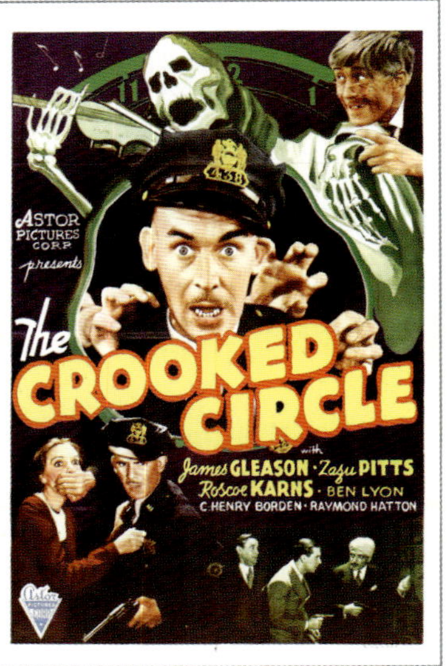

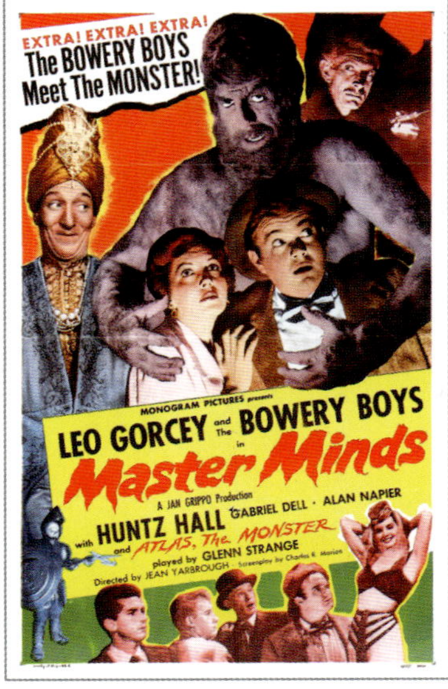

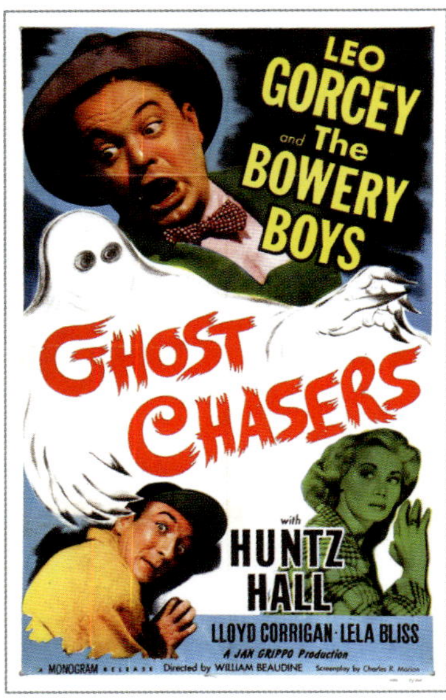

POVERTY ROW

While the Hollywood majors produced their epics and high-profile movies, filling the bottom half of the bill in the '30s and '40s was often the job of the smaller independent studios, referred to collectively as "Poverty Row." Companies such as Monogram Pictures churned out B-movies that may have had low budgets and second-tier or fading stars, but always had eye-catching posters. Westerns were popular, but horror stories allowed for plenty of outlandish shocks, thrills, and melodramatic nonsense for a minimal outlay. Fittingly, Monogram's old headquarters building in Los Angeles is still churning out outlandish nonsense: it's now owned by the Church of Scientology.

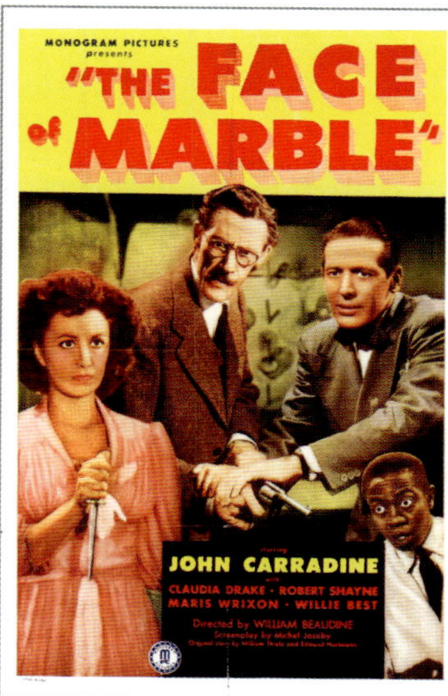
MONOGRAM PICTURES presents
"THE FACE of MARBLE"
JOHN CARRADINE
CLAUDIA DRAKE · ROBERT SHAYNE
MARIS WRIXON · WILLIE BEST
Directed by WILLIAM BEAUDINE

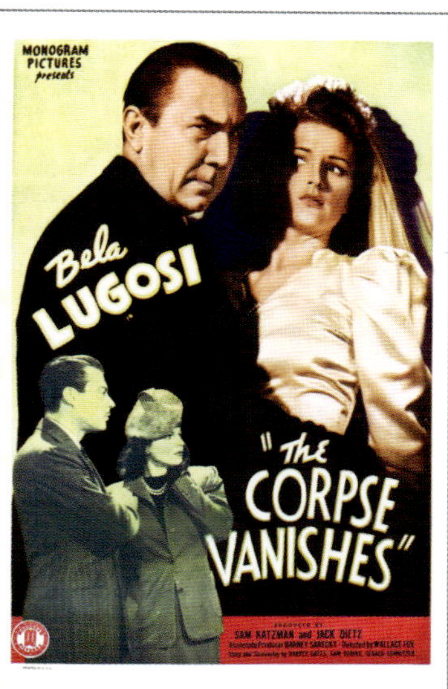
MONOGRAM PICTURES presents
Bela LUGOSI
"The CORPSE VANISHES"
SAM KATZMAN and JACK DIETZ

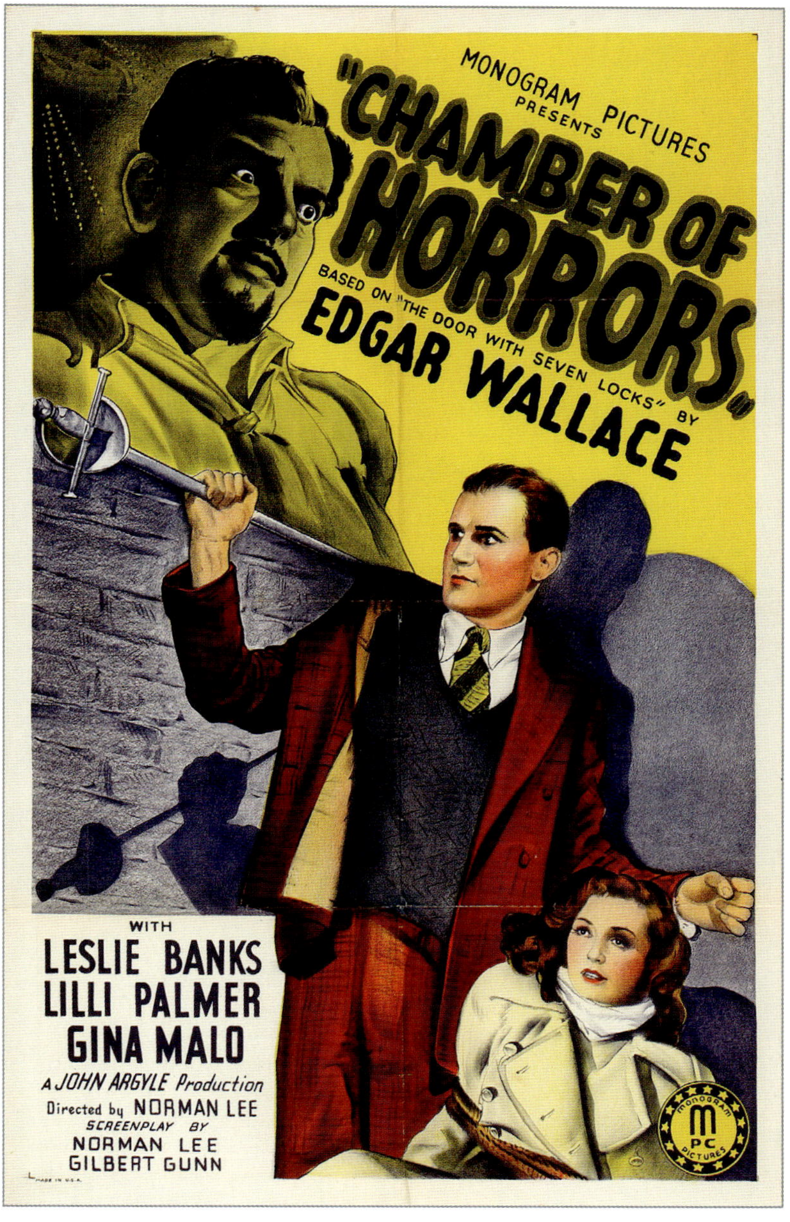
MONOGRAM PICTURES PRESENTS
"CHAMBER OF HORRORS"
BASED ON "THE DOOR WITH SEVEN LOCKS" BY
EDGAR WALLACE
WITH
LESLIE BANKS
LILLI PALMER
GINA MALO
A JOHN ARGYLE Production
Directed by NORMAN LEE
SCREENPLAY BY
NORMAN LEE
GILBERT GUNN
MONOGRAM MPC PICTURES

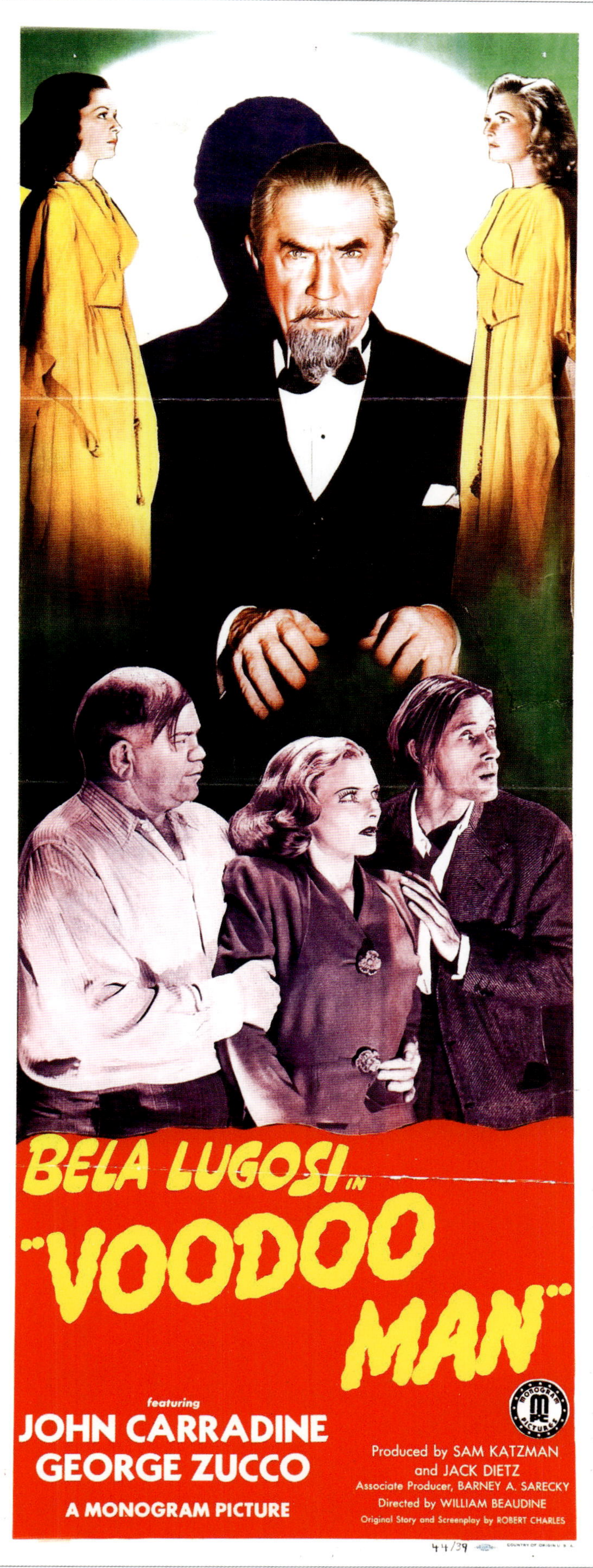
BELA LUGOSI IN
"VOODOO MAN"
featuring
JOHN CARRADINE
GEORGE ZUCCO
A MONOGRAM PICTURE
Produced by SAM KATZMAN
and JACK DIETZ
Associate Producer, BARNEY A. SARECKY
Directed by WILLIAM BEAUDINE
Original Story and Screenplay by ROBERT CHARLES
44/39

BELA'S BS

Playing the Count made Bela Lugosi (1882–1956) a star, first on Broadway and then in Universal's *Dracula* (1931), but sadly it was largely a case of diminishing returns. Soon enough, the only productions that would offer top billing were B-movies, which would often put him in Dracula-like poses on their posters—for example *Invisible Ghost* (1941) and the serial *The Whispering Shadow* (1933)—even if there were no vampires on screen. Lugosi ended his career featuring in oddities such as the bizarre British comedy *Mother Riley Meets the Vampire* (1952, represented here by its Belgian poster), and of course the legendary *Plan 9 from Outer Space* (1959), completed after his death by the ever-resourceful director Ed Wood, who padded out the scant footage of his star with interminable scenes of a supremely unconvincing "double" holding a cape in front of his face. For Lugosi though, as he once admitted, "Dracula never ends. I don't know whether I should call it fortune or a curse, but it never ends."

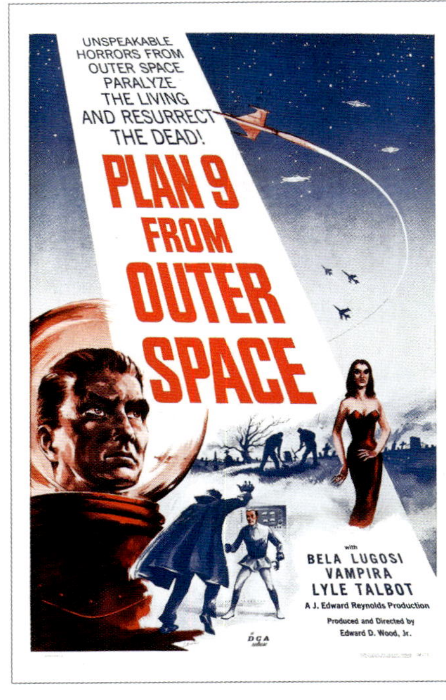

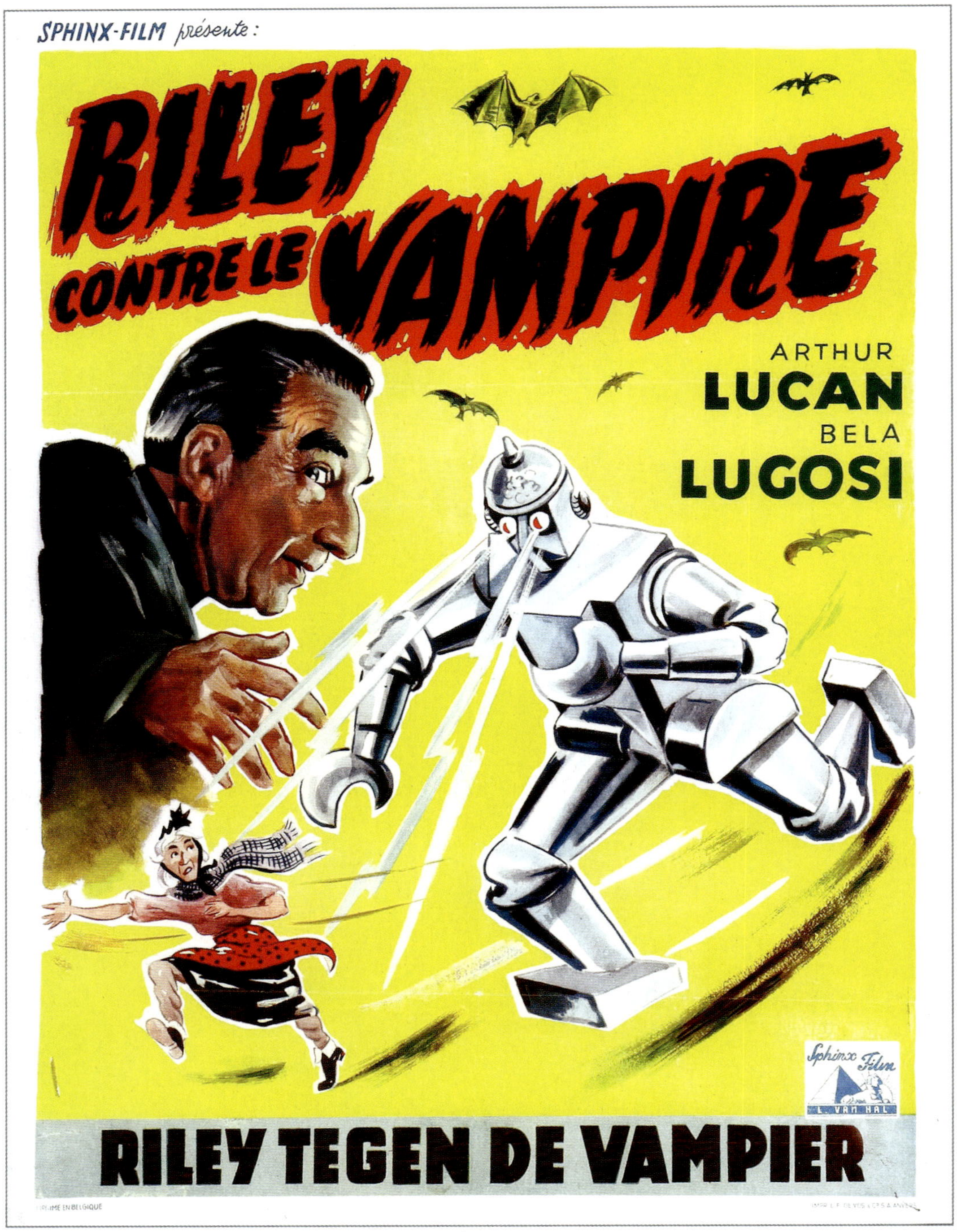

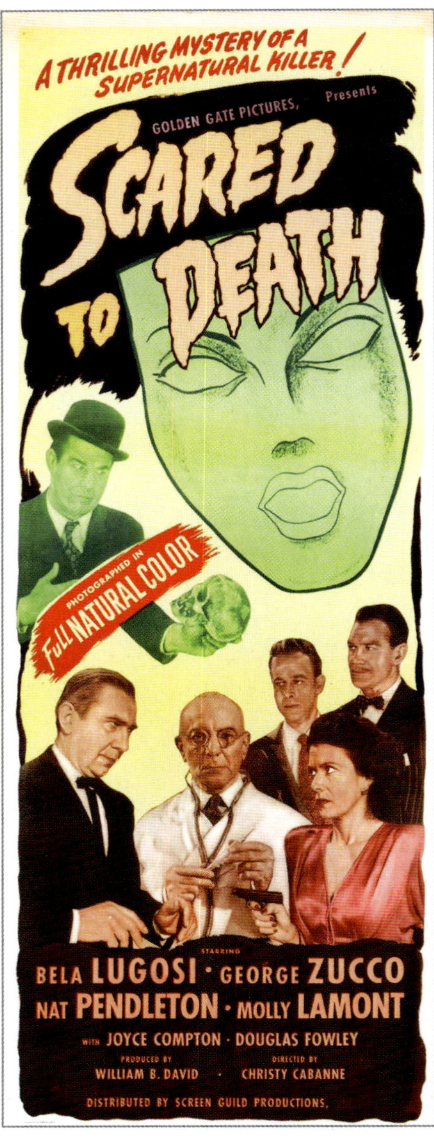

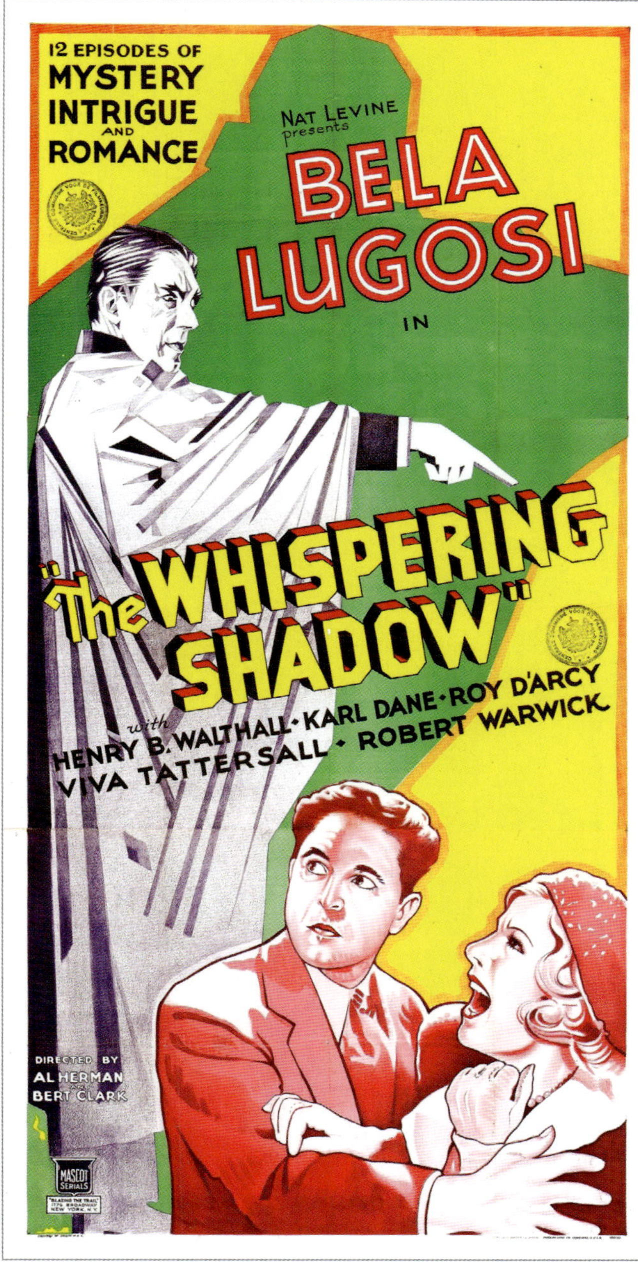
12 EPISODES OF
MYSTERY
INTRIGUE
AND
ROMANCE
NAT LEVINE
presents
BELA
LUGOSI
IN
"The WHISPERING
SHADOW"
with
HENRY B. WALTHALL · KARL DANE · ROY D'ARCY
VIVA TATTERSALL · ROBERT WARWICK
DIRECTED BY
AL HERMAN
BERT CLARK

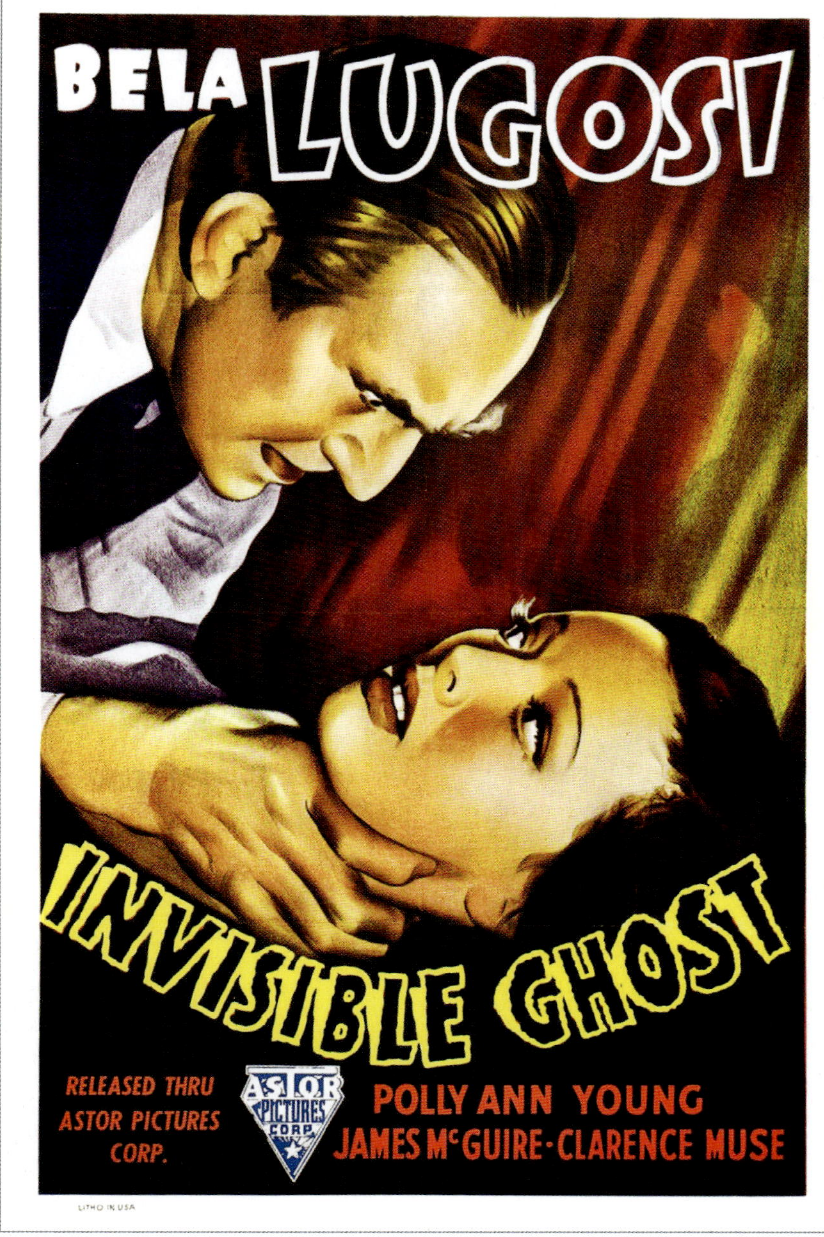
BELA LUGOSI
INVISIBLE GHOST
RELEASED THRU
ASTOR PICTURES
CORP.
POLLY ANN YOUNG
JAMES McGUIRE · CLARENCE MUSE
LITHO IN USA

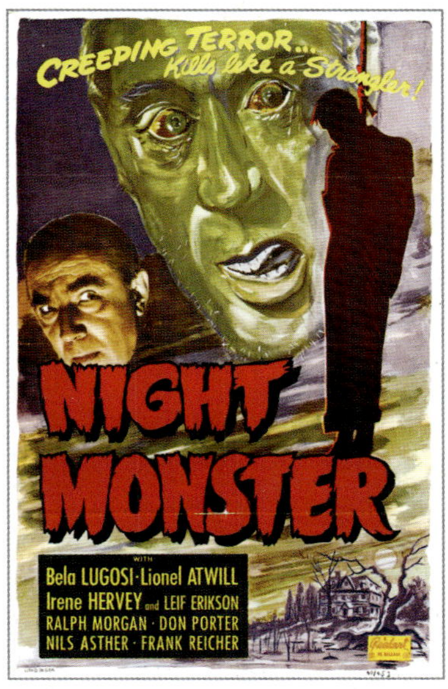
CREEPING TERROR... Kills like a Strangler!
NIGHT
MONSTER
Bela LUGOSI · Lionel ATWILL
Irene HERVEY and LEIF ERIKSON
RALPH MORGAN · DON PORTER
NILS ASTHER · FRANK REICHER

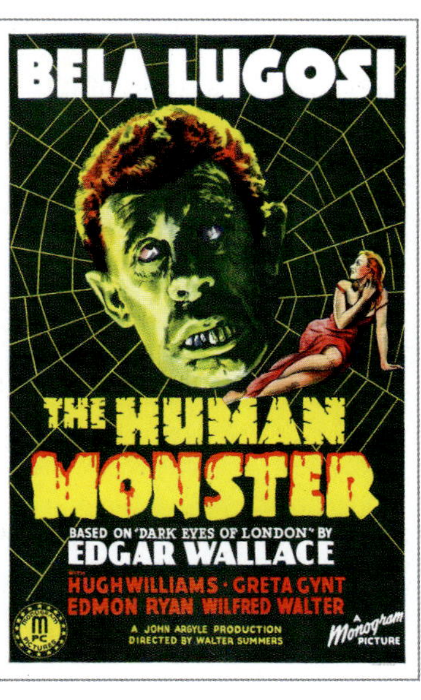
BELA LUGOSI
THE HUMAN
MONSTER
BASED ON "DARK EYES OF LONDON" BY
EDGAR WALLACE
HUGH WILLIAMS · GRETA GYNT
EDMON RYAN WILFRED WALTER
A JOHN ARGYLE PRODUCTION
DIRECTED BY WALTER SUMMERS
Monogram PICTURE

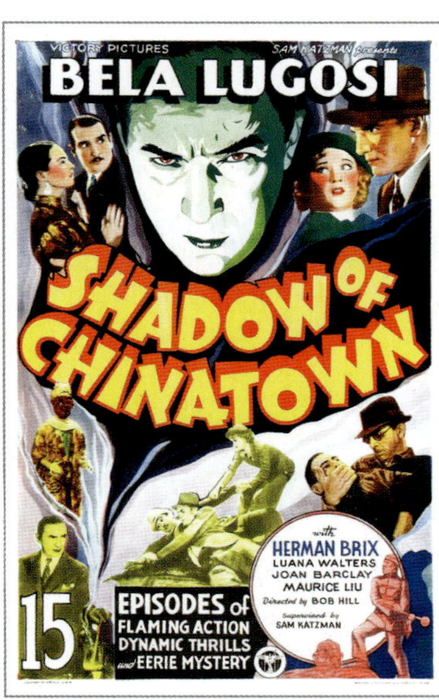
VICTORY PICTURES
SAM KATZMAN presents
BELA LUGOSI
SHADOW OF
CHINATOWN
with
HERMAN BRIX
LUANA WALTERS
JOAN BARCLAY
MAURICE LIU
Directed by BOB HILL
Supervised by
SAM KATZMAN
15
EPISODES of
FLAMING ACTION
DYNAMIC THRILLS
and EERIE MYSTERY

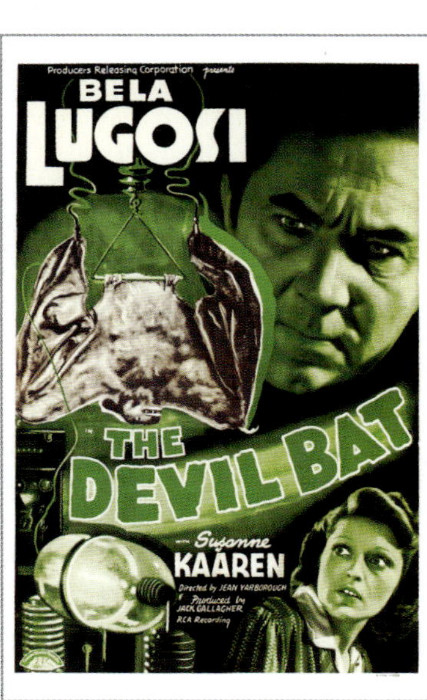
Producers Releasing Corporation presents
BELA
LUGOSI
THE
DEVIL BAT
Suzanne
KAAREN
Directed by JEAN YARBROUGH
Produced by
JACK GALLAGHER

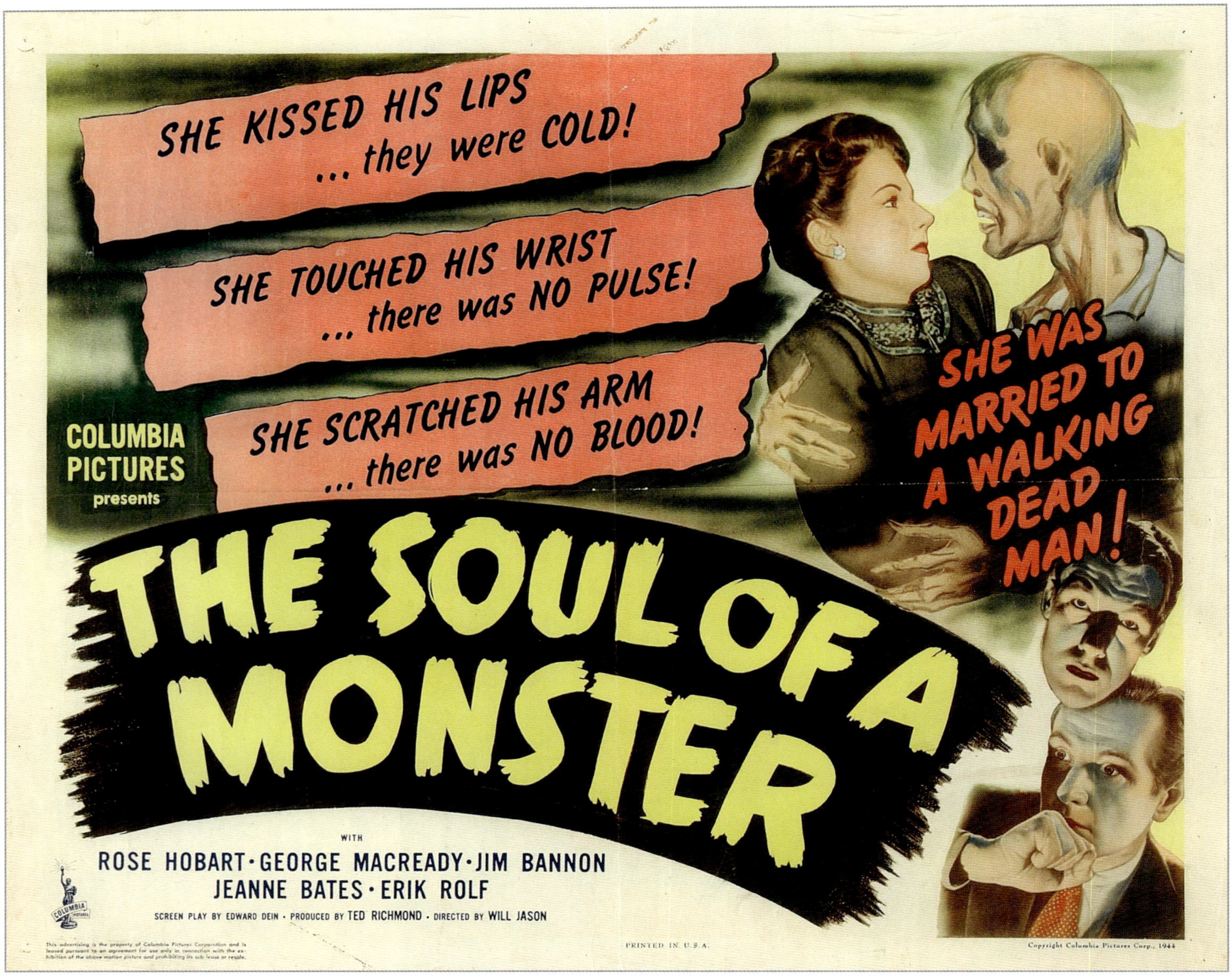

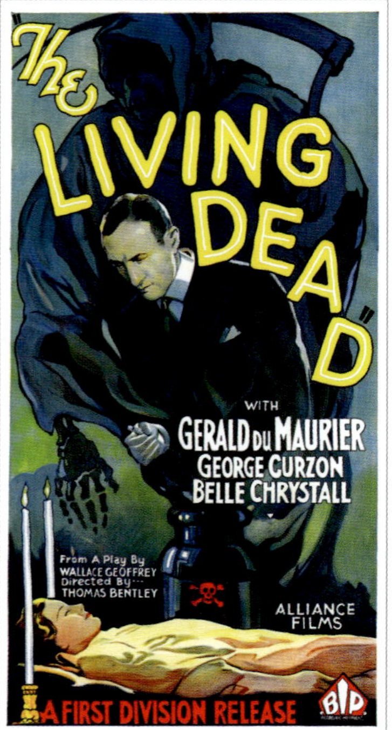

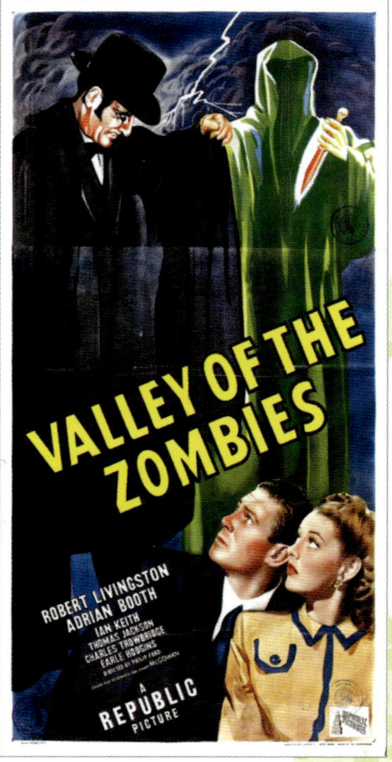

BIRTH OF THE LIVING DEAD

As this selection of stylish posters from the '30s and '40s proves, the Dead were both Living and Walking on screen long before the advent of George R. Romero's *Living Dead* film series, or the twenty-first-century TV phenomenon that is *The Walking Dead*. To be fair, these early zombies didn't tend to be rotting, ravenous flesh-eaters, and in 1932's *The Living Dead* they're actually still alive (but in a trance!). Boris Karloff's character in *The Walking Dead* (1936) is at least a reanimated corpse, but he talks, and is on a quest to find those who had him unjustly executed, rather than to find and eat intestines. The towering Darby Jones strikes a similar pose as a voodoo zombie on the posters for both the atmospheric *I Walked with a Zombie* (1943) and its tedious comic variant, *Zombies on Broadway* (1945).

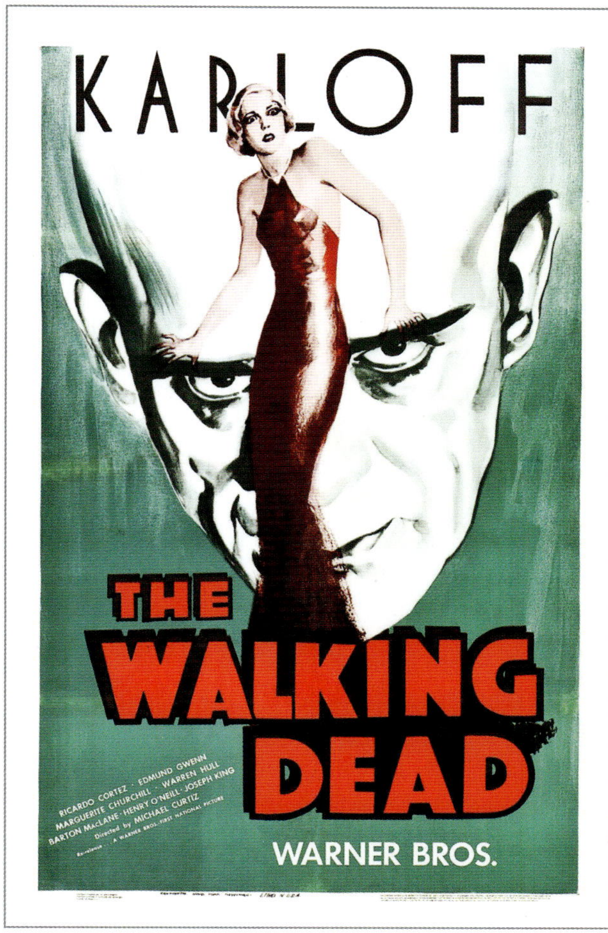
KARLOFF
THE WALKING DEAD
WARNER BROS.

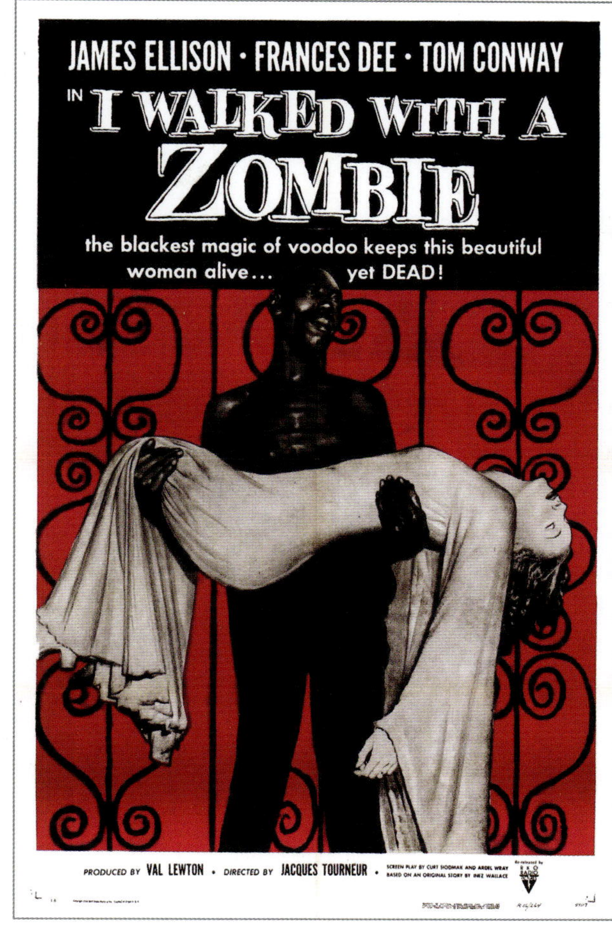
JAMES ELLISON · FRANCES DEE · TOM CONWAY
IN I WALKED WITH A ZOMBIE
the blackest magic of voodoo keeps this beautiful woman alive... yet DEAD!
PRODUCED BY VAL LEWTON · DIRECTED BY JACQUES TOURNEUR

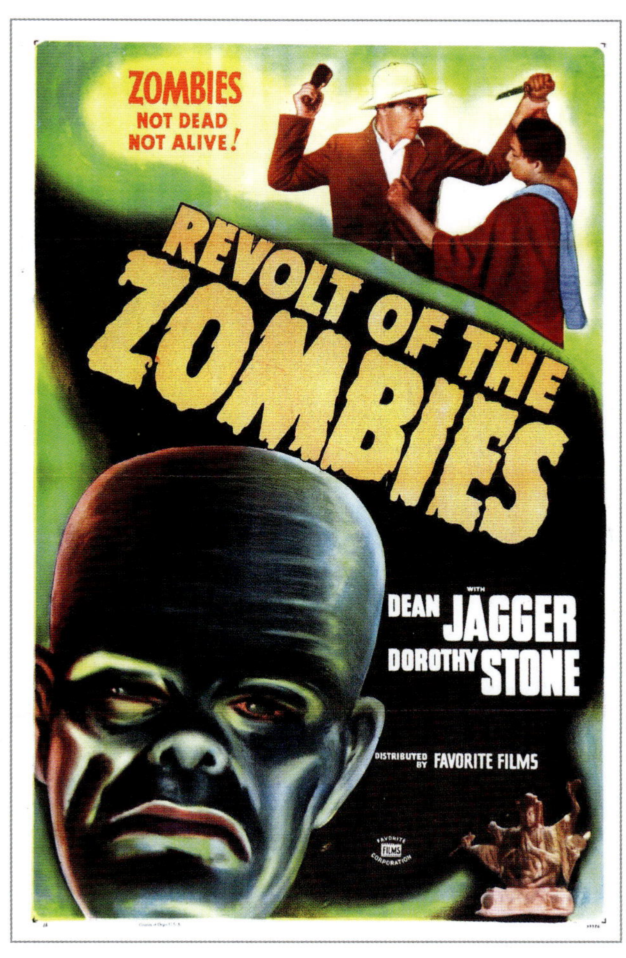
ZOMBIES NOT DEAD NOT ALIVE!
REVOLT OF THE ZOMBIES
DEAN JAGGER
WITH DOROTHY STONE
DISTRIBUTED BY FAVORITE FILMS

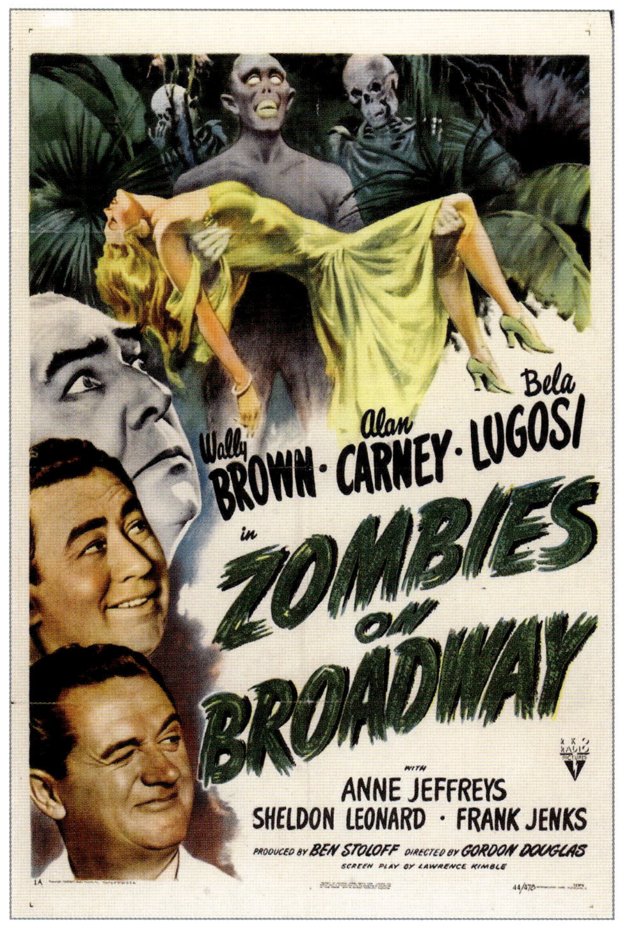
Wally BROWN · Alan CARNEY · Bela LUGOSI
in ZOMBIES ON BROADWAY
WITH ANNE JEFFREYS
SHELDON LEONARD · FRANK JENKS
PRODUCED BY BEN STOLOFF DIRECTED BY GORDON DOUGLAS
SCREEN PLAY BY LAWRENCE KIMBLE

CARRIED AWAY

A distressed or unconscious woman being carried away by an alien, robot, or monster (or indeed an alien robot monster) is a visual trope used endlessly on B-movie posters, not to mention pulp and comic book covers. Scholarly commentators have described it as representing a kind of dark foreplay; for poster artists, it was simply a striking image, often used when there was no such scene in the actual movie.

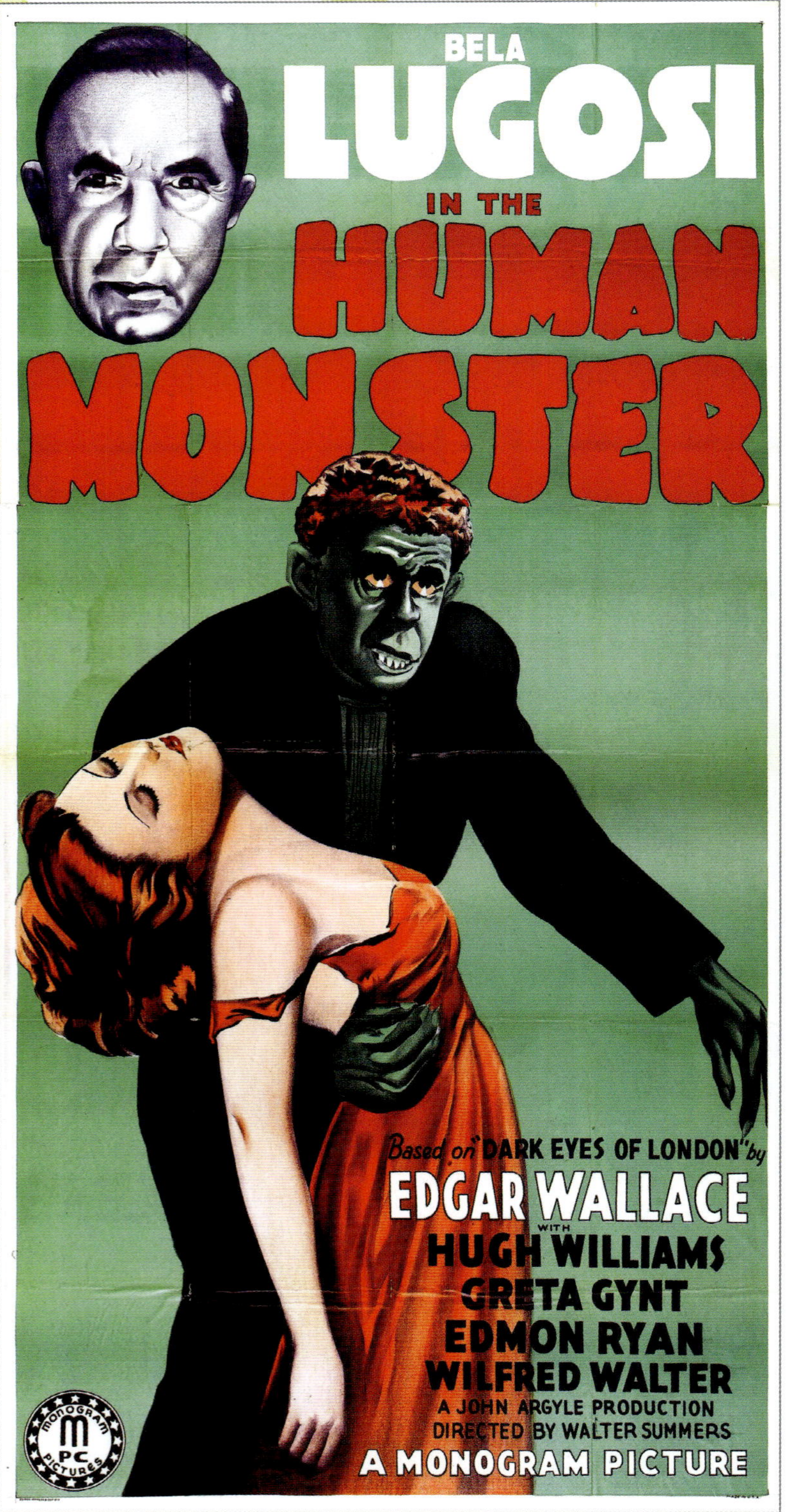

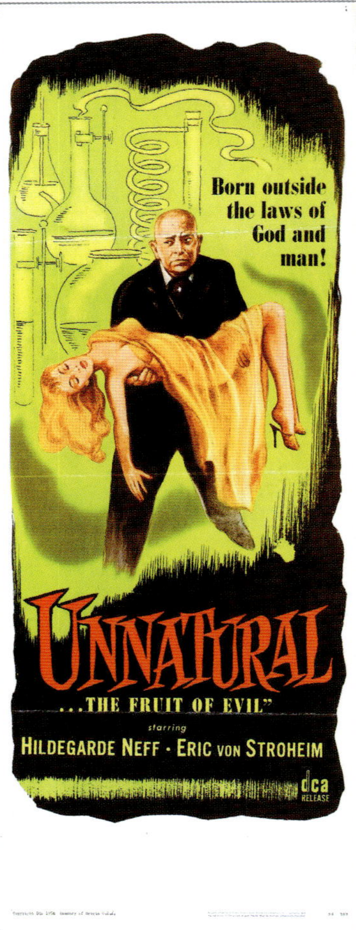

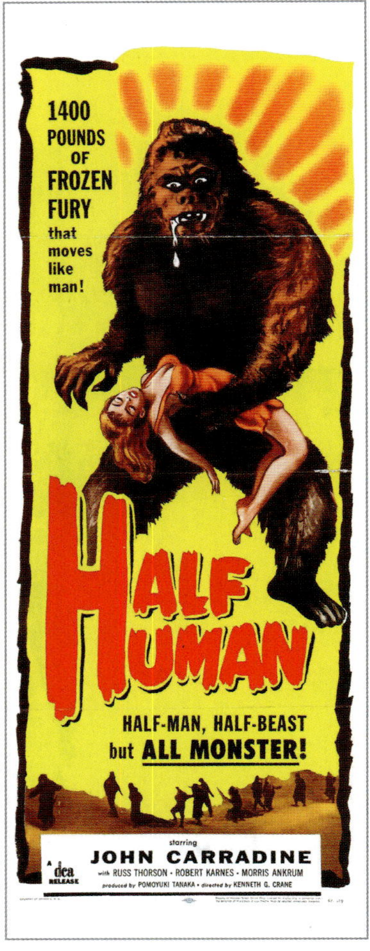

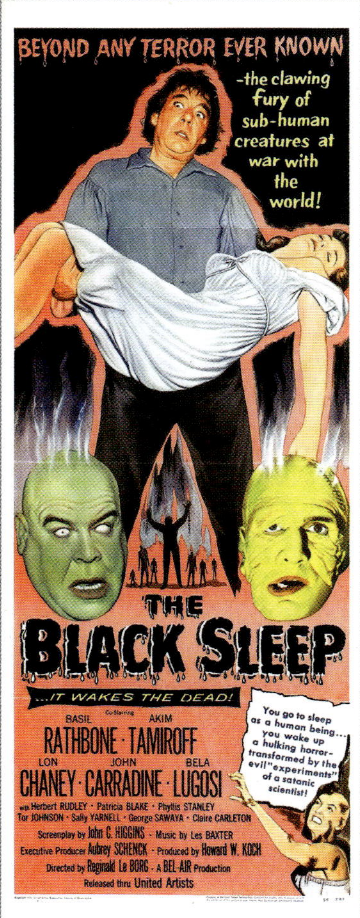

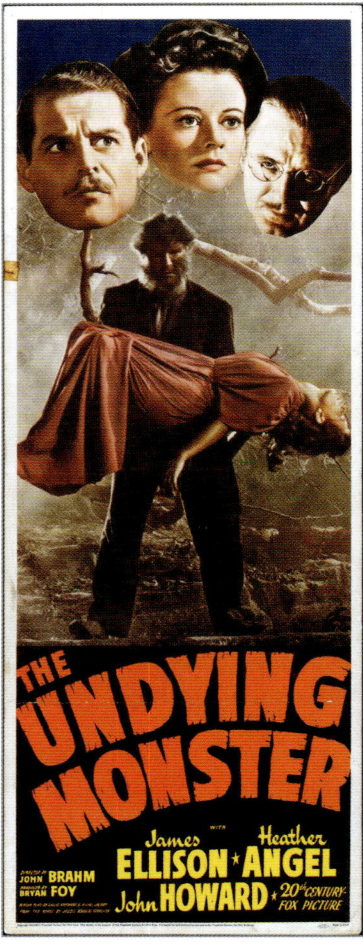

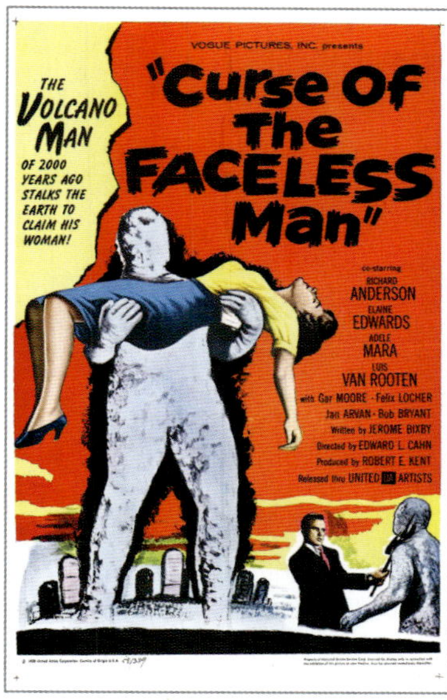

VOGUE PICTURES, INC. presents
THE VOLCANO MAN OF 2000 YEARS AGO STALKS THE EARTH TO CLAIM HIS WOMAN!
"Curse Of The FACELESS Man"
co-starring RICHARD ANDERSON ELAINE EDWARDS ADELE MARA LUIS VAN ROOTEN
with Gar MOORE · Felix LOCHER
Jan ARVAN · Bob BRYANT
Written by JEROME BIXBY
Directed by EDWARD L. CAHN
Produced by ROBERT E. KENT
Released thru UNITED ARTISTS

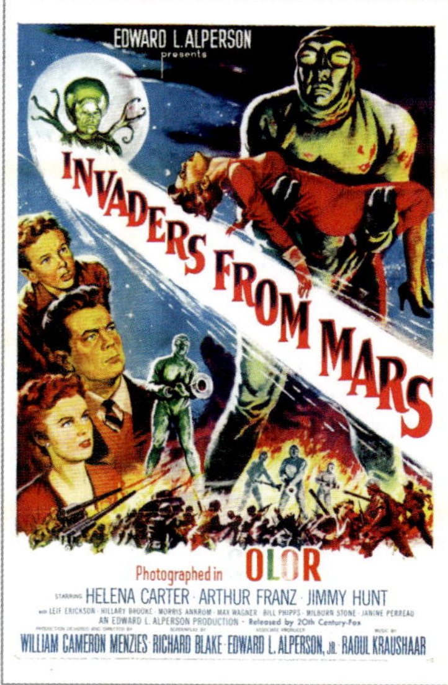

EDWARD L. ALPERSON presents
INVADERS FROM MARS
Photographed in COLOR
HELENA CARTER · ARTHUR FRANZ · JIMMY HUNT
AN EDWARD L. ALPERSON PRODUCTION · Released by 20th Century-Fox
WILLIAM CAMERON MENZIES RICHARD BLAKE EDWARD L. ALPERSON, JR. RAOUL KRAUSHAAR

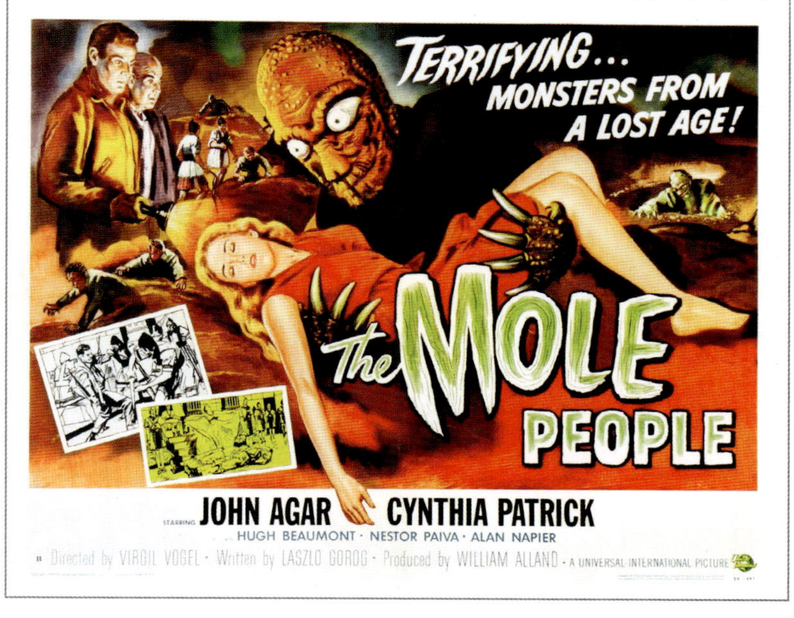

TERRIFYING... MONSTERS FROM A LOST AGE!
The MOLE PEOPLE
JOHN AGAR CYNTHIA PATRICK
HUGH BEAUMONT · NESTOR PAIVA · ALAN NAPIER
Directed by VIRGIL VOGEL · Written by LASZLO GOROG · Produced by WILLIAM ALLAND · A UNIVERSAL-INTERNATIONAL PICTURE

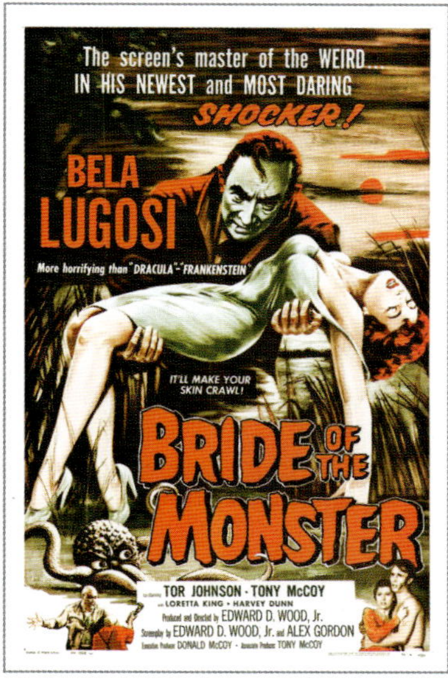

The screen's master of the WEIRD... IN HIS NEWEST and MOST DARING SHOCKER!
BELA LUGOSI
More horrifying than "DRACULA"-"FRANKENSTEIN"
IT'LL MAKE YOUR SKIN CRAWL!
BRIDE OF THE MONSTER
TOR JOHNSON · TONY McCOY
LORETTA KING · HARVEY DUNN
Produced and Directed by EDWARD D. WOOD, Jr.
Screenplay by EDWARD D. WOOD, Jr. and ALEX GORDON
Executive Producer DONALD McCOY · Associate Producer TONY McCOY

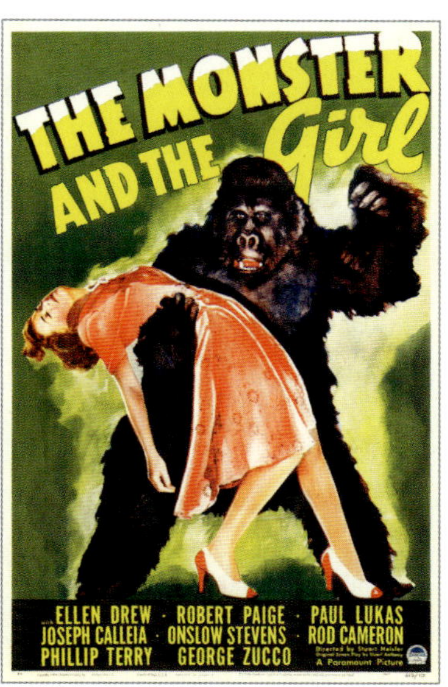

THE MONSTER AND THE Girl
ELLEN DREW · ROBERT PAIGE · PAUL LUKAS
JOSEPH CALLEIA · ONSLOW STEVENS · ROD CAMERON
PHILLIP TERRY · GEORGE ZUCCO
A Paramount Picture

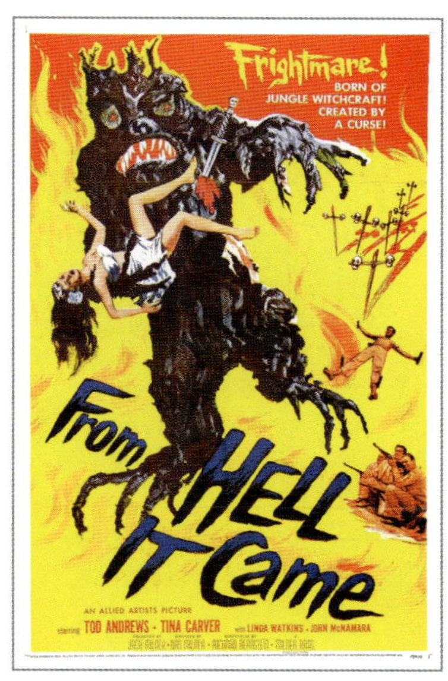

Frightmare!
BORN OF JUNGLE WITCHCRAFT! CREATED BY A CURSE!
From HELL IT Came
AN ALLIED ARTISTS PICTURE
TOD ANDREWS · TINA CARVER

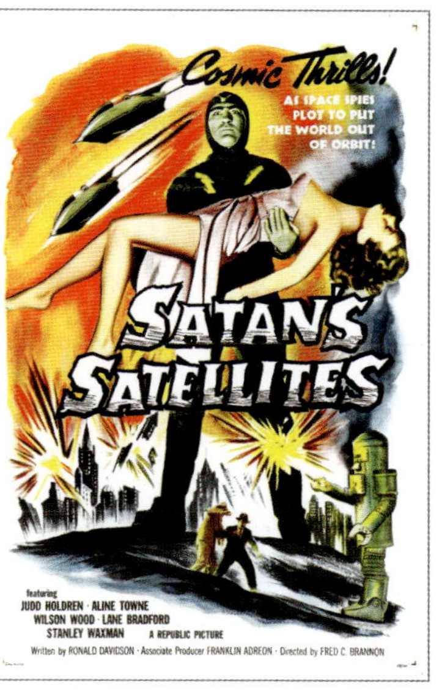

Cosmic Thrills!
AS SPACE SPIES PLOT TO PUT THE WORLD OUT OF ORBIT!
SATANS SATELLITES
JUDD HOLDREN · ALINE TOWNE
WILSON WOOD · LANE BRADFORD
STANLEY WAXMAN
A REPUBLIC PICTURE
Written by RONALD DAVIDSON · Associate Producer FRANKLIN ADREON · Directed by FRED C. BRANNON

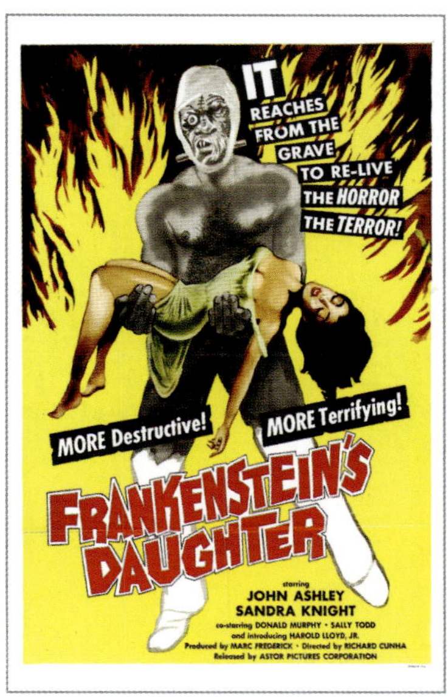

IT REACHES FROM THE GRAVE TO RE-LIVE THE HORROR THE TERROR!
MORE Destructive!
MORE Terrifying!
FRANKENSTEIN'S DAUGHTER
starring JOHN ASHLEY SANDRA KNIGHT
co-starring DONALD MURPHY · SALLY TODD
and introducing HAROLD LLOYD, JR.
Produced by MARC FREDERICK · Directed by RICHARD CUNHA
Released by ASTOR PICTURES CORPORATION

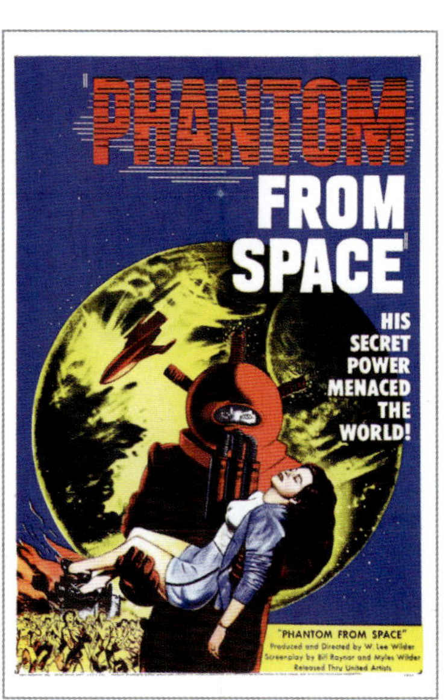

PHANTOM FROM SPACE
HIS SECRET POWER MENACED THE WORLD!
"PHANTOM FROM SPACE"
Produced and Directed by W. Lee Wilder
Screenplay by Bill Raynor and Myles Wilder
Released Thru United Artists

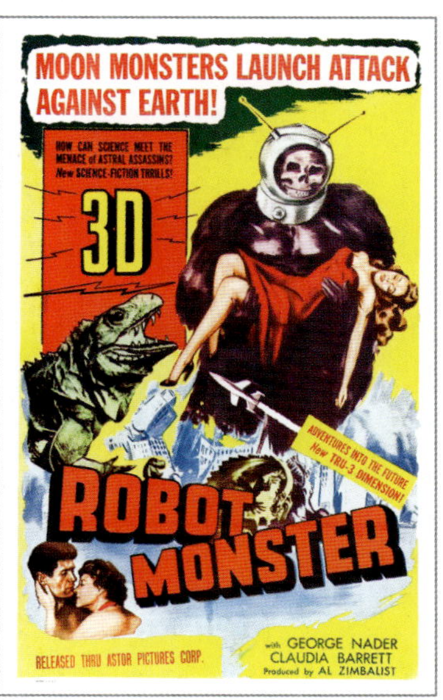

MOON MONSTERS LAUNCH ATTACK AGAINST EARTH!
3D
ADVENTURES INTO THE FUTURE
ROBOT MONSTER
RELEASED THRU ASTOR PICTURES CORP.
with GEORGE NADER
CLAUDIA BARRETT
Produced by AL ZIMBALIST

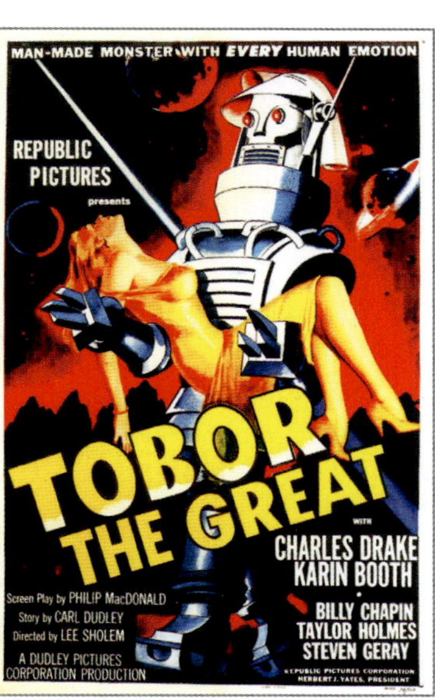

MAN-MADE MONSTER WITH EVERY HUMAN EMOTION
REPUBLIC PICTURES presents
TOBOR THE GREAT
with CHARLES DRAKE KARIN BOOTH
BILLY CHAPIN TAYLOR HOLMES STEVEN GERAY
Screen Play by PHILIP MacDONALD
Story by CARL DUDLEY
Directed by LEE SHOLEM
A DUDLEY PICTURES CORPORATION PRODUCTION
REPUBLIC PICTURES CORPORATION HERBERT J. YATES, PRESIDENT

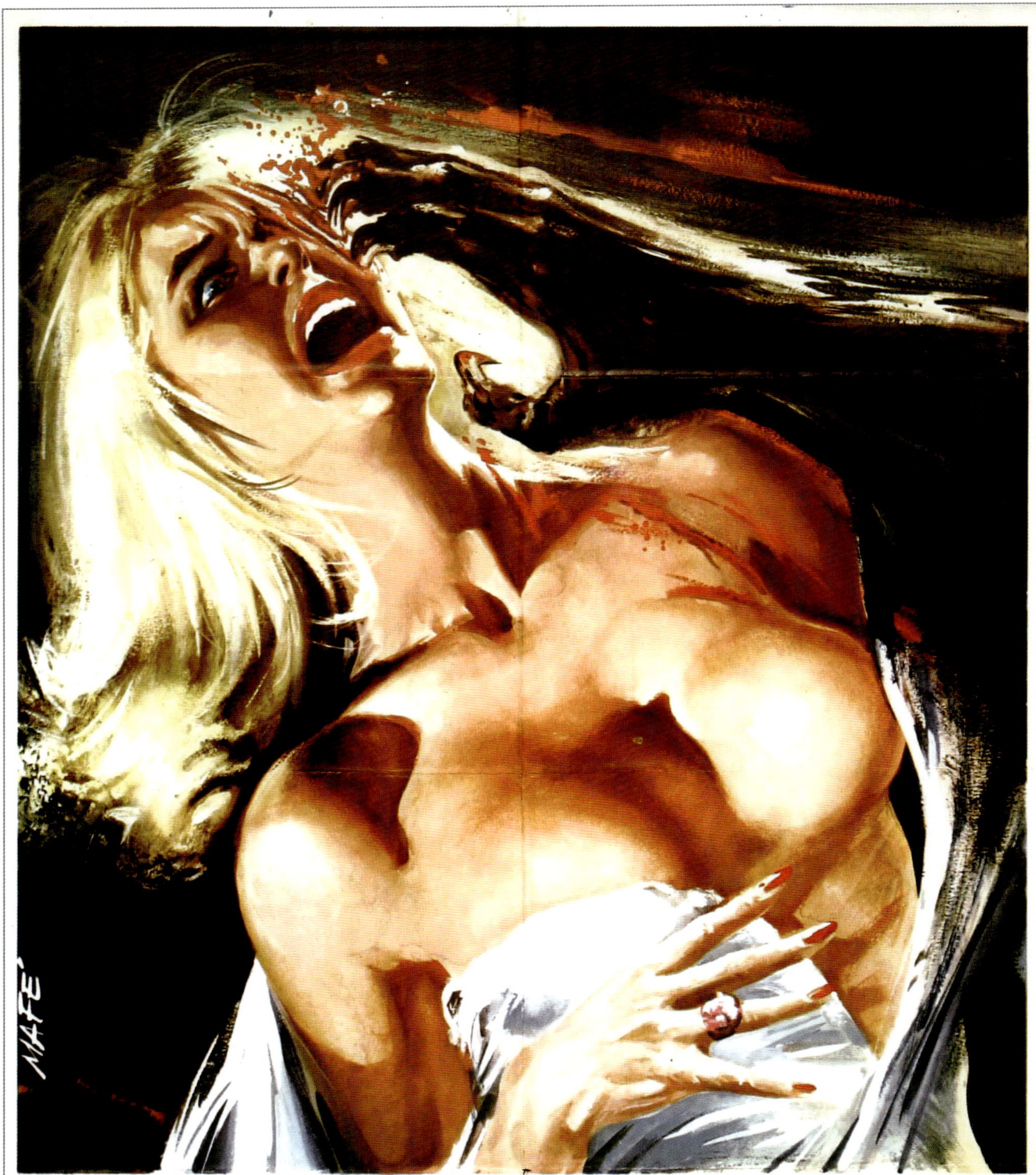

ARTIGLI

PETER CUSHING • SAMANTHA EGGAR • DONALD PLEASENCE • RAY MILLAND
SUSAN PENHALIGON regia: DENIS HEROUX
Un film prodotto dalla RANK ORGANISATION distribuito dalla MOVIE ENTERPRISE

EUROPEAN STYLE

While European film posters of any genre could deliver artistic accomplishments that their US counterparts struggled to match, it was horror movies that often inspired particularly beautiful, if unhinged, work. Biographical details of the illustrator known as Mafé are hard to come by, but his (or her) Italian poster (opposite) for British chiller *The Uncanny* (1977) is hands down the best produced for the film anywhere in the world. Vittorio Pisani's *foglio* for 1954's 3D Vincent Price vehicle *The Mad Magician* (*Il mostro delle nebbie*, overleaf) appears to have very little to do with the actual film, which is set in the 1800s, but is utterly spellbinding nonetheless.

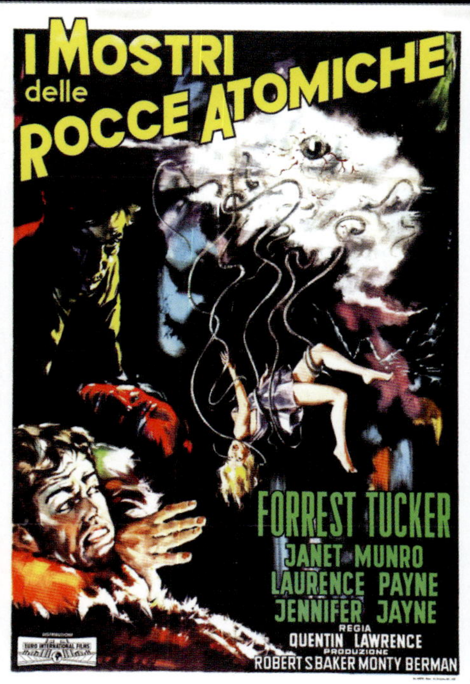

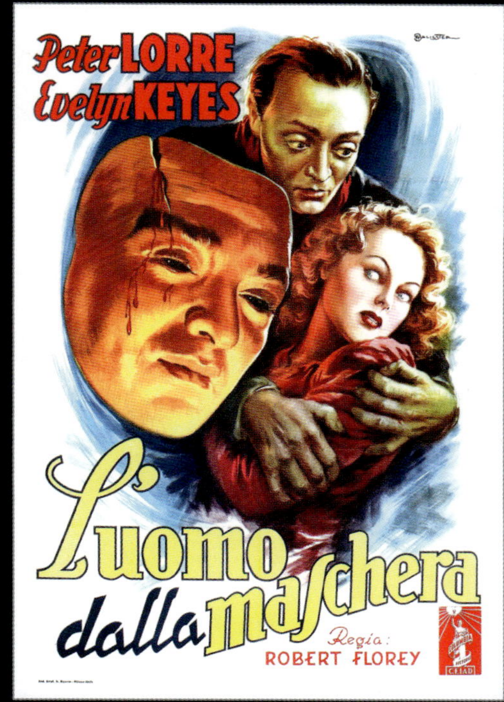

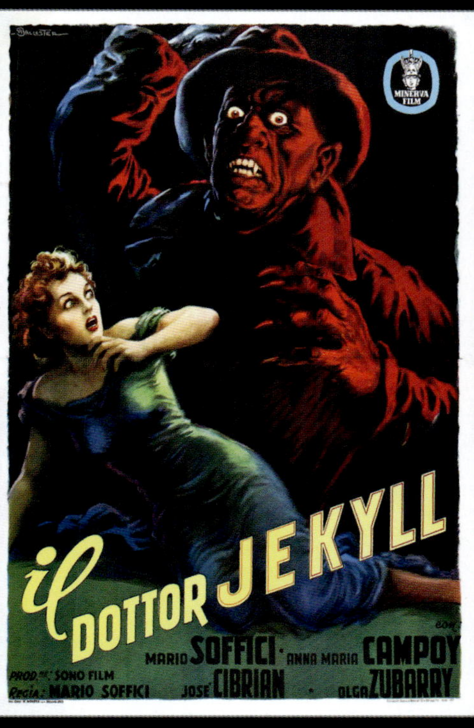

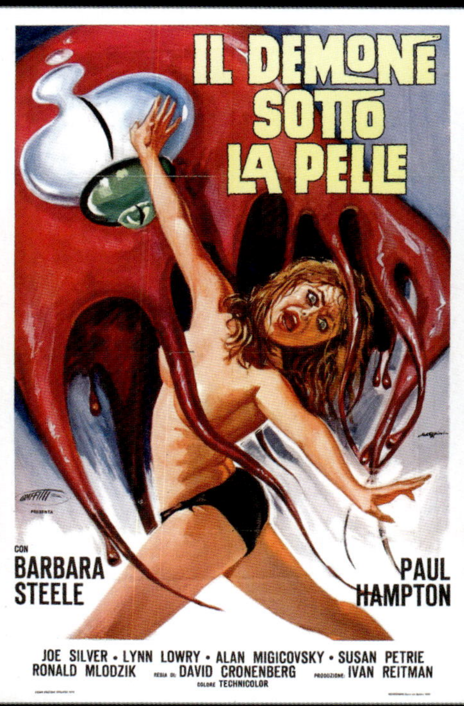

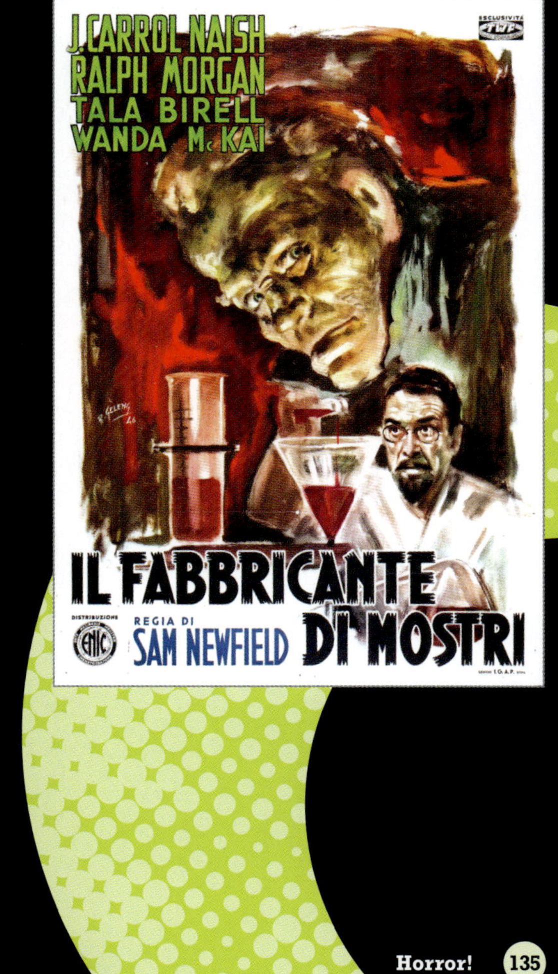

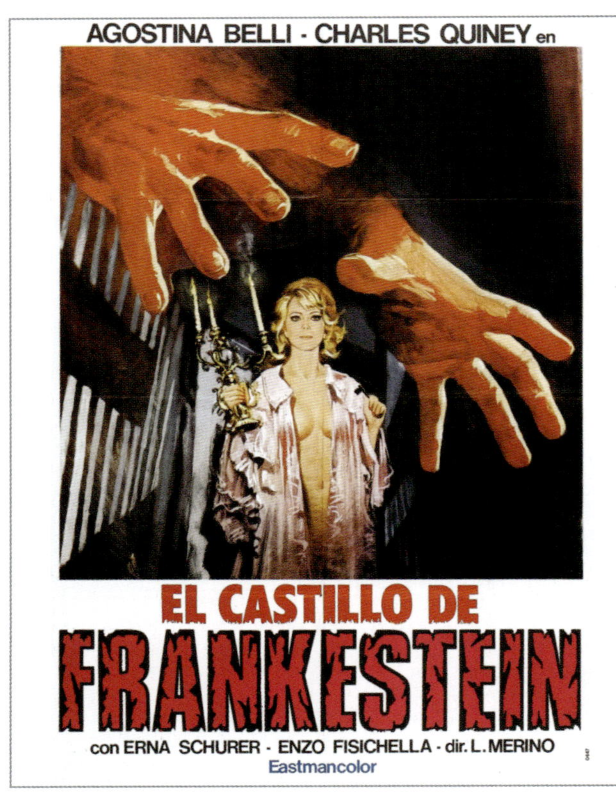
AGOSTINA BELLI · CHARLES QUINEY en
EL CASTILLO DE
FRANKESTEIN
con ERNA SCHURER · ENZO FISICHELLA · dir. L. MERINO
Eastmancolor

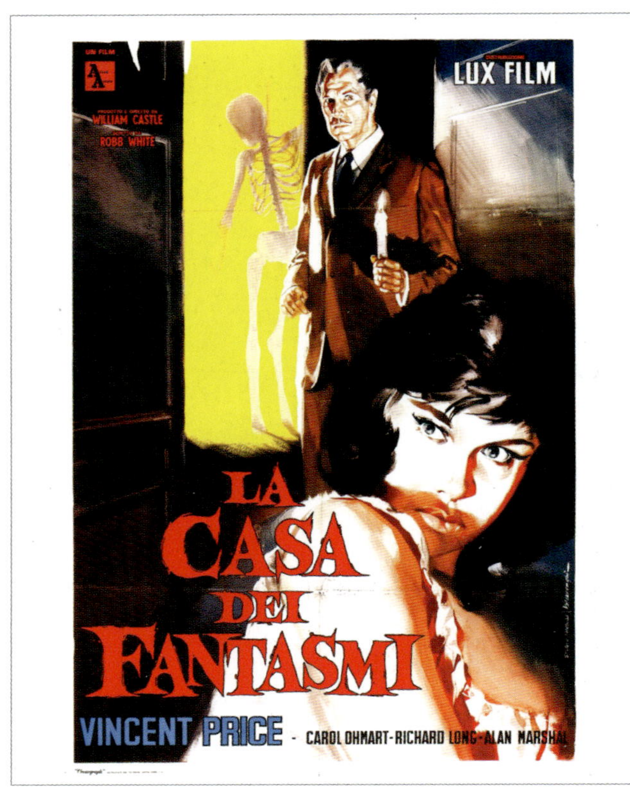
LUX FILM
WILLIAM CASTLE
ROBB WHITE
LA CASA DEI FANTASMI
VINCENT PRICE
CAROL OHMART · RICHARD LONG · ALAN MARSHAL

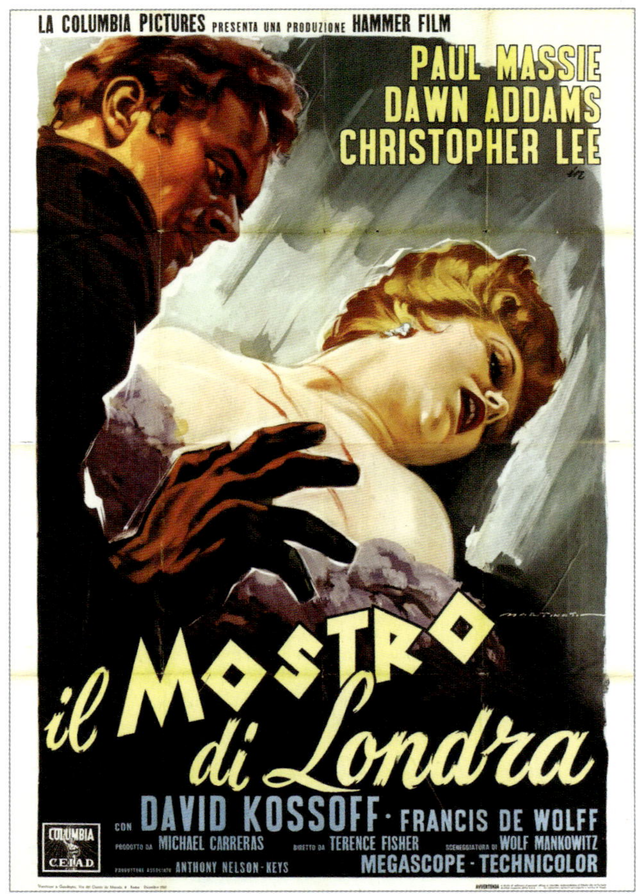
LA COLUMBIA PICTURES presenta una produzione HAMMER FILM
PAUL MASSIE
DAWN ADDAMS
CHRISTOPHER LEE
il Mostro di Londra
con DAVID KOSSOFF · FRANCIS DE WOLFF
prodotto da MICHAEL CARRERAS
diretto da TERENCE FISHER
sceneggiatura di WOLF MANKOWITZ
produttore associato ANTHONY NELSON-KEYS
MEGASCOPE · TECHNICOLOR
COLUMBIA
CEIAD

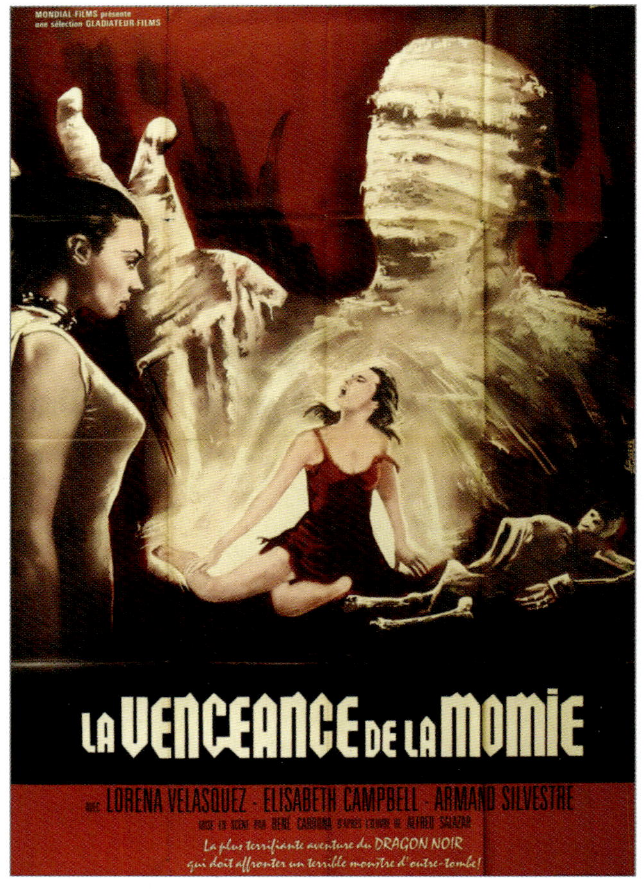
MONDIAL-FILMS présente
une sélection GLADIATEUR-FILMS
LA VENGEANCE DE LA MOMIE
avec LORENA VELASQUEZ · ELISABETH CAMPBELL · ARMAND SILVESTRE
La plus terrifiante aventure du DRAGON NOIR
qui doit affronter un terrible monstre d'outre-tombe!

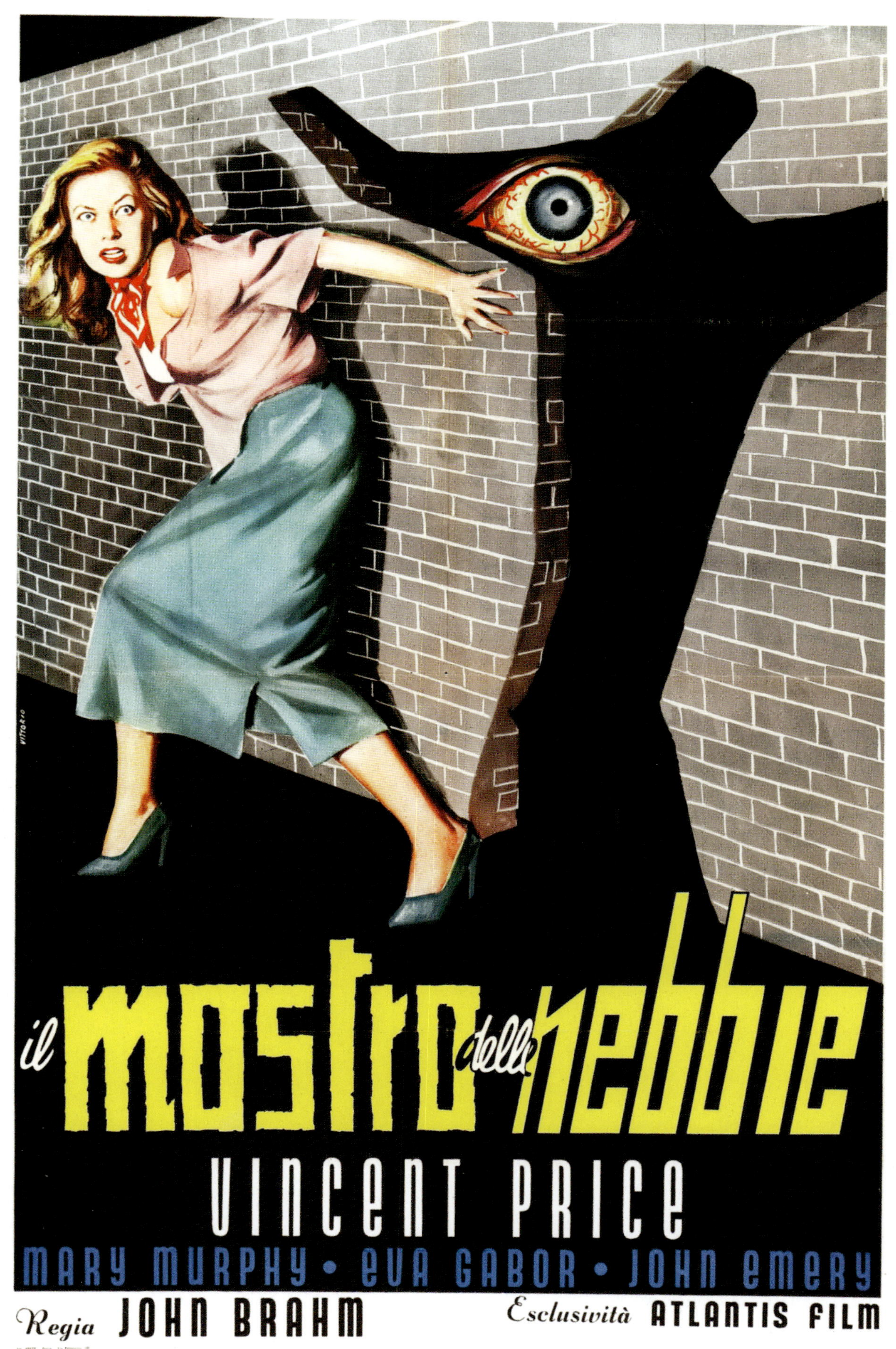
il mostro delle nebbie
VINCENT PRICE
MARY MURPHY • EVA GABOR • JOHN EMERY
Regia JOHN BRAHM
Esclusività ATLANTIS FILM
VITTORIO

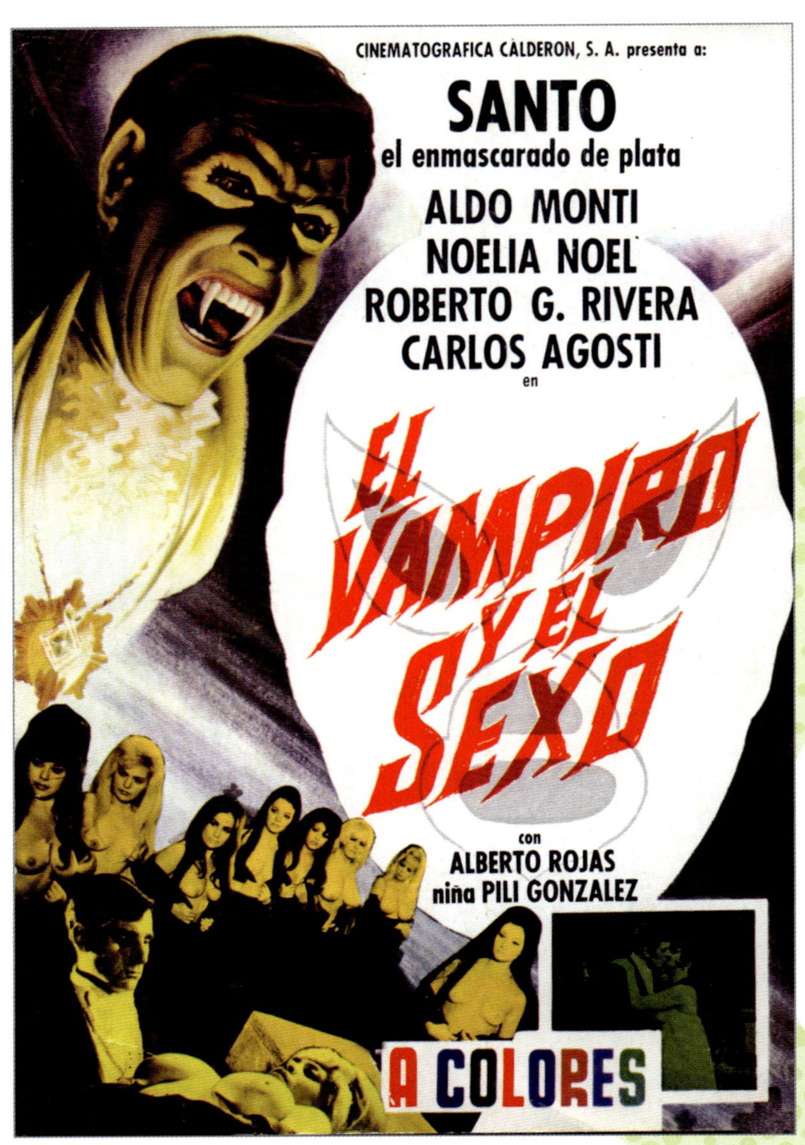

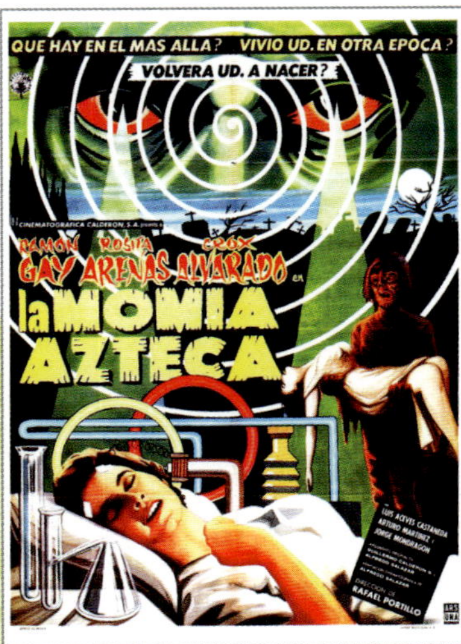

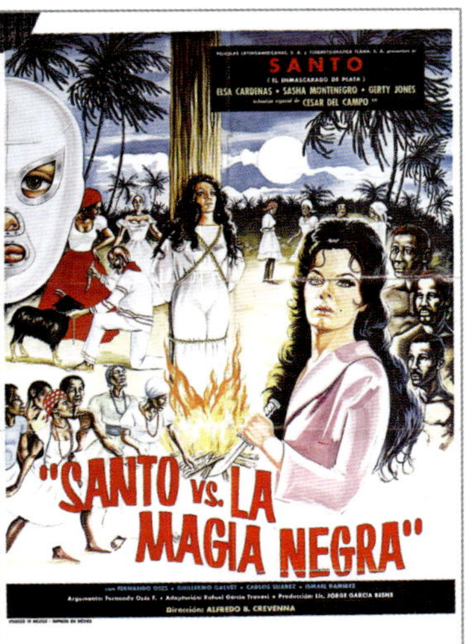

MEXICAN HORROR

Horror is well represented in the bewildering world of Mexploitation cinema, with some marvelously delirious movies (and posters) to enjoy, especially those featuring real-life masked wrestler El Santo facing off against local variants of the usual suspects, including Frankenstein's monster, vampires, mummies, werewolves, and zombies. One outing, *Santo y El tesoro de Drácula* (1967) was released outside Mexico in an extended cut as *El vampiro y el sexo*, with scenes of bare-breasted vampire ladies naughtily added in without Santo's consent (allegedly). When this long-forgotten "adult" version was unearthed in 2011 and scheduled for a film festival curated by director Guillermo del Toro, Santo's son stepped in to defend his late father's clean-cut-hero image, and blocked the screening.

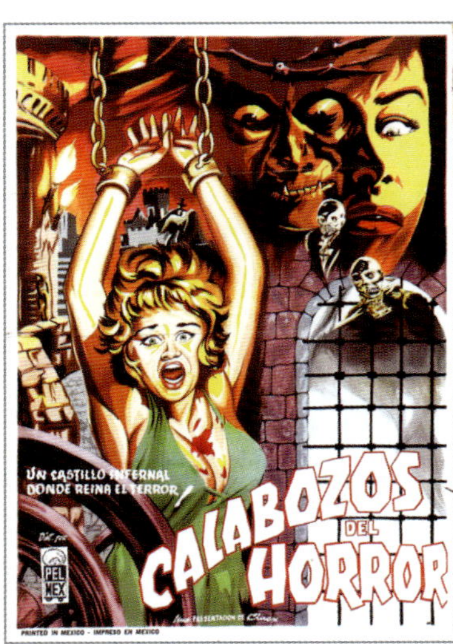

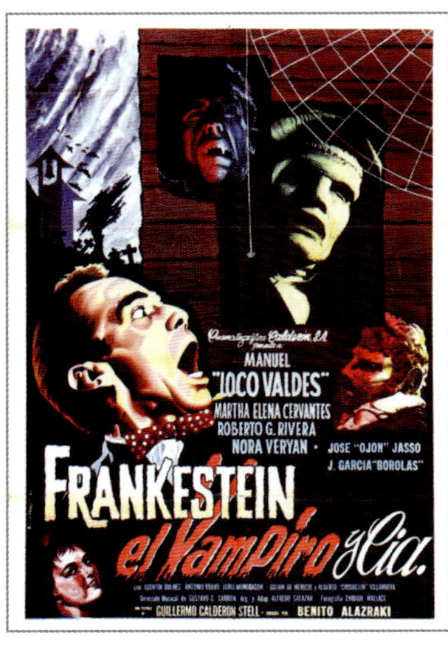

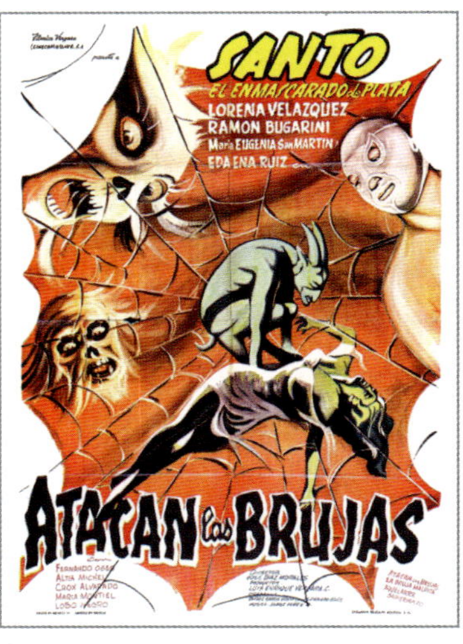

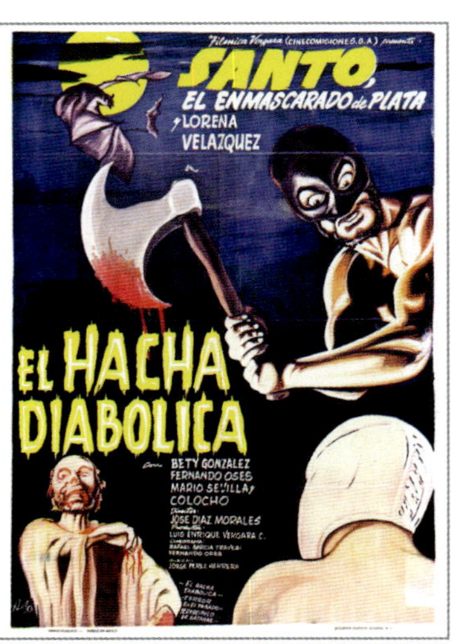

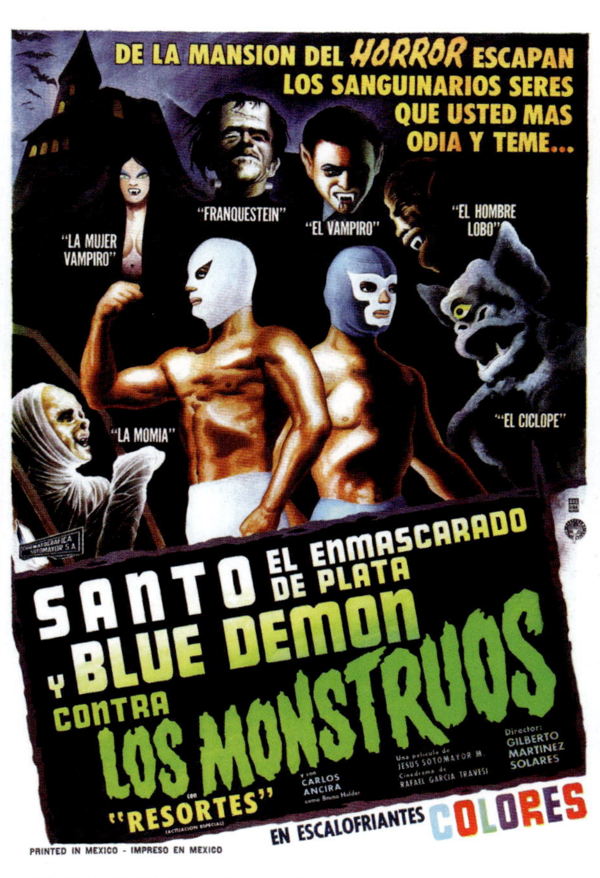
DE LA MANSION DEL HORROR ESCAPAN
LOS SANGUINARIOS SERES
QUE USTED MAS
ODIA Y TEME...
"FRANQUESTEIN"
"EL VAMPIRO"
"EL HOMBRE LOBO"
"LA MUJER VAMPIRO"
"LA MOMIA"
"EL CICLOPE"
SANTO EL ENMASCARADO DE PLATA
y BLUE DEMON
CONTRA
LOS MONSTRUOS
con "RESORTES"
y con CARLOS ANCIRA
Una película de JESUS SOTOMAYOR M.
Cinedrama de RAFAEL GARCIA TRAVESI
Director: GILBERTO MARTINEZ SOLARES
EN ESCALOFRIANTES COLORES
PRINTED IN MEXICO - IMPRESO EN MEXICO

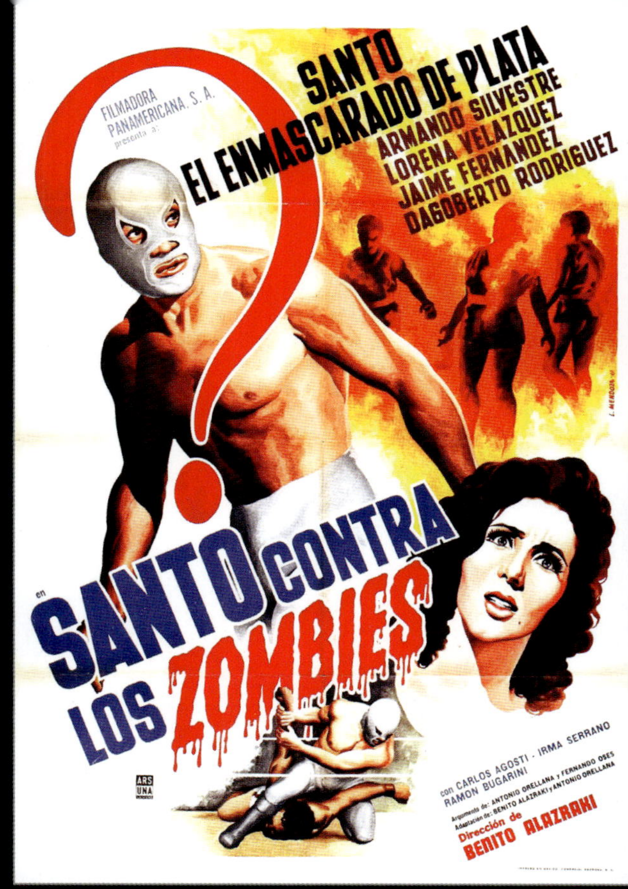
FILMADORA PANAMERICANA, S. A. presenta a:
SANTO
EL ENMASCARADO DE PLATA
ARMANDO SILVESTRE
LORENA VELAZQUEZ
JAIME FERNANDEZ
DAGOBERTO RODRIGUEZ
en SANTO CONTRA LOS ZOMBIES
con CARLOS AGOSTI - IRMA SERRANO
RAMON BUGARINI
Argumento de: ANTONIO ORELLANA y FERNANDO OSES
Adaptación de: BENITO ALAZRAKI y ANTONIO ORELLANA
Dirección de BENITO ALAZRAKI

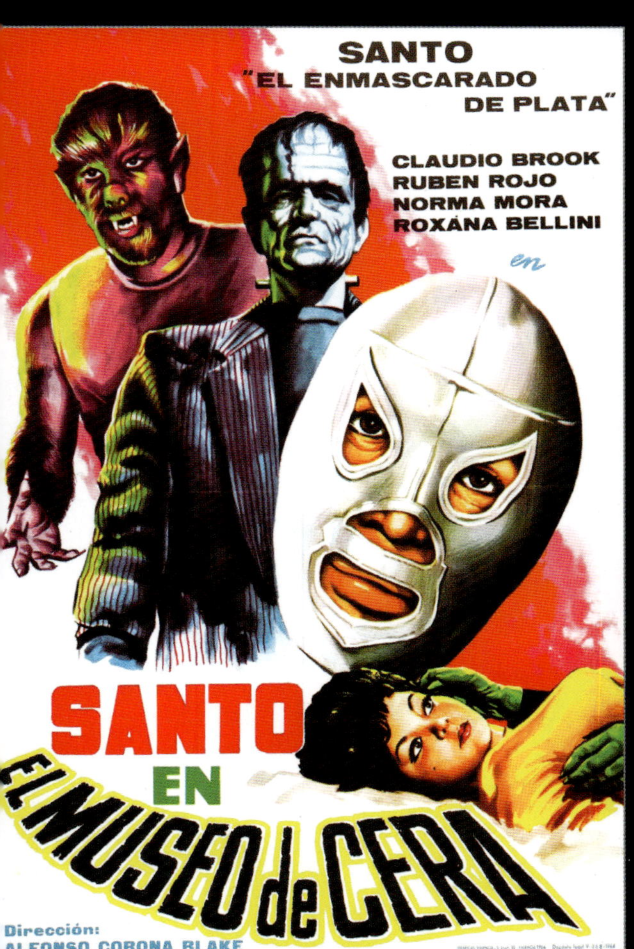
SANTO
"EL ENMASCARADO DE PLATA"
CLAUDIO BROOK
RUBEN ROJO
NORMA MORA
ROXANA BELLINI
en
SANTO
EN
EL MUSEO de CERA
Dirección:
ALFONSO CORONA BLAKE

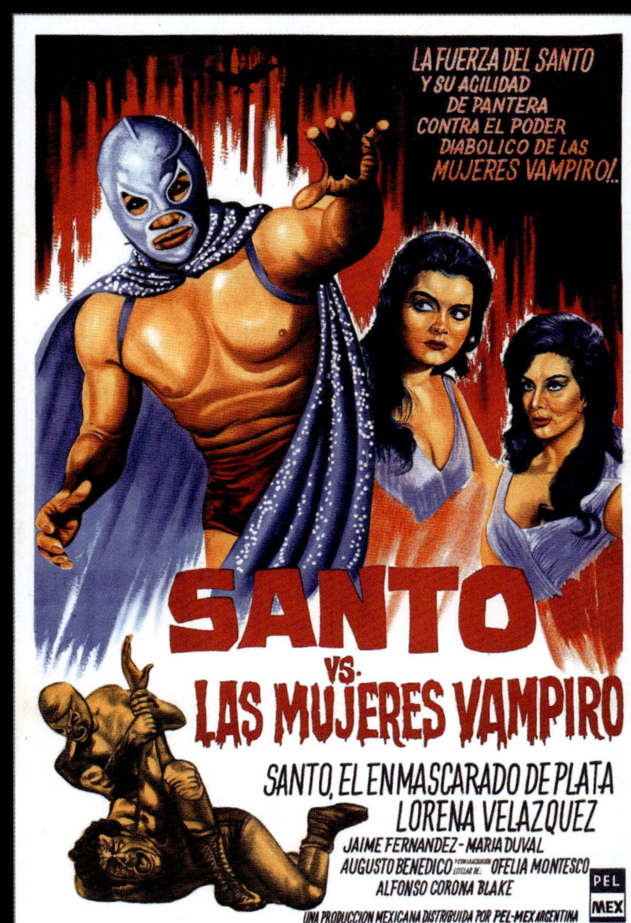
LA FUERZA DEL SANTO
Y SU AGILIDAD
DE PANTERA
CONTRA EL PODER
DIABOLICO DE LAS
MUJERES VAMPIRO!..
SANTO
vs.
LAS MUJERES VAMPIRO
SANTO, EL ENMASCARADO DE PLATA
LORENA VELAZQUEZ
JAIME FERNANDEZ - MARIA DUVAL
AUGUSTO BENEDICO - OFELIA MONTESCO
ALFONSO CORONA BLAKE
PEL MEX
UNA PRODUCCION MEXICANA DISTRIBUIDA POR PEL-MEX ARGENTINA

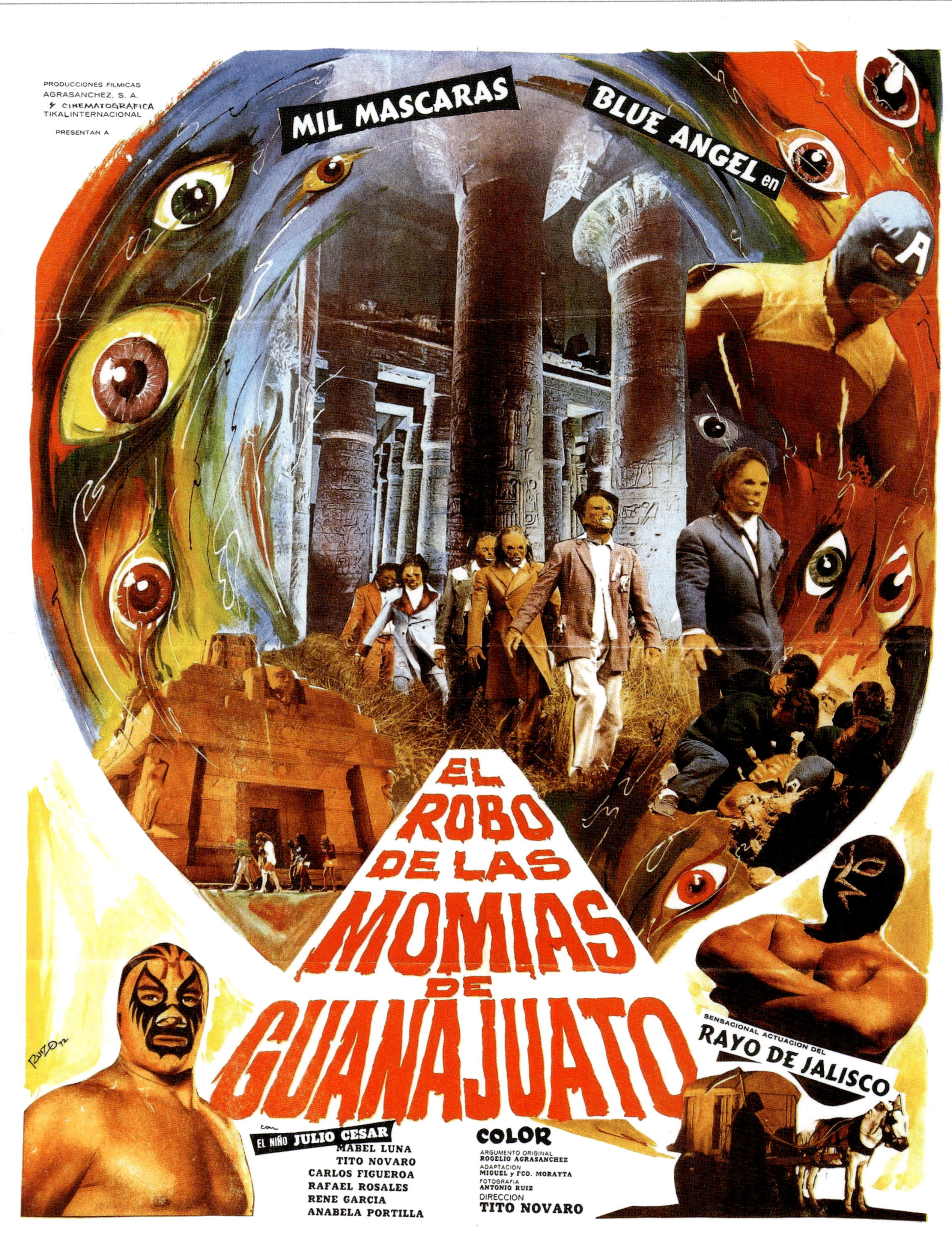
PRODUCCIONES FILMICAS
AGRASANCHEZ, S. A.
y CINEMATOGRAFICA
TIKALINTERNACIONAL
PRESENTAN A
MIL MASCARAS
BLUE ANGEL en
EL ROBO DE LAS MOMIAS DE GUANAJUATO
SENSACIONAL ACTUACION DEL
RAYO DE JALISCO
con
EL NIÑO JULIO CESAR
MABEL LUNA
TITO NOVARO
CARLOS FIGUEROA
RAFAEL ROSALES
RENE GARCIA
ANABELA PORTILLA
COLOR
ARGUMENTO ORIGINAL
ROGELIO AGRASANCHEZ
ADAPTACION
MIGUEL y FCO. MORAYTA
FOTOGRAFIA
ANTONIO RUIZ
DIRECCION
TITO NOVARO

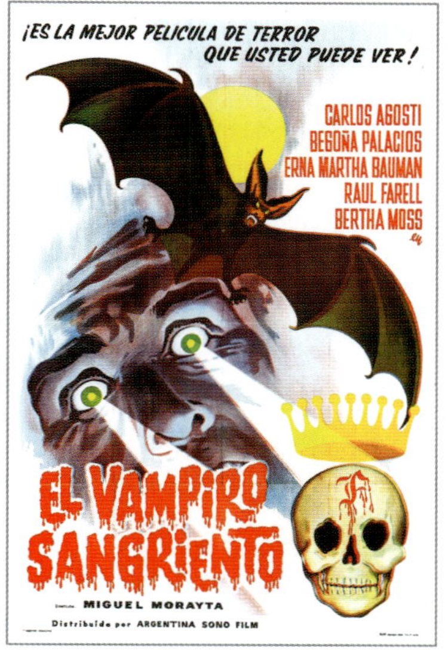
¡ES LA MEJOR PELICULA DE TERROR QUE USTED PUEDE VER!
CARLOS AGOSTI
BEGOÑA PALACIOS
ERNA MARTHA BAUMAN
RAUL FARELL
BERTHA MOSS
EL VAMPIRO SANGRIENTO
MIGUEL MORAYTA
Distribuido por ARGENTINA SONO FILM

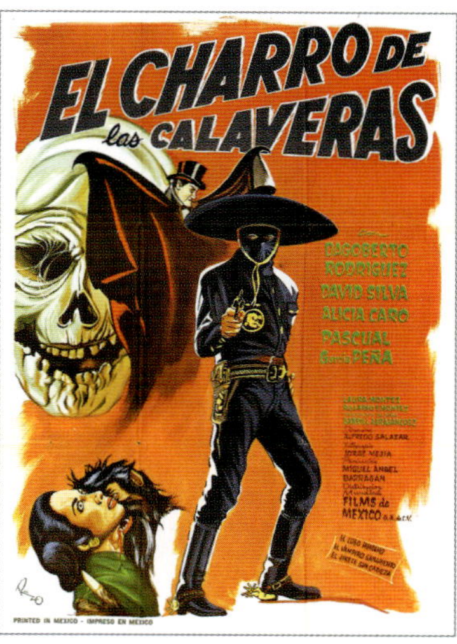
EL CHARRO DE las CALAVERAS
DAGOBERTO RODRIGUEZ
DAVID SILVA
ALICIA CARO
PASCUAL GARCIA PEÑA
FILMS de MEXICO
PRINTED IN MEXICO · IMPRESO EN MEXICO

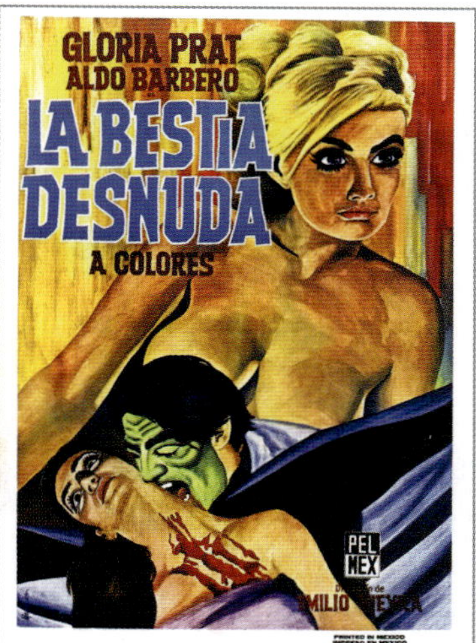
GLORIA PRAT
ALDO BARBERO
LA BESTIA DESNUDA
A COLORES
PEL MEX
PRINTED IN MEXICO
IMPRESO EN MEXICO

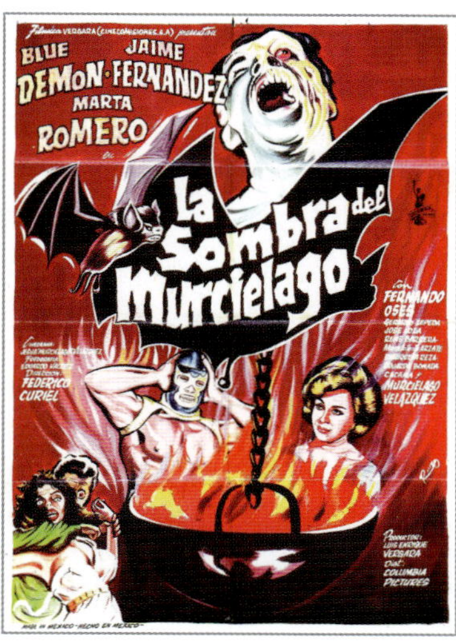
BLUE DEMON
JAIME FERNANDEZ
MARTA ROMERO
La Sombra del Murcielago
FERNANDO OSES
FEDERICO CURIEL

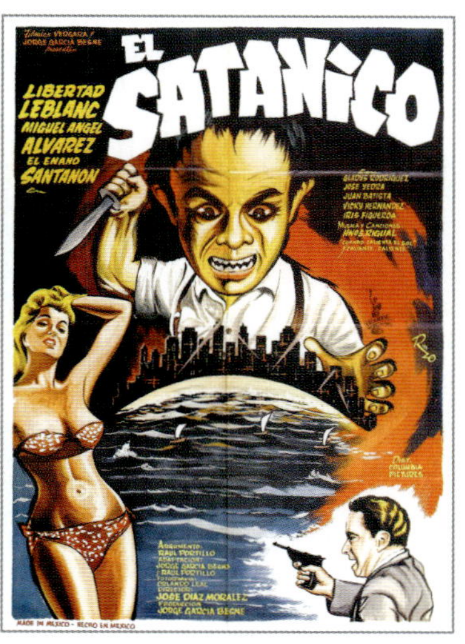
EL SATANICO
LIBERTAD LEBLANC
MIGUEL ANGEL ALVAREZ
EL ENANO SANTANON
JOSE DIAZ MORALES

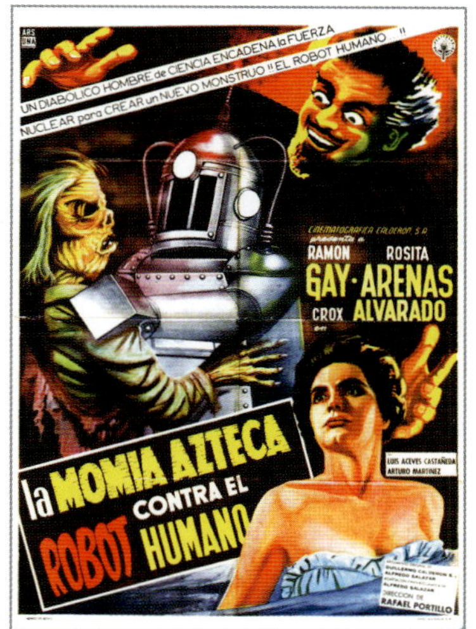
UN DIABOLICO HOMBRE DE CIENCIA ENCADENA LA FUERZA NUCLEAR para CREAR un NUEVO MONSTRUO !! EL ROBOT HUMANO !!
RAMON GAY
ROSITA ARENAS
CROX ALVARADO
la MOMIA AZTECA CONTRA EL ROBOT HUMANO
RAFAEL PORTILLO

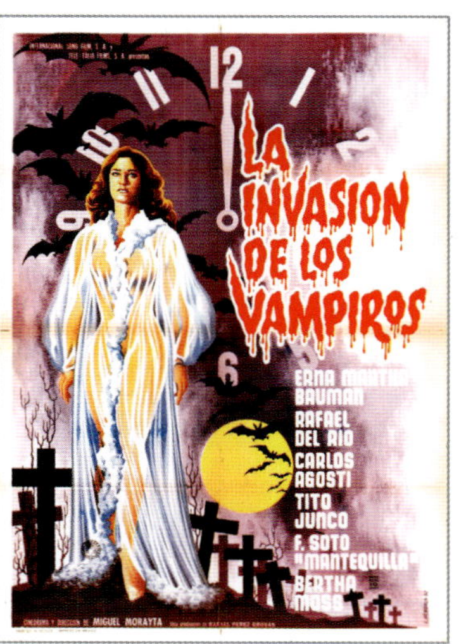
LA INVASION DE LOS VAMPIROS
ERNA MARTHA BAUMAN
RAFAEL DEL RIO
CARLOS AGOSTI
TITO JUNCO
F. SOTO "MANTEQUILLA"
BERTHA MOSS
MIGUEL MORAYTA

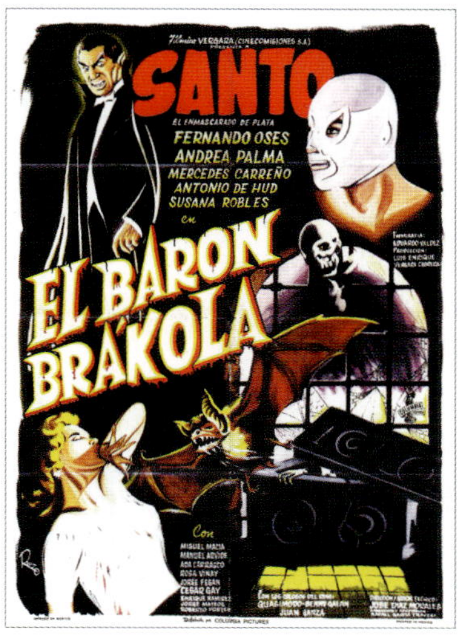
SANTO
EL ENMASCARADO DE PLATA
FERNANDO OSES
ANDREA PALMA
MERCEDES CARREÑO
ANTONIO DE HUD
SUSANA ROBLES
en
EL BARON BRAKOLA

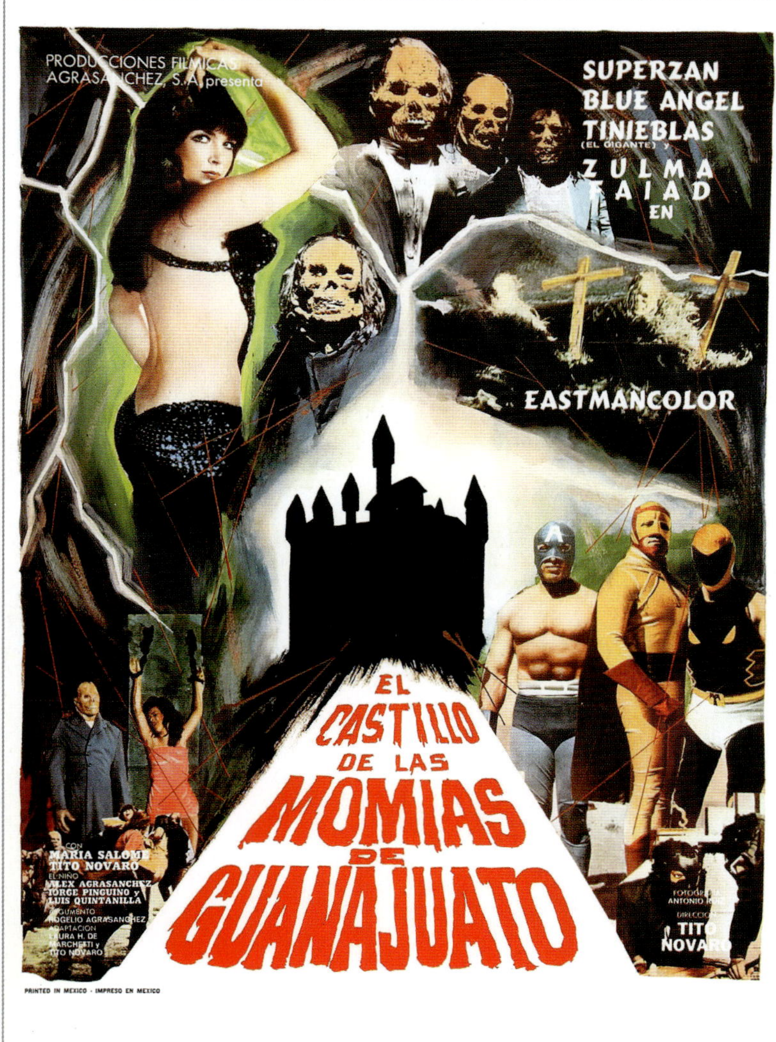
PRODUCCIONES FILMICAS AGRASANCHEZ, S.A. presenta
SUPERZAN
BLUE ANGEL
TINIEBLAS (EL GIGANTE) y
ZULMA FAIAD en
EASTMANCOLOR
EL CASTILLO DE LAS MOMIAS DE GUANAJUATO
CON MARIA SALOME
TITO NOVARO
EL NIÑO ALEX AGRASANCHEZ
JORGE PINGUINO y LUIS QUINTANILLA
ARGUMENTO ROGELIO AGRASANCHEZ
ADAPTACION LAURA H. DE MARCHESTI y TITO NOVARO
DIRECCION TITO NOVARO
PRINTED IN MEXICO · IMPRESO EN MEXICO

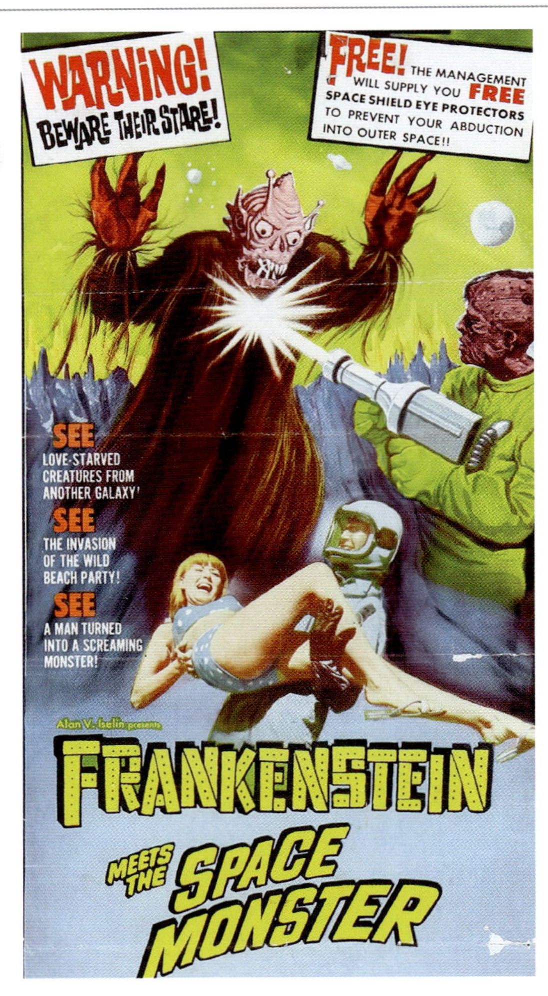

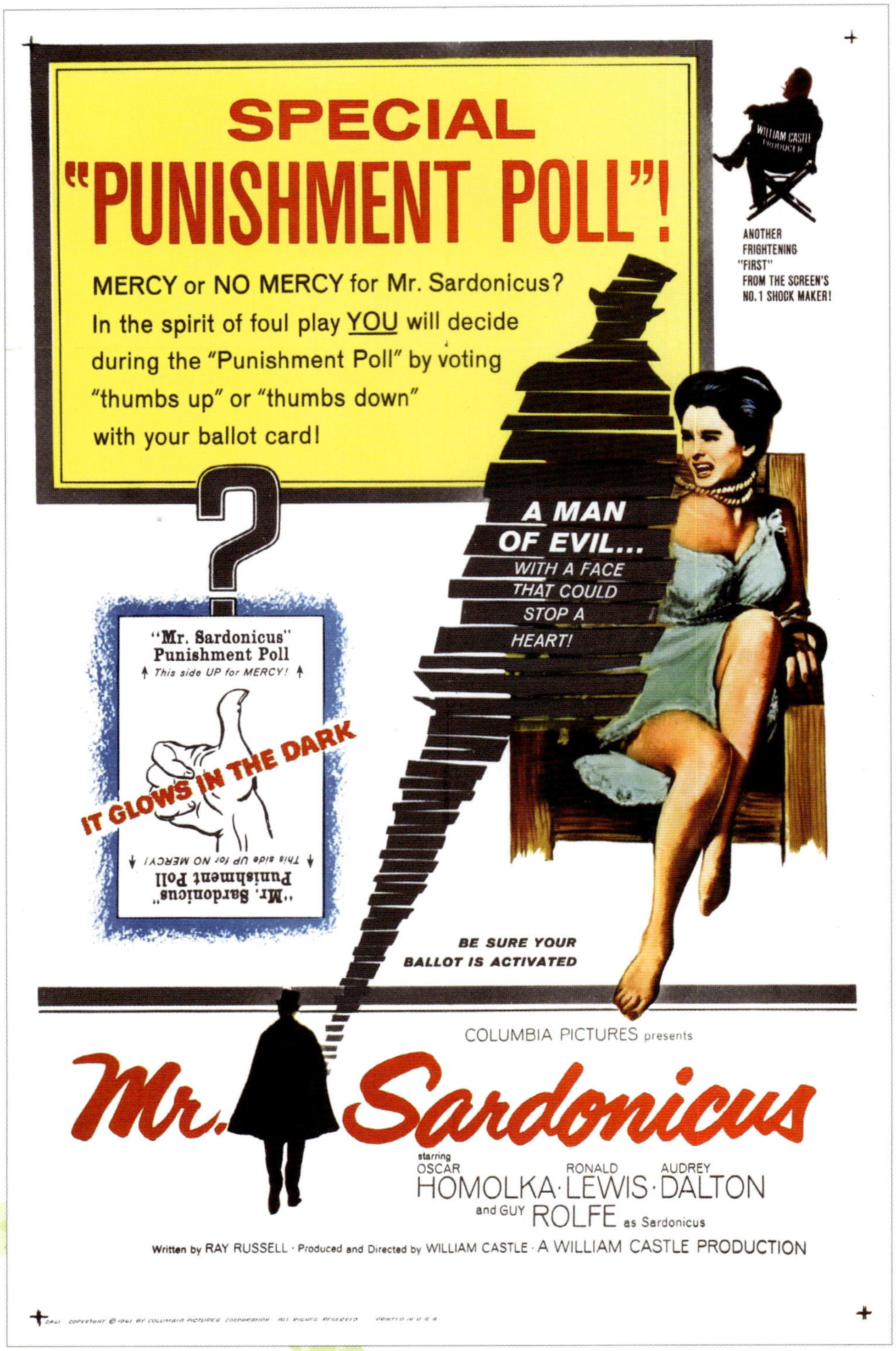

SPECIAL
"PUNISHMENT POLL"!
MERCY or NO MERCY for Mr. Sardonicus?
In the spirit of foul play YOU will decide
during the "Punishment Poll" by voting
"thumbs up" or "thumbs down"
with your ballot card!

ANOTHER FRIGHTENING "FIRST" FROM THE SCREEN'S NO. 1 SHOCK MAKER!

"Mr. Sardonicus" Punishment Poll
This side UP for MERCY!

IT GLOWS IN THE DARK

"Mr. Sardonicus" Punishment Poll
This side UP for NO MERCY!

A MAN OF EVIL... WITH A FACE THAT COULD STOP A HEART!

BE SURE YOUR BALLOT IS ACTIVATED

COLUMBIA PICTURES presents
Mr. Sardonicus
starring OSCAR HOMOLKA · RONALD LEWIS · AUDREY DALTON
and GUY ROLFE as Sardonicus
Written by RAY RUSSELL · Produced and Directed by WILLIAM CASTLE · A WILLIAM CASTLE PRODUCTION

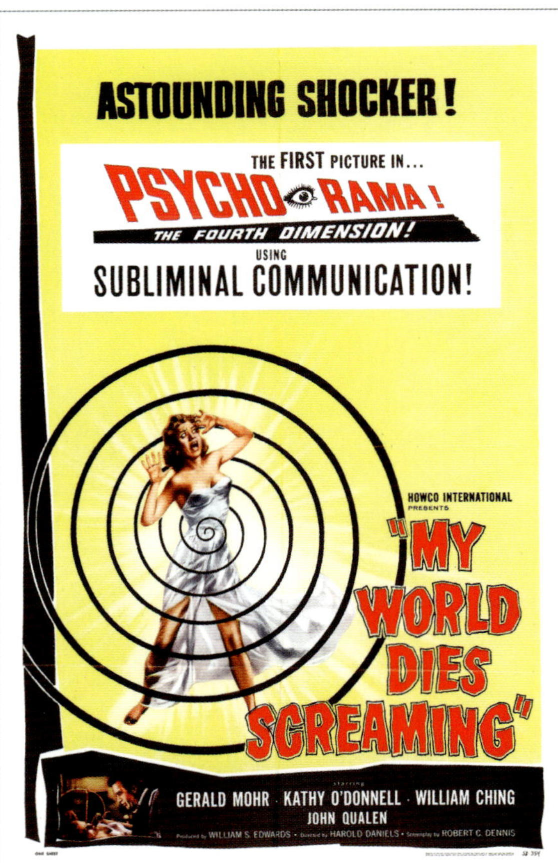

GIMMICKS

The history of filmed entertainment is in many ways the history of a succession of gimmicks designed to sell tickets. At first the picture alone was enough, but soon the new-fangled invention of "sound" was added, followed by color, 3D, CinemaScope, IMAX, and most recently, 48fps, which sounds very exciting even if 99 percent of filmgoers have no idea what it is. Exploitation filmmakers were rarely able to boast about being first with a big technological advance, but that didn't stop them using their posters to scream about amazing new innovations (as this and the following spread show), even if they essentially amounted a free mask to cover your eyes from the scary bits, or a complimentary bag to be sick into. *Castle of Evil*'s promise of "Funeral expenses guaranteed by a Major North American Insurance Co." for anybody dropping dead while watching the film made for a catchy tagline, though.

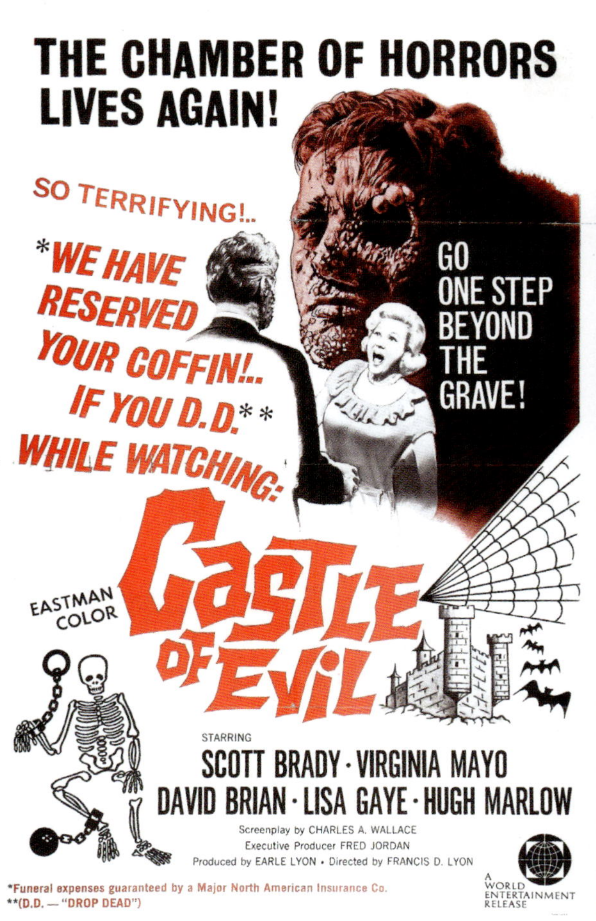
THE CHAMBER OF HORRORS
LIVES AGAIN!
SO TERRIFYING!..
*WE HAVE RESERVED YOUR COFFIN!.. IF YOU D.D.** WHILE WATCHING:
GO ONE STEP BEYOND THE GRAVE!
EASTMAN COLOR
CASTLE OF EVIL
STARRING
SCOTT BRADY · VIRGINIA MAYO
DAVID BRIAN · LISA GAYE · HUGH MARLOW
Screenplay by CHARLES A. WALLACE
Executive Producer FRED JORDAN
Produced by EARLE LYON • Directed by FRANCIS D. LYON
*Funeral expenses guaranteed by a Major North American Insurance Co.
**(D.D. — "DROP DEAD")
A WORLD ENTERTAINMENT RELEASE

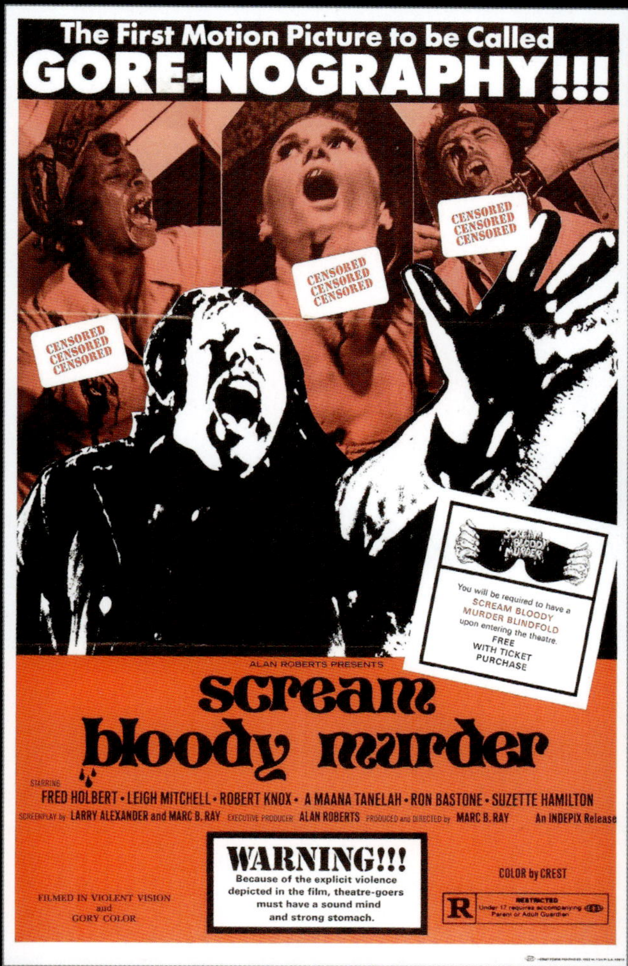
The First Motion Picture to be Called
GORE-NOGRAPHY!!!
CENSORED CENSORED CENSORED
CENSORED CENSORED CENSORED
CENSORED CENSORED CENSORED
You will be required to have a SCREAM BLOODY MURDER BLINDFOLD upon entering the theatre. FREE WITH TICKET PURCHASE
ALAN ROBERTS PRESENTS
scream bloody murder
STARRING
FRED HOLBERT · LEIGH MITCHELL · ROBERT KNOX · A MAANA TANELAH · RON BASTONE · SUZETTE HAMILTON
SCREENPLAY by LARRY ALEXANDER and MARC B. RAY EXECUTIVE PRODUCER ALAN ROBERTS PRODUCED and DIRECTED by MARC B. RAY
An INDEPIX Release
WARNING!!!
Because of the explicit violence depicted in the film, theatre-goers must have a sound mind and strong stomach.
FILMED IN VIOLENT VISION and GORY COLOR
COLOR by CREST
R RESTRICTED Under 17 requires accompanying Parent or Adult Guardian

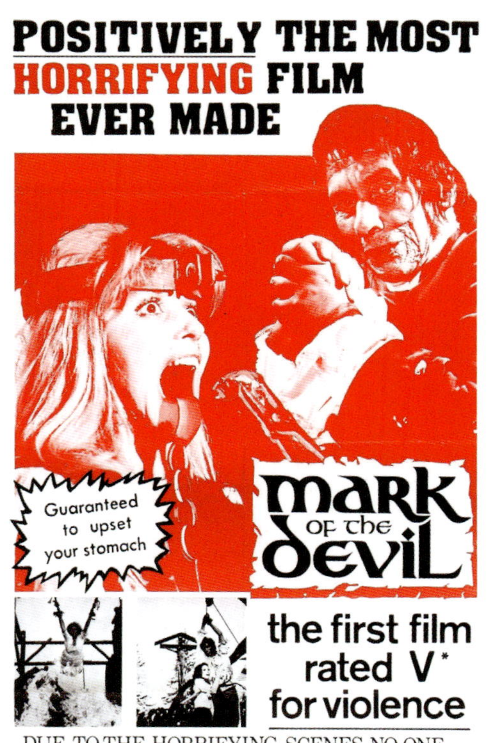
POSITIVELY THE MOST
HORRIFYING FILM
EVER MADE
Guaranteed to upset your stomach
MARK OF THE DEVIL
the first film rated V* for violence
DUE TO THE HORRIFYING SCENES NO ONE ADMITTED WITHOUT A VOMIT BAG
(available free at box office)
* ALL AGES ADMITTED / PARENTAL ESCORTS ENCOURAGED
DISTRIBUTED BY: HALLMARK RELEASING CORP.

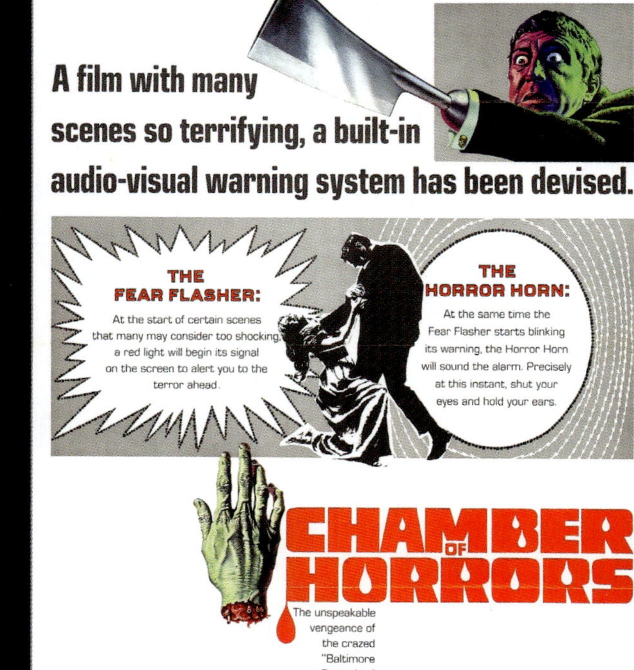
THE YEAR'S MOST STARTLING
ENTERTAINMENT INNOVATION!
A film with many scenes so terrifying, a built-in audio-visual warning system has been devised.
THE FEAR FLASHER:
At the start of certain scenes that many may consider too shocking, a red light will begin its signal on the screen to alert you to the terror ahead.
THE HORROR HORN:
At the same time the Fear Flasher starts blinking its warning, the Horror Horn will sound the alarm. Precisely at this instant, shut your eyes and hold your ears.
CHAMBER OF HORRORS
The unspeakable vengeance of the crazed "Baltimore Strangler."
STARRING
CESARE DANOVA · WILFRID HYDE-WHITE · LAURA DEVON · PATRICE WYMORE · SUZY PARKER
ALSO STARRING TUN TUN PHILIP BOURNEUF AND PATRICK O'NEAL AS "JASON"
Story by Ray Russell and Stephen Kandel • Produced and Directed by Hy Averback
Screenplay by Stephen Kandel
TECHNICOLOR® FROM WARNER BROS.

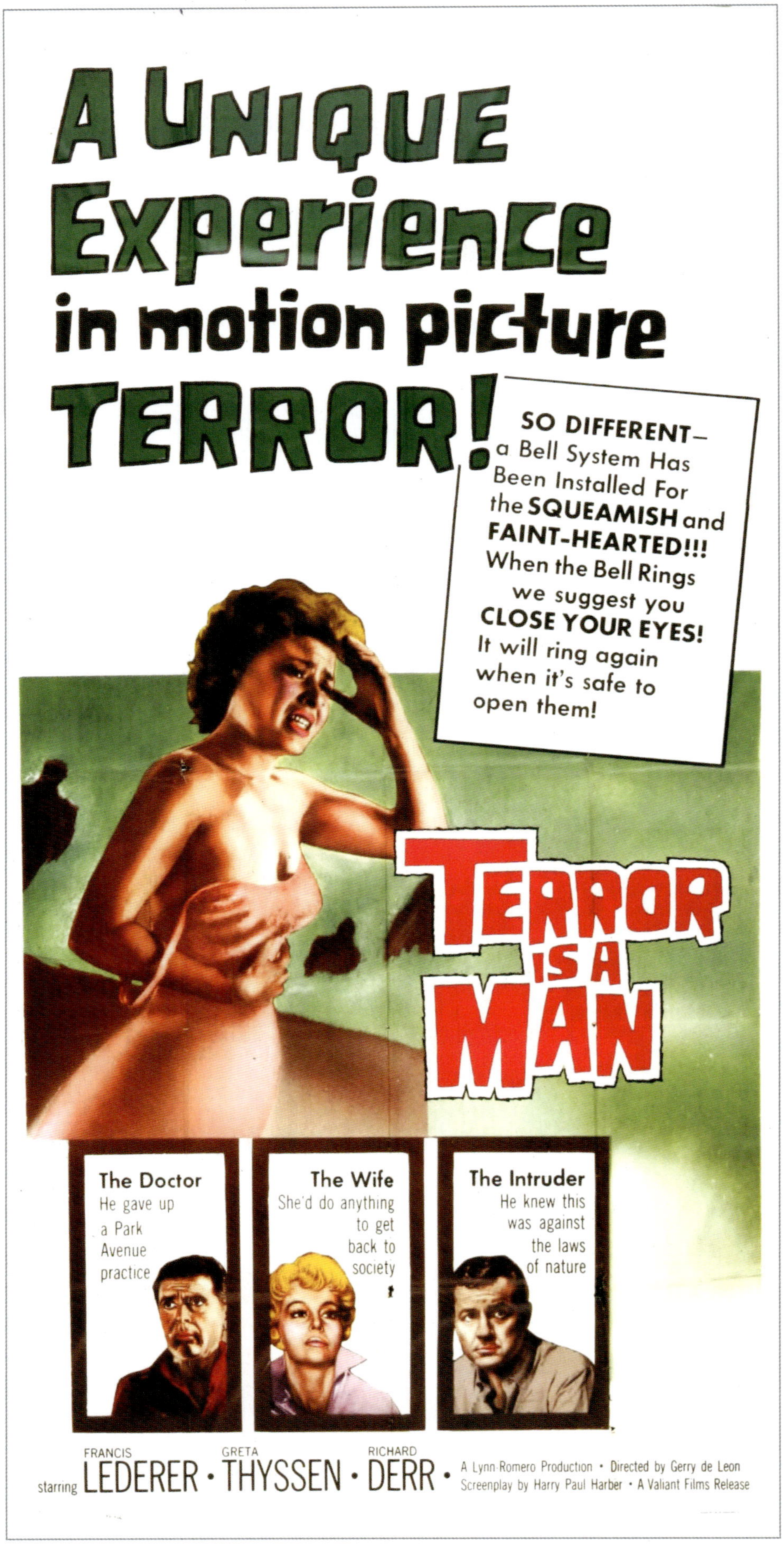

A UNIQUE
Experience
in motion picture
TERROR!

SO DIFFERENT—
a Bell System Has
Been Installed For
the **SQUEAMISH** and
FAINT-HEARTED!!!
When the Bell Rings
we suggest you
CLOSE YOUR EYES!
It will ring again
when it's safe to
open them!

TERROR IS A MAN

The Doctor
He gave up
a Park
Avenue
practice

The Wife
She'd do anything
to get
back to
society

The Intruder
He knew this
was against
the laws
of nature

starring FRANCIS LEDERER · GRETA THYSSEN · RICHARD DERR · A Lynn-Romero Production · Directed by Gerry de Leon
Screenplay by Harry Paul Harber · A Valiant Films Release

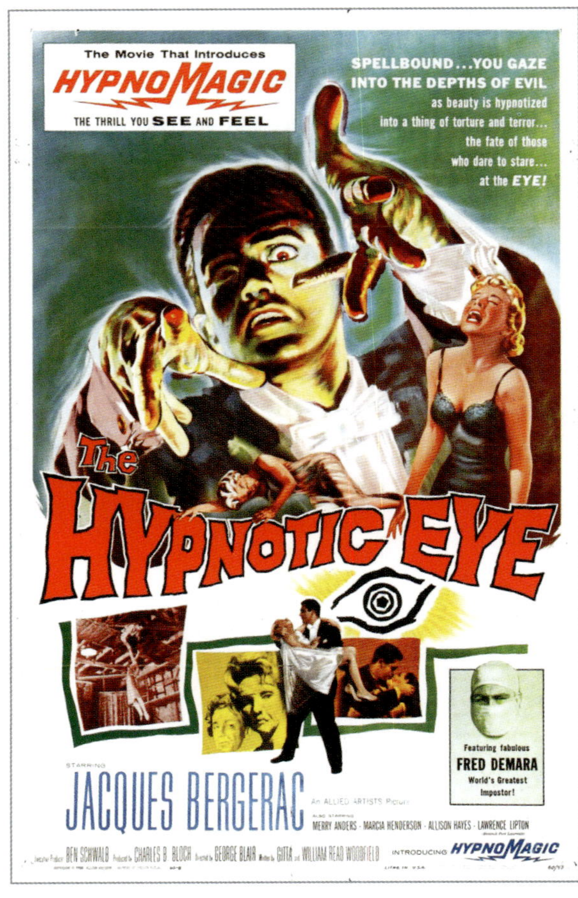

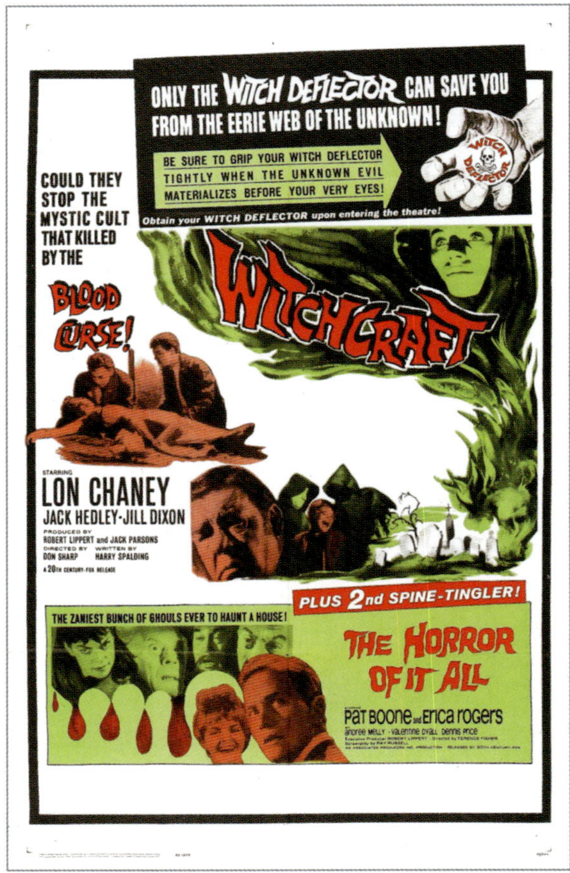

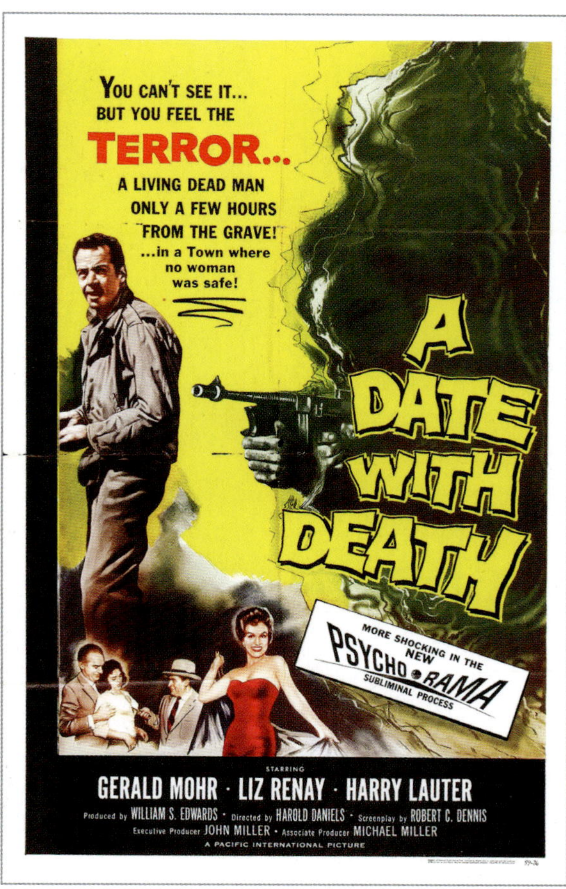
You can't see it... but you feel the
TERROR...
A living dead man only a few hours from the grave!
...in a Town where no woman was safe!
A DATE WITH DEATH
MORE SHOCKING IN THE NEW PSYCHO-RAMA SUBLIMINAL PROCESS
STARRING
GERALD MOHR · LIZ RENAY · HARRY LAUTER
A PACIFIC INTERNATIONAL PICTURE

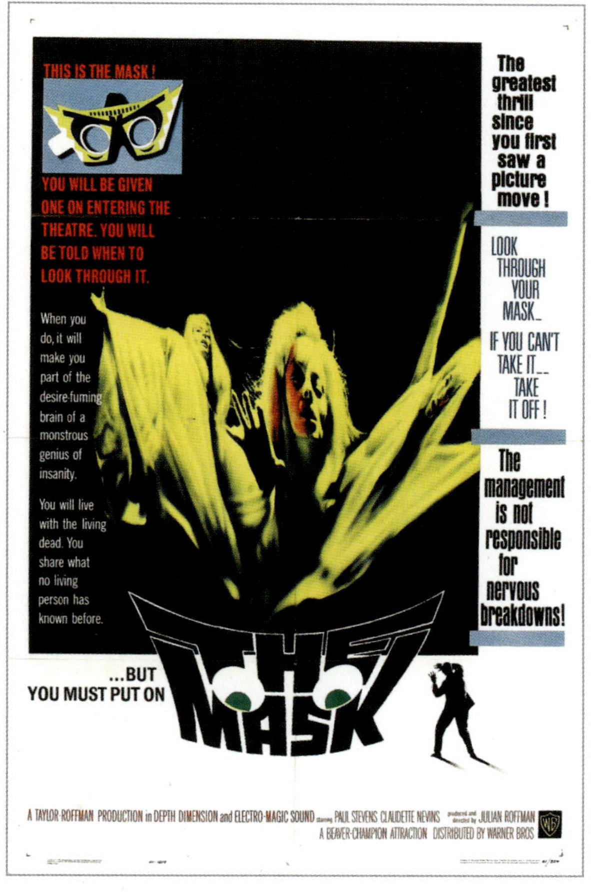
THIS IS THE MASK!
YOU WILL BE GIVEN ONE ON ENTERING THE THEATRE. YOU WILL BE TOLD WHEN TO LOOK THROUGH IT.
When you do, it will make you part of the desire-fuming brain of a monstrous genius of insanity.
You will live with the living dead. You share what no living person has known before.
The greatest thrill since you first saw a picture move!
LOOK THROUGH YOUR MASK... IF YOU CAN'T TAKE IT... TAKE IT OFF!
The management is not responsible for nervous breakdowns!
...BUT YOU MUST PUT ON
THE MASK

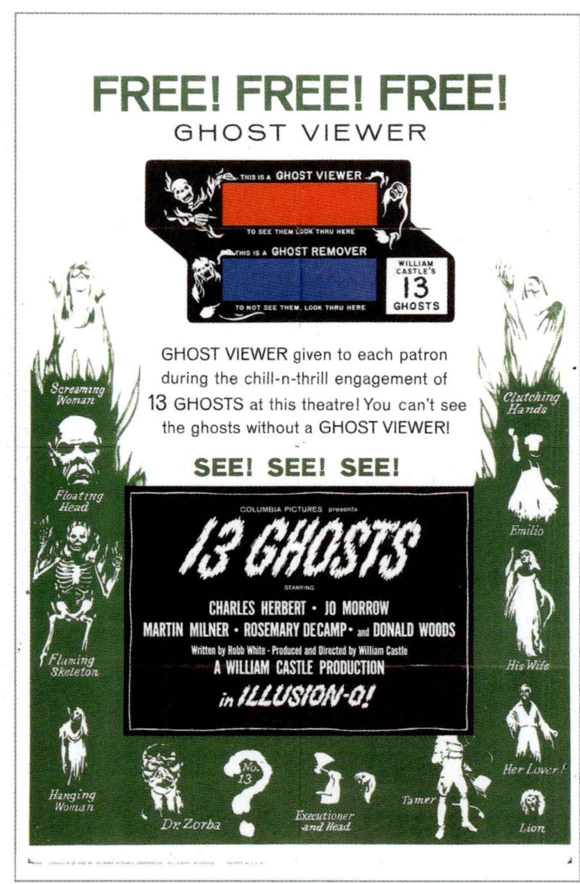
FREE! FREE! FREE!
GHOST VIEWER
THIS IS A GHOST VIEWER
THIS IS A GHOST REMOVER
WILLIAM CASTLE'S 13 GHOSTS
GHOST VIEWER given to each patron during the chill-n-thrill engagement of 13 GHOSTS at this theatre! You can't see the ghosts without a GHOST VIEWER!
SEE! SEE! SEE!
COLUMBIA PICTURES presents
13 GHOSTS
STARRING
CHARLES HERBERT · JO MORROW
MARTIN MILNER · ROSEMARY DECAMP · and DONALD WOODS
Written by Robb White · Produced and Directed by William Castle
A WILLIAM CASTLE PRODUCTION
in ILLUSION-O!
Screaming Woman
Clutching Hands
Floating Head
Emilio
Flaming Skeleton
His Wife
Hanging Woman
Her Lover!
Dr. Zorba
Executioner and Head
Tamer
Lion

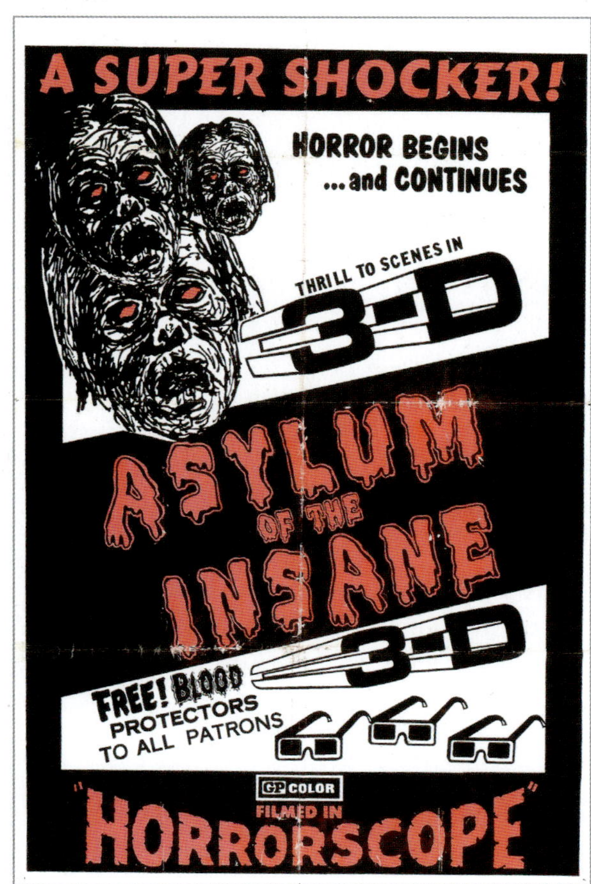
A SUPER SHOCKER!
HORROR BEGINS ...and CONTINUES
THRILL TO SCENES IN 3-D
ASYLUM OF THE INSANE
3-D
FREE! BLOOD PROTECTORS TO ALL PATRONS
CP COLOR
FILMED IN
"HORRORSCOPE"

KARLOFF THE UNCANNY

A starring role in Universal's *Frankenstein* (1931) made the mild-mannered British-born actor William Henry Pratt (1887–1969) a star, though of course the public knew him by his stage name, Boris Karloff. Scores of films followed, some great, some forgettable, but all eager to highlight him as the main draw in their advertising. The Italian poster for *Voodoo Island* (*L'isola stregata degli zombies*, 1957) even included a nicely painted image of Boris in his other great Universal role, *The Mummy* (1932), just to make sure moviegoers made the connection. He was still working, and still looming out of posters, right up until his death: overleaf is the moody Spanish poster for Michael Reeves's *The Sorcerers* (1967), along with one-sheets for his very last project, a quartet of Mexican horror movies filmed back-to-back in 1968. By then though, Karloff was too ill to travel, and shot all his scenes in Los Angeles.

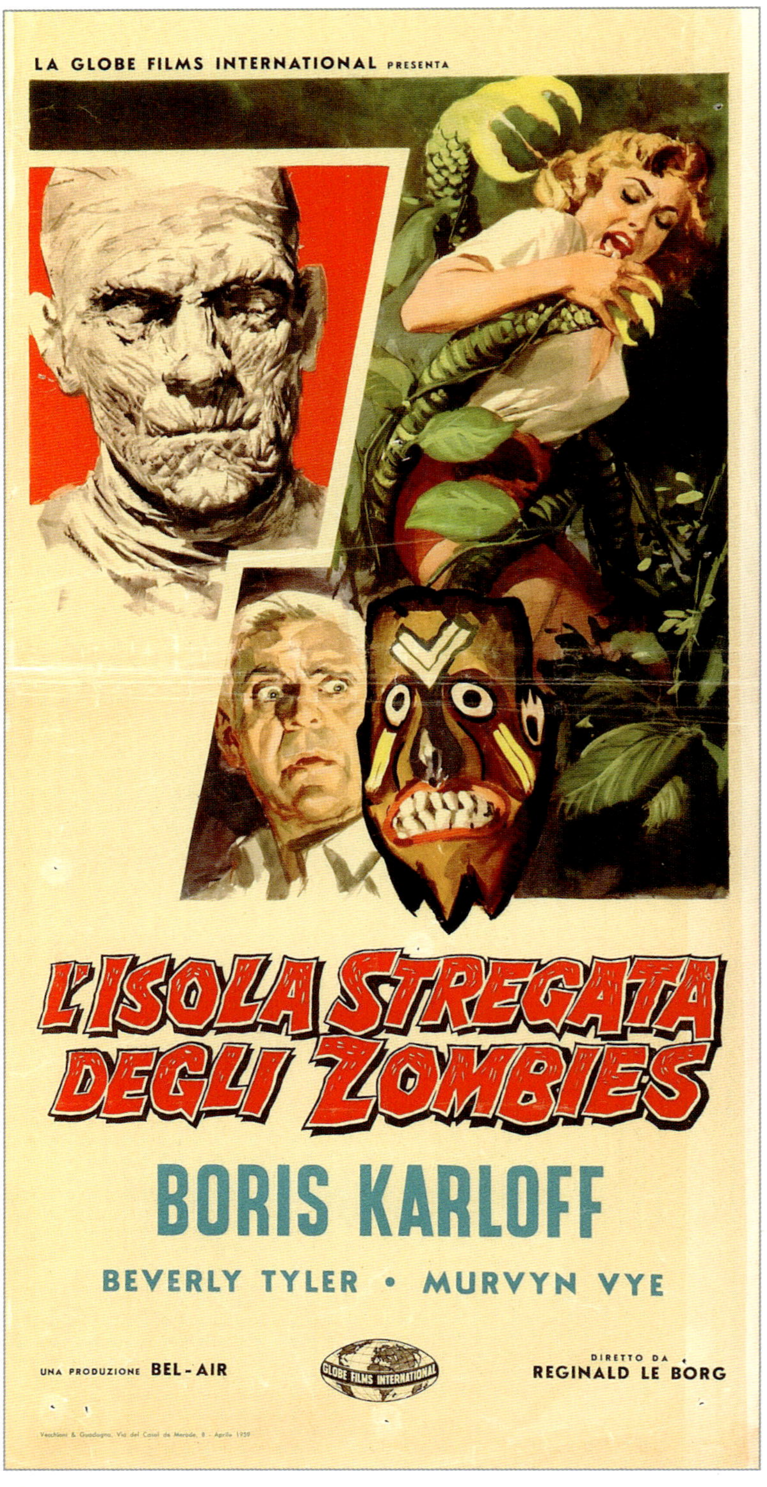

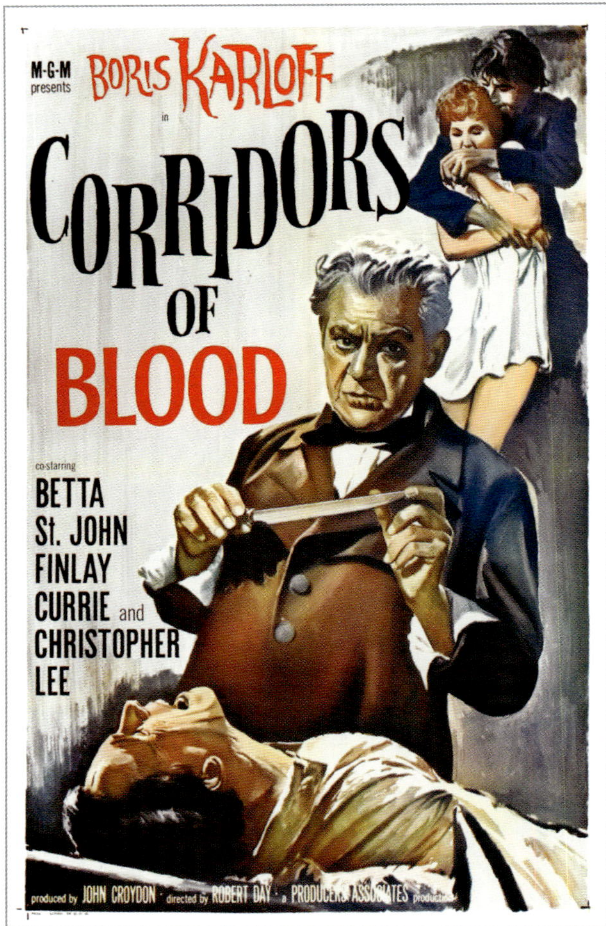

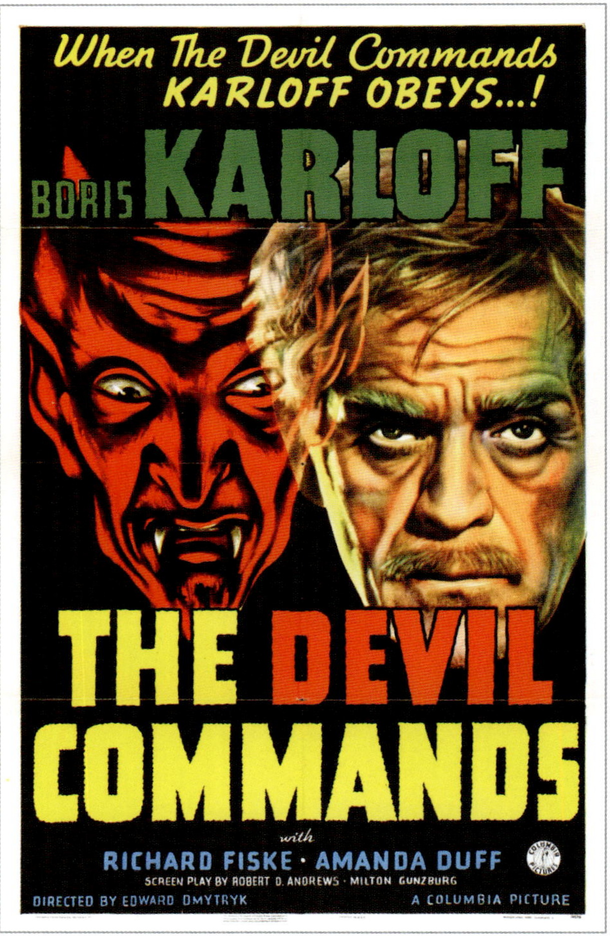

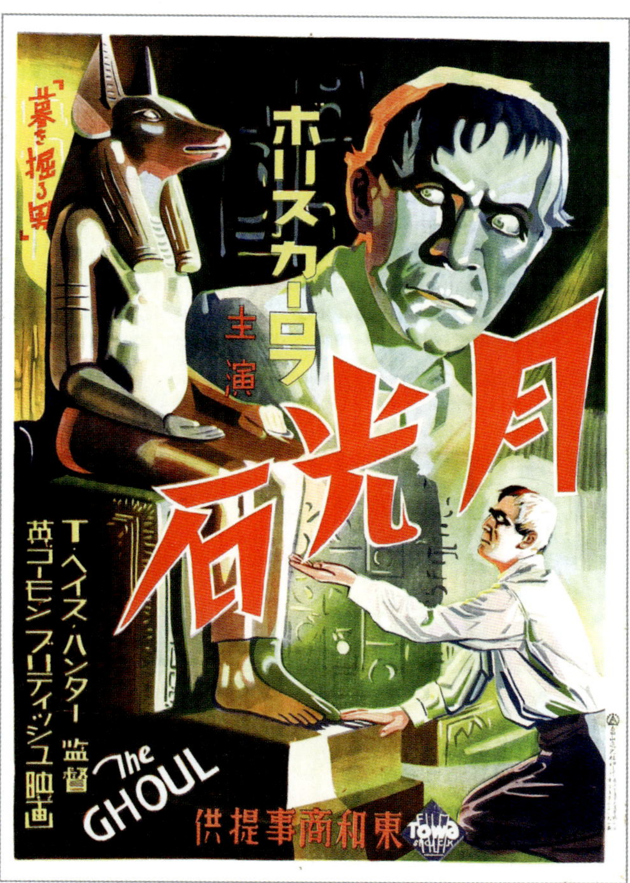
「墓を掘る男」
ボリス・カーロフ
主演
月光石
T・ヘイス・ハンター 監督
英ゴーモン ブリティッシュ映画
The GHOUL
東和商事提供

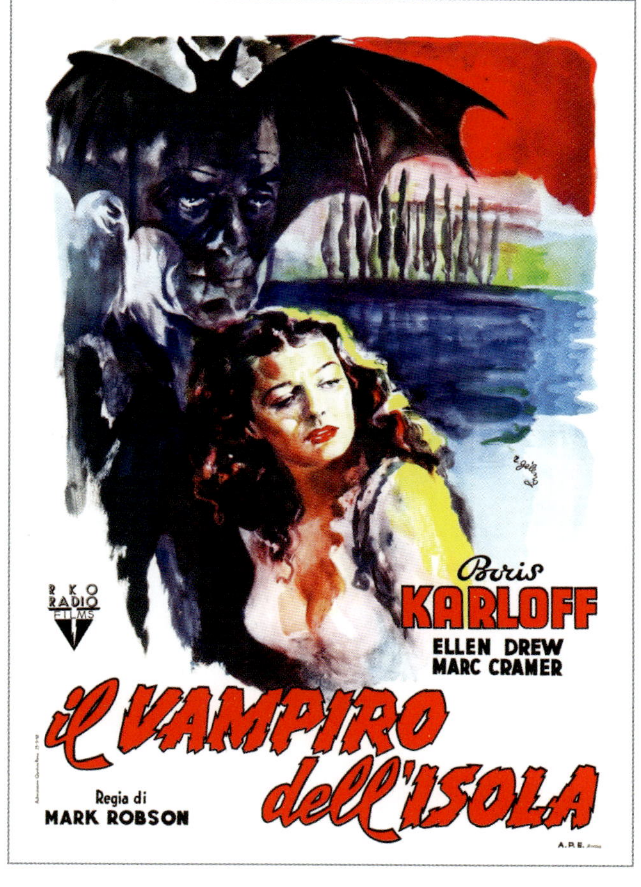
RKO RADIO FILMS
Boris
KARLOFF
ELLEN DREW
MARC CRAMER
il VAMPIRO dell'ISOLA
Regia di
MARK ROBSON

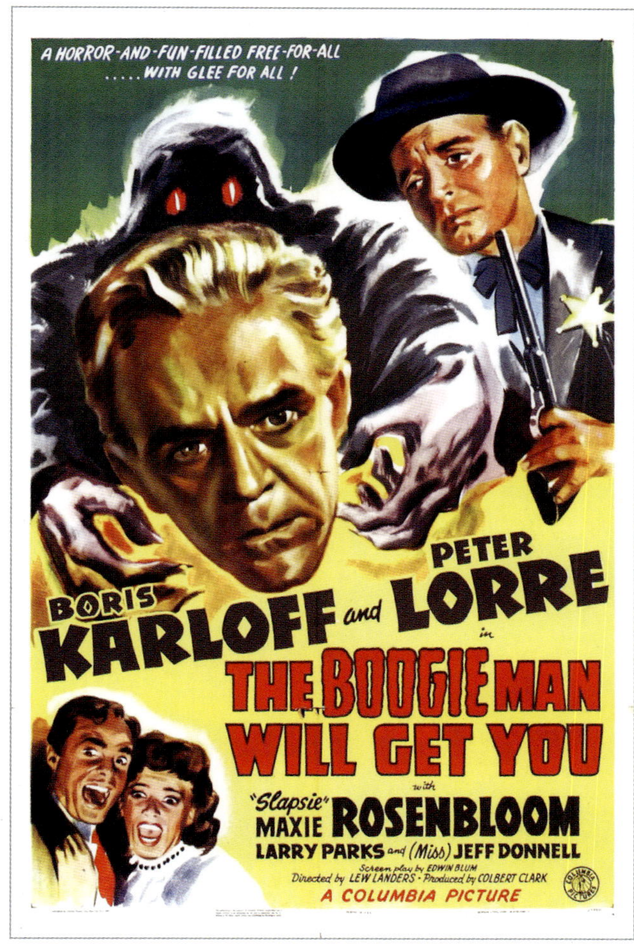
A HORROR-AND-FUN-FILLED FREE-FOR-ALL
.....WITH GLEE FOR ALL !
BORIS
KARLOFF and PETER LORRE
in
THE BOOGIE MAN WILL GET YOU
with
"Slapsie" MAXIE ROSENBLOOM
LARRY PARKS and (Miss) JEFF DONNELL
Screen play by EDWIN BLUM
Directed by LEW LANDERS · Produced by COLBERT CLARK
A COLUMBIA PICTURE

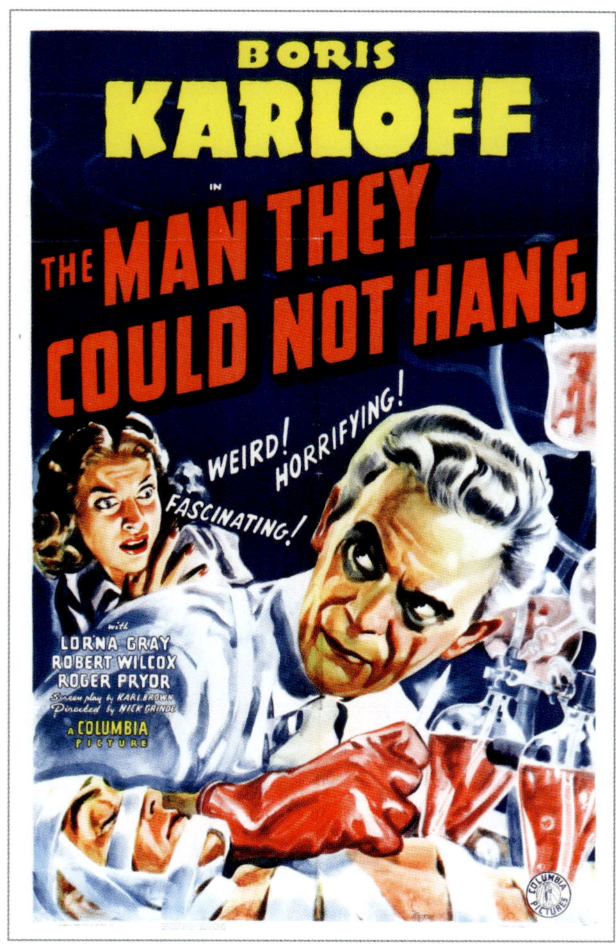
BORIS
KARLOFF
IN
THE MAN THEY COULD NOT HANG
WEIRD! HORRIFYING!
FASCINATING!
with
LORNA GRAY
ROBERT WILCOX
ROGER PRYOR
Screen play by KARL BROWN
Directed by NICK GRINDE
A COLUMBIA PICTURE

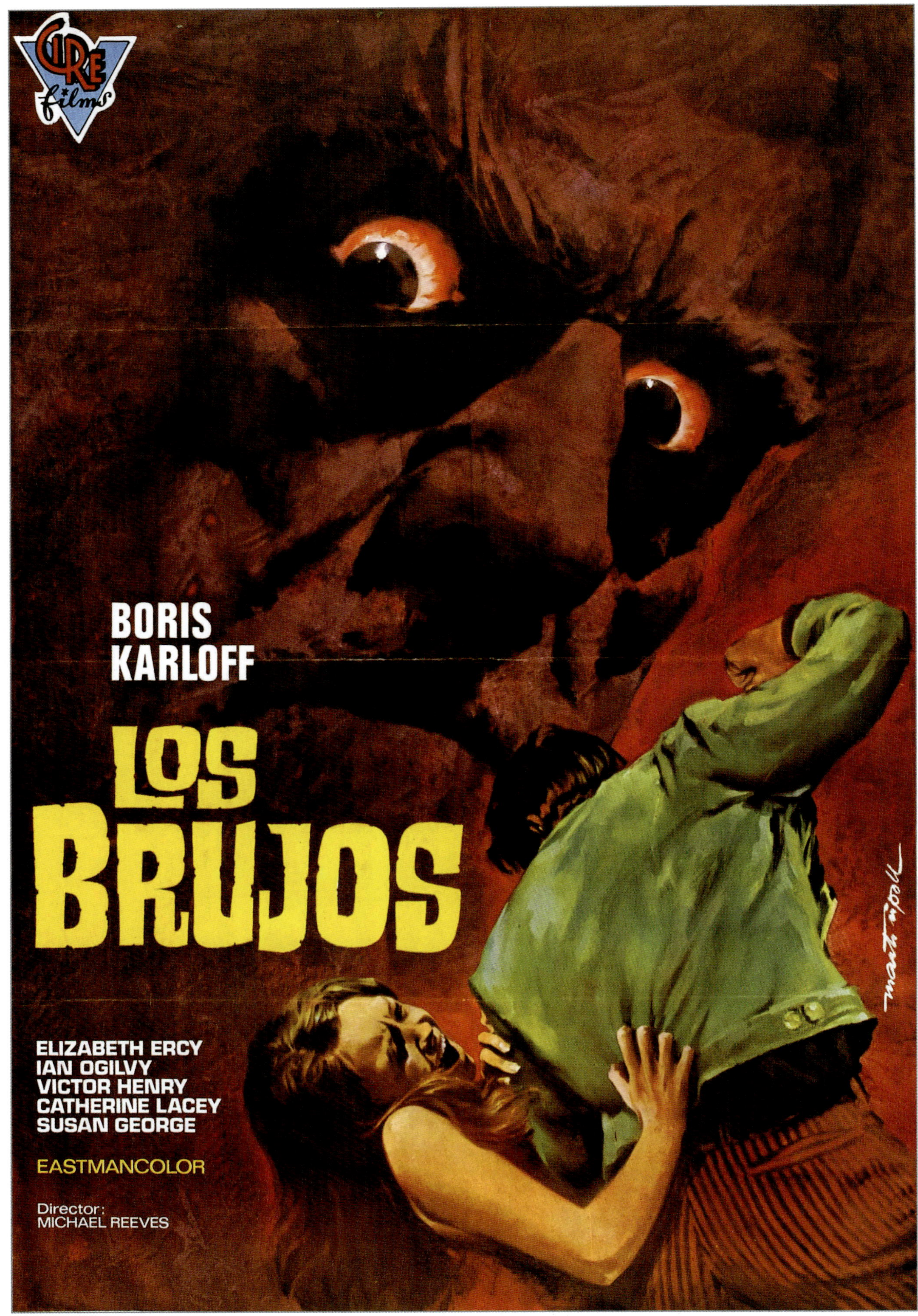
CIRE films
BORIS KARLOFF
LOS BRUJOS
ELIZABETH ERCY
IAN OGILVY
VICTOR HENRY
CATHERINE LACEY
SUSAN GEORGE
EASTMANCOLOR
Director:
MICHAEL REEVES

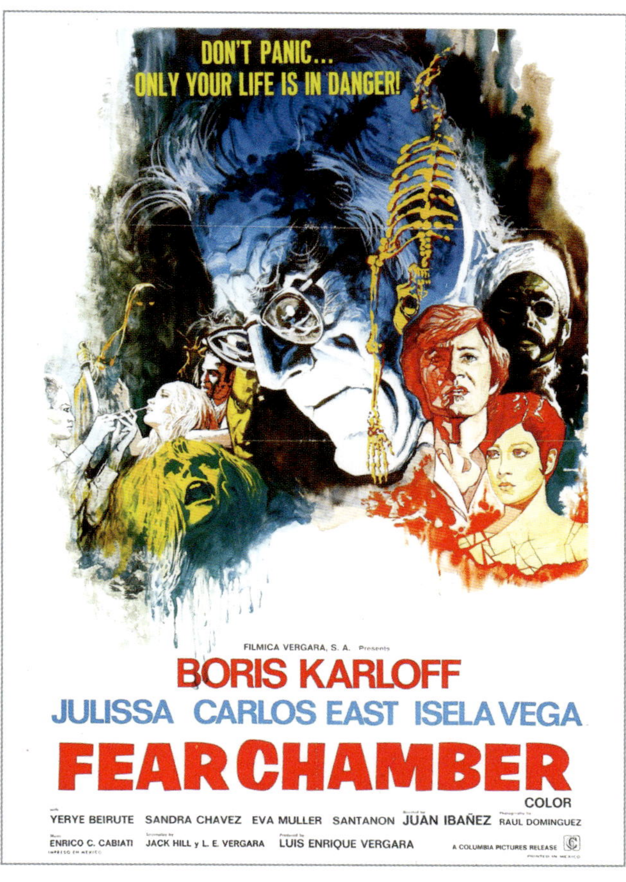
DON'T PANIC...
ONLY YOUR LIFE IS IN DANGER!
BORIS KARLOFF
JULISSA CARLOS EAST ISELA VEGA
FEAR CHAMBER
COLOR
YERYE BEIRUTE SANDRA CHAVEZ EVA MULLER SANTANON JUAN IBAÑEZ RAUL DOMINGUEZ
ENRICO C. CABIATI JACK HILL y L. E. VERGARA LUIS ENRIQUE VERGARA
A COLUMBIA PICTURES RELEASE

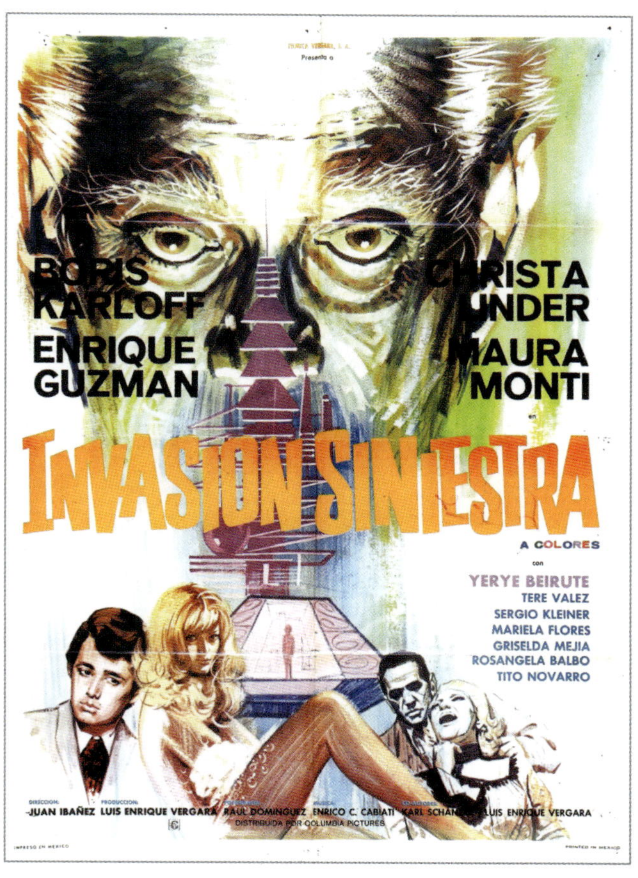
BORIS KARLOFF
CHRISTA LINDER
ENRIQUE GUZMAN
MAURA MONTI
INVASION SINIESTRA
A COLORES
YERYE BEIRUTE
TERE VALEZ
SERGIO KLEINER
MARIELA FLORES
GRISELDA MEJIA
ROSANGELA BALBO
TITO NOVARRO

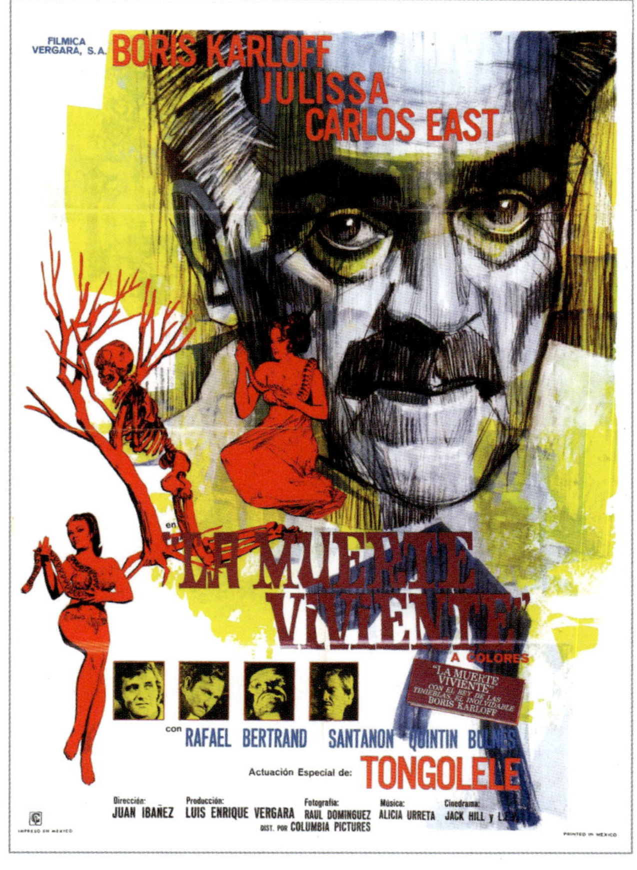
FILMICA VERGARA, S.A.
BORIS KARLOFF
JULISSA
CARLOS EAST
LA MUERTE VIVIENTE
A COLORES
RAFAEL BERTRAND SANTANON
Actuación Especial de: TONGOLELE
Dirección: JUAN IBAÑEZ
Producción: LUIS ENRIQUE VERGARA
Fotografía: RAUL DOMINGUEZ
Música: ALICIA URRETA
DIST. POR COLUMBIA PICTURES

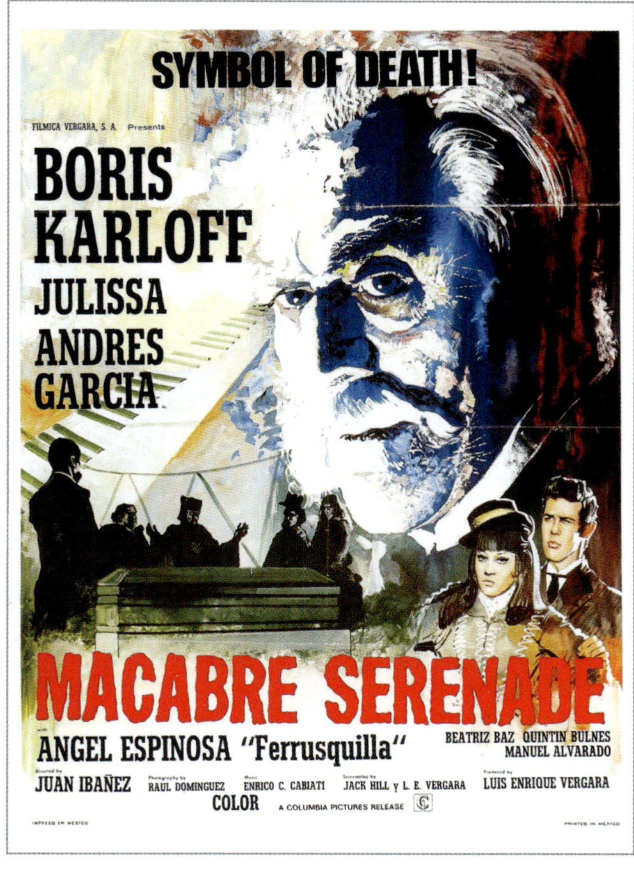
SYMBOL OF DEATH!
FILMICA VERGARA, S. A. Presents
BORIS KARLOFF
JULISSA
ANDRES GARCIA
MACABRE SERENADE
ANGEL ESPINOSA "Ferrusquilla"
BEATRIZ BAZ QUINTIN BULNES
MANUEL ALVARADO
JUAN IBAÑEZ RAUL DOMINGUEZ ENRICO C. CABIATI JACK HILL y L. E. VERGARA LUIS ENRIQUE VERGARA
COLOR
A COLUMBIA PICTURES RELEASE

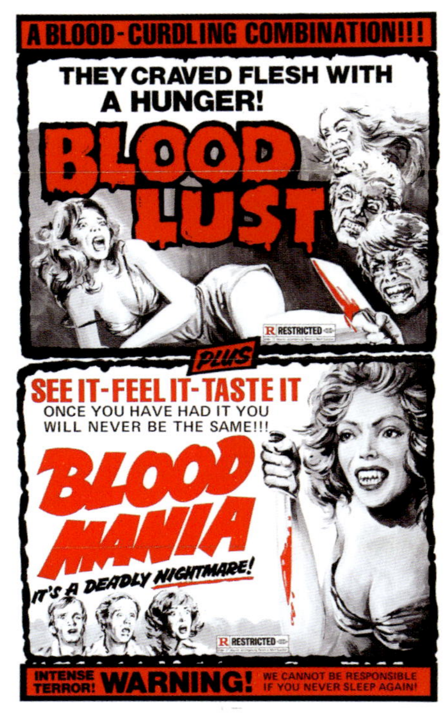
A BLOOD-CURDLING COMBINATION!!!
THEY CRAVED FLESH WITH A HUNGER!
BLOOD LUST
RESTRICTED
PLUS
SEE IT-FEEL IT-TASTE IT
ONCE YOU HAVE HAD IT YOU WILL NEVER BE THE SAME!!!
BLOOD MANIA
IT'S A DEADLY NIGHTMARE!
RESTRICTED
INTENSE TERROR! WARNING! WE CANNOT BE RESPONSIBLE IF YOU NEVER SLEEP AGAIN!

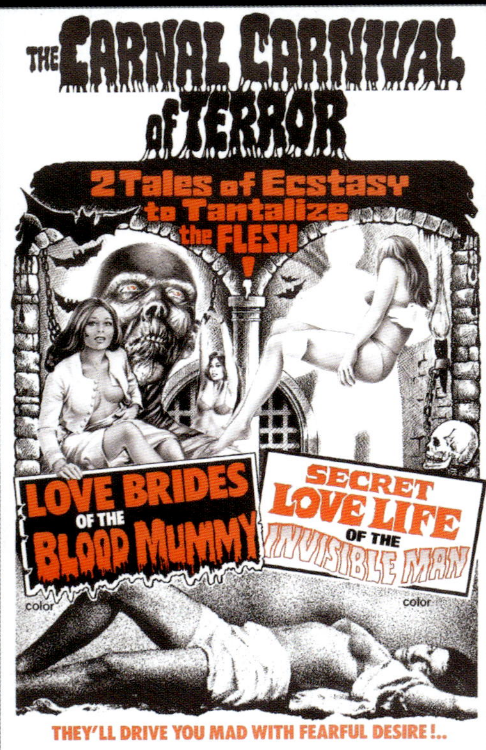
THE CARNAL CARNIVAL of TERROR
2 Tales of Ecstasy to Tantalize the FLESH!
LOVE BRIDES OF THE BLOOD MUMMY
color
SECRET LOVE LIFE OF THE INVISIBLE MAN
color
THEY'LL DRIVE YOU MAD WITH FEARFUL DESIRE!..

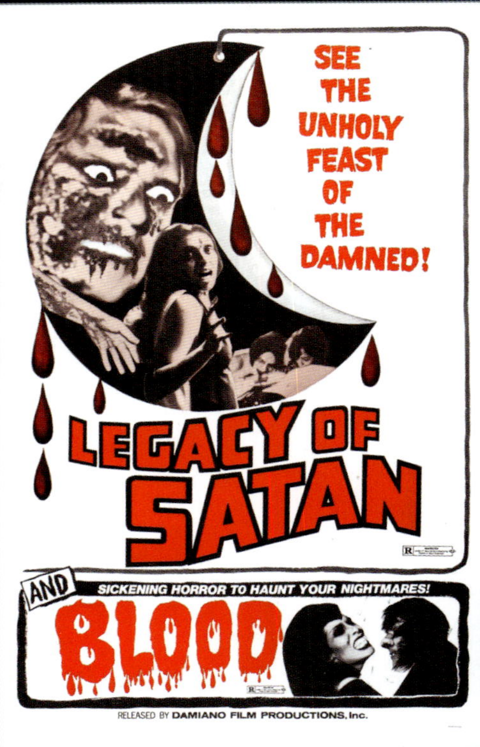
SEE THE UNHOLY FEAST OF THE DAMNED!
LEGACY OF SATAN
AND
SICKENING HORROR TO HAUNT YOUR NIGHTMARES!
BLOOD
RELEASED BY DAMIANO FILM PRODUCTIONS, Inc.

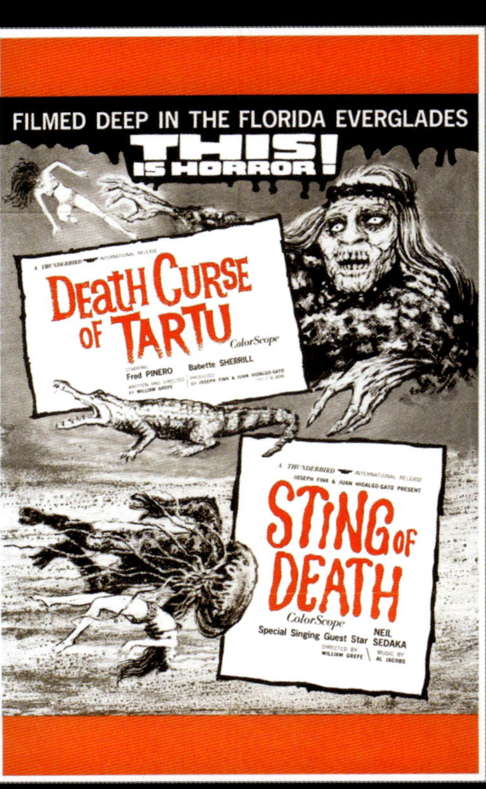
FILMED DEEP IN THE FLORIDA EVERGLADES
THIS IS HORROR!
DEATH CURSE OF TARTU
ColorScope
Fred PINERO
Babette SHERRILL
STING OF DEATH
ColorScope
Special Singing Guest Star NEIL SEDAKA

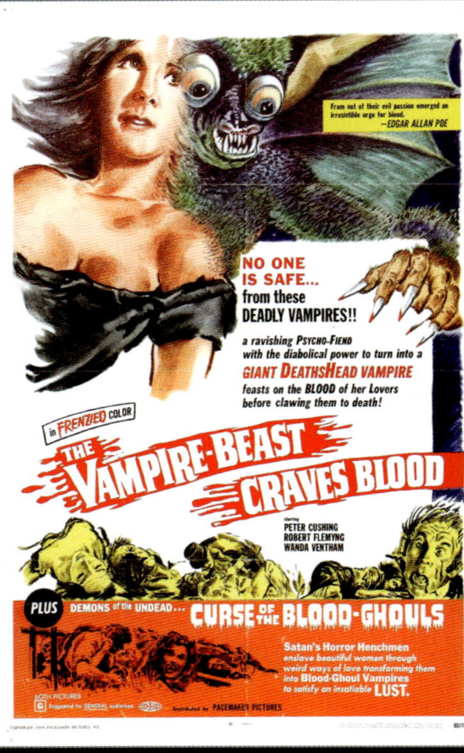
From out of their evil passion emerged an irresistible urge for blood.
—EDGAR ALLAN POE
NO ONE IS SAFE... from these DEADLY VAMPIRES!!
a ravishing PSYCHO-FIEND with the diabolical power to turn into a GIANT DEATHSHEAD VAMPIRE feasts on the BLOOD of her Lovers before clawing them to death!
in FRENZIED COLOR
THE VAMPIRE-BEAST CRAVES BLOOD
PETER CUSHING
ROBERT FLEMYNG
WANDA VENTHAM
PLUS
DEMONS of the UNDEAD... CURSE OF THE BLOOD-GHOULS
Satan's Horror Henchmen enslave beautiful women through weird ways of love transforming them into Blood-Ghoul Vampires to satisfy an insatiable LUST.
PACEMAKER PICTURES

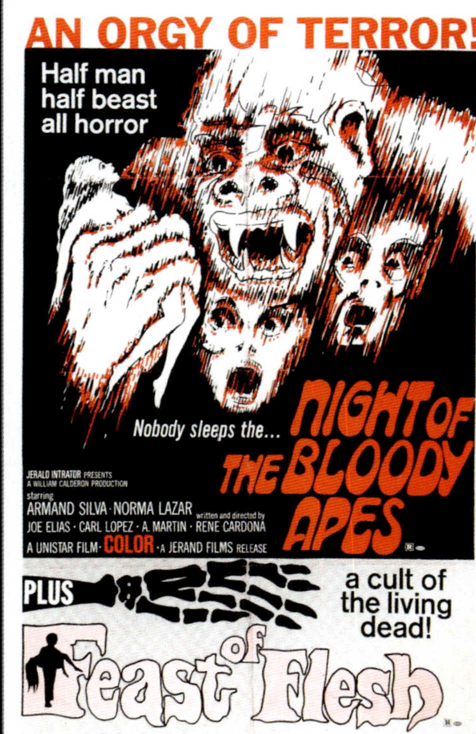
AN ORGY OF TERROR!
Half man half beast all horror
Nobody sleeps the...
NIGHT OF THE BLOODY APES
JERALD INTRATOR PRESENTS
A WILLIAM CALDERON PRODUCTION
starring
ARMAND SILVA · NORMA LAZAR
written and directed by
JOE ELIAS · CARL LOPEZ · A. MARTIN · RENE CARDONA
A UNISTAR FILM · COLOR · A JERAND FILMS RELEASE
PLUS
a cult of the living dead!
Feast of Flesh

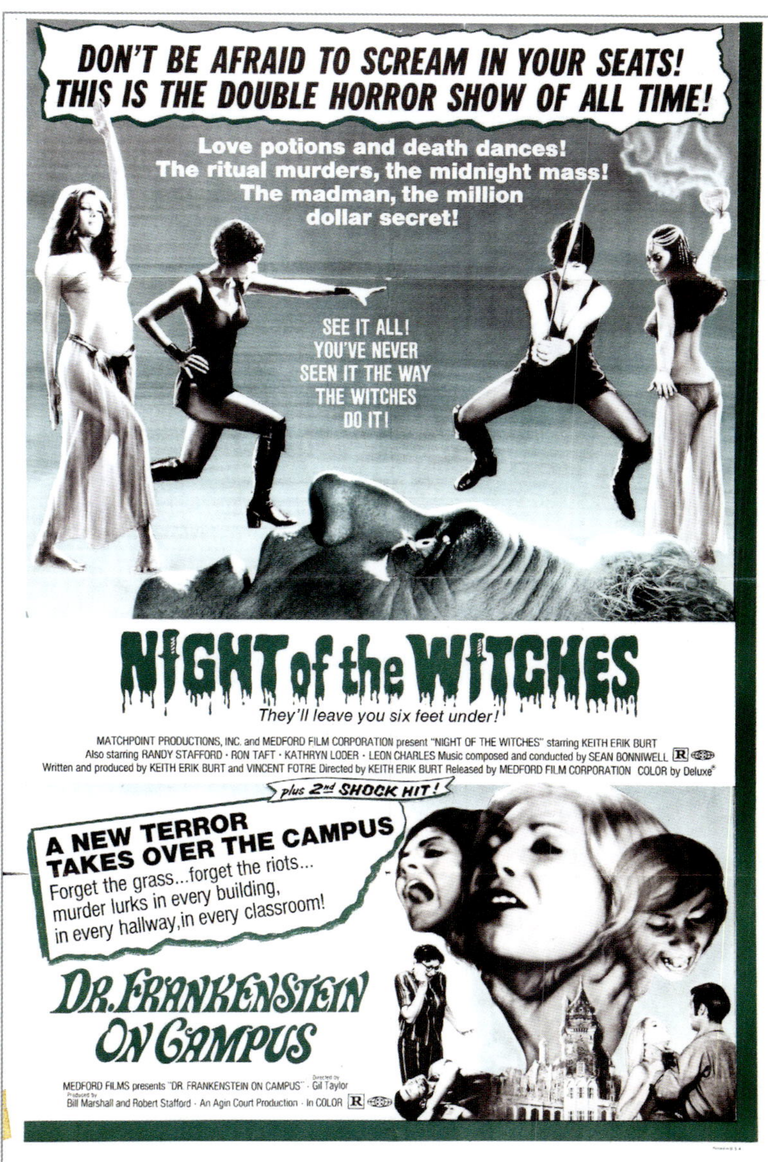

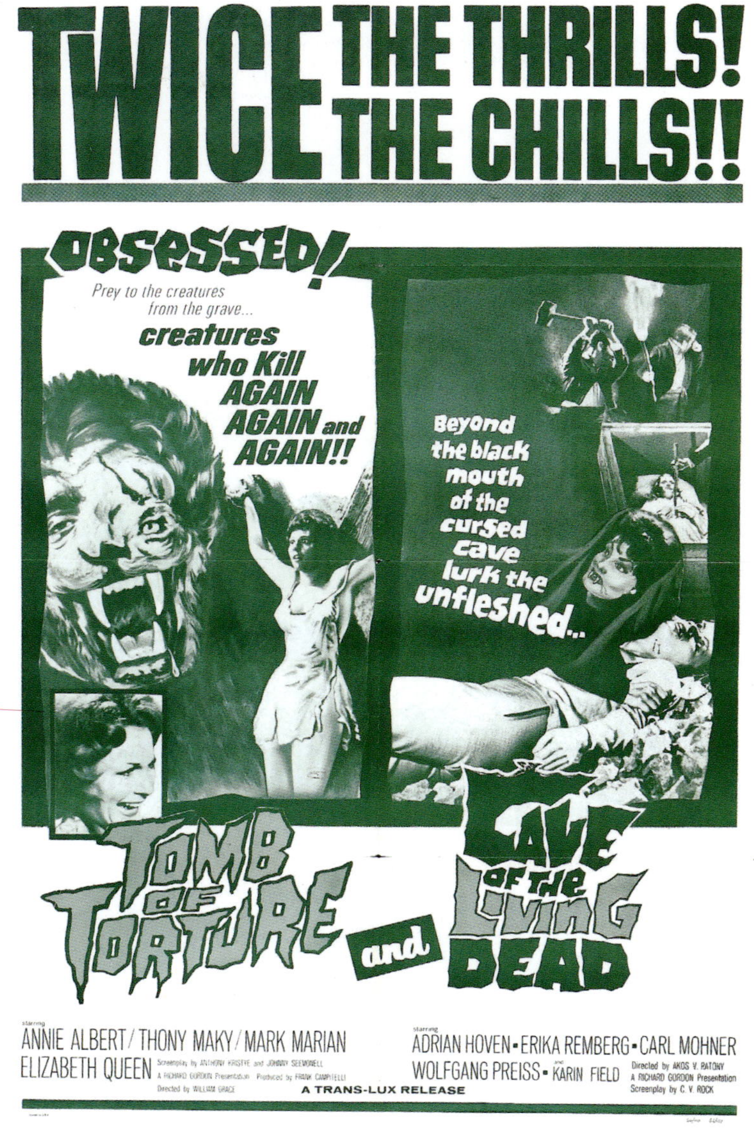

TWICE THE TERROR

What's better than one horror movie? Two horror movies of course, as these double bill posters are quick to point out. Sometimes it was a themed pairing, with the two films taking equal prominence in the advertising, such as with 1966's *Death Curse of Tartu* and *Sting of Death*, which were both filmed in the Florida Everglades. Other pairings retained a B-movie/main feature balance. *The Vampire-Beast Craves Blood*, given top billing by its US distributor in 1969, is better known by its original 1967 UK title, *The Blood Beast Terror*. Its star Wanda Ventham (seen on the poster) is these days better known for being Benedict Cumberbatch's mom.

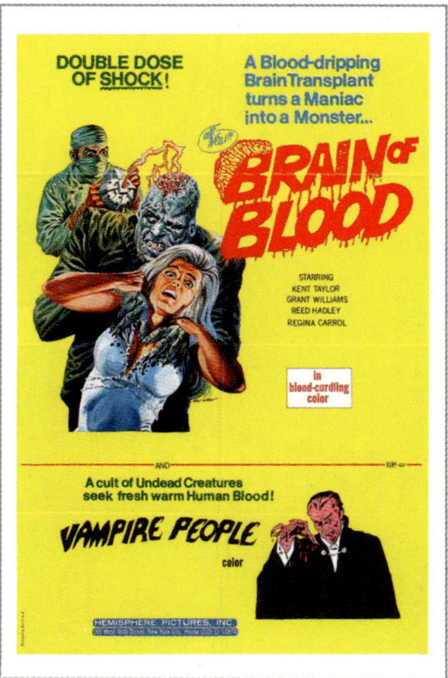

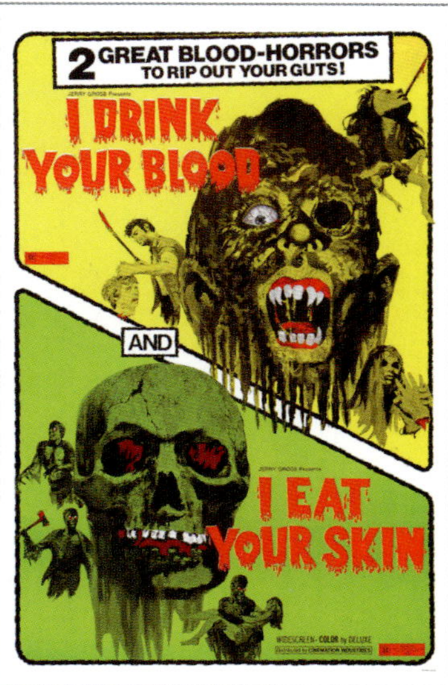

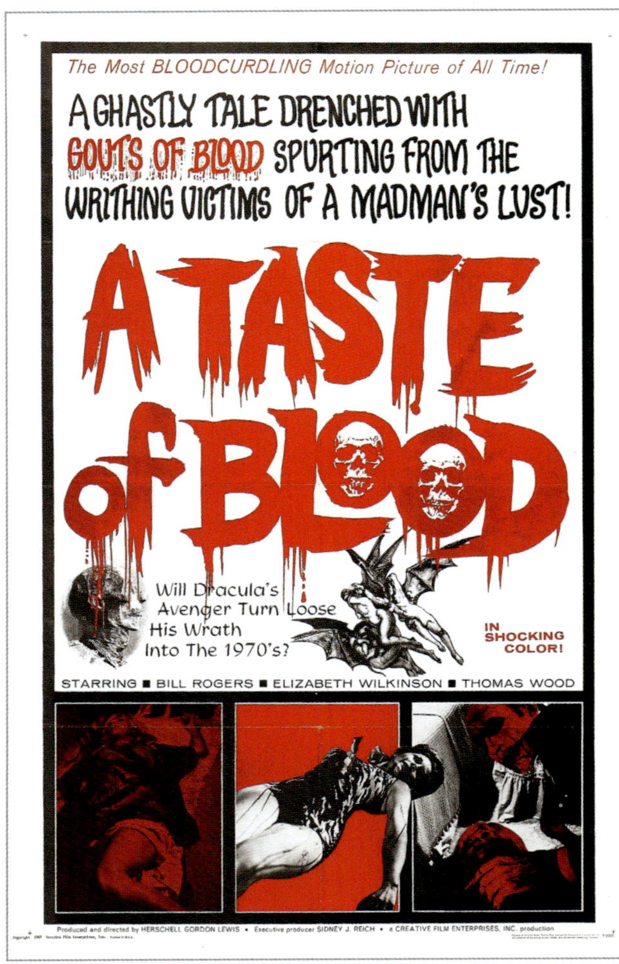

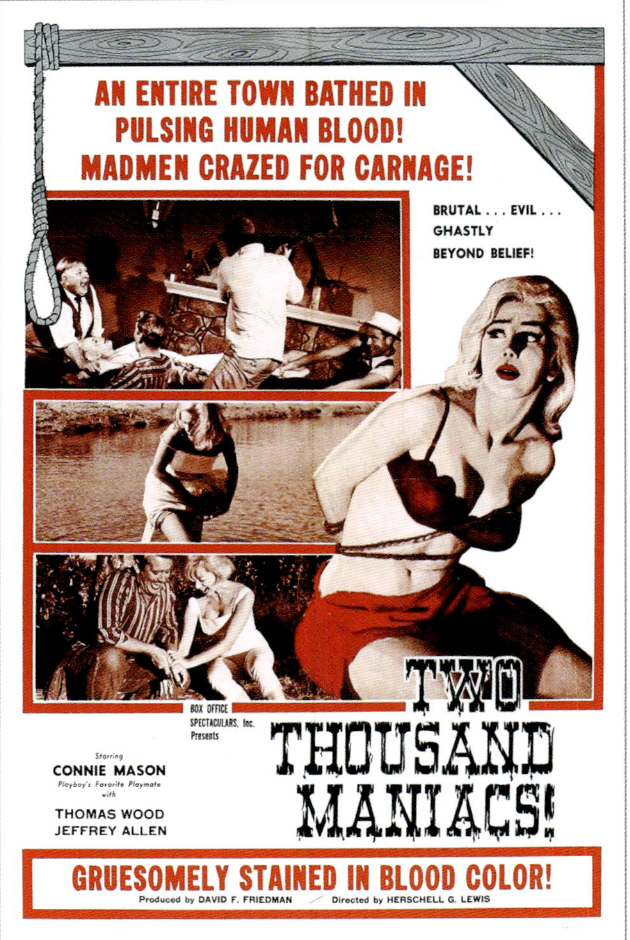

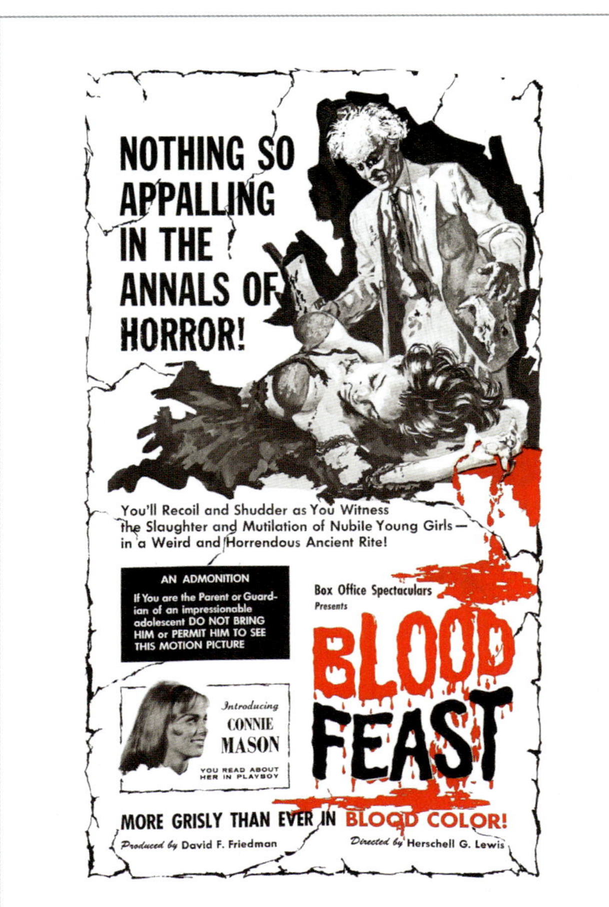

THE GODFATHER OF GORE

"Herschell Gordon Lewis is the man who put red meat into the American cinematic diet," says critic and exploitation movie connoisseur Joe Bob Briggs, adding that, "ultimately Herschell made Quentin Tarantino possible." Lewis started out directing "nudie cuties" with some success, but it was his aptly titled *Blood Feast* (1963) that really stabbed a nerve. Dismissed as "a blot on the American film industry" by the *Los Angeles Times*, its own director, an ex-English literature professor, likened it to "a Walt Whitman poem. It's no good, but it's the first of its kind, therefore it deserves recognition." Certainly, with its graphic dismemberment and a showstopping tongue removal, gore had never been this explicit on screen—and in full color, no less. For once, a poster tagline was on the money: there really hadn't been anything so appalling in the annals of horror. The "splatter" film had arrived. Audiences lapped it up, and equally blood-soaked follow-ups included *Two Thousand Maniacs!* (1964), *Color Me Blood Red* (1965), and *A Taste of Blood* (1967). In what is probably not a very surprising career development for someone who was an exploitation movie showman, Lewis became an in-demand advertising and copywriting consultant, and is now a member of the Direct Marketing Association Hall of Fame.

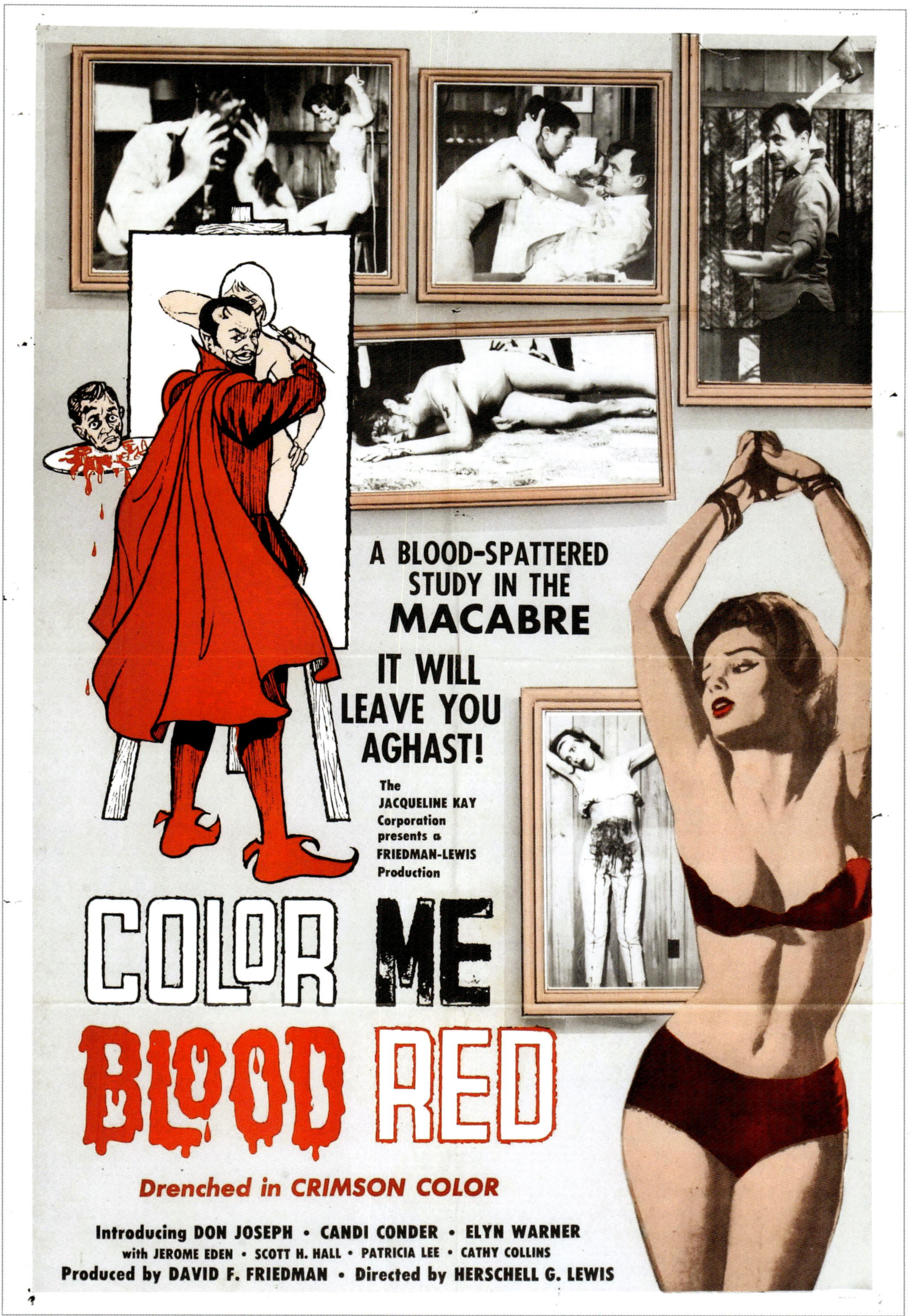
A BLOOD-SPATTERED STUDY IN THE MACABRE
IT WILL LEAVE YOU AGHAST!
The JACQUELINE KAY Corporation presents a FRIEDMAN-LEWIS Production
COLOR ME BLOOD RED
Drenched in CRIMSON COLOR
Introducing DON JOSEPH • CANDI CONDER • ELYN WARNER
with JEROME EDEN • SCOTT H. HALL • PATRICIA LEE • CATHY COLLINS
Produced by DAVID F. FRIEDMAN • Directed by HERSCHELL G. LEWIS

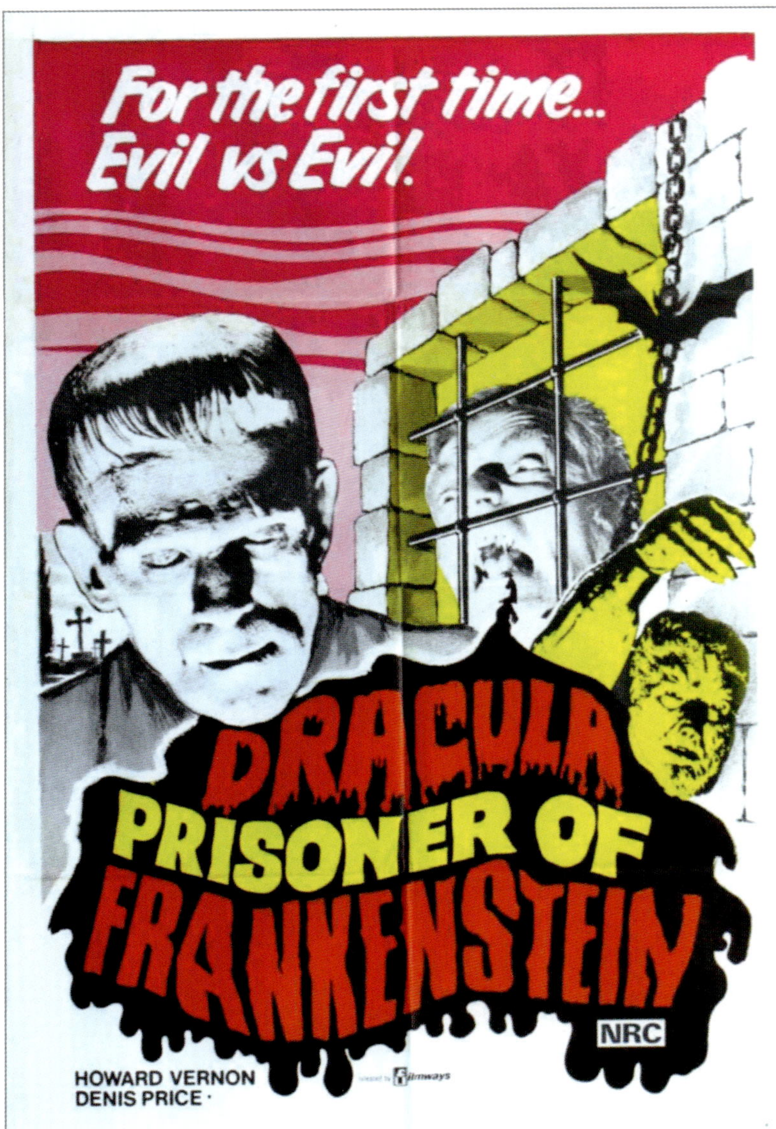

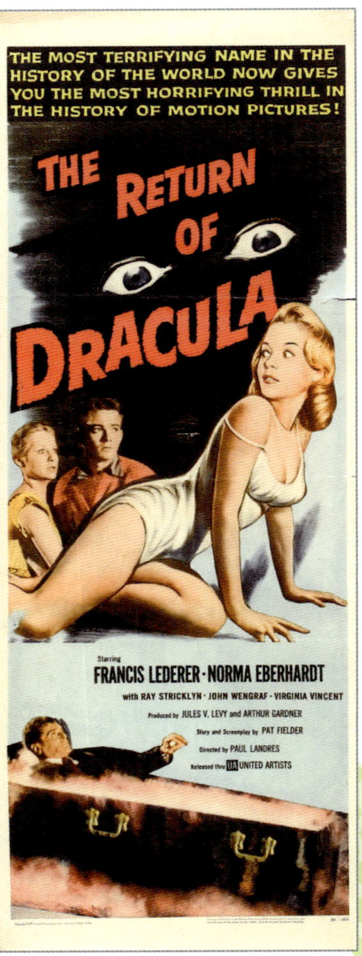

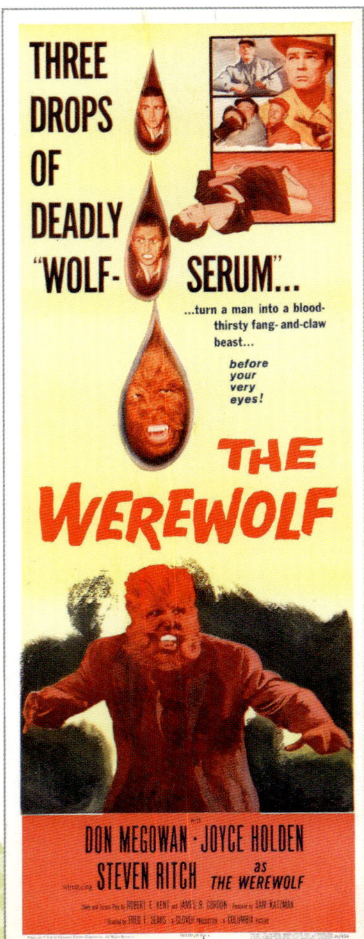

CASHING IN ON THE CLASSIC MONSTERS

The horror movie icons Dracula, Frankenstein's Monster, and the Wolf Man, as established by Universal in the '30s and reimagined by Hammer in the '50s and '60s, are (a few specific make-up designs aside) safely out of copyright. They are therefore fair game, leading to the never-ending deluge of vampire, Frankenstein, and werewolf exploitation movies, sampled here, that continues to this day. Sometimes filmmakers snagged the original stars for their versions. Sometimes the posters just pretended they had. Jesús "Jess" Franco did actually contract Christopher Lee for the title role of his well-intentioned but ultimately rather dull "faithful" Bram Stoker adaptation *Count Dracula* (1970), but whoever designed the Argentinean poster evidently preferred Bela Lugosi, so painted him instead. Meanwhile the poster for Franco's *Dracula, Prisoner of Frankenstein* (1972) thought it best to include an image of Boris Karloff. He's not in the film.

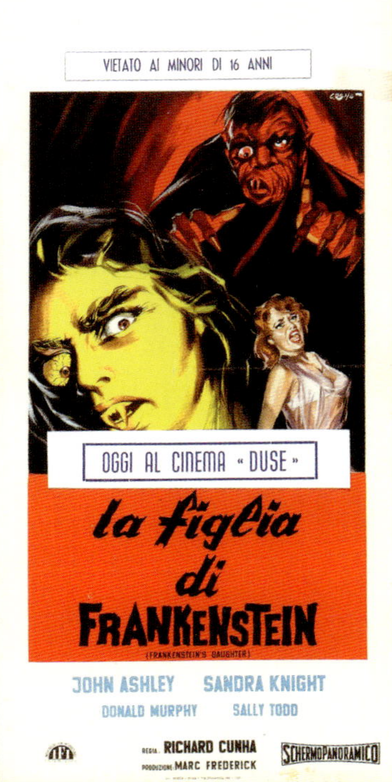

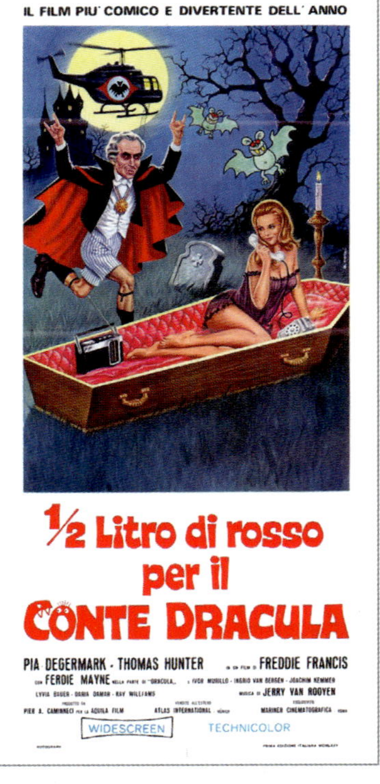

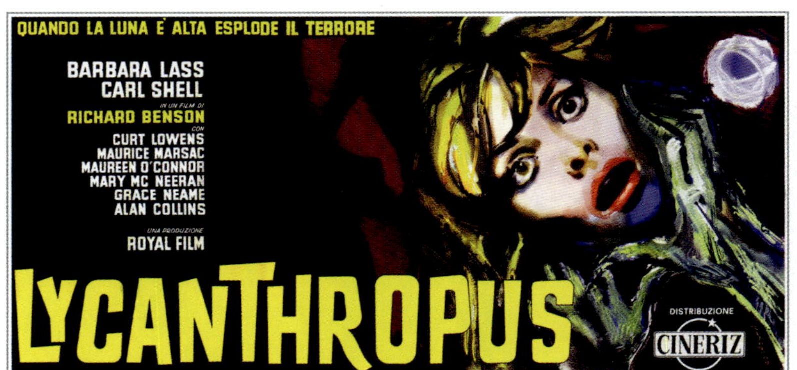

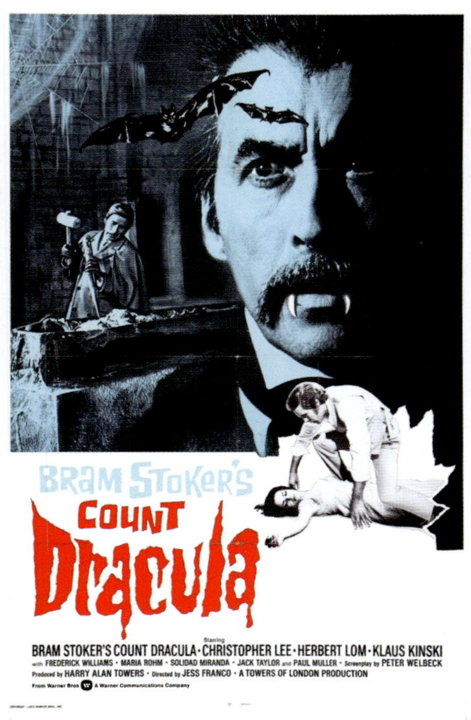
BRAM STOKER'S
COUNT
Dracula
BRAM STOKER'S COUNT DRACULA · CHRISTOPHER LEE · HERBERT LOM · KLAUS KINSKI
Produced by HARRY ALAN TOWERS · Directed by JESS FRANCO · A TOWERS OF LONDON PRODUCTION

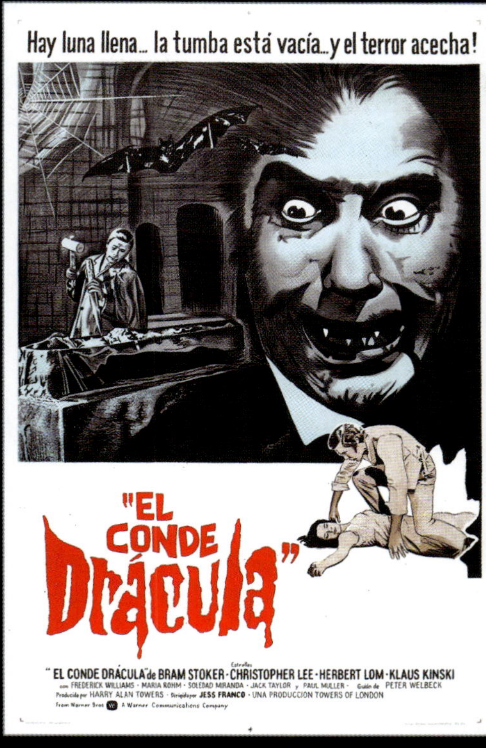
Hay luna llena... la tumba está vacía... y el terror acecha!
"EL CONDE Drácula"
"EL CONDE DRÁCULA" de BRAM STOKER · CHRISTOPHER LEE · HERBERT LOM · KLAUS KINSKI

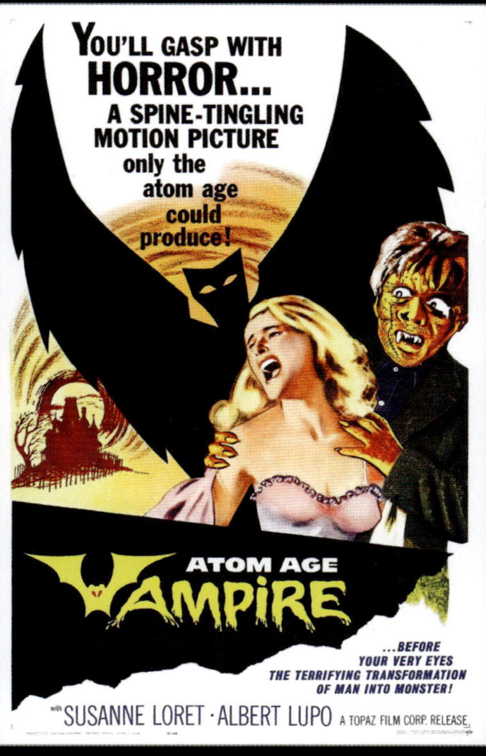
YOU'LL GASP WITH HORROR...
A SPINE-TINGLING MOTION PICTURE
only the atom age could produce!
ATOM AGE VAMPIRE
...BEFORE YOUR VERY EYES THE TERRIFYING TRANSFORMATION OF MAN INTO MONSTER!
with SUSANNE LORET · ALBERT LUPO A TOPAZ FILM CORP. RELEASE

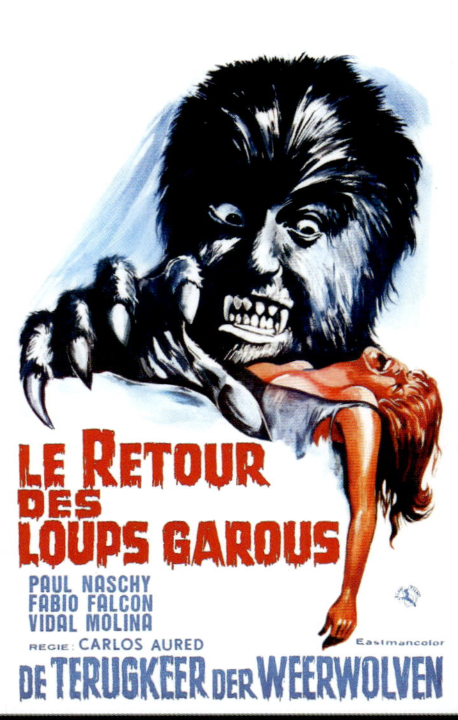
LE RETOUR DES LOUPS GAROUS
PAUL NASCHY
FABIO FALCON
VIDAL MOLINA
REGIE: CARLOS AURED
Eastmancolor
DE TERUGKEER DER WEERWOLVEN

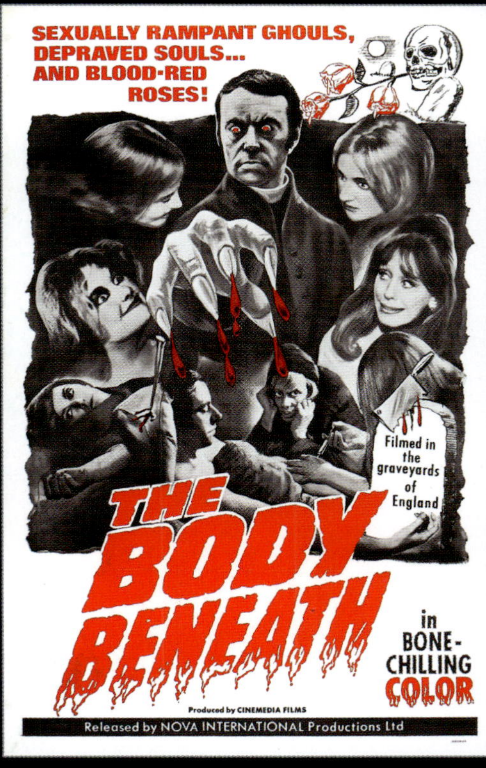
SEXUALLY RAMPANT GHOULS, DEPRAVED SOULS... AND BLOOD-RED ROSES!
Filmed in the graveyards of England
THE BODY BENEATH
in BONE-CHILLING COLOR
Produced by CINEMEDIA FILMS
Released by NOVA INTERNATIONAL Productions Ltd

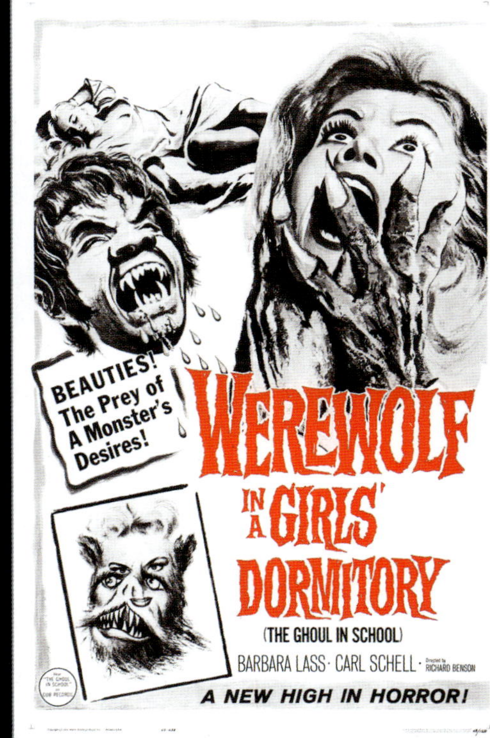
BEAUTIES! The Prey of A Monster's Desires!
WEREWOLF IN A GIRLS' DORMITORY
(THE GHOUL IN SCHOOL)
BARBARA LASS · CARL SCHELL · Directed by RICHARD BENSON
A NEW HIGH IN HORROR!

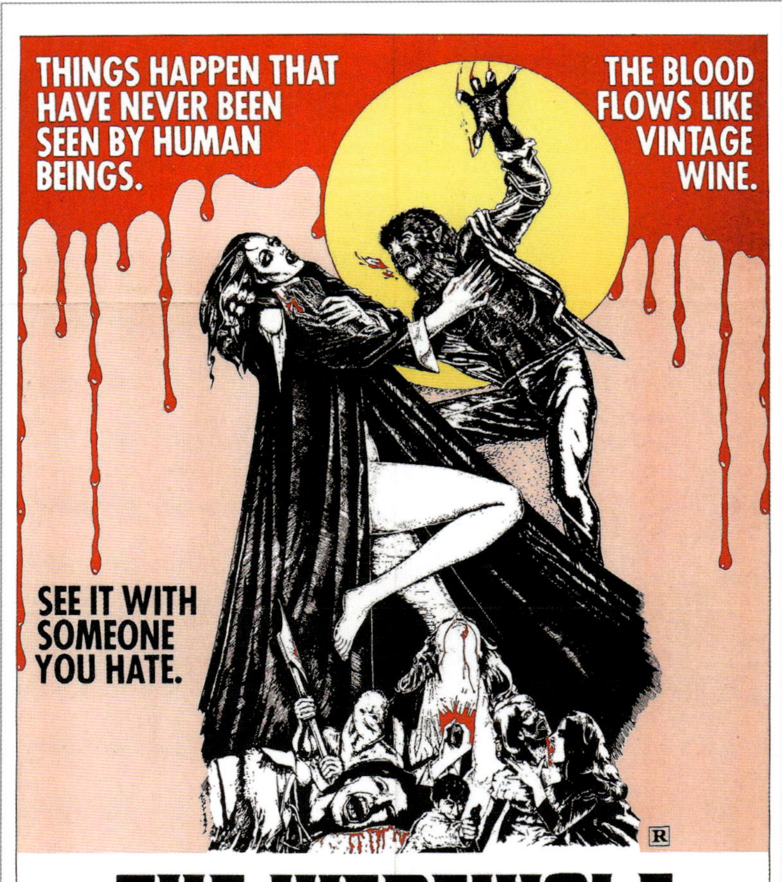
THINGS HAPPEN THAT HAVE NEVER BEEN SEEN BY HUMAN BEINGS.
THE BLOOD FLOWS LIKE VINTAGE WINE.
SEE IT WITH SOMEONE YOU HATE.
R
THE WEREWOLF vs. VAMPIRE WOMAN
Starring: PAUL NASH, GABY FUCHS, ANDREW REESE Directed By: LEON KLIM
Written By: JAMES MOLLIN & HENRY MUNK Presented By: 1ST LEISURE CORP.
A PLATA FILMS AND INTENT INTERNATIONAL PICTURE Released By: ELLMAN ENTERPRISES.

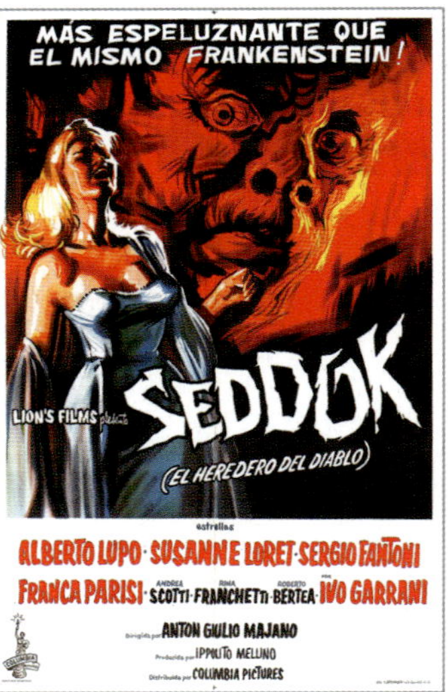
MÁS ESPELUZNANTE QUE EL MISMO FRANKENSTEIN!
LION'S FILMS presenta
SEDDOK
(EL HEREDERO DEL DIABLO)
estrellas
ALBERTO LUPO · SUSANNE LORET · SERGIO FANTONI
FRANCA PARISI · ANDREA SCOTTI · RINA FRANCHETTI · ROBERTO BERTEA · IVO GARRANI
Dirigida por ANTON GIULIO MAJANO
Producida por IPPOLITO MELLINO
Distribuida por COLUMBIA PICTURES

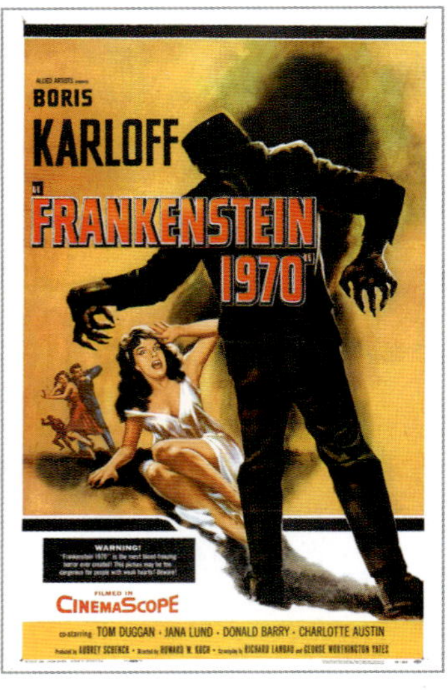
BORIS
KARLOFF
FRANKENSTEIN
1970
WARNING!
FILMED IN
CINEMASCOPE
co-starring TOM DUGGAN · JANA LUND · DONALD BARRY · CHARLOTTE AUSTIN

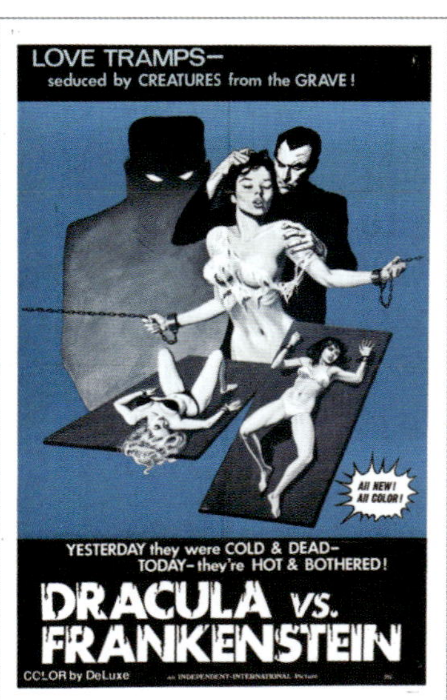
LOVE TRAMPS—
seduced by CREATURES from the GRAVE!
ALL NEW! ALL COLOR!
YESTERDAY they were COLD & DEAD–
TODAY– they're HOT & BOTHERED!
DRACULA vs. FRANKENSTEIN
COLOR by DeLuxe

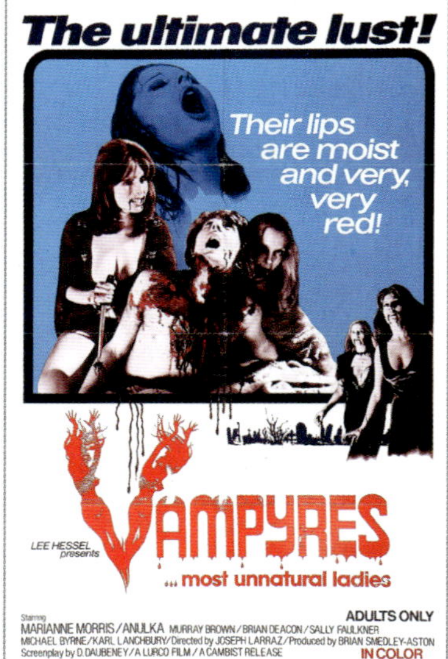
The ultimate lust!
Their lips are moist and very, very red!
LEE HESSEL presents
VAMPYRES
...most unnatural ladies
ADULTS ONLY
Starring
MARIANNE MORRIS / ANULKA MURRAY BROWN / BRIAN DEACON / SALLY FAULKNER
MICHAEL BYRNE / KARL LANCHBURY / Directed by JOSEPH LARRAZ / Produced by BRIAN SMEDLEY-ASTON
Screenplay by D. DAUBENEY / A LURCO FILM / A CAMBIST RELEASE
IN COLOR

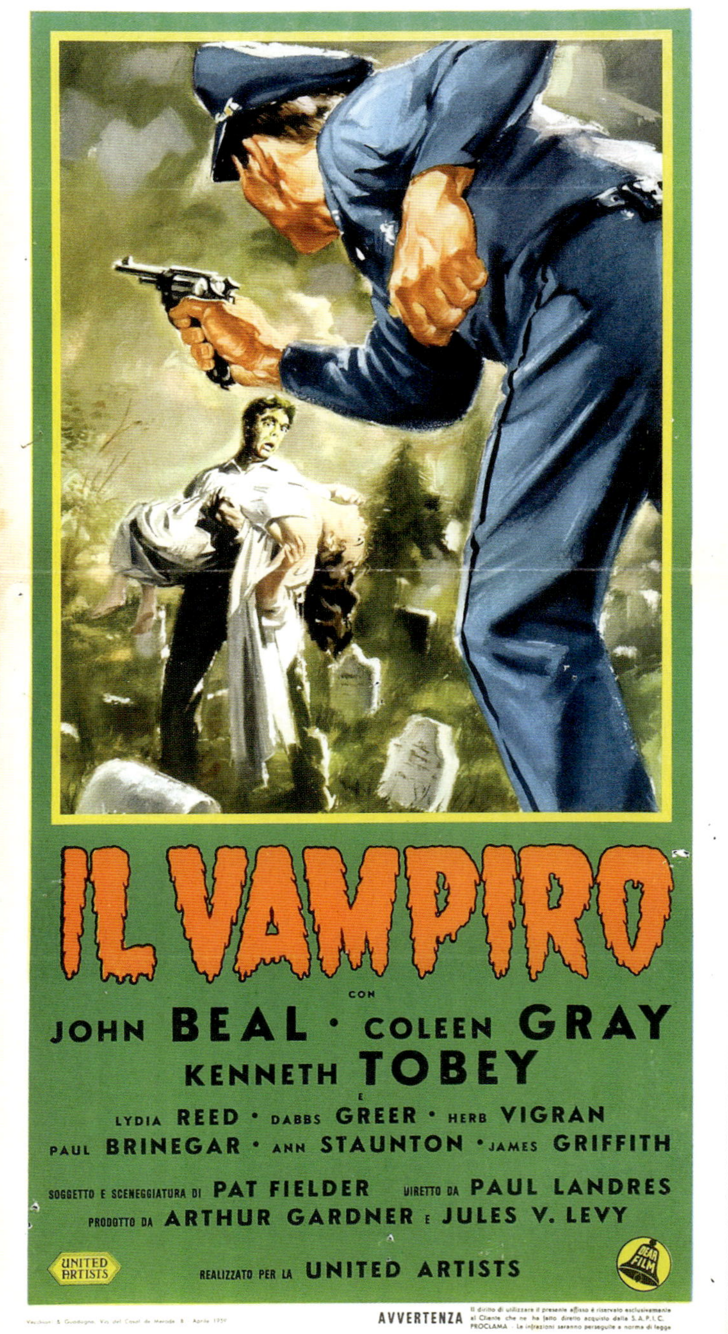
IL VAMPIRO
CON
JOHN BEAL · COLEEN GRAY
KENNETH TOBEY
E
LYDIA REED · DABBS GREER · HERB VIGRAN
PAUL BRINEGAR · ANN STAUNTON · JAMES GRIFFITH
SOGGETTO E SCENEGGIATURA DI PAT FIELDER DIRETTO DA PAUL LANDRES
PRODOTTO DA ARTHUR GARDNER E JULES V. LEVY
UNITED ARTISTS
REALIZZATO PER LA UNITED ARTISTS
AVVERTENZA

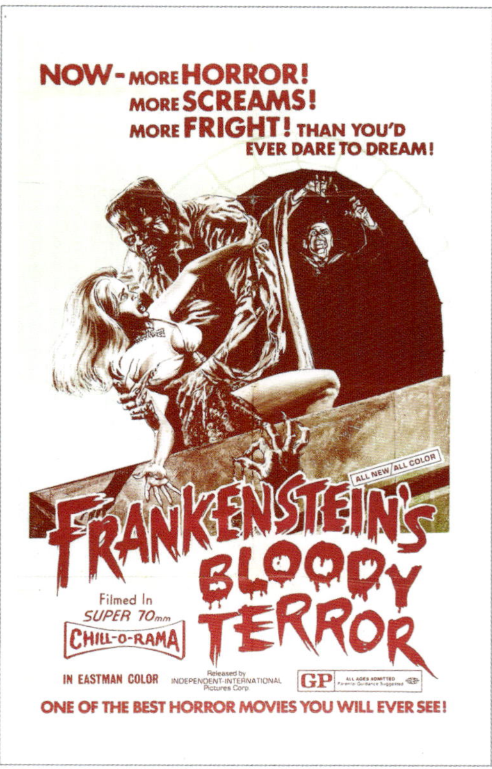
NOW - MORE HORROR!
MORE SCREAMS!
MORE FRIGHT! THAN YOU'D EVER DARE TO DREAM!
ALL NEW ALL COLOR
FRANKENSTEIN'S BLOODY TERROR
Filmed In SUPER 70mm CHILL-O-RAMA
IN EASTMAN COLOR
Released by INDEPENDENT-INTERNATIONAL Pictures Corp.
GP
ONE OF THE BEST HORROR MOVIES YOU WILL EVER SEE!

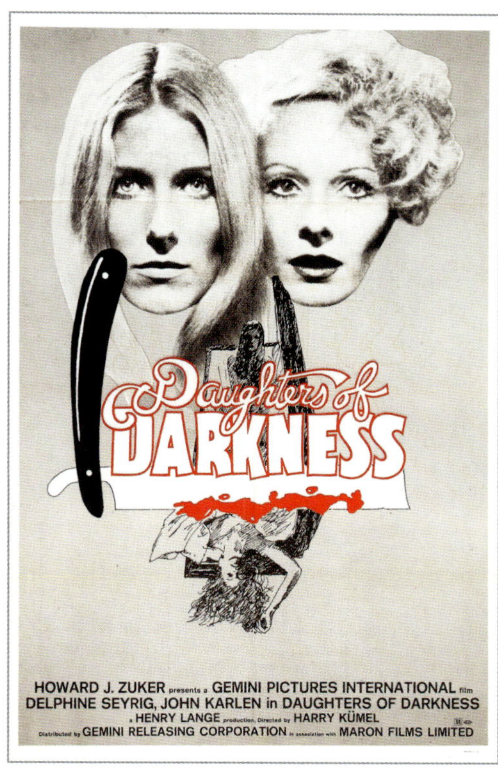
Daughters of DARKNESS
HOWARD J. ZUKER presents a GEMINI PICTURES INTERNATIONAL film
DELPHINE SEYRIG, JOHN KARLEN in DAUGHTERS OF DARKNESS
a HENRY LANGE production, Directed by HARRY KÜMEL
Distributed by GEMINI RELEASING CORPORATION in association with MARON FILMS LIMITED

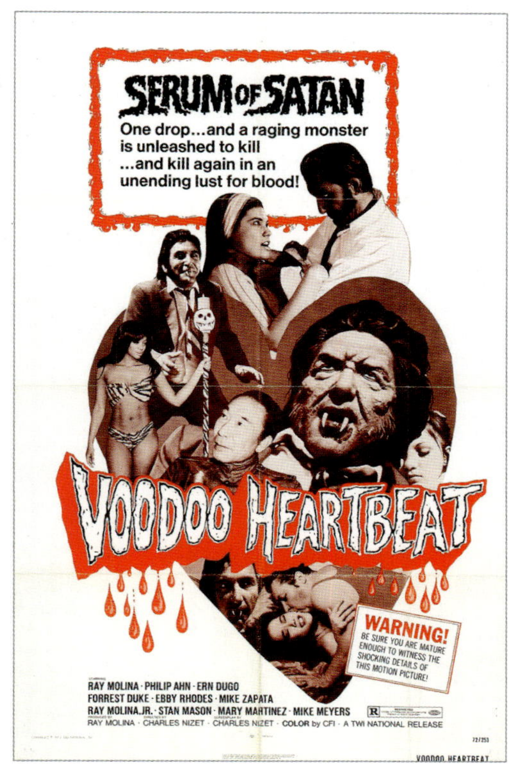
SERUM OF SATAN
One drop...and a raging monster is unleashed to kill ...and kill again in an unending lust for blood!
VOODOO HEARTBEAT
WARNING! BE SURE YOU ARE MATURE ENOUGH TO WITNESS THE SHOCKING DETAILS OF THIS MOTION PICTURE!
RAY MOLINA · PHILIP AHN · ERN DUGO
FORREST DUKE · EBBY RHODES · MIKE ZAPATA
RAY MOLINA, JR. · STAN MASON · MARY MARTINEZ · MIKE MEYERS
R
RAY MOLINA · CHARLES NIZET · CHARLES NIZET · COLOR by CFI · A TWI NATIONAL RELEASE

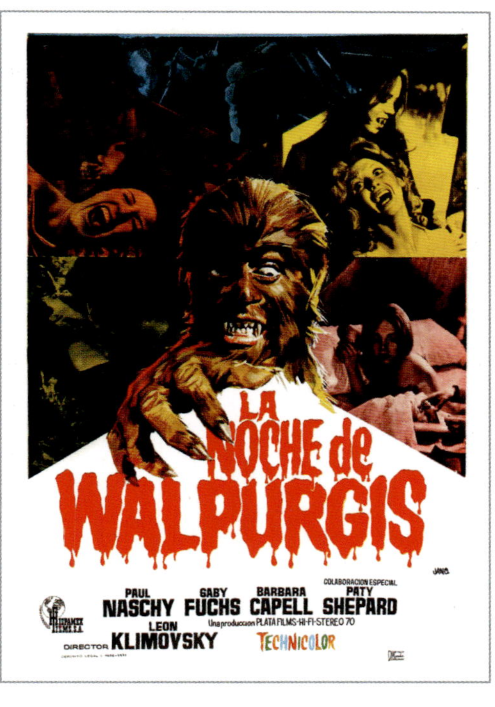
LA NOCHE de WALPURGIS
PAUL NASCHY
GABY FUCHS
BARBARA CAPELL
COLABORACION ESPECIAL PATY SHEPARD
Una produccion PLATA FILMS · HI-FI STEREO 70
DIRECTOR LEON KLIMOVSKY
TECHNICOLOR

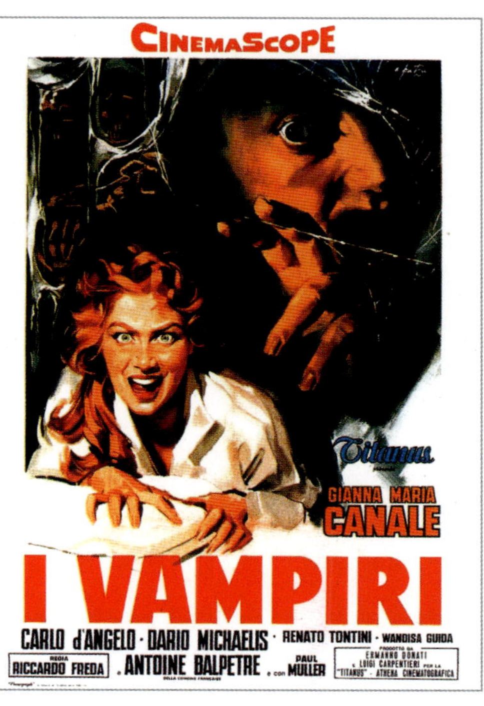
CINEMASCOPE
Titanus
GIANNA MARIA CANALE
I VAMPIRI
CARLO d'ANGELO · DARIO MICHAELIS · RENATO TONTINI · WANDISA GUIDA
REGIA RICCARDO FREDA
ANTOINE BALPETRE
e con PAUL MULLER
PRODOTTO DA ERMANNO DONATI e LUIGI CARPENTIERI PER LA "TITANUS" · ATHENA CINEMATOGRAFICA

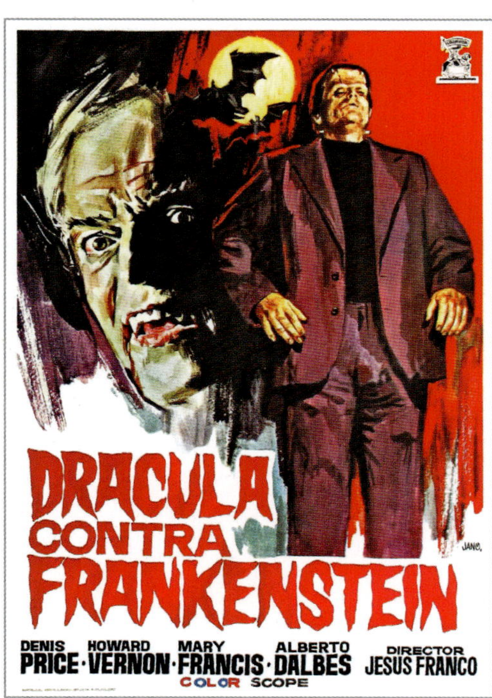
DRACULA CONTRA FRANKENSTEIN
DENIS PRICE · HOWARD VERNON · MARY FRANCIS · ALBERTO DALBES
DIRECTOR JESUS FRANCO
COLOR SCOPE

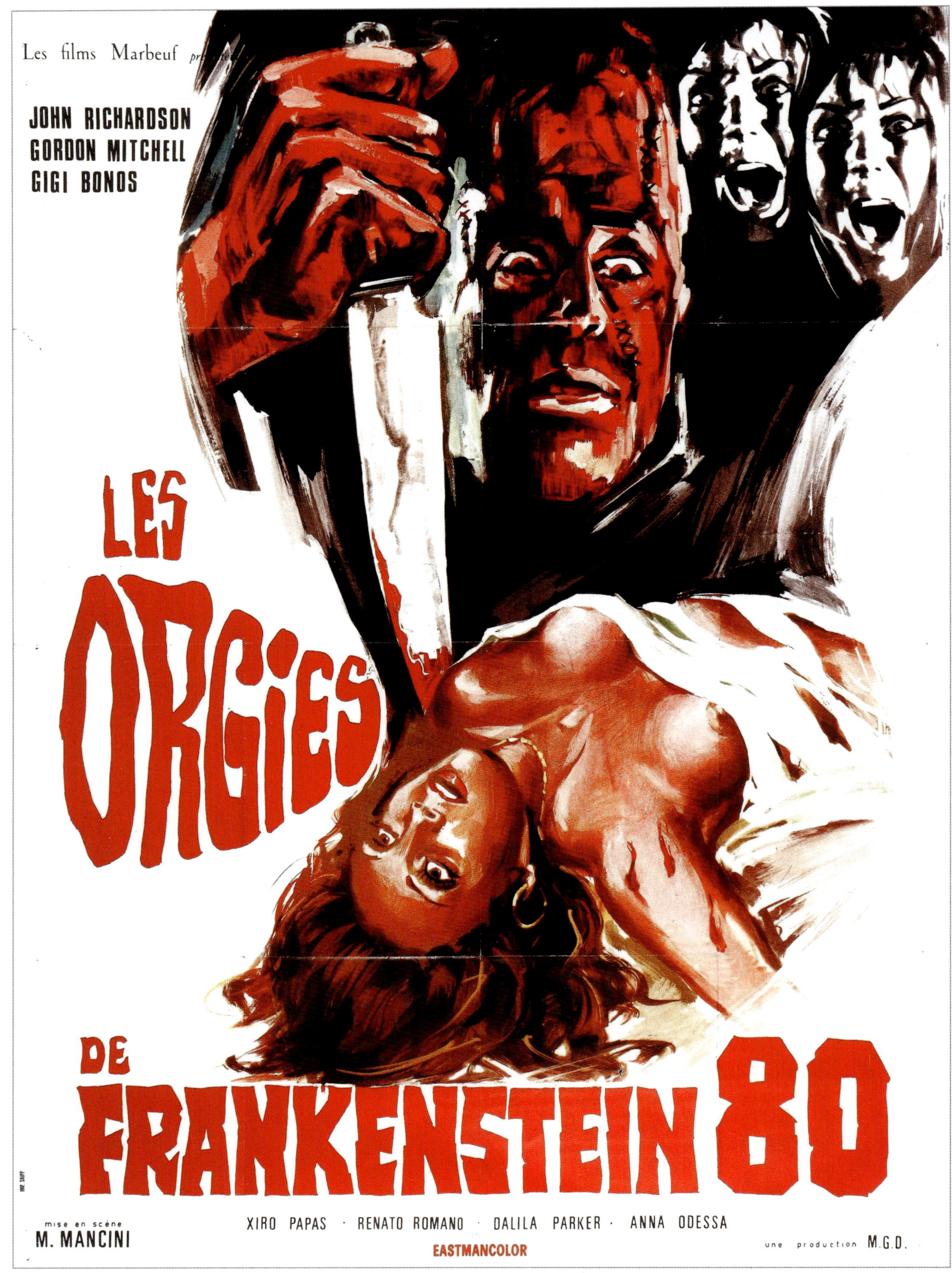
Les films Marbeuf présente
JOHN RICHARDSON
GORDON MITCHELL
GIGI BONOS
LES ORGIES DE FRANKENSTEIN 80
mise en scène
M. MANCINI
XIRO PAPAS · RENATO ROMANO · DALILA PARKER · ANNA ODESSA
EASTMANCOLOR
une production M.G.D.

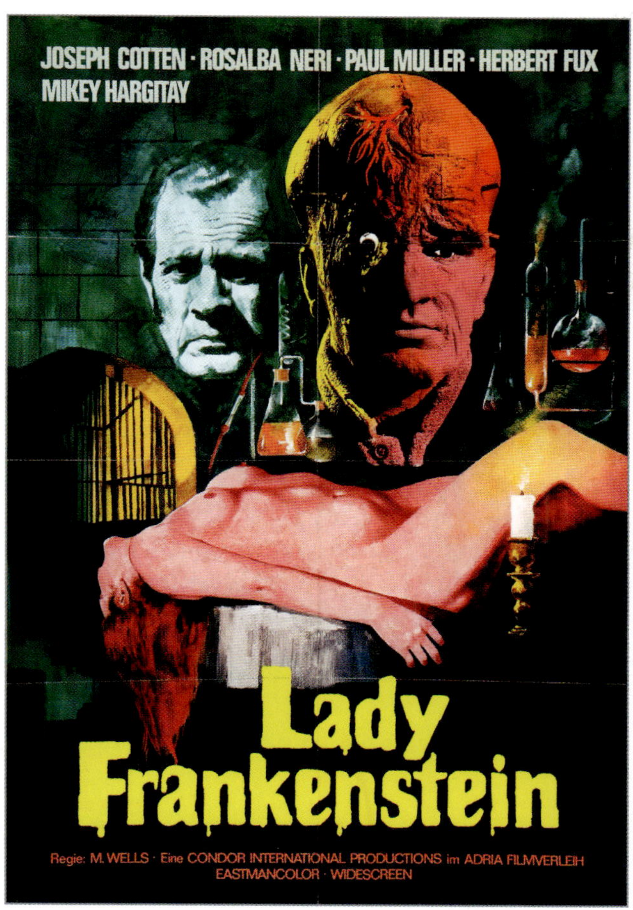
JOSEPH COTTEN · ROSALBA NERI · PAUL MULLER · HERBERT FUX
MIKEY HARGITAY
Lady Frankenstein
Regie: M. WELLS · Eine CONDOR INTERNATIONAL PRODUCTIONS im ADRIA FILMVERLEIH
EASTMANCOLOR · WIDESCREEN

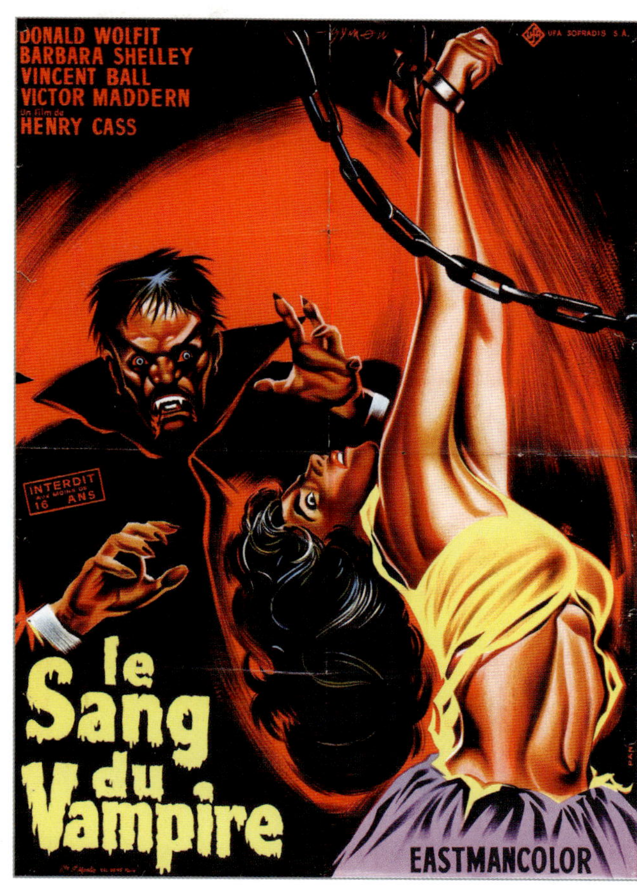
DONALD WOLFIT
BARBARA SHELLEY
VINCENT BALL
VICTOR MADDERN
Un film de
HENRY CASS
INTERDIT 16 ANS
le Sang du Vampire
EASTMANCOLOR

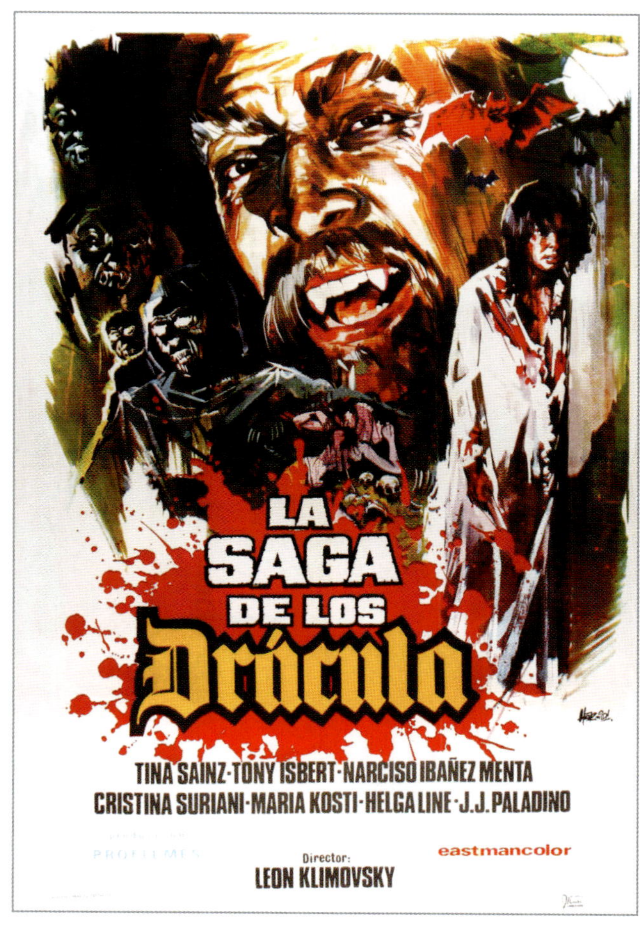
LA SAGA DE LOS Drácula
TINA SAINZ · TONY ISBERT · NARCISO IBAÑEZ MENTA
CRISTINA SURIANI · MARIA KOSTI · HELGA LINE · J.J. PALADINO
Director:
LEON KLIMOVSKY
eastmancolor

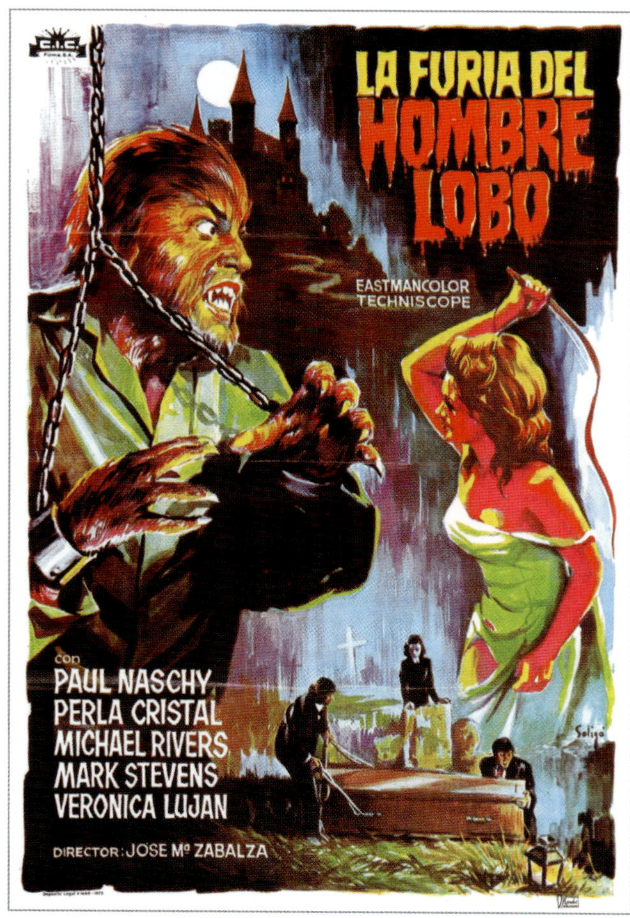
LA FURIA DEL HOMBRE LOBO
EASTMANCOLOR
TECHNISCOPE
con
PAUL NASCHY
PERLA CRISTAL
MICHAEL RIVERS
MARK STEVENS
VERONICA LUJAN
DIRECTOR: JOSE Mª ZABALZA

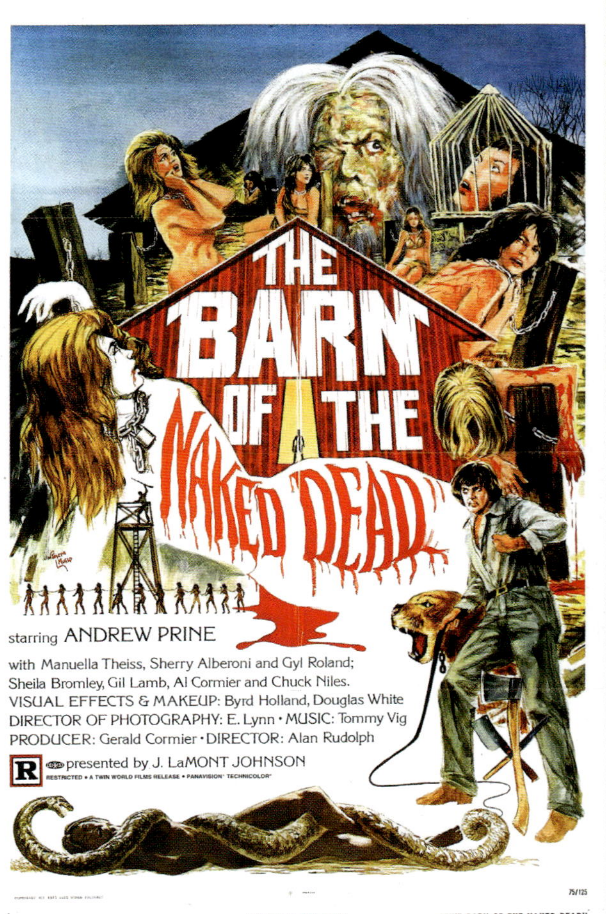

EXPLOITATION OF THE LIVING DEAD

The seismic impact of George R. Romero's zombiefest *Night of the Living Dead* ensured that similar titles quickly started to appear on posters. These days, producers (and their lawyers) protect every aspect of their movies to the fullest extent of the law; back in 1968, Romero's distributors forgot to put a copyrigh notice on prints of the film, meaning the whole thing fell into the public domain—"Living Dead" and variants thereof were therefore completely up for grabs. *Beyond the Living Dead* has also been released as *Terror of the Living Dead*, but is actually *La orgía de los muertos*, a 1973 Spanish film directed by José Luis Merino. One wonders why the US distributor didn't just adapt the original title into the even more titillating "Orgy of the Living Dead." Given its excellent poster, it would perhaps be churlish t point out that *The Dead Are Alive* (1972) doesn't actually feature any zombies. The same deficiency applies to both *House of the Living Dead* (1974) and *The Barn of the Naked Dead* (1974), though the latter is notable for being an early effort from the lauded director Alan Rudolph.

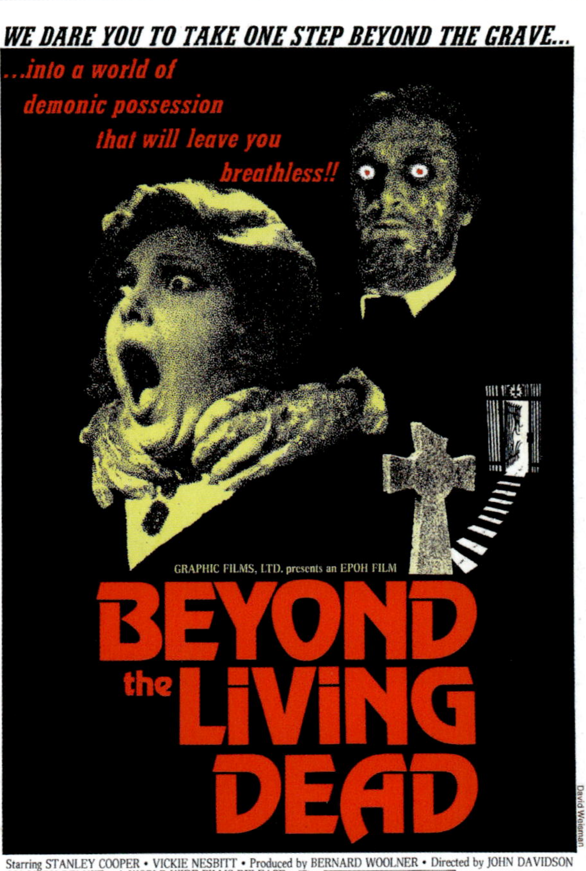

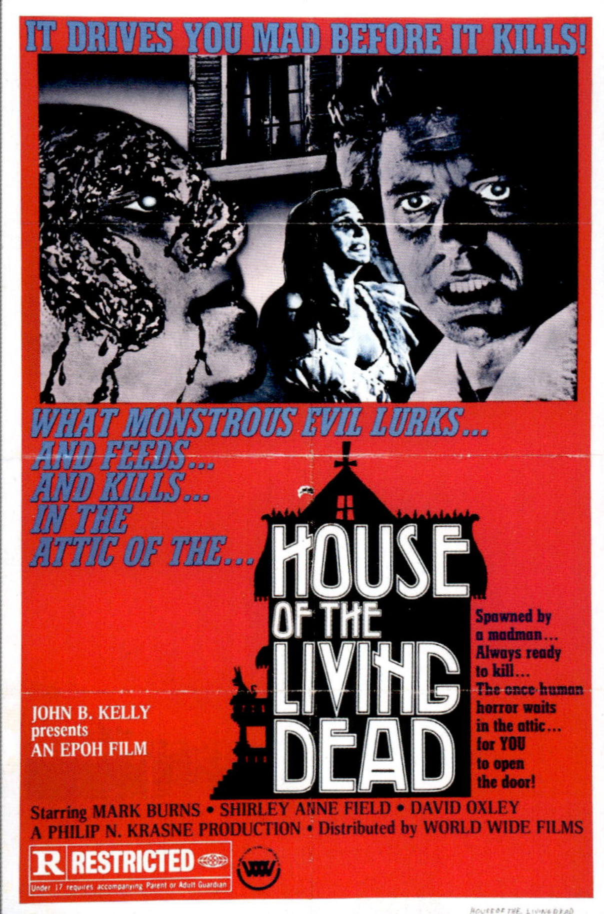

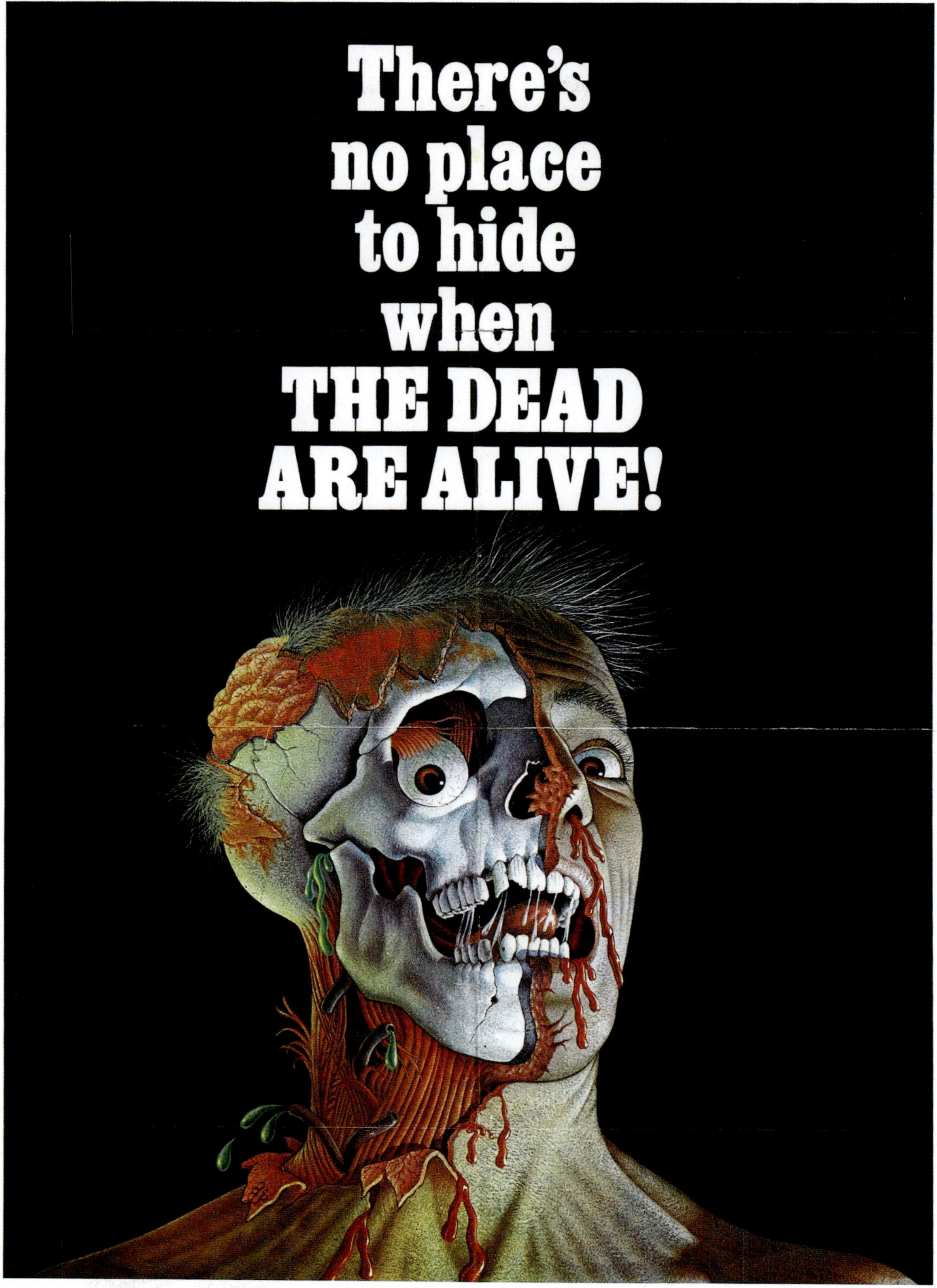
There's
no place
to hide
when
THE DEAD
ARE ALIVE!
NATIONAL GENERAL PICTURES Presents
ALEX CORD · SAMANTHA EGGAR · JOHN MARLEY THE DEAD ARE ALIVE
HORST FRANK and with NADJA TILLER Written by LUCIO BATTISTRADA and ARMANDO CRISPINO
Produced by MONDIAL TE. FI. Directed by ARMANDO CRISPINO Technicolor® A NATIONAL GENERAL PICTURES RELEASE
R RESTRICTED Under 17 requires accompanying Parent or Adult Guardian
COPYRIGHT © 1972 NATIONAL GENERAL PICTURES CORP.
72/163

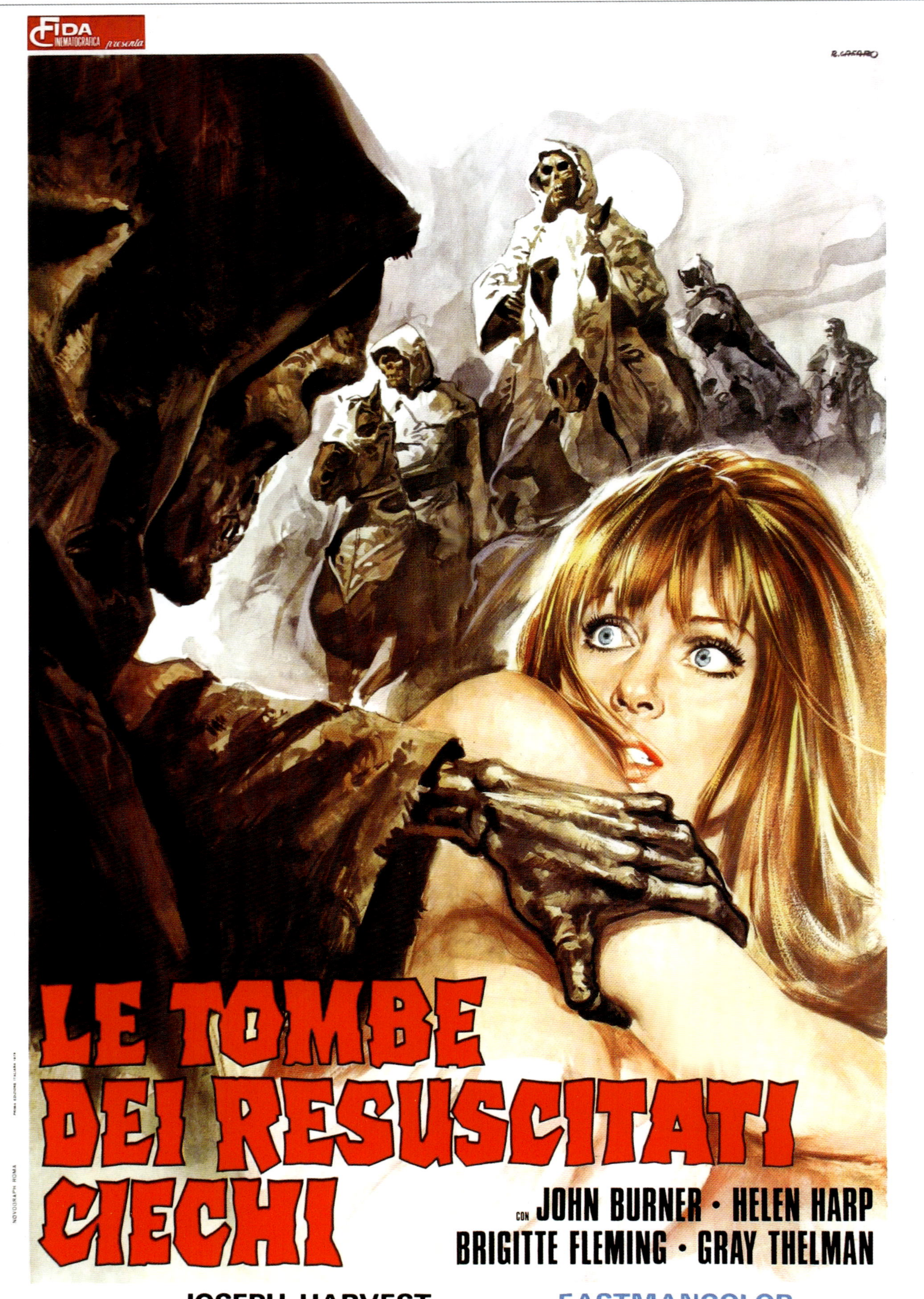
FIDA CINEMATOGRAFICA presenta
LE TOMBE DEI RESUSCITATI CIECHI
CON JOHN BURNER · HELEN HARP
BRIGITTE FLEMING · GRAY THELMAN
REGIA: JOSEPH HARVEST
EASTMANCOLOR
NOVOGRAPH ROMA

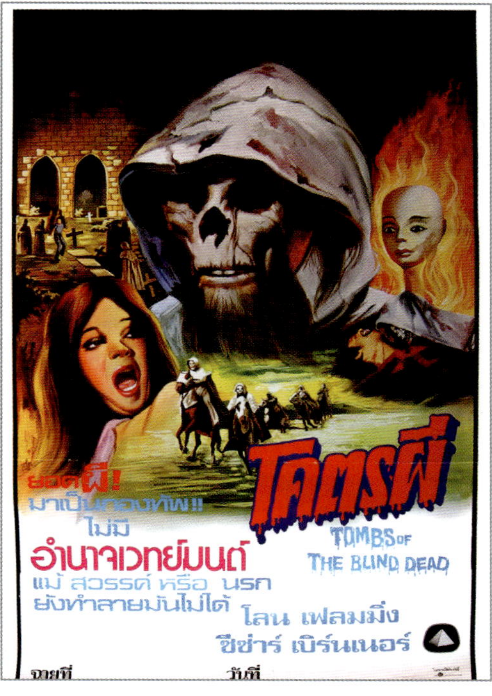

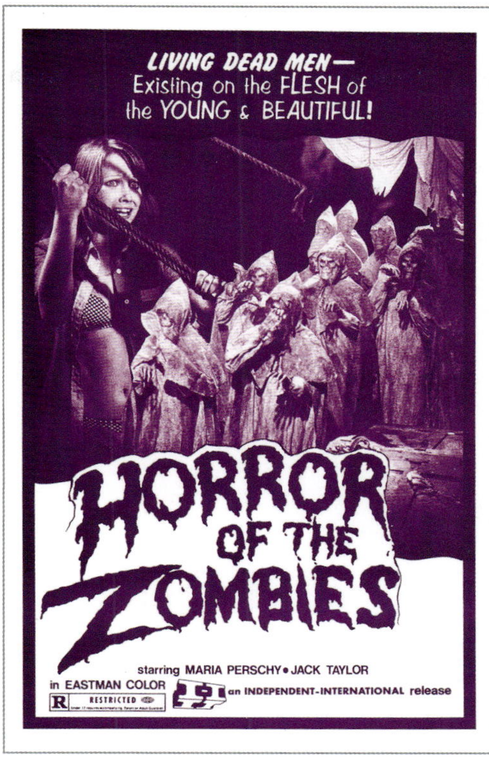

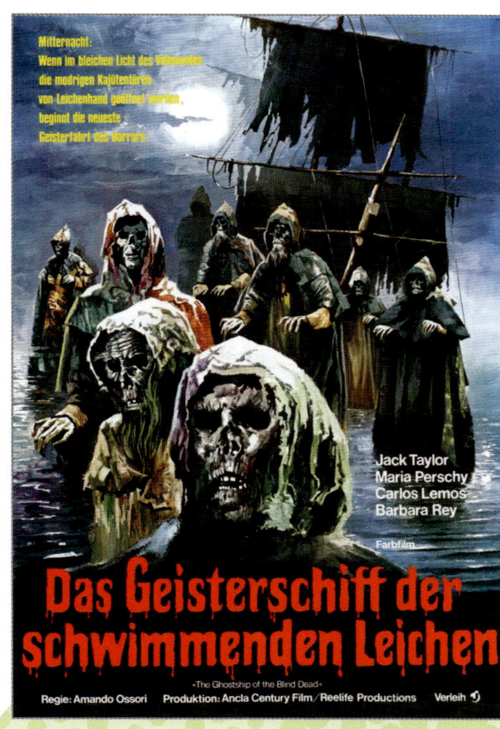

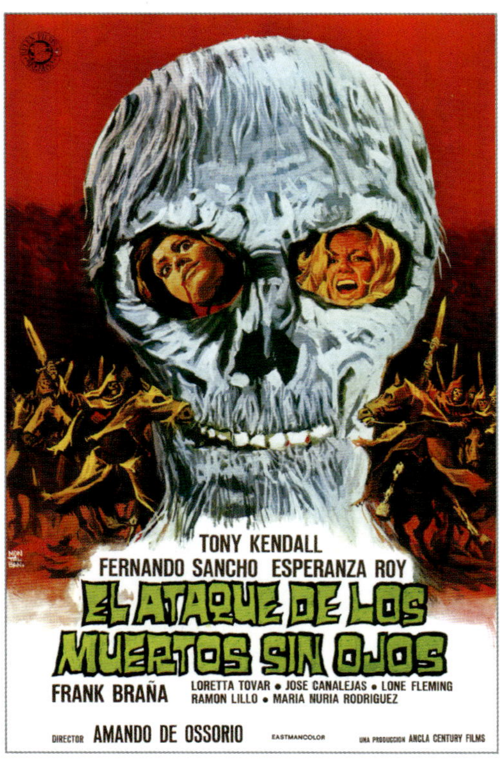

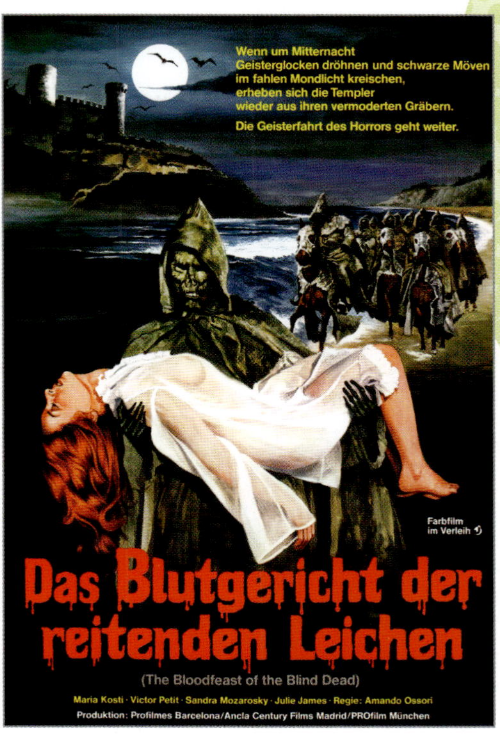

THE BLIND DEAD SERIES

Spanish director Amando de Ossorio's zombie movies featuring a bloodthirsty group of reanimated, ocularly challenged Knights Templar have been released and re-released under a bewildering number of titles around the world, too long to list here. Suffice to say there's a handy DVD box set grouping the quartet under the overall name that seems to have stuck: The Blind Dead. The zombies' slightly simian appearance inspired one genius/desperate US distributor to edit out any mention of the Templars from the first film, *Tombs of the Blind Dead* (1971), and release it to drive-ins as a *Planet of the Apes* "sequel"—*Revenge from Planet Ape*!

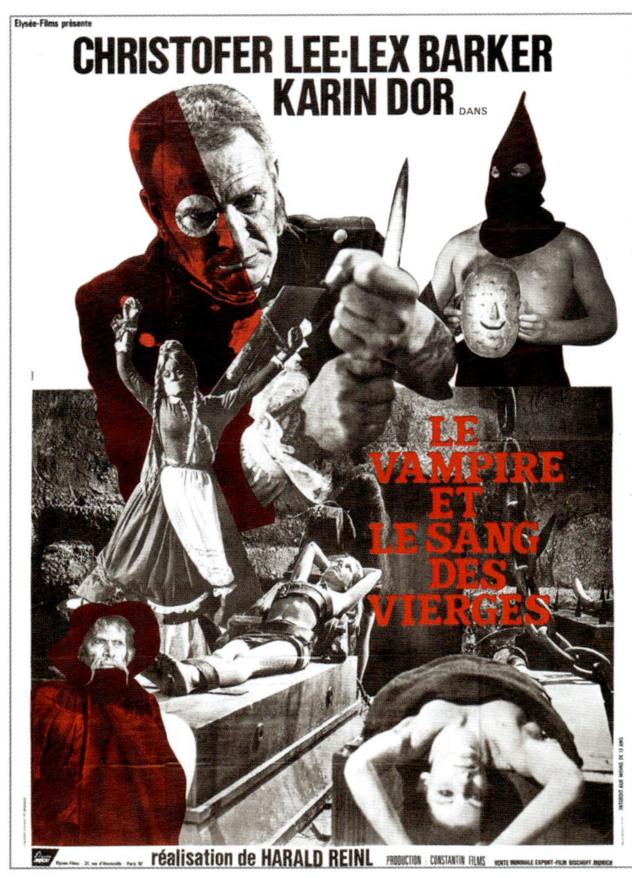

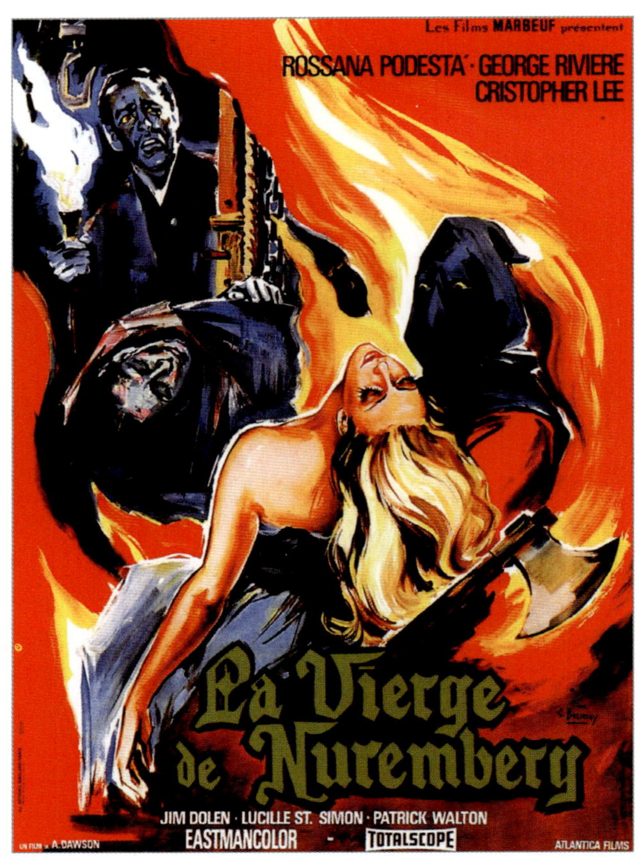

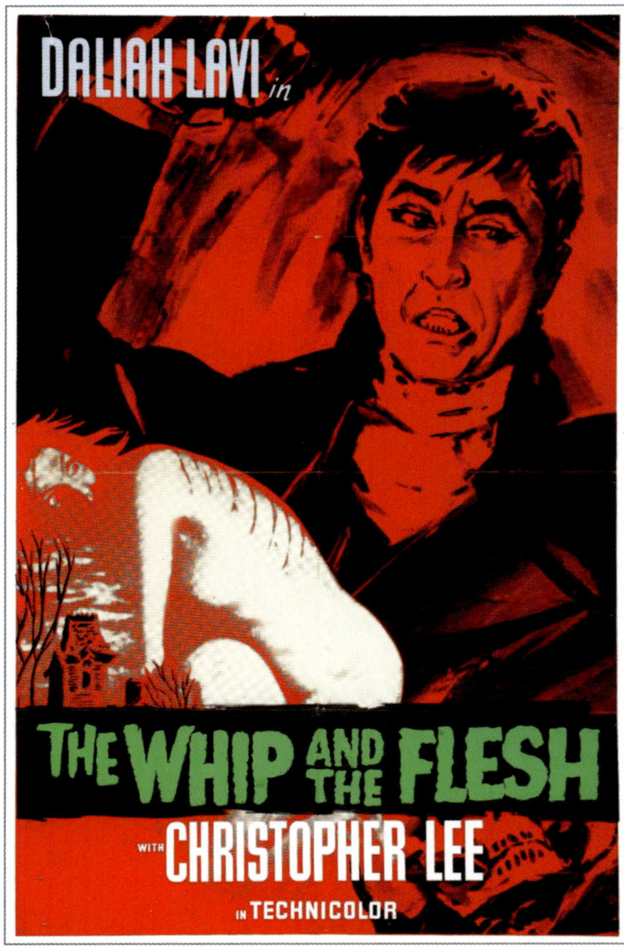

THE FACE OF CHRISTOPHER LEE

Sir Christopher Lee (1922–2015) loved to work. At a conservative estimate, he made over 200 screen appearances, yet still found time to learn to speak five languages fluently, write volumes of autobiography, and even record three heavy metal albums (he also sung opera). "Making films has never just been a job to me, it is my life," he once said, also admitting that, "there are frustrations—people who lie to you, people who don't know what they are doing, films that don't turn out the way you had wanted them to." It's unlikely that Lee would have counted any of the films illustrated here as particular highlights of his long career. *The Face of Fu Manchu* (1965) for example, with Lee as the titular nefarious "Yellow Peril," comes from an era before the phrase "political correctness" had been invented, and has not stood the test of time well at all. It does however have an impactful poster by Mitchell Hooks, who coincidentally painted the iconic art for another film featuring an Oriental nemesis: *Dr. No.* The Bond villain was also played by a Western actor in make-up (Joseph Wiseman), though 007 creator Ian Fleming initially suggested the part be played by his own cousin—Christopher Lee.

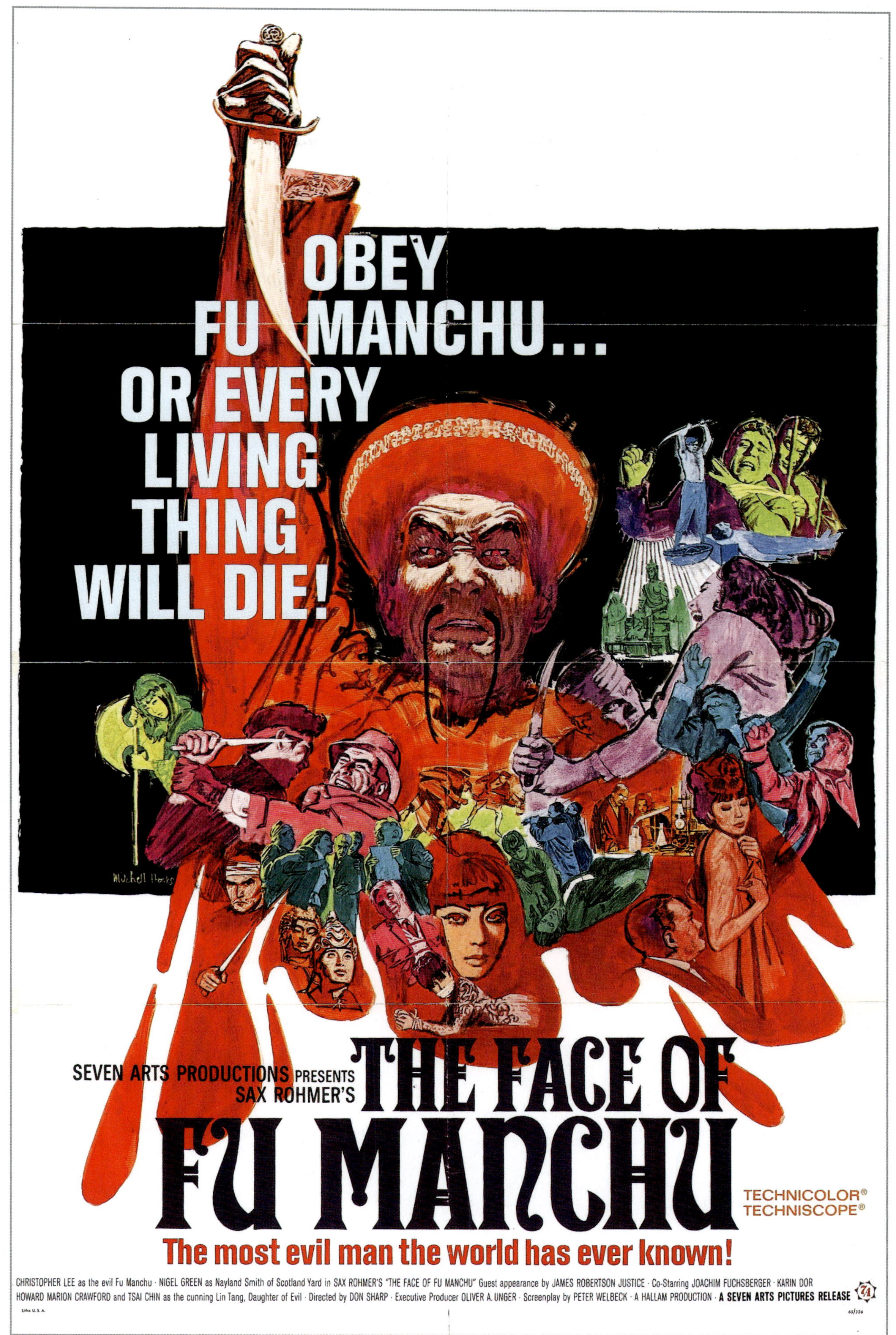
OBEY
FU MANCHU...
OR EVERY
LIVING
THING
WILL DIE!
SEVEN ARTS PRODUCTIONS PRESENTS
SAX ROHMER'S
THE FACE OF
FU MANCHU
TECHNICOLOR®
TECHNISCOPE®
The most evil man the world has ever known!
CHRISTOPHER LEE as the evil Fu Manchu · NIGEL GREEN as Nayland Smith of Scotland Yard in SAX ROHMER'S "THE FACE OF FU MANCHU" Guest appearance by JAMES ROBERTSON JUSTICE · Co-Starring JOACHIM FUCHSBERGER · KARIN DOR
HOWARD MARION CRAWFORD and TSAI CHIN as the cunning Lin Tang, Daughter of Evil · Directed by DON SHARP · Executive Producer OLIVER A. UNGER · Screenplay by PETER WELBECK · A HALLAM PRODUCTION · A SEVEN ARTS PICTURES RELEASE
Litho U.S.A.
65/326

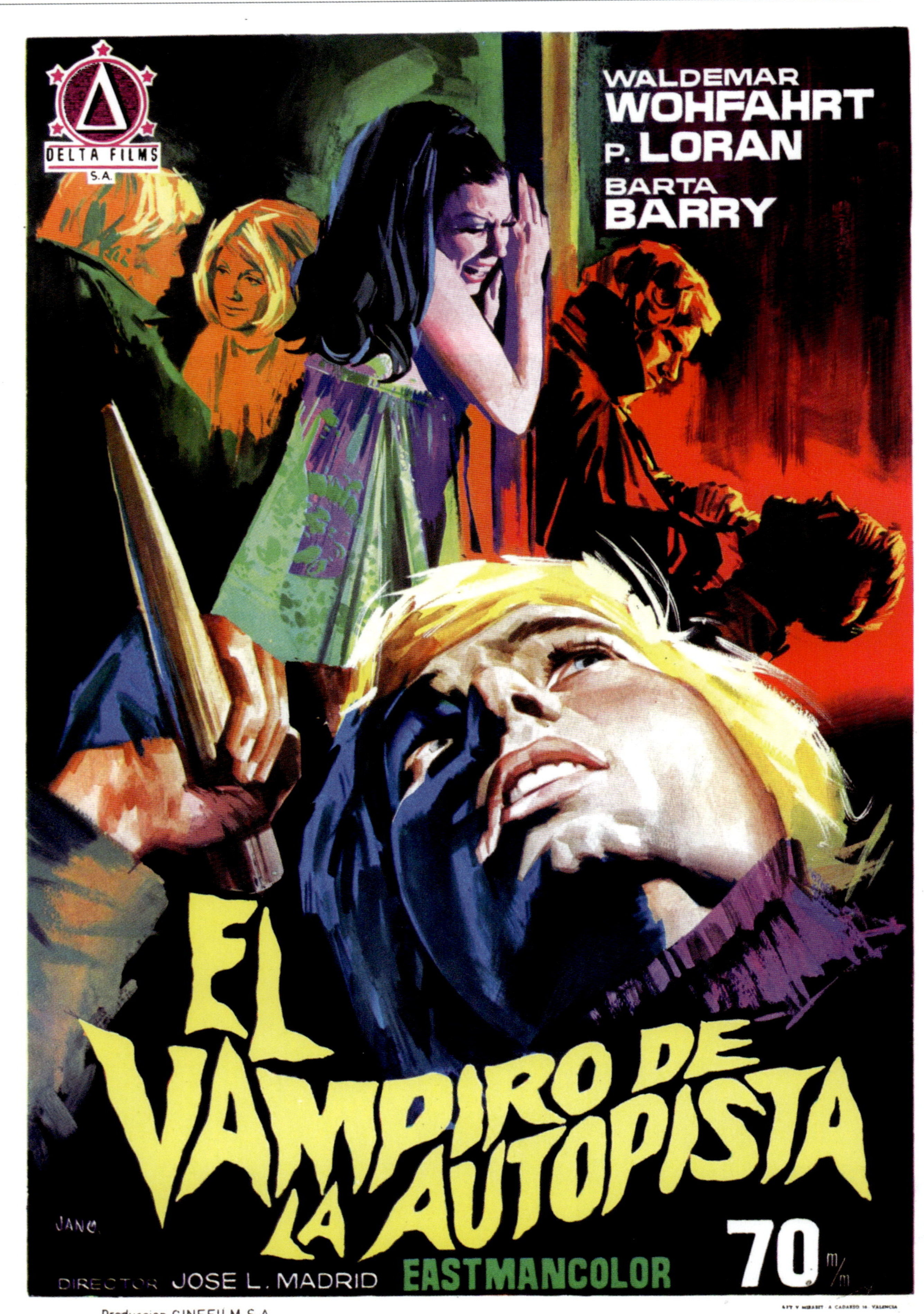
DELTA FILMS
S.A.
WALDEMAR
WOHFAHRT
P. LORAN
BARTA
BARRY
EL
VAMPIRO DE
LA AUTOPISTA
JANO
70 m/m
DIRECTOR JOSE L. MADRID
EASTMANCOLOR
Produccion CINEFILM S.A.

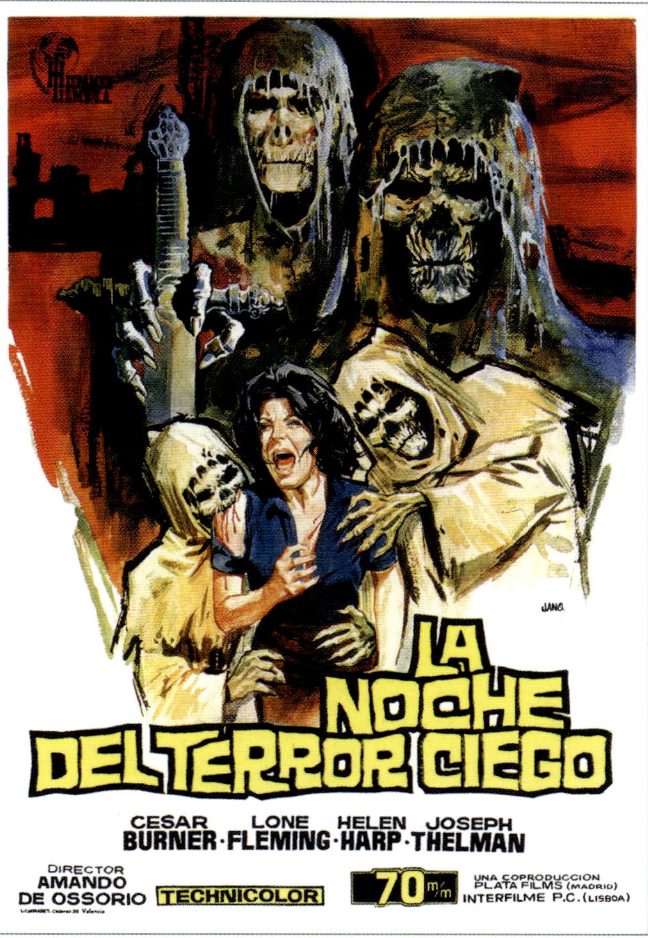

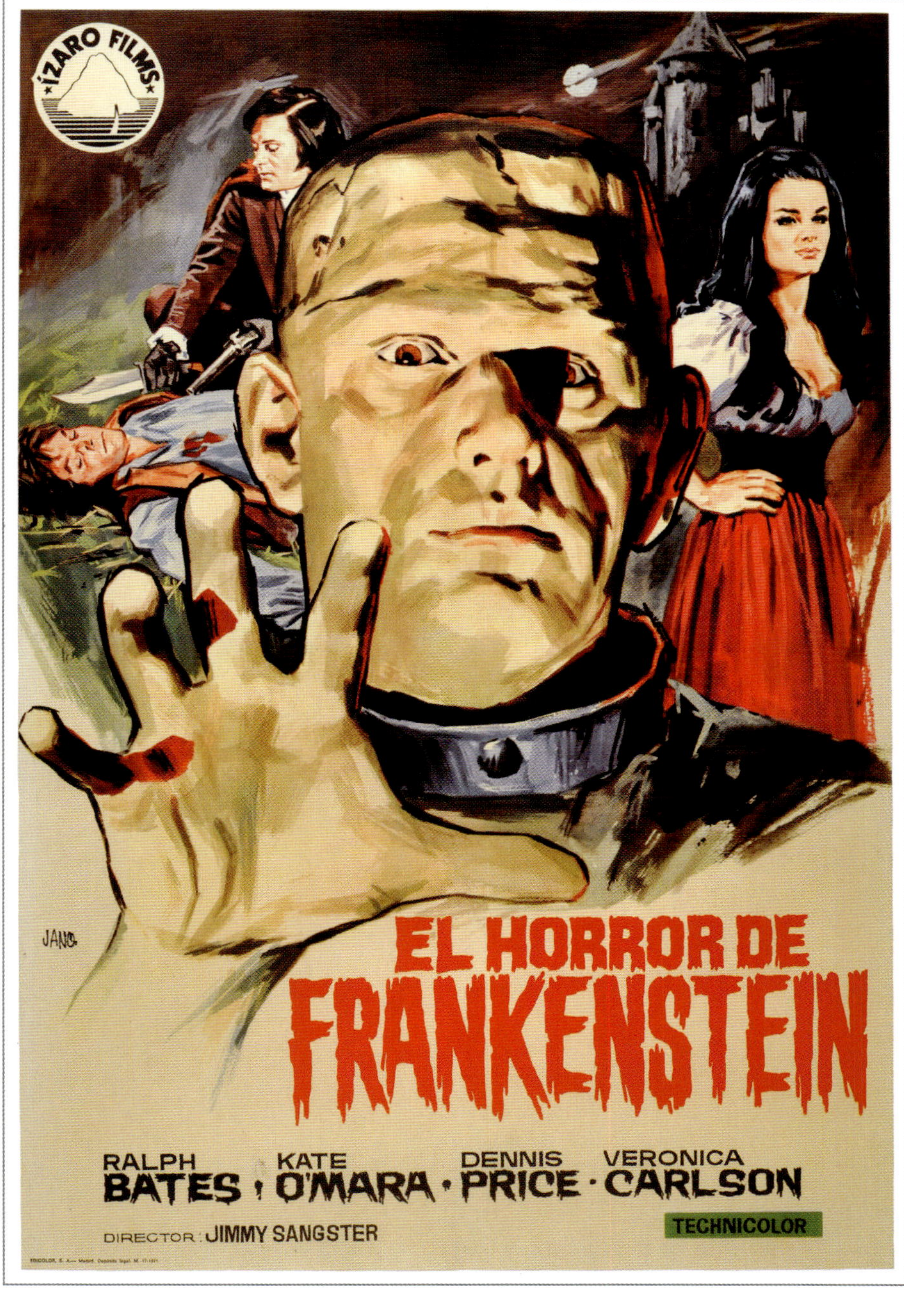

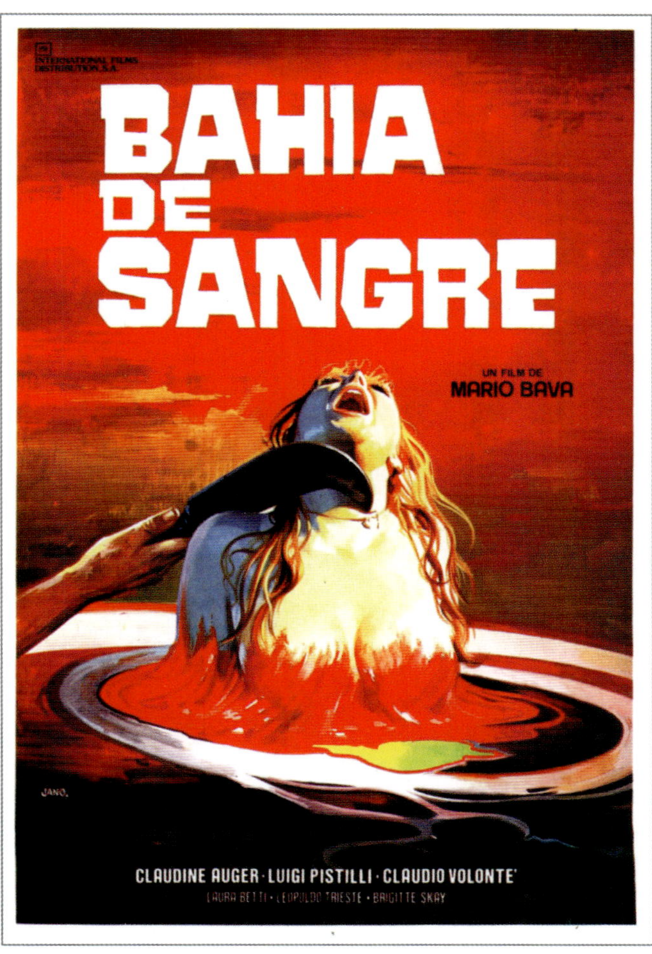

THE ART OF JANO

Francisco Fernández-Zarza Pérez (1922–1992), aka Jano, was a giant of Spanish movie art, who painted literally thousands of posters. As his pseudonym (Spanish for Janus) suggests, his style had more than one face, and he was equally at home illustrating mainstream movies like *The Wizard of Oz*, *Giant*, or *The Red Shoes* as he was with the slightly less refined fare showcased here, including José L. Madrid's *El vampiro de la autopista* (1970). The title translates as "The Vampire of the Highway," though the US distributor decided to call it, for reasons best known to itself, *The Horrible Sexy Vampire*. Sadly, the film could never hope to live up to Jano's stunning poster.

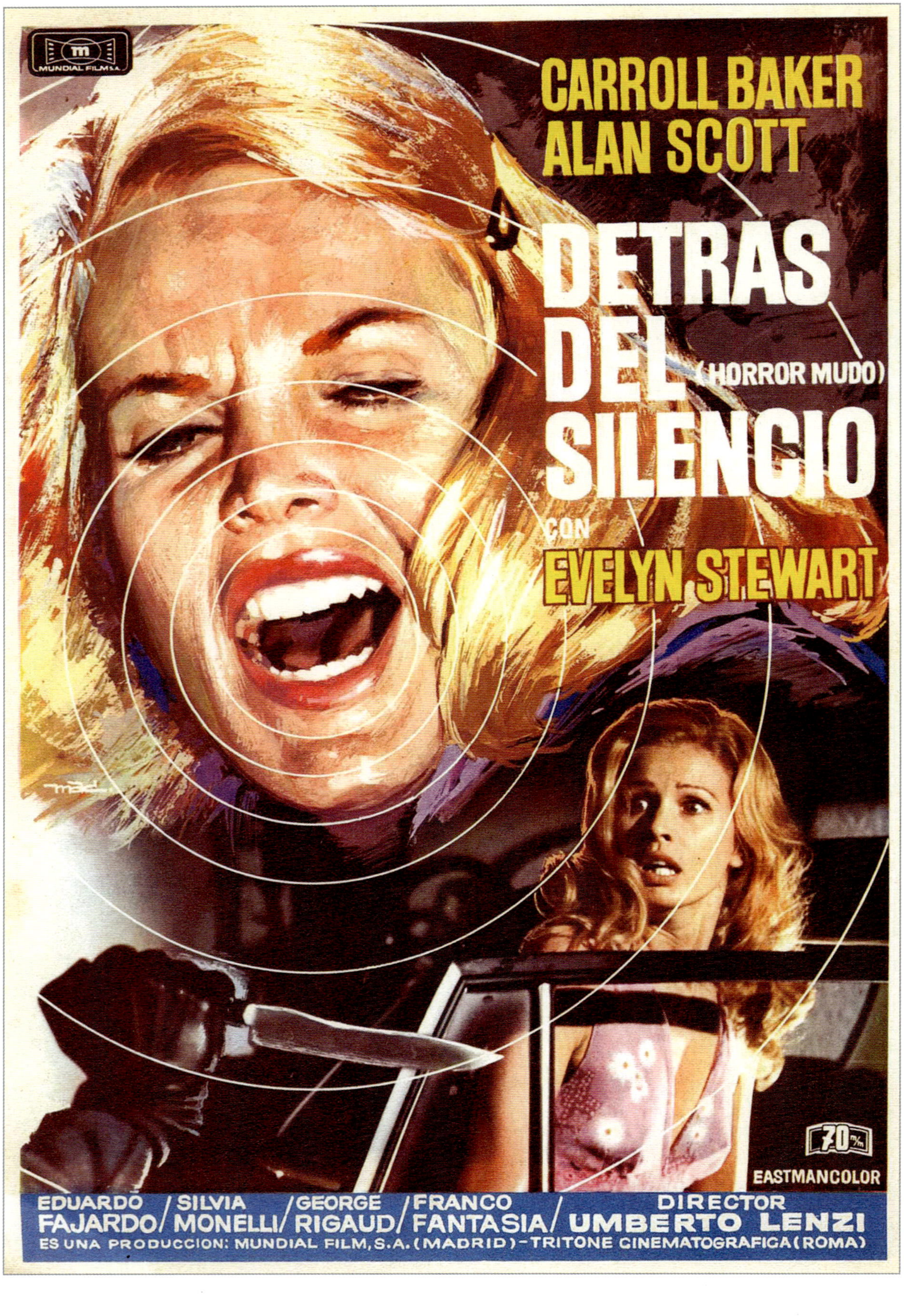

MUNDIAL FILM S.A.

CARROLL BAKER
ALAN SCOTT

DETRAS DEL SILENCIO (HORROR MUDO)

CON
EVELYN STEWART

70 m/m
EASTMANCOLOR

EDUARDO FAJARDO / SILVIA MONELLI / GEORGE RIGAUD / FRANCO FANTASIA / DIRECTOR UMBERTO LENZI

ES UNA PRODUCCION: MUNDIAL FILM, S.A. (MADRID) - TRITONE CINEMATOGRAFICA (ROMA)

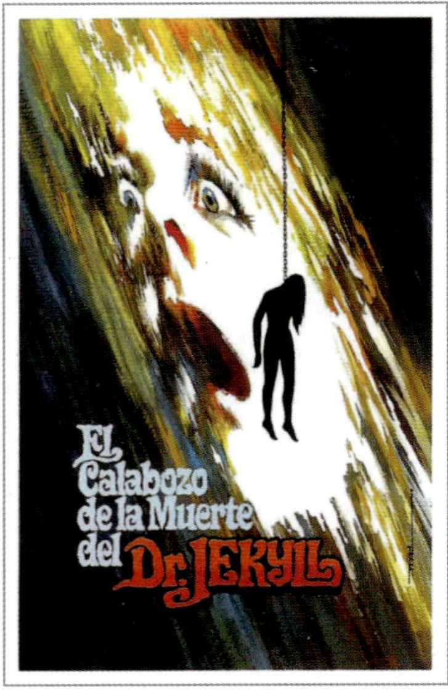

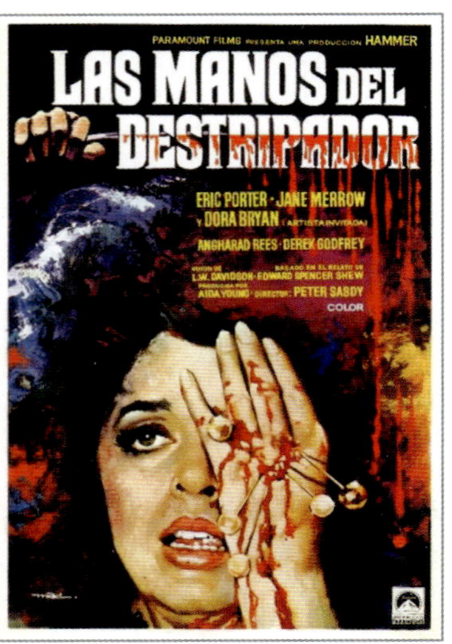

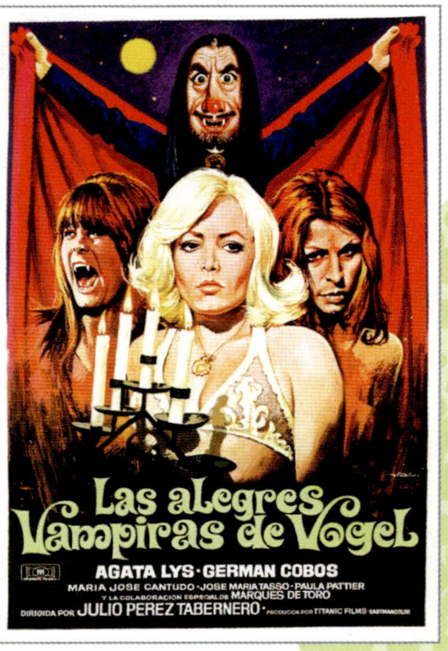

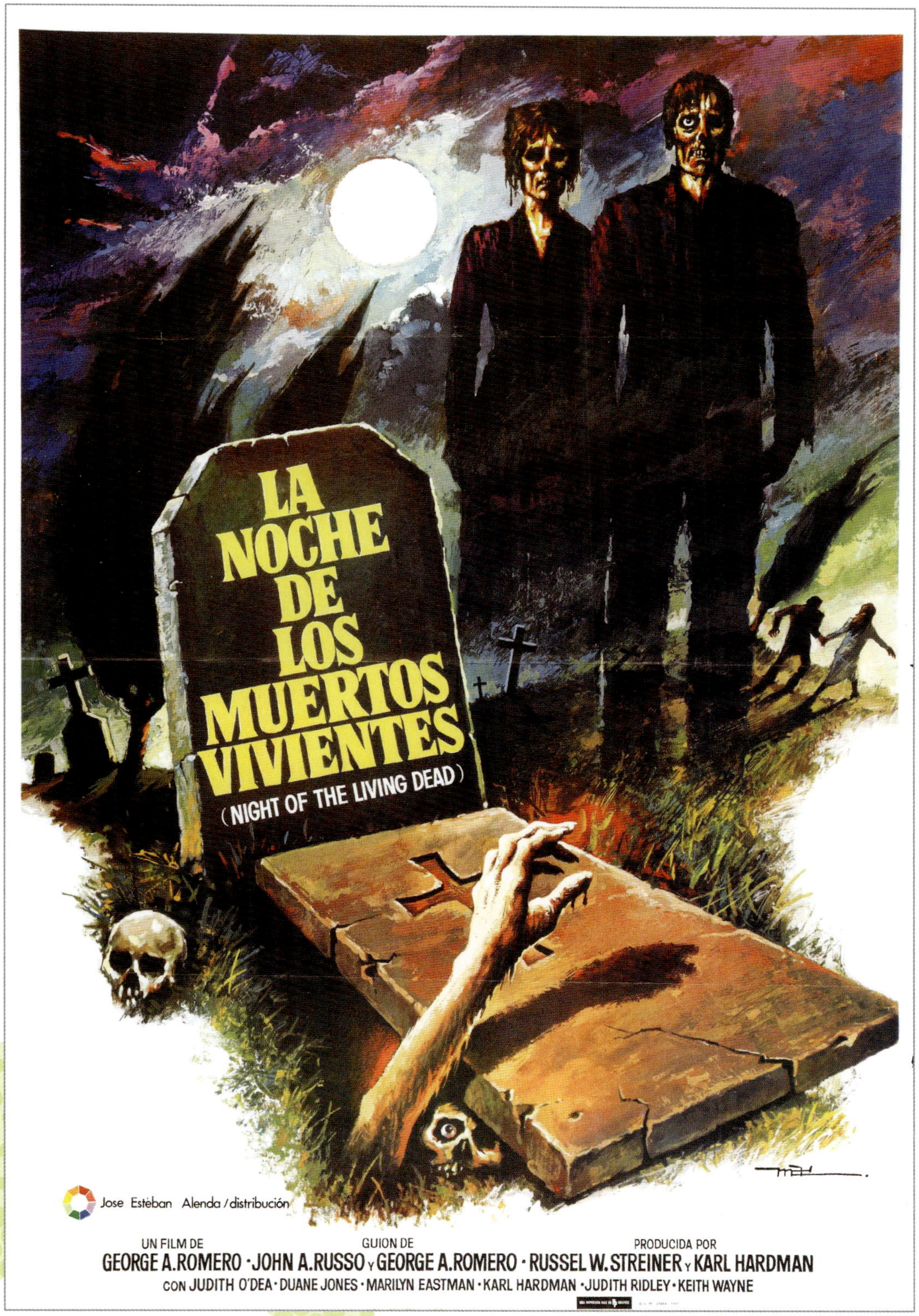

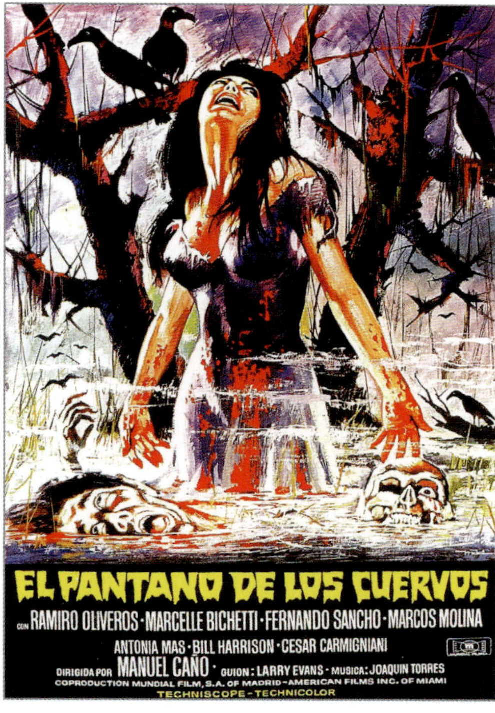

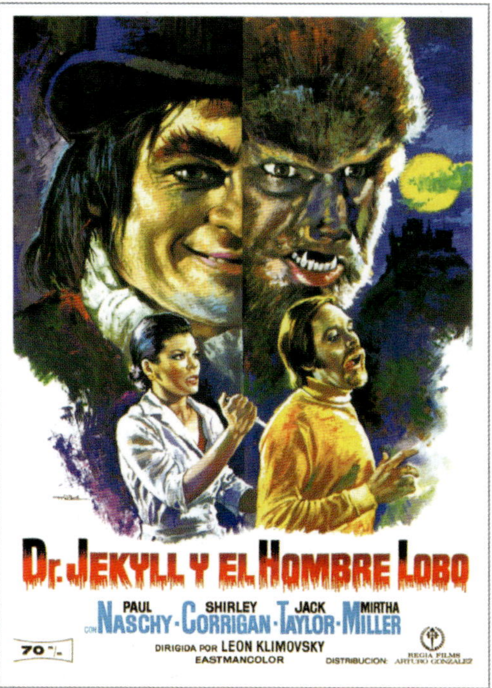

THE ART OF MAC AND MONTALBAN

The signatures of "MAC" and "Montalban" were ubiquitous on Spanish movie posters of all genres in the '60s and '70s. Both artists were hugely prolific, and their horror-related output often saw them at their best. For example MAC, aka Macario Gómez Quibus (showcased on this spread), painted a superbly creepy image for George R. Romero's *Night of the Living Dead* (1968), while José Montalbán Saíz (overleaf) did Ingrid Pitt and (part of) Peter Cushing proud on his poster for *The House That Dripped Blood* (1971). These elder statesmen of movie art are now hugely respected in their native country; in 2014 MAC was even awarded a medal by the Catalonian government for his services to culture.

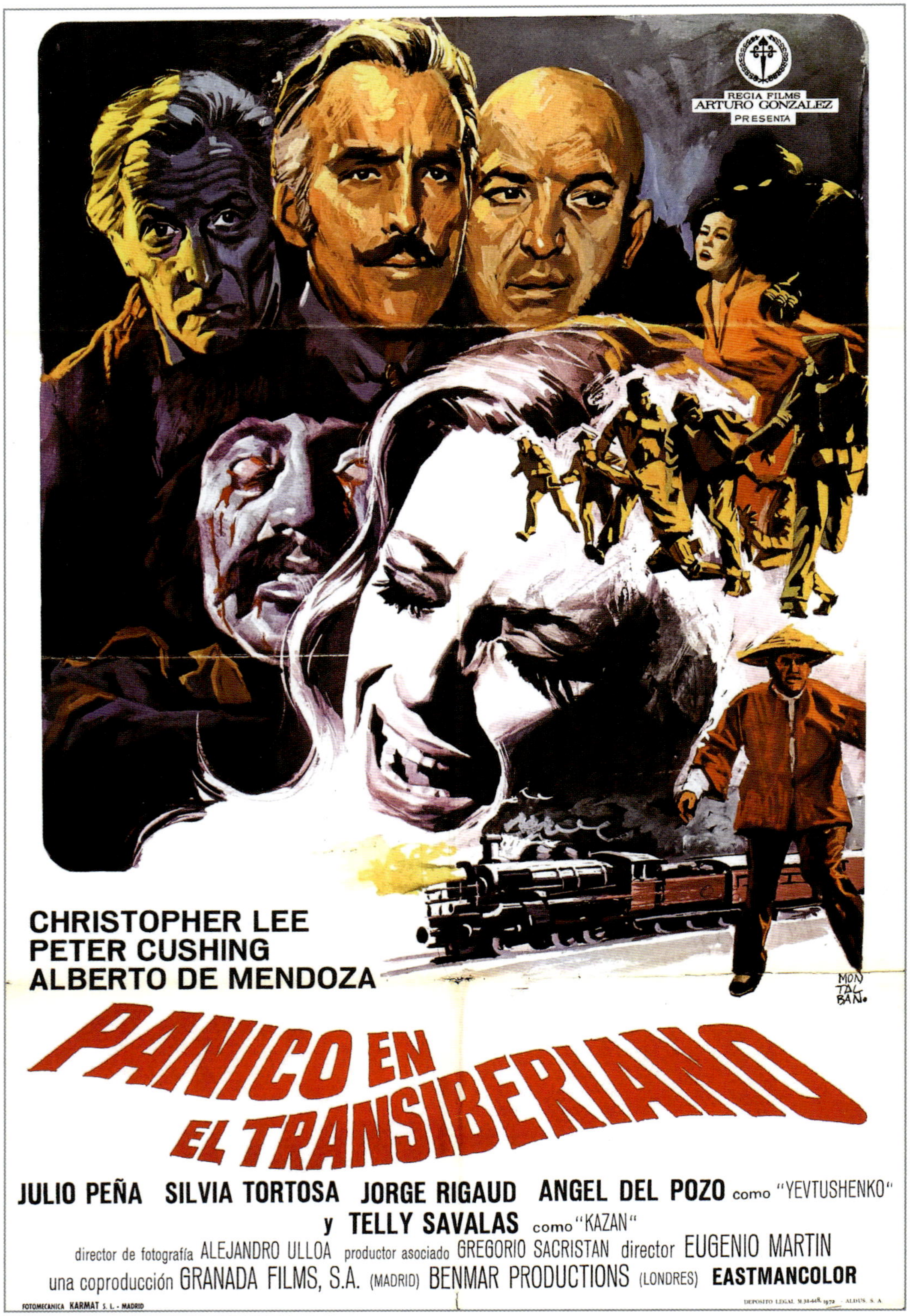

REGIA FILMS
ARTURO GONZALEZ
PRESENTA
CHRISTOPHER LEE
PETER CUSHING
ALBERTO DE MENDOZA
PANICO EN
EL TRANSIBERIANO
JULIO PEÑA SILVIA TORTOSA JORGE RIGAUD ANGEL DEL POZO como "YEVTUSHENKO"
y TELLY SAVALAS como "KAZAN"
director de fotografía ALEJANDRO ULLOA productor asociado GREGORIO SACRISTAN director EUGENIO MARTIN
una coproducción GRANADA FILMS, S.A. (MADRID) BENMAR PRODUCTIONS (LONDRES) EASTMANCOLOR
FOTOMECANICA KARMAT S. L. - MADRID

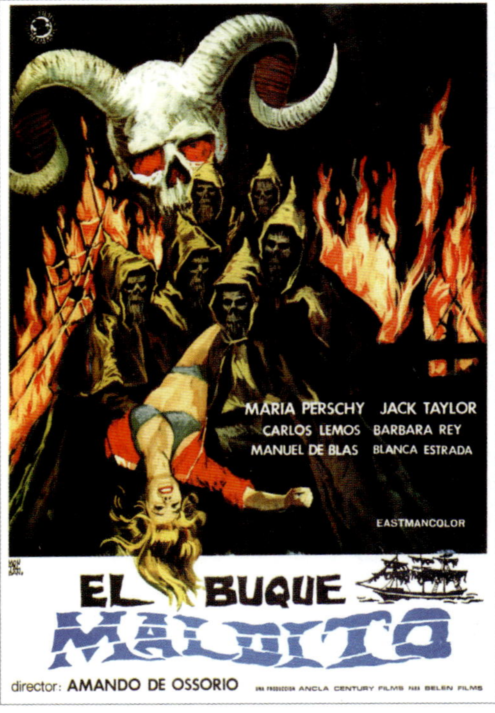

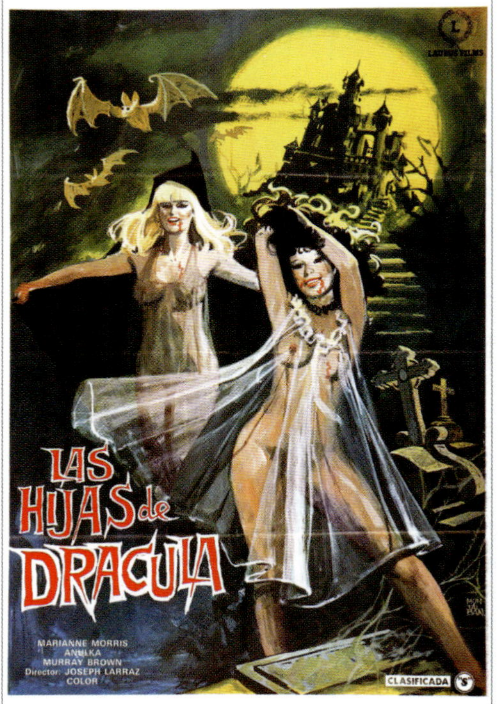

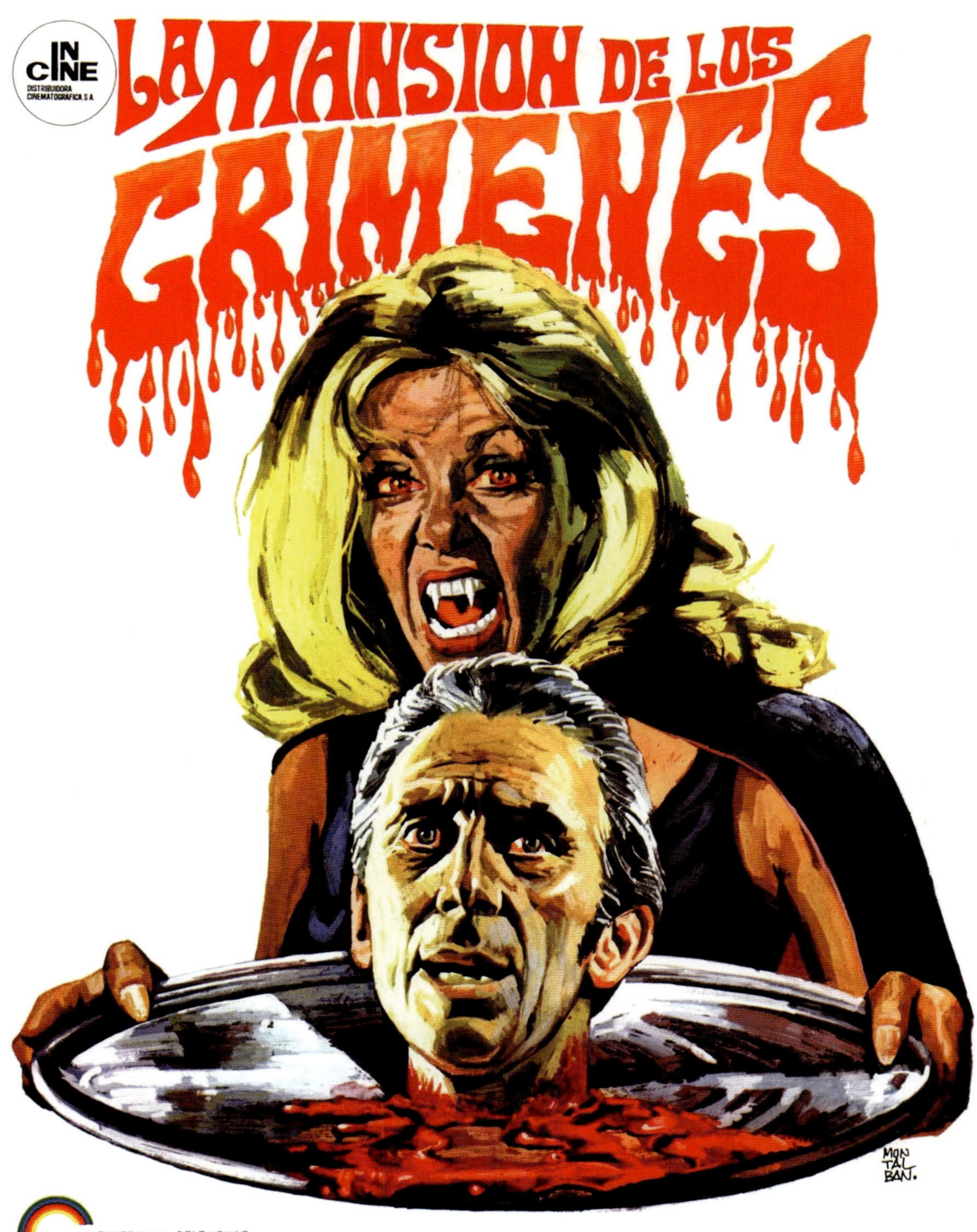

CINERAMA RELEASING

LA MANSION DE LOS CRIMENES CHRISTOPHER LEE • PETER CUSHING

NYREE DAWN PORTER • DENHOLM ELLIOTT • JON PERTWEE JOANNA DUNHAM - JOSS ACKLAND - JOHN BENNETT - JOHN BRYANS WOLFE MORRIS - TOM ADAMS E INGRID PITT como "CARLA"

productores ejecutivos PAUL ELLSWORTH Y GORDON WESCOURT • producida por MAX J. ROSENBERG Y MILTON SUBOTSKY • escrita por ROBERT BLOCH • dirigida por PETER DUFFELL • COLOR

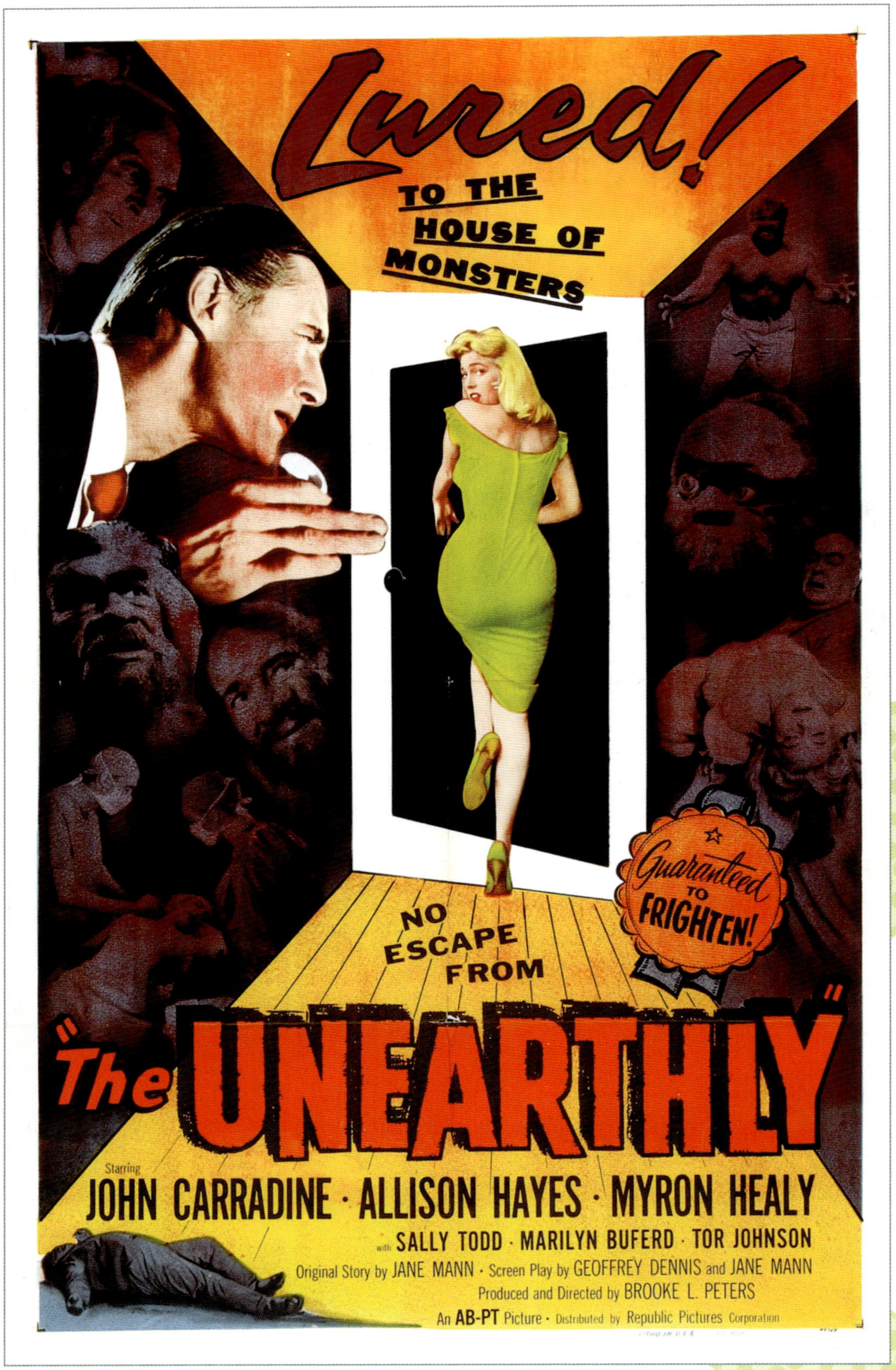

Lured!
TO THE
HOUSE OF
MONSTERS
NO
ESCAPE
FROM
Guaranteed TO FRIGHTEN!
"The UNEARTHLY"
Starring
JOHN CARRADINE · ALLISON HAYES · MYRON HEALY
with SALLY TODD · MARILYN BUFERD · TOR JOHNSON
Original Story by JANE MANN · Screen Play by GEOFFREY DENNIS and JANE MANN
Produced and Directed by BROOKE L. PETERS
An AB-PT Picture · Distributed by Republic Pictures Corporation

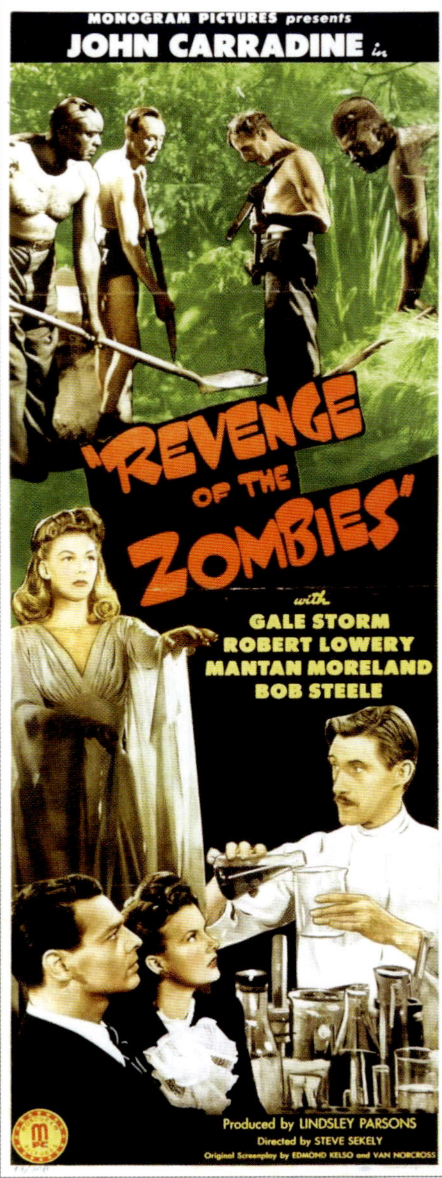

CARRADINE'S CAREER

John Carradine (1906–88) started in the movie business as a set designer for Cecil B. DeMille, before amassing so many acting credits that compiling a definitive filmography is no easy task—Carradine himself claimed he'd appeared in over 450 productions. He also claimed that he was screen-tested for both the Count in *Dracula* (1931) and the Monster in *Frankenstein* (1931), and while his profile was ultimately never as high as Lugosi or Karloff's, Carradine made his fair share of horror pictures, becoming an icon of the genre. He wasn't often top-billed though, as he is on the posters shown here. In a good example of a distributor aiming for different markets at different times, *Horror of the Blood Monsters* and *Space Mission to the Lost Planet* are actually the same movie, first released in 1970. The Philippines-shot *Vampire Hookers* (1978) is, according to one critic, "only watchable for those who appreciate enduring really bad movies, especially really bad movies with John Carradine, and we know how many of those exist."

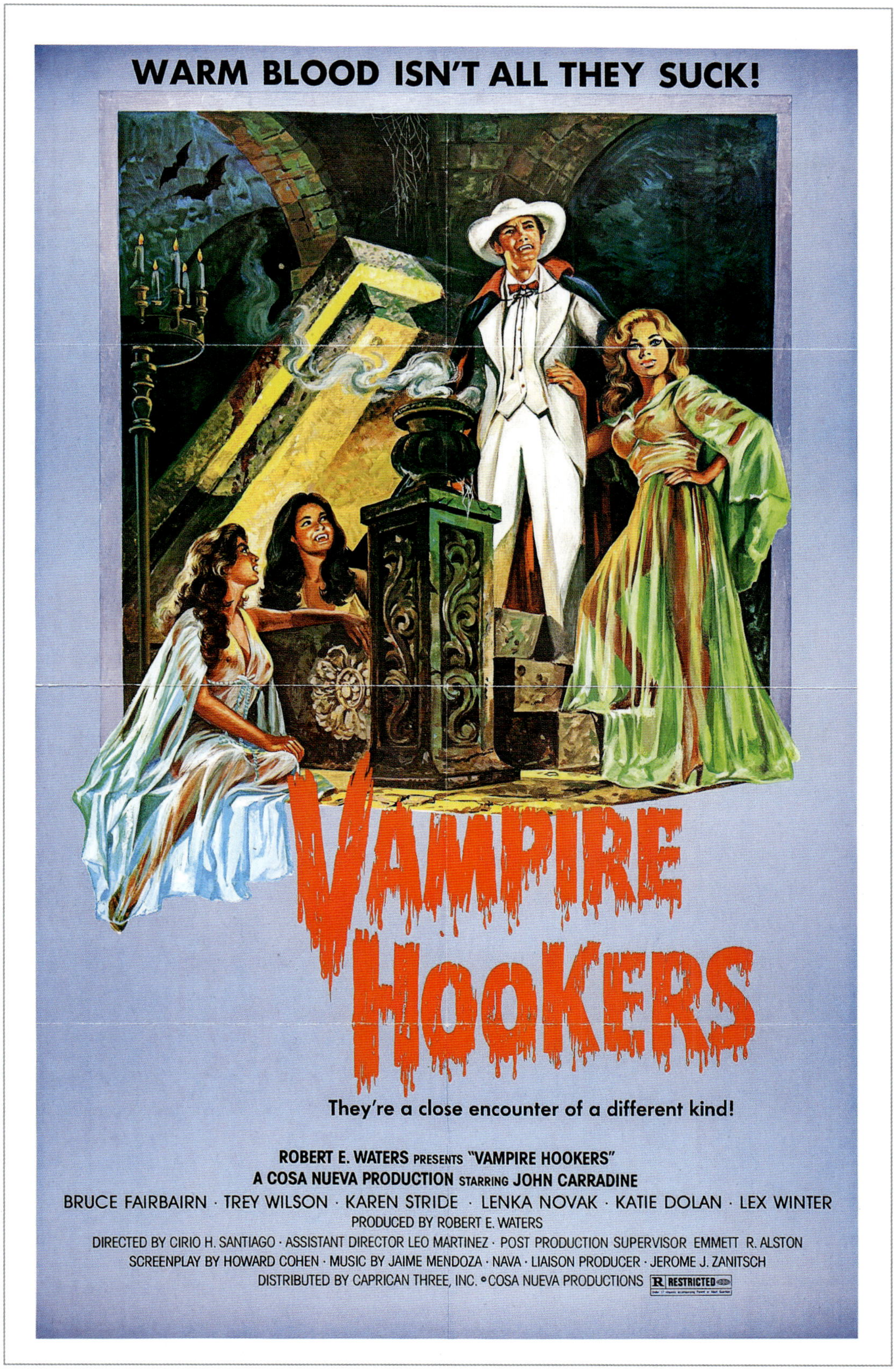

WARM BLOOD ISN'T ALL THEY SUCK!

VAMPIRE HOOKERS

They're a close encounter of a different kind!

ROBERT E. WATERS PRESENTS "VAMPIRE HOOKERS"
A COSA NUEVA PRODUCTION STARRING JOHN CARRADINE
BRUCE FAIRBAIRN · TREY WILSON · KAREN STRIDE · LENKA NOVAK · KATIE DOLAN · LEX WINTER
PRODUCED BY ROBERT E. WATERS
DIRECTED BY CIRIO H. SANTIAGO · ASSISTANT DIRECTOR LEO MARTINEZ · POST PRODUCTION SUPERVISOR EMMETT R. ALSTON
SCREENPLAY BY HOWARD COHEN · MUSIC BY JAIME MENDOZA · NAVA · LIAISON PRODUCER · JEROME J. ZANITSCH
DISTRIBUTED BY CAPRICAN THREE, INC. © COSA NUEVA PRODUCTIONS R RESTRICTED

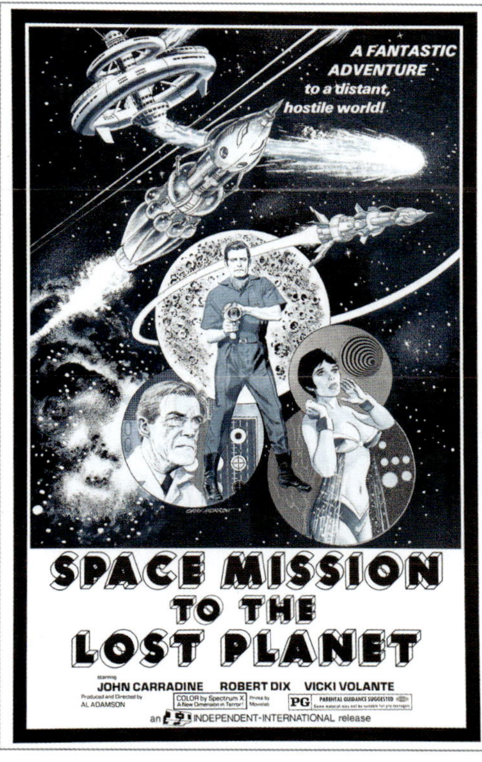

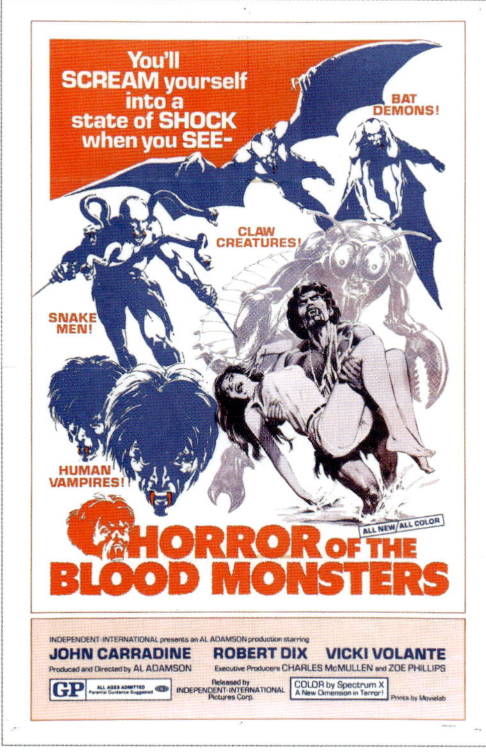

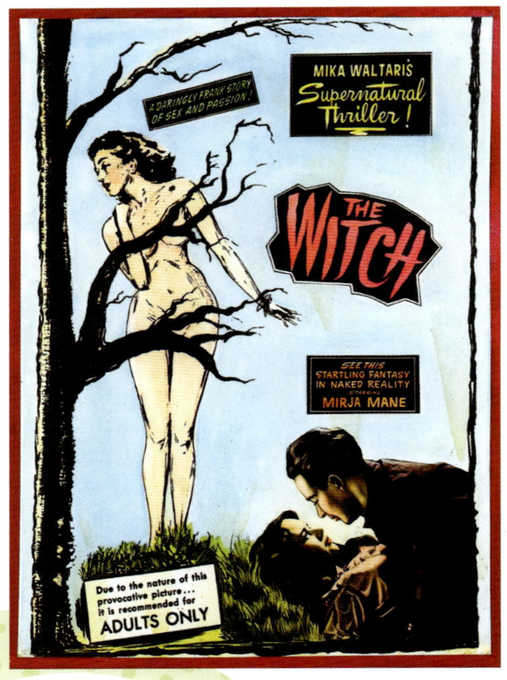

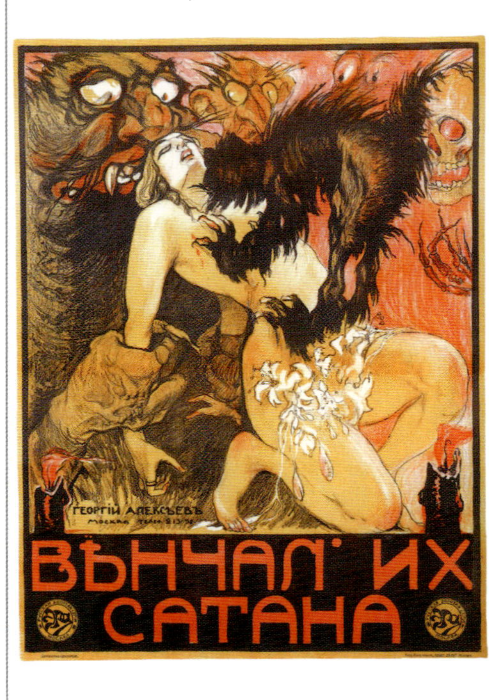

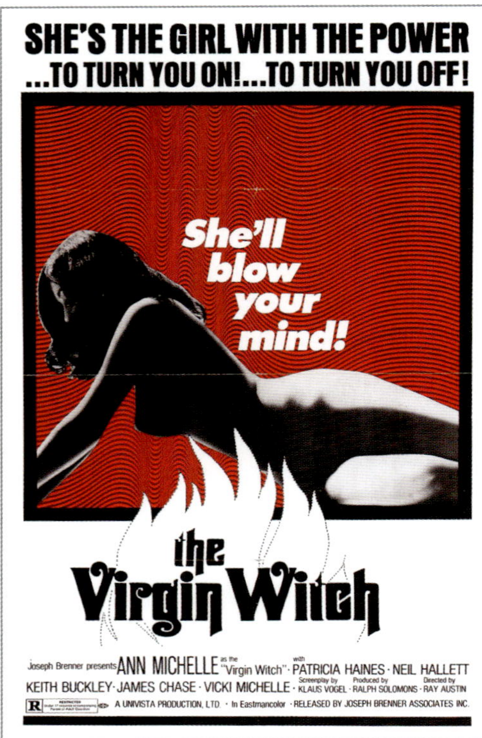

WITCHES

Witches, demon women, and other assorted brides of Satan (all preferably as naked as censors allow) have been on-screen favorites since almost the dawn of cinema. Georgi Alexeev's poster art for the Russian film *Venchal ikh satana* (Being Married by the Satan, 1917) has a touch of art deco style, but remains astoundingly graphic, even today—are those white flower petals, or . . . ? *The Witch Who Came from the Sea* (1976) is actually more of a horror-tinged psychological drama about sexual abuse, and doesn't feature a witch *per se*, but that didn't stop the unsigned one-sheet art including a supernatural-looking figure. That the piece is unsigned is perhaps no surprise, given that it is rather heavily indebted to a painting by the acclaimed fantasy artist Frank Frazetta, which had been published as the cover to the magazine *Vampirella* #11 in 1971.

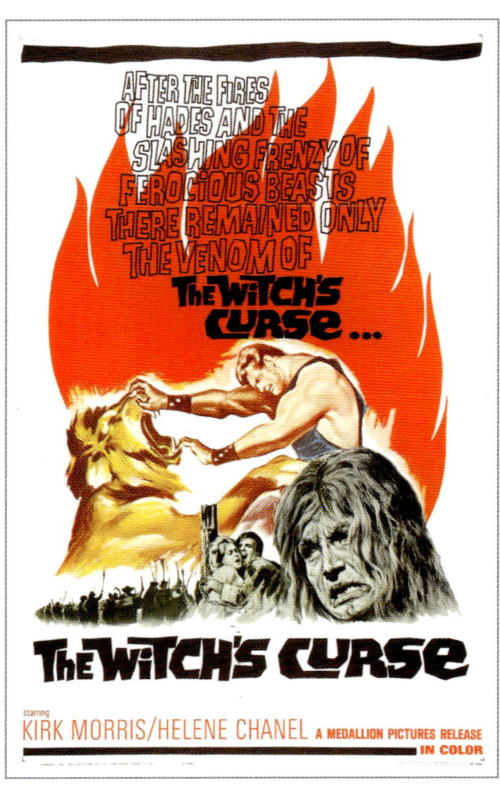

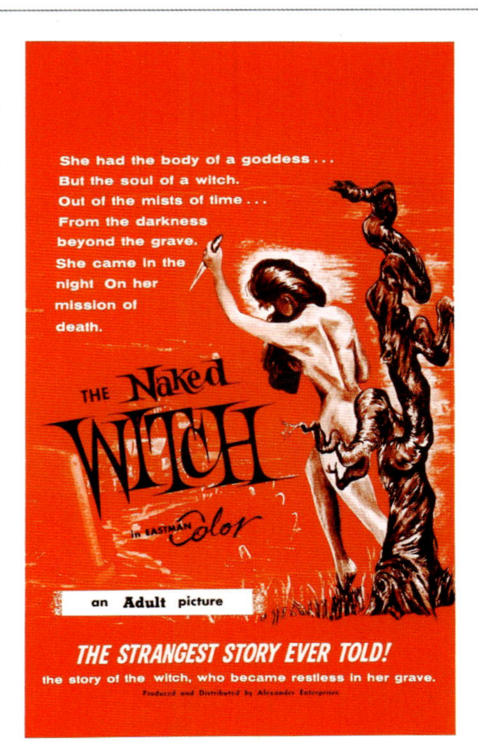

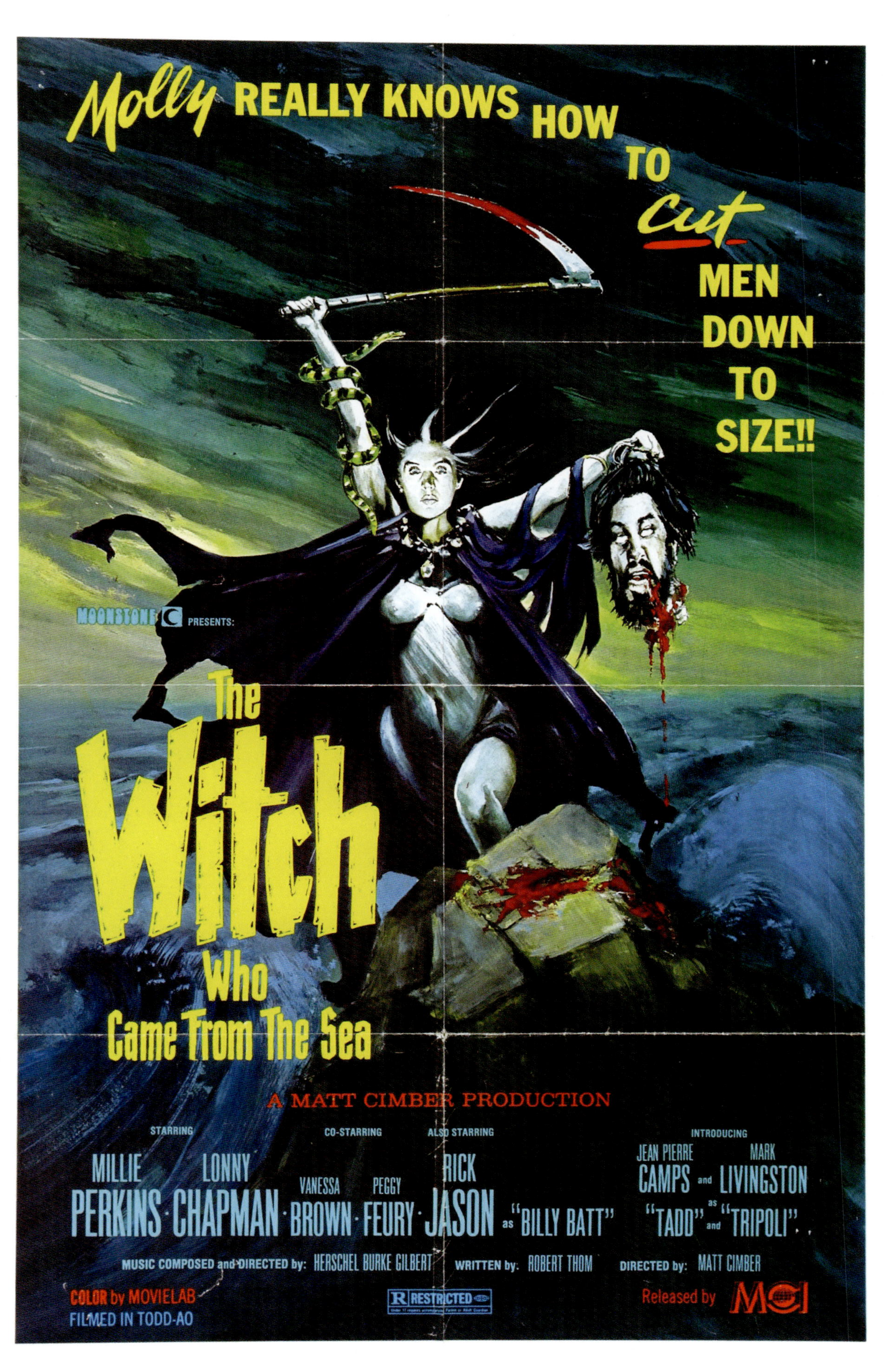
Molly REALLY KNOWS HOW TO Cut MEN DOWN TO SIZE!!
MOONSTONE PRESENTS:
The Witch Who Came From The Sea
A MATT CIMBER PRODUCTION
STARRING MILLIE PERKINS · LONNY CHAPMAN
CO-STARRING VANESSA BROWN · PEGGY FEURY
ALSO STARRING RICK JASON as "BILLY BATT"
INTRODUCING JEAN PIERRE CAMPS and MARK LIVINGSTON as "TADD" and "TRIPOLI".
MUSIC COMPOSED and DIRECTED by: HERSCHEL BURKE GILBERT
WRITTEN by: ROBERT THOM
DIRECTED by: MATT CIMBER
COLOR by MOVIELAB
FILMED IN TODD-AO
R RESTRICTED
Released by MCI

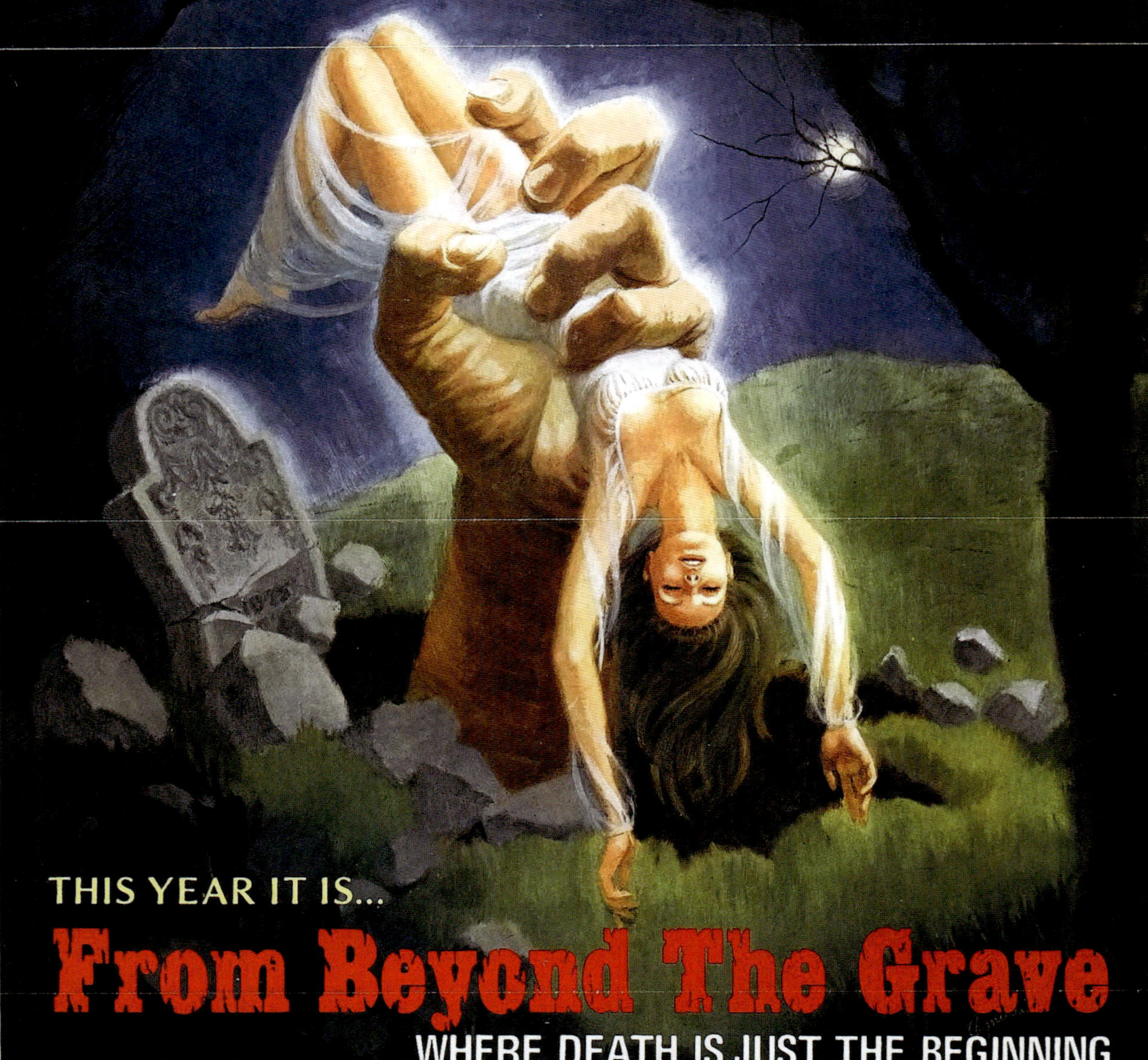
EVERY ONCE IN A WHILE
A HORROR FILM BECOMES A HORROR CLASSIC
In 1931, FRANKENSTEIN
In 1932, DRACULA
In 1968, ROSEMARY'S BABY
In 1974, THE EXORCIST
THIS YEAR IT IS...
From Beyond The Grave
...WHERE DEATH IS JUST THE BEGINNING
The Film You Will Remember All Your Life!
Starring
IAN BANNEN, IAN CARMICHAEL, PETER CUSHING, DIANA DORS, MARGARET LEIGHTON, DONALD PLEASENCE,
NYREE DAWN PORTER, DAVID WARNER Also Starring IAN OGILVY, LESLEY-ANNE DOWN • Associate Producer JOHN DARK
AN AMICUS PRODUCTION • Screenplay by ROBIN CLARKE and RAYMOND CHRISTODOULOU • Produced by MAX J. ROSENBERG and MILTON SUBOTSKY
Directed by KEVIN CONNOR • TECHNICOLOR®
A Howard Mahler Films Inc. Release
PG PARENTAL GUIDANCE SUGGESTED
SOME MATERIAL MAY NOT BE SUITABLE FOR PRE-TEENAGERS

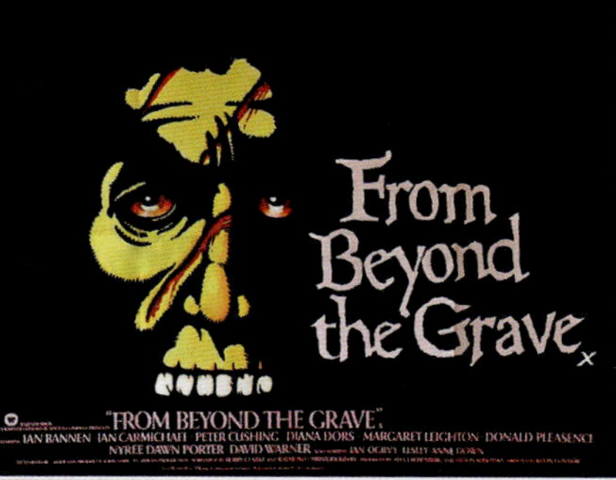

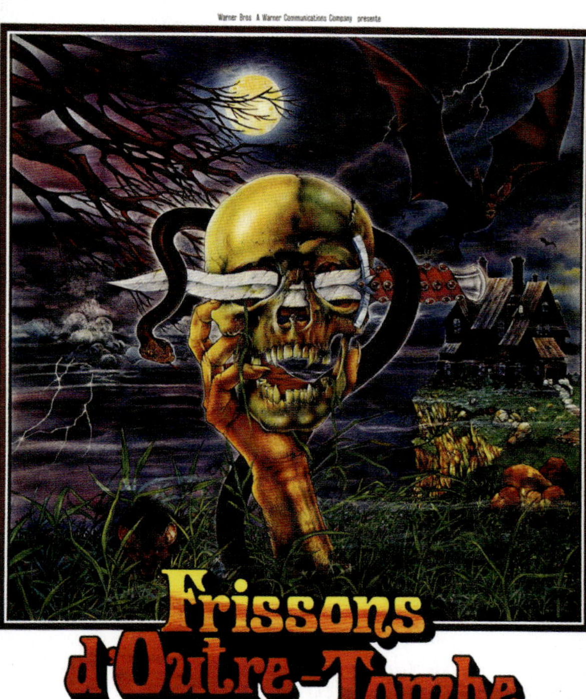

FIVE POSTERS, ONE FILM

Even in a world where hyperbole is the default style, it's still a ballsy move to definitively declare that your film is a horror classic on the level of *Dracula*, *Frankenstein*, *Rosemary's Baby*, and *The Exorcist*. While *From Beyond the Grave* (1974) has its fans, even the most fervent would be unlikely to put it in such rarified company. Still, if that poster helped grab a ticket sale or two, then it did its job. With an episodic plot based on several short stories by R. Chetwynd-Hayes, the film was the last of the "portmanteau" anthology titles released by British company Amicus Productions, and featured Peter Cushing as the proprietor of a spooky antiques shop whose customers tend to come to a sticky end. Not that you'd necessarily know that from its various effective but generic posters, including a US release as *The Creatures* which suggests a straightforward vampire flick. Only the Japanese poster highlights (some of) the impressive cast, which also included genre favorites Donald Pleasence and David Warner.

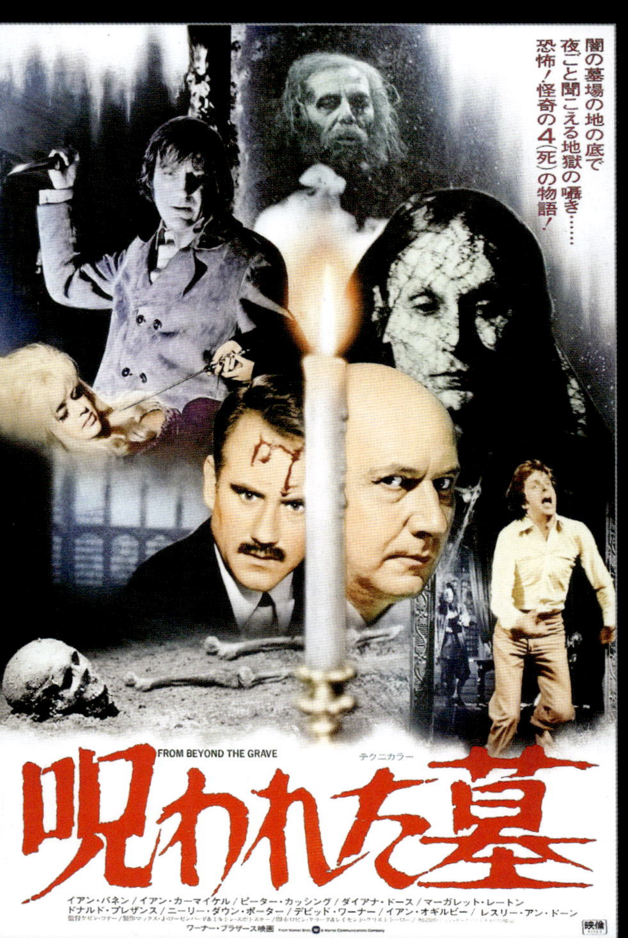

THE CREATURES

THEY CAME FROM BEYOND THE GRAVE!

THEY WEREN'T BORN... THEY WERE KICKED OUT OF HELL!!!

Starring IAN BANNEN, IAN CARMICHAEL, PETER CUSHING, DIANA DORS, MARGARET LEIGHTON, DONALD PLEASENCE, NYREE DAWN PORTER, DAVID WARNER Also Starring IAN OGILVY, LESLEY-ANNE DOWN Associate Producer JOHN DARK AN AMICUS PRODUCTION Screenplay by ROBIN CLARKE and RAYMOND CHRISTODOULOU Produced by MAX J. ROSENBERG and MILTON SUBOTSKY Directed by KEVIN CONNOR TECHNICOLOR

A Howard Mahler Films Inc. Release

PG PARENTAL GUIDANCE SUGGESTED
SOME MATERIAL MAY NOT BE SUITABLE FOR PRE-TEENAGERS

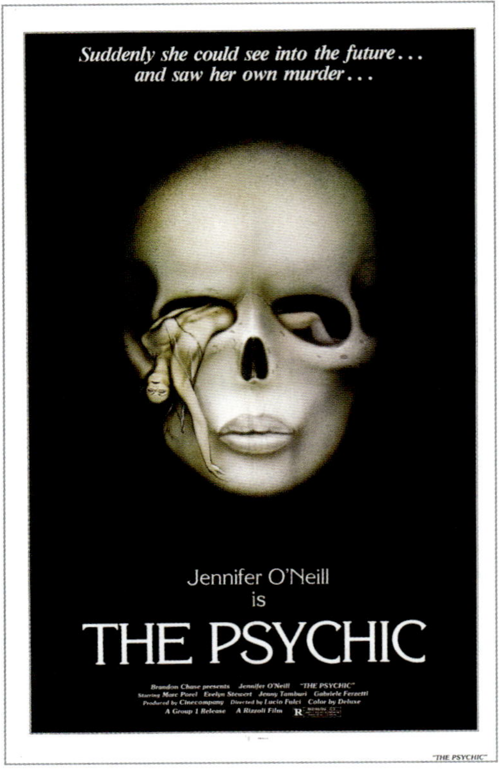

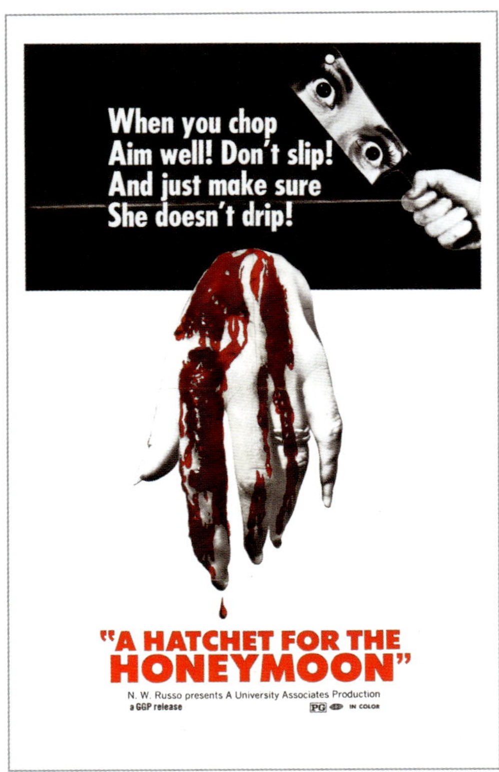

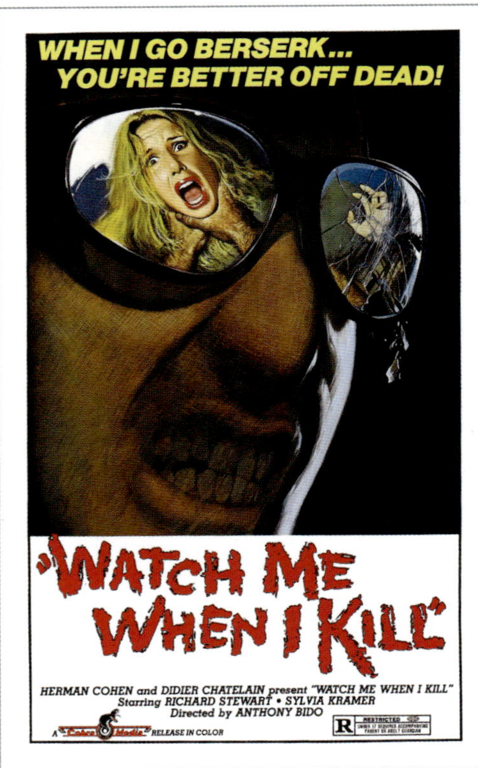

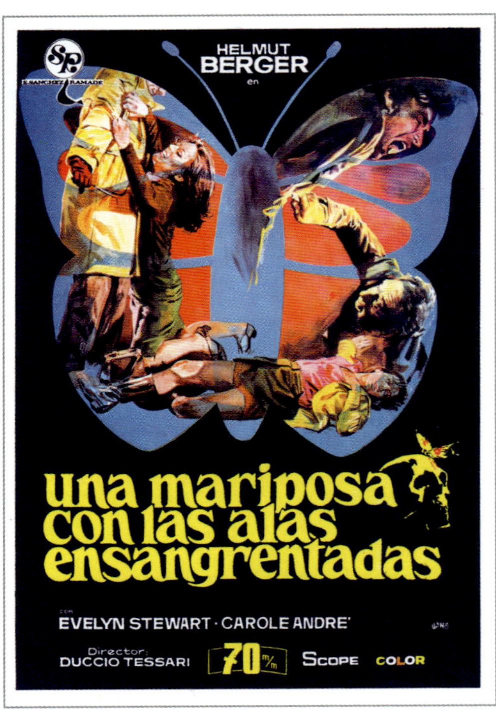

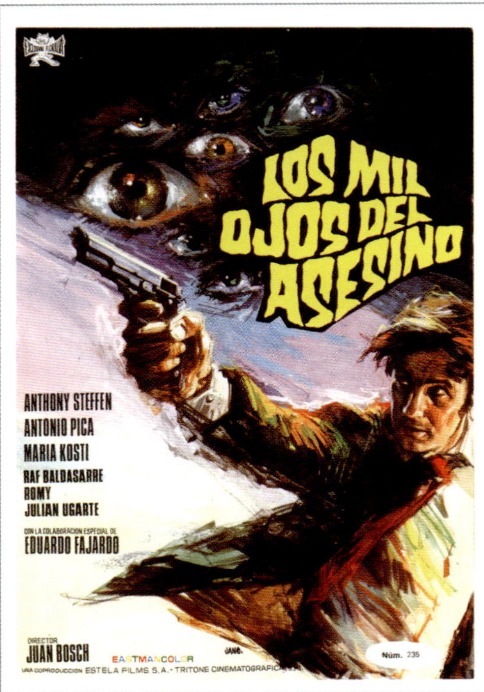

GIALLO

In 1929, the Italian publisher Mondadori began publishing cheap mystery pulp paperbacks with bright yellow covers. They were so popular that the local word for the color, *giallo*, soon became synonymous with "thriller." Fast-forward to the late '60s, and the term was being used outside Italy, but specifically in relation to a certain type of Italian-made murder mystery film, which usually featured multiple bloody killings, sometimes mixed with supernatural elements. While the prolific Umberto Lenzi's *Eyeball* (1975) can't claim to hit the artistic heights of fellow director Dario Argento's classic *gialli*, it does have a suitably eye-popping poster. The film's original title, *Gatti rossi in un labirinto di vetro*, translates as the somewhat more lyrical "Red Cats in a Labyrinth of Glass." No way the US distributor was going with that though.

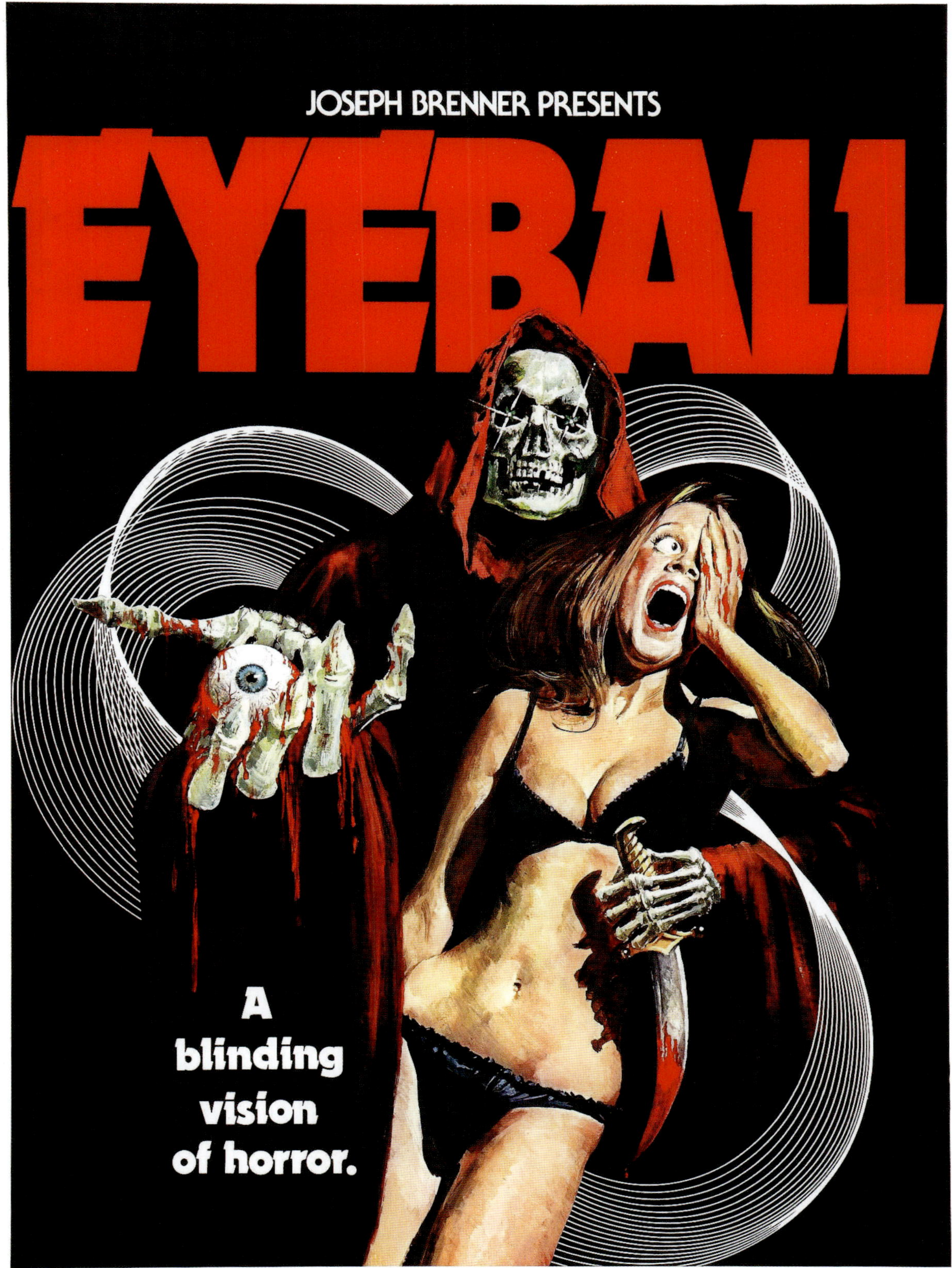
A STABBING NIGHTMARE BECOMES A LIVING TERROR!
JOSEPH BRENNER PRESENTS
EYEBALL
A blinding vision of horror.
JOSEPH BRENNER PRESENTS
"EYEBALL"
Starring
JOHN RICHARDSON · MARTINE BROCHARD · INES PELLEGRIN · SILVIA SOLAR · GEORGE RIGAUD
Directed by UMBERTO LENZI · Executive Producer JOSEPH BRENNER
A JOSEPH BRENNER ASSOCIATES, INC. RELEASE · IN COLOR
R RESTRICTED
UNDER 17 REQUIRES ACCOMPANYING PARENT OR ADULT GUARDIAN
Copyright © Magnusonic Devices, Inc.

FILIPINO HORROR

Horror movies shot in the Philippines often have an irresistible strangeness. As critic Scott Ashlin said of one obscure example, *The Deathhead Virgin* (1974), "A masked, harpoon-wielding, homicidal, aquatic, naked zombie girl is a rare and impressive thing indeed." While Christopher Lee did appear in the German film *The Blood Demon* (1967), thanks to a careless designer adapting an older double bill poster, he also apparently stars in the Filipino favorite *Mad Doctor of Blood Island* (1968), according to its re-release one-sheet (see the repeated photo of a stern-looking Lee, below). Rest assured, he's not in the film.

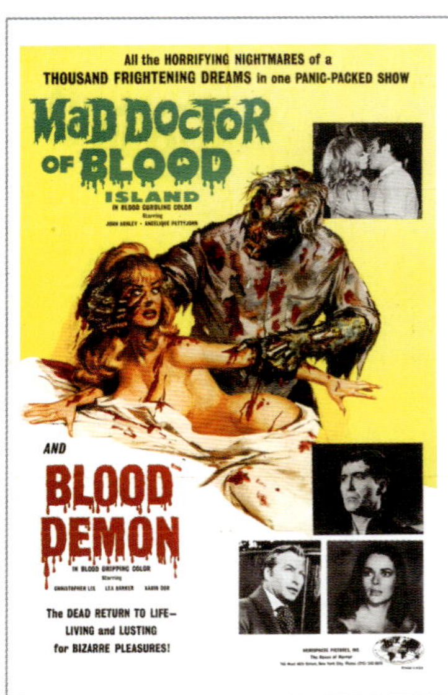

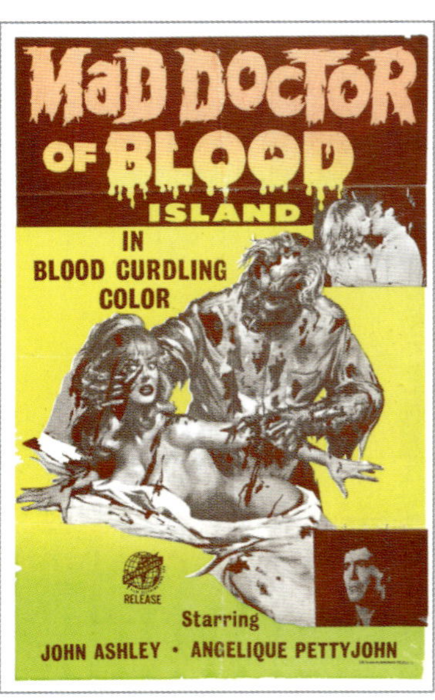

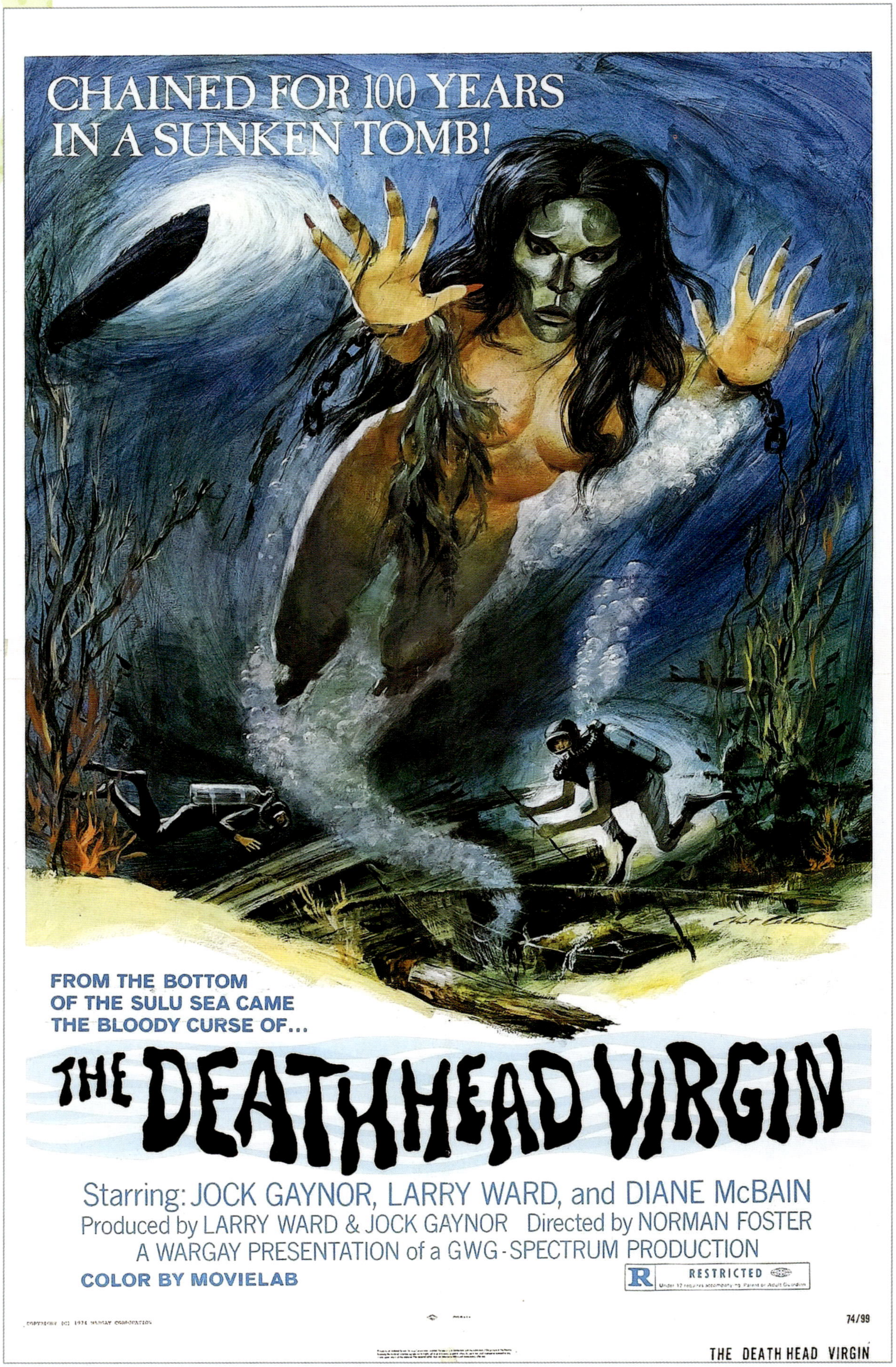

CHAINED FOR 100 YEARS
IN A SUNKEN TOMB!

FROM THE BOTTOM
OF THE SULU SEA CAME
THE BLOODY CURSE OF...

THE DEATHHEAD VIRGIN

Starring: JOCK GAYNOR, LARRY WARD, and DIANE McBAIN
Produced by LARRY WARD & JOCK GAYNOR Directed by NORMAN FOSTER
A WARGAY PRESENTATION of a GWG-SPECTRUM PRODUCTION
COLOR BY MOVIELAB

R RESTRICTED

74/99

THE DEATH HEAD VIRGIN

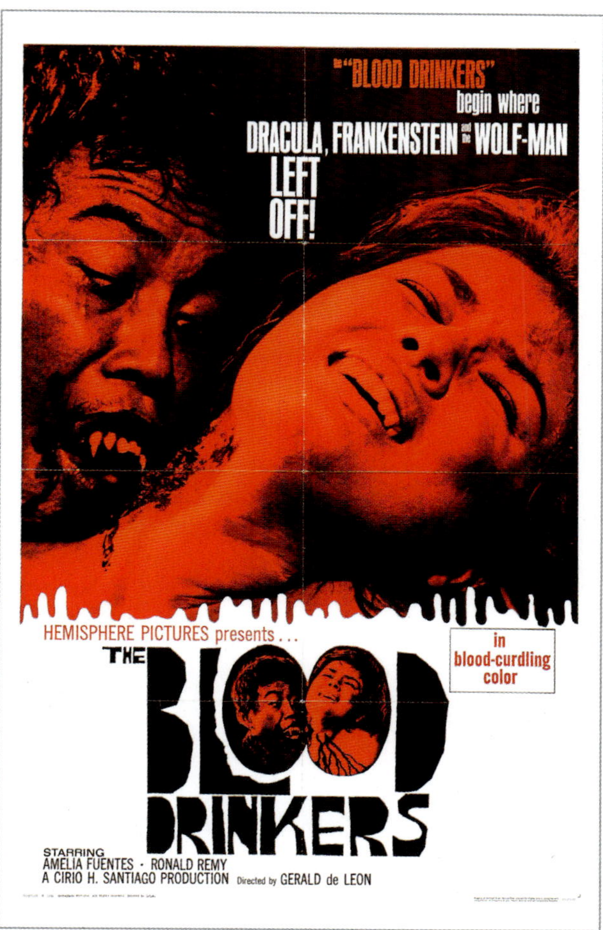

The "BLOOD DRINKERS" begin where
DRACULA, FRANKENSTEIN and the WOLF-MAN
LEFT
OFF!
HEMISPHERE PICTURES presents . . .
THE BLOOD DRINKERS
in blood-curdling color
STARRING
AMELIA FUENTES · RONALD REMY
A CIRIO H. SANTIAGO PRODUCTION Directed by GERALD de LEON

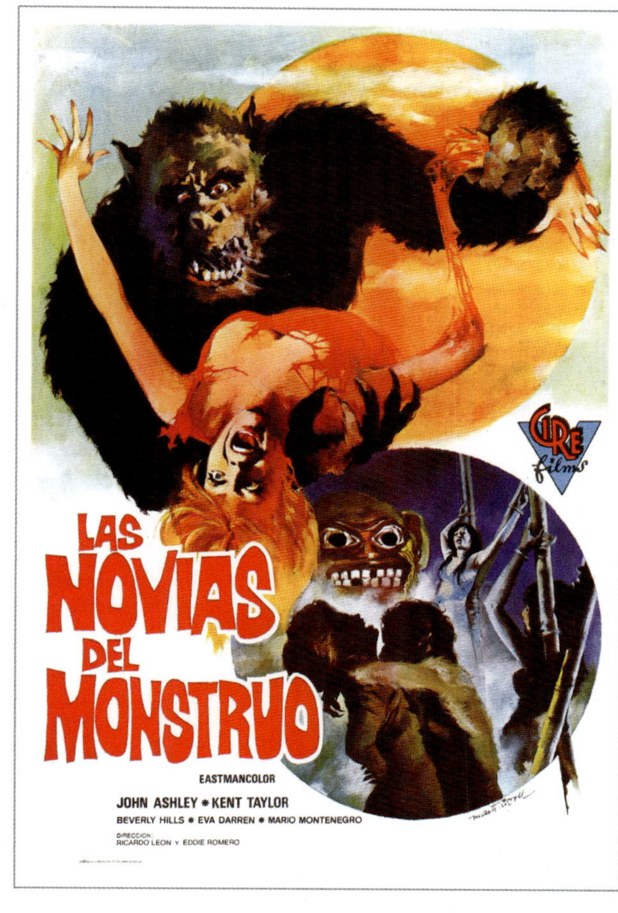

LAS NOVIAS DEL MONSTRUO
CIRE films
EASTMANCOLOR
JOHN ASHLEY ✱ KENT TAYLOR
BEVERLY HILLS ✱ EVA DARREN ✱ MARIO MONTENEGRO
DIRECCION
RICARDO LEON y EDDIE ROMERO

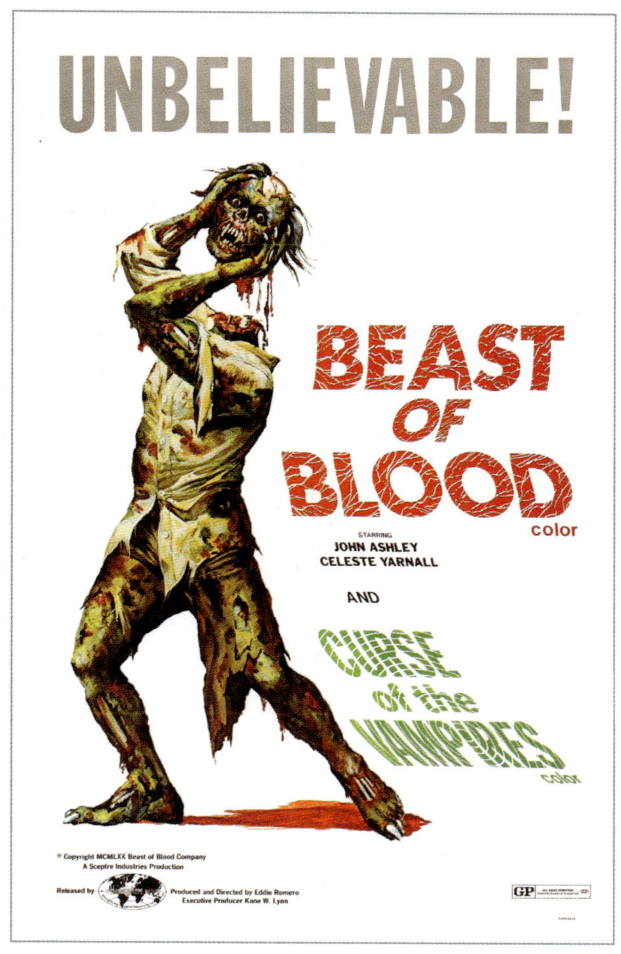

UNBELIEVABLE!
BEAST OF BLOOD
color
STARRING
JOHN ASHLEY
CELESTE YARNALL
AND
CURSE of the VAMPIRES
color
© Copyright MCMLXX Beast of Blood Company
A Sceptre Industries Production
Released by
Produced and Directed by Eddie Romero
Executive Producer Kane W. Lynn
GP

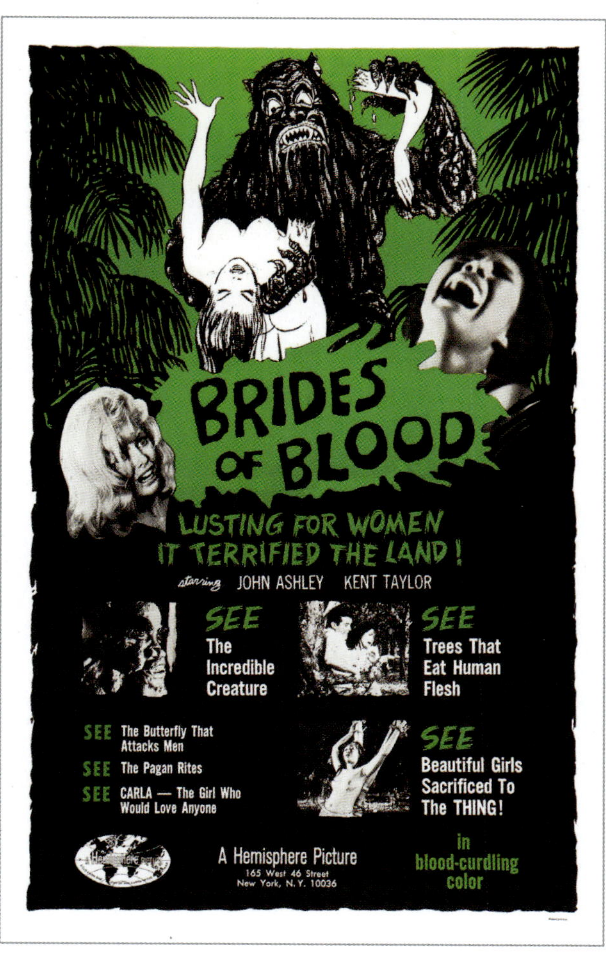

BRIDES OF BLOOD
LUSTING FOR WOMEN
IT TERRIFIED THE LAND!
starring JOHN ASHLEY KENT TAYLOR
SEE The Incredible Creature
SEE Trees That Eat Human Flesh
SEE The Butterfly That Attacks Men
SEE The Pagan Rites
SEE CARLA — The Girl Who Would Love Anyone
SEE Beautiful Girls Sacrificed To The THING!
A Hemisphere Picture
165 West 46 Street
New York, N.Y. 10036
in blood-curdling color

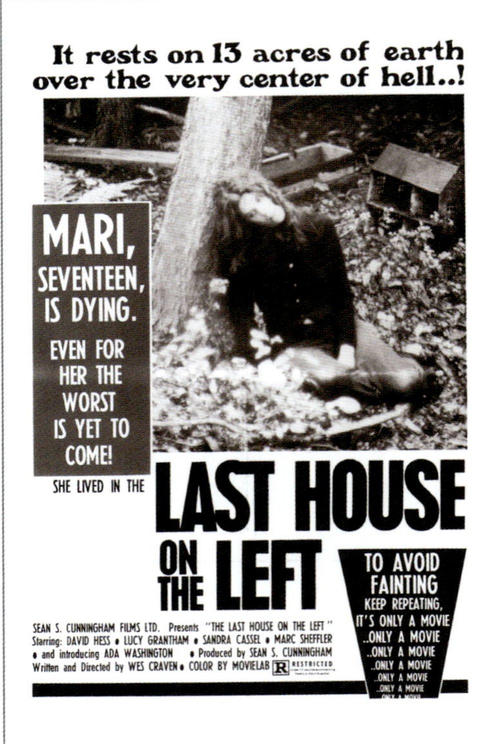

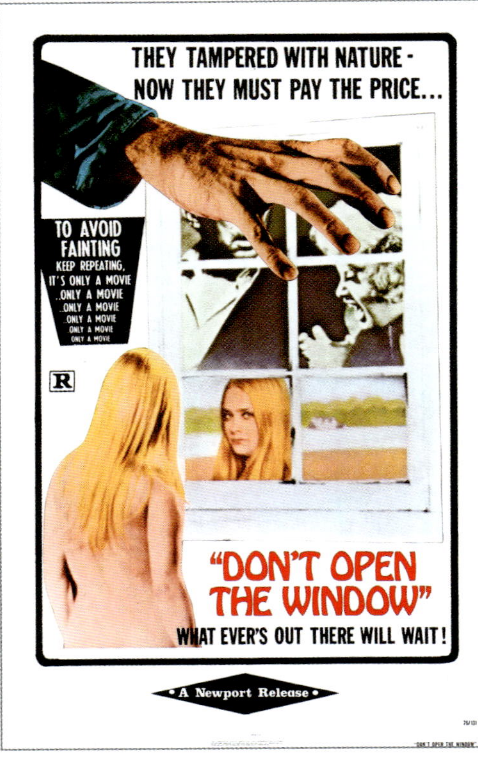

AFTER THE LAST HOUSE

Wes Craven's *The Last House on the Left* (1972) sticks in the mind for many reasons, not least the explicit violence that ensured it was banned in the UK for decades. It also has one of the catchiest, and most effective taglines in horror film history: "To avoid fainting keep repeating, it's only a movie . . . only a movie." It's no surprise then to see subsequent, unrelated productions referencing the catchphrase, the title, and even the poster design of the original film. *The New House on the Left* (1975) is particularly cheeky: as its original Italian title, *L'ultimo treno della notte*, suggests, it's pretty much house-free, and mostly takes place on a train. All's fair in love and movie marketing though; after all, very similar "It's only a movie" taglines were previously used for both William Castle's *Strait-Jacket* and Herschell Gordon Lewis's *Color Me Blood Red* back in the mid-'60s.

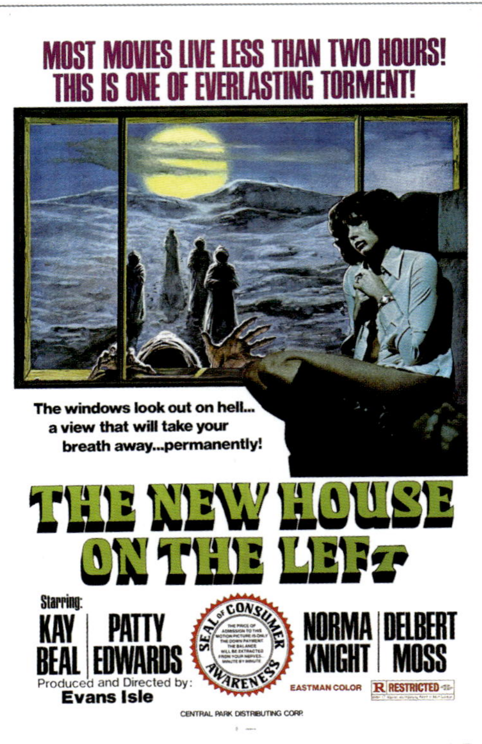

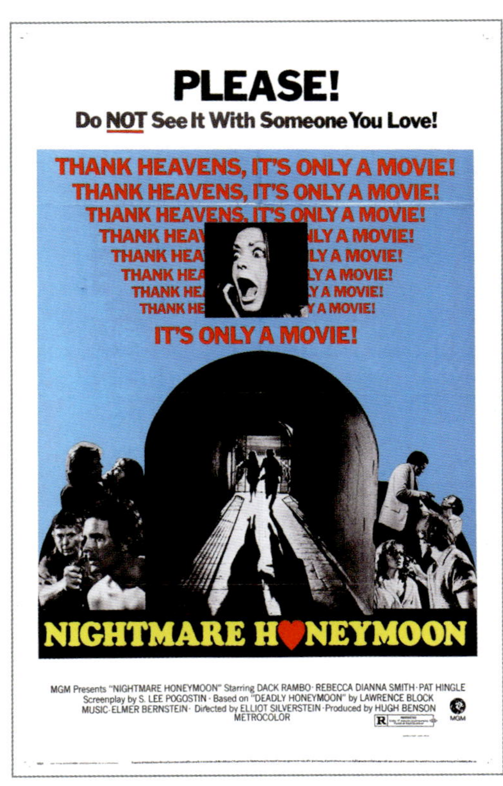

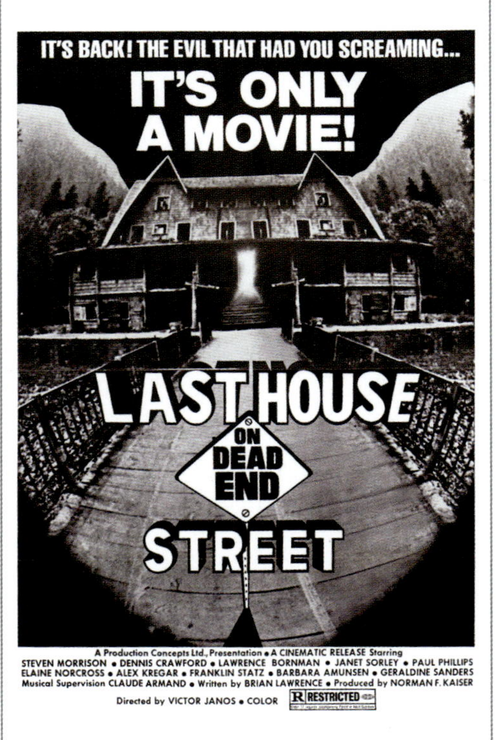

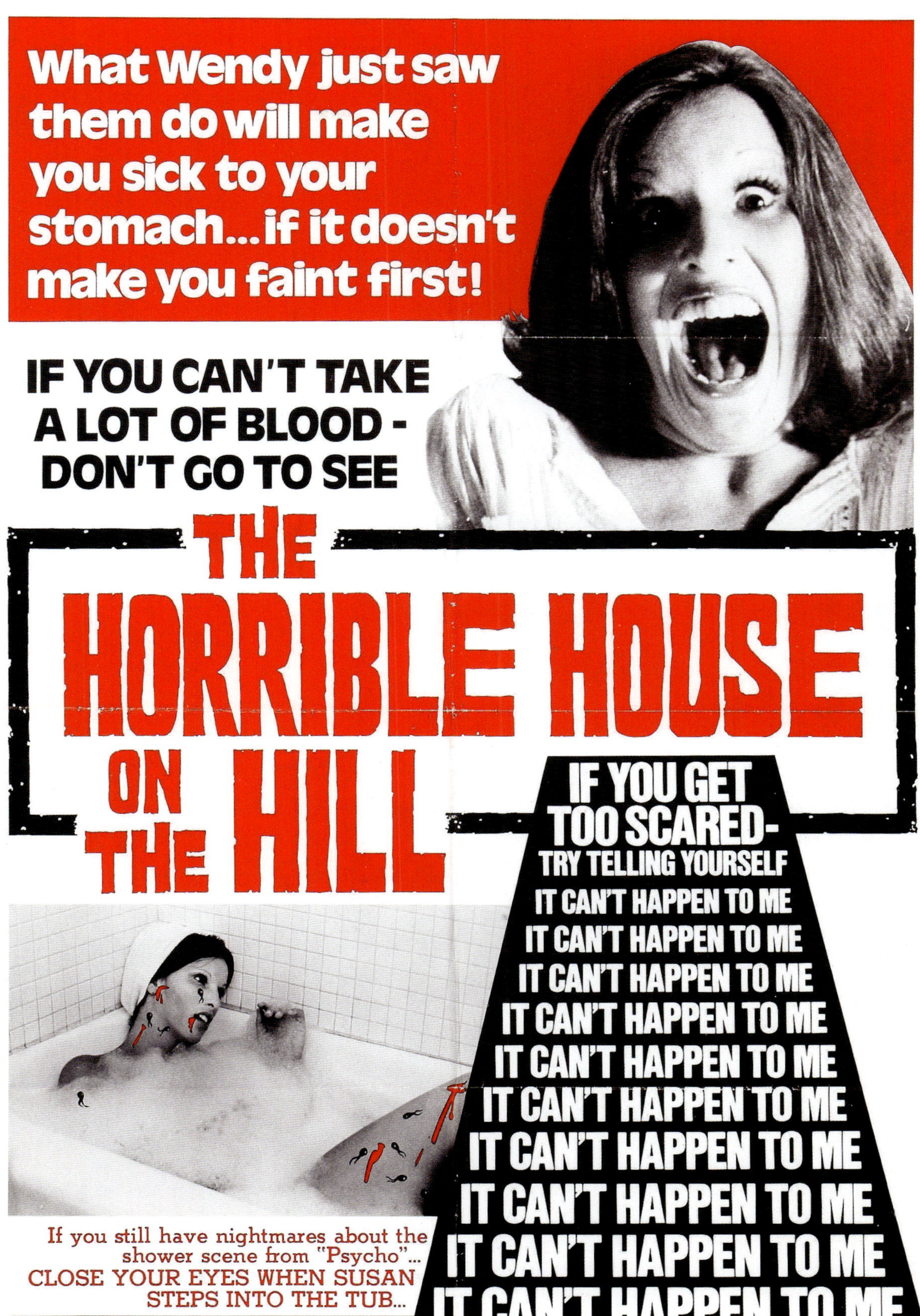
What Wendy just saw them do will make you sick to your stomach... if it doesn't make you faint first!
IF YOU CAN'T TAKE A LOT OF BLOOD - DON'T GO TO SEE
THE HORRIBLE HOUSE ON THE HILL
IF YOU GET TOO SCARED-
TRY TELLING YOURSELF
IT CAN'T HAPPEN TO ME
IT CAN'T HAPPEN TO ME
IT CAN'T HAPPEN TO ME
IT CAN'T HAPPEN TO ME
IT CAN'T HAPPEN TO ME
IT CAN'T HAPPEN TO ME
IT CAN'T HAPPEN TO ME
IT CAN'T HAPPEN TO ME
IT CAN'T HAPPEN TO ME
If you still have nightmares about the shower scene from "Psycho"...
CLOSE YOUR EYES WHEN SUSAN STEPS INTO THE TUB...
JERRY GROSS Presents "THE HORRIBLE HOUSE ON THE HILL" Starring GENE EVANS • SHELLEY MORRISON • SORREL BOOKE • Screenplay by JOHN DURREN
Produced by DYLAN JONES and MICHAEL BLOWITZ • Executive Producer JORDAN WANK • Directed by SEAN MacGREGOR • A BARRISTER PRODUCTION
Production Executive SANDRA BLOWITZ • Production Supervisor BERYL GELFOND
R RESTRICTED
Distributed by CINEMATION INDUSTRIES
COLOR

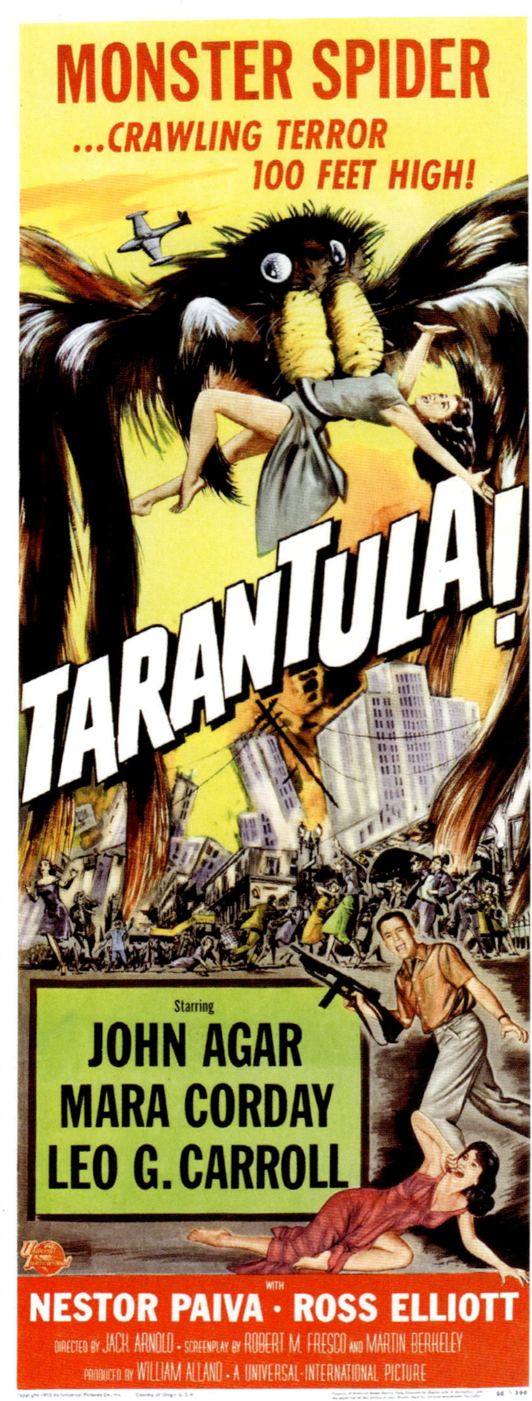

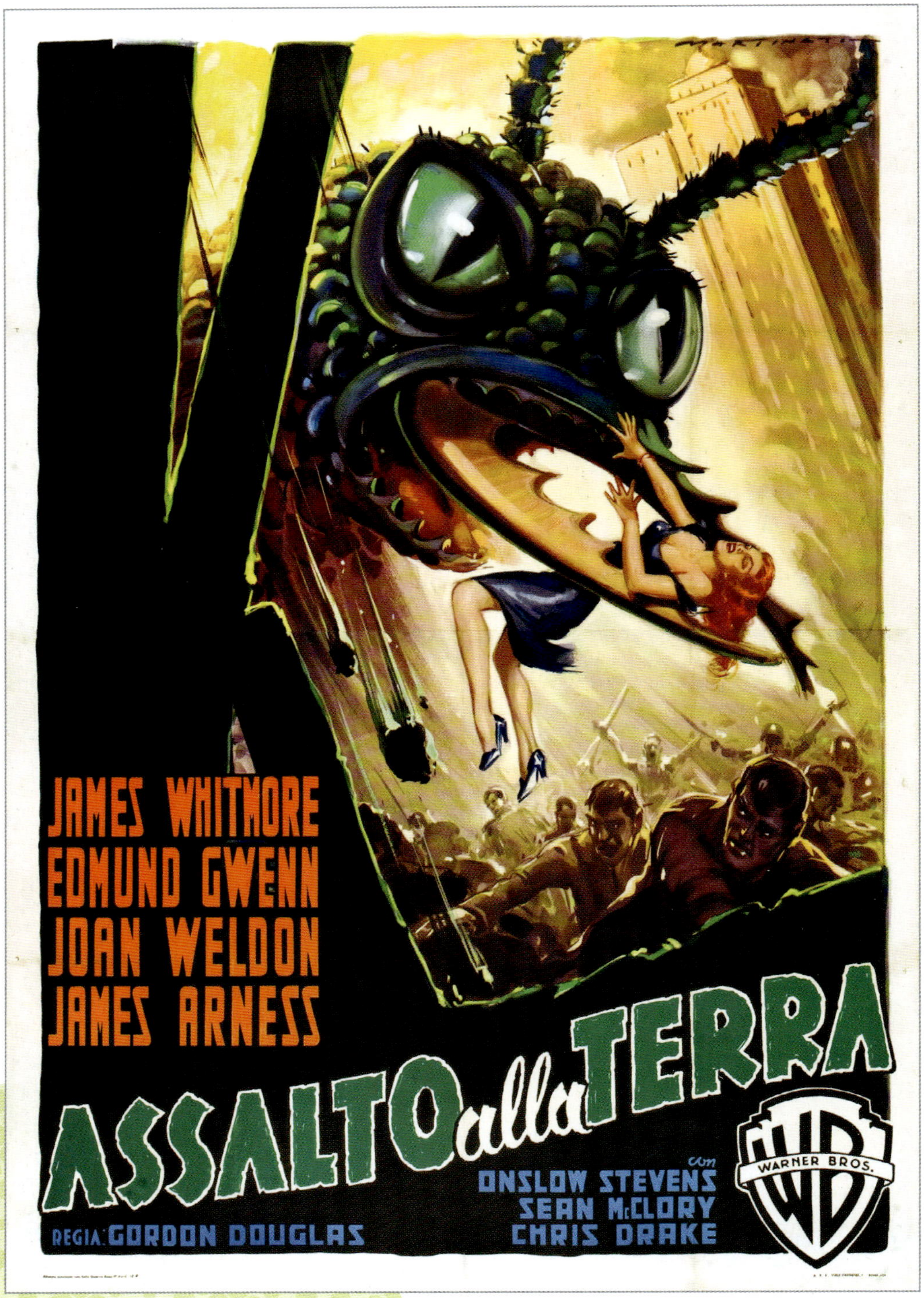

CREEPY CRAWLIES

If a spider is scary, then a *giant* spider (or bee, ant, praying mantis, et cetera) will be extra scary. That's how the reasoning often went anyway, though the monsters on the posters—such as Luigi Martinati's stunning *quattro-fogli* for the Italian release of *Them!* (*Assalto alla terra*, 1954)—were usually more effective than the ones on screen. *The Bees* (1978) didn't, as its somewhat uncouth one-sheet suggests, feature oversized insects, but it did have a plot in which John Saxon's hero suggests defeating the swarms by using a chemical to turn them gay. The one-sheet for *Kingdom of the Spiders* (1977) focuses on a sight more terrifying than killer arachnids: William Shatner over-acting.

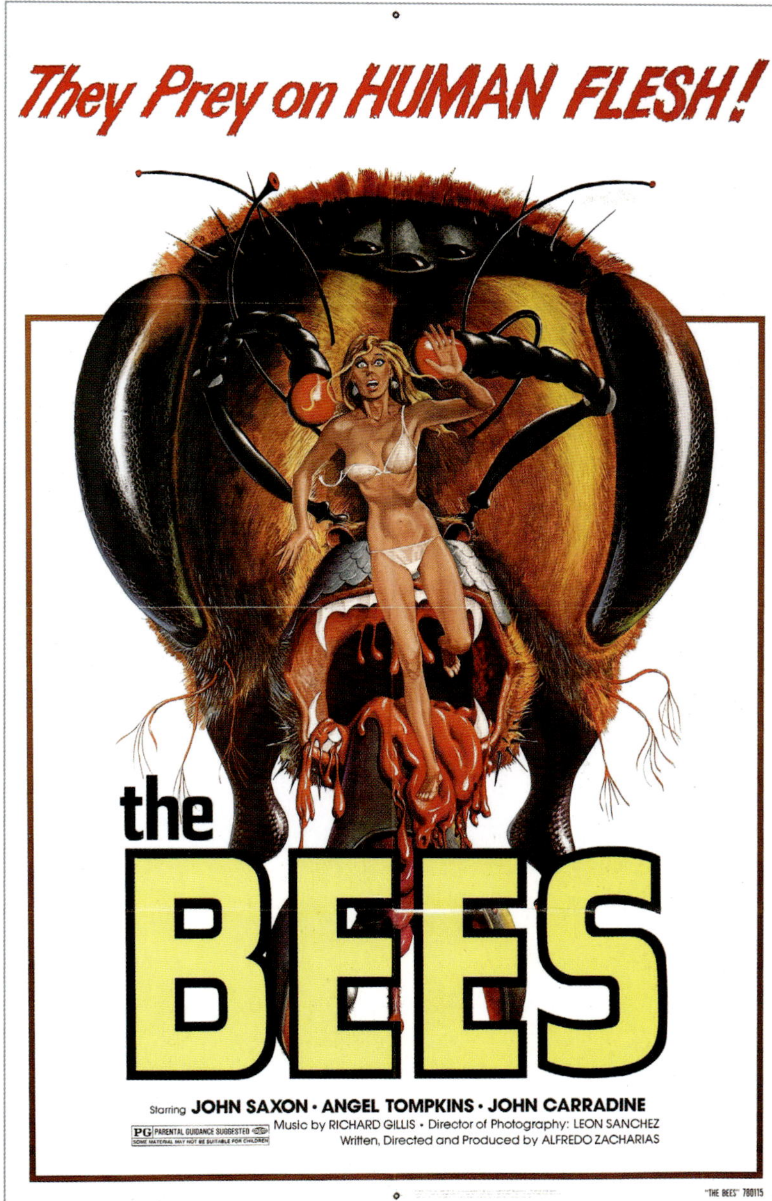
They Prey on HUMAN FLESH!
the BEES
Starring JOHN SAXON · ANGEL TOMPKINS · JOHN CARRADINE
Music by RICHARD GILLIS · Director of Photography: LEON SANCHEZ
Written, Directed and Produced by ALFREDO ZACHARIAS
PG PARENTAL GUIDANCE SUGGESTED

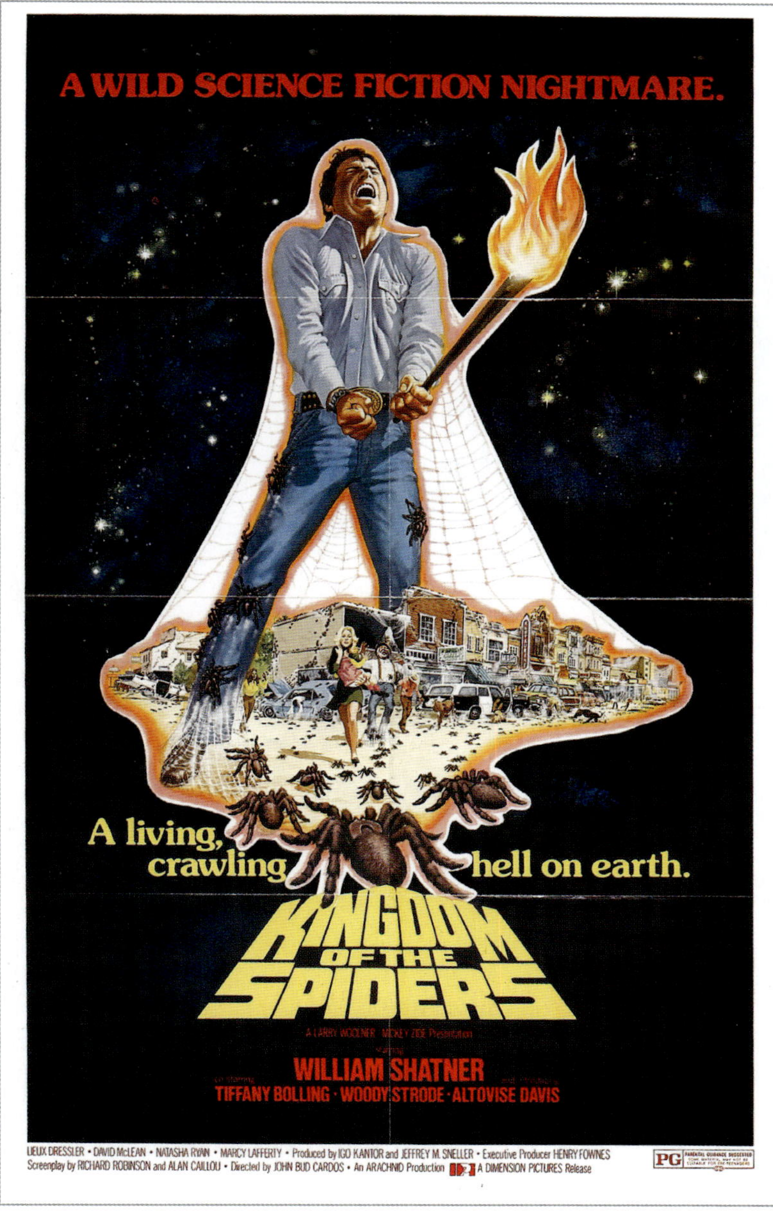
A WILD SCIENCE FICTION NIGHTMARE.
A living, crawling hell on earth.
KINGDOM OF THE SPIDERS
WILLIAM SHATNER
TIFFANY BOLLING · WOODY STRODE · ALTOVISE DAVIS

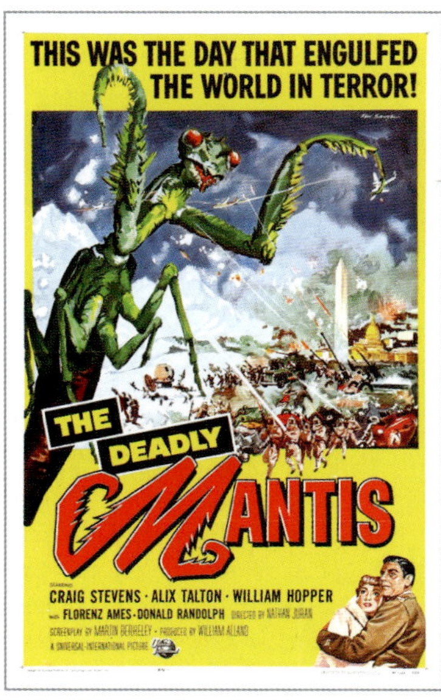
THIS WAS THE DAY THAT ENGULFED THE WORLD IN TERROR!
THE DEADLY MANTIS
CRAIG STEVENS · ALIX TALTON · WILLIAM HOPPER
FLORENZ AMES · DONALD RANDOLPH

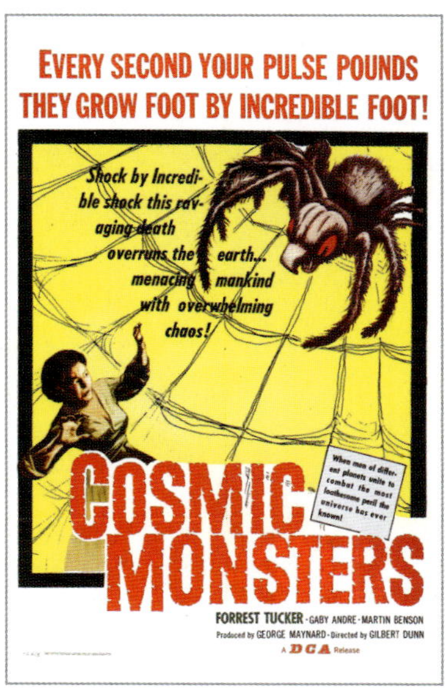
EVERY SECOND YOUR PULSE POUNDS
THEY GROW FOOT BY INCREDIBLE FOOT!
Shock by Incredible shock this ravaging death overruns the earth... menacing mankind with overwhelming chaos!
COSMIC MONSTERS
FORREST TUCKER
Produced by GEORGE MAYNARD · Directed by GILBERT DUNN
A DCA Release

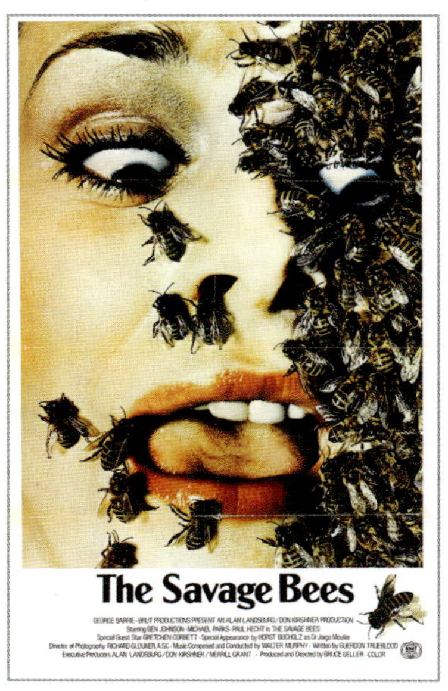
The Savage Bees

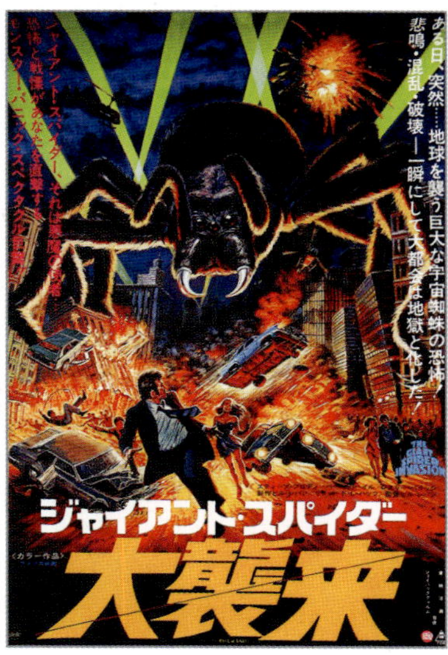
ジャイアント・スパイダー
大襲来

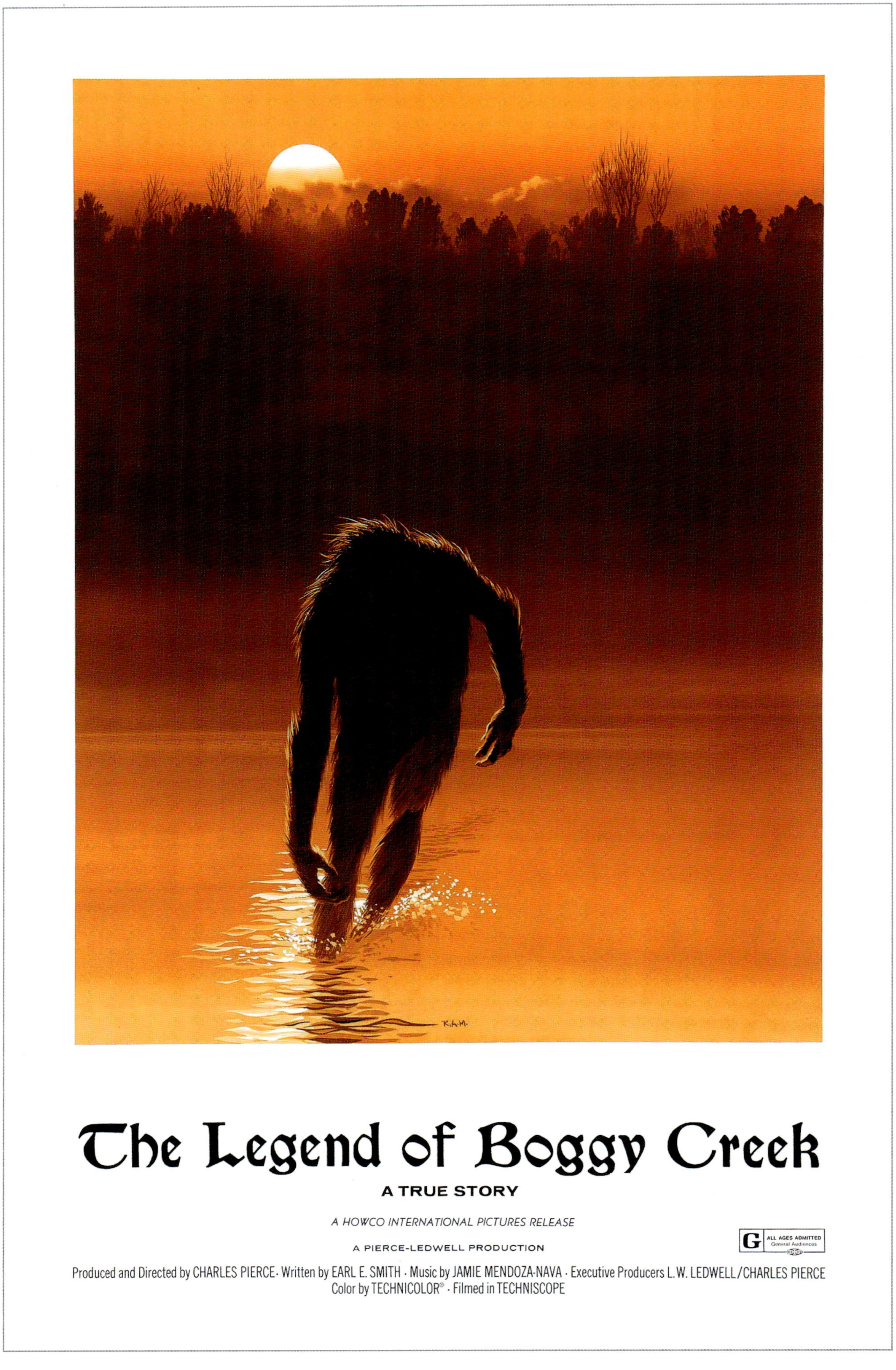

The Legend of Boggy Creek

A TRUE STORY

A HOWCO INTERNATIONAL PICTURES RELEASE

A PIERCE-LEDWELL PRODUCTION

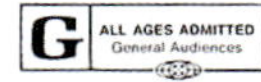

Produced and Directed by CHARLES PIERCE · Written by EARL E. SMITH · Music by JAMIE MENDOZA-NAVA · Executive Producers L. W. LEDWELL/CHARLES PIERCE
Color by TECHNICOLOR® · Filmed in TECHNISCOPE

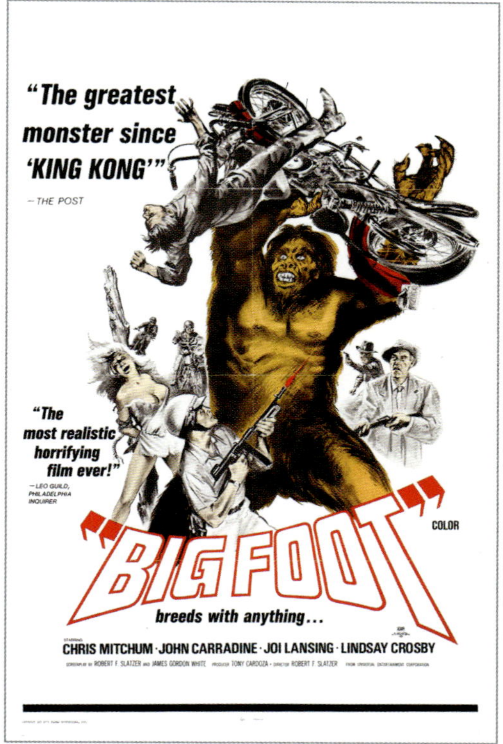

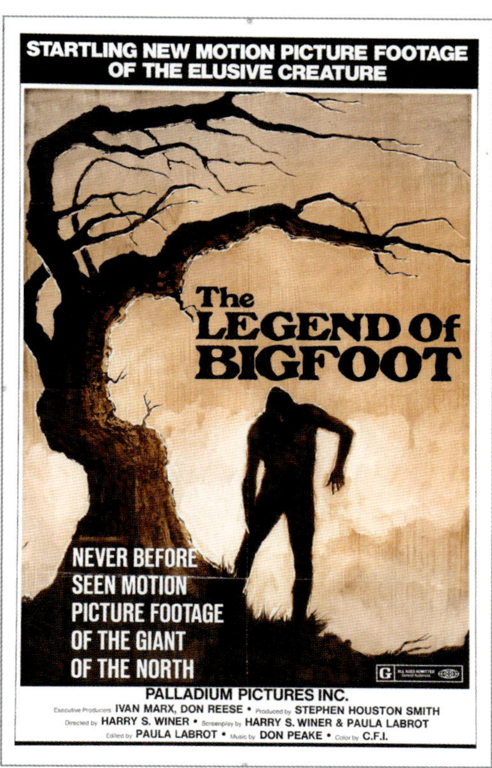

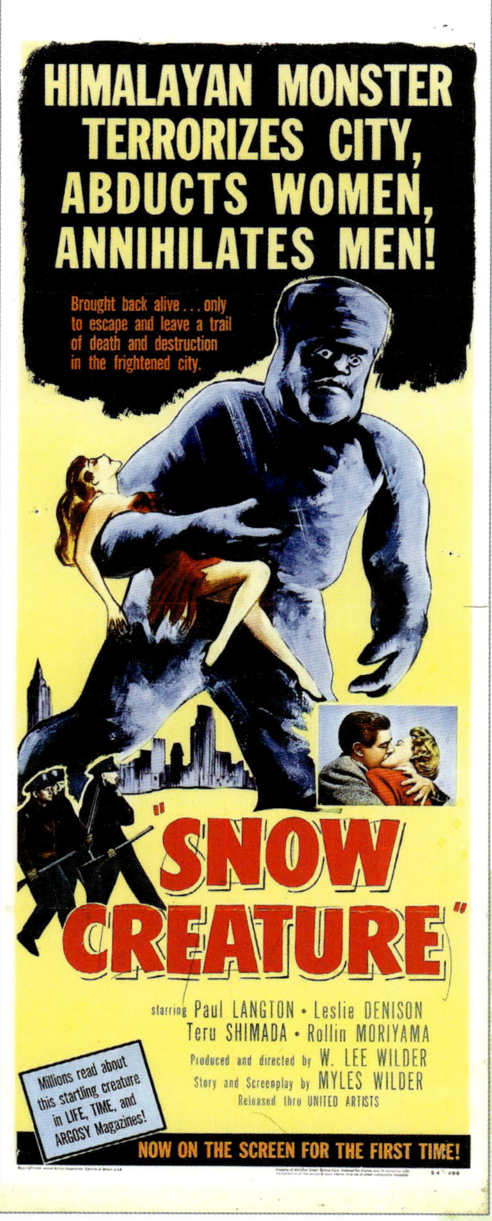

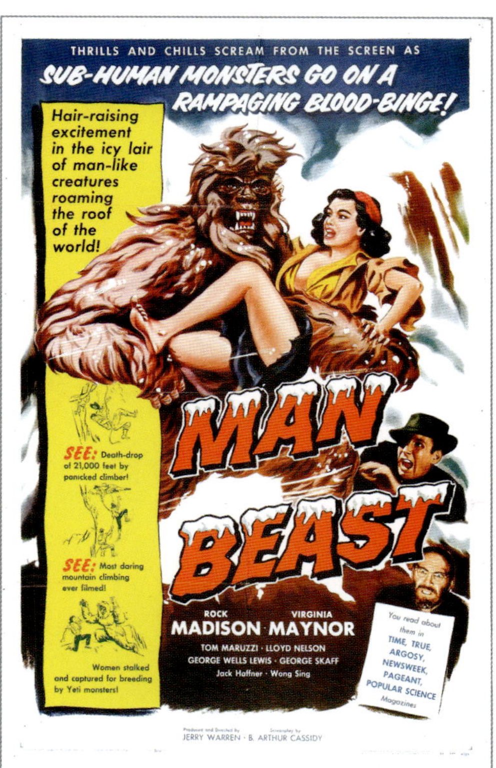

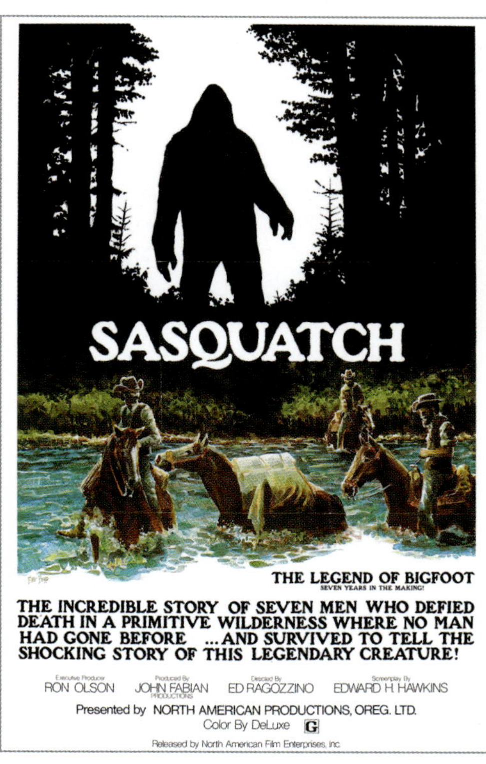

YETIS AND BIGFEET

While shambling ape-men of various hues had long been an exploitation staple, there was a chance to imbue them with a touch of "ripped-from-the-headlines" verisimilitude when reports of the Yeti began to filter out of the Himalayas in the early '50s. Similarly, the circulation of the instantly iconic home-movie footage of an alleged Sasquatch, shot by Roger Patterson in 1967, led to a rash of Bigfoot movies. One of the most successful, reportedly turning Charles B. Pierce's $160,000 budget into $4.8 million in North American theatrical rentals, was *The Legend of Boggy Creek* (1972), a docudrama with a terrific one-sheet painted by Ralph McQuarrie. If you've heard that name before, it's probably because of a little pre-production art job McQuarrie did a few years later: *Star Wars*.

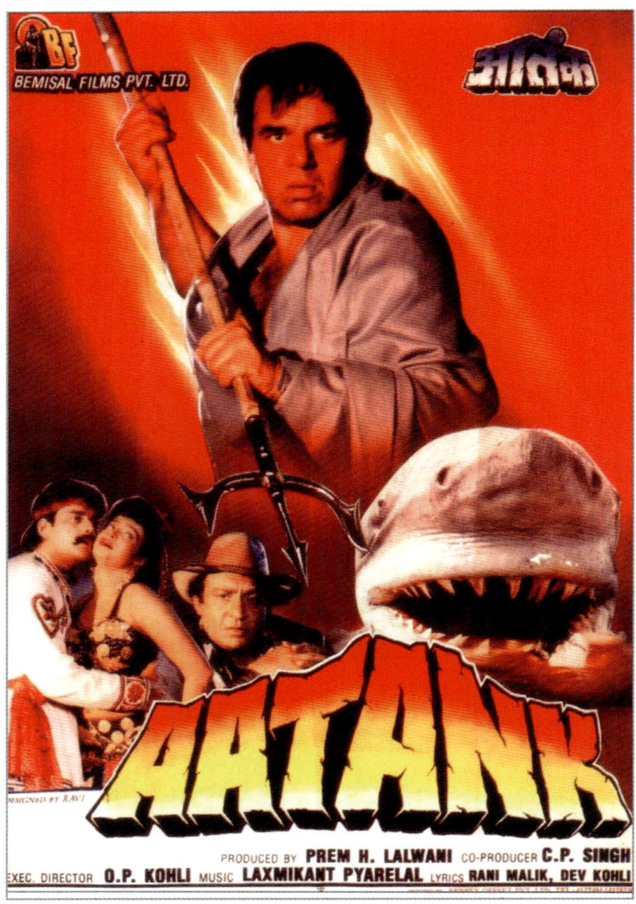

SONS OF JAWS

The phenomenal success of *Jaws* on its release in June 1975 amounted to nothing less than the birth of the modern summer blockbuster. Exploitation filmmakers were soon scrambling to the screen in its wake, though Cornel Wilde must be commended for actually beating Quint's crew to the screen by a couple of months. He scripted, directed, starred in, and even wrote the theme song for the April '75 release *Sharks' Treasure*, which featured, according to its poster, "100% real" shark footage. The following year's *The Jaws of Death*, in a similar dig at Spielberg's trickery, pointed out that no "mechanical sharks" had been used. This film even featured a twist, as Richard Jaeckel's protagonist was in league with the fishes: "In a moment of danger, deadly sharks once saved his life. Now he lives and kills as one of them, blood brother in a mysterious shark cult," the trailer explained, not at all bafflingly. The 1977 Mexican/English production *Tintorera* featured plenty of nudity as well as bloody deaths, while India's belated *Jaws* knock-off *Aatank* (1996), as is the Bollywood norm, had no nudity at all—but did have songs.

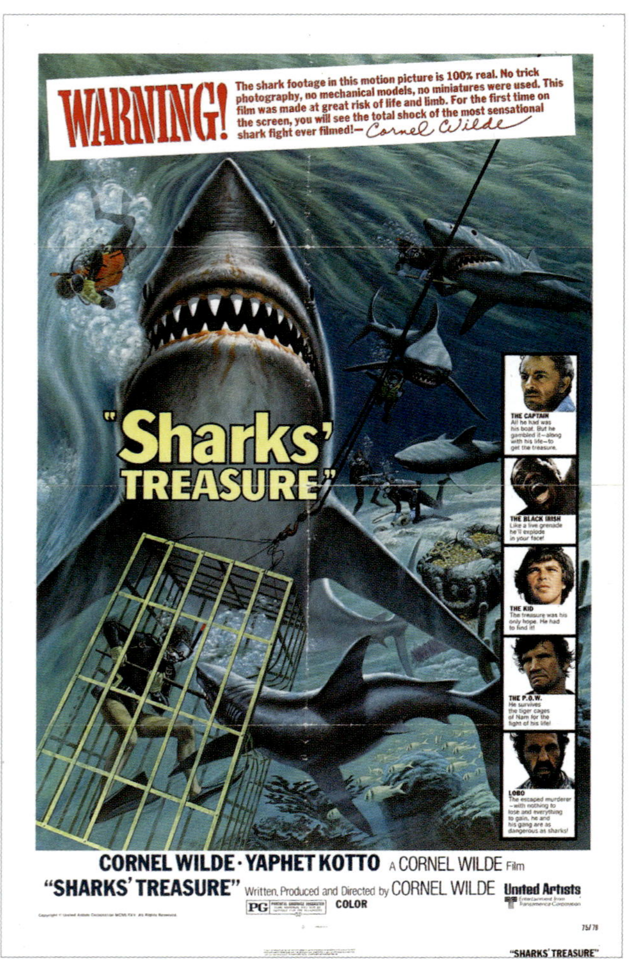

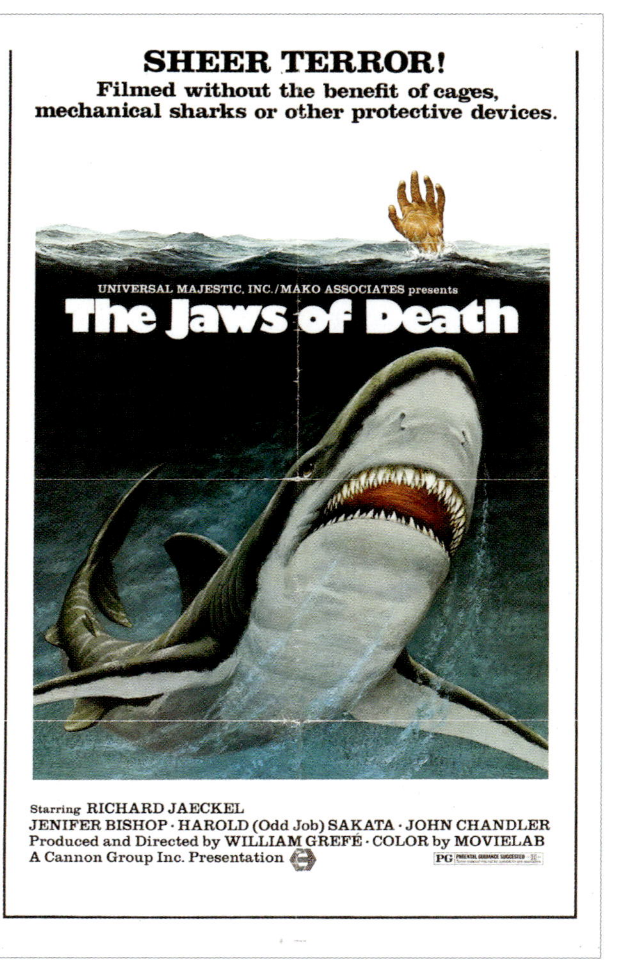

There's a monstrous killer churning up the sea...

TINTORERA

...Tiger Shark

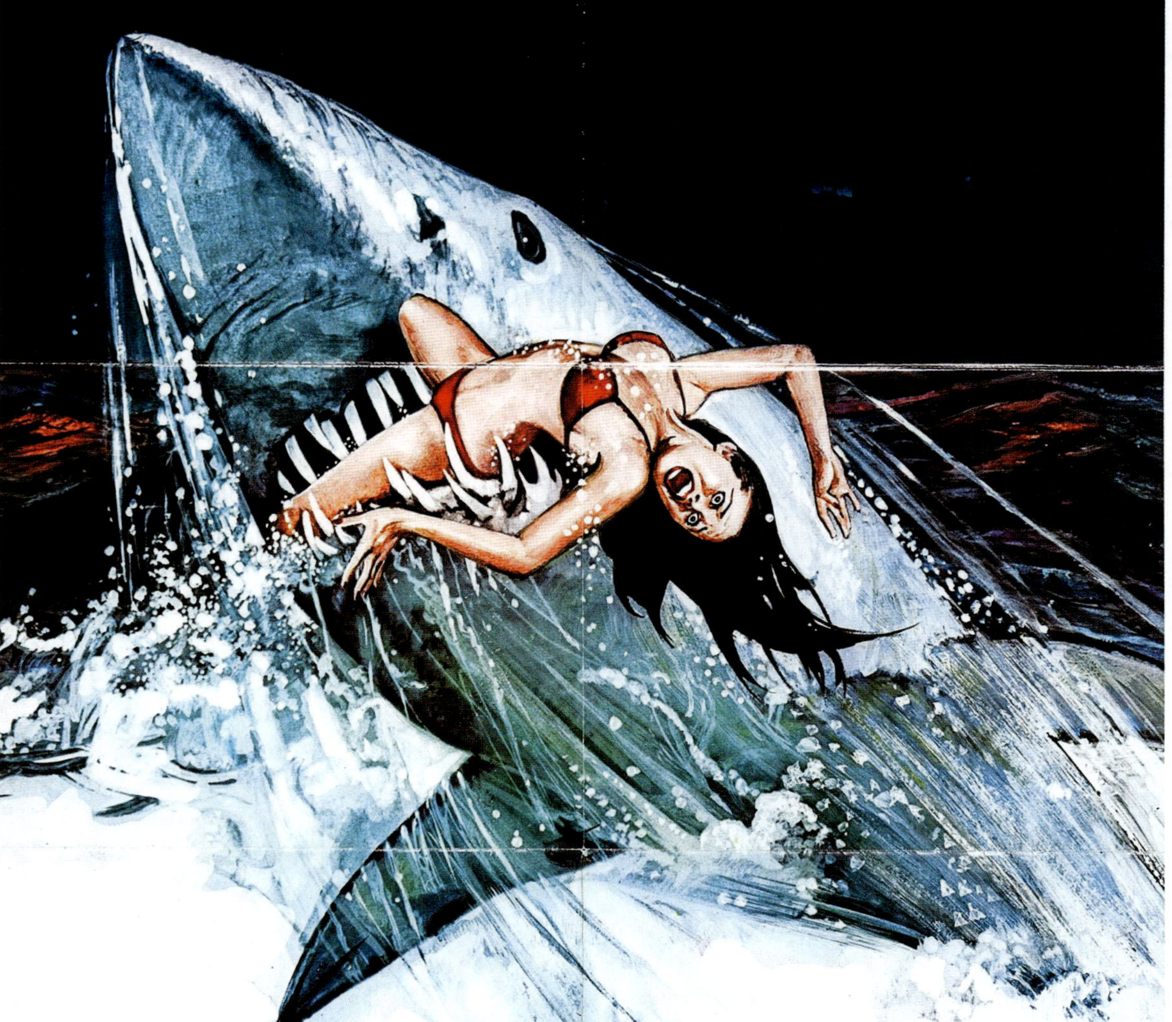

"TINTORERA" Starring SUSAN GEORGE • FIONA LEWIS • JENNIFER ASHLEY • HUGO STIGLITZ and ANDRES GARCIA
Directed by RENE CARDONA Jr. • Produced by GERALD GREEN • A HEMDALE Leisure Corporation and CONACINE Production
Music composed by BASIL POLEDOURIS Based on the bestseller by RAMON BRAVO
Released by United Film Distribution Company

R RESTRICTED
UNDER 17 REQUIRES ACCOMPANYING PARENT OR ADULT GUARDIAN

"TINTORERA"

ALL CREATURES GREAT AND SMALL

Contractual obligations can be tricky. The marketing department at MGM, presumably slack-jawed with incredulity after seeing an early cut of the film, did everything they could to hide the true nature of the oversized, mutant monsters in *Night of the Lepus* (from moviegoers who didn't read Latin, at least). They were legally required to credit the movie's source on the poster however, and so "Based Upon the Novel *The Year of the Angry Rabbit* by Russell Braddon" duly appeared, in the smallest print they could get away with. The 1972 production, featuring normal-sized domestic bunnies scampering around scale-model sets, was not a success. (You've probably seen some of it: it's on the TV when Neo goes to The Oracle's apartment in the first *Matrix* movie.) Plenty of other slightly scarier creatures have received the horror treatment over the years, especially in the post-*Jaws* era, but few have posters with the effective, elegant simplicity of *The Killer Shrews* (1959).

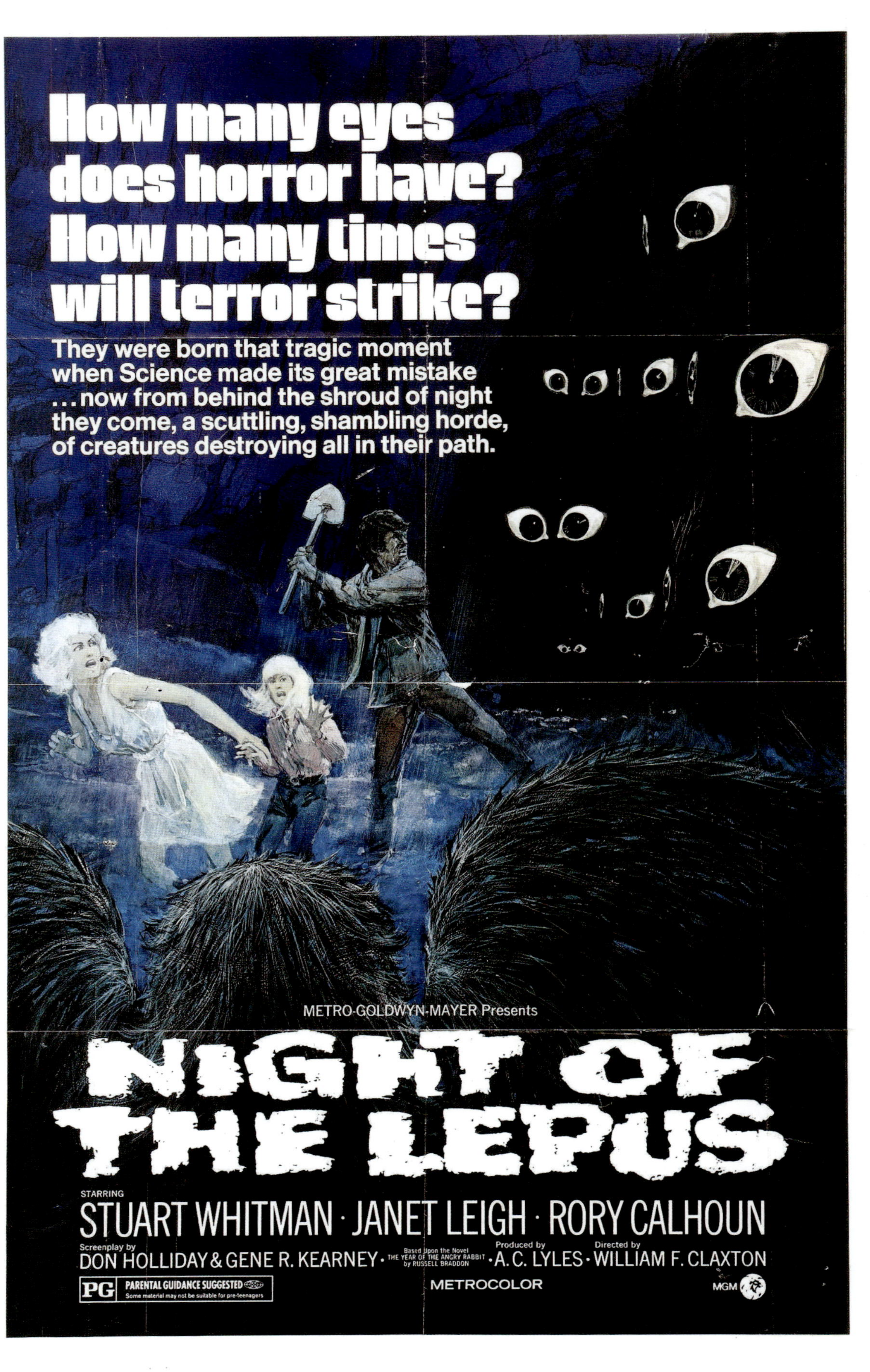

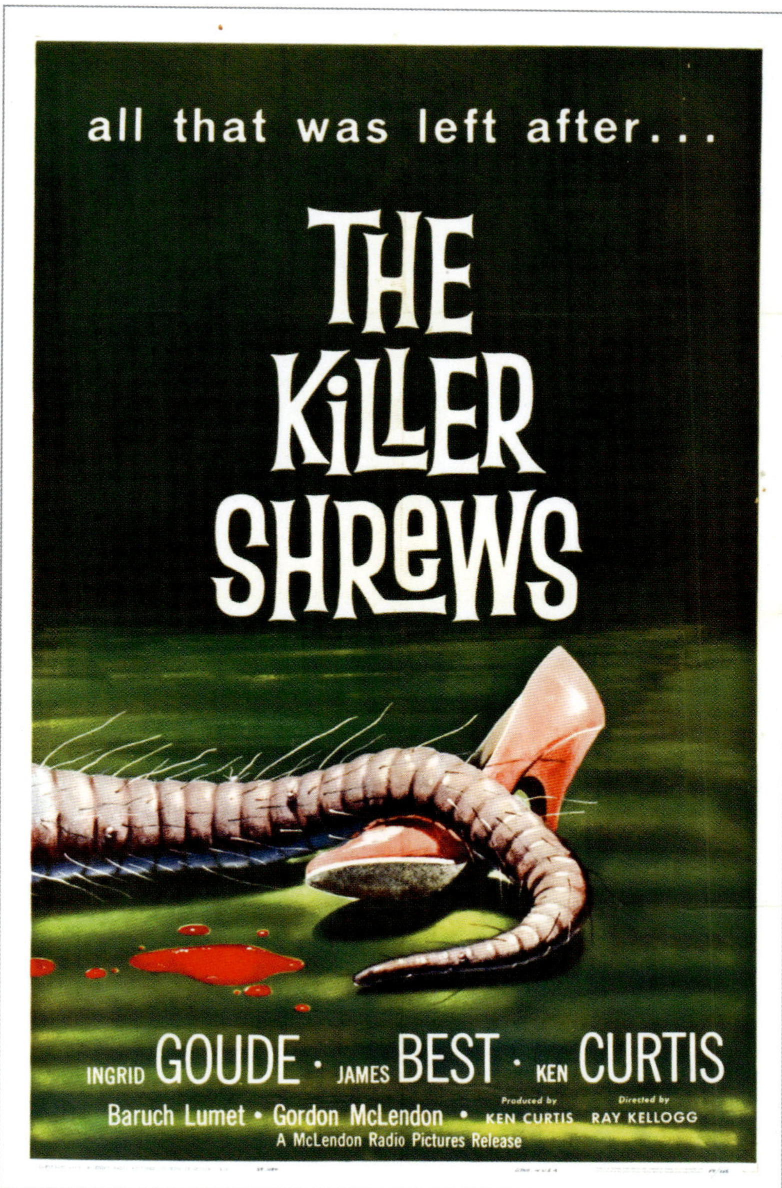
all that was left after...
THE KILLER SHREWS
INGRID GOUDE · JAMES BEST · KEN CURTIS
Baruch Lumet · Gordon McLendon · Produced by KEN CURTIS Directed by RAY KELLOGG
A McLendon Radio Pictures Release

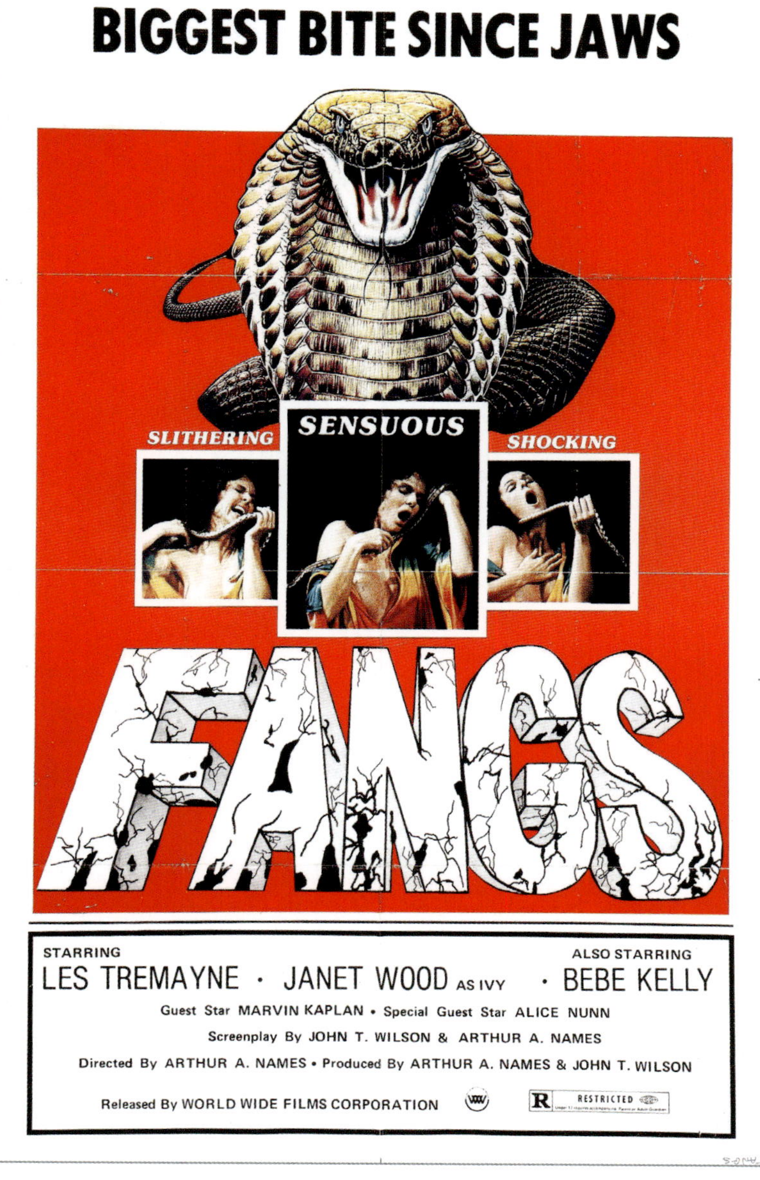
BIGGEST BITE SINCE JAWS
SLITHERING
SENSUOUS
SHOCKING
FANGS
STARRING
LES TREMAYNE · JANET WOOD AS IVY · ALSO STARRING BEBE KELLY
Guest Star MARVIN KAPLAN • Special Guest Star ALICE NUNN
Screenplay By JOHN T. WILSON & ARTHUR A. NAMES
Directed By ARTHUR A. NAMES • Produced By ARTHUR A. NAMES & JOHN T. WILSON
Released By WORLD WIDE FILMS CORPORATION
R RESTRICTED

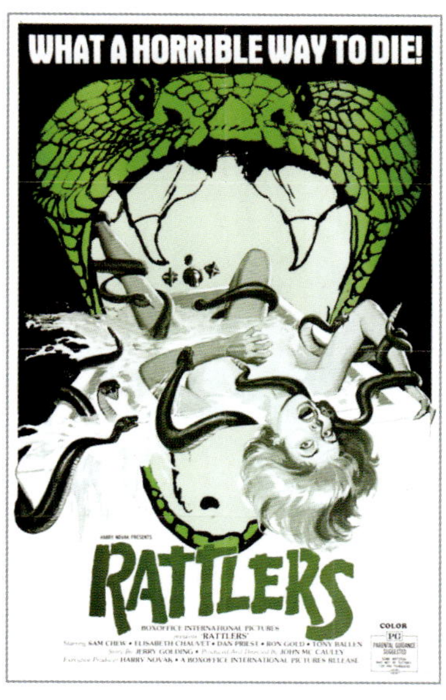
WHAT A HORRIBLE WAY TO DIE!
RATTLERS

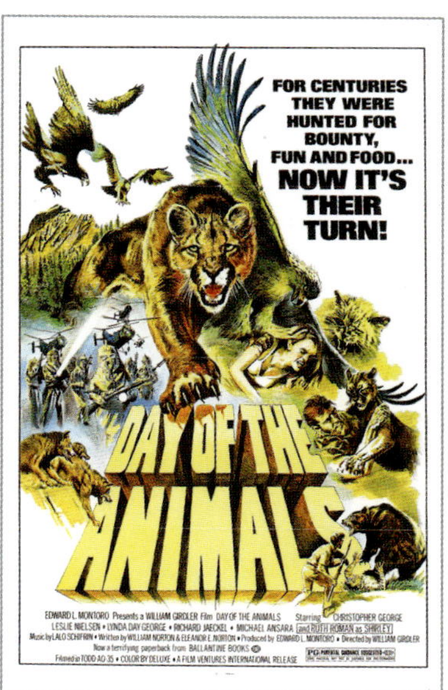
FOR CENTURIES THEY WERE HUNTED FOR BOUNTY, FUN AND FOOD... NOW IT'S THEIR TURN!
DAY OF THE ANIMALS

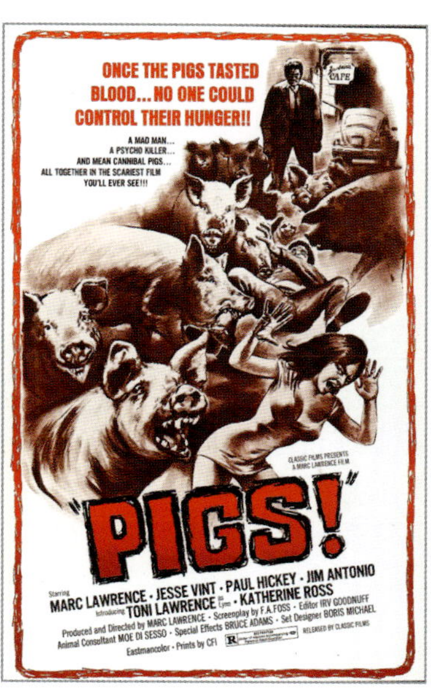
ONCE THE PIGS TASTED BLOOD... NO ONE COULD CONTROL THEIR HUNGER!!
PIGS!
MARC LAWRENCE · JESSE VINT · PAUL HICKEY · JIM ANTONIO
TONI LAWRENCE · KATHERINE ROSS

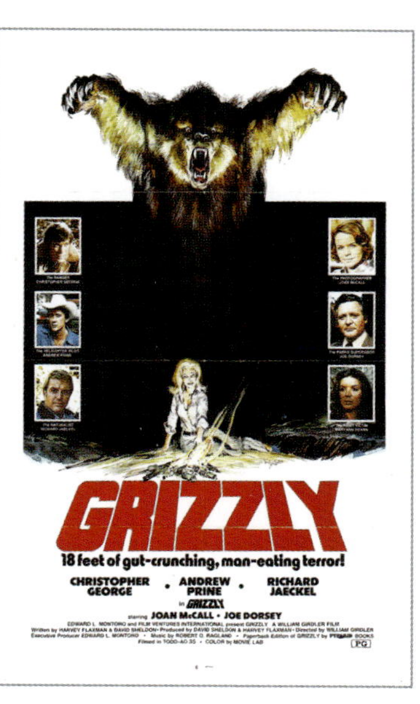
GRIZZLY
18 feet of gut-crunching, man-eating terror!
CHRISTOPHER GEORGE · ANDREW PRINE · RICHARD JAECKEL
JOAN McCALL · JOE DORSEY

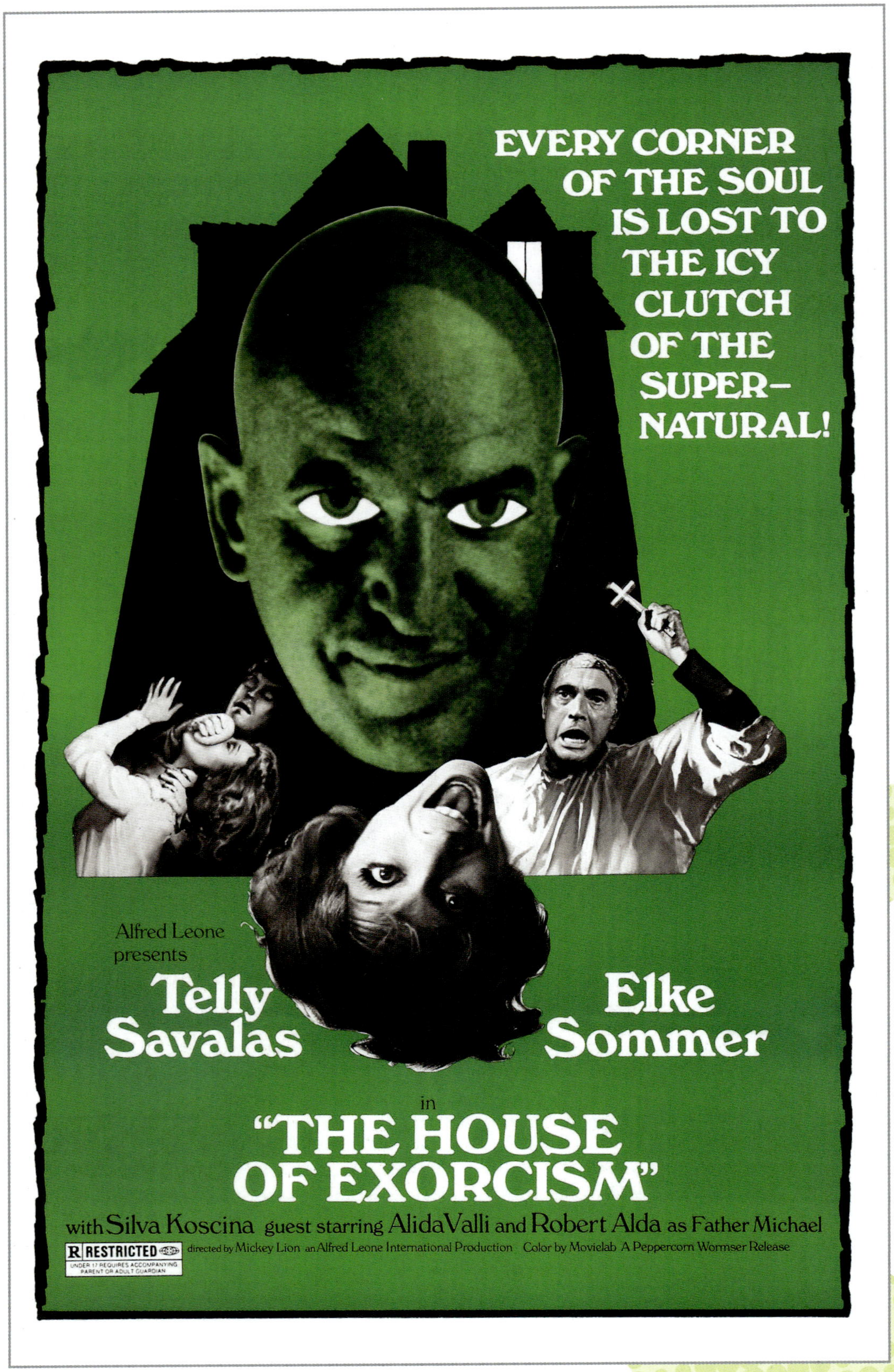

EVERY CORNER OF THE SOUL IS LOST TO THE ICY CLUTCH OF THE SUPER-NATURAL!

Alfred Leone presents

Telly Savalas

Elke Sommer

in

"THE HOUSE OF EXORCISM"

with Silva Koscina guest starring Alida Valli and Robert Alda as Father Michael

R RESTRICTED directed by Mickey Lion an Alfred Leone International Production Color by Movielab A Peppercorn Wormser Release

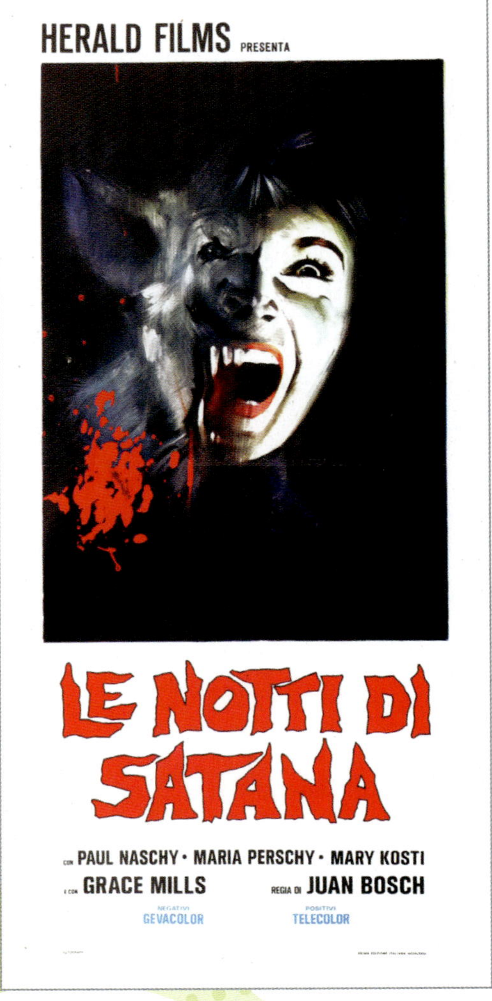

POSSESSED!

The blockbuster successes of *Rosemary's Baby* and especially *The Exorcist* ensured that Satan was kept busy with plenty of cash-ins and rip-offs. Few were as direct an homage to the latter as Turkey's *Şeytan* (1974), which was effectively an unofficial remake, head-spinning and all. *The House of Exorcism* (1975) was actually Mario Bava's 1973 Italian film *Lisa and the Devil*, completely re-edited and augmented with new exorcism footage for the eager US market. Bava was not amused, and took his name off the project: the poster credits the non-existent "Mickey Lion" as director. *Naked Evil* (overleaf) is from 1966: hat-tip to the canny exhibitor who scribbled "Black Exorcist!" onto the poster for a '70s screening.

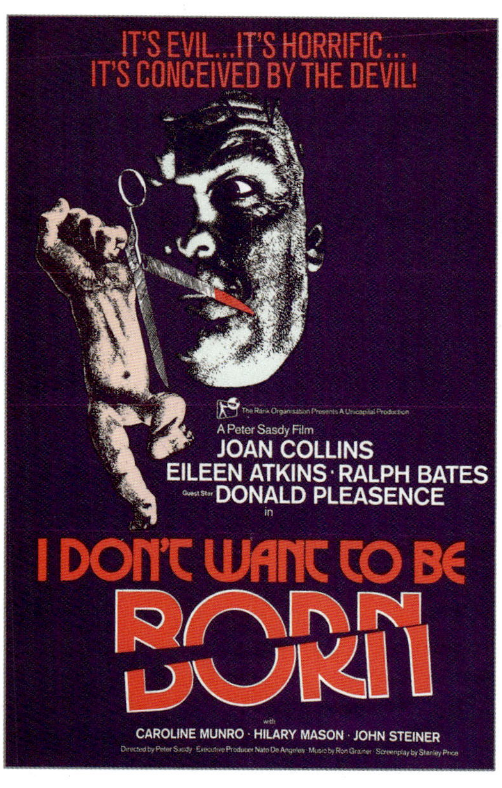
IT'S EVIL...IT'S HORRIFIC...
IT'S CONCEIVED BY THE DEVIL!
The Rank Organisation Presents A Unicapital Production
A Peter Sasdy Film
JOAN COLLINS
EILEEN ATKINS · RALPH BATES
Guest Star DONALD PLEASENCE
in
I DON'T WANT TO BE
BORN
with
CAROLINE MUNRO · HILARY MASON · JOHN STEINER
Directed by Peter Sasdy · Executive Producer Nato De Angeles · Music by Ron Grainer · Screenplay by Stanley Price

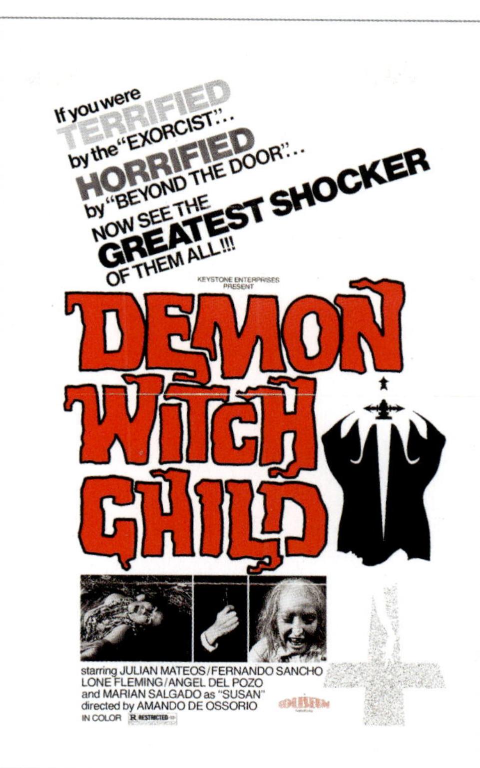
If you were
TERRIFIED
by the "EXORCIST"...
HORRIFIED
by "BEYOND THE DOOR"...
NOW SEE THE
GREATEST SHOCKER
OF THEM ALL!!!
KEYSTONE ENTERPRISES PRESENT
DEMON
WITCH
CHILD
starring JULIAN MATEOS / FERNANDO SANCHO
LONE FLEMING / ANGEL DEL POZO
and MARIAN SALGADO as "SUSAN"
directed by AMANDO DE OSSORIO
IN COLOR
R RESTRICTED

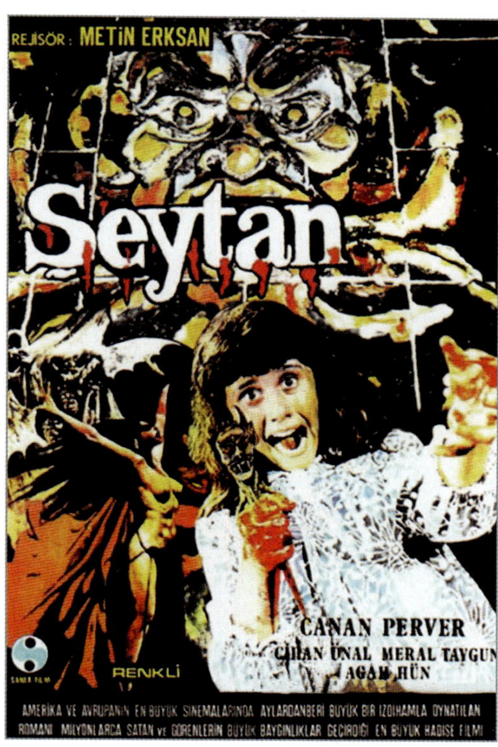
REJİSÖR: METİN ERKSAN
Şeytan
CANAN PERVER
CİHAN ÜNAL MERAL TAYGUN
AGAH HÜN
RENKLİ
AMERİKA VE AVRUPANIN EN BÜYÜK SİNEMALARINDA AYLARDANBERİ BÜYÜK BİR İZDİHAMLA OYNATILAN
ROMANI MİLYONLARCA SATAN ve GÖRENLERİN BÜYÜK BAYGINLIKLAR GEÇİRDİĞİ EN BÜYÜK HADİSE FİLMİ

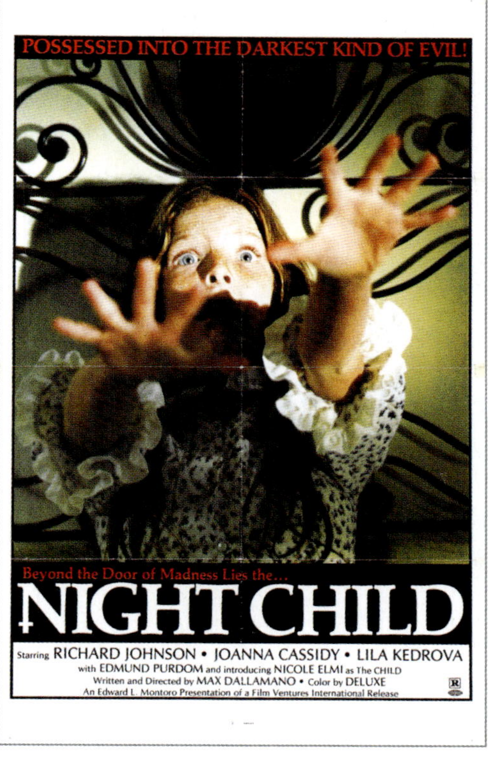
POSSESSED INTO THE DARKEST KIND OF EVIL!
Beyond the Door of Madness Lies the...
NIGHT CHILD
Starring RICHARD JOHNSON • JOANNA CASSIDY • LILA KEDROVA
with EDMUND PURDOM and introducing NICOLE ELMI as The CHILD
Written and Directed by MAX DALLAMANO • Color by DELUXE
An Edward L. Montoro Presentation of a Film Ventures International Release
R

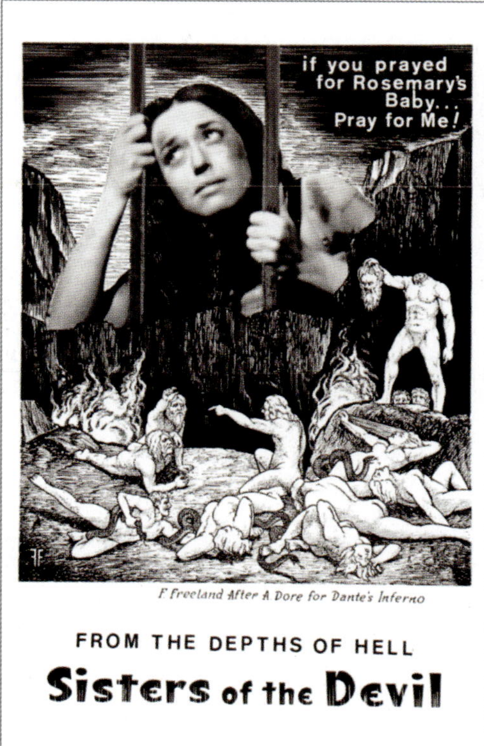
if you prayed
for Rosemary's
Baby...
Pray for Me!
F Freeland After A Dore for Dante's Inferno
FROM THE DEPTHS OF HELL
Sisters of the Devil

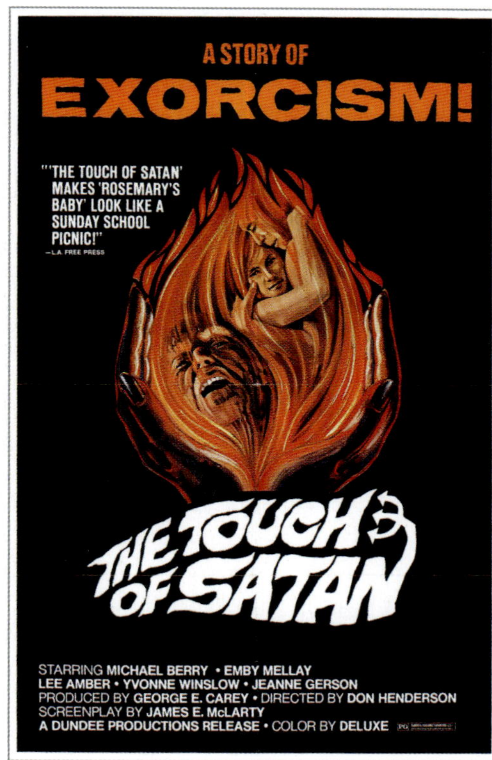
A STORY OF
EXORCISM!
"'THE TOUCH OF SATAN' MAKES 'ROSEMARY'S BABY' LOOK LIKE A SUNDAY SCHOOL PICNIC!"
—L.A. FREE PRESS
THE TOUCH OF SATAN
STARRING MICHAEL BERRY • EMBY MELLAY
LEE AMBER • YVONNE WINSLOW • JEANNE GERSON
PRODUCED BY GEORGE E. CAREY • DIRECTED BY DON HENDERSON
SCREENPLAY BY JAMES E. McLARTY
A DUNDEE PRODUCTIONS RELEASE • COLOR BY DELUXE

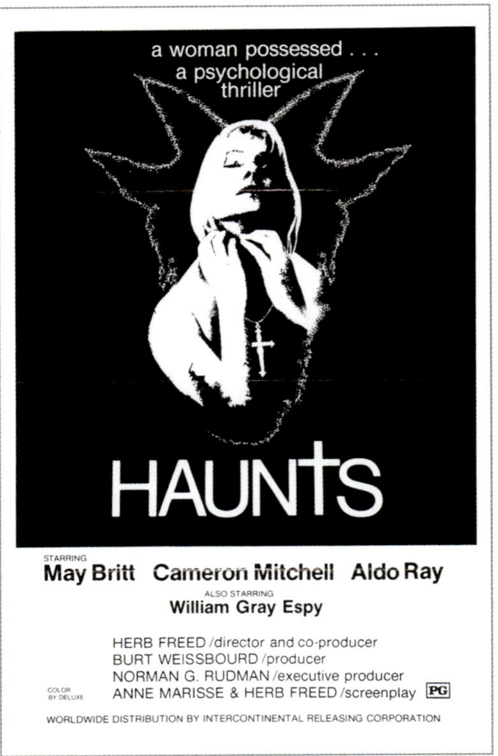
a woman possessed . . .
a psychological thriller
HAUNTS
STARRING
May Britt Cameron Mitchell Aldo Ray
ALSO STARRING
William Gray Espy
HERB FREED /director and co-producer
BURT WEISSBOURD /producer
NORMAN G. RUDMAN /executive producer
ANNE MARISSE & HERB FREED /screenplay
PG
WORLDWIDE DISTRIBUTION BY INTERCONTINENTAL RELEASING CORPORATION

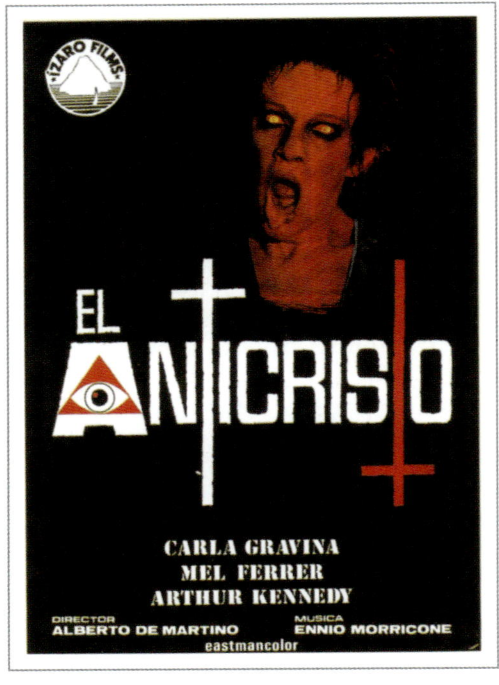
IZARO FILMS
EL ANTICRISTO
CARLA GRAVINA
MEL FERRER
ARTHUR KENNEDY
DIRECTOR
ALBERTO DE MARTINO
MUSICA
ENNIO MORRICONE
eastmancolor

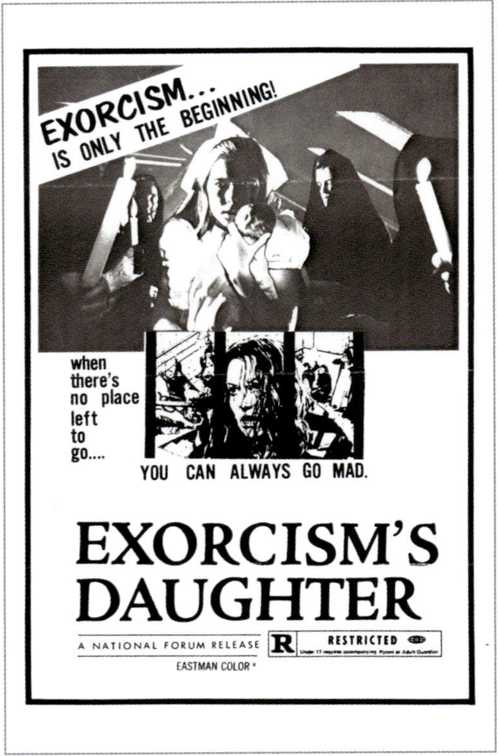
EXORCISM... IS ONLY THE BEGINNING!
when there's no place left to go....
YOU CAN ALWAYS GO MAD.
EXORCISM'S DAUGHTER
A NATIONAL FORUM RELEASE
R RESTRICTED
EASTMAN COLOR

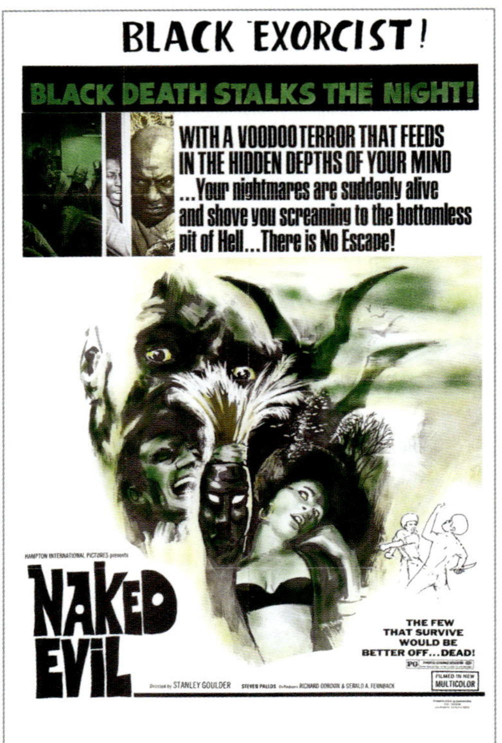
BLACK EXORCIST!
BLACK DEATH STALKS THE NIGHT!
WITH A VOODOO TERROR THAT FEEDS IN THE HIDDEN DEPTHS OF YOUR MIND ...Your nightmares are suddenly alive and shove you screaming to the bottomless pit of Hell...There is No Escape!
NAKED EVIL
THE FEW THAT SURVIVE WOULD BE BETTER OFF...DEAD!
STANLEY GOULDER
MULTICOLOR

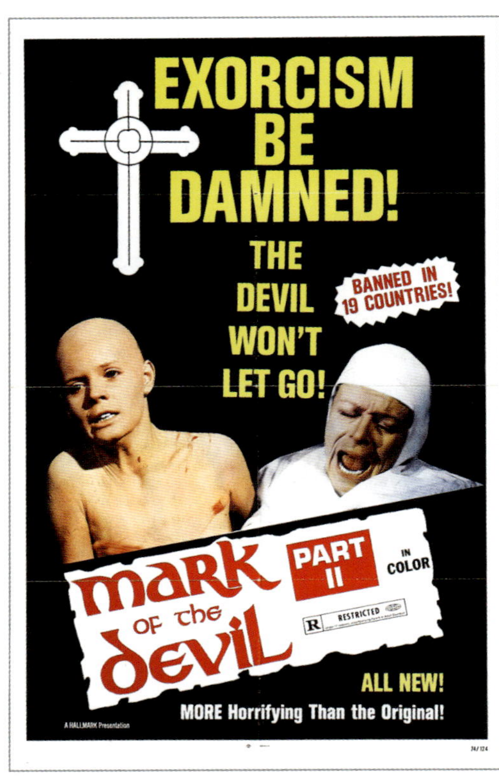
EXORCISM BE DAMNED!
THE DEVIL WON'T LET GO!
BANNED IN 19 COUNTRIES!
mark of the devil PART II
IN COLOR
R RESTRICTED
ALL NEW!
MORE Horrifying Than the Original!

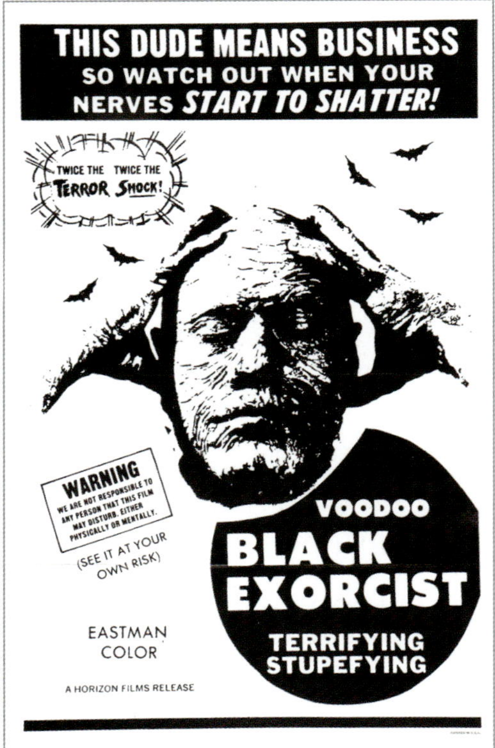
THIS DUDE MEANS BUSINESS
SO WATCH OUT WHEN YOUR NERVES START TO SHATTER!
TWICE THE TERROR TWICE THE SHOCK!
WARNING
(SEE IT AT YOUR OWN RISK)
EASTMAN COLOR
VOODOO
BLACK EXORCIST
TERRIFYING
STUPEFYING
A HORIZON FILMS RELEASE

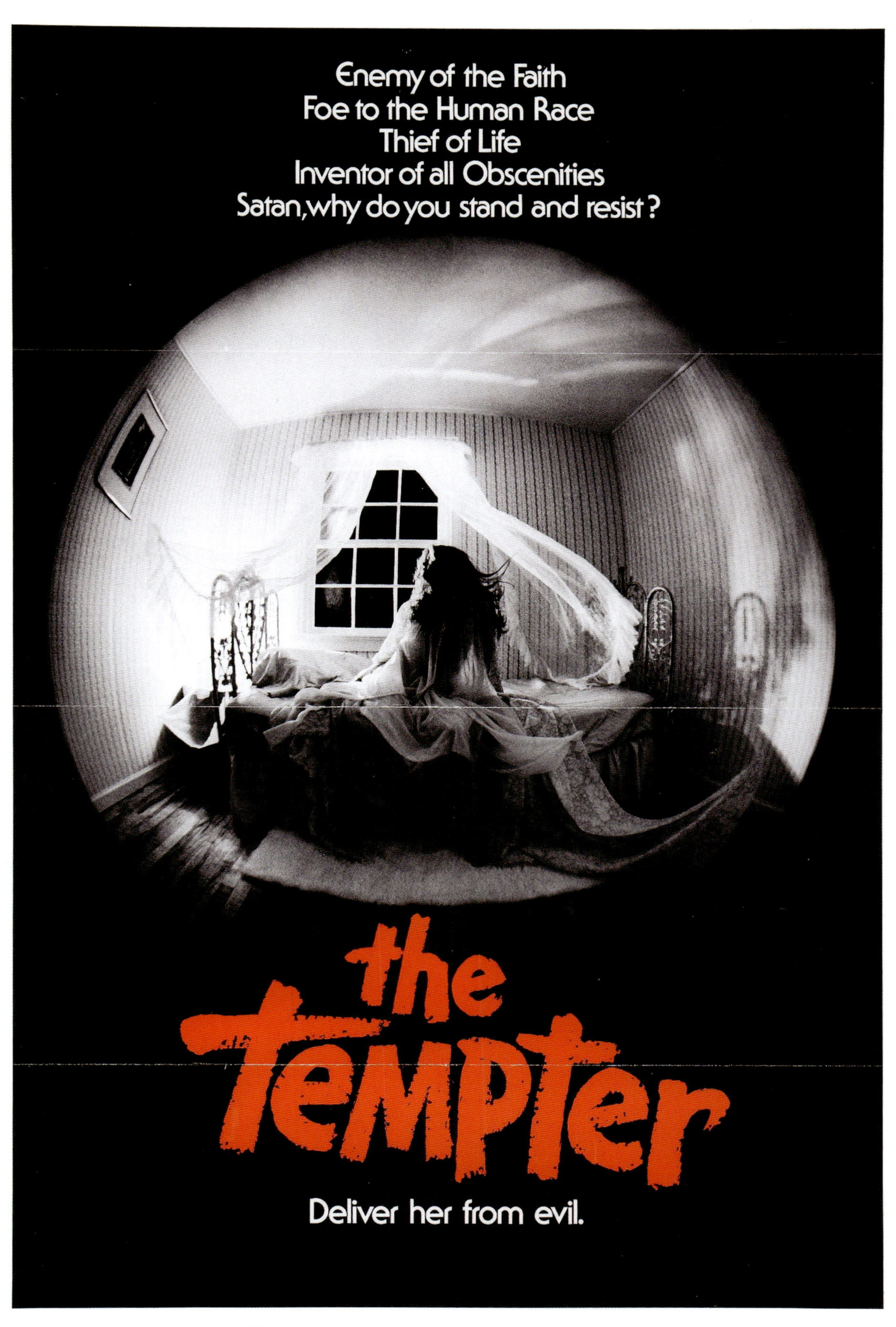
Enemy of the Faith
Foe to the Human Race
Thief of Life
Inventor of all Obscenities
Satan, why do you stand and resist?
the Tempter
Deliver her from evil.
AVCO EMBASSY PICTURES Release
R RESTRICTED

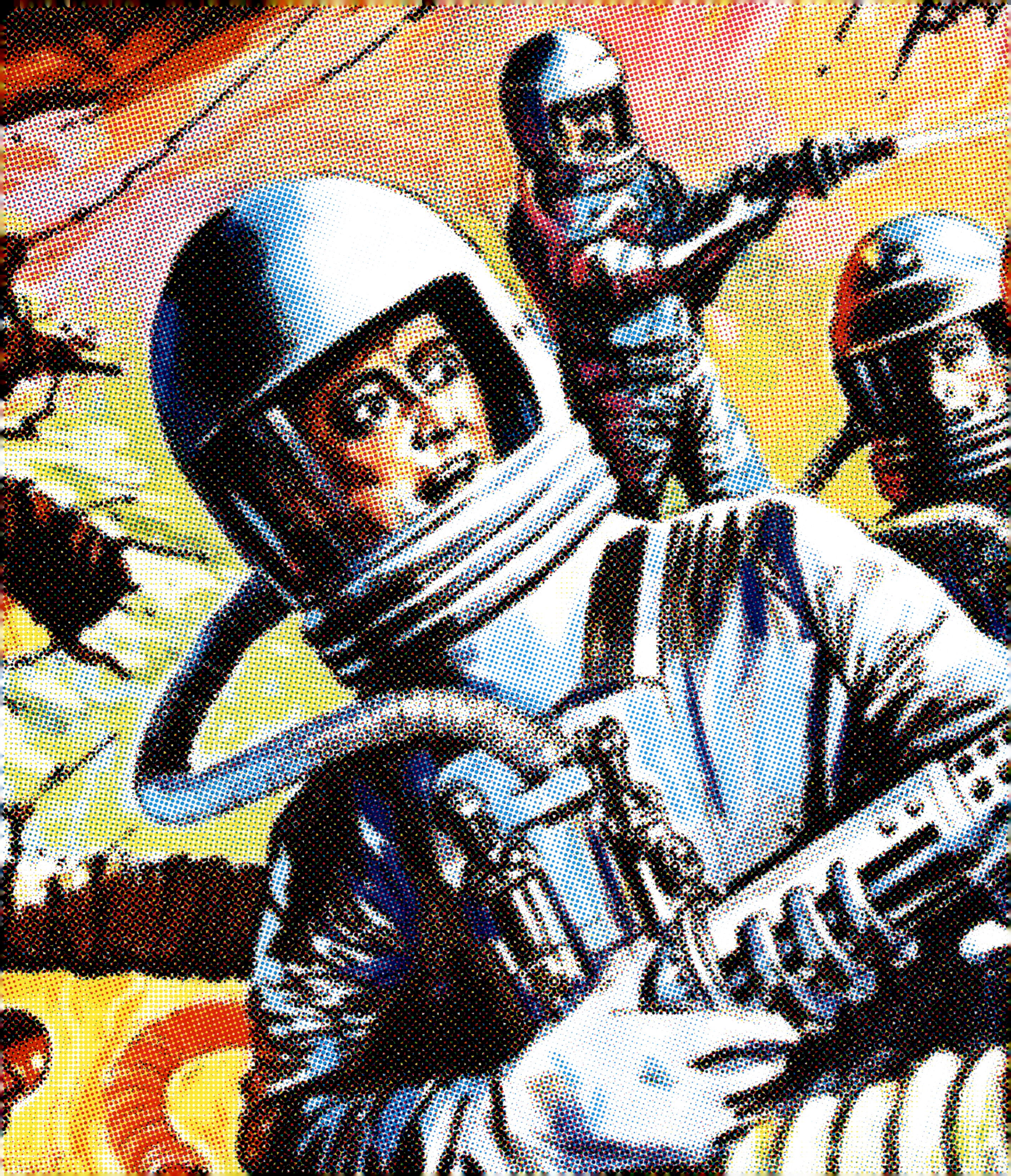

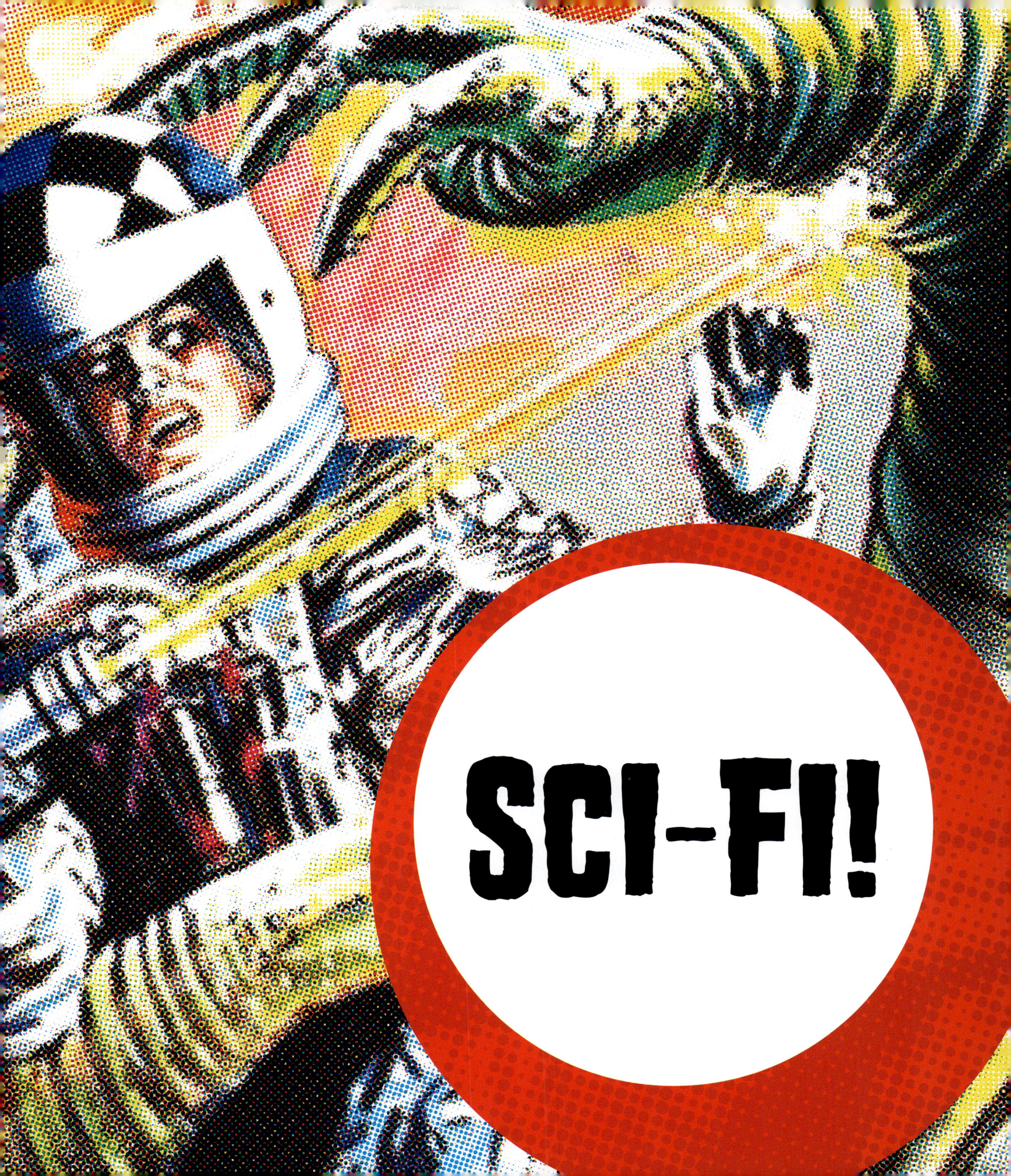
SCI-FI!

Kim Newman on

THE QUATERMASS XPERIMENT and DALEKS' INVASION EARTH 2150 A.D.

PREVIOUS SPREAD: Detail from the US one-sheet for *War Between the Planets* (1966).

OPPOSITE: The Italian *foglio* for *The Quatermass Xperiment* (1955), with gorgeous art by Carlantonio Longi.

BELOW: Hammer's film was released in the US as *The Creeping Unknown*, with a one-sheet featuring the zoo animals "absorbed" by the infected astronaut Carroon.

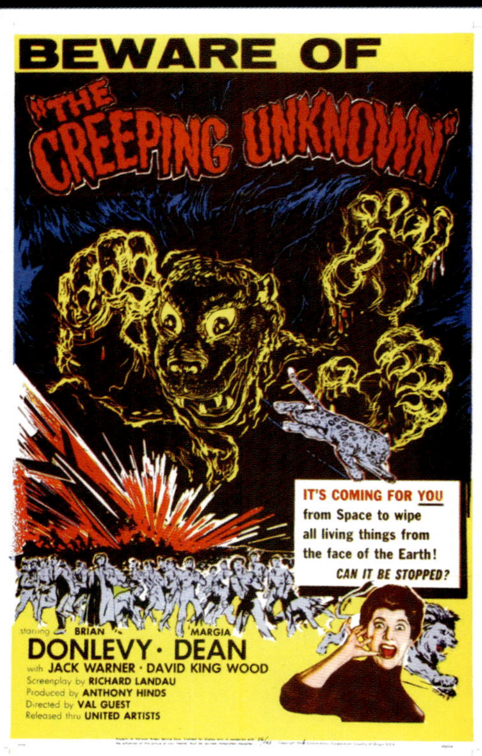

Science fiction cinema has always traded on a mix of wonder, scientific curiosity, and bred-in-the-bone paranoid terror. In the nineteenth century, Jules Verne and H.G. Wells imagined flying warships, voyages to the moon, monsters created by mad science, invisible men, lost worlds inside the Earth (with dinosaurs!), and travel through time.

Film science fiction in the 1930s and 1940s was inspired by comic strips like *Flash Gordon* and *Buck Rogers*, which followed Edgar Rice Burroughs by transplanting nineteenth century "lost city" adventures to other worlds where clanking robots, bizarre monsters, and sparkler-powered rocketships co-existed with imperiled princesses and wicked dictators. In the 1950s, fear of nuclear war, communism, and rock 'n' roll ran alongside cosy applications of super-science to domestic products (everything was advertised with "It's atomic!"). Movie screens were overwhelmed by flying saucers, giant bugs and reptiles, races of alien Amazons, mutating scientists, body-snatching infiltrators, and little green men (in black and white). In the 1960s and 1970s, resources studios would once have saved for Biblical epics or all-singing, all-dancing musicals were lavished on visionary works like Stanley Kubrick's *2001: A Space Odyssey* (1968) and super-produced pulp serials like George Lucas's *Star Wars* (1977). *Superman* (1978) added superheroes to the mix and *Alien* (1979) brought back the terrors from beyond space. Science fiction—once confined to kiddie matinees—began a long reign at the top of the box office, which continues into the twenty-first century.

British science fiction has always been calmer yet deeper, the gosh-wow enthusiasm of American space heroes like Flash Gordon set aside in favor of pipe-smoking boffins peering into cyclotrons and tutting over the dangers ahead. British television has been the source of major homegrown SF franchises. Manx author Nigel Kneale's world-saving rocketry guru Professor Quatermass first appeared in *The Quatermass Experiment* (1953), a BBC six-part serial that thrilled the nation in the early days of TV broadcasting. It was remade by Hammer Films as *The Quatermass Xperiment* (1955), the title capitalizing on

una tremenda avventura ai confini dell'impossibile

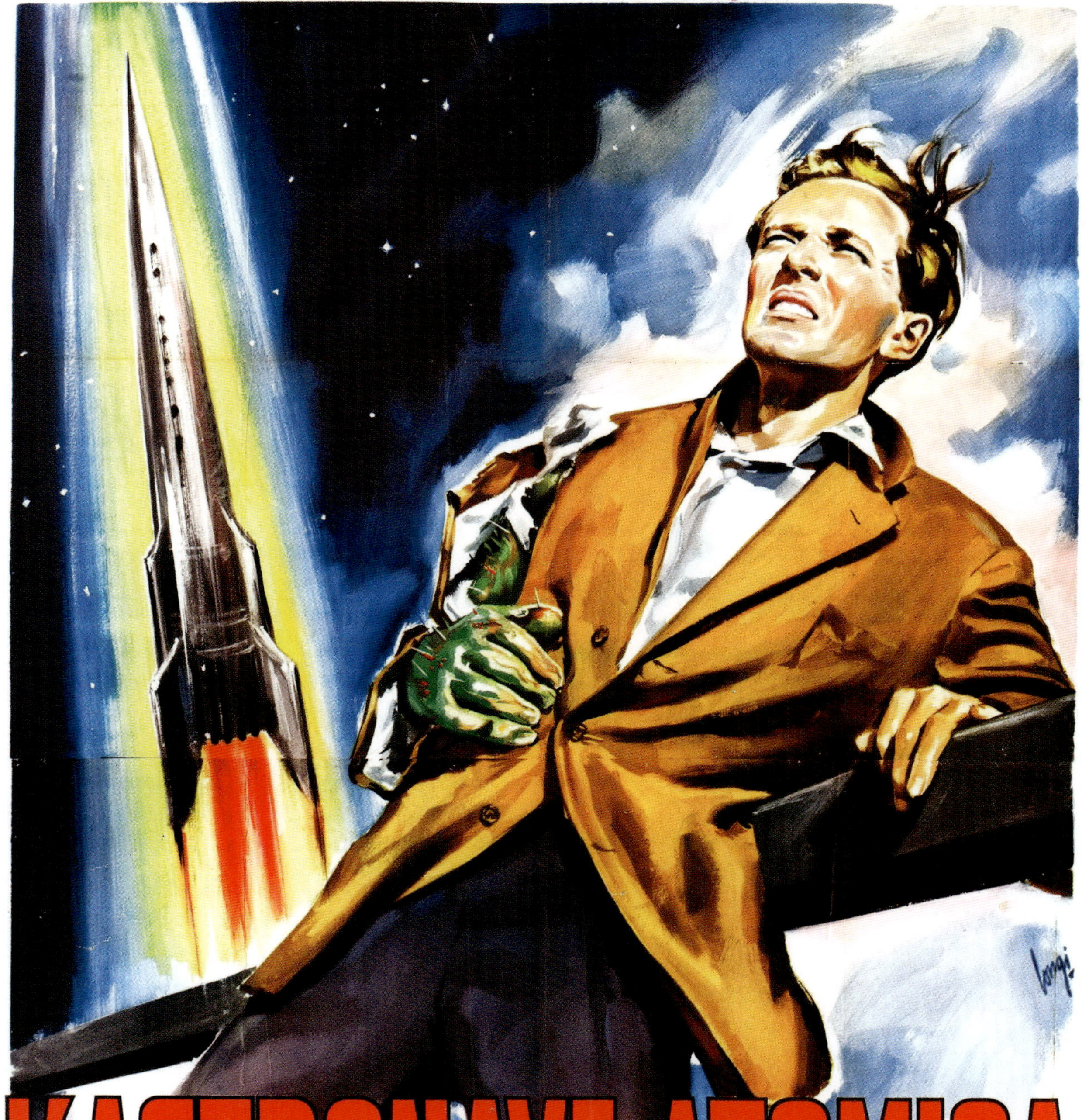

L'ASTRONAVE ATOMICA DEL DOTT. *Quatermass*

ESCLUSIVITA'
DAFNE
CINEMATOGRAFICA

BRIAN DONLEVY · JACK WARNER · RICHARD WORDSWORTH

DAVID KING WOOD - THORA HIRD - GORDON JACKSON

REGIA DI VAL GUEST

PRODUZIONE: ANTHONY HINDS
EXCLUSIVE FILMS

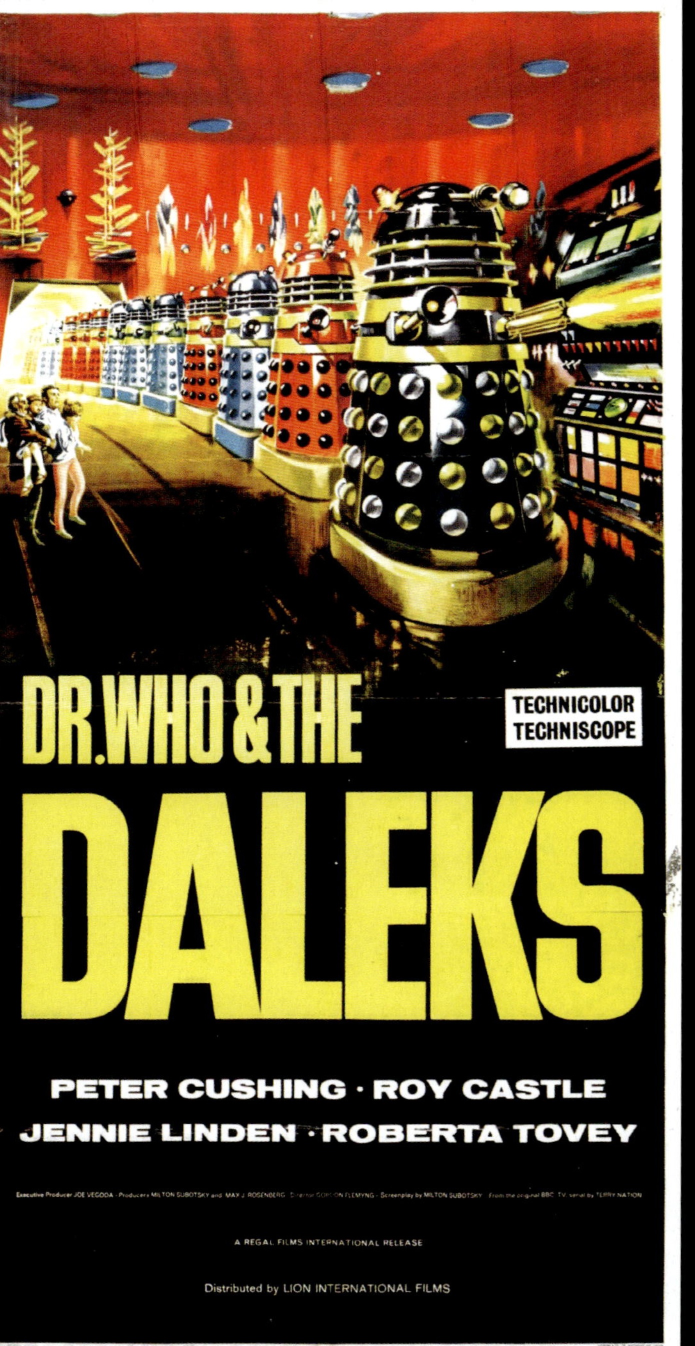

ABOVE: While the Dalek props built for the cinematic *Dr. Who and the Daleks* (1965) and its sequel were bigger than the ones that had appeared in the BBC TV series, they still stood shorter than the average human member of the cast, unlike the giants presented on this colorful but wildly inaccurate poster.

the X certificate required to protect children from the spectacle of infected astronaut Victor Carroon (Richard Wordsworth) transforming into a giant part-vegetable blob while shambling over noirish London bomb sites. In a riff on a famous scene from *Frankenstein* (1931), the monster has a tense encounter with an innocent little girl (Jane Asher) in the wasteland. In the TV serial, Quatermass successfully appeals to the monster's residual humanity and talks it into destroying itself to save the planet—a thoughtful finish Hammer dropped in favor of having the creature electrocuted in a shower of sparks like the Thing From Another World of the 1951 film.

Kneale disapproved of the casting of blunt, two-fisted American Brian Donlevy (who was actually Irish) as his sensitive scientist hero, but director Val Guest's stripped-down, streamlined cinema version remains a powerful, exciting, unsettling film. Mounted in high seriousness and using location shooting unavailable to the shot-as-live TV version, the film draws on the British cinema's tradition of quietly heroic war films and on-the-streets police movies (Jack Warner, famous as *Dixon of Dock Green*, represents Scotland Yard on the monster hunt) and was the first major British science fiction monster movie, climaxing in Westminster Abbey where Carroon has mushroomed into a giant pile of tentacular tripe with one last angry, staring eye. On release in Italy under the wonderful title *L'astronave atomica del dottor Quatermass* (The Atomic Spaceship of Dr Quatermass), the film benefited from a gorgeous poster featuring a streamlined 1950s rocket and the agonized astronaut with his cactus arm.

In 1963, Quatermass was succeeded as the BBC's premier SF hero by the first Doctor (William Hartnell), the time-traveling eccentric of *Doctor Who*, a show which set out to be educational and avoid bug-eyed monsters but caught on with child and adult audiences as soon as the Doctor encountered his most persistent enemies, the trundling, hateful cyborg fascist Daleks. Two colorful, charming, weirdly disturbing films were made from the first two Dalek-themed TV serials, both directed by Gordon Flemyng (who passed on the secret of making the sound effect of the Dalek spaceship to his actor son, Jason). *Dr. Who and the Daleks* (1965) and *Daleks' Invasion Earth 2150 A.D.* (1966) star Peter Cushing as a doddery Doctor, pitted against impressive, Day-Glo Daleks which dwarf the pepper pots of the BBC version. As with Quatermass, the films played down the intellectual content of the TV serials—though the hero was softened rather than toughened up, with Cushing playing the Doctor as a stooped old loveable uncle whereas Hartnell was at least initially a crotchety, ambiguous, perhaps even frightening figure.

The poster for *Daleks' Invasion Earth 2150 A.D.*, a stirring tale of resistance against the occupation of Earth by the Daleks and leather-and-helmet-clad zombie henchmen, conveys some of the excitement of the movie, with its lovingly

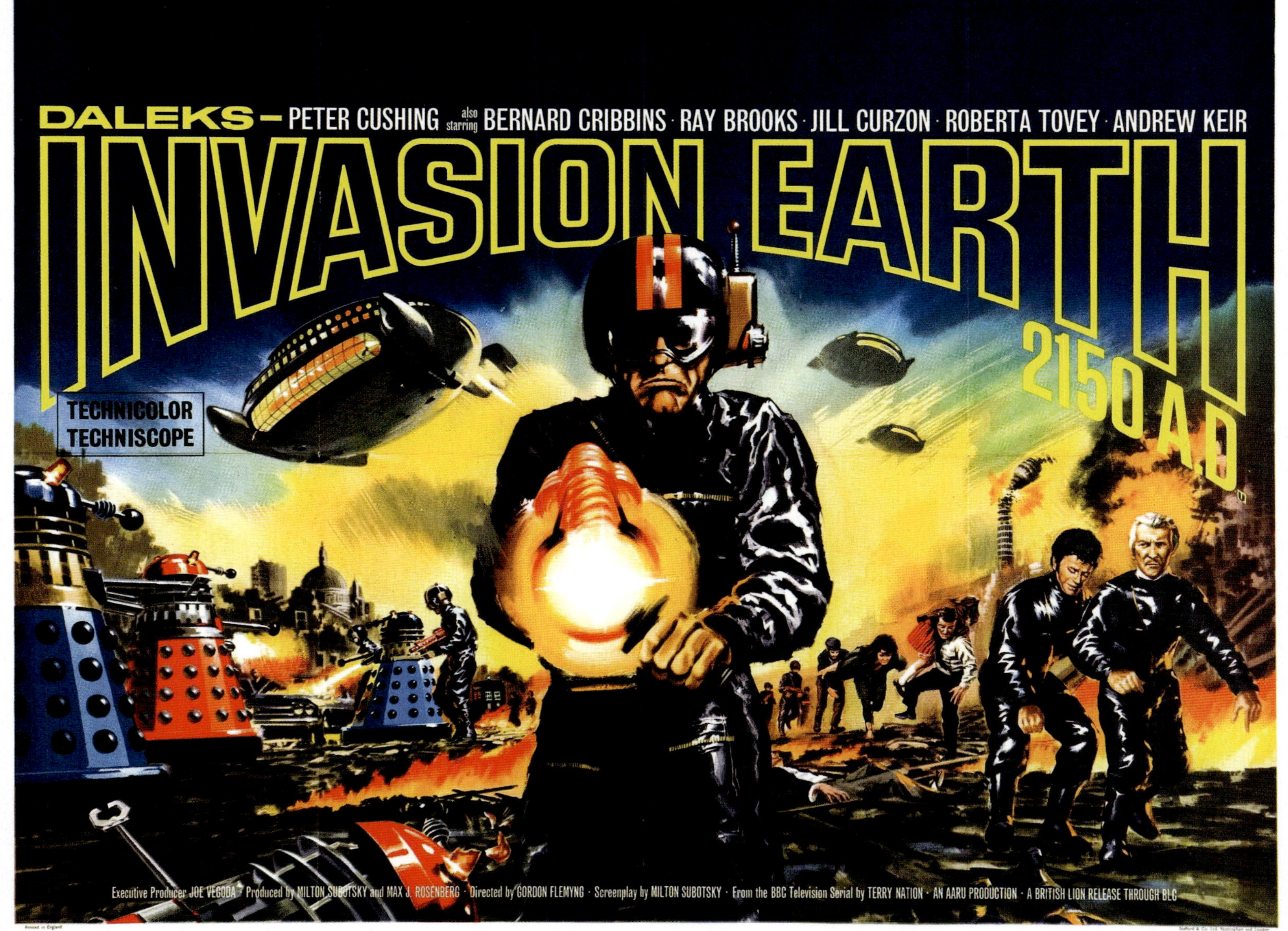

detailed alien ships (the film has only one), extermination-crazy Daleks, and a pitched battle in the ruins of London. The film is a *mélange* of elements from *The Time Machine* and *War of the Worlds*, with World War II references as London is blitzed again, an underground army manufacture homemade bombs, and there are black marketeers and collaborators ready to turn the heroes in to the alien overlords. It reproduces the startling cliffhanger of episode one of the TV version as a Dalek emerges from the waters of the Thames to menace the time-travelers, and boasts a stirring music score from Bill McGuffie (his leitmotif for the zombie-like Robomen is an uncanny precursor of Basil Poledouris's *RoboCop* theme). The Daleks were a craze in the 1960s—remaining a feature of the enduring *Doctor Who* franchise today—and these films offered them widescreen and panoramic action beyond the confines of black-and-white TV sets. Though inexpensive, *Daleks' Invasion Earth 2150 A.D.* is undeniably spectacular, climaxing with a mumbo-jumbo science trick as setting off a bomb affects the planet's magnetic field so the metal monsters are sucked screeching to the center of the Earth. ●

ABOVE: A Roboman attacks while London falls to the Daleks in Bill Wiggins's thrilling UK quad poster art for *Daleks' Invasion Earth 2150 A.D.* (1966). Top-billed star Peter Cushing is relegated to the far right.

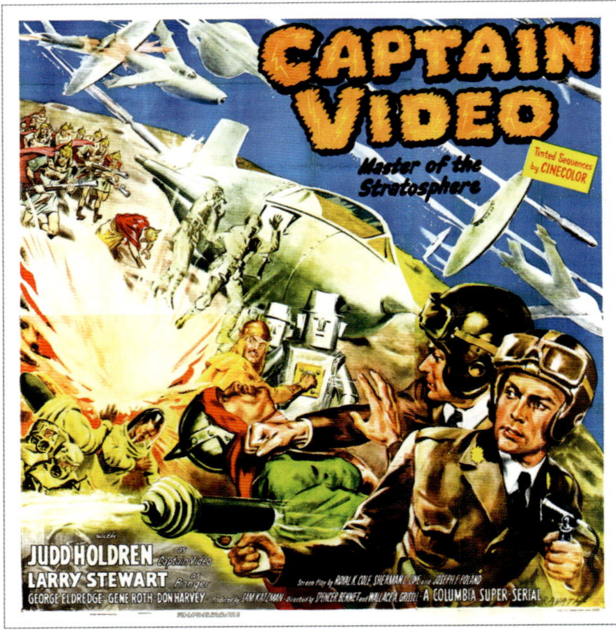

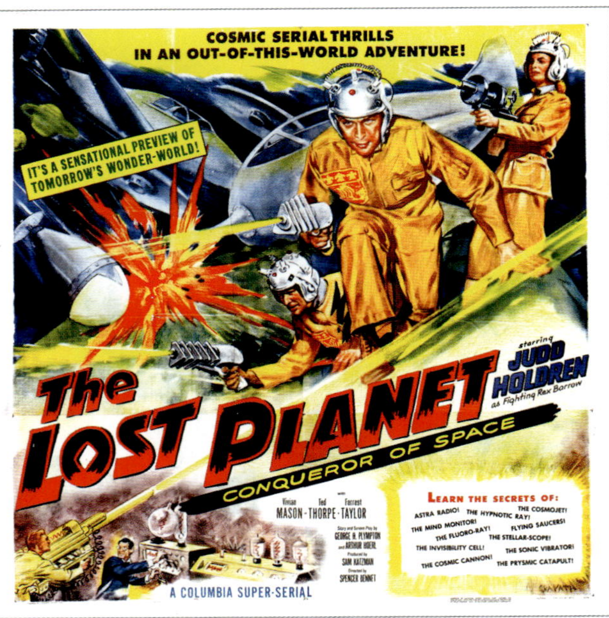

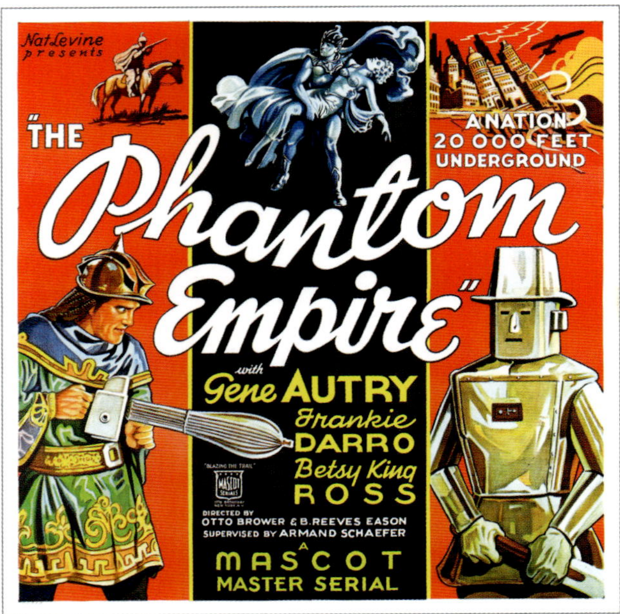

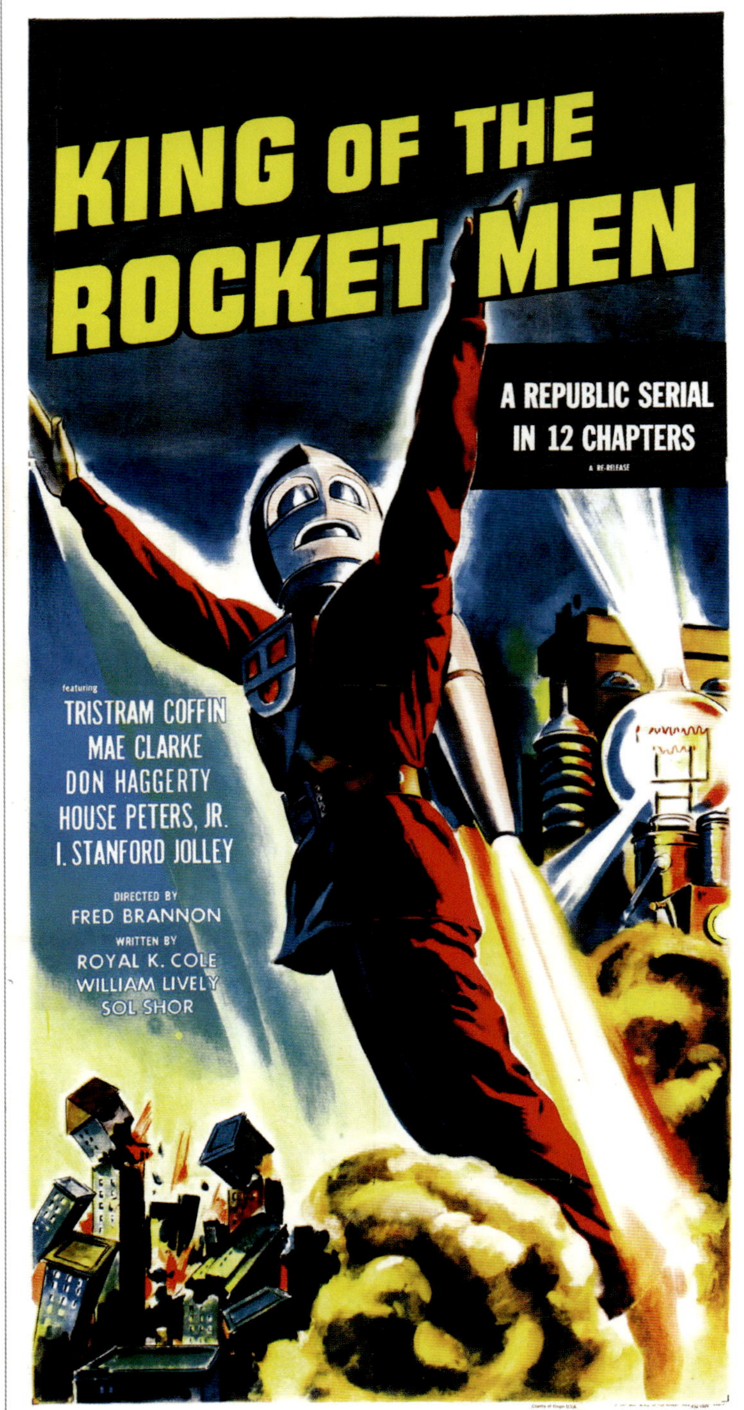

MORE SERIAL THRILLS

The sci-fi movie serial, a handful of examples of which are seen here, is the most successful film genre of all time. No, really: after all, what is the *Star Wars* saga if not a Saturday matinee serial writ large? George Lucas is happy to admit as much, and even gave his films chapter numbers (his decision to make an exciting bit of the story first, *Episode IV: A New Hope*, was proved correct when he finally got around to making the achingly dull *Episodes I* to *III* years later). In fact, *Star Wars* only exists because Lucas couldn't get hold of the rights to remake the apotheosis of the SF serial, *Flash Gordon*.

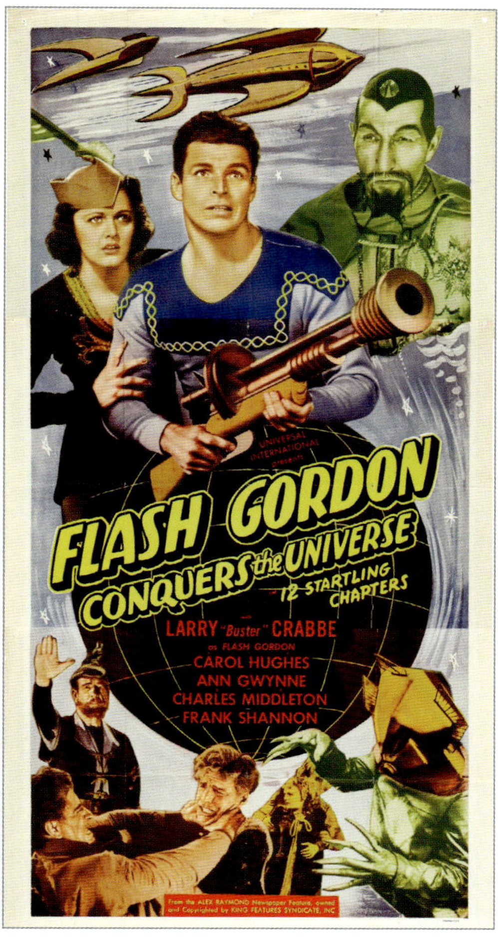
UNIVERSAL INTERNATIONAL presents
FLASH GORDON
CONQUERS the UNIVERSE
12 STARTLING CHAPTERS
LARRY "Buster" CRABBE
as FLASH GORDON
CAROL HUGHES
ANN GWYNNE
CHARLES MIDDLETON
FRANK SHANNON
From the ALEX RAYMOND Newspaper Feature, owned and Copyrighted by KING FEATURES SYNDICATE, INC.

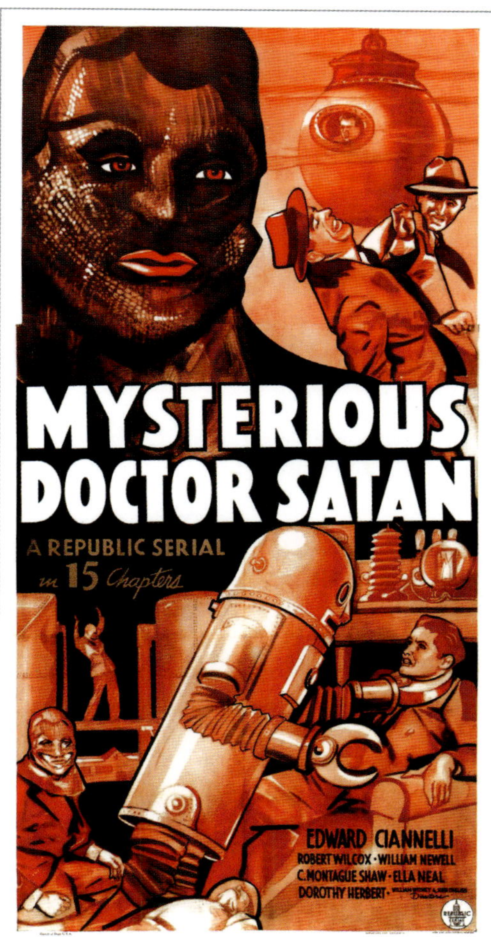
MYSTERIOUS
DOCTOR SATAN
A REPUBLIC SERIAL
in 15 Chapters
EDWARD CIANNELLI
ROBERT WILCOX · WILLIAM NEWELL
C. MONTAGUE SHAW · ELLA NEAL
DOROTHY HERBERT

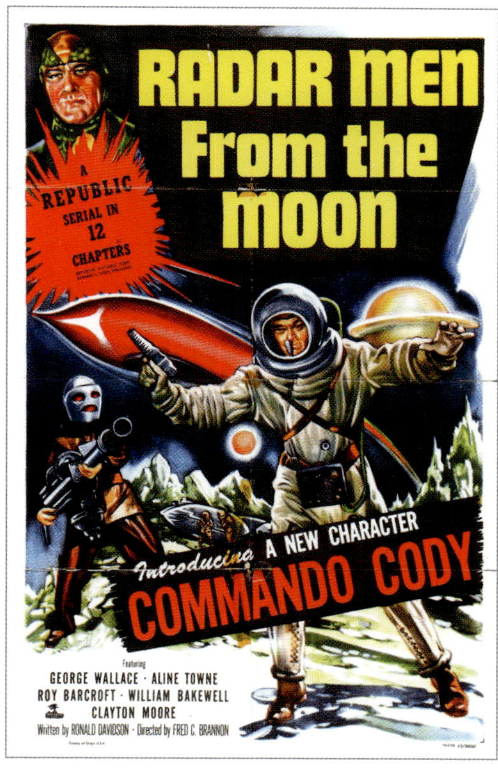
RADAR MEN
From the
moon
A REPUBLIC SERIAL IN 12 CHAPTERS
Introducing A NEW CHARACTER
COMMANDO CODY
featuring
GEORGE WALLACE · ALINE TOWNE
ROY BARCROFT · WILLIAM BAKEWELL
CLAYTON MOORE
Written by RONALD DAVIDSON · Directed by FRED C. BRANNON

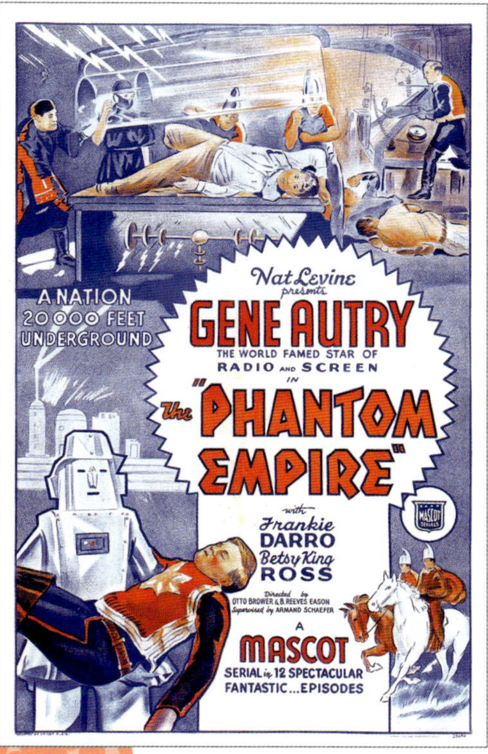
A NATION
20,000 FEET
UNDERGROUND
Nat Levine presents
GENE AUTRY
THE WORLD FAMED STAR OF
RADIO AND SCREEN
IN
"the PHANTOM
EMPIRE"
with
Frankie
DARRO
Betsy King
ROSS
Directed by
OTTO BROWER & B. REEVES EASON
Supervised by ARMAND SCHAEFER
A
MASCOT
SERIAL in 12 SPECTACULAR
FANTASTIC...EPISODES

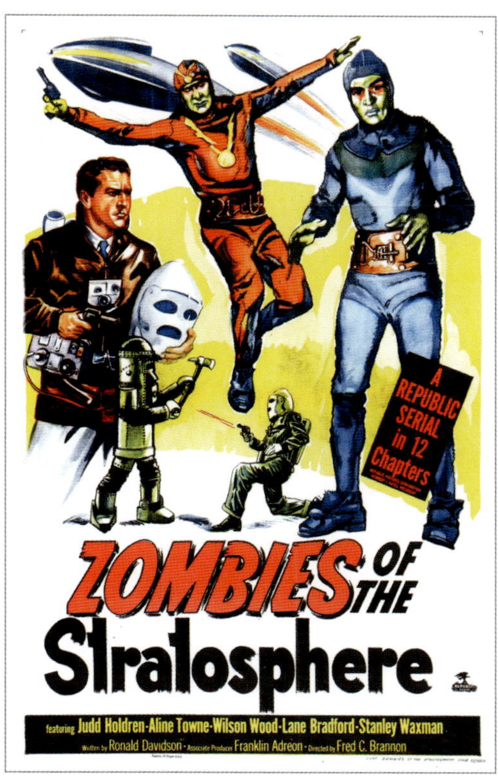
A REPUBLIC SERIAL in 12 Chapters
ZOMBIES OF THE
Stratosphere
featuring Judd Holdren · Aline Towne · Wilson Wood · Lane Bradford · Stanley Waxman
Written by Ronald Davidson · Associate Producer Franklin Adreon · Directed by Fred C. Brannon

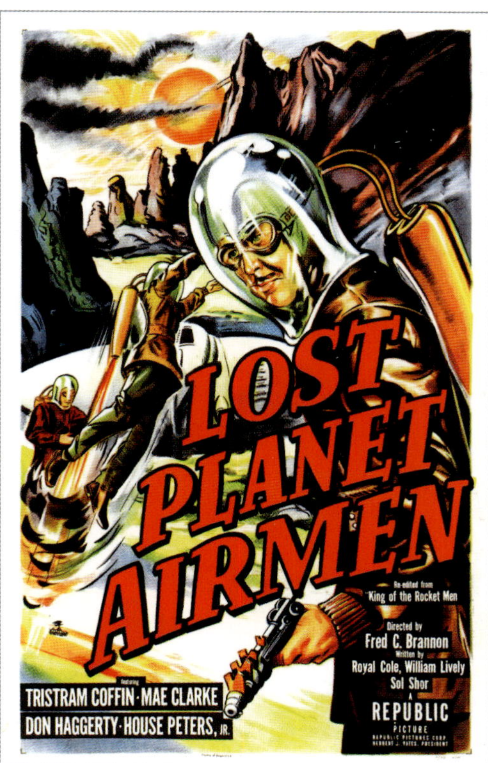
LOST
PLANET
AIRMEN
Re-edited from
King of the Rocket Men
Directed by
Fred C. Brannon
Written by
Royal Cole, William Lively
Sol Shor
featuring
TRISTRAM COFFIN · MAE CLARKE
DON HAGGERTY · HOUSE PETERS, JR.
A
REPUBLIC
PICTURE

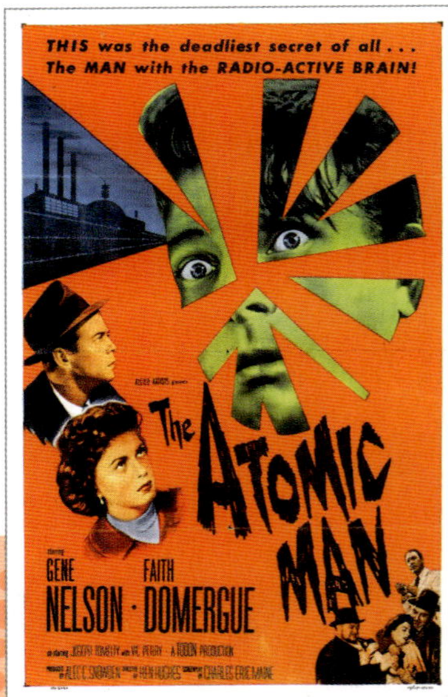

THE ATOMIC AGE

In a world where memories of the detonations at Hiroshima and Nagasaki were still fresh, anything related to the word "atomic" ensured a visceral reaction. Like *Godzilla* before it, *The H-Man* (1958), also produced by Japan's Toho Studios, was a monstrous threat caused by a nuclear explosion. The Mounties were up against a spy trying to launch atomic missiles in a 1953 Republic serial, and yes, they got their man. In the same year, the 1941 B-movie about an electricity-powered *Man-Made Monster* got a re-release under a more powerful, if inaccurate title. Distributors Realart knew *The Atomic Monster* would look much better on the poster.

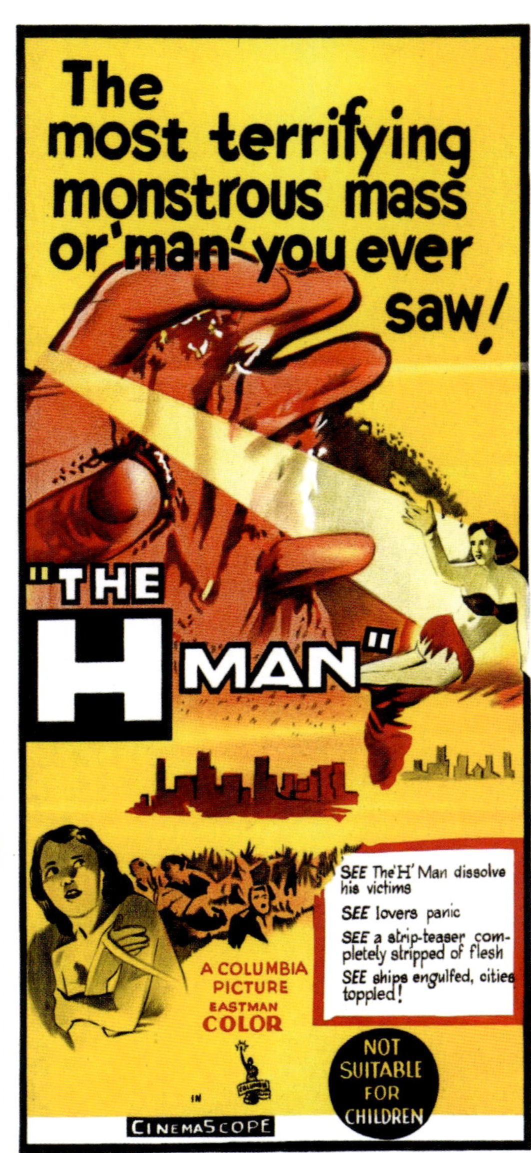

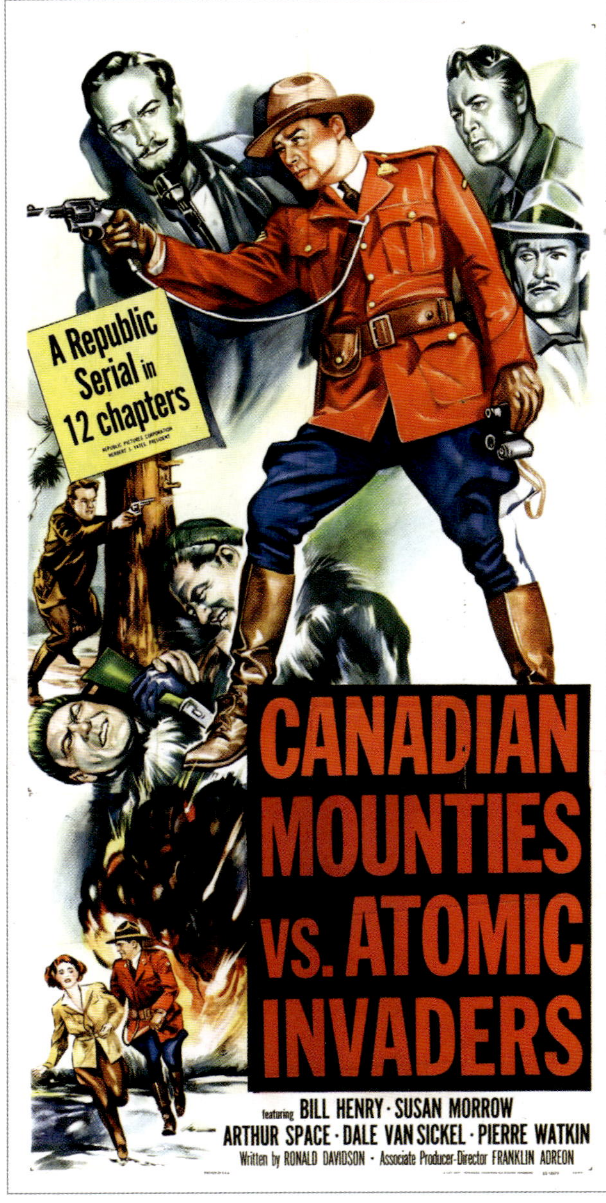

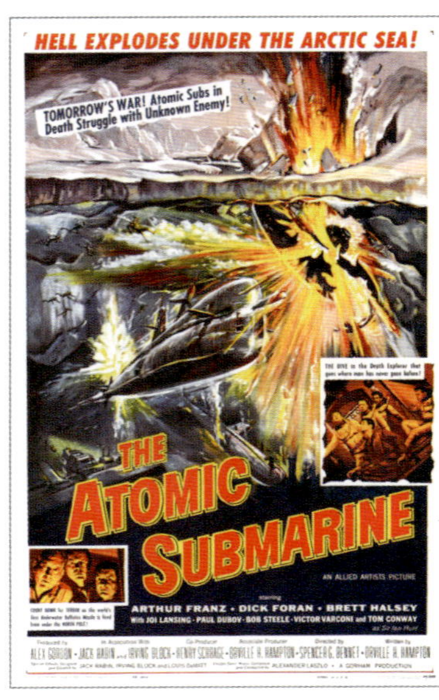

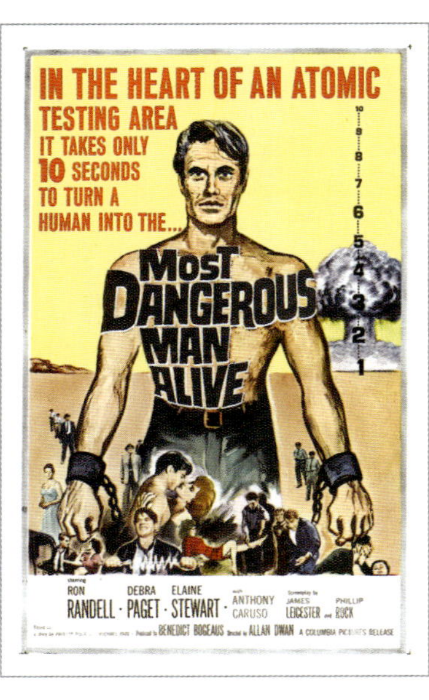

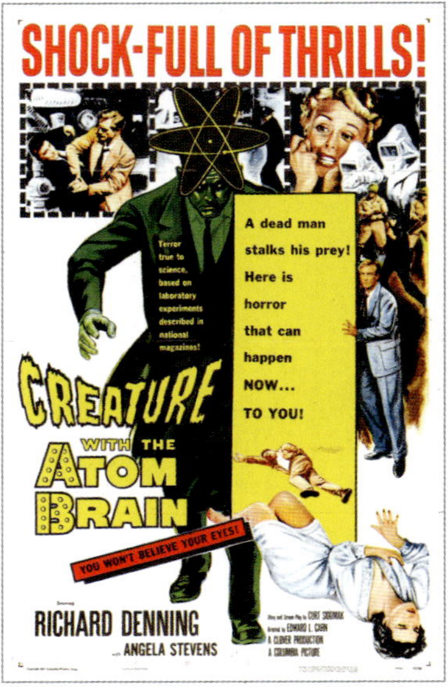

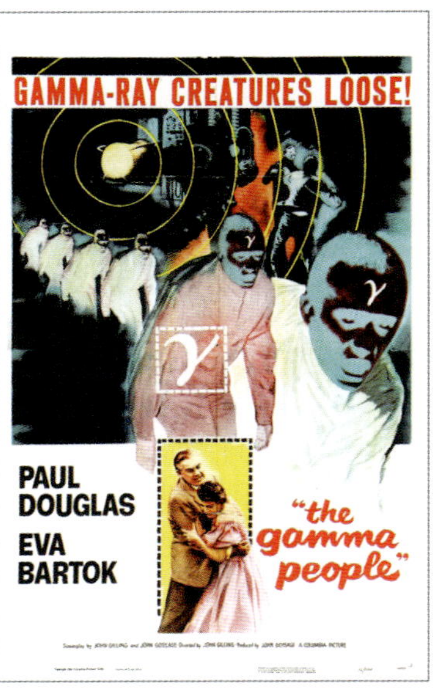

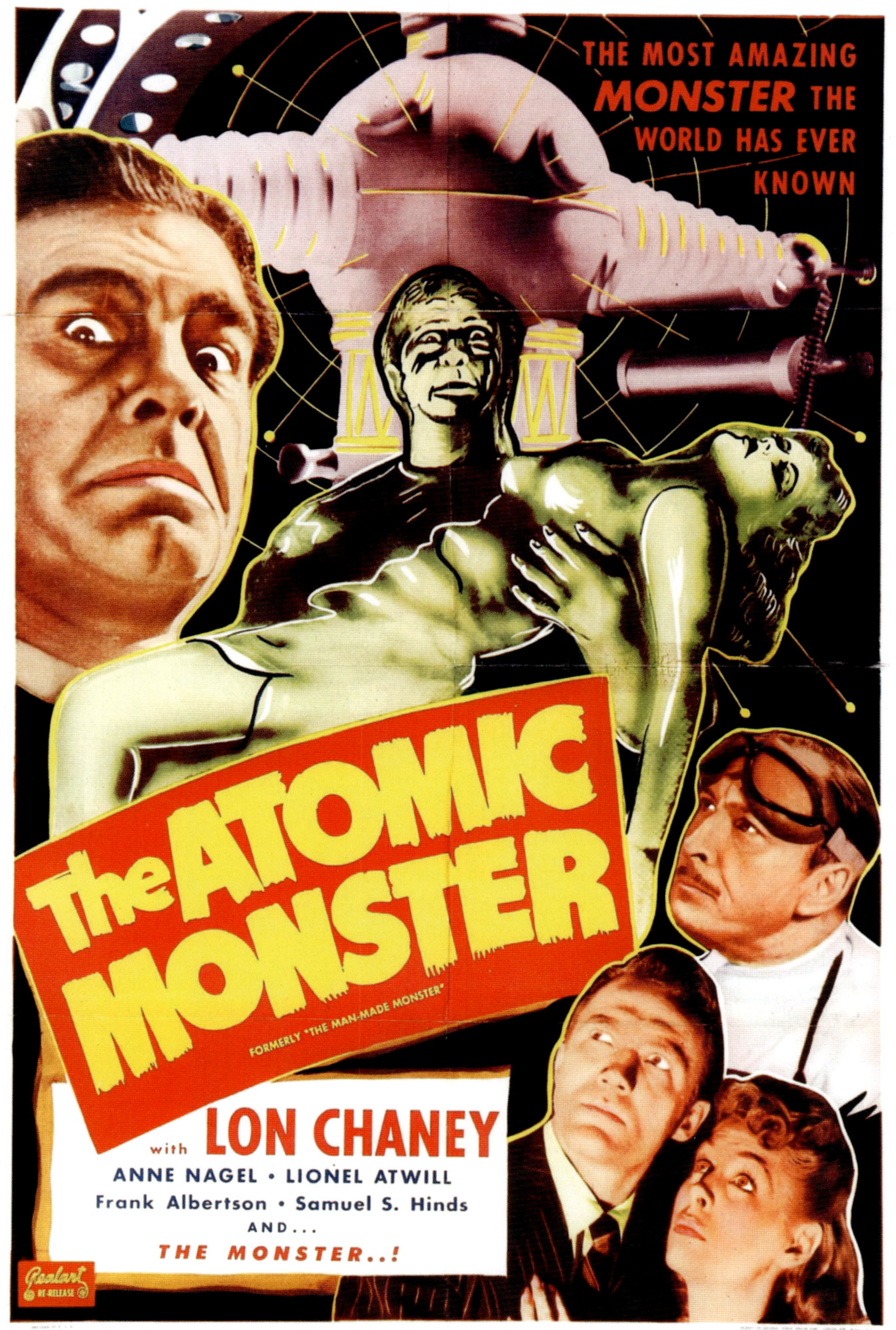
THE MOST AMAZING
MONSTER THE
WORLD HAS EVER
KNOWN
The ATOMIC MONSTER
FORMERLY "THE MAN-MADE MONSTER"
with LON CHANEY
ANNE NAGEL • LIONEL ATWILL
Frank Albertson • Samuel S. Hinds
AND...
THE MONSTER..!
Realart
RE-RELEASE

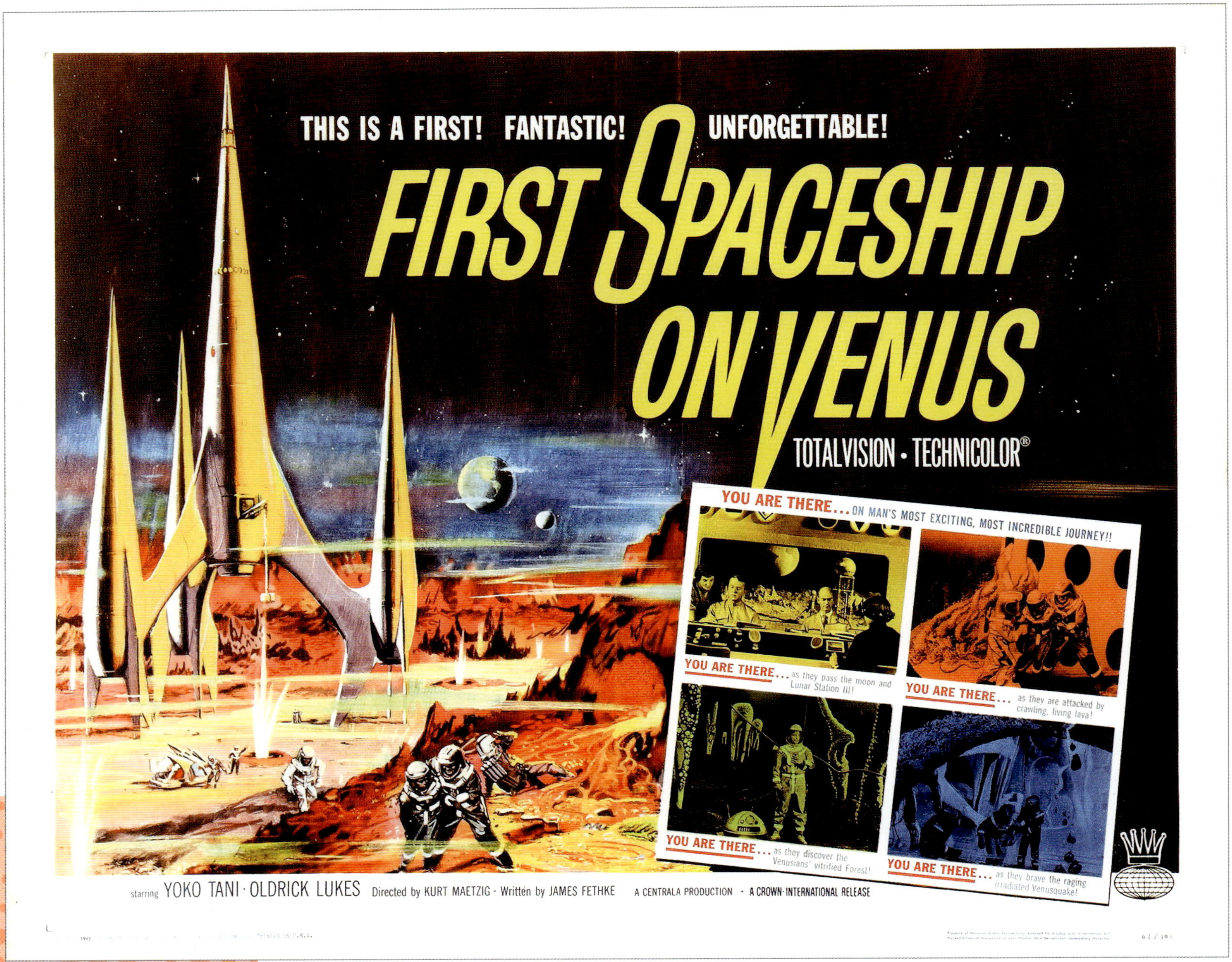

THIS IS A FIRST! FANTASTIC! UNFORGETTABLE!

FIRST SPACESHIP ON VENUS

TOTALVISION · TECHNICOLOR®

YOU ARE THERE... ON MAN'S MOST EXCITING, MOST INCREDIBLE JOURNEY!!

YOU ARE THERE... as they pass the moon and Lunar Station III!

YOU ARE THERE... as they are attacked by crawling, living lava!

YOU ARE THERE... as they discover the Venusians' vitrified Forest!

YOU ARE THERE... as they brave the raging irradiated Venusquake!

starring YOKO TANI · OLDRICK LUKES Directed by KURT MAETZIG · Written by JAMES FETHKE A CENTRALA PRODUCTION · A CROWN-INTERNATIONAL RELEASE

INTO SPACE

Even before the launch of Sputnik in 1957 got the space race fully underway, it seemed inevitable that mankind would be going into orbit, and would then choose to go to the moon, so it was up to filmmakers to stay ahead of the headlines. Some producers began to emphasize the "sci" over the "fi" in their space pictures, highlighting the "you are there" accuracy of the production (however wildly inaccurate it actually was). "Gravity zero! I've broken into outer space!" enthuses a character on the poster for *Riders to the Stars* (overleaf), which sounds odd to today's ears, but think about it: back in 1954 when the film was released, the term "zero gravity" had not been established in regular usage.

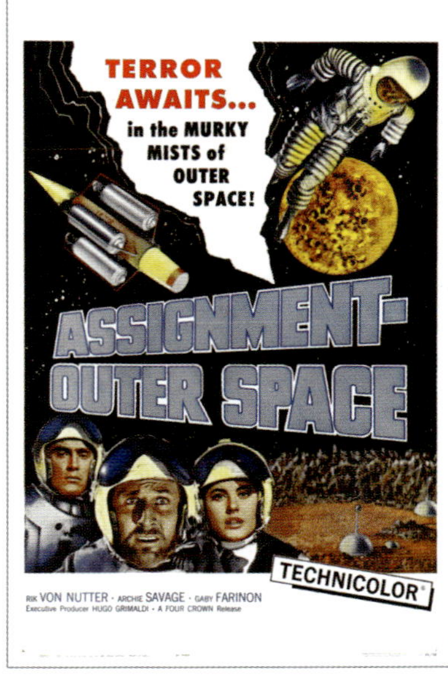

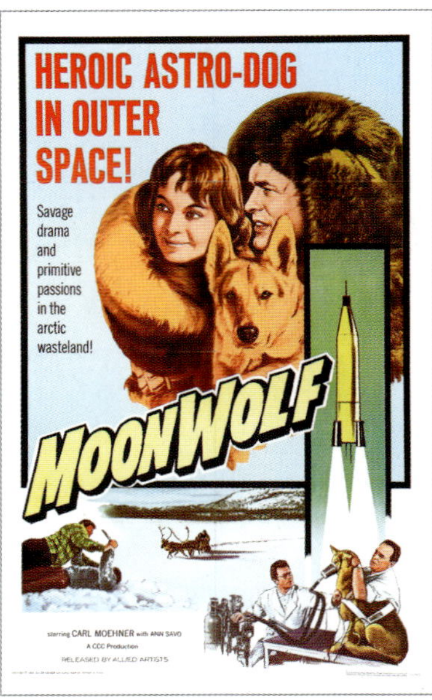

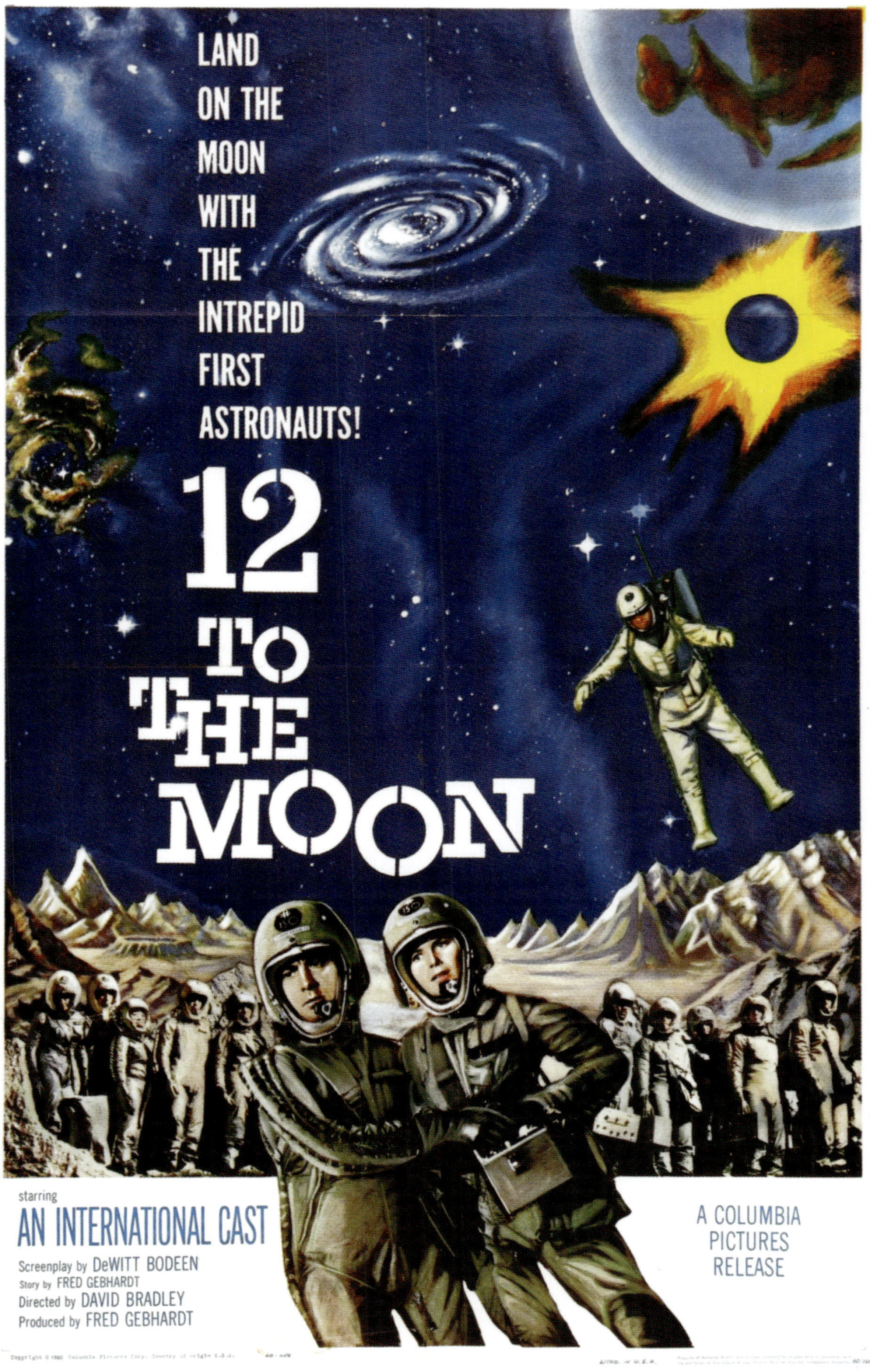

LAND ON THE MOON WITH THE INTREPID FIRST ASTRONAUTS!

12 TO THE MOON

starring

AN INTERNATIONAL CAST

Screenplay by DeWITT BODEEN
Story by FRED GEBHARDT
Directed by DAVID BRADLEY
Produced by FRED GEBHARDT

A COLUMBIA PICTURES RELEASE

MASSIMO BERNARDI E DIEGO SPATARO PRESENTANO PER LA ELEKTRA FILM
IN COLLABORAZIONE CON RALPH ZUCKER

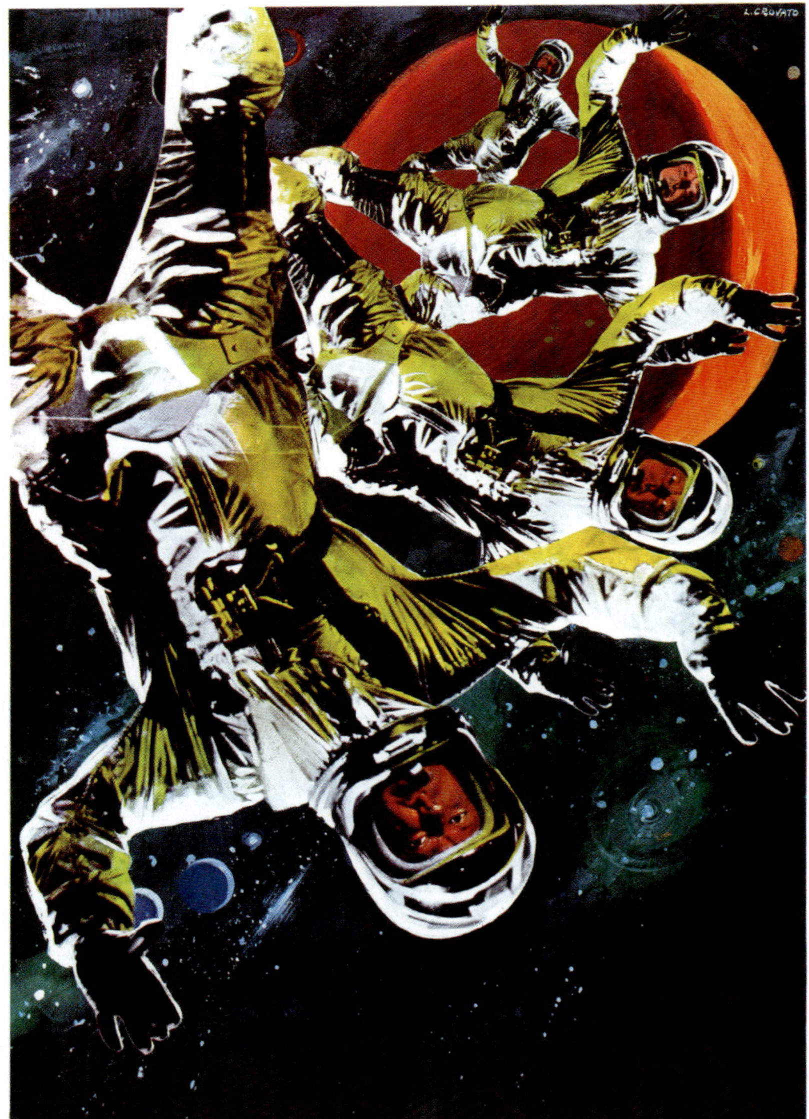

SOYUX-111
TERRORE SU VENERE

CON MICHAIL POSTNIKOW - OLDRICH LUKES
IGNACY MACHOWSKI E CON YOKO TANI NEL RUOLO DI «SUMIKO»
E CON OMEGA IL ROBOT REGIA DI KURT MAETZIG
UNA COPRODUZIONE VEB-DEFA
SUPERCOLOR - SISTEMA TECHNIMATION - STEREOSCOPE '70
FILMSERVICE ROMA ANNO DI PRIMA EDIZIONE 1972

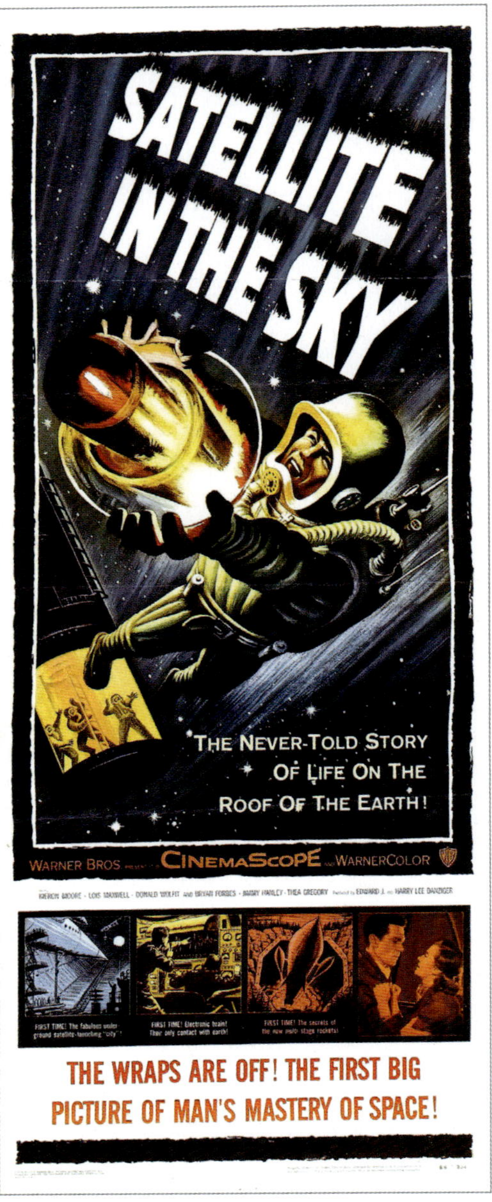

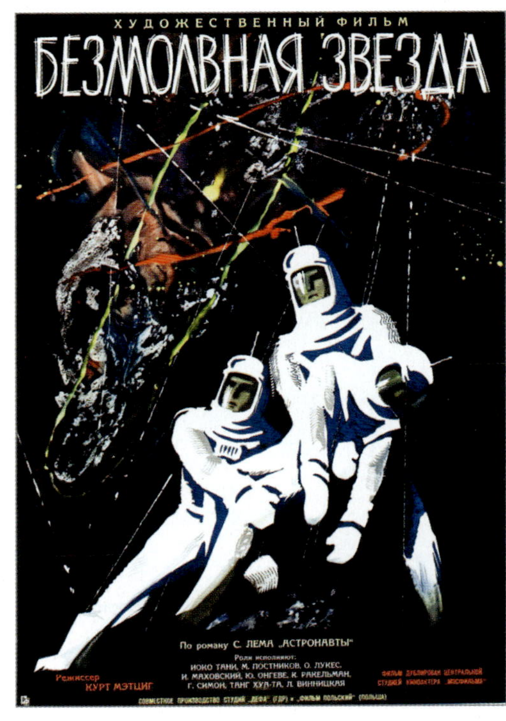

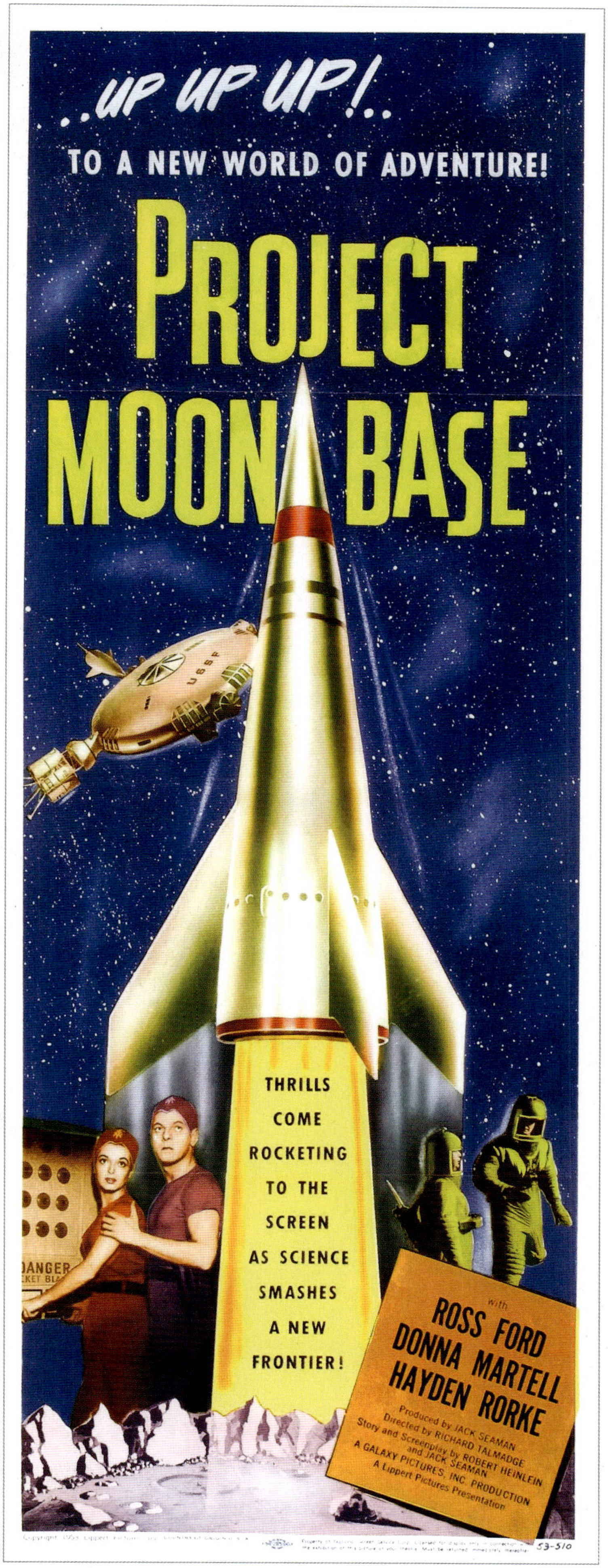

..UP UP UP!..

TO A NEW WORLD OF ADVENTURE!

PROJECT MOON BASE

THRILLS COME ROCKETING TO THE SCREEN AS SCIENCE SMASHES A NEW FRONTIER!

with
ROSS FORD
DONNA MARTELL
HAYDEN RORKE

Produced by JACK SEAMAN
Directed by RICHARD TALMADGE
Story and Screenplay by ROBERT HEINLEIN and JACK SEAMAN
A GALAXY PICTURES, INC. PRODUCTION
A Lippert Pictures Presentation

53-510

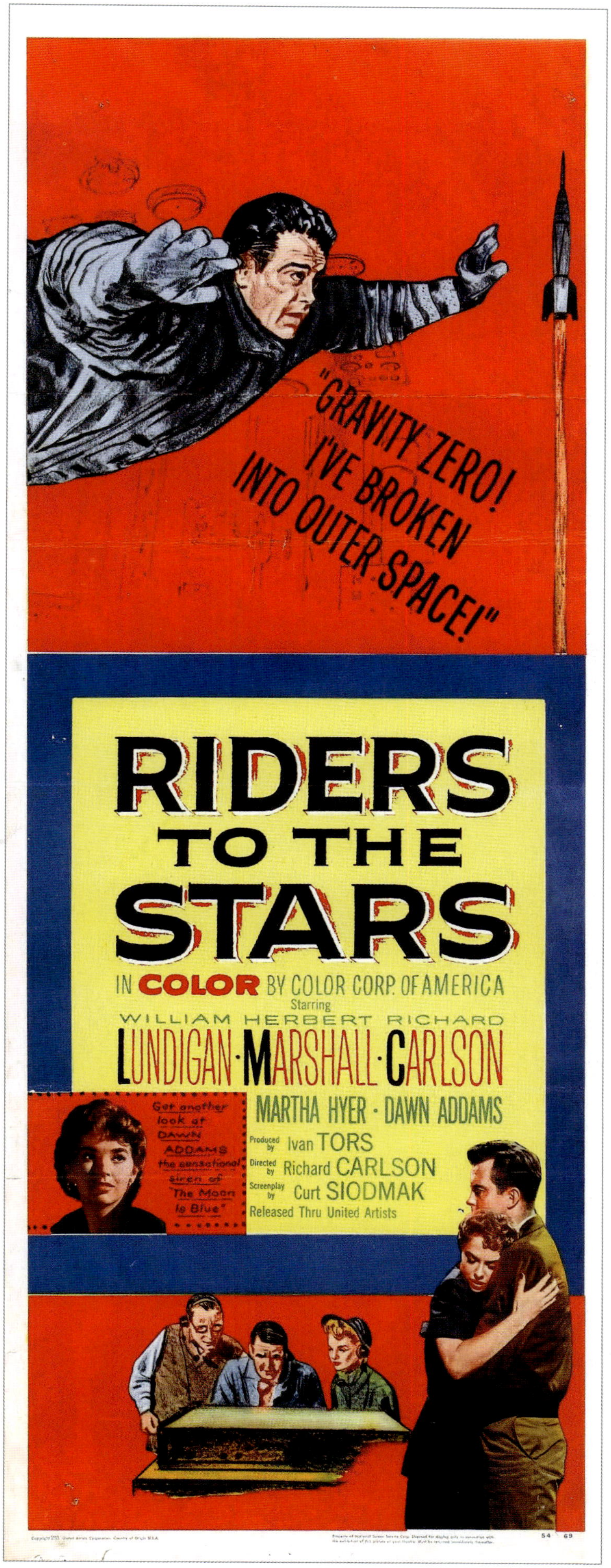

"GRAVITY ZERO! I'VE BROKEN INTO OUTER SPACE!"

RIDERS TO THE STARS

IN COLOR BY COLOR CORP. OF AMERICA
Starring
WILLIAM LUNDIGAN · HERBERT MARSHALL · RICHARD CARLSON
MARTHA HYER · DAWN ADDAMS

Get another look at DAWN ADDAMS the sensational siren of "The Moon Is Blue"

Produced by Ivan TORS
Directed by Richard CARLSON
Screenplay by Curt SIODMAK
Released Thru United Artists

54 69

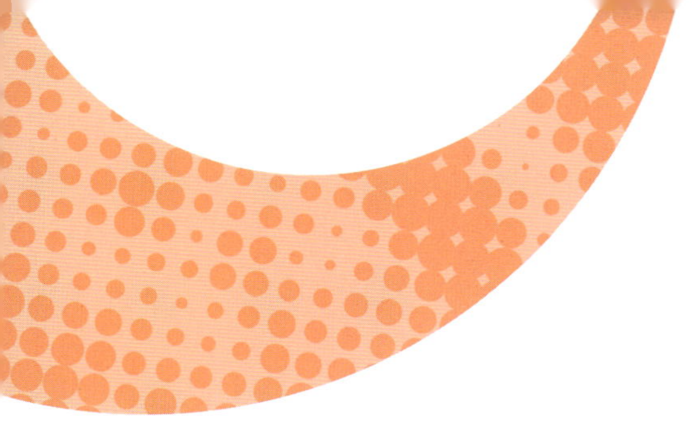

MARS

The movie business was mounting missions to the Red Planet way ahead of NASA's first probe. Decades before Matt Damon's marooned Martian was forced to "science the shit" out of his predicament, the posters for *Robinson Crusoe on Mars* (1964) proclaimed, "This film is scientifically authentic . . . it is only one step ahead of present reality!" It wasn't true then, and sadly still isn't today, but that mattered little to the producers of *Santo vs. la invasion de los marcianos* (Santo vs. the Invasion of the Martians, 1967), which cheekily aped its poster design, although the masked *lucha libre* hero doesn't brandish a raygun or indeed go to Mars in the film. He does wrestle plenty of Martians, though.

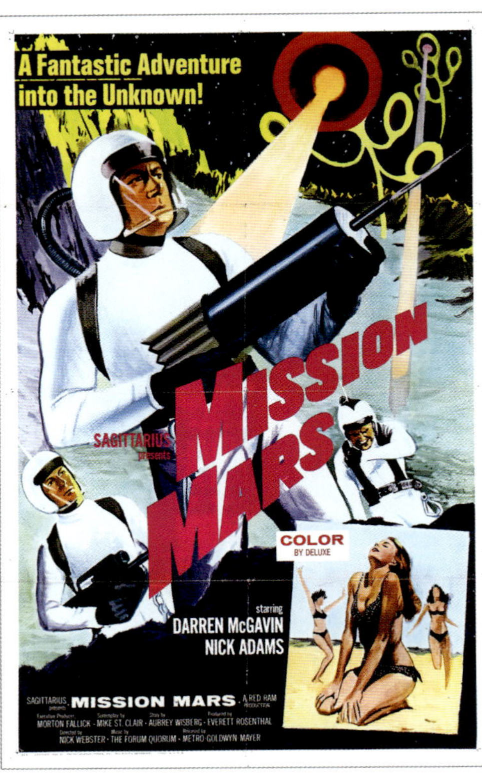

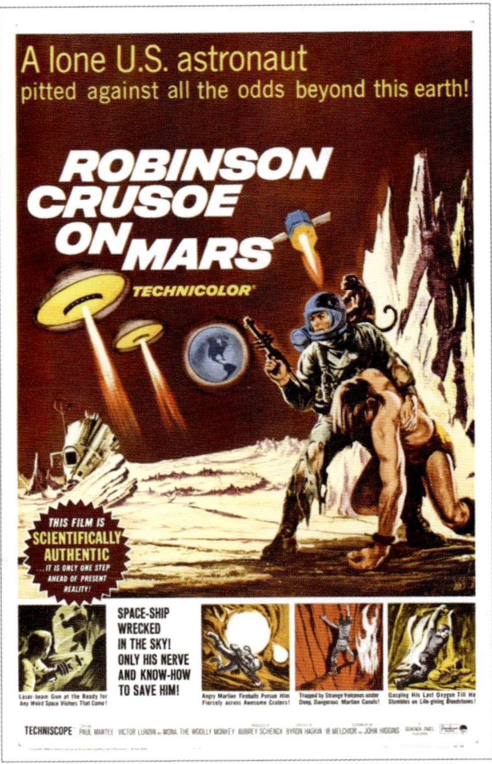

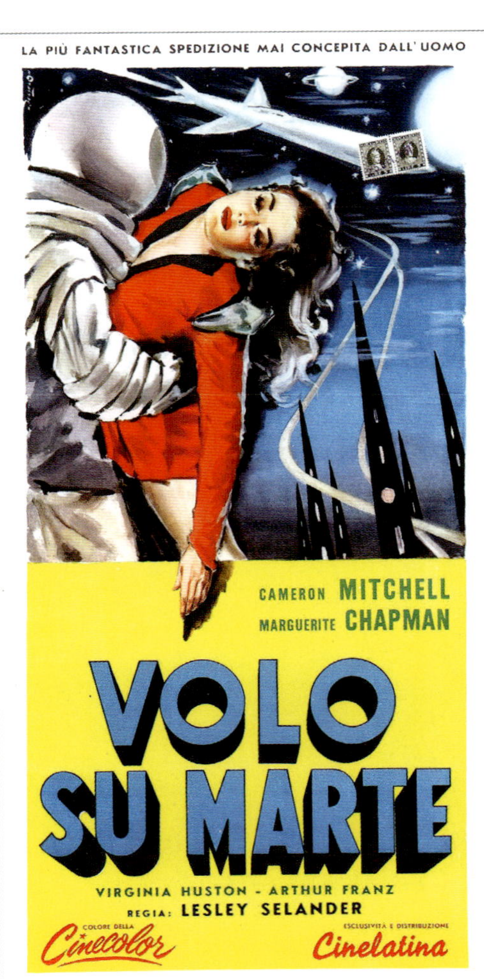

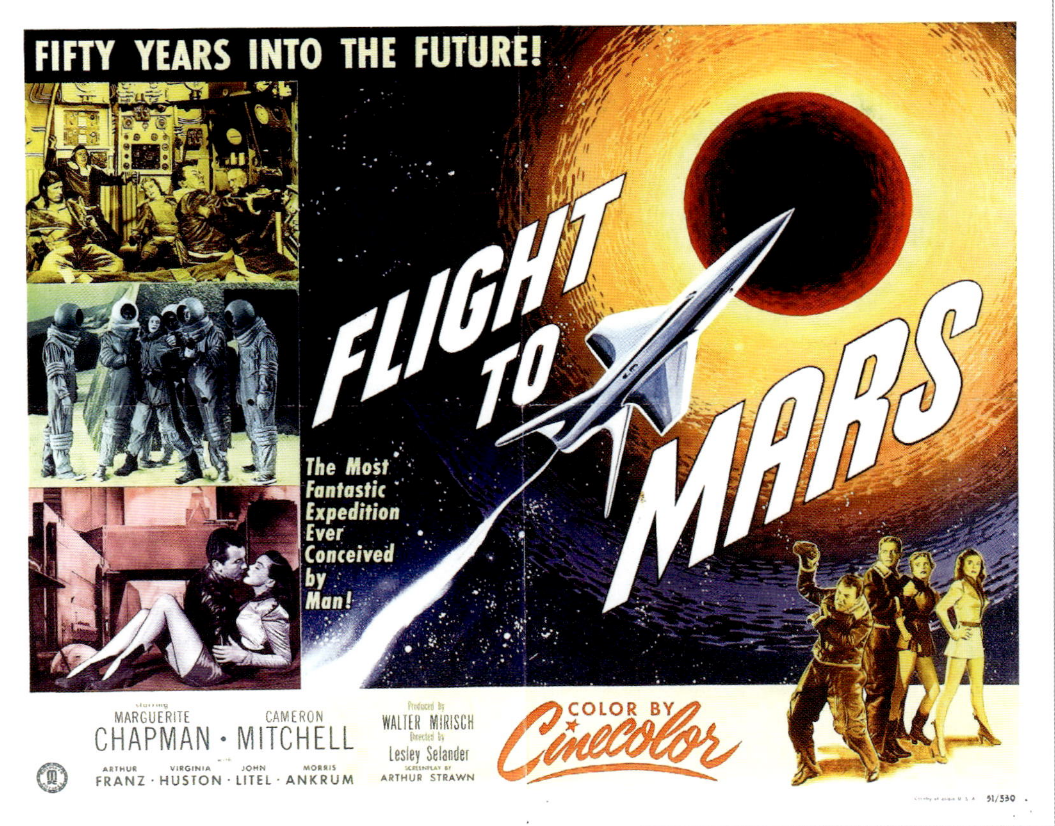

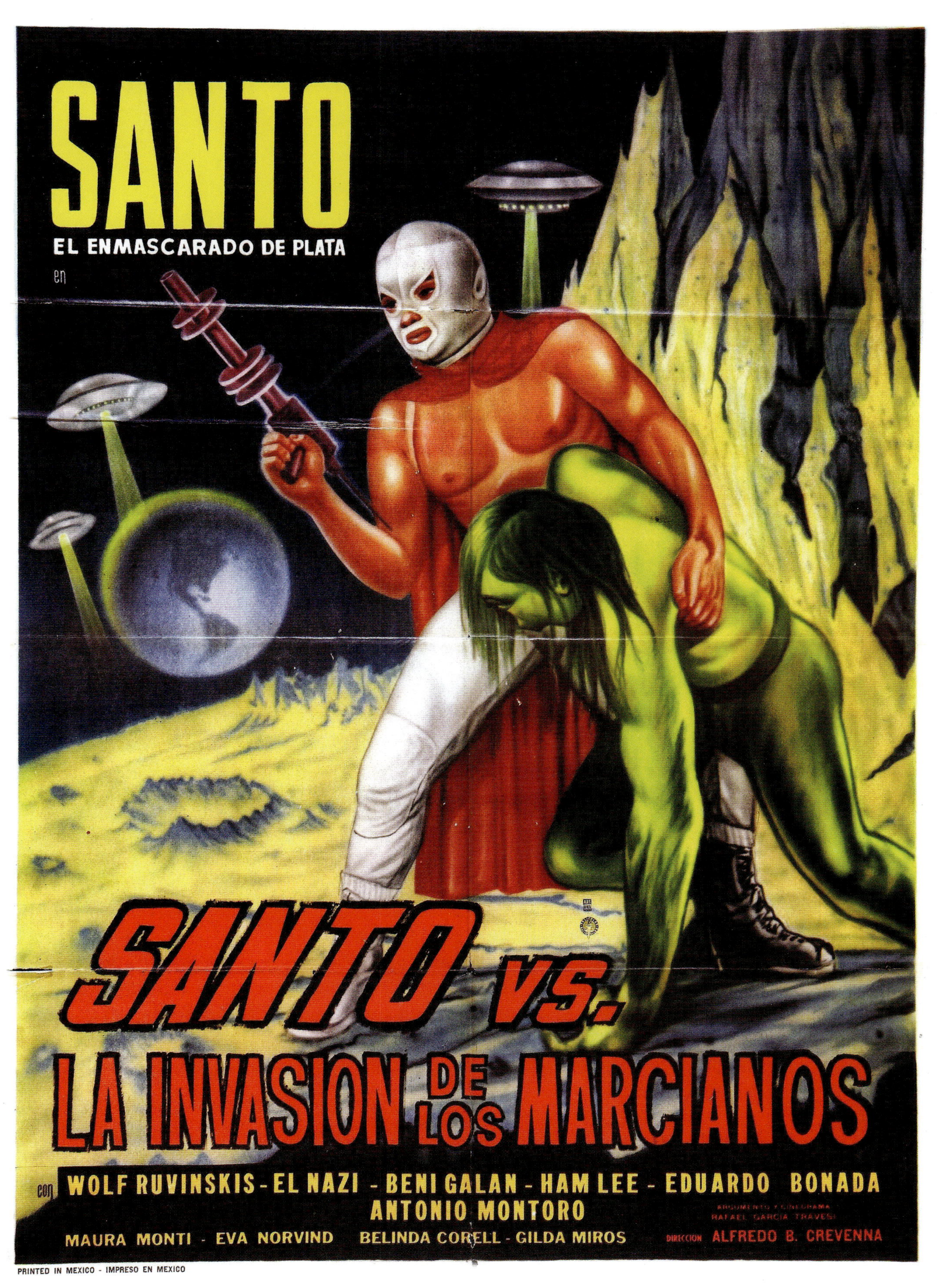
SANTO
EL ENMASCARADO DE PLATA
en
SANTO VS.
LA INVASION DE LOS MARCIANOS
con WOLF RUVINSKIS - EL NAZI - BENI GALAN - HAM LEE - EDUARDO BONADA
ANTONIO MONTORO
MAURA MONTI - EVA NORVIND BELINDA CORELL - GILDA MIROS
DIRECCION ALFREDO B. CREVENNA
PRINTED IN MEXICO - IMPRESO EN MEXICO

WOMEN FROM SPACE!

Even before *Star Trek* firmly entrenched the fact by adhering to it week-in, week-out, it had been established that outer space was as full of buxom women as it was of monsters. Foremost among them was Zsa Zsa Gabor in *Queen of Outer Space* (1958), a low-budget, not entirely serious film that recycled costumes from *Forbidden Planet*, and was praised by *Variety* as "a good-natured attempt to put some honest sex into science-fiction." The preening star was far from good-natured though. "She was not thoroughly professional, she didn't have her lines well prepared," remembered director Edward Bernds, adding that he never watched the film if it came on TV, as "Zsa Zsa Gabor still gives me a swift pain."

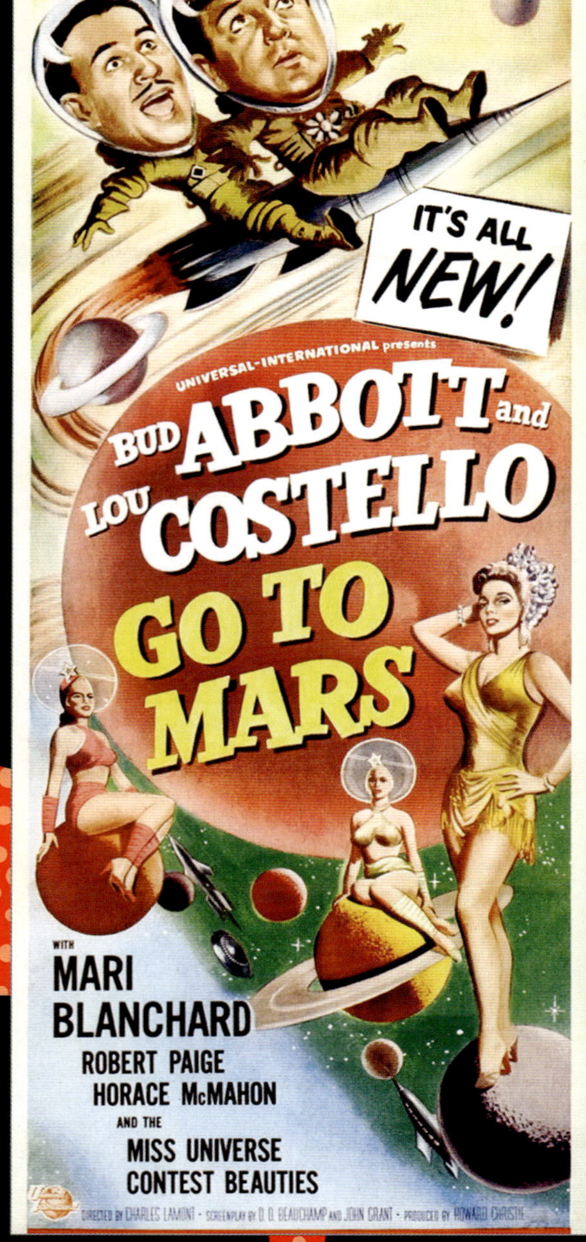

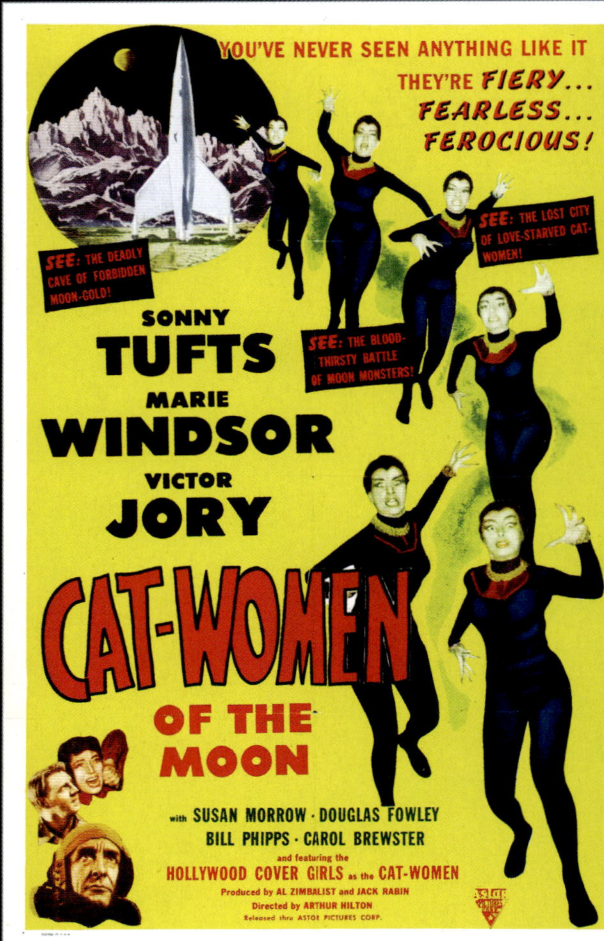

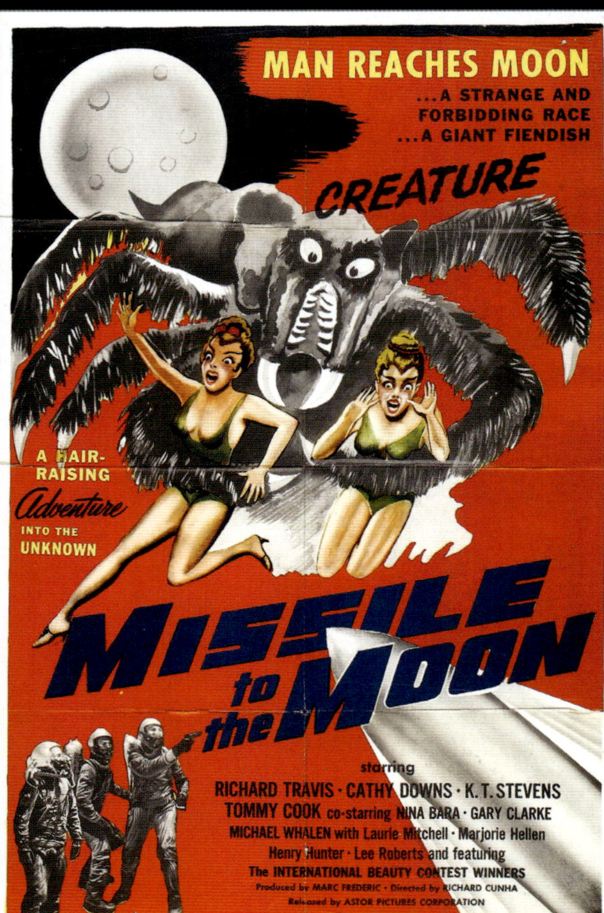

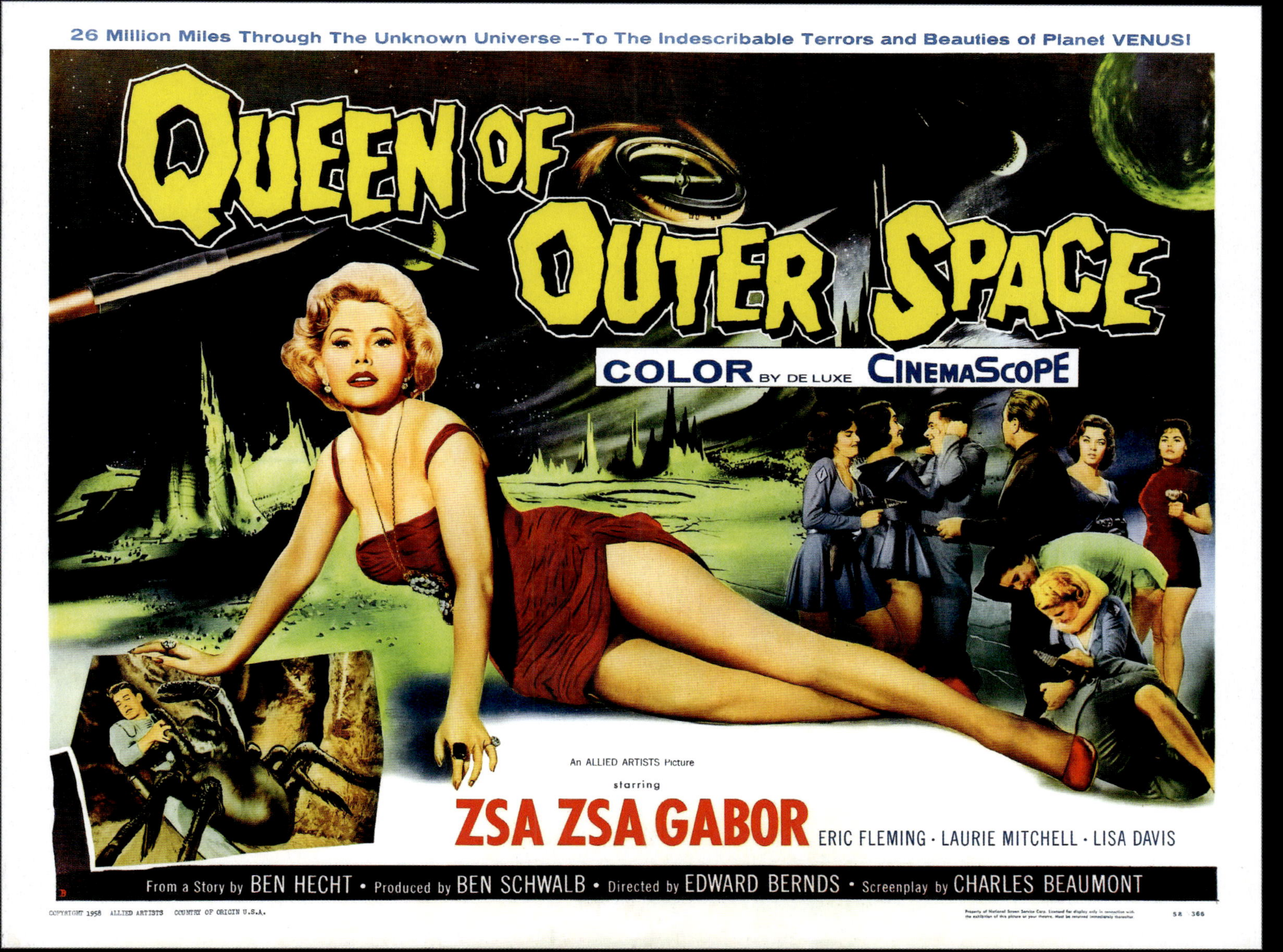

26 Million Miles Through The Unknown Universe -- To The Indescribable Terrors and Beauties of Planet VENUS!

QUEEN OF OUTER SPACE

COLOR BY DE LUXE CINEMASCOPE

An ALLIED ARTISTS Picture

starring

ZSA ZSA GABOR ERIC FLEMING · LAURIE MITCHELL · LISA DAVIS

From a Story by BEN HECHT • Produced by BEN SCHWALB • Directed by EDWARD BERNDS • Screenplay by CHARLES BEAUMONT

COPYRIGHT 1958 ALLIED ARTISTS COUNTRY OF ORIGIN U.S.A.

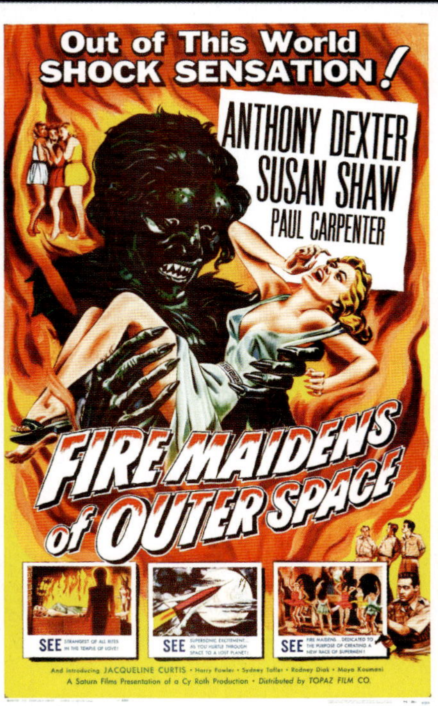

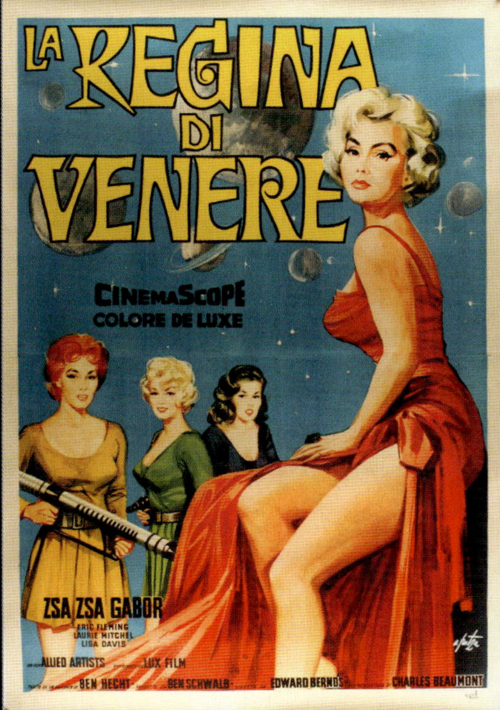

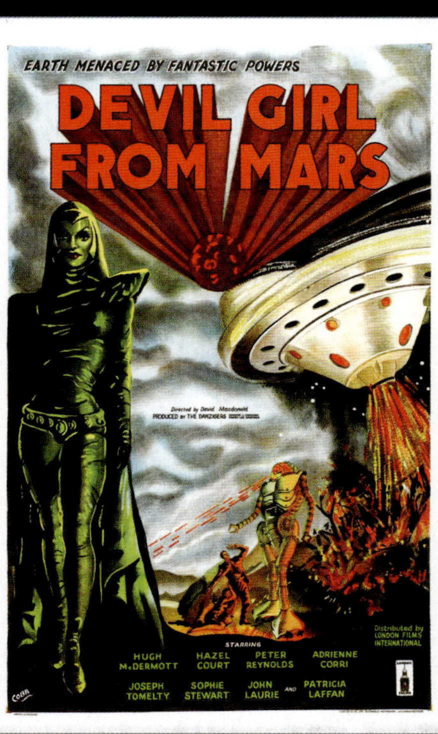

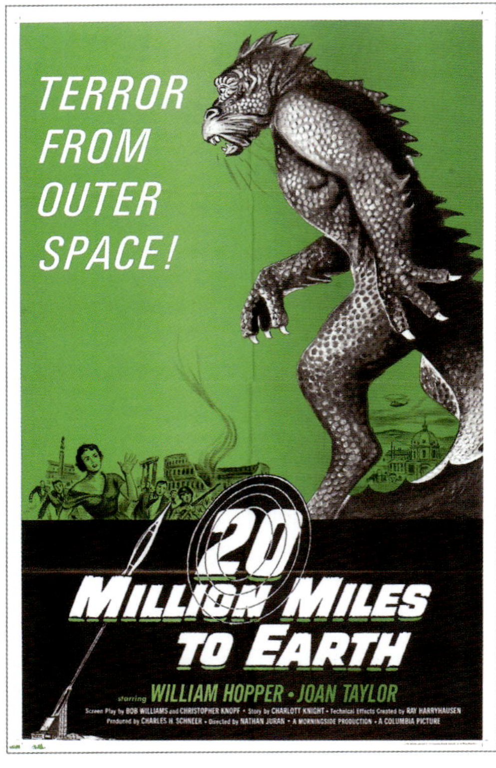

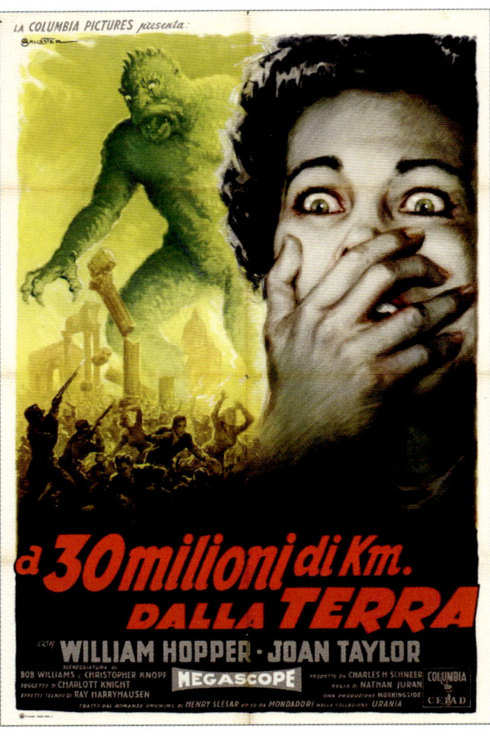

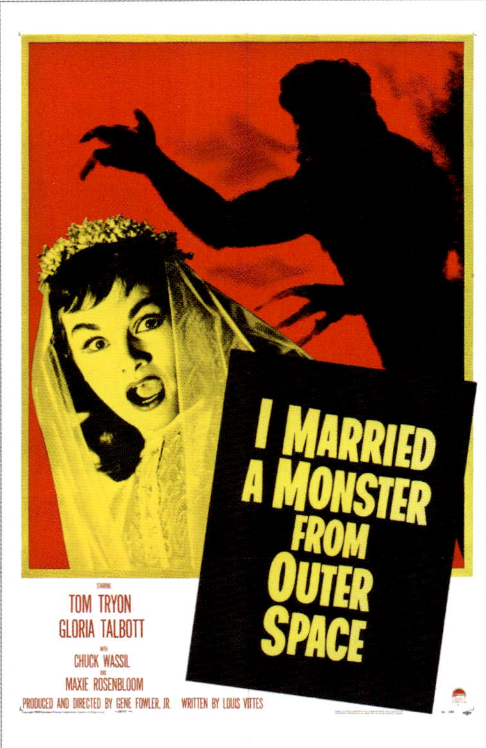

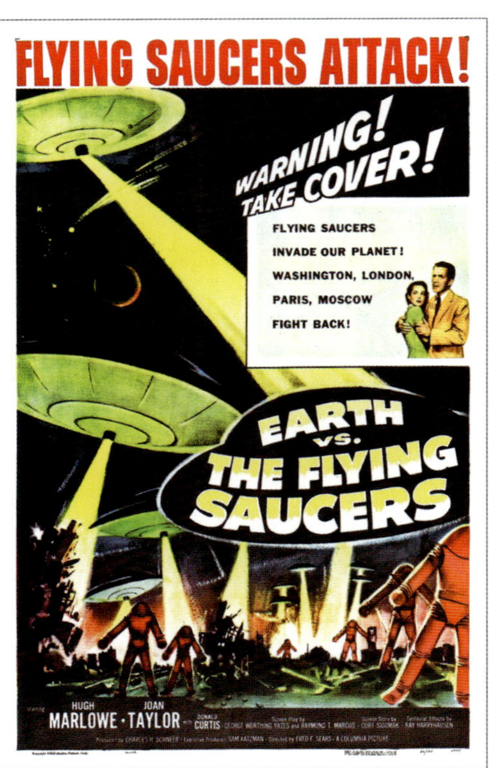

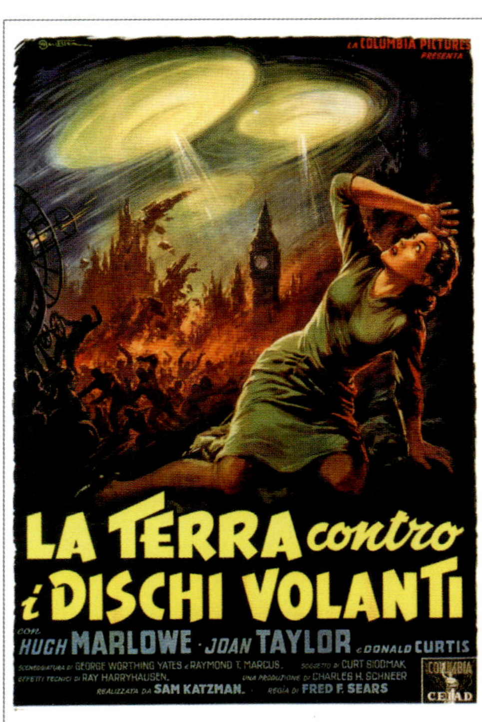

US VS. ITALY

Whether it was fashion, motorcars, or film posters, in the '50s you could rely on Italy to really elevate design to new heights of style. The rather functional US one-sheets shown here are utterly eclipsed by their amazing Italian counterparts. Anselmo Ballester's paintings for *Earth vs. the Flying Saucers* (1956) and *20 Million Miles to Earth* (1957) are working with the same basic elements as the American designs—actress Joan Taylor being menaced by saucers and Ray Harryhausen's giant monster respectively—but his compositions and stunning use of color ensure immense impact. M. Copizzi's *foglio* for *I Married a Monster from Outer Space* (1958) similarly transforms and augments a film still of a screaming Gloria Talbott into something genuinely eerie.

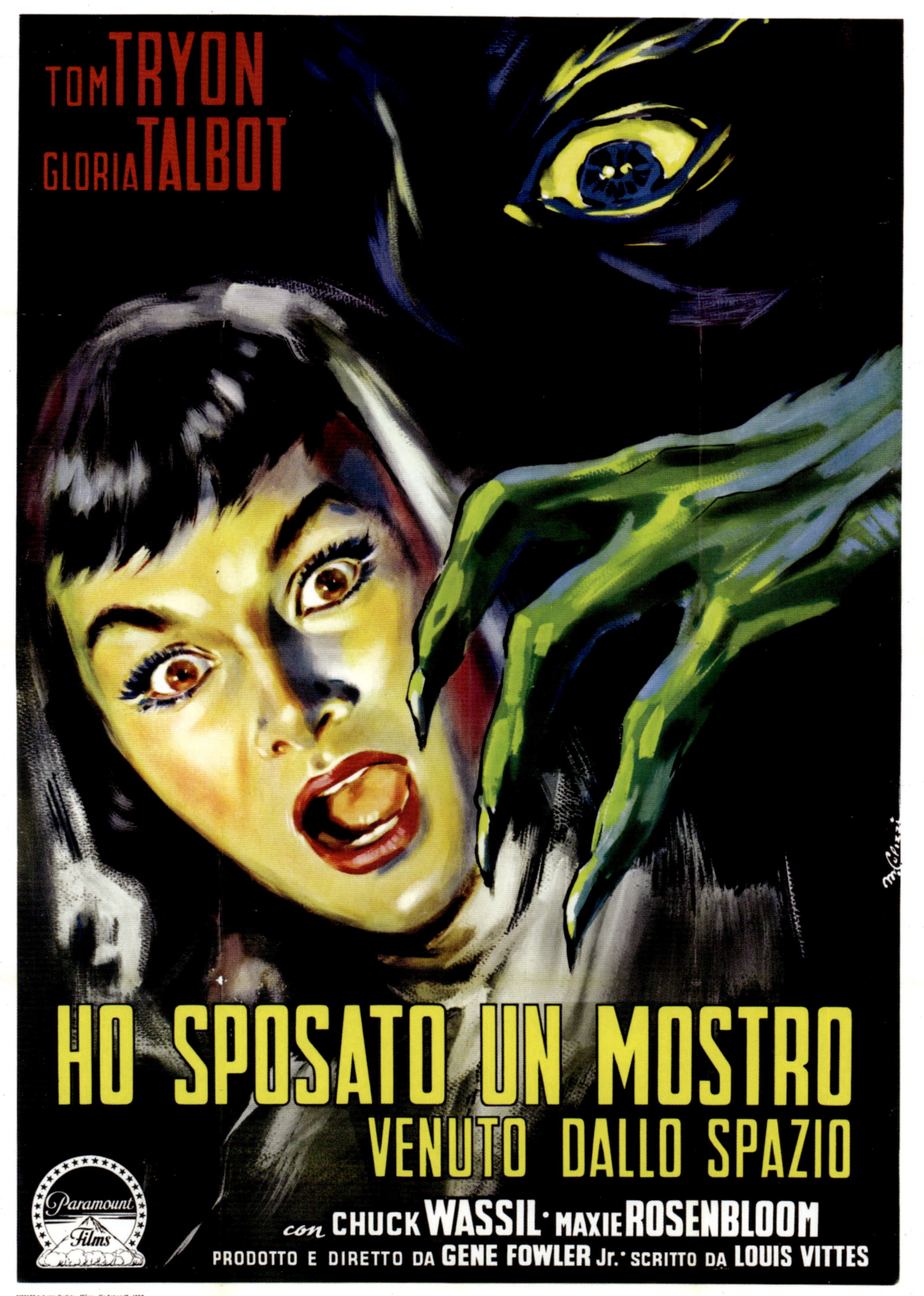
TOM TRYON
GLORIA TALBOT
HO SPOSATO UN MOSTRO
VENUTO DALLO SPAZIO
Paramount Films
con CHUCK WASSIL · MAXIE ROSENBLOOM
PRODOTTO E DIRETTO DA GENE FOWLER Jr. · SCRITTO DA LOUIS VITTES

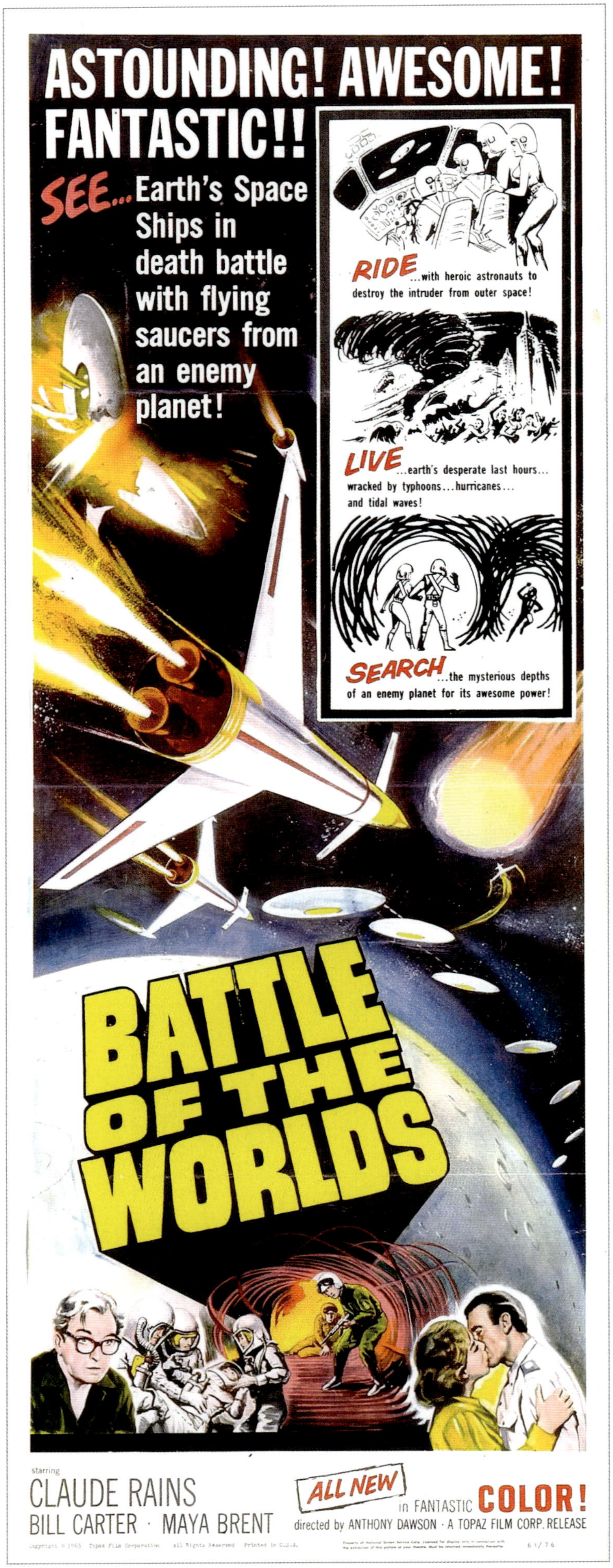

ASTOUNDING! AWESOME! FANTASTIC!!

SEE... Earth's Space Ships in death battle with flying saucers from an enemy planet!

RIDE ...with heroic astronauts to destroy the intruder from outer space!

LIVE ...earth's desperate last hours... wracked by typhoons...hurricanes... and tidal waves!

SEARCH ...the mysterious depths of an enemy planet for its awesome power!

BATTLE OF THE WORLDS

starring

CLAUDE RAINS

BILL CARTER · MAYA BRENT

ALL NEW in FANTASTIC COLOR!

directed by ANTHONY DAWSON · A TOPAZ FILM CORP. RELEASE

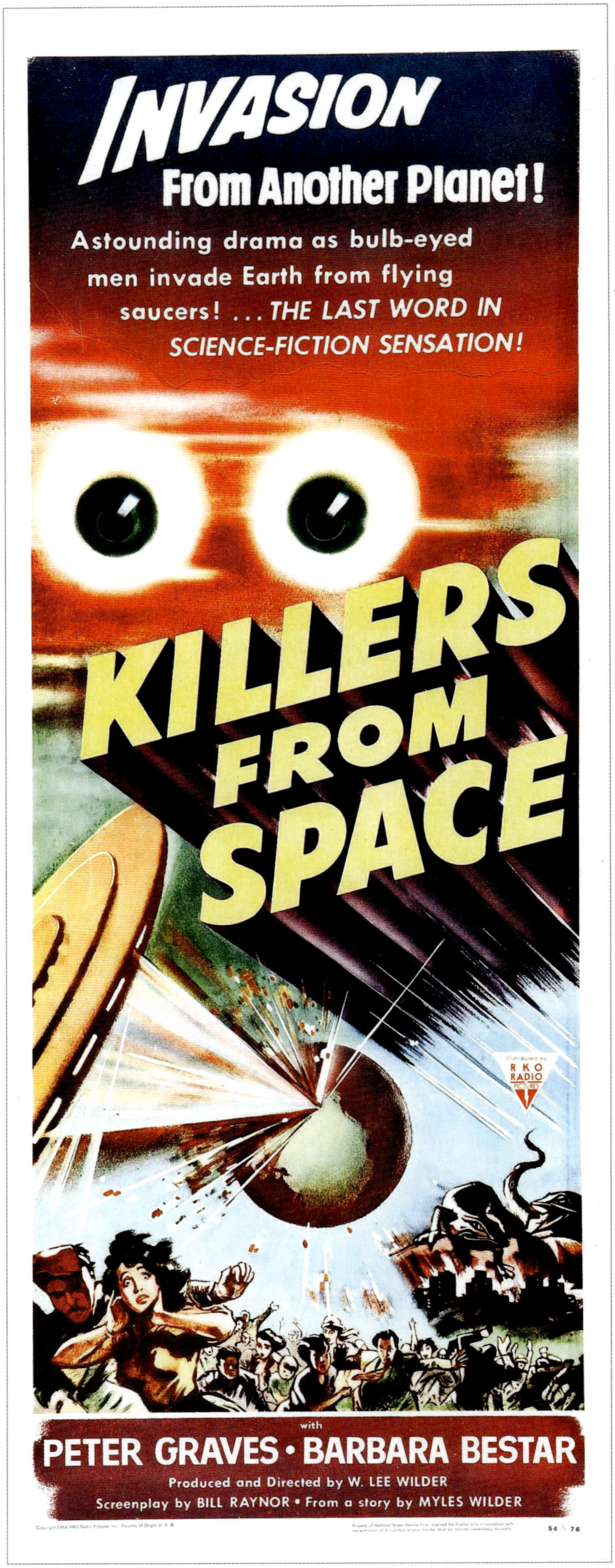

63/76

INVASION From Another Planet!

Astounding drama as bulb-eyed men invade Earth from flying saucers! ...THE LAST WORD IN SCIENCE-FICTION SENSATION!

KILLERS FROM SPACE

Distributed by RKO RADIO PICTURES

with

PETER GRAVES · BARBARA BESTAR

Produced and Directed by W. LEE WILDER

Screenplay by BILL RAYNOR • From a story by MYLES WILDER

54 \ 76

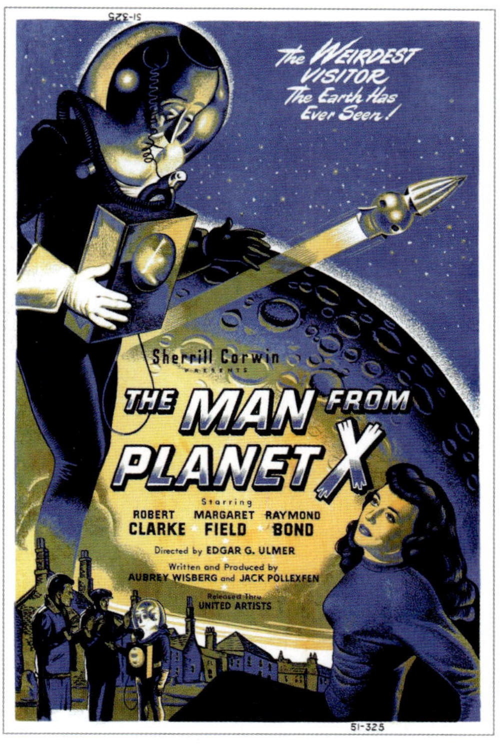

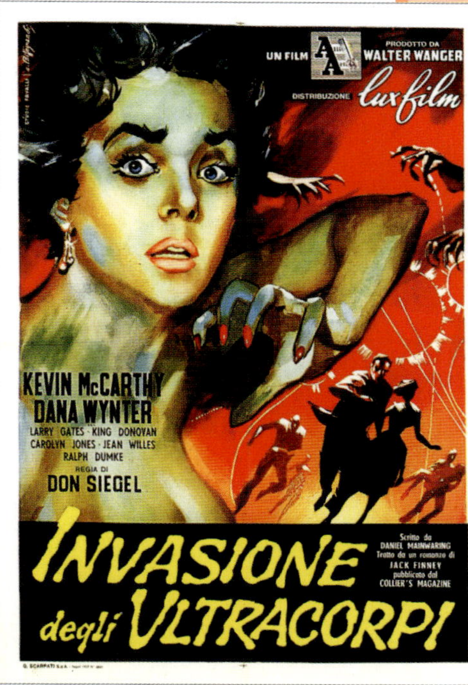

INVASION!

The USA in the 1950s was a paranoid place. Senator McCarthy's House Un-American Activities Committee and the FBI under J. Edgar Hoover were doing their best to convince the public that there was a "Red" under every bed, and the mounting tensions of the Cold War meant death from the skies was becoming a very real possibility. It's become a cliché to point out that the alien invasion movies from the period were really all about "the Commies," but that doesn't mean it isn't true . . . One film illustrated here, *Invasion, U.S.A.* (1952), eschewed saucers, Triffids, body snatchers, or bulb-eyed men, and simply showed an unnamed communist country attacking. The prominent puff quote on the poster from Hedda Hopper is no surprise: the famous gossip columnist had "named names" to McCarthy.

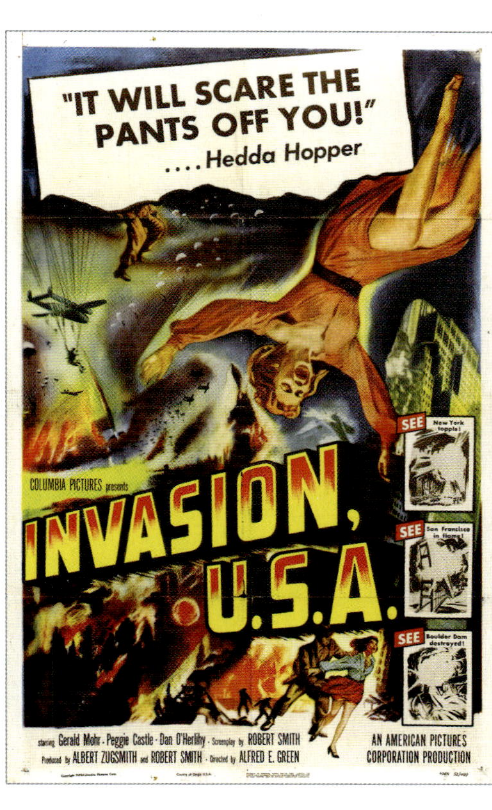

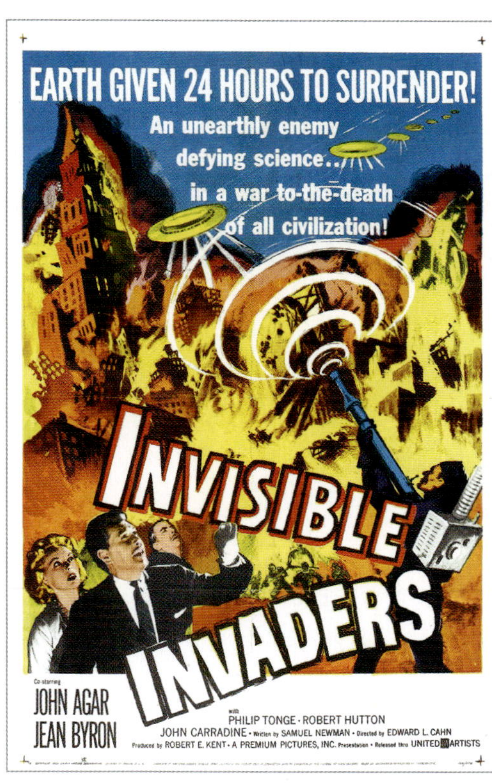

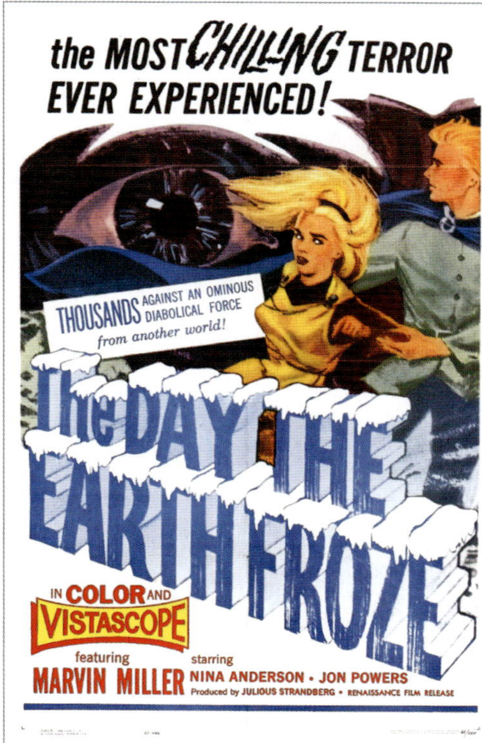

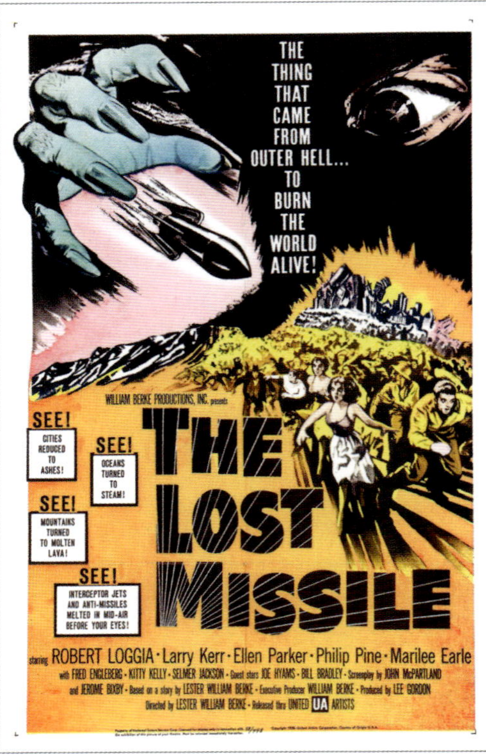
THE THING THAT CAME FROM OUTER HELL... TO BURN THE WORLD ALIVE!
WILLIAM BERKE PRODUCTIONS, INC. presents
SEE! CITIES REDUCED TO ASHES!
SEE! OCEANS TURNED TO STEAM!
SEE! MOUNTAINS TURNED TO MOLTEN LAVA!
SEE! INTERCEPTOR JETS AND ANTI-MISSILES MELTED IN MID-AIR BEFORE YOUR EYES!
THE LOST MISSILE
starring ROBERT LOGGIA · Larry Kerr · Ellen Parker · Philip Pine · Marilee Earle
Directed by LESTER WILLIAM BERKE · Released thru UNITED UA ARTISTS

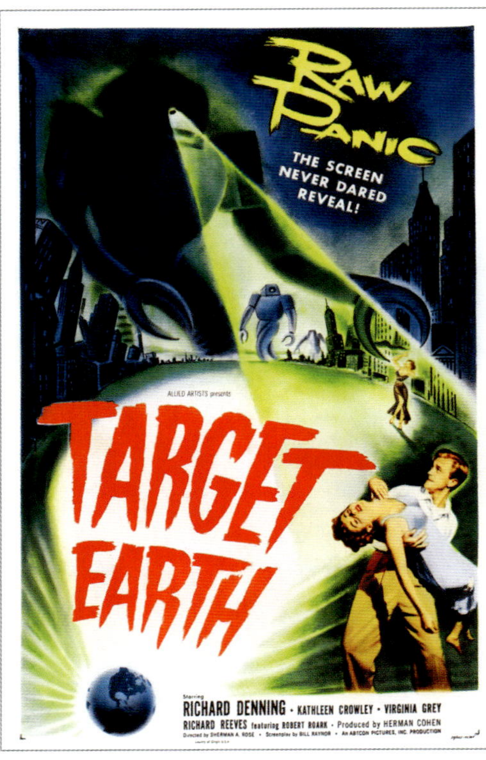
RAW PANIC
THE SCREEN NEVER DARED REVEAL!
TARGET EARTH
RICHARD DENNING · KATHLEEN CROWLEY · VIRGINIA GREY
RICHARD REEVES · Produced by HERMAN COHEN

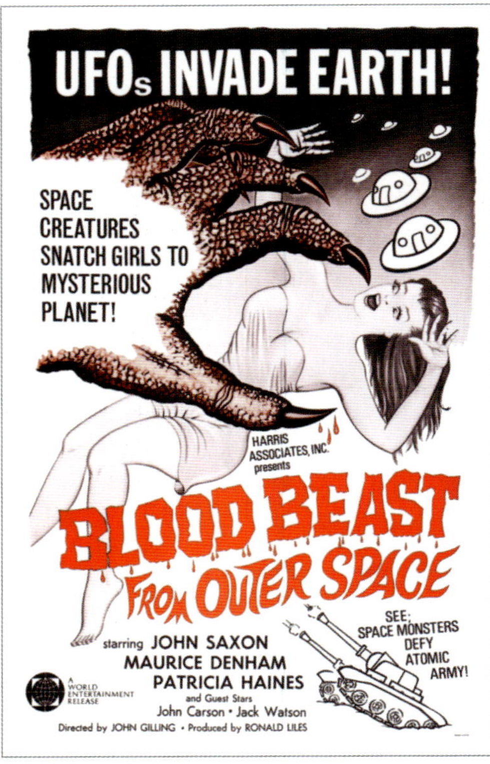
UFOs INVADE EARTH!
SPACE CREATURES SNATCH GIRLS TO MYSTERIOUS PLANET!
HARRIS ASSOCIATES, INC. presents
BLOOD BEAST FROM OUTER SPACE
SEE; SPACE MONSTERS DEFY ATOMIC ARMY!
starring JOHN SAXON
MAURICE DENHAM
PATRICIA HAINES
and Guest Stars
John Carson · Jack Watson
A WORLD ENTERTAINMENT RELEASE
Directed by JOHN GILLING · Produced by RONALD LILES

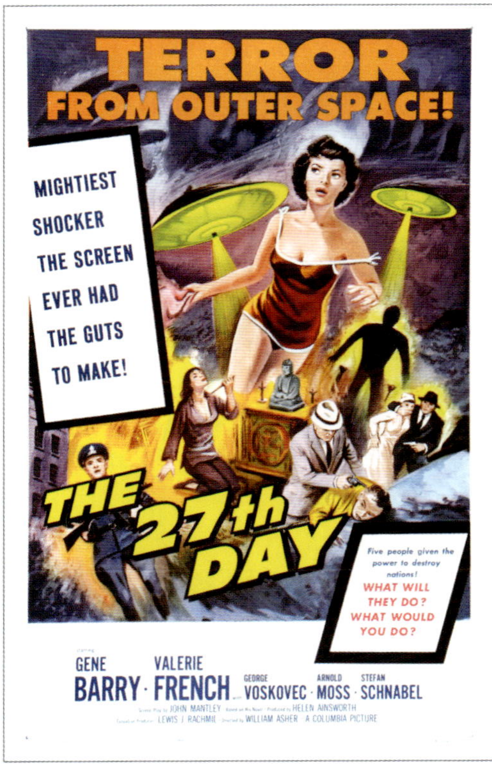
TERROR FROM OUTER SPACE!
MIGHTIEST SHOCKER THE SCREEN EVER HAD THE GUTS TO MAKE!
THE 27th DAY
Five people given the power to destroy nations! WHAT WILL THEY DO? WHAT WOULD YOU DO?
GENE BARRY · VALERIE FRENCH · GEORGE VOSKOVEC · ARNOLD MOSS · STEFAN SCHNABEL
A COLUMBIA PICTURE

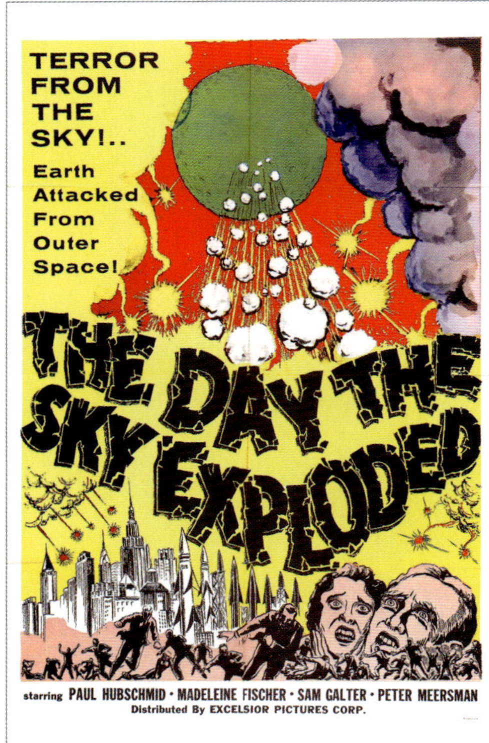
TERROR FROM THE SKY!..
Earth Attacked From Outer Space!
THE DAY THE SKY EXPLODED
starring PAUL HUBSCHMID · MADELEINE FISCHER · SAM GALTER · PETER MEERSMAN
Distributed By EXCELSIOR PICTURES CORP.

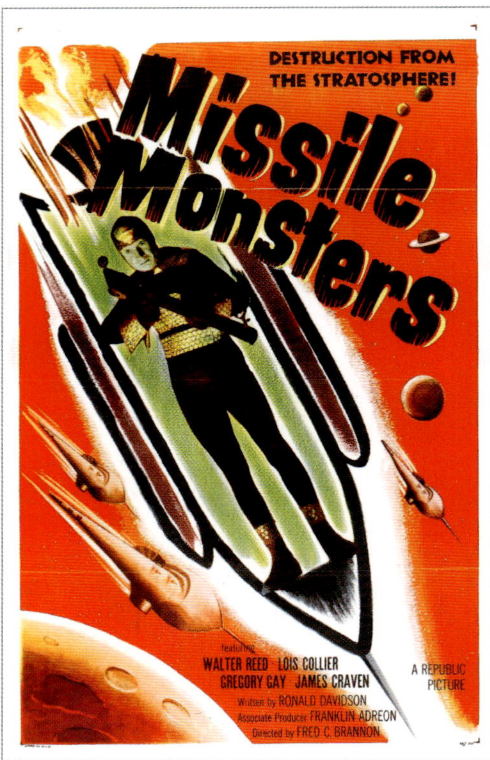
DESTRUCTION FROM THE STRATOSPHERE!
Missile Monsters
featuring WALTER REED · LOIS COLLIER
GREGORY GAY · JAMES CRAVEN
Written by RONALD DAVIDSON
Associate Producer FRANKLIN ADREON
Directed by FRED C. BRANNON
A REPUBLIC PICTURE

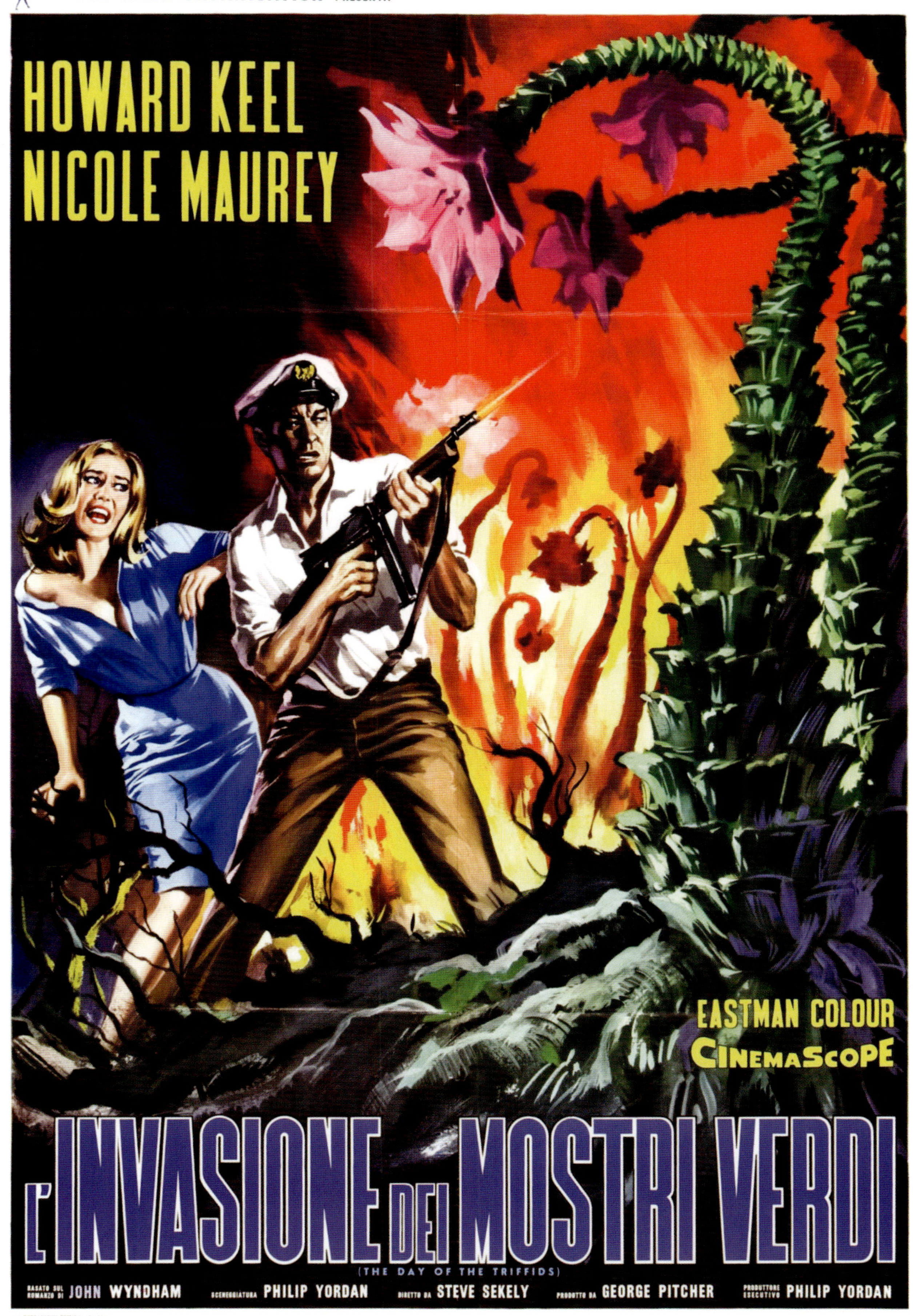
THE RANK ORGANISATION PRESENTA
HOWARD KEEL
NICOLE MAUREY
EASTMAN COLOUR
CINEMASCOPE
L'INVASIONE DEI MOSTRI VERDI
(THE DAY OF THE TRIFFIDS)
BASATO SUL ROMANZO DI JOHN WYNDHAM
SCENEGGIATURA PHILIP YORDAN
DIRETTO DA STEVE SEKELY
PRODOTTO DA GEORGE PITCHER
PRODUTTORE ESECUTIVO PHILIP YORDAN

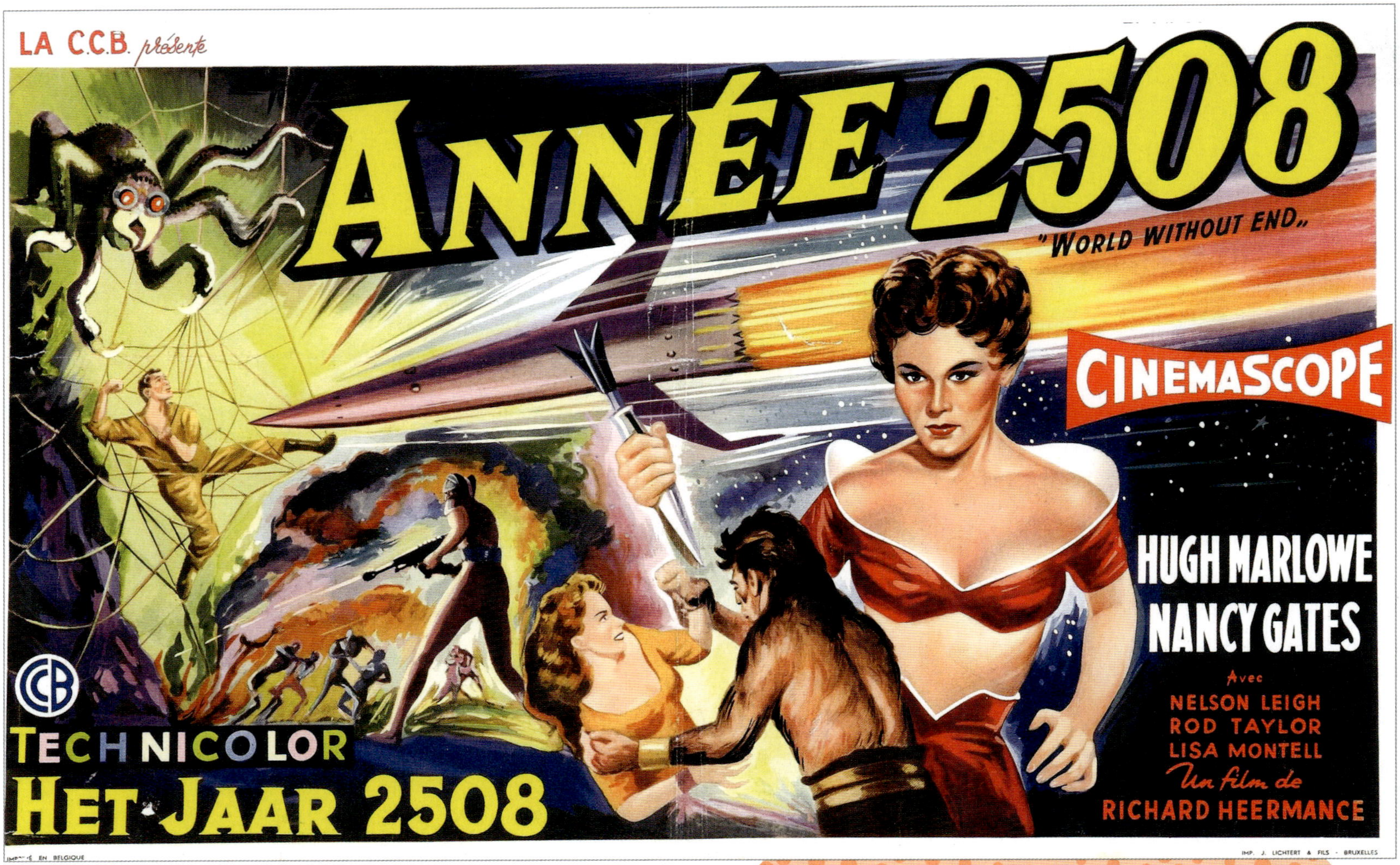

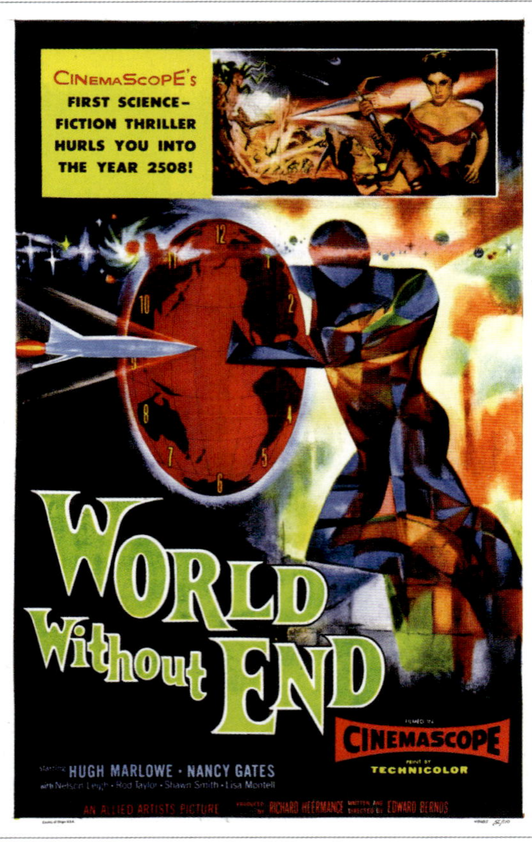

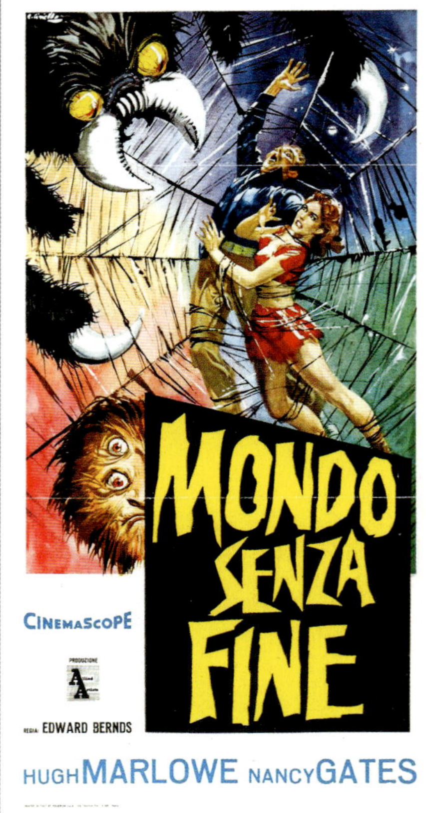

VARGAS GOES SCI-FI

World Without End (1956) is very much a B-movie. It recycles effects footage from 1951's *Flight to Mars*, and features a giant spider that looks great on the posters, but is a meter-long rubbery embarrassment in the actual film. Its plot, concerning travelers from the present era being flung forward in time to a future Earth where humankind has split into a beautiful, technologically advanced elite and a bunch of violent, primitive mutants is close enough to H.G. Wells's novel *The Time Machine* that his estate's lawyers reportedly got in touch. The film could boast a huge, A-list talent on the payroll though. According to his original contract, which surfaced at auction in 2013, the legendary pin-up artist Alberto Vargas (1896–1982) was paid the not inconsiderable sum of $1,500 for "full length water-color drawings of Nancy Gates, Lisa Montell and Shawn Smith, as we may direct in connection with our Photoplay." The results were turned into a stunning six-sheet, which proudly proclaimed, "Vargas interprets the women of the future."

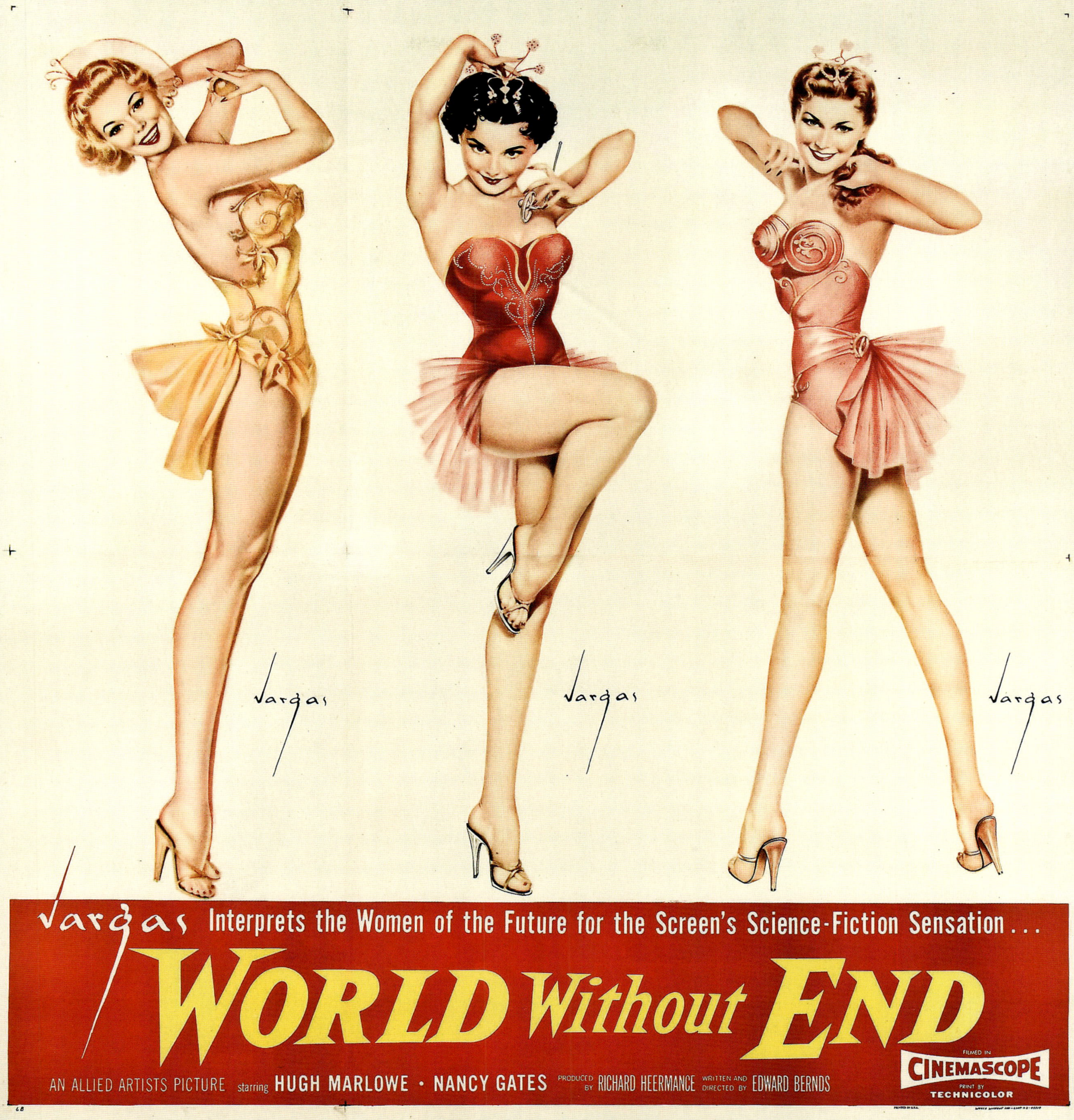

Vargas

Vargas

Vargas

Vargas Interprets the Women of the Future for the Screen's Science-Fiction Sensation . . .

WORLD Without END

AN ALLIED ARTISTS PICTURE starring HUGH MARLOWE · NANCY GATES PRODUCED BY RICHARD HEERMANCE WRITTEN AND DIRECTED BY EDWARD BERNDS

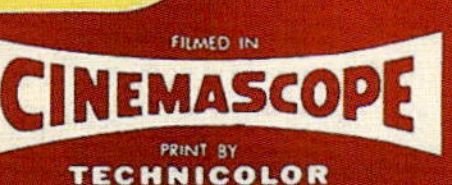

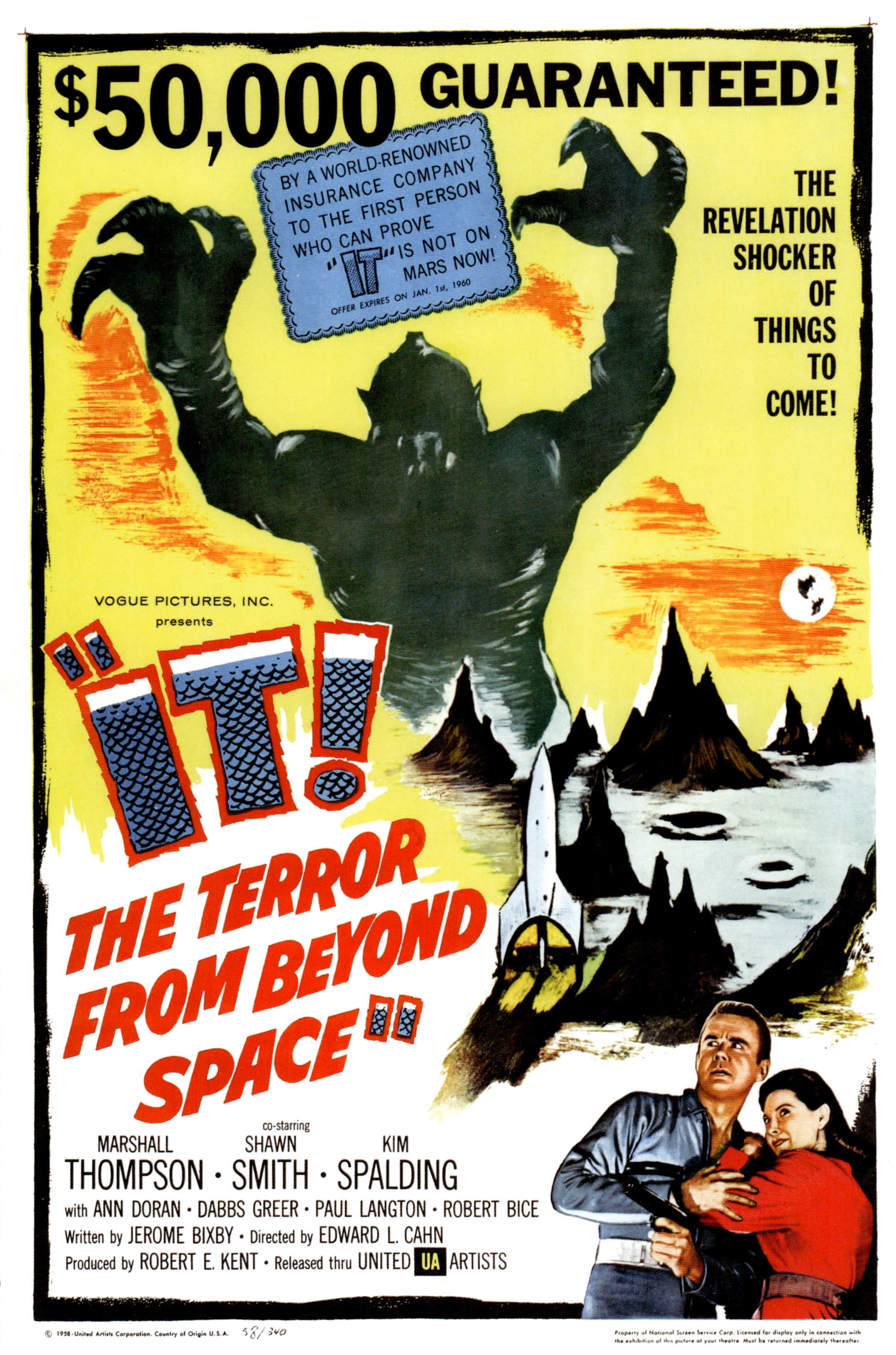
$50,000 GUARANTEED!
BY A WORLD-RENOWNED INSURANCE COMPANY TO THE FIRST PERSON WHO CAN PROVE "IT" IS NOT ON MARS NOW!
OFFER EXPIRES ON JAN. 1st, 1960
THE REVELATION SHOCKER OF THINGS TO COME!
VOGUE PICTURES, INC. presents
"IT!"
THE TERROR FROM BEYOND SPACE"
co-starring
MARSHALL THOMPSON · SHAWN SMITH · KIM SPALDING
with ANN DORAN · DABBS GREER · PAUL LANGTON · ROBERT BICE
Written by JEROME BIXBY · Directed by EDWARD L. CAHN
Produced by ROBERT E. KENT · Released thru UNITED UA ARTISTS
© 1958-United Artists Corporation. Country of Origin U.S.A.
58/340
Property of National Screen Service Corp. Licensed for display only in connection with the exhibition of this picture at your theatre. Must be returned immediately thereafter.

THE ORIGINAL ALIEN?

The list of *Alien*'s antecedents is a long one. Critics have traced the DNA of Ridley Scott's classic back to Mario Bava's *Planet of the Vampires*, the original *Creature from the Black Lagoon*, Agatha Christie's *And Then There Were None*, and *The Voyage of the Space Beagle* by A. E. van Vogt to name but a few (the latter author agreed, and sued 20th Century Fox for plagiarism; the case was settled out of court). Top of the list though is usually the atmospheric *It! The Terror from Beyond Space*, which does, it has to be said, feature the crew of an Earth-bound spaceship being picked off by a creature that hides in the ventilation ducts and is ultimately dispatched through an airlock (spoiler). On release back in 1958, *It!* was just another B-movie, albeit one with a cool monster and a rather ridiculous poster gimmick: that $50,000 wasn't going anywhere. Was it an influence though? *Alien* scriptwriter Dan O'Bannon allegedly once joked, presumably without a lawyer present, "I didn't steal from anybody, I stole from everybody!"

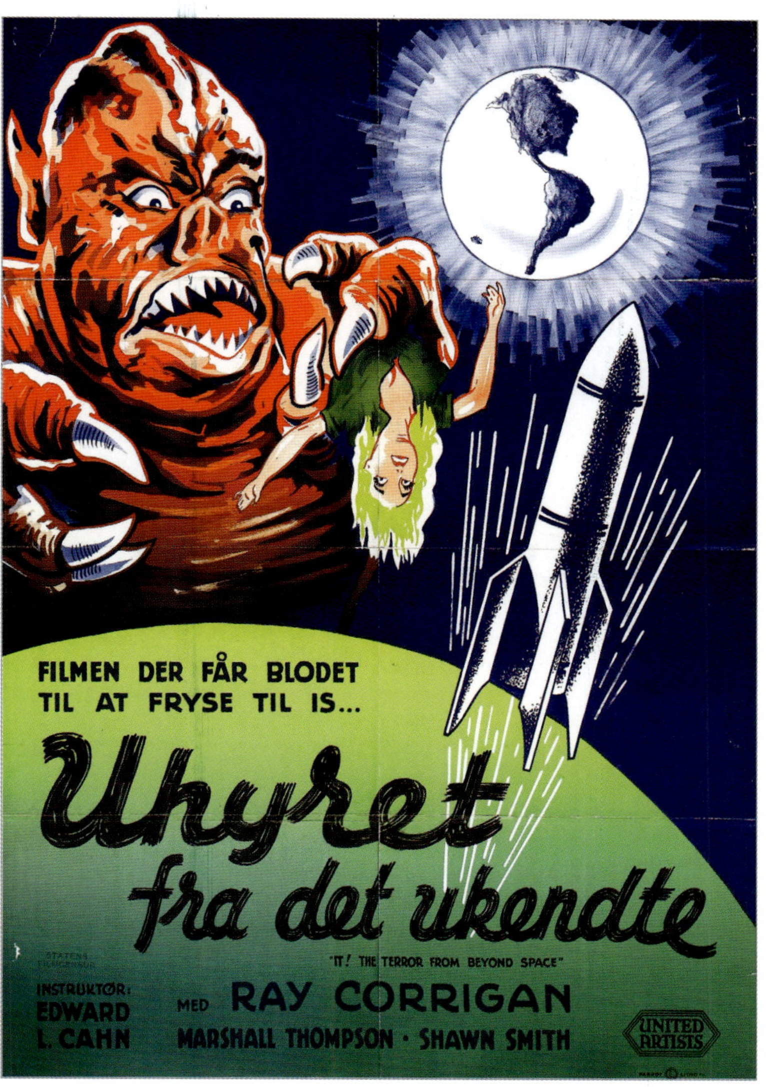

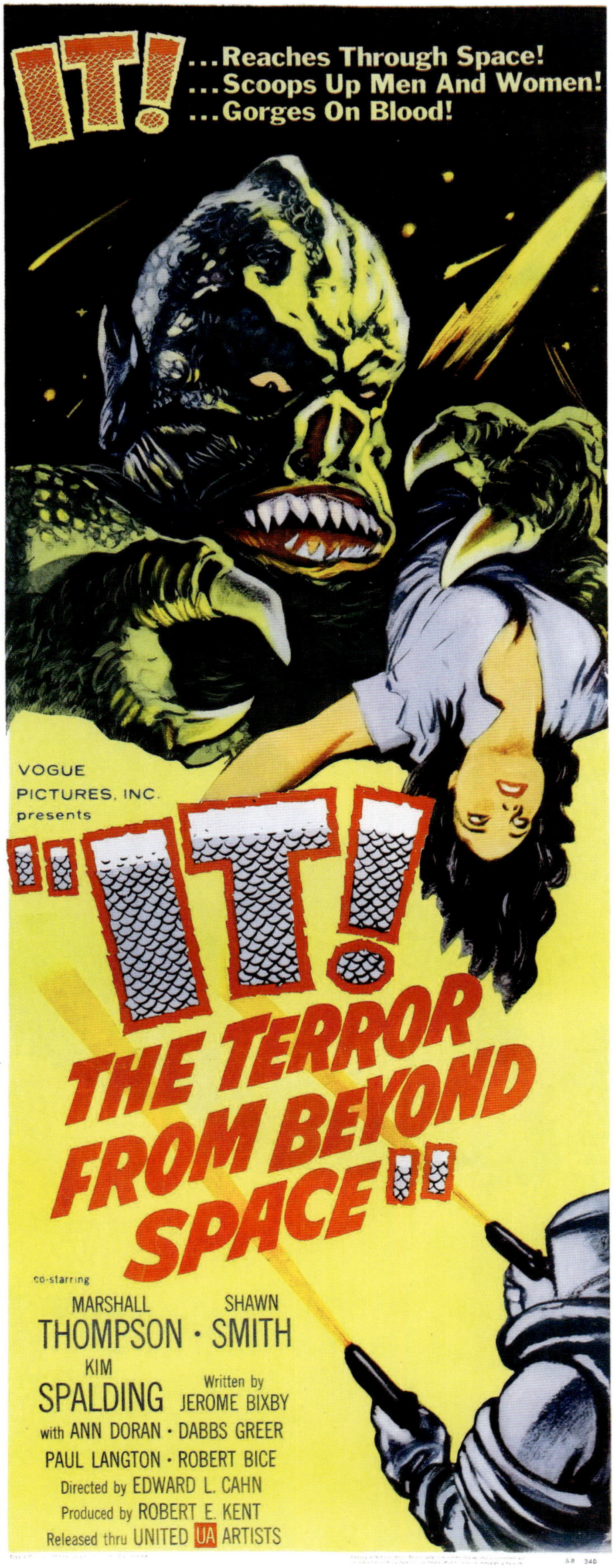

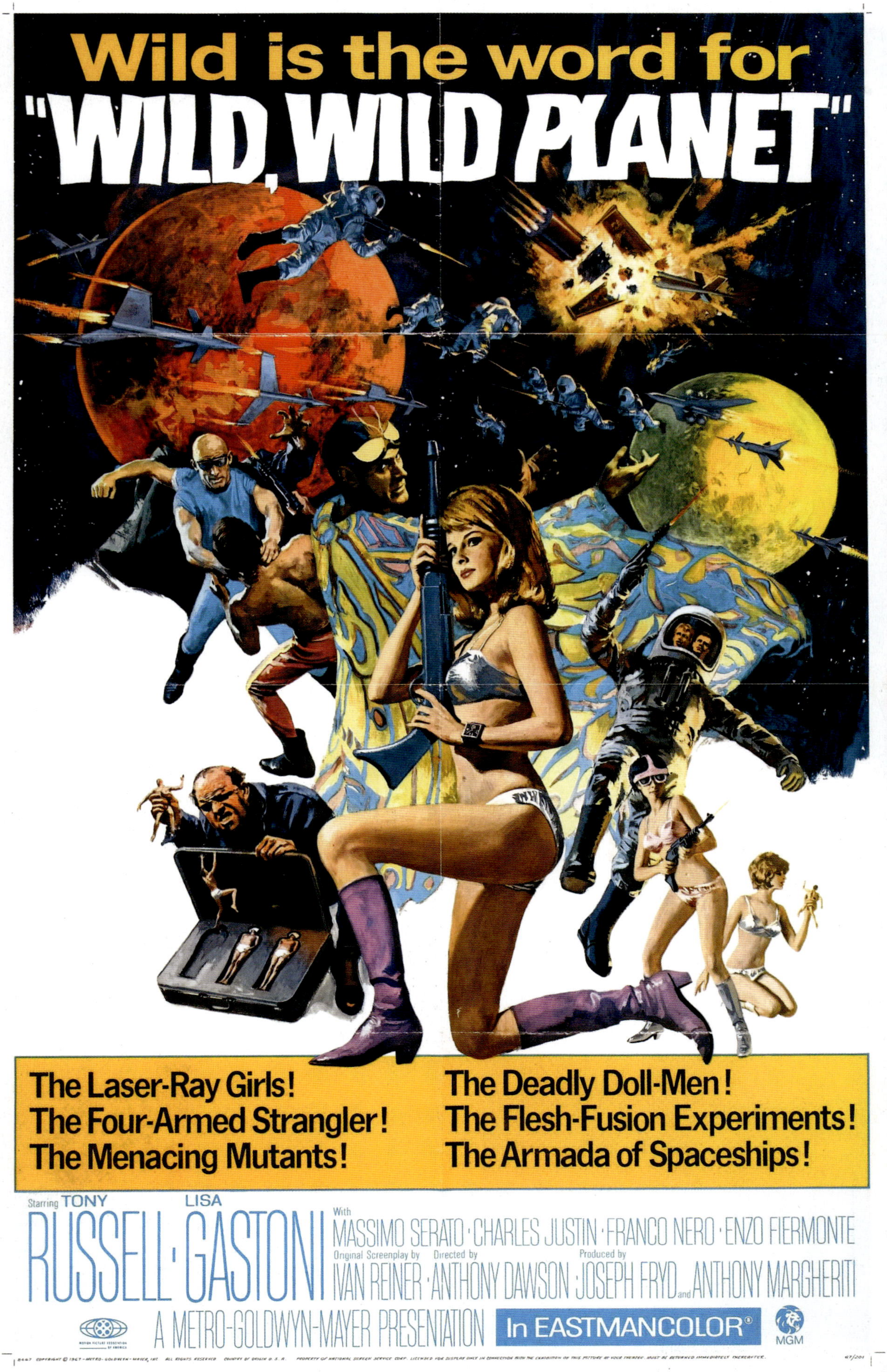

Wild is the word for

"WILD, WILD PLANET"

The Laser-Ray Girls!
The Four-Armed Strangler!
The Menacing Mutants!
The Deadly Doll-Men!
The Flesh-Fusion Experiments!
The Armada of Spaceships!

Starring TONY RUSSELL · LISA GASTONI

With MASSIMO SERATO · CHARLES JUSTIN · FRANCO NERO · ENZO FIERMONTE

Original Screenplay by IVAN REINER · Directed by ANTHONY DAWSON · Produced by JOSEPH FRYD and ANTHONY MARGHERITI

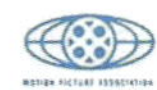

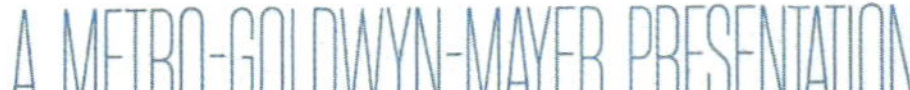

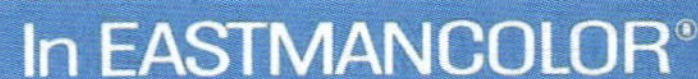

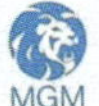

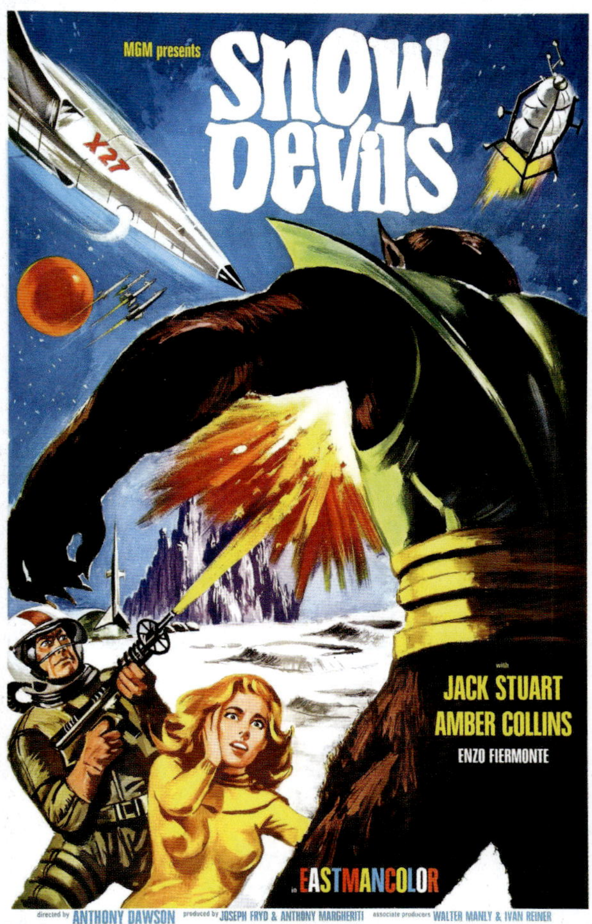

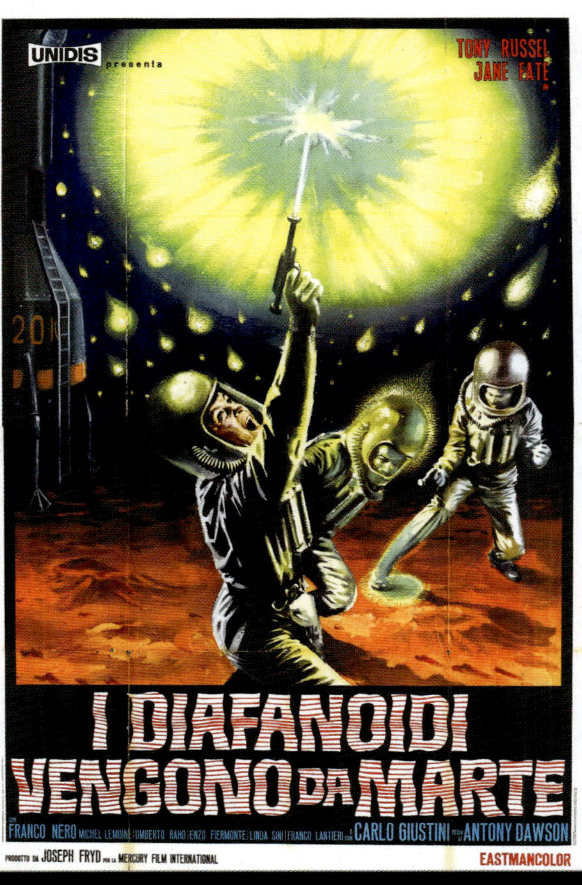

THE GAMMA ONE SERIES

By 1965, Italian director Antonio Margheriti (aka Anthony M. Dawson, 1930–2002) had established himself as a quick worker who could make good-looking films with very little money. No doubt having seen his accomplished 1960 space opera *Assignment Outer Space*, MGM did a deal with him to make some low-budget SF films, which they intended to sell direct to American television. The result was the Gamma One series, or quadrilogy if you will (to use the modern, post-*Alien* DVD-box-set term), all shot simultaneously in Italy in a mere three months, using the same sets and overlapping casts. Each film had a different, color-coded clapperboard, to avoid confusion in the editing room. *Wild, Wild Planet* (1966), *The War of the Planets* (1966, represented here by its Italian *foglio*), *War Between the Planets* (1966), and *Snow Devils* (1967) earned theatrical releases in the end, complete with colorful posters that summed up their stylish if somewhat crazy take on the genre.

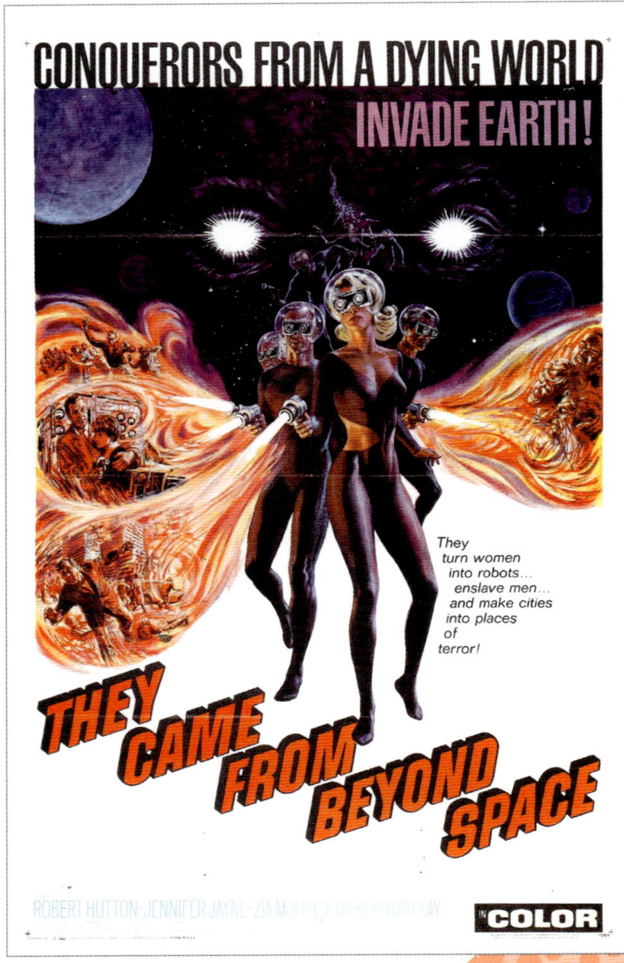

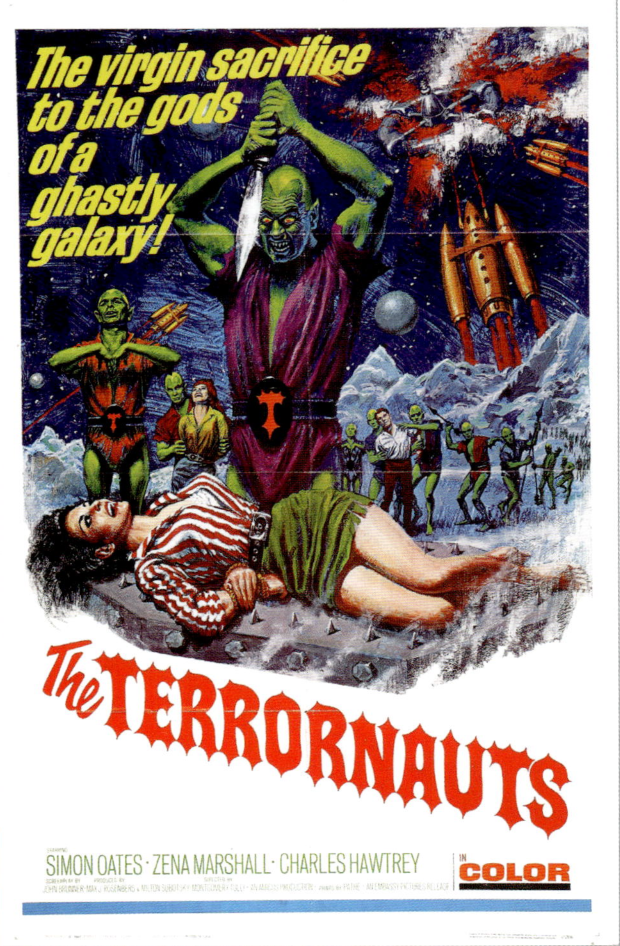

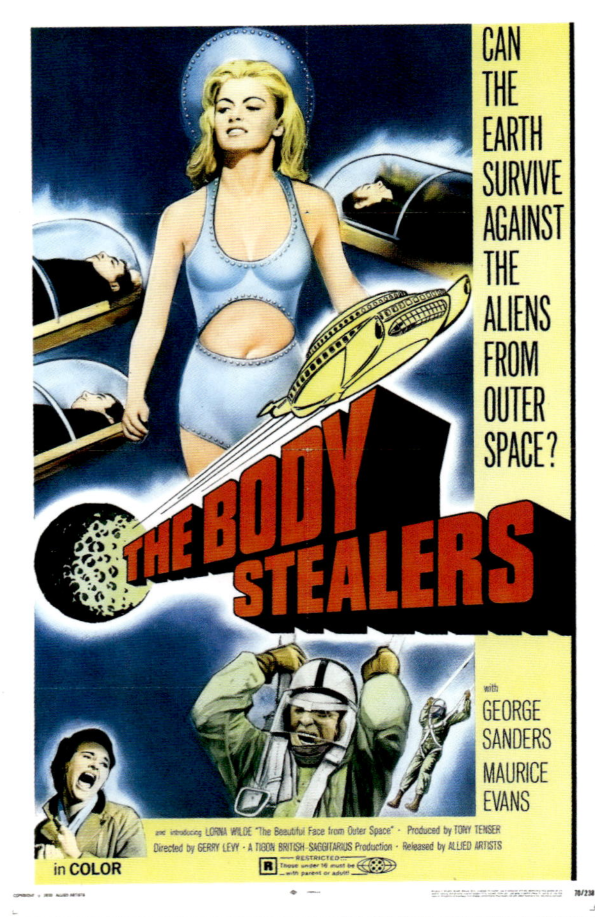

SFUK

As with the other subgenres covered in this book, the United Kingdom's film industry did its bit to supply the demand for sci-fi exploitation pictures. These US release one-sheets for UK productions are all rather effective, though the films in question are far from classic. *The Terrornauts* and *They Came from Beyond Space* were made back-to-back by Amicus Productions, the latter reusing some of the sets and props from the company's previous movie *Daleks' Invasion Earth 2150 A.D.* Released as a double bill in 1967 they flopped, though are worth tracking down today for a bit of campy fun—no film featuring *Carry On* comedy star Charles Hawtrey in a supporting role can be all bad. An element of Amicus's *Daleks' Invasion Earth 2150 A.D.* also cropped up in *The Body Stealers* (1969): the Dalek saucer ship appears in the climax (and on the poster). Star Lorna Wilde, "The Beautiful Face from Outer Space," was actually actress Pamela Conway, from Watford. *The Love Factor* (aka *Zeta One*, 1969) also features Hawtrey, and is ably described by legendary stuntman Vic Armstrong, who found himself working on the film early in his career: "It was a bit of science fiction hokum about some girls from outer space who are like the Sirens on the rocks, and entice men by wearing lingerie and suspender belts and then beat the crap out of them. It was as weird as it sounds, and very cheap." Armstrong went on to double Christopher Reeve as Superman and Harrison Ford as Indiana Jones, but back then was simply "very grateful to get the work."

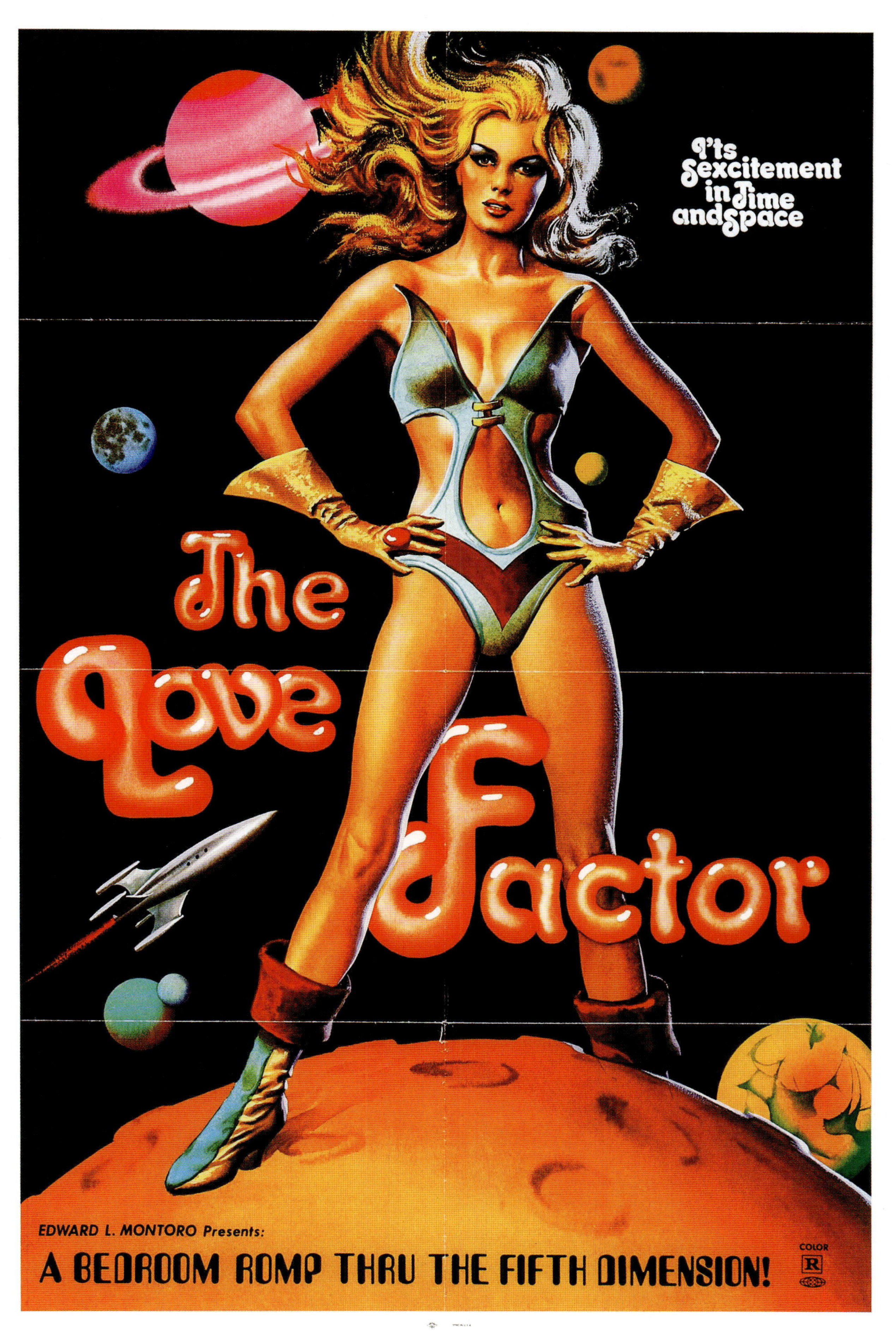

It's Sexcitement in Time and Space
The Love Factor
EDWARD L. MONTORO Presents:
A BEDROOM ROMP THRU THE FIFTH DIMENSION!
COLOR
R

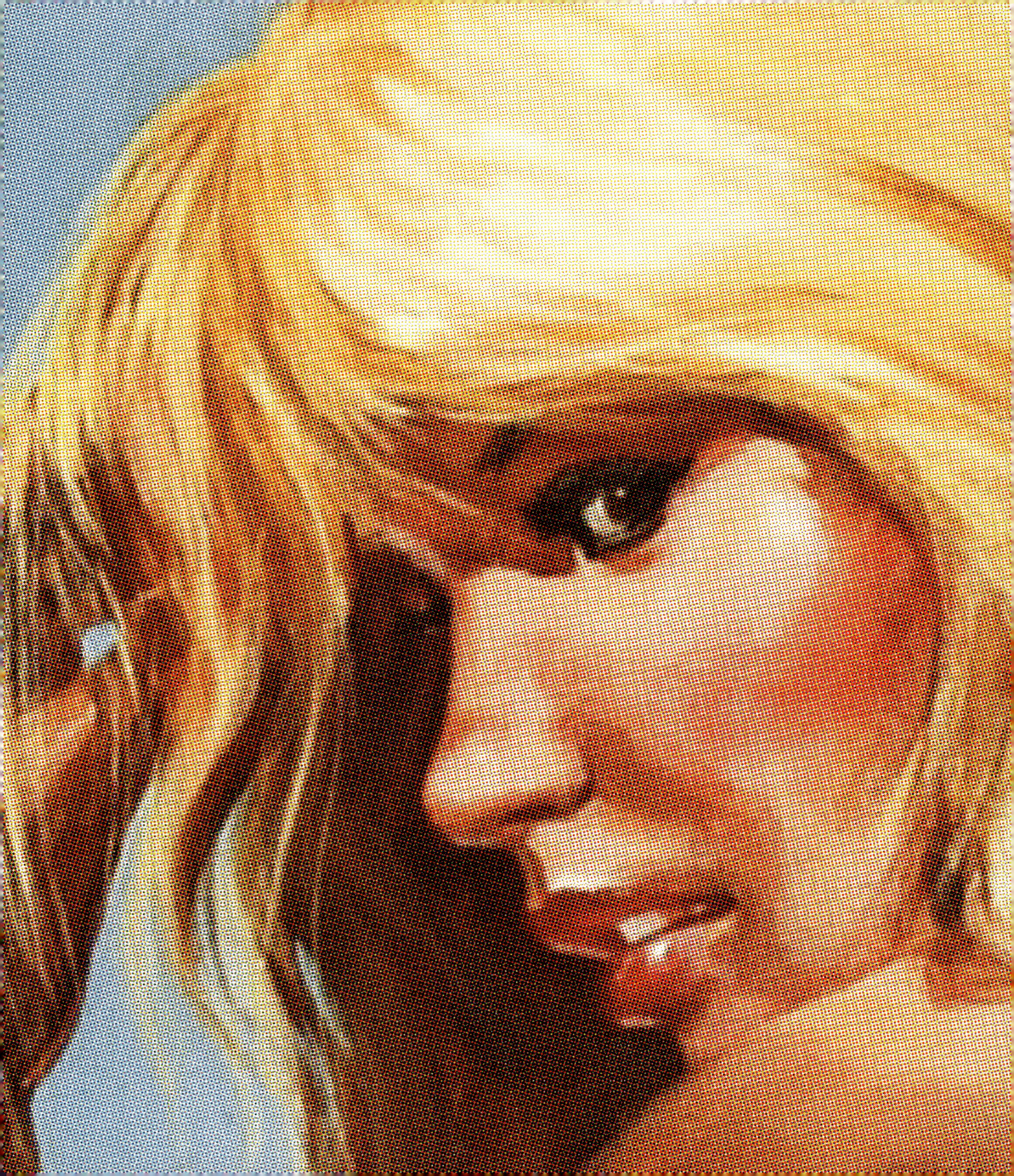

SEX!

Simon Sheridan on
DEEP THROAT and COME PLAY WITH ME

PREVIOUS SPREAD: Detail from the poster for *Sweet Cakes* (1976), a hardcore production directed by Howard Ziehm. Fellow director Wes Craven makes a brief, uncredited (and fully clothed) appearance in the film, playing a photographer.

OPPOSITE: The now iconic one-sheet for *Deep Throat* (1972), which helped usher "porno chic" into the mainstream.

BELOW: Puntastic poster for the lackluster softcore sequel *Deep Throat Part II* (1974).

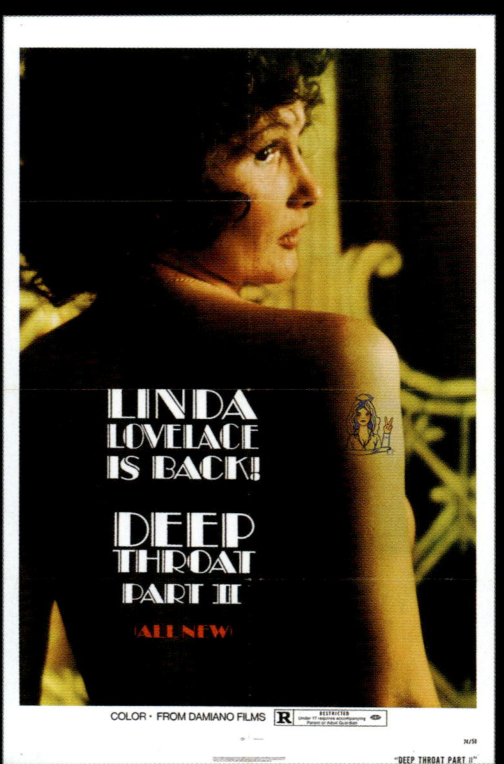

Prolific British commercial artist Tom Chantrell once joked that his poster artwork for sex films often provided greater thrills than sitting through the actual movies themselves. This might have been the case in Great Britain, but across the Atlantic X-rated pornography changed the way in which Americans went to the cinema. If horror movies had dominated exploitation cinema in the 1960s, then the 1970s was porn's decade. Suddenly sex films were more than just cheaply made titillating 8mm curiosities; they were feature-length color productions with storylines, professional casts and crews, and with one simple aim: to arouse an audience. Porn films exploded at the very moment when sexual liberation became a flashpoint for the most pronounced period of social and political upheaval since World War II.

Movies like *Boys in the Sand* (1971), *Behind the Green Door* (1972), and *Devil in Miss Jones* (1973) brought explicitness into the mainstream and—for a few gloriously hedonistic years—created the era of "porno chic," where pornography was favorably reviewed in the national press and discussed openly on TV. The burgeoning culture of big-screen porn also created a new breed of star performers, who stepped out of the anonymous world of stag movies and soon found themselves the objects of serious press interest. The likes of John Holmes, Marilyn Chambers, Georgina Spelvin, and Casey Donovan became almost as well known as their Hollywood counterparts. However, one film and one actress, above all others, challenged America's attitude toward pornography. Although 1972's *Deep Throat* was not the first hardcore production to secure a wide theatrical release in the US, it was unquestionably the first sexploitation film to enter the public consciousness and find a mass audience.

Starring New Yorker Linda Lovelace, *Deep Throat*'s undeniable hook was the actress's talent to perform spectacular fellatio. In the film's outlandish plot her character is only able to achieve orgasm through oral sex, since her clitoris is

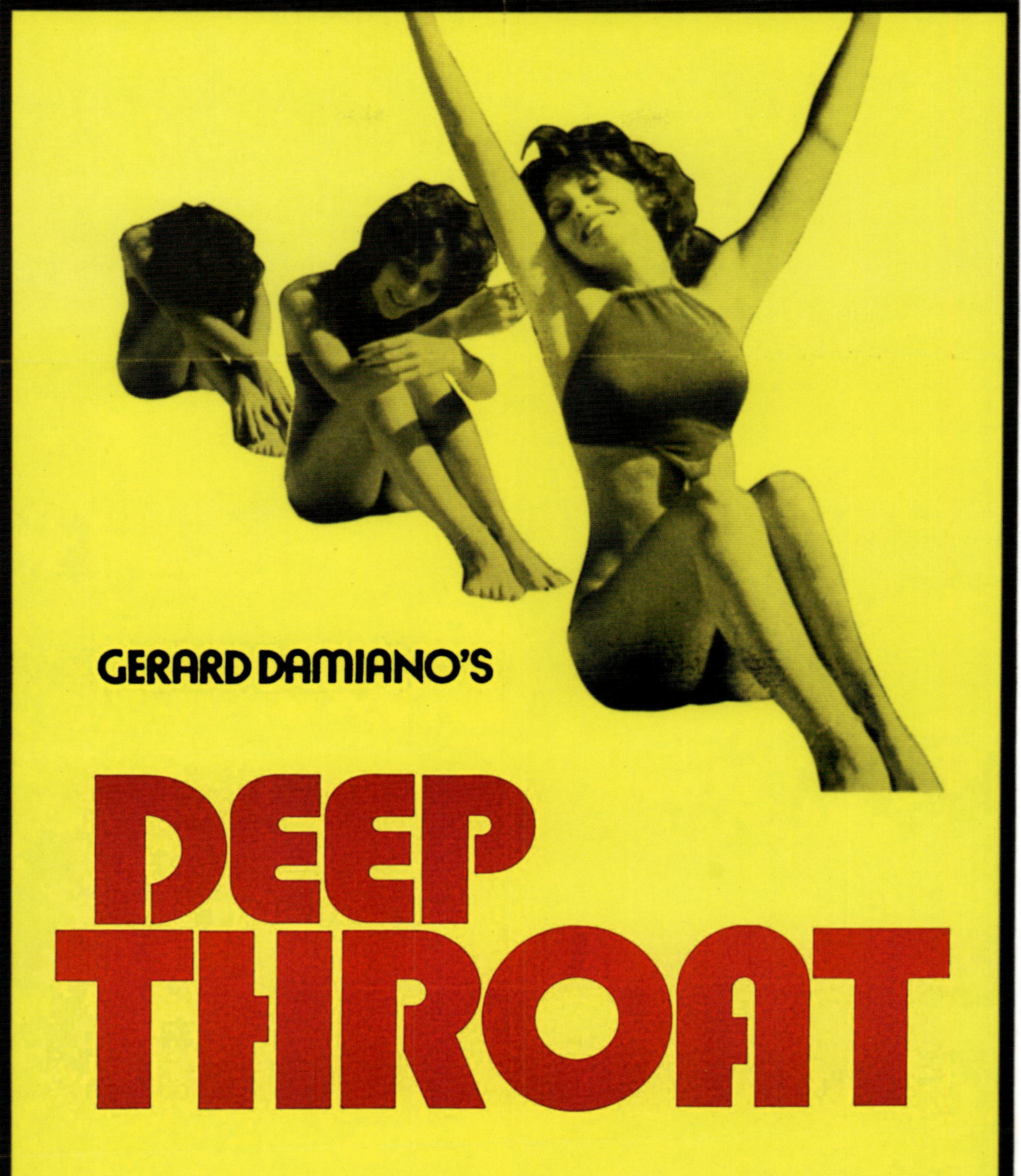
GERARD DAMIANO'S
DEEP
THROAT
HOW FAR DOES A GIRL HAVE TO GO
TO UNTANGLE HER TINGLE?
EASTMANCOLOR X ADULTS ONLY

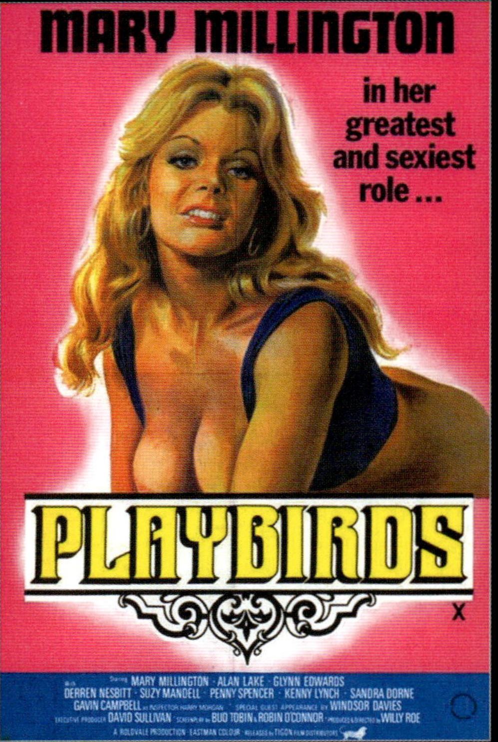

ABOVE: Mary Millington displays her charms in Tom Chantrell's art for *The Playbirds* (1978). Though "her greatest and sexiest role" gave her more screen time, the film could not surpass the success of the previous year's *Come Play with Me*.

where her epiglottis should be. Lovelace's skills played-up to America's greatest obsession of the 1970s, namely blow jobs. Directed by Gerard Damiano, and co-starring mustachioed rent-a-stud Harry Reems, *Deep Throat* was filmed on location over a single week, and had a budget of around $25,000. It has probably grossed in the region of $600 million since its June 1972 release, making it the most profitable US movie of all time.

The film made Lovelace a pop culture phenomenon. Al Goldstein, writing in the influential *SCREW* magazine, called *Deep Throat* "the very best porn film ever made" before adding that Lovelace had "the greatest mouth action in the annals of cock-sucking." Goldstein's purple prose was reprinted in its entirety in *Deep Throat*'s luxurious cinema pressbook. Additionally, the now iconic *Deep Throat* poster is a master class in understated symbolism, looking more like the cover of a keep fit manual promoting the health-giving properties of yoga. The artwork portrays Lovelace emerging triumphantly from a curled position to embrace the multitudinous joys of liberated womanhood.

Deep Throat begat a soulless softcore sequel in 1974, reuniting on-screen lovers Lovelace and Reems, but it didn't replicate the astonishing success of the original. However, its failure at the box office didn't dampen a succession of straight-to-video follow-ups and remakes in the '80s and '90s. Despite Lovelace's well-publicized stand against pornography in her later life, the enticing legend of *Deep Throat* endures even four decades later, and its tantalizing title remains shorthand for all forms of American sexploitation.

While the US was basking in cinematic emancipation, on the other side of the Atlantic the UK's desire for greater sexual freedom was still shackled by the authorities. Hardcore pornography was illegal and those who produced it or distributed it were punished with lengthy jail sentences. Although hardcore was banished from high street theaters, members-only cinema clubs flourished in every major British town where—for a while, at least—more explicit fare could be screened, including foreign imports like *Deep Throat*. Another porn movie that played to enthusiastic club audiences was *Miss Bohrloch* (1970), starring British actress Mary Maxted as an insatiable prostitute entertaining two male clients.

Born Mary Quilter in 1945, Maxted trained to be a veterinary nurse before graduating to porn in her twenties. In the early '70s she gave a series of unbridled performances in 8mm productions for director John Lindsay, and quickly emerged as Britain's foremost X-rated actress. Just like Linda Lovelace, Mary had ambitions beyond hardcore. In 1974 she met porn publisher David Sullivan, who changed her surname to "Millington" and made her the star attraction in his stable of girlie magazines. Such was Mary's incredible popularity that Sullivan quickly promoted her to movie star in his debut film, *Come Play with Me* (1977). The movie's slender plot concerned the naughty goings-on at a health farm staffed by nymphomaniac nurses. Despite her top-billing, Millington appeared only briefly, but Sullivan's infallible knack for publicity made *Come Play with Me* the most-talked about movie of the year.

The film premiered at the newly refurbished Moulin cinema in London's West End in April 1977 and broke box office records from day one, playing to packed houses and defiantly refusing to budge. The movie also played virtually every provincial cinema in the UK, and its beautiful poster depicting Mary and

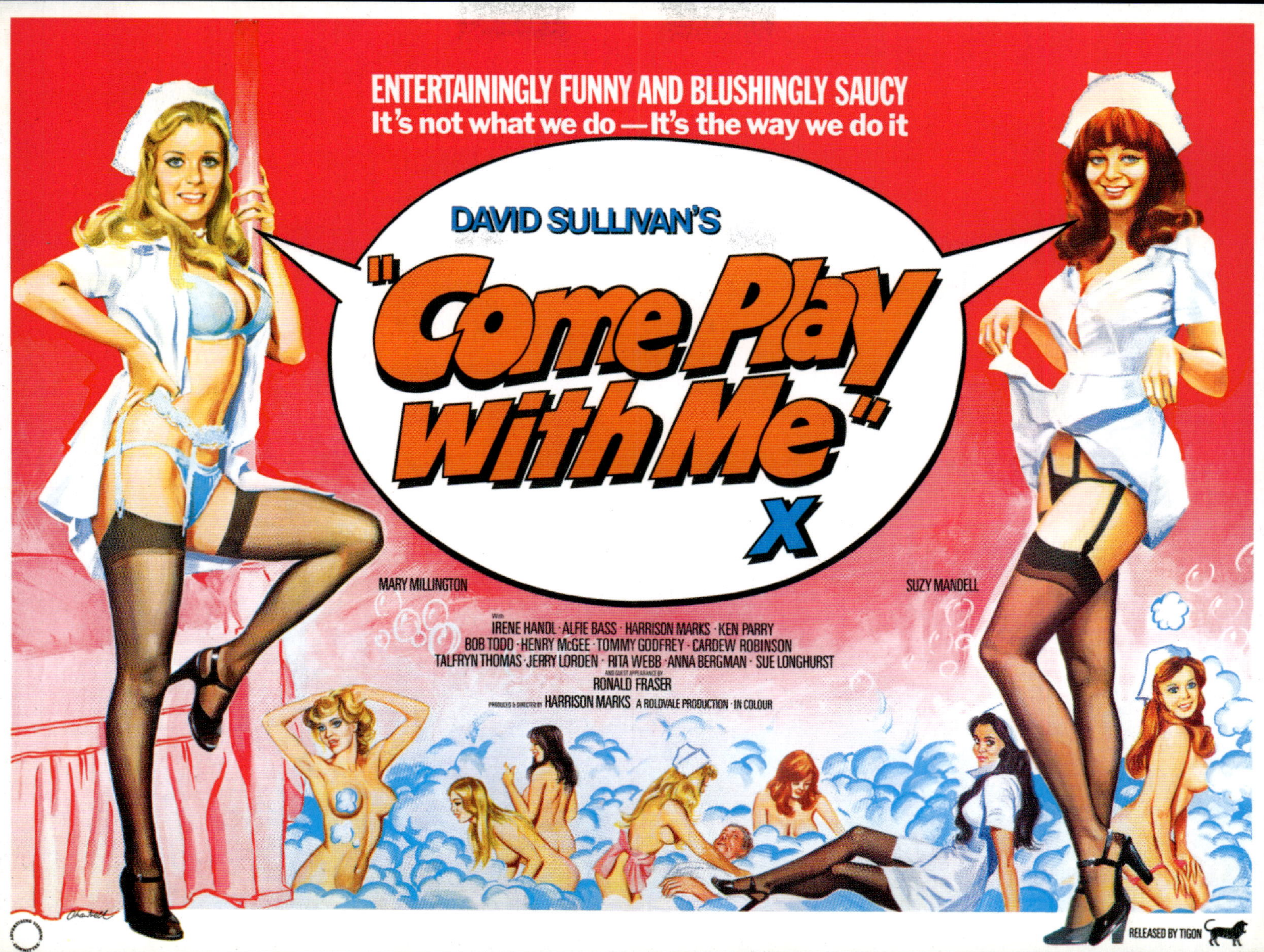

her co-star Suzy Mandel dressed in nurses' outfits (masterfully painted by Tom Chantrell), became one of the best-remembered images of the era.

The incredible longevity of *Come Play with Me* proved impossible to repeat, but a year later Mary returned to the big screen in *The Playbirds*, where she enjoyed a much expanded role playing—rather ironically—a policewoman who goes undercover in the porn industry. Mary never enjoyed any degree of crossover success in the US, although she was cast in Gerard Damiano's proposed 1978 movie *Love is Beautiful*, opposite male lead Harry Reems. Sadly, the film never got past the planning stages, and Mary only appeared in one further movie of note, the posthumously released Sex Pistols fantasy *The Great Rock 'n' Roll Swindle* (1980).

Tragically, in August 1979, Mary died aged just 33, the result of a drug overdose. Her desire to become a mainstream performer never materialized and the persecution she received at the hands of the British authorities had beaten her into submission. *Come Play with Me* out-lived her, however. It played continuously at the Moulin cinema until March 1981, notching up 201 unbroken weeks. It remains the longest-running British movie of all time. ●

ABOVE: *Come Play with Me*'s alluring UK quad was just one of the hundreds of posters painted by Tom Chantrell (1916–2001), the British artist fondly remembered for his work on Hammer and *Carry On* movies, and the UK poster for *Star Wars*. At his prolific height in the 1960s and '70s, he was producing multiple rough layouts and then the finished art for three entirely unconnected film posters each and every week.

BEATING THE CODE

Though there had been hardcore one-reelers and stag films since the birth of cinema, for a "legitimate" film to feature nudity and a sex scene was groundbreaking in the mid-1930s. The Czech/Austrian drama *Ecstasy* had originally been released in Europe in 1933, but when a US distributor tried to get approval from the moral guardians at the Production Code Administration in 1936, they came up against its boss Joseph Breen, who found the sight of Hedy Kiesler running naked around the countryside, and later simulating orgasm (even if it was just a close-up of her face) to be "highly—even dangerously—indecent." The film was eventually released, without Code approval, to independent "arthouses" in 1940. By this time Kiesler had moved to America and become Hollywood starlet Hedy Lamarr, as the bold and breathless US poster points out (international posters were somewhat more refined). *The Sin of Nora Moran* was released in America in late 1933, and so missed the strict enforcement of the Code that began in the US the following year. Though you'll look in vain for anything as explicit in the actual film (or indeed a lead actress with blonde hair), Alberto Vargas's art for the one-sheet is positively soaked in sex appeal. *Premiere* magazine deservedly voted it the second-best movie poster of all time.

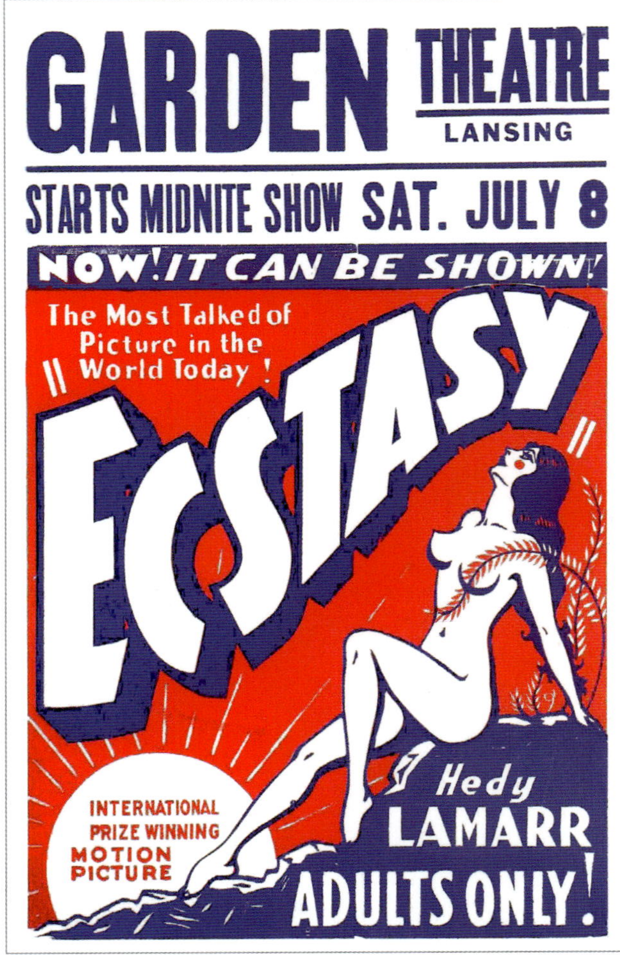

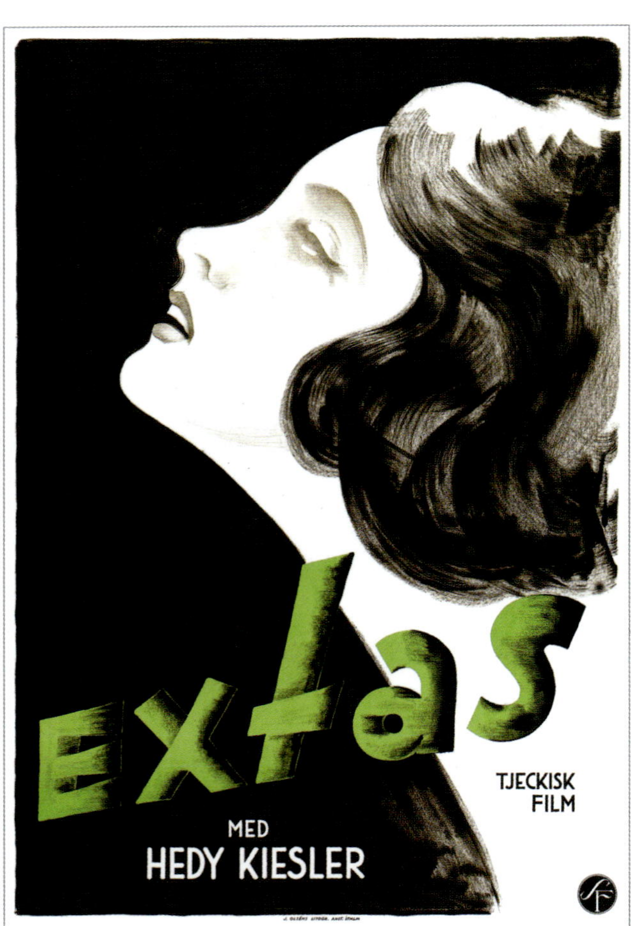

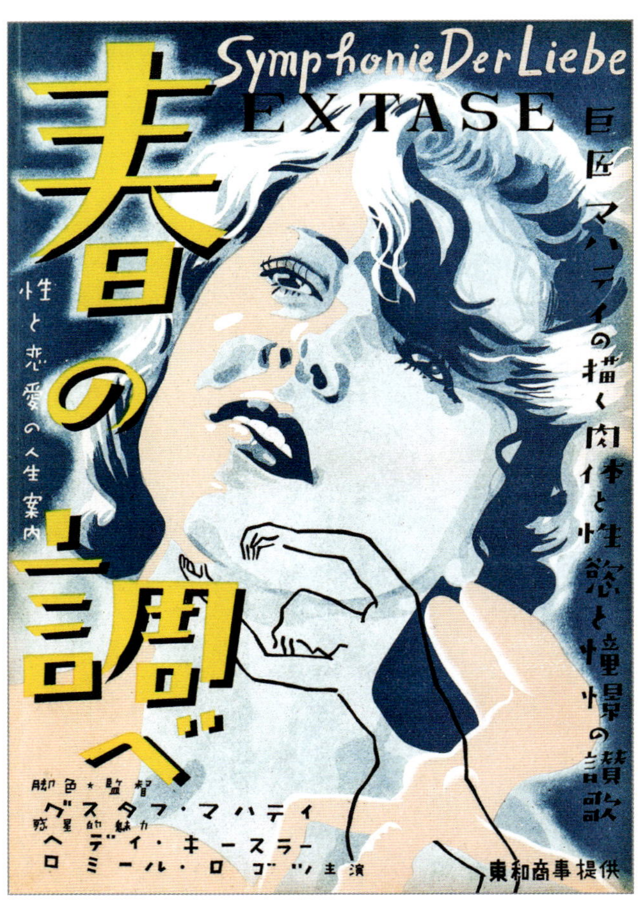

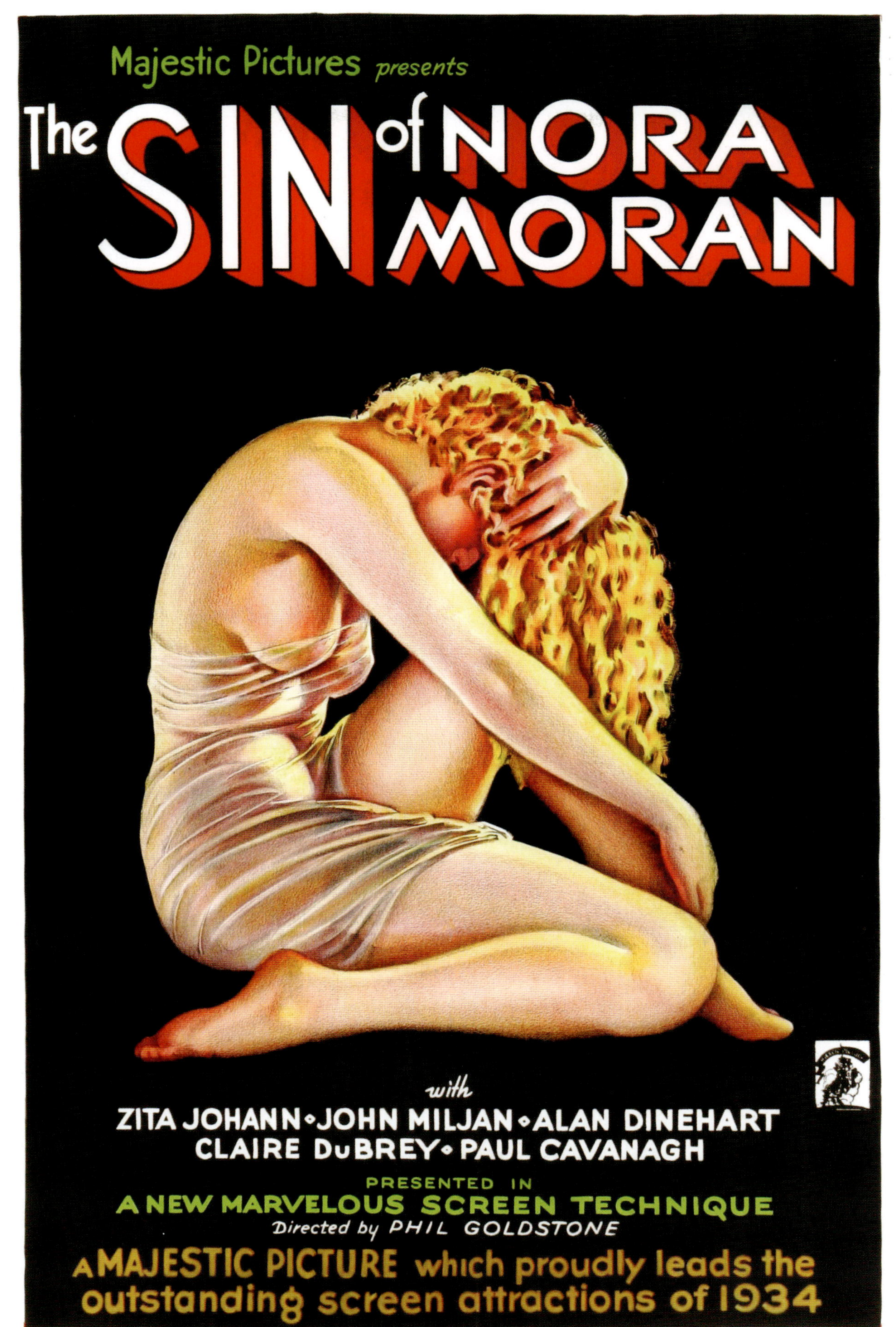
Majestic Pictures presents
The SIN of NORA MORAN
with
ZITA JOHANN • JOHN MILJAN • ALAN DINEHART
CLAIRE DuBREY • PAUL CAVANAGH
PRESENTED IN
A NEW MARVELOUS SCREEN TECHNIQUE
Directed by PHIL GOLDSTONE
A MAJESTIC PICTURE which proudly leads the
outstanding screen attractions of 1934

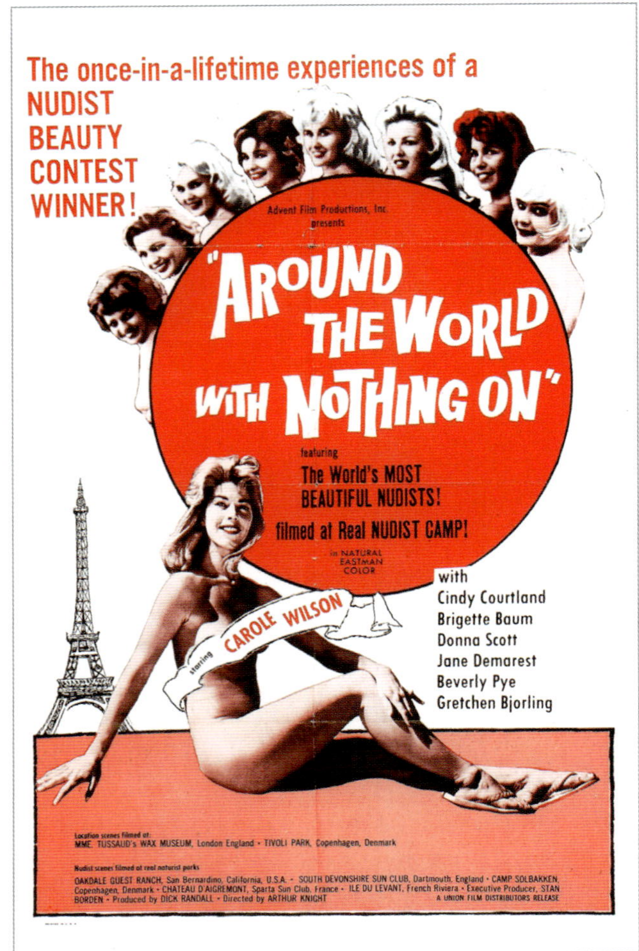
The once-in-a-lifetime experiences of a
NUDIST BEAUTY CONTEST WINNER!
Advent Film Productions, Inc. presents
"AROUND THE WORLD WITH NOTHING ON"
featuring
The World's MOST BEAUTIFUL NUDISTS!
filmed at Real NUDIST CAMP!
in NATURAL EASTMAN COLOR
starring CAROLE WILSON
with
Cindy Courtland
Brigette Baum
Donna Scott
Jane Demarest
Beverly Pye
Gretchen Bjorling
Location scenes filmed at:
MME. TUSSAUD's WAX MUSEUM, London England • TIVOLI PARK, Copenhagen, Denmark
Nudist scenes filmed at real naturist parks
OAKDALE GUEST RANCH, San Bernardino, California, U.S.A. • SOUTH DEVONSHIRE SUN CLUB, Dartmouth, England • CAMP SOLBAKKEN, Copenhagen, Denmark • CHATEAU D'AIGREMONT, Sparta Sun Club, France • ILE DU LEVANT, French Riviera • Executive Producer, STAN BORDEN • Produced by DICK RANDALL • Directed by ARTHUR KNIGHT
A UNION FILM DISTRIBUTORS RELEASE

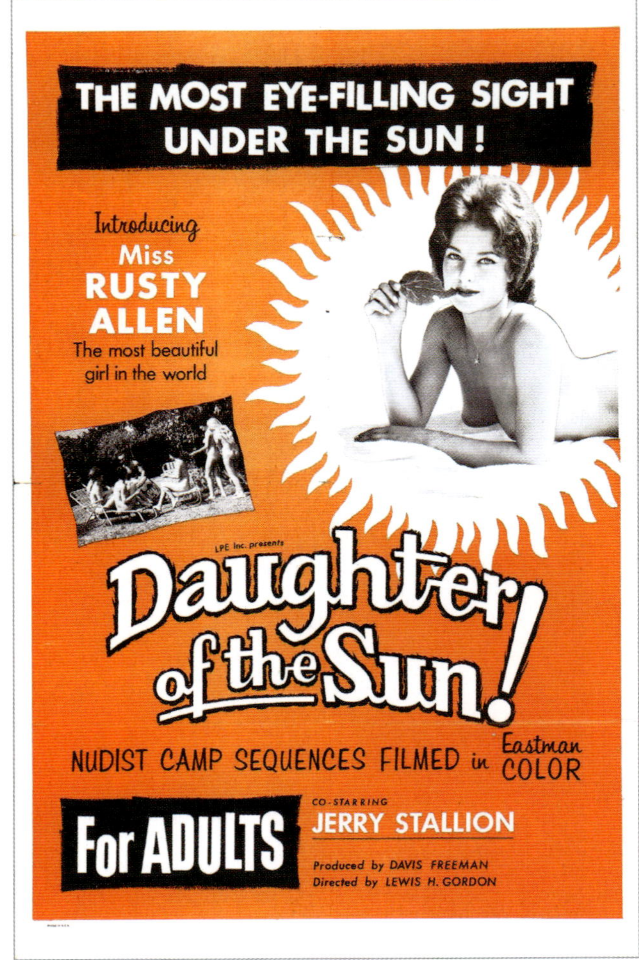
THE MOST EYE-FILLING SIGHT UNDER THE SUN!
Introducing
Miss
RUSTY ALLEN
The most beautiful girl in the world
LPE Inc. presents
Daughter of the Sun!
NUDIST CAMP SEQUENCES FILMED in Eastman COLOR
For ADULTS
CO-STARRING
JERRY STALLION
Produced by DAVIS FREEMAN
Directed by LEWIS H. GORDON

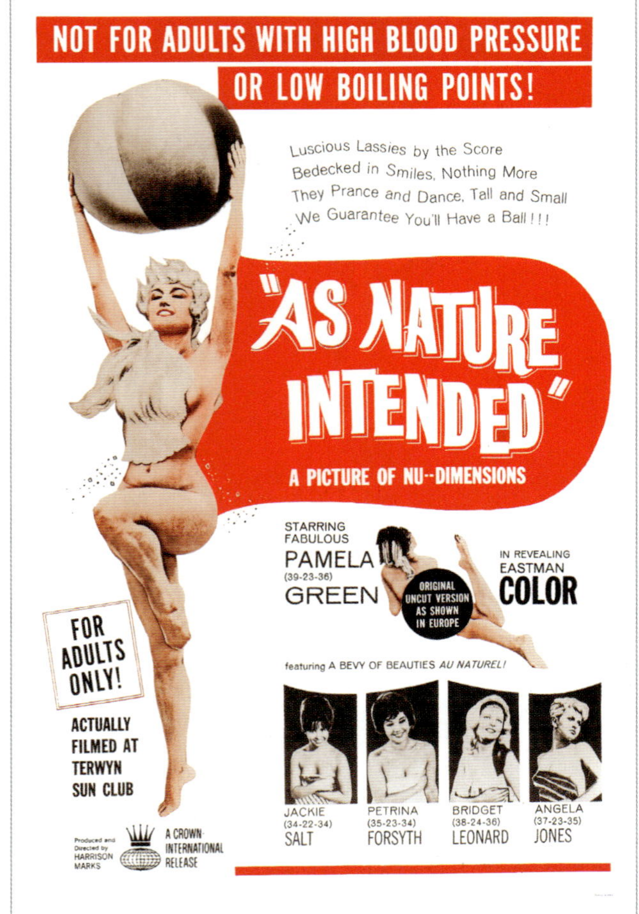
NOT FOR ADULTS WITH HIGH BLOOD PRESSURE
OR LOW BOILING POINTS!
Luscious Lassies by the Score
Bedecked in Smiles, Nothing More
They Prance and Dance, Tall and Small
We Guarantee You'll Have a Ball!!!
"AS NATURE INTENDED"
A PICTURE OF NU--DIMENSIONS
STARRING FABULOUS
PAMELA (39-23-36) GREEN
ORIGINAL UNCUT VERSION AS SHOWN IN EUROPE
IN REVEALING EASTMAN COLOR
FOR ADULTS ONLY!
ACTUALLY FILMED AT TERWYN SUN CLUB
featuring A BEVY OF BEAUTIES AU NATUREL!
JACKIE (34-22-34) SALT
PETRINA (35-23-34) FORSYTH
BRIDGET (38-24-36) LEONARD
ANGELA (37-23-35) JONES
Produced and Directed by HARRISON MARKS
A CROWN-INTERNATIONAL RELEASE

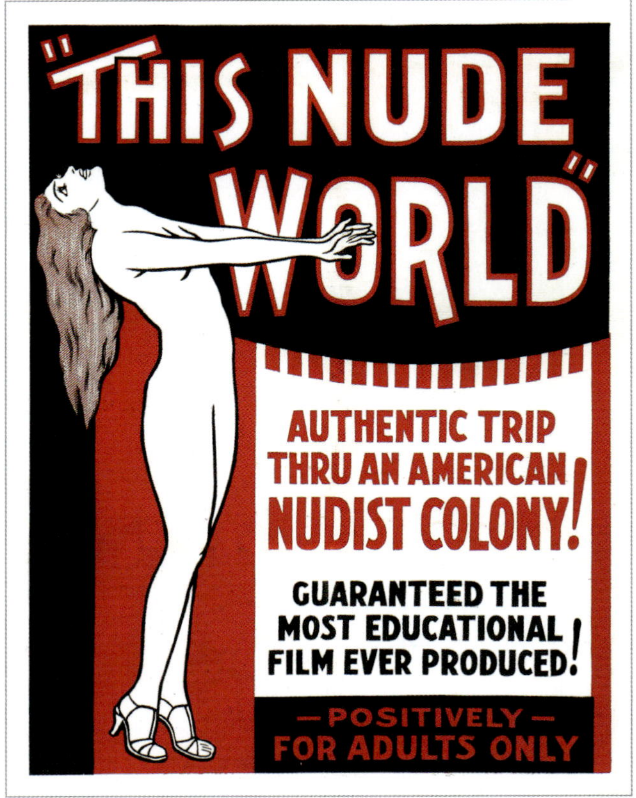
"THIS NUDE WORLD"
AUTHENTIC TRIP THRU AN AMERICAN NUDIST COLONY!
GUARANTEED THE MOST EDUCATIONAL FILM EVER PRODUCED!
—POSITIVELY— FOR ADULTS ONLY

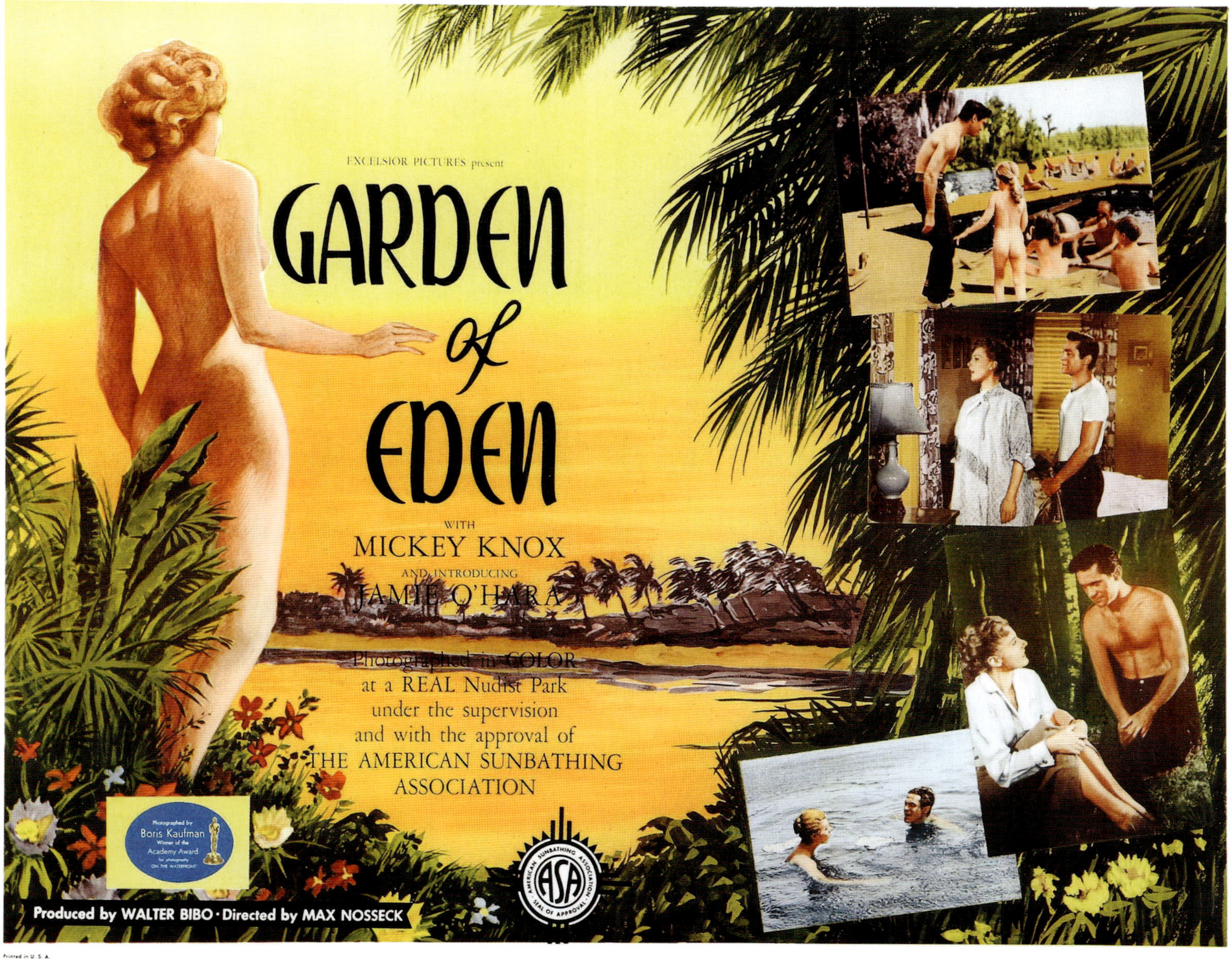

EXCELSIOR PICTURES present
GARDEN of EDEN
WITH
MICKEY KNOX
AND INTRODUCING
JAMIE O'HARA
Photographed in COLOR
at a REAL Nudist Park
under the supervision
and with the approval of
THE AMERICAN SUNBATHING
ASSOCIATION
Photographed by Boris Kaufman Winner of the Academy Award
AMERICAN SUNBATHING ASSOCIATION ASA SEAL OF APPROVAL
Produced by WALTER BIBO · Directed by MAX NOSSECK
Printed in U.S.A.

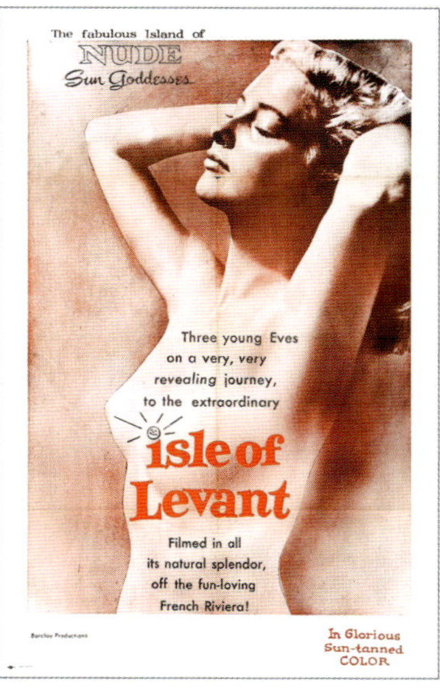

AS NATURE INTENDED

The opening text crawl of 1932's *This Nude World* gets right to it: "Who are these Nudists we've been hearing so much about? Do they meet and hold orgies by moonlight? Are they exotic and immoral? Are they trying to resurrect old pagan rites, or are they health fanatics?" It's the latter. The following rather dull hour of nudists cavorting healthily in various leafy settings is largely devoid of explicit nudity, except from behind (though to be fair there is a glimpse of a more exciting sort of bush 31 minutes in). There certainly isn't any sex, a trait shared by *Garden of Eden* (1954), which stood Excelsior Pictures in good stead when their nudist epic (in color!) came up against the New York State censors in court. Judge Charles Desmond found for the distributor, and summed up: "There is nothing sexy or suggestive about [the film] . . . nudists are shown as wholesome, happy people in family groups practicing their sincere but misguided theory that clothing . . . is deleterious to mental health." Judge Desmond's opinion of naturism aside, a legal ruling that nudity on screen was not obscene *per se*, had a huge impact on the exploitation business. The immediate upshot was *many* more nudist colony films, and now the door was open a crack, filmmakers would continue to push it . . .

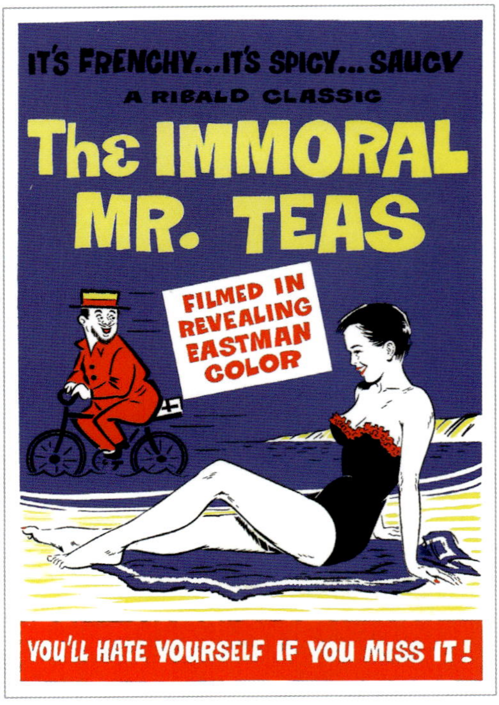

IT'S FRENCHY...IT'S SPICY...SAUCY
A RIBALD CLASSIC
The IMMORAL MR. TEAS
FILMED IN REVEALING EASTMAN COLOR
YOU'LL HATE YOURSELF IF YOU MISS IT!

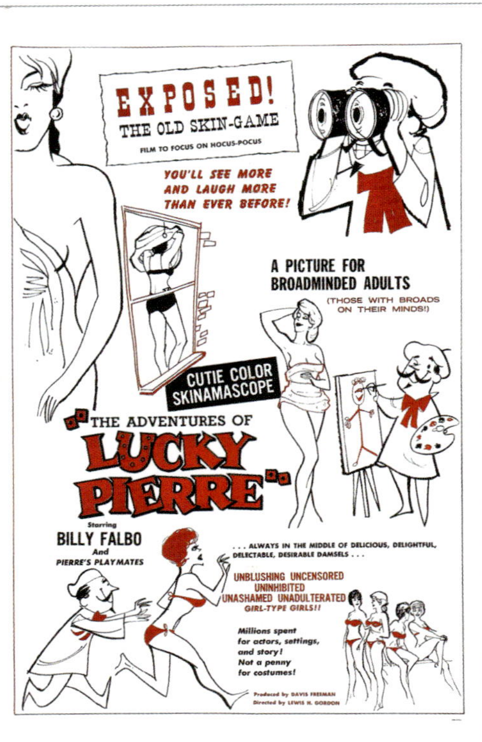

EXPOSED!
THE OLD SKIN-GAME
FILM TO FOCUS ON HOCUS-POCUS
YOU'LL SEE MORE AND LAUGH MORE THAN EVER BEFORE!
A PICTURE FOR BROADMINDED ADULTS
(THOSE WITH BROADS ON THEIR MINDS!)
CUTIE COLOR SKINAMASCOPE
THE ADVENTURES OF
LUCKY PIERRE
Starring
BILLY FALBO
And
PIERRE'S PLAYMATES
. . . ALWAYS IN THE MIDDLE OF DELICIOUS, DELIGHTFUL, DELECTABLE, DESIRABLE DAMSELS . . .
UNBLUSHING UNCENSORED
UNINHIBITED
UNASHAMED UNADULTERATED
GIRL-TYPE GIRLS!!
Millions spent for actors, settings, and story! Not a penny for costumes!
Produced by DAVIS FREEMAN
Directed by LEWIS H. GORDON

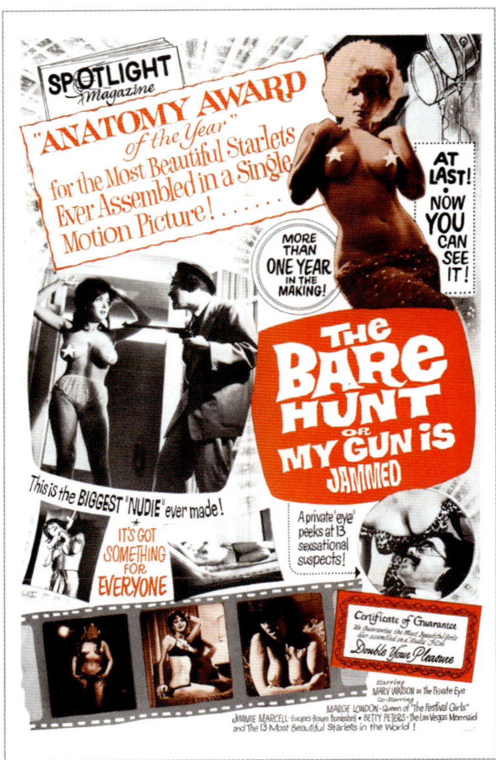

SPOTLIGHT Magazine
"ANATOMY AWARD of the Year" for the Most Beautiful Starlets Ever Assembled in a Single Motion Picture! . . . . . .
AT LAST! • NOW YOU CAN SEE IT!
MORE THAN ONE YEAR IN THE MAKING!
The BARE HUNT or MY GUN IS JAMMED
This is the BIGGEST "NUDIE" ever made!
IT'S GOT SOMETHING FOR EVERYONE
A private "eye" peeks at 13 sexsational suspects!
Certificate of Guarantee
Double Your Pleasure
Starring
MARV WATSON as The Private Eye
Co-Starring
MARGE LONDON - Queen of "The Festival Girls"
JIMMIE MARCELL - Europe's Bosom Bombshell • BETTY PETERS - The Las Vegas Mermaid
and The 13 Most Beautiful Starlets in the World!

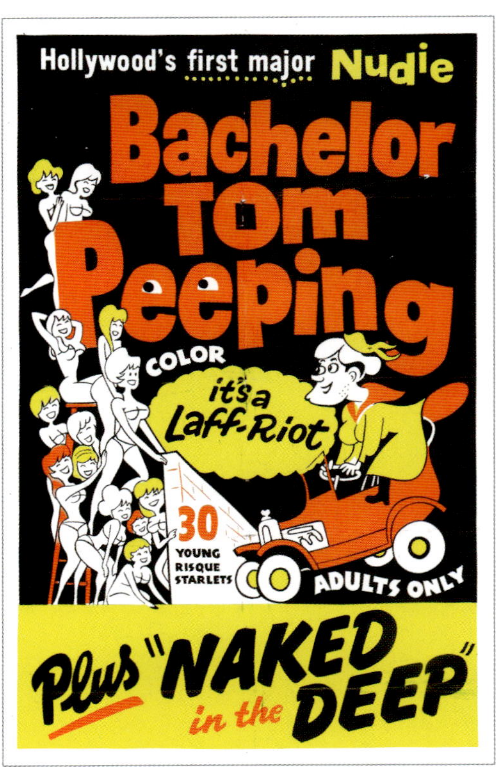

Hollywood's first major Nudie
Bachelor Tom Peeping
COLOR
it's a Laff-Riot
30 YOUNG RISQUE STARLETS
ADULTS ONLY
Plus "NAKED in the DEEP"

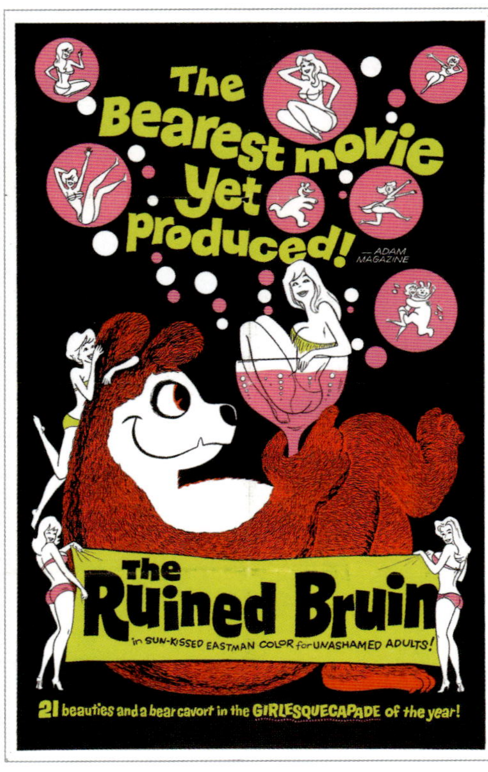

The Bearest movie yet produced!
—ADAM MAGAZINE
The Ruined Bruin
in SUN-KISSED EASTMAN COLOR for UNASHAMED ADULTS!
21 beauties and a bear cavort in the GIRLESQUECAPADE of the year!

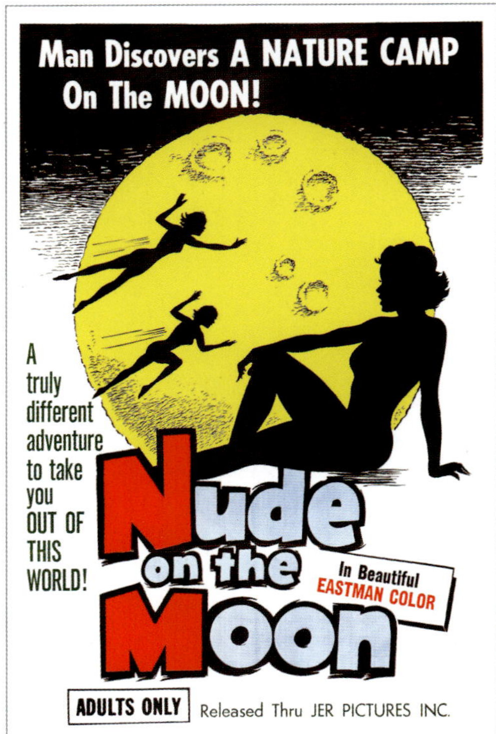

Man Discovers A NATURE CAMP On The MOON!
A truly different adventure to take you OUT OF THIS WORLD!
Nude on the Moon
In Beautiful EASTMAN COLOR
ADULTS ONLY
Released Thru JER PICTURES INC.

NUDIES

Even though filmmakers imported glamorous models to jump around on trampolines and play endless games of volleyball, pseudo-documentaries set in nudist camps could only go so far. Russ Meyer broke the mold in 1959 with *The Immoral Mr. Teas*, which ditched any pretense of being about naturism and simply presented a comic tale of a shy man hallucinating lots of naked ladies. It made a fortune, and the "nudie cutie" was born. 1962's Western-themed *Tonight for Sure* was less of a success, and was later dismissed by its own director as "an inane comedy, in which you saw a couple of boobs once in a while." Perhaps remembering his debut feature, Francis Ford Coppola (for it was he) featured scantily clad cowgirls again in *Apocalypse Now*.

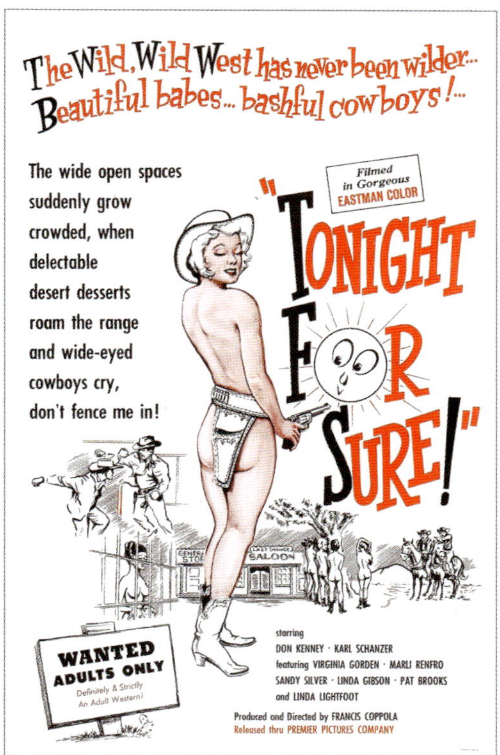

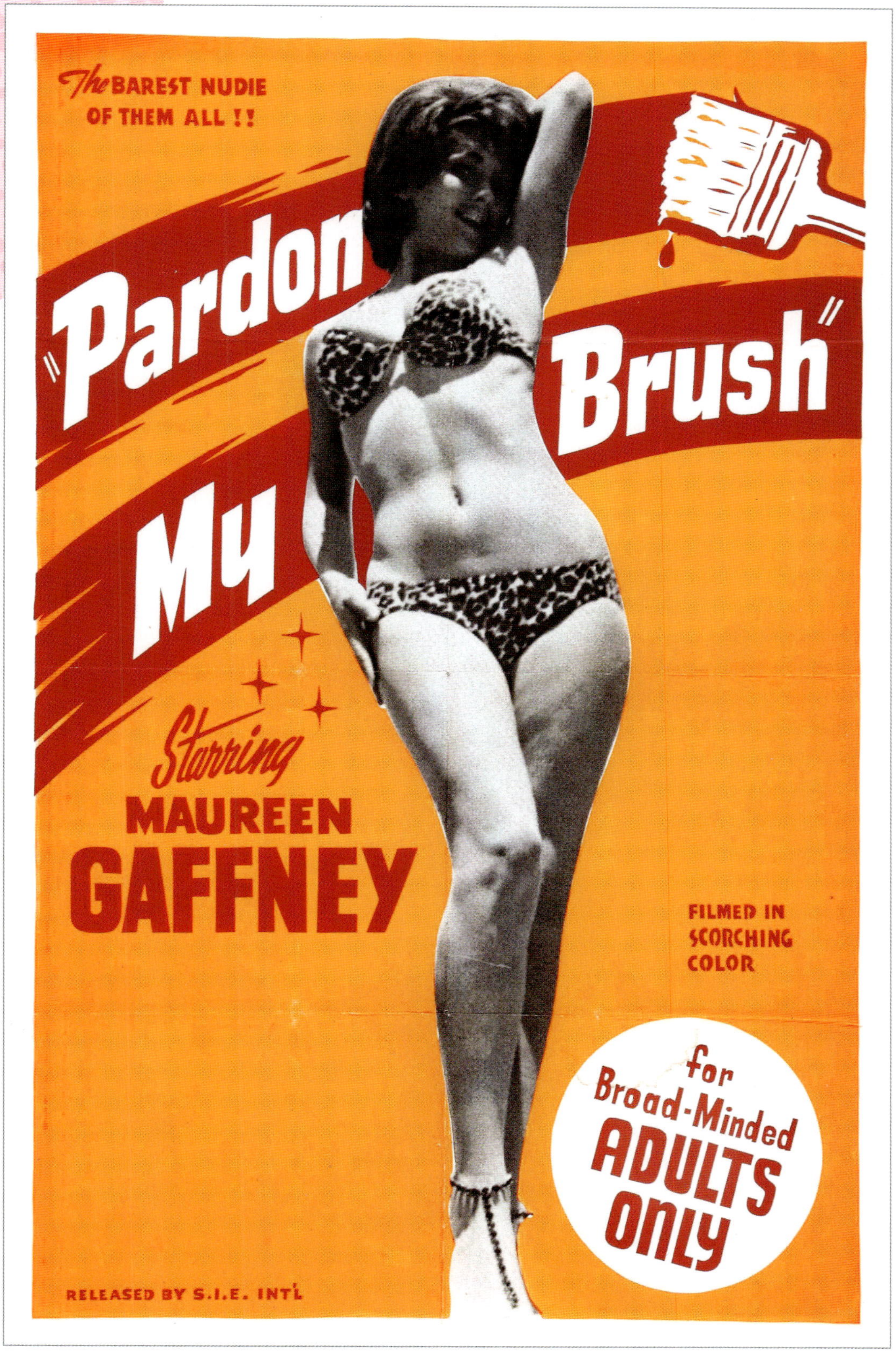

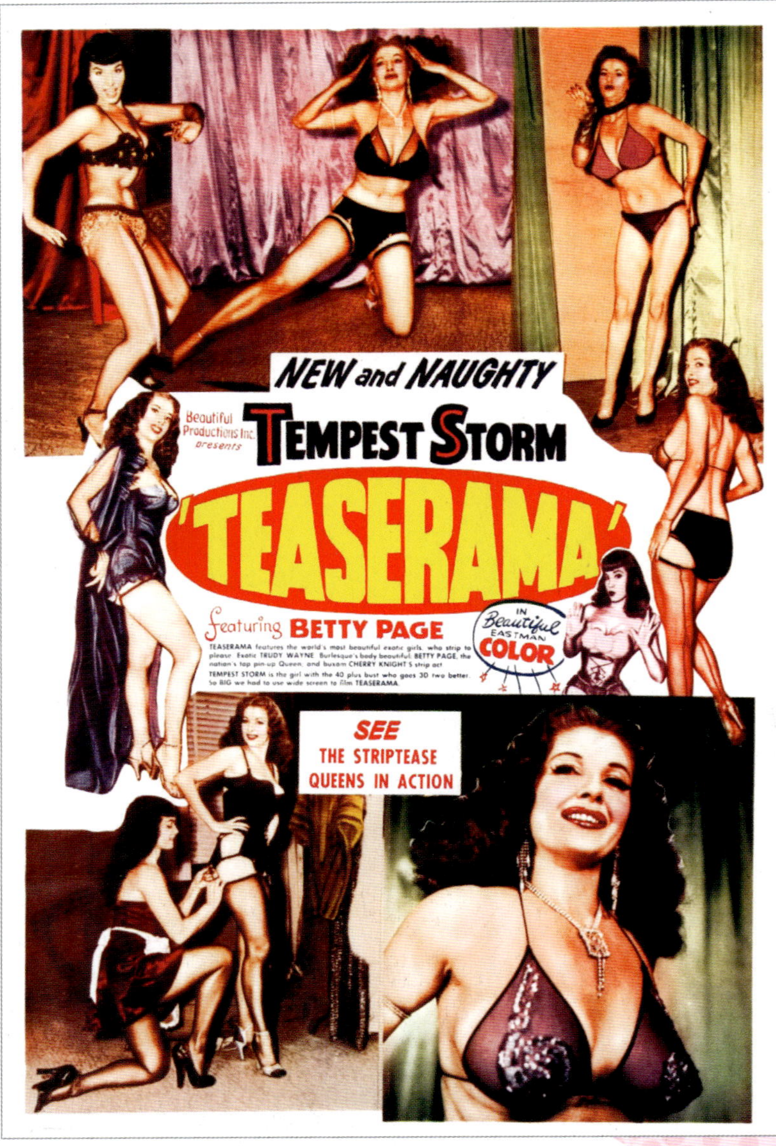

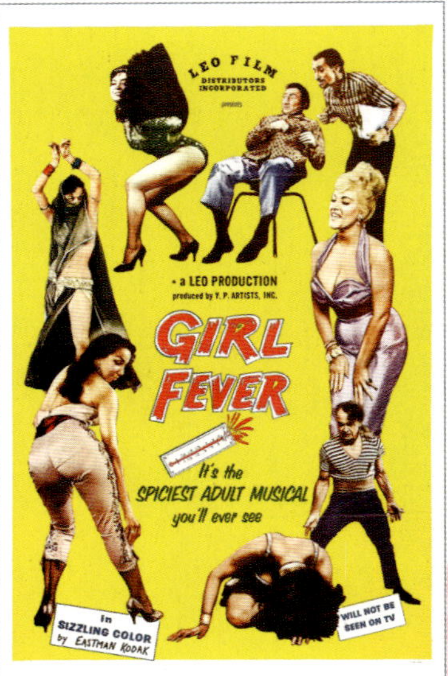

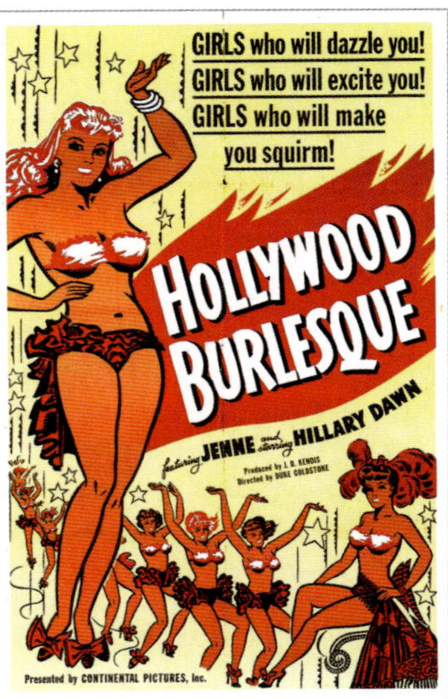

STRIPTEASE

Back in their 1940s and '50s heyday, the most in-demand striptease artists were limited by time and geography when it came to booking appearances. It's no surprise then that filmed performances also toured the country, with many of the biggest talents being immortalized on celluloid, including Tempest Storm, Lili St. Cyr, Bettie Page, and Evelyn "Treasure Chest" West (who had her "charms" insured by Lloyds of London for $50,000). *Teaserama* (1955) and its ilk were pretty basic, but they were often in color, and better than nothing until the real thing next came to town. "Proper" movies also cashed in on the world of nightclubs and strippers, though 39-inch Treasure Chest West was unimpressed by the star of one such production, *Too Hot to Handle* (1960, overleaf), sniping, "As far as Jayne [Mansfield] is concerned, she is way down on her erstwhile 38 bosom . . ."

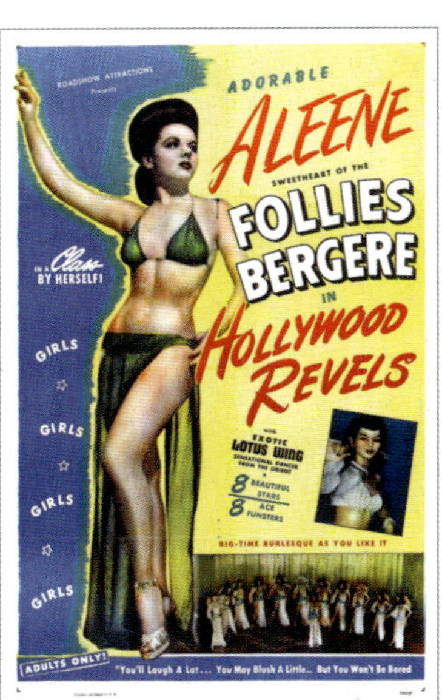

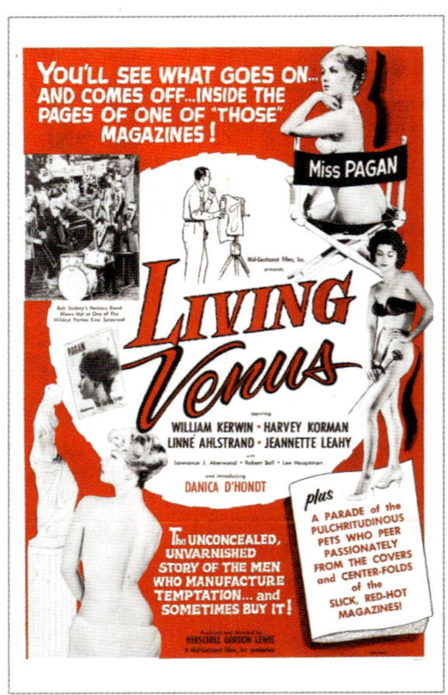

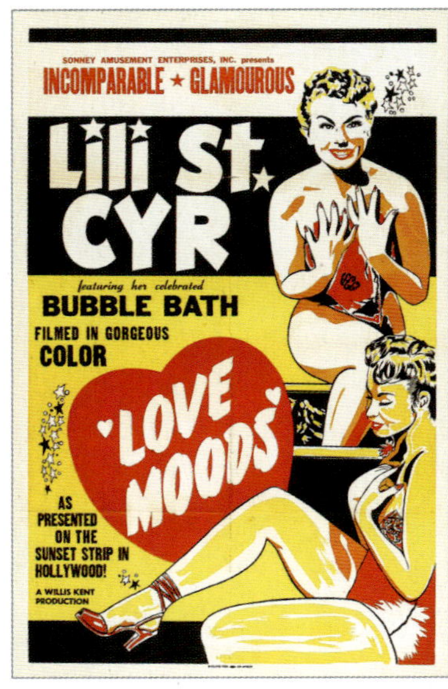

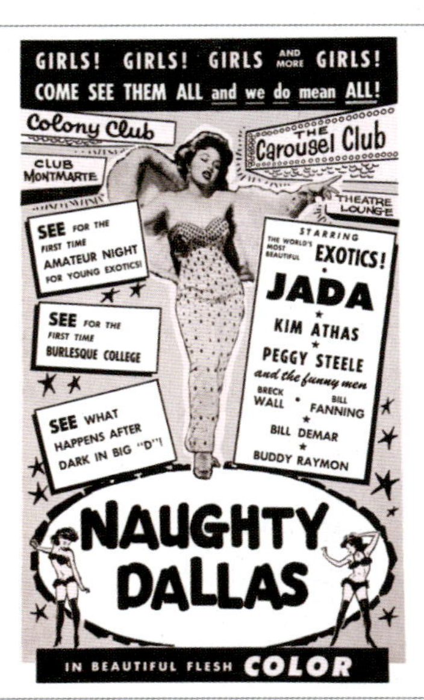

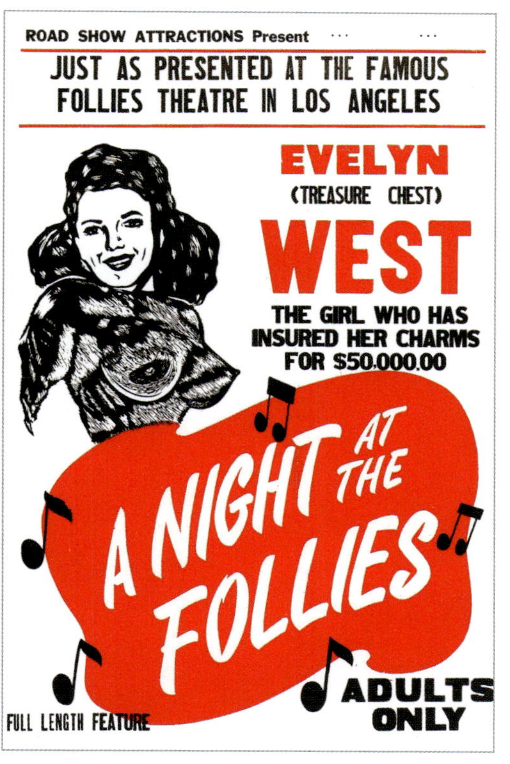
ROAD SHOW ATTRACTIONS Present
JUST AS PRESENTED AT THE FAMOUS
FOLLIES THEATRE IN LOS ANGELES
EVELYN
(TREASURE CHEST)
WEST
THE GIRL WHO HAS
INSURED HER CHARMS
FOR $50.000.00
A NIGHT AT THE FOLLIES
FULL LENGTH FEATURE
ADULTS ONLY

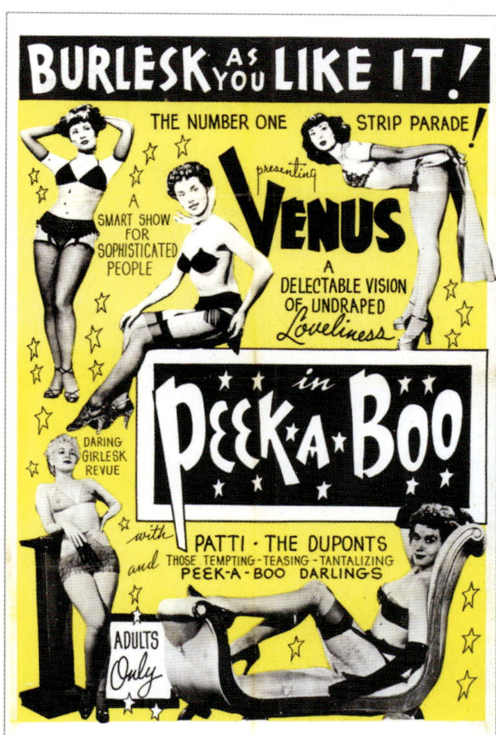
BURLESK AS YOU LIKE IT!
THE NUMBER ONE STRIP PARADE!
presenting
VENUS
A SMART SHOW FOR SOPHISTICATED PEOPLE
A DELECTABLE VISION OF UNDRAPED Loveliness
in
PEEK-A-BOO
DARING GIRLESK REVUE
with PATTI · THE DUPONTS
and THOSE TEMPTING-TEASING-TANTALIZING PEEK-A-BOO DARLINGS
ADULTS Only

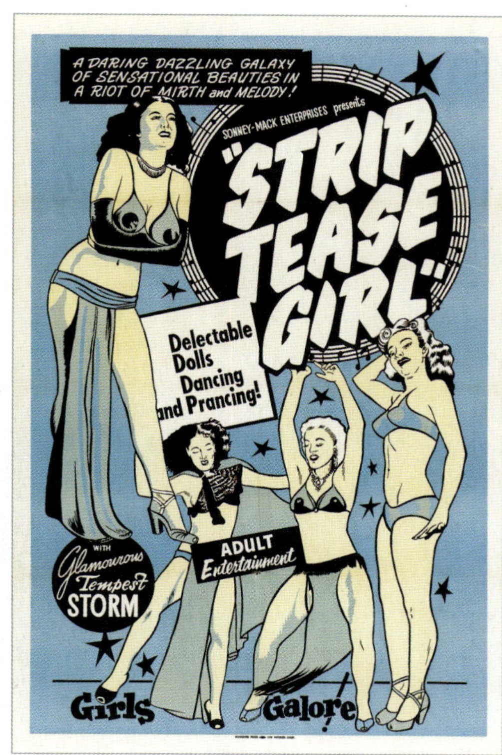
A DARING DAZZLING GALAXY
OF SENSATIONAL BEAUTIES IN
A RIOT OF MIRTH and MELODY!
SONNEY-MACK ENTERPRISES presents
"STRIP TEASE GIRL"
Delectable Dolls Dancing and Prancing!
WITH Glamourous Tempest STORM
ADULT Entertainment
Girls Galore!

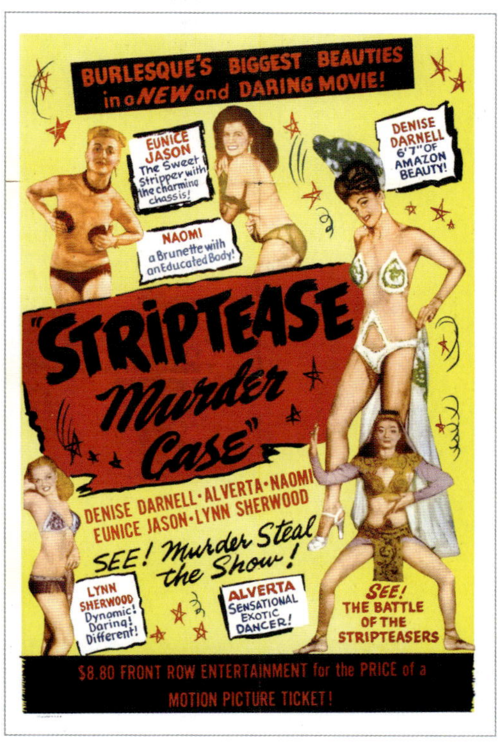
BURLESQUE'S BIGGEST BEAUTIES
in a NEW and DARING MOVIE!
EUNICE JASON The Sweet Stripper with the charming chassis!
DENISE DARNELL 6'7" OF AMAZON BEAUTY!
NAOMI a Brunette with an Educated Body!
"STRIPTEASE Murder Case"
DENISE DARNELL · ALVERTA · NAOMI
EUNICE JASON · LYNN SHERWOOD
SEE! Murder Steal the Show!
LYNN SHERWOOD Dynamic! Daring! Different!
ALVERTA SENSATIONAL EXOTIC DANCER!
SEE! THE BATTLE OF THE STRIPTEASERS
$8.80 FRONT ROW ENTERTAINMENT for the PRICE of a
MOTION PICTURE TICKET!

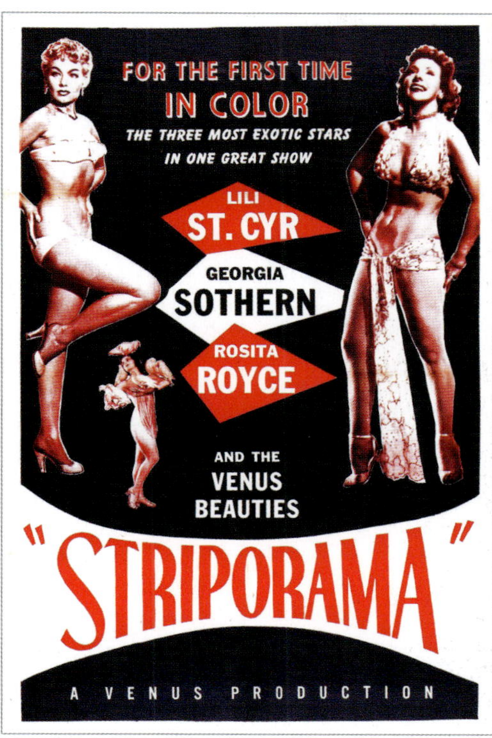
FOR THE FIRST TIME
IN COLOR
THE THREE MOST EXOTIC STARS
IN ONE GREAT SHOW
LILI
ST. CYR
GEORGIA
SOTHERN
ROSITA
ROYCE
AND THE
VENUS
BEAUTIES
"STRIPORAMA"
A VENUS PRODUCTION

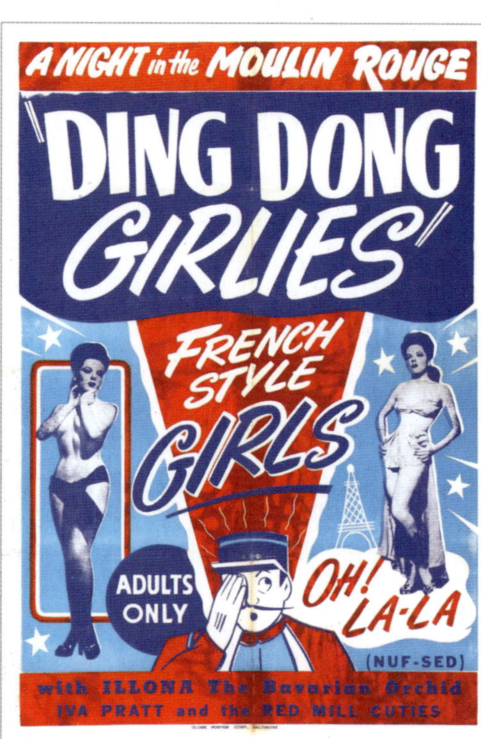
A NIGHT in the MOULIN ROUGE
"DING DONG GIRLIES"
FRENCH STYLE GIRLS
ADULTS ONLY
OH! LA-LA
(NUF-SED)
with ILLONA The Bavarian Orchid
IVA PRATT and the RED MILL CUTIES

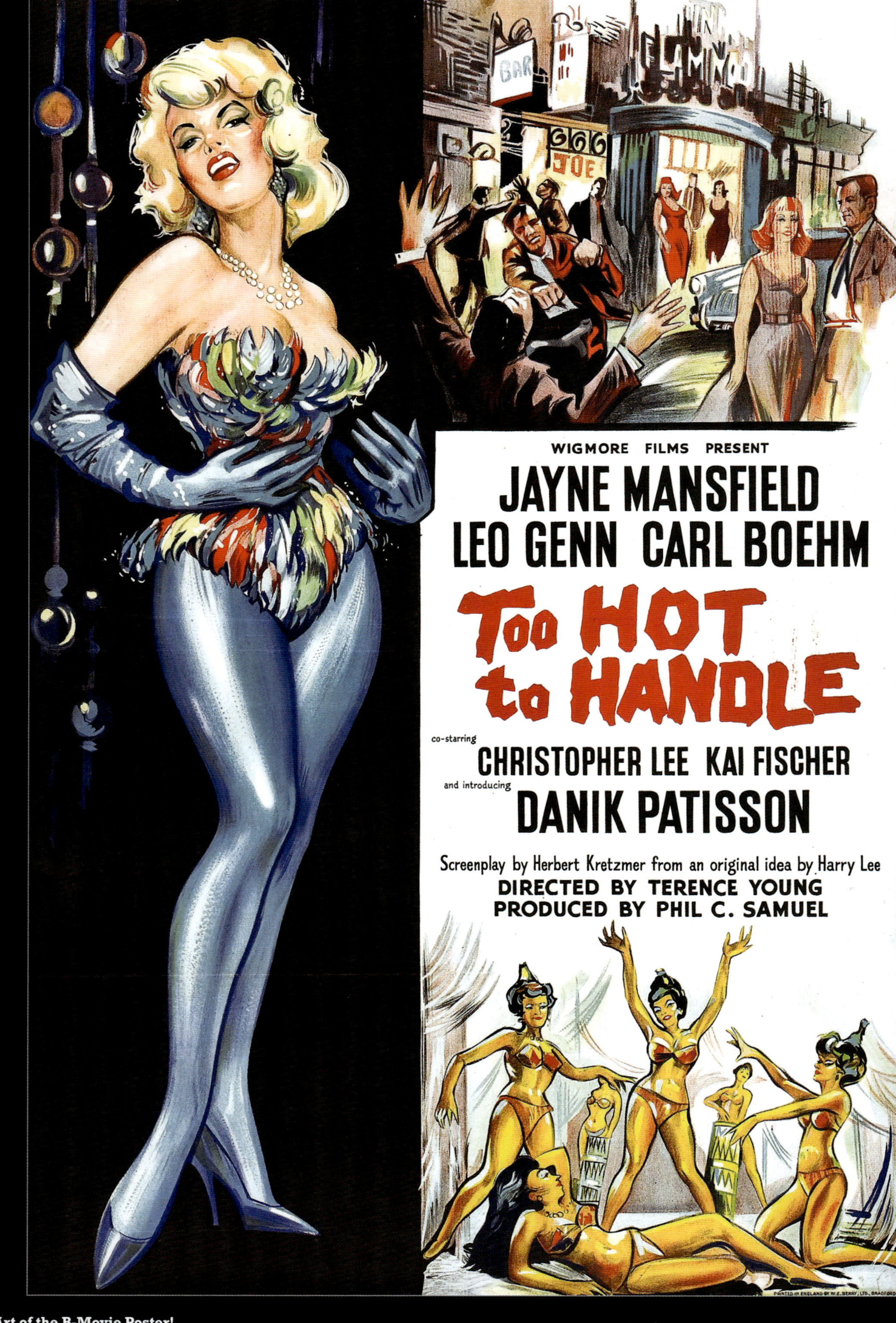
BAR
JOE
WIGMORE FILMS PRESENT
JAYNE MANSFIELD
LEO GENN CARL BOEHM
Too HOT to HANDLE
co-starring
CHRISTOPHER LEE KAI FISCHER
and introducing
DANIK PATISSON
Screenplay by Herbert Kretzmer from an original idea by Harry Lee
DIRECTED BY TERENCE YOUNG
PRODUCED BY PHIL C. SAMUEL

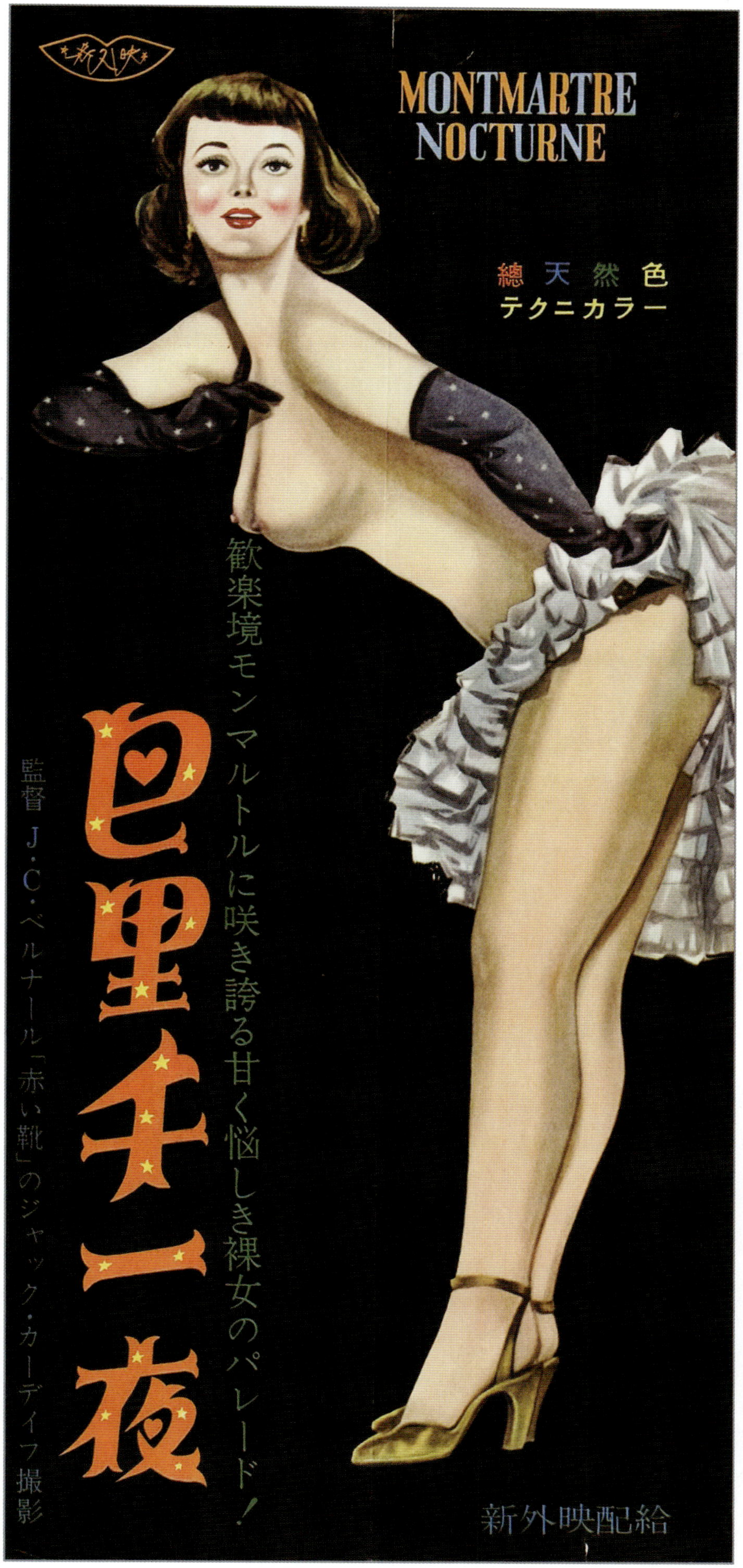

MONTMARTRE
NOCTURNE

總天然色
テクニカラー

歓楽境モンマルトルに咲き誇る甘く悩しき裸女のパレード！

巴里千一夜

監督 J・C・ベルナール「赤い靴」のジャック・カーディフ撮影

新外映配給

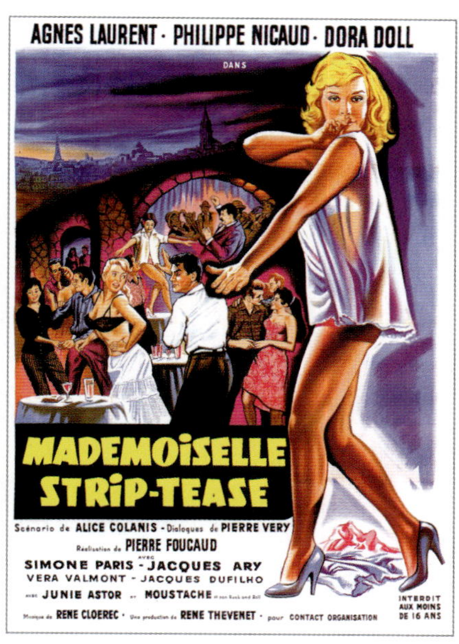

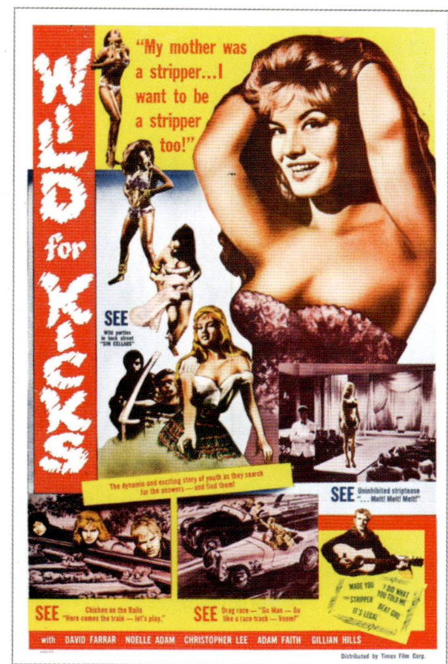

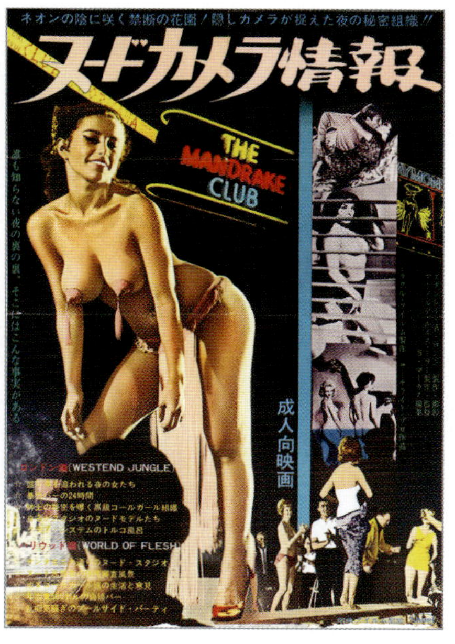

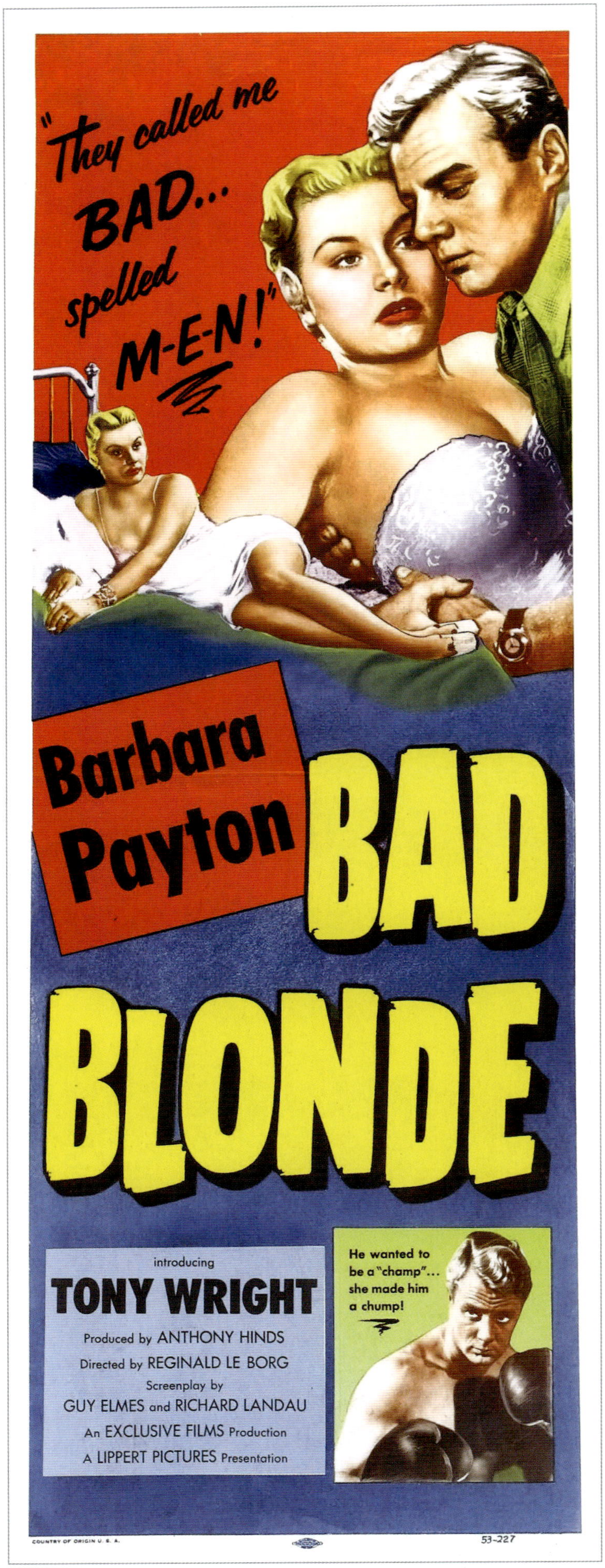

"They called me BAD... spelled M-E-N!"

Barbara Payton

BAD BLONDE

introducing

TONY WRIGHT

Produced by ANTHONY HINDS

Directed by REGINALD LE BORG

Screenplay by

GUY ELMES and RICHARD LANDAU

An EXCLUSIVE FILMS Production

A LIPPERT PICTURES Presentation

He wanted to be a "champ"... she made him a chump!

COUNTRY OF ORIGIN U. S. A.

53-227

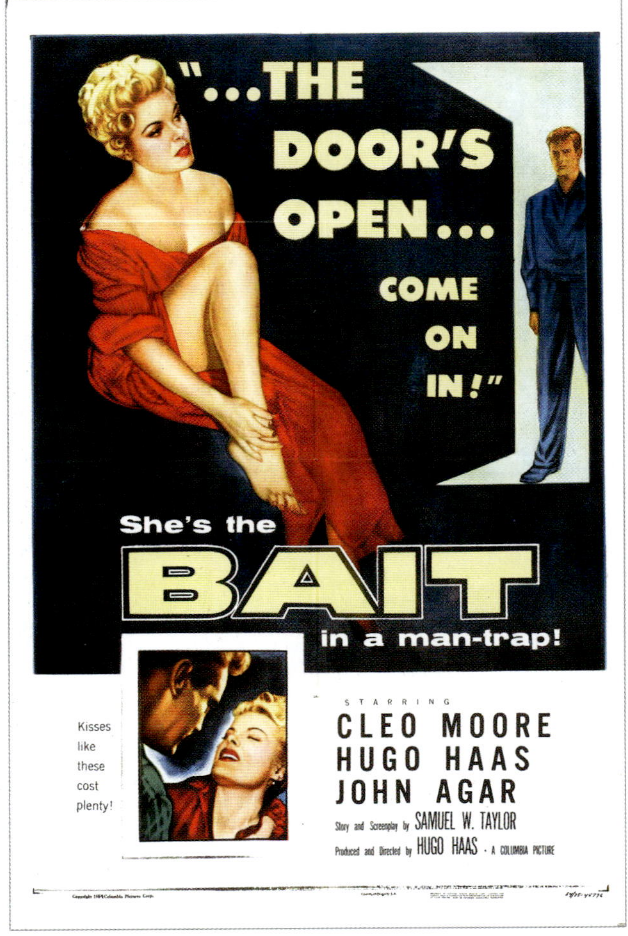

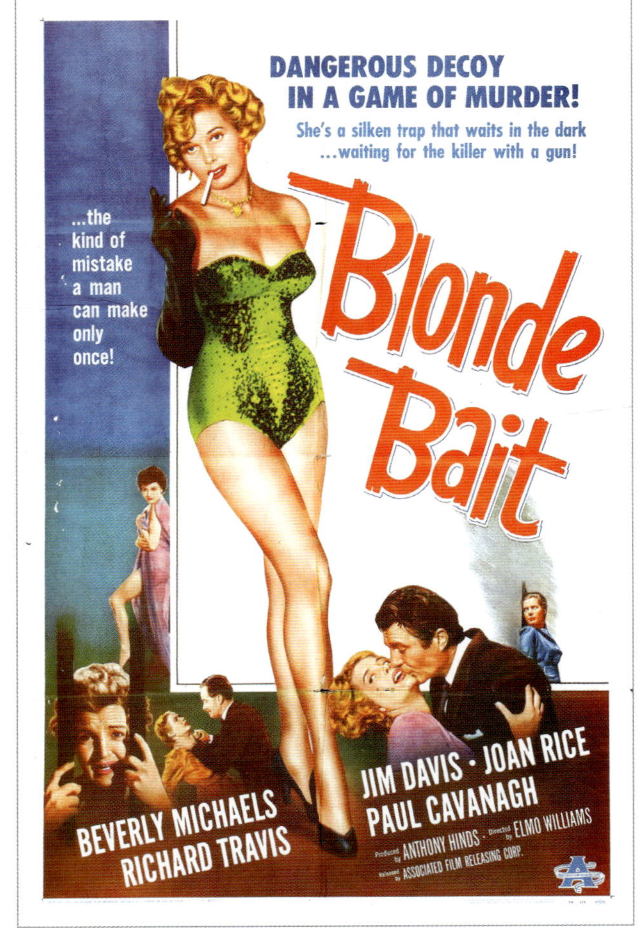

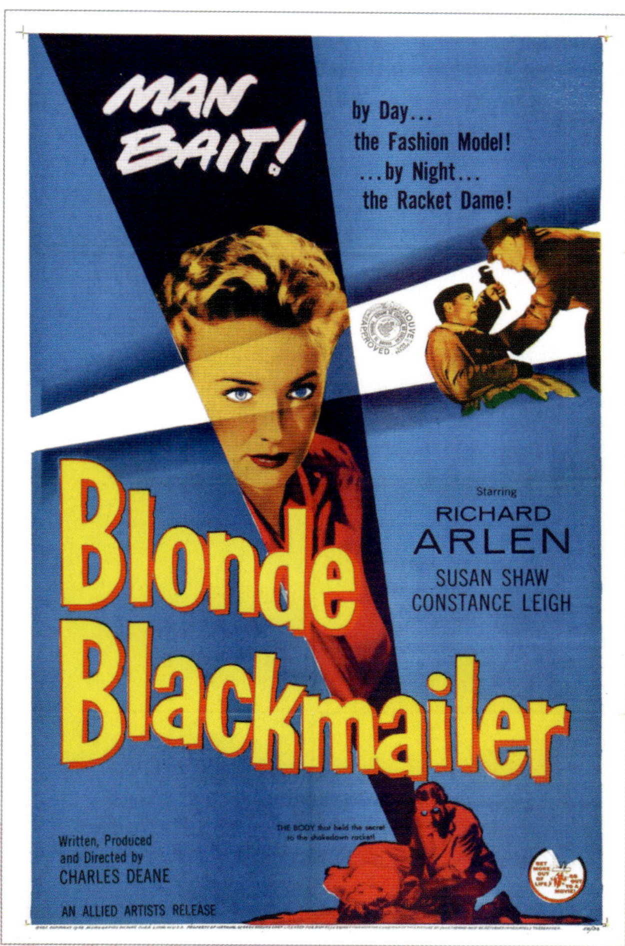

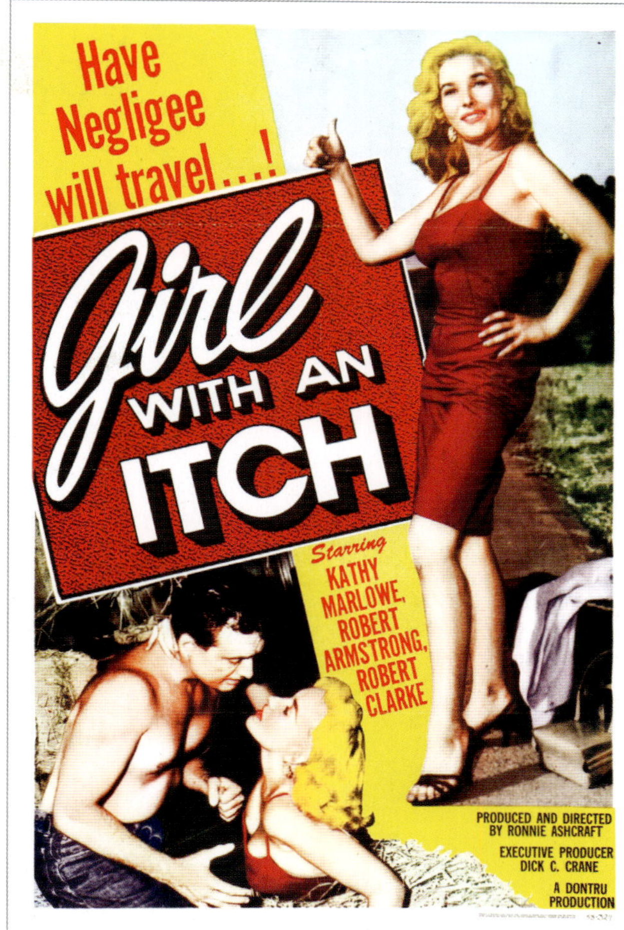

BAD GIRLS

"They called me BAD . . . spelled M-E-N!" purrs the memorable poster tagline for *Bad Blonde* (1953). This noir-ish drama about a boxer falling for a *femme fatale* was made in the UK by Hammer Films, where it was released as *The Flanagan Boy*. US distributors Lippert Pictures sexed-up the title to highlight its American star Barbara Payton, one of the many on-screen bombshells (usually blonde) tempting men off the straight and narrow during the '50s. In Payton's case, the bad behavior continued offscreen as well: a notorious party girl, she was married four times, lost custody of her son after exposing him to "unwholesome activities," and was eventually arrested on Sunset Boulevard for prostitution. Offered rehab, she proclaimed, "I'd rather drink and die," and duly did, aged 39. Diana Fluck, after understandably changing her name to Diana Dors, was promoted as the British answer to Marilyn Monroe in the likes of *Man Bait* (1952) and *Blonde Sinner* (1956), seen overleaf. Though she never made it big in the US, and was once denounced as a "wayward hussy" by the Archbishop of Canterbury, Dors ended up becoming a beloved agony aunt and chat show guest in her native country—she even got a prime front-row spot on the cover of The Beatles' *Sgt. Pepper*.

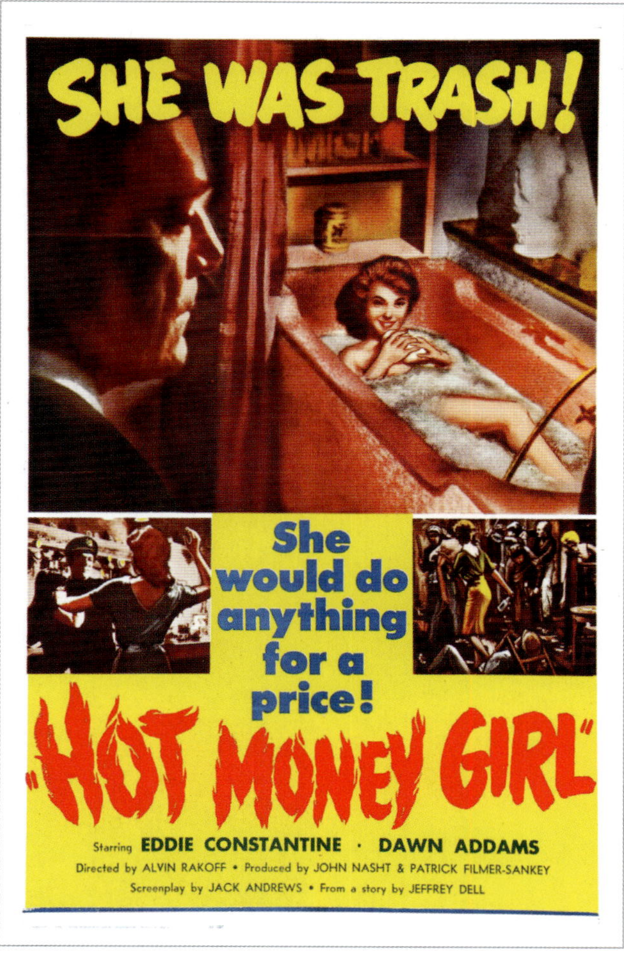

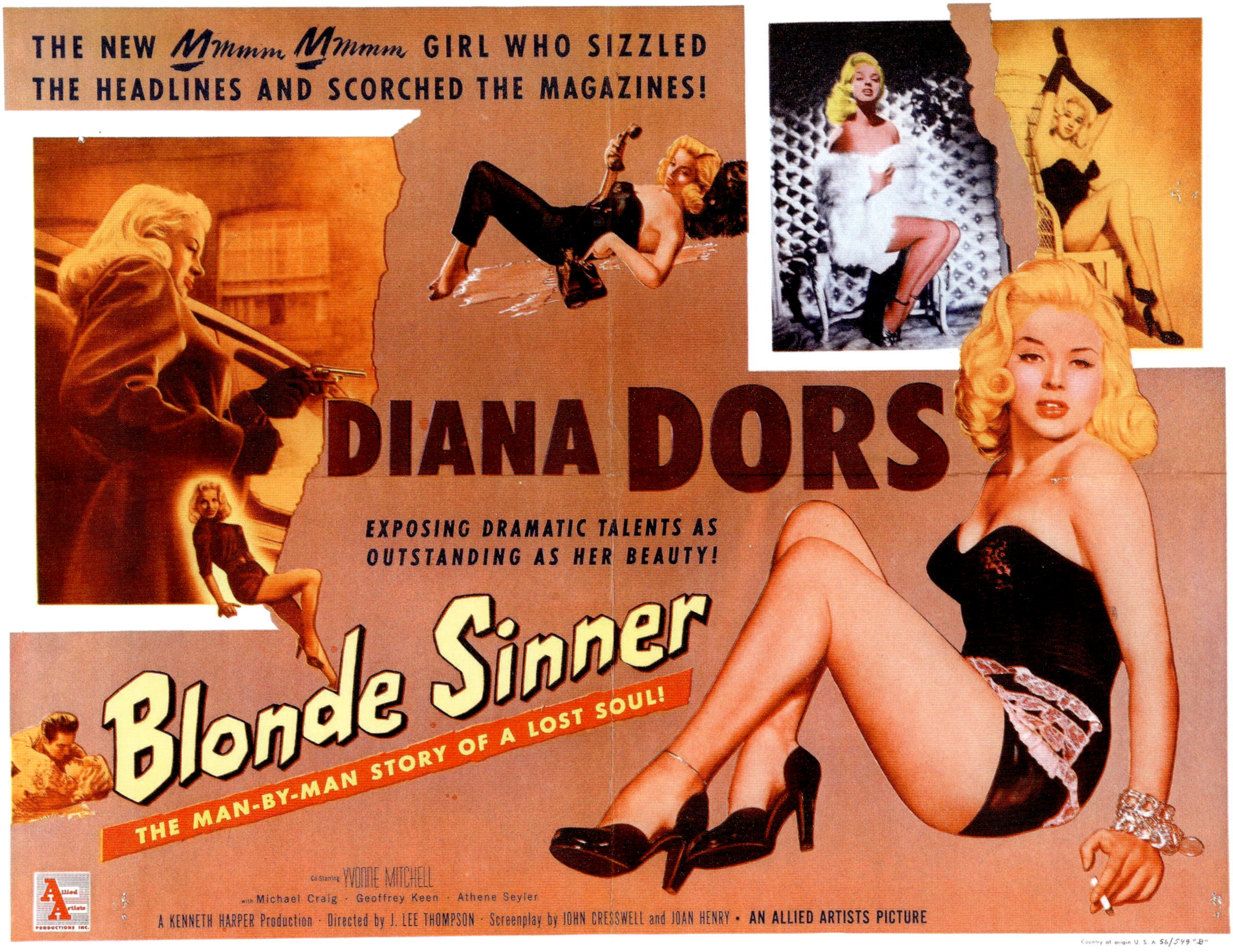

THE NEW Mmmm Mmmm GIRL WHO SIZZLED THE HEADLINES AND SCORCHED THE MAGAZINES!
DIANA DORS
EXPOSING DRAMATIC TALENTS AS OUTSTANDING AS HER BEAUTY!
Blonde Sinner
THE MAN-BY-MAN STORY OF A LOST SOUL!
Co-Starring YVONNE MITCHELL
with Michael Craig · Geoffrey Keen · Athene Seyler
A KENNETH HARPER Production · Directed by J. LEE THOMPSON · Screenplay by JOHN CRESSWELL and JOAN HENRY · AN ALLIED ARTISTS PICTURE

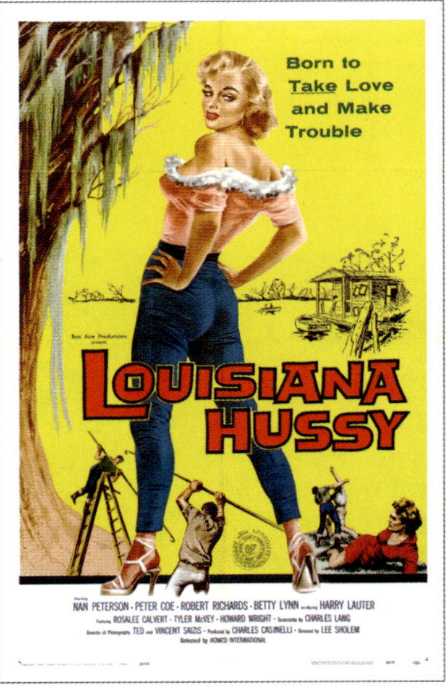
Born to Take Love and Make Trouble
LOUISIANA HUSSY
NAN PETERSON · PETER COE · ROBERT RICHARDS · BETTY LYNN · HARRY LAUTER

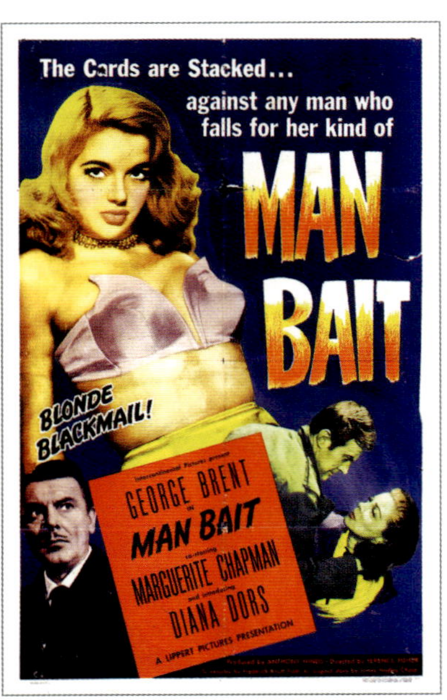
The Cards are Stacked...
against any man who falls for her kind of
MAN BAIT
BLONDE BLACKMAIL!
GEORGE BRENT
MAN BAIT
MARGUERITE CHAPMAN
DIANA DORS
A LIPPERT PICTURES PRESENTATION

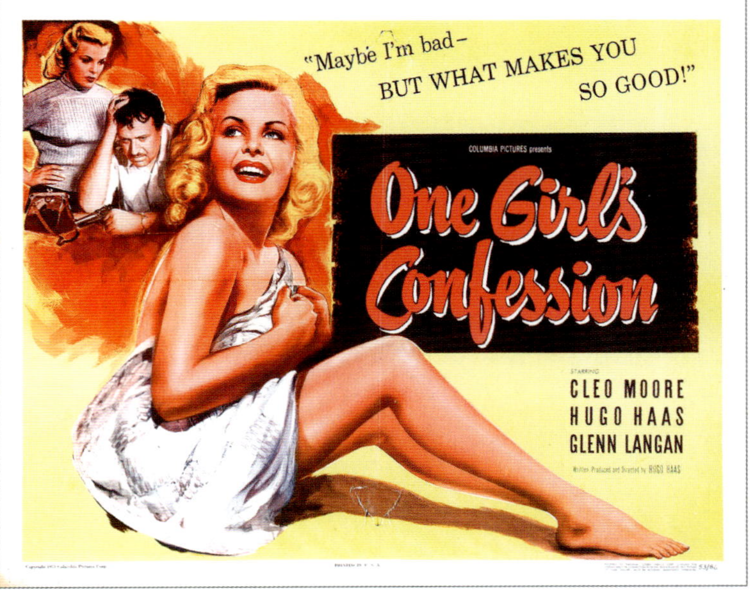
"Maybe I'm bad – BUT WHAT MAKES YOU SO GOOD!"
COLUMBIA PICTURES presents
One Girl's Confession
CLEO MOORE
HUGO HAAS
GLENN LANGAN

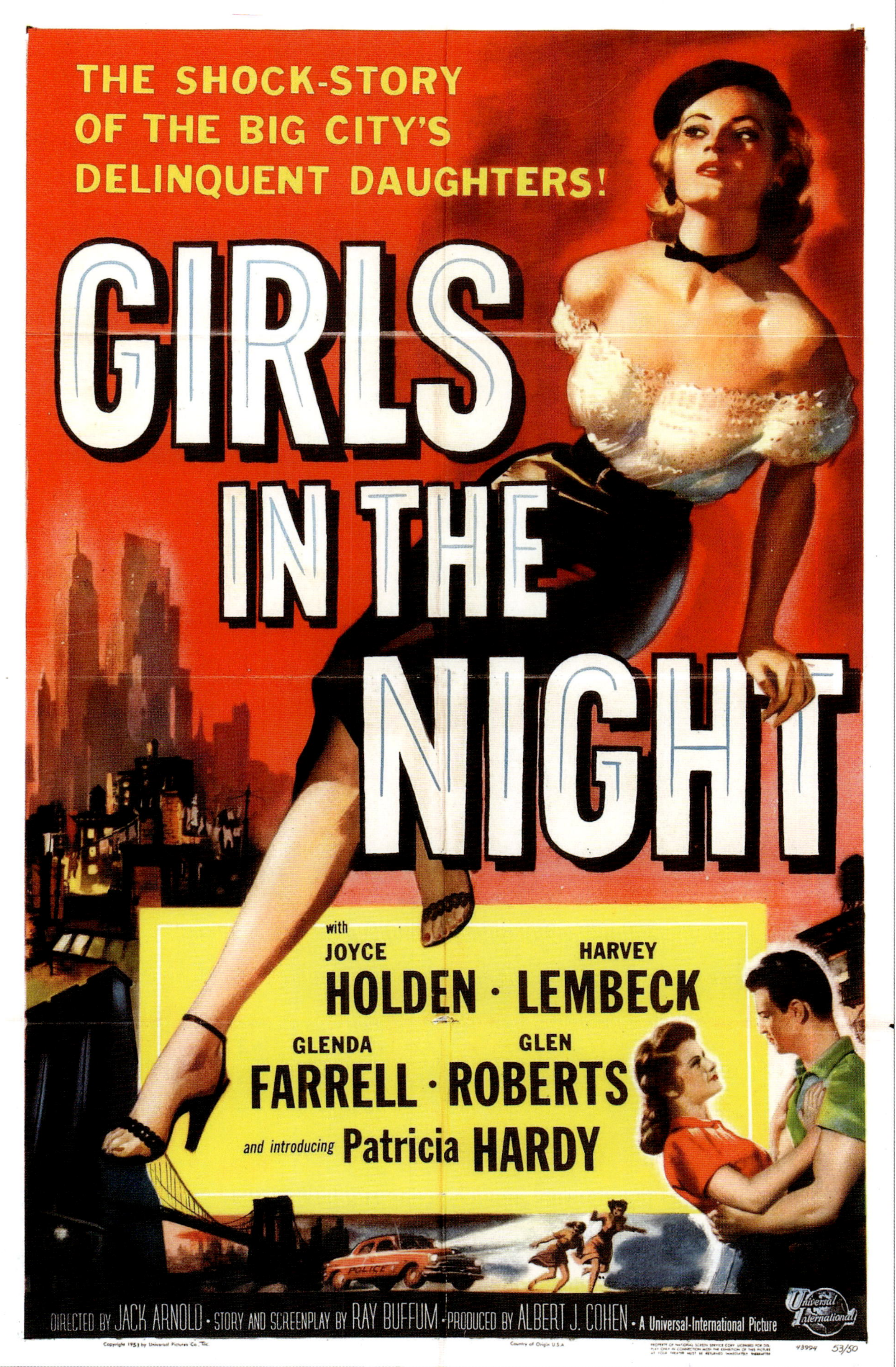
THE SHOCK-STORY
OF THE BIG CITY'S
DELINQUENT DAUGHTERS!
GIRLS
IN THE
NIGHT
with
JOYCE
HOLDEN · LEMBECK
HARVEY
GLENDA
FARRELL · ROBERTS
GLEN
and introducing Patricia HARDY
POLICE
DIRECTED BY JACK ARNOLD · STORY AND SCREENPLAY BY RAY BUFFUM · PRODUCED BY ALBERT J. COHEN · A Universal-International Picture
Universal International

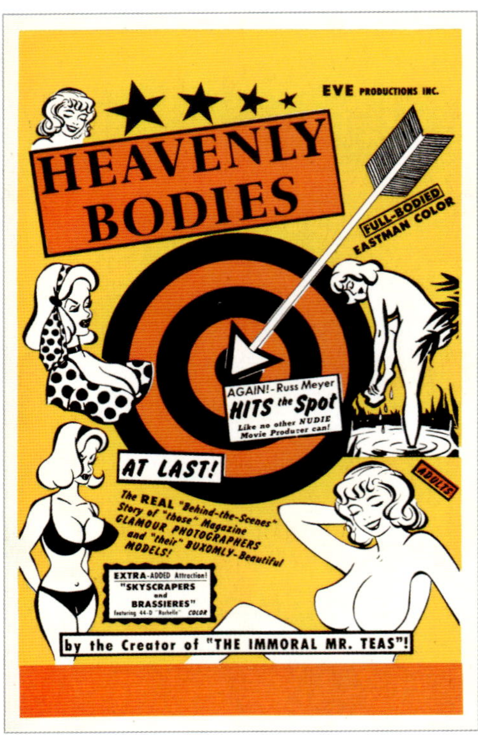

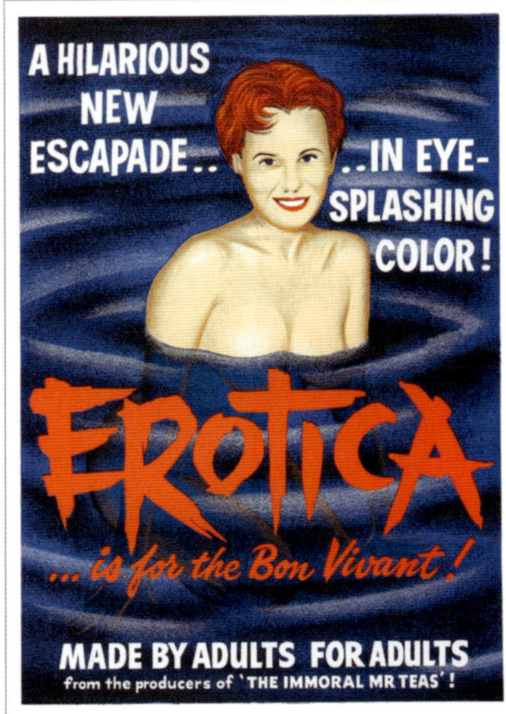

THE BREAST OF RUSS MEYER

Russ Meyer (1922–2004) used to tell the story of how he lost his virginity. While serving as a combat photographer during World War II, he met Ernest Hemingway one night in a French brothel. Learning that the young cameraman was a first-timer, the great writer generously offered to pay for a prostitute. Meyer, in a move that pretty much sums up the key to his subsequent success as a sexploitation auteur, chose the one with the biggest boobs. "Most of my films have women who have large breasts," he once pointed out (presumably for the benefit of blind people), adding the important caveats that, "They must be cantilevered. They must be defying gravity . . . Big, big, big. Casting a long shadow." "King of the Nudies" reads Meyer's gravestone, and he was.

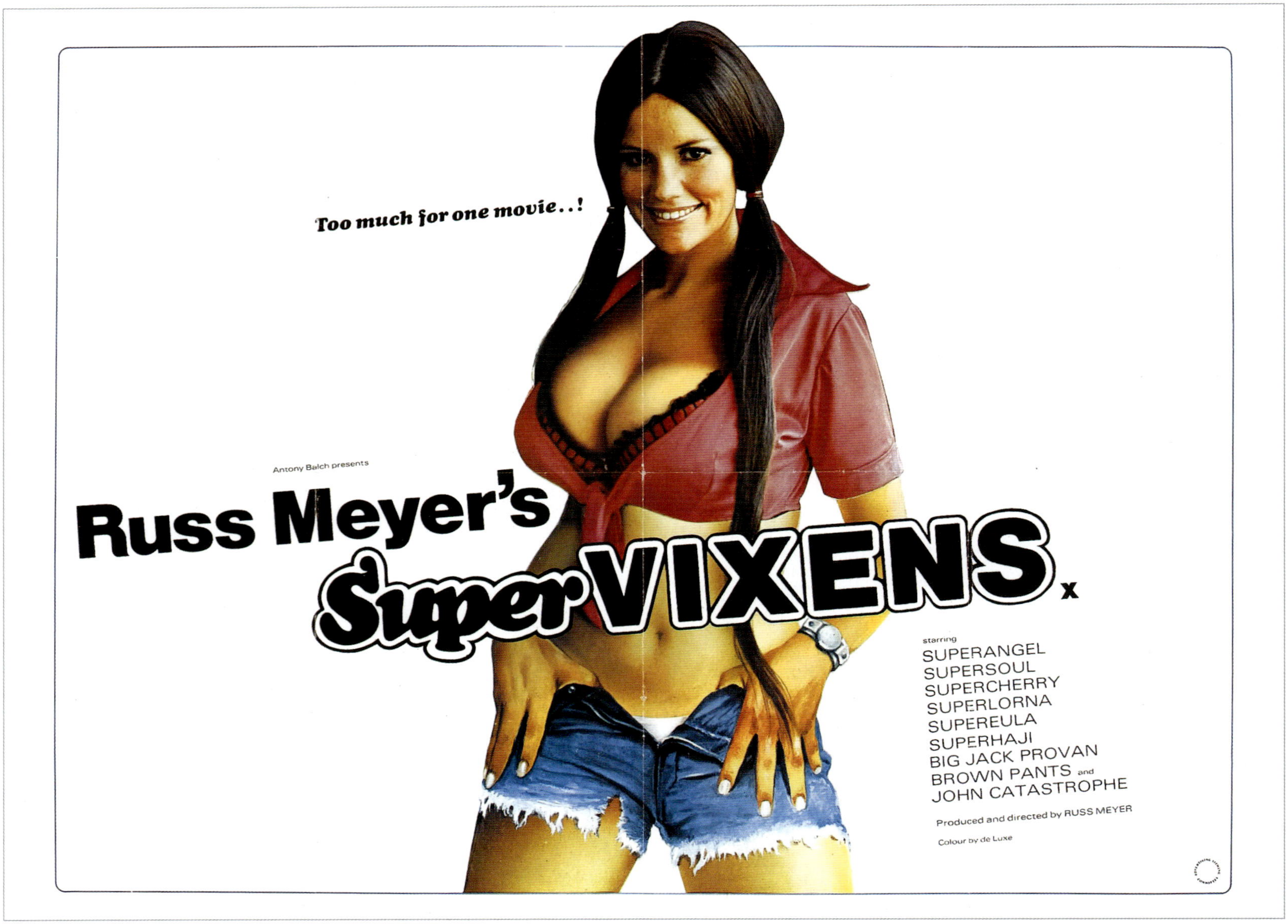

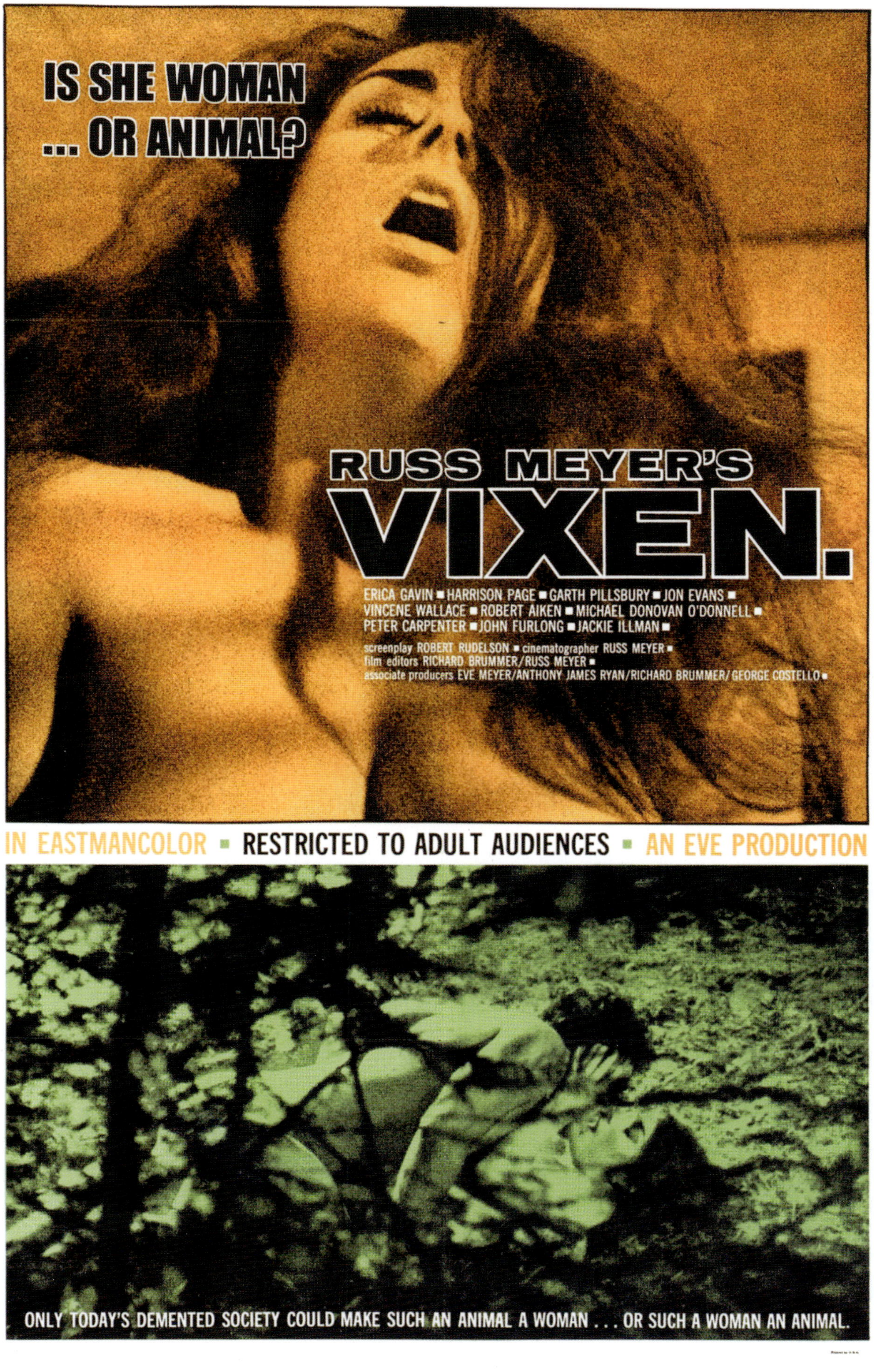

IS SHE WOMAN
... OR ANIMAL?

RUSS MEYER'S
VIXEN.

ERICA GAVIN ■ HARRISON PAGE ■ GARTH PILLSBURY ■ JON EVANS ■
VINCENE WALLACE ■ ROBERT AIKEN ■ MICHAEL DONOVAN O'DONNELL ■
PETER CARPENTER ■ JOHN FURLONG ■ JACKIE ILLMAN ■

screenplay ROBERT RUDELSON ■ cinematographer RUSS MEYER ■
film editors RICHARD BRUMMER/RUSS MEYER ■
associate producers EVE MEYER/ANTHONY JAMES RYAN/RICHARD BRUMMER/GEORGE COSTELLO ■

IN EASTMANCOLOR ■ RESTRICTED TO ADULT AUDIENCES ■ AN EVE PRODUCTION

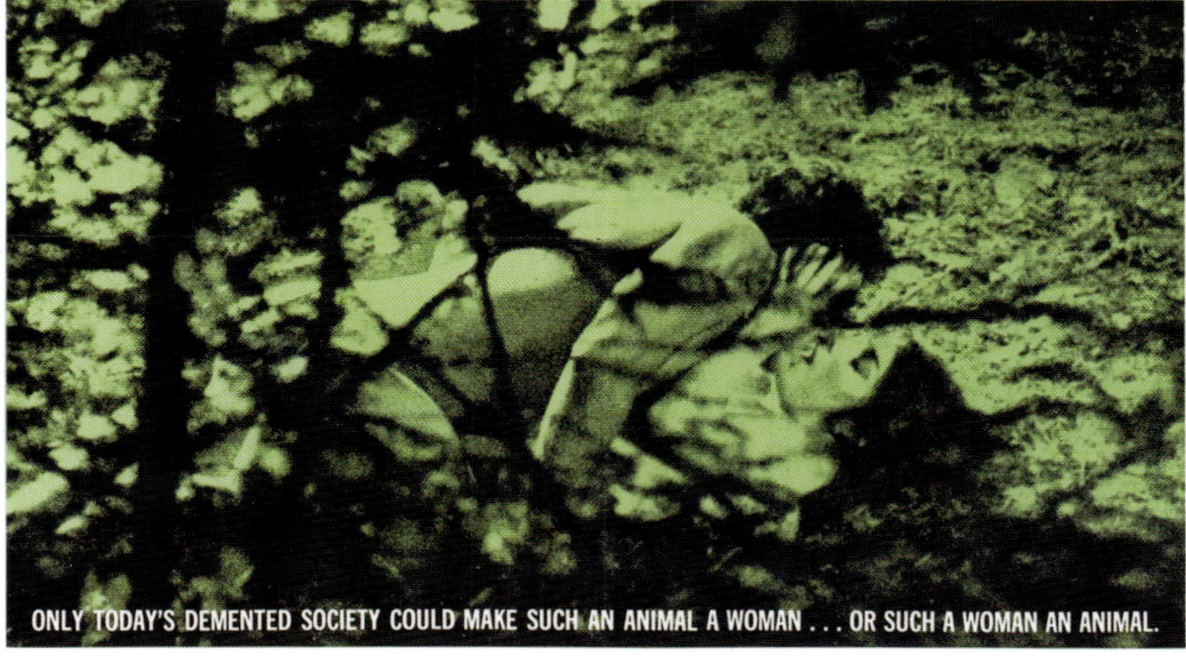

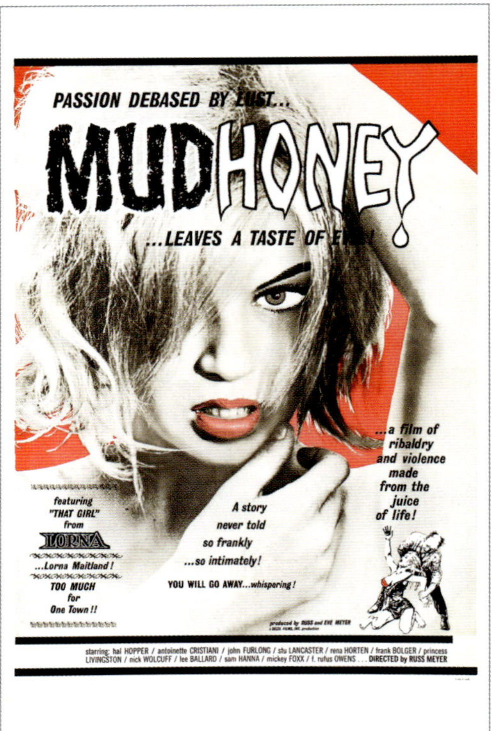
PASSION DEBASED BY LUST...
MUDHONEY
...LEAVES A TASTE OF EVIL!
...a film of ribaldry and violence made from the juice of life!
featuring "THAT GIRL" from LORNA ...Lorna Maitland! TOO MUCH for One Town!!
A story never told so frankly ...so intimately!
YOU WILL GO AWAY...whispering!

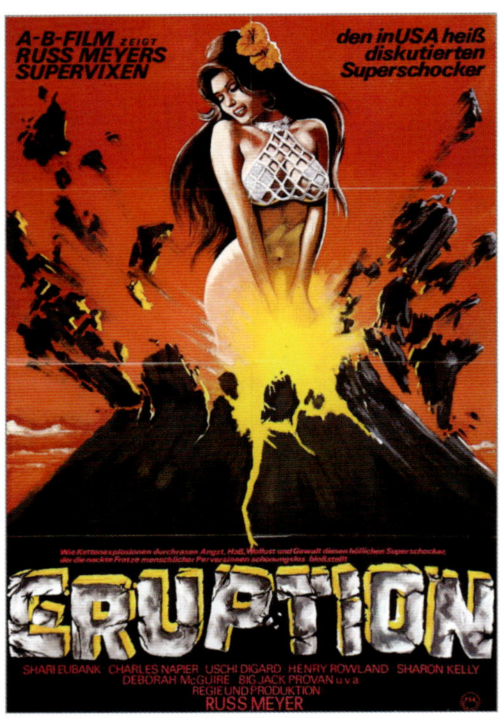
A-B-FILM ZEIGT RUSS MEYERS SUPERVIXEN
den in USA heiß diskutierten Superschocker
ERUPTION
SHARI EUBANK CHARLES NAPIER USCHI DIGARD HENRY ROWLAND SHARON KELLY
DEBORAH McGUIRE BIG JACK PROVAN u.v.a.
REGIE UND PRODUKTION
RUSS MEYER

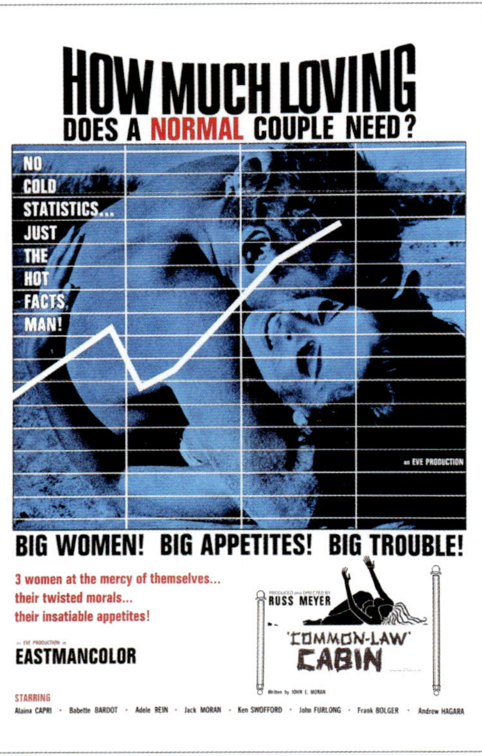
HOW MUCH LOVING DOES A NORMAL COUPLE NEED?
NO COLD STATISTICS... JUST THE HOT FACTS, MAN!
BIG WOMEN! BIG APPETITES! BIG TROUBLE!
3 women at the mercy of themselves...
their twisted morals...
their insatiable appetites!
EASTMANCOLOR
RUSS MEYER
COMMON-LAW CABIN
STARRING

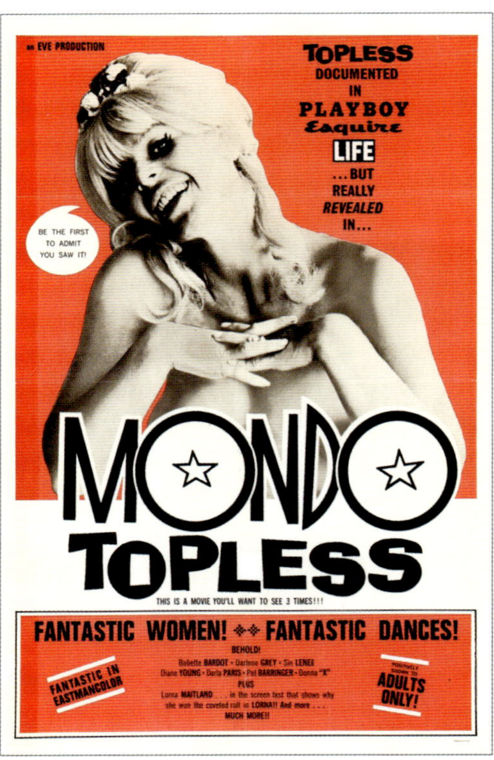
an EVE PRODUCTION
TOPLESS DOCUMENTED IN PLAYBOY Esquire LIFE ...BUT REALLY REVEALED IN...
BE THE FIRST TO ADMIT YOU SAW IT!
MONDO TOPLESS
THIS IS A MOVIE YOU'LL WANT TO SEE 3 TIMES!!!
FANTASTIC WOMEN! FANTASTIC DANCES!
FANTASTIC IN EASTMANCOLOR
ADULTS ONLY!

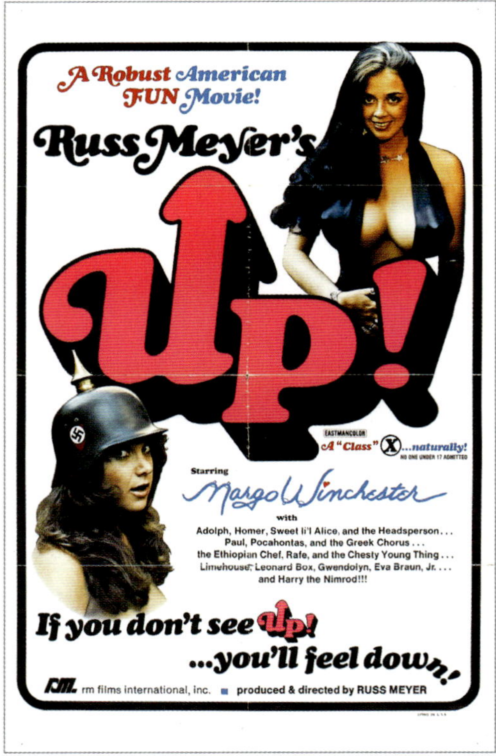
A Robust American FUN Movie!
Russ Meyer's
up!
A "Class" X ...naturally!
Starring
Margo Winchester
with
Adolph, Homer, Sweet li'l Alice, and the Headsperson...
Paul, Pocahontas, and the Greek Chorus...
the Ethiopian Chef, Rafe, and the Chesty Young Thing...
Limehouse, Leonard Box, Gwendolyn, Eva Braun, Jr....
and Harry the Nimrod!!!
If you don't see up!
...you'll feel down!
rm films international, inc. produced & directed by RUSS MEYER

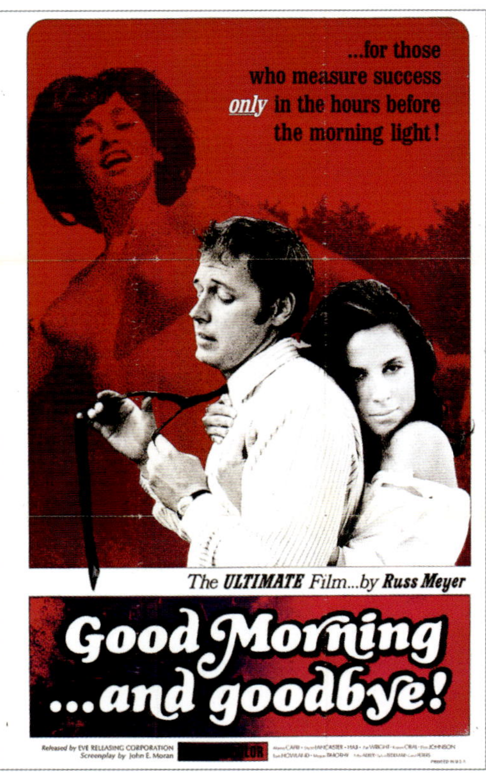
...for those who measure success only in the hours before the morning light!
The ULTIMATE Film...by Russ Meyer
Good Morning ...and goodbye!

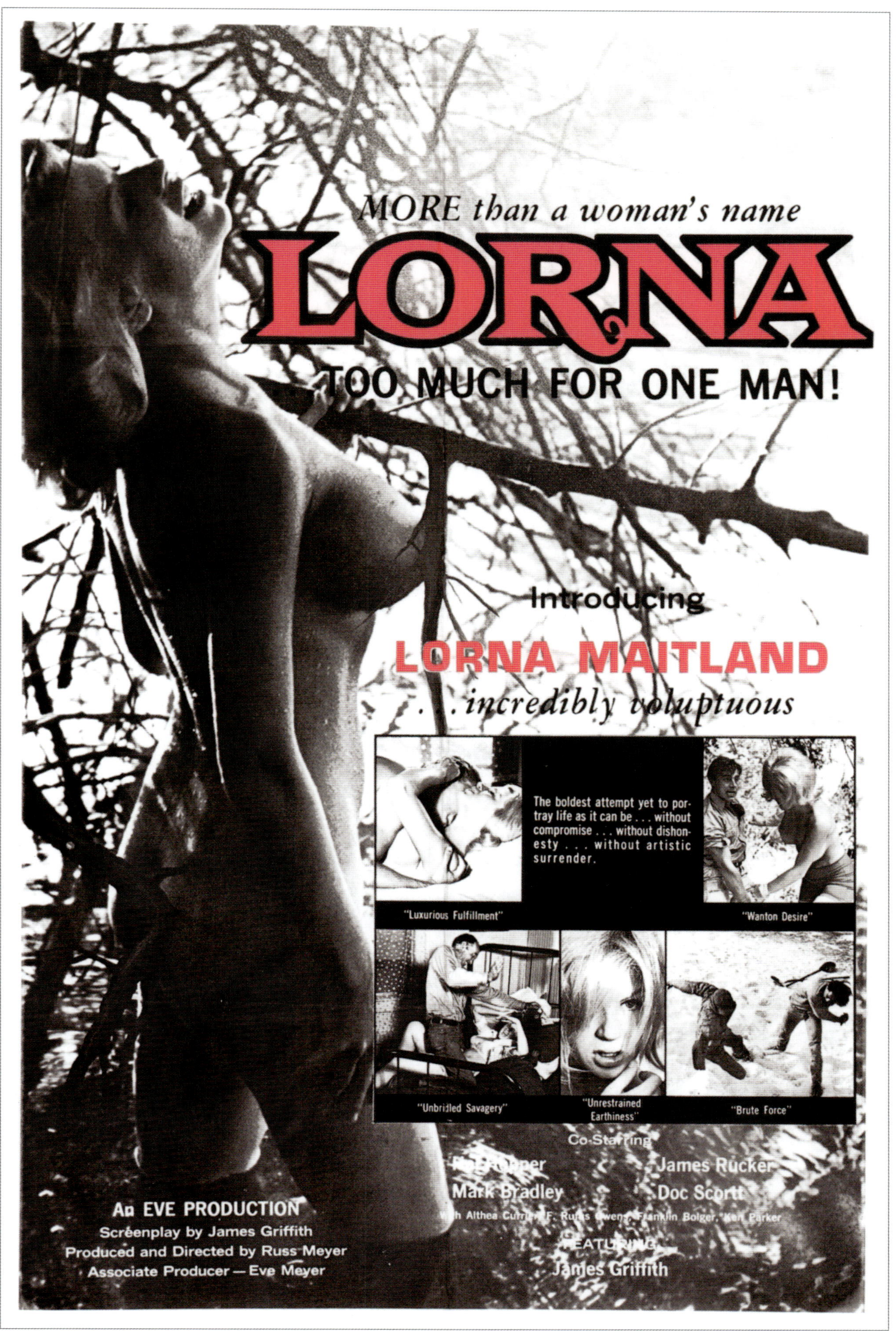
MORE than a woman's name
LORNA
TOO MUCH FOR ONE MAN!
Introducing
LORNA MAITLAND
. . . incredibly voluptuous
The boldest attempt yet to portray life as it can be . . . without compromise . . . without dishonesty . . . without artistic surrender.
"Luxurious Fulfillment"
"Wanton Desire"
"Unbridled Savagery"
"Unrestrained Earthiness"
"Brute Force"
Co-Starring
James Rucker
Mark Bradley
Doc Scortt
James Griffith
An EVE PRODUCTION
Screenplay by James Griffith
Produced and Directed by Russ Meyer
Associate Producer — Eve Meyer

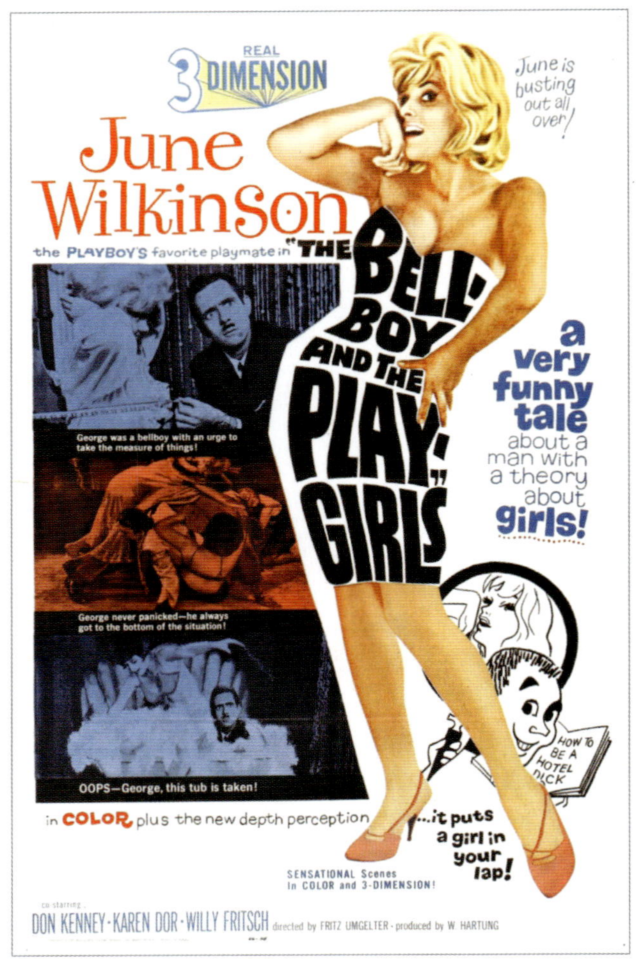
REAL
3 DIMENSION
June is busting out all over!
June Wilkinson
the PLAYBOY'S favorite playmate in "THE BELL-BOY AND THE PLAY-GIRLS"
a very funny tale about a man with a theory about girls!
George was a bellboy with an urge to take the measure of things!
George never panicked—he always got to the bottom of the situation!
OOPS—George, this tub is taken!
HOW TO BE A HOTEL DICK
in COLOR plus the new depth perception
...it puts a girl in your lap!
SENSATIONAL Scenes in COLOR and 3-DIMENSION!
co-starring
DON KENNEY · KAREN DOR · WILLY FRITSCH directed by FRITZ UMGELTER · produced by W. HARTUNG

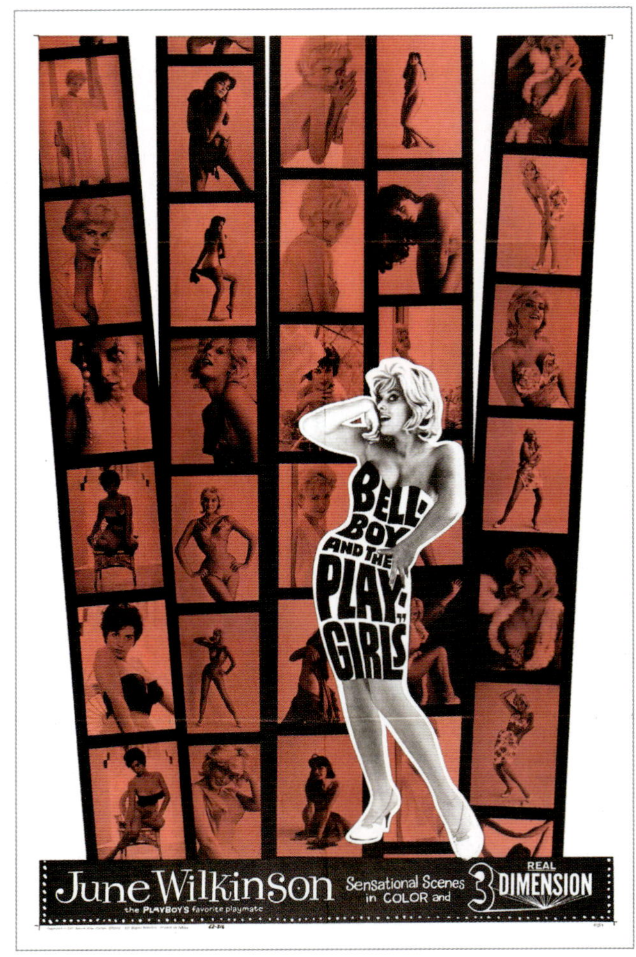
BELL-BOY AND THE PLAY-GIRLS
June Wilkinson
the PLAYBOY'S favorite playmate
Sensational Scenes in COLOR and
REAL
3 DIMENSION

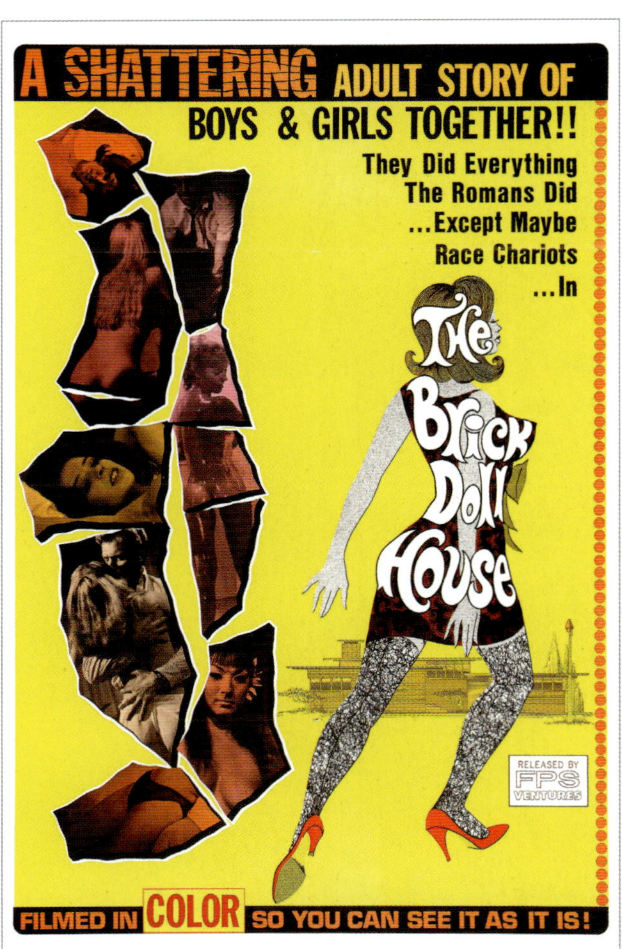
A SHATTERING ADULT STORY OF BOYS & GIRLS TOGETHER!!
They Did Everything
The Romans Did
...Except Maybe
Race Chariots
...In
The Brick Doll House
RELEASED BY
FPS
VENTURES
FILMED IN COLOR SO YOU CAN SEE IT AS IT IS!

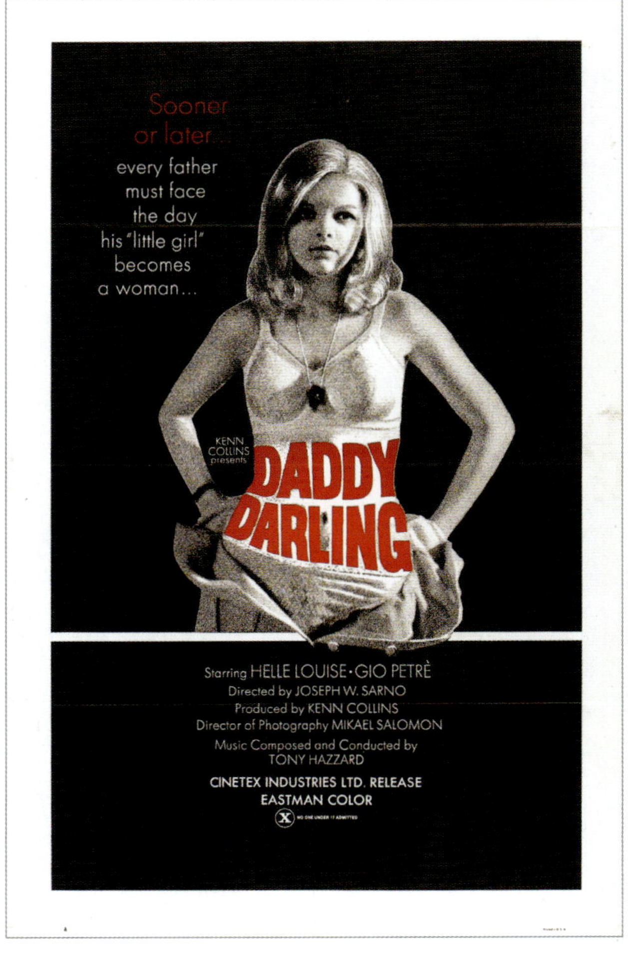
Sooner or later...
every father must face the day his "little girl" becomes a woman...
KENN COLLINS presents
DADDY DARLING
Starring HELLE LOUISE · GIO PETRÈ
Directed by JOSEPH W. SARNO
Produced by KENN COLLINS
Director of Photography MIKAEL SALOMON
Music Composed and Conducted by
TONY HAZZARD
CINETEX INDUSTRIES LTD. RELEASE
EASTMAN COLOR
X

A LADY OF LETTERS

Mixing groovy fonts with the female form was often a feature of '60s design, and while the trend is generally considered to have reached its apotheosis in the concert posters for bands such as The Grateful Dead created by Wes Wilson, it filtered down into the exploitation film industry too, with varying degrees of success. The poster for 1967's achingly hip and happening documentary *Mondo Mod* encouraged viewers to "Freak out with the go-high scene," reverting to a more conservative typeface to advise, "Parents: If you don't understand your children see this motion picture!" These days, the film is mostly notable for being an early credit for two future legends of cinematography: László Kovács and Vilmos Zsigmond. Similarly, cool posters aside, *The Bellboy and the Playgirls* (1962) will never be entirely forgotten, since this American re-edit of the German film *Mit Eva fing die Sünde an* was augmented with extra footage shot by a young Francis Ford Coppola.

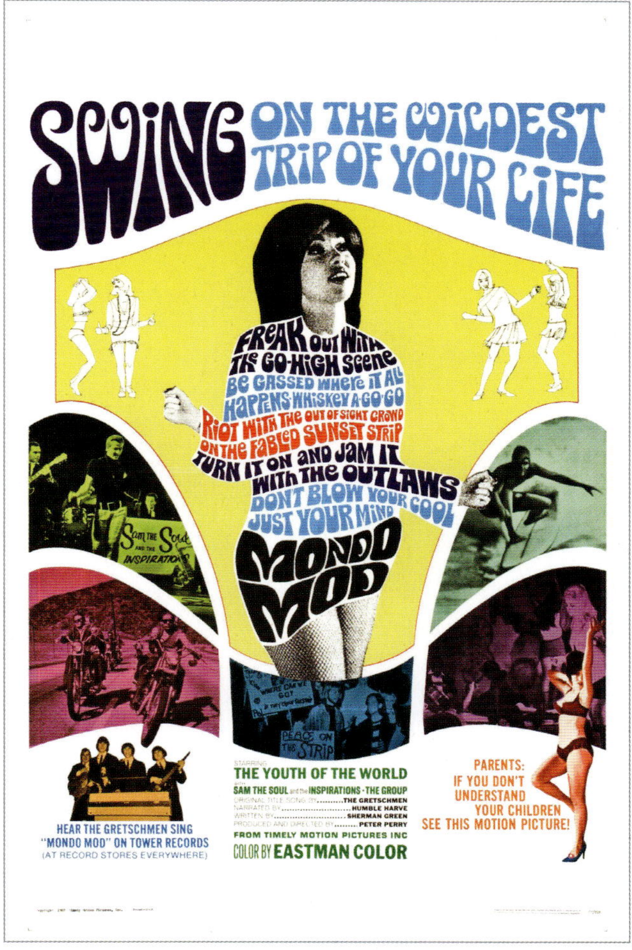

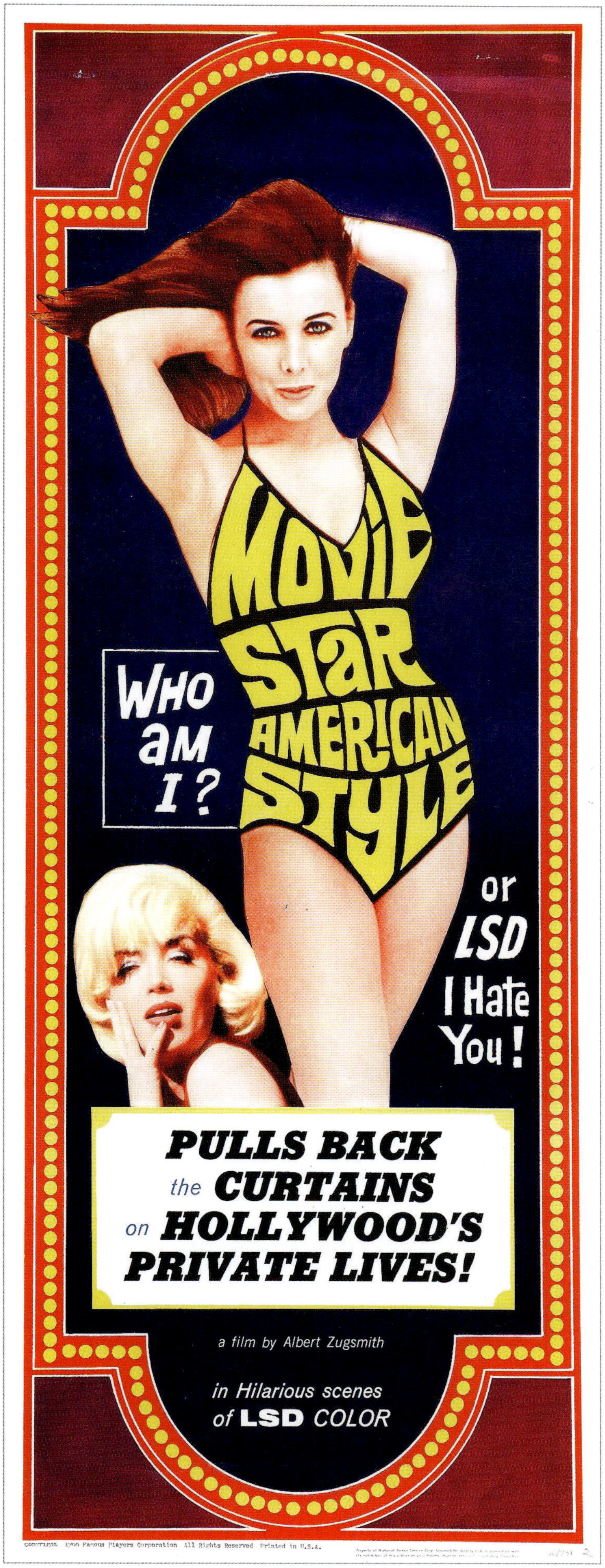

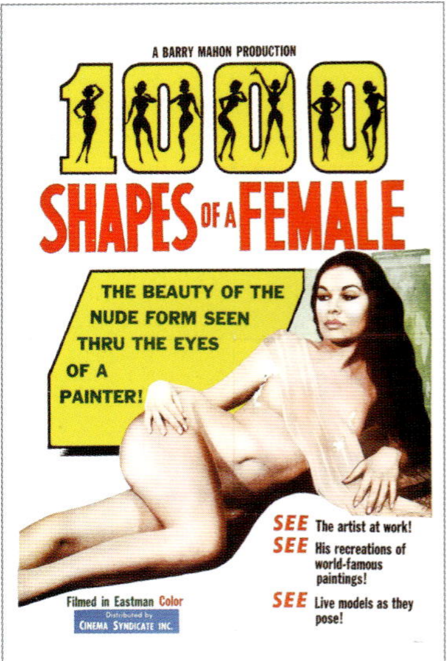

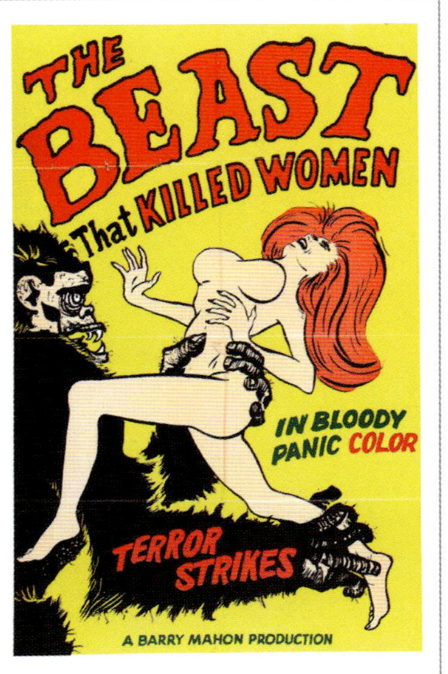

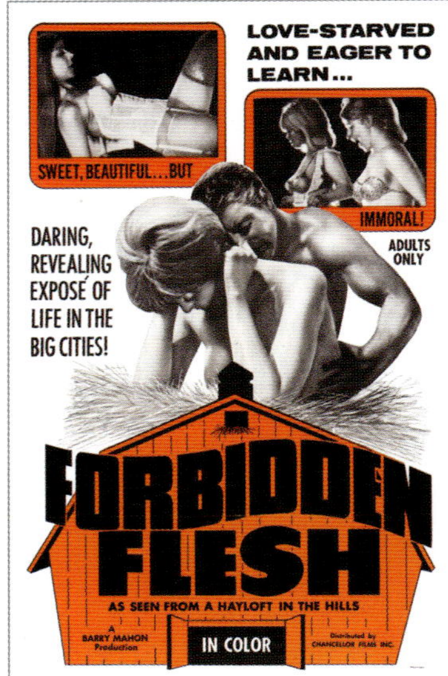

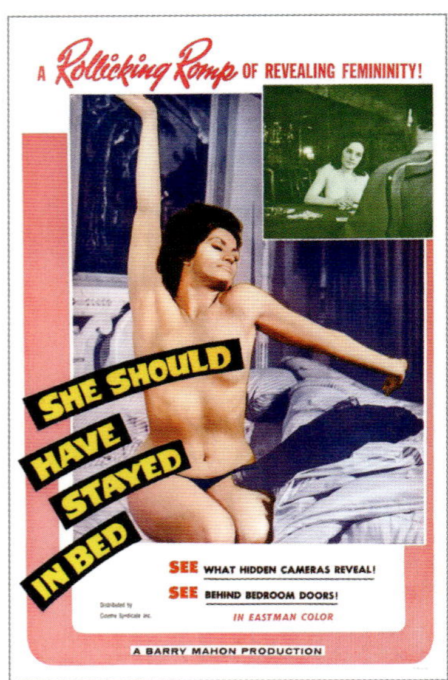

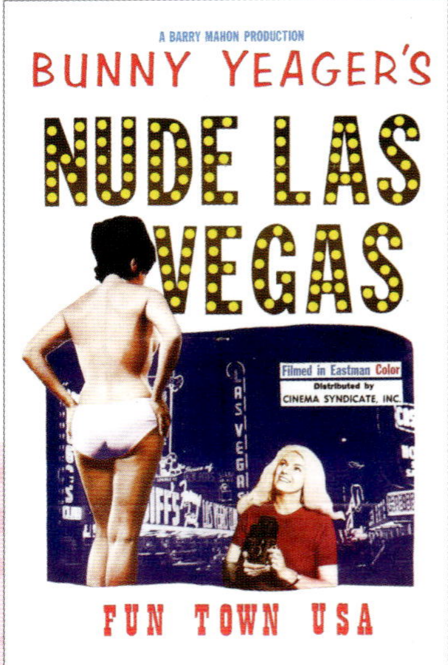

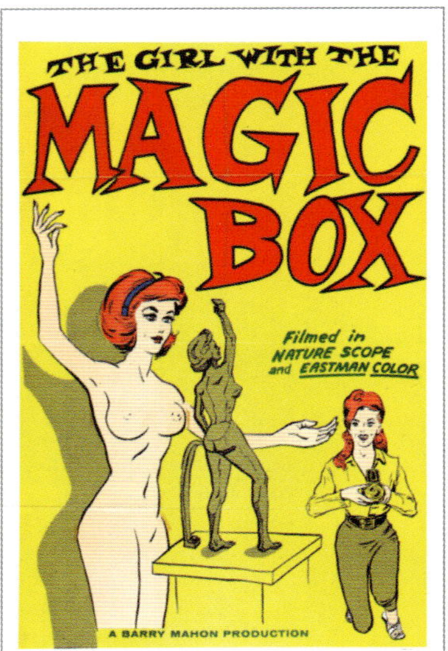

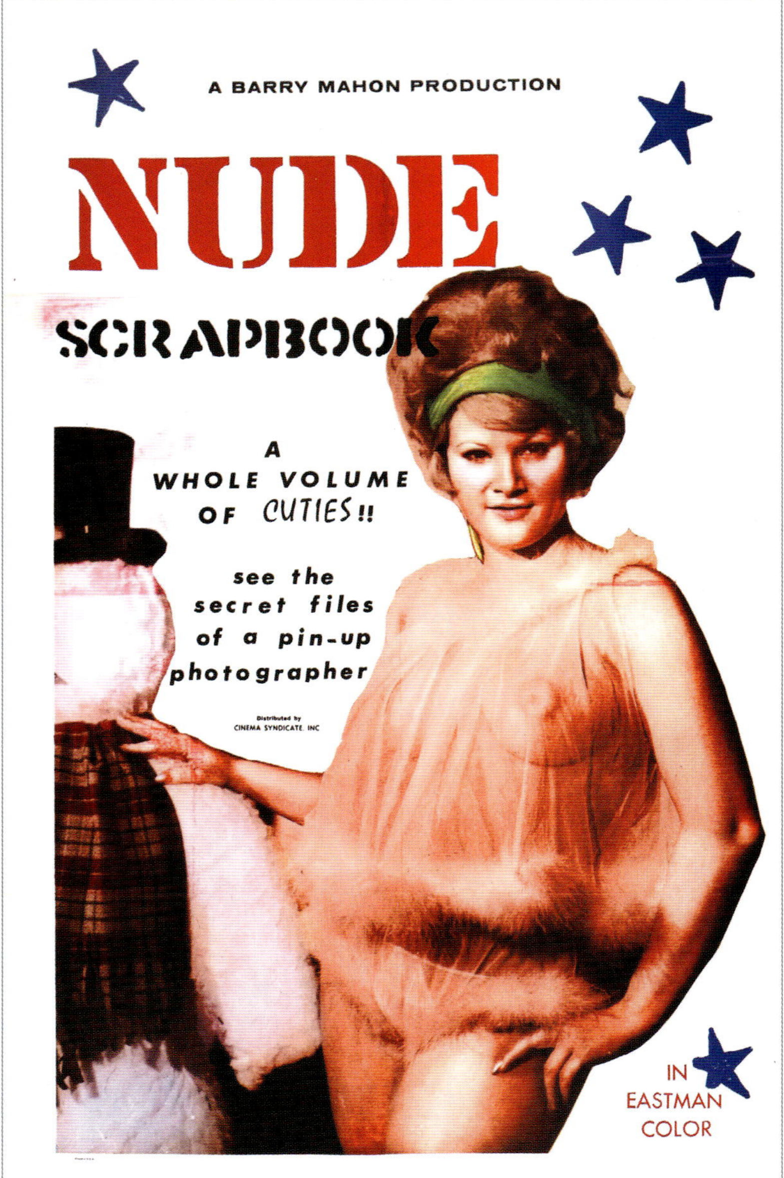

A BARRY MAHON PRODUCTION

The prolific American producer and director Barry Mahon (1921–99) has got one of those "you couldn't make it up" life stories. Having learned to fly while still at college, he volunteered for the British Royal Air Force in WWII, and flew Spitfires before being captured and imprisoned in Stalag Luft III (though only for a while: Steve McQueen's character in *The Great Escape* is loosely based on Mahon). He was later Errol Flynn's personal pilot and manager, and as a producer he pioneered the use of computer spreadsheets to plan, schedule, and budget feature films. As these simple but direct posters show, he specialized in what he himself admitted were "referred to commonly as exploitation pictures because the advertising generally oversells what you see when you get inside."

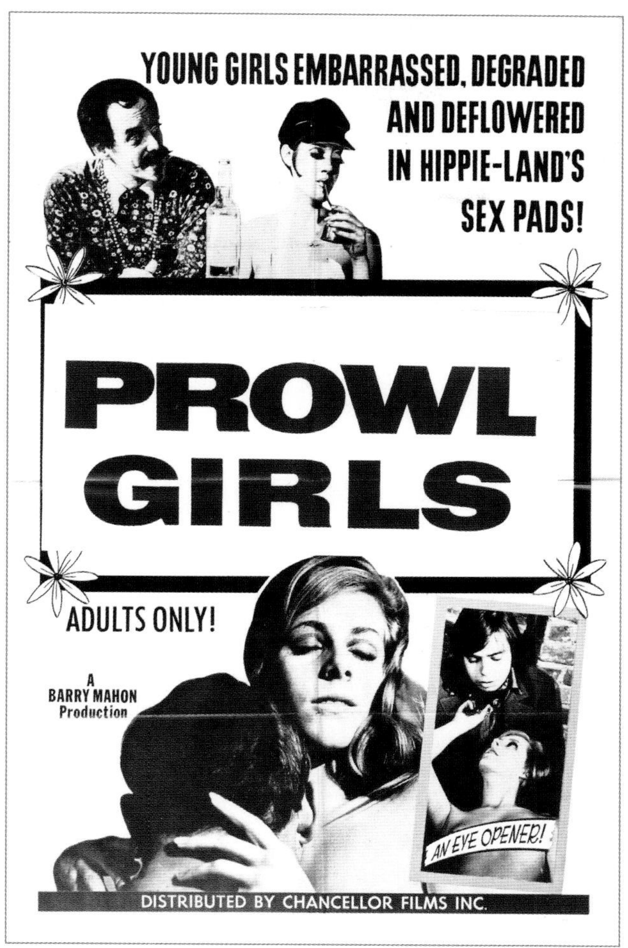
YOUNG GIRLS EMBARRASSED, DEGRADED AND DEFLOWERED IN HIPPIE-LAND'S SEX PADS!
PROWL GIRLS
ADULTS ONLY!
A BARRY MAHON Production
AN EYE OPENER!
DISTRIBUTED BY CHANCELLOR FILMS INC.

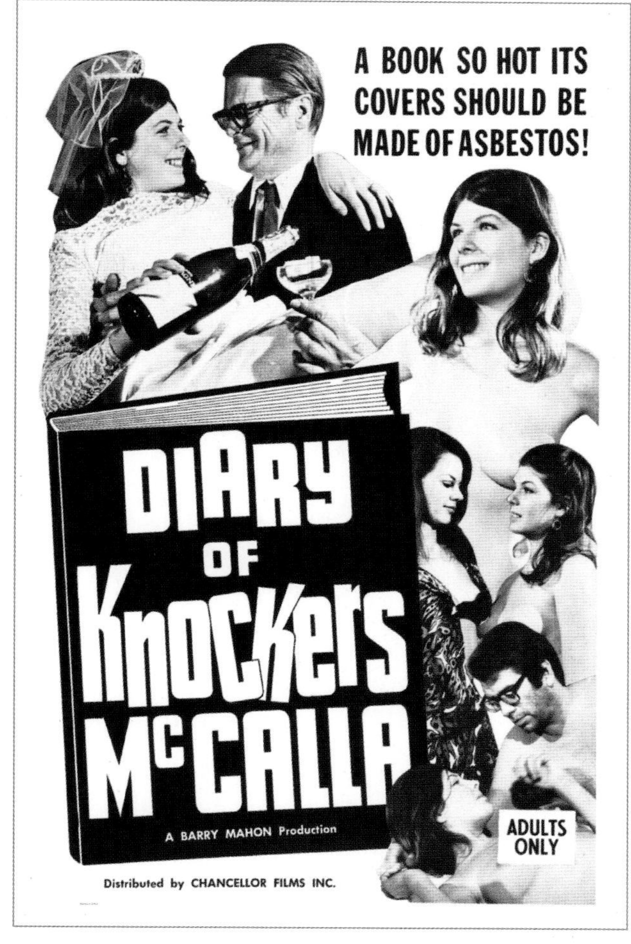
A BOOK SO HOT ITS COVERS SHOULD BE MADE OF ASBESTOS!
DIARY OF KNOCKERS McCALLA
A BARRY MAHON Production
ADULTS ONLY
Distributed by CHANCELLOR FILMS INC.

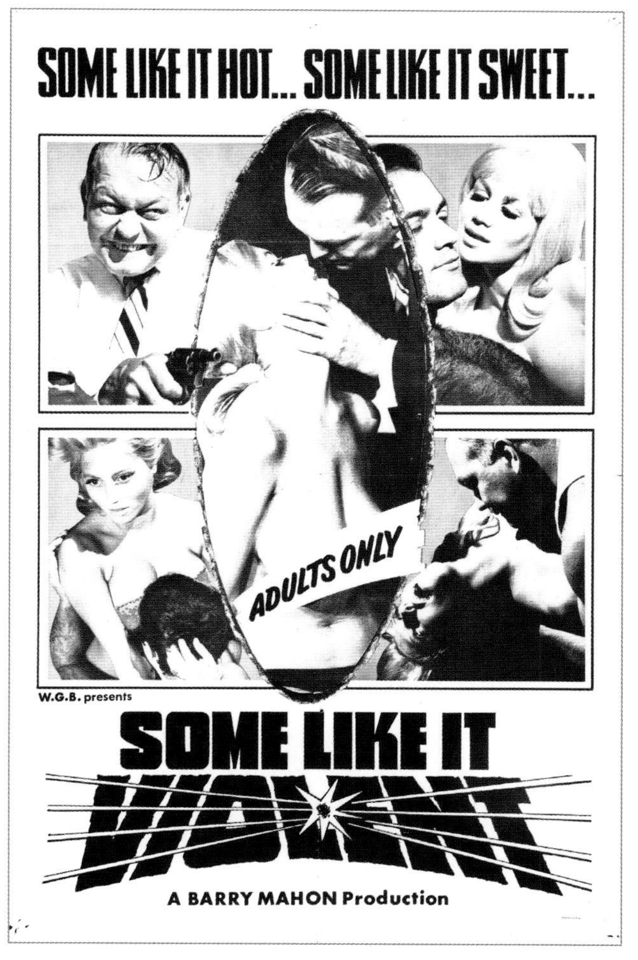
SOME LIKE IT HOT... SOME LIKE IT SWEET...
ADULTS ONLY
W.G.B. presents
SOME LIKE IT VIOLENT
A BARRY MAHON Production

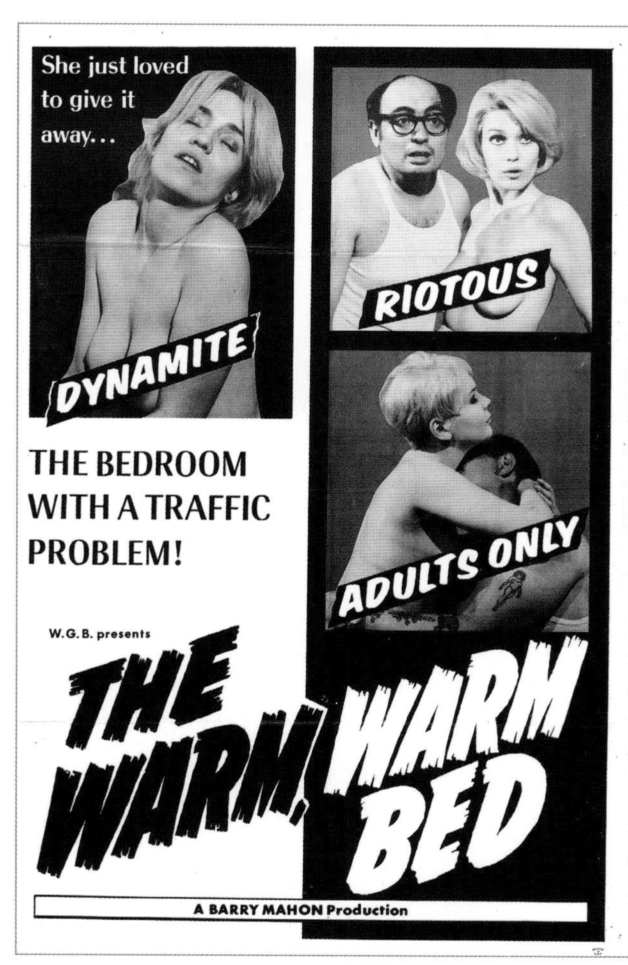
She just loved to give it away...
DYNAMITE
RIOTOUS
THE BEDROOM WITH A TRAFFIC PROBLEM!
ADULTS ONLY
W.G.B. presents
THE WARM, WARM BED
A BARRY MAHON Production

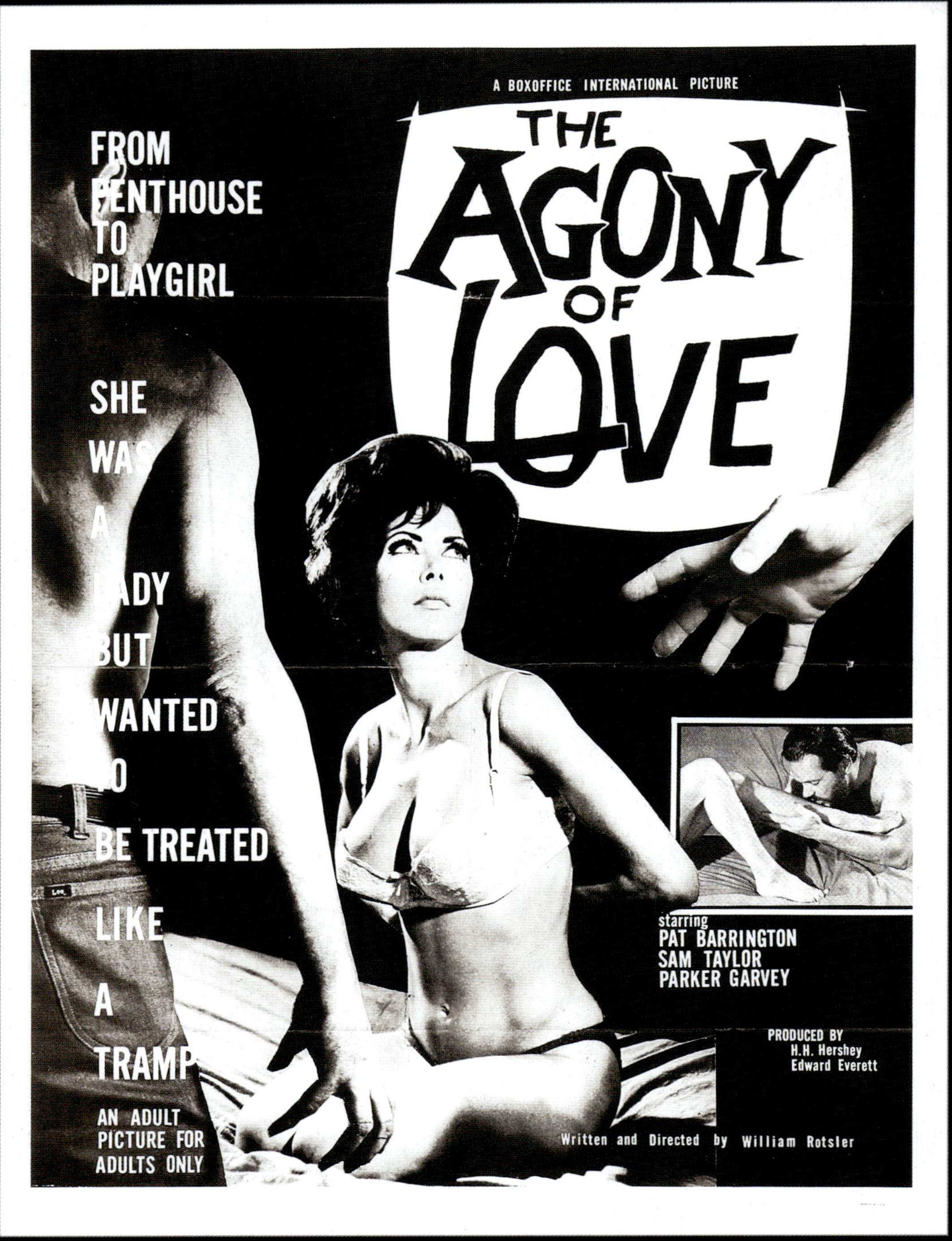

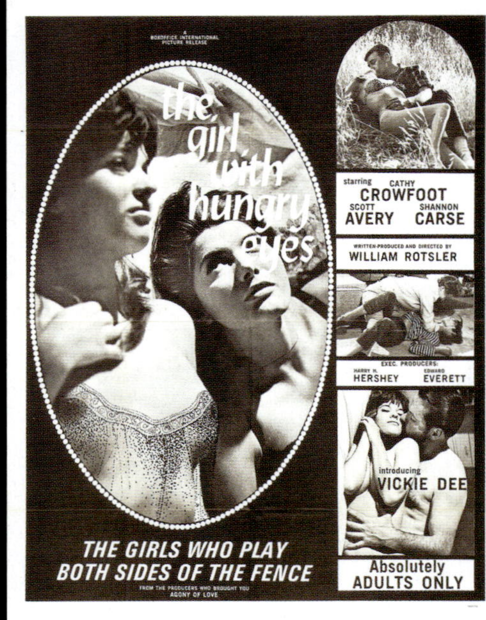

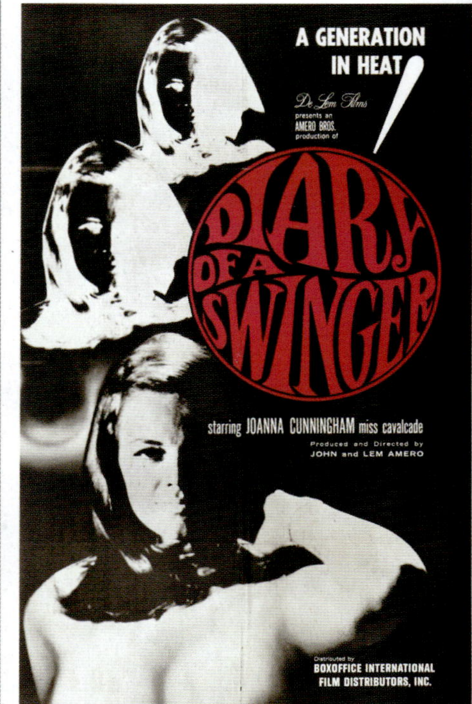

BOXOFFICE INTERNATIONAL

For Harry Novak (1928–2014), it was simple: "I guess I was just a born exploitationer. I liked to take something that had nothing and build it into something." His company Boxoffice International Pictures was a major producer and distributor in the '60s and '70s, not least of the wave of increasingly explicit but not quite hardcore sexploitation films seen here, which nevertheless, as one poster boasts, aimed to "shake the moral code of human existence." *Agony of Love* and *The Girl With the Hungry Eyes* were shot together in 1966. As Novak was eager to point out, "shooting two pictures back-to-back is like buying a chocolate ice cream soda—getting ice cream and soda for the same price."

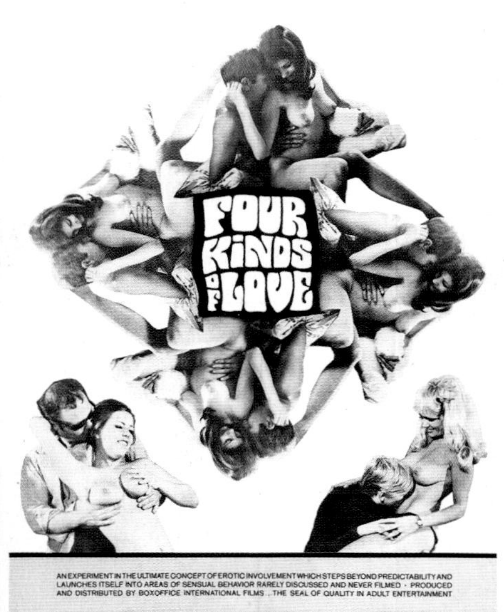

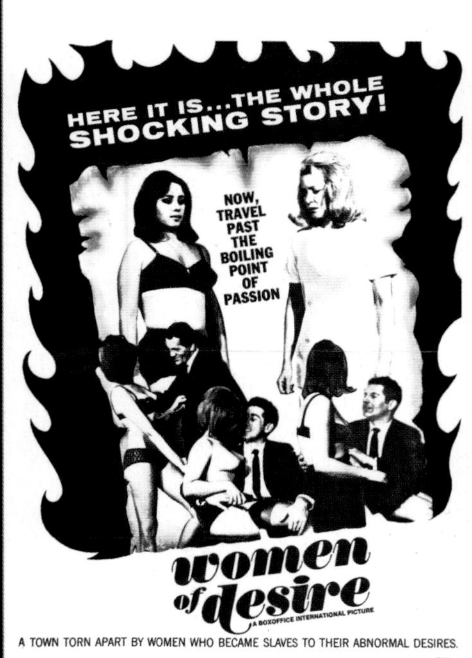

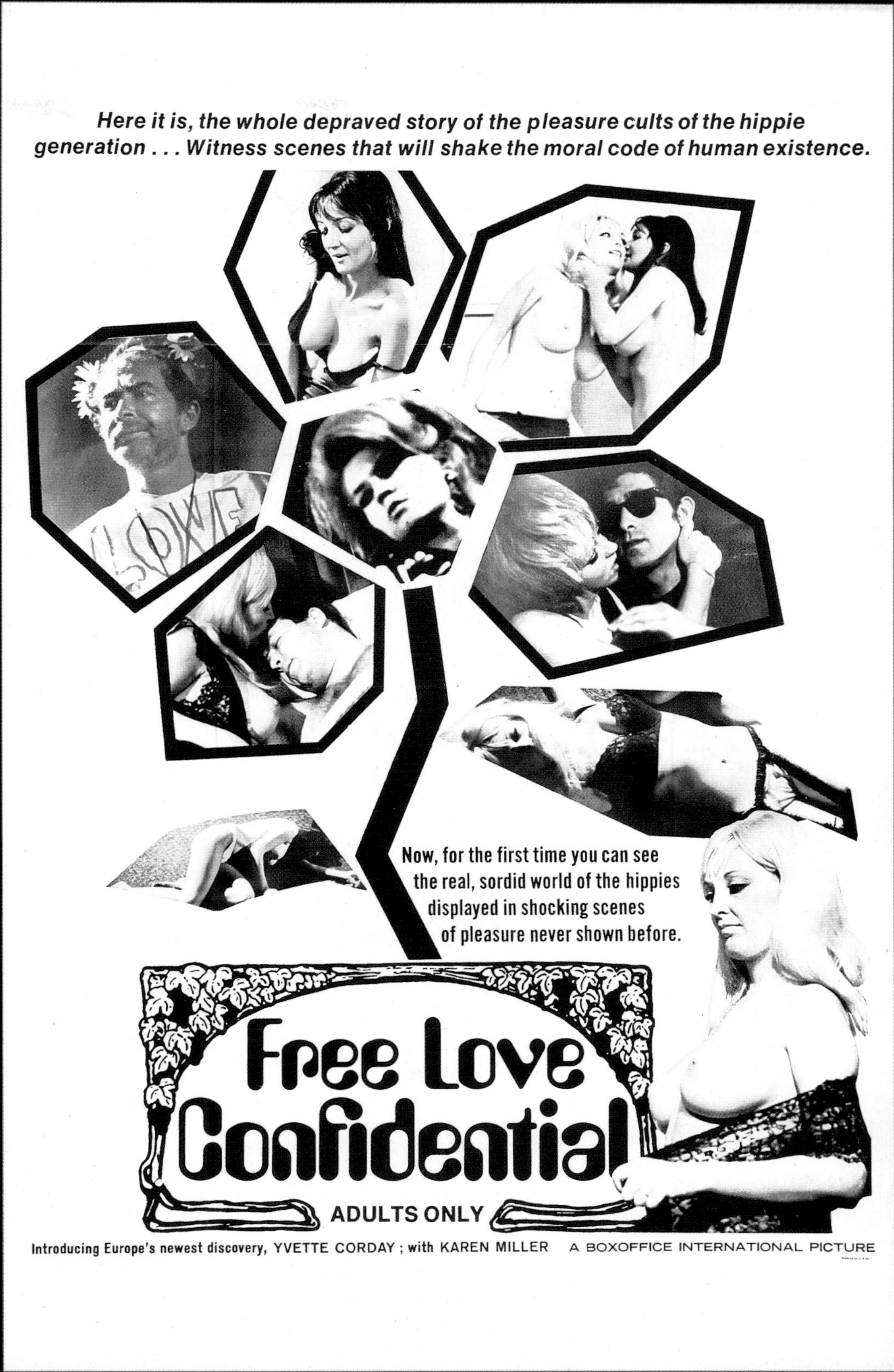

Here it is, the whole depraved story of the pleasure cults of the hippie generation . . . Witness scenes that will shake the moral code of human existence.

Now, for the first time you can see the real, sordid world of the hippies displayed in shocking scenes of pleasure never shown before.

Free Love Confidential

ADULTS ONLY

Introducing Europe's newest discovery, YVETTE CORDAY ; with KAREN MILLER A BOXOFFICE INTERNATIONAL PICTURE

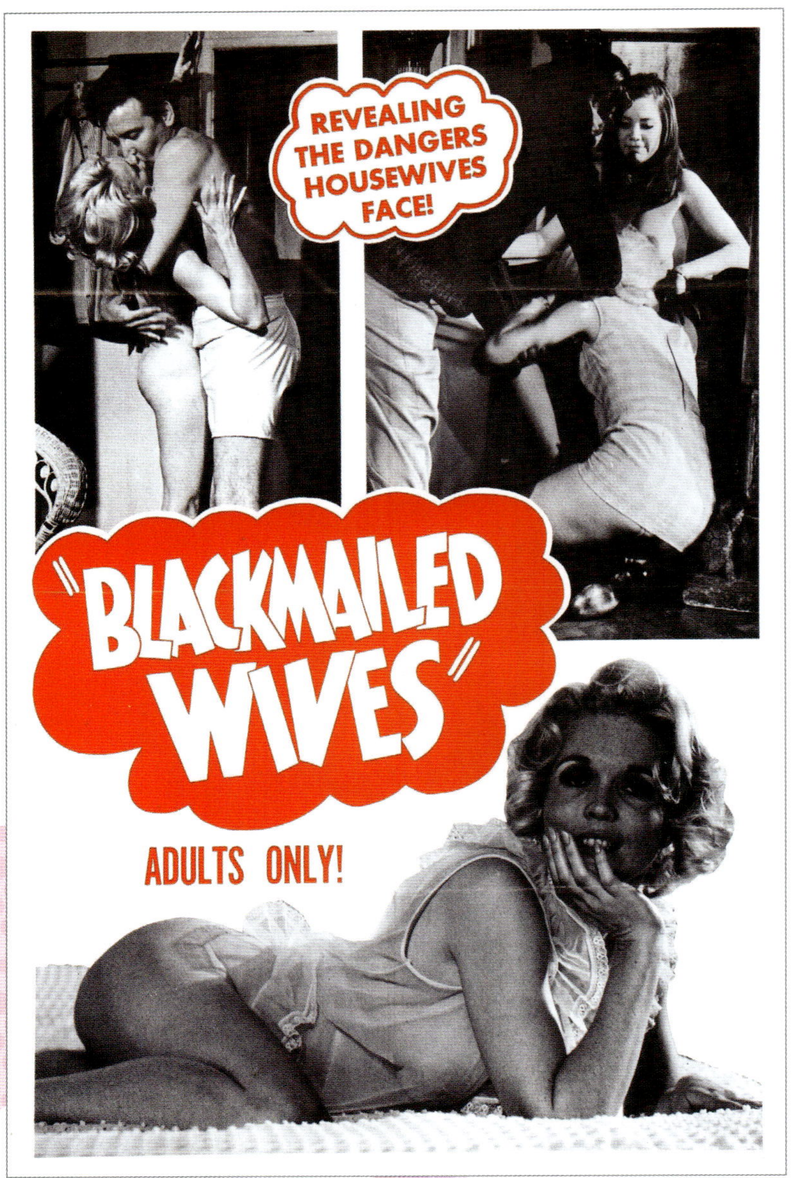

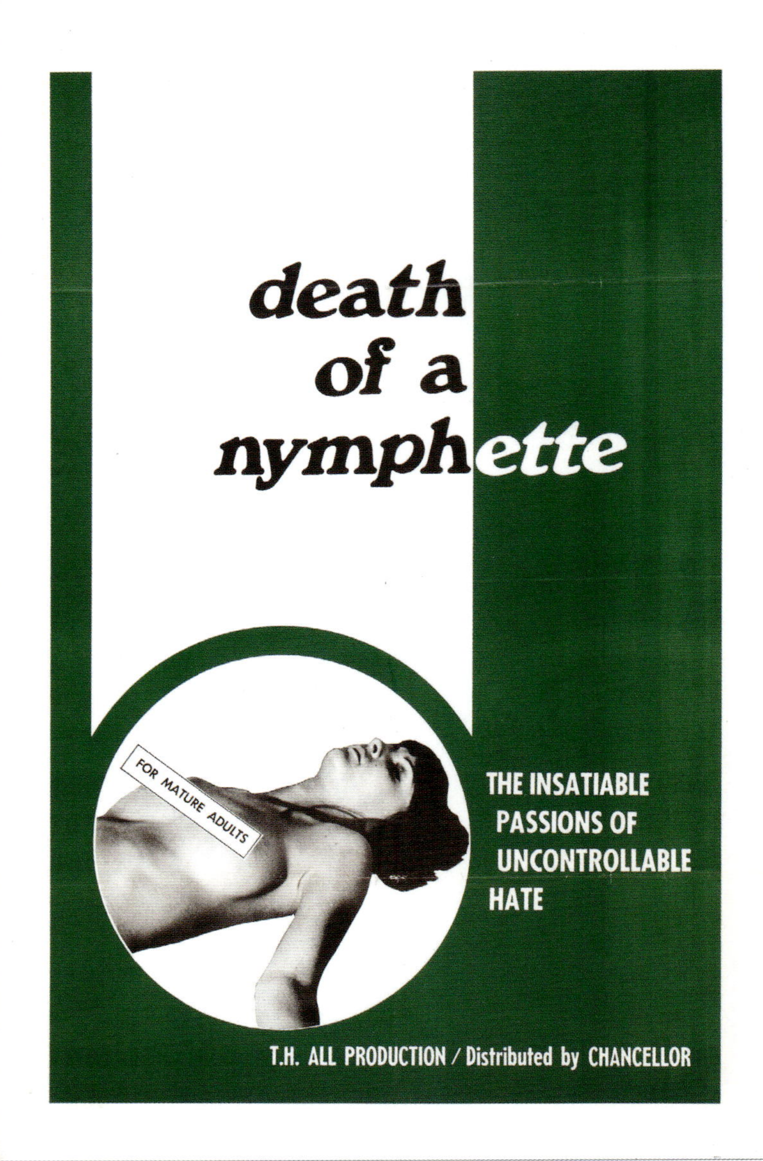

'60s SEX

As the plentiful smut over the next few pages shows, the '60s saw an explosion of sexploitation films. While they still evaded the censors by stopping short of full, explicit sex, many of them dispensed with the simpler pleasures of the "nudie cutie" in favor of a hard-edged, violent tone—with blunt posters to match. Film historian (and director of cult horror flick *Frankenhooker*) Frank Henenlotter put forward an interesting theory on the birth of the "roughie": "One day you have nudie cuties, the next you have roughies, and there doesn't seem to be much of a gap in between . . . It was as if the audiences for these films were almost immediately frustrated at watching beautiful women but not being able to touch them . . . So if you can't touch them, what? Beat them up?" Whether this concept of what the academic writer Cynthia J. Miller described as "a kind of venting of violence against the unobtainable [sex] object" is true or not, audiences certainly lapped up a steady diet of S&M, abduction, torture, and what *Death of a Nymphette* (1967) soberly described as "the insatiable passions of uncontrollable hate."

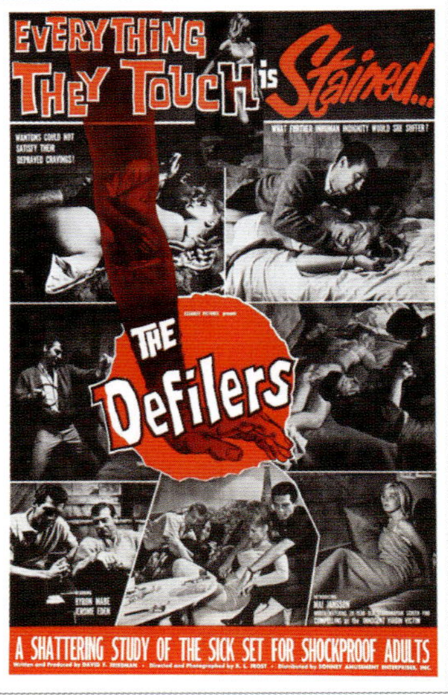

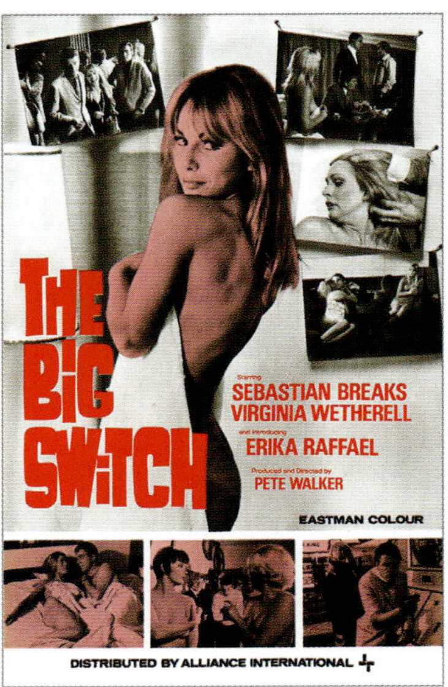

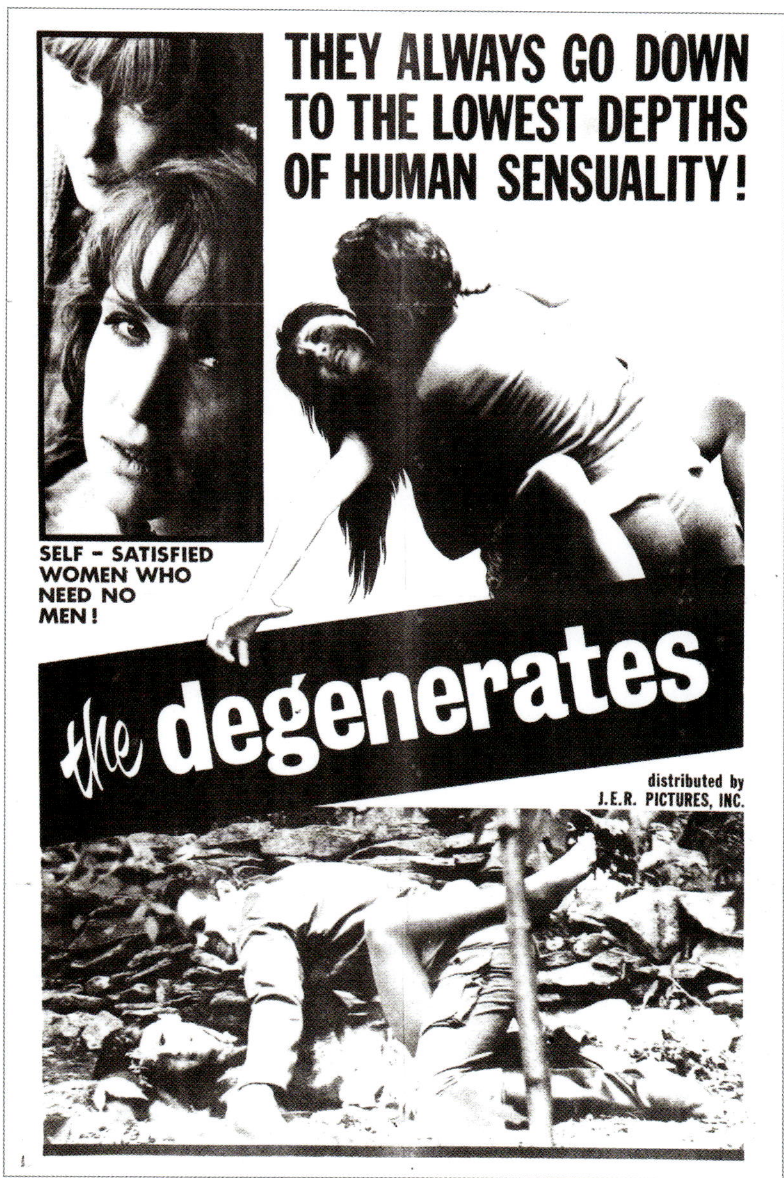
THEY ALWAYS GO DOWN TO THE LOWEST DEPTHS OF HUMAN SENSUALITY!
SELF - SATISFIED WOMEN WHO NEED NO MEN!
the degenerates
distributed by J.E.R. PICTURES, INC.

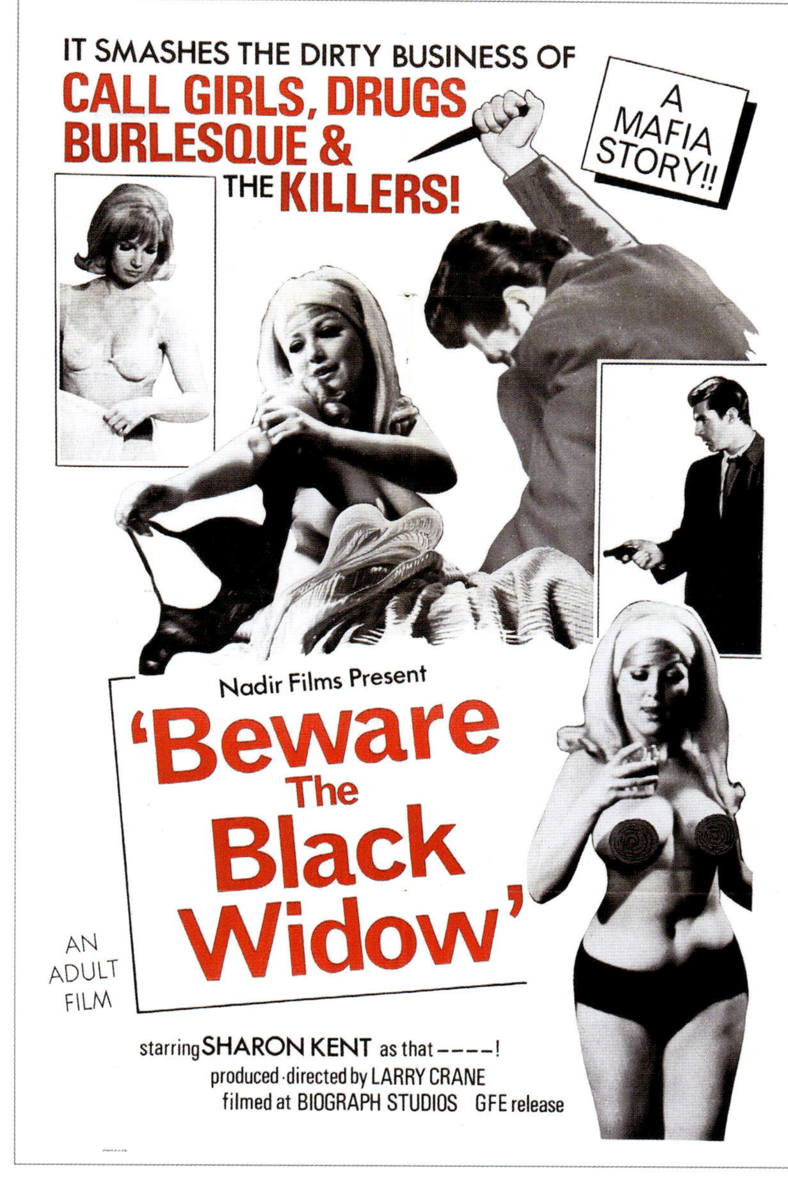
IT SMASHES THE DIRTY BUSINESS OF
CALL GIRLS, DRUGS BURLESQUE & THE KILLERS!
A MAFIA STORY!!
Nadir Films Present
'Beware The Black Widow'
AN ADULT FILM
starring SHARON KENT as that ----!
produced·directed by LARRY CRANE
filmed at BIOGRAPH STUDIOS GFE release

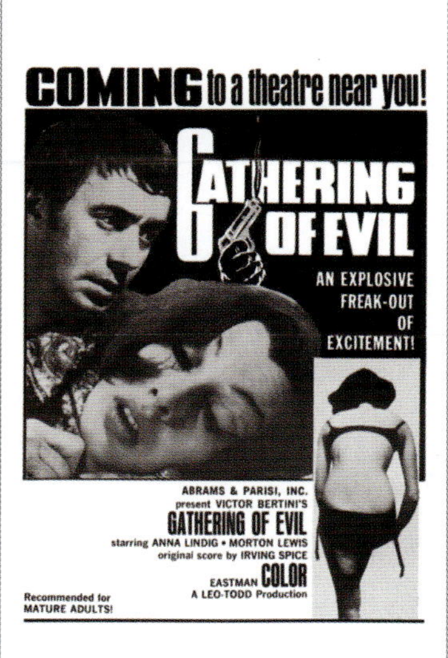
COMING to a theatre near you!
GATHERING OF EVIL
AN EXPLOSIVE FREAK-OUT OF EXCITEMENT!
ABRAMS & PARISI, INC.
present VICTOR BERTINI'S
GATHERING OF EVIL
starring ANNA LINDIG • MORTON LEWIS
original score by IRVING SPICE
EASTMAN COLOR
A LEO-TODD Production
Recommended for MATURE ADULTS!

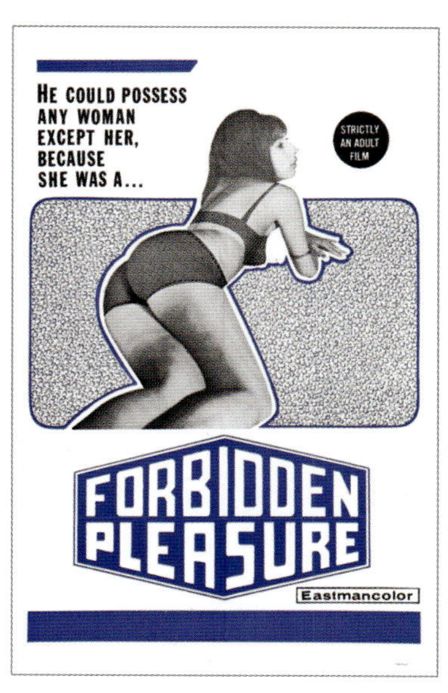
HE COULD POSSESS ANY WOMAN EXCEPT HER, BECAUSE SHE WAS A...
STRICTLY AN ADULT FILM
FORBIDDEN PLEASURE
Eastmancolor

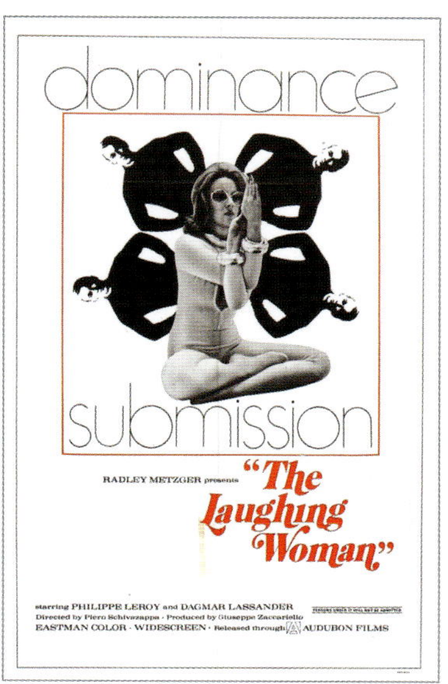
dominance
submission
RADLEY METZGER presents "The Laughing Woman"
starring PHILIPPE LEROY and DAGMAR LASSANDER
Directed by Piero Schivazappa · Produced by Giuseppe Zaccariello
EASTMAN COLOR · WIDESCREEN · Released through AUDUBON FILMS

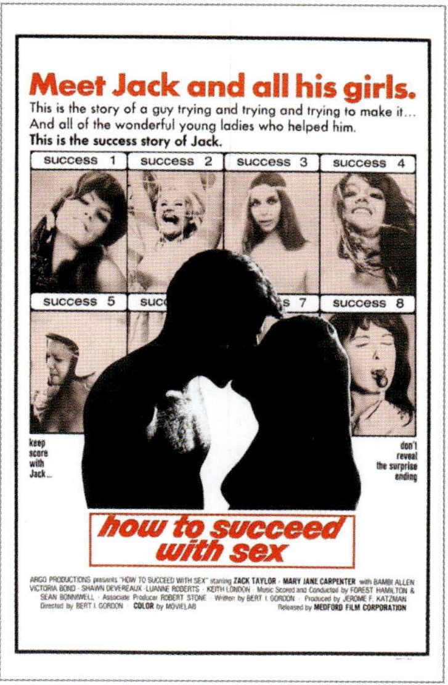
Meet Jack and all his girls.
This is the story of a guy trying and trying and trying to make it...
And all of the wonderful young ladies who helped him.
This is the success story of Jack.
success 1
success 2
success 3
success 4
success 5
success 8
keep score with Jack...
don't reveal the surprise ending
how to succeed with sex
Released by MEDFORD FILM CORPORATION

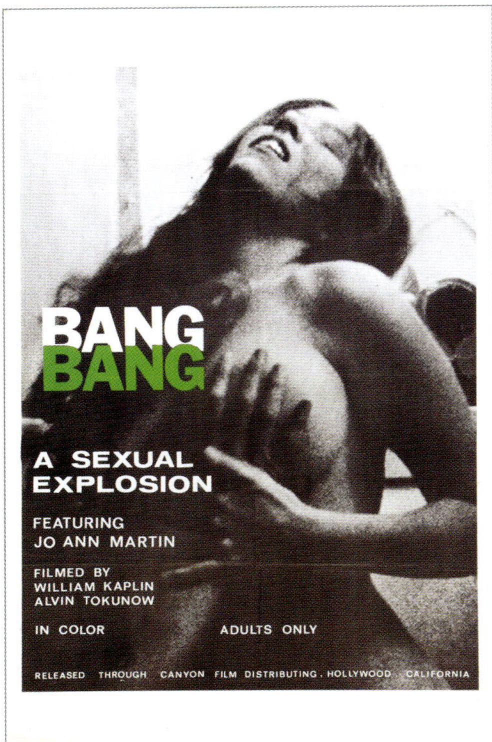
BANG
BANG
A SEXUAL EXPLOSION
FEATURING
JO ANN MARTIN
FILMED BY
WILLIAM KAPLIN
ALVIN TOKUNOW
IN COLOR
ADULTS ONLY
RELEASED THROUGH CANYON FILM DISTRIBUTING . HOLLYWOOD . CALIFORNIA

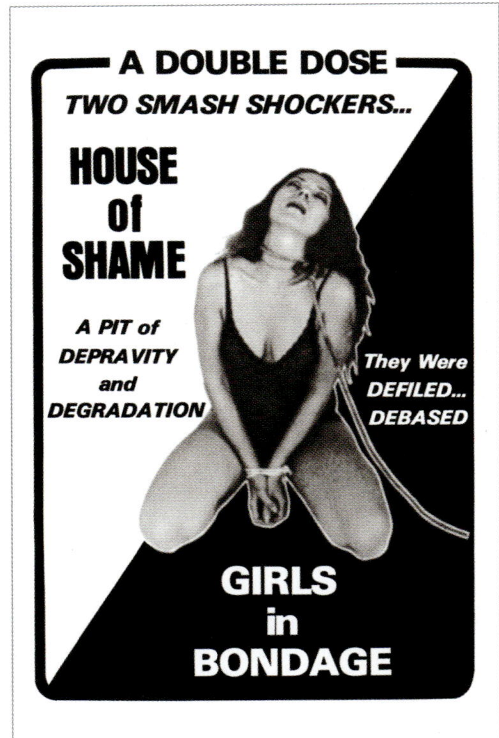
A DOUBLE DOSE
TWO SMASH SHOCKERS...
HOUSE of SHAME
A PIT of DEPRAVITY and DEGRADATION
They Were DEFILED... DEBASED
GIRLS in BONDAGE

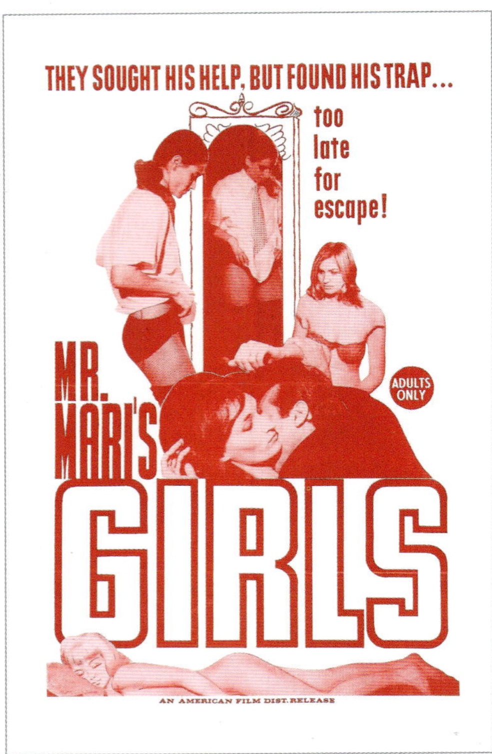
THEY SOUGHT HIS HELP, BUT FOUND HIS TRAP...
too late for escape!
ADULTS ONLY
MR. MARI'S GIRLS
AN AMERICAN FILM DIST. RELEASE

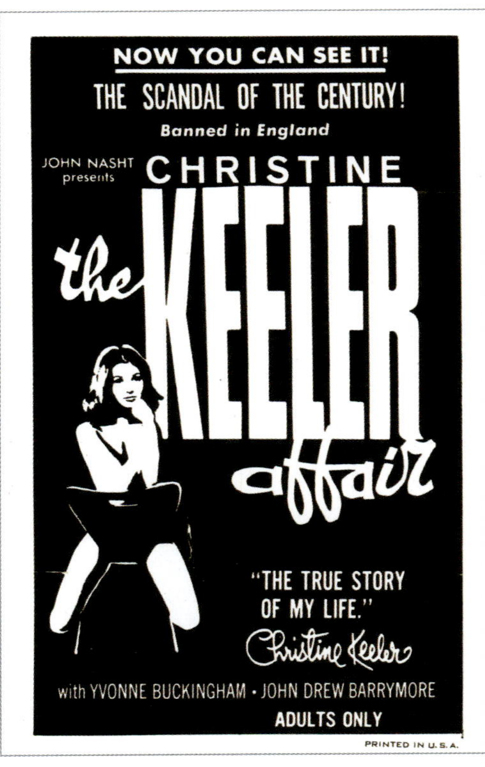
NOW YOU CAN SEE IT!
THE SCANDAL OF THE CENTURY!
Banned in England
JOHN NASHT presents
CHRISTINE
the KEELER affair
"THE TRUE STORY OF MY LIFE."
Christine Keeler
with YVONNE BUCKINGHAM • JOHN DREW BARRYMORE
ADULTS ONLY
PRINTED IN U.S.A.

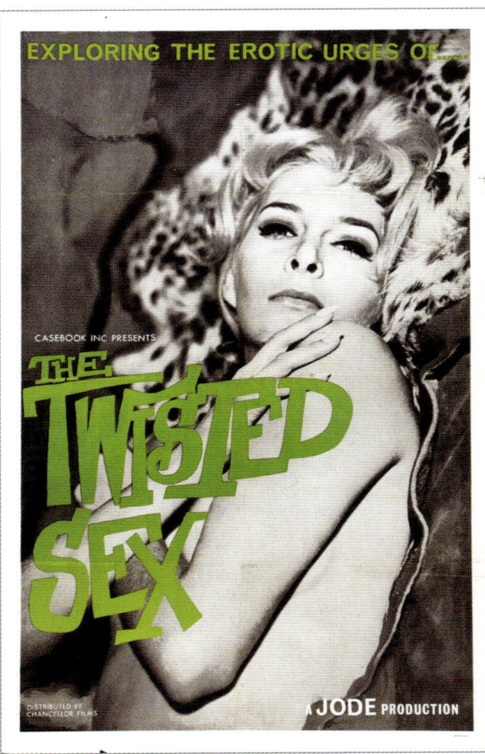
EXPLORING THE EROTIC URGES OF...
CASEBOOK INC PRESENTS
THE TWISTED SEX
A JODE PRODUCTION

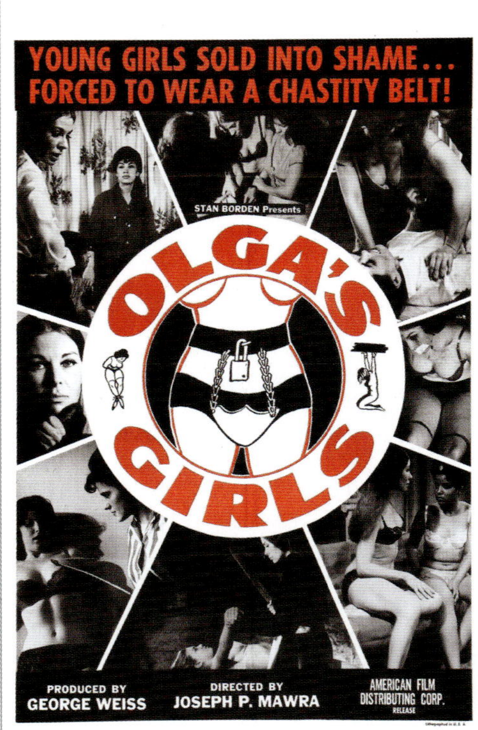
YOUNG GIRLS SOLD INTO SHAME...
FORCED TO WEAR A CHASTITY BELT!
STAN BORDEN Presents
OLGA'S GIRLS
PRODUCED BY GEORGE WEISS
DIRECTED BY JOSEPH P. MAWRA
AMERICAN FILM DISTRIBUTING CORP. RELEASE

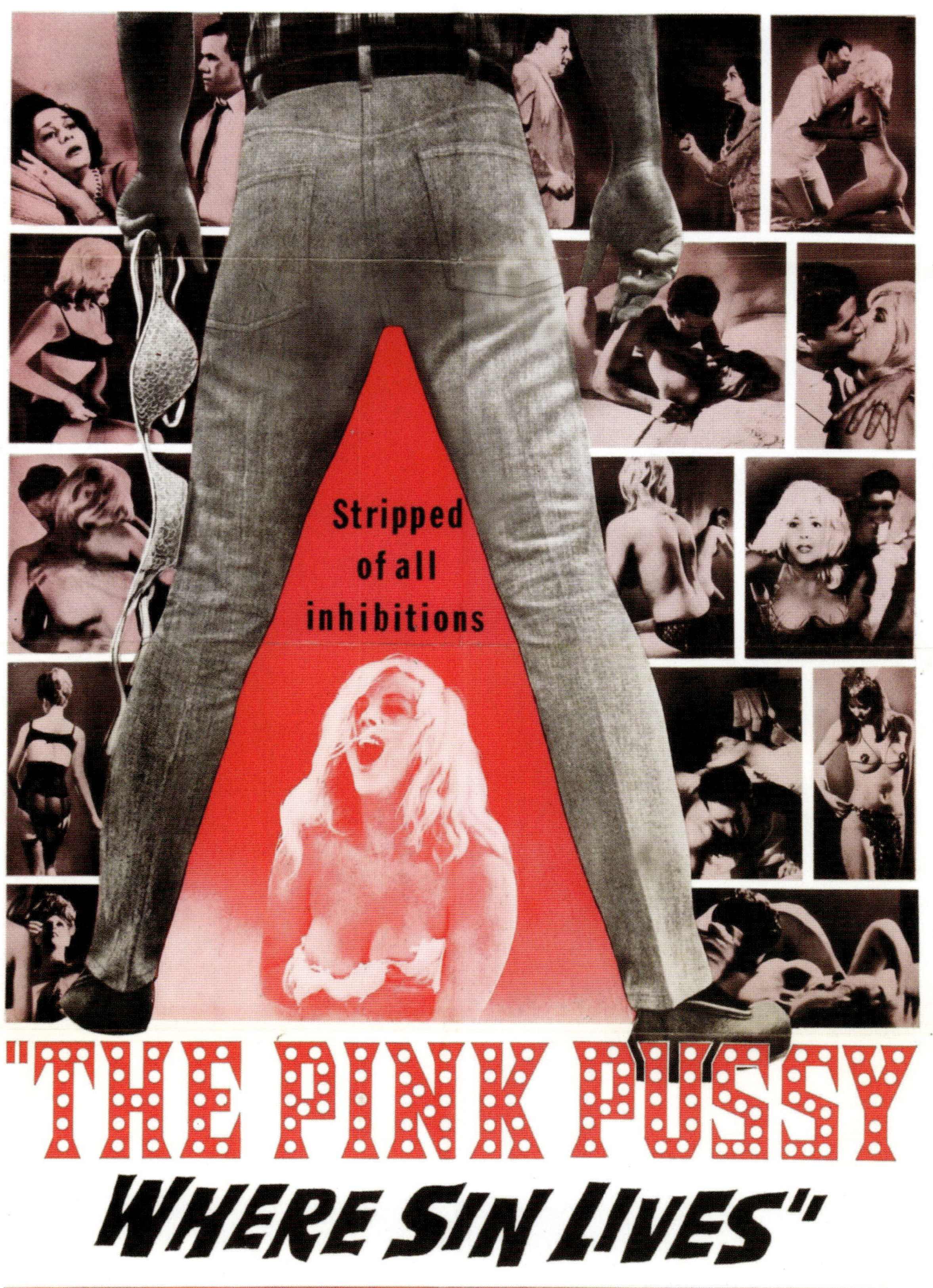
THE HOT-BED OF PLEASURE!
Stripped of all inhibitions
"THE PINK PUSSY
WHERE SIN LIVES"
Starring LIBERTAD LEBLANC Produced by EMILE SPLITZ Written and Directed by ALBERT DUBOIS Distributed by CAMBIST FILMS

GOING MAINSTREAM

Though the 22 million claimed by its Italian poster is probably over-egging it a bit, a very great number of Americans went to see *Deep Throat* (1972). After the Swedish drama *I Am Curious (Yellow)* brought graphic nudity and (simulated) sex to mainstream US movie theaters in 1969, it was just a matter of time until the hardcore "Golden Age of Porn" dawned. Following *Deep Throat*'s wide opening and *Behind the Green Door* in 1972, the popularity of "porno chic" ensured that *Devil in Miss Jones* ended up as the tenth biggest grosser of 1973 in the US (just one spot below Roger Moore's debut as 007 in *Live and Let Die*). Viewers of *Linda Lovelace Meets Miss Jones* (1975) were left frustrated though: despite the title, they didn't share a scene in what was a cash-in compilation of old footage.

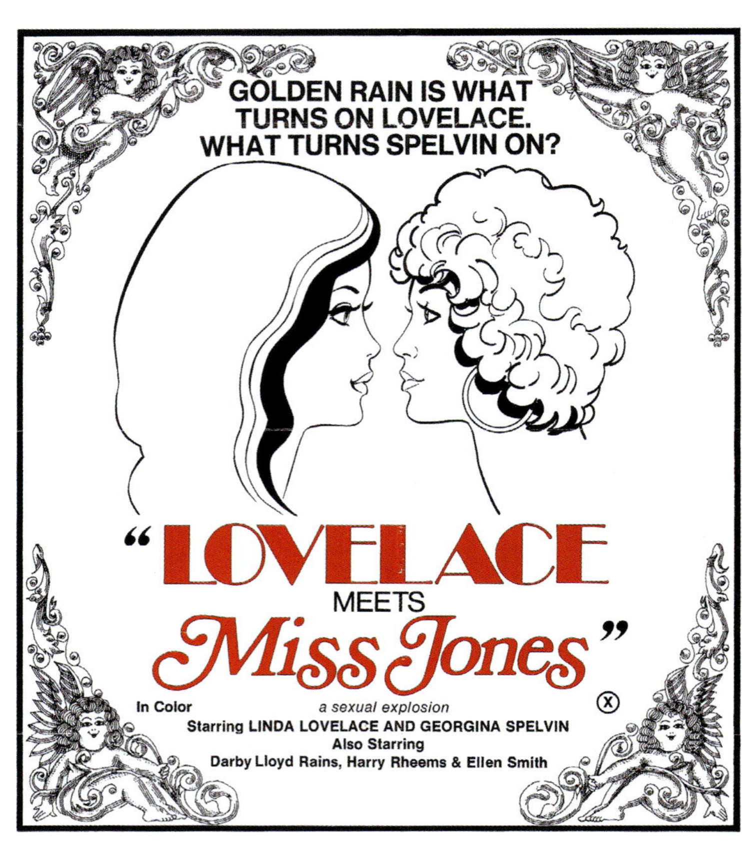

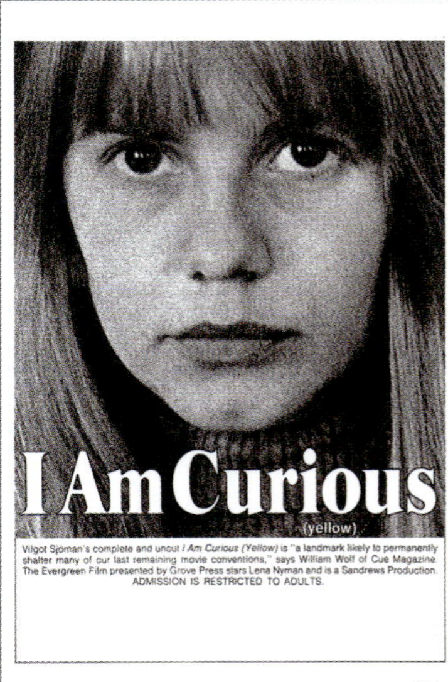

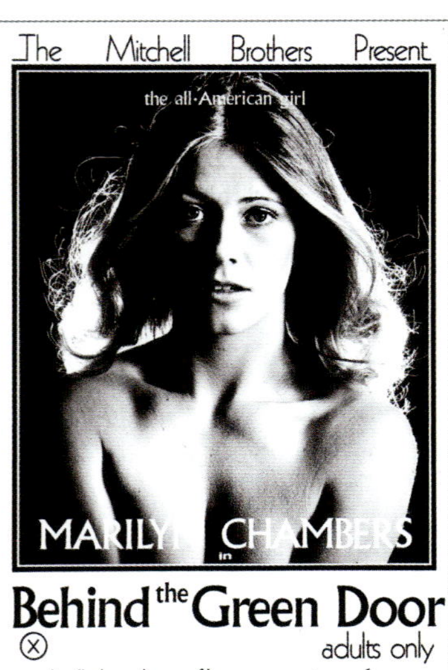

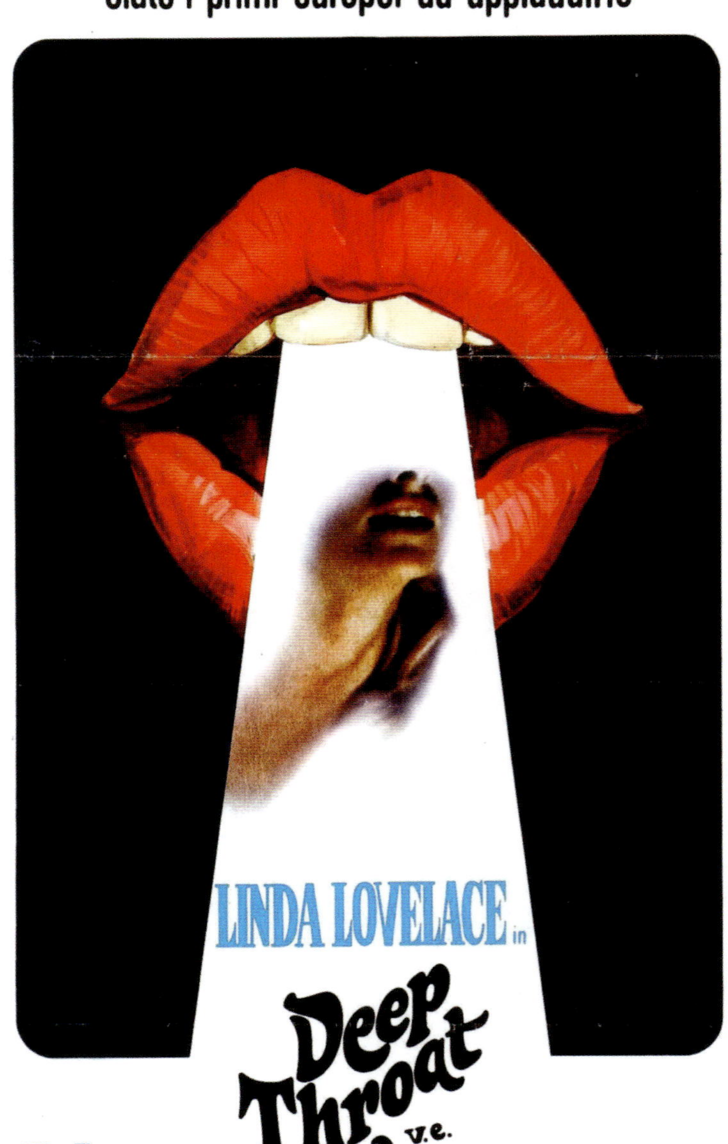

"May the bluenoses leave it lay for the pleasure of those whose taste it is.

STANDS PHOTOGRAPHICALLY HEAD AND SHOULDERS ABOVE 'THROAT'...AND MORE VARIED! THE FIRST TEN MINUTES ACHIEVE MODIGLIANI TONES. THE CAST IS ENTHUSIASTIC...GEORGINA SPEVLIN MAKES A MARK ON YOUR EMOTIONS!"

Judith Crist, *NEW YORK MAGAZINE*

"The Most Interesting Film of its Kind to Date!

BECAUSE IT DISSOLVES THE DISTINCTION BETWEEN SEX FILMS AND ART FILMS. GEORGINA SPEVLIN'S PERFORMANCE WAS REMARKABLY PERSUASIVE!"

Charles Michener/*NEWSWEEK*

"The 'Devil in Miss Jones' is Unique, Surprising, Provocative!

EXCEPTIONALLY WELL FILMED AND ACTED—AS WELL AS LUSTILY PERFORMED, AND GOES ANOTHER BIG STEP TOWARD BRIDGING THE GAP BETWEEN SERIOUS ART FILMS AND THOSE PREVIOUSLY LABELED SEXPLOITATION."

Bruce Williamson/*PLAYBOY*

"The Picture is a Sensation!

A BREATHTAKING EROTIC ODYSSEY, THE LIKES OF WHICH HAS NEVER BEEN SO STRONGLY DEPICTED ON THE SCREEN. IF MARLON BRANDO CAN BE PRAISED FOR GIVING HIS ALMOST-ALL IN 'LAST TANGO IN PARIS,' ONE WONDERS WHAT THE REACTION WILL BE TO MISS JONES' LEAD, GEORGINA SPEVLIN, WHOSE PERFORMANCE IS SO NAKED, IT SEEMS TO BE A MASSIVE INVASION OF PRIVACY. THE FINALE TAKES JEAN-PAUL SARTRE'S 'NO EXIT' TO A LOGICAL, AND SURPRISINGLY MORALISTIC EXTREME."

Addison Verrill/*VARIETY*

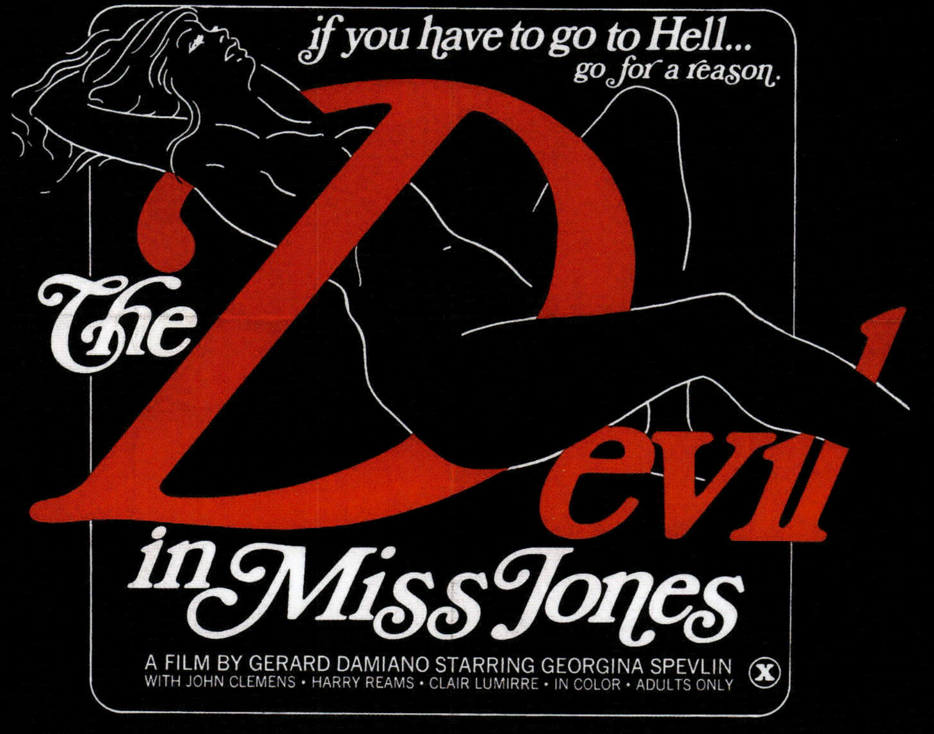

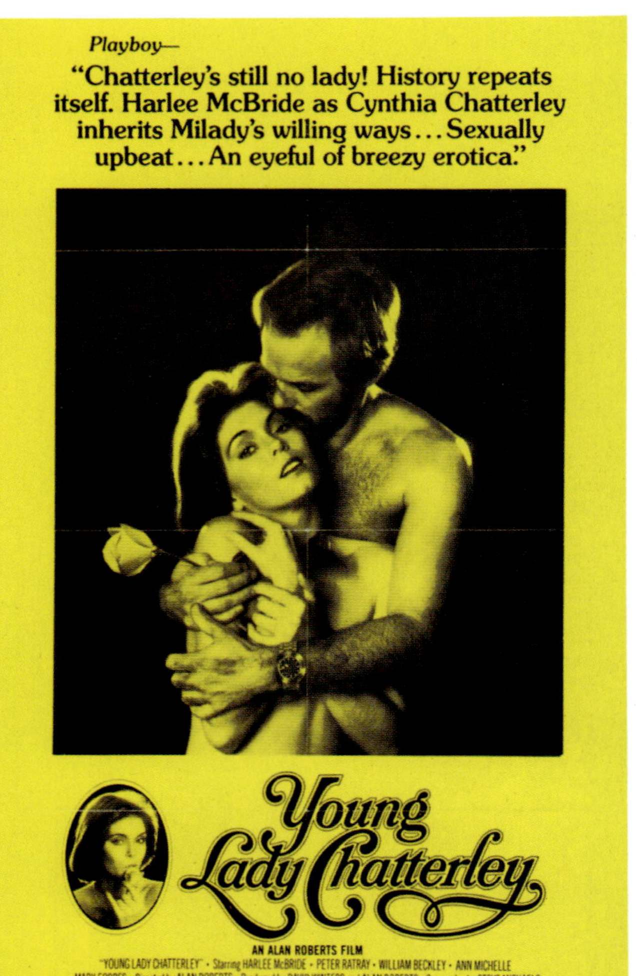

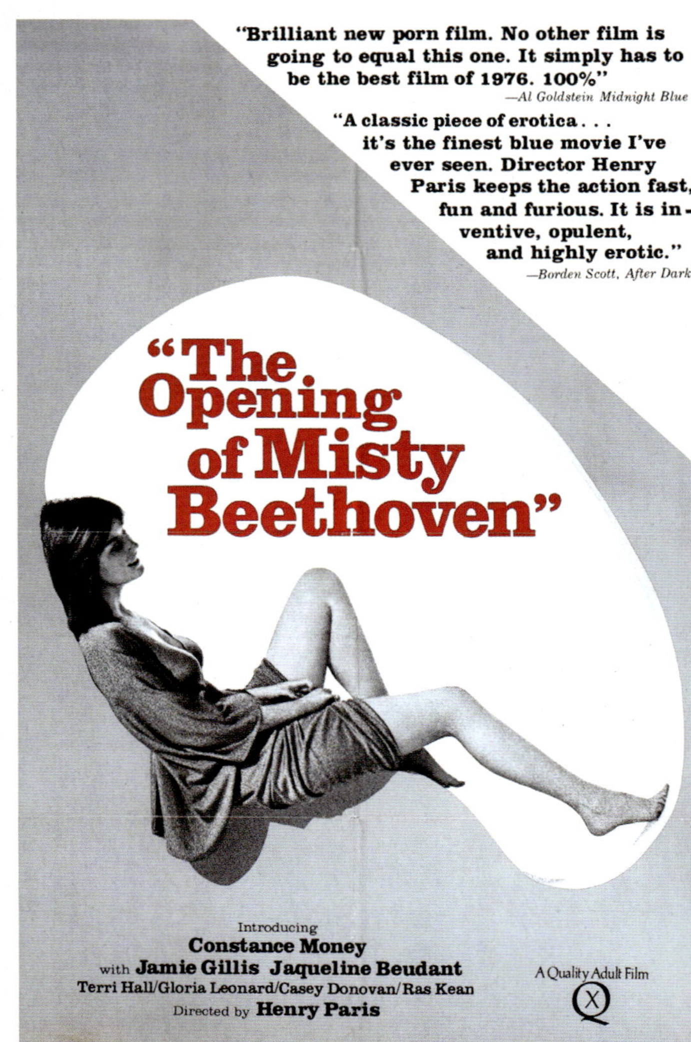

STAY CLASSY

With hardcore now penetrating the mainstream, distributors were keen to legitimize the product by festooning their posters with quotes from "proper" reviewers, such as *Playboy*, *Variety*, and Al Goldstein, the founder of *SCREW* magazine and host of the public access cable TV show *Midnight Blue*, whose early championing of *Deep Throat* helped to open the floodgates in the first place. Some were trying it on though, like the unattributed "quote" on the one-sheet for *Rendezvous with Anne* (1976), which, to make matters worse, evidently wasn't proofread. Though it doesn't feature a quote, let's pause to celebrate the re-release poster for the well-reviewed *Young Lady Chatterley* (1977), featuring possibly the purest, most perfect porn film title of all time: *Naked Young Lady*.

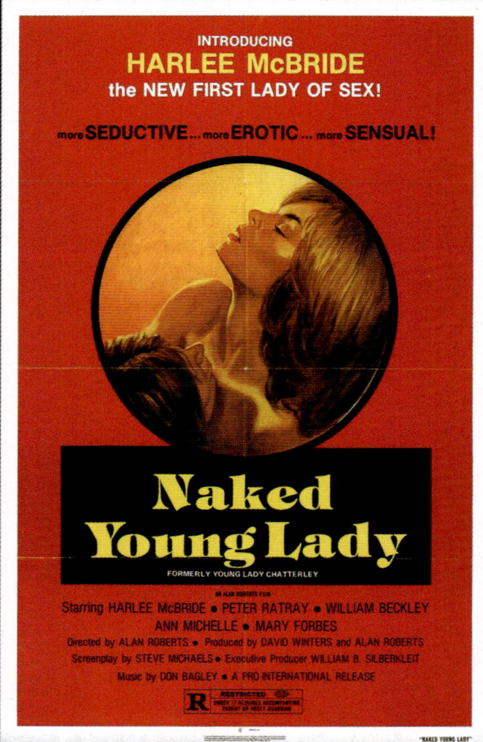

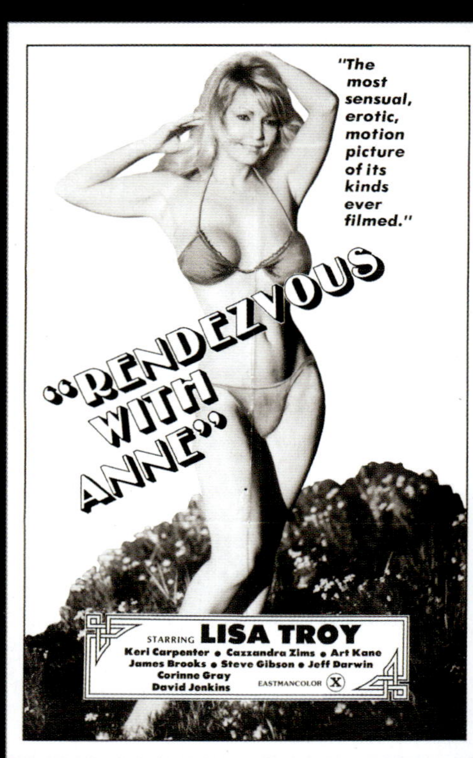

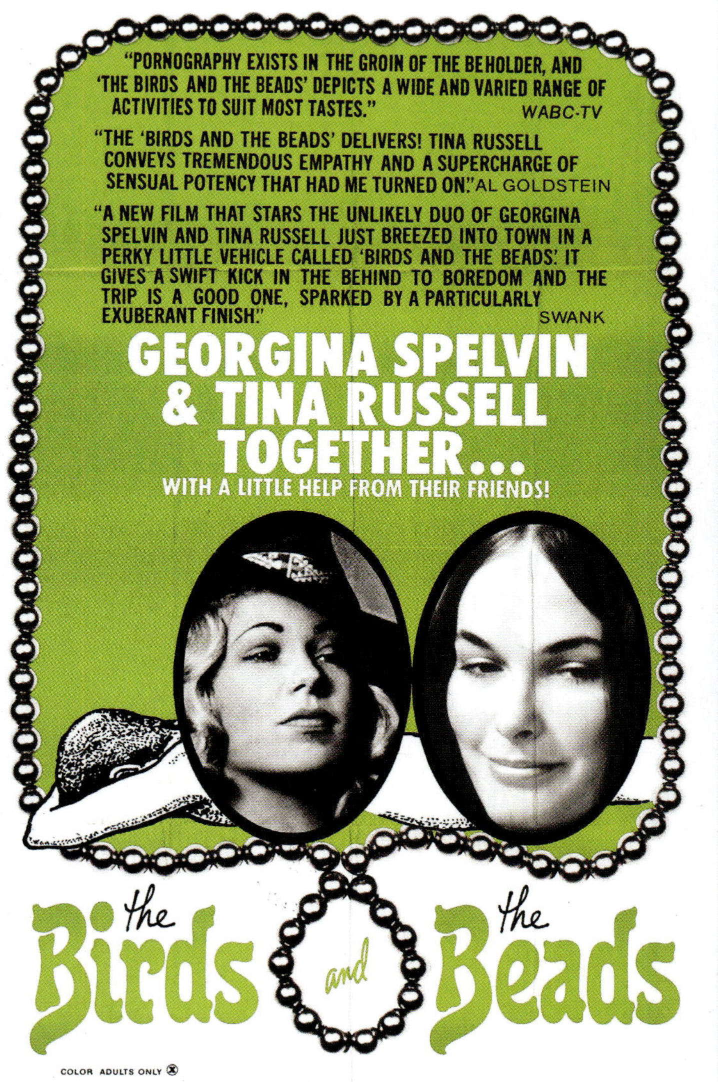

"PORNOGRAPHY EXISTS IN THE GROIN OF THE BEHOLDER, AND 'THE BIRDS AND THE BEADS' DEPICTS A WIDE AND VARIED RANGE OF ACTIVITIES TO SUIT MOST TASTES." WABC-TV
"THE 'BIRDS AND THE BEADS' DELIVERS! TINA RUSSELL CONVEYS TREMENDOUS EMPATHY AND A SUPERCHARGE OF SENSUAL POTENCY THAT HAD ME TURNED ON." AL GOLDSTEIN
"A NEW FILM THAT STARS THE UNLIKELY DUO OF GEORGINA SPELVIN AND TINA RUSSELL JUST BREEZED INTO TOWN IN A PERKY LITTLE VEHICLE CALLED 'BIRDS AND THE BEADS.' IT GIVES A SWIFT KICK IN THE BEHIND TO BOREDOM AND THE TRIP IS A GOOD ONE, SPARKED BY A PARTICULARLY EXUBERANT FINISH." SWANK
GEORGINA SPELVIN & TINA RUSSELL TOGETHER...
WITH A LITTLE HELP FROM THEIR FRIENDS!
the Birds and the Beads
COLOR ADULTS ONLY

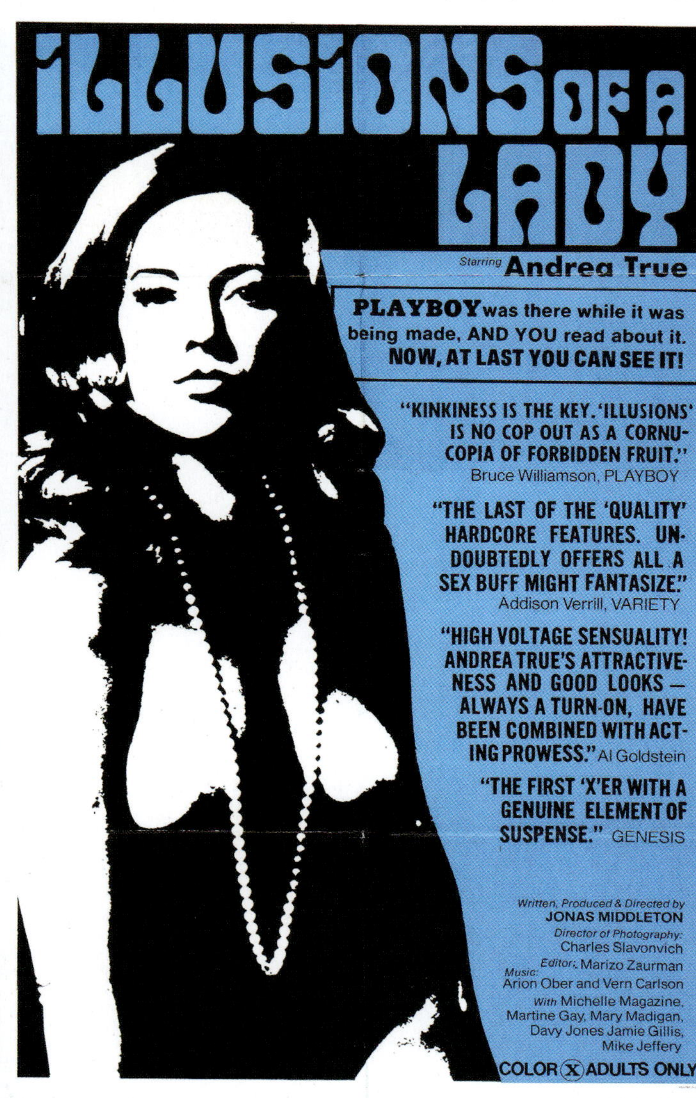

ILLUSIONS OF A LADY
Starring Andrea True
PLAYBOY was there while it was being made, AND YOU read about it. NOW, AT LAST YOU CAN SEE IT!
"KINKINESS IS THE KEY. 'ILLUSIONS' IS NO COP OUT AS A CORNUCOPIA OF FORBIDDEN FRUIT." Bruce Williamson, PLAYBOY
"THE LAST OF THE 'QUALITY' HARDCORE FEATURES. UNDOUBTEDLY OFFERS ALL A SEX BUFF MIGHT FANTASIZE." Addison Verrill, VARIETY
"HIGH VOLTAGE SENSUALITY! ANDREA TRUE'S ATTRACTIVENESS AND GOOD LOOKS — ALWAYS A TURN-ON, HAVE BEEN COMBINED WITH ACTING PROWESS." Al Goldstein
"THE FIRST 'X'ER WITH A GENUINE ELEMENT OF SUSPENSE." GENESIS
Written, Produced & Directed by JONAS MIDDLETON
Director of Photography: Charles Slavonvich
Editor: Marizo Zaurman
Music: Arion Ober and Vern Carlson
With Michelle Magazine, Martine Gay, Mary Madigan, Davy Jones Jamie Gillis, Mike Jeffery
COLOR X ADULTS ONLY

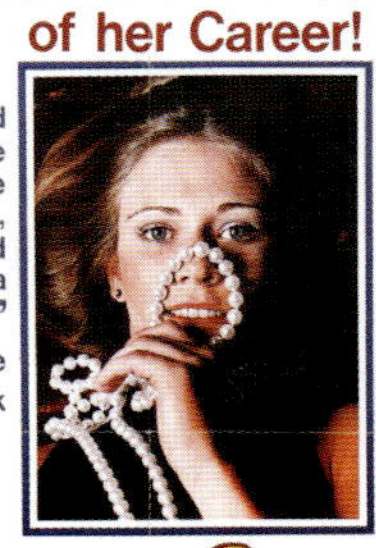
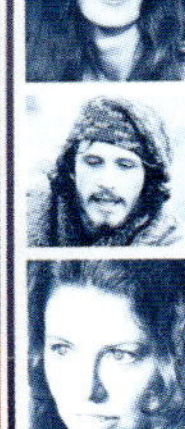
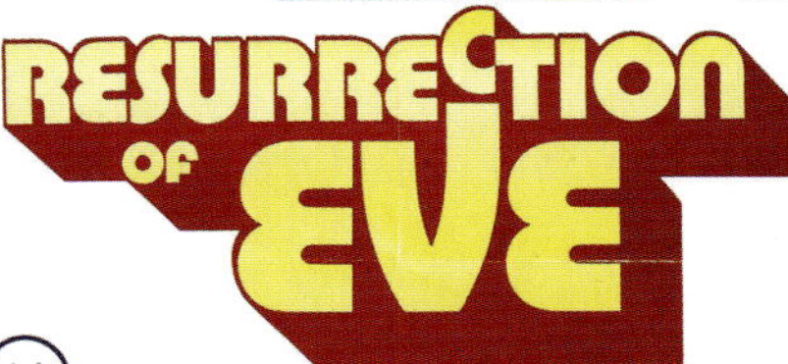

Marilyn Chambers
From 'Behind the Green Door' to the Performance of her Career!
"Everyone agreed she has the feminine luminescence of a Marilyn Monroe, and the wit and presence of a Katherine Hepburn...."
—SHOW Magazine New York
RESURRECTION OF EVE
X A Mitchell Brothers Film Group Production
Starring Marilyn CHAMBERS Mathew ARMON Johnnie KEYES Mimi MORGAN
With Special Guests the NICKELETTES · the TUBES · ERIC NORD Music by Richard Wynkoop

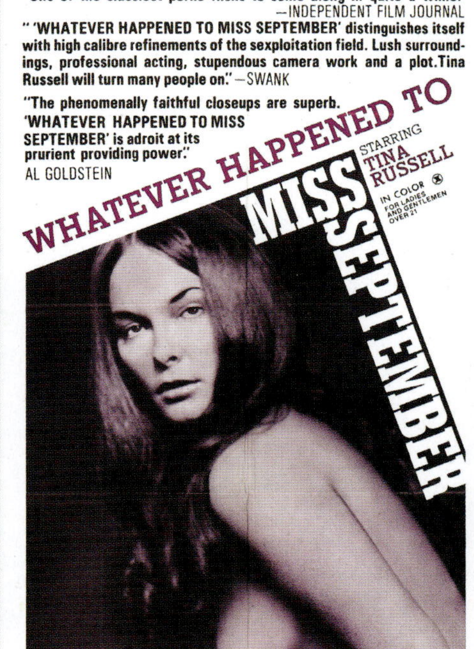

"One of the classiest porno flicks to come along in quite a while." —INDEPENDENT FILM JOURNAL
"'WHATEVER HAPPENED TO MISS SEPTEMBER' distinguishes itself with high calibre refinements of the sexploitation field. Lush surroundings, professional acting, stupendous camera work and a plot. Tina Russell will turn many people on." —SWANK
"The phenomenally faithful closeups are superb. 'WHATEVER HAPPENED TO MISS SEPTEMBER' is adroit at its prurient providing power." AL GOLDSTEIN
WHATEVER HAPPENED TO MISS SEPTEMBER
STARRING TINA RUSSELL
IN COLOR FOR LADIES AND GENTLEMEN OVER 21

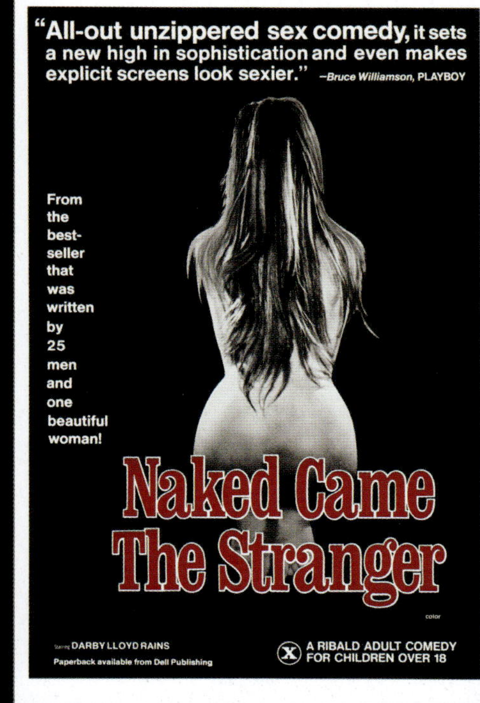

"All-out unzippered sex comedy, it sets a new high in sophistication and even makes explicit screens look sexier." —Bruce Williamson, PLAYBOY
From the best-seller that was written by 25 men and one beautiful woman!
Naked Came The Stranger
Starring DARBY LLOYD RAINS
Paperback available from Dell Publishing
X A RIBALD ADULT COMEDY FOR CHILDREN OVER 18

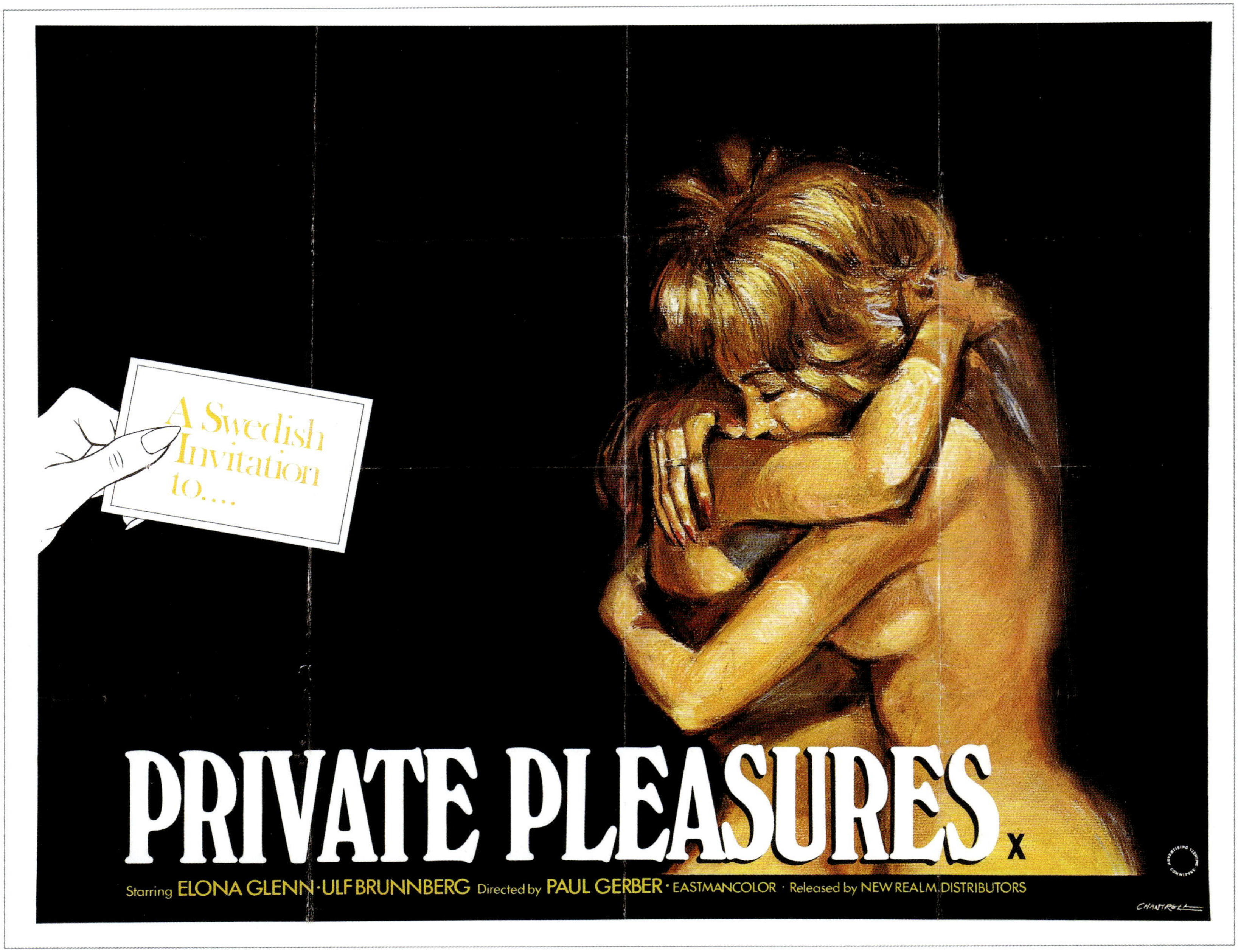

A Swedish Invitation to....

PRIVATE PLEASURES X

Starring ELONA GLENN · ULF BRUNNBERG Directed by PAUL GERBER · EASTMANCOLOR · Released by NEW REALM DISTRIBUTORS

CHANTRELL

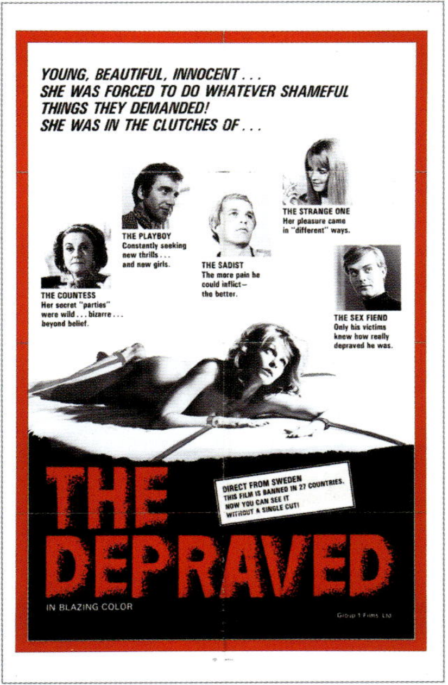

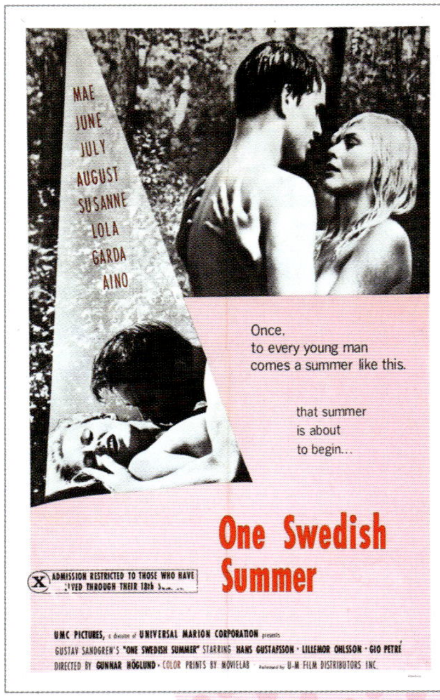

THE FASCINATION WITH SWEDEN

In the years before the Muppets, it was a scientifically proven fact (probably) that during word association games, the most popular response to "Swedish" was "sex." Everyone knew that Sweden was a *smörgåsbord* of lust—movie posters said so. "A Swedish Invitation" offers the British quad poster for *Private Pleasures* (aka *I lust och nöd*, 1976), complete with tasteful art by Tom Chantrell hinting at the lesbian finale. An early trailblazer, seen overleaf, was the softcore epic *Inga* (1968). Written and directed by an American (Joseph W. Sarno), but shot in Sweden, it was one of the first movies to be released in the US with the then newly minted X rating.

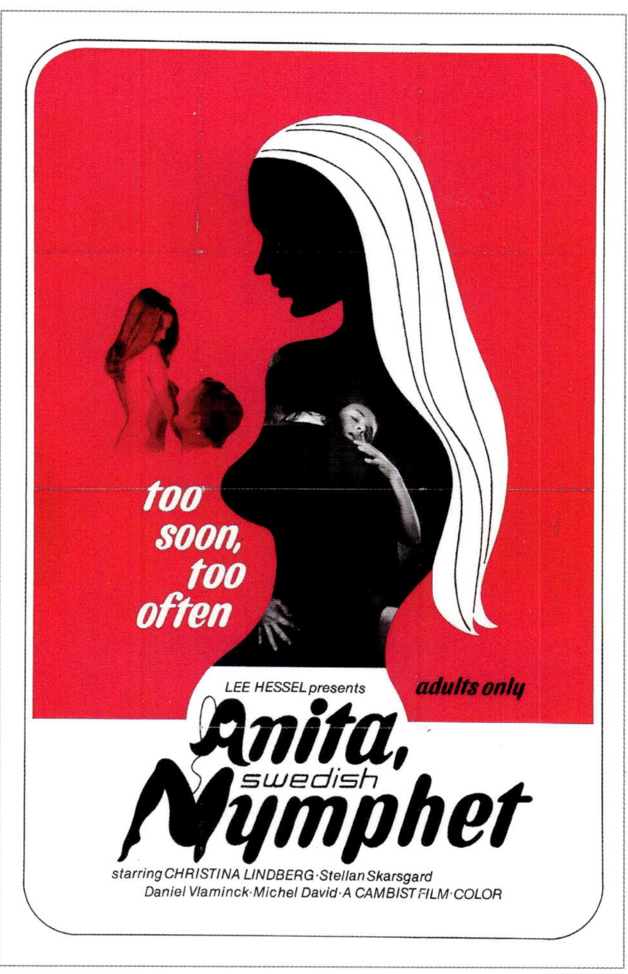
too soon, too often
LEE HESSEL presents
adults only
Anita, swedish Nymphet
starring CHRISTINA LINDBERG · Stellan Skarsgard
Daniel Vlaminck · Michel David · A CAMBIST FILM · COLOR

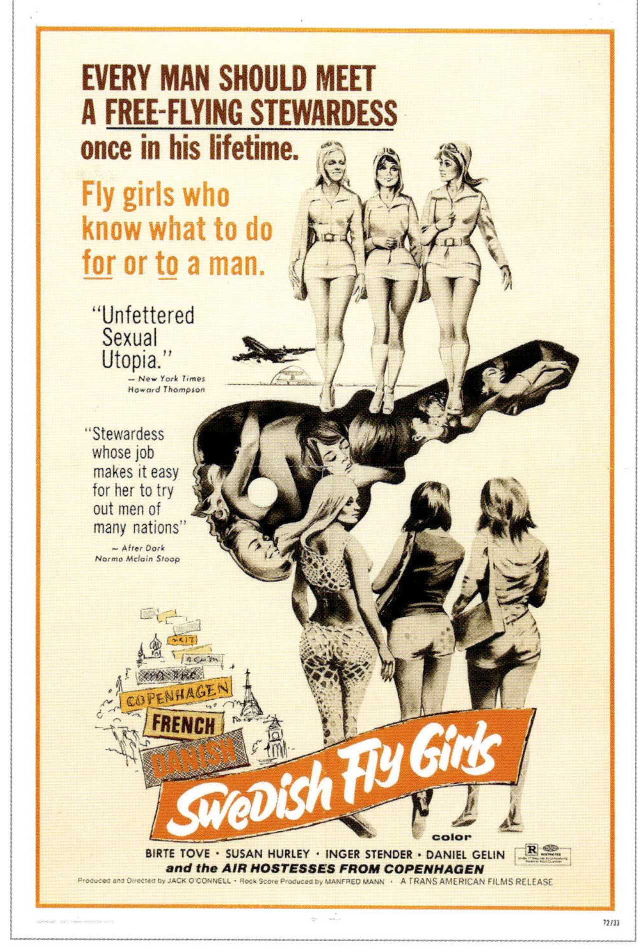
EVERY MAN SHOULD MEET
A FREE-FLYING STEWARDESS
once in his lifetime.
Fly girls who know what to do for or to a man.
"Unfettered Sexual Utopia."
— New York Times Howard Thompson
"Stewardess whose job makes it easy for her to try out men of many nations"
— After Dark Norma Mclain Stoop
COPENHAGEN
FRENCH
DANISH
Swedish Fly Girls
color
BIRTE TOVE · SUSAN HURLEY · INGER STENDER · DANIEL GELIN
and the AIR HOSTESSES FROM COPENHAGEN
Produced and Directed by JACK O'CONNELL · Rock Score Produced by MANFRED MANN · A TRANS AMERICAN FILMS RELEASE
72/33

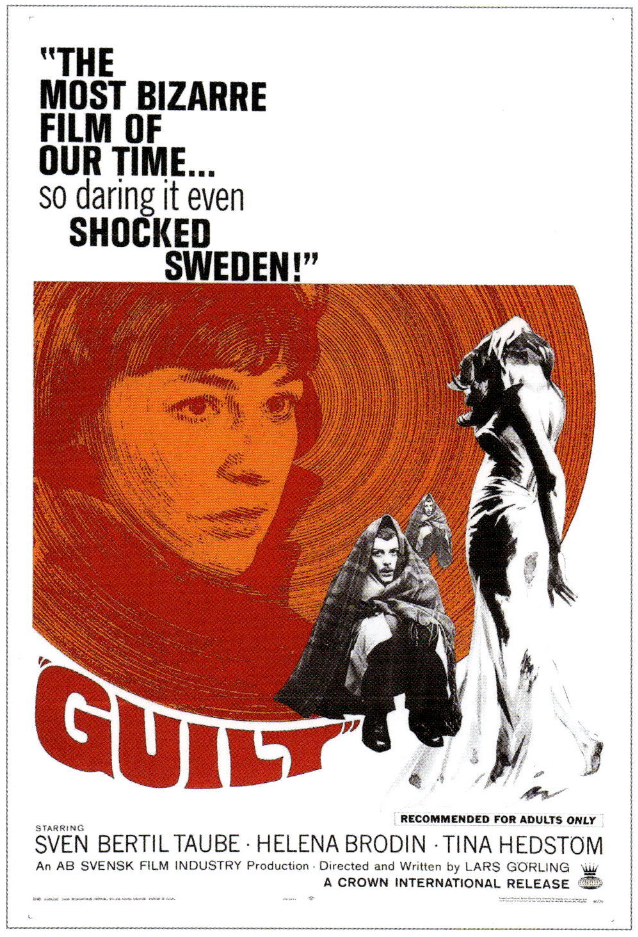
"THE MOST BIZARRE FILM OF OUR TIME... so daring it even SHOCKED SWEDEN!"
"GUILT"
RECOMMENDED FOR ADULTS ONLY
STARRING
SVEN BERTIL TAUBE · HELENA BRODIN · TINA HEDSTOM
An AB SVENSK FILM INDUSTRY Production · Directed and Written by LARS GORLING
A CROWN INTERNATIONAL RELEASE

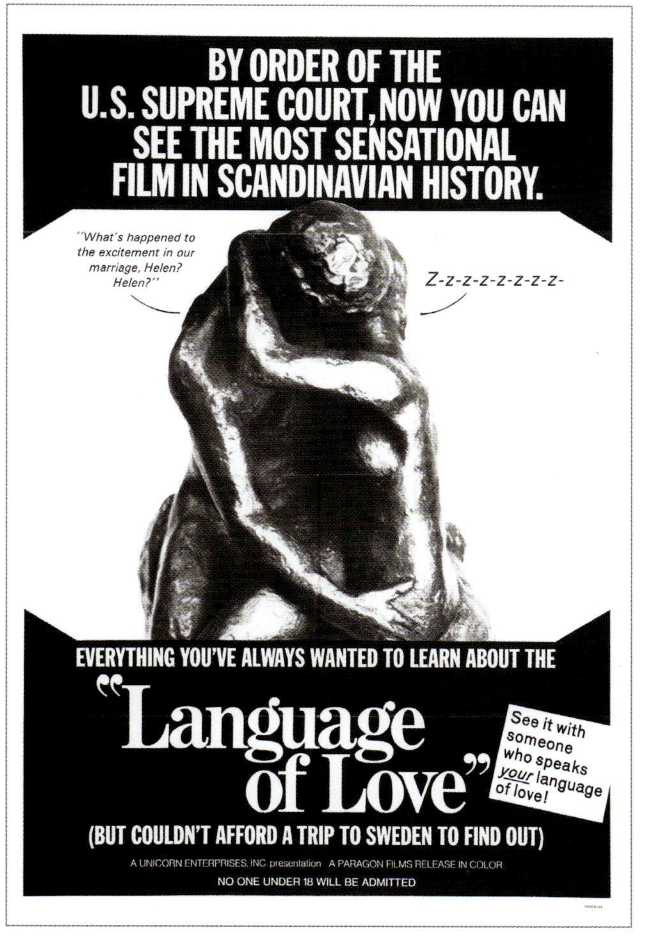
BY ORDER OF THE U.S. SUPREME COURT, NOW YOU CAN SEE THE MOST SENSATIONAL FILM IN SCANDINAVIAN HISTORY.
"What's happened to the excitement in our marriage, Helen? Helen?"
Z-z-z-z-z-z-z-z-
EVERYTHING YOU'VE ALWAYS WANTED TO LEARN ABOUT THE
"Language of Love"
See it with someone who speaks your language of love!
(BUT COULDN'T AFFORD A TRIP TO SWEDEN TO FIND OUT)
A UNICORN ENTERPRISES, INC. presentation · A PARAGON FILMS RELEASE IN COLOR
NO ONE UNDER 18 WILL BE ADMITTED

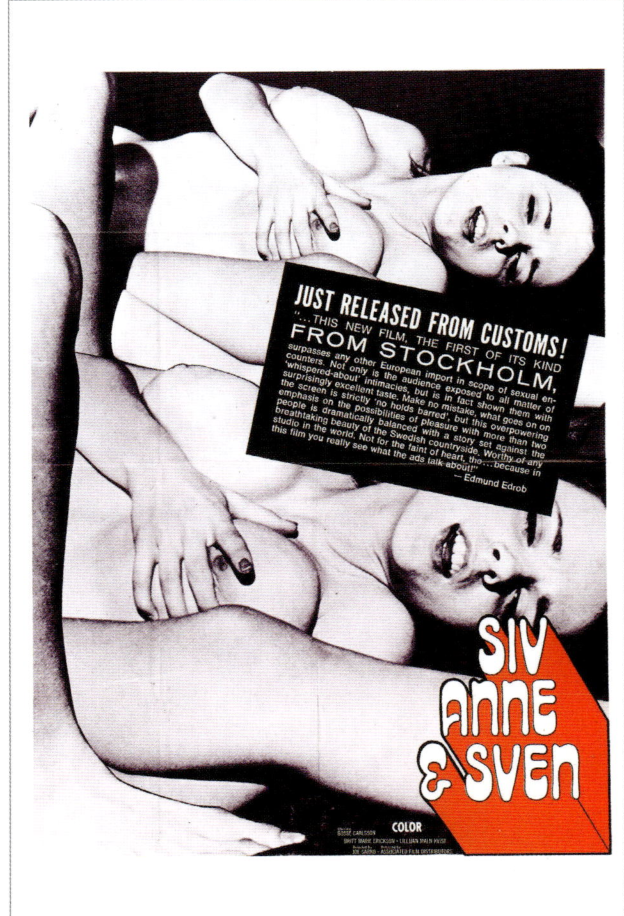
JUST RELEASED FROM CUSTOMS!
"...THIS NEW FILM, THE FIRST OF ITS KIND FROM STOCKHOLM, surpasses any other European import in scope of sexual encounters. Not only is the audience exposed to all matter of 'whispered-about' intimacies, but is in fact shown them with surprisingly excellent taste. Make no mistake, what goes on on the screen is strictly 'no holds barred', but this overpowering emphasis on the possibilities of pleasure with more than two people is dramatically balanced with a story set against the breathtaking beauty of the Swedish countryside. Worthy of any studio in the world. Not for the faint of heart, tho...because in this film you really see what the ads talk about!"
— Edmund Edrob
SIV ANNE & SVEN
COLOR

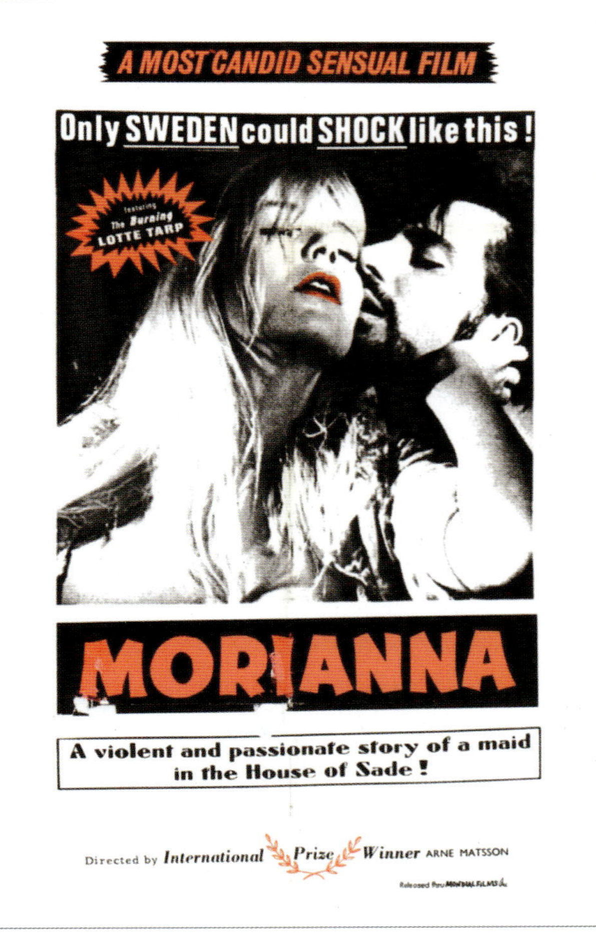
A MOST CANDID SENSUAL FILM
Only SWEDEN could SHOCK like this!
The Burning LOTTE TARP
MORIANNA
A violent and passionate story of a maid in the House of Sade!
Directed by International Prize Winner ARNE MATSSON

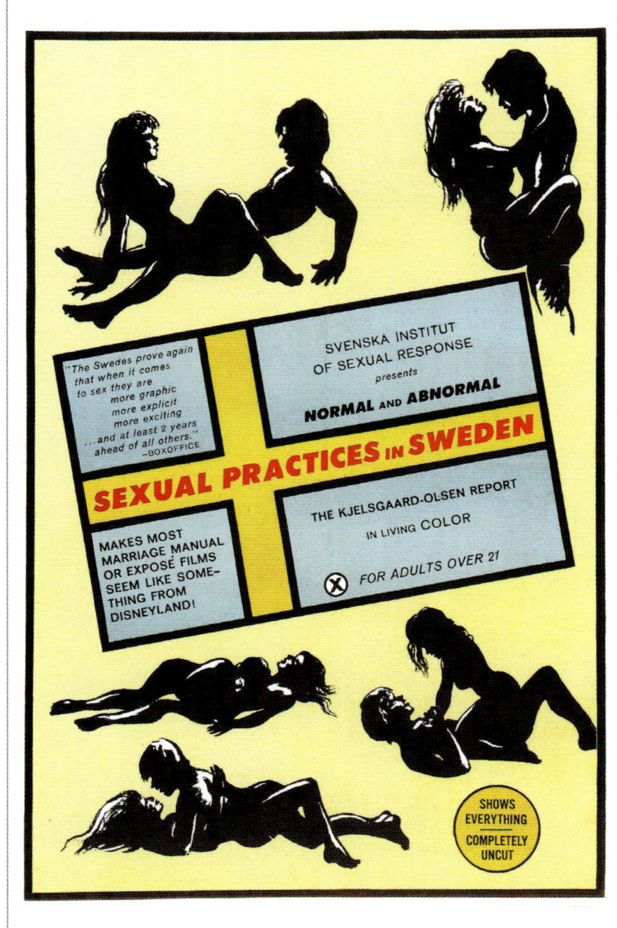
"The Swedes prove again that when it comes to sex they are more graphic more explicit more exciting ...and at least 2 years ahead of all others." –BOXOFFICE
SVENSKA INSTITUT OF SEXUAL RESPONSE
presents
NORMAL AND ABNORMAL
SEXUAL PRACTICES IN SWEDEN
THE KJELSGAARD-OLSEN REPORT
IN LIVING COLOR
FOR ADULTS OVER 21
MAKES MOST MARRIAGE MANUAL OR EXPOSÉ FILMS SEEM LIKE SOMETHING FROM DISNEYLAND!
SHOWS EVERYTHING
COMPLETELY UNCUT

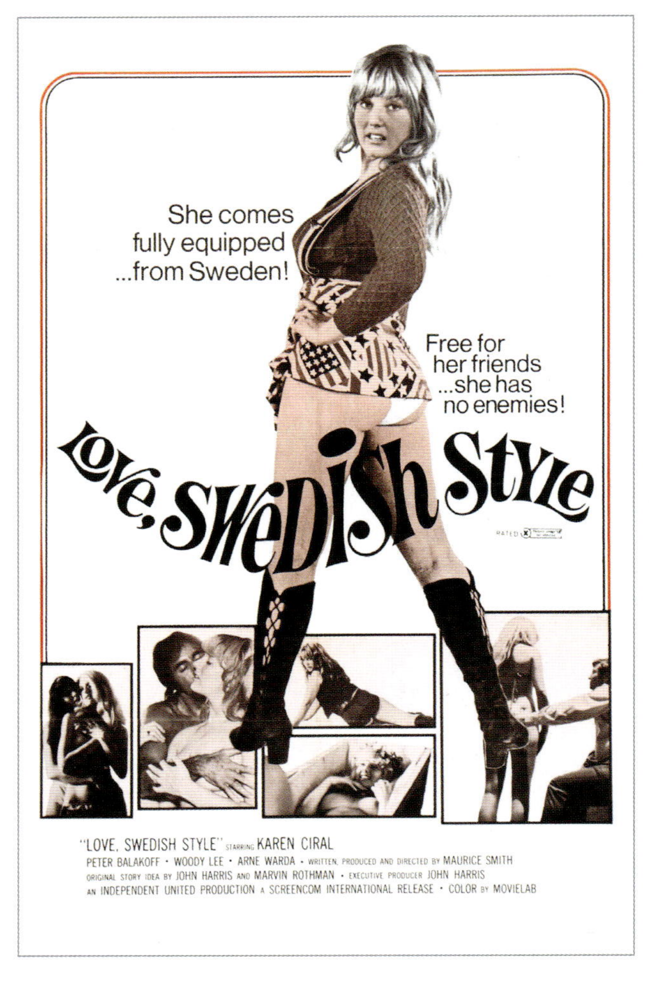
She comes fully equipped ...from Sweden!
Free for her friends ...she has no enemies!
LOVE, SWEDISH STYLE
"LOVE, SWEDISH STYLE" STARRING KAREN CIRAL
PETER BALAKOFF • WOODY LEE • ARNE WARDA • WRITTEN, PRODUCED AND DIRECTED BY MAURICE SMITH
ORIGINAL STORY IDEA BY JOHN HARRIS AND MARVIN ROTHMAN • EXECUTIVE PRODUCER JOHN HARRIS
AN INDEPENDENT UNITED PRODUCTION A SCREENCOM INTERNATIONAL RELEASE • COLOR BY MOVIELAB

"Inga is so graphic, I could have sworn the screen was smoking."
—N.Y. Daily Column

"If I were to describe in detail what goes on in 'Inga', I'd get arrested."
—Robert Salmaggi, WINS Radio

"'I Am Curious, Yellow' is banned in this country and 'Inga' is not. In 'Inga'... the sexual activity is... more tantilizing."
—David Goldman, WCBS Radio

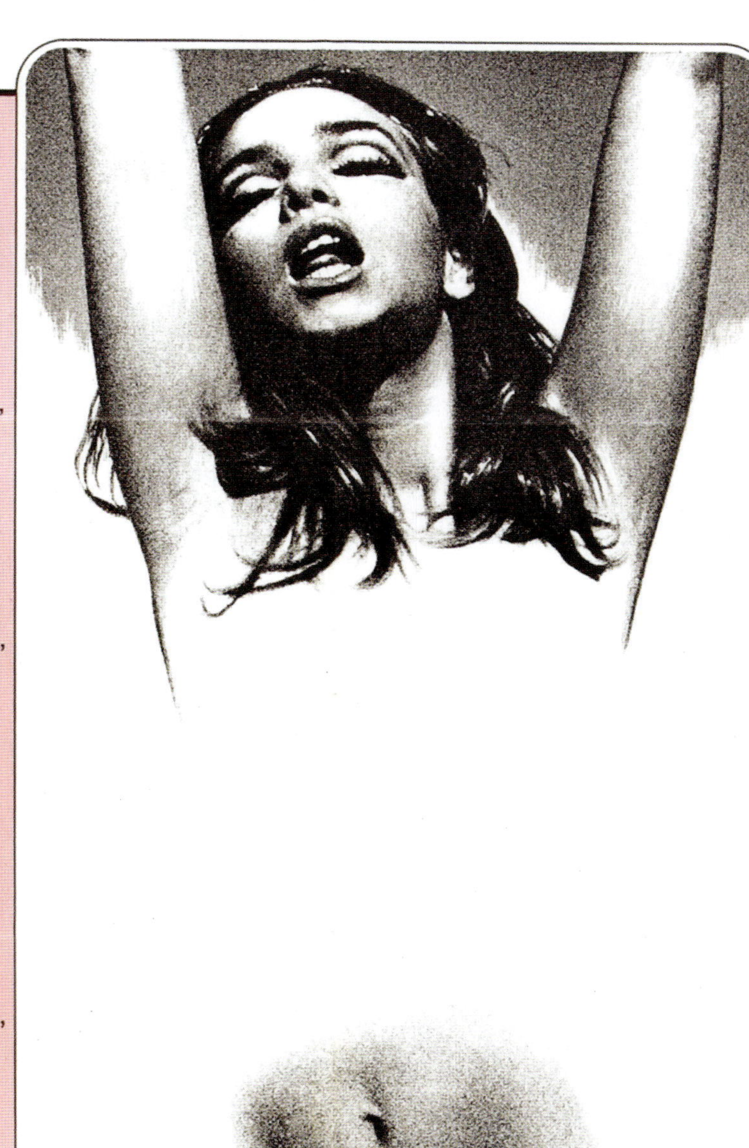

Starring
MARIE LILJEDAHL
with
MONICA STROMMERSTEDT
THOMAS UNGEWITTER
LASSEN CASTEN
A CANNON Production
Music Composed and Conducted by
CLAY PITTS
Co-Produced by
ROBERT BRANDT
Produced by
DONALD DENNIS
AN INSKAFILM, Ltd. Picture
A CINEMATION INDUSTRIES Release

From Sweden... the classic female concept

JERRY GROSS and NICHOLAS DEMETROULES
PRESENT

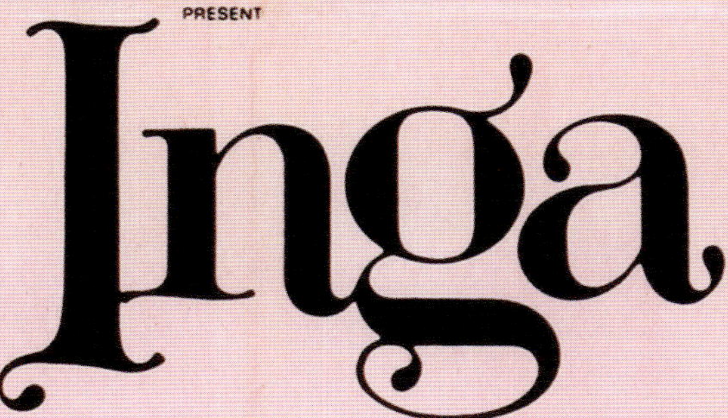

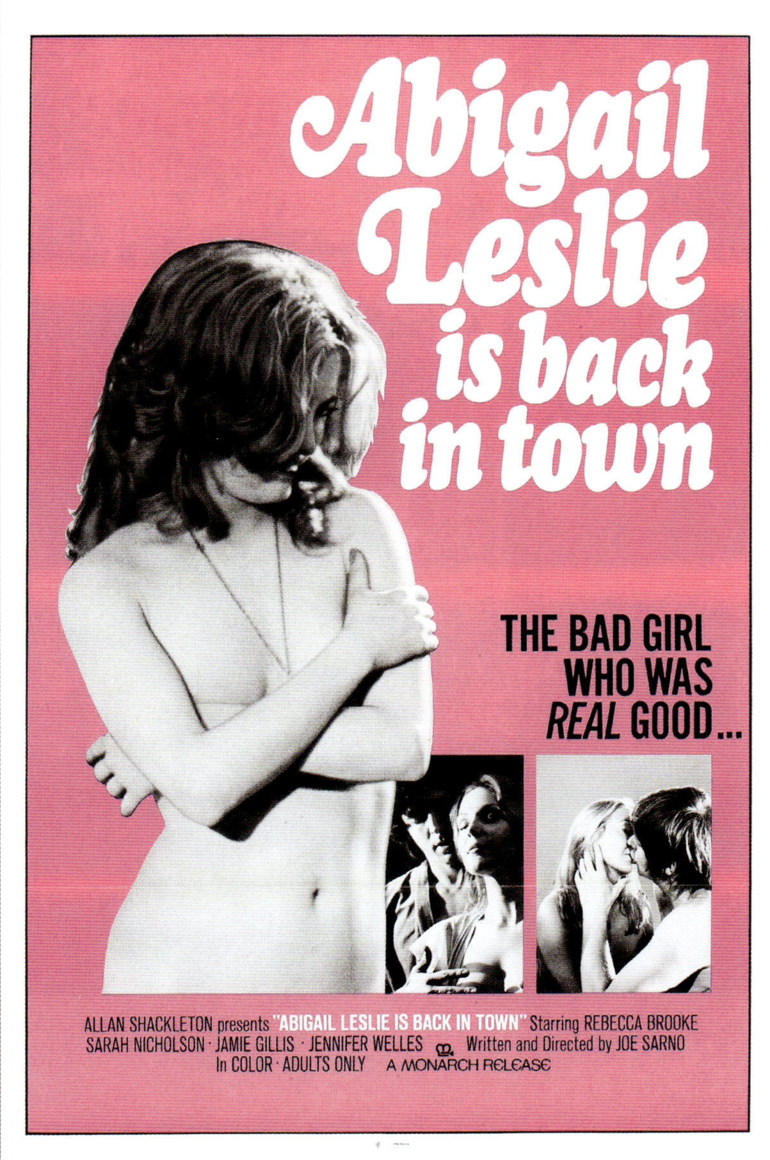

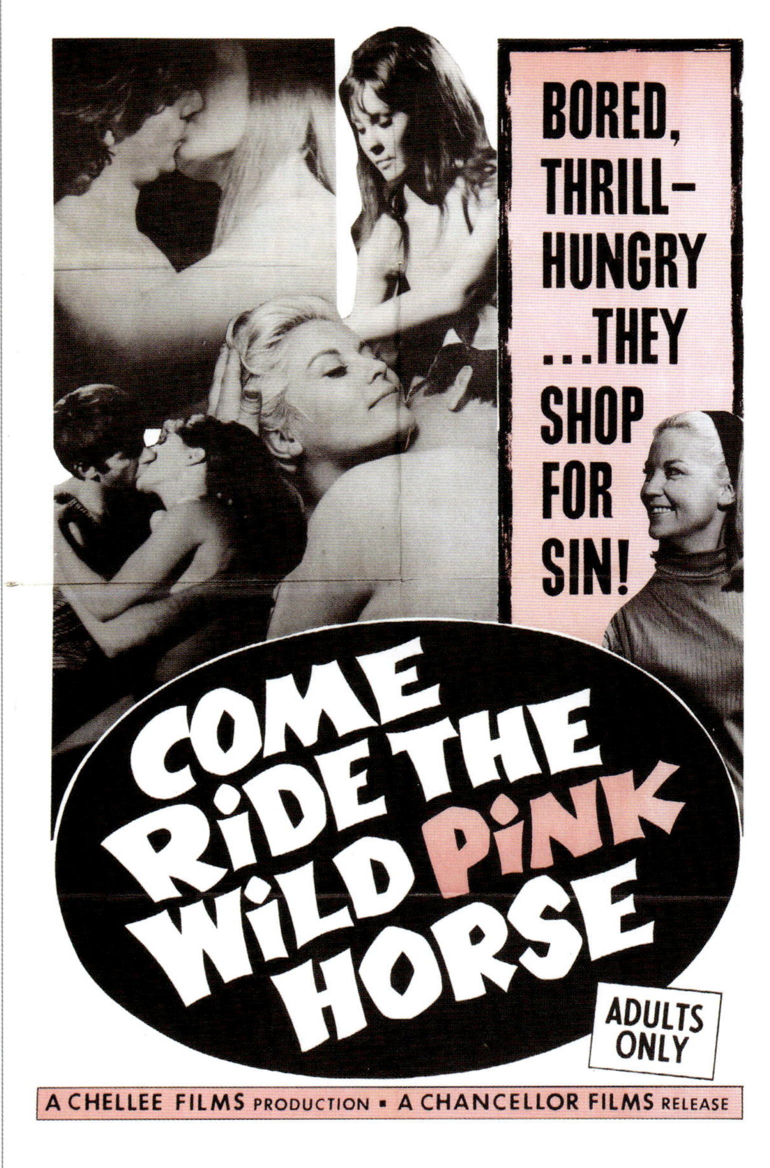

JOSEPH SARNO

Though he's best known as "the Ingmar Bergman of porn" thanks to *Inga* and his other Swedish-made films, writer and director Joseph W. Sarno (1921–2010) was a prolific pioneer of sexploitation in his native America, from his first adult feature *Nude in Charcoal* (aka *The Secret of Venus*, 1961) to his late-period pseudonymous hardcore work. While its fantastic one-sheet promises more than the film delivers, *Sin You Sinners* (1963), with its stark black-and-white photography and plot centered on a mother-and-daughter conflict, was an early example of Sarno's approach. "I went for the ragged, realistic look more than anything, and I was more interested in psychology and character development than most of the other filmmakers at that time," Sarno explained. Richard Corliss, in his obituary for *Time* magazine, agreed: "If not exactly a feminist, Sarno certainly understood women. He was less a sexploitationist than a psychiatrist—an acute observer of the horny heart."

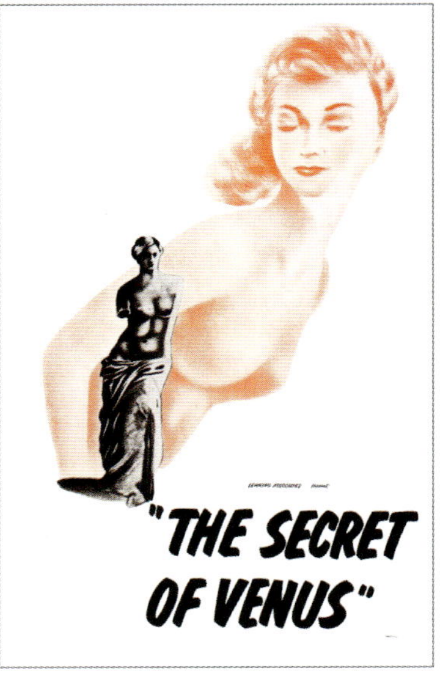

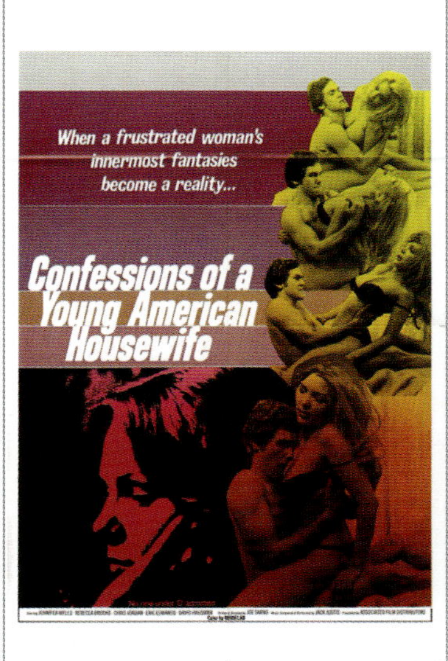

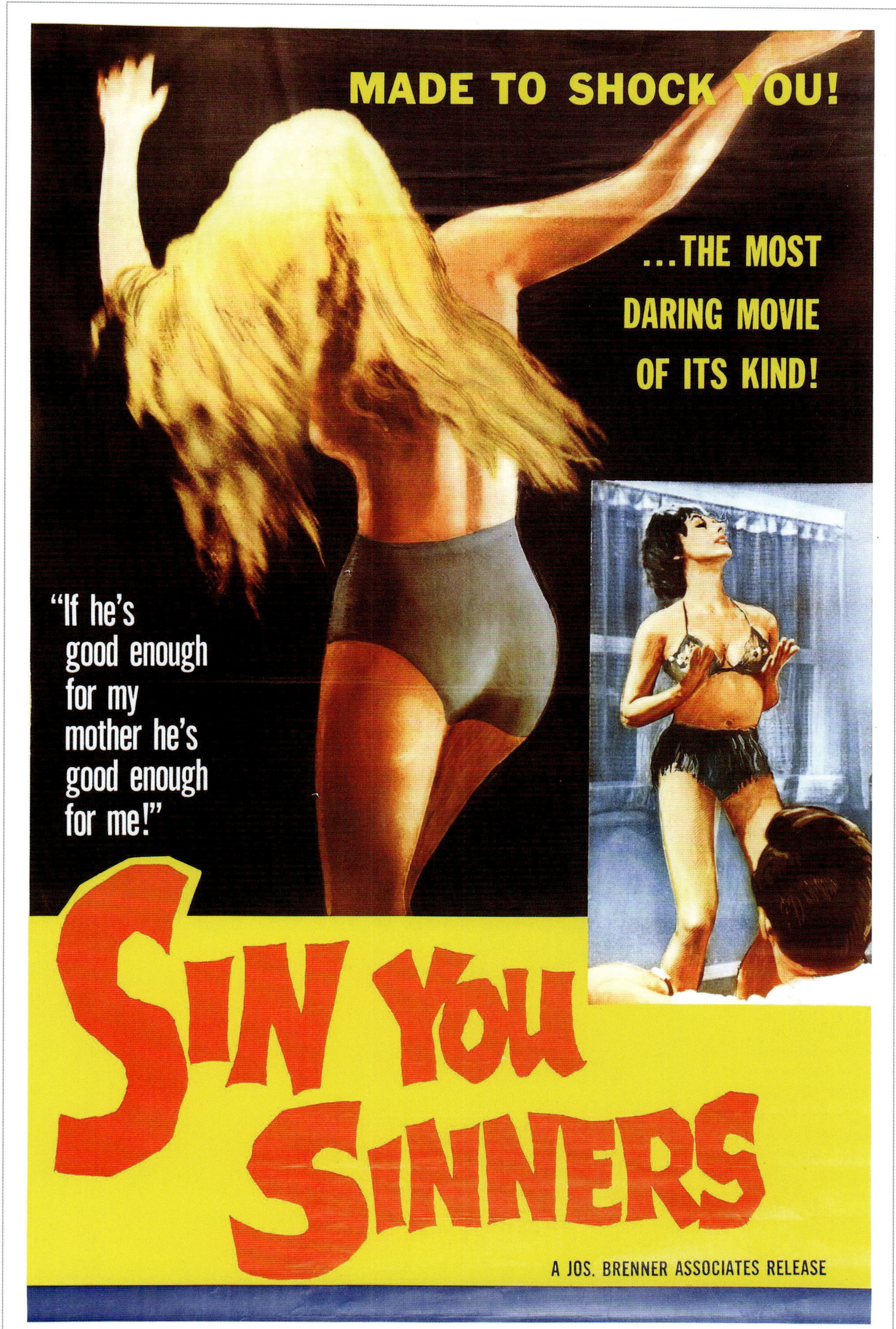
MADE TO SHOCK YOU!
...THE MOST DARING MOVIE OF ITS KIND!
"If he's good enough for my mother he's good enough for me!"
SIN YOU SINNERS
A JOS. BRENNER ASSOCIATES RELEASE

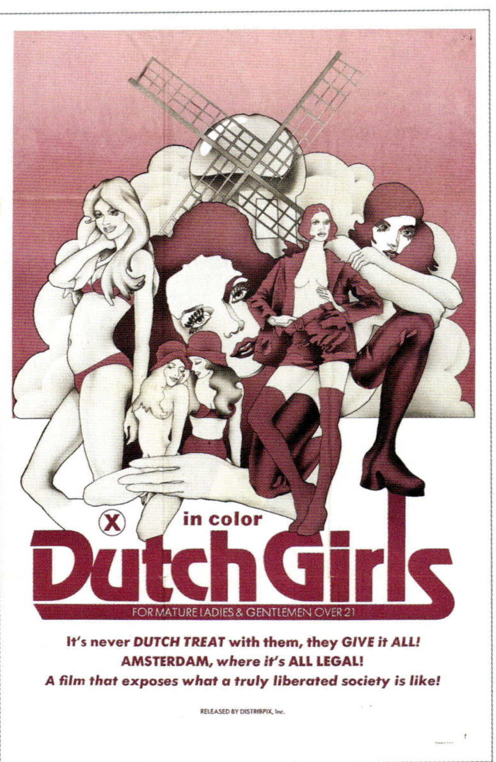

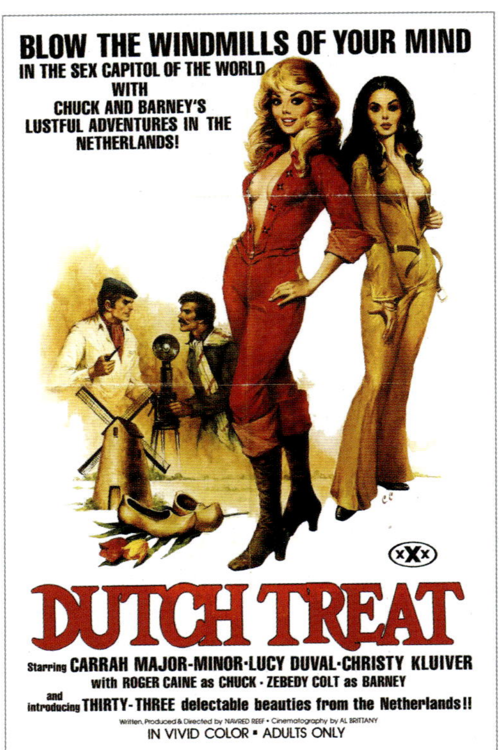

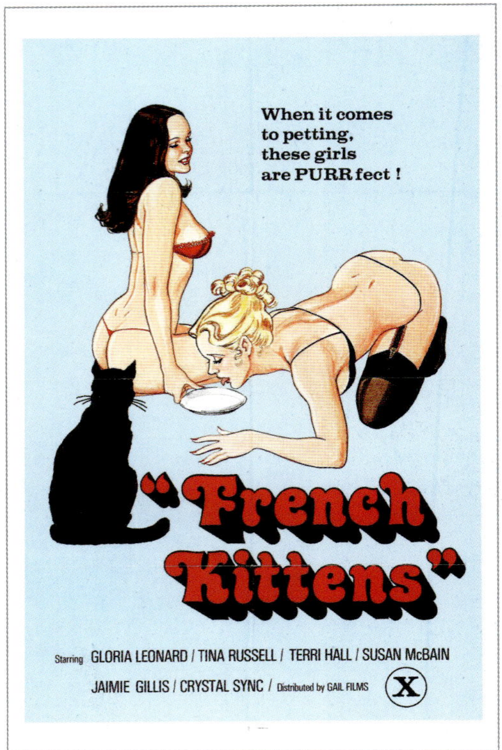

MORE FOREIGN FANCIES

When Noel (son of Rex) Harrison recorded the beautiful song "The Windmills of Your Mind" in 1968, little did he know that within a decade it would be reduced to a punch line on a sexploitation movie poster. *Dutch Treat* (1977) adds in a "Netherlands" pun, and pictures of a windmill, tulips, and clogs for good measure—no, this isn't Sweden, but the girls are still up for anything, including the top-billed "Carrah Major-Minor" (remember 1977 was when that iconic poster of Farrah Fawcett-Majors was smiling from millions of bedroom walls). French ladies also have a certain "ooh la la," including the star of *French Pussycat* (1972), "the sweetest French Pastry since Pussy Galore!" Never mind that Sybil Danning was Austrian, and the Bond character was not from France either: Elaine Gignilliat's art of a French maid playing with her pussy is what you're looking at.

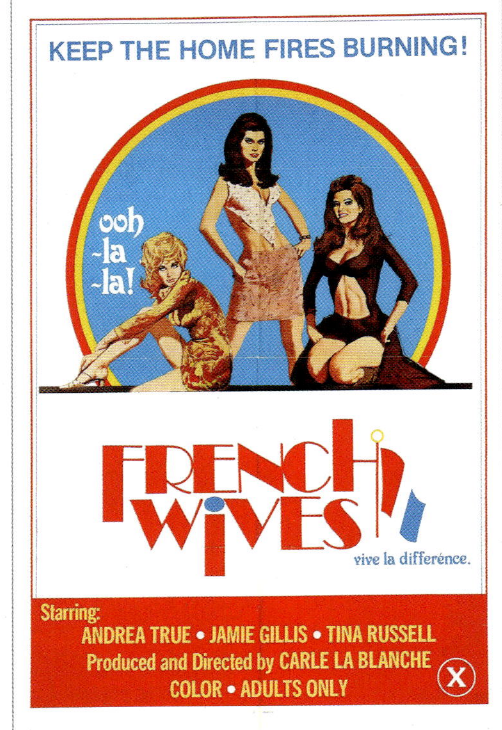

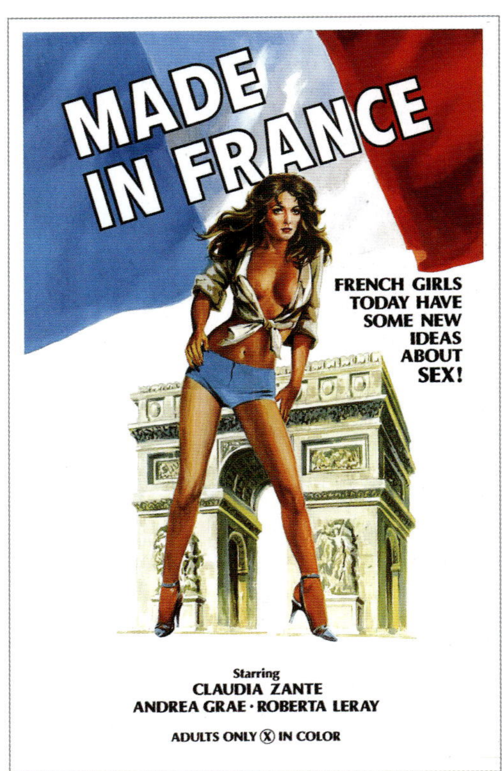

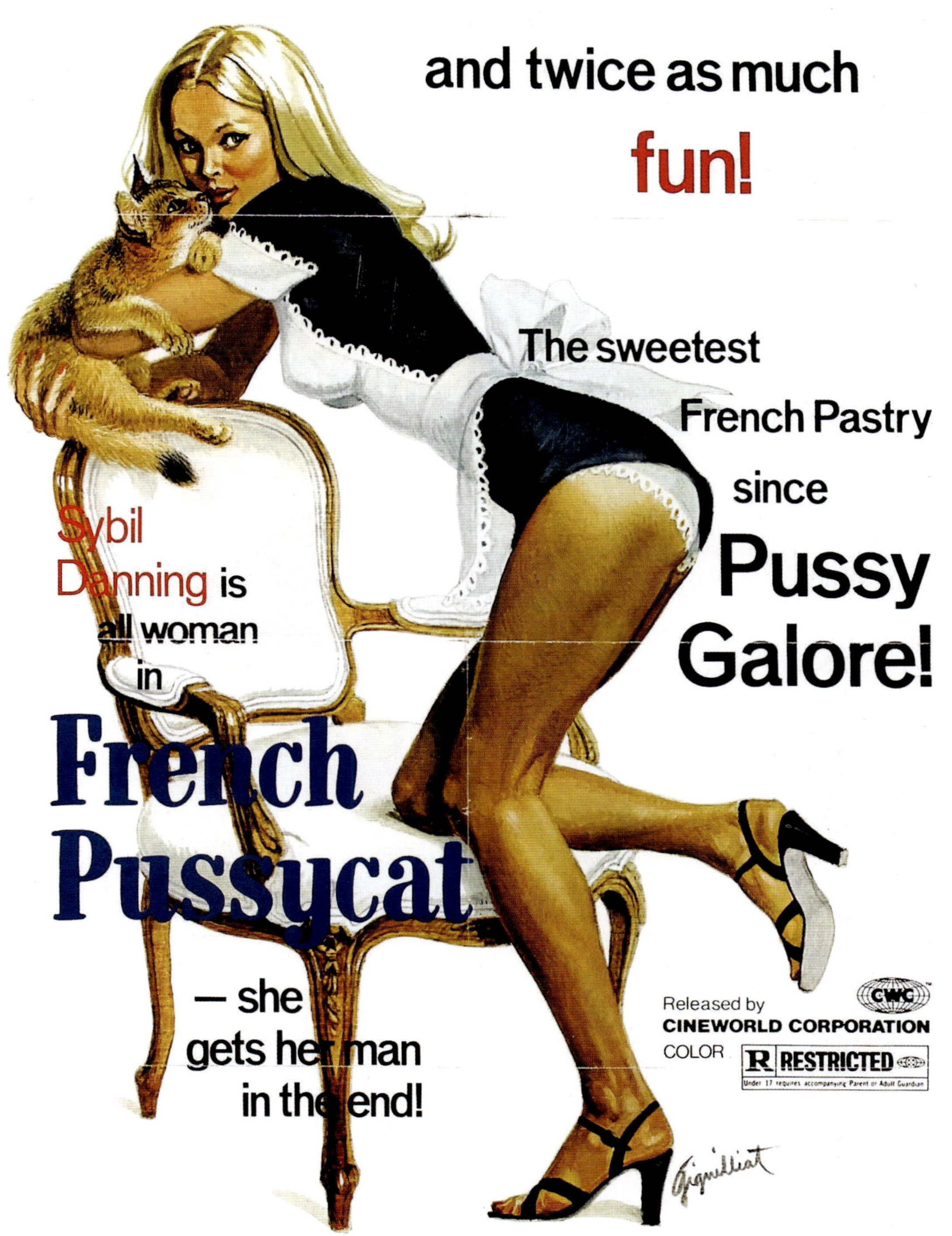
Cute as a kitten...
and twice as much
fun!
The sweetest
French Pastry
since
Pussy
Galore!
Sybil
Danning is
all woman
in
French
Pussycat
— she
gets her man
in the end!
Released by
CINEWORLD CORPORATION
CWC
COLOR
R RESTRICTED
Under 17 requires accompanying Parent or Adult Guardian
starring Sybil Danning Katie Buchele Marlene Appel
Produced by Elio Romano Written and Directed by Henry Billian

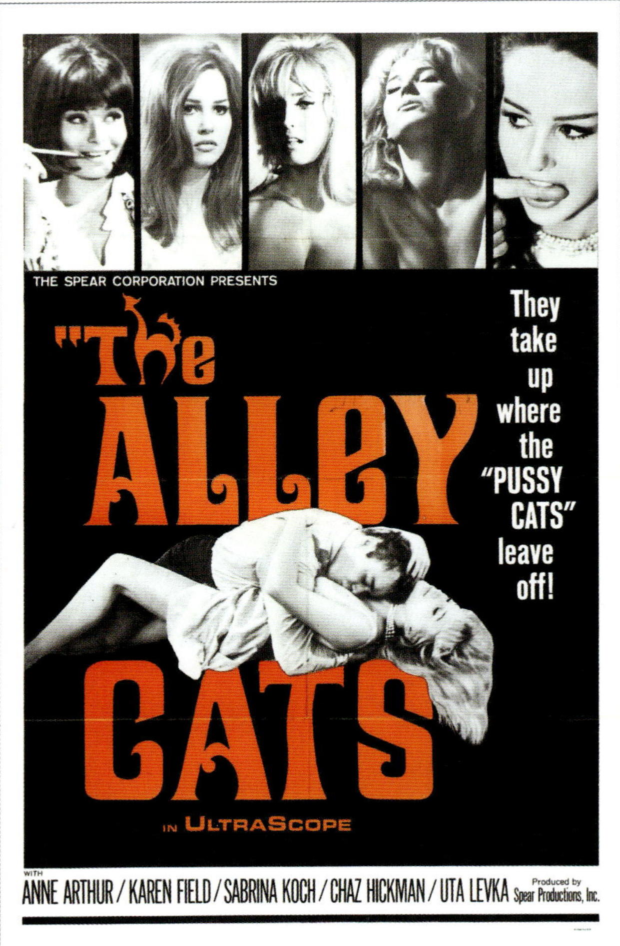
THE SPEAR CORPORATION PRESENTS
"The ALLEY CATS"
They take up where the "PUSSY CATS" leave off!
IN ULTRASCOPE
WITH ANNE ARTHUR / KAREN FIELD / SABRINA KOCH / CHAZ HICKMAN / UTA LEVKA
Produced by Spear Productions, Inc.

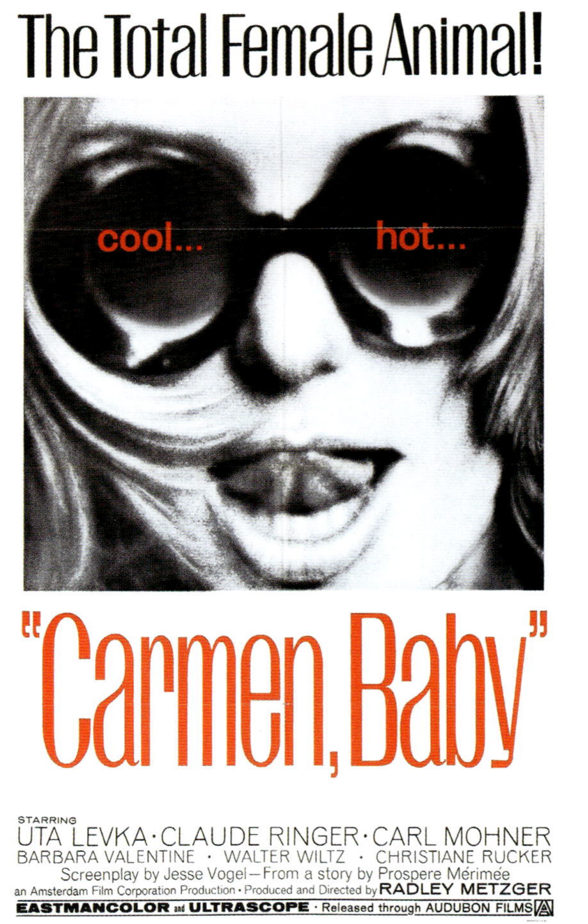
The Total Female Animal!
cool...
hot...
"Carmen, Baby"
STARRING UTA LEVKA · CLAUDE RINGER · CARL MOHNER
BARBARA VALENTINE · WALTER WILTZ · CHRISTIANE RUCKER
Screenplay by Jesse Vogel—From a story by Prospere Mérimée
an Amsterdam Film Corporation Production · Produced and Directed by RADLEY METZGER
EASTMANCOLOR and ULTRASCOPE · Released through AUDUBON FILMS

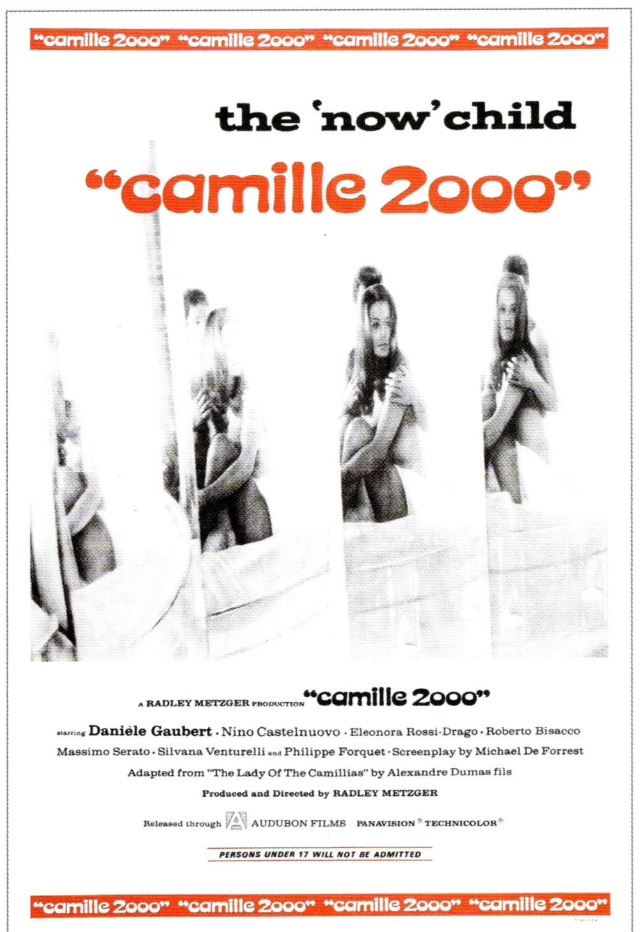
"camille 2000" "camille 2000" "camille 2000" "camille 2000"
the 'now' child
"camille 2000"
A RADLEY METZGER PRODUCTION "camille 2000"
starring Danièle Gaubert · Nino Castelnuovo · Eleonora Rossi-Drago · Roberto Bisacco
Massimo Serato · Silvana Venturelli and Philippe Forquet · Screenplay by Michael De Forrest
Adapted from "The Lady Of The Camillias" by Alexandre Dumas fils
Produced and Directed by RADLEY METZGER
Released through AUDUBON FILMS PANAVISION® TECHNICOLOR®
PERSONS UNDER 17 WILL NOT BE ADMITTED
"camille 2000" "camille 2000" "camille 2000" "camille 2000"

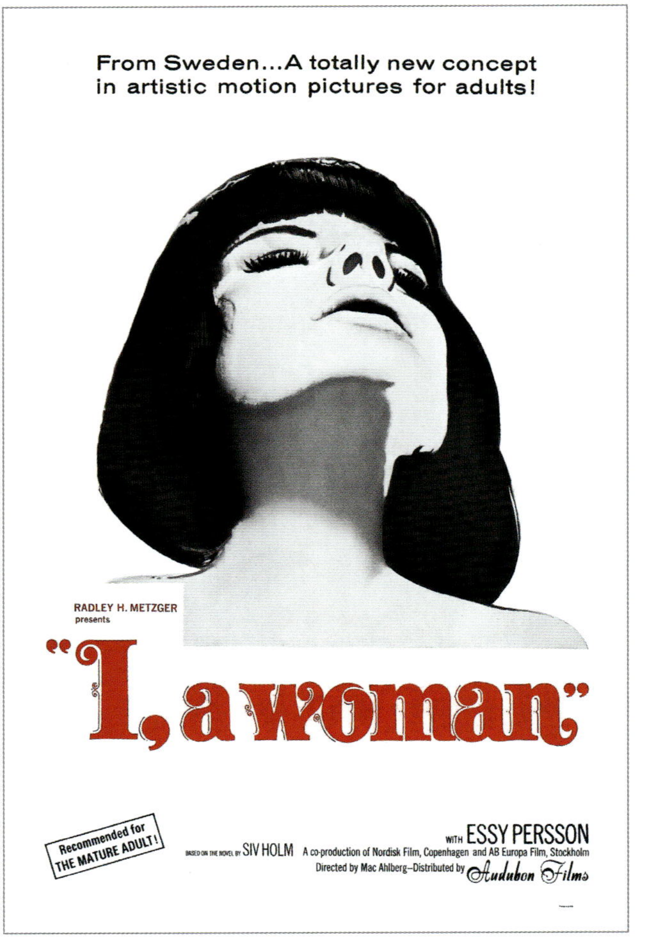
From Sweden...A totally new concept in artistic motion pictures for adults!
RADLEY H. METZGER presents
"I, a woman"
Recommended for THE MATURE ADULT!
WITH ESSY PERSSON
BASED ON THE NOVEL BY SIV HOLM A co-production of Nordisk Film, Copenhagen and AB Europa Film, Stockholm
Directed by Mac Ahlberg—Distributed by Audubon Films

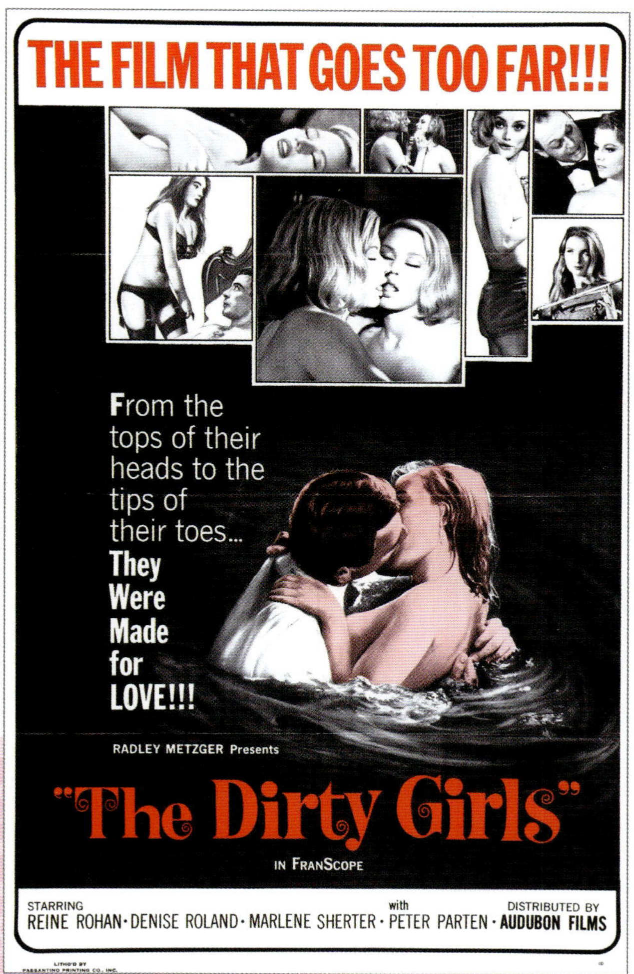

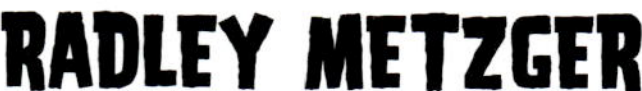

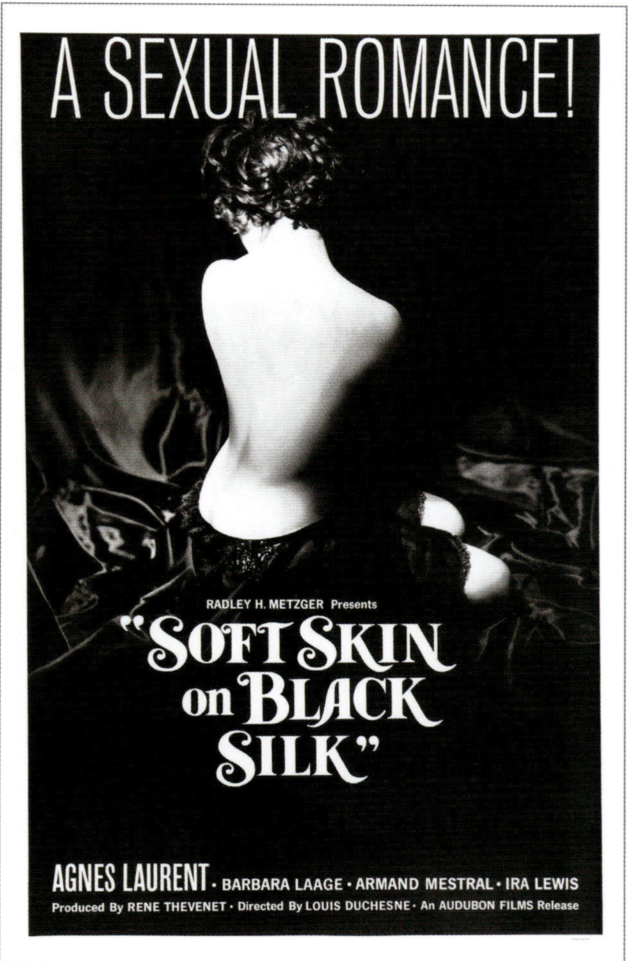

RADLEY METZGER

Beautiful cinematography. Elegant production design. Witty scripts. Rarely the qualities adult films are renowned for, unless your name is Radley Metzger. Starting out in the business as an editor, Metzger first found major success re-editing European films for the US market. His distribution company Audubon Films' release of the Swedish erotic drama *I, a Woman* (1965) reportedly made $4 million, and went a long way to open up the audience for sexploitation in America. As the trade paper *Variety* pointed out, the film "freed itself from the exploitation houses . . . invaded suburbia and immediately struck paydirt." Metzger's own films as a director, and later the hardcore features under his *nom de porn* Henry Paris, were classy affairs with high production values and some big name fans: *The Lickerish Quartet* (1970) was praised as "an outrageously kinky masterpiece" by Andy Warhol. Aiming for quality was the best way to sell sex to the "young marrieds" of "polite society," according to Metzger. "If you take a little [something], as Mary Poppins said, to make the medicine go down, if you couch it in something entertaining—hopefully, witty and well-photographed—it's a lot easier to take."

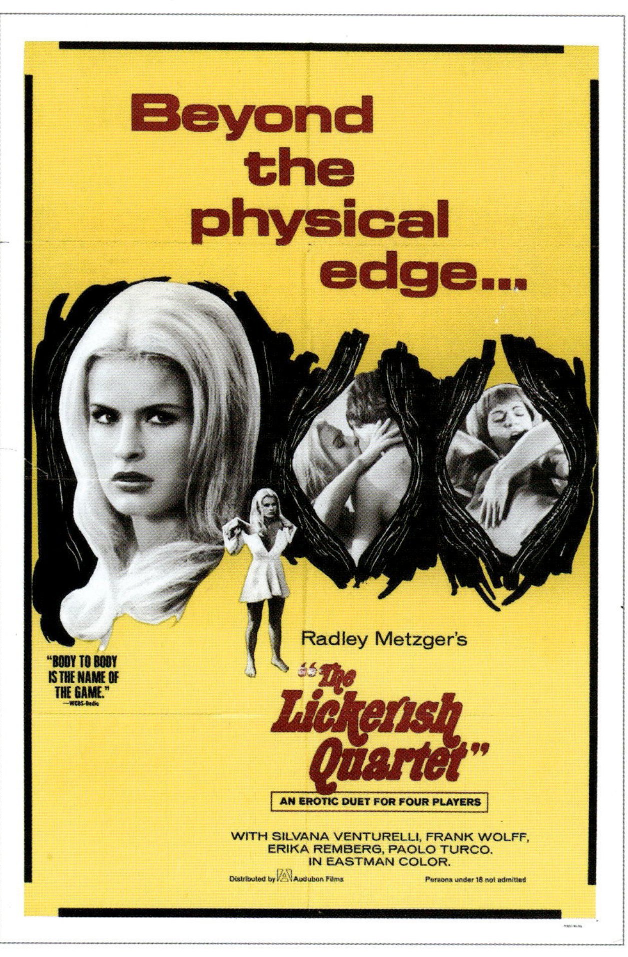

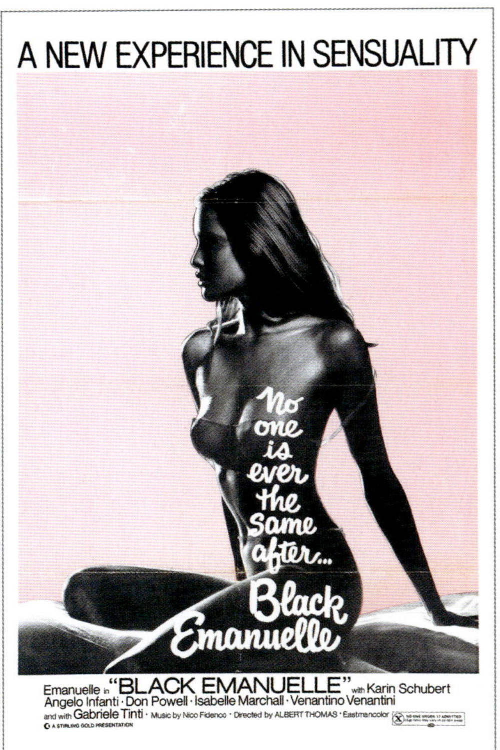
A NEW EXPERIENCE IN SENSUALITY
No one is ever the same after...
Black Emanuelle
Emanuelle in "BLACK EMANUELLE" with Karin Schubert
Angelo Infanti · Don Powell · Isabelle Marchall · Venantino Venantini
and with Gabriele Tinti · Music by Nico Fidenco · Directed by ALBERT THOMAS · Eastmancolor
A STIRLING GOLD PRESENTATION

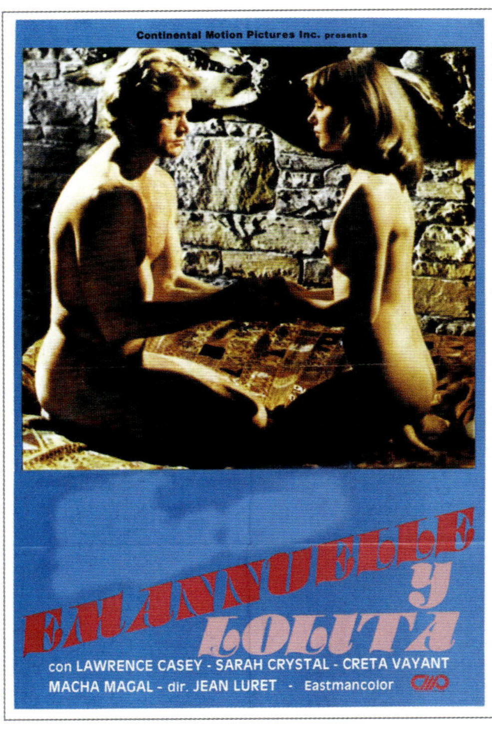
Continental Motion Pictures Inc. presents
EMANNUELLE y LOLITA
con LAWRENCE CASEY - SARAH CRYSTAL - CRETA VAYANT
MACHA MAGAL - dir. JEAN LURET - Eastmancolor

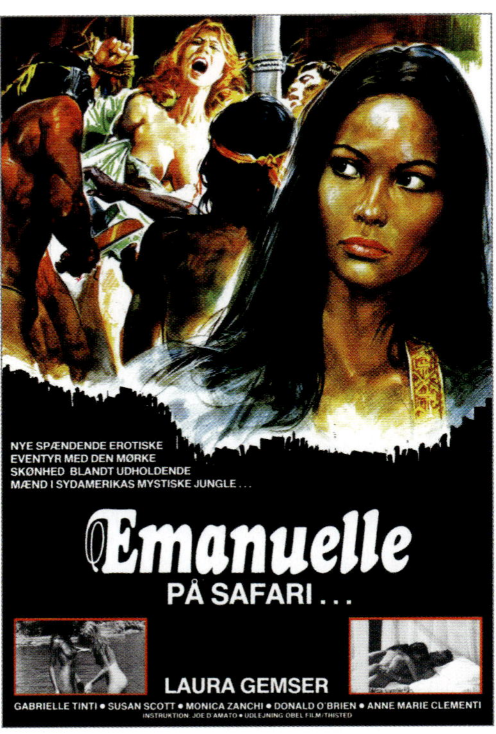
NYE SPÆNDENDE EROTISKE
EVENTYR MED DEN MØRKE
SKØNHED BLANDT UDHOLDENDE
MÆND I SYDAMERIKAS MYSTISKE JUNGLE . . .
Emanuelle
PÅ SAFARI . . .
LAURA GEMSER
GABRIELLE TINTI • SUSAN SCOTT • MONICA ZANCHI • DONALD O'BRIEN • ANNE MARIE CLEMENTI
INSTRUKTION: JOE D'AMATO • UDLEJNING OBEL FILM/THISTED

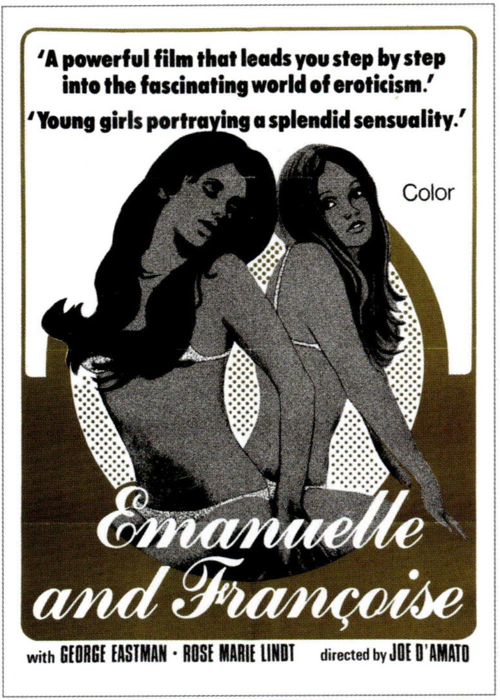
'A powerful film that leads you step by step into the fascinating world of eroticism.'
'Young girls portraying a splendid sensuality.'
Color
Emanuelle and Françoise
with GEORGE EASTMAN · ROSE MARIE LINDT directed by JOE D'AMATO

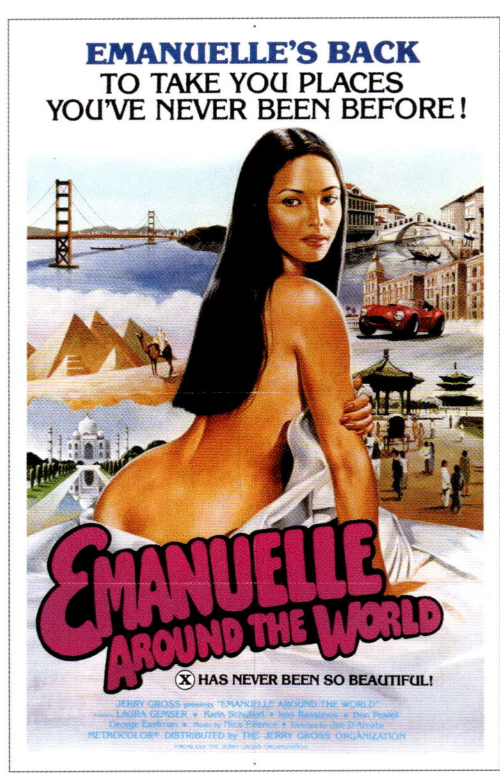
EMANUELLE'S BACK
TO TAKE YOU PLACES
YOU'VE NEVER BEEN BEFORE!
EMANUELLE AROUND THE WORLD
X HAS NEVER BEEN SO BEAUTIFUL!
JERRY GROSS presents "EMANUELLE AROUND THE WORLD"
METROCOLOR DISTRIBUTED by THE JERRY GROSS ORGANIZATION

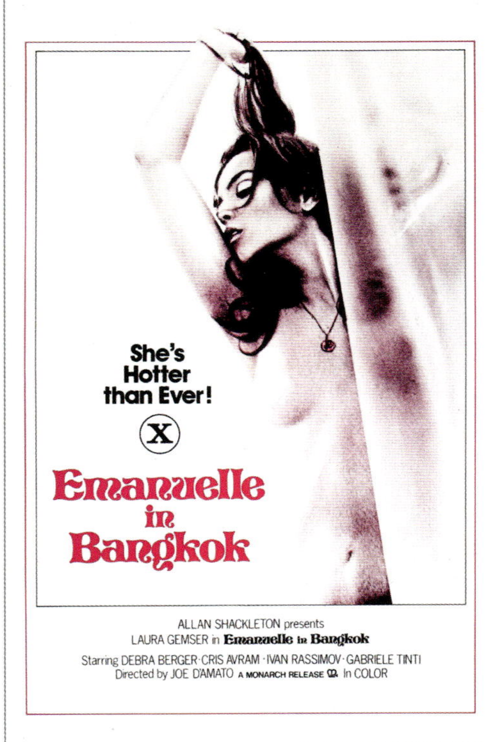
She's Hotter than Ever!
X
Emanuelle in Bangkok
ALLAN SHACKLETON presents
LAURA GEMSER in Emanuelle in Bangkok
Starring DEBRA BERGER · CRIS AVRAM · IVAN RASSIMOV · GABRIELE TINTI
Directed by JOE D'AMATO A MONARCH RELEASE In COLOR

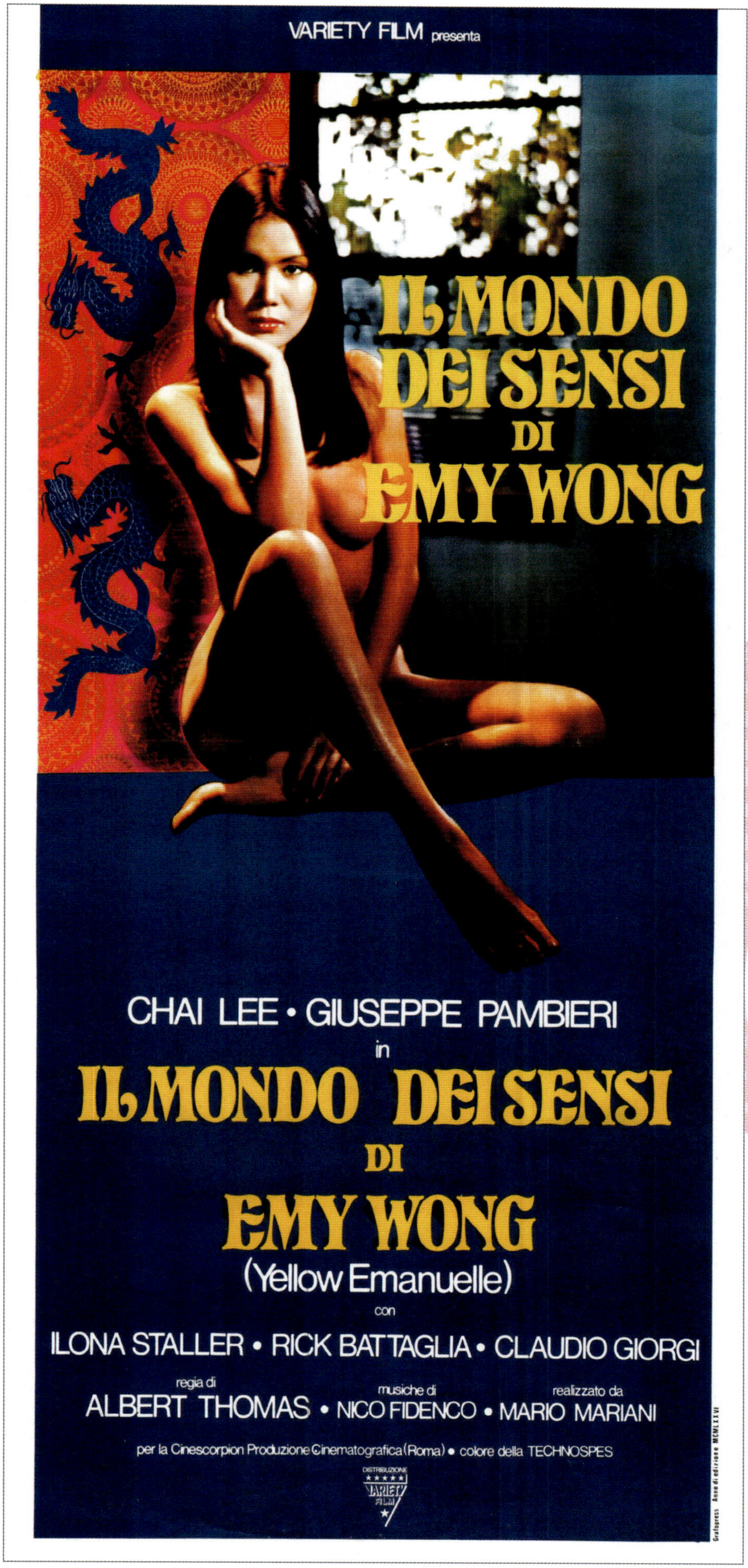

VARIETY FILM presenta

IL MONDO DEI SENSI DI EMY WONG

CHAI LEE • GIUSEPPE PAMBIERI

in

IL MONDO DEI SENSI DI EMY WONG

(Yellow Emanuelle)

con

ILONA STALLER • RICK BATTAGLIA • CLAUDIO GIORGI

regia di ALBERT THOMAS • musiche di NICO FIDENCO • realizzato da MARIO MARIANI

per la Cinescorpion Produzione Cinematografica (Roma) • colore della TECHNOSPES

DISTRIBUZIONE VARIETY FILM

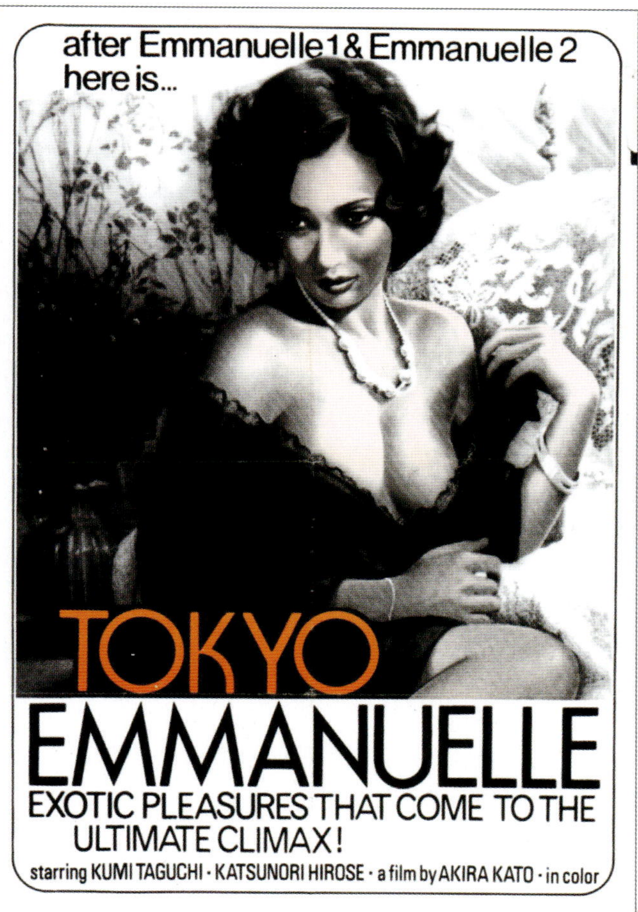

THE FURTHER ADVENTURES OF EMANUELLE

The stylish French softcore feature *Emmanuelle* (1974) was a huge hit around the world, making a star of Sylvia Kristel, and launching a series of official sequels and TV spinoffs which ran well into the twenty-first century. There were also plenty of *un*official sequels and spinoffs, from exploitationers who often craftily dropped an "m" from the name to avoid any copyright infringement unpleasantness. Add in the otherwise unconnected films which had opportunistic re-releases with the word Emanuelle (or Emmanuelle, or indeed Emannuelle) stuck into the title, and there's a shelfload of sexual encounters in various foreign locales to sit through. While the long list of Kristel stand-ins included Chai Lee (better known for *The Benny Hill Show*) and Kumi Taguchi, foremost among their number was the Indonesian-born Laura Gemser, who starred in a whole series of films beginning with *Black Emanuelle* in 1975. "It seemed like one long, long movie that didn't end," Gemser later remembered. "It was always the same story, the same things happened . . . With all the strange situations I get in, I always had to get myself undressed to get something. Any excuse is good to get naked!"

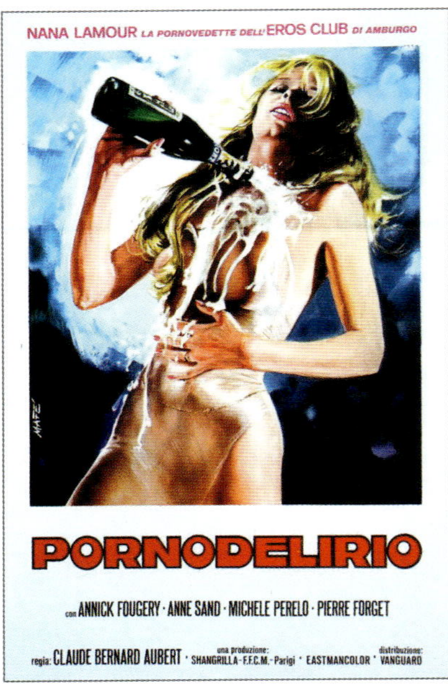

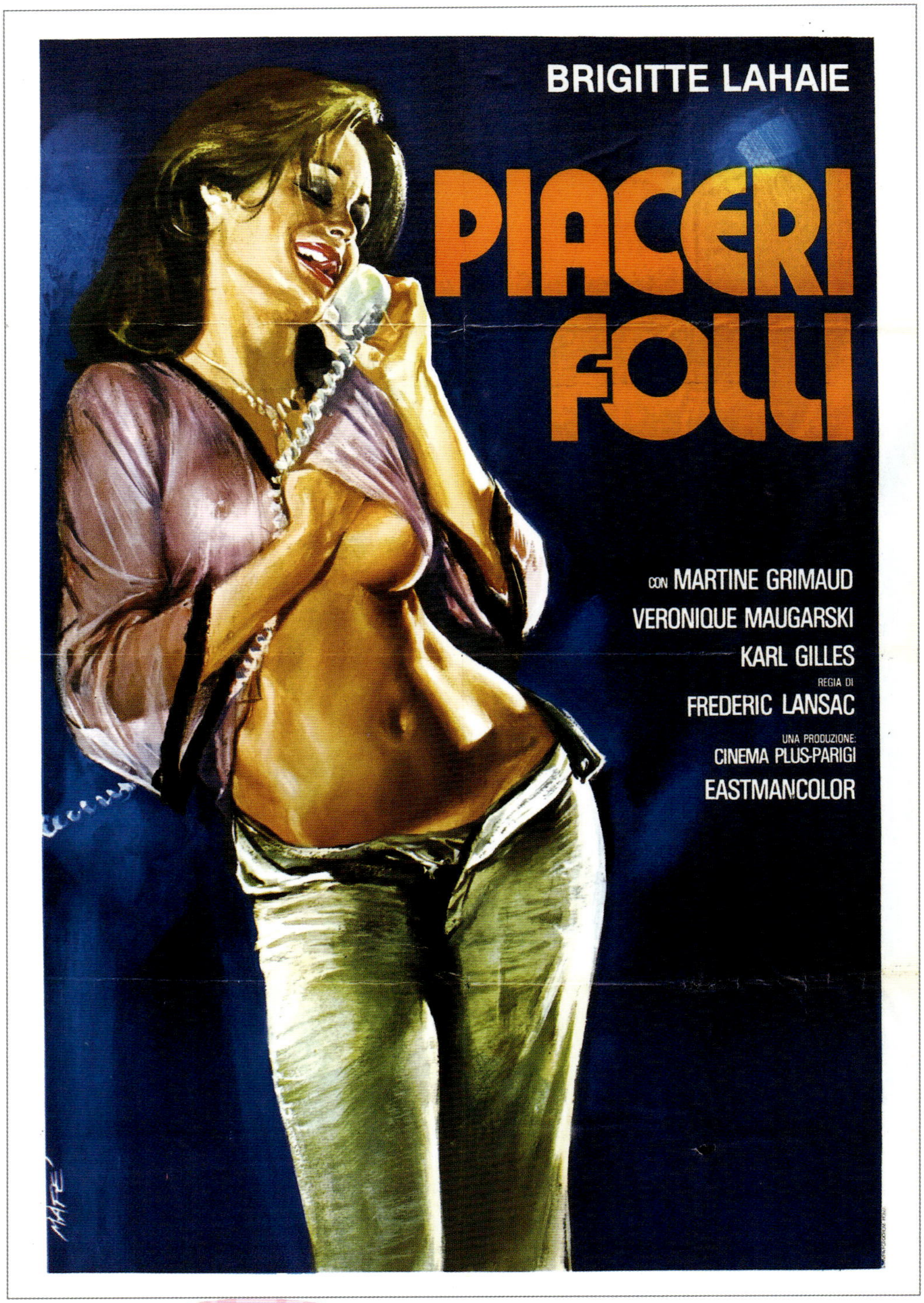

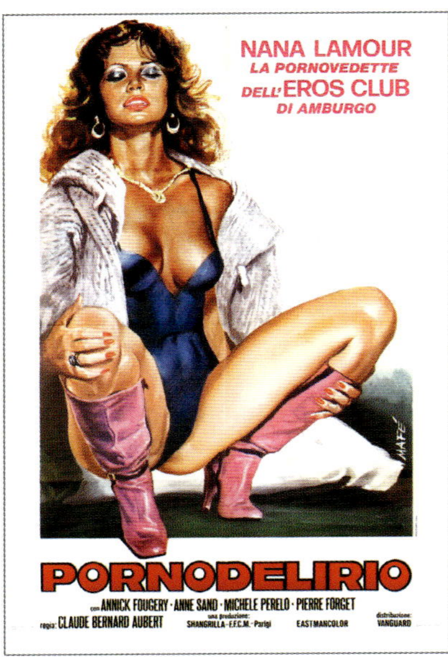

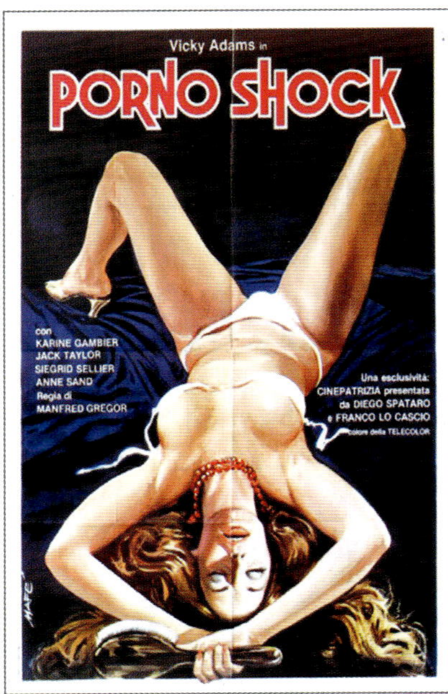

THE ART OF MAFÉ

"How can so little be known about an artist so great?" the popular online magazine *Pulp International* wailed in 2011, though the lack of any readily available biographical details didn't stop its editor anointing the (presumably) Italian artist Mafé as "the greatest illustrator of X-rated posters ever." The website went on to ably sum up the appeal: Mafé's posters are "a far cry from the gynecological tab A into slot B collages of modern porno art . . . In our opinion the poster for *Piaceri Folli* [1977, shown opposite, far right] is one of the most successful we've ever seen. If the mission was to create something both provocative and striking while still being classy, this is a grand slam." This editor can only agree. If he (or she, but let's face it, probably he) is still with us, will the real Mafé please stand up?

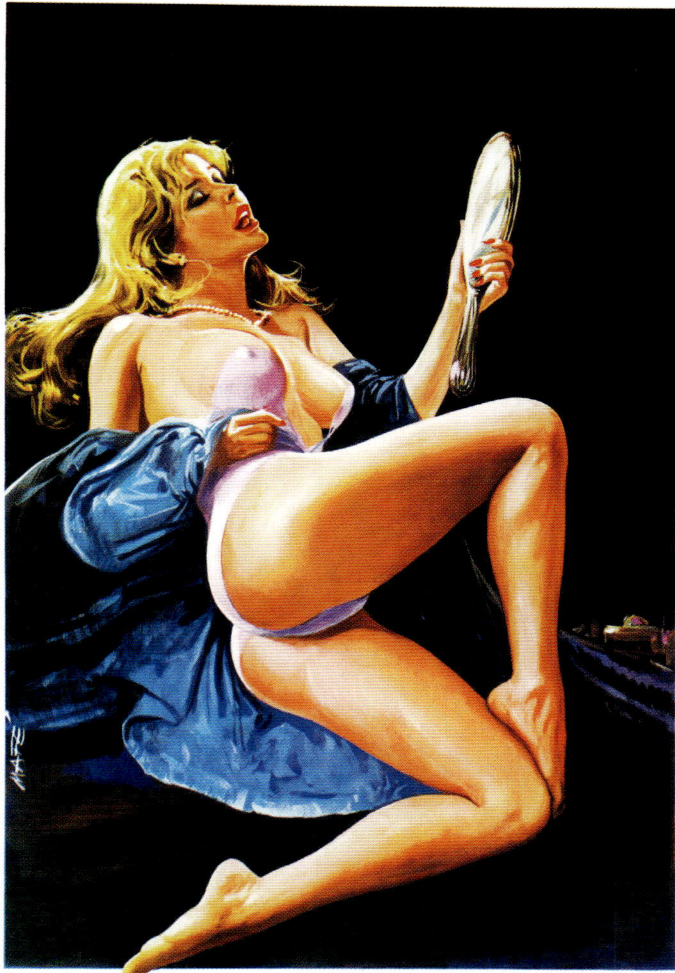

Vicky Adams in

PORNO SHOCK

con
KARINE GAMBIER - JACK TAYLOR
SIEGRID SELLIER - ANNE SAND

Regia di
MANFRED GREGOR

Una esclusività: CINEPATRIZIA presentata
da DIEGO SPATARO e FRANCO LO CASCIO
colore della TELECOLOR

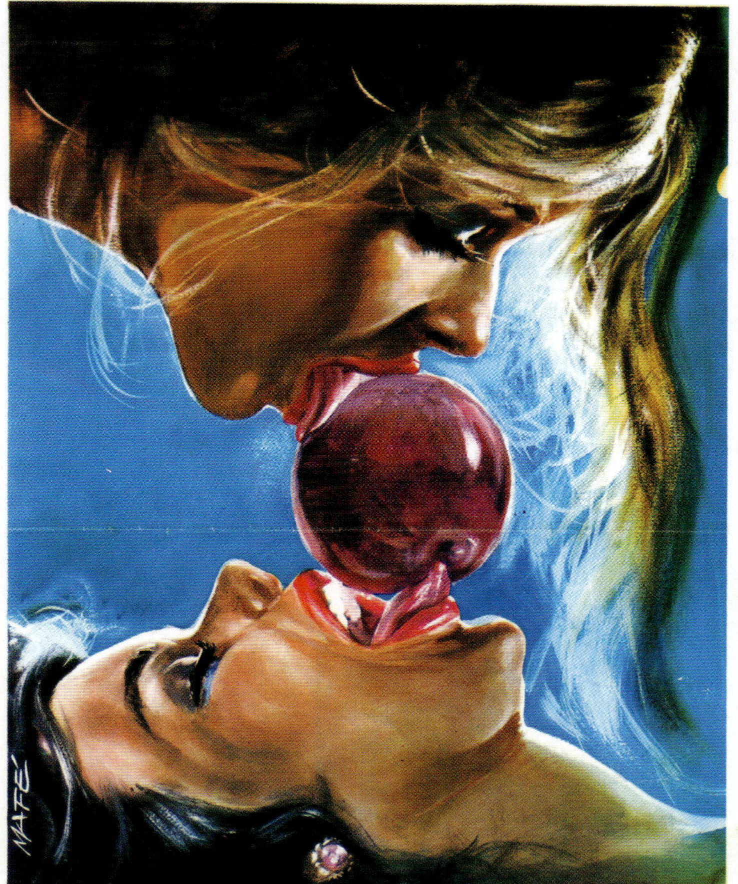

BRIGITTE LAHAIE

PIACERI FOLLI

CON MARTINE GRIMAUD - VERONIQUE MAUGARSKI - KARL GILLES - REGIA DI FREDERIC LANSAC
UNA PRODUZIONE: CINEMA PLUS-PARIGI - EASTMANCOLOR

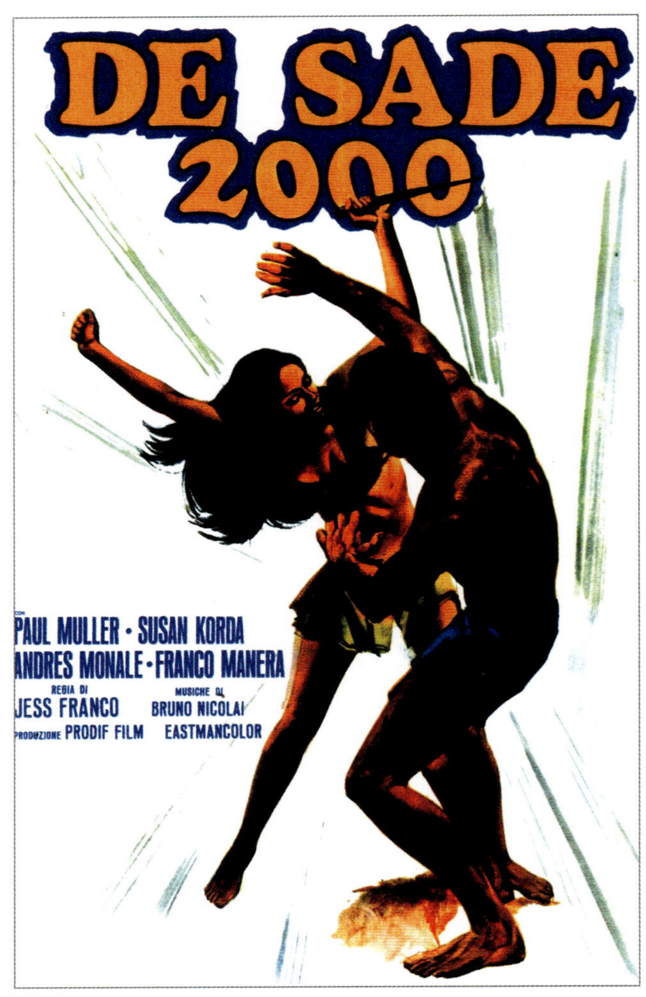

DE SADE

Rather like Giacomo Casanova, it's often forgotten these days that Donatien Alphonse François, Marquis de Sade, was a real, historical personage. His writings, full of violent—or rather, sadistic—sexual fantasies, are no longer widely read, but given that he died in 1814, they are all out of copyright. His work is therefore free to adapt, and his name can be slapped onto sexploitation film posters with abandon. The US movie *Invitation to Ruin* (1968, represented here by its Japanese poster) was a sleazy contemporary tale of girls being kidnapped and tortured in a basement, but according to its promotional puffery was nothing less than, "Eroticism in the tradition of De Sade." Jess Franco directed *Marquis de Sade: Justine* (1968) and *De Sade 2000* (aka *Eugenie de Sade*, 1969), the first of which could at least claim to be (loosely) based on de Sade's writing, and featured Klaus Kinski in the role he was born to play: the Marquis himself. Were de Sade around today though, he would surely gravitate toward Alex de Renzy's eye-wateringly graphic *Femmes de Sade* (1976), a film full of acts which are frankly too indecent to describe here.

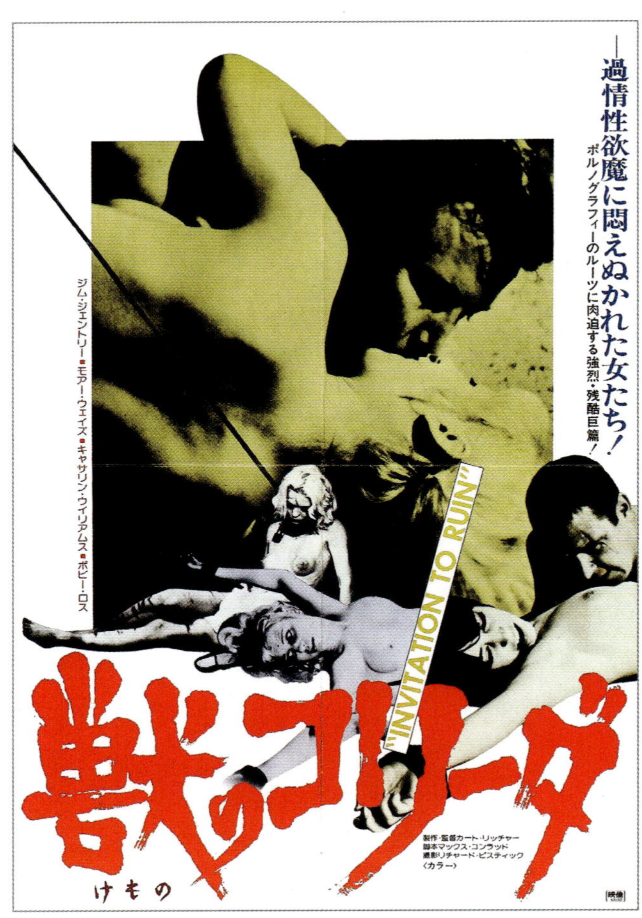

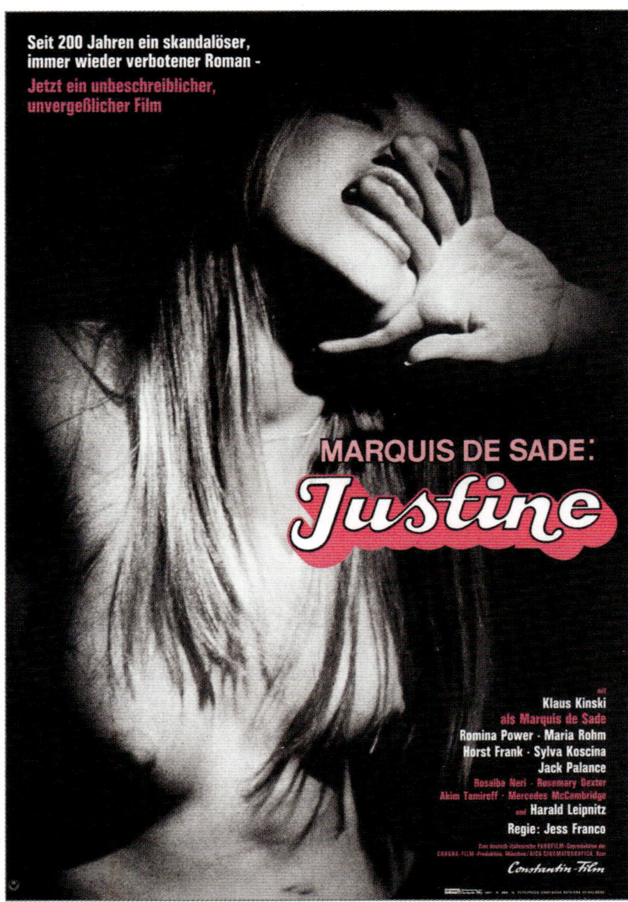

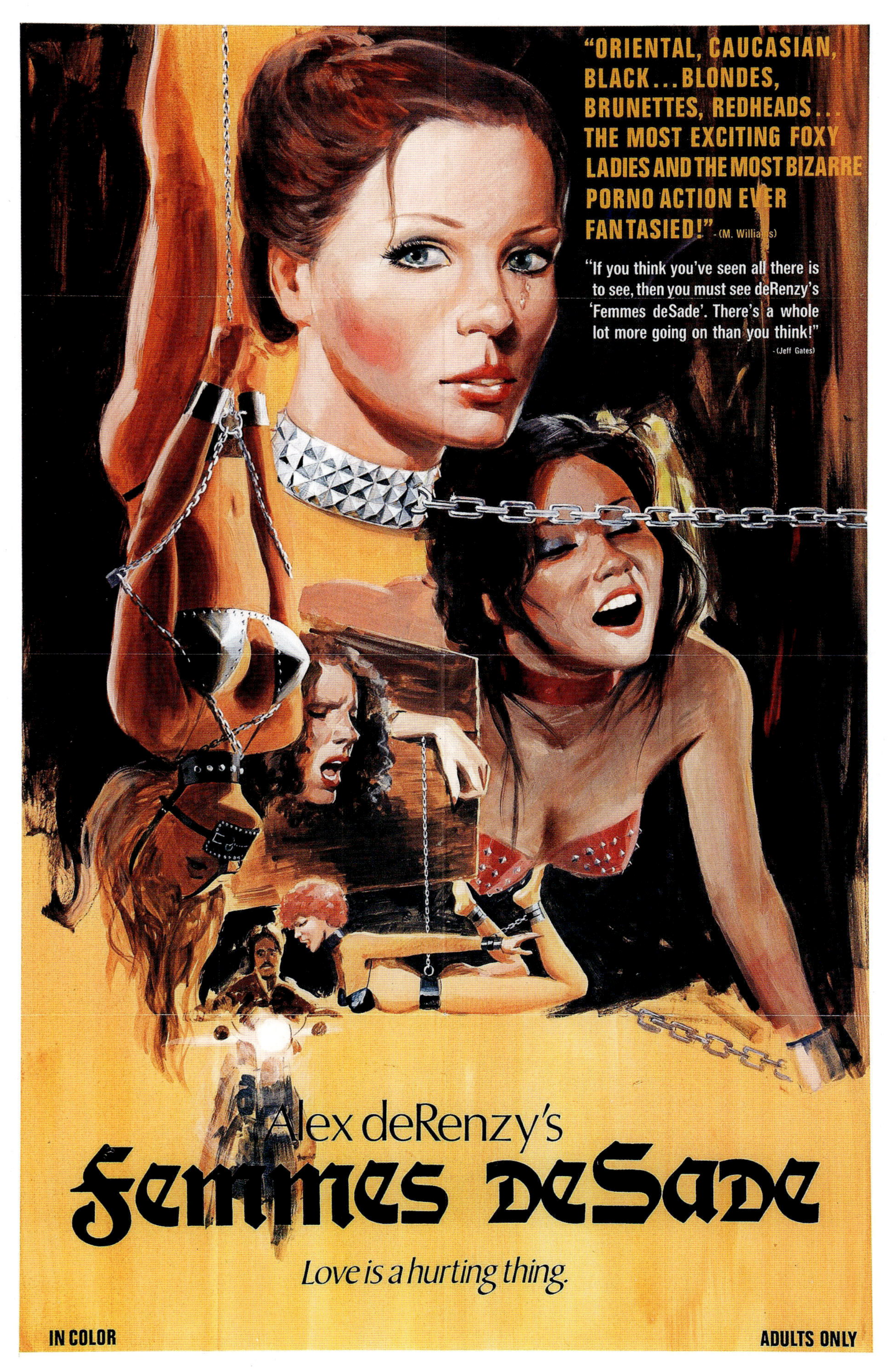
"ORIENTAL, CAUCASIAN, BLACK... BLONDES, BRUNETTES, REDHEADS... THE MOST EXCITING FOXY LADIES AND THE MOST BIZARRE PORNO ACTION EVER FANTASIED!" - (M. Williams)
"If you think you've seen all there is to see, then you must see deRenzy's 'Femmes deSade'. There's a whole lot more going on than you think!" - (Jeff Gates)
Alex deRenzy's
Femmes deSade
Love is a hurting thing.
IN COLOR
ADULTS ONLY

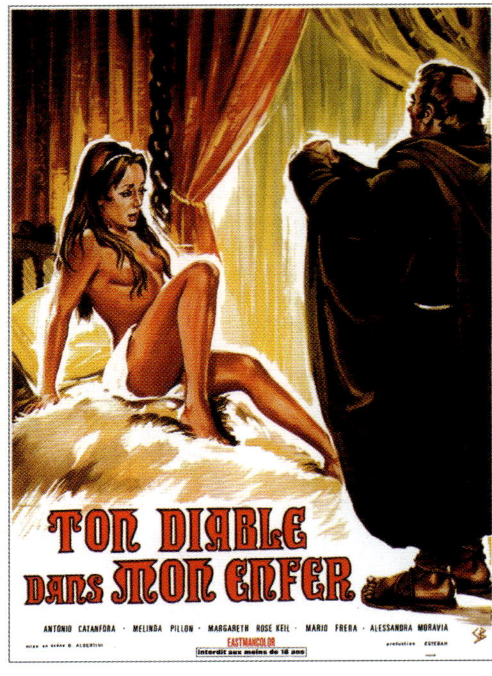

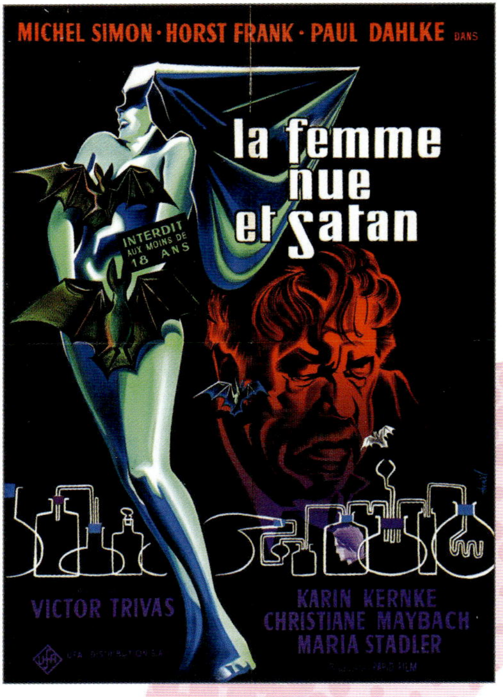

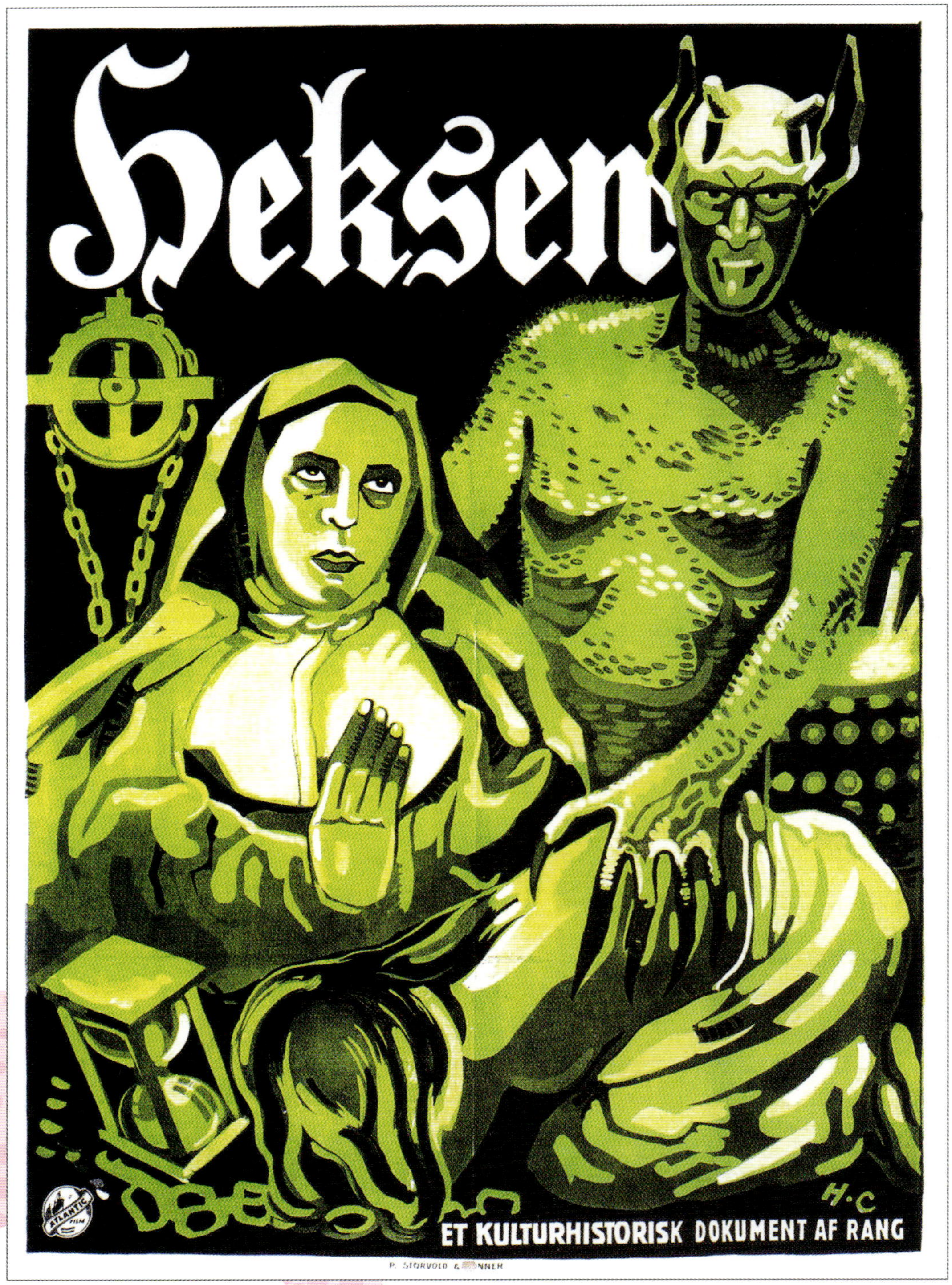

NUNSPLOITATION

Häxan (1922) is a straight-faced drama/documentary about medieval witch-hunts, and reportedly was the most expensive silent movie ever made in Sweden. However lofty the film's intent, its Danish poster (seen above) featuring Satan sticking his tongue out, apparently taking a nun from behind, appeals to baser instincts—a heady mix of sex, violence, and convents which later became known as nunsploitation. The subgenre reached the height of its popularity in the '70s, especially after Ken Russell's *The Devils* (1971) brought misbehaving nuns (albeit historically accurate ones) defiantly to the screen. Jess Franco's *The Demons* (1972) and Gianfranco Mingozzi's *Flavia* (1974), represented here by their German posters (opposite page, below left and right), also claimed to be inspired by historical events, and still pack a punch, especially in their uncensored versions. The same can sadly not be said of Russell's masterpiece: his original director's cut is still awaiting a proper release!

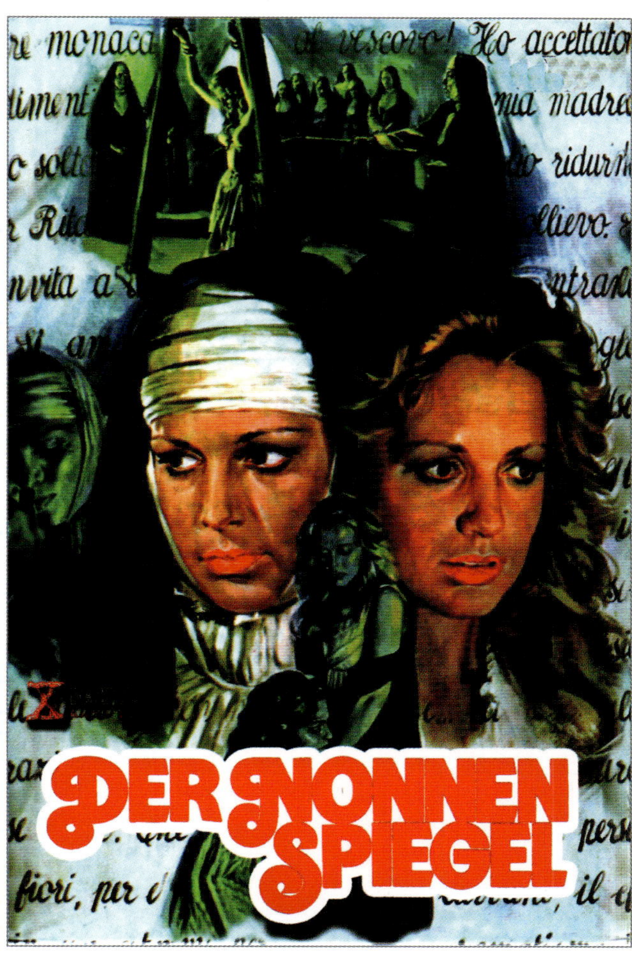
DER NONNEN SPIEGEL

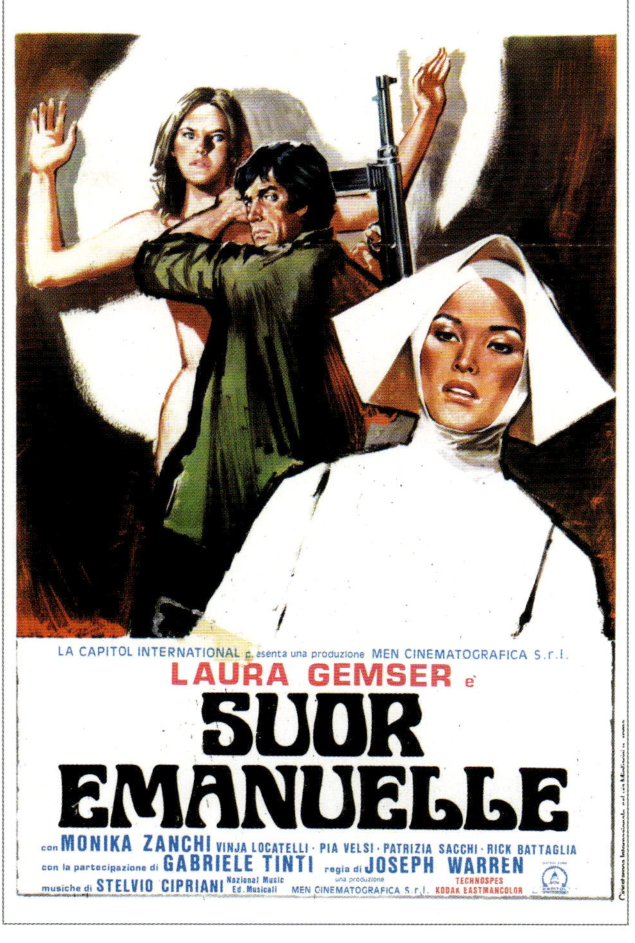
LA CAPITOL INTERNATIONAL presenta una produzione MEN CINEMATOGRAFICA S.r.l.
LAURA GEMSER è
SUOR EMANUELLE
con MONIKA ZANCHI VINJA LOCATELLI · PIA VELSI · PATRIZIA SACCHI · RICK BATTAGLIA
con la partecipazione di GABRIELE TINTI regia di JOSEPH WARREN
musiche di STELVIO CIPRIANI Nazional Music Ed. Musicali
una produzione MEN CINEMATOGRAFICA S.r.l.
TECHNOSPES KODAK EASTMANCOLOR

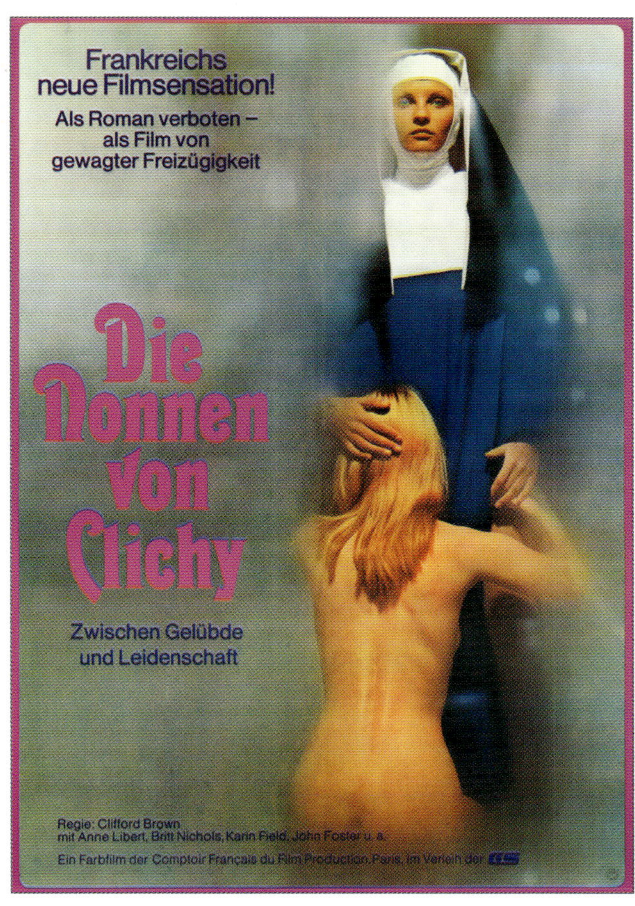
Frankreichs neue Filmsensation!
Als Roman verboten – als Film von gewagter Freizügigkeit
Die Nonnen von Clichy
Zwischen Gelübde und Leidenschaft
Regie: Clifford Brown
mit Anne Libert, Britt Nichols, Karin Field, John Foster u. a.
Ein Farbfilm der Comptoir Français du Film Production, Paris, im Verleih der

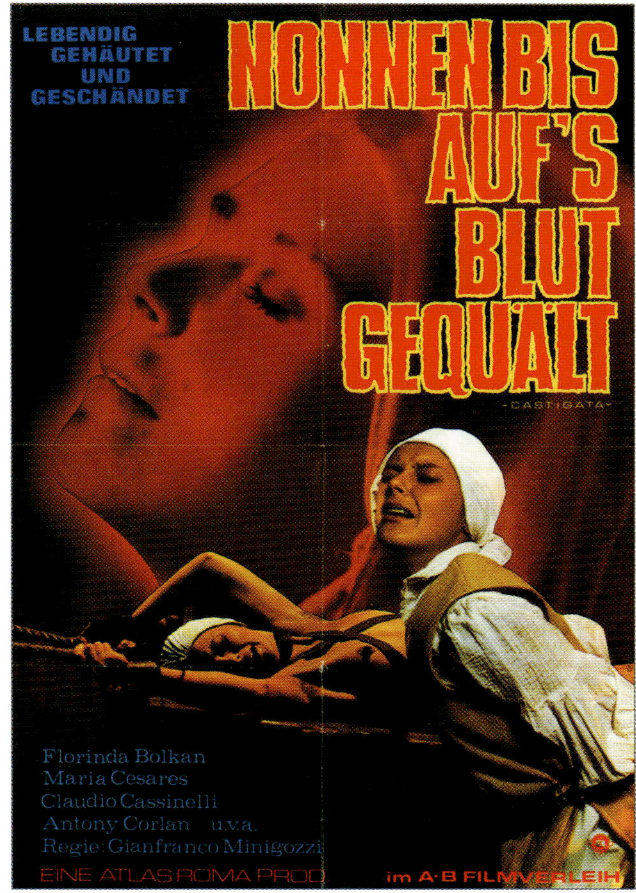
LEBENDIG GEHÄUTET UND GESCHÄNDET
NONNEN BIS AUF'S BLUT GEQUÄLT
-CASTIGATA-
Florinda Bolkan
Maria Cesares
Claudio Cassinelli
Antony Corlan u.v.a.
Regie: Gianfranco Minigozzi
EINE ATLAS ROMA PROD.
im A·B FILMVERLEIH

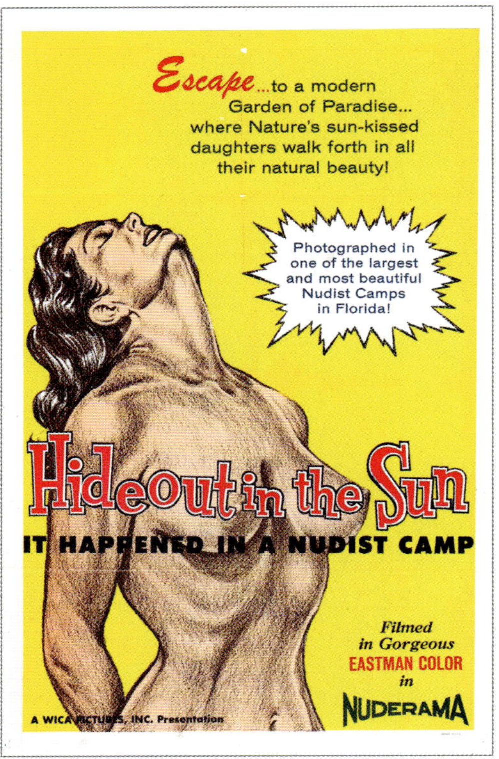
Escape...to a modern Garden of Paradise... where Nature's sun-kissed daughters walk forth in all their natural beauty!
Photographed in one of the largest and most beautiful Nudist Camps in Florida!
Hideout in the Sun
IT HAPPENED IN A NUDIST CAMP
Filmed in Gorgeous EASTMAN COLOR in
NUDERAMA
A WICA PICTURES, INC. Presentation

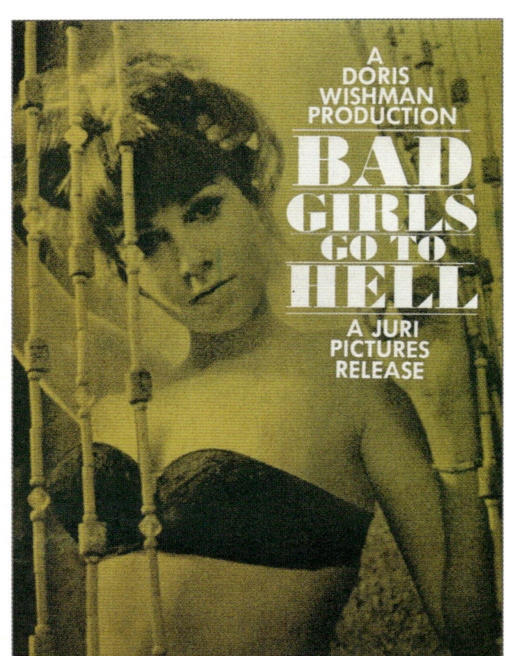
A DORIS WISHMAN PRODUCTION
BAD GIRLS GO TO HELL
A JURI PICTURES RELEASE

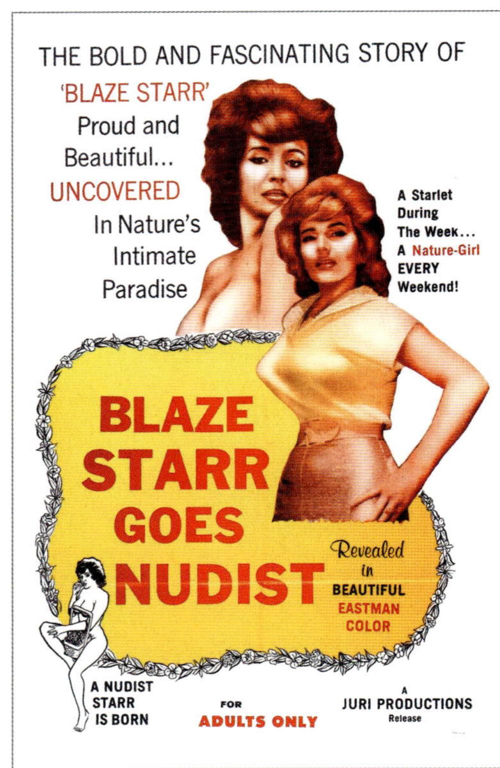
THE BOLD AND FASCINATING STORY OF
'BLAZE STARR' Proud and Beautiful...
UNCOVERED In Nature's Intimate Paradise
A Starlet During The Week... A Nature-Girl EVERY Weekend!
BLAZE STARR GOES NUDIST
Revealed in BEAUTIFUL EASTMAN COLOR
A NUDIST STARR IS BORN
FOR ADULTS ONLY
A JURI PRODUCTIONS Release

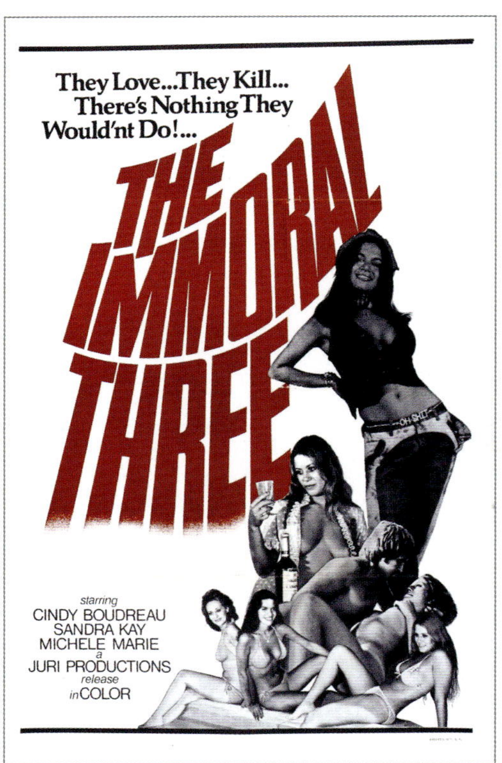
They Love...They Kill... There's Nothing They Would'nt Do!...
THE IMMORAL THREE
starring
CINDY BOUDREAU
SANDRA KAY
MICHELE MARIE
a
JURI PRODUCTIONS
release
in COLOR

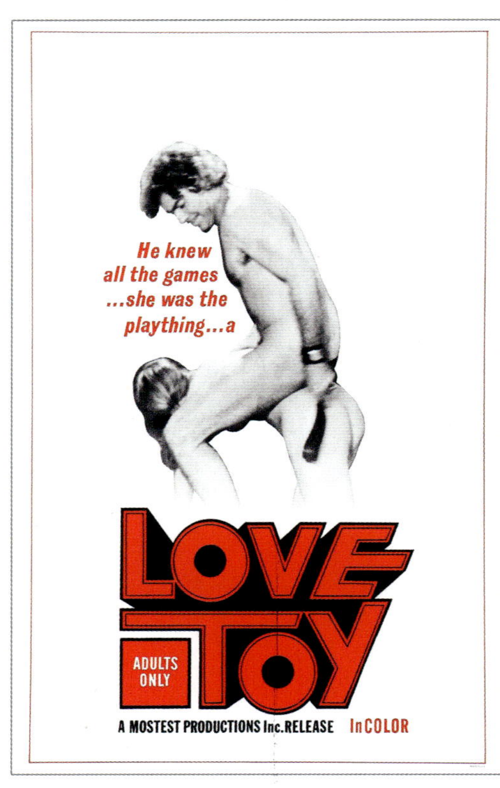
He knew all the games ...she was the plaything...a
LOVE TOY
ADULTS ONLY
A MOSTEST PRODUCTIONS Inc. RELEASE
In COLOR

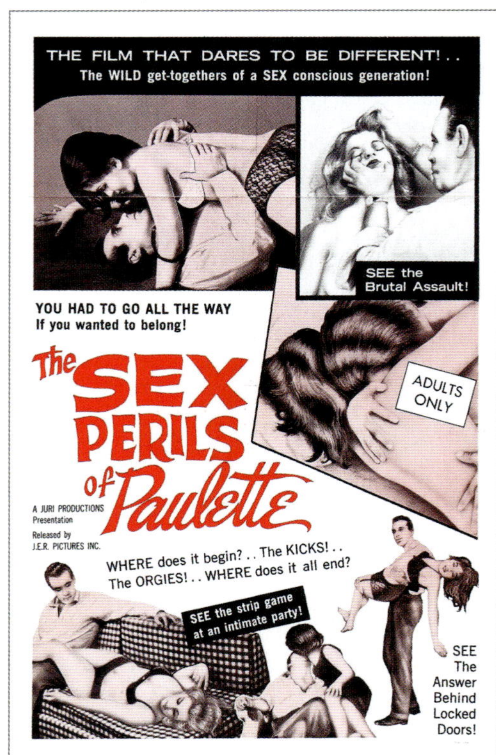
THE FILM THAT DARES TO BE DIFFERENT!..
The WILD get-togethers of a SEX conscious generation!
SEE the Brutal Assault!
YOU HAD TO GO ALL THE WAY
If you wanted to belong!
The SEX PERILS of Paulette
ADULTS ONLY
A JURI PRODUCTIONS Presentation
Released by J.E.R. PICTURES INC.
WHERE does it begin?.. The KICKS!.. The ORGIES!.. WHERE does it all end?
SEE the strip game at an intimate party!
SEE The Answer Behind Locked Doors!

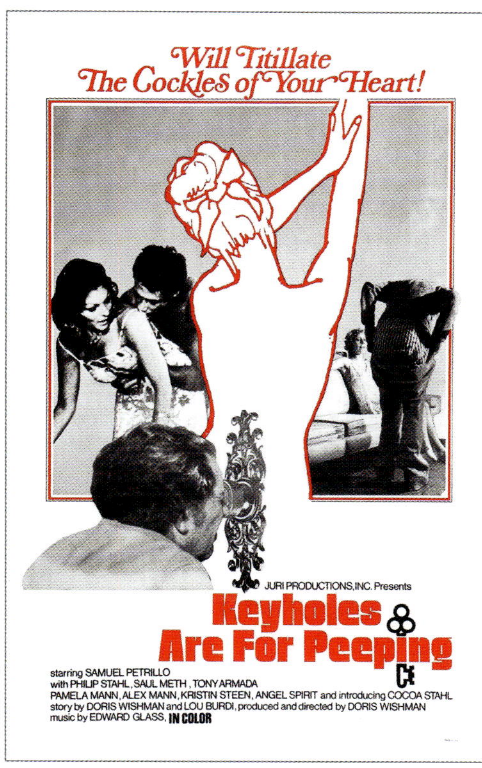

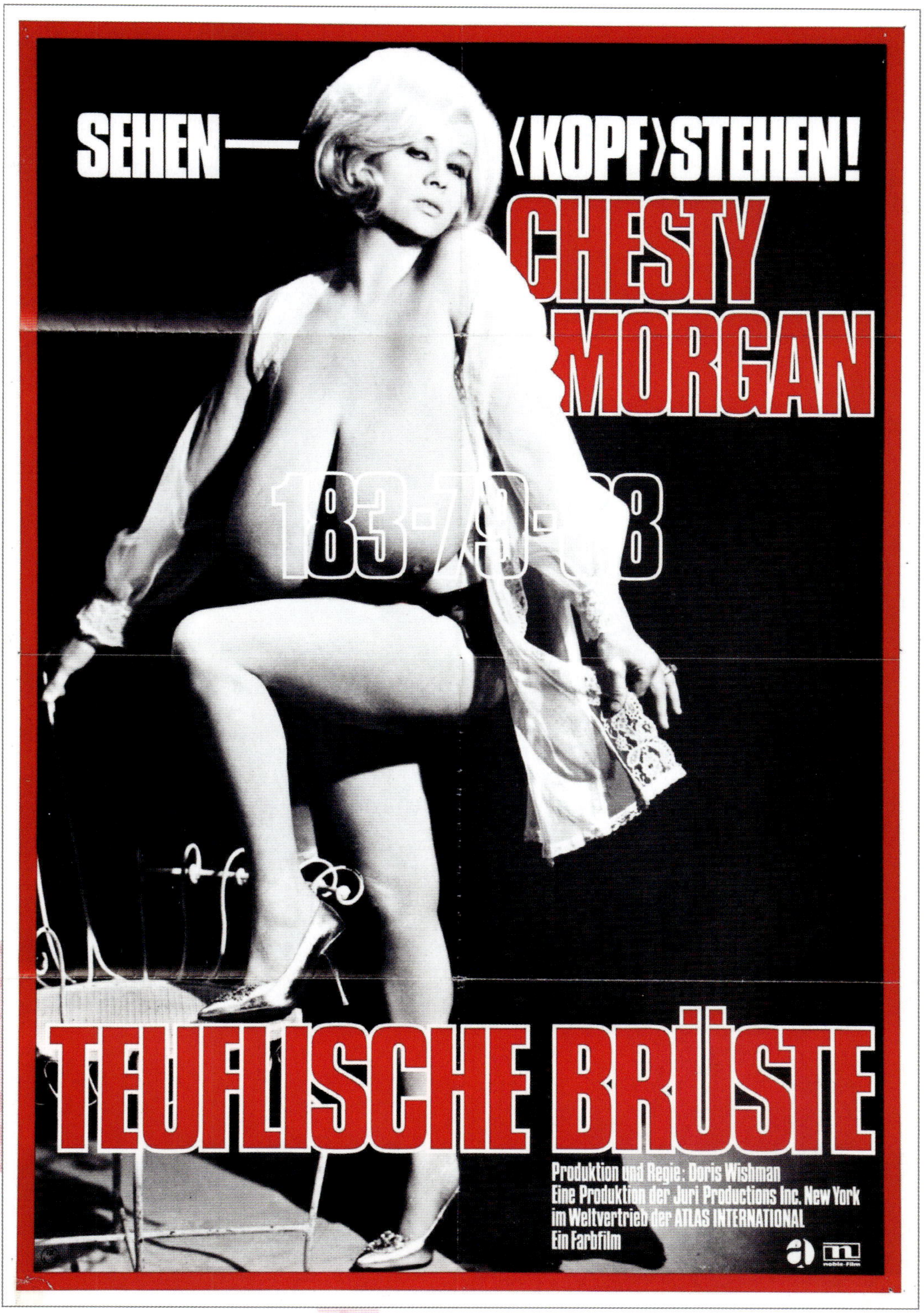

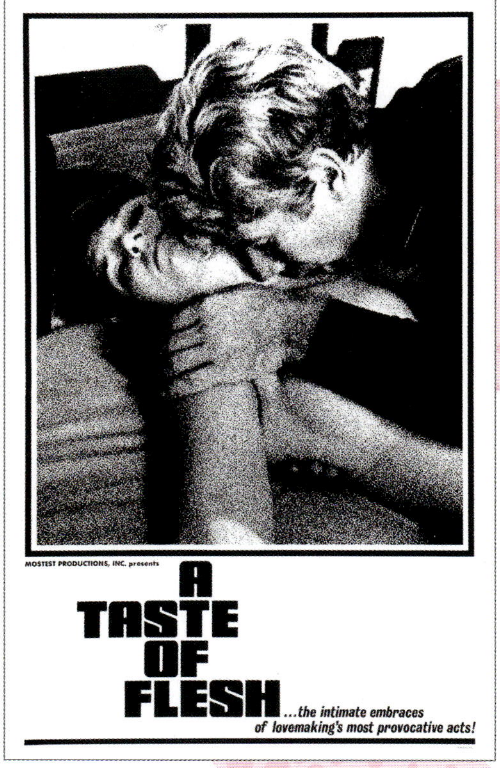

THE QUEEN OF EXPLOITATION

Movie critic Joe Bob Briggs once described Doris Wishman as "the greatest female exploitation film director in history," and it's hard to argue with that, especially when you consider this 4'11" force of nature usually wrote, cast, produced, and edited her films as well. Borrowing $10,000 from her sister to shoot her debut *Hideout in the Sun* (1960), Wishman went on to make 30 films in total, including more nudies, "roughies" such as *Bad Girls Go to Hell* (1965), and two 1974 vehicles for Chesty Morgan and her all-natural 73-inch bust, *Deadly Weapons* and *Double Agent 73*. "I made all my films with love and care and Wishman blood and no money," she said. "You need a gimmick and then you shoot. It was fun." Doris Wishman died in 2002, aged somewhere between 80 and 90 (no one was quite sure), having just completed a production entitled *Dildo Heaven*. "After I die I will be making movies in hell!" she used to claim, and you'd be foolish to doubt her.

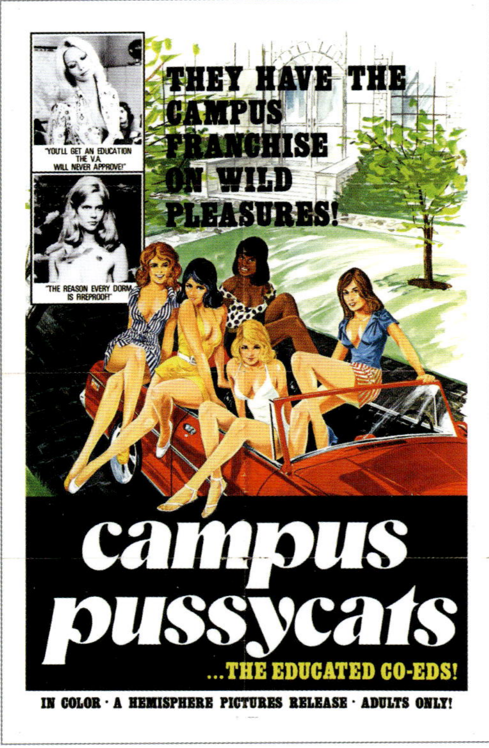
THEY HAVE THE CAMPUS FRANCHISE ON WILD PLEASURES!
"YOU'LL GET AN EDUCATION THE V.A. WILL NEVER APPROVE!"
"THE REASON EVERY DORM IS FIREPROOF!"
campus pussycats
...THE EDUCATED CO-EDS!
IN COLOR · A HEMISPHERE PICTURES RELEASE · ADULTS ONLY!

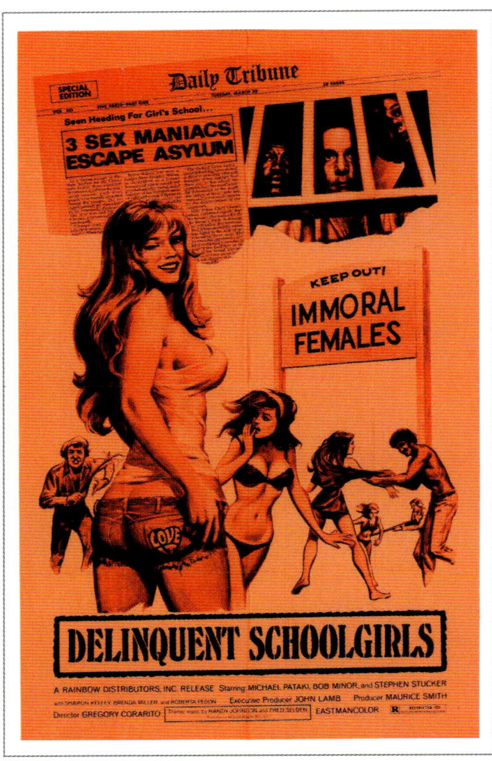
Daily Tribune
SPECIAL EDITION
Seen Heading For Girl's School...
3 SEX MANIACS ESCAPE ASYLUM
KEEP OUT!
IMMORAL FEMALES
LOVE
DELINQUENT SCHOOLGIRLS
A RAINBOW DISTRIBUTORS, INC. RELEASE Starring MICHAEL PATAKI, BOB MINOR, and STEPHEN STUCKER
Executive Producer JOHN LAMB Producer MAURICE SMITH
Director GREGORY CORARITO
EASTMANCOLOR

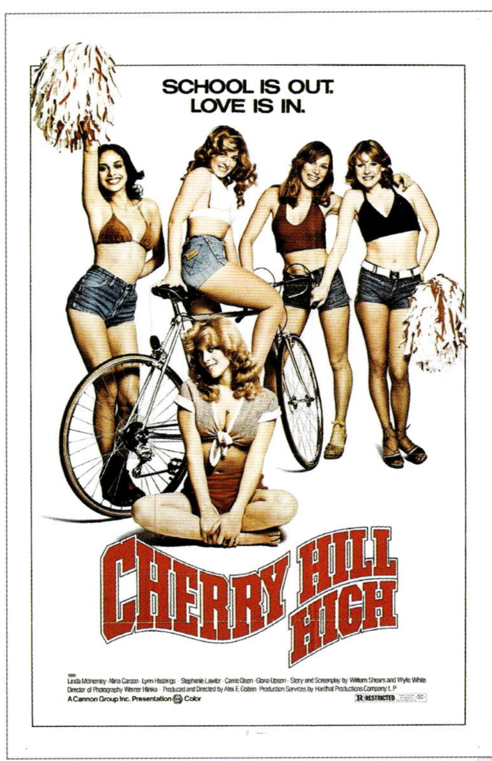
SCHOOL IS OUT. LOVE IS IN.
CHERRY HILL HIGH
A Cannon Group Inc. Presentation Color

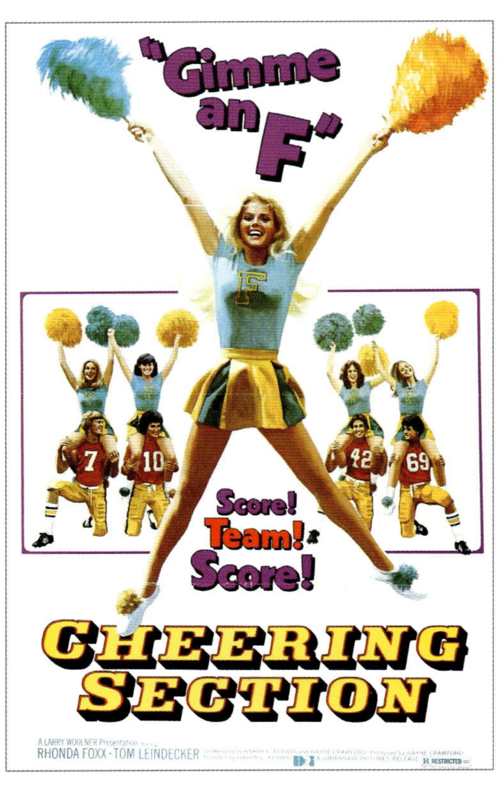
"Gimme an F"
F
7
10
42
69
Score! Team! Score!
CHEERING SECTION
RHONDA FOXX · TOM LEINDECKER

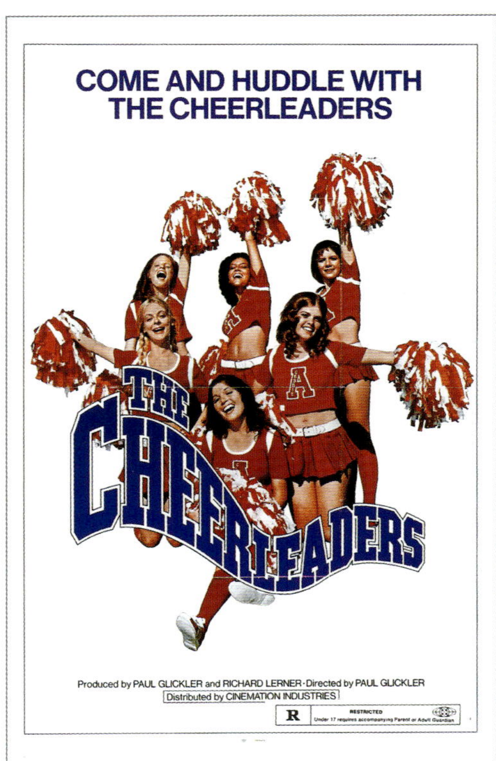
COME AND HUDDLE WITH THE CHEERLEADERS
THE CHEERLEADERS
Produced by PAUL GLICKLER and RICHARD LERNER · Directed by PAUL GLICKLER
Distributed by CINEMATION INDUSTRIES
R RESTRICTED
Under 17 requires accompanying Parent or Adult Guardian

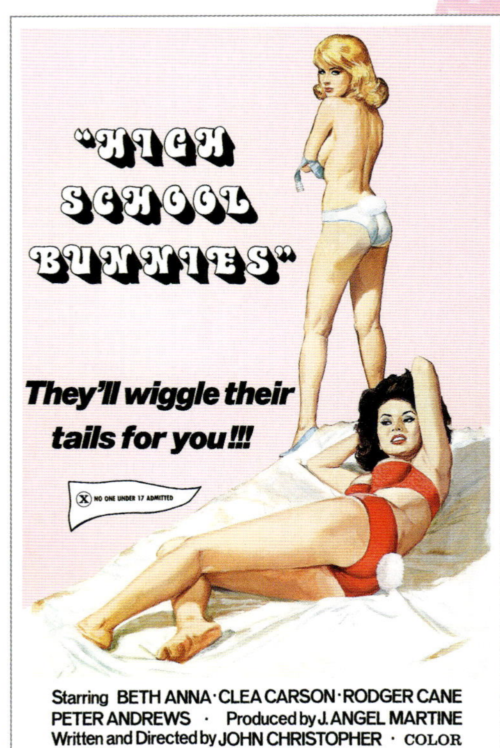
"HIGH SCHOOL BUNNIES"
They'll wiggle their tails for you!!!
X NO ONE UNDER 17 ADMITTED
Starring BETH ANNA · CLEA CARSON · RODGER CANE
PETER ANDREWS · Produced by J. ANGEL MARTINE
Written and Directed by JOHN CHRISTOPHER · COLOR

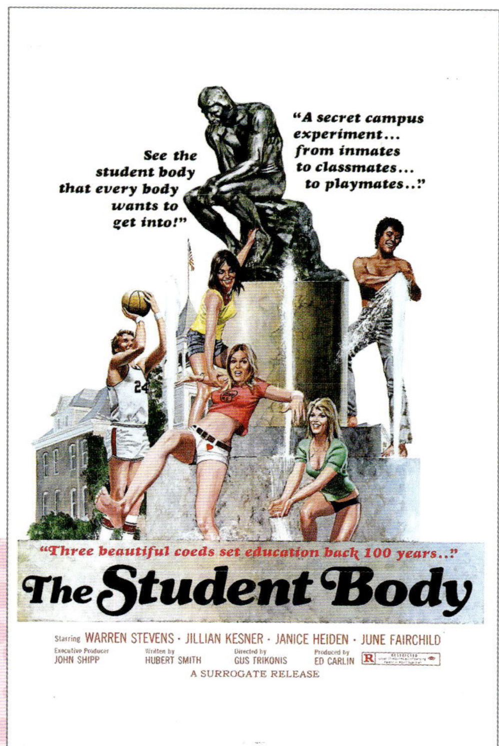

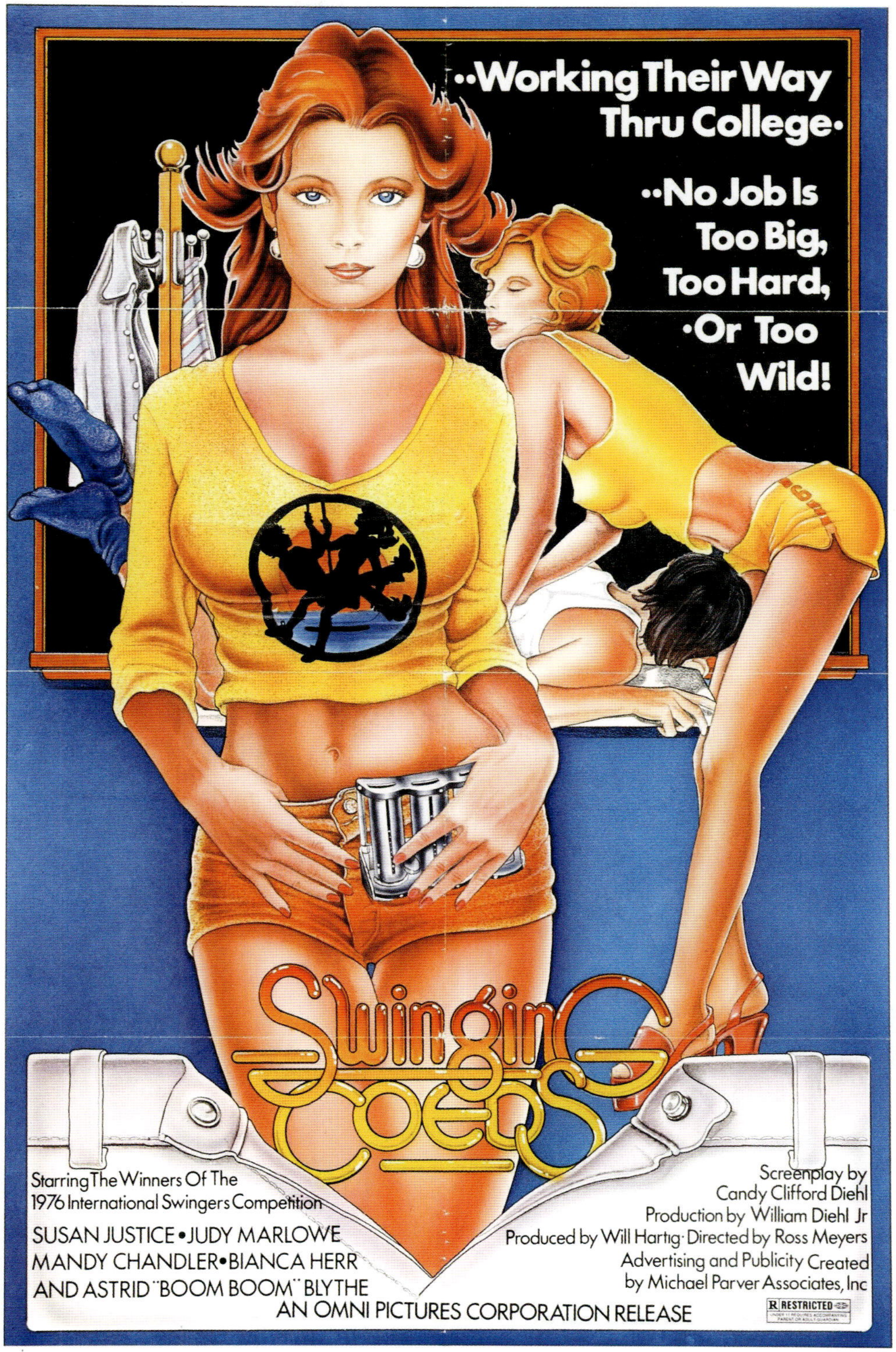

BACK TO SCHOOL

From the innocent antics of the UK's *St. Trinian's* movies to the Japanese vending machines purporting to sell their used panties (yes, really), the image of the sexy high school/college student, of age and desperate to learn the ways of love, is a fetish worldwide. In the US, countless hard and softcore releases have played up the stereotype, from the cheerleaders of *Cheering Section* (1977)—"Gimme an 'F'"—to the stars of *The Student Body* (1976), classily advertised with the tagline, "See the student body that every body wants to get into!" Viewers of *Swinging Coeds* expecting American college girls would be disappointed: this 1976 US release was actually a dubbed version of the 1972 pseudo-documentary *Mädchen, die nach München kommen*. In a particularly flagrant exploitation move, distributors Omni Pictures employed completely made-up cast and crew names to hide the movie's German origins. Alas, those trying to find further credits for Astrid "Boom Boom" Blythe (winner of the equally non-existent International Swingers Competition) will come up empty.

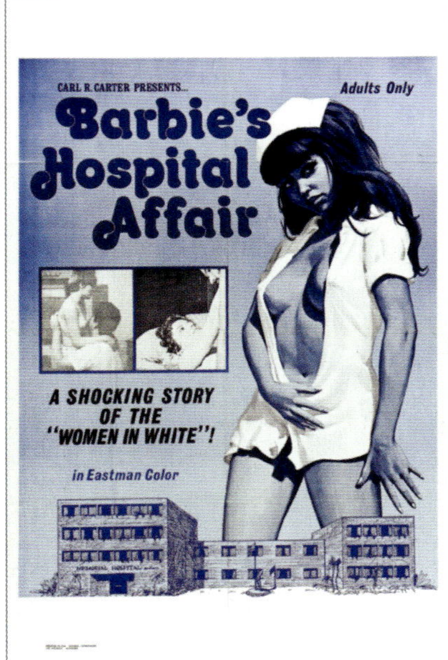

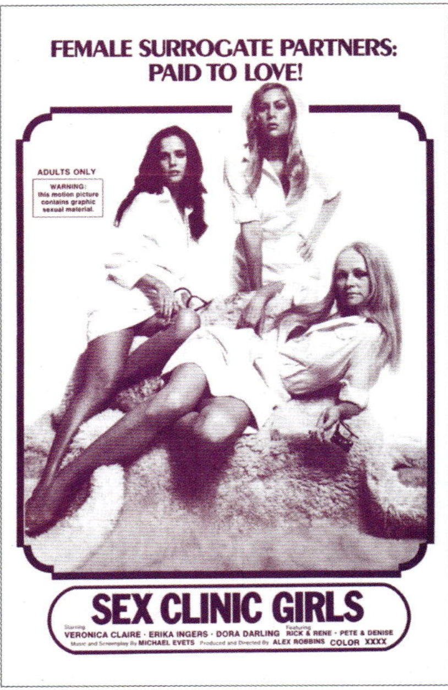

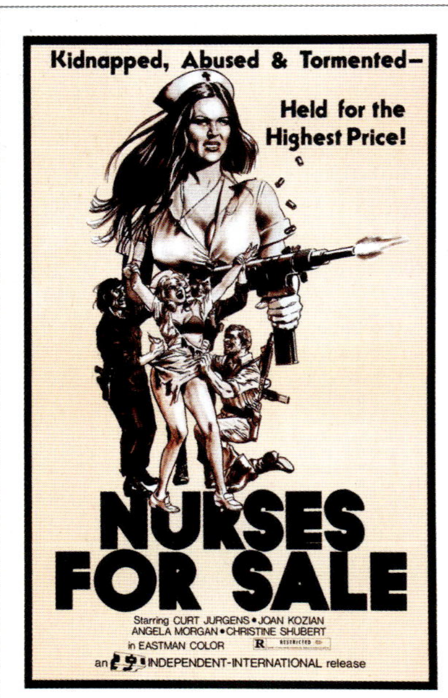

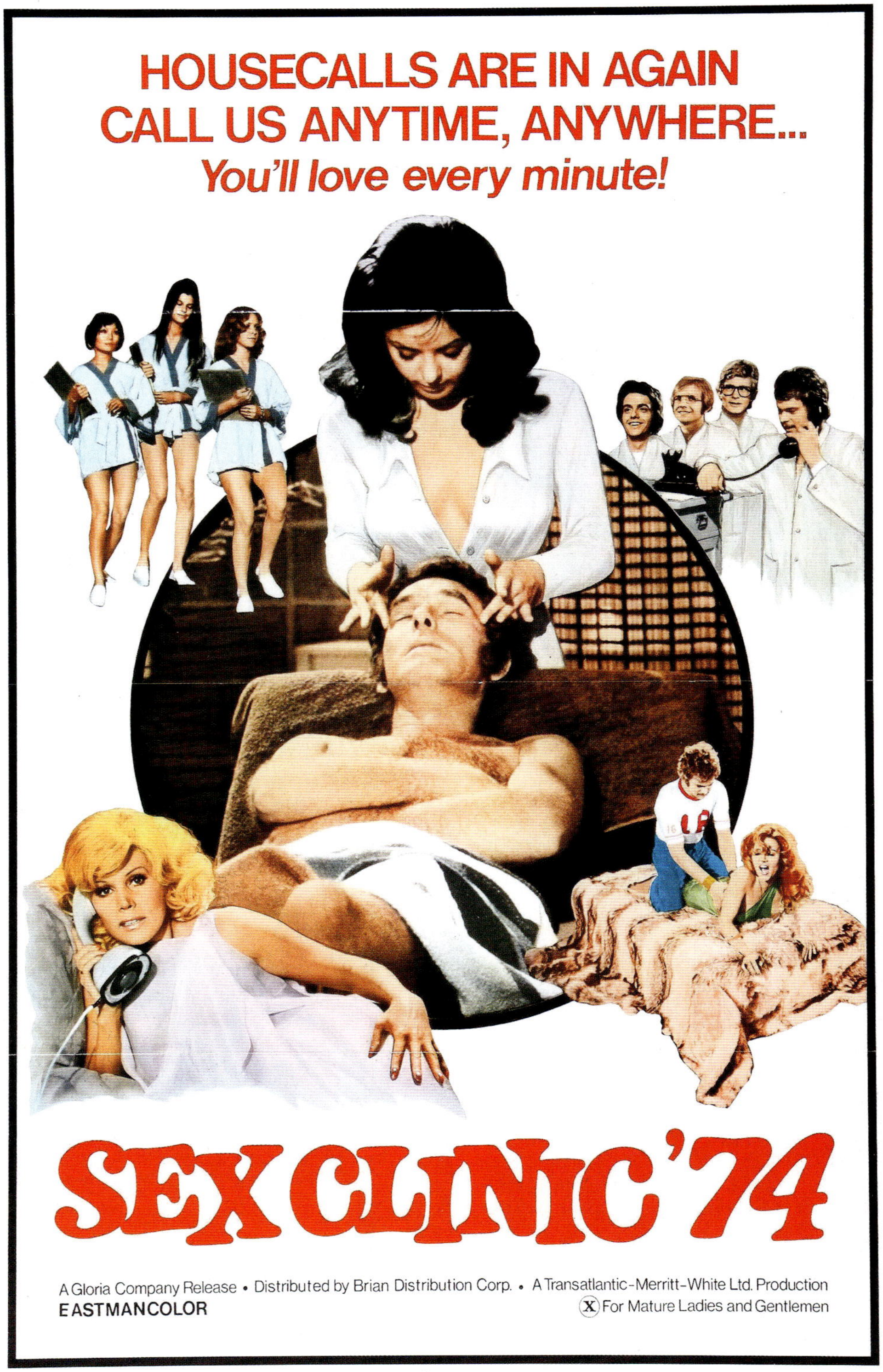

NAUGHTY NURSES

Whether it's high culture (Hemingway's *A Farewell to Arms*) or not-so-high culture (*The Benny Hill Show*), the sexy nurse has long been a fantasy mainstay. Sure enough, there are plenty of sexploitation movies featuring women in tight white uniforms, and usually out of them as well. The American poster for *L'Infermiera* (aka *The Sensuous Nurse*, 1975) promises that, "Ursula bares all." Red-blooded fans of the *Dr. No* star will be pleased to know that she actually does, at some length, in this Italian sex comedy, which also throws in nudity from another ex-Bond girl, Luciana Paluzzi (Fiona in *Thunderball*) for good measure. As one online reviewer was moved to opine: "Ursula Andress's naked body is one of those things that make you believe in God."

Ursula Andress

will melt your thermometer

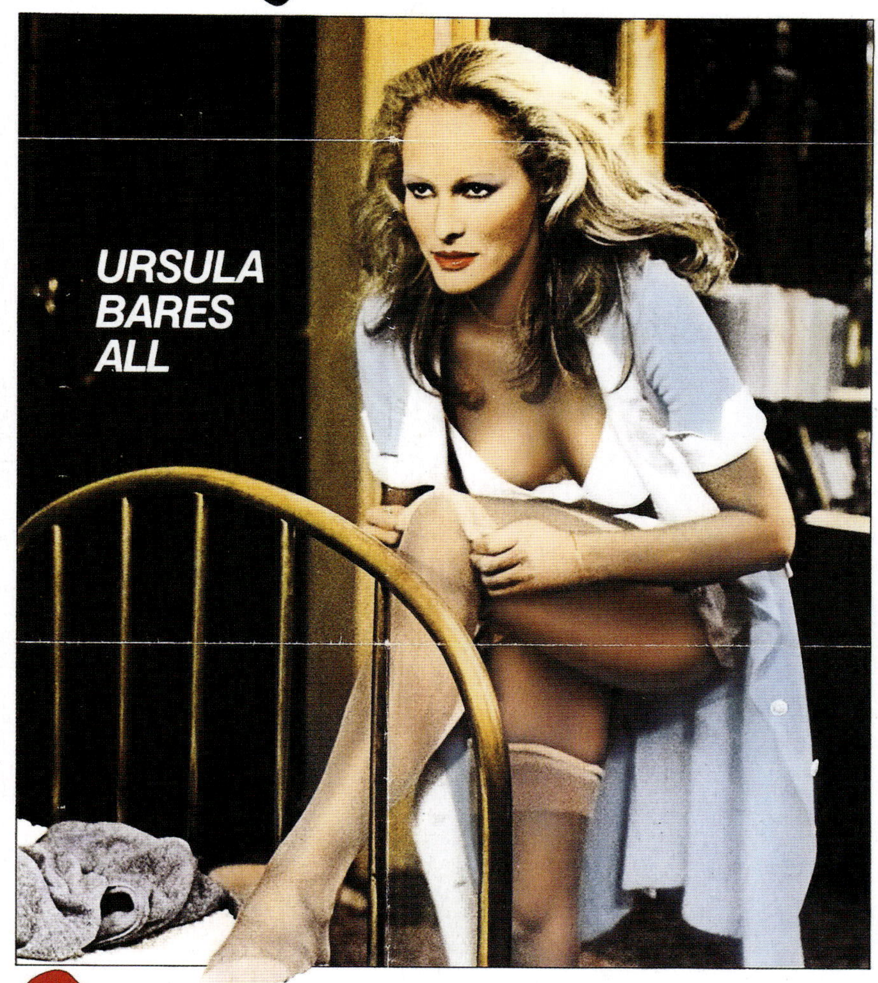

The Sensuous

NURSE

WARNING!

Due to the visual content of this film, the taking of photographs is strictly forbidden.

ALSO STARRING JACK PALANCE

A MID-BROADWAY PRODUCTIONS, INC. RELEASE

R RESTRICTED

Under 17 requires accompanying Parent or Adult Guardian

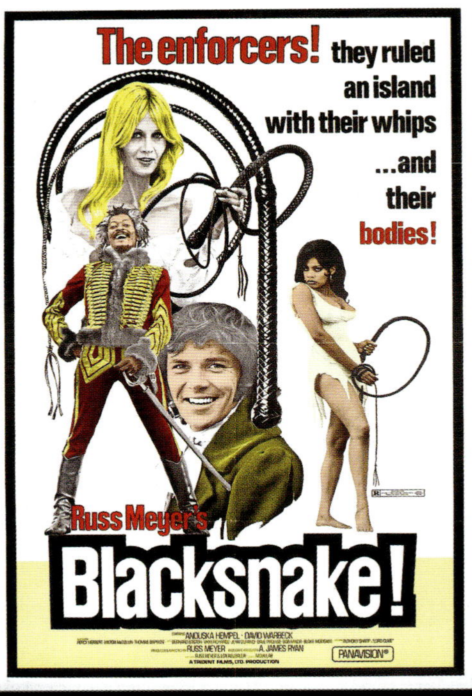

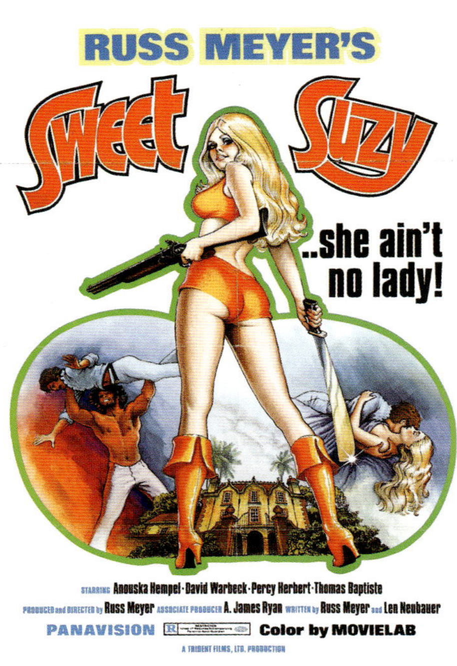

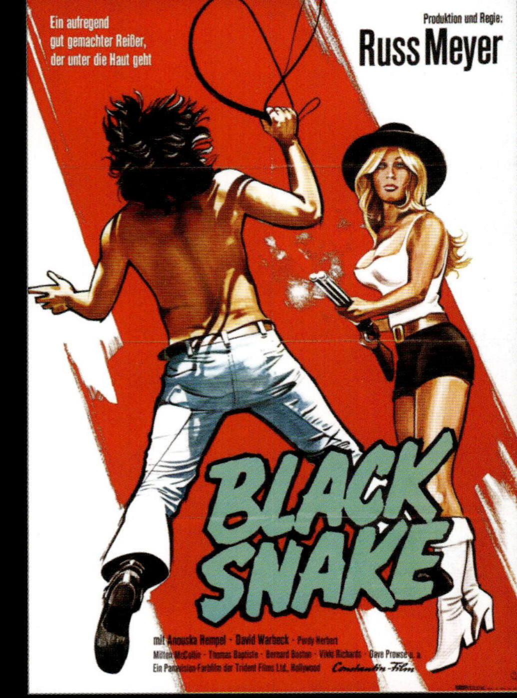

BLACKSNAKE!

"Boisterous action from opening scene to mind-bending climax!" promises Voiceover Man in the trailer for 1973's *Black Snake*. While there's plenty going on in this heady mix of period plantation drama, blaxploitation, and sex (with a zombie subplot), it's an atypical Russ Meyer outing, and one he was never happy with: "It had a skinny leading lady and she was British [Anouska Hempel]. It was a costume movie. Like everything you could possibly do wrong, I did." Various releases tried different titles, with different approaches on the posters—the Italian title, "Raw Meat," with striking art by Luca Crovato, being arguably the most effective. Ultimately though, as Meyer admitted, "we ended up with a film that blacks and whites both hated. The only place it did good business was in Little Rock. Little Rock's a great town for me."

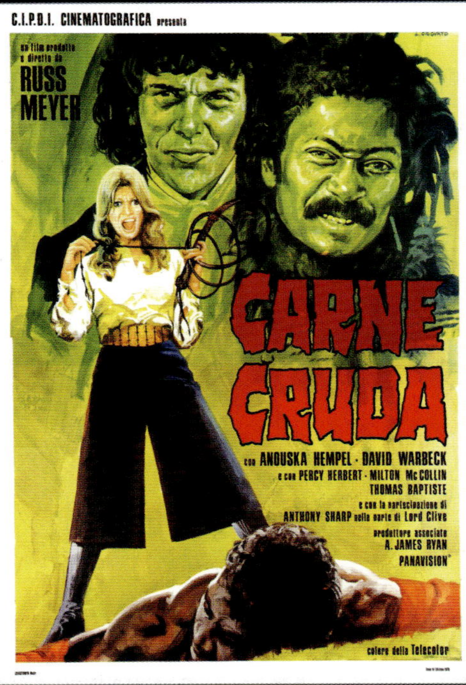

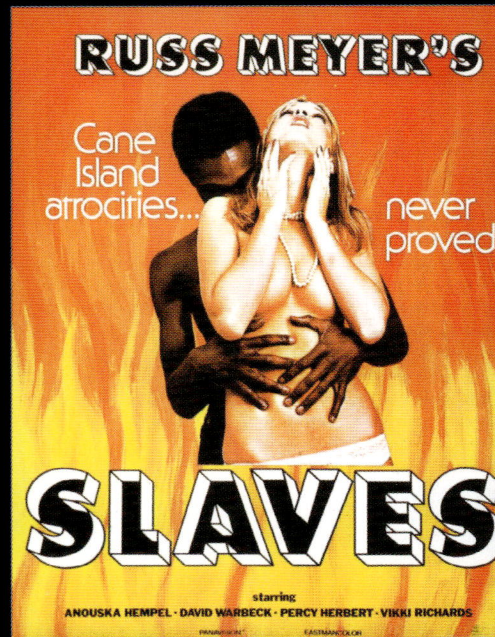

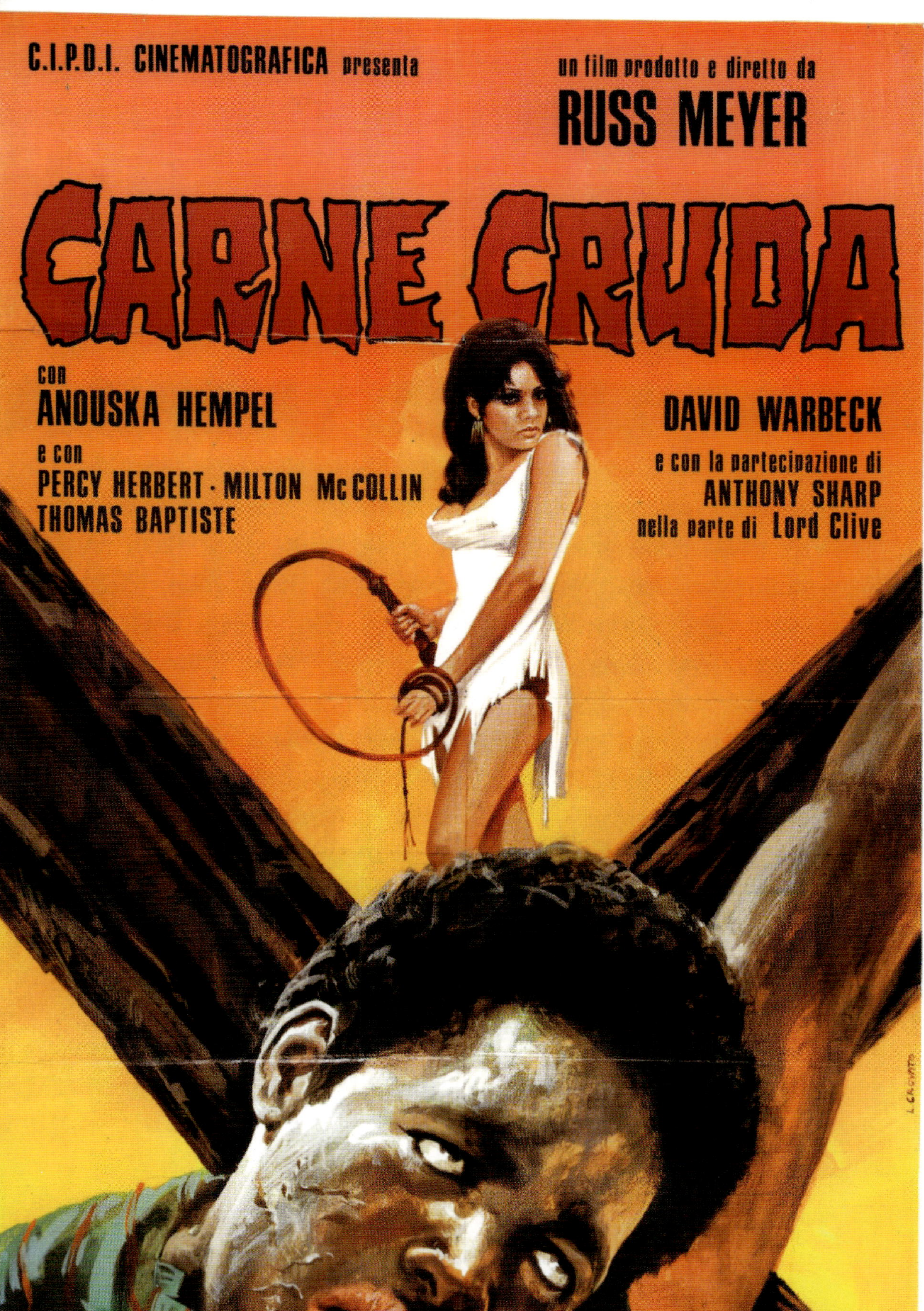
C.I.P.D.I. CINEMATOGRAFICA presenta
un film prodotto e diretto da
RUSS MEYER
CARNE CRUDA
con
ANOUSKA HEMPEL
DAVID WARBECK
e con
PERCY HERBERT · MILTON McCOLLIN
THOMAS BAPTISTE
e con la partecipazione di
ANTHONY SHARP
nella parte di Lord Clive
produttore associato A. JAMES RYAN · PANAVISION® · colore della Telecolor
SELESTAMPA Roma
Anno di Edizione 1974

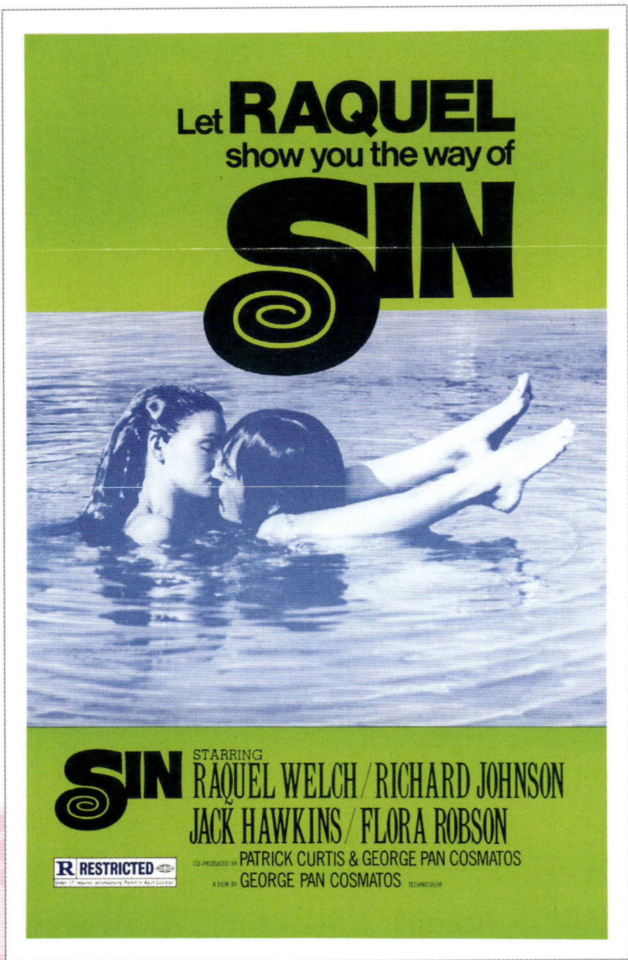

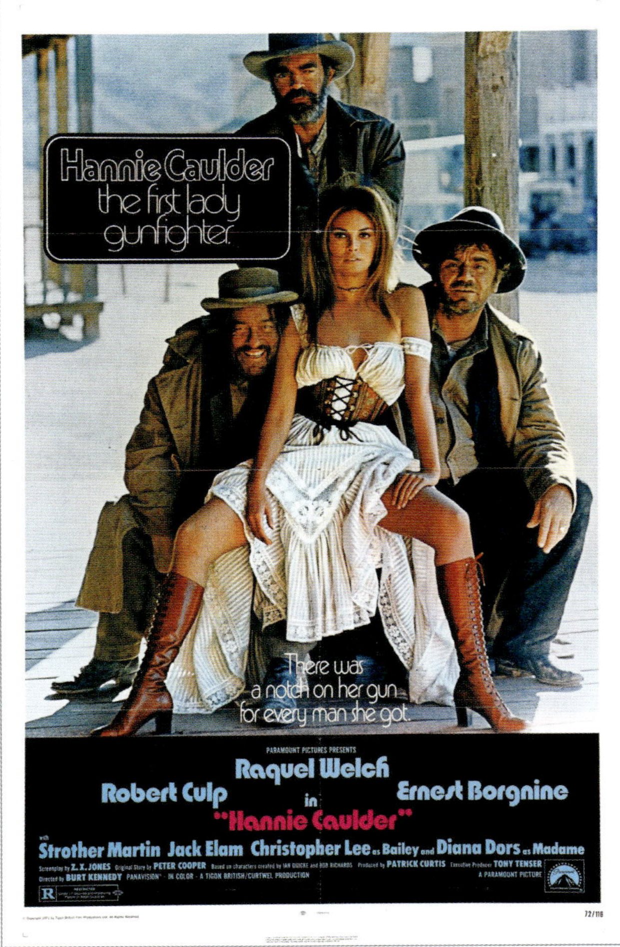

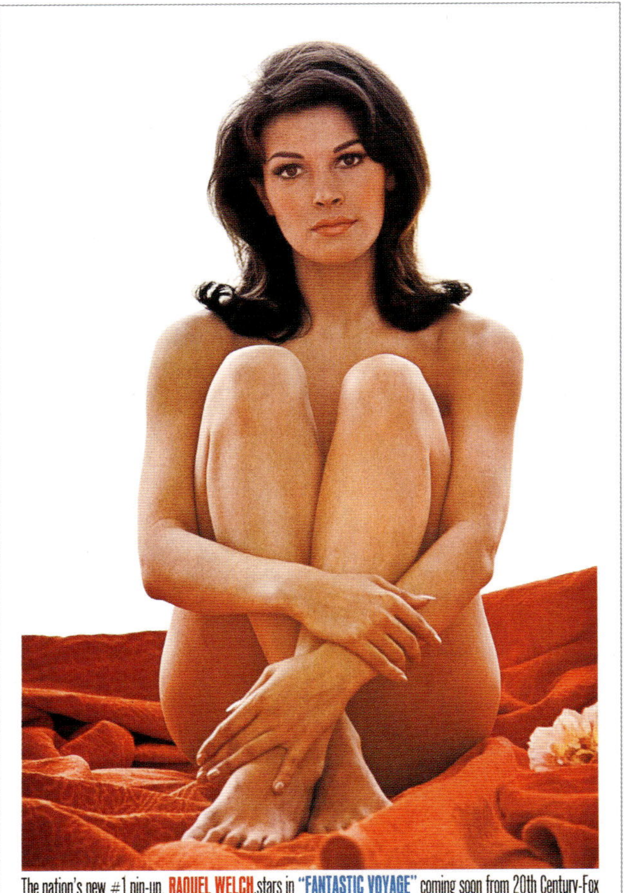

RAQUEL!

In the '60s and '70s, mainstream sex symbols didn't come much bigger than Raquel Welch. Launched in 1966 by the one-two punch of 20th Century Fox's *Fantastic Voyage* and Hammer's *One Million Years B.C.* (in which she wore what even *Time* magazine had to admit was one of the "Top 10 Bikinis in Pop Culture"), Welch parlayed her clout in the industry into starring roles in some interesting movies alongside the fluff, none less so than *Hannie Caulder* (1971), an ahead-of-its-time female revenge Western cited by Tarantino as an influence on *Kill Bill*. Less successful though was the previous year's *The Beloved*, a turgid adultery drama filmed in Cyprus. It was released as *Sin* in some countries, and eventually emerged in the US as *Restless*, with a poster which—surprise!—has very little to do with the actual film.

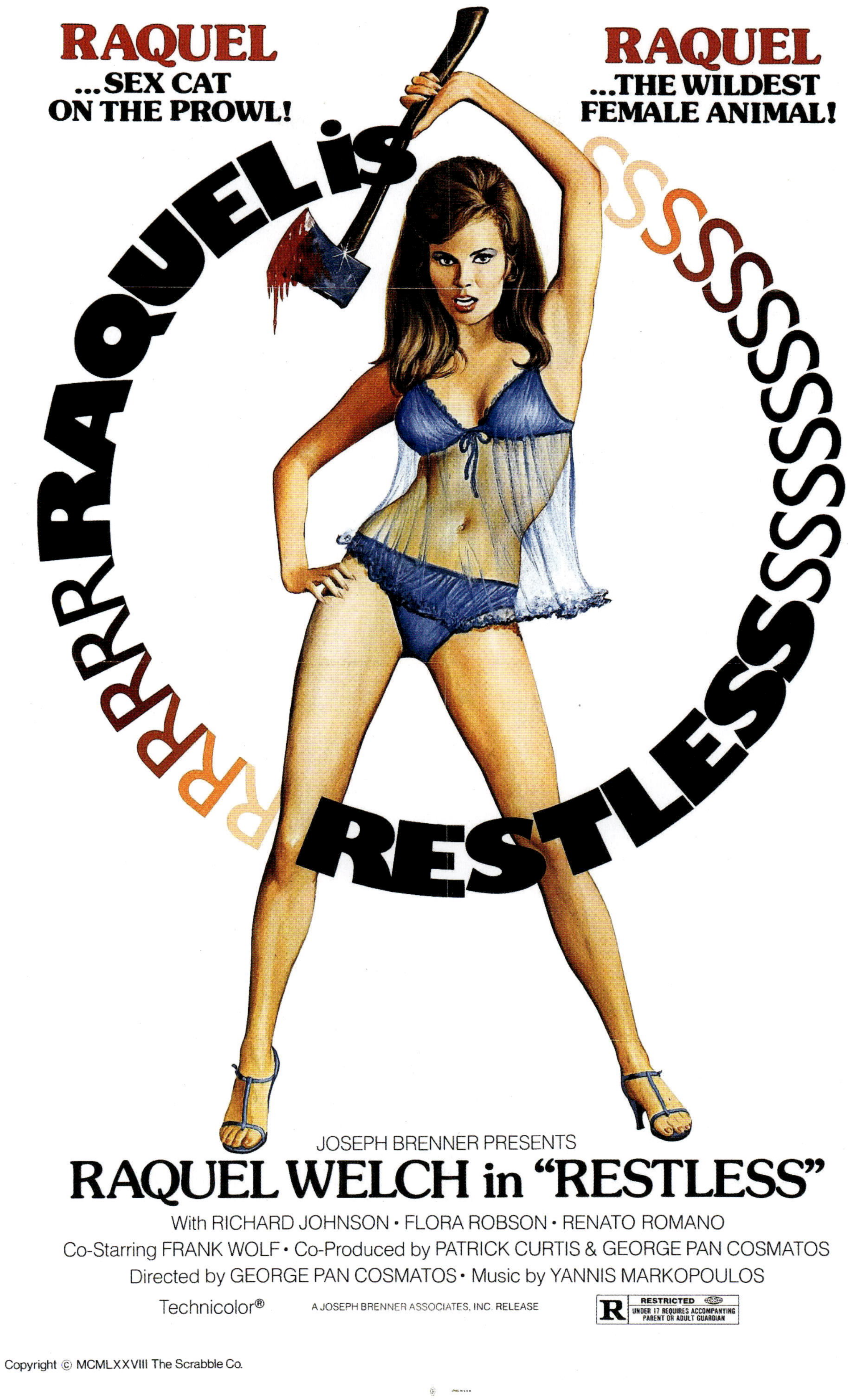

RAQUEL
...SEX CAT
ON THE PROWL!

RAQUEL
...THE WILDEST
FEMALE ANIMAL!

RRRRRRRRAQUEL is SSSSSSSSSSSSSSRESTLESS

JOSEPH BRENNER PRESENTS

RAQUEL WELCH in "RESTLESS"

With RICHARD JOHNSON • FLORA ROBSON • RENATO ROMANO

Co-Starring FRANK WOLF • Co-Produced by PATRICK CURTIS & GEORGE PAN COSMATOS

Directed by GEORGE PAN COSMATOS • Music by YANNIS MARKOPOULOS

Technicolor®

A JOSEPH BRENNER ASSOCIATES, INC. RELEASE

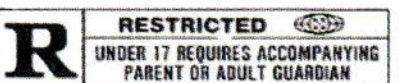

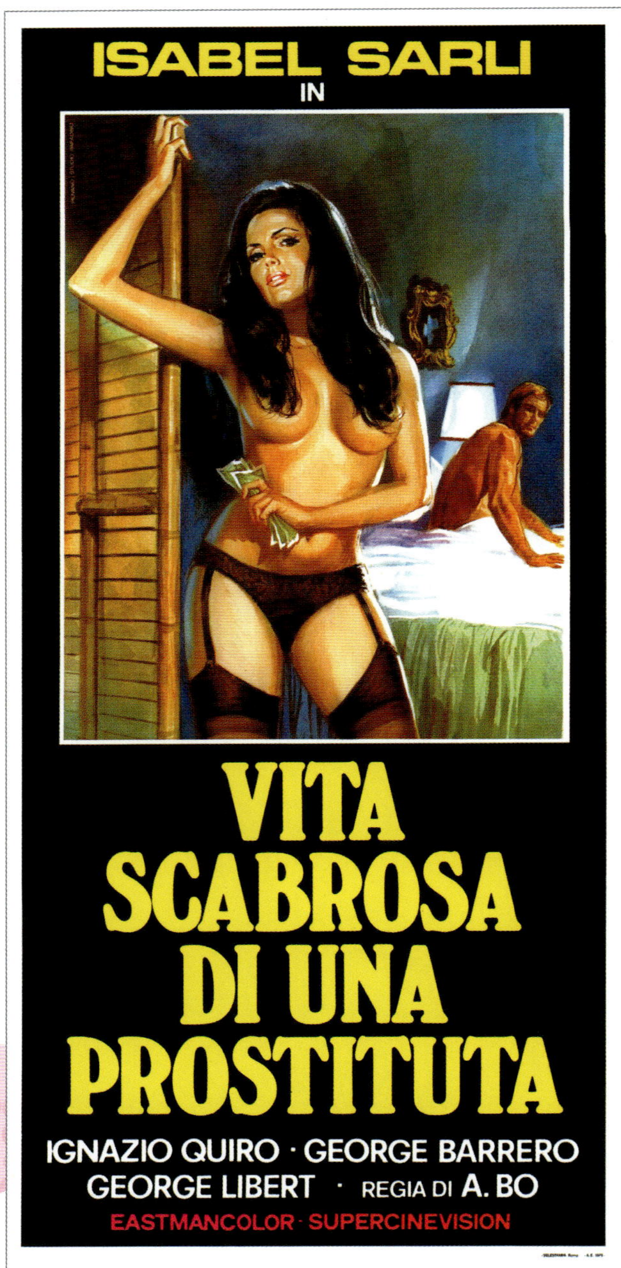

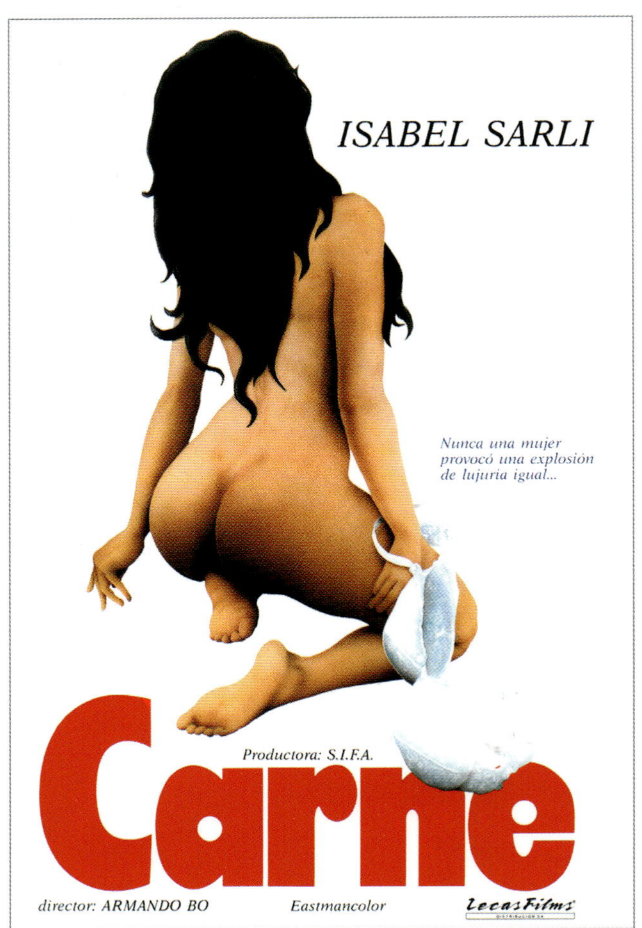

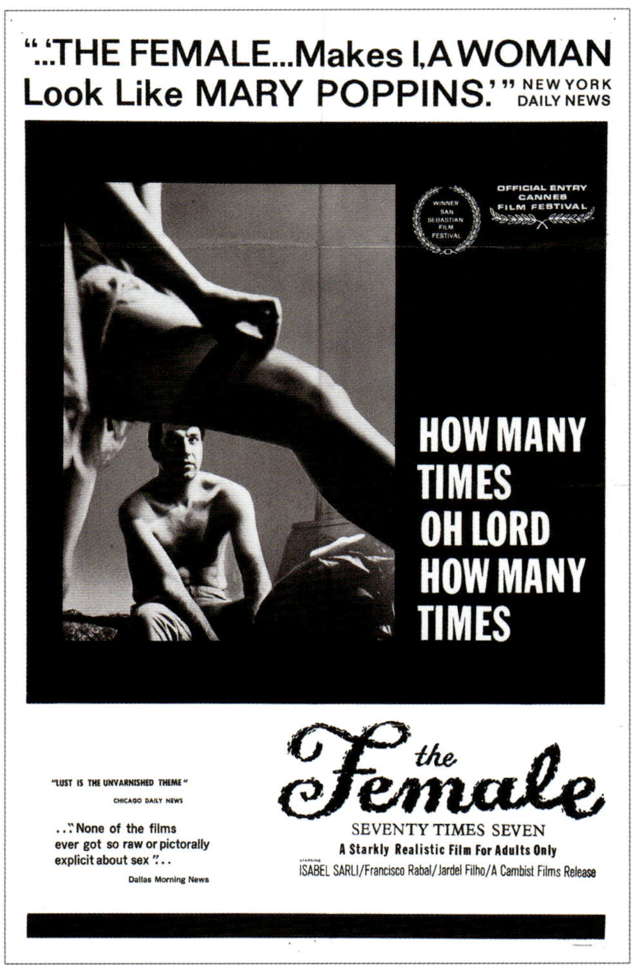

ISABEL SARLI

"Makes Racquel [sic] Welch look like Twiggy standing backward," was the opinion of one critic, and while the anatomical logic behind that statement is slightly baffling, there's no denying that the Argentine star Isabel Sarli spent a lot of time showing off said remarkable anatomy in the 27 lurid films she made with her husband, director Armando Bó. John Waters was a fan, admitting that his *Pink Flamingos* "stole" from Sarli's *Fuego* (1969), adding that she "inspired us all to a life of cheap exhibitionism, exaggerated sexual desires and a love for all that is trash-ridden in cinema. We salute you, Isabel Sarli, a truly outstanding woman in film." Her home country holds her in similarly high regard: in 2012 then-President Christina Kirchner appointed Sarli as Argentine Ambassador of Popular Culture. Beat that, Racquel.

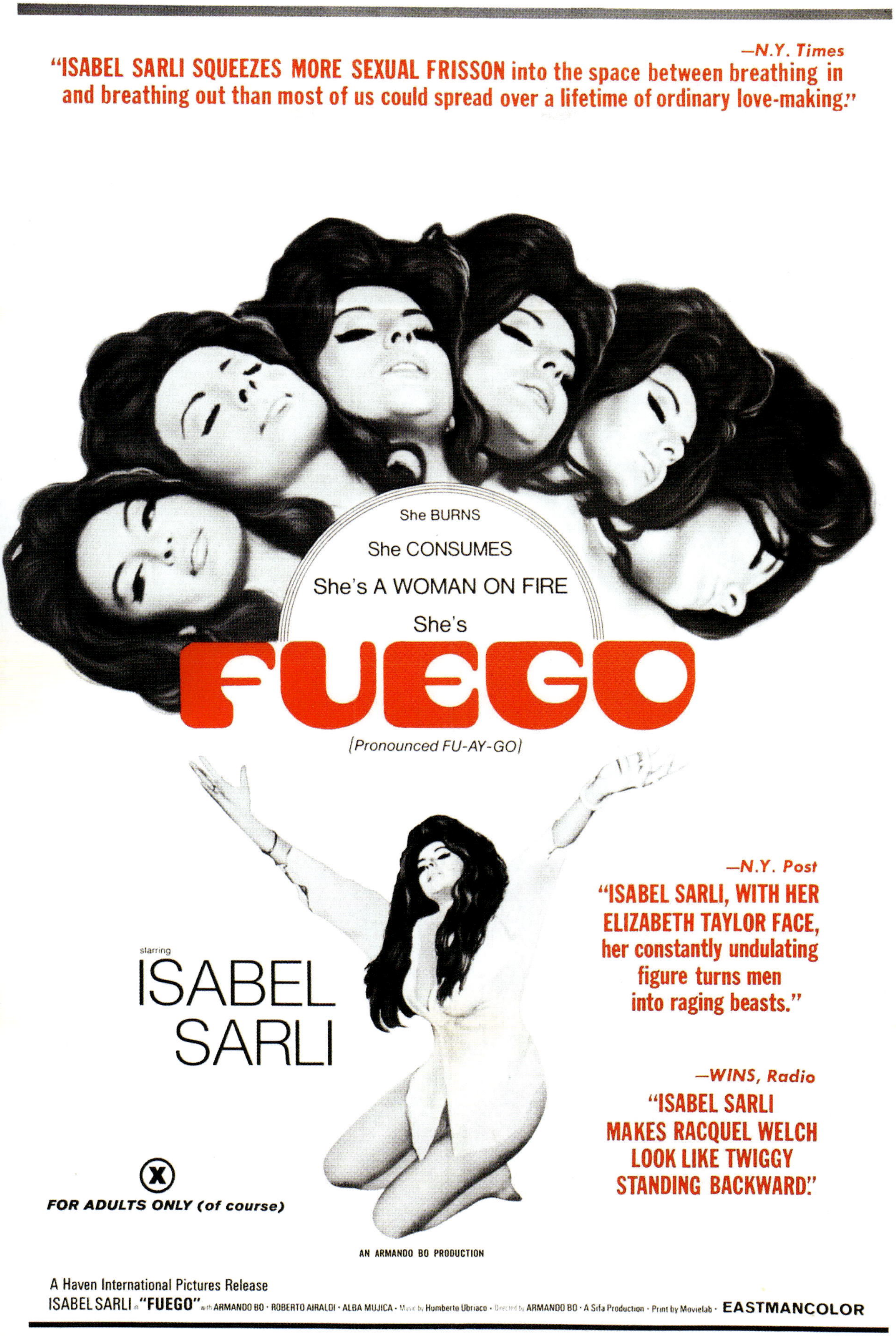

—*N.Y. Times*

"ISABEL SARLI SQUEEZES MORE SEXUAL FRISSON into the space between breathing in and breathing out than most of us could spread over a lifetime of ordinary love-making."

She BURNS

She CONSUMES

She's A WOMAN ON FIRE

She's

FUEGO

(Pronounced FU-AY-GO)

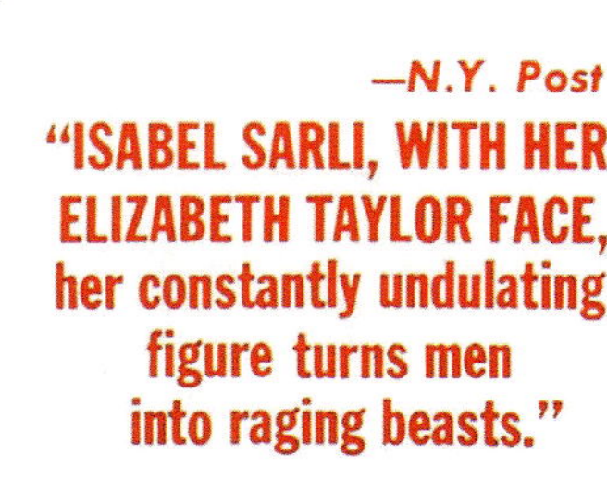

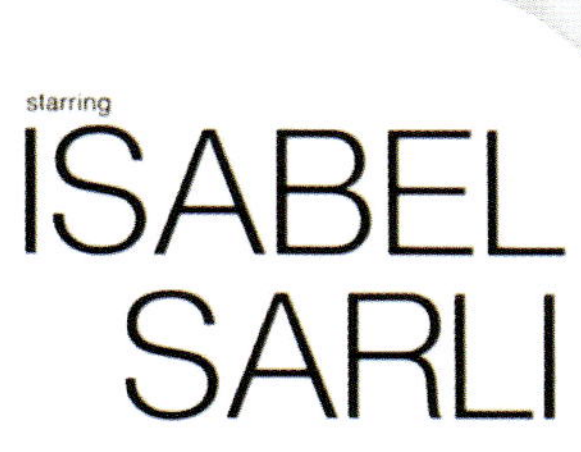

—*WINS, Radio*

"ISABEL SARLI MAKES RACQUEL WELCH LOOK LIKE TWIGGY STANDING BACKWARD."

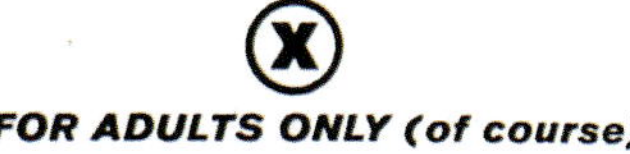

AN ARMANDO BO PRODUCTION

A Haven International Pictures Release

ISABEL SARLI in **"FUEGO"** with ARMANDO BO · ROBERTO AIRALDI · ALBA MUJICA · Music by Humberto Ubriaco · Directed by ARMANDO BO · A Sifa Production · Print by Movielab · **EASTMANCOLOR**

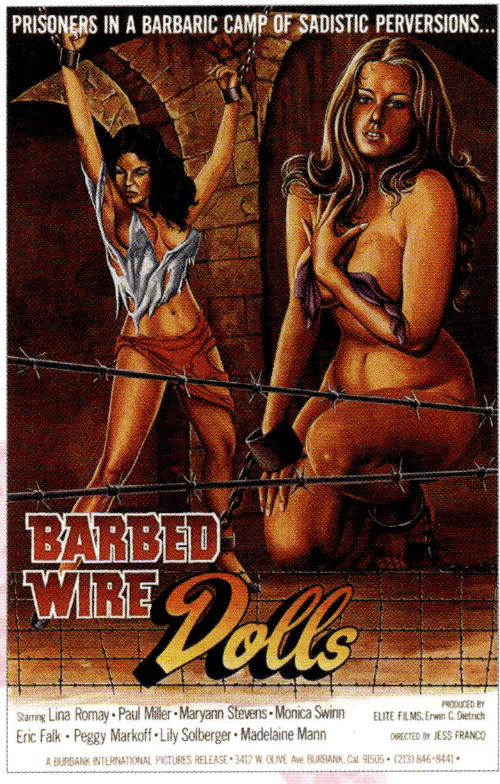

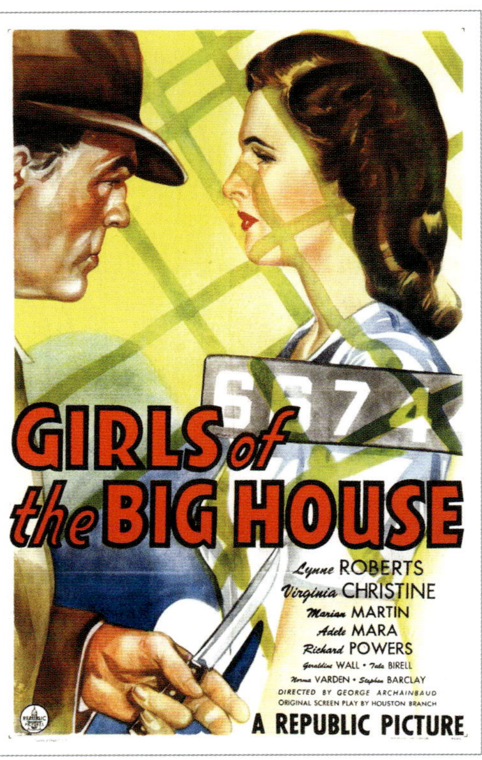

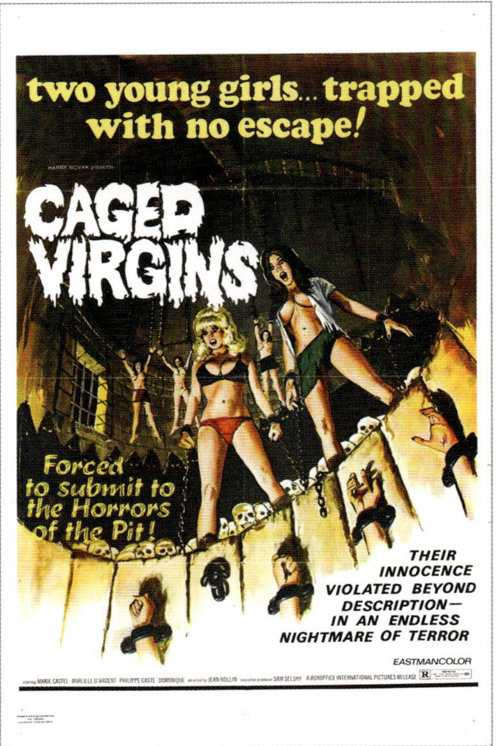

INCARCERATED

Whether it's being locked up in a reform school, put behind bars in a prison, chained to a dungeon wall, or tortured in a maniac's basement, incarceration is a constant danger for women in exploitation movies. Ida Lupino starred as a wicked warden in *Women's Prison* (1955), an early example of a subgenre that was still going strong, with added explicit lesbianism and violence, in Jess Franco's *Barbed Wire Dolls* (1975). Jean Rollin's dreamlike horror film better known as *Requiem for a Vampire* (1971) was given a US release by Harry Novak's Boxoffice International under the somewhat blunter title *Caged Virgins*, with a poster that played down the supernatural elements of the plot (which features vampire bats doing unmentionable things to said virgins). Jano's poster for the Spanish asylum melodrama *Las Melancholias* (aka *House of Insane Women*, 1971) masterfully captures its demented excesses.

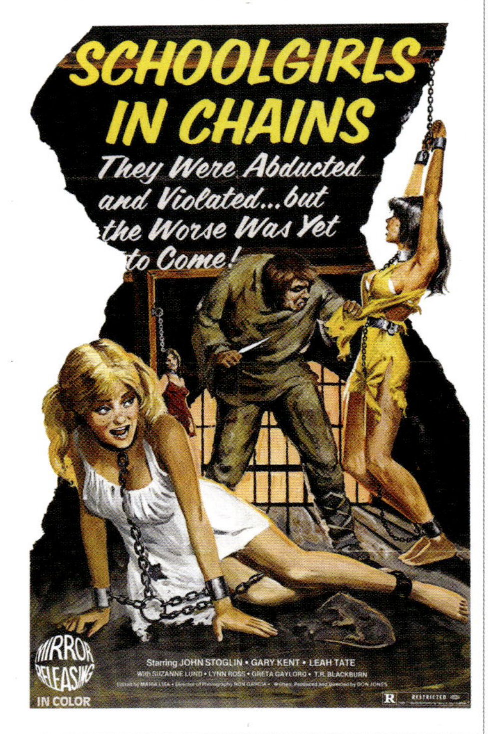

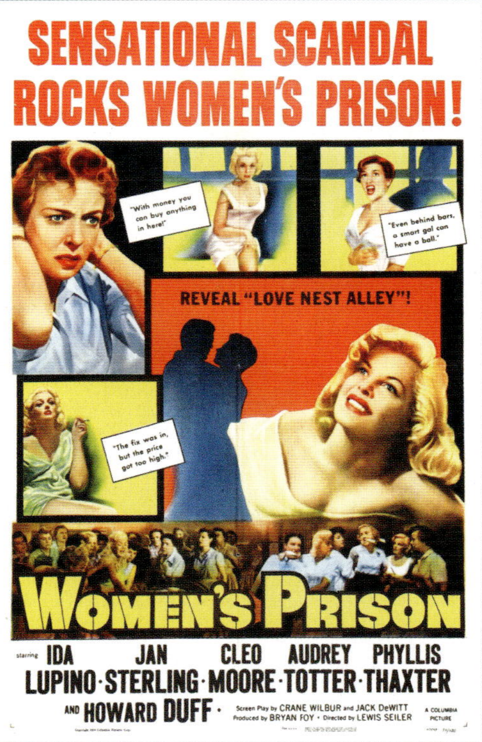

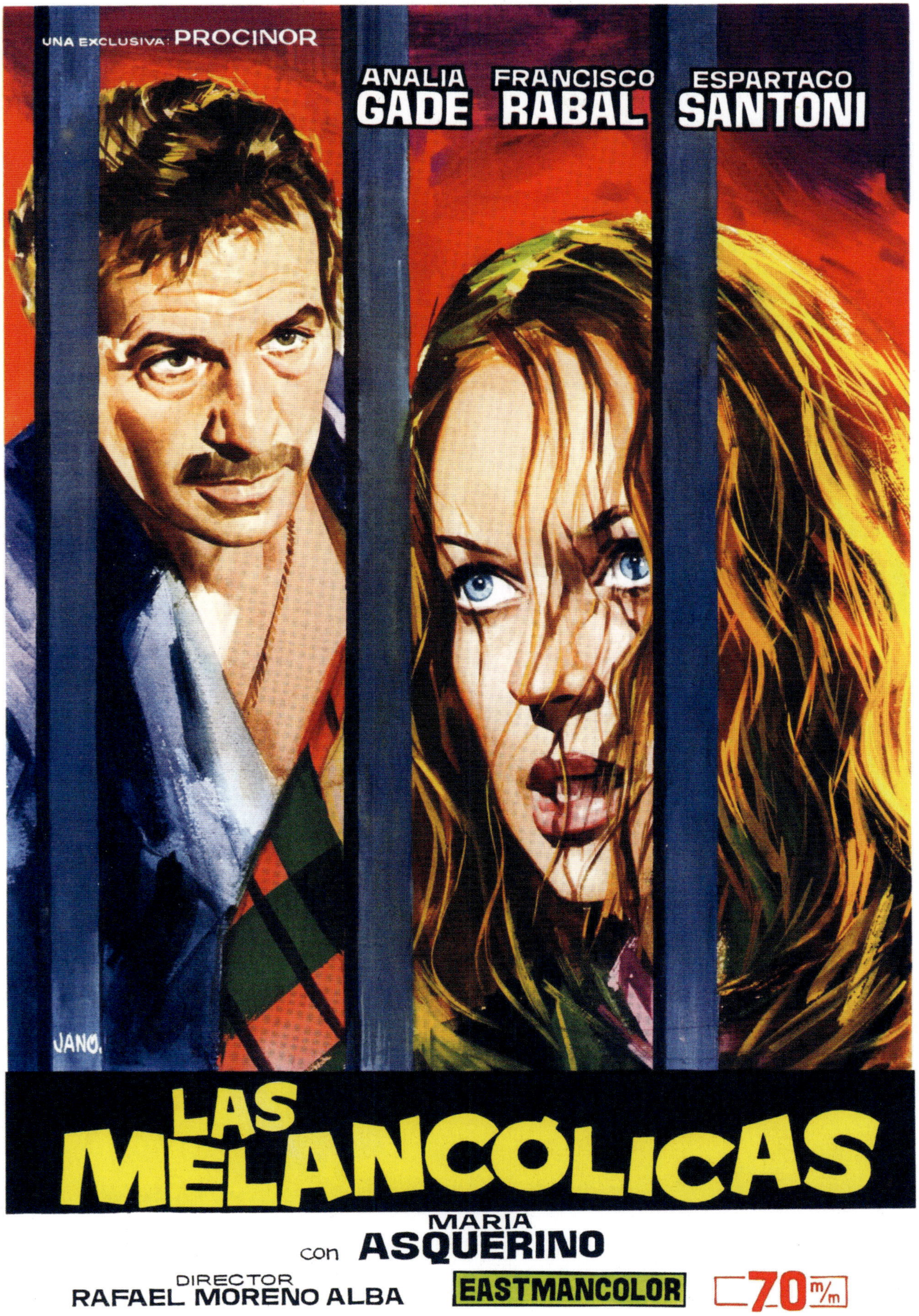

UNA EXCLUSIVA: PROCINOR

ANALIA GADE FRANCISCO RABAL ESPARTACO SANTONI

JANO.

LAS MELANCÓLICAS

con MARIA ASQUERINO

DIRECTOR RAFAEL MORENO ALBA

EASTMANCOLOR

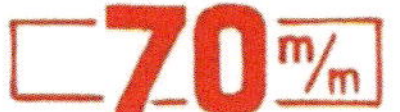

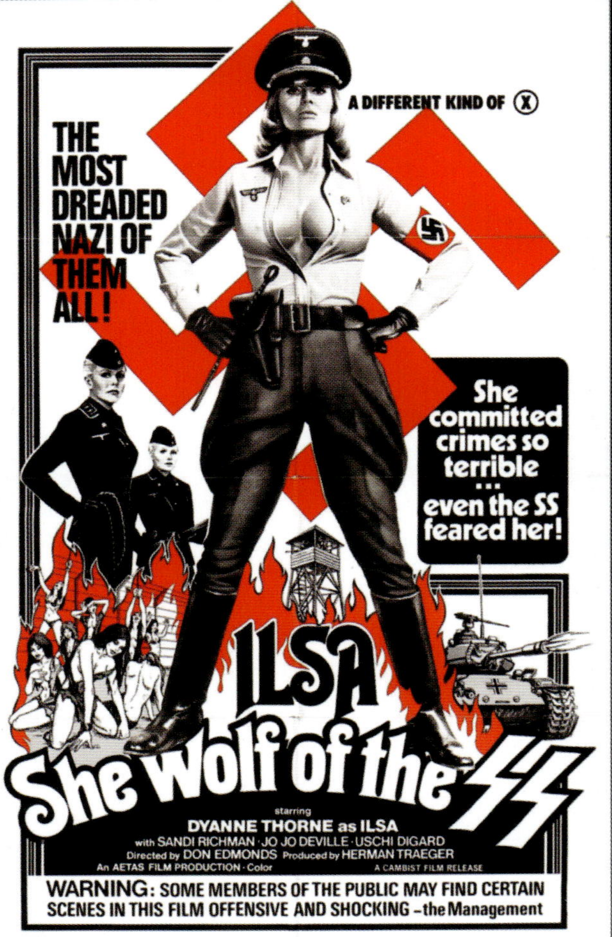

A DIFFERENT KIND OF X
THE MOST DREADED NAZI OF THEM ALL!
She committed crimes so terrible ... even the SS feared her!
ILSA
She wolf of the SS
starring
DYANNE THORNE as ILSA
with SANDI RICHMAN · JO JO DEVILLE · USCHI DIGARD
Directed by DON EDMONDS Produced by HERMAN TRAEGER
An AETAS FILM PRODUCTION · Color
A CAMBIST FILM RELEASE
WARNING: SOME MEMBERS OF THE PUBLIC MAY FIND CERTAIN SCENES IN THIS FILM OFFENSIVE AND SHOCKING –the Management

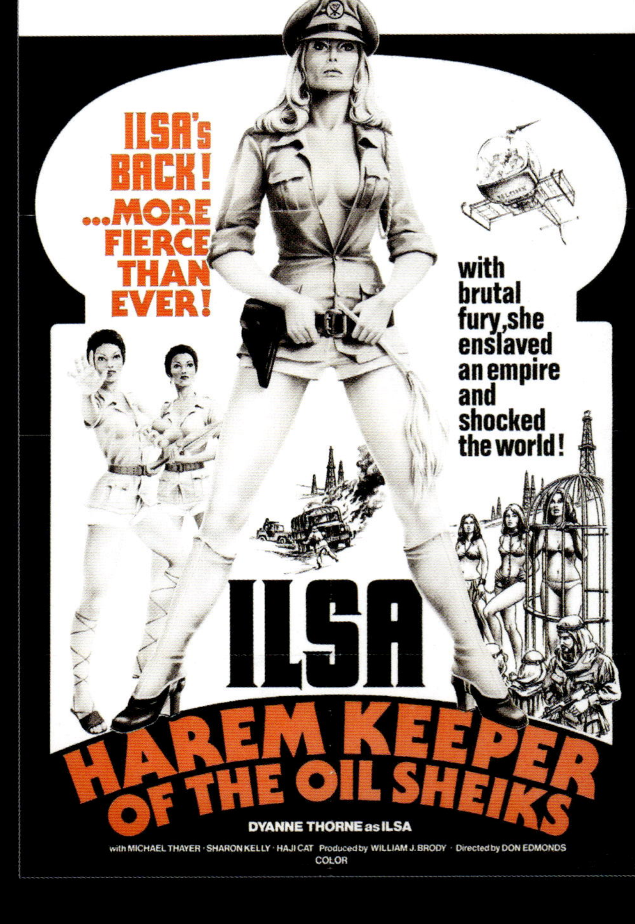

ILSA's BACK! ...MORE FIERCE THAN EVER!
with brutal fury, she enslaved an empire and shocked the world!
ILSA
HAREM KEEPER OF THE OIL SHEIKS
DYANNE THORNE as ILSA
with MICHAEL THAYER · SHARON KELLY · HAJI CAT Produced by WILLIAM J. BRODY · Directed by DON EDMONDS
COLOR

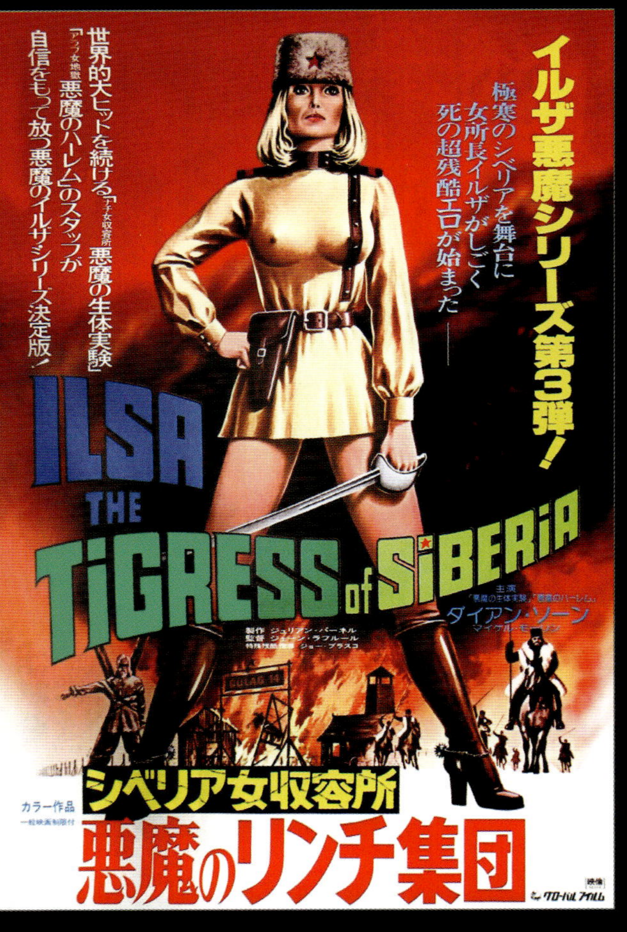

イルザ悪魔シリーズ第3弾!
極寒のシベリアを舞台に
女所長イルザがしごく
死の超残酷エロが始まった——
世界的大ヒットを続ける「ナチ女収容所 悪魔の生体実験」
「アラブ女地獄 悪魔のハーレム」のスタッフが
自信をもって放つ悪魔のイルザシリーズ決定版!
ILSA
THE
TiGRESS of SiBERiA
主演
ダイアン・ソーン
製作 ジュリアン・パーネル
カラー作品
シベリア女収容所
悪魔のリンチ集団

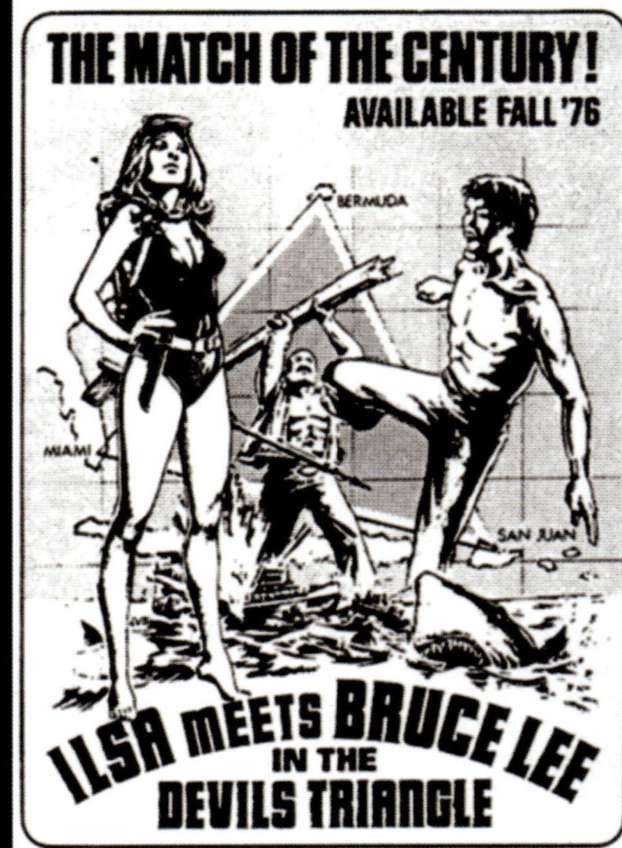

THE MATCH OF THE CENTURY!
AVAILABLE FALL '76
BERMUDA
MIAMI
SAN JUAN
ILSA MEETS BRUCE LEE
IN THE
DEVILS TRIANGLE

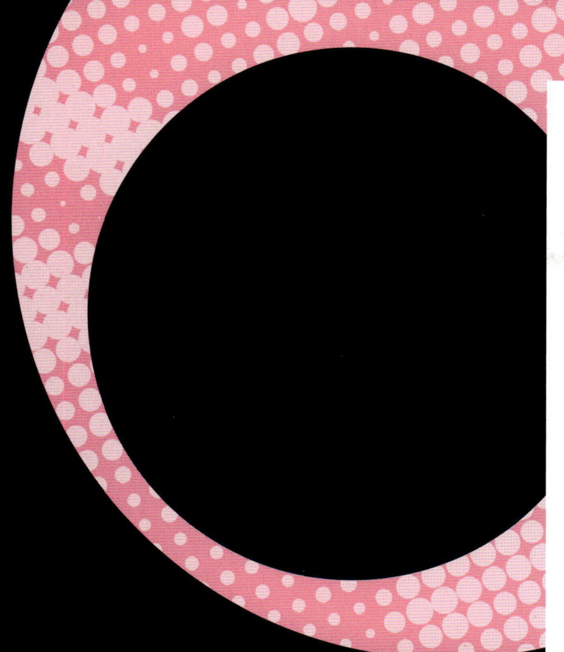

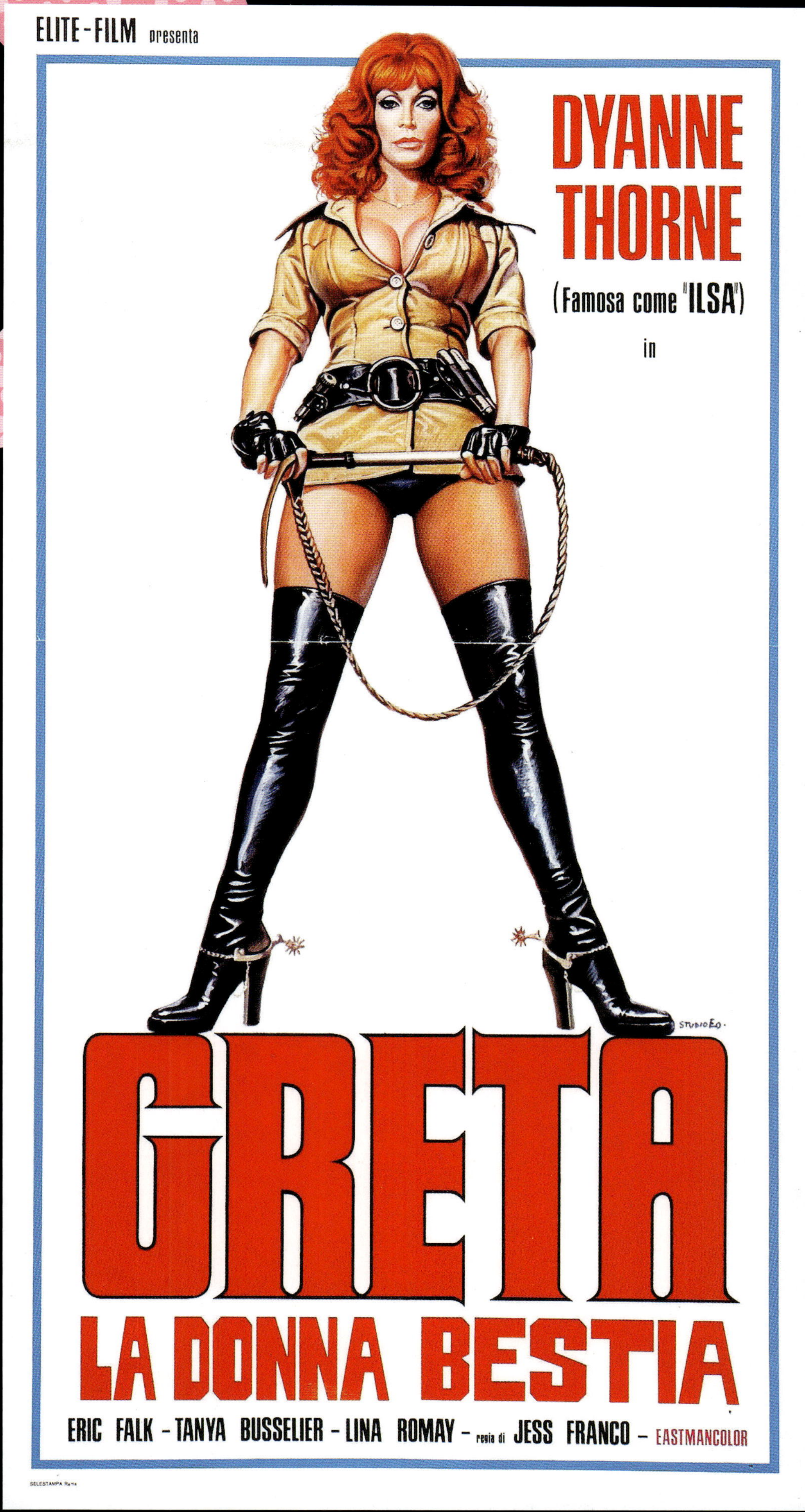

ILSA!

"The script was trash, but the character seduced me. A chance to portray a real person who was an animal, and yet a charmer, with a history of heinous crimes—shocking, but after a week of contemplation, I said, 'Yes'." It was a fateful decision. Dyanne Thorne's riveting performance as a torture camp Kommandant in *Ilsa, She Wolf of the SS* (1975)—inspired by the real-life "concentration camp murderess" Ilse Koch—made her forever the Queen of Naziploitation. *Ilsa, Harem Keeper of the Oil Sheiks* (1976) and *Ilsa, the Tigress of Siberia* (1977) followed, as did *Greta, Haus ohne Männer* (1977), which was not technically an Ilsa picture, but nevertheless used the by-then iconic legs akimbo pose on its Italian poster (and was later re-released as *Ilsa, the Wicked Warden*). Sadly, the almost unbearably cool concept of *Ilsa Meets Bruce Lee in the Devil's Triangle* never got beyond some basic teaser art. "There was never a script," Thorne remembers. "It was never written, only discussed. I was told to study martial arts, which I did. They were going to use an actor going by the name of Bruce Li. It would have been fun but it didn't happen." None of the sequels that *were* made actually featured her playing a Nazi—as Thorne herself notes, she was, "A *Nazi* once, *nasty* always!"—but it's bursting out of an SS uniform that she'll be best remembered. These days, as befits someone with a PhD in comparative religion, Thorne is an ordained minister conducting "scenic outdoor weddings" in Las Vegas.

ELITE-FILM presenta

DYANNE THORNE

(Famosa come "ILSA")

in

GRETA

LA DONNA BESTIA

ERIC FALK - TANYA BUSSELIER - LINA ROMAY - regia di JESS FRANCO - EASTMANCOLOR

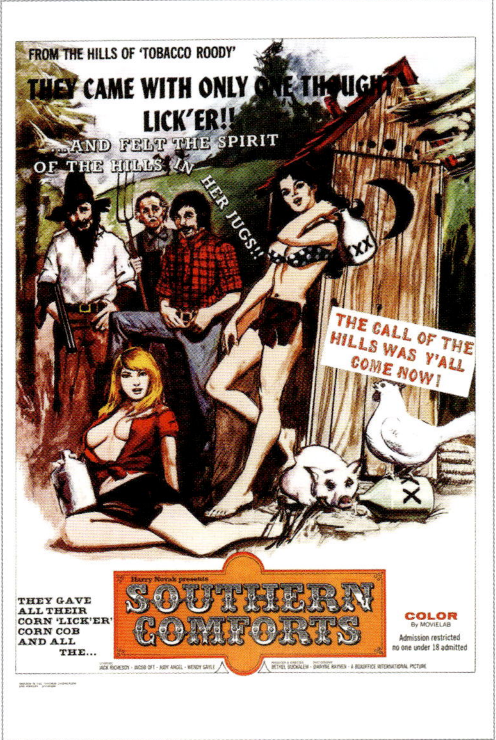

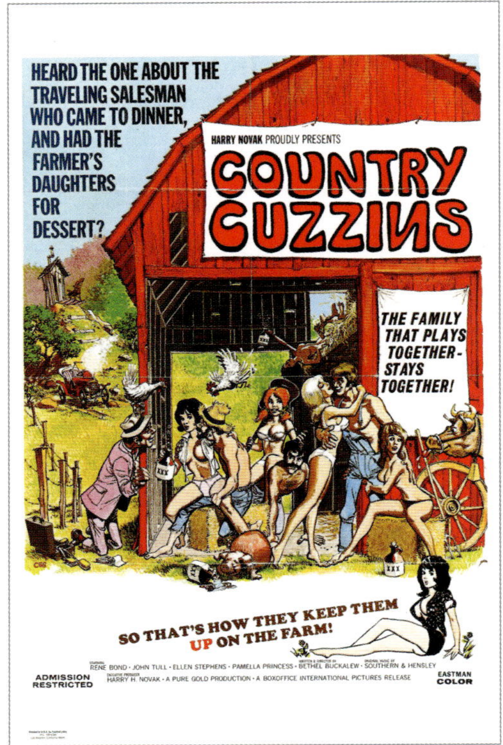

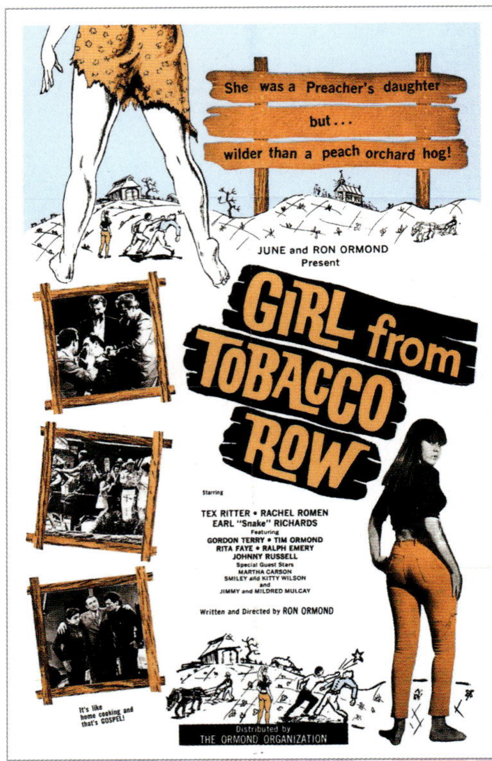

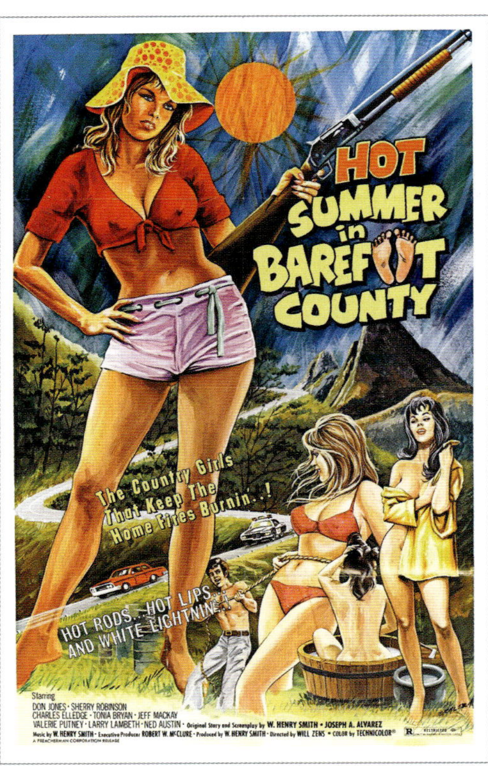

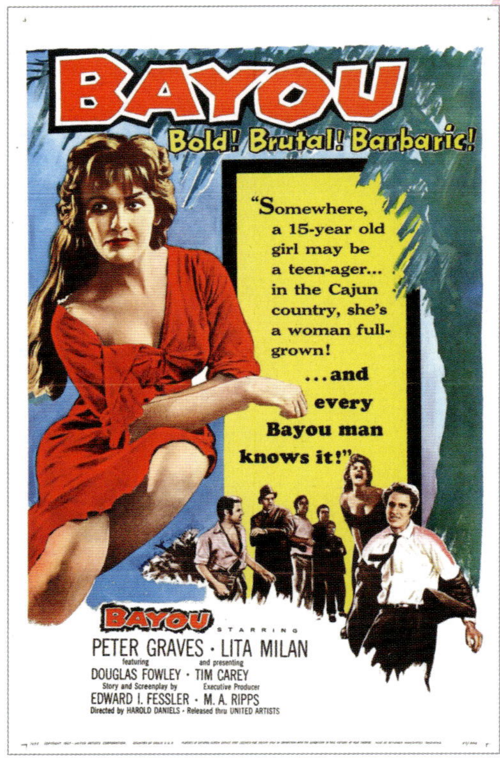

HICKSPLOITATION

They do things different down South. There are rules, not least that during car chases, as hick flick historian Scott Von Doviak points out, "stepping on the gas pedal will cause spirited banjo music to erupt on the soundtrack." There must also be moonshine, redneck sheriffs, and loose women, the latter often in very tight shorts—as the poster for 1974's *Hot Summer in Barefoot County* shows, "Daisy Dukes" were a fashion statement years before the sanitized version of hicksploitation hit the small screen in *The Dukes of Hazzard*. Actor Paul Walsh has fond memories of the good ol' boy epic he co-starred in, *Redneck Miller* (1976): "We had a blast makin' this thing. Seems like it took about two weeks to shoot. Tarantino owns it now and I really hope he releases it on DVD before my Mom dies. She would *love* it."

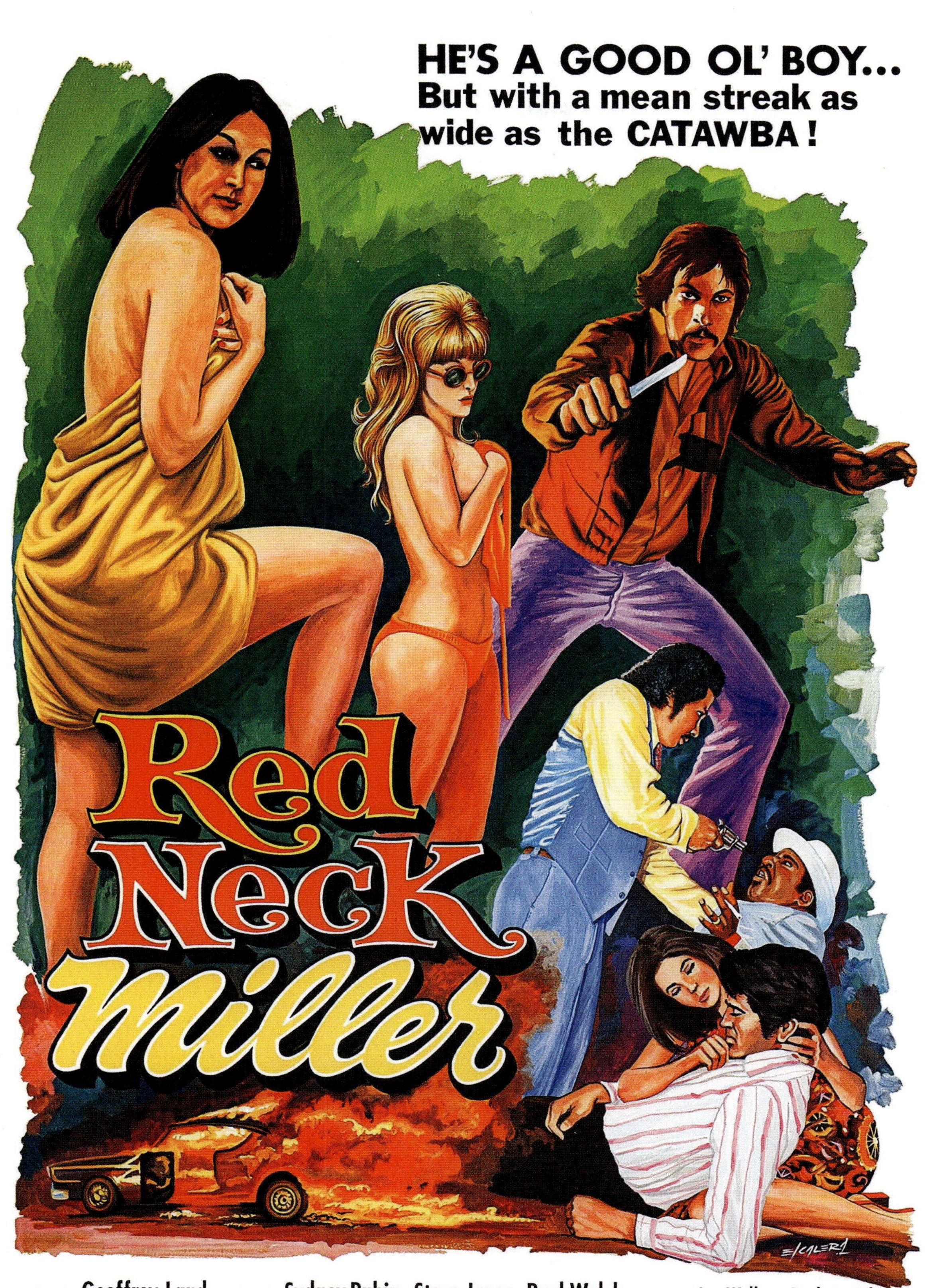
HE'S A GOOD OL' BOY...
But with a mean streak as wide as the CATAWBA!
Red Neck Miller
Starring Geoffrey Land • Co-Starring Sydney Rubin • Steve Jones • Paul Walsh Also Starring Lou Walker • Paulette Gibson Angel Sande • Marcel Cobb with Charles Elledge • Sid Rancer • Linda Hammond • Charles Leonard • Allan 'Mitch' Miller
Original Story & Screenplay W. Henry Smith • Joseph A. Alvarez • Director of Photography Austin McKinney
Film Editor Julie Tanser • Executive Producers Ulmer S. Eaddy, Jr. • W. Henry Smith • Produced by W. Henry Smith
Directed by John Clayton • Original Music by W. Henry Smith • Dan Knight • Allan Miller • Bruce 'Sonny' – COLOR
R

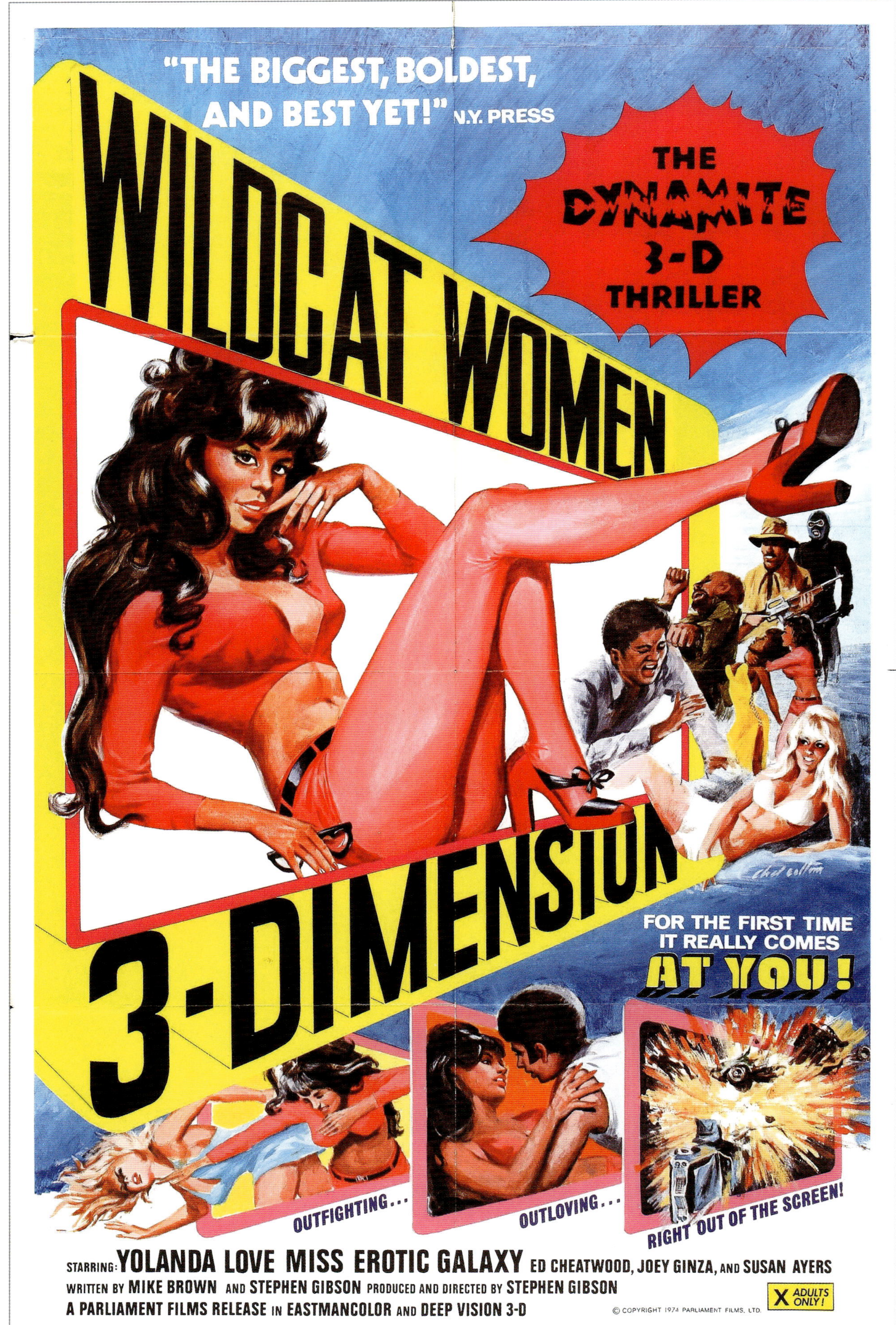
"THE BIGGEST, BOLDEST, AND BEST YET!" N.Y. PRESS
WILDCAT WOMEN
THE DYNAMITE 3-D THRILLER
3-DIMENSION
FOR THE FIRST TIME IT REALLY COMES
AT YOU!
OUTFIGHTING...
OUTLOVING...
RIGHT OUT OF THE SCREEN!
STARRING: YOLANDA LOVE MISS EROTIC GALAXY ED CHEATWOOD, JOEY GINZA, AND SUSAN AYERS
WRITTEN BY MIKE BROWN AND STEPHEN GIBSON PRODUCED AND DIRECTED BY STEPHEN GIBSON
A PARLIAMENT FILMS RELEASE IN EASTMANCOLOR AND DEEP VISION 3-D
© COPYRIGHT 1974 PARLIAMENT FILMS, LTD.
X ADULTS ONLY!

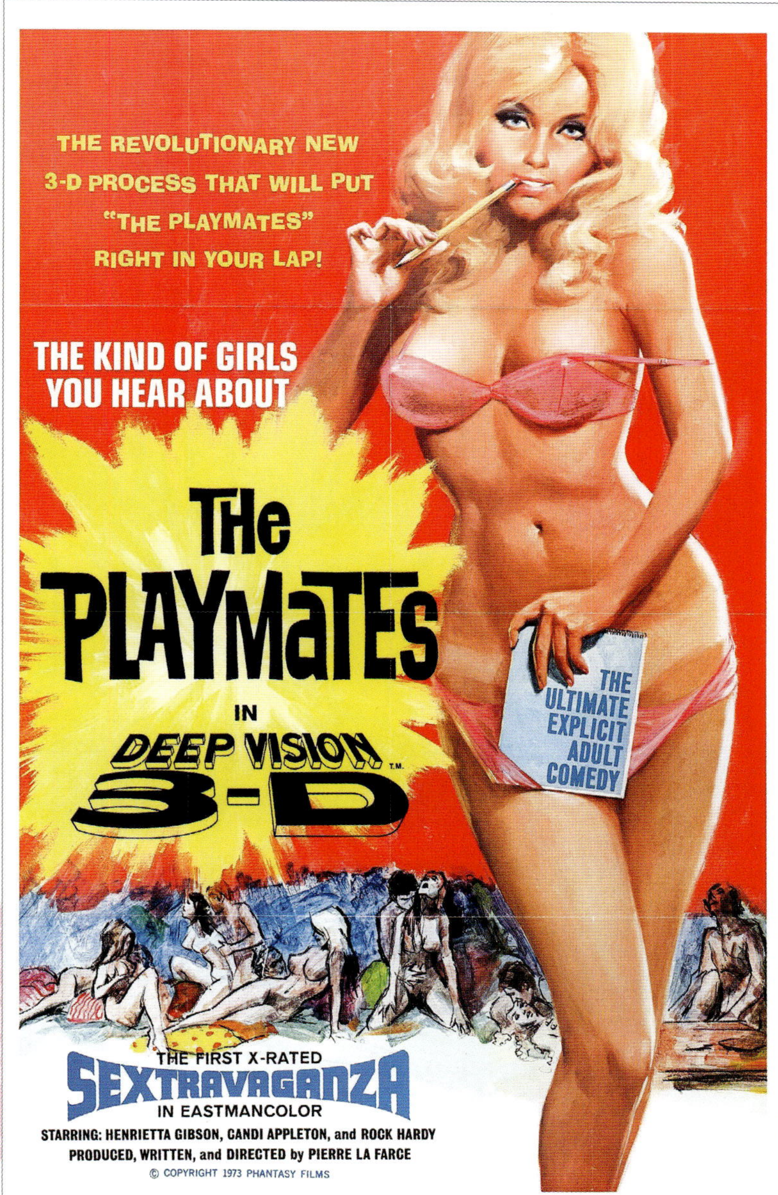

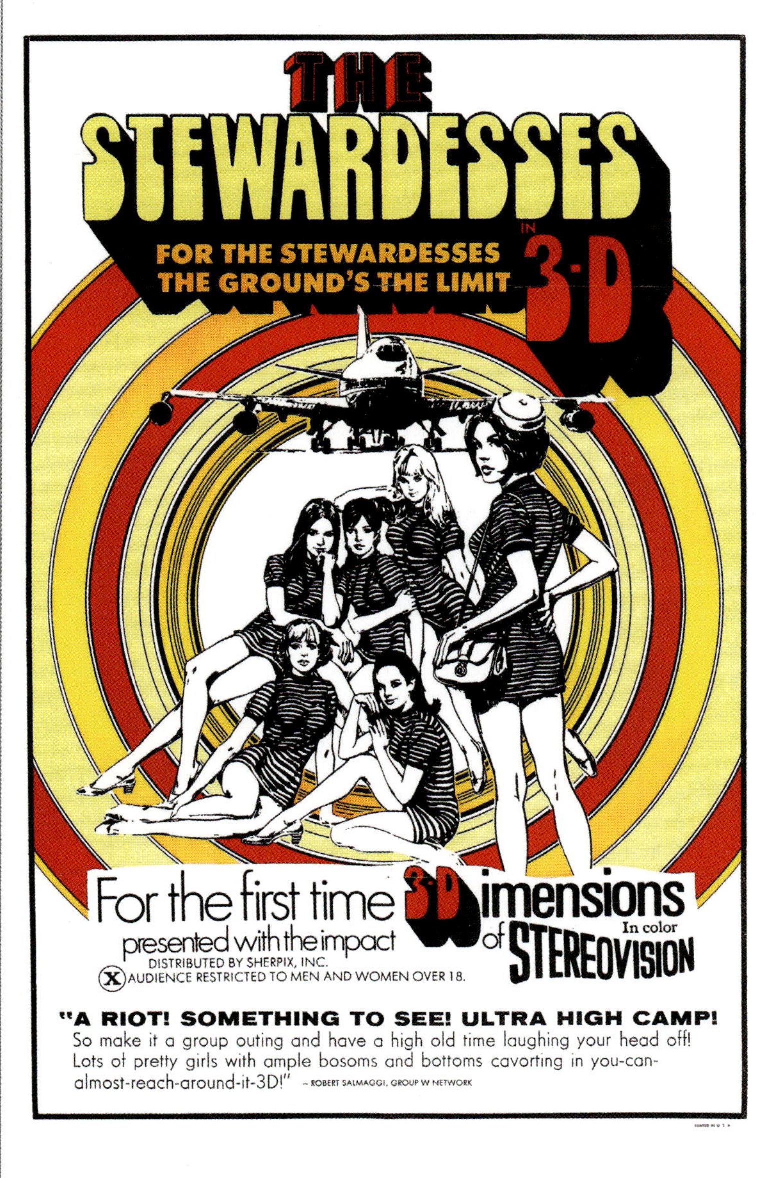

IN YOUR FACE!

"Lots of pretty girls with ample bosoms and bottoms cavorting in you-can-almost-reach-around-it-3D!" marvels the poster for *The Stewardesses*, summing up the irresistible attraction of sexploitation in three dimensions. This 1969 movie introduced a new single-strip, 35mm 3D process dubbed StereoVision, and proved so popular (in both hardcore and later softcore versions) that it reportedly ended up grossing 300 times its original $100,000 budget. The hardcore *Black Lolita* had an edited softcore release as *Wildcat Women* (1975), but its cheapskate 3D (shot with a polychromatic lens) was, like its incomprehensible plot, simply headache-inducing.

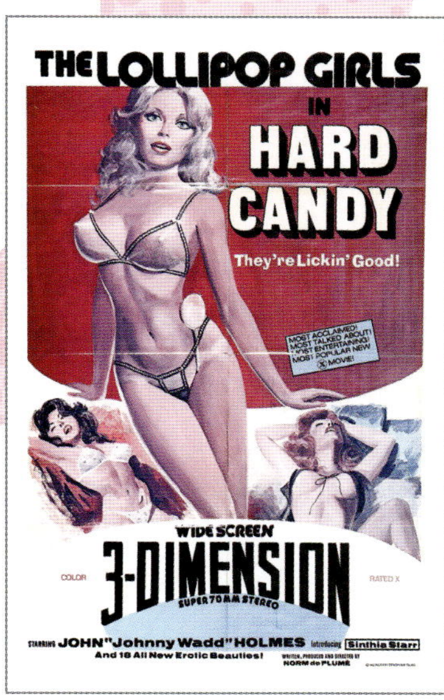

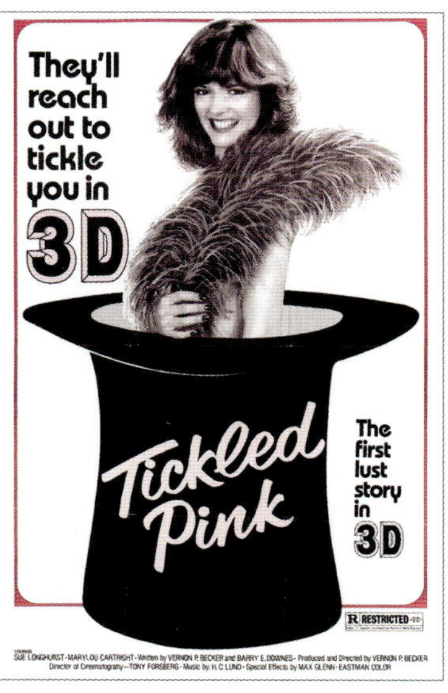

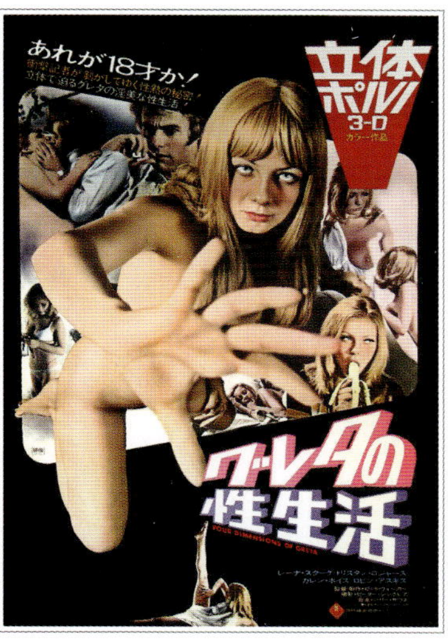

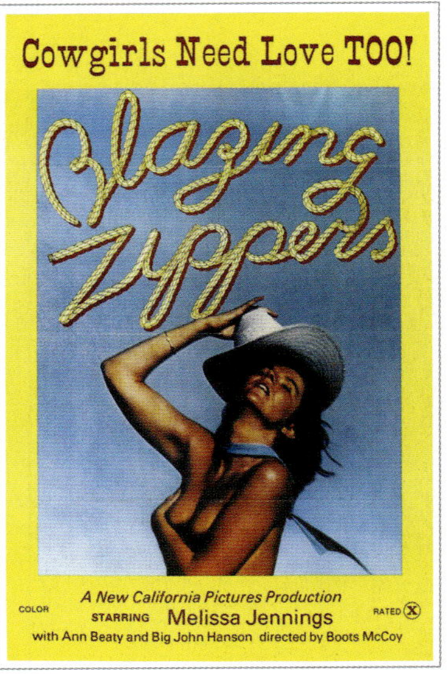

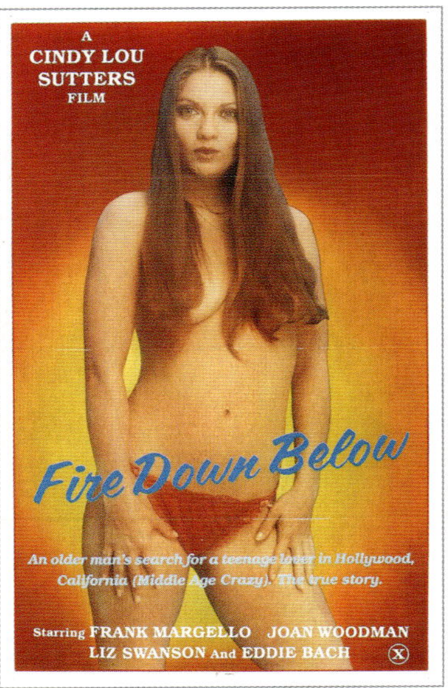

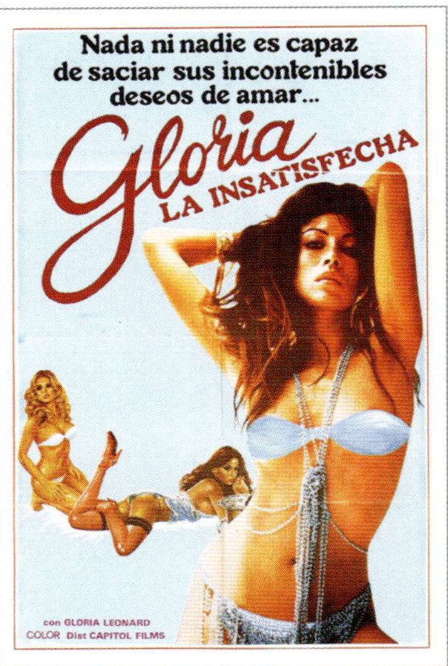

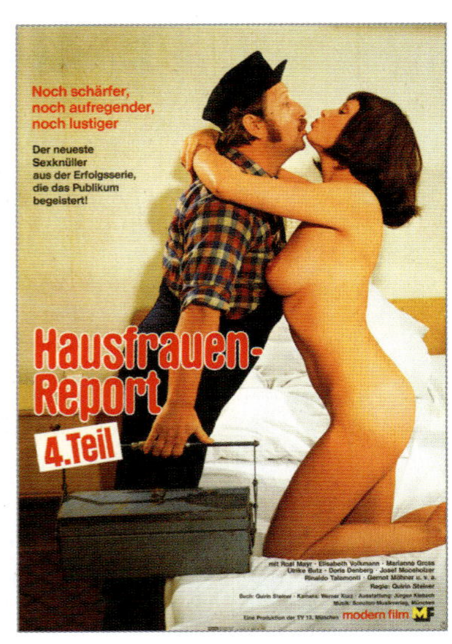

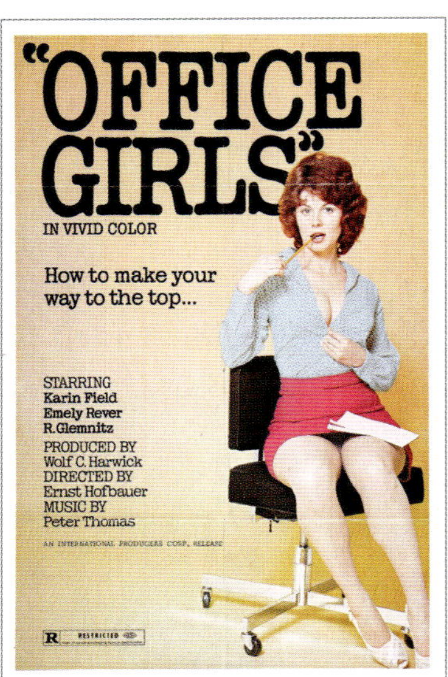

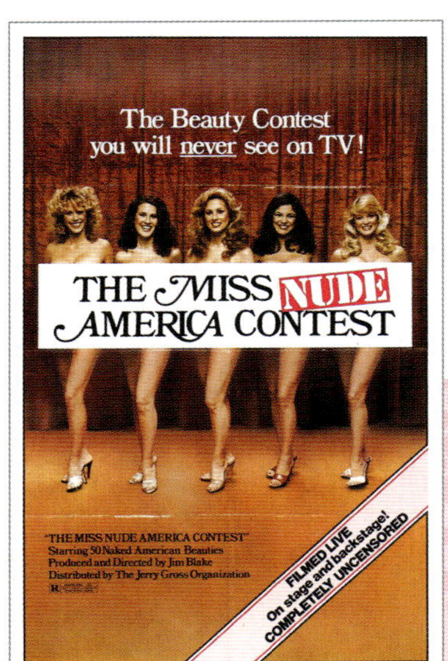

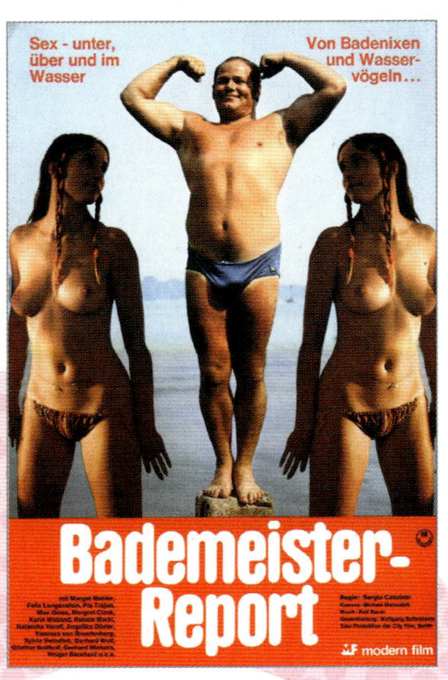

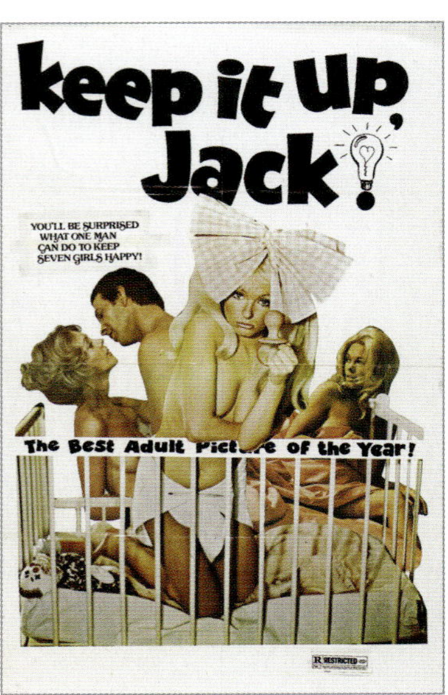

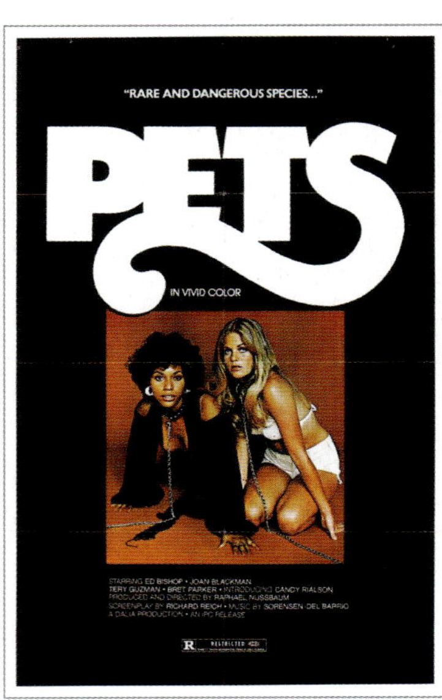

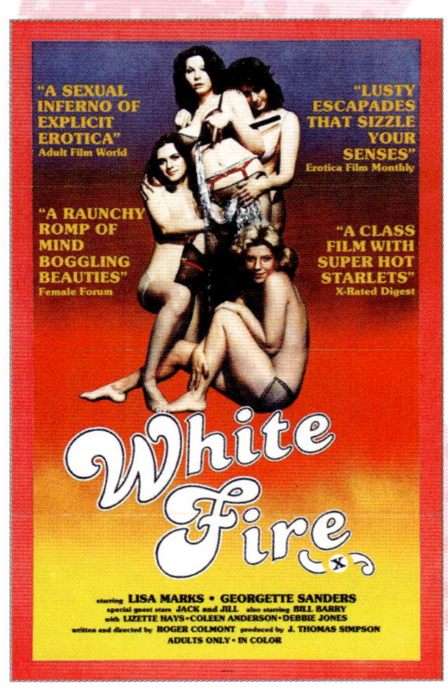

THE '70s IN COLOR

In the early part of the '70s, it was still worth pointing out to the viewers when an exploitation film wasn't shot in black and white: "In vivid color" reads the tagline on the posters for both *Office Girls* (1971) and *Pets* (1973). By the end of the decade, color was the norm, both on screen and on the posters. Thanks to more affordable four-color printing, having a mono or two-tone one-sheet became an artistic decision, not a budgetary necessity. The rise of the color photo-based poster began in earnest, with sexploitation producers often simply aping the look of the top-shelf magazine pictorials their stars also appeared in. Marie Ekorre, star of *The Keyhole* (aka *Nøglehullet,* 1974), was indeed a *Penthouse* centerfold as the poster boasts, though she was actually from Sweden. Her surname is the Swedish for "squirrel." Feel free to insert your own joke here.

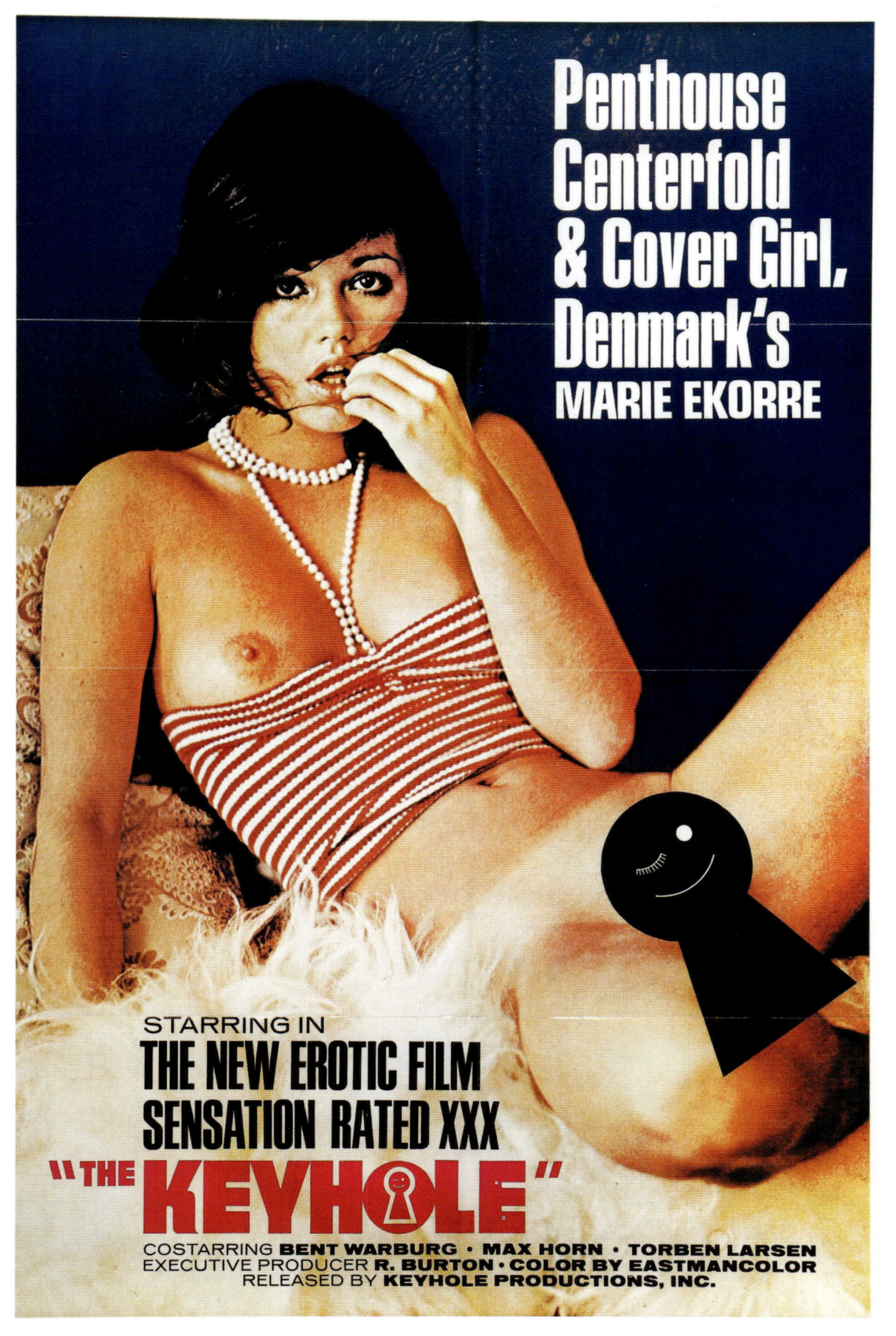
Penthouse
Centerfold
& Cover Girl,
Denmark's
MARIE EKORRE
STARRING IN
THE NEW EROTIC FILM
SENSATION RATED XXX
"THE KEYHOLE"
COSTARRING BENT WARBURG · MAX HORN · TORBEN LARSEN
EXECUTIVE PRODUCER R. BURTON · COLOR BY EASTMANCOLOR
RELEASED BY KEYHOLE PRODUCTIONS, INC.

OUT-BLAZING BLAZING SADDLES

THIS YEAR'S MAD, MAD WORLD OF
SHEER LUNACY AND COMPLETE INSANITY

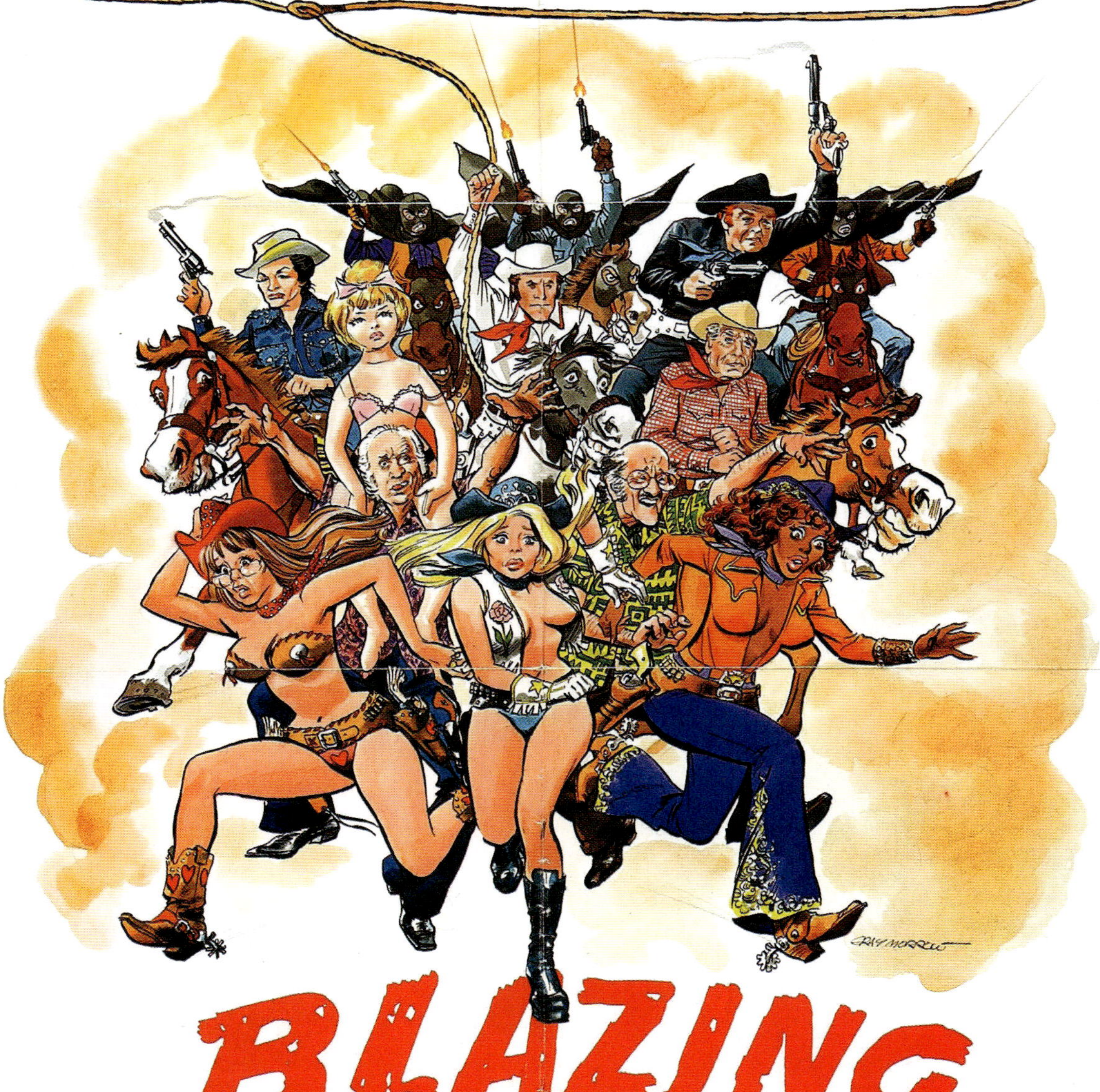

BLAZING
STEWARDESSES

a SAMUEL M. SHERMAN production

Starring YVONNE DE CARLO · BOB LIVINGSTON · DON 'RED' BARRY

Geoffrey Land & STEWARDESSES Connie Hoffman · Regina Carrol · T. A. King

Special Guest Stars THE RITZ BROS.—HARRY & JIMMY RITZ

Directed by
AL ADAMSON
IN METROCOLOR

Exec. Producer
DAN Q. KENNIS

Assoc. Producer
IRWIN PIZOR

R RESTRICTED

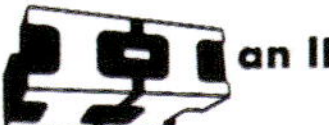

an INDEPENDENT-INTERNATIONAL Picture

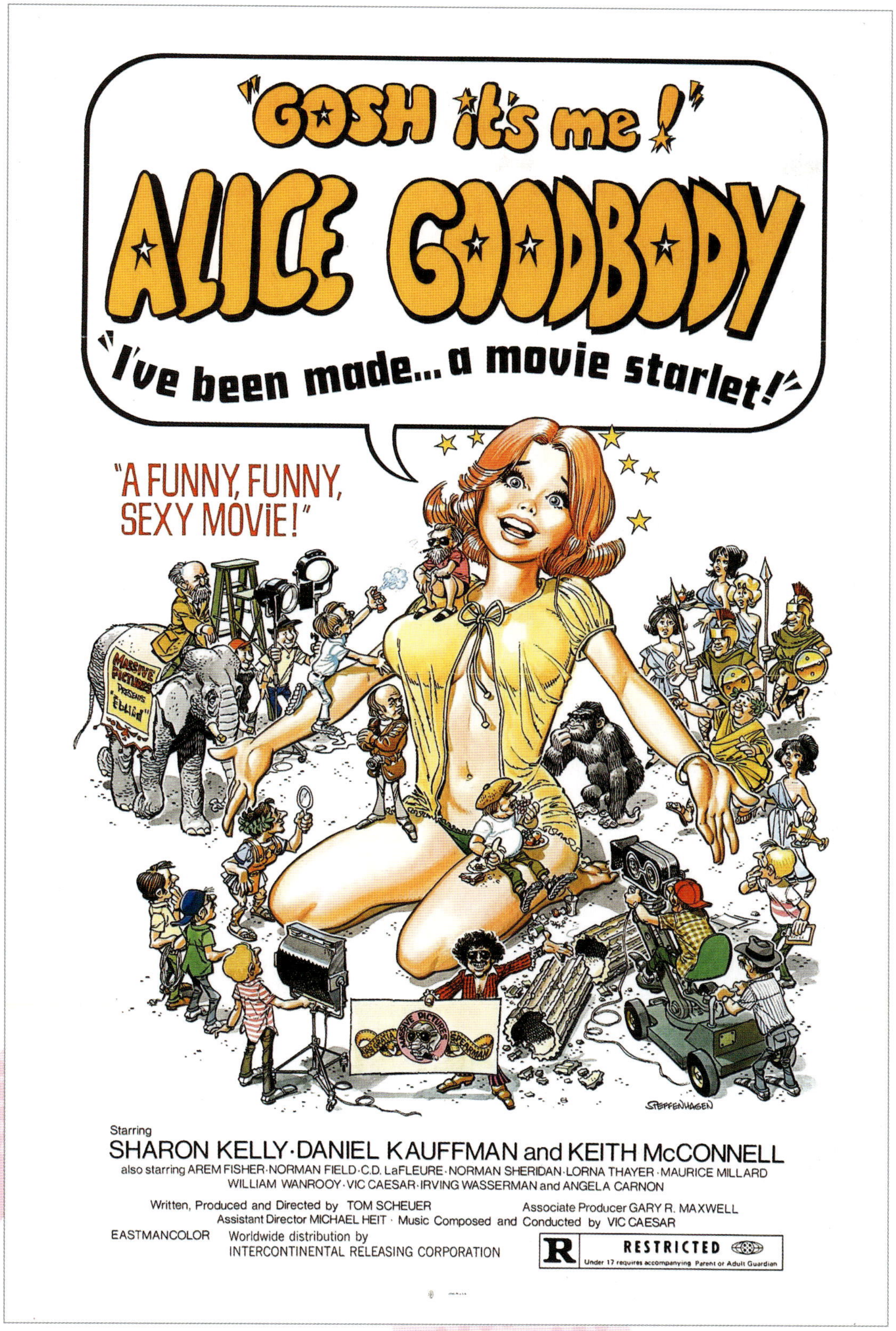

"GOSH it's me!"
ALICE GOODBODY
"I've been made... a movie starlet!"

"A FUNNY, FUNNY, SEXY MOVIE!"

Starring
SHARON KELLY · DANIEL KAUFFMAN and KEITH McCONNELL
also starring AREM FISHER · NORMAN FIELD · C.D. LaFLEURE · NORMAN SHERIDAN · LORNA THAYER · MAURICE MILLARD
WILLIAM WANROOY · VIC CAESAR · IRVING WASSERMAN and ANGELA CARNON
Written, Produced and Directed by TOM SCHEUER
Associate Producer GARY R. MAXWELL
Assistant Director MICHAEL HEIT · Music Composed and Conducted by VIC CAESAR
EASTMANCOLOR
Worldwide distribution by INTERCONTINENTAL RELEASING CORPORATION
R RESTRICTED
Under 17 requires accompanying Parent or Adult Guardian

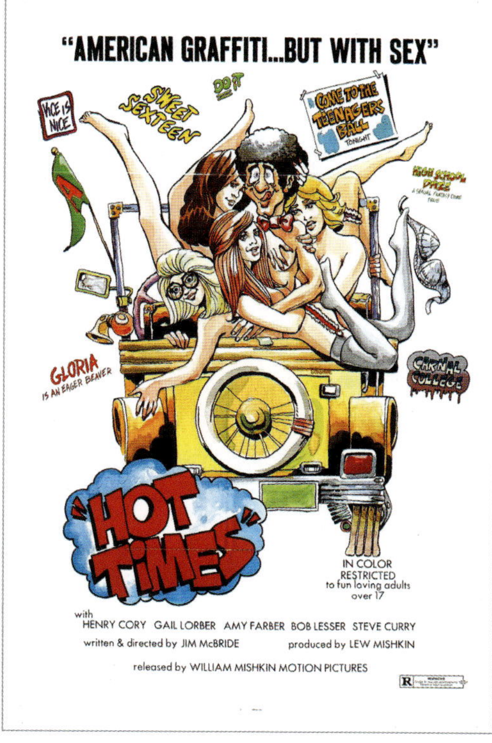

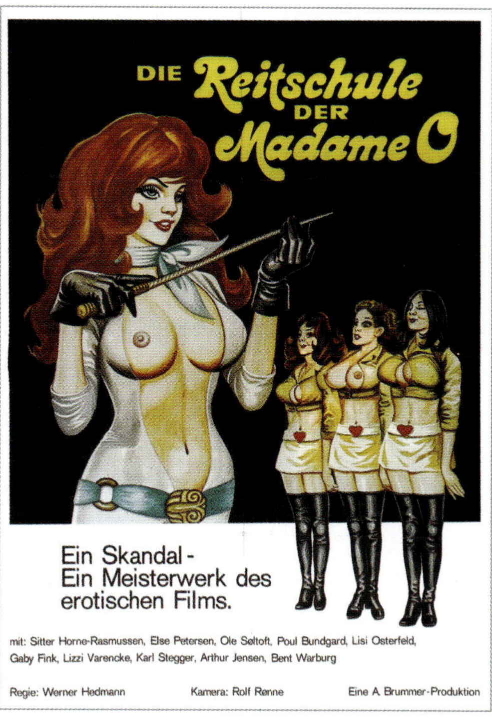

CARTOON STYLE

Why have a cartoon-style poster for a live-action film? Being able to feature unfeasibly large breasts is certainly one advantage, but sometimes the choice is a little more calculated. "*American Graffiti* . . . But with sex" is the first thing you read on the poster for *Hot Times* (1974), and to drive the point home, the unsigned artwork is attempting to ape the style of Mort Drucker's one-sheet for George Lucas's blockbuster from the year before. In addition to the obvious nod to Mel Brooks's 1974 hit *Blazing Saddles*, the poster for *Blazing Stewardesses* (1975) also references *It's a Mad, Mad, Mad, Mad World* (1963), with art by Gray Morrow that recalls the similarly chaotic crowd drawn by Jack Davis on the one-sheet for that '60s comedy epic. Davis, like Mort Drucker, was a big-name caricaturist, best known for his contributions to *Mad* magazine; prolific comicbook artist Morrow was probably more affordable.

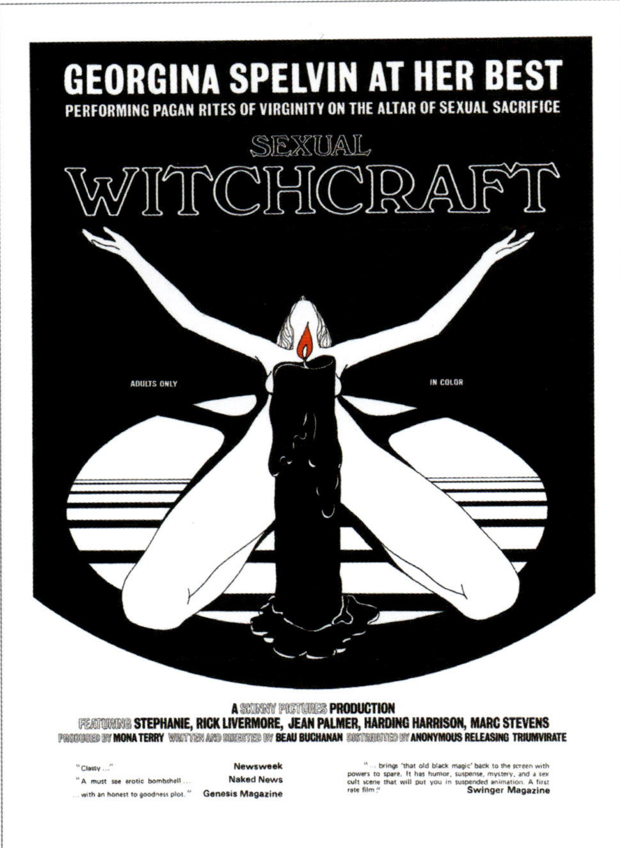

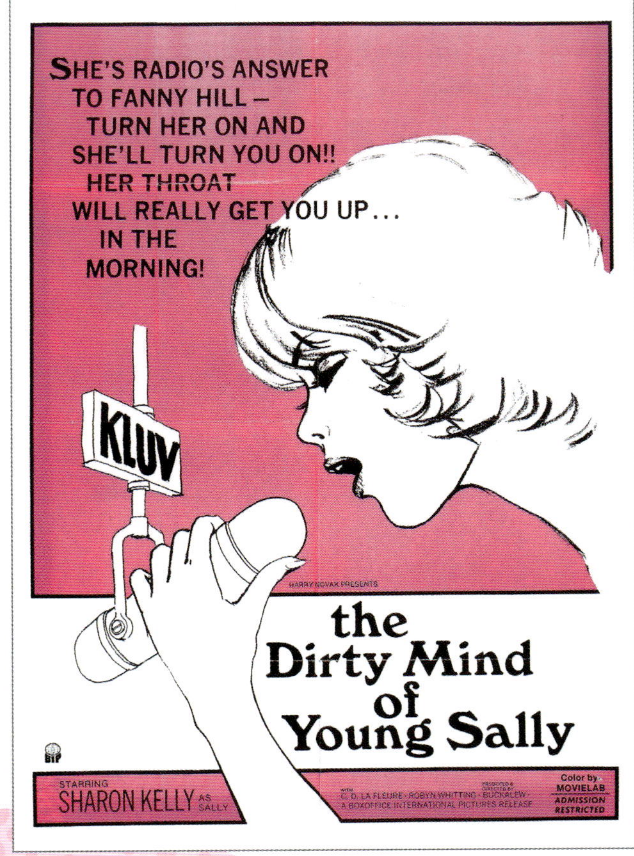

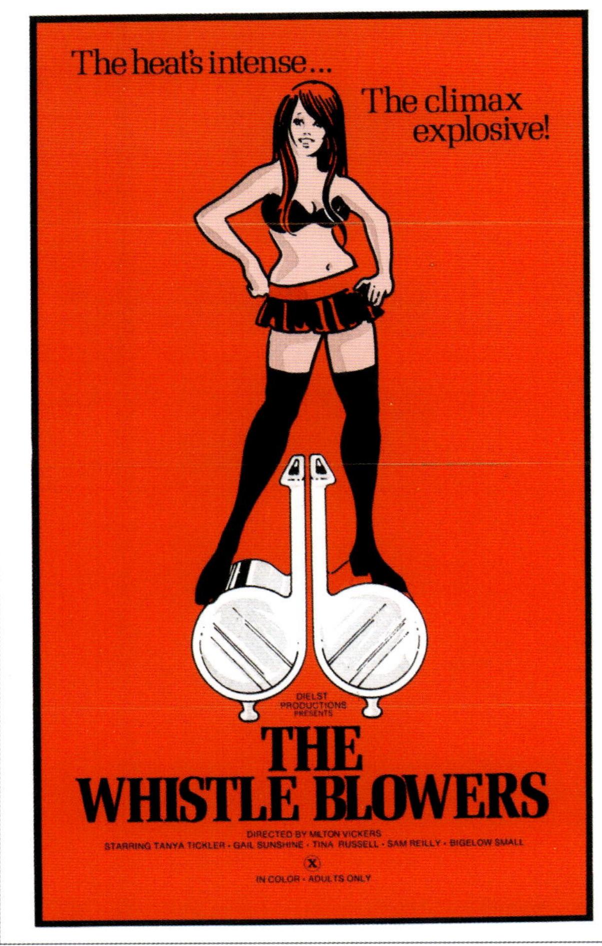

BY DESIGN

The "can you see what we did there?" school of poster design should never be underestimated. Sure, it's a bit obvious, but sometimes that is just what's needed to connect with a potential viewer. Take the one-sheet for *The Dirty Mind of Young Sally* (1973). As online reviewer The Primal Root (not his real name) has noted, it features "the illustrated image of a woman fondling a radio mic as if it were an engorged wang-doodle she's about to show her uvula off to. Proving not only does young Sally have a dirty mind, the target audience has one as well." *Exactly*. The poster for the same year's *Sexual Witchcraft* offers a different wang-doodle substitute, and promises *Devil in Miss Jones* star "Georgina Spelvin at her best," but on-screen, the sex scenes were brief. As the blogger Bloody Pit of Horror (also not his real name) pointed out, "Perhaps that's why *Newsweek* called it 'classy,' but for a typical porn viewer, this is going to be a disappointment." While the poster for yet another 1973 movie, *The Whistle Blowers*, won't win any awards, the design for the otherwise-forgotten Swedish Zola "adaptation" *Nana* (1970) is rather artful, and has aged remarkably well for a poster approaching its half century.

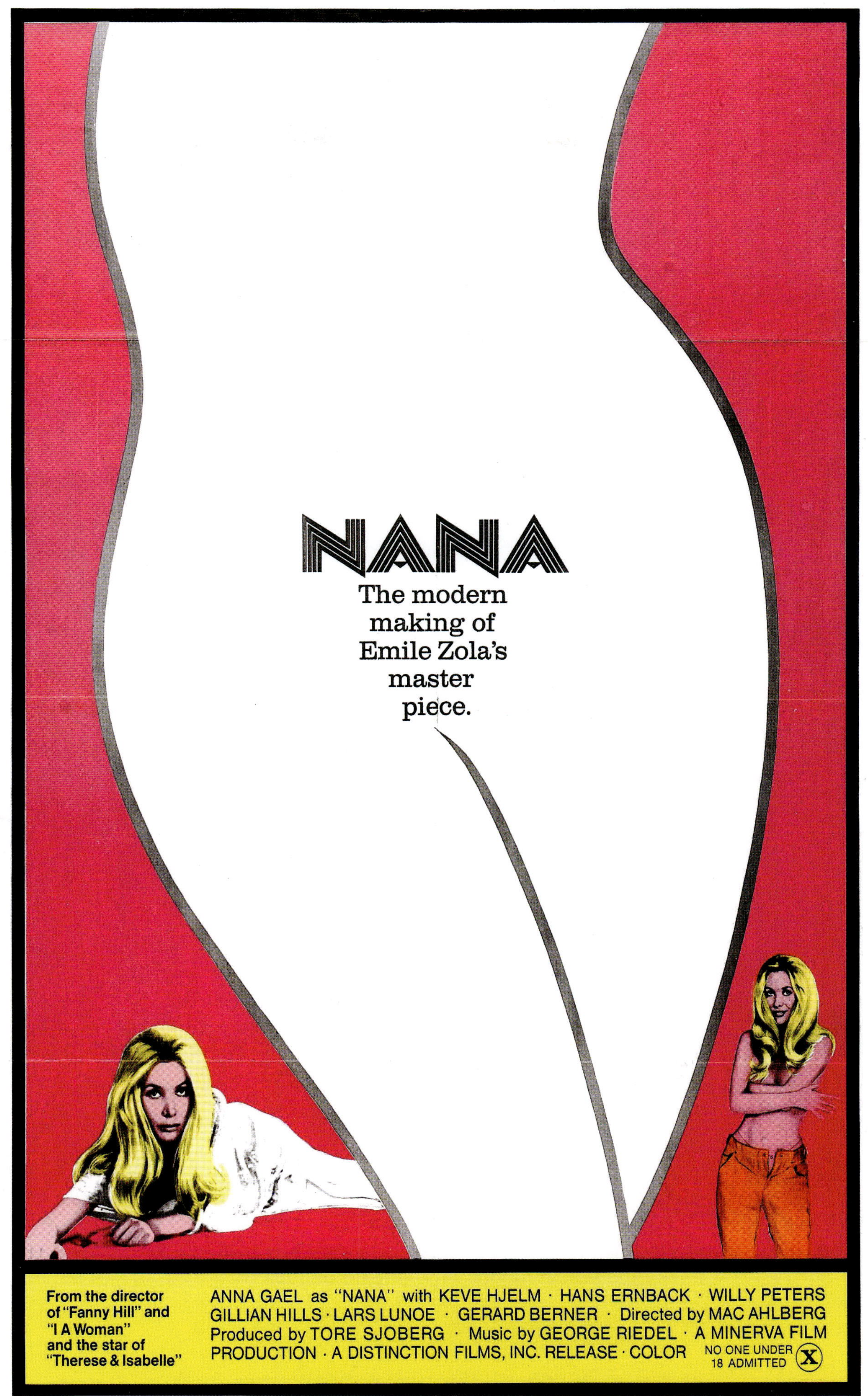
NANA
The modern making of Emile Zola's master piece.
From the director of "Fanny Hill" and "I A Woman" and the star of "Therese & Isabelle"
ANNA GAEL as "NANA" with KEVE HJELM · HANS ERNBACK · WILLY PETERS
GILLIAN HILLS · LARS LUNOE · GERARD BERNER · Directed by MAC AHLBERG
Produced by TORE SJOBERG · Music by GEORGE RIEDEL · A MINERVA FILM
PRODUCTION · A DISTINCTION FILMS, INC. RELEASE · COLOR
NO ONE UNDER 18 ADMITTED
X

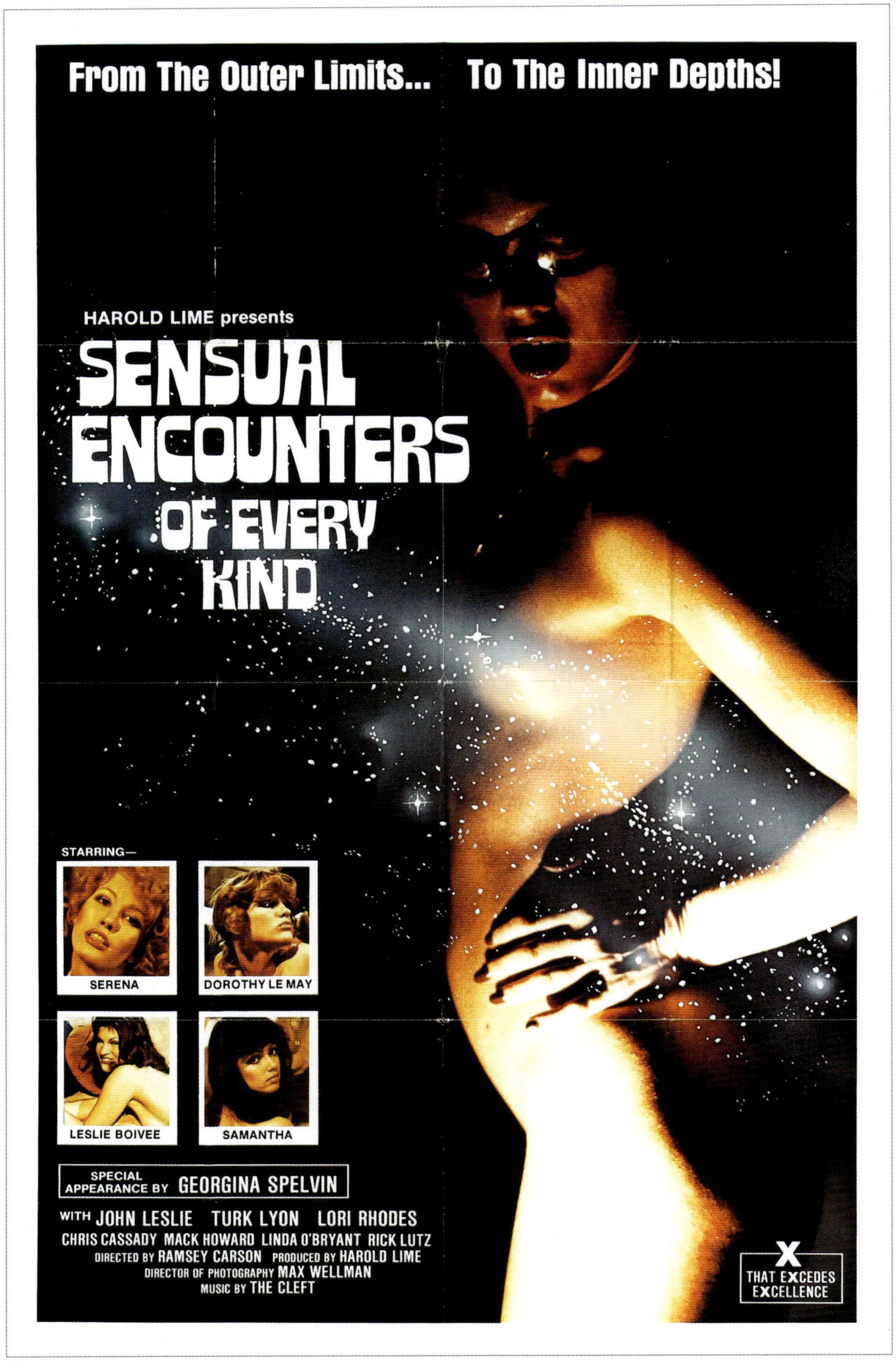

From The Outer Limits... To The Inner Depths!

HAROLD LIME presents

SENSUAL ENCOUNTERS OF EVERY KIND

STARRING—

SERENA

DOROTHY LE MAY

LESLIE BOIVEE

SAMANTHA

SPECIAL APPEARANCE BY GEORGINA SPELVIN

WITH JOHN LESLIE TURK LYON LORI RHODES
CHRIS CASSADY MACK HOWARD LINDA O'BRYANT RICK LUTZ
DIRECTED BY RAMSEY CARSON PRODUCED BY HAROLD LIME
DIRECTOR OF PHOTOGRAPHY MAX WELLMAN
MUSIC BY THE CLEFT

X
THAT EXCEDES EXCELLENCE

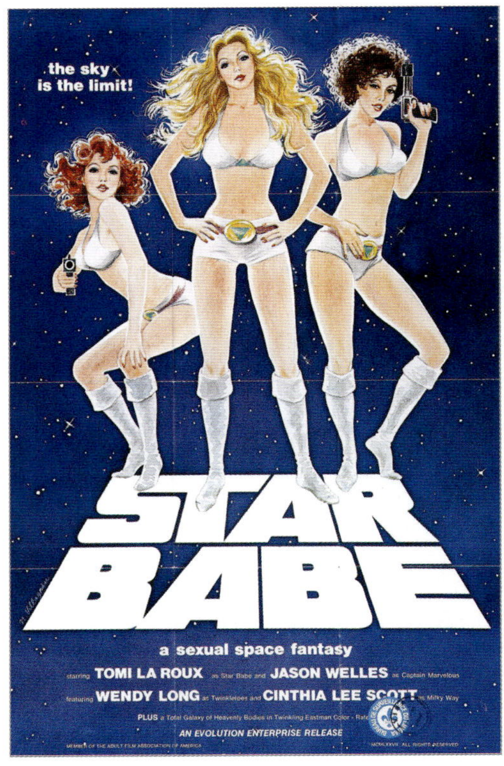

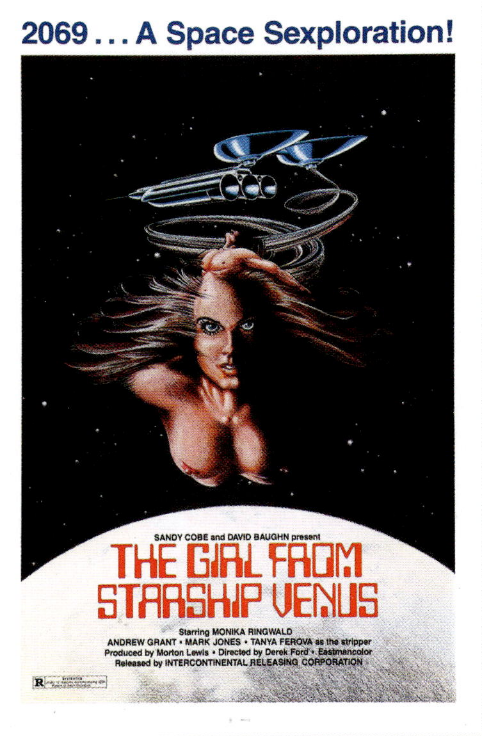

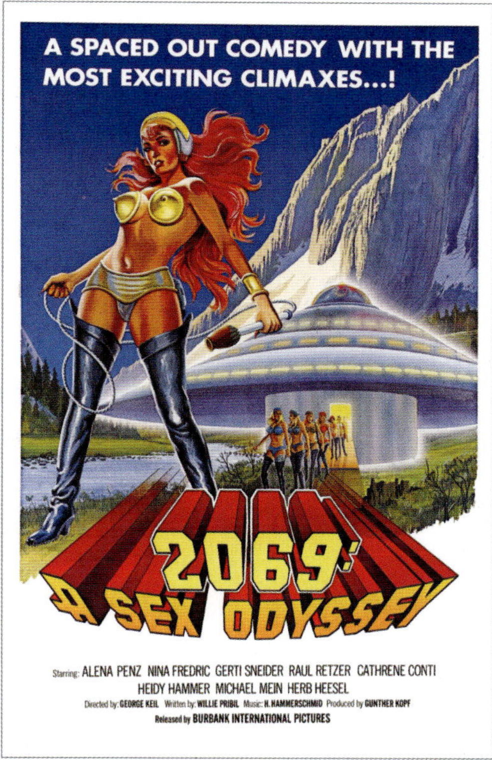

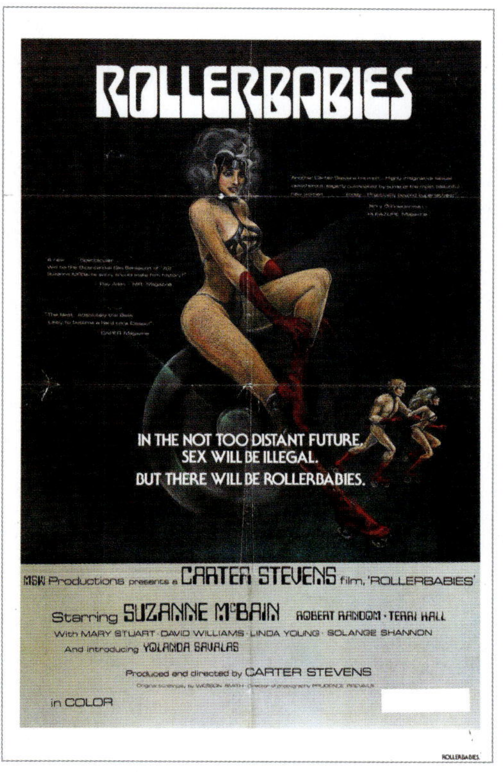

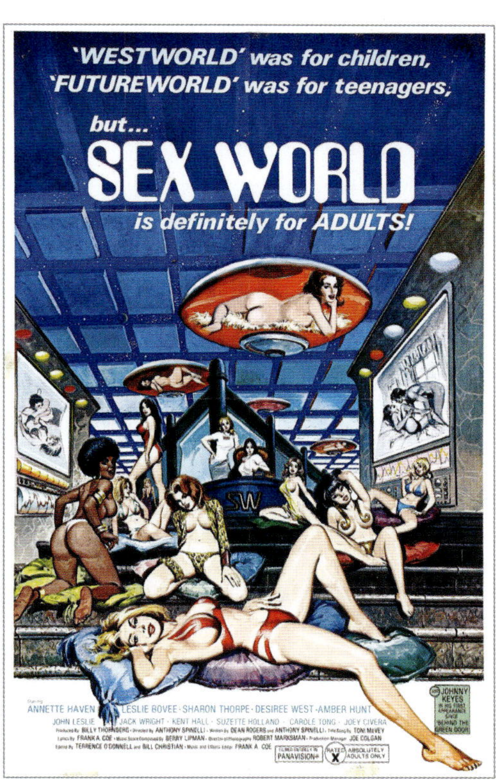

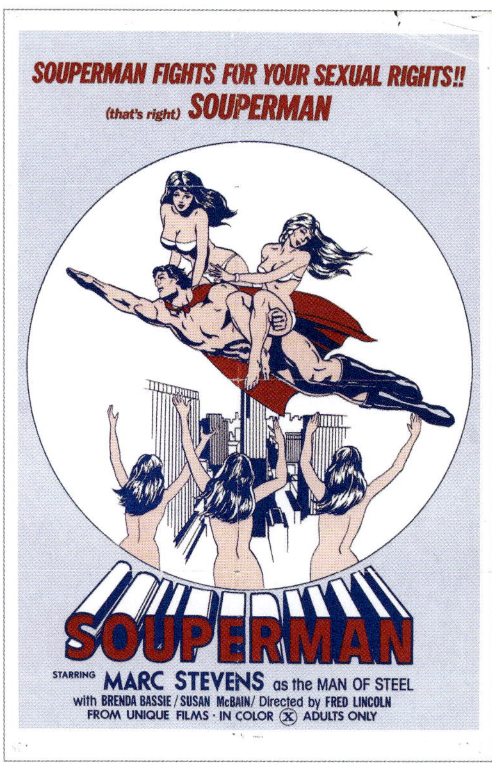

LOOKS FAMILIAR

It is a truth universally acknowledged, that a Hollywood producer in possession of a big hit movie will not be in want of a porn-a-like parody of same. An XXX "homage" will always pop up, sometimes even before the mainstream version appears: for example, Marc Stevens hit the screen as *Souperman* (aka Clark Bent) in 1976, a couple of years before Christopher Reeve flew in. The sci-fi crazes post *2001: A Space Odyssey* and especially *Star Wars*/*Close Encounters of the Third Kind* proved a particularly rich seam of inspiration, as seen here. The pornographers are still at it of course, with more recent hits including *Shaving Ryan's Privates* and the posh period piece *Down On Abby*.

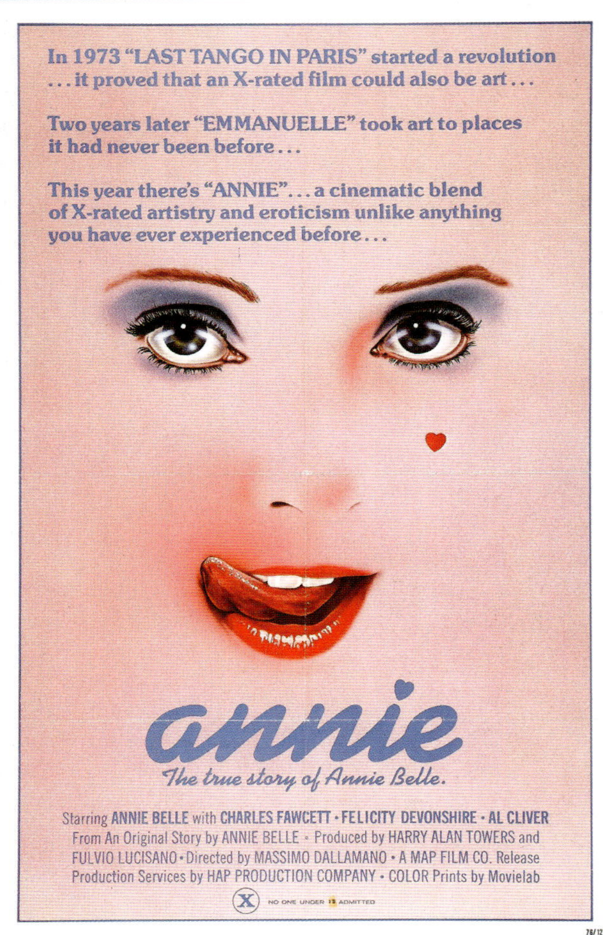

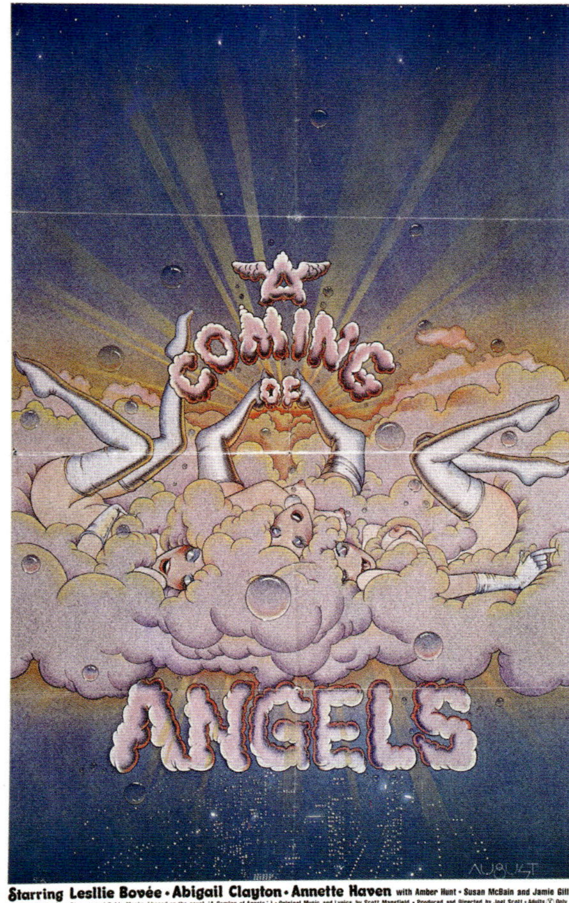

HIGH ART

Porn movies don't tend to merit printed posters any more. Indeed, with online streaming now the preferred delivery method, it's rare for them to actually receive a physical release in a box with a printed cover. Even if a "cover" or "key art" is designed for online use, it will invariably be photographic. Why commission an artist to paint a picture when you can just show photos? (Especially if you can heavily retouch those photos in a computer to ensure the desired effect.) Back in the '70s, there was still a demand for the idealized image that an artist with a working knowledge of anatomy could produce with a brush. Among the few artists of such posters who signed their work and can be traced today, Elaine Gignilliat stands tall. Her accomplished oil painting of Annette Haven for *Reflections* (1977) is a bit of a departure though—Gignilliat is best known for her rather more chaste romance novel covers.

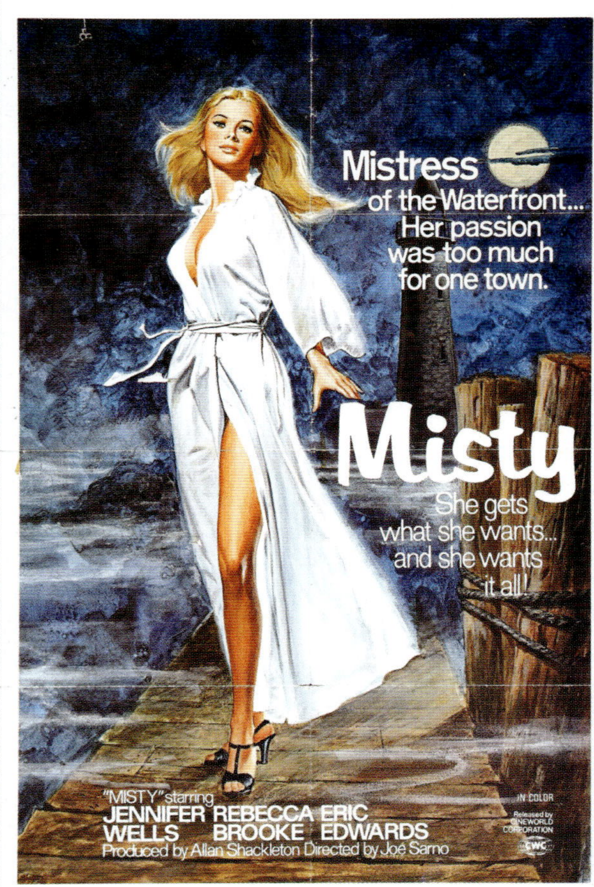

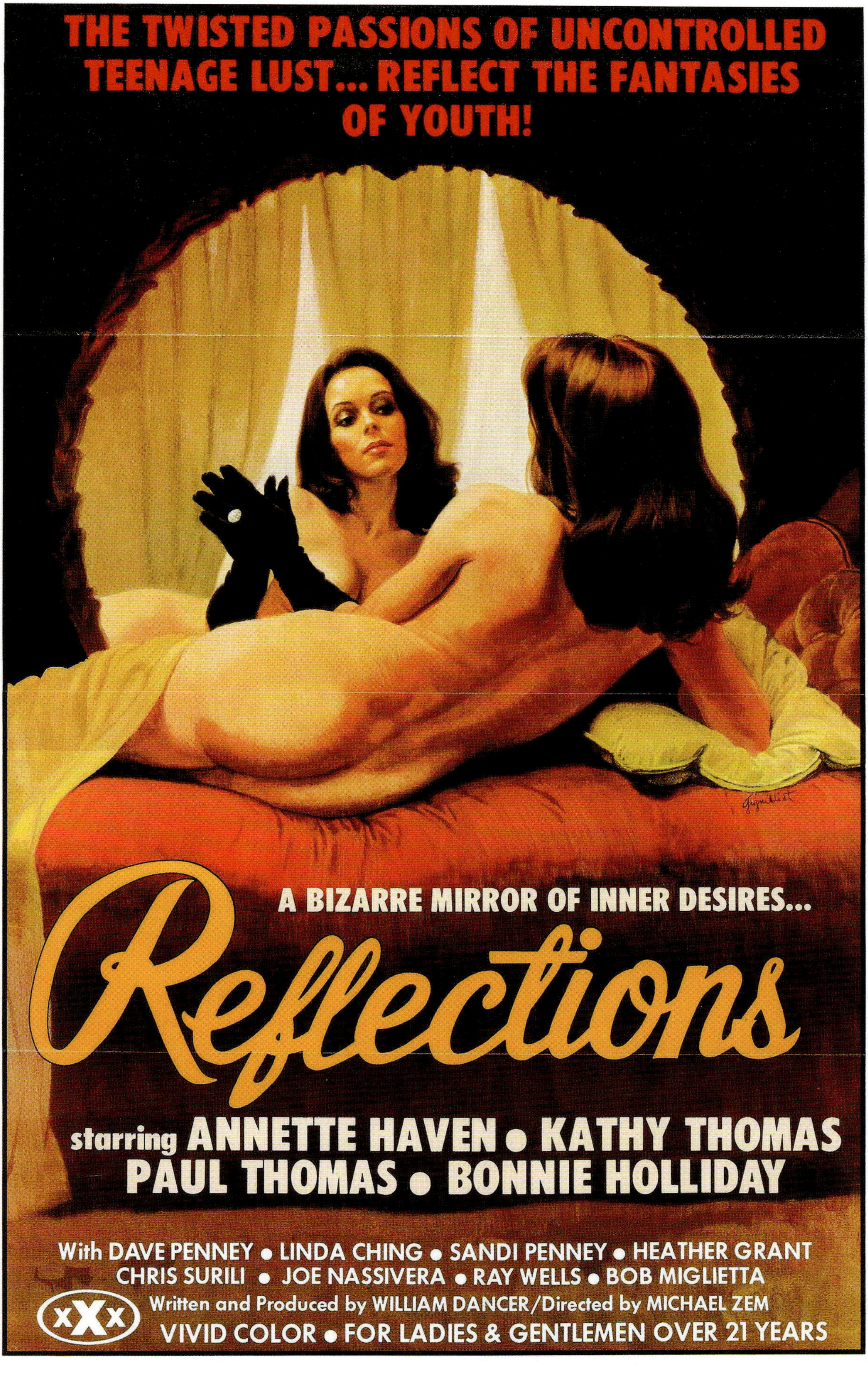

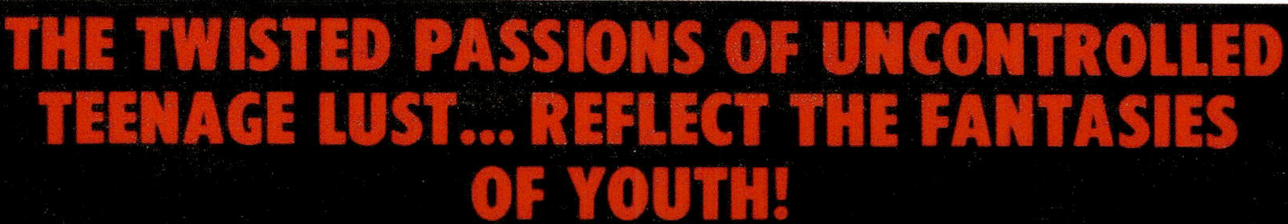

A BIZARRE MIRROR OF INNER DESIRES...

Reflections

starring **ANNETTE HAVEN • KATHY THOMAS**
PAUL THOMAS • BONNIE HOLLIDAY

With DAVE PENNEY • LINDA CHING • SANDI PENNEY • HEATHER GRANT
CHRIS SURILI • JOE NASSIVERA • RAY WELLS • BOB MIGLIETTA

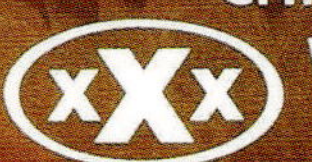

Written and Produced by WILLIAM DANCER/Directed by MICHAEL ZEM
VIVID COLOR • FOR LADIES & GENTLEMEN OVER 21 YEARS

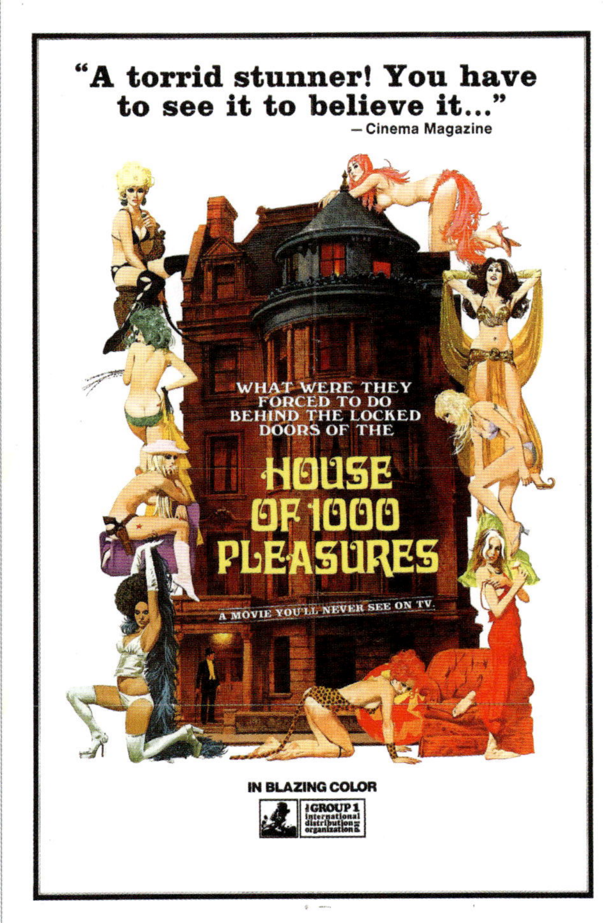

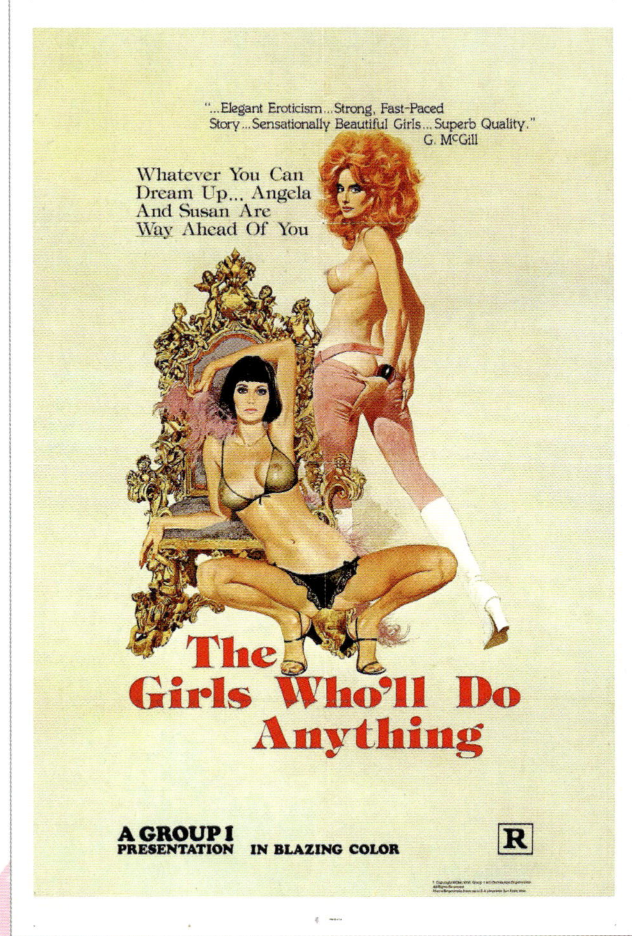

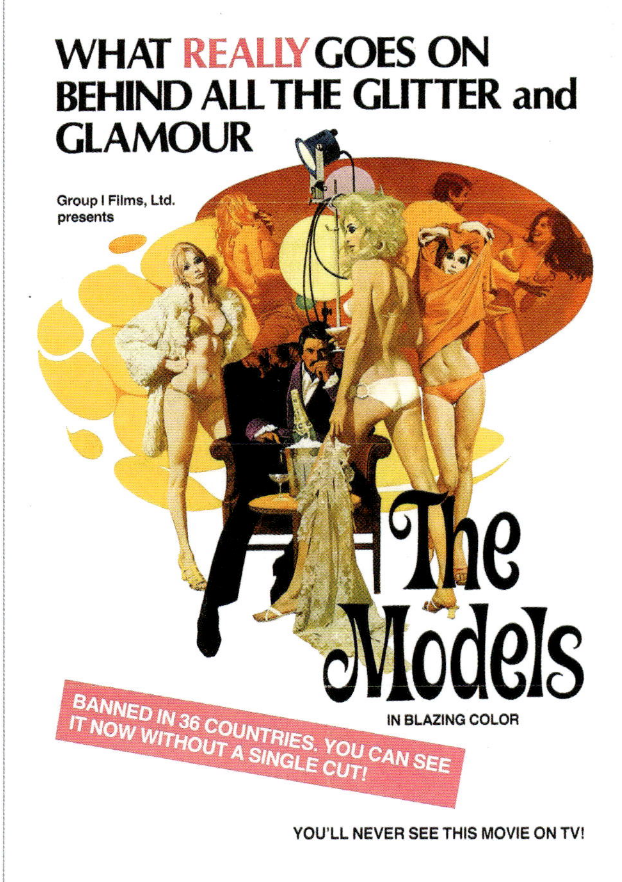

THE ART OF ROBERT McGINNIS

You may not know his name, but you know his art. Robert McGinnis's film poster work includes *Breakfast at Tiffany's*, *Barbarella*, and all the James Bond movies from *Thunderball* to *The Man with the Golden Gun*. Add to that over 1,200 paperback covers, and you have a Titan of the medium, one of the true greats, whose mastery of the female form is often imitated, but rarely bettered. It's a surprise then to see him illustrating these mid-'70s US one-sheets for a bunch of now-forgotten softcore flicks, but presumably it was a well-paid gig, and he had a gap in his schedule. Group 1 Distributors were lucky to get him, and the results have his trademark sexy elegance. Still working as he approached his 90s, McGinnis lamented in a 2015 interview that modern film posters "don't have that human warmth, the strengths and the weaknesses of a painter or an artist. I can't knock computer art and the work that they do because it's just so imaginative and wonderful. But that flavor is gone." Sobering words. McGinnis was trying to be polite, but as modern movie poster design moves inexorably toward soulless collages of market research-driven Photoshopped mush, the flavor is, indeed, gone. It is all the more important then to appreciate, and celebrate, the posters that have gone before.

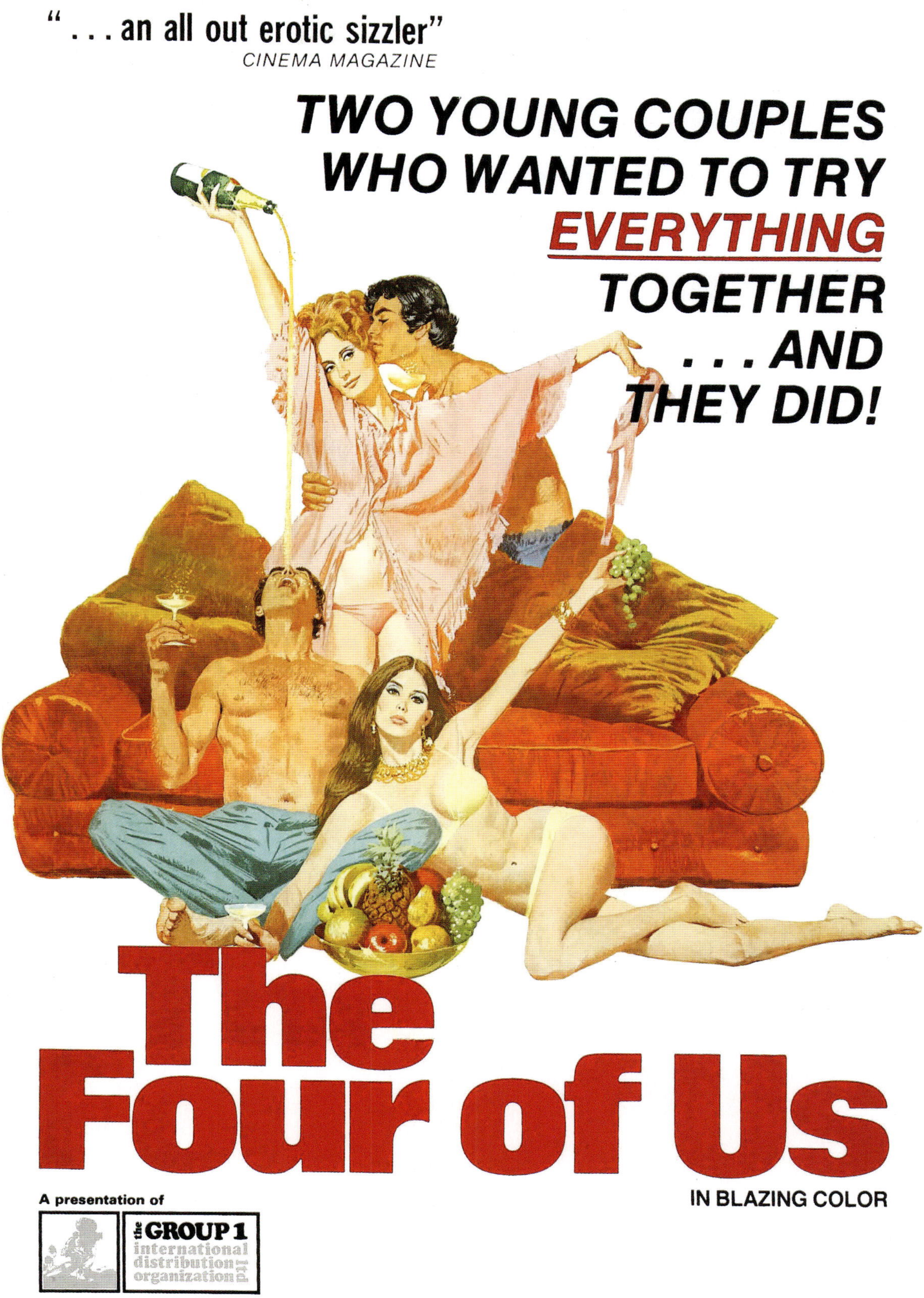

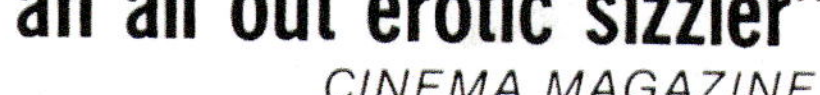

CINEMA MAGAZINE

TWO YOUNG COUPLES WHO WANTED TO TRY EVERYTHING TOGETHER ...AND THEY DID!

The Four of Us

IN BLAZING COLOR

A presentation of

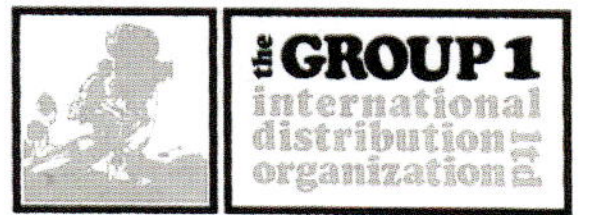

INDEX

CONTRIBUTORS

STEPHEN JONES lives in London, England. He is the winner of three World Fantasy Awards, five Horror Writers Association Bram Stoker Awards, three International Horror Guild Awards, and 21 British Fantasy Awards, as well as being a recipient of the HWA Lifetime Achievement Award and a Hugo Award nominee. A former television producer/director and genre movie publicist and consultant (the first three *Hellraiser* movies, *Nightbreed* etc.), he has written and edited more than 140 books, including *The Art of Horror*, *Fearie Tales: Stories of the Grimm and Gruesome*, *A Book of Horrors*, the *Zombie Apocalypse!* series, and the annual *Best New Horror* series. You can visit his website at *www.stephenjoneseditor.com*

ADAM NEWELL, who curated this book (and wrote the mini features scattered throughout its pages), is a longtime editor and project manager of movie and art-related books. Titles he's helped bring to print over the years include Stephen Jones's *The Art of Horror*, Gallery 1998's *Crazy 4 Cult: Cult Movie Art*, Scott C's *The Great Showdowns*, Olly Moss's *Silhouettes From Popular Culture*, Marcus Hearn's *The Art of Hammer*, and Pete Tombs's *Mondo Macabro: Weird & Wonderful Cinema Around the World*.

KIM NEWMAN is a writer, critic, and broadcaster. His many books include the award-winning series of *Anno Dracula* vampire novels, the BFI Classic volumes on *Doctor Who*, *Cat People* and *Quatermass and the Pit*, the *BFI Companion to Horror* (as editor), *Nightmare Movies: Horror On Screen Since the 1960s*, *Apocalypse Movies: End of the World Cinema*, and *Ghastly Beyond Belief* (written with Neil Gaiman). He is a regular contributor to *Video Watchdog*, and his column "Kim Newman's Video Dungeon" appears in *Empire* magazine. His website is at *www.johnnyalucard.com*

ERIC SCHAEFER is a professor of Visual and Media Arts at Emerson College in Boston. He holds a Ph.D. in Radio–Television–Film from the University of Texas, Austin and is the author of *"Bold! Daring! Shocking! True!": A History of Exploitation Films, 1919-1959* and editor of the collection *Sex Scene: Media and the Sexual Revolution*. He has published and presented widely on historical aspects of adult films ranging from early exploitation movies to hardcore.

SIMON SHERIDAN is a writer, broadcaster, and filmmaker. He has long held an active interest in all aspects of British pop culture (the 1960s and 1970s variety in particular) and his encyclopedic knowledge runs the gamut of "X"-rated cinema right through to modern music and cheerful TV nostalgia. His books include *Come Play with Me: The Life and Films of Mary Millington*, The *A-Z of Classic Children's Television*, *The Complete Kylie*, *The Complete ABBA*, and *Keeping the British End Up*: *Four Decades of Saucy Cinema*. On British television Simon has appeared in a variety of documentaries, and his debut movie, *Respectable—The Mary Millington Story*, which he wrote, produced, and directed, was released to UK cinemas in April 2016. His website is at *www.simonsheridan.com*

PETE TOMBS was born in London and grew up watching Hammer films before discovering Paul Naschy and Euro horror at the long gone Dalston Odeon. Life was never the same again! He is the author of the books *Immoral Tales: Sex and Horror Cinema in Europe 1956-84* (with Cathal Tohill) and *Mondo Macabro: Weird & Wonderful Cinema Around the World*, and runs the Mondo Macabro video label together with Andy Starke. He is a partner in the UK production outfit Rook Films.

VERN writes about movies at *www.outlawvern.com*, with an emphasis on lowbrow action. He is the author of the film criticism books *Seagalogy: A Study of the Ass-Kicking Films of Steven Seagal* and *"Yippee Ki-Yay Moviegoer!"—Writings on Bruce Willis, Badass Cinema and Other Important Topics*, as well as the novel *Niketown*, and the upcoming *Worm On a Hook*. He lives in Seattle.

ACKNOWLEDGMENTS

The Editor would like to thank all the contributors, for their enthusiastic co-operation on this project.
Thanks are also due to Adam Ferguson, Sharon Gosling, Marcus Hearn, Martin Stiff, and especially Mikhail Ilyin.

SOURCES

Even with 1,000 posters, this book can only begin to illuminate the nether regions of exploitation cinema. There's so much more to discover, and the sources below, all of which proved very useful in compiling the present volume, will help continue the journey. While specialist DVD/Blu-ray labels like Something Weird and Mondo Macabro have impressive catalogs to explore, it's also worth pointing out that quite a few of the films featured in this book have fallen into the public domain, and can be found and watched online, entirely legally.

BOOKS:

Armstrong, Vic, with Robert Sellers, *The True Adventures of the World's Greatest Stuntman*. Titan Books, 2012

Cline, John, and Robert E. Weiner (Eds), *From the Arthouse to the Grindhouse: Highbrow and Lowbrow Transgression in Cinema's First Century*. Scarecrow Press, 2010

Doherty, Thomas, *Teenagers and Teenpics: The Juvenilization of American Movies in the 1950s*. Temple University Press, 2002

Greene, Doyle, *Mexploitation Cinema: A Critical History of Mexican Vampire, Wrestler, Ape-man and Similar Films, 1957-1977*. McFarland, 2005

Lewis, John E., and Tony Michels, *Hollywood V. Hard Core: How the Struggle Over Censorship Created the Modern Film Industry*. New York University Press, 2002

McDonough, Jimmy, *Big Bosoms and Square Jaws: The Biography of Russ Meyer, King of the Sex Film*. Jonathan Cape, 2005

Marshall, John, *Buy Me Quick! The Films of Harry Novak*. Forthcoming.

O'Dowd, John, *Kiss Tomorrow Goodbye, The Barbara Payton Story*. BearManor Media, 2006

Peary, Gerald, *Quentin Tarantino Interviews*. University Press of Mississippi, 2013

Phillips, Gene D., *Godfather: The Intimate Francis Ford Coppola*. The University Press of Kentucky, 2013

Polito, Robert, *Hollywood & God*. University of Chicago Press, 2009

Rhodes, Gary D. (Ed), *Horror at the Drive-In: Essays in Popular Americana*. McFarland, 2008

Schaefer, Eric, *"Bold! Daring! Shocking! True!": A History of Exploitation Films, 1919-1959*. Duke University Press, 1999

Tohill, Cathal and Pete Tombs, *Immoral Tales: Sex and Horror Cinema in Europe 1956-84*. Titan Books, 1995

Tombs, Pete, *Mondo Macabro: Weird and Wonderful Cinema Around the World*. Titan Books, 1997

Von Doviak, Scott, *Hick Flicks: The Rise and Fall of Redneck Cinema*. McFarland, 2004

Weaver, Tom, *Interviews with B Science Fiction and Horror Movie Makers*. McFarland, 2006

NEWSPAPERS AND MAGAZINES:

Film Comment (July/August 1980: Russ Meyer interview by Ed Lowry and Louis Black

Providence Evening Bulletin (29 October, 1971: Henry Silva interview by Jack Major)

Motion Picture Magazine (1926: Elmer Clifton interview)

The New York Times (various reviews; 2 May, 2010 Joe Sarno obit. by William Grimes)

Rolling Stone (August, 1986: Jack Nicholson interview by Fred Schruers)

Spin (May 1998: Doris Wishman interview by Joy Williams)

The Telegraph (4 August, 2013: Christopher Lee interview by Tim Walker)

Time (17 May, 2010 obit. of Joseph W. Sarno by Richard Corliss; 7 August 2010 Isabel Sarli article by Richard Corliss)

Vanity Fair (October, 1919: "The Ex-Vampire" by Theda Bara)

FILMS:

A Hard Look (2000). Documentary about the Emmanuelle movies, and indeed the Emanuelle movies.

Herschell Gordon Lewis: The Godfather of Gore (2010)

WEBSITES:

1000misspenthours.com
Alienseries.wordpress.com
Antoniomargheriti.com
Ascenicwedding.com
Avclub.com
Blaxploitationpride.org
Boopedia.com
Britmovie.co.uk
Cinematerial.com
Dangerousminds.net
Dvddrive-in.com
Dvdverdict.com
Filmmakermagazine.com
Herschellgordonlewis.com
Horrorcultfilms.co.uk
IMDB.com
Io9.gizmodo.com
Junglefrolics.blogspot.co.uk
learnaboutmovieposters.com
Major-smolinski.com
Mondomacabrodvd.com
Montalban-art.com
Popmatters.com
Pulpinternational.com
Retrocrush.com
Rogerebert.com
Santostreet.com
Selvedgeyard.com
Sensesofcinema.com
Slantmagazine.com
Somethingweird.com
Stofilbloggen.wordpress.com
Techinasia.com
Thebloodypitofhorror.blogspot.co.uk
The-unknown-movies.com
Trashcinemacollective.com
Tripwiremagazine.co.uk
Univers-mac.blogspot.com.es
Variety.com
Videowatchdog.com
Wipfilms.net
Wrongsideoftheart.com
Youtube.com

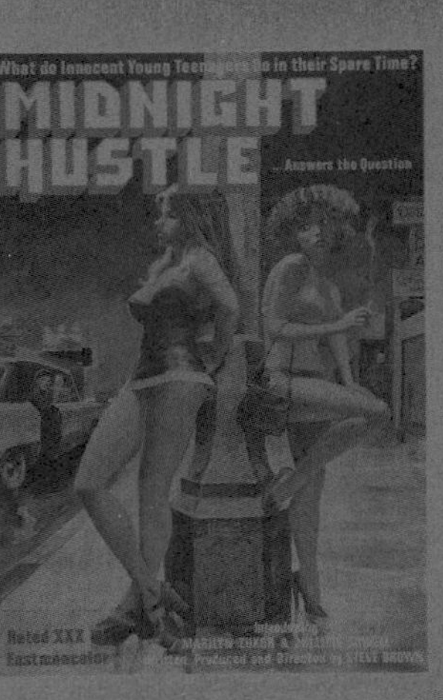
What do Innocent Young Teenagers do in their Spare Time?
MIDNIGHT HUSTLE
...Answers the Question

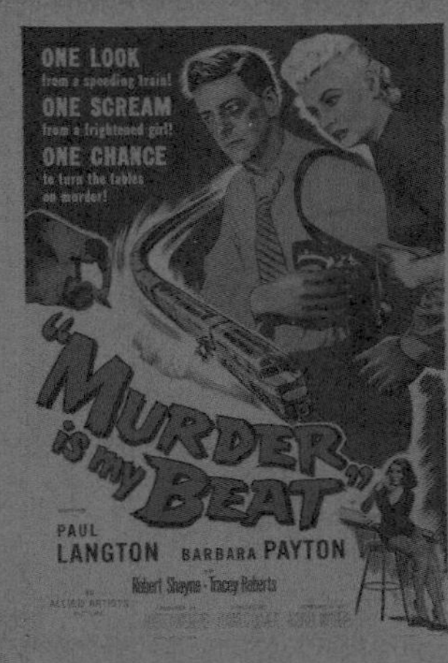
ONE LOOK
from a speeding train!
ONE SCREAM
from a frightened girl?
ONE CHANCE
to turn the tables on murder!
"MURDER is my BEAT"
PAUL LANGTON BARBARA PAYTON
Robert Shayne · Tracey Roberts

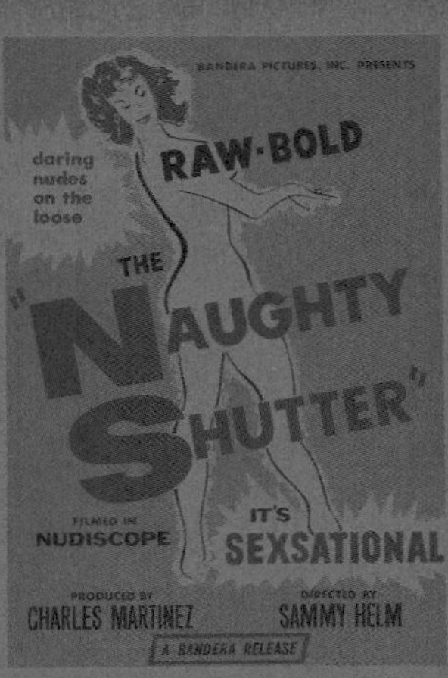
BANDERA PICTURES, INC. PRESENTS
daring nudes on the loose
RAW·BOLD
THE "NAUGHTY SHUTTER"
FILMED IN NUDISCOPE
IT'S SEXSATIONAL
PRODUCED BY CHARLES MARTINEZ
DIRECTED BY SAMMY HELM
A BANDERA RELEASE

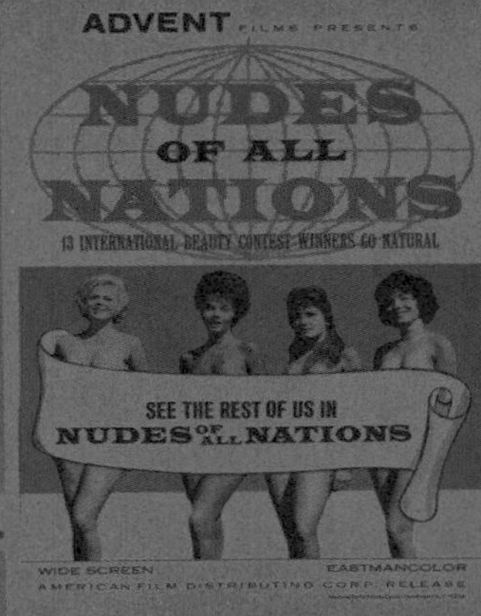
ADVENT FILMS PRESENTS
NUDES OF ALL NATIONS
SEE THE REST OF US IN
NUDES OF ALL NATIONS
WIDE SCREEN
EASTMANCOLOR

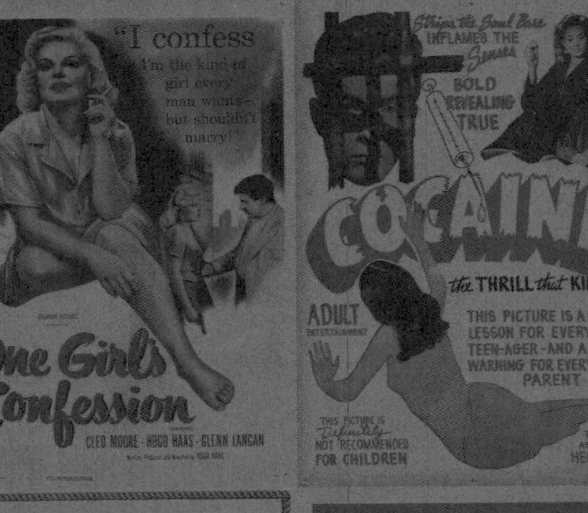
"I confess I'm the kind of girl every man wants—but shouldn't marry!"
One Girl's Confession
CLEO MOORE · HUGO HAAS · GLENN LANGAN
BOLD
REVEALING
TRUE
COCAINE
the THRILL that KIL
ADULT ENTERTAINMENT
THIS PICTURE IS A LESSON FOR EVERY TEEN-AGER AND A WARNING FOR EVERY PARENT
NOT RECOMMENDED FOR CHILDREN

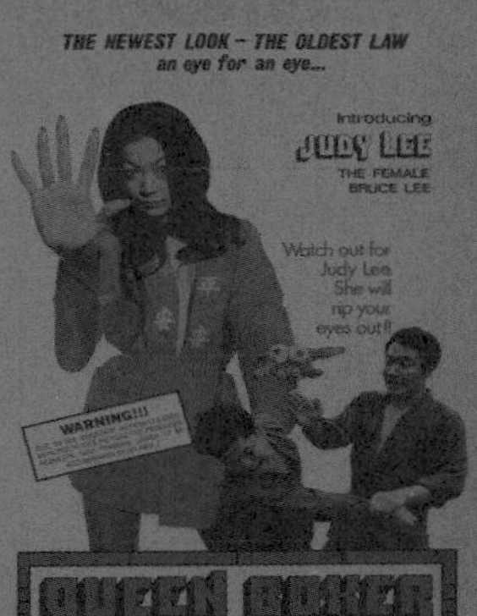
THE NEWEST LOOK – THE OLDEST LAW
an eye for an eye...
Introducing JUDY LEE
THE FEMALE BRUCE LEE
Watch out for Judy Lee
She will rip your eyes out!!
WARNING!!!
QUEEN BOXER

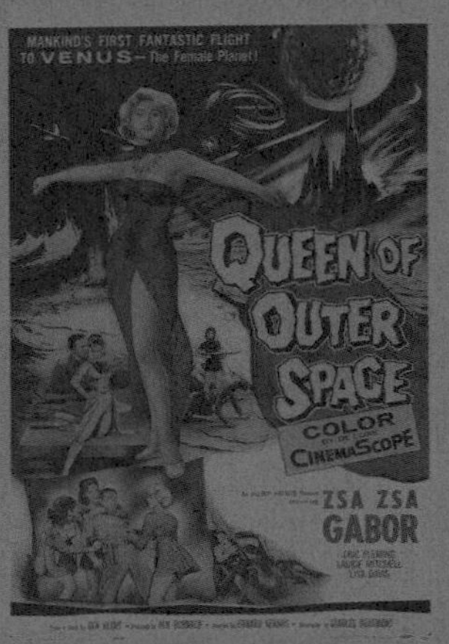
MANKIND'S FIRST FANTASTIC FLIGHT TO VENUS – The Female Planet!
QUEEN OF OUTER SPACE
COLOR
CINEMASCOPE
ZSA ZSA GABOR

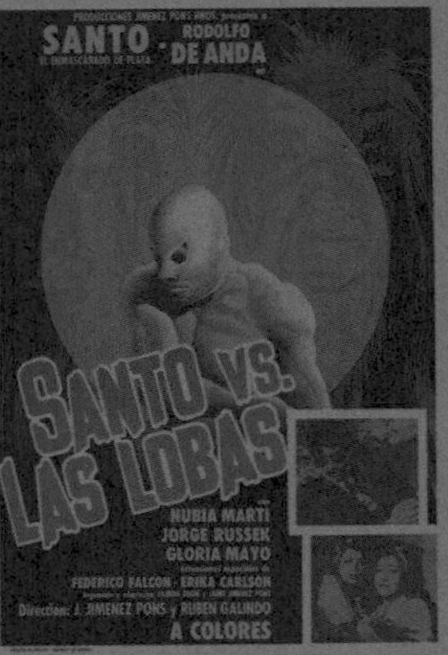
SANTO
RODOLFO DE ANDA
SANTO VS. LAS LOBAS
NUBIA MARTI
JORGE RUSSEK
GLORIA MAYO
FEDERICO FALCON · ERIKA CARLSON
A COLORES

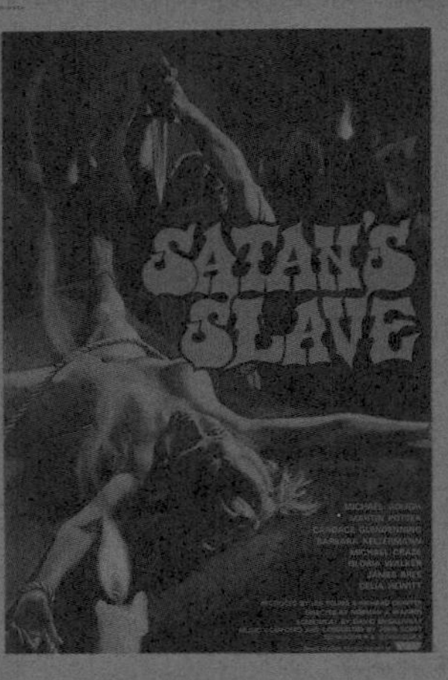
SATAN'S SLAVE

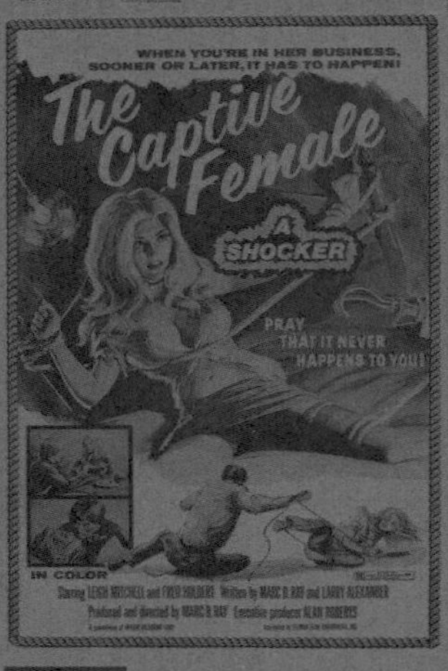
WHEN YOU'RE IN HER BUSINESS, SOONER OR LATER, IT HAS TO HAPPEN!
The Captive Female
A SHOCKER
PRAY THAT IT NEVER HAPPENS TO YOU!
IN COLOR

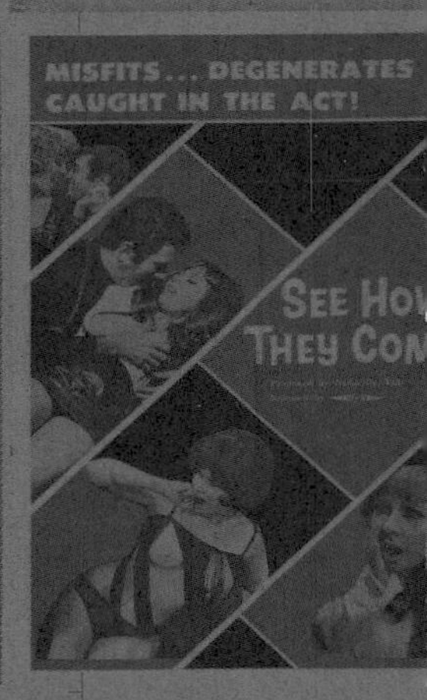
MISFITS ... DEGENERATES
CAUGHT IN THE ACT!
SEE HOW
THEY COM

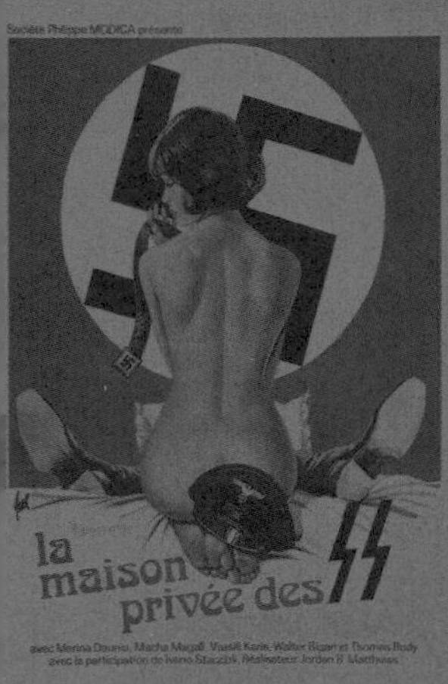
la maison privée des SS

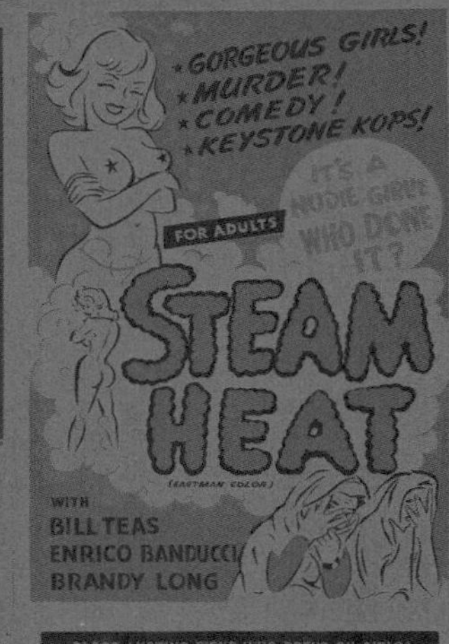
★GORGEOUS GIRLS!
★MURDER!
★COMEDY!
★KEYSTONE KOPS!
IT'S A NUDIE-GIRLIE WHO DONE IT?
FOR ADULTS
STEAM HEAT
WITH
BILL TEAS
ENRICO BANDUCCI
BRANDY LONG

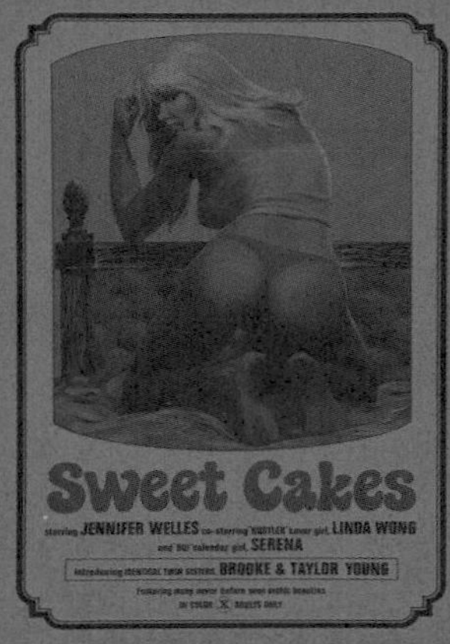
Sweet Cakes
JENNIFER WELLES
LINDA WONG
SERENA
BROOKE & TAYLOR YOUNG

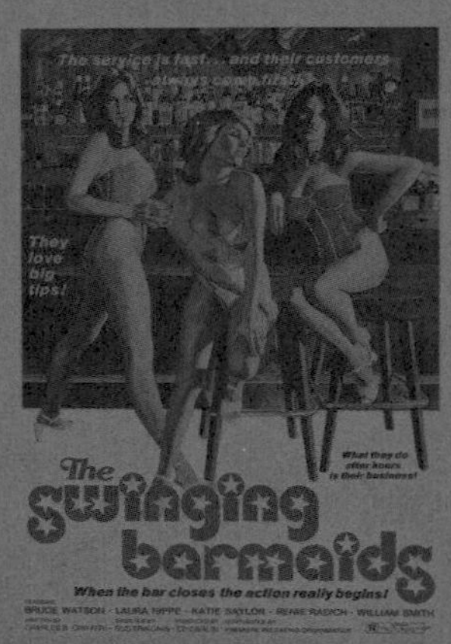
They love big tips!
The swinging barmaids
When the bar closes the action really begins!

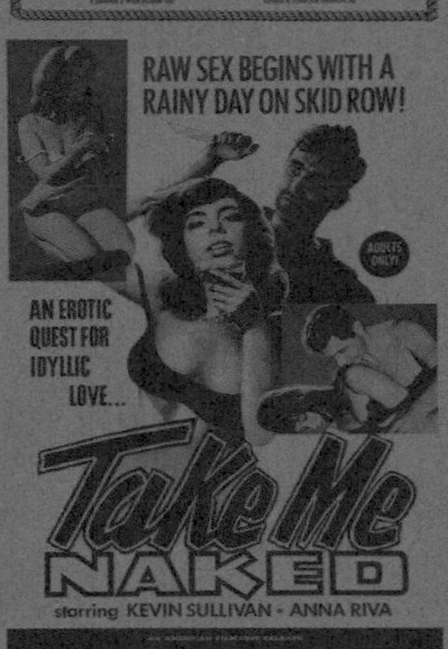
RAW SEX BEGINS WITH A RAINY DAY ON SKID ROW!
AN EROTIC QUEST FOR IDYLLIC LOVE...
ADULTS ONLY
Take Me NAKED
starring KEVIN SULLIVAN · ANNA RIVA

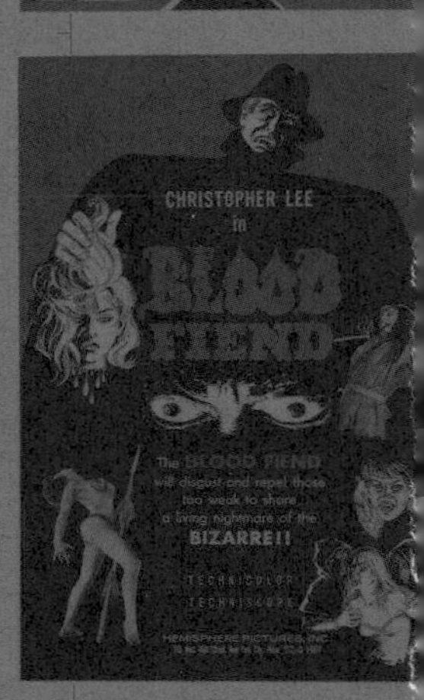
CHRISTOPHER LEE
in
BLOOD FIEND
BIZARRE!!

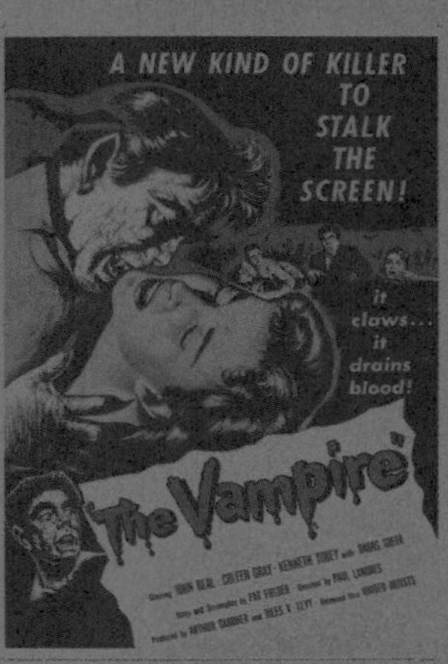
A NEW KIND OF KILLER TO STALK THE SCREEN!
it claws... it drains blood!
"The Vampire"

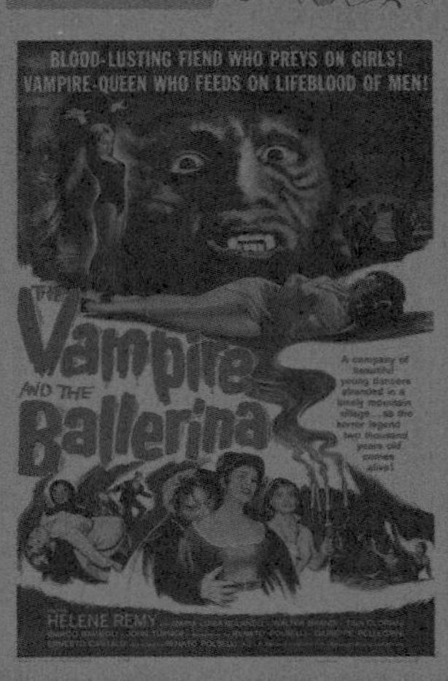
BLOOD-LUSTING FIEND WHO PREYS ON GIRLS!
VAMPIRE-QUEEN WHO FEEDS ON LIFEBLOOD OF MEN!
The Vampire AND THE Ballerina
HELENE REMY

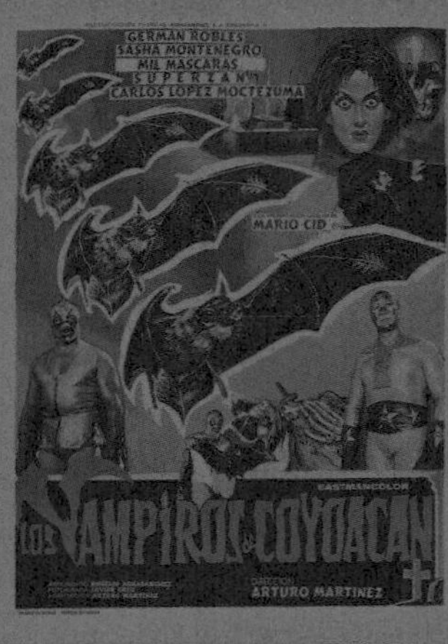
GERMAN ROBLES
SASHA MONTENEGRO
MIL MASCARAS
SUPERZAN
CARLOS LOPEZ MOCTEZUMA
MARIO CID
LOS VAMPIROS DE COYOACAN
ARTURO MARTINEZ

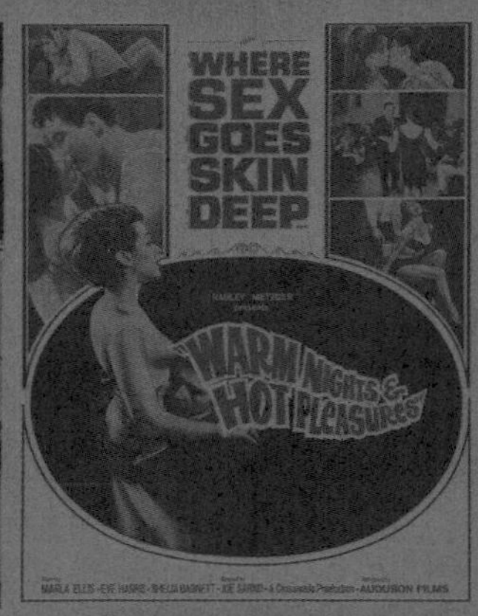
WHERE SEX GOES SKIN DEEP
WARM NIGHTS & HOT PLEASURES

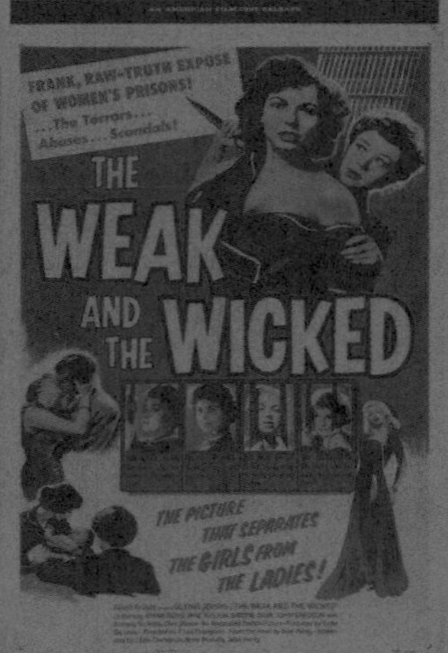
FRANK, RAW-TRUTH EXPOSÉ OF WOMEN'S PRISONS!
...The Terrors... Abuses... Scandals!
THE WEAK AND THE WICKED
THE PICTURE THAT SEPARATES THE GIRLS FROM THE LADIES!

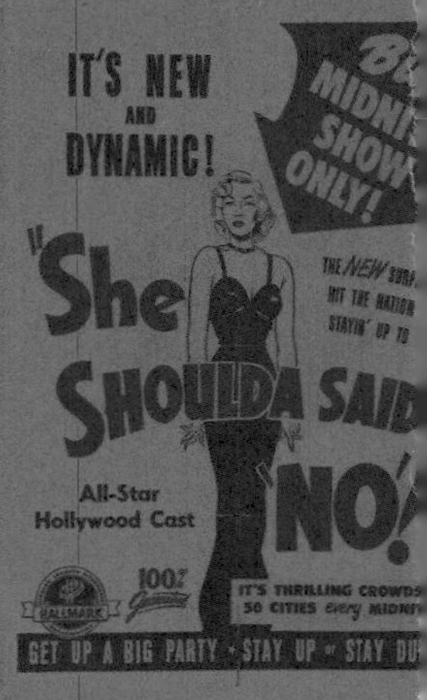
IT'S NEW AND DYNAMIC!
MIDNIGHT SHOWS ONLY!
"She Shoulda Said NO!"
All-Star Hollywood Cast
GET UP A BIG PARTY · STAY UP · STAY OU